Director of Publications and Marketing: Nancy M. Perrin, M.A., CAE
Publications Project Manager: Wendi S. Kishi, B.A.
Copy Editor: S. Jane Thomas, B.S.
Editorial Assistant: Scott M. Faubion, B.A.

For order information or questions, write or call:
Pharmacoeconomics and Outcomes: Applications for Patient Care, Second Edition
American College of Clinical Pharmacy
3101 Broadway, Suite 650
Kansas City, MO 64111
816-531-2177
816-531-4990 (Fax)
accp@accp.com

Printed in the United States of America.

ISBN: 1-880401-78-9

Welcome from the Editorial Board

Health care reform and technological advances are creating changes in how health care interventions are evaluated. Throughout the past two past decades, cost containment has at times appeared to overshadow clinical assessments. However, the overarching goal of understanding both the costs and consequences of interventions is ultimately being acknowledged. Clinical endpoints are still necessary, of course, but are no longer sufficient to make fully informed patient care decisions. It is not appropriate to make a decision primarily based on cost. Outcomes assessment provides the means to incorporate both clinical endpoints and economic data (the costs and consequences) to fully and more properly evaluate pharmaceutical products and services.

Outcomes assessment-specifically pharmacoeconomic outcomes, such as cost-effectiveness analysis and health-related quality-of-life evaluations-is a subject typically lacking in the formal educational backgrounds of the vast majority of practicing clinical pharmacists. Among the principal reasons for this lack are: 1) these are still relatively new and evolving fields for which published methodologies are presently at a stage of consensus development; 2) the body of peer-reviewed published literature is relatively sparse compared to other fields; and 3) the number of specialists qualified to teach these subjects is limited to a rather small group of individuals who have conducted primary research, were formally trained, or otherwise developed expertise through practical experience. Yet, there is a well-identified need for self-advancement in these areas, fostered by mounting economic pressures. Health care reform is forcing practitioners to refocus their efforts beyond cost-containment to the demonstration of value. This can, in part, be achieved by measuring and managing patient outcomes. Pharmacists have recognized the need to become better educated and familiar with these methodologies so as to use them for the benefit of their patients and their health care systems. Indeed, just as pharmacokinetics was an opportunity for clinical pharmacy in the 1970s, pharmacoeconomics and outcomes assessments may open up new avenues in this decade and beyond.

In response to this need, in 1996 ACCP served as the springboard for the development of the first edition of Pharmacoeconomics and Outcomes: Applications for Patient Care. This four-part series was a unique, curricular-based certificate program designed for guided self-study. The second edition has followed a slightly different format. Pharmacoeconomics and Outcomes: Applications for Patient Care, Second Edition, is an updated version, that incorporates only the most pertinent curriculum from the first edition into one textbook and takes into account the various changes in health care and the advancements in the disciplines of outcomes and pharmacoeconomics that have occurred since 1996. This revised textbook is designed to equip various health care practitioners, especially pharmacists, with a working knowledge and pragmatic understanding of the application of these techniques in their practice settings.

Pharmacoeconomics and Outcomes: Applications for Patient Care, Second Edition, is divided into 23 chapters, spanning a variety of relevant areas, including health care system reform; the principles, techniques, and methods of economic and humanistic outcomes assessments (with pertinent examples and problem exercises); case studies that allow readers to use these data to inform drug decision-making as well as evaluate and justify clinical pharmacy services. The goal of this textbook is to develop the participant's knowledge and skills needed to apply the concepts and methods of pharmacoeconomics and outcomes research to make drug therapy decisions within their healthcare organizations. The curriculum is directed primarily at practitioners, students of colleges of pharmacy, and industry pharmacists who require an effective working knowledge of pharmacoeconomics and outcomes research. The book is designed to not only impart knowledge but also stresses development of skills and application of material. These goals are accomplished using written text, exercises designed to illustrate and apply the textbook material, annotated references, and multiple-choice self-assessment questions with the answers explained. In addition, a companion book consisting of in-depth, practical application case studies that reinforce the textbook curriculum is available.

This has been a rather ambitious undertaking and we believe this textbook will be of immediate value to practitioners in a variety of practice settings. Continuing self-education, both in general and in this specific area of outcomes assessment, is necessary for the profession to minimally survive and optimally thrive in the increasingly competitive environment of a reforming health care system. We recognize, and indeed experience directly, the demands placed on individuals who conduct research, practice, and teach in these fields. Therefore, we are appreciative of and empathetic to the sacrifices made by the authors who developed and revised the chapters and case studies for which there are painfully few templates from which to model. We, the editors, as well as the authors, reviewers, and ACCP staff have worked diligently to develop this textbook. We believe this information is pertinent to the continually evolving health care system. And who better to develop such a text than the members and staff of ACCP, who for 25-plus years have endeavored to be the preeminent voice of clinical pharmacy. In fact, developing this book has been educational for us and, for the most part enjoyable! Aided by the tools described in this text and demonstrated in this companion case study book, you have the opportunity to justify the value of your profession to the health care system and to society. We sincerely hope you benefit from this series and go on to further your expertise in this field.

Pharmacoeconomics and Outcomes: Applications for Patient Care, Second Edition Editorial Board

TreeAge Software

Acknowledgements

Development and publication of Pharmacoeconomics and Outcomes: Applications for Patient Care, Second Edition is made possible through a generous educational grant from our corporate contributor, Aventis. ACCP is deeply grateful for their significant support in helping produce this second edition.

TABLE OF CONTENTS

TOOLS FOR MEASURING HUMANISTIC OUTCOMES

MEASURING HEALTH STATUS

Answers

THE STRUCTURE OF THE UNITED STATES HEALTH CARE DELIVERY SYSTEM

Jack E. Fincham, Ph.D.

Outline

I. Uniqueness of the United States health care system

II. Regulatory aspects
- A. Governmental controls
  - 1. Regulation
    - a. State
      - i. Health regulatory boards (e.g., boards of pharmacy, medicine, and nursing)
      - ii. Various state agencies
    - b. Federal
      - i. Food and Drug Administration
      - ii. Federal Trade Commission
      - iii. Drug Enforcement Administration

III. Institutions
- A. Hospitals
  - 1. General
  - 2. Private, for profit
  - 3. Governmental
    - a. Local
    - b. State
    - c. Federal
  - 4. Specialty
- B. Long-term care facilities
  - 1. Skilled nursing facilities
  - 2. Intermediate care nursing facilities
  - 3. Assisted living facilities
- C. Ambulatory care centers
  - 1. Patterns of ambulatory care use
- D. Home health care
- E. Subacute care

IV. Professions
- A. Physicians
- B. Physician extenders
- C. Pharmacists
  - 1. Education and training

        2. Person power issues
        3. Practice options
    D. Nurses
    E. Allied Health Professions

V. Managed care
    A. Managed care organizations
        1. Health maintenance organizations
        2. Preferred provider organizations
        3. Exclusive provider organizations
        4. Physician-hospital organizations
        5. Management service organization
    B. Integrated models
    C. Hybrids

VI. Health care financing
    A. Costs of care
        1. Current expenditures
        2. Patient cost-shifting
        3. Consumer influence
        4. Estimated future trends
    B. Public payment plans
        1. Medicaid
        2. Medicare
        3. Future of public programs
            a. Stressors
            b. Force of demographics
    C. Private payment plans

VII. Patterns of disease
    A. The impact of patterns of disease
        1. Health and disease
            a. Morbidity
            b. Mortality
        2. Prevention
        3. Treatment patterns
    B. Special challenges
        1. Access issues
        2. Uninsured
        3. Underinsured

VIII. Personal health behaviors
    A. Health seeking behavior
        1. Mediators
            a. Advertising and promotion
    B. Patient actions
        1. Self-medication
        2. Compliance
            a. Initial noncompliance
            b. Partial compliance
            c. Persistence
            d. Hypercompliance
    C. Unintended outcomes
        1. Adverse drug effects and drug errors
    D. Future health demands and opportunities
    E. Other influences
        1. Microbial resistance
        2. Biotechnology
        3. Patient specific therapies

IX. Summary

Learning Objectives

1. Differentiate the varying components of the United States health care system that contribute to its uniqueness.
2. Evaluate the various portals from which patients can seek care in the United States health care system, including institutions, ambulatory care options, and home health care.
3. Discuss the current and future health care professional person power needs in the United States.
4. Recognize the importance of the varying interactions required of health professionals in the health care delivery system.
5. Recognize the influence of managed care on the delivery of health-related services in the United States
6. Understand the financing mechanisms for payment for the delivery of health care in the United States.
7. Analyze the patterns of morbidity and mortality affecting the United States population.
8. Realize the importance of self-care and personal health decisions on the use of health care services.

Abbreviations in this chapter

ADL	Activities of daily living
AIDS	Acquired immune deficiency syndrome
COX	Cyclooxygenase
DEA	Drug Enforcement Administration
DTC	Direct-to-consumer
EPO	Exclusive provider organization
FDA	Food and Drug Administration
FTC	Federal Trade Commission
GDP	Gross domestic product
HIV	Human immunodeficiency virus
HMO	Health maintenance organization
ICF	Intermediate care facility
IPA	Independent practice association
LTCF	Long-term care facility
MCO	Managed care organization
MSO	Management service organization
NACDS	National Association of Chain Drugstores
NCPA	National Community Pharmacists Association
NP	Nurse practitioner
OTC	Over the counter
PA	Prior approval
PBM	Pharmacy benefit managers
PHO	Physician-hospital organization
PPO	Preferred provider organization
RN	Registered nurse
SNF	Skilled nursing facility
VA	Veterans Affairs

Uniqueness of the United States Health Care System

When considering the unique structure of the United States health care system, it is necessary to analyze many components, including: governmental regulatory and monitoring segments, various delivery points for obtaining care, health person power requirements now and in the future, the current and future impact of managed care, the financing of health care, patterns of disease, and personal health behaviors and actions. Considering these disparate aspects of the United States system is important because the structure of health care and the delivery of services also are disjointed. In fact, when considering all the aspects that pertain to the United States health care system, it may not appear to be a system at all, but rather simply the aggregate sum of differing parts.

What is becoming increasingly important is the need to analyze patterns of health care expenditures and evaluate their impact on health conditions and disease states. Patterns of morbidity dictate where resources should be provided. Specialty services are designed to treat commonly occurring conditions. For example, due to the prominence of cardiovascular disease in the United States, research conducted by the major pharmaceutical manufacturers has focused on agents to treat hypertension, heart failure, hypercholesterolemia, and other cardiovascular diseases. Delivery of services to treat other conditions also follows needs existing due to patterns of morbidity and mortality. In other words, is there more of a need for primary care or specialty services? In addition, required services for varying population components (e.g., young vs. the elderly) may necessitate that limited resources be parsed out undemocratically. The strength of analytical tools, such as pharmacoeconomic analyses, will guide many difficult decisions now and in the future. It is hoped that data driven decision-making will allow for enhanced delivery and better use of the many components of health care delivery in the United States.

Regulatory Aspects

Governmental Controls

Regulation

State

Health Regulatory Boards. States have varying mechanisms to protect the public health through regulation of health professions. Some states have "super" regulatory boards that deal with all health professions within a state. The majority of states have individual regulatory boards overseeing each specific profession. These state boards of pharmacy deal with pharmacy rules and regulations within the state, serve as a semi-judicial entity for disciplining pharmacists and pharmacies, monitor the registration and reciprocation of pharmacy licenses, and serve to protect the public health. These boards regularly require that a public member (nonpharmacist) serve on the board. These boards are made up of political appointees put in place through the respective office of the governor for the specific states.

Appointees for the board of pharmacy positions typically serve a 3-year period, with the option for a renewal term if so desired by the governor making the appointment. Winds of change affect politics and political appointees, so as a governor seeks reelection or a lame duck governor leaves office, a board member may not be reappointed by a newly elected governor. Most states strive to have representatives from varying practice locales serve on boards (e.g., health system, community chain, and community independent pharmacist practitioners).

State boards that regulate nursing, medicine, and allied health may have the potential to impact pharmacists through varying regulations that detail the scope of practice for the affected professions. Scope of practice acts that enable the delivery of primary care by nonphysicians may include or exclude pharmacists. Prescribing privileges may be extended to nontraditional providers (e.g., nurse practitioners [NPs] and physician assistants), and the respective health professions boards monitor the oversight of such prescribing or other professional activities. In the case of one regulatory board enabling expanded roles (e.g., NP prescribing), another board (i.e., pharmacy) also has oversight responsibilities for monitoring the prescribing as to appropriateness.

Various State Agencies. States also have other boards or agencies that influence the practice of health professionals through varying regulations or policies. These agencies may include departments of health, health and environment, or other health professions regulatory bodies that specify how certain activities must be conducted. In addition, state Medicaid programs specify how pharmacists, pharmacies, and others bill for services, provide nondispensing products, and stipulate minimum requirements for patient counseling and education.

Federal

Food and Drug Administration. The United States Food and Drug Administration (FDA) approves labeled indications of new drug entities, reviews the safety profile of newly submitted drugs, and monitors the adverse effect profile of all drugs on the market in the United States. The FDA also regulates the advertising and promotion of prescription drugs in the United States marketplace. As a component of this regulation, the FDA monitors all aspects of professional as well as direct-to-consumer advertising.

Federal Trade Commission. The Federal Trade Commission (FTC) also oversees advertising and promotion of over-the-counter (OTC) nonprescription products. Thus, regarding drug use, there are two federal agencies with oversight responsibilities for drug use: the FDA and the FTC. The former deals with prescription drugs, and the latter deals with OTC products and advertising and promotion.

Drug Enforcement Administration. The Drug Enforcement Administration (DEA), founded in 1973, is an agency of the United States Justice Department that oversees the use of scheduled drugs (schedules II, III, IV, and V) in the United States. Purchase of schedule II narcotic and non-narcotic agents is made only through use of DEA required forms that all pharmacies in the United States must use. In addition, this agency is charged with oversight of the illicit use of drugs (i.e., legitimate drugs used illegally, and illicit street drugs used illegally) in the United States and territories. Before the agency assumed its current name, the entity was known as the Bureau of Narcotic and Dangerous Drugs. Formerly, the agency was much more involved in monitoring misuse of legitimately intended narcotic and non-narcotic drugs. Monitoring of oxycodone usage has been a priority of the DEA for some time. An explosion of illegitimate drugs has occurred in the United States, the DEA has become more and more short staffed and has had to spend much more time dealing with the importation, distribution, and use of drugs of abuse (e.g., methamphetamine, methylenedioxymethamphetamine [ecstasy], and cocaine).

Institutions

Hospitals

There were 36.4 million hospital discharges in the United States during 2000. Hospitals vary in location, type of ownership, and level of services provided. Payment for hospital services continues to be the largest cost component of health care services.

General

General hospitals far and away are the largest hospital type in the country. General hospitals are nonspecialized facilities that allow for patients with most medical conditions to be treated. Depending on the size of the facility and medical staffing, the range of services may vary from neonatal to geriatric in scope.

Private, for Profit

For profit hospitals are designed to provide institutional services ranging from general to specialty in nature for a profit to shareholders. These facilities also may vary in size and level of services provided. HCA, Inc. and Humana are two examples of for profit entities that own hospitals in various parts of the United States.

Governmental

Local

Local hospitals may be managed and supported by communities, counties, or municipalities. These facilities are nonprofit in terms of ownership. These facilities may range in capacity from less than 10 to hundreds or thousands. A range of service may be provided depending on the facility size and medical staff capabilities.

State

Varying states also operate hospitals. Every state that has a penitentiary has a hospital or clinic associated with it. In addition, there may be facilities for the developmentally disabled, or for those with mental conditions requiring confinement. States also may operate general hospitals in conjunction with cities or municipalities. States maintain ownership over teaching hospital facilities.

Federal

Each branch of the armed services maintains hospital facilities throughout the United States. Also the Veterans Affairs (VA) maintains hospitals throughout the country. Federal prisons have hospitals associated with each facility. There also are federal psychiatric hospitals.

Specialty

Specialty hospitals may provide specialized treatment for any of the following:

- Obstetrics and gynecology
- Pediatrics
- Psychiatry
- Orthopedics
- Oncology
- Rehabilitation
- Cardiovascular
- Other possibilities

Long-term Care Facilities

The elderly (age 65 years and older) make up the largest age segment of residents in long-term care facilities (LTCFs). The percentage of the population classified as elderly is expected to increase from 13 percent of the population in 2000 to 20 percent by 2030. Although only 5 percent of the elderly reside in LTCFs, the cost of long-term care is significant now and will increase in the future. The sheer number and increasing longevity of the elderly account for the rapid increase in spending for long-term care in the United States.

The vast majority (more than 80 percent) of nursing home care is funded through public coffers by the Medicare and Medicaid programs. Medicare long-term care coverage is funded through Medicare Part A of payment for skilled nursing facility (SNF) care. This SNF care is associated with postoperative or posthospitalization care rehabilitation services. Medicaid nursing facility care, or intermediate care facility (ICF) service, is provided to Medicaid eligible recipients. Slightly more than 50 percent of LTCFs are part of a chain of like facilities. The balance is privately or governmentally owned and operated. Sporadic abuse in LTCFs has received public attention and subsequent political scrutiny. The awareness of the occurrence of abuse has focused attention on the need to more closely monitor the quality of care provided in LTCFs.

Skilled Nursing Facilities

There are slightly more than 53,000 SNF only beds in the United States, more than 600,000 dual certification beds (could be either SNF or ICF), and more than 1 million total Medicare stays in the United States per year. Roughly 8 percent of long-term care reimbursement in the United States is for SNF care.

Intermediate Care Nursing Facilities

A total of close to 70 percent of the cost of long-term care is is for ICF services. There are more than 1 million Medicaid only ICF beds in the United States, and close to 2 million ICF Medicaid patients in the country. Occupancy rates approach 90 percent for ICF facilities.

Assisted Living Facilities

According the National Center for Assisted Living, there are 28,000 assisted living facilities in the United States housing more than 1 million people. The "typical" assisted living resident is an 83-year-old woman (the average age of all assisted living residents is 83 years). The average man-woman ratio in assisted living residences is 26:74 percent. The average size of an assisted living residence is 43 units and ranges from three units to 200 units. The average number of residents in a facility is 40, with a range of one to 175 resident. The "typical" assisted living resident stays in a residence an average of 35 months. Almost 26 percent of all assisted living residents need no assistance with activities of daily living (ADL). On average, residents need help with 1.7 ADL.

A total of 22 states have existing licensing regulations using the term "assisted living," and 11 states have created task forces or processes to make recommendations for developing assisted living rules. A total of 35 states reimburse, or plan to reimburse, for assisted living or board and care as a Medicaid service. The greatest demand for senior housing occurs with people with lower incomes. Of the number of individuals who estimate their annual incomes to be less than $20,000, a total of 8.7 percent are elderly living in seniors housing.

Ambulatory Care Centers

Ambulatory care centers are an amalgamation of treatment clinics that may include specialized clinics offering anticoagulation, oncology, diabetes, primary care or family practice, cardiac care, asthma or pulmonary, human immunodeficiency virus (HIV)/acquired immune deficiency syndrome (AIDS), lipid control, or smoking cessation care services. The clinics may be associated with a group practice physician office, a hospital-related series of clinics, or free standing owned or operated by varying entities. In several ambulatory care practice settings, pharmacists have begun to practice within physician offices. These nondispensing roles allow pharmacists access to both patients and physicians to help monitor drug prescribing and patient drug therapy regimens in close proximity to physicians and other caregivers.

Patterns of Ambulatory Care Use

According to the 2000 summary of the National Ambulatory Medical Care Survey, during 2000, an estimated 823.5 million visits were made to physician offices in the United States, with an overall rate of 300 visits per 100 patients. One-fourth of the visits were to a general or family practitioner, and 15 percent were to an internist. Blood pressure measurement was the leading diagnostic screening procedure performed. Referral from another physician was the reason for the visit in 17 percent of the cases. Medicare or Medicaid was the expected source of payment for 30 percent of the visits. Two-thirds of the office visits involved drugs therapy. In communications reported between physicians and patients or patient representatives: the most common therapeutic classification mentioned was cardiovascular and the most common generic drug mentioned was acetaminophen.

Home Health Care

There are about 14,000 home health and hospice care agencies in the United States. In the late 1990s, there were about 3 million home health care patients visited annually in the country. Between 1992 and 1998, there was an increase of 53 percent in the number of home health care visits. The top four categories for patient visits are: cardiovascular disease, cerebrovascular disease, musculoskeletal system, and respiratory. Oncology visits are still among the top 10 reasons for visits, but actually declined between 1990 and 2000.

Subacute Care

Subacute care is a fairly new form of institutional care that merges hospital-type services with the skilled operation of a nursing facility to reduce the cost of services while maintaining quality of care. Long-term care facilities are dedicating entire wings, even entire facilities, to provide high-tech, hospital-like care to seriously ill patients of all ages at a lower cost compared with hospital-based facilities.

Subacute care is comprehensive inpatient care designed for patients who have an acute illness, injury, or exacerbation of a disease process. It is goal-oriented treatment rendered immediately after, or instead of, acute hospitalization. Services are provided for patients needing extensive wound care, intensive rehabilitation, cardiac care, and/or pain management. The provision of subacute care grew dramatically during the 1990s. There are between 35,000 and 45,000 subacute care beds in LTCFs in the United States. The majority of subacute units have been opened since 1990.

Professions

Physicians

There are more than 700,000 allopathic physicians (M.D.) in the United States, and more than 40,000 osteopathic physicians (D.O.) in the United States. There are numerous physician specialties, with the top five being family practice, internal medicine, obstetrics and gynecology, general surgery, and psychiatry.

Physician Extenders

There are more than 30,000 physician assistants in the United States. The largest number within a state are in New York (3998) and California (3370), and the lowest number within a state are in Mississippi (42).

Pharmacists

Education and Training

As of January 2002, there were 83 schools and colleges of pharmacy in the United States, enrolling about 36,000 students in first professional degree programs. Twenty-eight of these schools were in private institutions, and 55 were public institutions. Only four schools continue to offer the B.S. in pharmacy degree, all 83 schools offer the doctor of pharmacy (Pharm.D.) degree. Sixty-four of these schools offer graduate programs in the pharmaceutical sciences (M.S. and Ph.D.).

Residency and fellowship opportunities are plentiful for graduates to pursue specialization after graduation. Competition is keen for attracting graduates due to the present shortage of pharmacists in the country. No region is exempt from the shortage, it is especially acute in the South, Southeast, Southwest, and Western United States.

Person Power Issues

In response to the shortage of pharmacists in the United States, the United States Department of Health and Human Services through the Health Resources and Services Administration, Bureau of Health Professions, prepared a report for Congress (The Pharmacist Workforce: A Study of the Supply and Demand for Pharmacists). The supply of pharmacists in the United States is projected to increase from about 196,000 in 2000 to 224,500 in 2010. Among additional findings of this report are the following conclusions:

"While the overall supply of pharmacists has increased in the past decade, there has been an unprecedented demand for pharmacists and for pharmaceutical care services, which has not been met by the currently available supply. This current shortage may reflect an extension of a less serious shortage reported during the 1988 to 1994 period."

The report goes on to summarize the extent and ramifications of the pharmacist shortage. The report notes:

"The most striking evidence of a pharmacist shortage, and the extent of the shortage, are the:

- demonstrably increased vacancy rates, difficulties in hiring, and other phenomena commonly associated with shortages; and
- unprecedented increases in the volume and range of activities demanded of today's pharmacist. The increased volume is manifested most convincingly by the sharply increased number of prescriptions filled each year in retail settings. The increased range is manifested by the substantially expanded roles and responsibilities of pharmacists in both retail and institutional settings."

"Factors identified as contributing to the shortage include:

- increased use of prescription medications;
- market growth and competition among retail pharmacies, resulting in increased pharmacist positions, expanded store hours, and new store openings; expansions in pharmacy practice and pharmacists' roles and professional opportunities;
- increased access to health care and the increased number of health care providers authorized to prescribe medications;
- changes in the pharmacist workforce, including the greater number of women pharmacists and their shorter work patterns; and
- the double impact of increased insurance coverage for prescription drugs, resulting in an increase in both prescription volume and the number of third-party payment issues that need to be resolved."

The impact of the shortage and consequences for the profession and society are summarized in the report as:

- "Consequences of the shortage include a negative impact on the profession and the public resulting in:

- reduced time for pharmacists to provide patient counseling—a role of increasing importance in light of the expanded use and complexity of medications;
- job stress, inadequate working conditions, and reduced professional satisfaction due to longer working hours and lesser flexibility in scheduling, and introducing fatigue-related factors that increase the potential for medications error;
- service restrictions particularly affecting underserved or otherwise vulnerable sectors of the population such as the elderly, residents of rural communities, individuals with mental illness who are on medications, and persons dependent on publicly supported services, such as Native Americans and veterans;
- recruitment of pharmacy practice faculty away from schools and colleges of pharmacy, hampering schools' ability to increase class size."

Any report written, including this report to Congress, makes assumptions about the future. However, since this report was released in 2000, many of the projections have in fact materialized.

Practice Options

Practice options for pharmacists have never been better or more varied than they are at present. Opportunities for pharmacists are enhanced with residency and fellowship training. The shortage of pharmacists has accentuated the concerns about filling these post-Pharm.D. training options. Many excellent opportunities are vacant because of the number of options graduating pharmacists currently have as they enter the profession. As pharmacists acquire skills through these programs, whether the programs are clinically oriented, pharmacoeconomic based, or practice focused, they can then pursue outstanding careers in numerous pharmacy practice portals.

The increase in managed care activities in the recent past subsequently has increased pharmacist activities in varied environments. Pharmacist participation in disease management programs and error reduction activities portends the need for pharmacists to be better engaged in disease management activities and programs. Increasing automation and use of supportive personnel has allowed pharmacists to better apply clinical skills in direct care patient settings.

Collaborative practice models also have opened doors for pharmacists by allowing pharmacists to practice along side physicians in practice settings. Pharmacist may review patients' drugs and therapeutic regimens, provide educational services for physicians and staff, and counsel patients along with other services. Pharmacists in collaborative practice arrangements also have been allowed to prescribe limited drugs under protocols that must be approved by physician colleagues.

Nurses

The health care system is experiencing a nursing shortage that is every bit as significant as is the pharmacist shortage. The United States Department of Health and Human Services Bureau of Health Professions in nursing staffing surveys has found a shortage of young people choosing careers in nursing. In the recent past, the average age of registered nurses has increased. For example, according to the Bureau of Health Professions, in 1980, 52.9 percent of registered nurses (RNs) were younger than 40 years of age; in 2000, 31.7 percent were younger than 40. In 1980, 26 percent of RNs were younger than 30 years of age, but by 2000, less than 10 percent were younger than 30 years of age.

The growth of the number of NPs as physician extenders in providing primary care has been dramatic in the past decades. Nurse practitioners see patients, provide care, prescribe drugs regimens, and work in institutional and ambulatory environments. Nurse practitioners have been accepted by patients and providers as primary caregivers. Insurers see NPs as a less costly provider of primary care.

Allied Health Professions

According to published data from the Bureau of Health Professions, Office of Research and Planning, the number of allied health professionals increased from 750,000 in 1970 to 2.32 million in the late 1990s. This increase of 210 percent in a generation has been led by increases in ancillary dental professionals, medical laboratory workers, health information specialists, occupational therapists, physical therapists, and speech pathologists and audiologists.

Managed Care

Managed Care Organizations

The structure of managed care organizations (MCOs) can take many forms and has evolved throughout the years as more and more pressure to reduce expenditures in the health care system has mounted. The emergence and growth of the managed care industry has been seen as both a boon and a bust; the perception varies by the impact MCOs have had on the varying professions. As pharmacists in ambulatory settings have seen operating margins decrease and the numbers of drug benefit plans explode, frustration with MCOs and their intent to reduce expenditures for drugs has mounted expeditiously. Pharmacy benefit managers (PBMs) operate in the system with a complex array of copayments and deductibles required of patients. Pharmacy benefit managers offer a tiered payment scheme for patients. If a patient receives a prescription for a generic drug, the copayment may be a flat amount such as $5 per prescription. A brand name drug with a generic available may require a higher copayment amount such as $10. A brand name drug with no generic available may require the patient to pay a higher amount for the prescription such as $20. Coverage for nonapproved labeled indications of a drug (e.g., for cosmetic purposes) may be nonexistent. Other expensive therapies may require prior approval (PA) from the MCO plan personnel before the drug is eligible for reimbursement. Many MCOs and PBMs currently are using this three-tier formulary payment system. In the near future, these three-tier systems likely will expand to include four- and five-tier formulary systems to manage continually rising drug costs and the onslaught of biotechnology prescription products. Often in drug formulary listings, the MCO indicates the relative expense of a drug option by placing multiple dollar signs ($) next to the drug. The more dollar signs present, the more expensive the drug. Some MCOs have sent formulary listings with such notations to patients so they are aware of the varying costs of drug alternatives.

In other cases, the patient may be required to pay a certain percentage of the cost of each prescription. This percentage may vary depending on the drug type (e.g., generic, brand name with a generic available, and brand name with no generic available). The pharmacy is reimbursed by the PBM based on the cost of the drug plus professional fee. In the recent past, the payment for the cost of the drug has decreased and the amount paid for the professional fee has shrunk steadily.

Health Maintenance Organizations

Health maintenance organizations (HMOs) have existed since the 1930s. Some HMOs received governmental support for formation during the Nixon administration in the early 1970s. The premise for HMO existence is the combining of delivery of health services and insurance for such services under one umbrella. Through this combination of delivery and insurance, it has been hoped that costs of care delivery would decrease. Health maintenance organizations typically can contract with either group practice medical practices or operate with a staff model. There are four traditional models of HMOs: staff model, group model, network, and independent practice association (IPA). In the staff model HMO, physicians are considered employees. The group practice may be an independent group of physicians contracting with several HMOs as well as servicing private pay patients. In the network model, HMOs contract with numerous multispecialty group practices to expand geographic coverage. In the IPA model, the HMO contracts with solo or specialty practices. Physicians are compensated on a fee-for-service basis. Health maintenance organizations typically contract with select health system institutions to provide hospital-based services for enrolled patients. In reality, there are few HMOs at present that fit into these traditional categories, more than likely, a mixture of the categories is the norm at present.

Preferred Provider Organizations

Preferred provider organizations (PPOs) are a form of insurance plan that further limits points of care provision for a defined population of enrolled patients. The number of primary and specialty care providers may be reduced to limit patient access to care. Select hospitals also may be chosen for patient use to try to decrease the cost of care.

Exclusive Provider Organizations

Exclusive provider organizations (EPOs) are a form of PPO that even further limits the number of care providers and institutions providing services for a defined population of enrolled patients. This form of PPO seeks to contain costs by ratcheting down the cadre of physicians and the number of institutions where patients can obtain care. The lines that distinguish HMOs and PPOs have blurred as both organizations have begun to offer more and more services similar to each another (i.e., HMOs with point-of-service offerings so patients can skip the "gatekeeper" referral process required to visit a specialist).

Physician-Hospital Organizations

Physician-hospital organizations (PHOs) are jointly owned organizations of hospitals and affiliated physicians on staff. The PHO contracts with HMOs to provide a range of services for enrollees. The PHO enables negotiating, contracting, and marketing on behalf of the involved parties.

Management Service Organizations

Management service organizations (MSOs) exist to serve disparate entities (e.g., physicians, group practices, and/or other health service providers) by providing practice management, administrative, billing, and other support-type services. Each separate entity maintains autonomy over services provided; however, sharing administrative expenses can occur through the use of the MSO.

Integrated Models

Integrated systems of care work within a network that is set to provide a comprehensive continuum of care for a defined population. Through incentives and in some cases disincentives, the integrated system is held accountable for performance of the components within the integrated model. Provision of a range of services from outpatient to inpatient is contractually agreed on in a competitive environment.

Hybrids

Hybrids can contain elements of any of the above managed care structural models. Governmental programs, such as Medicaid, in several states use hybrid models. In these situations, patients are directed to specific providers (e.g., group practices and pharmacies) and specific health systems for institutional care.

Other government programs, such as the VA, offer services in a hybrid fashion. For-profit companies, such as Humana Military Health care, provide hybrid services for varying segments of the United States Tricare managed care model. In this instance, the care is provided for enrolled, eligible patients (i.e., active duty military or retired veterans) and dependents in a networked model containing varying service providers within the VA system.

Other programs may segment, or carve out, specific services to be provided to patients in a hybrid fashion. For example, mental health services for enrolled patients in Medicaid programs may be required to obtain care from select providers and institutions on either an inpatient or outpatient basis.

Health Care Financing

Costs of Care

Current Expenditures

In 2000, health expenditures accounted for about 13.2 percent of the gross domestic product (GDP) in the United States. In 2001, projected expenditures for health were 14 percent of the GDP. The percentage had remained close to 13 percent for a decade or so. Also, it is estimated that a full 50 percent of the costs of acute care are consumed by 5 percent of the population. National health spending in 2000 increased 6.9 percent from 1999. Medicare expenditures for

2000 were $224 billion, which accounted for 38 percent of public spending, and 17 percent of total expenditures for health care services. Medicaid spending reached $202 billion in 2000, an increase of 8.9 percent from 1999. In 2000, Medicaid spending accounted for 15.5 percent of total health spending.

Increases in expenditures for health services were fueled by several categories in which large increases in expenditures were evident.

- Prescription drugs. Prescription drug spending increased by 17.3 percent in 2000. Per capita prescription filling was 10.5 per person in 2000 up from 8.3 per person in 1995.
- Nursing homes. Expenditures for nursing care increased by 3.3 percent in 2000. Government spending for nursing home care amounted to 61 percent of total nursing home expenditures in 2000, and the majority of these funds came from the Medicaid program (48 percent).
- Hospitals. Spending for hospital services increased by 5.1 percent in 2000, reaching the amount of $412 billion. Hospital services as a percentage of total expenditures in the health care system have decreased from 42 percent in 1982 to 32 percent of total costs in 2000.

As the economy across the United States has spiraled into a tailspin, the public expenditures for health care became an item exposed to increasing scrutiny. The Medicare and Medicaid programs have always been politically charged, but they are even more so when economic factors are depressed to the extent that they are currently.

Patient Cost-shifting

Shifting of costs from payers to patients is occurring at a precipitous pace. The problem is not just that employers are dropping coverage, but that they are shifting premium costs to workers. According to a 1999 report by the Kaiser Family Foundation, between 1985 and 1995 the proportion of workers making no direct contribution to premiums for worker-only coverage dropped by 30 percent, from 64 percent to 33 percent. Another study found that the average premium contribution by workers for employee-only coverage rose 284 percent from 1988 to 1996. The increase for family coverage was 146 percent. As coverage becomes more expensive, more and more workers are unable to afford it.

Higher out-of-pocket costs greatly diminish affordability. Increasing cost-sharing requirements, limits on benefits and managed care denials also are shifting financial burdens from payers (employers) to workers and their families. This patient shifting (cost-shifting) is a major reason why a majority of Americans challenge the assumption that managed care has been successful in reducing health care costs. Managed care may have reduced the increase of expenditures and attempted to increase efficiency in the system, but for patients, costs have increased.

Consumer Influence

Many bills have been introduced in the federal and state legislatures to set in place a patient bill of rights. These bills have been advocated by consumer groups, and challenged vigorously by managed care entities.

Estimated Future Trends

It is projected that national health expenditures will reach $2.8 trillion in 2011. This is an annual increase of 7.3 percent between 2001 and 2011. This level of spending will amount to 17 percent of the GDP in the United States, and be 2.5 percent higher than the projected increase in the GDP over that period of time. An increase in the elderly population of the United States combined with newer technologies and escalating costs of care will further increase spending on health care in the United States.

Public Payment Plans

Health insurance and the process of obtaining health insurance are undergoing tremendous change. Partly due to demand and partly to do extreme cost drivers, the United States system of insurance for health care is becoming increasingly contentious and political. Economic downturns or expansions do not seem to ease this apparent societal point of conflict. The basic fact is that insurance and delivery of health care is both personal and yet public due to demands for financing at both the state and federal level. As individuals are affected and families are impacted, the debate swirling around health insurance becomes even more personal. Public demands centering on Medicaid and Medicare are but two examples of how these programs have become more and more visible in the public arena.

Medicare and Medicaid now account for more than 80 percent of the public expenditures for personal health services. Medicaid expenditures have increased dramatically in recent years, which in turn has caused budget catastrophes for many states. In some states, managed care programs have been used to try to limit rising costs. These efforts have resulted in minor impacts on spending in the Medicaid program. They have been minor simply because more than 90 percent of spending in Medicaid programs has been for traditional fee-for-service services. In addition, long-term care expenditures account for more a significant portion of Medicaid spending and usually are not covered by managed care plans. When cutbacks to services are implemented, the impact on access to quality patient care is a major concern.

Medicaid

Medicaid is a jointly funded federal and state program designed to provide health care for the poor (economically needy) and disabled (medically needy). Medicaid-eligible recipients include the blind and disabled, the aged poor and families with dependent children if one parent is absent, unemployed, or unable to work. Federally mandated required services for Medicaid recipients include inpatient and outpatient hospital care, physician visits, laboratory services, radiology services, and nursing facility care. Coverage for prescription drugs is an optional component of Medicaid services. Federal funding to states is set on a cost-sharing basis, based on the state's per capita income, where wealthier states obtain less than 50 percent and poorer states obtain more than 50 percent of the federal distribution. Although an outpatient prescription program is not mandated by federal regulations, it is an option provided by most states.

In the instance where a patient may have coverage under both Medicare and Medicaid policies, Medicaid is always the payer of last resort. Also, in the case where a patient may have Medicaid coverage as well as other forms of private health insurance coverage, Medicaid is the payer of last resort. Other forms of payment coverage must be expended before Medicaid coverage is applied in any dual coverage situation.

Medicare

Medicare is solely financed by the federal government. Medicare enrolls eligible individuals regardless of income. Eligibility is extended to individuals who are older than 65 years of age, or to patients with end-stage renal disease regardless of age or income. Medicare beneficiaries are covered by the Social Security Amendment passed in 1965, which extended health care services to all people 65 years of age and older. Medicare Part A coverage includes inpatient hospital care, SNF care, hospice, and home health care, with deductibles and limits placed on each area. Payment for intermediate care provided in LTCFs is not covered by Medicare. Medicare beneficiaries also are eligible for Part B coverage, which, for a relatively small health insurance premium, allows senior citizens to obtain extended coverage for physician services, outpatient hospital services, home health care services and a limited number of outpatient drugs (e.g., hepatitis B vaccine, immunosuppressant drugs, epoetin, pneumococcal and influenza vaccine, and some oral cancer drugs). Payment for drugs in hospitals is allowed for Medicare patients. However, other payment for drugs, including outpatient drugs coverage, is not available through Medicare insurance.

Currently, the debate about a prescription drug benefit for Medicare enrollees is focused and intense. Each of the two major political parties in the United States has a plan before Congress for coverage of outpatient prescription drugs. Professional practitioner pharmacy organizations, such as the National Community Pharmacists Association (NCPA), and trade organizations, such as the National Association of Chain Drugstores (NACDS), oppose current proposals for reasons varying from limits on access to certain pharmacies to use of a PBM for claims processing. Other organizations in pharmacy, because of their representing groups that may play a role in such payment schemes, have not taken a stand one way or the other on these plans.

Future of Public Programs

Stressors

Inevitable stressors impact the future of public programs in the United States health care system. These stressors may include:

- Economic considerations
- Technology
- Age-related changes

As the economy in the United States experienced turbulence since the events of September 11, 2001, enormous pressure was placed on the financial viability of publicly funded health-related programs. Budgets in virtually every state were under siege, Medicaid programs were facing huge cuts never before seen. As reimbursement levels for services provided by health professionals, institutions, and caregivers spiral downward and as demand for services increases, something must give in the future for programs to continue to provide quality health care services. As more technological advances have entered the health care arena, costs have increased. Technological advances in drug delivery portend even higher costs for drugs in the future.

The advancing age of our population in the United States accentuates the demand for publicly funded health care services and places additional burdens on the funding for such programs. An enormous percentage of costs in the Medicare program occurs as individuals are treated in the last months of their lives; as the number affected in the Medicare program increase, these costs will further escalate. The addition of a Medicare drug benefit, although necessary, will more than likely cause costs associated with Medicare to increase exponentially.

Force of Demographics

Through consideration of the sheer number of the elderly and the political clout they will wield, the shape of health insurance programs provided for the elderly, and purchased by the elderly will be vastly different than what is currently in place.

Because of the rapid increase in the elderly population, the ways of defining the elderly are rapidly changing. Rather than simply referring to everyone older than 65 years of age as "old", it is now acceptable to categorize the elderly as follows:

- Young old age: 65–74 years of age
- Middle old age: 75 - 84 years of age
- Old old age: 85 years of age and older.

The fastest growth segment of these three categories is the old old age group. In 1995, it was estimated that there were 60,000 individuals 100 years or age or older; by 2035, it is estimated that there will be 1 million individuals 100 years of age or older.

Private Payment Plans

Within the next several years, a series of proposals from the major, for-profit insurance companies in the United States, if enacted, will change employee health insurance options in a significant manner. The companies are Aetna, CIGNA, Humana, United Health Group, and Wellpoint Health Network. This new type of health plan will be a complex menu of premiums, copayments, and deductibles. Employees will be provided with a fixed amount of money to spend on health care, and be required to shop for care that they need. Medical savings accounts will be combined with catastrophic-illness insurance for employees and dependents for costs that exceed a large deductible.

These plans propose to shift costs to employees who use more health care services. In effect, this model is similar in nature to other forms of insurance (e.g., homeowners, renters, and automobile owners) that shift costs from those who use little of the insurance services to those who use more. Thus, the more health care services that you use, the more you will be expected to pay, and the amount of reserve funds through insurance that the individual has will be diminished quickly.

It certainly remains to be seen if the public will accept such a shift in the concept of what health insurance means in the United States. The provision of health services for Medicaid clients and Medicare enrollees through "social insurance" models (publicly funded programs) may be less palatable for taxpayers if their own ability to pay for health care is eroded through such proposals as previously discussed.

Patterns of Disease

The Impact of Patterns of Disease

Health and Disease

Morbidity

As one would assume, the incidence of disease closely follows subsequent death due to the leading causes of morbidity in the United States. Cardiovascular disease has the largest impact on morbidity and mortality statistics. There are in excess of 57 million Americans with cardiovascular disease, accounting for a staggering expenditure of $260 billion annually. The presence of AIDS is a significant influence on morbidity, although the incidence and the number of deaths due to AIDS has leveled off, the prevalence continues to increase. The subsequent sequelae of AIDS (e.g., infectious diseases) certainly affects other causes of death as well. The current patterns of morbidity and mortality in the United States are a reflection of several converging factors. The population of the United States is aging, and as the average age increases, patients are more apt to acquire diseases that are common in advancing age.

Mortality

According to data from the United States Department of Health and Human Services, the 10 leading causes of death in the United States for 1999 were (total number of deaths equals 2.4 million):

1. Diseases of the heart: 725,192 (30.3 percent)
2. Malignant neoplasms: 549,838 (23 percent)
3. Cerebrovascular diseases: 167,366 (7 percent)
4. Chronic lower respiratory disease: 124,181 (5.2 percent)
5. Accidents (unintentional injuries): 97,860 (4.1 percent)
6. Diabetes mellitus: 68,399 (2.9 percent)
7. Influenza and pneumonia: 63,730 (2.7 percent)
8. Alzheimer's disease: 44,536 (1.9 percent)
9. Nephritis, nephritic syndrome and nephrosis: 35,525 (1.5 percent)
10. Septicemia: 30,680 (1.3 percent)
11. All other causes (20.2 percent)

As a comparison, the preliminary data for 2000 do not vary from this listing and ranking of causes of death. The presence of a disease on this list may belie the significance of the disease. The presence of a disease being on this list may belie just how significant the disease is in fact. For example, there are 600,000 occurrences of stroke in the United States annually; 167,366 people die; there are currently 4.6 million stroke survivors in the United States.

There are other significant causes of death that, although they might not reach the incidence level necessary for a top 10 listing, are nevertheless major mortality factors. For example, there are more than 30,000 suicides in the United States per year. Drug treatment preceding the despondency leading to suicide may or may not avert the tragedy, but it is something that health professionals could and should consider. It also should be noted that in 2000, there were more than 16,000 homicides in the United States. Drug treatment may not have a role in homicide prevention, but this dire number of untimely deaths is a tragic commentary on the rate of crime in the United States and effect on the United States society.

Prevention

Prevention remains the key to many chronic health problems. For example, the chief avoidable cause of death in the United States is tobacco use. More than 500,000 Americans die from tobacco use and subsequent smoking-related morbidity every year. Another 50,000 die from the effects of second hand or environmental smoke. Despite these alarming data points, 3000 adolescents begin to smoke every day. The impact of smoking on cardiovascular, cerebrovascular, respiratory, and cancer-related morbidity and mortality is enormous. The influence of these disease states on patient morbidity and mortality could be attenuated with this preventive action (smoking cessation) alone. Although tobacco use is not listed as one of the top mortality causes, causes of death secondary to cigarette smoking are among the top 10 leading causes of death (i.e., cardiovascular, cerebrovascular, and neoplasms).

In addition, the impact of diet on cardiovascular, cerebrovascular, and cancer-related mortality is significant as well. There is an epidemic of obesity in the United States and the influence of obesity on morbidity and mortality is significant. Unhealthy food additives (e.g., excessive sodium, saturated fats, and carbohydrates) and inappropriate dietary intake place an enormous health burden on society.

Prenatal care in the United States is exquisite for those who can afford it, or for those with proper insurance. For the rest of Americans who do not possess the ability to pay for care, prenatal care is substantially substandard. This bimodal access to proper prenatal and perinatal services leaves many exceedingly disadvantaged; the long-term consequences of this lack of proper care from the beginning of life have been devastating for both mothers and offspring.

Treatment Patterns

Because of the varied delivery points for care in the United States, complete identification of treatment patterns is difficult in the United States. A consortium of federal agencies has targeted preventable health activities that could significantly improve the health of Americans. The publication of Healthy People 2000 and the subsequent update, Healthy People 2010, targeted several leading health indicators that require prompt and sustained attention to reduce further health complications for patients in the future. These health indicators are:

- Physical activity
- Overweight and obesity
- Tobacco use
- Substance abuse
- Responsible sexual behavior

- Mental health
- Injury and violence
- Environmental quality
- Immunization
- Access to health care

Prevention efforts aimed at reducing the impact of these indicators on the health of the population can dramatically postpone expensive care in the future for affected patients. Conversely, lack of attention to forestalling the effects of these indicators will have an increasing effect on the health of those affected.

Special Challenges

Access Issues

Many factors may impact the ability of individuals to access the health care system. Factors such as insurance availability, race, gender, patient choice, and patient-provider communication all play a role. A significant number of Americans remain uninsured. Without a doubt, health insurance coverage affects access to care. An estimated total of 40 percent of adults and 25 percent of children without health insurance have no regular source of health care. Race has played a role in access to health care, and many underrepresented minorities can relate instances where race has played a role in the care delivered to them. Racial and ethnic minorities are more likely to be uninsured, even if economic factors are even. Women not only use the health care system more frequently than men do, but they do so in a more efficient manner. Women use the health care system more advantageously than men. Patients also may use the health care system differently based on their own care seeking preferences. Finally, the ability of providers to communicate with patients, and the quality of the communication between the parties affects how patients can access caregivers, sources of information, and institutional services that may be required.

Uninsured

A disturbing trend related to health coverage for Americans has intensified in the past decades. The number of people in the United States without health care coverage increased to 38.4 million in 2000. Although about 70 percent of Americans receive health insurance benefits, and the elderly have coverage through Medicare, millions remain uninsured due to the lack of an employee health insurance benefit or because they simply cannot afford the costs of insurance.

Demographic variables significantly influence the uninsured population in the United States. More than 80 percent of those who are uninsured in the United States are from families with one full-time or part-time worker, but the worker is without health insurance as an employee benefit. In 2000, 16 percent of Americans (nonelderly) were uninsured. This percentage grew throughout the 1990s despite a period of record economic growth. Low-wage workers simply cannot afford high premiums that accompany health insurance coverage. The percentage of coverage is even lower (33 percent) for low-wage workers (less than $20,000 annually) without insurance. The type of business also affects insurance coverage, almost 30 percent of workers in small business (less than 25 employees) lack insurance. Although racial and ethnic subpopulations account for 33 percent of the United States population, they make up about 50 percent of the uninsured. Finally, geography plays a role as well, the lowest percentage of uninsured individuals resides in Connecticut (7 percent), and the largest percentage (27 percent) resides in New Mexico. Uninsured rates vary within states as well; uninsured populations are especially high among the poor in southern and western states in the United States. In these states, 33 percent or more of low-income populations are uninsured.

Underinsured

About 13 percent of people with insurance coverage do not fill prescriptions annually because of the cost of drugs and lack of complete coverage for prescription drugs; 17 percent cannot pay their recurring health bills. This trend has led to what is termed a "consumer driven" health care system because people have to pay for services out of pocket and they must choose what services to obtain, thus driving the market for services based on the services for which they can pay.

Personal Health Behaviors

Health-seeking Behavior

Mediators

Advertising and Promotion

The direct-to-consumer (DTC) advertising and promotion of drugs through print, radio, and television media has reached an all time level of exposure and expenditure. Once manufacturers were allowed to advertise prescription drugs directly to consumers, expenditures for these promotion efforts increased yearly and dramatically. Recently, as the intensity and frequency of DTC advertisements have increased, the issue of such advertising has become more and more a focus of attention and criticism. One of the criticisms is that the general public seeing these advertisements may not have a full appreciation of what the advertised drug is used to treat, and why treatment with the drug may or may not be beneficial. It also is difficult in the short time that the advertisement is seen or heard to provide a complete and necessary discussion of the risk-to-benefit profile of the advertised drug.

Many contend that the rising percentage of health expenditures pertaining to prescription drug use is a directed result of consumer advertisements for prescription drugs. This classic "push" and "pull" marketing scheme has driven use and demand of prescription drugs. "Push" marketing refers to classic promotional efforts aimed at prescribers, decision-makers, and dispensers. "Pull" marketing refers to advertisements geared to cause consumers to demand prescription drug prescribing by their physicians.

Two agents entering the marketplace in the past several years are examples of how this phenomenon has affected the channel of distribution of prescription drugs in the United States. The antiarthritic drugs rofecoxib (Vioxx) and celecoxib (Celebrex) have been heavily advertised and promoted (COX)-2 inhibitors. Express Scripts (a major PBM) has stated that the use of these two new agents has far exceeded the narrow therapeutic classification use that would allow for their prescribing. In fact, the advertising of these two agents to consumers has been the subject of a critical New York Times article in 2002. However, patients seem to like DTC advertising, and physicians grudgingly acknowledge that DTC does provide information to patients. Manufacturers suggest that DTC informs and educates patients who might not otherwise be exposed to important information through other means. In the final analysis, only patients and their actions can refute or provide evidence either way regarding DTC.

Patient Actions

Self-medication

Self-medication can be defined broadly as a decision made by a patient to consume a drug with or without the approval or direction of a health professional. Self-medication activities on the part of patients have increased throughout the past decades. Over-the counter access to more drugs that were previously prescription, advertising, and convenience of access of products all have served to boost self-medication activities.

Patient use of self-selected products potentially can have enormous benefits for patients and others. Through the rational use of drugs, patients may avoid more costly therapies or services. Self-medication allows patients to have some autonomy in health decisions, which can be positive if the autonomy is an informed process, allowing beneficial outcomes for patients. Manufacturers and retailers also can benefit from an increased level of self-medication activities.

Self-medication also has a downside. When patients consume drugs without direction or explanation of proper indications, the effectiveness of other drugs taken may be eroded or worse yet, patients may suffer unnecessary adverse drug effects. Products are switched from prescription to OTC status with increasing frequency, and more often than not drugs are switched to increase sales and exposure to wider population bases. When drugs are switched from prescription to OTC, many drug benefit plans no longer cover the drug through payment plans.

Compliance

Compliance can take various forms and can fluctuate throughout time. Compliance behavior may include initial noncompliance, partial compliance, persistence, and hypercompliance. Patient compliance is not an "either or" phenomenon. Patients may vary in their compliance behavior throughout time and may take differing concurrently prescribed drugs in an inefficient manner. Thus, they may be 100 percent compliant with some drugs, and much less compliant with other drugs consumed.

The average rate of compliance across patient subgroups and therapeutic categories is estimated to be 50 percent. This percentage is abysmal regardless of reasons for noncompliance.

Initial Noncompliance

The patient receives a written prescription, transfers it to a pharmacy or has the prescription phoned to a pharmacy, but does not wait or return to pick up the filled prescription. Patients who do not present written prescriptions for filling could be included in this group. Estimates for this type of initial noncompliance range from 3 percent to 20 percent.

Partial Compliance

Partial compliance refers to the process of consuming some of the drugs as prescribed by the physician or physician extender, but not taking the precise amount prescribed. It has been suggested that in some instances, 100 percent compliance may be an unreasonable expectation. For example, in the case of a mildly hypertensive patient, 75–80 percent of the regimen consumed may be enough to maintain normotension. However, if the dosage form is extended release or a once daily regimen, taking only 75–80 percent may be a prescription for disaster. Obviously, if a patient does not take oral contraceptives as prescribed on a daily basis, the intended action of the regimen may not be achieved.

Persistence

Persistence is the aspect of compliance whereby a patient complies with a prescribed and dispensed regimen precisely and continues to do so throughout time. Such compliance also may refer to achieving a therapeutic end point, such as normotension for hypertensive patients.

Hypercompliance

Hypercompliance is the situation whereby a patient takes a prescribed and dispensed drugs at a level over and above the recommended and intended dosing interval.

Unintended Outcomes

Adverse Drug Effects and Drugs Errors. The prevalence and significance of adverse drug effects has received increased scrutiny recently and will no doubt continue to be scrutinized. A 1999 report by the Institute of Medicine estimated that between 44,000 and 98,000 avoidable deaths annually result from medical errors in institutional settings. Drug misuse represents the largest category of medical errors in the health care system. Drug misuse leads to about 200,000 deaths per year in all settings and accounts for $300 billion in costs annually.

Future Health Demands and Opportunities

As it becomes more and more possible that an outpatient drug benefit will be enacted for Medicare recipients, spending for health services may increase even more. Whereas in the past patients may have been hesitant to seek care because of lack of ability to pay for drugs, they may now be more willing to seek care for underlying health problems. As this unmet need reaches the health care system, more and more services will be required; in addition, an increasing expectation will be placed on pharmacists to monitor the outpatient drug therapies of patients in a similar fashion as is done in LTCFs and hospitals. Increased use of services will more than likely also impact pharmacists practicing in LTCFs and health system venues.

Other Influences

Microbial Resistance

Certain infectious diseases require notification to either state departments of health or the United States Centers for Disease Control and Prevention. Thus, both state-specific patterns and general countrywide patterns of outbreaks can be monitored, and highly infectious pockets of infection can be contained. Public health epidemiology has always been challenging, but the emergence of drug-resistant strains of bacteria (e.g., tuberculosis) and the increased ability for personal mobility across countries and continents have further impeded efforts to control infectious disease outbreaks. The overuse of antibiotics has been suggested to increase expenditures for prescription drugs by $5 billion annually. Preventable nosocomial infections claim from 20,000 to 60,000 lives per year and account for $18 billion in unnecessary expenditures.

Biotechnology

The emergence of genomics, proteomics, and resultant targeted therapies will alter the landscape of therapeutics in an irreversible fashion. The development of new drugs is changing dramatically from previous models and methods. These changes in drug discovery have altered the landscape of the pharmaceutical industry, academic research, and the prescribing and use of these new drugs. No one involved in any and all related aspects to this profound change in drug discovery will be unaffected by these changes. These fundamental changes are occurring due to changes in how drugs are discovered, delivered to patients through dosage forms, and how they work in the body. Physicians and pharmacists will need to examine and reexamine what they know about drugs and their effects; payers and insurers will be under increasing pressure to control drug expenditures. Patients will use ever more costly drugs with ever narrower therapeutic uses. Legislatures at the state and federal levels will be dealing with pharmaceuticals that are more costly but more effective, if used properly, for use with governmental programs such as Medicare and Medicaid.

Patient-specific Therapies

At the turn of the 20th century, the German bacteriologist Paul Ehrlich started the quest for "magic bullets" or specific curative drugs that would provide operative control of disease. Central to this quest has been gaining an understanding of drug, "target" structure, and function; the development of drug delivery strategies to achieve controlled release; and targeting of drugs to specific sites in the body. Recent developments that are revolutionizing this field of the pharmaceutical sciences include the identification of multiple metabolic isoenzymes, the importance of transporters in drug disposition, and the emergence of pharmacogenetics and pharmacogenomics.

The science of drug formulation has moved from hand-rolled pills and individually compounded dosage forms at the start of the 20th century to an era of high-speed tablet presses and encapsulation machines that turn out thousands of dosage forms per minute. Programmable, pulsatile delivery devices that control release and target "magic bullets" to specific sites in the body are now a reality. Deoxyribonucleic acid can be delivered to cell nuclei using liposomal delivery devices. With the 21st century still in its infancy, scientists are working toward developing tissue scaffolds for regeneration of organs. These advances in technology have been achieved through the development of the science of physical pharmacy in the mid-part of the 20th century, a better understanding of physiology, and advances in molecular and cell biology.

Summary

The complexity of the United States health care system will not diminish in the future. Inevitably, the future no doubt will contain economic stressors that affect the provision of health care. For example, the inclusion of a Medicare drug benefit will increase the complicated nature of delivery and financing of health care in the United States. More, and medically complicated, patients will challenge resources and delivery mechanisms. Subsequently, because of the continued increase in health care expenditures and prescription drugs costs, pharmacoeconomics should play an ever increasing role in future health care decisions to ensure the most efficient use of sparse resources.

Annotated Bibliography

1. Anderson RN. Deaths: leading causes for 1999. National vital statistics reports. Hyattsville, MD: National Center for Health Statistics, 2001; 49(11).

   These two elaborate compendia produced by the United States Department of Health and Human Services, Centers for Disease Control and Prevention, National Center for Health Statistics detail the causes of death in America. Ranking causes of death remains a popular option for presenting mortality statistics. This ranking of mortality indicators is accompanied by a cross tabulation of statistics related to demographic factors that include gender, race, age, and International Classification of Diseases indication.

2. Cherry DK, Woodwell DA. National ambulatory medical care survey: 2000 Summary. Advance data from vital and health statistics. Hyattsville, MD: National Center for Health Statistics, 2002,. Report No. 328.

   This report described ambulatory care visits made to physician offices in the United States in 2000. Statistics are presented on selected characteristics of the physician's practice, the patient, and the visit. Highlights of trends in physician office visit use from 1997 to 2000 also are presented. During 2000, an estimated 823.5 million visits were made to physician offices in the United States, and an overall rate of 300.4 visits per 100 people. One-half of these visits were made to the patients' primary care providers. The proportion of visits with at least one prescription for cardiovascular-renal drugs, hormones, or metabolic/nutrient drugs has increased since 1997.

3. Fuchs V R. What's ahead for health insurance in the United States? N Engl J Med 2002; 346:1822–4.

   This thoughtful treatise details the shift in focus driven by major insurers to have consumers become much more accountable for health care service decisions. The accountability of consumers will ensue because of limits that will be placed on the amount of funds available for use within a certain year. This financial disincentive for patients due to limits on available payment sources will impact providers within the health care system. Whether this scheme will diminish quality, lower costs, and impact access to care remains to be seen. The concept of health insurance accountability being considered (similar to automobile, home owners, or other types of insurance) is vastly different than the social insurance concept that typically surrounds health care delivery.

4. Holmer AF. Direct-to-consumer advertising—strengthening our health care system. N Engl J Med 2002;346:526–8.

   In this article, the president of the Pharmaceutical Research and Manufacturers of America attempts to make the case for the importance and need for direct-to-consumer (DTC) advertising for prescription drugs. The author disagrees that DTC advertising bypasses physicians. He asserts that the purpose of DTC advertising is to promote a dialogue between physicians and patients. He also suggests that the physician-patient relationship is strengthened and that patient compliance can be enhanced through DTC advertising. He posits that the DTC advertising phenomenon is a result of consumers pushing to obtain more information about their health care and decisions affecting their health. He concludes by suggesting that DTC advertising is here to stay, and because of this, the United States health care system is strengthened.

5. Rosenthal MB, Berndt ER, Donohue JM, Frank RG, Epstein AM. Promotion of prescription drugs to consumers. N Engl J Med 2002;346:498–505.

   After examining data on spending for promotional purposes and sales of prescription drugs, the authors conclude that although the use of DTC advertising has grown disproportionately to other forms of promotion, it continues to account for a small proportion of total promotional efforts. They suggest that physicians must assist patients in evaluating health-related information obtain through DTC advertising.

6. Wolfe SM. Direct-to-consumer advertising—education or emotion promotion? N Engl J Med 2002;346:524–6. [Erratum: N Engl J Med 2002;346:1424.]

   The author is critical of DTC advertising in this treatise. He concludes that the education of patients—or physicians—is too important to be left to the pharmaceutical industry with its pseudoeducational campaigns designed, first and foremost, to promote drugs. He concludes that Public Health Service agencies, such as the National Institutes of Health and the Food and Drug Administration (FDA), along with medical educators in schools and residency programs, must move much more forcefully to replace tainted drug company "education" with scientifically based, useful information that will stimulate better conversations between doctors and patients and lead to true empowerment.

This series of articles (References 4-6), and/or correspondence is a prime example of the controversy surrounding the promotion of prescription drugs directly to consumers. The amount of money that is spent, the subsequent need to raise the price of pharmaceuticals, and the merit of such marketing is discussed in pointed terms. The pros and cons of the advertising are discussed and debated by impartial observers, those with a vested interest (e.g., pharmaceutical association representatives), and academicians in a free-flowing fashion. The prevalence and frequency of these advertisements (e.g., print, radio, and television) belie the argument that these advertisements are in place simply to provide education to patients.

7. Reducing the costs of poor-quality health care through responsible purchasing leadership. Midwest Business Group on Health. Chicago, 2002.

   This report details the problems pervasive in the health care system that are a result of lack of attention paid to quality control mechanisms. The report suggests that 30 percent of health care expenditures (about $390 billion annually) are made to cover the costs of poor-quality care that is provided. Furthermore, it is estimated that 33 percent of this total is paid by employers (purchasers) on behalf of covered employees or dependents. The authors estimate that 200,000 deaths are a result of because of drug misuse, and as much as $300 billion is spent because of drug misuse. The purchaser of care can impact the problem through prudent decisions about policies, coverage, and benefits allowed.

8. Heffler S, Smith S, Won G, Clemens MK, Keehan S, Zezza M. Health spending projections for 2001-2011: the latest outlook. Faster health spending growth and a slowing economy drive the health spending projection for 2001 up sharply. Health Aff (Millwood) 2002 Mar-Apr;21(2):207–18.

   This actuarially based assessment and series of projections are updated repeatedly to factor in variable that fluctuate from year to year. For example, the effects of the September 11, 2001, tragedy have impacted the consequences of many facets of daily life, including use of health care services. These projections are just that, the future cannot be predicted, however using a sound methodology, the authors equate current factors and resultant effects on health care costs with those that might occur in the future. This is a usual to use for considering the impact of variables on the percentage of the United States Gross Domestic Product (GDP) that is spent on health care.

9. Hoffman C, Pohl MB. Health insurance coverage in America. Washington, D.C.: The Kaiser Commission on Medicaid and the Uninsured, 2002.

   This report presents the disturbing, epidemic incidence of uninsured and underinsured patients currently in place in America. The number and percentage of uninsured residents has grown precipitously in the past decade despite a record period of sustained economic growth in the United States. A disturbing 16 percent of the nonelderly are uninsured in America. Four out of five of the uninsured are in working families. Not surprising, low-wage workers are at a greater risk of being uninsured as are unskilled laborers, service workers, and small business employees. Statistics are presented buttressing the argument that lack of insurance has a dramatic effect on access to care. Uninsured families with children are at a heightened level of risk due to lack of access to preventive and acute care services.

10. Report to Congress. The pharmacist workforce: a study of the supply and demand for pharmacists. Rockville, MD: Department of Health and Human Services, Health Resources and Services Administration, Bureau of Health Professions, 2000.

    This compilation of the factors affecting the pharmacist workforce is a good source of information for anyone trying to understand the present and future demand for pharmacists in the United States. Principal findings of the report include: the shortage is acute in direct patient care settings; the demand for pharmacists will likely continue unabated through the next decade; the shortage could hinder the ability of pharmacists to reduce drugs errors; despite the emergence of more than 10 new schools of pharmacy in the recent past, the shortage continues; and the shortage has impacted and intensified the competition for pharmacists with postgraduate training.

11. Spillman BC, Lubits J. The effect of longevity on spending for acute and long-term care. N Engl J Med 2002;342:1409–15.

In the United States, the effect of longevity on expenditures for acute care differs from its effect on expenditures for long-term care. Acute care expenditures, primarily for physician and hospital services increase at a reduced rate as the age of death increases. Expenditures for long-term care increase at an accelerated rate. Increases in longevity after 65 years of age may result in greater spending for long-term care, but the number of elderly people has more important effect on total spending.

12. Fincham JE. Nicotine addiction. In Popovich N, ed. Handbook of Nonprescription

Drugs, 13th ed. Washington, D.C.: American Pharmaceutical Association, 2002, 997–1014.

More than 500,000 deaths occur annually in the United States due to tobacco-related sequelae. A national health objective for the year 2010 is to reduce cigarette smoking from a level of 24 percent in 1998 to 12 percent of the adult population. Despite this aggressive goal, cigarette smoking among adults in the United States in 1999 was estimated to be 23.5 percent. Even though advances have been made in curtailing the increase in smoking prevalence, cigarette smoking remains the chief avoidable cause of death in the United States. Higher levels of smoking occur with adults between 18 and 24 years of age with a level of 27.9 percent, and the lowest level reported for those older than 65 years of age with a rate of 10.6 percent. More men than women smoke, and those achieving higher levels of education smoke less than those with lower education levels. Significant impacts on smoking behavior must occur if this goal is to be reached.

Self-Assessment Questions

1. If patients pay a flat $5 for each generic prescription they have filled in a pharmacy as part of their pharmacy health benefit, this is classified as a which one of the following?
   A. Deductible.
   B. Copayment.
   C. Coinsurance.
   D. Maximum allowable cost product.

2. In the public sector (in the Medicaid program), payment for outpatient prescription drugs is which one of the following?
   A. Mandatory.
   B. Subject to pharmacy benefit manager (PBM) approval.
   C. Optional.
   D. Never covered.

3. In pharmacy third-party programs, which one of the following is the most common reimbursement method of paying pharmacies?
   A. The acquisition cost of the product dispensed.
   B. A dispensing or professional fee.
   C. Acquisition cost of the product dispensed plus a dispensing or professional fee equals the reimbursement.
   D. Acquisition cost of the product dispensed minus a dispensing or professional fee plus a dollar amount to be determined.

4. Which one of the following statements is true concerning the goals of PBMs in the United States health care system?
   A. Pharmacists have universally and positively accepted PBMs as a vital means to reduce drug costs in the United States health care system.
   B. Pharmacy benefit managers attempt to reduce expenditures for pharmaceuticals through reducing reimbursement levels for pharmacies.
   C. Each of the national pharmacy organizations in the United States has endorsed PBMs as playing the pivotal role in any Medicare outpatient drug benefit program.
   D. Up to this point, state Medicaid programs in the U.S have only used PBMs to reduce drug costs.

5. Which one of the following populations represents the largest group of users of long-term care facilities (LTCFs)?
   A. Pediatric (0–4 years).
   B. Adolescent populations (13–17 years).
   C. Young and middle-aged adults (24–65 years).
   D. Elderly (age 65 and older).

6. After reviewing the available drugs to treat depression in a managed care formulary, you come across the notation prior approval (PA) next to a listing. That notation means which one of the following to you?
   A. The drug is never covered in the plan.
   B. The drug requires a step therapy before use.
   C. There is a generic substitute available for the drug.
   D. The use of the drug must be approved by plan personnel before use.

7. When considering the following listings along side a series of drugs in a managed care formulary, which one of the following drugs is the least expensive?
   A. Drug A, $.
   B. Drug B, $$.
   C. Drug C, $$$.
   D. Drug D, $$$$.

8. Which one of the following represents how many deaths per year that occur in the United States due to smoking-related morbidity?

   A. More than 500,000.
   B. More than 5 million.
   C. More than 50 million.
   D. Less than 200,000.

9. Of the types of hospitals in the United States, which one of the following is the largest from the standpoint of numbers of facilities?

   A. General.
   B. Specialty.
   C. Psychiatric.
   D. Rehabilitation.

10. In which one of the following segments is a 78-year-old patient classified?

    A. Middle aged.
    B. Young old age.
    C. Middle old age.
    D. Old old age.

TYPES OF ECONOMIC AND HUMANISTIC OUTCOMES ASSESSMENTS

Kathleen M. Bungay, Pharm.D.;
and Lisa A. Sanchez, Pharm.D.

Outline

Frequent misuse and misunderstandings exist regarding what pharmacoeconomics is and what it encompasses. This chapter will assist readers in clarifying their understanding of pharmacoeconomics and lead to an increased understanding of its principles, methods, and applications.

I. Definitions
   A. Pharmacoeconomics—typically defined as the description and analysis of the costs and consequences of pharmaceuticals and pharmaceutical services and its effects on individuals, health care systems, and society. These costs and consequences typically include both economic and humanistic assessments.
      1. A division of outcomes research. However, not all outcomes research is pharmacoeconomic research.
   B. Outcomes research—more broadly defined as studies that attempt to identify, measure, and evaluate the end results of health care services in general; includes not only clinical effects, but also economic and humanistic outcomes such as functional status, well-being, and satisfaction with care. Proponents of outcomes research believe that all three types of outcomes should be measured. (Reference: Figure 1. Components of Contemporary Clinical Decision Making; Reference: Table 1. Some Economic and Humanistic Pharmacoeconomic Evaluations)

II. A proposed model for outcomes evaluations
   A. Proposed that evaluation of drug therapy and related services should always include assessments of economic, clinical, and humanistic outcomes.
   B. The economic, clinical, and humanistic outcome (ECHO) model organizes outcomes of medical care along three general dimensions: clinical, economic, and humanistic.
      1. Economic outcomes—direct, indirect, and intangible costs compared with the consequences of medical treatment alternatives.
      2. Clinical outcomes—medical events that occur as a result of disease or treatment (outside the scope of this program).
      3. Humanistic outcomes—consequences of disease or treatment on patient functional status, or quality of life, measured along several dimensions, e.g., physical functioning, social functioning, general health perceptions and well-being. (Reference: Figure 2. The Conceptual Model: Economic, Clinical, and Humanistic Outcome [ECHO] Model)
   C. The ECHO model recognizes intermediary outcomes
      1. Economic outcomes have intermediaries introduced from the clinical and humanistic side of the model.
         a. From the clinical side are direct costs of medical care associated with each treatment, not just the direct cost of the pharmaceutical products; laboratory testing, emergency department visits, inpatient hospitalizations, and costs of retreatment from product failure also included.
         b. From humanistic side are the indirect, or productivity costs associated with the time lost from work.

        c. Direct nonmedical costs for transportation to the hospital, or physicians office for treatment also included.
    2. Humanistic outcomes have intermediaries that affect the individual's subjective evaluation of outcomes.
        a. Examples of the intermediaries are listed here and in Figure 3: side effects; efficacy/effectiveness; patient's willingness or ability to pay; adherence to drug regimen (compliance); patient's knowledge; drug dosing schedules. (Reference: Figure 3. Alternative conceptualizations of the relationship between therapeutic interventions and outcomes)

III. Economic outcomes assessment
  A. Costs
    1. Costs—the resources consumed by a program or treatment alternative. Costs must be identified, relevant to the perspective(s) chosen, prior to measurement and comparison.
        a. Direct medical costs—costs incurred for medical products and services used for the prevention, detection, and treatment of a disease.
            i. Examples: hospitalization, drugs, laboratory testing, supplies
                a) Fixed costs represent overhead costs
                b) Variable costs—vary as a function of volume
        b. Direct nonmedical costs—costs for nonmedical services that are the result of illness or disease, but do not involve purchasing medical services.
            i. Examples: special food, transportation for health care, family care
        c. Indirect costs—costs of morbidity and mortality resulting from illness or disease.
            i. Examples: lost productivity, premature death
                a) Human capital method
                b) Willingness to pay
        d. Intangible costs—costs of pain, suffering, grief, and other nonfinancial outcomes of disease and medical care.
        e. Incremental costs—additional costs incurred to obtain an additional unit of benefit from an alternative strategy.
        f. Opportunity costs—money spent on one resource that cannot be spent for other purposes; the value of the next best use that is forgone.
  B. Consequences
    1. Positive versus negative
        a. Full evaluations must measure both desirable and undesirable outcomes.
    2. Intermediate versus final
        a. Intermediate outcomes are commonly used to demonstrate clinical efficacy because their usage reduces the costs and time required to conduct a clinical trial.
    3. Balancing costs and consequences is the essence of pharmacoeconomic evaluation.
  C. Perspectives: The pharmacoeconomic question being asked usually determines the appropriate perspective or viewpoint to be used. (Reference: Figure 4. Potential Perspectives for Pharmacoeconomic Evaluations)
    1. Patient—the ultimate consumer of health care services. Costs, from patients' perspective, are essentially what they pay for a product or service (the portion not covered by insurance).
    2. Provider—the health care professional or care organization; costs from this perspective are the actual costs of providing a product or service, regardless of the charge.
    3. Payer—insurers, government, or employers; the cost to the payer are the charges for health care products and services allowed (reimbursed) by the payer.
    4. Society—costs include patient morbidity and mortality costs, and the overall costs of giving and receiving medical care.
    5. Controversy in choosing perspective
        a. Many researchers assert that society is the best perspective for all economic evaluations.
  D. Exercise 3: Cost-identification
  E. Misuse of pharmacoeconomic terms: Many have demonstrated that pharmacoeconomic terminologies are commonly misused.
  F. Economic Assessments: The basic task of economic evaluations is to identify, measure, value, and compare the costs and consequences of the alternatives being considered.
    1. Partial economic evaluation include a simple descriptive tabulation of outcomes or resources consumed.
    2. Full economic evaluation helps to assess the economic benefit of a program, service, or treatment.
        a. Requires two distinguishing features of economic evaluation.
            i. Comparison of two or more treatment alternatives.
            ii. Both costs and consequences of the alternatives are examined.
        b. Limitations of full economic analyses. (Reference: Table 2. Common Economic Evaluation Methodologies)
    3. Cost of illness (COI)

   a. Definition—involves identifying all the direct and indirect costs of a particular disease or illness within a health care system.
   b. Yields a total cost of a disease that can be compared to the cost of implementing a prevention or treatment strategy.
4. Cost-minimization analysis (CMA)
   a. Definition—compares the costs of two or more treatment alternatives that have a demonstrated equivalence in therapeutic outcome (i.e., therapeutically equivalent alternatives).
   b. Results expressed as a total cost per treatment alternative; allows for separate examination of the relevant cost components.
   c. Used to determine the least costly alternative.
5. Cost-benefit analysis (CBA)
   a. Definition—method to compare the costs and benefits of treatment alternatives or programs; costs and benefits expressed in monetary terms.
   b. Results are expressed as either a cost-to-benefit ratio, or as the net cost or benefit.
   c. Example: if cost for treatment is $100 and value of outcome of treatment is $1000, cost-benefit ratio is: benefit ÷ cost = $1000 ÷ $100 = 10/1 benefit of $1 million and cost of $100,000 also yields cost-benefit ratio of 10/1
   d. Used to compare treatment alternatives or programs, particularly when deciding how to allocate scarce resources.
6. Cost-effectiveness analysis (CEA)
   a. Definition—method to compare treatment alternatives, or programs where cost is measured in monetary terms and consequences in units of effectiveness or natural units.
      i. May be less expensive, and at least as effective as the comparator.
      ii. May be more expensive while providing an additional benefit worth the additional cost.
      iii. May be less expensive and less effective when the extra benefit is not worth the extra cost.
   b. Results are expressed as average cost-effectiveness ratios, or as the incremental cost of using one alternative over another.
   c. For example: drug A has 90 percent cure rate, drug B has 95 percent cure rate; drug A costs $50,000 to treat 100 patients, drug B costs $100,000 to treat 100 patients
   d. Calculation of cost-effectiveness ratios:
      drug A costs $50,000/100 patients ÷ 90 cures/100 patients = $555/cure
      drug B costs $100,000/100 patients ÷ 95 cures/100 patients = $1053/cure
   e. Calculation of incremental cost-effectiveness ratio:
      $100,000 - $50,000
      95 cures - 90 cures
      = $10,000/additional cure with drug B
   f. Used to compare competing programs or treatment alternatives that differ in therapeutic outcome
7. Cost-utility analysis (CUA)
   a. Definition—method to compare treatment alternatives or programs where costs are measured in monetary terms and outcome is expressed in terms of patient preferences or quality of life.
   b. Results are expressed as dollars per quality-adjusted life-year (QALY) gained, or some other patient-weighted utility measure.
   c. Used to compare treatments or programs using terms of patient preference, or quality of health care, or when outcomes cannot be expressed in monetary terms.

G. Exercise 4: Selection of Economic Evaluation Methods

IV. Techniques for analysis

A. Discounting
1. Definition—an analysis that adjusts (reduces) future costs and consequences to reflect present fiscal value.
2. Discounting costs—based on the time value of money; because the value of money decreases over time, future costs must be adjusted (discounted) to present time values.
3. Discount rate—discount rate of 3–8 percent should be used (often reflective of current interest rates used by banking institutions).

B. Sensitivity analysis
1. Definition—an analysis that tests robustness of study conclusions; sensitive variables (or assumptions) are varied over a range of plausible results and the impact on study results is observed.
2. Variables include percent efficacy (or effectiveness), incidence of specific adverse drug reactions, and dominant costs.

C. Decision analysis
1. Definition—an explicit, quantitative, and prescriptive approach to choosing between competing treatment alternatives or programs.

2. Tool used in decision analysis is a decision tree; allows for the graphic presentation of treatment alternatives, outcomes, and probabilities. (Reference: Figure 5. Decision Tree)

D. Incremental cost analysis

1. Definition—an analysis that examines the extra cost of one program or treatment alternative relative to the additional effect provided by that alternative.
2. formula: $\frac{\text{Cost B} - \text{Cost A}}{\text{Effect B} - \text{Effect A}}$

V. Applied Pharmacoeconomics

A. Definition—putting pharmacoeconomic principles, methods and theories into practice to assess the value of pharmaceutical products and services used in "real-world" practice settings.

B. Primary application—to inform local decision making.

1. Specific applications of economic assessments
   a. Formulary management
   b. Clinical guidelines
   c. Drug use policies
   d. Service or program evaluation
   e. Individual patient treatment decisions

VI. Humanistic Outcomes Assessment

A. Background

1. Measurement of health
   a. Case study

B. Evolution of today's health status outcome measures

1. During the 1940s, physicians first began to measure patient functioning;
   a. Karnofsky Functional Status for Patients with Cancer
   b. New York Heart Association Classification
2. When social science methods and clinical expertise came together in the 1970s, the first modern health-status questionnaires emerged.
   a. Quality of Well-Being Scale,
   b. Sickness Impact Profile,
   c. Health Perceptions Questionnaire,
   d. Older Americans Resources and Services (OARS) questionnaire
3. The next generation developed in the 1980s and 90s
   a. Health Insurance Experiment (HIE) health surveys
   b. Duke-UNC Health Profiles
   c. Nottingham Health Profile
   d. Medical Outcomes Study health surveys, including the SF- 36 Health Survey
4. Variations in medical care in small areas
   a. Typically traced to the work of John Wennberg, who uncovered a phenomenon known as small-area variation.
   b. Wennberg and colleagues noticed large disparities in the rates of various medical procedures in different geographic areas.
5. The Rand HIE
   a. In 1990, health expenditures accounted for 12.4 percent of GNP, whereas that proportion was 4 percent in 1980, and the rate of growth was exceeding the rate of inflation, questions surfaced.
   b. This quandary prompted the federal government to support a large-scale controlled trial, now known as HIE.
      i. One purpose of the HIE was to learn whether the direct cost of medical care, when borne by consumers, affects their health.
      ii. Presented one of the first major challenges for measuring health status.
      iii. A consequence of this challenge resulted in one of the most extensive applications of psychometric theory and methods (long used in educational testing), to the development and refinement of health status surveys.
      iv. The measurement goal in the HIE was to construct the best possible scales for measuring a broad array of functioning and well-being concepts.
      v. HIE demonstrated the potential of scales, constructed from self-administered surveys, as reliable and valid tools for assessing changes in health status.
      vi. It left two questions unanswered:
         a) Can methods of data collection and scale construction work in sicker and older populations?
         b) Could scales that are more efficient be constructed?

vii. The answer to these questions was the challenge accepted by the Medical Outcomes Study (MOS) investigators.

6. Medical Outcomes Study
   a. Two-year observational study designed to help understand how specific components of the health care system affected the outcomes of care.
   b. Original purpose was to develop more practical tools for monitoring patient outcomes, and their determinants, in routine practice using state-of-the-art psychometric techniques.
7. Agency for Health Care Policy and Research (AHCPR)/Agency for Healthcare Research and Quality (AHRQ)
   a. To enhance the quality, appropriateness, and effectiveness of health care services and access to services, the federal government established AHCPR (Omnibus Budget Reconciliation Act of 1989).
      i. The act, sometimes referred to as the Patient Outcomes Research Act, called for the establishment of a broad-based, patient-centered outcomes research program.
   b. In 1999, the agency was reauthorized as AHRQ.

C. Evaluating the Quality of Care
   1. Structure denotes the attributes of the settings in which care occurs. Evaluations of structure address the relatively stable characteristics of the providers of care, of the tools and resources they have at their disposal, and of the physical and organizational settings in which they work.
   2. Process of care denotes what is actually done in giving and receiving care. It includes the patient's activities in seeking care and carrying it out, as well as the practitioner's activities in making a diagnosis and recommending, or implementing, treatment.
   3. Outcomes of care denote the effects of care on the health status of patients and populations. Improvements in patients' knowledge and salutary changes in patients' behaviors are included under a broad definition of health status, and so is the degree of each patient's satisfaction with care.

D. Definitions
   1. Quality of Life
      a. Quality of life refers to an evaluation of all aspects of our lives, including where and how we live, how we play, and how we work.
   2. Health
      a. Health is one of 12 domains of life to be considered when researching and evaluating overall quality of life.
      b. The other 11 domains are listed in Table 3 and include: community; education; family life; friendships; housing; marriage; nation; neighborhood; self; standard of living; and work.
   3. Health-related quality of life
      a. Encompasses only those aspects of life that are dominated, or significantly influenced by personal health or activities performed to maintain, or improve health.
      b. Is a specifically focused area of investigation within the larger field of health services and quality-of-life research. Standardized questionnaires are used to capture health-related quality-of-life data.
      c. The term health-related quality of life was adopted by researchers to set their research apart from the more global concept of quality of life, and to more accurately reflect the scope of their research.

E. Measurement
   1. Measurement is a set of numbers or rules used to quantify a physical attribute. Examples of measurement devices are rulers, thermometers, and scales.
   2. Health has distinct components that must be measured and interpreted individually to fully understand health at a given time, as well as changes over time.
      a. Clues about the components are found in the definitions of health offered by the World Health Organization, as well as in dictionaries.
         i. The World Health Organization has defined health as a state of complete physical, social, and mental well-being, not merely the absence of disease or infirmity.
         ii. Dictionary definitions also identify both physical and mental dimensions of health. The former pertains to the body and bodily needs, the latter to the mind and, particularly, to the emotional and intellectual status of the individual.
         iii. Health connotes completeness, where nothing is missing from the person; it also connotes proper function, where all is working efficiently. The dictionary also suggests well-being, soundness, and vitality as important components of health.
      b. Both World Health Organization and dictionary definitions provide precedents for the dimensionality of health and, specifically, for the distinction between physical and mental health.
      c. Two features of these definitions are crucial
         i. The dimensionality of health.
         ii. The existence of a full range of health states, ranging from disease to well-being.
   3. Range of measurement

    a. Many measurement scales artificially restrict the range of individual differences enumerated. Consistent with a disease orientation, most disease-specific measures emphasize the negative end of the health continuum.
    b. Figure 7 illustrates how both the positive and negative ends of the range might be considered when evaluating mental health status.

F. Measurement strategy
  1. To provide an assessment of health-related quality of life, one of three approaches is usually taken.
    a. Focus on general health status
    b. Disease-specific-focused on specific aspects of the disease under study.
    c. Both generic and disease specific.
  2. Though measurement strategies may be slightly different, there are some commonly agreed upon and frequently measured general health concepts.
    a. Physical functioning
    b. Mental functioning
    c. Social and role functioning
    d. General health perceptions

G. General health status measures
  1. Not disease or disorder specific.
  2. Relevant to all ages, races, sexes, and socioeconomic backgrounds.
  3. Permit examination of treatment benefits in comparable units.
  4. Advantages
    a. Used for monitoring patients with more than one condition.
    b. Can compare patients with different conditions by providing a common yardstick.
    c. Used to assess the relative benefits of different treatments.
    d. The same measures can be appropriately applied to both general (well) and patient (sick) populations; can be used with people of any age, gender, or race.
  5. Disadvantages
    a. Do not cover areas of health status that are important to particular groups of patients who may experience specific improvements or disabilities in functioning due to their disease state.
    b. Need to use additional questionnaires for disease- or condition-specific set of questions.
    c. Not specific to any particular disease state; not able to capture symptoms or domains specifically related to one disease state (e.g., dexterity with arthritis). (Reference: Table 5 lists these key health concepts and indicates how they might be assessed)

VII. Components Common to Many General Health Status Measures

A. Physical functioning
  1. Physical functioning as it relates to health-related quality-of-life assessment typically refers to the limitations, or disability, experienced by the patient over a defined period.
  2. Questions focus on observable and important physical limitations easily noticed and evaluated by the patient or observer.

B. Social and Role Functioning
  1. Social functioning
    a. Social functioning is defined as the ability to develop, maintain, and nurture mature social relationships.
      i. Frequency of social contacts.
      ii. Nature of those contacts within the social network or community.
  2. Role functioning
    a. Concerned with the impact health has on a person's ability to meet the demands of that person's normal life role. Work for pay, homemaking duties, and schoolwork are all covered by questions asking about this concept.
    b. Identify everyday role situations or activities that can be directly affected or limited by disease, illness, or treatment.
    c. Whereas most role limitations are due to physical health problems, role limitations are observed both in the presence, and in the absence of, physical limitations.

C. Mental Health
  1. Disease often affects behavioral, as well as physical aspects of a person's life. General health status assessments, therefore, usually include questions covering aspects of psychological health.

D. General Health Perceptions
  1. General health perceptions address the person's overall beliefs and evaluations about his or her health.

VIII. Disease-Specific Health Status Instruments

A. Some limitations or problems with patients' health are unique to their specific disease state.

B. Batteries of questions were designed for use with specific patient populations, and are used to supplement a general health status instrument.
C. These more narrowly focused disease-specific measures request detailed information about the impact a specific disease, and its treatment, have on the patient, from the patient's perspective.
D. In addition, using disease-specific measures allows inclusion of questions of specific interest.
E. Among some specific areas previously investigated with disease-specific questionnaires are sexual functioning, nausea and vomiting, pain, cancer, arthritis, epilepsy, HIV infection, anxiety and depression, asthma, and rhinitis.

IX. Psychometric Theory
A. The underlying theory that supports the design of health surveys, consisting of scales measuring attributes of a person or a population's health.
B. Same theories that support the creation of educational measurements (e.g., Standardized Achievement Tests).
C. A person who studies these theories and conducts research or measurement of such attributes as intelligence, pain, mental well-being, or functioning is usually a doctorate level research psychologist and can be known as a psychometrician.
D. In recent years has produced, in the health sciences literature devoted to measuring health status, a daunting array of already available scales.
E. Perhaps the most common error committed by clinical researchers is to dismiss the existing scales too lightly, and embark on the development of a new instrument with an unjustifiably optimistic and naïve expectation that they can do better.
F. A comprehensive set of standards, widely used in the assessment of psychology and education, is the manual called Standards for Educational and Psychological Tests, published by the American Psychological Association (1974).

X. Psychometric Considerations
A. Psychometrics is the science of testing questionnaires to measure attributes of individuals.
B. It is used in the field of health assessment to translate people's behavior, feelings, and personal evaluations into quantifiable data.
C. These data, once captured, must be both relevant and correct if they are to provide useful insights into health-related quality of life.
   1. Reliability—the relationship between true variation and random error. Evaluations assess the consistency and repeatability of measurement.
   2. Validity—refers to the extent to which differences in scale scores reflect the true differences in the individuals studied.
   3. Useful scales must be sensitive to change, and be accepted by the investigators and respondents.

XI. Use of Patient-Reported Health Status
A. Monitoring the health of populations.
B. Evaluating health care policy.
C. Conducting clinical trials of alternative treatment.
D. Designing systems for monitoring and improving health care outcomes.
E. Individual Patient Care Decisions
   1. Controversies in using health status assessments.
   2. Contributions of technology and modern test theory to the use of health status instruments.
   3. Advances in using health status assessments for individual patient care decisions.
      a. Standardized measures capturing patient perspectives are likely to become more acceptable as a piece of evidence of which providers and their patients can make decisions about treatment and a treatment's efficacy.
      b. Mature theoretical models, sophisticated measurement techniques, and enhanced technology for use in measurement, make the routine use of individual patient results in their own care more promising than ever before.
   4. Two practical concerns of the critics of use of health-related quality-of-life assessments in individual patient care are:
      a. Respondent burden and;
      b. Reliability of scores obtained from shorter questionnaires.
   5. Modern test theory offers the potential for individualized, comparable assessments for the careful examination and application of different health status measures.
      a. One such theory is Item Response Theory (IRT). Researchers report that IRT has a number of potential advantages over the currently used Classical Test Theory in assessing self-reported health outcomes.
      b. Applications of the IRT models are ideally suited for implementing computer adaptive testing. IRT methods are also reported to be helpful in developing better health outcome measures, and in assessing change over time.

6. Patients increasingly have more access to computer technology. It is becoming more practical to use assessments using a computer.
    a. Patients answering questions about a health status concept using dynamic assessment technology are requested only to complete the number of questions needed (minimizes response burden) to establish a reliable estimate.
    b. The resulting scores for an individual are estimated to meet the clinical measures of precision.

XII. Case Study Continued

XIII. Patient Satisfaction

A. Another outcome suggested by a popular quality-of-care model for how to evaluate the quality of health care is that of patient satisfaction.

B. Empirical studies show that patients' expressions of dissatisfaction are potent predictors of disenrollment from a physician or a health plan.

C. A consumer's evaluation of the care received, known as consumer evaluation or patient satisfaction, is both similar and different from a patient's assessment of health status.
    1. The same psychometric techniques are used to obtain information, and to evaluate the accuracy of the information.
    2. The science of obtaining the information is similar.
    3. The information is unique and different from what is asked about health status.
    4. Both reports and ratings are used in patient satisfaction surveys.
        a. Reports are descriptions.
        b. Ratings are evaluations that require a judgment by the evaluator (patient).

D. There are many different patient satisfaction surveys available.
    1. Attributes that are commonly evaluated, regardless of the care setting include:
        a. The clinician's scientific knowledge and skill;
        b. The quality of clinician-patient communications;
        c. The provision of humane interpersonal treatment;
        d. And the degree of the patient's trust in the care provider.

E. One setting in which patient satisfaction surveys are becoming increasingly important is that of primary care.
    1. Four distinguishing and shared multiple characteristics are considered essential and unique to this area of health care and provide attributes that can be evaluated by patients. These characteristics include:
        a. Accessibility to care;
        b. Continuity of care;
        c. The comprehensiveness of care and;
        d. How well a patient's care is integrated into a coherent and continuing whole.

XIV Other Measures of Outcomes

A. The concept of work functioning must be included as an outcome to meet the evaluation needs of employers, who have become a significant form in health care.

B. The ability to quantify the constituent parts of the losses in work productivity is growing in importance, and will undoubtedly be an important measured health domain.

XV. Conclusion

Learning Objectives

1. Identify and define the terminology and basic components of health economics, outcomes research, and pharmacoeconomics.
2. Differentiate between full and partial economic evaluations.
3. Define direct, indirect, intangible, incremental, and opportunity costs, and classify them based on the perspective taken.
4. Discuss the controversies related to the perspective taken for an economic analysis.
5. Discuss the controversies related to discounting costs and benefits.
6. Differentiate between the application of outcomes research results to system decisions and individualization of patient therapy.
7. Discuss the identification and measurement of appropriate outcomes in health economics research.
8. Understand the evolution and scientific basis for the use of patient self-reported health status assessments.
9. Characterize contemporary developments in content, measurement, and uses of personal health measures.
10. Distinguish between population-based and individual level measures of health.
11. Understand the basic concepts underlying the measurement of health-related quality of life.
12. Differentiate between generic and disease-specific health-related quality-of-life instruments.
13. Discuss uses of health status assessments with other health care professionals.
14. Understand the technological improvements going on in the field of health status measurement.

Abbreviations in this chapter

ACER	Average cost-effectiveness ratio
AHCPR	Agency for Health Care Policy and Research
AHRQ	Agency for Healthcare Research and Quality
CBA	Cost-benefit analysis
CEA	Cost-effectiveness analysis
COI	Cost of illness
CMA	Cost-minimization analysis
CUA	Cost-utility analysis
ECHO	Economic, clinical, humanistic outcomes
HIE	Health Insurance Experiment
HRQOL	Health-related quality of life
IRT	Item Response Theory
MOS	Medical Outcomes Study
MOS SF-36	Medical Outcomes Study, short form, 36 items
OARS	Older Americans Resources and Services
QALY	Quality-adjusted life-year

Introduction

Frequent misuse of pharmacoeconomic terms abounds. Misconceptions, such as pharmacoeconomics equals cost-containment, and pharmacoeconomics compromises clinical decision making, have lead to apprehension by many health care professionals as they evaluate the economic and humanistic outcomes of health care products and services. Pharmacoeconomics is not about determining the cheapest health care alternatives, but is about determining those alternatives that provide the best health care outcome per dollar spent. This chapter should assist in clarifying many of these misconceptions, leading to an increased understanding of pharmacoeconomic principles, methods, and its application to health care today.

Definitions

Pharmacoeconomics typically is defined as the description and analysis of the costs and consequences of pharmaceuticals and pharmaceutical services, and its impact on individuals, health care systems, and society. Pharmacoeconomics is a division of outcomes research and, typically, addresses both economic and humanistic outcomes. However, not all outcomes research is pharmacoeconomic research.

Outcomes research is more broadly defined as studies that attempt to identify, measure, and evaluate the end results of health care services. As depicted in Figure 1, not only clinical effects, but also economic and humanistic outcomes are included. Thus, proponents of outcomes research believe in measuring, not only the clinical and cost impacts of health care, but also the outcomes that take the patient's perspective into account. Some of the economic and humanistic outcomes to be addressed are listed in Table 1.

Economic, Clinical, and Humanistic Outcomes Model

It has been proposed that the evaluation of drug therapy and related services should include an assessment of economic, clinical, and humanistic outcomes (ECHO) model

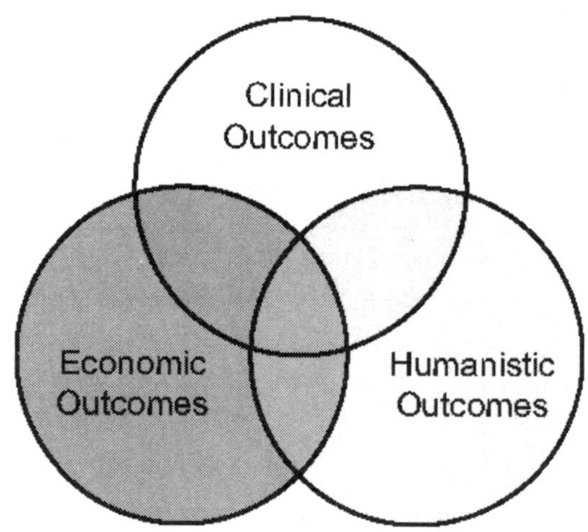

Figure 1. Components of Contemporary Clinical Decision-Making

Table 1. Some Economic and Humanistic Pharmacoeconomic Evaluations

Economic Evaluations	Humanistic Evaluations
Cost-of-illness	Quality of Life
Cost-minimization analysis	Patient preferences
Cost-benefit analysis	Patient Satisfaction
Cost-effectiveness analysis	Willingness-to-pay
Cost-utility analysis	

(see Reference 13). In their proposed model, the ECHO model, depicted in Figure 2, it is assumed that the outcomes of medical care can be classified along these three dimension. Clinical outcomes are defined as medical events that occur as a result of disease or treatment. Economic outcomes are defined as direct, indirect, and intangible costs, compared with the consequences of medical treatment alternatives. Humanistic outcomes are defined as the consequences of disease or treatment on patient functional status, or quality of life. Multiple variables important for understanding the value of alternatives exist within each type of outcome. The authors propose that all three of these outcomes need to be balanced simultaneously to assess value.

Some of the many variables that need to be balanced are intermediate outcomes, or intermediaries. The ECHO model proposes some examples of intermediaries. The economic outcomes have intermediaries introduced from the clinical and humanistic side of the model. The clinical outcomes have intermediaries introduced from the direct costs of medical care associated with each treatment. These intermediaries include the costs of laboratory testing, emergency department visits and inpatient hospitalizations, and costs of retreatment from product failures. As you can see, these costs are more than just the direct costs of pharmaceutical products. Direct nonmedical costs for transportation to the hospital or physician's office for treatment also must be included. Humanistic outcomes have intermediaries, including indirect costs such as time lost from work, that must be added.

Additional humanistic intermediaries are proposed. Examples of these intermediaries include adverse reactions, efficacy or effectiveness of a drug, the patients' willingness or ability to pay, patient compliance, patient knowledge, and dosing requirements such as frequency of administration. Figure 3 depicts a suggested framework for the relationship between the choice of a therapeutic agent and humanistic outcome. Before improvements in health status and patient satisfaction were widely recognized as goals of therapy, the decision about the success of an intervention was based on a favorable balance between the effectiveness and the safety from the clinician's point of view. In this model, effectiveness and safety are no longer the only factors considered to evaluate success. The effects of symptom

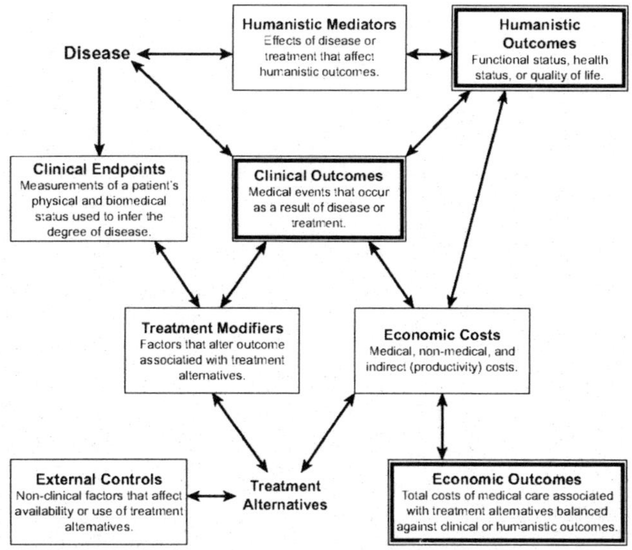

Figure 2. The Conceptual Model: Economic, Clinical, and Humanistic Outcomes (ECHO) Model.
Reprinted with permission from Kozma CM, Reeder CE, Shulz RM. Economic, clinical, and humanistic outcomes: a planning model for pharmacoeconomic research. Clin Ther 1993;15:1121–32.

relief and adverse events, from the patient's perspective, become the main measure of success. For example, even though selective serotonin-reuptake inhibitors are shown to be very effective in the treatment of depression, some patients report insomnia and nightmares. On a depression rating scale, the patient may achieve a score that indicates relief from the symptoms of depression. Patients may simultaneously report in a self-administered health-related quality-of-life (HRQOL) questionnaire they have low vitality and low scores in role-functioning, both indicating poor functioning from the patient's viewpoint. When the patient is questioned about the low scores, it could be discovered that she is a single parent who needs to maintain a job to support her children. Her job requires concentration and alertness during the day, and the drug, although effective and seemingly safe, interferes with her daily functioning, and what is important to her.

Another intermediate factor is the patient's ability, or willingness, to pay for the prescribed therapy. The patient's perception of the effectiveness, or experience, of side effects on health status, as well as financial constraints, can influence willingness to continue to purchase the drug. Nonadherence to therapy, a significant problem with drugs effectiveness, can actually have a positive effect on functional health status as perceived by the patient. The relationship of compliance to outcomes is of growing importance as the study of health status and patient satisfaction matures. It is impossible to establish a relationship between a therapeutic intervention, and its outcome, without the assurance that the patient has taken the prescribed therapy. In addition to willingness to pay and compling, patients' knowledge of their therapy and the dosing schedule influence the humanistic outcomes and each other. Even though many of these relationships are

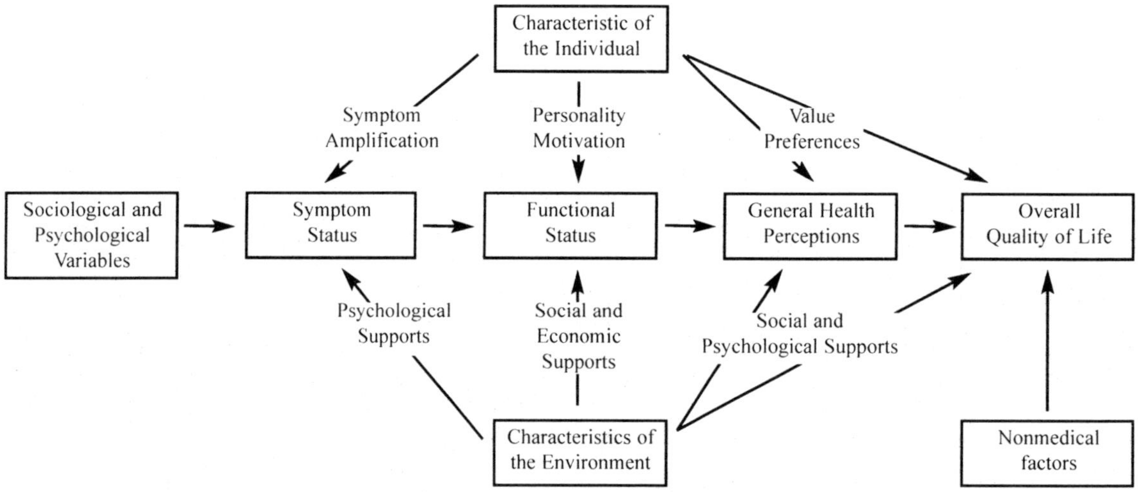

Figure 3. Relationships among measures of patient outcome in a HRQOL conceptual model.
Wilson IB, Cleary PD. Linking clinical variables with health-related quality of life. A conceptual model of patient outcomes. JAMA 1995;273(1):59–65. Reprinted with permission.

studied, there is much room for advancement in understanding the relationships of each of these intermediate variables to humanistic outcomes.

The methods of pharmacoeconomic evaluation strive to assess the value of pharmaceutical products and services, and incorporate several types of outcomes, including those of a clinical, economic, and humanistic nature, in assessing this value to the health care system. This series focuses on the assessment of economic and humanistic outcomes and its applications to patient care. The assessment of clinical outcomes is beyond the scope of the series, and will be addressed in global terms only.

Costs

Traditional cost-containment measures are not always synonymous with improved patient care. Thus, attention has turned toward demonstrating the value of health care. It is critical that the health care products and services used in today's institutions and organizations achieve the highest possible benefit from the dollars spent. Quantification of the value of health care products and services, especially pharmaceuticals, is critical today.

Before a full discussion of the methods of economic evaluation can take place, it is important to examine closely the various categories of costs and consequences that can be included in an economic evaluation. A full evaluation of the relevant costs and consequences differentiates pharmacoeconomics from traditional cost-containment strategies and drug use evaluations. Costs are defined as the value of the resources consumed by a program or treatment alternative. Consequences are defined as the effects, outputs, and outcomes of the program or treatment alternative. This section focuses on identifying, measuring, and comparing the costs, or economic outcomes of health care interventions.

A comparison of two or more treatment alternatives should extend beyond a simple comparison of drug acquisition costs. Cost categories that need to be considered include direct, indirect, and intangible costs. Other costs often discussed in pharmacoeconomic evaluations include opportunity and incremental costs. Including these various cost categories, when appropriate, will provide a more accurate estimate of the total economic impact of a health care program, or treatment alternative, on a specific population, organization, or patient. Each of these types of cost categories are discussed in greater detail.

Direct Costs

Direct costs are the resources consumed in the prevention, detection, or treatment of a disease or illness. These costs can be divided into direct medical and direct nonmedical costs. Direct medical costs quantify the fundamental transactions associated with medical care, and are the costs that contribute to the portion of gross national product spent on health care. An example of costs associated directly with health care interventions include hospitalizations, drugs, medical supplies and equipment, laboratory and diagnostic testing, and physician visits.

Direct medical costs can be further subdivided into fixed and variable costs. Fixed costs represent the overhead costs that are relatively constant and not readily influenced at the treatment level. Thus, they are typically not included in most pharmacoeconomic evaluations. Some examples of fixed costs are those incurred for heat, rent, and lighting. Variable costs, on the other hand, vary as a function of volume and include drugs, fees for a professional service, and supplies. Thus, as a greater number of services are used, more funding must be consumed to provide these services. Shifts in variable costs are particularly important as a means of assessing the cost-effectiveness of a treatment alternative.

Some controversy exists as to whether personnel costs should be considered as fixed or variable costs. For example, in a hospital setting, one might ask whether switching from a treatment that requires administration 4 times daily to one administered once daily truly saves time for pharmacy technicians, pharmacists, and nurses. Some argue that staffing of these personnel is relatively constant, regardless of the number of patients or number of doses, and that such a change would not cause the hospital to lay off personnel. Others feel that an intervention, such as the one described, frees time for these personnel to perform other activities that provide value and, thus, should be treated as a variable cost. Certainly in this time of "downsizing" or "rightsizing," personnel are often viewed as variable costs by administrators.

Direct nonmedical costs also contribute a significant portion to the total direct cost of a treatment alternative. These are the costs for nonmedical services that are the result of illness or disease, but do not involve the purchase of medical services. Thus, these costs are consumed to purchase services other than medical care, and include resource expenditures borne by patients in seeking care. For example, direct nonmedical costs may include transportation to and from health care facilities, extra trips to the emergency department, attendant child or family care expenses, special diets or clothes, and various other out-of-pocket expenses.

Indirect Costs

Indirect costs are also necessary to consider in the full economic evaluation of a program or treatment alternative. Indirect costs are a less obvious, but no less important source of resource consumption, especially from the perspective of the patients. Indirect costs are those costs that result from morbidity and mortality. These costs are related to changes in production capacity that result from disease or health care interventions. Morbidity costs are costs incurred from missing work, that is, lost productivity. Mortality costs are the costs incurred due to premature death.

To estimate indirect costs, two techniques typically used are the human capital method, and the willingness-to-pay method. Each method attempts to estimate different types of costs. The human capital approach attempts to value morbidity and mortality losses based on an individual's earning capacity. Thus, the value of a life is directly related to income. To estimate the earnings foregone or gained as a result of the illness, the human capital approach uses standard labor wage rates. Because all segments of the population do not have the same level of earnings, using this approach raises an ethical dilemma. Some individual groups such as the elderly, children, and the homeless earn virtually nothing at all. Thus, valuing "imputed" wages of some segments of the population may be an acceptable means of more fairly assigning a value to indirect costs.

In the willingness-to-pay approach, patients are explicitly asked how much money they would be willing to spend to reduce the likelihood of illness. The values obtained through this method are often unreliable because there may be up to 200-fold differences in valuations of life due to pay estimates that are not realistic relative to ones ability. It should be noted that while the willingness-to-pay approach incorporates indirect and intangible costs, the human capital approach considers only changes in work loss and productivity due to morbidity and mortality.

Intangible Costs

Intangible costs are probably the most difficult costs to measure. Intangible costs are those costs incurred that represent nonfinancial outcomes of disease and medical care, and which are not properly expressed in monetary terms. Examples of intangible costs include pain, suffering, inconvenience and grief. Typically, these types of costs are identified in an economic analysis, but often not formally quantified. These costs can either be presented as a caveat in the discussion of the results of an economic evaluation or converted into a common unit of outcome measurement such as a quality-adjusted life-year (QALY).

Incremental Costs

As medical interventions become increasingly intense, costs typically increase. However, due to the economic principle of decreasing incremental returns, the additional outcome gained per additional dollar spent typically decreases. At some point of increasing expenditures, there may be no additional benefits, or even a reduction in outcome. Thus, incremental costs may be another way to assess the economic impact of a program or treatment alternative on a population. Incremental costs represent the additional cost that a program or treatment alternative imposes over another, compared to the additional effect, benefit, or outcome it provides. In other words, incremental costs are the extra costs required to purchase an additional unit of effect.

Opportunity Costs

If a resource is used to purchase a program or treatment alternative, then the opportunity to use it for another purpose is lost. This is referred to as an opportunity cost. This cost represents what could have been produced or purchased with the same resources if the treatment alternative in question was not purchased. In other words, opportunity cost is the value of the alternative that was forgone.

Consequences

Full pharmacoeconomic analyses provide an assessment of the efficiency, and are determined according to the amount of output per unit of input, of one alternative versus another. Compared to the costs of the inputs, the outcomes, or consequences of a disease and its treatment, comprises an equally important component of this research. Although the assessment of costs is relatively similar across the various methods, the manner in which consequences are assessed represents the key distinction among these techniques. Regardless of the method used, good assessments of relative consequences of competing alternatives allows researchers to balance the costs of a program or treatment with their consequences or benefits.

Positive versus Negative Consequences

Most often, benefits of drug therapy are characterized in terms of beneficial effects to the patient. However, a comprehensive assessment of benefits will address both positive and negative effects of competing alternatives. Positive consequences may translate into life-years gained, cases cured, disability days avoided, and improved functional status and well-being. Conversely, because drug products are not devoid of adverse effects, negative consequences also may result. Negative consequences can include harmful side effects, exacerbation of disease, drug toxicity, treatment failure, or even death. Thus, the balancing of positive and negative consequences is critical. For example, the consequences component of an analysis of an aminoglycoside would reflect not only the positive consequences associated with curing an infection, but the potential negative consequences associated with drug toxicities, such as nephrotoxicity.

Intermediate versus Final Consequences

Intermediate consequences are commonly used in clinical trials to demonstrate clinical efficacy because their use reduces the cost and time required to conduct a clinical trial. For example, achieving a decrease in low-density lipoprotein cholesterol levels achieved with a lipid-lowering agent is an intermediate consequence. This intermediate outcome serves as a proxy for more relevant final outcomes, or consequences, expressed as a decrease in myocardial infarction rate and an increase in lives saved. Intermediate consequences are used often in cost-effectiveness analyses as proxies predictive of final consequences of interest. The challenge lies in finding intermediate outcome indicators that can reliably predict long-term effects.

Balancing Costs and Consequences

Balancing costs and consequences is the essence of pharmacoeconomic evaluation. Regardless of the method of economic evaluation used, the objective of pharmacoeconomic research is to provide information regarding the relative value of treatment alternatives through an explicit attempt to balance the costs and consequences of each alternative. Typically, results of this approach will be reported in terms of a cost per unit of effect. The primary distinction among the various methods of economic evaluation rests in the valuation of the consequence side of the equation. This chapter summarizes specific methodological approaches of balancing costs and consequences. Subsequent chapters describe each method in greater detail.

Perspectives

Many perspectives are possible in the economic and humanistic evaluation of medical care. Perspective refers to the point of view from which the economic analysis is performed. These perspectives, or viewpoints, will influence the costs and consequences identified, measured, and compared for a program or treatment alternative. An economic evaluation can be conducted from a single perspective, or multiple perspectives. Common perspectives include those of the patient, provider, payer, and society. The value of a treatment alternative will be heavily dependent on the point of view taken. A variety of perspectives are shown in Figure 4.

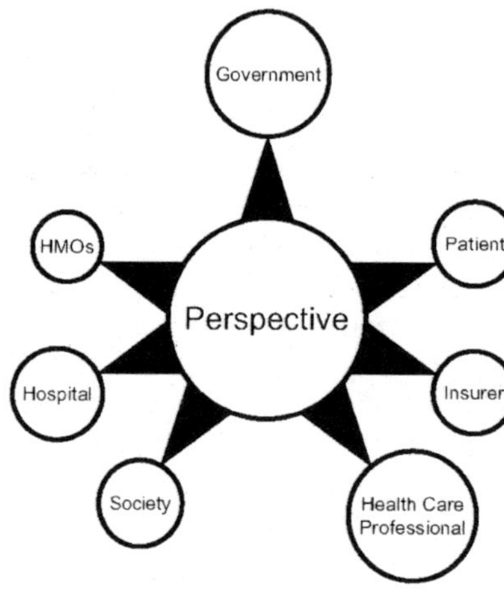

Figure 4. Potential Perspectives for Pharmacoeconoic Evaluations

Patient Perspective

Patients are the ultimate consumers of health care services. Costs from the perspective of patients are essentially what they pay for a product or service, that is, the portion not covered by insurance. Other costs incurred due to illness or treatment, including morbidity and mortality costs, may be captured using this perspective. Consequences from a patient's perspective are the clinical effects of a program or treatment alternative. Costs from a patient's perspective might include insurance co-payments and out-of-pocket drug costs. Also, indirect costs, in terms of health-related work and living limitations are also important from the patient perspective. Additionally, patients are concerned with the positive and negative consequences of a given treatment. The patient's perspective should be considered when assessing the impact of drug therapy on quality of life, or if a patient will pay out-of-pocket expenses for a health care service.

Provider Perspective

Costs from the provider's perspective are the true expense of providing a product or service, regardless of the charge. Few providers are prepared to identify and measure their true economic costs. Charge data may be more readily available, but are usually not reflective of the true costs of health care. Providers can be hospitals, managed care organizations, or private practice physicians. The primary costs from a provider's perspective are of a direct nature. For example, drugs, hospitalization, laboratory tests, supplies, and salaries of health care professionals may be appropriately identified and measured from a provider's perspective. Indirect costs, on the other hand, may be less important from the provider perspective since these expenses are not realized by the provider. When making formulary management, or drug use policy decisions, the viewpoint of the health care organization should dominate. The exception would be when making decisions for a Medicaid or Medicare formulary where the government, or societal perspectives, should dominate.

Payer Perspective

Payers include insurance companies, the government, or employers. Medicare, Blue Cross/Blue Shield, and Motorola are all examples of payers. The costs to the payer are those charges for health care products and services allowed, or reimbursed, by the payer. Again, the primary cost from a payer's perspective are direct costs. However, indirect costs, such as lost workdays and decreased productivity also may contribute to the total cost of health care to the payer. For example, if a patient has peptic ulcer disease, his or her employer may lose the patient's services for 30 days out of the work year. This represents an indirect cost to the employer, who incurs the loss of 30 productive days for this employee. The payer's perspective should be used when insurance companies and employers are contracting with managed care organizations, or selecting employee health care benefits.

Societal Perspective

Society is another potential perspective for pharmacoeconomic evaluations. This perspective is the broadest of all perspectives because it is the only one that considers the benefit to society as a whole. Many researchers assert that society is the best perspective for all economic evaluations. In general, all direct and indirect costs are included in an economic evaluation performed from a societal perspective. Costs from a societal perspective include patient morbidity and mortality costs, and the overall costs of giving and receiving medical care. Also, the perspective that dominates in the health economic literature is that of society. From a societal perspective, all of the important costs and consequences an individual member of society could experience may be included in a complete evaluation of a health care program or treatment alternative. In countries with nationalized medical systems, society is the predominant perspective.

Controversy in Choosing a Perspective

There is some controversy surrounding the issue of a study perspective. Many researchers assert that society is the only relevant, as well as the best perspective from which to conduct an economic analyses from. However, in the United States these studies can be very resource intensive, in terms of time and money. Further, in the real world, organizations may need to focus solely on a single perspective to obtain the data necessary to inform timely decision-making on a local level. Regardless of the perspective chosen, perspective is fundamental because all costs and consequences identified, measured and compared will depend on it.

Exercise 3: Cost Identification

Now let's apply some of the principles of economic outcomes evaluation to a "real world" practice setting, such as your own. Please turn to Exercise 3: Cost Identification.

Now that you have identified the costs and consequences relevant to the perspectives chosen, we can proceed with learning about the appropriate methods to measure and compare competing health care products and services. For further information about cost identification, you may want to turn to the answer section of your workbook to read how you might have responded.

Misuse of Pharmacoeconomic Terms

No phenomenon has contributed more to the confusion surrounding pharmacoeconomic terminology than the indiscriminate use of these terms in the health care literature. Several studies were conducted in recent years documenting this misuse of economic terminology. Undoubtedly, the most commonly misused term is "cost-effective." The issue was first raised when in 1986 when various misinterpretations of the term cost-effective were reported in the New England Journal of Medicine (see Reference 6). Once common misinterpretation equates cost-effectiveness with "cost-savings." A second misinterpretation equates cost-effectiveness with being "most effective." Both of these interpretations are incorrect, as each considers only one-half of the cost versus consequences.

Economic Assessments

The fundamental task of economic evaluations is to identify, measure, value, and compare the costs and consequences of the alternatives being considered. The two distinguishing features of economic evaluations are that there is a comparison of two or more treatment alternatives, and that both costs and consequences of the alternatives are examined. Pharmacoeconomic evaluations may consist of either partial or full economic evaluations. In general, a full economic evaluation encompasses both of these important features, whereas a partial economic evaluation addresses only one of these features.

Full Evaluations

Full economic evaluations are necessary to comprehensively assess the economic costs and benefits of program and treatment alternatives. Full economic evaluations include cost-minimization analysis (CMA), cost-benefit analysis (CBA), cost-effectiveness (CEA), and cost-utility analysis (CUA). Although each of these methods vary in several important ways, they can all provide a comprehensive analysis of both the costs and consequences of evaluated alternatives. Full economic evaluations are necessary for evaluating an intervention as part of a resource allocation decision. They are also useful for determining what drugs to include, or exclude, to or from a formulary list, or as part of a disease management program.

Limitations of Full Economic Analyses

Full economic evaluations do have some limitations. Each method for comparing costs and consequences has its own distinct limitations and assumptions associated with it, thus, practitioners must be aware of these. Further, although the quality and usefulness of the information is much greater with a full economic evaluation, the amount of time and effort necessary to conduct the evaluation is also much greater.

Various methods of economic evaluation are listed in Table 2 and include cost-of-illness (COI) evaluation, CMA, CBA, CEA, and CUA. Each method, except COI, is used to

Table 2. Common Economic Evaluation Methodologies

Methodology	Cost Unit	Outcome Unit
Cost-of-illness	Dollars	Not assessed
Cost-minimization	Dollars	Assumed to be equivalent in comparative groups
Cost-benefit	Dollars	Dollars
Cost-effectiveness	Dollars	Natural units or units of effect
Cost-utility	Dollars	Quality-adjusted life years or other utility

compare competing programs or treatment alternatives. Also, they are similar in that they measure cost in dollars, but differ in their measurements of outcomes and applications. The purpose of this section is to introduce these methods to readers. A more complete in-depth discussion of each of these methodologies is presented in upcoming chapters.

Partial Evaluations

Partial economic evaluations examine only a portion of the costs versus the consequences question. They may include only a simple descriptive tabulation of outcomes or resources consumed. If only consequences or costs of a program's service or treatment are described, then the evaluation illustrates a simple outcome or cost description and is not considered a full evaluation (which evaluates both costs and consequences and compares them to other treatment options). For example, a study in which the costs and consequences are described, but not compared to alternative options, is referred to as a cost-outcome analysis. Other examples of partial evaluations include efficacy evaluations and cost analyses. A cost analysis compares the costs of two or more alternatives without regard to outcome.

Cost of Illness

A COI evaluation identifies and estimates the overall cost of a particular disease in a defined population. This method, often referred to as burden of illness, measures the direct and indirect costs associated with a specific disease or illness. The costs of many diseases in the United States are estimated, including diabetes mellitus, peptic ulcer disease, and cancer.

By identifying the direct and indirect costs of an illness, one can determine the relative value of a treatment or prevention strategy. For example, by determining the cost of a particular disease to society, the costs of a prevention strategy could be subtracted to yield the cost-benefit of implementing this strategy nationwide. Cost-of-illness is not used to compare competing treatment alternatives, but to provide an estimation of the financial burden of a disease. Thus, the value of prevention and treatment strategies can be measured against this illness cost. This economic evaluation methodology is further examined and described in Chapter 6.

Cost-minimization Analysis

Cost-minimization analysis is a tool used to compare two or more treatment alternatives that are equal in efficacy. Cost-minimization analysis compares the costs of treatment alternatives in dollars. Outcomes are not compared because of the underlying assumption that the treatment alternatives are therapeutically equivalent. Thus, the primary focus of this analysis is to determine the least costly alternative.

Cost-minimization analysis is a relatively straightforward and simple method for comparing competing programs or treatment alternatives. However, if no evidence exists to support the therapeutic equivalence of the alternatives being compared, another method should be used. It should be noted that CMA only shows a cost-savings of one treatment or program over another. An example of the appropriate use of CMA would be to compare a brand-name product to a generic equivalent. Because the outcomes associated with the two drugs are equivalent, costs alone can be compared. Cost-minimization analysis also may be useful when comparing therapeutic agents in the same therapeutic class, assuming that they have demonstrated equivalency in safety and efficacy. The costs of these agents would be identified, measured, and compared. However, the costs must extend beyond those for drug acquisition, and should include all relevant costs incurred for preparing, administering, and monitoring the drugs. This economic evaluation methodology is further examined and discussed in Chapter 7.

Cost-benefit Analysis

Costs and outcomes, or benefits, are both valued in monetary units when performing a CBA. In a CBA, the benefits accrued from a program or intervention, and all of the costs of providing a program or intervention, are identified and converted into equivalent dollars in the year they will occur.

Results of these analyses are typically expressed as either a cost-benefit ratio, or a net cost or benefit. For example, if the cost associated with a treatment is \$100, and the outcome resulting from the treatment is valued at \$1000, then the cost-benefit ratio, would be expressed as the benefit (\$1000) divided by the cost (\$100) or as 10:1. This ratio could be interpreted as a treatment alternative that produces \$10 of benefit for every \$1 spent. Alternatively, by subtracting the costs, \$100, from the benefits, \$1000, these results could be expressed as a \$900 net benefit. Thus, when comparing two treatment alternatives, the alternative with the greatest cost-benefit ratio, or net benefit, would be considered the most efficient use of resources. It should be noted that the results of a CBA are most commonly expressed as a net cost or benefit, because it is sometimes misleading to simply compare ratios. A program that costs \$100,000 and results in a benefit of \$1,000,000 also yields a cost-benefit ratio of 10:1. However, the relative magnitude of these costs and benefits are dramatically different from others that yields 10:1.

The appropriate time to use CBA is when comparing treatment alternatives or programs where outcome can be expressed in monetary terms. Using CBA, treatment alternatives with different outcomes also can be compared because they are converted into the common denominator of dollars. Cost-benefit analysis may be an appropriate method to use when justifying and documenting the value of an existing pharmacy service, or the potential worth of a new one. Cost-benefit analysis may be particularly useful when allocating scarce funds to competing programs. This economic evaluation methodology is further examined and discussed in Chapter 8.

Cost-effectiveness Analysis

When treatment alternatives are not therapeutically equivalent, or when it is not desirable to express outcomes in monetary units, CEA may provide a more comprehensive evaluation method. Cost is measured in monetary units and outcomes are expressed in terms of obtaining a specific therapeutic objective. These outcomes are expressed in physical, natural, or nondollar units such as cases cured, lives saved, or mm Hg drop in blood pressure. Cost-effectiveness analysis allows researchers to summarize the health benefits and resources used by competing programs so that policy-makers can choose among them. The difference between a cost-effective alternative and one with cost-savings is that cost-savings refers to a competing alternative that is less expensive. However, a cost-effective alternative does not always mean the comparator is less expensive. In fact, a product or service may be considered cost-effective compared to competing alternatives if one of the following three conditions are met. First, a cost-effective alternative may be less expensive, and at least as effective as its comparator. Second, a cost-effective alternative may be more expensive while providing an additional benefit that is worth the additional cost. Third, a cost-effective alternative may be less expensive and less effective in those cases where the extra benefit is not worth the extra cost.

Cost-effectiveness analysis attempts to reveal the optimal alternative, which may not always be the least costly alternative, for accomplishing a desired objective. In this regard, cost-effectiveness need not be cost reduction, but instead should be considered as cost optimization. Cost-effectiveness analysis provides the means to determine and promote the most efficient drug therapy. Another way to say this is that CEA seeks to identify the alternatives that yield the best health care outcome per dollar spent.

The results of a CEA can be expressed either as the average cost-effectiveness ratio (ACER), or as the incremental cost-effectiveness ratio. Average cost-effectiveness ratios represent the average cost of obtaining a specific therapeutic outcome, spread over a large population. An incremental cost-effectiveness ratio represents the additional cost, and additional benefit, when one option is compared to the next most expensive or intensive option.

The decision to use average versus incremental cost-effectiveness ratios is controversial. An ACER reflects the cost per benefit of a new strategy independent of other alternatives, whereas an incremental cost-effectiveness ratio reveals the cost per unit of benefit of switching from one treatment strategy that may already be in operation to another treatment strategy.

Making a formulary management decision regarding whether to add drug A or drug B to the formulary can best illustrate this concept. Imagine drug A is an antibiotic with a 90 percent efficacy, or cure rate, with a total treatment cost for 100 patients of $50,000. The ACER of drug A is calculated by dividing the cost, $50,000, by the outcome, 90 cures, to yield an ACER of $555 per cure. Drug B has a 95 percent cure rate and costs $100,000 to treat 100 patients, yielding an ACER of $1053 per cure.

To determine the incremental cost-effectiveness ratio, or additional cost required to obtain additional cures with drug B, the cost of drug A, $50,000, is subtracted from the cost of drug B, $100,000, and this is then divided by the cures from drug A, 90, subtracted from the cures resulting from drug B, 95. Thus, the incremental cost for each additional cure with drug B is $50,000 divided by five cures or $10,000 per cure.

($100,000 - $50,000)
(95 - 90 cures)
= $10,000 per cure

Using the ACER, it appears that the additional benefit gained by using drug B costs $498 per cure, which is the difference between the ACERs of drug B and drug A. However, this cost represents the difference per patient, spread over the 100 patients that were treated. Only the incremental cost-effectiveness ratio allows you to pose the question of whether one additional cure is worth spending $10,000 when a cure with drug A can be achieved for $555. The decision to use drug A or B is often dependent on the severity of the infection. A cost of $10,000 to cure one case of otitis media may be deemed excessive by a pharmacy and therapeutics committee, but it may be acceptable to use drug B in cases of life-threatening sepsis.

Cost-effectiveness analysis is useful when comparing competing programs or treatment alternatives that differ in therapeutic or clinical outcome. By calculating a summary measurement of efficiency, alternatives with different costs, efficacy rates, and safety rates can be fairly compared along a level playing field. This economic evaluation methodology is further examined and discussed in the Cost-Effectiveness Analysis chapter.

Cost-utility Analysis

At times, it is desirable to include a measure of patient preference, or quality of life, when comparing competing treatment alternatives. Using CUA, the costs of a treatment alternative are expressed in monetary terms and outcomes or consequences are expressed in terms of patient preference or quality-adjusted life-years. Cost-utility analyses can compare cost, quality, and the quantity of patient years. This method is useful when evaluating programs or alternatives that are life-extending, yet with significant side effects, such as cancer chemotherapy, and those that produce reductions in morbidity, rather than mortality, such as occurs with the treatment or arthritis.

The results of a CUA are most often expressed as a cost per QALY gained, or some other health state utility measurement. Quality-adjusted life-years represent the number of full years at full health that are valued equivalently to the number of years as experienced. For example, a full year of health in a disease-free patient would equal 1.0 QALY, while a year spent receiving dialysis might be valued significantly lower, perhaps as a 0.5 QALY.

Because QALYs and other utility measures are highly subjective measurements, there is a lack of agreement on which scales should be used to measure utility. Also, quantifying patient preferences or quality of health care outcomes is complex; thus, CUA may be limited in scope of application from a managed care or institutional perspective. However, when quality of life is the most important health outcome being examined, CUA is a method one may consider to use. This economic evaluation methodology is further examined and described in Chapter 10.

Exercise 4: Selection of Economic Evaluation Methods

Now to assess the understanding of the previous material, one must build on the case study presented earlier in Exercise 3. Please refer to Exercise 4: Selection of the Appropriate Economic Evaluation.

Now that economic evaluation techniques for the problem have been selected, turn to the answer section of the workbook for more information about selection of proper economic evaluation methodologies. To begin to learn about methods necessary to assess the strength of the findings. Often, it is critical to perform specific analyses to present and test the economic evaluation results properly. These analyses include discounting, sensitivity analysis, decision analysis, and incremental cost analysis. Each of these will be discussed.

Techniques for Analysis

Discounting

Discounting, or adjusting for differential timing, should be performed if the costs and consequences of program and treatment alternatives accrue during different periods of at least 1 year in duration. To be fair and for accurate comparison, the costs and consequences of various alternatives should be evaluated at the same point in time. Discounting will assist in ensuring a fair and complete comparison is possible.

When costs, or consequences of a program or treatment alternative, will occur in the future, these costs and consequences should be reduced or discounted to be more reflective of current fiscal values. Many investigators will repeat the analyses, varying the discount rates, to examine the effects on costs and consequences. Although, there is no standard discount rate specifically recommended for pharmacoeconomic evaluations, current banking interest rates are often viewed as a benchmark. Many investigators recommend that net costs should be discounted to their present value using a rate of 3–8 percent per annum. However, the modal rates used in economic evaluation of health care products and services appear to be about 5 percent.

Sensitivity Analysis

A standard approach for managing uncertainty in an economic evaluation is to perform a sensitivity analysis. Because of the methodological controversies and the almost universal need to make assumptions when conducting economic evaluations, sensitivity analysis is an essential component of any pharmacoeconomic evaluation. Sensitivity analysis is a tool that tests the robustness of economic evaluation results and conclusions. Underlying assumptions or sensitive variables are varied over a range of plausible results. Holding other evaluation parameters constant, the study results are then recalculated. If changing the values of specific variables does not substantially alter the results, one has more confidence in the original findings. Thus, sensitivity analysis provides a measure of robustness, which also may enhance extrapolation of the results.

Variables include those that are clinically relevant. For example, a drug's rate of efficacy, incidence of adverse drug reactions, and dominant cost values may be varied. A sensitivity analysis may reveal at what point one drug gains or loses a cost-effective advantage and due to what variables. Also, the threshold value for changing a drug-use decision may be revealed through sensitivity analysis.

Decision Analysis

Decision analysis is a technique often used in pharmacoeconomic evaluations to structure the logical and chronological order of the analysis. This technique represents an explicit, quantitative, and prescriptive approach to choosing among treatment alternatives. Decision analysis is a systematic, quantitative method of describing clinical problems, identifying possible courses of action, assessing the probability and value of outcomes, and finally making a calculation to select the optimum course of action. Because making drug therapy decisions usually involves these steps, a decision analysis approach often provides a valuable way of structuring many pharmacoeconomic evaluations, especially CEAs.

The tool used in decision analysis is a decision table or decision tree. A decision tree, shown in Figure 5, allows investigators to graphically display all treatment alternatives being compared, the relevant outcomes associated with these alternatives, and the probabilities of these outcomes occurring in a patient population. This tree can allow for the algebraic conversion of all of these variables into one summary

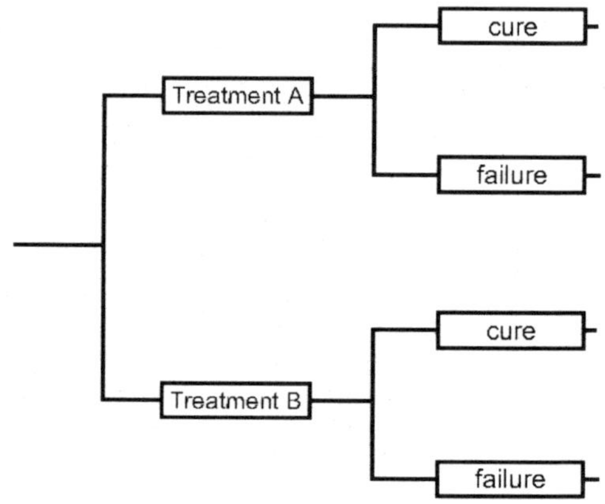

Figure 5. Decision Tree

measurement, often a cost-effectiveness ratio, to allow for a meaningful comparison of two or more treatment alternatives.

Incremental Cost Analysis

Although the results of economic evaluations are often expressed as averages, it is often more instructive and informative to assess the incremental costs. Incremental cost analysis assesses the additional cost that one treatment, service, or program imposes over another compared with the additional benefits or successes it provides. Thus, incremental analysis focus on the additional costs and additional clinical outcomes of alternative strategies. Incremental cost analysis should be considered for any economic assessment method as a further means of evaluating the data.

Incremental cost analysis is useful when prioritizing health care programs or services for policy decision making. This analysis also may be more useful than average summary measures of efficiency when assessing the value of an alternative that is more expensive but has a greater effect. Thus, incremental cost analysis can be used to answer the question "Is the extra effect worth the extra cost?"

Applied Pharmacoeconomics

Much of the focus of pharmacoeconomics to date is on defining terminology and refining methods and techniques of analyses. Unfortunately, not as much effort is placed on how to apply these methods in the real world to assist pharmacy practitioners and administrators to inform decisions at a local level. Applied pharmacoeconomics is defined as putting pharmacoeconomic principles, methods, and theories into practice to quantify the "value" of pharmacy products and pharmaceutical care services used in "real-world" environments.

There are many benefits that can be realized by applying pharmacoeconomic principles and methods to pharmacy and medical practices. Economic assessments can assist in balancing cost and outcome when determining the most efficient use of health care products and services. When assessing the value of an existing health care service, or the potential worth of implementing a new one, these methods are useful. In general, the application of pharmacoeconomic principles is viewed as a tool to assist health care decision-makers to make better health care decisions. The appropriate application of pharmacoeconomic principles and methods facilitates systematic quantification of the value of health care products and services.

Primary Application of Pharmacoeconomics

The primary application of economic assessments is for contemporary clinical decision making. Common drug use decisions, including formulary management, practice guidelines, drug policy, individual patient treatment, and resource allocation, can be supported using pharmacoeconomic techniques. Economic outcomes data can be powerful tools in determining and promoting the most efficient use of drugs in institutions and organizations. The use of pharmacoeconomics to support each of these decision types is discussed further.

Specific Applications of Economic Evaluations

Formulary Management

Although a formulary is often viewed as a cost-containment tool, it does not always represent a list of the least expensive alternatives. In fact, the purpose of many formularies today is to optimize therapeutic outcomes while controlling costs. Therefore, formulary management decisions should extend beyond evaluating only safety and efficacy, or drug acquisition costs, and include an assessment of the value of health care products and services.

Pharmacoeconomics can assist in determining and supporting various formulary management decisions by providing data regarding which agents are the most efficient for a particular hospital or managed care organization. These data can influence the following formulary decision options:

- Inclusion of newly marketed or other target drugs;
- Exclusion of newly marketed or other target drugs;
- Inclusion, with restriction, of newly marketed or other agents;
- Deletion of drugs from the formulary;
- Curtailing the use of nonformulary items;
- Influencing physician prescribing patterns.

Economic outcomes data can provide critical support for these various formulary decision options.

Practice/Clinical Guidelines

In our current cost-conscious health care environment, it may not be sufficient to determine the treatment alternatives that are the best value, or the most cost-effective. It is also important to determine the best way to use these treatment alternatives in hospitals and managed care organizations. Development of drug use guidelines, policies, or protocols can assist in influencing prescribing and promoting the most cost-effective and desirable use of drugs.

The recent expansion of the outcomes movement fostered by the Agency for Health Care Policy and Research (AHCPR) has sought to standardize the parameters of medical care nationally though decreasing procedural variance, improving therapeutic outcomes, and increasing the appropriateness of medical services paid for by third-party insurers. Although there are many diseases and conditions that have no guideline initiatives, many hospitals and managed care organizations are working to develop guidelines specific to their setting. Pharmacoeconomic principles and methods can be used to determine the treatment alternatives and dosing regimens that are the best value for patients, hospitals, organizations, and payers. A drug use guideline based on a rigorous pharmacoeconomic evaluation may have increased acceptance by other health care practitioners.

Drug Use Policy

At an institution, organization, or government level, policies regarding the appropriate use of health care products and services are made. These policies may be implemented to promote the most efficient use of health care products and services, especially pharmaceuticals. Successful policies can have a significant impact on influencing physician prescribing patterns and the provision of high-quality patient care for the resources available.

A successful drug policy should use the results of pharmacoeconomic evaluations for its development. The health care professionals who may be affected by this policy should be consulted in the policy development phase. Adequate time and resources must be spent on the strategic implementation of the policy. Furthermore, educational strategies should be used, including verbal, written, and on-line communication. However, a policy will only be as successful as the pharmacoeconomic data, implementation, and educational strategies chosen.

Service or Program Resource Evaluation

The principles and methods of pharmacoeconomics can be useful in determining the value of an existing pharmacy or medical service, or estimating the potential worth of implementing a new service. With fewer health care resources available at most hospitals and managed care organizations, competition for these resources has increased. The determination of economic outcomes can provide the means to demonstrate that a specific pharmacy service maximizes the resources allocated to it by hospital administration.

Through the use of pharmacoeconomic methods like CBA, the return on investment, or other benefits produced by one service, can be compared to another service. Practitioners and administrators can use these data to make more informed resource allocation decisions.

Individual Patient Treatment

When applying the principles and methods of economic outcomes assessment to practice, the most important, but also the most difficult application, is the decision about an individual patient's therapy. Most pharmacoeconomic studies, by design, evaluate different patient groups. Thus, it can be difficult to translate the results to an individual who may not exactly parallel the study group's characteristics. Traditionally, clinical decisions have included assessments of the safety and efficacy, or the clinical outcomes, of drug therapy. Today's decisions also should consider economic and humanistic outcomes of drug therapy.

As our awareness expands from considering just safety, efficacy, and cost in clinical decision making, we also should begin to account for the human consequences. Many researchers, pharmaceutical manufacturers, insurers, employer groups, government agencies, physician groups, and clinicians are now taking an active interest in using pharmacoeconomic principles to measure and monitor humanistic outcomes of health care.

Humanistic Outcome Assessments

In the past decade or so, the situation in clinical research has become more complex. The effects of new drugs or surgical procedures on quantity of life are likely to be marginal. Conversely, there is an increased awareness of the impact of health care on the quality of human life. Therapeutic efforts in many disciplines of medicine, especially those increasing numbers who care for patients with chronic, long-term disease states, are directed equally, if not primarily, to improvement of the quality life, not the quantity of life.

With therapeutic efforts focusing more on improving patient function and well-being, the need increases to understand the relationships between traditional clinical and HRQOL, especially since it is increasingly used as an outcome in clinical trials, effectiveness research, and research on the quality of care. Factors that have facilitated this increased usage include the accumulating evidence that measures of health status are valid and reliable. In an effort to promote a better understanding of linking clinical variables to HRQOL, a valuable distinction between basic clinical medicine and social science approaches to patients' health has been published (see Reference 31). Their model linking clinical variables with HRQOL, includes five levels or subdivisions: biological and physiological factors; symptoms; functioning; general health perceptions; and overall quality of life.

Case Study

A 72-year-old white male with a history of diabetes mellitus, coronary artery disease, hypertension, and emphysema is seen in a general medicine clinic with complaints of increasing shortness of breath and chest pressure. He was seen 8 weeks previously for similar complaints, at which time verapamil 80 mg/3 times/day was prescribed. The patient stated that he took the verapamil for about 10 days, but discontinued therapy because "it was not working." Since then, he noted a gradual decline in his exercise tolerance. He had previously been able to walk one city block without symptoms, but he now becomes short of breath and feels "chest heaviness" when walking across the room. The patient denies palpitations and orthopnea, but does state that he has not been sleeping well lately. His social history is that of a widower who lives with his daughter and one grandson. He denies alcohol use and he quit smoking 5 years ago. Physical examination reveals an elderly, pale, thin male sitting comfortably in a chair. His blood pressure is 135/90 mm Hg, his heart rate is 80 beats per minute, and his respiratory rate is 16 breaths per minute. His lungs are clear and his cardiac examination is normal. There is no evidence of ascites or pedal edema.

Take a few minutes to think about what is missing from the case that would improve your understanding of this patient and his health.

Common to all of health status assessment tools is a theoretical framework that views the measurement of biologic functioning as an essential, but inadequate component for comprehensively evaluating health. Beyond the documentation of organ system function lies the need to assess general well-being and behavioral functioning. This broader assessment of health is seen as necessary because basic biologic abnormalities can extend into a person's behavioral functioning and sense of well-being, disrupting the person's HRQOL. The impact a disease can have on a person's life can be likened to a rock dropped into the center of a still pond as depicted in Figure 6. Ripples are sent out over the entire surface of the water or the entirety of life, extending far beyond central organ dysfunction. All of the outer circles are eventually affected and need to be addressed in a HRQOL assessment to have a comprehensive understanding of a patient's condition.

Missing from the case, as presented, is information about this patient's functioning, how he is doing, how he gets around, how he feels, what his social situation and support system consists of, and level of functioning to which he expects to return.

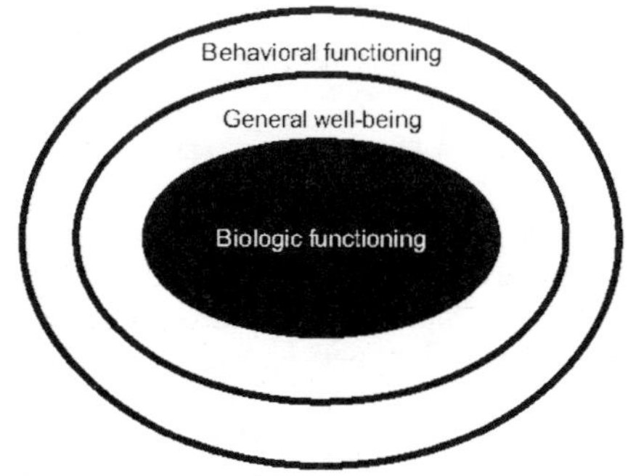

Figure 6. Health Status Concepts
Reprinted with permission from Ware JE.
Conceptualizing and measuring generic health outcomes. Cancer 1991;67(suppl 3):774–9.

Evolution of Today's Health Status Outcome Measures

During the 1940s, physicians first began to measure patient functioning; the Karnofsky Functional Status for Patients with Cancer and the New York Heart Association Classification were among the instruments developed during that period. The first health-status measures distinguished among functional states and included symptoms, anatomic findings, occupational status, and daily living activities. Studies began in the 1950s when clinicians examined the functional status of patients with severe disabilities. When social science methods and clinical expertise came together in the 1970s, the first modern health-status questionnaires emerged. The early tools were quite long, but the data they captured were valid, reproducible, and relevant. The focus was multidimensional, providing assessments of physical, psychological, and social health. The development, refinement, and use of the early instruments helped to establish the foundation for today's studies. Typical measures of this period include the Quality of Well-Being Scale, the Sickness Impact Profile, the Health Perceptions Questionnaire, and the Older Americans Resources and Services (OARS) questionnaire; they were used in health services and clinical research as outcome measures. The next generation developed in the 1980s and 90s were the Rand Health Insurance Experiment (HIE) health surveys, the Duke-UNC Health Profiles, the Nottingham Health Profile, and the Medical Outcomes Study (MOS) health surveys, including the SF- 36 Health Survey. For a more detailed discussion of the history and development of health status assessment, see the *Proceedings of the Advances in Health Assessment Conference:* Palm Springs, California. For a more exhaustive list of questionnaires, readers are directed to Spilker.

Variations in Medical Care in Small Areas

The impetus for research on rationality of processes in health care delivery, an issue that the field of outcomes research and guidelines development are meant to address, typically is traced to the work of John Wennberg, who uncovered a phenomenon known as small-area variation. In brief, Wennberg and colleagues noticed large disparities in the rates of various medical procedures in different geographic areas. The differences could not be attributed to differences in the populations, but instead appeared to indicate differences in physician cultures of different regions, where certain treatment strategies became the norm. For example, a 10-fold difference in rates of tonsillectomy was observed just within the six New England states.

The Rand HIE

When it became apparent in the United States, in 1990, that health expenditures accounted for 12.4 percent of the GNP, whereas that proportion was 4 percent, in 1980, and that the rate of growth of health care expenditures was exceeding the rate of inflation, as well as growth in our economy, questions surfaced. Does spending more buy better health? In individual cases, the answer may be an obvious yes or no, but in the population as a whole as of 1983, the point of diminishing (or absent) returns was difficult to identify. This quandary prompted the federal government to support a large-scale controlled trial, now known as the HIE.

One purpose of the HIE was to learn whether the direct cost of medical care, when borne by consumers, affects their health. The researchers found that the more people had to pay for medical care, the less of it they used. Free care had no effect on major health habits that are associated with cardiovascular disease and some types of cancer. Secondly, the study detected no effects of free care for the average enrollee on any of the five general self-assessed health measures.

In addition to these remarkable findings, the HIE presented one of the first major challenges for measuring health status. A consequence of this challenge resulted in one of the most extensive applications of psychometric theory and methods (long used in educational testing), to the development and refinement of health status surveys. Researchers developed or adapted measures to evaluate the effect of cost sharing on health status. At that time, the comprehensive set included four distinct categories—general health, health habits, physiological health, and the risk of dying from any cause related to risk factors. General health was operationally defined as—physical functioning, role functioning, mental health, social contacts, and health perceptions.

The measurement goal in the HIE was to construct the best possible scales for measuring a broad array of functioning and well-being concepts; it demonstrated the potential of scales, constructed from self-administered surveys, as reliable and valid tools for assessing changes in health status. However, it left two questions unanswered: Can methods of data collection and scale construction work in sicker and older populations? In addition, could scales that are more efficient be constructed? The answer to these questions was the challenge accepted by the MOS investigators.

Medical Outcomes Study

The MOS was a 2-year observational study designed to help understand how specific components of the health care system affected the outcomes of care. One of the two original purposes of the MOS was to develop more practical tools for monitoring patient outcomes, and their determinants, in routine practice using state-of-the-art psychometric techniques. The study, and its many implications and conclusions, are mentioned here for completeness, but any of the multiple publications resulting from this study should be consulted for further details.

Agency for Health Care Policy and Research Agency for Healthcare Research and Quality

To enhance the quality, appropriateness, and effectiveness of health care services and access to these services the federal government in Public Law 101-239 (Omnibus Budget Reconciliation Act of 1989) established the Agency for Health Care Policy and Research (AHCPR). The act, sometimes referred to as the Patient Outcome Research Act, called for the establishment of a broad based, patient-centered outcomes research program. In addition to the traditional measures of survival, clinical endpoints and disease–and treatment-specific symptoms and problems, the law mandated measures of "functional status and well-being and patient satisfaction." In 1999, then President Clinton signed the Health Care Research and Quality Act, reauthorizing AHCPR as the Agency for Healthcare Research and Quality (AHRQ) until the end of fiscal year 2005. Presently, its mission is to improve the outcomes and quality of health care, reduce its costs, address patient safety and medical errors, and broaden access to effective services and improve the quality of health care services.

However, there is a difference between quality-of-life assessment and quality of care assessment. Evaluating and improving the quality of health care services includes improving a patient's health status, but the two are not synonymous. Quality health status outcomes are one facet of defining quality health care, though arguably an ultimate outcome.

Evaluating the Quality of Care

The best measure of quality is not how well or how frequently a medical service is given, but how closely the result approaches the fundamental objectives of prolonging life, relieving distress, restoring functioning, and preventing disability. Lembeche PA. Am J Public Health 1952;42:276–86.

Before attempting to assess the quality of care, either in general, or in any particular situation, it is necessary to come to an agreement on what constitutes quality. To measure quality without a firm foundation of prior agreement on how to define it is to court disaster. The author of a well-established conceptual model suggests measuring quality by observing the performance of other health professionals (see Reference 5). The health professional's management of a clearly definable episode of illness in a given patient is defined as the simplest unit of care. It is possible to divide this management into two domains: the technical and the interpersonal. Technical care is the application of the science and technology of medicine and other health sciences, to the management of a personal health problem. Its accompaniment is the management of the social and psychological interactions between the client and the practitioner. Technical care has been called "the science of medicine" and its counterpart, interpersonal care, is often referred to as "the art of medicine." Assessment of the quality of health care has been classified into three categories. They are structure, process, and outcome. The following section will describe what each of these categories represents, who is involved in the evaluation, and what methods are used to monitor each. Each will be illustrated using an example from a pharmacy practice setting.

Structure of Care

Structure denotes the attributes of the settings in which care occurs. Evaluations of structure address the relatively stable characteristics of the providers of care, of the tools and resources they have at their disposal, and of the physical and organizational settings in which they work. This includes the attributes of material resources, such as facilities, equipment, and money; of human resources such as the number and qualifications of personnel; and of organizational structure such as medical staff organization, methods of peer review, and methods of reimbursement. The concept of structure includes the human, physical, and financial resources that are needed to provide medical care. The term embraces the number, distribution, and qualifications of professional personnel, and so too the number, size, equipment, and geographic disposition of hospitals and other facilities. But the concept also goes beyond the factors of production to include the ways in which the financing and delivery of health services are organized, both formally and informally. The presence of health insurance is an aspect of structure. Structure includes the organization of the medical staff in a hospital, and the presence or absence of a quality review effort. To summarize, the basic characteristics of structure are that it is relatively stable, that it functions to produce care, or is a feature of the environment of care, and that it influences the kind of care provided. Inspectors, engineers, architects, national licensing boards, and medical boards complete evaluation of the quality of the structure of a health system. The measurement of structure has many different units. For example, the number of licensed physicians, assurance that all practicing physicians are licensed, and that the building conforms to fire and safety codes are all measures of structure. Researchers have proposed examples of structure criteria by which to evaluate the quality of pharmaceutical care (see Reference 9). These criteria are numerous and include a variety of characteristics, some of which are the presence of appropriate drug information references, having sufficient inventory and record-keeping capabilities, having adequate physical space, availability of trained technicians, and financial stability.

Process of Care

The *process* of care denotes what is actually done in giving and receiving care. It includes the patient's activities in seeking care and carrying it out, as well as the practitioner's activities in making a diagnosis and recommending or implementing treatment. The primary objective of evaluation is to examine a set of activities that go on within and between practitioners and patients. Quality of the process of care is viewed as normative behavior. The norms are derived either from the science of medicine, or the ethics and values of society. Measurements of process are determined by previous scientific research and discoveries and through published literature that defines accepted standards. Most evaluations of the process of care have roots in peer review. One example of how the system monitors processes through the use of Peer Review Standard Organizations for physician peer review. In this system, peers have developed, discovered, or otherwise set precedents for practice standards that become accepted by the medical community. The evaluation of process is then conducted by applying those accepted practice standards to the applicable health care professionals. A judgment concerning the quality of the process is made either by direct observation or by review of recorded information. Dispensing drugs to a patient is one measure of the process of pharmaceutical care. In one proposed strategy, there are both technical and interpersonal aspects to this process of care (see Reference 5). The technical responsibilities of the pharmacist include gathering prescription information, entering the prescription into a computer, reviewing the patient's profile, obtaining the drug from stock, labeling the drug container, assessing if the correct drug and dosage is prescribed, checking for drug allergies and drug interactions, monitoring for adverse events, and assessing if the patient is adherent to their regimen. In this example, the interpersonal skills of listening, being empathetic to the patient, being friendly, and showing concern and consideration are equally important elements of the process of dispensing a drug.

Outcomes of Care

The *outcomes* of care denote the effects of care on the health status of patients and populations. Improvements in patients' knowledge and salutary changes in patients' behaviors are included under a broad definition of health status, and so is the degree of each patient's satisfaction with care. Although most health professionals agree that quality outcomes are a goal of care, little emphasis is placed on their evaluation, and even less on documenting achievement of success. Because patient knowledge, behaviors, and satisfaction are the outcomes of interest, patients are the best sources of information for evaluating these outcomes. These patient-based evaluations are accomplished by using surveys that are scientifically designed and tested for reliability and validity. Surveys also may be interviewer administered or take place by telephone. The use of patients' assessments of their care and their health has received increased attention over the past few decades. Currently, patient self-administered questionnaires are used for making health care policy decisions as well as in clinical practice. However, the methods used to create these questionnaires predate the current awareness in the health care community.

Definitions

Quality of Life refers to an evaluation of all aspects of our lives, including such things as where we live, how we live, how we play, and how we work. Health-related quality of life encompasses only those aspects of life that are dominated or significantly influenced by personal health or activities performed to maintain or improve health.

Health-related quality of life1 is a specifically focused area of investigation within the larger field of health services and quality of life research. Standardized questionnaires are used to capture health-related quality of life data in a variety of research settings. These standardized questionnaires may be self-administered, or completed via telephone or personal interview, by observation, or by postal survey. More recently, computers and Internet technology have become a mode of administration. Health is just one of 12 domains of life that are considered when researching and evaluating a person's overall quality of life. The other 11 domains are listed in Table 3 and include community, education, family life, friendships, housing, marriage, nation, neighborhood, self, standard of living, and work. The term HRQOL was adopted by researchers to set their research apart from the more global concept of quality of life and to more accurately reflect the scope of their research.

Measurement

Now that we have defined HRQOL, and know what it is that we want to measure, we need to discuss a mechanism for achieving this goal. *Measurement* is a set of numbers or rules used to quantify a physical attribute. Examples of measurement devices are rulers, thermometers, and scales. Think for a moment how you might go about measuring a table. To measure a table, you need to measure the attributes of that table so you can describe it to someone who has never seen it. You would say that it has four legs, that each leg is 10 inches high, and that the table is 4 feet long and 3 feet wide. Width, length, and height are all attributes of the table. In the same way, physical functioning and mental health are attributes of health. One cannot just expect to be able to

Table 3. Twelve Domains of Life

Community	Marriage
Education	Nation
Family Life	Neighborhood
Friendships	Self
Health	Standard of Living
Housing	Work

measure health—you need to measure the attributes of health. An important feature of health is its dimensionality.

Health has distinct components that must be measured and interpreted individually to fully understand health at a given point in time, as well as changes over time. Clues about the components can be found in the definitions of health offered by the World Health Organization as well as in dictionaries. The World Health Organization has defined *health* as a state of complete physical, social, and mental well-being, not merely the absence of disease or infirmity. Dictionary definitions also identify both physical and mental dimensions of health. The former pertains to the body and bodily needs, the latter to the mind, and particularly, to the emotional and intellectual status of the individual. Health connotes completeness, where nothing is missing from the person; it also connotes proper function, where all is working efficiently. The dictionary also suggests well-being, soundness, and vitality as important components of health. Thus, both the World Health Organization and dictionary definitions provide clear precedents for the dimensionality of health and, specifically, for the distinction between physical and mental health. Empiric evidence in support of this distinction is also quite convincing. To summarize, two features of these definitions are crucial; namely, the dimensionality of health and the existence of a full range of health states ranging from disease to well-being.

Many measurement scales artificially restrict the range of individual differences enumerated. Consistent with a disease orientation, most disease specific measures emphasize the negative end of the health continuum. The result is a substantial loss of information. The situation is analogous to a scale for measuring weight that ends at 100 pounds. All objects weighing more are assigned the same score. This would be satisfactory in a world where nothing weighed more than 100 pounds or where differences greater than 100 pounds were irrelevant. Figure 7 illustrates how both the positive and negative ends of the range might be considered when evaluating mental health status. In measuring health, just as in measuring the table, it is important to be able to express each attribute in relationship to the others. To do this, a complete strategy is needed.

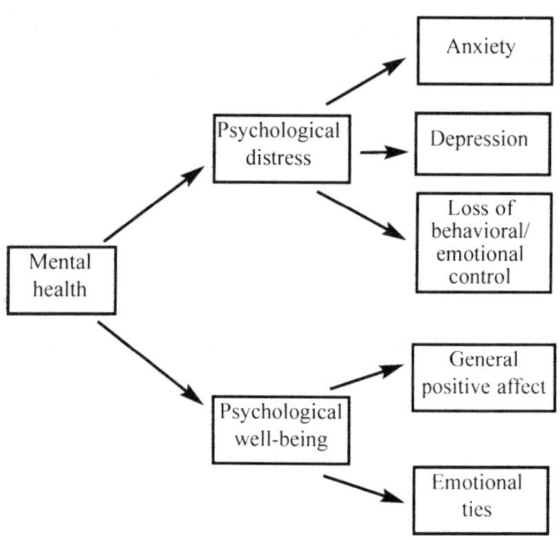

Figure 7. Positive and negative ends of mental health status

Measurement Strategy

To provide an assessment of HRQOL, one of three approaches is usually taken. Researchers can either select tools that focus on general health status, or they can chose tools that are more narrowly focused on specific aspects of the disease under study. For a comprehensive picture of patients' HRQOL, it is often desirable to include both types of assessment tools in research projects having a HRQOL objective. As mentioned, it is important to remember that health is a multidimensional concept that extends over a wide range of a continuum. For example, measurement of mental health necessitates inclusion of both negative and positive ends of the spectrum. Measurement of physical health should include elucidation of vigorous activities as well as basic functions such as bathing and dressing oneself.

Though measurement strategies for different health status instruments may be slightly different, there are some commonly agreed upon and frequently measured general health concepts that can be identified and discussed. These concepts are 1) physical functioning; 2) mental functioning; 3) social and role functioning; and 4) general health perceptions. By denoting a measure as a general health status measure, it is understood that the questions are not disease or disorder specific, and they cover a range of health states from a life-threatening condition to an overall sense of well-being. General measures evaluate aspects of health relevant to all ages, races, sexes, and socioeconomic backgrounds and permit examination of treatment benefits in comparable units.

Medical outcomes study researchers compared and reported the functional status and well-being of patients with chronic conditions using general health measures (see Reference 27). The authors reported the usefulness of generic (nondisease specific) health measures for monitoring progress and for use as outcomes in studies of patients with chronic conditions. The authors maintain that there are several advantages of general measures of functional status and well-being over disease specific measures. Among these, they note, first, they are useful for monitoring patients with more than one condition, and secondly, for comparing patients with different conditions by providing a common yardstick. Lastly, the same measures can be appropriately applied to both general (well) and patient (sick) populations with the advantage of comparing patient groups (sicker) against the healthy standard of a general population.

Commonly Measured Domains of Health in General Health Status Assessment

General health status instruments evaluate aspects of health relevant to all ages, races, sexes, and socioeconomic backgrounds. Questions in a general health status questionnaire are not defined by the disease or disorder under study. These questions have historically covered the full range of the state of disease or illness, and have therefore emphasized the negative end of the health continuum. Increasingly, this limitation in older general health status instruments is being recognized and outcomes researchers are now constructing general health status tools that extend measurements into the well-being end of the health spectrum. General health status tools are, by definition, multidimensional and evaluate at least four key health concepts, which include physical functioning, social and role functioning, mental health, and general health perceptions. Table 4 lists these key health concepts and indicates how they might be assessed.

Physical Functioning

Physical functioning, as it relates to HRQOL assessment, typically refers to the limitations, or disability, experienced by the patient over a defined period. The questions focus on observable and important physical limitations easily noticed and evaluated by the patient or observer. Among such limitations are difficulties in walking, eating, or dressing. In the past, questions concentrated on the negative end of the physical functioning continuum and provided no insight into the well range of physical functioning where activities such as playing sports and running might be noted. Measures of physical functioning should not be confined only to limitations and disabilities. Rather, these measures also should include questions regarding activities of daily living, energy level, satisfaction with physical condition, and ability to perform all levels of activities ranging from the most basic to the most vigorous. Without questions covering the entire continuum of this domain, only those people with physical limitations or disabilities will be identified, evaluated, and segmented for research purposes; any differences among respondents without significant physical limitations or disabilities will be lost by assessments that do not include the well end of the range. In addition to physical limitations, specific concepts often included in general health status questions about physical abilities, days in bed, bodily pain, and more recently, physical well-being. Table 5 delineates these components of the physical domain, and how they are incorporated into a variety of general health assessment instruments.

Social and Role Functioning

Although social and role functioning are often thought of as a single entity and used interchangeably, they are distinct concepts in terms of HRQOL. Social functioning questions address the extent to which a person participates in social interactions, and also the satisfaction derived from these interactions and from the social network that person has established. Role functioning questions are concerned with those duties and responsibilities that are limited by an individual's health.

Social Functioning

Social functioning is defined as the ability to develop, maintain, and nurture mature social relationships. Social well-being is separated into two areas that include the frequency of social contacts and the nature of those contacts within the social network or community. Both of these areas must be considered together. Evaluating only the frequency of contacts in isolation from the nature of those contacts may offer no insight or the wrong insight into the person's state of social functioning; therefore, including a person's assessment of the adequacy of his or her social network is essential when evaluating social functioning in the context of HRQOL. It is known that belonging to a community, family, or neighborhood provides a strong sense of being wanted, loved, and valued, and has significant influence on assessments of mental health, as well as on social health.

Role Functioning

Role functioning as a component of health is concerned with the impact health has on a person's ability to meet the demands of that person's normal life role. Work for pay, homemaking duties, and schoolwork are all covered by questions asking about this concept. A role function assessment should identify everyday role situations or activities that can be directly affected or limited by disease, illness, or treatment. Whereas most role limitations are due to physical health problems, it has been noted that role limitations are observed both in the presence and in the absence of physical limitations.

Mental Health

Disease often affects the behavior, as well as the physical aspects of a person's life. General health status assessments, therefore, usually include questions covering aspects of psychological health. These questions typically focus on the frequency and intensity of symptoms of psychological distress. Anxiety and depression are common themes in mental health components of general health status instruments, but scales focusing only on these two concepts do not adequately cover the full mental health continuum. Perceptions of psychological well-being, life satisfaction, and cognitive functioning are also needed if a comprehensive assessment of the mental health domain by a health-related quality of life instrument is to be achieved. Although general health status questionnaires covering the mental health domain are not intended for use as diagnostic tools, some questions are used as screens for certain disorders such as depression.

General Health Perceptions

General health perceptions address the person's overall beliefs and evaluations about his or her health. Questions covered in this area focus on each person's health preferences, values needs, and attitudes. Assessments of general health perceptions are necessary because they allow consideration of individual differences in reactions to pain, perceptions of difficulty, the level of effort required, or the degree of worry or concern about health. Unlike questions that focus on measures of limitations, pain, and dysfunction to assess other health domains of interest, questions covering general health perceptions address positive feelings. These questions can be positively framed, thereby allowing the full spectrum of HRQOL to be evaluated.

Table 4. Summary of Information About Widely Used General Health Surveys

	QWB	SIP	HIE	NHP	QLI	COOP	EURO-QOL	DUKE	MOS FWBP	MOS SF-36
CONCEPTS										
Physical functioning	•	•	•	•	•	•	•	•	•	•
Social functioning	•	•	•	•	•	•	•	•	•	•
Role functioning	•	•	•	•	•	•	•	•	•	•
Psychological distress		•	•	•	•	•	•	•	•	•
Health perceptions (general)			•	•	•	•	•	•	•	•
Pain (bodily)		•	•	•		•	•	•	•	•
Energy/fatigue	•		•	•				•	•	•
Psychological well-being			•					•	•	•
Sleep		•		•				•	•	
Cognitive functioning		•						•	•	
Quality of Life						•			•	
Reported health transition						•			•	
CHARACTERISTICS										
Administration method (S = self, I = interviewer, P = proxy)	I, P	S, I, P	S, P	S, I	S, P	S, I	S	S, I	S, I	S, I, P
Scaling method (L = Likert, R = Rasch, T = Thurstone, U = utility)	U	T	I	T	L	L	U	L	L	L, P
Number of questions	107	136	86	38	5	9	9	17	149	36
Scoring options (p = profile, SS = summary scores, SI = single index)	SI	P,SS,SI	P	P	SI	P	SI	P, SI	P	P, SS

QWB = Quality of Well-Being Scale (1973)

SIP = Sickness Impact Profile (1976)

HIE = Health Insurance Experiment surveys (1979)

NHP = Nottingham Health Profile (1980) (1992)

QLI = Quality of Life Index (1981) (1992)

COOP = Dartmouth Function Charts (1987)

EUROQOL = European Quality of Life Index (1990)

DUKE = Duke Health Profile (1990)

MOS FWBP = MOS Functioning and Well Being Profile

MOS SF-36 = MOS 36-Item Short -Form Health Survey

Reprinted with permission from Ware JE. The status of health assessment 1994. Annu Rev Public Health 1995;16:327–54.

Advantages of generic health status measures are that they can be used to assess the relative burden of different conditions, and to assess the relative benefits of different treatments. The questionnaires can be used with people of any age, gender, or race. For example, elderly patients with arthritis and young patients with hypertension can be asked the same questions without suspicion that their age or disease state differences will confound their answers. In a general health status instrument, patients may be asked if they believe their health is excellent, very good, good, fair, or poor. A general questionnaire would not ask about nausea related to cancer chemotherapy treatment, but may ask if the patient is less energetic, or more calm and peaceful.

Disadvantages of generic instruments are that, by design, they do not cover areas of health status that are important to specific groups of patients who may experience specific improvements, or disabilities, in functioning due to their disease state. For instance, general health status questionnaires do not include self-esteem, a concept that is very important to patients with cystic fibrosis. For this reason, additional types of questionnaires that consider a disease- or condition-specific set of questions were designed for many disease states.

Disease-specific Health Status Instruments

Some limitations or problems with patients' health are unique to their specific disease state. For this reason, batteries of questions were designed for use with specific patient populations, and are used to supplement a general health status instrument. These more narrowly focused disease-specific measures request detailed information about the impact of a specific disease and the effect of treatment on the patient, from the patient's perspective. While items in both general health status measures and in disease-specific measures may appear to ask the same question, those in a disease-specific tool are phrased to direct patients to think about their disease, its symptoms, or its treatment, rather than the disease or limitations in general. In addition, using disease-specific measures allows inclusion of questions of specific interest. Among some specific areas previously investigated with disease-specific questionnaires are: sexual functioning; nausea and vomiting; pain; cancer; arthritis; epilepsy; HIV infection; anxiety and depression; asthma, and rhinitis.

Psychometric Theory

The design of health surveys, consisting of scales measuring the attributes of a person or a population's health, are supported by an underlying theory known as psychometric theory. Health status scales development also can be viewed as a unique application of the design and theory that support the creation of educational measurements for instance, Standardized Achievement Tests. A person who studies these theories and conducts research or measurement of such attributes as intelligence, pain, mental well-being, or functioning, is usually a doctorate level research psychologist and can be known as a *psychometrician.*

One readily apparent feature of health sciences literature devoted to measuring health status is the daunting array of already available scales. Paradoxically, if you proceed a little further to find an instrument for your intended purpose, you may conclude that none of the existing scales is quite right. Many researchers tend to magnify the deficiencies of existing measures and underestimate the effort required to develop an adequate new measure. Perhaps the most common error committed by clinical researchers is to dismiss the existing scales too lightly, and embark on the development of a new instrument with an unjustifiably optimistic and naïve expectation that they can do better. The development of scales requires considerable investment of both mental and fiscal resources. A comprehensive set of standards, widely used in the assessment of psychology and education, is the manual called Standards for Educational and Psychological Tests, published by the American Psychological Association (1974). In addition to these standards, there are a number of compendia of measuring scales.

Psychometric Considerations

The literature is ever expanding with reports of general health and disease-specific, HRQOL research. As with any field of research, the studies reported in the literature meet various levels of scientific rigor. Readers of these reports must have a basic understanding of psychometrics to draw proper conclusions from HRQOL findings.

Psychometrics is the science of testing questionnaires to measure attributes of individuals. It is used in the field of health assessment to translate people's behavior, feelings, and personal evaluations into quantifiable data. These data, once captured, must be both relevant and correct if they are to provide useful insights into HRQOL. Two psychometric properties that any measurement scale or instrument must possess include reliability and validity. In addition, useful scales must be sensitive to change and be accepted by the investigators and respondents. When measuring reliability, the scientist is concerned with the relationship between true variation and random error. Evaluations assess the consistency and repeatability of measurement. Validity refers to the extent to which differences in scale scores reflect the true differences in the individuals studied. Whereas the goal is to elicit observed differences that are indeed true differences among respondents, factors such as how the measure is administered, who administers the form, where it is administered, and when it is administered, can affect responses across groups of study participants, and, therefore, can add a degree of uncertainty to the findings of a HRQOL assessment.

Use of Patient-reported Health Status

Applications of general health surveys are numerous, and include monitoring the health of general populations, evaluating health care policy, conducting clinical trials of alternative treatments, designing systems for monitoring and improving health care outcomes, and making clinical decisions in medical practice. Standardized health surveys have the potential to become new laboratory tests in medical practice. Without these tests, patient functioning, and well-being affected by disease and treatment, are unlikely to be discussed during a typical medical visit. Two-thirds to three-fourths of adults in the United States have reported that physicians rarely, or never, ask about the extent of their limitations in performing everyday activities, even in the presence of chronic conditions. As a result, clinicians may not be well-informed about their patient's functional status, well-being, or changes over time. Scientists have proposed that one solution might be to standardize functional and well-being assessments for every medical practice. Such routine assessments could be useful for a number of reasons. They would ensure that all important dimensions of functional status and well-being are considered consistently. They would detect, explain, and track changes in functional capacity over time. Third, their use would make it possible

Table 5. Items Measuring Generic Health Concepts

Concepts	Definition	Abbreviated items*
Physical		
Physical limitations	Limitations in performance of self-care, mobility, and physical activities	Needs help with bathing, dressing, in bed chair, couch, for most of day Does not walk at all
Physical abilities	Ability to perform everyday activities	Able to walk uphill, up stairs Able to participate in sports, strenuous activities
Days in bed	Confinement to bed due to health problems	During past 30 days, number of days health keeps one in bed all day or most of day
Bodily pain	Ratings of the intensity, duration frequency of bodily pain and limitations in usual activities due to pain	During the past 3 months, how much pain one has had How much pain interfered with thing
Physical well-being	Personal evaluation of physical condition	Ratings of physical shape or condition
Mental		
Anxiety/depression	Feelings of anxiety, nervousness, tenseness, depression, moodiness downheartedness	Depressed or very unhappy Bothered by nervousness, or nerves
Psychological well-being	Frequency and intensity of general positive affect	Happy, pleased, satisfied with life Wakes up expecting an interesting day Feels cheerful, lighthearted
Behavioral/emotional control	Control of behavior, thoughts, and feelings during specified period	Feels emotionally stable Loses control of behavior, thoughts, feelings Laughs or cries suddenly
Cognitive functioning	Orientation to time and place, memory, attention span, and alertness	Feels confused, forgets a lot, makes more mistakes than usual
Social and role		
Interpersonal contacts	Frequency of visits with friends and relatives Frequency of telephone contacts with close friends or relatives during specific periods of time	Number of friends visited Going out less often to visit people How often on telephone with close friends/relatives in past month
Social resources	Quantity and quality of social ties, network	Number of close friends, people to talk with
Role functioning	Freedom from limitations in performance of usual role activies (e.g., work, housework, school) due to poor health	Limited in kind or amount of major role activity Working shorter hours Health causes problems at work Unable to work because of health
General health perceptions		
Current health	Self-rating of health at present	In general, is health excellent, good, fair or poor?
Health outlook	Expectations regarding health in the future	I expect to have a very healthy life

Adapted with permission of Ware JE. The Health Institute, New England Medical Center, Boston, MA.

to better consider the patient's total functioning when choosing among therapies. They would guide the efficient use of community resources and social services, and fifth, they could more accurately predict the course of chronic disease. Such data would make it possible for clinicians to better inform patients about the tradeoffs involved in alternative treatments. A great potential exists for standardized measures of functional status and well-being administered routinely and incorporated into existing clinical databases. Meyer and associates published an example of experiences with the use of a short-form general health status measure in a dialysis unit. The clinicians involved in this project related that patients' scores enhance, rather than simply summarize, the collective understanding of a conscientious dialysis team.

In the dialysis unit, health status surveillance revealed new information that was qualitatively different from other assessments made in the care of these patients. The authors suggested that patient-based health status assessment can improve the management of individual patients, and can contribute to the epidemiology of treatment of endstage renal disease. Health status assessment offers a language in which to phrase experiences that the individual patient may find difficult to express, or may not even think to formulate, or remember, unless prompted. It provides a thread along which to reconstruct experiences. By objectifying the patient's subjective experiences, health status assessment makes the experience more accessible to the staff who shares responsibility for care. It puts the patient's experience on their agenda for discussion, even when the technical aspects of care do not compete for attention.

Advantage of Health Status Assessment Information

Self-administered surveys allow patients a voice in their care. It permits the patient to communicate to those caring for them, about what matters most. This may be information that one needs to know, but does not have time to elicit. Analogously to providing a common language for patients and health professionals, the general HRQOL information also can provide a standard, or a common language, for different disciplines of health professionals. For example, a Nephrologist and a Psychiatrist can use a common metric to discuss a dialysis patient's emotional health. A standardized method of asking patients about their functioning and well-being can be efficiently used in treatment decisions, and as a monitoring parameter for efficacy and toxicity. The information also may be a tool, or indicator, for compliance assessments.

Health-related quality of life can be used to add important information to the evaluation of the effectiveness of an intervention. For example, does the 34-year-old otherwise healthy woman, diagnosed with depression, who just started an antidepressant feel better or worse? One could just simply ask her that question when you see her 4 weeks after the start of her therapy. As pharmacists, we commonly ask, "Are you having any side effects?" If the patient tells you she has diarrhea, you may form an impression of that diarrhea, which seems like a mild side effect. However, having her answer survey questions about her functioning can reveal how trivial or nontrivial the impact of her diarrhea is to her everyday activities. What would happen if her diarrhea limits her ability to function as the checkout person in the grocery store? She cannot leave her post frequently to go to the bathroom, and if she does, she could be fired and not be able to provide for her two young children that she is raising alone. The patient sees the limitation imposed by diarrhea as considerable, and knowing a little more about her functioning conveys a bit of a different message to us than just knowing she is having diarrhea. A discussion using information from a patient self-administered health status survey also could lead to the patient revealing that she has decided to stop taking her drugs. She did not think it was working, and the diarrhea was not worth the hassle.

Advances in Health Status Assessments for Individual Patient Care Decisions

Standardized measures capturing patient perspectives on their physical functioning, social and role functioning, mental health, and general health perceptions are likely to become more acceptable as an additional piece of evidence on which providers, and their patients, can make decisions about treatment and the treatment's efficacy. Mature theoretical models, sophisticated measurement techniques, and enhanced technology for use in measurement, make the routine use of individual patients results in their own care more promising than ever before.

Two practical concerns of the critics of use of HRQOL assessments in individual patient care are: 1) respondent burden; and 2) reliability of scores obtained from shorter questionnaires. Current researchers struggle with the competing demands invoked by the everyday use requiring shorter forms and the reliability of a result obtained from fewer questions. Specifically, concerns are raised about the reliability of the result, and the interpretation, since with popular outcomes measures the standard error around a single person estimate is large and not satisfying enough to ensure stable conclusions.

Modern test theory offers the potential for individualized, comparable assessments for the careful examination and application of different health status measures. One such theory is Item Response Theory (IRT). Researchers report that IRT has a number of potential advantages over the currently used Classical Test Theory in assessing self-reported health outcomes. Applications of the IRT models are ideally suited for implementing computer adaptive testing. IRT methods are also reported to be helpful in developing better health outcome measures, and in assessing change over time.

Patients increasingly have more access to computer technology. It is becoming more practical to use assessments using a computer. Patients answering questions about a health status concept, using dynamic assessment technology, are requested only to complete the number of questions needed (minimizes response burden) to establish a reliable estimate. The resulting scores for an individual are estimated to meet the clinical measures of precision.

In summary, the study of HRQOL requires a multidimensional approach. Assessments should include components that evaluate, at a minimum, the health concepts of physical, social and role functioning, mental health, and perception of general health. Additionally, the full continuum of these concepts should be included, from the most limited, to the healthiest. Approaches to capture HRQOL data include the self-administered questionnaire (paper and pencil, or computer), personal and telephone interviews, observation, and a postal survey. The assessment instruments must possess acceptable reliability, validity, and sensitivity, and the investigators, as well as the participants, must accept them. Psychometrics is an essential part of HRQOL research, especially in today's research environment that requires shorter, more focused measures.

Existing health outcomes measures, drawn from classic test theory and emerging approaches based on item response theory, offer exciting opportunities for appreciably expanded applications in biomedical and health services research, clinical practice, decision making, and policy development. The research agenda of measurement scientists includes challenges to: 1) refine and expand measurement techniques that rely on IRT; 2) improve measurement tools to make them more culturally appropriate for diverse populations, and more conceptually and psychometrically equivalent across such groups; 3) address long standing issues in preference- and utility-based approaches, particularly in the elicitation of preference responses and scoring instruments; and 4) enhance the ways in which data from outcomes measurement tools are calibrated against commonly understood clinical and lay metrics, are interpreted, and are made useable for different decision-makers.

With the advances in measurement that promise to continue, knowledgeable clinicians will become the transportation for these measures to include in patient care. It is suggested interpretation is, in part, an issue of familiarity, and repeated applications of measures can lead to a better understanding. Ideally, a better understanding of what patients tell their providers about their health status can be used for decision making, which require the patients to more actively and routinely participate in their own care.

Case Study Continued

Now back to the case of Mr. A to consider the following questions. You have stumbled on the results of a questionnaire filed in the outpatient chart. Apparently, the patient filled one out at his last visit in the clinic, about 8 weeks ago, dated Oct. 1, 1995. There was another questionnaire filled out earlier today, Dec. 7, 1995, in the clinic. The results of these questionnaires are listed at the end of this section, as Appendices A and B. Please look at the scores for each of the scales and the changes in the scores. There is a brief interpretation guide attached as Appendix C. For another point of comparison of this patient's scores, you also can use the normative values supplied in Appendix D. There are three sets of values listed. The first set is for the general United States population, the second is for the population in Mr. A's age range, and the third is for patients with similar medical conditions. Take some time now to interpret the results of these questionnaires. What other questions do you have for this patient? Think of at least four additional questions. Reflect on the differences between your questions earlier in this section and those you are asking now.

After questioning Mr. A, you find that this month is the second anniversary of his wife's death. He is very sad about this, and is feeling that he wants to give up now. How does this information change your original plan and problem list? Appendix E gives Mr. A's scores 1 year after this clinic visit, dated December 5, 1996, for comparison.

Patient Satisfaction

Another outcome suggested by a well-accepted model for how to evaluate the quality of health care, is that of patient satisfaction (see Reference 5). During the last decade, organization-wide quality improvement efforts in both service and manufacturing sectors of the United States have embraced consumer evaluations of goods and services as a way to monitor product quality. In the health care setting, consumer satisfaction surveys have evolved, from marketing tools, to measures of quality of the product or service delivered. Empirical studies show that patients' expressions of dissatisfaction are potent predictors of disenrollment from a physician or a health plan. Studies of satisfaction with physicians have documented the importance of access, communication, technical quality, and interpersonal quality of care. The concept of assessing patient satisfaction is introduced here and explored further in Chapter 16.

A consumer's evaluation of the care received, known as *consumer evaluation*, or *patient satisfaction*, is both similar and different from a patient's assessment of health status. The same psychometric techniques are used to obtain information, and to evaluate the accuracy of the information. The science of obtaining the information is similar. However, the information that is requested of the patients, that is, the consumers, is unique and very different from what is asked about health status. Both reports and ratings are used in patient satisfaction surveys. Reports are descriptions, whereas ratings are evaluations that require a judgment by the evaluator. For instance, a patient may be asked how long the wait was before being seen by the physician, which is a report; the patient also may be asked if the wait was too long, requiring a judgment.

There are many different patient satisfaction surveys available. Attributes that are commonly evaluated, regardless of the care setting, include the clinician's scientific knowledge and skill, the quality of clinician-patient communications, the provision of humane interpersonal treatment, and the degree of the patient's trust in the care provider. One setting in which patient satisfaction surveys are becoming increasingly important is that of primary care. Four distinguishing and shared multiple characteristics are considered essential and unique to this area of health care, and provide attributes that can be evaluated by patients. These characteristics include accessibility to care, continuity of care, the comprehensiveness of care, and how well a patient's care is integrated into a coherent and continuing whole. As competition in the health care market has increased, many health care delivery organizations have come to view patient satisfaction as an important consumer supplied indicator of quality and a potential benchmarking device when studied over time.

Other Measures of Outcomes

Those seeking to evaluate the impact of the health care system on the health of an individual or population are forced to include multiple outcomes to accommodate both external and internal needs. So far this chapter has focused on economic outcomes and humanistic outcomes. Within the humanistic outcomes category, the basic concepts included in assessments of health status and patient satisfaction were identified. However, as noted, the identification of perspective is important. In the restructuring of health care, the perspective of the employer has become a significant force. To meet the evaluation needs of employers, the concept of work functioning must be included as an outcome. For example, in 1990, the cost of depression to society was estimated to be $44 billion. Of this, $11.7 billion was attributed to reductions in productive capacity, due to excess absenteeism. The ability to quantify the constituent parts of the losses in work productivity is developmental. However, it is growing in importance, and will undoubtedly be an important measured health domain.

Traditionally, simple measures that ask the patient about lost days from work and days in bed were used to measure work functioning. Many popular health status measures include questions on limitations in daily work activities. However, these concepts are still in need of further development. A conceptual basis for measuring the ability to function in work roles may be found in the recent disability literature. Within this literature, disability encompasses the total inability to work, as well as the less severe limitations in work-role functioning. The Institute of Medicine and the World Health Organization, in the development of terminology and classification systems for disability and functional limitations, have established a fundamental instrument development guideline. They suggest that a person's ability to function in work roles will result from two sets of variables: 1) the characteristics of that person's illness or impairment; 2) the requirements of the work situation. Both of these areas are presently under study.

Conclusion

The methods of pharmacoeconomic evaluation strive to assess the value of health care in terms of outcomes of a clinical, economic, and humanistic nature. This chapter has provided several key definitions and concepts that will be built on in later chapters of this book. Further discussion of how to actually perform and apply the results of economic methodologies will be presented in detail as well. Detailed information regarding the conduct and application of humanistic outcomes assessments will be presented in Chapters 14 and 18.

Because "quality-of-life" represents the broadest range of human experiences, use of this general term in the health field has led to considerable confusion, particularly because of the overlap with the more specific concept, health status. To make the meaning more specific and retain the important aspects of life quality, the term "health-related "quality-of-life" is both useful and important.

Annotated Bibliography

1. Barr JT, Schumacher GE. Applying decision analysis to pharmacy management and practice decisions. Top Hosp Pharm Manage 1994;13:60–71.

   In this paper, decision analysis is presented and applied to a typical management situation. Decision analysis is an explicit, quantitative, and prescriptive approach for choosing among alternative outcomes. Literature examples of using pharmacy-related decision analysis are provided, including its use in formulary additions, cost-effectiveness analysis, drug therapy evaluation, therapeutic drug monitoring, and health policy issues.

2. Bootman JL, Townsend RJ, McGhan WF. Principles of pharmacoeconomics, 2nd ed. Cincinnati: Harvey Whitney Books Company, 1996.

   Designed principally for the student as an introduction to pharmacoeconomics, the authors present various techniques, tools, and strategies used to evaluate the economic contribution of specific drug therapies at a policy level and for individual patients. Chapters 6 and 7 will be of particular interest to readers seeking information on outcomes measurement, as overviews of cost-utility analysis and health-related quality of life (HRQOL) measurement, respectively, are presented. The bibliographies in these chapters include many of the key theoretical and empiric citations for these two approaches to measurement. This book is a good starting point for those who wish to read further.

3. Crane VS. Economic aspects of clinical decision-making: applications of clinical decision analysis. Am J Hosp Pharm 1988;45:548–53.

   Clinical decision analysis as a basic tool for decision making is described, and potential applications of decision analysis in six areas of clinical practice are identified in this paper. Applications of clinical decision analysis in the areas of diagnostic testing, patient management, product and program selection, research and education, patient preferences, and health care-policy evaluation are described. Decision analysis offers health professionals a tool for making quantifiable, cost-effective clinical decisions, especially in terms of clinical outcomes.

4. Detsky AS, Nagiie IG. A clinician's guide to cost-effectiveness analysis. Ann Intern Med 1990;113:147–54.

   The authors describe how cost-effectiveness analysis can be used to help set priorities for funding health care programs. For each intervention, the costs and clinical outcomes associated with that strategy must be compared with an alternate strategy for treating the same patients. This paper also discusses the distinction between cost-effectiveness analysis and incremental cost-effectiveness analysis. If an intervention results in improved outcomes, but also costs more, the incremental cost per incremental unit of clinical outcome should be calculated and the incremental cost-effectiveness ratios ranked to set funding priorities. By using this list, the authors maintain the person responsible for allocating resources can maximize the net health benefit for a target population derived from a fixed budget. Because clinicians should participate in policy-making, they must understand the role of this technique in setting funding priorities and allocating health care resources.

5. Donnabedian A. The quality of care: how can it be assessed? JAMA 1988;260:1743–8.

The author states that although much is known about assessing quality, much remains to be known. Before assessment can begin, one must decide how quality is to be defined. It is further asserted that quality depends on a number of factors: 1) whether one assesses only the performance of practitioners or also the contributions of patients and of the health care system; 2) how broadly health and responsibility for health are defined; 3) whether the maximally effective or optimally effective care is sought; and 4) whether individual or social preferences define the optimum. The need for more detailed information about the causal linkages among structural attributes of health care settings, the processes of care, and the outcomes of care is discussed. The author states the components or outcomes of care to be sampled must be specified, appropriate criteria and standards formulated, and the necessary information obtained to assess quality. Definitions of structure, process, and outcomes are given.

6. Doubilet P. The use and misuse of the term "cost-effective" in medicine. N Engl J Med 1986;314:253–6.

This paper describes the inconsistencies in the definitions and interpretations of the term cost-effectiveness by authors in medical literature sources. Cost-effectiveness criteria vary considerably and the following interpretations are discussed: 1) cost-effectiveness is equivalent to "cost-savings;" 2) the more effective therapy is also the most cost-effective therapy; 3) cost-effectiveness is the option that is cost-saving while providing equal or better health; 4) cost-effective therapy is that having an outcome worth its corresponding cost relative to competing alternatives. The first two interpretations are incorrect because they only examine one side of the cost-effectiveness equation. The third and fourth interpretations can both be considered correct interpretations of the term. The authors stress it is imperative to standardize terms, such as cost-effectiveness to enhance its usefulness and application to health care policy and clinical decision-making.

7. Drummond MF, Stoddart GL, Torrance GW. Methods for the economic evaluation of health care programmes, 2nd Ed. Oxford: Oxford University Press, 1997.

This second edition of a landmark textbook, originally published in 1986, discusses in detail the methodological principles of economic evaluation in health care and has been used in courses teaching economic evaluation. The text is not structured like a standard textbook, with detailed discussion of theoretical concepts, but rather concentrates on practical methodological issues that evaluators need to resolve in undertaking an economic evaluation.

8. Eisenberg JM. Clinical economics: a guide to the economic analysis of clinical practices. JAMA 1989;262:2879–86.

This paper discusses the tools of economics that can be applied to the analysis of medical practice. The focus of the analysis is to improve physicians' choices of ways to use social and individual resources for clinical interventions in the hope of improved health. Types of economic evaluations including cost-identification, cost-effectiveness, cost-benefit, and cost-utility analyses are presented. In addition, useful discussions on study perspectives and determination of health care costs are provided.

9. Farris KB, Kirking DM. Assessing the quality of pharmaceutical care II: applications of concepts of quality assessment from medical care. Ann Pharmacother 1993;27:215-23. Bungay KM, Wagner AK. Comment: assessing the quality of pharmaceutical care. Ann Pharmacother 1993;27:1542.

The authors propose a framework to facilitate quality assessment of pharmaceutical care. The structure-process-outcome paradigm is presented as a framework for quality assessment of pharmaceutical care. It is recommended that structure be assessed at periodic intervals because it identifies the potential for the provision of quality care. The process of care should be documented, and it is recommended that these variables be linked to outcomes before either structure or process is used to make inferences about the quality of pharmaceutical care. Outcomes assessment will require an interdisciplinary approach. Examples of structure and process criteria are provided for use as a model to integrate pharmaceutical care into a health care system. The editorial comments discuss possible additions to the author's published choices of health outcomes variables.

10. Freund DA, Dittus RS. Principles of pharmacoeconomic analysis of drug therapy. PharmacoEconomics 1992;1:20–32.

This paper outlines some of the basic principles of pharmacoeconomic analysis. The authors recommend that every analysis should have an explicitly stated perspective, which, unless otherwise justified, should be a societal perspective. Various methods of economic evaluations are reviewed. A discussion of modeling frameworks, such as influence diagrams and decision trees, is also included.

11. Hatoum HT, Freeman RA. The use of pharmacoeconomic data in formulary selection. Top Hosp Pharm Manage 1994;13:47–53.

This paper encourages pharmacists to improve their knowledge and use of pharmacoeconomic data in formulary selection. Changes in the formulary selection process, particularly concerning use of cost-containment strategies, are described. An overview is presented of the origin, as well as the potential impact of pharmacoeconomic data upon formulary management. The need to balance the economic benefit with the clinical advantages for any proposed new drug for formulary inclusion remains the most critical decision to be made by pharmacists.

12. Katz DA, Welch HG. Discounting in cost-effectiveness analysis of healthcare programmes. PharmacoEconomics 1993; 3:276–85.

This paper discusses the application of discounting to economic evaluations. Discounting is described as a technique used to make fair comparisons of programs whose costs and outcomes occur at different times. The agreements and disagreements among health economists regarding the need for discounting, and the procedures for discounting costs and benefits are presented. The authors also describe the method of constant rate discounting, which uses the same rate to discount costs and benefits.

13. Kozma CM, Reeder CE, Shulz RM. Economic, clinical, and humanistic outcomes: a planning model for pharmacoeconomic research. Clin Ther 1993;15:1121–32.

This paper describes a theoretical framework for identifying, collecting, and using outcomes data to assess the value of pharmaceutical treatment alternatives. The Economic, Clinical, and Humanistic Outcomes model depicts the value of a pharmaceutical product or service as a combination of traditional clinical-based outcomes with more contemporary measures of economic efficiency and quality. The model should assist health services researchers in planning, conducting, and evaluating pharmaceutical products and services from a multidimensional perspective. This framework represents a comprehensive framework for medical decision-making.

14. Lee JT, Sanchez LA. Interpretation of "cost-effective" and soundness of economic evaluations in pharmacy literature. Am J Hosp Pharm 1992;48:2622–7.

    Interpretations of the term "cost-effective" in the pharmacy literature are discussed. Sixty-five studies evaluating cost issues were identified in the pharmacy literature. The adequacy of these studies was evaluated according to ten methodologic criteria. In 36 (55 percent) articles, "cost-savings" was incorrectly equated to "cost-effectiveness." Of the 10 criteria, only 50 percent or more of the studies evaluated satisfied three. Criteria least often satisfied dealt with the identification of relevant costs and consequences of each strategy, discounting, incremental analysis, and sensitivity analysis. The authors conclude that many pharmacoeconomic studies incorrectly used the term cost-effective and inadequately addressed basic methodologic components.

15. Meyer KM, Espindle DM, DeGiacomo JM, Jenuleson CS, Kurtin PS, Davies AR. Monitoring dialysis patients' health status. Am J Kidney Dis 1994;24:267–79.

    The authors report 3 years experience with quarterly assessments of self-reported health of dialysis outpatients using the Medical Outcomes Study, short form, 36 items (MOS SF-36). Program logistics and results are described, including reliability coefficients, standard deviations, and standard errors of measurement for the MOS SF-36 in this patient population. Two case reports compare information obtained from the MOS SF-36 with the dialysis team's assessments of the patient, as recorded in the medical record. The comments of two patients on reviewing their MOS SF-36 results are also summarized. Patient reactions to the health status assessment program are explored, and potential benefits and areas for further work are outlined. The authors report that serial measurement of dialysis patients' health status allowed for recognition of clear patterns in individual patient's responses. Patterns sometimes suggested that the patient was either substantially more or less impaired than the dialysis team had thought. Changes in these patterns, both transient and protracted, frequently exceeded 95 percent confidence intervals for patient-level scores.

16. Pathak DS, MacKegian LD. Assessment of quality of life and health status selected observations. J Res Pharm Econ 1992;9:31–52.

    This paper focuses on conceptual and methodological issues involved in the definition and measurement of the construct of HRQOL. Conceptual issues discussed include quality of life versus HRQOL, defining HRQOL, need for a comprehensive framework to investigate the construct HRQOL, and demographic characteristics as determinants of HRQOL. Methodological issues discussed are new psychometric terms versus traditional terms, multi-attribute utility measurement and external validation, measurement of value versus utility, and time-related phenomena and the assessment of temporary and cyclical health states. Because these conceptual and methodological issues remain unresolved, caution is recommended in applying current assessment methods to set health care priorities. It is proposed that the true value of HRQOL assessments resides not in the final values obtained through such assessments, but in the explication of the process used in the valuation of subjective outcomes that cannot be adequately captured by objective measure.

17. Sanchez LA. Pharmacoeconomics and formulary decision-making. Pharmaco-Economics 1996;8(Suppl 2):S16–25.

    This paper describes how pharmacoeconomic data can be used to support various formulary management decisions. For example, these data can support the inclusion or exclusion of a drug on, or from, the formulary and support practice guidelines that promote the most cost-effective, or optimal use, of pharmaceutical products. Various strategies, including using published pharmacoeconomic studies, using economic modeling techniques, and conducting local pharmacoeconomic research, can be used to incorporate pharmacoeconomics into formulary decision making. Criteria for evaluating the pharmacoeconomic literature, suggestions for using economic models and suggested guidelines for conducting pharmacoeconomic projects are discussed. Furthermore, the process for formulary action and the influence of pharmacoeconomics on formulary management in a United States hospital are presented in this paper.

18. Sanchez LA. Expanding the role of pharmacists in pharmacoeconomics: how and why? PharmacoEconomics 1994; 5:367–75.

    The purpose of this paper is to illustrate the value of pharmacoeconomics in modern, pharmacy-practice settings, motivate pharmacists to expand their current roles to include pharmacoeconomics, and provide strategies for incorporating pharmacoeconomics into traditional pharmacy roles. Strategies, including use of published pharmacoeconomic literature, economic modeling and local pharmacoeconomic research, are presented.

19. Sanchez LA, Lee JT. Use and misuse of pharmacoeconomic terms: a definitions primer. Top Hosp Pharm Manage 1994;13:11–22.

    Given the current cost-conscious health care environment, pharmacists must now be able to assess the effect of an agent from safety, efficacy, and value considerations. This article describes the various methodologies that may be used in performing pharmacoeconomic analyses and highlights the use and misuse of pharmacoeconomic terminology. Case studies relating the use of these methods to the pharmacy practice setting are presented. The technical nuances of the various methods are explained to promote a better understanding of the appropriate use of these techniques and the terminology used to describe them.

20. Schrogie JJ, Nash DB. Relationship between practice guidelines, formulary management, and pharmacoeconomic studies. Top Hosp Pharm Manage 1994;13:38–46.

    This paper describes how pharmacy and therapeutics committees can use pharmaco-economic and outcomes studies as tools to evaluate and implement clinical guidelines for patient care. Ways in which the results of studies can help optimize the clinical effects and control the costs of drug therapy are discussed. The use of these data to assist in positioning products in competitive environments is described. A four-part classification of research studies is offered as an aid to strategic research planning.

21. Spilker B, ed. Quality of life and Pharmacoeconomics in Clinical Trials 2nd ed. Philadelphia, PA: Lippincott Williams & Wilkins Publishers, 1996. Revised edition of Quality of Life Assessment in Clinical Trials (1990).

A comprehensive reference for clinical investigators who conduct quality of life assessments. The volume is divided into 11 sections: introduction to the field; standard scales, tests, and approaches; specific scales, tests, and measures; choosing and administering tests and treatments; analyzing, interpreting, and presenting data; special perspectives on quality of life issues; cross-cultural and cross-national issues; health policy issues; special populations to assess quality of life; specific problems and diseases; and pharmacoeconomics. Expanded to four times its predecessor's size and scope, the Second Edition reflects the rapid progress made worldwide in quality of life assessment and the growing importance of quality of life issues and pharmacoeconomics in health care decision-making. The editor has assembled more than 200 experts from diverse clinical, research, and social science disciplines to provide a comprehensive reference on the methodology, interpretation, and use of quality of life and pharmacoeconomic studies. The Second Edition features all-new sections on pharmacoeconomics and on crucial health policy issues such as outcomes research. The greatly expanded coverage of quality of life assessment includes a new section on cross-cultural and cross-national issues, more detailed information on specific tests, scales, and measures, and more comprehensive guidelines on choosing and administering tests and treatments and analyzing, interpreting, and presenting data.

22. Streiner DL, Norman GR. Health measurement scales: a practical guide to their development and use. 2nd ed. New York: Oxford University Press, 1999.

This is the second edition initiated in recognition of significant developments in the field of measurement since its first printing. This book is organized in chronological sequence according to the order that someone faced with the problem of developing a new instrument might encounter topics. Chapter 2 provides an overview of the criteria that the authors recommend be used to assess any measurement instrument. By reviewing this section, the reader should be able to peruse the literature to see if any available instrument is suitable. In the remaining chapters, the authors assume an unsuccessful search, and provide detailed information regarding the steps involved in developing a new scale. Finally, the appendices provide additional resources for locating further information about health status measurement, including an annotated bibliography of references for existing scales.

23. Udvarhelyi S, Colditz GA, Rai A, et al. Cost-effectiveness and cost-benefit analyses in the medical literature. Ann Intern Med 1992;116:238–44.

The objective of this paper was to determine whether published cost-effectiveness and cost-benefit analyses have adhered to basic analytic principles. Seventy-seven articles published either from 1978-1980 or 1985-1987 in general medical, surgical, and medical subspecialty journals were reviewed based on six fundamental principles of economic evaluations. The study results revealed that only three of the 77 articles reviewed met all six principles. Articles in general medical journals were more likely to use analytic methods appropriately. The authors concluded that greater attention should be devoted to ensuring the appropriate use of analytic methods for economic analyses, and readers should make note of the methods used when interpreting the results of economic analyses.

24. Katz S, Akpom CA, Papsidero JA, Weiss ST. Measuring the health status of populations. In: Berg RL, ed. Health status indexes: proceedings of a conference conducted by Health Services Research. Chicago: Hospital Research and Educational Trust, 1972:39.

In this article, the history of population and individual-level health measurement is reviewed. Key issues facing the field in the early 1970s are examined.

25. McDowell I, Newell C. Measuring health: a guide to rating scales and questionnaires, 2nd ed. New York: Oxford University Press, 1996.

An update of the 1987 edition, this text provides an overview of the field of health status assessment, including the history, techniques, and future directions of measurement. The authors review 88 rating scales and questionnaires that measure physical disability, social health, psychological well-being, depression, mental status, pain, general health status, and quality of life. The description of each scale or questionnaire includes its purpose, conceptual basis, reliability, validity, and a copy of the measure.

26. Patrick DL, Erickson P. Health status and health policy: allocating resources to health care. New York: Oxford University Press, 1993.

Patrick and Erickson propose and explicate the Health Resource Allocation Strategy as a process for comparing costs and outcomes of alternative options when selecting medical and health care interventions with the greatest benefit in relation to cost. They provide a guide to the development and application of health status and quality of life measures, emphasizing those based on utility theory, and they examine contemporary uses of such measures, including preventing disease and promoting health, assessing the cost-benefit of technology, and improving access to care. A compilation of disease-specific measures appears in Chapter 5; the appendix illustrates four utility-based indexes: Disability/Distress Index; Health Utilities Index; Quality of Well-Being Scale; and the EuroQol instrument. The glossary defines key terms.

27. Stewart AL, Ware JE Jr., eds. Measuring functioning and well-being: the Medical Outcomes Study approach. Durham, NC: Duke University Press, 1992.

In this book, the authors provide a comprehensive account of a broad range of self-reported measures of functioning and well-being developed for the Medical Outcomes Study, a large-scale investigation of how patients fare with health care in the United States. Many of these measures were derived from those used in earlier health policy research, including the Health Insurance Experiment (HIE). The authors address conceptual and methodologic issues involved in measuring physical, social, and role functioning; psychological distress and well-being; general health perceptions; energy and fatigue; sleep; and pain. Information is also presented on the construction, reliability, and validity of each measure, along with administration, scoring, and interpretation guidelines. The appendix includes copies of each measure; a glossary defines key terms; and the bibliography offers citations for most of the articles and books in health status assessment and related measurement methods for the past 50 years.

28. Testa MA, Simonson DC. Assessment of quality-of-life outcomes. N Engl J Med 1996;334:835–40.

Quality of life assessments and a conceptual scheme of quality of life are reviewed in this article. The article also addresses properties of measurement scales, selecting an assessment instrument, and interpreting quality of life effects.

29. Manning WG, Leibowitz A, Goldberg G, et al. A controlled trial of the effect of a prepaid group practice on use of services. N Engl J Med 1984; 310:1505–10.

This is an important paper, reporting results of the Rand HIE. The HIE was the first, and still the largest, randomized health services research study ever conducted. Patients were randomly assigned to fee-for-service or health maintenance organization plans to study differences in service use and health outcomes associated with these systems. The article reports the findings with respect to use. Overall expenditures on services were lower in the health maintenance organizations, attributable primarily to differences in rates of hospitalization. The study found that health maintenance organization patients were hospitalized 40 percent less than equivalent fee-for-service patients. Ambulatory care use was similar in the two systems. Subsequent research has validated these findings, both the magnitude and nature of the use differences.

30. Ware JE, Rogers WH, Davies AR, et al. Comparison of health outcomes at a health maintenance organization with those of fee-for service care. Lancet 1986;1:1017–22.

This landmark article from the Rand HIE shows that the health outcomes associated with managed care differ for patients at different levels of illness and socioeconomic status. In particular, the authors report that outcomes in managed care were worse for patients who were poor and sick at the outset of the study. For nonpoor and/or well patients, managed care had beneficial health effect.

31. Wilson IB, Cleary PD. Linking clinical variables with health-related quality of life. A conceptual model of patient outcomes. JAMA 1995; 273(1):59–65.

This article provides the clinician with an introduction to health services research concepts. In this article, the authors present a conceptual model, a taxonomy of patients outcomes that categorizes measures of patient outcome according to the underlying health concepts they represent and porpoises specific causal relationships between different health concepts, thereby integrating the two models of health described. This article is valuable to clinicians in practice, and in research settings since it discusses the conceptual intersection of those two worlds.

32. Wennberg J, Gittelson A. Variations in medical care among small areas. Sci Am 1982;246:120–34.

This is a valuable paper in which the phenomenon of small-area variation associated with six surgical procedures are described. It is one of the first empiric studies of small-area variation in the United States. The authors studied the rates of selected procedures in the six New England states. The results provide powerful evidence that area norms, rather than universally shared scientific criteria, determine medical treatments provided to patients. This field of work led to the call for research, including clinical practice guideline development, health outcomes research, and cost-effectiveness analysis of medical interventions, to try to bring greater rationality to medical care.

Conferences

A variety of conferences have been convened since the early 1970s to address issues of health status measurement—theoretical, conceptual, empiric, and historical. The published proceedings from these conferences include many of the now-classic articles in the health measurement field, and their citation lists contain many others. The following publications direct the interested reader to these sources.

1. Berg RL, ed. Health status indexes: proceedings of a conference conducted by health services research. Chicago: Hospital Research and Educational Trust, 1973.
2. Fowler FJ, ed. The proceedings of the Conference of Measuring the Effects of Medical Treatment. Med Care 1995;33(4): supplement.
3. Health status indexes: work in progress. Health Services Res 1976; 11(4): special issue.
4. Katz S, ed. The Portugal conference: measuring quality of life and functional status in clinical and epidemiological research. J Chronic Dis 1987;40(6): special issue.
5. Lohr KN, ed. Advances in health status assessment: conference proceedings. Med Care 1989;27(3): supplement.
6. Lohr KN, ed. Advances in health status assessment: fostering the application of health status measures in clinical settings—proceedings of a conference. Med Care 1992:30(5): supplement.
7. Lohr KN, Ware Jr JE, eds. Proceedings of the advances in health assessment conference. J Chronic Dis 1987;40: supplement 1.
8. Patrick DL, Chiang YP, eds. Health Outcomes Methodology: Symposium Proceedings. Med Care 2000;38(9): supplement II.

Self-Assessment Questions

1. Proponents of outcomes research believe that which one of the following is true?
   A. Outcomes research is synonymous with pharmacoeconomics.
   B. We should measure not only the clinical and cost impacts of health care, but also the outcomes that take the patients perspective into account.
   C. Only clinical effects, and not functional status or well-being, should be included as outcomes.
   D. All outcomes research is pharmacoeconomic research.

2. The economic, clinical, and humanistic outcomes (ECHO) model recognizes the existence of intermediate outcomes. Which one of the following is an example of an intermediate outcome?
   A. A patient's physical functioning or mental well-being.
   B. A specific laboratory value.
   C. The total cost of hospitalization.
   D. Adherence to a drug regimen.

3. Which one of the following statements best describes economic outcomes?
   A. The direct, indirect, and intangible costs compared with the consequences of medical treatment alternatives.
   B. The medical events that occur as a result of a disease or treatment.
   C. The consequences of a disease or treatment on a patient's functional status or quality of life.
   D. The cost-savings associated with a disease or treatment alternative.

4. Which one of the following best represents a direct medical cost?
   A. Pain.
   B. Transportation.
   C. Mortality.
   D. Medical professional time.

5. Lost productivity is an example of which one of the following cost categories?
   A. Direct medical cost.
   B. Direct nonmedical cost.
   C. Indirect cost.
   D. Intangible cost.

6. Which one of the following statements regarding the perspective of economic evaluations is true?
   A. Economic evaluations are valid only if conducted from a single perspective.
   B. Economic evaluations can be conducted from multiple perspectives.
   C. Economic evaluations should only be conducted from the perspective of the patient.
   D. Society is the only valid perspective for economic evaluations.

7. From the perspective of a provider, which one of the following is a direct cost of health care?
   A. The amount paid out-of-pocket by patients directly to their physicians for a clinic visit.
   B. The patient charge for a visit to an emergency department.
   C. The prescription cost of insulin at the community pharmacy.
   D. The salary of the clinical pharmacist who monitors a patient's therapy.

8. From the perspective of an employer, indirect costs are best described by which one of the following?
   A. Hospitalization costs borne by the patient.
   B. Drug effects on patient functioning.
   C. Loss of patient income associated with missed workdays.
   D. Family caregiving costs.

9. The costs and consequences of health care can be different depending on the perspective of the evaluation. Costs from a patient's perspective are best described as which one of the following?
   A. Essentially, what patients are charged for a product or service.
   B. Essentially, the true cost of providing a product or service, regardless of the charge.
   C. Essentially, the charges allowed for a health care product or service.
   D. Essentially, the cost of giving and receiving medical care, including patient morbidity and mortality.

10. Which one of the following constitutes a full economic evaluation?
    A. Two antibiotics are compared and relative cure rates are determined.
    B. The costs for treatment of hypertension by general practice physicians, versus pharmacists, are considered in light of the blood pressure control achieved.
    C. The costs and efficiency of treatment of hypercholesterolemia with a new HMG-CoA reductase inhibitor are determined.
    D. The acquisition costs of two therapeutically equivalent antihypertensive agents are compared.

11. Which one of the following is an example of a partial economic evaluation?
    A. A comparison of the costs and consequences of two alternatives.
    B. A cost-utility analysis.
    C. A comparison of the costs of two equally effective alternatives.
    D. A quality of life comparison of multiple treatment alternatives.

12. Which one of the following is true of partial economic evaluations?
    A. Partial evaluations should be performed as components of full economic evaluations.
    B. Partial evaluations assess all important components necessary for a complete economic analysis.
    C. Partial evaluations may provide a description of the costs, or consequences, of competing alternatives.
    D. Partial evaluations compare the costs and consequences of two treatments.

13. Which one of the following statements is *not* true about cost-minimization analysis?
    A. Cost-minimization analysis is a tool used to compare the costs of two or more treatment alternatives.
    B. Cost-minimization analysis shows only a cost-savings of one treatment alternative over another.
    C. Cost-minimization analysis measures costs of treatment alternatives in dollars and a assumes comparable efficacy.
    D. Cost-minimization analysis is a method to be used when no evidence exists to support the therapeutic equivalence of two or more treatment alternatives.

14. When conducting a cost-benefit analysis (CBA), the results are best expressed as which one of the following?
    A. Cost-benefit ratio.
    B. Average cost per utility.
    C. cost-savings.
    D. Incremental cost ratio.

15. When quantifying the value of a clinical pharmacy service, which one of the following economic evaluation methods is the best to use?
    A. Cost-benefit analysis.
    B. Cost-effectiveness analysis.
    C. Cost-minimization analysis.
    D. Cost-utility analysis.

16. Which one of the following statements does not describe a cost-effective treatment alternative?
    A. Less expensive and less effective, where the lost benefit was worth the extra cost.
    B. Less expensive and at least as effective.
    C. More expensive with an additional benefit worth the additional cost.
    D. Less expensive and less effective, where the extra benefit is not worth the extra cost.

17. A cost-effectiveness analysis would be best applied to which one of the following situations?
    A. When comparing two or more treatment alternatives that differ in clinical outcome.
    B. When comparing two or more treatment alternatives that are equal in clinical outcome.
    C. When comparing two or more treatment alternatives that differ in humanistic outcome.
    D. When comparing two or more treatment alternatives that differ in cost.

18. Which one of the following statements best describes an incremental cost-effectiveness ratio?
    A. A summary measurement of efficiency.
    B. The cost per benefit of a new strategy, independent of other treatment alternatives.
    C. The cost to obtain an extra benefit realized when switching from one strategy to another.
    D. The cost per quality-adjusted life-year (QALY) gained.

19. When comparing treatment alternatives, which one of the following is the most correct application for cost-utility analysis?
    A. Alternatives that are life-extending with serious side effects.
    B. Alternatives that differ in cost.
    C. Alternatives that differ in efficacy and safety.
    D. Alternatives that are similar in clinical and humanistic outcomes.

20. Which one of the following statements about discounting is not true?
    A. When costs and consequences of a treatment alternative occur in the future, they should be reduced to reflect current fiscal value.
    B. Discounting is the process of adjusting for differential timing.
    C. There is one standard discount rate that should be used in pharmacoeconomic analyses.
    D. Comparisons of programs or treatment alternatives should be made at the same time.

21. Which one of the following statements regarding discounting is true?
    A. Researchers should always use a 5 percent discount rate.
    B. Costs incurred today to initiate a new program should be discounted.
    C. Discounting can be useful when comparing acute and long-term treatment strategies.
    D. Benefits should not be discounted.

22. The primary reason to perform a sensitivity analysis is to accomplish which one of the following?
    A. Test the robustness of the economic evaluation conclusions.
    B. Reveal sensitive variables of the economic evaluation.
    C. Uncover the range of plausible values.
    D. Allow for a meaningful comparison of treatment alternatives.

23. Which one of the following statements is *not* true regarding the application of pharmacoeconomics to pharmacy practice?
    A. Pharmacoeconomics can be a powerful tool for determining the most efficient use of drugs.
    B. Pharmacoeconomics can assist pharmacy and therapeutics committees in incorporating clinical, economic, and humanistic outcomes of drug therapy into formulary management decisions.
    C. Pharmacoeconomics can provide data to support individual patient treatment and resource allocation decisions.
    D. Use of pharmacoeconomic data ensures that organizational drug-use policies will influence physician prescribing patterns.

24. Which one of the following formulary decision options would be *least* influenced by the inclusion of pharmacoeconomic data?
    A. Inclusion or exclusion of newly marketed agents.
    B. Inclusion with restriction of newly marketed agents.
    C. Deletion of drugs from the formulary.
    D. Determination of the least expensive to purchase alternative.

25. Which one of the following is true regarding health and quality of life?
   A. Quality of life is encompassed by a person's lifestyle, including work and economic status.
   B. Health or HRQOL refers only to those aspects of life dominated, or significantly influenced, by personal health or activities performed to maintain health.
   C. Quality of life is divided into physical and mental dimensions of functioning and well-being.
   D. The concept of health includes marital status, education, and religious beliefs.

26. Which one of the following activities is a dimension of general health status measurement?
   A. Carrying a bag of groceries.
   B. Physical functioning.
   C. Playing sports.
   D. Bathing or dressing.

27. Which one of the following pairs illustrates two opposite extremes of mental well-being? These two attributes can be used to describe the range of a mental health continuum.
   A. Psychological distress and physical distress.
   B. Physical distress and psychological well-being.
   C. Psychological well-being and psychological distress.
   D. High physical energy and physical weariness.

28. Which one of the following features could be described as one of the most striking differences between traditional clinical measures of a patient's health and measures of health status?
   A. The source of the data is patient self-administered questionnaires.
   B. The collection of data from patients is a new phenomenon, whereas collection of laboratory data dates back many years.
   C. Clinicians can use the clinical data, but not health status data, in decision-making.
   D. Clinical data are "hard data", whereas, health status data are not as scientifically rigorous in their standards of measurement.

29. The following are characteristics of a good scale for measuring health status. Which one of the following is true of generic/general health status measures, but *not* true of disease specific measures?
   A. The concepts can be measured in patients of all ages, races, and socio-demographic characteristics.
   B. The concepts being measured include all possible dimensions of health for a patient population.
   C. The measurement framework extends across the entire range of a dimension, from disease to well-being.
   D. The measurement must be sensitive to change over time to be used in clinical practice.

30. The categorization of structure, process, and outcome published in the early 1960s (see Reference 5) was designed to evaluate which one of the following?
   A. Patients satisfaction with care.
   B. The quality of health care.
   C. Health policy changes.
   D A patients self-assessment of the health care system.

31. Which one of the following best describes a difference between patient satisfaction and health status?
   A. Patient satisfaction results are required for accreditation by JCAHO; health status results are not.
   B. Health status measurements of functioning and well-being are required by law for drug approval; patient satisfaction results are not.
   C. Patient satisfaction is measured with a combination of reports and ratings; health status doesn't use ratings.
   D. Health status is measured using psychometric techniques; patient satisfaction is not.

32. It has been proposed that one solution to increase clinicians' information about the functional status, well-being, and changes over time of their patients might be to standardize these assessments in everyday medical practice. Such routine assessments could be useful for all except which one of the following purposes?
   A. To replace the need for referral to specialists in assessment of functional or emotional problems.
   B. To detect, explain, and track changes in functional capacity over time.
   C. To make it possible to better consider the patients total functioning when choosing among therapies.
   D. As guidance for efficient use of community resources and social services.

33. Which one of the following are *not* characteristics of the measurement and use of individual level patient self-reported health status information?
   A. Standardized method of asking patients about their functioning and well being can be efficiently used in treatment decisions and as a monitoring parameter for efficacy and toxicity of treatment.
   B. Concerns have been raised about the reliability and interpretation of the results from individual, patient-level, health status information.
   C. Modern psychometric test theory, such as Item Response Theory, offers potential for individual patient-level, health status assessment, and use in clinical care.
   D. Existing health outcome assessments drawn from classic test theory can no longer be used.

Appendix A

MOS SF-36™ HEALTH SURVEY

SITE: 1 DATE: 10-01-1995

ID: 12345986500 SEX: Male AGE: 65-74

HEALTH SCORES

Physical Functioning	(PF)	Vitality	(VT)
Role Physical	(RP)	Social Functioning	(SF)
Bodily Pain	(BP)	Role Emotional	(RE)
General Health	(GH)	Mental Health	(MH)

■ = INITIAL (I) ▒ = PREVIOUS (P) ■ = CURRENT (C) 10-01-1995

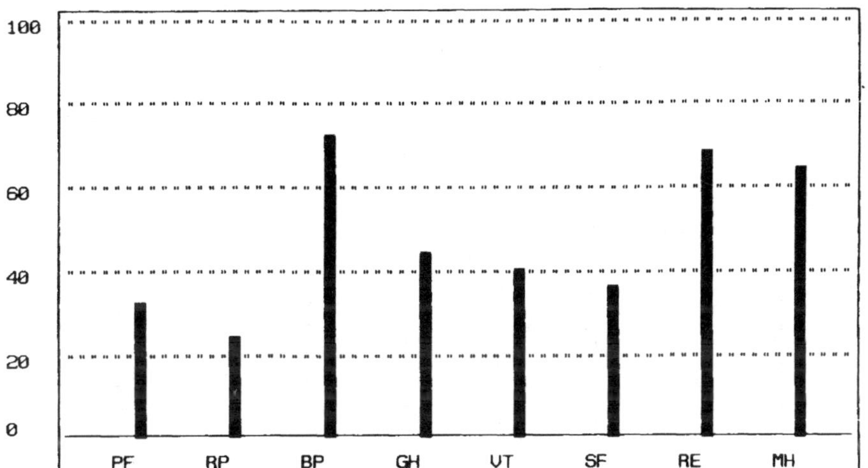

	PF	RP	BP	GH	VT	SF	RE	MH
I	----	----	----	----	----	----	----	----
P	----	----	----	----	----	----	----	----
C	30.0	25.0	74.0	45.0	40.0	37.5	66.7	64.0

LIMITATIONS GRID

	I	P	C
Physical Limitation			■
Emotional Limitation			
Role Disability			■
Personal Evaluation			

REPORTED CHANGE IN HEALTH

	I	P	C
Much better now			
Somewhat better now			
About the same			—
Somewhat worse now			■
Much worse now			

DATA QUALITY

	INITIAL	PREVIOUS	CURRENT 10-01-1995
VERSION USED	----	----	STANDARD
OVERALL QUALITY	----	----	EXCELLENT
ITEMS COMPLETE (%)	----	----	100.0
CONSISTENCY OF RESPONSES (%)	----	----	100.0

Ware, J.E., Snow, K.K., Kosinski, M. SF-36(R) Health Survey: Manual and Interpretation Guide. Lincoln, RI: QualityMetric Incorporated, 1993, 2000.

Appendix B

MOS SF-36™ HEALTH SURVEY

SITE: 1 DATE: 12-07-1995

ID: 12345986500 SEX: Male AGE: 65-74

HEALTH SCORES

Physical Functioning	(PF)	Vitality	(VT)
Role Physical	(RP)	Social Functioning	(SF)
Bodily Pain	(BP)	Role Emotional	(RE)
General Health	(GH)	Mental Health	(MH)

■ = INITIAL (I) 10-01-1995 ▒ = PREVIOUS (P) ■ = CURRENT (C) 12-07-1995

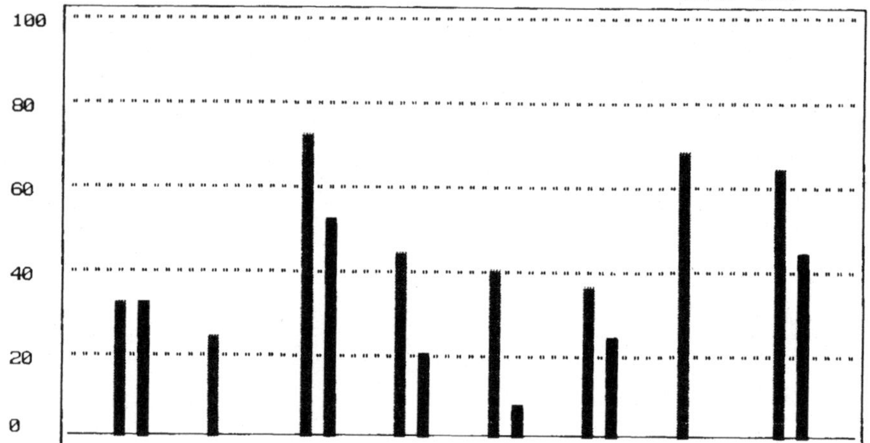

	PF	RP	BP	GH	VT	SF	RE	MH
I	30.0	25.0	74.0	45.0	40.0	37.5	66.7	64.0
P	----	----	----	----	----	----	----	----
C	30.0	0.0	52.0	20.0	10.0	25.0	0.0	44.0

LIMITATIONS GRID

I P C

Physical Limitation ....
Emotional Limitation ....
Role Disability ....
Personal Evaluation ....

REPORTED CHANGE IN HEALTH

I P C

Much better now ....
Somewhat better now .....
About the same ....
Somewhat worse now ......
Much worse now ....

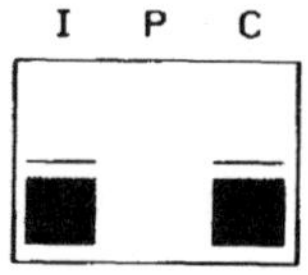

DATA QUALITY

	INITIAL 10-01-1995	PREVIOUS	CURRENT 12-07-1995
VERSION USED	STANDARD	----	STANDARD
OVERALL QUALITY	EXCELLENT	----	SATISFACT
ITEMS COMPLETE (%)	100.0	----	100.0
CONSISTENCY OF RESPONSES (%)	100.0	----	93.3

Ware, J.E., Snow, K.K., Kosinski, M. SF-36(R) Health Survey: Manual and Interpretation Guide. Lincoln, RI: QualityMetric Incorporated, 1993, 2000.

Appendix C

SF-36 HEALTH STATUS SURVEY RESULTS:
INTERPRETATION GUIDE FOR INDIVIDUAL PATIENT REPORTS (RT Version 1.0)

About the SF-36

The SF-36 (Short-Form, 36 Item) Health Survey is a patient-based, generic health status assessment survey that obtains patients' assessments of their functioning and well-being (how they feel), and perceptions of their health in general. The SF-36 has been used to assess the health status of both general and chronic disease populations. Its reliability in these populations has been documented, and its validity in relation to such clinical indicators as presence or absence of disease, severity within disease category, and changes in disease-related symptoms over time has been demonstrated by investigators.

The information about a patient's functional status and well-being obtained with the SF-36 can be useful in assessing and obtaining a better understanding of a patient's overall health status. Data obtained with the SF-36 should be interpreted within the context of all other information available about the patient.

SF-36 Scoring

The SF-36 measures eight different health concepts, each of which is scored on a scale from 0 to 100. Points in between are percentages of the total possible score. All scales are scored so that a higher score indicates better health. For instance, on the Bodily Pain scale, a higher score indicates <u>less</u> pain, and on the Physical Functioning scale, a higher score indicates <u>better</u> physical functioning. Each item in the SF-36 belongs to, and is used in the scoring of, only one of the eight scales. The table below lists each health concept and indicates the meaning of low and high scores for each concept.

Interpreting the Report

Background

The patient's ID (medical record or encounter) number, gender and age range, and the date on which the patient completed the SF-36, are indicated just below the report title *(MOS SF-36 Health Survey).*

Health Scores

This section reports the patient's scores on each of the eight health concepts (commonly referred to as the eight SF-36 *scales*). Scale scores for each of three possible time points are displayed. A histogram format is used to indicate the eight scale scores at each point in time.

- The scale names (and their corresponding abbreviations in parentheses) are indicated above the graph. Scale abbreviations are used to indicate the corresponding bar in the histogram.
- Initial (I), previous (P), and current (C) dates of survey completion are shown underneath the time point legend. Previous date indicates the most recent date of survey completion before the current administration.
- The vertical axis ranges from 0 to 100 (the range for each SF-36 scale). The horizontal axis lists each scale (by its abbreviation).
- Initial, previous, and current scale scores are listed below the bar(s) corresponding to that scale. "NA" is indicated if a score could not be calculated for a scale on a particular date (scale scores cannot be calculated for a given scale if less than half of the items comprising that scale are completed). **NOTE:** "0.0" is a possible scale score.

Confidence Intervals

Confidence intervals are particularly useful in evaluating changes in SF-36 scores over time and in comparing a patient's scores to benchmark scores. The size of the 90 percent confidence interval (CI) around an individual patient's score ranges between +/- 10 points for the Physical Functioning scale and +/- 23 points for the Role Emotional scale. For any one scale, one would be correct 90 percent of the time or more in concluding that a change truly occurred or a difference truly exists if the difference between the scores being compared exceeds the 90 percent CI for that scale.

Health Concept (Scale Name Bolded)	Lowest Possible Score (0)	Highest Possible Score (100)	Confidence Interval*
Physical Functioning	Limited a lot in performing all physical activities including bathing or dressing	Performs all types of physical activities including the most vigorous without limitations due to health	+/- 10
Role limitations due to physical problems	Problem with work or other daily activities as a result of physical health	No problems with work or other daily activities as a result of physical health	+/- 19
Bodily Pain	Very severe and extremely limiting pain	No pain or limitations due to pain	+/- 12
General Health	Believes personal health is poor and likely to get worse	Believes personal health is excellent	+/- 15
Vitality	Feels tired and worn out all of the time	Feels full of pep and energy all of the time	+/- 13
Social Functioning	Extreme and frequent interference with normal social activities due to physical and emotional problems	Performs normal social activities without interference due to physical or emotional problems	+/- 21
Role limitations due to Emotional problems	Problems with work or other daily activities as a result of emotional problems	No problems with work or other daily activities as a result of emotional problems	+/- 23
General Mental Health	Feelings of nervousness and depression all of the time	Feels peaceful, happy, and calm all of the time	+/- 12

Ware, J.E., Snow, K.K., Kosinski, M. SF-36(R) Health Survey: Manual and Interpretation Guide. Lincoln, RI: QualityMetric Incorporated, 1993, 2000.

Limitations Grid

This grid is a visual representation of four dichotomous summary limitation indicators. The indicators identify limitations patients reported in four different health categories. The limitation indicators and their criteria for activation are: Physical Limitation (PF<100), Emotional Limitation (MH<53), Role Disability (RP<100 or RE<100) and Personal Evaluation (GH<56). When an indicator is "activated," a black box appears across from the indicator name, under the appropriate date of survey administration.

Reported Change in Health

This section of the report reports how a patient rates their general health in comparison to a year ago (if the standard version of the SF-36 is used) or a week ago if the acute version is used). (See discussion of the Standard and Acute versions in the Data Quality section, below.) Response options appear on the left, and responses on initial, previous, and current administrations are indicated in a box on the right. The length of the bar corresponds to the degree to which the patient rates his or her general health compared to the past: a longer bar above the "about the same" line indicates greater improvement, while a longer bar below the line indicates greater worsening of general health. If the patient reported that their health is "about the same", an asterisk appears across from this response option.

Data Quality

This section indicates the SF-36 version administered during the current administration (standard or acute). The two versions differ in the recall period used in the items included in the RP, BP, VT, SF, RE, and MH scales. The standard version uses a 4 week recall period, whereas the acute version uses a 1 week recall period. The standard version is most frequently used. General population norms and confidence intervals are available on the standard version only.

The Data Quality section also indicates a rating of the overall quality of the data, the percent of items complete and the percent consistency of responses based on the current administration. *Item completeness* and *response consistency*, two indicators of data quality, are assessed each time a patient completes the SF-36. The closer each of these percentages is to 100 percent, the better the data quality. Item completeness is assessed by calculating the percent of items completed by the patient. Response consistency is assessed by evaluating 15 pairs of items for agreement in the pattern of responses. Taking these two indicators into account, the data quality of each SF-36 form is assigned a rating of *Excellent, Satisfactory, or Problematic*. (See next column for interpretation of problematic data.)

Missing / Double Marks and Inconsistency Report

If there are any missing data (percent items complete<100) or inconsistent responses (percent consistency<100), then a second page is printed. The top of the page notes which questions were not answered or had multiple responses (and are therefore considered missing). The bottom of the page indicates which of the 15 consistency checks were failed. The numbers listed above the inconsistency check box represent the questions involved in the consistency check. For example, if a patient responds "all of the time" to both questions 9a ("Did you feel full of pep?") and 9i ("Did you feel tired?"), then a check mark is listed under "9a vs 9i" because these responses are inconsistent.

Interpreting Problematic Data

- On a given date for a given patient, any of the following conditions result in a data quality rating of Problematic:
  1. Less than half of the items were completed for one or more of the scales, resulting in one or more missing scale scores.
  2. Inconsistent response pattern (response consistency ≤85 percent).
  3. Combination of both 1 and 2.
- A low response consistency (percent) could mean two things:
  1. The patient had difficulty understanding the questions.
  2. The patient was not paying attention to the way he/she responded to some or all of the questions (random answers).
- Items complete (percent) and response consistency (percent) can help identify patients who repeatedly have trouble completing the form and/or have trouble responding in a consistent manner.

Treat Problematic Data with Caution

Problematic data are by nature less reliable. This is especially true if there is a problem with response consistency. It is often useful to examine the individual items causing the inconsistent responses for individual patients.

References

1. Ware JE, Jr., Sherbourne C. A 36-item short-form health survey (SF-36): I. Conceptual framework and item selection. Med Care 1992, 30:6.
2. Ware JE. SF-36 Health Survey Manual and Interpretation Guide. The Health Institute, New England Medical Center, Boston MA, 1993.
3. Response Technologies, Inc. The RT 2000/SF-36 Report Formats. © 1992 Response Technologies, Inc.

Appendix D

Normative Values

NORMS FOR THE GENERAL U.S. POPULATION, TOTAL SAMPLE

Total Sample
(N=2,474)

	PF	RP	BP	GH	VT	SF	RE	MH
Mean	84.15	80.96	75.15	71.95	60.86	83.28	81.26	74.74
25th Percentile	70.00	50.00	61.00	57.00	45.00	75.00	66.67	64.00
50th Percentile *(median)*	90.00	100.00	74.00	72.00	65.00	100.00	100.00	80.00
75th Percentile	100.00	100.00	100.00	85.00	75.00	700.00	100.00	88.00
Standard Deviation	23.28	34.00	23.69	20.34	20.96	22.69	33.04	18.05
Range	0-100	0-100	0-100	5-100	0-100	0-100	0-100	0-100
% Ceiling	38.79	70.85	31.85	7.40	1.50	52.32	71.01	3.91
% Floor	0.84	10.33	0.58	0.00	0.52	0.64	9.61	0.00

Ages 65 & over
Males (N=293)

	PF	RP	BP	GH	VT	SF	RE	MH
Mean	65.79	59.72	68.76	58.62	57.80	79.66	76.94	77.37
25th Percentile	45.00	25.00	51.00	47.00	40.00	62.50	66.67	68.00
50th Percentile *(median)*	75.00	75.00	72.00	62.00	60.00	100.00	100.00	84.00
75th Percentile	90.00	100.00	84.00	77.00	75.00	100.00	100.00	92.00
Standard Deviation	28.31	42.51	25.37	22.05	22.55	26.00	37.48	17.42
Range	0 100	0-100	0-100	5-100	0-100	0-100	0-100	16 100
% Ceiling	6.6	45.9	22.8	1.8	1.7	50.7	68.3	7.6
% Floor	3.0	24.4	0.9	0.0	1.0	1.5	14.9	0.0

NORMS FOR COMORBID CONDITIONS: CHRONIC OBSTRUCTIVE PULMONARY DISEASE (COPD) WITH HYPERTENSION

	PF	RP	BP	GH	VT	SF	RE	MH
Mean	56.91	34.38	54.82	45.29	44.95	71.82	59.73	68.06
25th Percentile	35.00	0.00	31.00	35.00	30.00	62.50	0.00	56.00
50th Percentile *(median)*	61.11	25.00	52.00	42.00	50.00	75.00	66.67	72.00
75th Percentile	80.00	75.00	72.00	60.00	55.00	100.00	100.00	84.00
Standard Deviation	29.14	38.73	26.14	18.94	19.55	31.40	44.61	19.68
Range	0-100	0-100	10-100	5-87	0-90	0-100	0-100	13-100
% Ceiling	5.88	14.12	10.59	0.00	0.00	32.94	48.24	2.35
% Floor	2.35	42.35	0.00	0.00	1.18	2.35	27.06	0.00

Ware, J.E., Snow, K.K., Kosinski, M. SF-36(R) Health Survey: Manual and Interpretation Guide. Lincoln, RI: QualityMetric Incorporated, 1993, 2000.

Appendix E

MOS SF-36™ HEALTH SURVEY

SITE: 1 DATE: 12-05-1996

ID: 12345986500 SEX: Male AGE: 65-74

HEALTH SCORES

Physical Functioning	(PF)	Vitality	(VT)
Role Physical	(RP)	Social Functioning	(SF)
Bodily Pain	(BP)	Role Emotional	(RE)
General Health	(GH)	Mental Health	(MH)

■ = INITIAL (I) 10-01-1995 ▒ = PREVIOUS (P) 12-07-1995 ■ = CURRENT (C) 12-05-1996

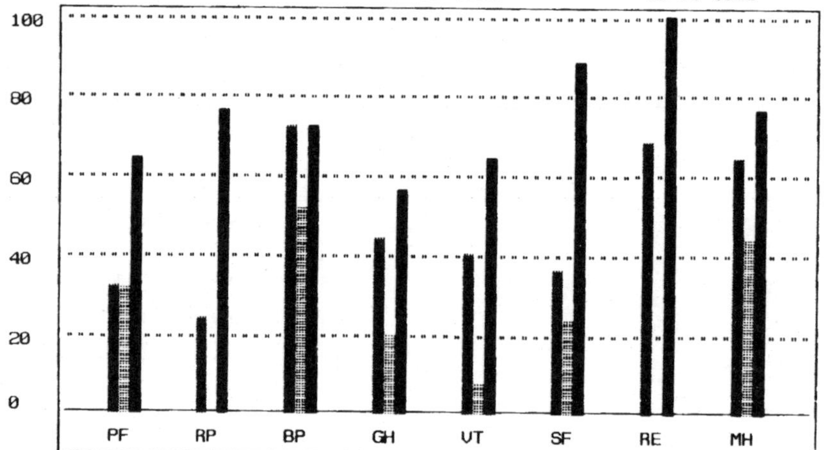

	PF	RP	BP	GH	VT	SF	RE	MH
I	30.0	25.0	74.0	45.0	40.0	37.5	66.7	64.0
P	30.0	0.0	52.0	20.0	10.0	25.0	0.0	44.0
C	65.0	75.0	74.0	57.0	65.0	87.5	100.0	76.0

LIMITATIONS GRID

I P C

Physical Limitation ....
Emotional Limitation ....
Role Disability ....
Personal Evaluation ....

REPORTED CHANGE IN HEALTH

I P C

Much better now ....
Somewhat better now .....
About the same ....
Somewhat worse now ......
Much worse now ....

DATA QUALITY

	INITIAL 10-01-1995	PREVIOUS 12-07-1995	CURRENT 12-05-1996
VERSION USED	STANDARD	STANDARD	STANDARD
OVERALL QUALITY	EXCELLENT	SATISFACT	EXCELLENT
ITEMS COMPLETE (%)	100.0	100.0	100.0
CONSISTENCY OF RESPONSES (%)	100.0	93.3	100.0

Ware, J.E., Snow. K.K., Kosinski, M. SF-36(R) Health Survey: Manual and Interpretation Guide. Lincoln, RI: QualityMetric Incorporated, 1993, 2000.

INVESTIGATING THE OUTCOMES RESEARCH QUESTION

Jane T. Osterhaus, Ph.D.
J. Gregory Boyer, Ph.D.

Outline

I. Why pharmacoeconomic assessments
    A. A way to measure value, regardless of the system of health care
    B. A way to measure and document the value of pharmaceutical products and services
    C. Outcomes research is critical to the future of pharmacy practice
        1. Vital to demonstrate pharmacist effectiveness
        2. Vital to document overall benefit of an intervention
        3. Vital to determine a national standard for pharmaceutical care
        4. What is not measured cannot be managed

II. Asking the question
    A. Define the problem
        1. Asking the right question helps increase the utility of outcomes research
        2. Research process is cyclical
        3. Practitioners role is essential for framing the research question
        4. Review the literature to see who else has addressed the question
    B. Define objectives
        1. A broad problem will result in broadly defined objectives
        2. At least one objective should be quantifiable
        3. One primary and multiple secondary objectives are acceptable
    C. Identify alternatives
        1. Broad problems lead to broad objectives which lead to many alternatives
        2. Not all alternatives need be limited to pharmaceuticals or even health
    D. Formulate research hypothesis
        1. Null hypothesis
            a. For every null hypothesis there is an alternative
            b. Data obtained will test the null hypothesis
    E. Establish a framework
        1. Prioritize objectives
        2. Consider what can be done within the problem or research question identified
            a. Be realistic
            b. Identify alternatives that are feasible now
        3. Consider both processes and outcomes of care
            a. Process and outcomes are not mutually exclusive aspects of care
        4. Consider dependent and independent variables
            a. Research hypothesis implies dependent variable of research
            b. Dependent variable is the end point to study
            c. Differences between dependent variables and outcomes

III. Identification, measurement and valuation of resources and outcomes

- A. Resources used
  - 1. Identifying resources
    - a. Do not immediately go to an administrative database and look at costs
    - b. Identify what variables are needed before collecting anything
    - c. Identify the resources in terms of what is actually being used
  - 2. Measuring resources
    - a. The perspective from which the question is to be answered is critical when it is being determined how resources are measured
    - b. Count resources in the units of service required to produce the intended benefit
    - c. Watch for substitution of resources
    - d. Watch for migration of resources
    - e. Some resources are difficult to separate
      - i. Overhead
      - ii. Technologies that produce multiple outcomes
      - iii. Personnel time
  - 3. Valuing resources
    - a. Market values of goods and services are used to value resources in health care
    - b. Opportunity costs are theoretically the best value measure; however, market value is perfectly acceptable and is what people tend to understand
    - c. Do not confuse charges and costs
    - d. Sources of cost or charge data
    - e. Scrutinize the source of the cost or charge data
- B. Outcomes
  - 1. Identifying outcomes
    - a. Three types of outcomes of interest: clinical, humanistic, and economic
    - b. Each outcome type is not mutually exclusive
    - c. Identifying clinical outcomes
      - i. Death also is an outcome
      - ii. Pharmacotherapeutic outcomes are those that the pharmacists actually control
      - iii. Pharmaceutical care outcomes represent the contribution of drug therapy in addressing the overall clinical outcome
      - iv. Clinical indicators and intermediate outcomes are separate from clinical outcomes
        - (a) Used when final outcomes either are not readily identified or the times required for the outcome to occur is lengthy
        - (b) In some cases, the intermediate outcomes represent the outcomes for which the pharmacist should be held accountable
        - (c) It is important to determine the confidence one has in linking intermediate and final outcomes
    - d. Identifying economic outcomes
      - i. Direct medical resources used to provide a service or achieve an outcome, including health care providers' time, laboratory services, and diagnostic procedure
      - ii. health-related quality of life
      - iii. patient satisfaction
      - iv. reduced activity days
  - 2. Measuring outcomes
    - a. Measure them in the best units
    - b. Sources of process and outcomes data will vary
    - c. Depends on the study's perspective
    - d. Types of outcomes of interest
      - i. Clinical outcomes: data may be obtained from the patient, the provider, or the medical record
      - ii. Economic: data may be obtained from the patient, administrative databases, the provider, or medical charts
      - iii. Humanistic: data should come from the patient; in some cases, patient proxies

(e.g., caregivers, parents, or spouses) are used to estimate quality of life

(a) Copyright issues

(b) Modifications of instruments

e. Data accuracy should be verified

i. Source documents

ii. Patient is source of quality of life, satisfaction data

3. Valuing outcomes

a. Market value does not necessarily exist on the outcome side of the equation

b. The lack of a commonly accepted metric makes it difficult to combine outcomes

c. Approaches discussed in the literature are fairly contentious

i. Human capital approach

ii. Willingness to pay

iii. Utilities

d. Currently, outcomes may be best left disaggregated and reported in units best for the measure

e. Once dollars are spent, the value of life is certainly implied; the decisions one makes indicate the minimum amount life is worth

IV. Select a study design

A. Study design is important because it will affect several parts of the evaluation process

1. Cost of the evaluation
2. Time required to conduct the evaluation
3. Accuracy of the information gained
4. Complexity of administering the evaluation
5. Ease of defending the subsequent decisions made based on the evaluation

B. Variability and the study of groups

1. Law of large numbers
2. Variability among populations

C. Choose the study population carefully

D. Data requirements will indicate whether retrospective or prospective sources are appropriate

1. Resource use

a. Administrative databases

b. Patient/provider surveys

c. Medical records

2. Quality of life

a. Patients

b. Proxies

c. Copyright issues, instrument modifications

3. Clinical measures

a. Medical records

b. Providers

V. Study designs

A. Experimental designs

1. Piggyback randomized, controlled trials
2. Economic clinical trials

B. Observational designs

1. Claims data analysis

C. Simulation designs

1. Decision tree models
2. Markov models

D. Combination designs

E. Validity

1. Biases to internal validity affect the accuracy of the results of the study as they apply to those who participated in the study

a. Patient selection bias

b. Crossover bias

c. Errors in measurement of outcomes

d. Errors in ascertainment of exposure to technology

2. Biases to external validity affect the generalizability of the results to other settings
a. Differences among people studied versus people with whom the results will be applied
3. All designs are affected by biases, but the patterns are different for different designs
F. Choice of study design must take potential biases into account
1. Cannot escape subjective judgments
2. Recognize
3. Put into context
4. Learn from the literature
G. Data from experimental studies
1. Necessary, but not always sufficient to make treatment decisions
2. Useful starting point for continual evaluation of interventions
3. Safety and efficacy aspects address appropriateness, which must be known before quality can be addressed
H. Problems in existing outcomes research limit the value of the findings
I. One study is not likely to answer all questions
J. Make a timeline
1. Estimate how long it should take to conduct a study given the design selected

VI. Collect data
A. Patients are the only people who can provide certain information
1. Consider patient needs when determining how to collect data
B. Many different ways to collect data
1. Paper and pencil
2. Optical scan forms
3. Direct computer entry and telephone remote data entry
4. Interview
5. Observation

VII. Analyze data
A. Develop data analysis plan before the study starts
B. Clearly state what is to be studied
1. Limit the amount of data collected
2. If it is unknown how a certain variable will be analyzed or used, do not collect it
C. Keep analysis plan simple
1. Limit the number of questions asked
D. Level of statistics needed to conduct an analysis depends on the data collected and the goals of the analysis
1. Evaluate patients
a. What is the status?
b. What is the baseline assessment?
2. Discriminate among patients
a. Does this quality-of-life instrument discriminate among various severity levels of patients with asthma?
b. Can clinicians move patients from one severity level to another by appropriately treating them?
3. Predict how patients may act
a. Can clinicians predict a patient's annual level of resource use based on a general health-related quality-of-life score?
F. Distribution of data also is determined by the type of analysis
1. Clinical analysis
2. Economic analysis
a. Health care resource use is likely to be skewed
b. Use incremental costs, depending on whether comparing within or among interventions
3. Humanistic analysis
a. For existing health-related quality-of-life instruments, analyze according to the recommendations of the developers
b. Patient satisfaction instruments also should be scored according to the developer's recommendations
c. Validity is an ongoing process
4. Get help if it is needed

VIII. Discount results

A. If a study runs more than a year, the costs and the benefits should be discounted
   1. Discounting benefits is controversial
B. Discount rate used can affect results
   1. Intervention that costs $1,000 at Year 1; benefit estimated to be $2,000 at Year 10. At a 5 percent discount rate, present value is $1,228 and net benefit is $228; at a 10 percent discount rate, the net benefit is negative

IX. Conduct sensitivity analysis
A. Uncertainty in pharmacoeconomic studies is no different than some of the uncertainty that occurs in clinical trials
B. Uncertainty due to random events and uncertainty due to lack of knowledge occur in pharmacoeconomic studies
   1. Uncertainty due to random events is statistically predictable
   2. Uncertainty due to lack of knowledge is addressed through sensitivity analysis
C. A Sensitivity analysis indicates one of three things:
   1. An assumption significantly affects a conclusion
   2. An assumption does not significantly affect a conclusion
   3. Establishes a minimum or maximum value that a variable must have for an intervention to appear worthwhile
D. Identifies the important variables on which a sensitivity analysis was conducted
   1. Confidence in those values should be discussed, as that can affect generalizability of results

X. Ethical Issues
A. Investigational review board
   1. Prospective study
      a. Before study starts
      b. Ensures patients are not put at undue risk
      c. Ensures consent form fully discusses risks and benefits of the study
   2. Retrospective study
      a. Institutions should review the protocol
      b. Different institutions have different policies regarding the notification of patients
      c. Contact an IRB member for clarification regarding institutional policies
B. Analysis of claims data
   1. Ongoing United States Congressional oversight regarding human subject protections
   2. Patient identifiers must be removed from the database before any analysis is initiated
   3. Understanding of current institutional standard operating procedures is critical
C. Patient questionnaires
   1. Usually requires some IRB review
   2. In many cases, review can be expedited
   3. Often, completion of a survey itself is considered the patient's indication of informed consent

XI. Interpret study results
A. Value of a benefit may vary
B. Interpretation of health-related quality-of-life and economic data
   1. What is a meaningful change?
      a. Relate quality-of-life scores to other clinical or economic measures
      b. Use sensitivity analysis
      c. Effect size, other measures

XII. Conclusion

Learning Objectives

1. Outline a strategy for designing a pharmacoeconomic or outcomes research question.
2. Understand the importance of establishing a research framework.
3. Discuss common pitfalls that create unintentional biases when conducting pharmacoeconomic evaluations in practice.
4. Understand how study design affects the evaluation process.
5. Outline the steps involved in conducting a pharmacoeconomic evaluation.

Abbreviations in this chapter

AWP	Average wholesale price
FDA	Food and Drug Administration
FEV_1	Forced expiratory volume in 1 second
IRB	Investigational Review Board

Introduction

Pharmacoeconomics uses a series of tools that assist in making objective decisions. These tools provide supportive information to providers, formulary committees, and patients. The tools do not always come with easy-to-use directions, and, in fact, can be misused and misinterpreted if used incorrectly. If applied properly, the tools can assist in more efficient and appropriate use of health care resources. A key to applying these tools properly is asking the right question and developing a practical approach to answering the question.

This chapter introduces a strategy to consider when faced with a pharmacoeconomic or outcomes assessment question. The strategy is intended to be applicable to projects conducted in clinical practice or in clinical research. This chapter focuses on how to ask a question that is answerable, and how to initiate and conduct studies with an economic or humanistic focus.

The link between pharmaceutical care and pharmacoeconomics also is discussed. The increasing implementation of pharmaceutical care, especially in ambulatory settings, has increased the importance of evaluating the impact of alternative systems of care. Evaluating the impact of pharmaceutical care in a manner that produces meaningful results is a methodological challenge; however, evaluation of these systems is an important determinant of their success.

Why Pharmacoeconomic Assessments?

Why should pharmacists/clinicians care about pharmacoeconomics and why should pharmacoeconomic evaluations be conducted in various practice settings? Several different types of health care reform initiatives are being implemented in this country, both at the state and national levels. A prescription drug benefit for Medicare was a 2000 campaign promise of both major presidential candidates. States are wrestling with the cost of prescription drug programs, and as each state struggles with budget deficits, cuts to various health care programs are a major focus of discussion. Of great concern is whether there is good value for money in the costs invested in every aspect of health care. Everybody wants a way to measure value, regardless of the system implemented. Pharmaceuticals and pharmacy services are no exception; a means of measuring and documenting the value of pharmaceutical products and services is expected.

Specifically, patients and other health care decision-makers are faced with new technologies that are perceived to be expensive. Efficacy may have been clearly demonstrated, but how is it determined whether there is value in the investment in pharmaceutical products or in pharmaceutical services relative to other treatment options? There is a need to rationally evaluate the costs and consequences of these interventions.

Traditionally, many health care coverage decisions, such as formulary selections, were made in closed situations. Greater transparency in decision-making is more apparent as patients or their designates use the media or the courts to force health care organizations to provide them with treatment options for which patients think (or hope) they may benefit. Providers need a way to demonstrate and justify the decisions made. If one has a rational set of tools that can be used to assist in making these decisions, it is going to be easier to justify decisions made.

Outcomes research studies the end results of medical care. Pharmacists have a strong basis in clinical therapeutics and are familiar with the clinical basis of disease and how to treat patients' clinical symptoms. Outcomes research encourages the expansion from the one-dimensional clinical perspective to include measures of humanistic and economic end points. To completely describe the outcomes of care, clinical, economic, and humanistic parameters must be measured simultaneously.

Outcomes research also is critical to the future of pharmacy practice. It is perceived to be vital for demonstrating pharmacist effectiveness, documenting the overall benefit of an intervention and determining a responsible national standard for pharmaceutical care. Pharmaceutical care has been defined as the responsible provision of drug therapy for the purpose of achieving definite outcomes. To operationalize that definition, the costs and consequences of pharmaceutical products and services need to be measured. Pharmacists have an opportunity to evaluate the systems of pharmaceutical care using pharmacoeconomic methods, which provides an opportunity to evaluate in three dimensions the impact of the associated products and services.

Asking the Question

Define the Problem

The first step in solving a problem is to define the problem clearly. Stating the problem up front seems rather obvious, but it is not always done. Much time and energy are wasted trying to answer poorly defined questions. A problem can be defined in broad terms, such as premature death in the United States. That may be difficult to get a hold of, but that problem can be narrowed to premature death associated with some type of medical condition, such as asthma. The narrower the problem, the easier it is to address. Another problem might be the impact of rheumatoid arthritis on patients' functional status. The source of the question may be quite variable, it may be in response to a research article, a practical question from a patient care center, or a question from patients.

Asking the question properly increases the utility of outcomes research. Do not assume no one has ever asked a question; rather, review the literature to see if anyone else has addressed it.

The feasibility and usefulness of an outcomes management system has been evaluated. This study was initiated by a managed care consortium, a group of employers and their health care partners who were working cooperatively to assess outcomes in usual practice situations. Initial information on outcomes predictors was found to be "interesting" to providers and payers, but it did not provide information about specific aspects of the process of care that could be altered to improve outcomes. The managed care consortium identified a set of questions to guide the next phase of its outcomes project. These questions are applicable elsewhere, and if answered, will improve the value of outcomes research. There is a role for pharmacy in all of these questions. For example, one question asks, "How do deviations from accepted treatment recommendations relate to patient outcomes and changes in outcomes over time?" Other questions relate access to service and variations in practice to patient outcomes and satisfaction. Table 1 lists the complete set of questions.

Table 1. Examples of Outcomes Research Questions

- How does control of access to services affect patient outcomes and patient satisfaction?
- How do deviations from accepted treatment recommendations relate to patient outcomes and changes in outcomes over time?
- How do variations in practice style, follow-up visit intervals, use of monitoring tests and procedures, and discussion of treatment options affect patient outcomes and satisfaction?
- How does patients' confidence in their ability to manage their chronic disease and level of knowledge relate to health status and satisfaction?

State Objectives

After the problem has been stated, the next step is to define the objectives. A broad problem will result in broadly defined objectives. If premature death is a problem, an objective could be to reduce premature death or, more narrowly, reduce premature death associated with asthma. A broad objective is to reduce poor compliance rates; a narrower objective is to reduce poor compliance rates associated with metered-dose inhaler use in patients with asthma. (An even narrower objective restricts the age of the asthma patients to be studied.) A broad objective is to improve the functional status of patients with rheumatoid arthritis. A narrower objective is to evaluate the impact of a specific disease modifying antirheumatic drug on the functional status of patients with moderate to severe rheumatoid arthritis.

At least one objective should be quantifiable. Intangible objectives are important, but they create measurement challenges. Consider hospice care, for example. An objective of hospice care is to provide patients who have terminal illnesses an opportunity to die with dignity. That is a valuable, but also intangible, objective. A secondary objective in evaluating hospice care might be the reduction of health care resources associated with managing patients with terminal illnesses. That reduction in health care resources is certainly much more measurable, but it is not the primary objective of hospice care. It is appropriate to have one primary and multiple secondary objectives associated with the question.

Identify Alternatives

Next, identify the alternatives. Broad problems lead to broad objectives, which naturally lead to many alternatives. If a problem is broadly defined, some of these alternatives are not going to be limited to health. Airport safety could affect premature death; so could environmental issues and immunization programs. From a pharmaceutical care perspective, think about the alternatives, but do not necessarily limit thinking to only pharmaceutical alternatives. Other options may be proper to consider. For example, if thinking about treating gastroesophageal reflux disease, lifestyle modification may be appropriate; or for managing osteoarthritis, joint replacement surgery versus pharmacotherapy may be responsible alternatives. It is important to balance the variety of potential alternatives with the reality of studying all alternatives and the feasibility of using the alternatives. Essentially, a research hypothesis needs to be clearly stated. The hypothesis statement should contain two or more variables that are measurable and should specify how the variables are related.

Establish a Framework

The intent behind this practical approach to investigating the question is to establish a framework for the analysis. Prioritize the objectives. Consider the hospice example; although this objective is an intangible, the primary objective of a hospice is to allow patients to die with dignity. The secondary objective is to reduce health care costs associated with such patient management. Prioritize objectives first; then consider how to quantify them.

When establishing the framework, consider what can be done within the problem or research question identified. Be realistic; identify the alternatives that are feasible now. This helps focus on the pertinent question, and when it comes to analyzing data, the quantity of data should be manageable. However, there is nothing wrong with being a futurist and looking outside of the box. What would happen if pharmacists were given the right to prescribe? What would happen if pharmacists were given the right to modify dosage regimens without going back to the physician? Although the scope of thinking should not be limited, it is important to recognize that some of these changes may not happen in individual practice settings in the short-term.

It is important to consider both the processes and the outcomes of care as the framework is being developed. Process and outcomes are not mutually exclusive aspects of care; in fact, linking process to outcome is the ultimate goal. Defining the process means identifying the resources used to treat a condition or to provide a certain level of services. If process and outcomes are not linked, a complete picture of the issue is not seen. For example, if a patient presents to a clinic with a diagnosis of migraine and reports being treated with an analgesic, the process is known. The patient did receive a treatment, but the outcome of that treatment is unknown. If there is no documentation of the patient response, the provider may think the patient has adequate relief because no further treatment was requested. However, the patient may think this is the best that can be done, and so will not seek additional treatment. In this example, the process is known, but the outcome is not. It is difficult to use this information in a meaningful way because it is incomplete.

On the other hand, if only the outcome is known, the results are not much better. If a patient says, "My migraine medication does not work," you have no idea whether the patient has actually been evaluated, whether there has been any type of diagnostic procedure performed, or whether the patient has actually received treatment. The patient-reported outcome is known, but it is not known what did or did not happen to reach that outcome. This information needs to be linked back to the measures of process of care. It is critical to be able to link process and outcome.

As another example, consider asthma. Suppose the relationship between patient compliance and outcomes of asthma therapy is raised as a question. To understand the issue, some basic facts about asthma must be collected. Table 2 lists specific categories of clinical, economic, and humanistic variables that should be considered when approaching a question. Decide how to define asthma patients and how to differentiate them from patients with chronic obstructive pulmonary disease. Pediatric patients need to be differentiated from adult patients. The symptoms and diagnosis of asthma must be defined so that the appropriate patients are observed. Treatments used to manage asthma will need to be outlined.

Humanistic and economic baseline patterns also are important to understand. Determine the level of resource use, such as hospitalizations and emergency department visits, among patients with asthma and decide if the level of compliance could affect such resource use. The burden of illness, in terms of the impact of asthma on health-related quality of life and possible associations between health-related quality of life and compliance should be considered.

The cost of the illness to parents who have children with asthma also is important. How well is the link between asthma-related processes of care and asthma-related outcomes established? This may all seem like a lot of information to collect, but if the goal is to determine whether compliance affects asthma outcomes, it is critical to have a benchmark, otherwise it will not be known if change has occurred. Collecting information at baseline is a pharmacoeconomic study in and of itself, and is a good place to start. The Cost-of-Illness Analysis chapter discusses this topic more fully.

Table 2. Key aspects of Asthma Burden of Illness

Type of Outcome	Key Aspects
Clinical	Definition and etiology
	Symptoms and diagnosis
	Appropriate drugs, dose
	Potential adverse events, drug interactions
	Natural history
Economic	Hospitalizations
	Emergency department visits
	Ambulance services
	Physician visits
	Laboratory costs
	Productivity
Humanistic	Quality of life impact
	Patient
	Caregiver
	Parent
	Satisfaction with treatment
	Reduced activity days

Asking the Question

- Define the problem as clearly as possible
- State the objectives, remembering a narrower objective may be easier to explore than a broader objective
- Identify alternatives that are realistic and could feasibly be implemented and state a research hypothesis
- Establish a framework based on the priority of each study objective.

Identification Measurement and Valuation of Resources and Outcomes

Assuming that a problem has been identified and objectives surrounding the problem have been stated, the next step is to consider the input and output associated with the problem. The following sections discuss how to identify, measure, and value both resources and outcomes.

Resources Used

Identifying Resources

When thinking about the resources used to provide a specific process of care, first identify the resources in terms of what is actually being used. Identify each component, such as prescription drugs, pharmacists' time, emergency department visits, and diagnostic procedures, then separately identify what variables define these components. Once the variables are defined, the data collection follows.

Measuring Resources

The perspective from which the question is to be answered is critical when determining how resources are measured. Multiple perspectives can be taken; it could be the institution; the patient; or the provider of care. Several different perspectives may need to be considered when measuring and valuing resources. The perspective taken to investigate the research question should be stated prospectively as it determines what resources are important to measure. For example, if the perspective of the study were that of a patient with asthma, the important resources to measure might be doses of an inhaler taken or frequency of nighttime awakenings. If this same example, if the perspective were that of the formulary committee, the resources to measure might focus on the per dose costs of two different drugs and the administration frequency needed to control the patient's asthma symptoms.

To measure resources, count the units of service required to produce the intended benefit, such as hours of work, hospital days, or number of diagnostic tests. In some cases, it is important to watch for substitution of resources. At some settings, pharmacy technicians fill unit dose trays. In others, pharmacists perform that task. In the ambulatory setting, the issue may be whether pharmacists or technicians are actually performing the tasks of filling prescriptions. If pharmacists are filling prescriptions when someone at a lesser wage could actually provide that same service at the same level, the impact of such substitution needs to be considered. If it is unlikely that pharmacy technicians are going to be available to provide this service, look at it from the perspective of the pharmacist actually providing the service. However, in the future, it may be useful to note that technicians could provide that support.

Migration of resources also can occur. If two interventions for managing a condition are compared, remember that other interventions also may be used. For example, when comparing amoxicillin and cephalexin for managing otitis media in an observational study, it is possible that patients are migrating to amoxicillin/clavulanate or zithromycin. If a study aim is to shift patients from cephalexin to amoxicillin, also be aware of shifts elsewhere. Migration is a big concern when only costs are considered because costs might drop for one or both treatments studied, whereas use increases for a third agent that was not being measured. Migration also should be monitored in a drug use review, especially if one drug is being studied as opposed to an entire class or therapeutic group indicated in managing a condition. In addition, migration should be considered in a benchmarking study and, in general, in any study that has a time factor for which there is no control group. If using a traditional clinical trial design where patients are randomized to one treatment or another, and the regimens are more tightly controlled, migration is less likely to be an issue.

Some resources are difficult to measure. Consider overhead. When considering the costs of providing pharmaceutical care services, the office or cubicle from which that service is provided has a cost associated with it. This cost could be estimated in terms of rent paid or the opportunity cost of the office (i.e., what is the next best use of the space?). Some technologies produce multiple outcomes. If blood is drawn for serum electrolytes, a wealth of information can be obtained from that one blood sample. The potassium concentration may be all that is needed, and not all those other results, yet the charge of running the laboratory is the same.

When thinking about measuring resources used, it is important to differentiate between the amount of time spent providing care that affects the question at hand relative to the total time at work. If nurses administer drugs and a drug that is administered 4 times/day is compared to a drug that is administered 1 time/day, nursing drug dispensing time can be reduced if all other things remain equal. However, it may be argued that in the big scheme of things, overall nursing costs will not be "saved" unless the number of nurses on staff is reduced. However, that nurse might be freed up and assigned to other duties, increasing the efficiency of the system or improving the quality of care. The changes that occur should be measured, and, at a minimum, the immediate and long-term implications for nursing or any other personnel should be discussed.

Valuing Resources

Fortunately, on the resource side of the equation, there are market values for goods and services. A certain amount of money is paid for prescription drugs and laboratory procedures. When valuing these resources, it is appropriate to use the market value. Opportunity costs are theoretically the best source of valuation; however, market value is perfectly acceptable.

Be careful not to confuse charges and costs. When studying an issue from the perspective of an institution, the costs to the institution are what is important, not what is charged to insurance companies or patients. Charges are not equal to costs. It is important to specify which parameter is being used because it can influence the results and interpretation of a study. The challenge with collecting institutional costs is that many institutions have relatively unsophisticated accounting procedures, making true costs difficult to identify. In addition, some institutions will deliberately subsidize certain areas, making cost-to-charge ratios difficult to apply. Finally, volunteer time and other free services are sometimes ignored when measuring costs, and they should not be.

Charge data may be useful if the perspective taken is that of the patient or a third-party payer. The patient perspective includes charges for services paid out of pocket; any copayments for prescriptions and physician visits; and any nonreimbursable expenses, such as massage therapy, acupuncture, or over-the-counter products. A third-party payer's perspective might include charges less a percentage that might be negotiated due to a volume discount. Any amount paid directly by the patient, such as a deductible, also is excluded from the third-party payer's perspective.

If cost data are accessible, and the institutional or provider perspective is of interest, those data should be used. In the absence of true cost data, there are other sources of data for monetary valuations. A commonly used proxy for cost data are the average wholesale price (AWP). However, the AWP is not an accurate proxy of cost data because there is probably not an institution in the United States paying AWP for its drugs. So, although AWP is a standard, it may not be realistic. Another data source often used to approximate cost data are an institution's administrative billing records. These data are actually better termed 'charge' data because each value includes an institutional markup. Scrutinize the source of the cost or charge data and consider how much confidence can be placed in the appropriateness of the source. When there is a lack of confidence in the monetary valuations, a sensitivity analysis should be undertaken. The sensitivity analysis serves as a means to explore various assumptions and help establish a level of confidence in the study results.

Outcomes

Identifying Outcomes

There are three types of outcomes of interest: clinical, humanistic, and economic. These types of outcomes are discussed in chapters 3, 5, and 16 of this course material. Each outcome type is not mutually exclusive. Figure 1 demonstrates the overlap of the outcome dimensions. Fortunately, it is not critical to characterize each outcome as being one of the three. It is important to accurately capture key outcomes of interest. Pain could be a clinical outcome, (e.g., intensity, duration, and frequency) or it could be a humanistic outcome (e.g., how does pain affect the ability to function?). What is important to remember is the importance of evaluating beyond one dimension. All three dimensions need to be considered; therefore, look as broadly as possible at the types of outcomes that could be of interest. Outcomes of interest also may be a function of the study's perspective.

Figure 1.
Overlap of outcomes dimensions

ED = emergency department
FEV_1 = forced expiratory volume in 1 second
ICU = intensive care unit

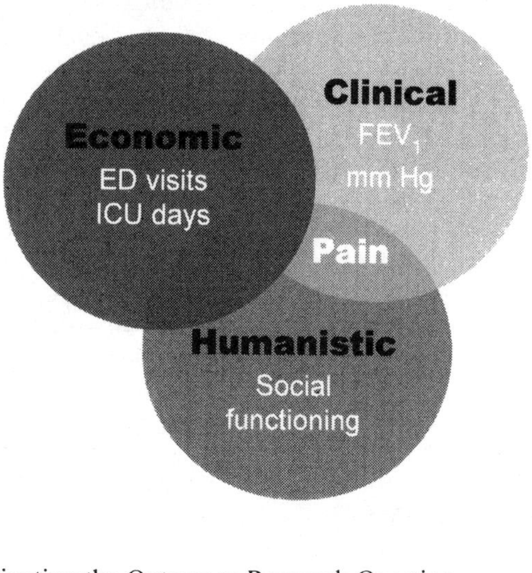

In a study of asthma outcomes, affect on health-related quality of life may be important to the patient, but of secondary importance to the provider. Patient satisfaction may be an important measure to an accrediting body.

Identifying Clinical Outcomes

In pharmaceutical care, four specific types of clinical outcomes are identified: curing a disease, reducing or eliminating symptoms, slowing a disease process, and preventing a disease. These outcomes, along with defined pharmacotherapeutic outcomes, span the three dimensions of clinical, economic, and humanistic end points. Pharmacotherapeutic outcomes, as listed in Table 3, are those that the pharmacists can actually affect. These oucomes include making sure that the patient gets the right drug, in the right quantity, at the right time, and that the likelihood of adverse events and drug interactions is minimized. The types of outcomes defined in the pharmaceutical care system (e.g., that the patient has the right drug for the right indication) have clinical implications, but also have economic implications because the patient should not pay for something not needed. Defined outcomes also have humanistic implications because if the patient gets the right drug and is taking it correctly, quality of life can be affected in a positive, or perhaps a negative, way. Pharmaceutical care outcomes fit nicely into the three types of outcomes of interest and represent the contribution of drug therapy in addressing overall clinical outcomes.

Clinical indicators can be separated from clinical outcomes and may be considered intermediate outcomes. Forced expiratory volume in 1 second (FEV_1), hemoglobin A_{1c}, and blood pressure changes are all physiologic measures often used to evaluate clinical response. There is interest in these physiologic measures because they represent the inner workings of a human being and may provide a link to the clinical outcome. Was the FEV_1 associated with an asthma exacerbation? Did a patient's nonadherence to therapy result in exacerbation of diabetes symptoms?

Other outcomes of interest include treatment successes. How many patients with community-acquired pneumonia who were treated with a specific antibiotic were actually cured? Death also is an outcome. It is not necessarily a positive outcome, but it serves as a reminder of the need to look at both positive and negative outcomes when trying to measure and identify them.

These intermediate outcomes can be used when final outcomes either are not readily identified or it takes too long to measure them. An example is the treatment of hypertension. If patients are adherent, and their blood pressure is reduced, their probability of stroke in 15 or 20 years is reduced. The measure of blood pressure serves as an intermediate marker, which is appropriate because the link between reducing blood pressure and avoiding a stroke is established.

That is not necessarily the case for many other conditions. When other intermediate outcomes are considered, such as patient adherence to therapy, it is important to determine the confidence in linking intermediate and final outcomes.

In some cases, the intermediate outcomes represent the outcomes for which the pharmacist should be held accountable. The broader outcomes, such as treatment success, represent the goals of the health care team managing the patient. It is appropriate, at times, to state that the outcome of interest, which the pharmacist controls, is an intermediate one. For example, ensuring the patient gets the drug, is an important, but intermediate outcome over which the pharmacist is more likely to have a direct impact. It would be ideal to know the link between the intermediate outcome and the final outcome. That literature is, unfortunately, not overwhelming. As that literature broadens, the intermediate end points that are reliable indicators of long-term outcomes will become more evident. If intermediate outcomes are going to be used, such as measures of patient adherence, it is important to note how strong the link is between the intermediate outcome and the final outcome.

Identifying Economic Outcomes

Economic outcomes include the direct medical resources used to provide a service or achieve an outcome, including health care providers' time, laboratory services, and diagnostic procedures. By providing pharmaceutical services in a specific area of ambulatory or institutional care, these services may reduce resource needs in other areas, such as nursing time or physician time. These shifts in resources are important to document and certainly can have an impact on whether measured results affect overall management of a condition.

Patient productivity as an indirect cost also is an economic measure. The indirect costs of some conditions may be much greater than the direct medical costs. This fact has been demonstrated with rheumatoid arthritis, where patients' lost productivity is much greater than the costs of the medicines and medical care they receive. Migraine headaches also have higher indirect than direct costs. Depending on the perspective from which the study is conducted (e.g., the patient, an employer, or an insurance company), indirect costs of care may be an important issue. Although a specific hospital or institution may currently be less interested in indirect costs, as more systems focus on patient satisfaction and attempt to differentiate their services from others, indirect costs of care could increase in importance. Caregiver costs also may be important to consider, depending on the condition of interest.

Identifying Humanistic Outcomes

Humanistic outcomes include but are not limited to quality of life, functional status, and patient satisfaction. Quality of life is a multidimensional concept (see the following chapters: Data Sources and Tools for Measuring Humanistic Outcomes, Measuring Health Status, Patient Satisfaction, Measuring Work Outcomes, Interpretation of Humanistic Assessments, Using Patient-Based Assessments for Individual Patient Care, and Evaluating Humanistic Outcomes Literature). Depending on the research question, different health-related quality-of-life dimensions may be of specific interest, such as social functioning, physical functioning, or well-being. Patient preference for one health state versus another also is a humanistic measure and is discussed more completely in the Cost-Utility Analysis chapter. Patient satisfaction with care is another outcome that is of great interest to many health care systems. System administrators want to know whether patients are satisfied with the care they receive because there is a relationship between member turnover and satisfaction with care. Questionnaires have been developed to measure patient satisfaction with pharmacy services. Other questionnaires have been developed to measure patient satisfaction with services on a more global basis. These are discussed in detail in the Patient Satisfaction chapter.

Reduced activity days also may be considered a humanistic measure. This measure is sometimes separated from lost productivity because it is a much broader measure. Children who have illnesses and miss school have reduced activity days. People not in the paid workforce, whether they are staying home to take care of children or are independently wealthy and do not have to work, still can have reduced activity days. This is classified as a humanistic measure because patients typically prefer to be able to perform activities fully as opposed to performing them at a reduced level. In addition, although lost productivity can be estimated monetarily based on wages, the same cannot be estimated easily for reduced activity days. No specific monetary amount can be applied to this variable. The concept of symptom-free days recently has emerged as a way to describe and value treatment outcomes. Symptom-free days is a frequent outcome measure in asthma studies in that it provides a key patient-based measure of asthma control.

Measuring Outcomes

When measuring outcomes, they should be counted in the best units. Try to collect all variables in a common metric, such as dollars, even though it may seem more efficient. Information should be collected in the most natural, obvious units. For example, the number of asthma exacerbations may be a clinical outcome and is captured as total number of exacerbations; the number of physician visits might be an economic outcome, captured as the number of visits, and then a cost per visit may be applied to the number of visits; and the number of days of reduced activity a humanistic outcome, captured as number of days. Measuring health-related quality of life should be achieved using appropriate disease-specific (e.g., Asthma Quality-of-life questionnaire) or general (e.g., Medical Outcomes Study, short form-36) health-related quality-of-life questionnaires.

The sources of process and outcomes data will vary, depending on the perspective from which the study is conducted and on the types of outcomes of interest. Clinical data may be obtained from the patient, the provider, or the medical record. Administrative files sometimes are an adequate source of data for an outcomes study. Resource use data may be obtained from the patient, administrative databases, the provider, or medical charts. The best source for health-related quality-of-life data is clearly the patient, although in some cases patient proxies, such as caregivers, parents, and spouses, are used to estimate quality of life.

If retrospective data are to be used, (administrative or otherwise), the accuracy of the data should be verified. Some institutions routinely validate their databases. In other cases, it may be sufficient to take a sample from the database and using patient charts, confirm that the chart and claims data agree. For example, did this patient, in fact, have an endoscopy when she was charged for it? Such an effort provides an element of confidence in the data. The accuracy of the data collected is critical when it comes time to discuss and defend results and make decisions based on the results.

Valuing Outcomes

Valuing outcomes is the reason the question being studied was asked in the first place. Unfortunately, unlike resources that have market values for goods and services, a common denominator does not necessarily exist on the outcomes side of the equation. The lack of a commonly accepted metric makes it difficult to combine outcomes. If the goal is to conduct a cost-benefit analysis, a monetary value must be placed on all outcomes, including life. Approaches discussed in the literature for valuing life are fairly contentious. The human capital approach looks at how much money people might earn throughout their lifetimes, and assumes that is their value to society. A problem with the human capital approach is people who have little or no income or income potential have little or no worth. An additional problem with the human capital approach is that women would often be valued less than men.

Willingness to pay is another approach that asks, "What are you willing to pay to avoid a certain health event, such as a heart attack or a stroke?" People tend to respond based on how much money they earn. Measuring utilities, another way to value outcomes, is discussed more fully in the Cost-Utility Analysis chapter.

If all outcomes were collapsed into a monetary or other single unit, the generalizability of the results would likely be limited. Currently, outcomes may be best left disaggregated and reported in units best for the measure. Consider using money saved for measuring economic outcomes, lives saved or limbs saved may be appropriate for clinical measures; and patient discomfort may be a good humanistic measure. Clinicians are able to cope with disaggregated measures. For example, they do not add up a weight of 150 pounds, a diastolic blood pressure of 80 mm Hg, and a temperature of 98.6°F and conclude that 328.6 equals health. They look at each separately. However, once a certain amount of dollars is spent treating patients, the value of life is certainly implied. By intervening, health care providers say life is worth at least as much as the cost of the intervention and, thus, are setting at least a minimum value on the worth of that life.

Identification, Measurement, and Valuing Resources

- Identify resources actually being used
- Measure resources from the perspective taken in the study and in their natural units (i.e., hours and days)
- Value resources in a clear, transparent way
- Identify outcomes of interest and consider the multidimensionality of these outcomes
- Measure outcomes in appropriate units
- Value outcomes in metrics that make sense, which may or may not be a monetary unit

Select a Study Design

The study design used to estimate costs and consequences of an intervention will affect the cost of the evaluation, the time required to conduct the evaluation, the accuracy of the information gained, the complexity of administering the evaluation, and the ease of defending the subsequent decisions made based on the evaluation. To make decisions about an intervention, whether it is a drug or a service, estimate the magnitude of the benefits and risks. As examples, this magnitude may be represented clinically as mean improvement in FEV_1 and a decreased incidence of headache or humanistically as mean improvement in health-related quality of life measured by the Asthma Quality-of-life Questionnaire. The degree of uncertainty about such estimates also should be provided. The uncertainty might be represented as the standard deviation or variance about the improvement in quality of life or FEV_1. Both the estimate of the effect and the range of uncertainly are important. It makes a big difference if an intervention reduces the risk of having a stroke by 5 percent or 50 percent, or if the variance of those estimates is ± 5 percent or ± 20 percent.

When considering study design, the processes and outcomes that should be measured and valued should be identified. The processes and outcomes will clearly depend on the question asked and the perspective taken. Once the types of resources needed and outcomes are identified, sources of data should be considered. Resource use information is frequently found in a database or in patient medical records. If quality of life is the focus, data probably will not be found in a database, but will need to be collected prospectively from patients or their proxies. Clinical measures can sometimes be found retrospectively in databases or medical records, but often they must be collected prospectively as well. It is important to think about what needs to be collected to answer the questions being asked; otherwise it may be tempting to let the existing data drive the decision.

Depending on the type of study, sample size (number of patients or number of observations) needs to be considered. The sample size needed is a function of the primary question that is being asked. If the study does not have enough subjects, the confidence interval for the outcome of interest is too wide to allow any useful interpretations. As the number of subjects increases, the confidence interval narrows, as will the confidence in the conclusions. However, too many subjects provides a narrow confidence interval, but it may be narrower than is needed. The traditional approach to estimating sample size is based on statistical significance of the primary outcome measure. The following must be specified: the smallest effect of the outcome to be detected, the type (i.e., type I is the willingness to accept the null hypotheses when, in fact, it is false, type II is the willingness to reject the null hypotheses when, in fact, it is true), error rates, and the design of the study.

All study designs for evaluating interventions provide information. They range from asking one person for an expert opinion to conducting a randomized, double-blind, placebo-controlled, clinical trial. However, there is a tendency to place different weights on information from different sources. Some sources are more likely to have problems with internal validity, others with external validity. Some methods are likely to provide more precise estimates of effect and variance. Two studies may provide similar results, but sometimes the logistics of collecting information are different. Time intervals between an intervention and the observed consequences must be considered. Also of importance is how frequently the data are collected in a study. A 12-month study of data collected only at its beginning and ending can provide different information than can the same study with data collected at monthly intervals. Thus, selecting a suitable study design is an important step when conducting an evaluation. There are three broad types of study designs used: experimental, observational, and simulations.

Experimental Designs

Experimental designs encompass classical experimental designs, including both prospectively and retrospectively conducted economic, clinical trials; randomized, controlled clinical trials; modified, quasi-experimental designs; and pre- and post-tests. Figure 2 illustrates these experimental designs.

Piggyback, Randomized, Controlled Trials

An experimental design used commonly in the pharmaceutical industry is to "piggyback" collection of resource use, and often health-related quality of life, onto a randomized, controlled trial, as displayed in Figure 3. At the completion of the trial, resource use across treatment groups is compared. When health-related quality-of-life measures have been included, changes across groups also are compared. This method is most useful when assessing treatment for conditions with relatively short clinical courses where study protocols are closely related to actual clinical practice. Sepsis and acute renal failure are disease states amenable to a piggyback trial.

An advantage of this design is that the randomized, controlled trial is recognized as having good internal validity and high scientific rigor, which makes it a standard of the industry in the drug approval process. Also because the trial already may be funded to determine safety and efficacy, piggybacking presents a relatively inexpensive way to collect economic and health-related quality-of-life data. In addition, as more decision-makers across the globe demand expanded levels of outcomes data, the study may become less of a piggyback and more of a three-dimensional outcomes study.

In general, randomized, clinical trials are well suited for the evaluation of quality of life and functional status. However, there are disadvantages associated with this piggybacking. Because of the rigors of the clinical portion of the trial, resource use is often protocol-driven. For example, a study protocol typically dictates inclusion and exclusion of specific types of patients, when these patients return for clinic visits, and drugs and procedures used. In addition, certain adverse events could result in hospitalization, whereas, in day-to-day clinical practice, the same adverse event might well be treated on an outpatient basis. Another disadvantage is that this design assesses efficacy, performance in the clinical trial setting under ideal conditions, as opposed to effectiveness and performance in everyday clinical practice under less than ideal conditions. In this situation, resources saved or expended and outcomes observed may be an accurate reflection of neither actual practice patterns nor the true patient populations.

The piggybacked randomized, controlled, clinical trial may not have sufficient power to obtain statistical significance in the area of cost-effectiveness and health-related quality of life. Typically, adequate numbers of patients are enrolled to statistically evaluate narrowly defined safety and efficacy end points. However, economic end points are not normally distributed and have large variances. Such end points require larger sample sizes to determine statistical differences among treatment arms than are needed to show differences in clinical end points. Some researchers now determine *a priori* the sample size needed to adequately assess differences in both economic and clinical outcomes within the randomized, clinical trial setting.

Economic Clinical Trials

The "gold standard" design for assessment of outcomes is probably the prospective, randomized, economic, clinical trial or naturalistic trial where assessment of the decision to initiate a therapeutic option occurs longitudinally. This design offers the opportunity to observe the effects of a therapy on economic and humanistic outcomes in conjunction with clinical practice patterns in a specific practice setting. Like any large-scale longitudinal clinical trial, this design requires considerable resources in the way of financial support, time, and a large study population.

Figure 2.
Experimental study designs used for economic evaluations
RCT = randomized, controlled trial

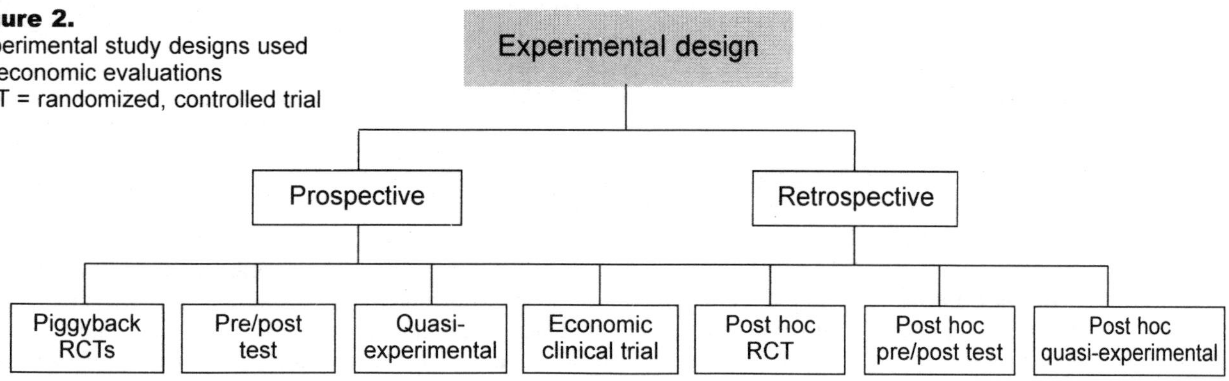

Figure 3.
Randomized, clinical trial design with piggyback economic and health-related quality-of-life assessments

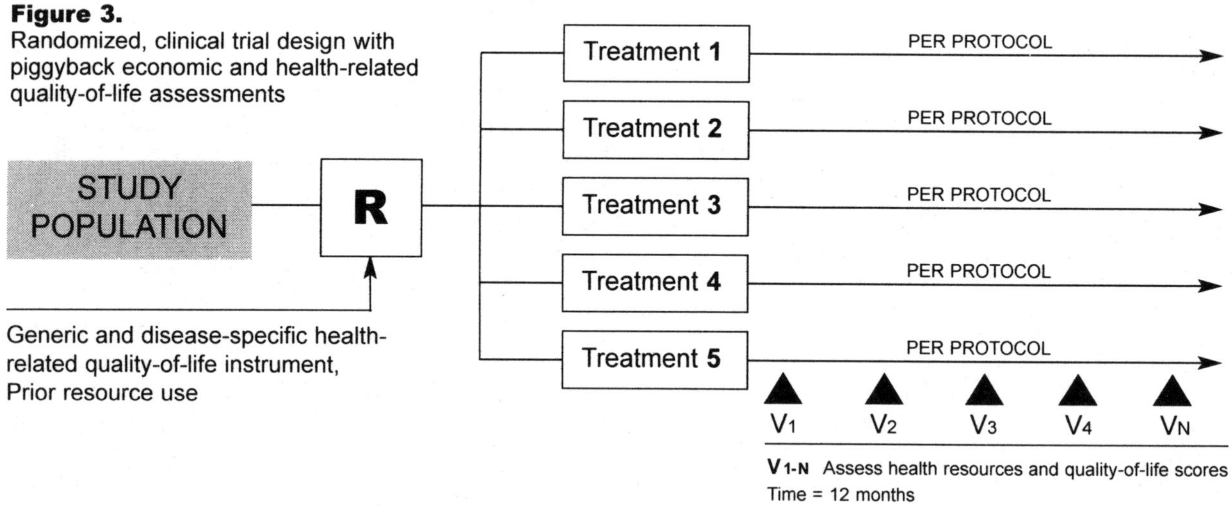

On examination of Figure 4, it is seen that in this design randomization occurs in the clinic setting. Patients are assigned to a study arm where they receive a specific treatment. The usual course of clinical practice proceeds in this setting. Patients might not be adherent to therapy, may have their dose or therapy changed or discontinued by the clinician, or might experience adverse events. Any number of possibilities may occur as part of routine practice. This design allows the researcher to investigate actual practice without adhering to the restrictions often imposed by a randomized, controlled protocol. This design allows for observation and collection of clinical, health resource use, and quality-of-life data at predetermined time points throughout the study. This trial is superior to the randomized, controlled, piggyback design for collecting economic data because it maximizes external validity and generalizability to the practice site. However, there is some loss of internal validity that occurs with this design. To ensure patient safety, such a study could not be carried out until the Food and Drug Administration (FDA) has approved the treatments involved for marketing.

Naturalistic trials, although optimal for outcomes research, do have certain disadvantages. To provide adequate statistical power, large study populations are required to find differences among treatment groups. These studies typically are conducted longitudinally and may last 2, 3, or more years. Large study samples followed over lengthy periods are costly to conduct. In addition, attribution of effects to the study treatments can be problematic because of the relaxed restrictions on use of other drugs and procedures in this design.

Observational Designs

A second group of designs includes observational studies, which are used frequently in the discipline of epidemiology. This group includes case-control designs, cohort designs, and claims data analysis. These designs are observational because comparisons of outcomes are made among study groups based on observed differences in an uncontrolled setting.

Observational designs are useful in assessing treatment outcomes for conditions such as cardiovascular disease; diabetes; human immunodeficiency virus (HIV); and other chronic, long-term illnesses when it is not feasible to conduct a longitudinal, clinical trial due to time constraints or lack of resources. These types of designs also may be selected when experimental studies are not possible or are unethical. However, with the exception of the prospective cohort, quality-of-life outcomes are unable to be assessed when using these methods. One specific type of observational design, claims data analysis, is discussed in detail in the next section.

Claims Data Analysis

Assessment of a large, automated database is a commonly adopted method of describing burden of illness in a given population. Within certain limitations, this design may be used to compare costs of episodes of illness associated with various treatment choices.

A "closed" system of care is required for effective use of this analysis. Closed systems are those in which all of a patient's medical care is provided by one center or organization. Examples include staff-model health maintenance organizations, state Medicaid programs, and some hospital systems. A closed system allows the researcher to have access to information about diagnoses, clinic visits, treatment data, hospitalizations, drugs, and laboratory tests. A hypothetical study design using a closed system database is depicted in Figure 5. By extracting data from the system database for patients with particular treatments or diagnosis codes, a pool of individuals can be gathered for study. Once groups of patients have been identified, data of interest can be gathered retrospectively. Groups may then be compared to one another for assessment of end points associated with various drugs and treatments used.

Increasing numbers of hospitals and managed care organizations are linking various departmental systems together, allowing consistent access across administrative databases. Linking provides access to resource use and billing and pharmacy, laboratory, and clinical databases,

Figure 4.
Prospective economic clinical trial design

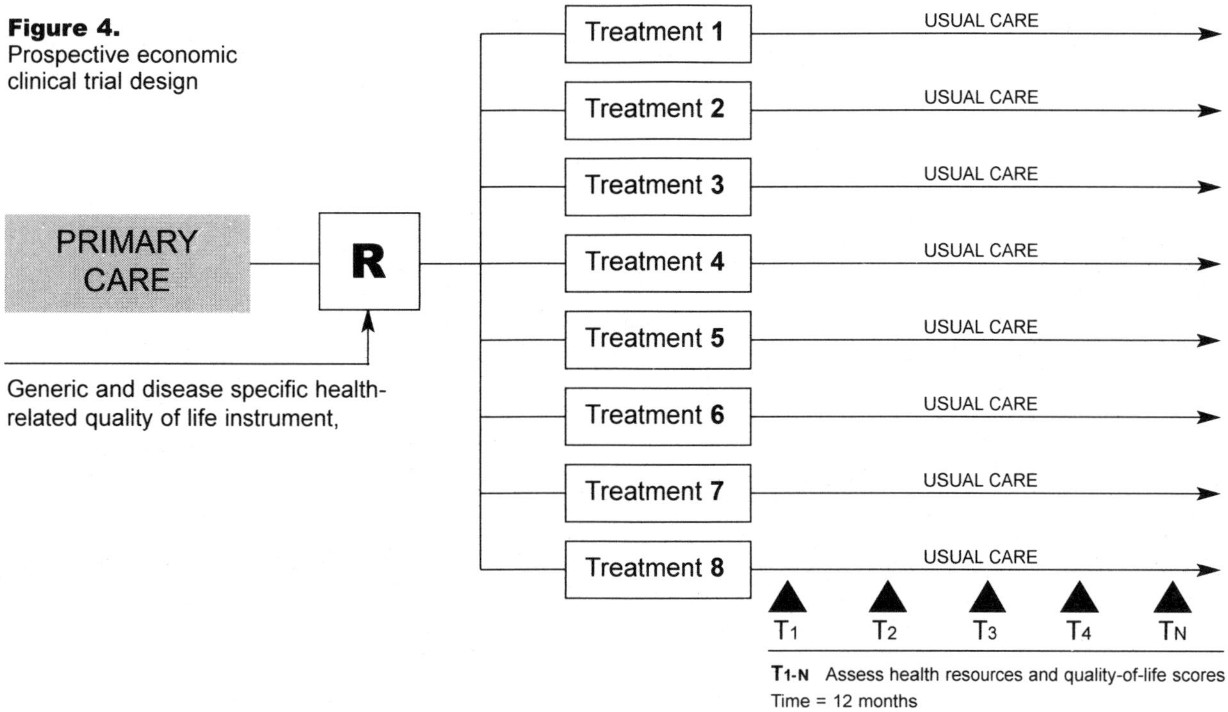

providing a wealth of data. Linking data systems is crucial to facilitate effective database analyses.

Use of hospital data systems presents numerous challenges. In a small hospital setting, the numbers of patients treated for a specific disease or with a particular drug may not be large enough to make efforts worthwhile. In addition, the ability to collect complete data depends on accurate coding of the data when it is entered into the database. However, data found in a hospital data system likely will not contain information on actual clinical or humanistic outcome, but will be limited to clinical procedures administered, drugs ordered and consumed, and laboratory test reported.

Simulation Designs

A third family of designs often combines data from the medical literature, traditional clinical trials, meta-analyses of clinical trails, epidemiologic studies, and expert opinion. Modeling techniques aim to simulate actual clinical practice patterns and final health outcomes. Modeling makes it possible to estimate treatment costs and outcomes when conducting a prospective or observational study is impractical. The modeling framework is typically a mathematical, computer-based portrayal of the problem.

Modeling techniques have advantages and limitations, as do all research designs. Modeling is inexpensive compared to the cost of conducting an experimental or observational study. A model is flexible and can be adapted to represent most diseases and treatments over long periods of time. However, models are only as good as the literature on which they are based. Models relying on incomplete data are limited in use and credibility.

Modeling techniques are more widely accepted in European countries than in the United States. Decision-makers typically are concerned that model parameters can be manipulated to produce any desired outcome. For these reasons, when using a simulation model, adopt model assumptions carefully and clearly state these assumptions. Uncertainty in assumptions of probabilities, costs, and outcomes must be addressed by means of a sensitivity analysis. Modeling is discussed further in the Decision Analysis and Markov Modeling chapters.

Decision Tree Models

The decision tree model is a good simulation choice when there is a need to examine treatments for acute or short-term illnesses. Decision trees also are useful when the clinical decision is complex and there is a significant level of uncertainty in the available information.

This method of analysis is a common and important tool used by outcomes researchers. The framework allows for flexibility in analysis because sensitivity analysis can be applied to key variables, spanning a realistic range of clinical probabilities or economic costs, to help provide the researcher with a best- and worst-case scenario. This form of analysis is a fundamental tool often used in cost-effectiveness analysis. Construction of decision trees is discussed in detail in the Decision Analysis chapter.

Markov Models

A Markov model or process may be applied to a decision tree to enhance the flexibility of the tree design. The fundamental reason for selecting a Markov process is to approach a modeling problem in which the same thing can occur over and over, or when the characteristics of a future event change with time. Markov processes involve creation of a network of health states where the probabilities of moving from one state to another are modeled. Progressing patients from one state to another may simulate a cohort of patients. Each state is associated with specific outcomes and

Figure 5.
Hypothetical study design using an automated database design

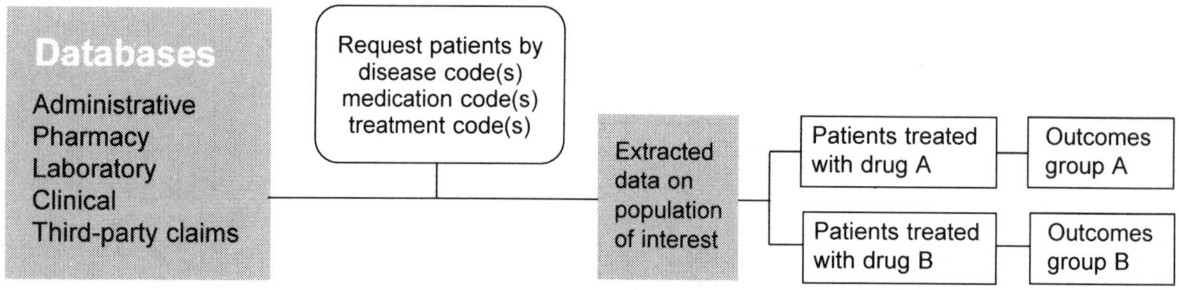

costs that are incurred as patients move through the model. See the Markov Modeling chapter for more detail.

Combination Designs

Depending on the issues in question, available resources, and time constraints, it may be necessary or useful to use a combination of techniques in the design of an evaluation. Multiple combinations of data may be used in the modeling process by grouping data from prospective, observational, and simulation designs, providing estimates of costs and final outcomes. This is a common approach used in pharmacoeconomic analyses.

Validity

Each type of study design has its own inherent biases. Biases to internal validity affect the accuracy of the results of the study, potentially blurring the effect of the intervention. Biases to external validity affect the generalizability of the results to other settings. An example of bias to internal validity includes patient selection bias, where patients in two comparison groups differ in ways that could affect the outcome of interest (i.e., one group may be sicker than the other). Other types of bias to internal validity include crossover bias, where patients in one group mistakenly receive the intervention being studied in the other group; errors in measurement of outcomes; and errors in ascertainment of exposure, where patients' past characteristics are misclassified. Examples of external validity biases include differences among people studied versus people with whom conclusions are extrapolated. For example, one group may be older or sicker. These vulnerabilities of different study designs to different biases, which are presented in Table 4, show that all designs are affected by biases, with different patterns for different designs.

A randomized, clinical trial's strength is that patient bias is minimized due to randomization. However, the randomized, clinical trial's weakness lies in issues of external validity. Randomized, clinical trials may be vulnerable to population biases and to the intensity and quality of care received in a trial relative to that received in actual practice settings. Whether efficacy or effectiveness is being measured also

Table 4. Susceptibility of Various Designs to Biases

	INTERNAL VALIDITY				EXTERNAL VALIDITY	
Design	Patient Selection	Crossover	Error in Measurement of outcomes	Error in Ascertainment of exposure	Population	Technology
RCT	0	++	+	0	++	++
Non-RCT	+	+	+	0	+	+
CCS	++	0	+	+++	0	0
Comparison of clinical series	+++	0	+	0	+	+
Databases	++	0	++	++	0	0

0 implies minimal vulnerability to a bias
+++ implies high vulnerability to a bias
CCS = case-control studies; RCT = randomized, controlled trials.
Reprinted with permission from Eddy DM. Should we change the rules for evaluating medical technologies? In: Gelljns AC, ed. Modern methods of clinical investigation. Washington, D.C.: National Academy Press, 1990.

must be considered. Databases and case control studies tend to draw from real populations, but misspecification can be a significant concern. Because it is impossible to escape subjective judgments in dealing with biases, they must be recognized and put into context. The choice of study design must take potential biases into account.

Again, learn from the literature. Most clinical outcomes data currently come from experimental, clinical trials. However, a common criticism from health care managers is that clinical trials do not have a realistic focus and, therefore, are not useful for decision-making. In contrast, some researchers argue that the only way to obtain accurate information is from a randomized, controlled, clinical trial. Clinical trial data are necessary but not always sufficient to make informed treatment decisions. Such trials do provide a useful starting point for continual evaluation of interventions. The clinical study design has some shortcomings that must be acknowledged; conversely, the shortcomings of studies that lack randomization, are not blinded, and lack controls also must be acknowledged. If the safety and efficacy profile of a pharmaceutical or other intervention is not understood, trying to conduct any outcomes research on the product is difficult to imagine. Safety and efficacy aspects actually address appropriateness, which must be known before quality can be addressed. Clinical trials can be used as a springboard to move from evaluating efficacy to effectiveness.

Table 5. Limitations of Recent Pharmacy Outcomes Research Literature

- Clinicians rate their own performance or the performance of their students
- Comparison groups are inadequate or missing
- Basic population characteristics are inadequate or missing
- Data collection methods lack consistency. New measures are created for many projects
- Generalizability is limited when only one or two pharmacists are evaluated
- Process measures not outcomes are common end points, the end points are short term
- Intermediate outcomes often selected over final outcomes (OK when there is a strong link, but not always the case)
- Data quality is a potential problem

The literature, although important to understand, does not always provide answers to the questions being asked. For pharmaceutical care research questions, a review of recent pharmacy outcomes research literature illustrates problems that limit the value of existing research. These limitations are listed in Table 5. If time and resources are to be invested in answering a research question, taking the time to ensure that the right question is asked and considering the strengths and weaknesses of the study design are imperative. The study design selected is based on tradeoffs. One study is not likely to answer all questions. Clinical outcomes of interest, such as cure of a disease, palliation of symptoms, and prevention of a condition, are known and typically can be described. However, they are not necessarily the sole responsibility of the pharmacist. The pharmacist has responsibility for pharmacotherapeutic outcomes that need to be consistent with and linked to clinical outcomes. The study design chosen to address a specific problem needs to take pharmacists responsibility for specific outcomes into consideration. For example, a tool was created to measure the impact of pharmacist interventions in a Hansen's disease clinic. Pharmacists identified a problem in patient care. After assessment of the problem, initial methodology for monitoring compliance was developed, the method was validated, and the relationship between therapeutic response and compliance was demonstrated. The pharmacists findings led to the inclusion of the compliance monitoring program as a regular part of this Hansen's disease clinic. The United States Public Health Service provides reimbursement for both the analytical and consultative functions of this compliance program because pharmacists demonstrated both to be essential. Once a study design is selected, a time line should be developed to determine how long it should take to conduct the study. Certainly, if a questionnaire must be developed, time to pretest and refine the questionnaire should be included. By thinking about the time commitment up front, frustration with timing issues that tend to appear in the middle of a project can be avoided.

Select a Study Design

- Choose a study design that appropriately supports the research question, the availability of the data, the time allowed for the research, and the funds available
- Consider factors that might bias the research, such as patient selection, measurement error, generalizability from population providing the findings to population in which these findings will be applied

Collect Data

Some data may be collectible through clinical or administrative databases. In this case, it might be a matter of obtaining access to specific computer files. Other data may need to come directly from patients. Looking at a patient to determine the amount of pain the patient is experiencing or the patient's level of satisfaction with a recent health encounter will not work. That information is not likely to consistently reside in a computer file either. Patients are the only source for such information.

Patients can respond reliably to information in questionnaires, as long as time is taken to design the questionnaires properly. Most patients are impressed that someone takes time to ask them questions about how they feel about their illness or their treatment because, historically, that aspect of care has been ignored. If patients are to be a source of information, their needs should be considered when determining how to collect the data. For example, elderly patients may have difficulty completing standardized forms or entering information directly into a computer.

Data can be collected prospectively in many ways. "Paper and pencil" is the most inexpensive approach initially, although at the end of the study someone has to enter that information into a computer database so it can be analyzed. Optically scanned data collection instruments also can be created. Although the initial costs of using optical scanning may be higher, data entry costs can be reduced because a machine reads the data. Direct computer entry and telephone remote data entry are other means of data collection that reduce the human element involved in entering data. An advantage of the paper-and-pencil method is that questions can easily be added. Once an optical scan form is developed, it is difficult to customize further. Use of computer touch screen technology requires longer lead time to prepare and test before it is ready for use with patients, but it can be ideal for patients who may have difficulty holding a pencil (e.g., patients with rheumatoid arthritis or osteoarthritis). Interviewing patients also is an option; it is time consuming and one of the more expensive ways of collecting data. However, in some cases, it is the most reasonable means of collecting data. Observing behavior is another means of collecting data, depending on the question at hand. Consider the potential bias that is created if people know their behavior is being observed. Data sources and tools for collecting humanistic outcomes are discussed more fully in the Data Sources and Tools for Measuring Humanistic Outcomes chapter.

Collect Data

- Obtain access to existing data sources if using secondary data
- Capture primary data using a method appropriate to the study design and from a representative sample of the patient population under study

Analyze Data

By developing a plan for data analysis before the study starts, the amount of data collected is kept realistic and usually minimized. By collecting only the data needed, a great deal of time and effort can be saved.

Keep the analysis plan simple. The level of statistics needed to conduct an analysis depends on the data collected and the goals of the analysis. Data are analyzed to evaluate patients, to discriminate among patients, or to try to predict how patients may act. If the goal is to evaluate patients, questions asked might include: are their differences in annual costs between patients with rheumatoid arthritis who are newly diagnosed versus those who have had the disease for more than 5 years? What differences exist in health-related quality of life between patients who have more severe disease compared to those with less severe disease? Descriptive statistics are often useful at this evaluative stage. Discrimination among patients might involve determining whether a health-related quality-of-life instrument can differentiate among patients based on levels of severity or presence or absence of a disease, or whether patients can be moved from one severity level to another based on appropriate treatment. If the goal is to predict behavior, a question might be: Can a patient's annual level of resource use based on a general health-related quality-of-life score be predicted? Predicting how patients might act is the most challenging of the three approaches and typically requires more complex statistical procedures and more data.

The level of analysis is driven not only by the question asked, but also by the type of data collected. The distribution of the data helps determine the type of analysis required. For example, health care resource use is likely to be skewed. A few patients may account for a large percentage of the resource. In that situation, a mean may not be the appropriate way to present the results; medians may be better. It also is important to provide some indication of the variance surrounding the midpoint. Knowing that the mean length of hospital stay for a group of 50 patients is 9 days is difficult to put in context without knowing the variance. If the mean length of stay is 9 days with a range of 0 to 60 days, consider if the mean represents the data well. If three of these patients each were hospitalized for 60 days, these patients would represent 40 percent of the total days in hospital; thus to assume that the average patient requires 9 days in the hospital is misleading. Reporting that the median number of hospital days is 4 provides the user with a better sense of the patient population. For this reason, providing the median and the range might be the best way to summarize the data.

For economic analyses, it is important to look at incremental costs (i.e., the additional cost incurred in providing a level of service or intervention relative to another). Several types of economic analyses may be applicable to the question to be investigated.

For those embarking on analysis of health-related quality-of-life measures, this discussion assumes that quality-of-life instruments used have been developed previously by other parties. In that case, it is important to analyze that instrument according to the developers' recommendations. Because validity is an ongoing process, it is important to assess the instrument's validity characteristics as well. This validity is addressed more completely in the Measuring Health Status and Interpretation of Humanistic Assessments chapters. A valid and reliable instrument is necessary before looking at the humanistic responses of the instrument. Patient satisfaction instruments also should be scored according to the developer's recommendations.

When creating an instrument, a scoring algorithm that makes sense should be chosen. There are many people interested in statistics whose expertise can be tapped. Textbooks also are available for those who need a refresher course in statistics.

Analyze Data

- Plan the data analysis up front
- Ensure that the appropriate data are being captured to support the analysis and that all data captured are being used (i.e., no data are being captured unnecessarily)

Discount Results

Discounting is discussed only briefly because it is discussed in greater detail in the Sensitivity Analysis chapter. If a study runs more than a year in length, it is necessary to discount the costs and the benefits associated with that study. The reason for doing this is related to the time value of money. People like instant gratification and want to be compensated for things they put off enjoying. People put money in the bank and collect interest on it at the end of the year, but most people probably would not put much money in the bank if the bank were not paying interest. In the same manner, if money is invested up front for treating hypertension, the results of reduced incidence of stroke are not seen until later; discounting the results as if they occurred in the current time period allows comparison of the results with other investment opportunities. The controversy associated with discounting benefits is that it is difficult to put off health-related quality of life. Improvements in quality of life now cannot necessarily be traded off for better improvements later. However, if benefits are not discounted along with costs, the rational decision-maker will always put off investing in any health intervention because the same amount at some future time will always look like more than when it is discounted to present value.

The discount rate used can affect the results. For example, an intervention that costs $1,000 at year 1 will have benefits estimated to be $2,000 at year 10. Using a 5 percent discount rate, the present value is $1,228, so the net benefit is $228. At a 10 percent discount rate, the net benefit is negative, which could definitely alter the perception of a program's value.

Discount Results

- Consider discounting study results if the time horizon warrants

Conduct a Sensitivity Analysis

Just as in clinical trials, uncertainty in pharmacoeconomic studies must be addressed. In clinical trials, power calculations are generated to estimate the sample size needed to observe differences among treatment groups with a certain degree of confidence. Uncertainty exists due to random events and due to lack of knowledge of certain factors. Uncertainty due to random events is statistically predictable, and can be addressed in the statistical analysis. However, uncertainty due to lack of information presents other challenges.

What if the discount rate should change? What if the number of patients who visit an emergency department changes with time? The way uncertainty due to lack of information is addressed is through sensitivity analysis. Sensitivity analyses allows the question, What if? What if the number of physician visits changes? What if the discount rate is 7 percent instead of 5 percent?

A sensitivity analysis indicates one of three things. First, it can demonstrate substantial dependence of a conclusion on an assumption. If results vary widely when a specific assumption is challenged, obviously there will be less confidence in the results of that study. Second, it can demonstrate that an assumption does not significantly affect a conclusion. If the results do not change much, then it may be concluded that it is not necessary to spend a lot of time measuring that specific variable; because the measurement does not change the conclusions significantly, there can be less concern with the precision of that measure. Such results should increase confidence in the conclusions drawn. Third, a sensitivity analysis also can help establish a minimum or maximum value that a variable must have for an intervention to appear worthwhile. If providing pharmacy services to a specific area in a hospital, as few as 4 or 5 hours a day or as many as 12 hours might need to be provided to actually demonstrate value to the patients.

When interpreting and presenting study findings, it is important to identify the important variables on which a sensitivity analysis is conducted. Confidence in those values should be assessed because the confidence in the values can affect the generalizability of the results. In addition, if the analysis contains some assumptions known to be controversial, such as willingness-to-pay estimates or discounting benefits at a high rate, those assumptions should be subjected to a sensitivity analysis. Sensitivity analysis is more completely discussed in the Sensitivity Analysis chapter.

Conduct a Sensitivity Analysis

- Conduct a sensitivity analysis to test key assumptions, to identify key variables that might warrant extra attention, or to establish a range of acceptable findings

Consider Ethical Issues

Anytime a patient is to be involved in a research project, ethical issues need to be considered. Before a prospective study starts, an investigational review board (IRB) must review the protocol to ensure that patients are not put at an undue risk and that, through the consent form, they are fully apprised of the risks and benefits of the study. If a study is conducted retrospectively, some institutions will still want to review the protocol. Different institutions have different policies regarding notification of patients. When in doubt, contact an IRB member for clarification.

Analysis of claims data typically does not warrant notification of each individual included in the database, as long as patient identifiers are removed before any analysis is initiated. However, issues of patient privacy and protection of patient records have arisen. Ensure the access or analysis is acceptable to the institution's IRB. In general, access is granted if the analysis in no way allows the identification of any individual patient.

Sending questionnaires directly to patients, whether they are health-related quality-of-life questions or patient satisfaction questions, usually requires some IRB review, although in many cases it can be expedited because the risk to the patient is minimal. Frequently, the completion of a survey itself is considered the patient's indication of informed consent, as long as patients are informed in a cover letter that their responses are anonymous and that there will be no repercussions if they choose not to participate. When in doubt, always consult the institution's IRB.

Consider Ethical Issues

- Ensure patients are not put at an unnecessary risk
- Identify who must grant approval to conduct this research and secure that approval

Interpret Study Results

Study results need to be put in context. It is a good idea to take a step back and look at the study from different perspectives. The study design, the patient population, the study setting, and a host of other factors all can affect the conclusions drawn. Was the patient population studied similar to other patients not included in the trial? What were the limitations of the study? How generalizable are the results? When interpreting pharmacoeconomic study results, it is important to remember that the value of a benefit may vary across individuals or among generations. Clinicians may be familiar with interpreting clinical data and throughout time are able to put such results in context quickly. They may look at studies reporting intermediate measures such as FEV_1 or blood pressure and have a sense of whether the results are good or bad. Economic and humanistic measures, because they are still new, are not necessarily viewed in the same light. The researcher may need to help put such measures in context until the information is used more consistently in heath care decision-making.

Interpreting quality-of-life data is important but not necessarily a measure clinicians know how to apply to patient care. What does a change mean? Relating quality-of-life scores to other clinical or economic measures may provide an additional anchor on which to present quality-of-life data. However, health-related quality-of-life measures something different than clinical and economic measures, so there would not be a perfect correlation. Interpretation of humanistic assessments is more fully discussed in the Interpretation of Humanistic Assessments chapter.

Interpreting economic measures is a challenge, in part because of the skewness associated with resource use and of the difficulty in assigning meaningful costs to resources. If the difference between two groups of patients is 2 days in the intensive care unit, such a difference may not be statistically significant but the cost differential may be notable. This is where sensitivity analysis can be useful to help put the resource use issues into perspective.

Interpret Study Results

- Ensure the conclusions drawn from the study are supported by the study results
- Detail the study's limitations so as not to overstate the strength of the study conclusions

Conclusions

Ten steps have been identified that can serve as a useful guide in creating a study protocol to address an outcomes question. These steps are summarized in Table 6.

Table 6. Ten General Principles of Analysis

- Define problem
- State objectives
- Identify alternatives
- Analyze benefits/effectiveness
- Analyze costs
- Differentiate perspective of analysis
- Perform discounting
- Analyze uncertainties
- Address ethical issues
- Interpret results

Source: Office of Technology Assessment, Washington, D.C., 1980

Pharmacoeconomic research, if used appropriately, will provide increased confidence in health care decisions. Certainly, as these tools are adopted, it is possible to have greater transparency in decision-making.

Measuring outcomes is clearly complex, but it is essential to managing complete patient care. Care cannot be fully managed if there is no way to measure it. Outcomes need to be linked to the specific practices provided to actually improve the quality and efficiency of the pharmaceutical care system specifically, and the health care system, in general. Asking the right questions and following through with appropriate studies linking outcomes and processes of care will assist decision-makers in the quest for information on which to base decisions.

Annotated Bibliography

1. American Pharmaceutical Association. Patient outcomes of pharmaceutical interventions: a scientific foundation for the future. Invitational Conference of the American Pharmaceutical Association. November 13–14, 1994; Washington, D.C.

   The papers and recommendations included in this book are based on six questions identified in an effort to advance the research base underpinning patient outcome-oriented pharmacy practice. The questions may serve as a benchmark for discussion and education as the science of outcomes research evolves and as pharmacy begins to embrace formal outcomes assessments.

2. Bootman JL, Townsend RJ, McGhan WF, eds. Principles of Pharmacoeconomics, 2nd ed. Cincinnati, OH: Harvey Whitney Books Co., 1996.

   The second edition of this book is a greatly expanded version of the first and includes discussions on pharmacoeconomic research in clinical trials, medical centers, community practice, and managed health care settings. The information is relevant for researchers, practitioners, and students; however, the primary audience is the beginning researcher. The book should stimulate health care providers and researchers to generate more pharmacoeconomic research and apply the results to prevent and treat disease.

3. Cody RP, Cody R, Smith JK. Applied Statistics and the SAS Programming Language, 4th ed. Englewood Cliffs, NJ: Prentice Hall, 1997.

   The book is split into three sections: a tutorial section that serves as an introduction to programming with SAS software; the main text which describes common statistical tests, how to run them with SAS software, and how to interpret the results; and an SAS programming section, which shows common problems in data manipulation and how to solve the problems using SAS software.

4. Cook TD, Campbell DT. Quasi-Experimentation: Design and Analysis for Field Settings. Boston: Houghton Mifflin Company, 1979.

   The authors present some quasi-experimental designs and features that can be used in many social research settings. The designs serve to probe causal hypotheses about a variety of issues in applied research. Each design is assessed in terms of validity, and general conclusions are drawn about the strengths and limitations of each design. Also discussed are randomized experiments, which are possible in field research if obstacles for using random assignment are overcome. The book does not address health care issues specifically, but the principles discussed apply to health care situations.

5. Eddy DM. Should we change the rules for evaluating medical technologies? In: Gelijns AC, ed. Modern Methods of Clinical Investigation. Washington, D.C.: National Academy Press, 1990.

   This book chapter includes a discussion of the tradeoffs that need to be made when considering study design issues. The author points out that a variety of factors need to be considered when determining study design, such as costs, logistics, and the relative amount of precision needed. The pros and cons of randomized, clinical trials are compared with case control and cohort studies. This chapter is a nice summary of study design issues that are sometimes ignored.

6. Kozma CM, Reeder CE, Schulz RM. Economic, clinical, and humanistic outcomes: a planning model for pharmacoeconomic research. Clin Ther 1993;15:1121–32.

   This paper proposes a theoretical framework for identifying, collecting, and using outcomes data to assess the value of pharmaceutical treatment alternatives. The economic, clinical, and humanistic outcomes model depicts the value of a product or service as a combination of traditional clinical-based outcomes with more contemporary measures of economic efficiency and quality. The model should assist researchers and practitioners in planning, conducting, and evaluating pharmaceutical products and services from a multidimensional perspective.

7. Rector TS, Hatton RC. Statistical concepts and methods used to evaluate pharmacotherapy. In: Carter BL, Angaran DM, Lake K, Raebel MA, eds. Pharmacotherapy Self-Assessment Program, 2nd ed. Biostatistics, Research Design and Literature Evaluation Strategies, Drug Information Technologies and Strategies, Drug Regulatory Process, Accreditation and Regulation of the Medication Use System: Selected Aspects. Kansas City, MO: American College of Clinical Pharmacy, 1996, 25–48.

   The section on biostatistics in this book serves as a useful primer for those who need to become acquainted or reacquainted with various aspects of statistical analysis. Brief sections discuss statistics for nominal, ordinal, and interval measures. The focus is on clinical measures, which can serve as a useful place to start before moving into economic and humanistic measures.

8. Salant P, Dillman DA. How to Conduct Your Own Survey. New York: John Wiley & Sons, Inc., 1994.

   This book brings the process of conducting surveys within the reach of people who need survey information, but have no formal survey training. The book explains how surveys work and what makes them accurate. Step-by-step decisions that must be made while conducting a survey are described, including whether a survey is even appropriate. Simple designs and straightforward solutions are emphasized.

9. Steinwachs DM, Wu AW, Skinner EA. How will outcomes management work? Health Aff 1994;13:153–62.

   The authors describe the implementation of two outcomes programs in a health care system. Although some results are presented, the more interesting topic is the implementation process, which is described along with the inherent challenges encountered. The importance of choosing the right issue to study is demonstrated, along with the importance of ensuring that the targeted recipients of the data have an understanding of their meaning.

10. Wright J. Research design and literature evaluation. In: Carter BL, Angaran DM, Lake K, Raebel MA, eds. Pharmacotherapy Self-Assessment Program, 2nd ed. Biostatistics, Research Design and Literature Evaluation Strategies, Drug Information Technologies and Strategies, Drug Regulatory Process, Accreditation and Regulation of the Medication Use System: Selected Aspects. Kansas City, MO: American College of Clinical Pharmacy, 1996, 53–71.

    The author reviews clinical research design in a concise and understandable way. Bias and validity, as well as methods for minimizing them, are discussed. All the major study designs are described from both a research and literature evaluation standpoint. This is a good starting point for learning about this topic.

11. Spilker B, ed. Pharmacoeconomics and Quality of Life in Clinical Trials. New York: Raven Press, 1995.

    A comprehensive volume that provides a useful overview of quality-of-life instruments for a variety of disease states, along with special issues for consideration for those interested in incorporating humanistic outcomes assessments in clinical trials.

12. Hopkins, WG. A new view of statistics. Internet Society for Sport Science: *http://www.sportsci.org/resource/stats/*. Accessed October 2002.

    This is a helpful Web site that explains statistical issues in an understandable fashion. This article was written for sports science, but is clearly applicable here; it includes formulas for estimating sample size and conducting a variety of statistical tests (see *http://www.sportsci.org/resource/stats/ssdetermine.html*).

Self-Assessment Questions

1. Which one of the following is the first step when initiating the research process?
   A Determine what data are available.
   B. Determine the question.
   C. Determine the desired answer.
   D. Determine the study perspective.

2. Which one of the following best describes why it is critical to link processes to outcomes?
   A. It is impossible to measure outcomes without processes.
   B. It is impossible to measure processes without outcomes.
   C. Processes and outcomes are not mutually exclusive aspects of care; knowing both allows rational decisions to be made.
   D. Processes and outcomes are mutually exclusive aspects of care; knowing one or the other allows decisions to be made more quickly.

3. All except which one of the following are examples of bias to internal validity?
   A. Patient selection.
   B. Differences among people studied and people about whom conclusions should be drawn.
   C. Ascertainment of exposure.
   D. Errors in outcome measurement.

4. Which one of the following is an example of bias to external validity?
   A. Crossover.
   B. Patient selection.
   C. Population bias.
   D. Error in measurement of outcomes.

5. Which one of the following is the preferred source of health-related quality-of-life data?
   A. Patient.
   B. Administrative databases.
   C. Caregiver.
   D. Medicaid databases.

6. Study design affects all except which one of the following?
   A. The cost of the evaluation.
   B. The time required to conduct the evaluation.
   C. The importance of the study.
   D. The accuracy of the information gained.

7. Which one of the following is true when measuring outcomes in a study?
   A. Outcomes should be measured in their most natural units.
   B. The same data source should be used for all outcomes.
   C. Outcomes should be measured in monetary units.
   D. Outcomes must be measured before resources are determined.

8. When measuring resources used in an evaluation comparing Drug A and Drug B, which one of the following describes a potential source of error?
   A. Substitution of resources that occurs if a pharmacy technician begins performing some tasks performed by a pharmacist at the beginning of the study.
   B. Migration of resources that occurs if more people are treated with Drug A than Drug B.
   C. Substitution of resources that occurs if more people are treated with Drug B than Drug A.
   D. Migration of resources that occurs if a pharmacy technician begins performing some tasks performed by a pharmacist at the beginning of the study.

9. All except which one of the following is a goal of a study analysis?
   A. To evaluate patients.
   B. To discriminate among patients.
   C. To predict how patients may act.
   D. To incriminate patients based on their actions.

10. It is important to establish a research framework before beginning a study because of which one of the following?
   A. Without a framework funding would not be received.
   B. A framework forces the prioritization of study results.
   C. A framework focuses the researcher on what can be accomplished.
   D. A framework requires the researcher to measure both process and outcomes.

DATA SOURCES FOR ECONOMIC OUTCOMES ANALYSES

Nelda E. Johnson, Pharm.D.

Outline

This chapter assists readers in identifying and selecting the best sources for cause and outcomes data for conducting health economics projects.

I. Criteria for selecting data sources
   A. Types of data
      1. Economic data
         a. direct medical costs (hospitalizations, drugs, laboratory tests)
         b. nonmedical costs (indirect and intangible costs)
      2. Patient outcomes data
         a. clinical response to therapy
         b. quality of life
         c. patient satisfaction
   B. Research question being asked
      1. Clearly defined hypothesis or study description is necessary
      2. Helps to define costs, outcomes, and data sources
   C. Perspective used for the study
      1. The specific perspective is the point of view for the study
      2. Helps to define the types of costs that should be measured
      3. Provides direction for selecting data source
   D. Access to the data
      1. Permission must be obtained to access and use financial data
      2. Some organizations readily grant permission
      3. Informed consent may be needed for measuring patient outcomes
   E. Resources available for the study
      1. Some analyses may require special funding
      2. Depends on data sources and study design

II. Major sources of data
   A. External data sources
      1. Published studies
         a. need to be critically evaluated
         b. may be useful in modeling analyses
      2. Medical claims and administrative databases
         a. limited clinical outcomes data
         b. rarely contain quality of life or patient satisfaction data
   B. Internal data sources
      1. Cost and outcomes data obtained directly from the organization
      2. Useful if sufficient numbers of patient cases exist
      3. Drug use evaluation data can be a useful source

III. Frequently used data sources
   A. Hospital data
      1. Cost-accounting systems
         a. financial data
         b. patient data may include demographics, morbidity, mortality, and length-of-stay data
      2. Ease of access and level of detail available varies widely (see Table 1)
      3. Must understand differences between actual hospital cost data and patient charge data
         a. hospital cost data should be used if perspective is the provider
         b. patient charges are rarely paid in full by third-party payers
      4. Resource use data are used to compare data across hospitals
   B. Data from managed care organizations
      1. Medical and pharmacy claims databases
         a. available in most managed care organizations
         b. must understand the details of claims data (see Table 2)
   C. Government databases
      1. Medicare and Medicaid
      2. Available from the United States Department of Health and Human Services Office of Statistics and Data Management
      3. They are large data sets available on CD-ROM or magnetic tapes
      4. Require computer disk space and programming time
      5. Usually used in grant-based research projects
   D. Private consultants
      1. Usually use proprietary data sources that they have developed
      2. May be costly to access

IV. Advantages and limitations of using databases
   A. Advantages of database research
      1. Provides a large sample size
      2. Avoids expensive data collection and data entry
      3. Data collection is unobtrusive to patients and providers
      4. Facilitates tracking patient costs over long periods
   B. Database limitations
      1. Patients have not been randomly assigned to treatments
      2. Not possible to confirm cause and effect relationships
      3. Data may be missing because of inadequate coding or data entry
      4. Often lack clinical detail

V. Conclusion
   A. Many factors may influence the selection of a data source for economic outcomes analyses

Learning Objectives

1. Identify and select appropriate data sources for health economics research projects.
2. Understand the advantages and disadvantages of using automated databases for health economics research.
3. Differentiate between hospital cost and charge data.
4. List the criteria for selecting a data source for an economic outcomes analysis.

Data Sources for Economic Outcomes Analyses

Researchers use a variety of administrative and cost-accounting data to determine the costs and outcomes associated with health care services. This chapter assists readers in identifying and selecting the best sources for cost and outcomes data for different types of health economics projects.

Criteria for Selecting Data Sources

Several important factors should be considered before an appropriate data source for an economic outcomes analysis is selected. Some of the factors that are discussed in this chapter include types of data appropriate for the study, the specific research question being asked, the perspective that will be used for the study, the ability to access the data source, and the resources available to spend on the study.

Types of Data

First, clinicians must focus on understanding the different types of data that can be used in an economic outcomes analysis. A thorough understanding of these data types helps the researcher select the best data source. One type of data that is always needed for an analysis is economic data. The most easily measured and most commonly available economic data are the direct medical costs incurred in treating a medical condition. Direct medical costs are those costs associated with providing medical care to patients and include resources, such as hospitalizations, physician office visits, diagnostic procedures, laboratory tests, and drug use. These direct medical costs are best obtained either directly from a health care provider or from the insurance or claims processing center that pays for these services.

Other types of cost data that may be included in an economic outcomes analysis include the patients' out-of-pocket expenses for health care, changes in patients' levels of productivity, and other intangible costs, such as pain and suffering. These types of patient data are not readily available from health care organizations and, instead, must be obtained directly from patients in a prospective study. These data elements are important for an outcomes study, especially if the perspective is that of the patient or society; however, they are more difficult to obtain and are not always available in the literature.

Other types of data elements important for economic outcomes studies are measures of patient outcomes. Patient outcomes may include clinical response to therapy or humanistic outcomes, such as quality of life or patient satisfaction. Data for clinical outcomes can be obtained from the medical literature or from patients' medical records; however, quality of life and patient satisfaction data usually are obtained from patient surveys because these data are not routinely collected or recorded.

Research Question Being Asked

A clearly defined hypothesis or description of the study problem is one of the key factors that helps narrow the focus of the study and determine the appropriate data source. For instance, if a study is designed to evaluate differences in quality of life with two pharmaceutical products, the data will have to be collected prospectively, preferably in a randomized study. If the analysis is designed to evaluate the economic impact of a product used in elderly patients, then a data source containing information from a significant number of elderly patients needs to be used.

Perspective Used for the Study

The specific perspective used for the study is another helpful factor for deciding which types of costs should be included in an economic analysis. A clearly defined perspective also provides direction for selecting the appropriate sources of data. For example, if a pharmaceutical product is used primarily in an acute hospital setting, a study conducted from the perspective of the hospital should measure actual hospital costs using data from the hospital's cost-accounting system. It would be misleading to use charge data, because these data do not represent the actual costs incurred by the hospital.

If the perspective used for the study is that of an integrated health care system, the study should include not only the hospital costs, but also the total cost of care, including hospital readmissions, physician office visits, laboratory testing, and outpatient drug costs. From an insurer's perspective, the amounts paid for medical and pharmaceutical products and services are of greatest importance, not the hospital's cost data. The amounts paid can be obtained from managed care and insurance claims databases. To obtain data from an employer's perspective, special studies would have to be conducted to measure lost time from work or changes in productivity. If the perspective used is that of the patient or of society, it is important to measure costs and outcomes from the patients' points of view. These might include out-of-pocket costs, such as copayments for drugs, and measures of quality of life and patient satisfaction with care.

Access to the Data

Another factor that may influence the type of data used in a study is the ability to access the data. Most health care organizations consider their cost data to be proprietary, so it is usually necessary to obtain permission to access these data. Gaining permission can be accomplished most easily by working directly with an administrator who can authorize access. Some organizations are more willing than others to share financial data for the purpose of conducting health economic studies. For patient outcomes data, such as quality of life, it may be necessary to obtain permission from patients through informed consent if the data are being collected solely for research purposes.

Resources Available for the Study

Depending on the data sources selected for the study, special funding or additional resources, such as computer programming or data analyst skills, may be needed. This is particularly true for large studies or those that require accessing a large computer database to retrieve cost or clinical information. If additional resources are not available for the study, this may, in some cases, limit the data sources or scope of the study.

Major Sources of Data

There are two main sources of data for health economic studies; they include external sources which are outside the health care organization and internal sources from within the organization.

External Data Sources

External data sources include published studies and external databases. Published studies can serve as useful data sources, especially for analyses that incorporate modeling or decision analysis techniques. Clinicians must carefully scrutinize the quality of the published study and determine if drug therapy in the study was comparable to how the drug will be used in their own organizations. Guidelines for assessing the quality of pharmacoeconomic analyses are available in the literature. Patient outcomes data can be extracted from the published literature and combined with an organization's own cost data using standard methods for economic analyses.

Other external data sources are medical claims databases, such as those available from Medicare and Medicaid. These types of databases usually contain limited clinical and patient outcomes data. Few have quality of life or patient satisfaction data.

Internal Data Sources

A useful source of both cost and outcomes data is the organization in which the analysis is conducted. Health care organizations that have sufficient numbers of patients receiving the therapy of interest can access their own internal data sources to determine both financial and outcomes data. Care should be exercised if there are few patients from which to draw the sample because the sample may not be representative of the patient population. When a health care organization has too few cases, the data can be evaluated in a preliminary fashion. However, a full analysis also should include data from an external data source.

Data may be available from several different areas within a health care organization, including patients' medical records (for clinical outcomes data), financial and administrative databases (for cost outcomes data), quality assessment activities (for patient satisfaction measures), and drug use evaluations (for specific responses to a particular drug). Drug use evaluations also serve as a good starting point to identify patients who have received a particular therapy and can be used to assess additional outcomes and resource use data that can be useful in an economic analysis.

Frequently Used Data Sources

Some of the commonly used sources to obtain data for economic outcomes studies are hospitals, managed care organizations, government databases, and private consultants. Because each organization usually has its own specialized information system, those wishing to conduct economic analyses within a health care organization must work closely with those who are most familiar with the system. This applies to hospital systems, managed care organizations, pharmacy benefit management companies, and insurers. Even within one health care system, a variety of computerized information systems may be used. The best way to become familiar with the data sources is to obtain a sample of the data and begin to conduct a pilot analysis. This helps assess the completeness of the data and the feasibility of using it for a full economic analysis.

Hospital Data

Hospital information systems usually contain detailed cost and resource use data for each hospital admission. These systems also may contain limited information about patient outcomes, including morbidity and mortality or severity of illness data. The ease with which hospital data are accessed and the level of detail available vary widely among different hospital systems. Some of the data elements commonly available from a sophisticated hospital information system are outlined in Table 1.

Table 1. Examples of Hospital Data

Medical Record Information	Billing Information	Admission/Discharge Information
Demographics	Number of products received	Length of stay
Diagnosis codes	Number of tests received	Type of admission (routine or urgent)
Procedure codes	Departmental costs	Place of admission (emergency department, scheduled admission)
Physician information	Total hospital costs	Discharge disposition (to home, transferred, deceased)
Severity of illness rating	Total hospital charges	

Before hospital data are used in an economic analysis, a clear distinction between the use of actual hospital cost data and patient charge data should be made. Patient charges are the amount of money requested by the hospital for the services provided. These charges are rarely paid in full because most hospital contracts allow the hospital to be paid either a daily rate or a rate based on a discount of charges. Charge data was used quite frequently in the past; more recently, this type of data has come into disfavor because it is recognized that little relationship exists between actual hospital costs and the amounts charged for hospital services. It is only appropriate to use charge data when the full charges are paid. Because Medicare, Medicaid, and third-party payers do not pay full charges, and there are few patients who do pay full charges, it is rarely appropriate to use charge data in an economic outcomes analysis. Actual hospital costs more accurately reflect the financial impact to the hospital and should be used whenever possible, especially if the study is conducted from the perspective of the hospital. If the study is conducted from the perspective of society or from a third-party payer, the appropriate economic measure to use would be the amount paid out for the service.

In those cases where charge data are all that is available, it is recommended that the cost-to-charge ratio for the institution be obtained from the financial officer. This number is the ratio between what it costs to provide care and what is charged for that care for the institution overall. Using this ratio can help to change the charge data into something that approximates cost data, on average. This practice is most useful when comparing two alternatives within the same setting. It is less useful when combined with cost data from other sources.

Data from hospital cost-accounting systems can be used to determine how many resources were consumed during a hospitalization and include factors such as the amount of nursing time used, the number of intensive care days, the number of laboratory and diagnostic tests, and the drugs used. By collecting this type of resource use data, standardized costs can be applied and the data can be analyzed. Another way resource use data can be useful is to apply the organization's own cost data to published resource use data so that the financial impact of a therapy or service can be calculated for the organization.

Hospital medical records also serve as a rich data source for obtaining detailed clinical information about patients. However, collecting data through chart review is a labor-intensive activity and subject to errors during data extraction. It also requires entry into a database for further analysis. These labor-intensive steps usually limit the number of charts that can be reviewed unless additional funding or resources are available to support this type of data collection process.

Data from Managed Care Organizations

Medical and pharmacy claims data from managed care organizations frequently are used as data sources for economic outcomes analyses. Managed care claims data are particularly helpful if the perspective used for the study is that of a third-party payer and if the drug is primarily used in the outpatient setting. But before attempting to access and use this type of data in an economic analysis, clinicians must have a thorough understanding of the managed care plan and the types of claims data that are available. Table 2 lists some types of demographic and claims information that is typically available.

Table 2. Managed Care Claims Data Elements

Enrollee Information	Claims Information
Demographics	Primary care physician visits
Diagnosis codes	Hospitalizations
Procedure codes	Emergency department visits
Physician information	Laboratory claims
Date of enrollment	Prescription claims

Different levels of detail for clinical and economic data may be available, based on how the health care plan and the database are organized. For instance, if primary care physicians are paid a set fee on a capitated basis for each health care member per month, the managed care claims database may not contain specific claims for each time a member is seen by his or her primary care physician. In other plans, physicians may submit encounter forms that contain the patient's diagnoses and procedure information for each visit. Encounters can be counted as resources used; however, because physicians are not paid for each visit in a capitated plan, no dollar amount is paid out by the organization. When conducting economic research using managed care claims data, clinicians must decide in advance how to handle this type of data because it can influence the results of the study.

One other factor to consider before using managed care claims data is that the medical and pharmacy claims are not always integrated into a single database. Instead, pharmacy prescription claims often are contracted to an external pharmacy benefit management company and exist in a separate database. In this case, it is necessary to obtain the pharmacy data and then merge them with the medical claims data before a full economic analysis can be conducted.

Before analyzing the claims data, the quality of the data should be reviewed to determine if there are missing data or duplicate entries. Whether members in the plan were continuously enrolled during the time frame for the study also must be evaluated. Database query tools can greatly expedite the process for doing this. For organizations without automated methods to analyze the data, additional support, such as programming or data management, may be necessary.

Government Databases

Medicare and Medicaid data files can be obtained from the United States Department of Health and Human Services Office of Statistics and Data Management. These are large data sets available on CD-ROM or magnetic tapes that require significant computer disk space and programming time to analyze. As such, they usually are used in projects funded by grants or by research-based organizations.

Private Consultants

A growing number of consulting companies provide useful data for health economic studies using proprietary data sources they have developed or purchased. These data sources can be useful when data for a specific type of patient population are needed, such as for cancer or acquired immune deficiency syndrome. However, the fees charged to access these specially created data sources may be significant and require additional funding for the study.

Advantages and Limitations of Using Databases

Advantages of Database Research

Using databases for economic outcomes studies offers several advantages. First, such a method makes it possible to obtain a large sample size and avoid the expense associated with conducting primary data collection, such as chart reviews. It also obviates the time and expense associated with entering the data into a database before the analysis. Because data collection is unobtrusive to patients and providers, it will not result in behavioral changes simply because a study was being conducted. Because of the longitudinal nature of databases, they also facilitate tracking patients' health experiences and costs back over time. These types of data have an advantage in that it represents ordinary medical practice, rather than the selective patient populations that exist in randomized, clinical trials.

Database Limitations

One of the major limitations of using databases for health economic evaluations is that patients are not randomly assigned to a treatment regimen, which may create certain biases in the data. For example, if physicians only prescribe an expensive drug with fewer adverse events to patients who are at high risk for the event or to patients for whom other therapies have failed, a bias is created in the sample of patients who received that drug. An economic analysis may find that patients who received the drug used more resources because they were at higher risk for adverse events compared to patients who received other drugs.

Because database analyses are always retrospective and patients are not randomly assigned to different treatments, it is not possible to confirm cause and effect relationships. For instance, an economic analysis may show that hospital costs and length of stay decreased after a new antibiotic was added to the formulary. However, these changes may have been because of other factors, such as implementation of a critical pathway during the same time frame.

Database studies must be carefully designed to control for confounding variables, including patient differences such as comorbidities or different severities of illness. In addition, data obtained from databases must be carefully examined to determine if any key data elements are missing and to look for problems of inadequate or inaccurate coding procedures. It is commonly known that procedures and diagnoses codes often are subject to "upcoding." This means that patients may be assigned codes that maximize financial reimbursement for the medical services provided. In health care systems where procedure and diagnosis codes are not used for reimbursement purposes, little incentive exists for the health care providers to routinely submit accurate diagnosis and procedure codes.

Conclusion

This chapter describes some of the factors that influence the selection of data sources for conducting economic outcomes analyses. It also provides readers with information to assist in identifying and selecting the best sources for cost and outcomes data for different types of health economics projects.

Annotated Bibliography

1. Anderson F. Why is the pharmaceutical industry investing increasing amounts in health economic evaluations? Int J Technol Assess Health Care 1995;11:750–61

   This article contains a good description of the reasons pharmaceutical companies conduct and invest in health economic studies. Several potential uses of economic studies are described in this European-based opinion paper, and include prioritizing in-house research projects, providing criteria for pharmaceutical pricing, serving as a basis for registration of new pharmaceuticals, assisting in reimbursement and price negotiations, serving as a strategic marketing instrument, and assisting in the transition to over-the-counter drugs.

2. Davidoff AJ, Powe NR. The role of perspective in defining economic measures for the evaluation of medical technology. Int J Technol Assess Health Care 1996;12:9–21.

   This is a comprehensive article in which the authors appropriately discuss the special issues surrounding how cost data are obtained and analyzed, with consideration for the different perspectives that might be used in an economic analysis.

3. Johnson N, Weir G. Using databases to conduct outcomes research. Pharm Ther 1994;19:840–7.

   Various types of databases used to assess and compare economic outcomes data are discussed in this publication. A case example is provided and the steps for conducting database research are outlined.

4. Jones JK. Inpatient data bases. In: Strom BL, ed. Pharmacoepidemiology. New York: Churchill Livingstone, Inc., 1989.

   The data elements and process for data integration when using hospital databases for research purposes are well described in this chapter. In addition, this chapter discusses the advantages and disadvantages of using hospital records for research purposes.

5. Kozma CM, Kirchdoerfer LJ. Obtaining pharmacoeconomic data in health care organizations. Top Hosp Pharm Manage 1994;13:23–30.

The authors provide examples of the variables necessary to conduct pharmacoeconomic analyses and describe the types of data needed for these studies. They provide descriptive examples using hospitals, physicians' offices, and pharmacies as possible data sources for pharmacoeconomic research.

6. Lewis NH, Patwell JT, Briesacher BA. The role of insurance claims databases in drug therapy outcomes research. Pharmacoeconomics 1993;4:323–30.

   The authors synthesize information about how claims databases can be used for pharmacoeconomics research and discuss the advantages and disadvantages of various database sources.

7. Reeder CE, Kozma CM, McCollam AR. Overview of pharmaceutical outcomes, pharmacoeconomics, and quality of life. In: Ito SM, Blackburn S, eds. A pharmacist's guide to principles and practices of managed care pharmacy. Alexandria, VA: Foundation for Managed Care Pharmacy, 1995.

   The database requirements and linkages necessary in managed care to conduct pharmacoeconomic and outcomes research are discussed in this chapter. The authors list some of the problems with using managed care claims databases, such as inadequate database linkages and inappropriate database design, that make it difficult to conduct research using these sources. They also suggest that these problems will diminish as newer databases are developed and refined.

8. Swartz M, Young DW, Siegrist R. The ratio of costs to charges: how good a basis for estimating costs? Inquiry 1995;32:476–81.

   This study evaluated the accuracy of costs derived from the ratio of costs to charges. The investigators found that hospital charges were not a good basis for determining relative hospital costs. They urge health care researchers to use caution when accurate estimates of costs are important. However, the cost-to-charge ratio may be acceptable for some cross-hospital comparisons.

9. U.S. Congress, Office of Technology Assessment. Congress of the United States. Identifying health technologies that work: searching for evidence. Publication No. OTA-H-608, Washington, DC: U.S. Government Printing Office, September 1994.

   This extensive report was prepared in response to a request by the Senate Committee on Labor and Human Resources. It was undertaken to examine what the federal government gets out of its investment in health technology research and to understand how its investment could be improved. Included in this book are reports of the possibilities and limitations of current methods and sources for evaluating health technologies. Potential deficiencies in the current methods of collecting data are addressed.

Self-Assessment Questions

1. Which one of the following is an important factor to consider before selecting a data source for an economic outcomes analysis?
   A. The price of the drug.
   B. Perspective used for the study.
   C. Patient compliance.
   D. Input from private consultants.

2. From which one of the following sources should outcomes data, such as measures of quality of life, be obtained?
   A. The patient.
   B. Databases.
   C. Chart review.
   D. Claims.

3. Data from published economic outcomes analyses are a useful source of data if which one of the following is true?
   A. Data analysis techniques were used.
   B. Data were collected internally.
   C. Permission for accessing the data was obtained.
   D. The study was appropriately conducted and the results are applicable to the clinical setting.

4. Cost and outcomes data obtained from within the organization should be used cautiously if which one of the following occurred?
   A. Charge data are greater than cost data.
   B. A prospective study was conducted.
   C. Few patients received the treatment of interest.
   D. Resources are limited.

5. Which one of the following is the best way to become familiar with the type of data available from a particular source?
   A. Publish a pharmacoeconomic analysis.
   B. Obtain a data extract and conduct a preliminary analysis.
   C. Find the limitations of the data source.
   D. Calculate cost to charge ratios.

6. Which one of the following types of data are commonly available from hospital financial information systems?
   A. Quality of life.
   B. Patient satisfaction.
   C. Mortality rates.
   D. Cost and resource use data.

7. Which one of the following best describes the differences between hospital costs and hospital charges?
   A. Hospital costs are a more accurate measure of hospital resources used.
   B. Patient charges are the most accurate measure of hospital resources used.
   C. Patient charges are the amount of money that insurance companies usually pay the hospital.
   D. Hospital costs cannot be used in an economic analysis because it is not possible to obtain these data.

8. Which one of the following is an important consideration before using managed care claims data for an economic analysis?
   A. Capitated contracts are not commonly used in managed care organizations.
   B. Formulary decisions are made based only on prescription drug costs.
   C. Medical claims and pharmacy claims data are not usually integrated into one database.
   D. Database query tools are not particularly helpful.

9. Which one of the following is an advantage of using databases for economics research?
   A. The data are always retrospective.
   B. Patients were randomly assigned to treatment options.
   C. It is possible to identify specific cause and effect relationships to assess drug use.
   D. The data represent drug use in usual clinical practice.

10. Researchers using databases as a source of economic data must do which one of the following?
    A. Conduct prospective studies.
    B. Develop primary data collection tools.
    C. Use research designs that control for confounding variables.
    D. Obtain informed consent from each person whose data are extracted.

COST-OF-ILLNESS ANALYSIS

By Emily Cox, PhD

Outline

I. Cost of Illness
- A. Cost-of-illness analysis measures the economic burden of disease and illness on society
  - 1. includes direct medical and non-medical costs consumed in treating and caring for those afflicted with disease;
  - 2. indirect costs associated with productivity losses due to disease morbidity and mortality;
  - 3. and psychosocial or intangible costs associated with changes in the quality of one's life due to the disease.
- B. COI analysis can determine within each disease category, the distribution of resources across cost categories (direct, indirect and intangible) to assess how and where health care resources are being allocated
- C. used to identify and set priorities for policy making
  - 1. can assist policy makers in establishing priorities for research funding or target disease categories for prevention campaigns
- D. can help direct the allocation of research funds toward diseases exacting a large economic burden on society
  - 1. highlighting the economic burden of disease lends credence to an organizations' plea for donations in the "fight for a cure"
- E. used by advocacy groups to lobby Congress for greater research funding
- F. used by pharmaceutical companies to estimate the potential economic impact of their product used in pricing policies
- G. COI studies do not provide any indication of whether resources are being used effectively or efficiently, but can provide a baseline for pharmacoeconomic methodologies designed to assess effectiveness or efficiency.
  - 1. example: cost-benefit analysis of immunization programs often involve an estimation of the cost of the disease (Haemophilus influenzae or varicella). The benefit of the vaccination program is then calculated as the decrease in the cost of disease associated with preventing the disease.

II. Methodology
- A. Scope of the analysis
  - 1. can be comprehensive: estimating the full economic burden of illness and disease on society for a broad spectrum of diseases
  - 2. or narrow: estimating one component of the economic burden of one particular disease within a limited geographic area
    - i. example: estimation of the direct costs of hypertension within a managed care organization
- B. Prevalence versus incidence based approach to measuring cost-of-illness
  - 1. prevalence: the proportion of individuals in a population who have a disease in a specified period of time, usually one year
  - 2. incidence: the number of new events or cases of disease that develop in a population of individuals at risk over a specified time interval,
    - i. incidence based analysis measure the costs over the lifetime of the individual with the condition or disease; from diagnosis to cure or death
    - ii. more difficult and used less frequently due to the information requirements
      - (a) information requirements: disease progression, survival probabilities, current and future projections of incidence rates, current and future treatment patterns
      - (b) most appropriate for diseases where the costs and complications of the disease occur long term (e.g., diabetes and hypertension)
      - (c) provides a more accurate baseline for estimating the benefit of a new treatment or preventive programs whose benefits may accrue over many years

3. prevalence-based approach

i. estimates the cost of disease within a specific period of time for all individuals diagnosed with the disease regardless of the time since diagnosis

ii. most appropriate for diseases or illnesses whose effect can be measured during the time period of the analysis, usually a year

C. Defining the disease

1. use existing disease definitions within the literature

2. one resource is the ICD-9-CM disease coding system

i. classifies disease into major disease categories

ii. used in the US in cause-of-death coding and required for reporting diagnoses and diseases to all US Public Health Service and the Centers for Medicare and Medicaid Services (CMS), formerly the Health Care Financing Administration programs.

3. Understanding the characteristics of the disease

i. episodic, chronic or acute; what is the probability of survival: these factors are important in determining the time-line for analysis

4. demographic profile of patients (e.g., prevalence by age, gender, ethnicity)

i. important in the calculation of indirect costs due to productivity losses

III. Costs

A. Direct costs

1. medical care expenditures for diagnosis, treatment, continuing care, rehabilitation, and terminal care, and non-medical expenditures.

i. example: hospitalization, outpatient clinical care, nursing home care, home health care, services of primary physicians, specialists, dentist, and other health professionals, drugs and drug sundries, and rehabilitation counseling and other rehabilitation costs, such as those for prostheses, appliances, eyeglasses, hearing aids, speech devices, etc., necessary to prevent or overcome illness-related impairments

2. other relevant disease related direct costs

i. expenditure for research, training, construction, and administrative functions necessary for prevention and treatment of the disease

3. other non-medical direct costs

i. For example: cost of travel time, time lost from work by family members and caregivers, loss of opportunities for promotion and education due to illness resulting in reduced productivity

ii. costs are often difficult to estimate and rarely included in cost-of-illness analysis

4. data sources

i. resource use: collected prospectively through survey methods or monitoring patients' use of medical resources over time; or retrospectively via large database analysis

B. Indirect costs:

1. measures the loss in productivity due to morbidity and mortality associated with disease

2. productivity: the decrease in economic output (GNP) resulting from the loss of an individual from the work force either as a result of death or morbidity

i. proxy used is an individual's earnings or market wage

ii. costs are captured as days of lost work in the case of temporary disability or net present value of an individual's potential earnings stream in the case of permanent disability or death

3. method: human capital approach

i. most often used to estimate productivity losses associated with disease morbidity and mortality

ii. measures a person's productive contribution to society through his/her earnings stream

iii. disadvantage

(a) fails to take into consideration imperfections within the labor market. (e.g., job discrimination)

iv. underestimates the value of women, the young, the elderly and minorities

v. does not capture the value of non-market activities from housekeeping or volunteer work

4. method: willingness-to-pay (WTP)

i. used less frequently

ii. method: asks individuals hypothetical questions regarding their "willingness-to-pay" to reduce their probability of death or morbidity

iii. advantage:

(a) claims to measure the entire range of indirect and intangible benefits: productivity and the cost of pain and suffering

iv. disadvantage:

(a) difficult to apply

(b) assumes that individuals can comprehend and respond to questions involving small changes in the risk of significant events

(c) affected by earnings: lower income earners tend to be willing to pay less than higher income earners

C. Intangible or Psychosocial Costs

1. measures the effect disease has on one's quality of life.

i. example: the emotional stress from losing one's job, or the fear and anxiety experienced as a result of being diagnosed with a terminal illness

ii. quality of life instruments can measure these intangible aspects of disease

iii. assigning a cost to the intangible aspects of disease is difficult and are rarely included in cost-of-illness analysis

iv. when quality of life is an important factor, researchers should consider including this information as a separate component of the analysis

D. Summing It All Up

1. per-patient costs are then multiplied by the prevalence of the condition or annual incidence rates

2. data sources on prevalence and incidence

i. published studies and reports

ii. national surveys

(a) published by the National Center for Health Statistics

IV Examples from the literature

A. Cost of Back Pain: Tulder et al (1995)

1. utilized a prevalence based approach to estimate the direct and indirect costs associated with back pain in the Netherlands

2. data on resource utilization and costs obtained through a variety of national published findings

3. resource use identified through ICD-9 coding system thought to represent back pain

4. mortality costs were not included due to the low risk of death

5. costs of absenteeism: calculated as the total number of sick days multiplied by the mean cost of one sick day

6. costs of disablement: estimated by multiplying the total days of disability with the mean daily pension in 1991

7. no estimation of the cost of back pain for non-wage earners was included (children, housewives and the unemployed) nor were intangible costs associated with pain and grief

8. results: total direct medical costs of back pain $US367.6 million; total indirect costs $US4.6 billion; $US3.1 billion due to absenteeism and $US1.5 billion represented by disablement:

i. total indirect costs represented 93% of the total cost; this highlights the substantial economic burden back pain has on the labor economy

9. critiques:

i. sensitivity analysis was not conducted on estimates where assumptions were made

ii. caution should be exercised in relying solely upon ICD-9 coding systems to determine resource use due to miscoding and other inconsistencies inherent with databases

B. Alzheimer's disease: Rice, et al. (1993)

1. prevalence based approach to estimate the total formal and informal care costs of Alzheimer's disease

2. based upon a sample of community and institutionalized patients in California

3. costs associated with productivity losses were not estimated

4. formal care services: defined as those services "rendered for a price in the traditional medical and social service marketplace" included costs for hospital, nursing home care, physician services, social services, medications, and other items or services associated with the care of the Alzheimer's patient

i. charges were used as a proxy for costs

5. informal care services: services that fall outside of the labor market and for which providers are not reimbursed are those provided by caregivers to assist the patient with activities of daily living (ADL), and instrumental activities of daily living (IADL)

6. results: annual average per person cost for caring for an Alzheimer's patient was about $47,000 ($47,083 for community and $47,591 for institutionalized patients)

7. seventy-three percent of the total costs for community patients were represented by informal costs; 88% of the total costs of caring for institutionalized patients were represented by formal care costs

8. a good example of how, within a disease category, differences in the pattern of cost-of-illness exist by setting and/or severity of disease

C. Alzheimer's disease: Ernst and Hay (1994)

1. present per-case, prevalence and lifetime estimates of the costs of Alzheimer's disease in 1991

2. costs categories identified were nursing home care, mental hospital, community care, physicians' services (diagnosis and regular care) hospitalization and caregiver costs

3. the authors do estimate the lost labor income of Alzheimer's patients discounted at 4%: estimated at $50,380 per person
4. use secondary data sources to estimate costs
5. lifetime costs based upon the assumption that patients diagnosed with Alzheimer's would survive on average 4.3 years for women and 3.3 years for men
6. results: per patient direct costs of $47, 581 and total costs of $173,932 per year; prevalence figures multiplied by direct and total costs per patient costs to obtain estimates of total costs

V. CONCLUSION
A. Case Study: Calculation of the cost-of-migraine within a managed care organization
1. See the Case Study in *Pharmacoeconomics and Outcomes: Applications for Patient Care, Case Studies* to complete this activity

Learning Objectives

1. Discuss the purpose of cost-of-illness analysis.
2. Differentiate between cost-of-illness analysis and pharmacoeconomic analyses.
3. Contrast prevalence-based and incidence-based methods of conducting cost-of-illness analysis.
4. Discuss the methods used to estimate indirect costs in cost-of-illness analysis and advantages and disadvantages of each.
5. Discuss how to define a disease or condition.

Abbreviations in this chapter

AIDS	Acquired immune deficiency syndrome
ADL	Activities of daily living
CMS	Centers for Medicare and Medicaid Services
GNP	Gross national product
HIV	Human immunodeficiency virus
IADL	Instrumental activities of daily living
ICD-9	International Classification of Disease, 9th Revision
ICD-9-CM	International Classification of Disease, 9th Revision, Clinical Modification

Cost of Illness

The United States continues to spend more per capita on health care than any other industrialized nation. In 2000 alone, the nation spent $1.3 trillion on health care or $4637 per person, representing 13.2 percent of the nation's economy (gross national product [GNP]). This amount represents a 7 percent growth in expenditures from 1999, a rate expected to continue to grow through 2011. If this forecast is correct, the nation's spending for health care is expected to reach $2.8 trillion. These trends in health care expenditures represent an enormous economic burden to society. A logical question that follows reports of these spending trends is: "What are we paying for?" One way to answer this question is to break costs down by expenditure category. Government estimates suggest that of the $1.3 trillion spent in 2000, $422 billion went for professional services, including physician and clinical services, dental and other personal health care; and $122 billion was spent on prescription drugs. Another way to better understand where our health care dollars are being spent is through cost-of-illness analysis.

Cost-of-illness analysis measures the economic burden of disease and illness on society. The measurement of this economic burden incorporates direct medical and nonmedical costs consumed in treating and caring for those afflicted with disease, indirect costs associated with productivity losses due to disease morbidity and mortality and psychosocial or intangible costs associated with changes in the quality of a patient's life due to the disease. Cost-of-illness analysis differs from pharmacoeconomic analysis in a couple of ways. First, in cost-of-illness analysis the unit of analysis is a condition or disease rather than an intervention; second, the methods differ in their purpose of analysis. In cost-of-illness analysis, the goal is to determine the economic burden of a disease on society, whereas the goal in pharmacoeconomics analyses is to elicit which intervention provides the most efficient allocation of resources. Therefore, the results of cost-of-illness analysis allow decision-makers to assess how and where health care and other resources are being allocated within a disease category or across a spectrum of diseases.

An important contribution to the understanding of cost-of-illness analysis came in 1967 when Dorothy Rice calculated the cost of illness for eight major diagnostic categories: neoplasms; mental, psychoneurotic, and personality disorders; diseases of the nervous system and sense organs; diseases of the circulatory system; diseases of the respiratory system; diseases of the digestive system; diseases of the bones and organs of movement; injuries, and an 'all other' category. For each diagnostic category, direct medical expenditures, including hospital care, nursing home care, physicians' services, dentists' services, nursing care, and other professional services, were estimated. Productivity losses associated with each disease category also were estimated.

An update of these early estimates was again conducted using health expenditure data from 1980. In this update, direct and indirect costs were estimated for the 16 major diagnostic categories of the International Classification of Diseases, Ninth Revision, Clinical Modification (ICD-9-CM). Estimates also were provided for men and women and for two age groups (65 years of age and older, and younger than 65 years of age). The total economic cost of illness in 1980 was estimated at $455 billion, 46 percent of which was represented by direct costs, 15 percent represented by morbidity and 39 percent of costs associated with mortality. In 1980, costs related to diseases of the circulatory system had the greatest economic burden at $85 billion, followed by the cost of injuries and poisonings at $83 billion. Figure 1 presents the distribution of these costs across nine of the 16 diagnostic categories and illustrates the variability in the distribution of costs. For example, a majority of costs associated with injuries and poisonings and neoplasms are related to reductions in productivity due to premature death or mortality (68 percent and 63 percent, respectively). This distribution is contrasted to the cost of diseases of the genitourinary system where direct medical costs comprise 80 percent of all costs. Reasons for the differences in cost-distribution are varied and can be attributed to differences in the demographic makeup of the population, treatment availability, and probability of death or permanent disability across diagnoses.

These types of studies provides valuable information on patterns of health care expenditures by disease or illness category and highlights the productivity losses due to disease within the United States. However, the purpose in conducting cost-of-illness analysis is not only to become more informed as a nation on how health dollars are being spent, but also to identify and set priorities for policy-making. Cost-of illness studies can assist policy-makers in establishing priorities for research funding or to target disease categories for health prevention campaigns. For example, identifying the substantial mortality costs associated with injuries and poisonings can direct funding efforts toward prevention campaigns, such as poison prevention week, programs to educate parents and children on how to avoid common household injuries, or highway safety programs to reduce motor vehicle accidents.

Cost-of-illness analysis can identify diseases exacting a large economic burden on society, both in terms of the number of people afflicted and costs of treatment and care. Highlighting the economic burden of disease lends credence to an organization's plea for donations in the "fight for a cure". This information also is used by advocacy groups to lobby Congress for greater research funding. More recently, cost-of-illness studies have been used by pharmaceutical companies to serve as a baseline in estimating the economic impact of their product.

Cost-of-illness studies do not, in and of themselves, provide any indication of whether resources are being used effectively or efficiently. However, they can provide a baseline for pharmacoeconomic methodologies designed to assess effectiveness or efficiency. Cost-of-illness analyses are used in cost-benefit and cost-effectiveness analyses to obtain baseline measures in the assessment of the economic impact of preventive or treatment programs. For example, cost-benefit analysis of immunization programs often involve estimating the cost of the disease (*Haemophilus influenzae* or varicella) that the vaccine would hope to eradicate. The benefit of the vaccination program is then

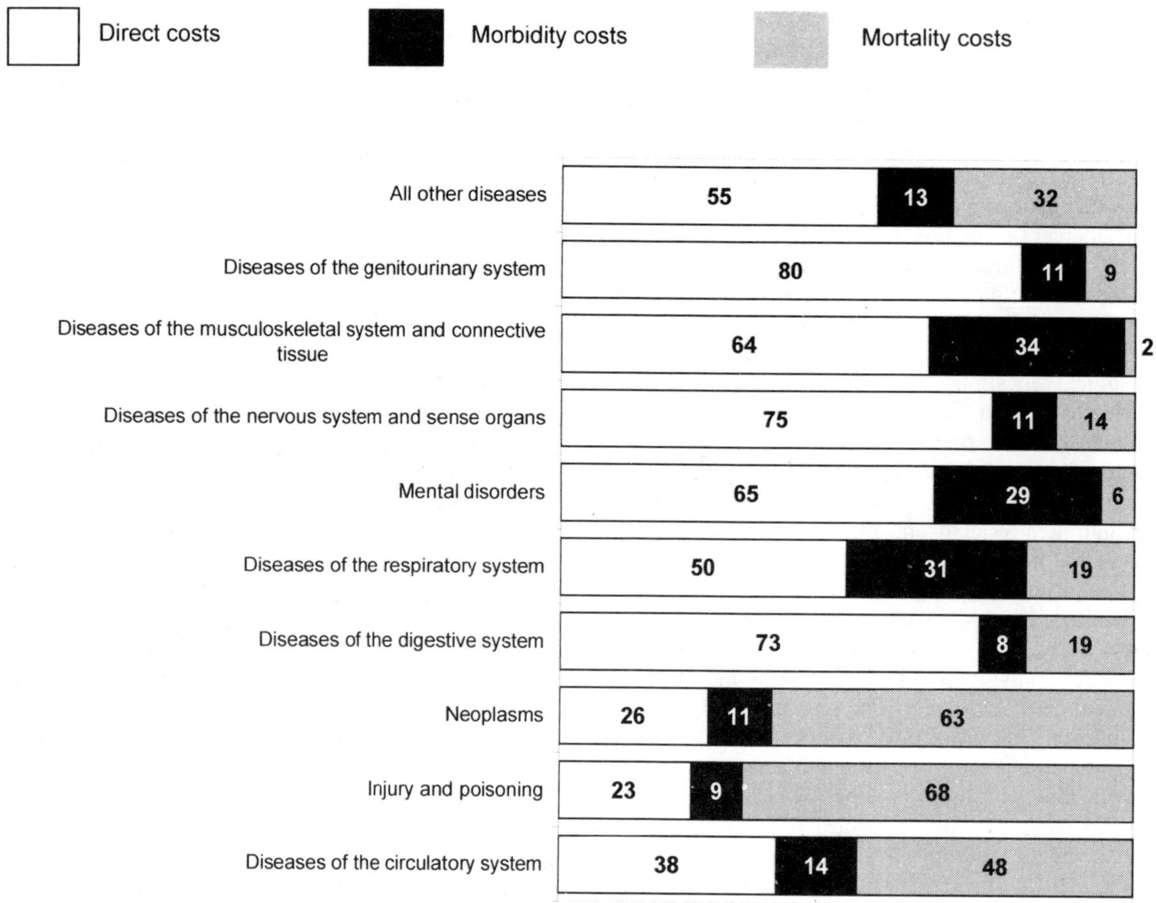

Figure 1: Percent distribution of economic costs of illness, by diagnosis and type of cost: 1980

calculated as the decrease in the cost of disease associated with preventing the occurrence of disease.

Methodology

Cost-of-illness studies measure the direct, indirect (morbidity and mortality), and intangible costs associated with disease or illness. The scope of cost-of-illness analysis can be comprehensive, estimating the full economic burden of illness and disease on society for a broad spectrum of diseases. The scope also can be narrow, estimating one component of the economic burden (e.g., direct medical costs for one particular disease within a limited geographic area). An example in this instance is a cost-of-illness analysis of hypertension within a managed care organization. The estimate of costs is based on the number and demographic profile of patients with hypertension within the health plan's membership. If the analysis were to be conducted from the health plan's perspective, the calculation of costs may focus on direct medical expenditures alone rather than the costs of lost productivity because the health plan is not likely to be directly affected by the lost productivity of its subscribers.

Prevalence Versus Incidence

There are two general approaches used to measure cost-of-illness: the prevalence-based approach and the incidence-based approach. Prevalence and incidence are epidemiological terms representing measures of disease frequency. Prevalence measures the proportion of individuals in a population who have a disease in a specified time period, usually 1 year. Incidence is a measure of the number of *new events* or cases of disease that develop in a population of individuals at risk over a specified time interval, again, typically 1 year.

Incidence-based cost-of-illness analysis calculates lifetime disease costs, from diagnosis to cure or death. This approach tends to be more difficult to estimate due to the information requirements needed to calculate lifetime costs. Incidence-based costing requires knowledge of disease progression, survival probabilities, current and future projections of incidence rates, and current and future treatment patterns. This information is often difficult to obtain for many diseases and assumptions have to be made. Although difficult to estimate, incidence-based costing may be more useful to policy-makers particularly for chronic conditions where the costs and complications of the disease occur long term (e.g., acquired immune deficiency syndrome [AIDS], diabetes, and hypertension). Incidence-based costing also provides a more accurate baseline for estimating the benefit of a new treatment or preventive program whose benefits may accrue over many years. The benefit of preventing disease or delaying progression is the lifetime disease costs averted. Measuring this benefit using a prevalence-based approach provides only a partial assessment of the total benefit from treatment.

Currently, most cost-of-illness analyses are conducted using a prevalence-based approach. Prevalence-based cost-of-illness studies estimate the cost of disease within a specified time period for all individuals diagnosed with the disease regardless of the time since diagnosis. Prevalence-based cost-of-illness studies for chronic diseases would, thus, include costs for newly diagnosed patients as well as patients in later stages of their disease.

Defining the Disease

One of the first steps in conducting cost-of-illness analysis is a clear definition and understanding of the disease in question. As a guide, researchers should rely on existing disease definitions or classification systems, such as those developed for neoplasms by the National Cancer Institute. Researchers also should be familiar with the ICD-9-CM disease coding system. The ICD-9-CM is based on the official version of the World Health Organization's International Classification of Disease, 9th Revision (ICD-9). The ICD-9 scheme classifies diseases into major disease categories, such as diseases of the nervous system and sense organs, and diseases of the circulatory or respiratory system. In addition, each major disease category contains hundreds of subcategories. The ICD-9-CM classification scheme is used in the United States in cause-of-death coding and is required for reporting diagnoses and diseases to all United States Public Health Service and Center for Medicaid and Medicare Service (CMS) programs. The ICD-9 codes are found within medical claims data and are used to identify patients with a particular condition.

In addition to defining the disease, it is imperative to understand the epidemiological characteristics of the disease: is it episodic? chronic or acute? what is the probability of survival for individuals diagnosed with the disease? does the condition worsen over time or remain stable? These factors are important in determining the time line over which to examine costs. For example, in calculating the costs associated with migraine, an important task is estimating the number of migraine episodes experienced by patients in a given time period. Because migraines are an episodic event, choosing too short a time frame of analysis could underestimate the number of migraine episodes, thus underestimate the costs of treatment. The demographic profile of those afflicted with the disease also is an important factor to consider. Does the disease afflict primarily the aged or the young? what is the incidence or prevalence in males versus females? The patient demographic profile is important in the calculation of indirect costs due to productivity losses.

Costs

Direct Costs

Direct costs include the medical care expenditures for diagnosis, treatment, continuing care, rehabilitation, and terminal care, as well as nonmedical expenditures. In general, direct costs have been defined as those costs used to prevent or overcome illness-related impairments. These costs include hospitalization; outpatient clinical care; nursing home care; home health care; physician, specialists, dentists, and other health professionals services; drugs and drug sundries; and rehabilitation counseling and other rehabilitation costs, such as those for prostheses, appliances, eyeglasses, hearing aids, and speech devices. In addition to treatment- or diagnosis-specific direct costs, other direct costs are relevant from a societal perspective in the calculation of total disease costs. These costs include expenditures for research, training, construction, and administrative functions necessary for preventing and treating the disease.

Measurement of direct medical costs requires a knowledge of the treatment pattern of the disease. This information can be gathered directly by survey methods or by monitoring patients' use of medical resources over a specified time period. For example, in a study calculating the lifetime costs of treating people with the human immunodeficiency virus (HIV), information on the services received by patients with HIV was obtained directly from patient surveys. The survey collected information from March 1991 through August 1992 from 26 sites in 10 cities. The study also estimated costs for four stages of HIV in recognition of the different level of intensity of resource consumption within each stage of the disease.

Information on patterns of resource consumption also can be gathered retrospectively through large database analysis or from published studies and reports. In a study estimating the economic and social costs of Alzheimer's disease, the authors cite a variety of published sources used to estimate the number of physician visits per year by patients with Alzheimer's disease. For many diseases, there exist recommended treatment protocols developed by professional organizations which can be used as a basis to estimate resource consumption. The National Heart, Lung, and Blood Institute publishes recommendations on the detection, evaluation, and treatment of high blood cholesterol. The institute also publishes data on the prevalence of hypertension in the United States.

Managed care organizations can use their own databases to determine not only the prevalence of a particular disease within their own population but also resource use (e.g., hospitalization stays, physician visits, urgent care visits, and laboratory testing). This process involves identifying patients through ICD-9 codes and evaluating their resource use over time. The limitation in this approach is that patients often suffer from multiple conditions, and determining which costs are associated with the disease or condition of interest can be difficult.

Other nonmedical direct costs also should be considered in cost-of-illness calculation. These costs include the cost of travel time, time lost from work by family members and caregivers, loss of opportunities for promotion and education due to illness resulting in reduced productivity. To obtain an accurate measure of these costs, patient level data should be collected, including patient logs or direct surveys. Collecting these data can be costly and time consuming, and, as a result, these data are seldom included in cost-of-illness analysis. However, for certain diseases, these costs may be an important factor in capturing the burden of disease and illness. In these instances, some discussion of these costs is warranted if no attempt to measure them is made.

Indirect Costs

The indirect costs of illness are measured by the loss in productivity due to morbidity and mortality associated with disease. Productivity is measured as the decrease in economic output (e.g., GNP) resulting from the loss of an individual from the work force either as a result of death or morbidity. The proxy used to measure this decrease in economic output is a person's earnings. These costs are captured as days of lost work in the case of temporary disability or net present value of an individual's potential earnings stream in the case of permanent disability or death.

Labor is a valuable economic resource to an individual and to society which necessitates its inclusion in the calculation of cost-of-illness analysis. Disease and illness can have an enormous impact on the productive capacity of individuals within society. Disease morbidity can cause a person to lose time from work temporarily or permanently due to severe disability.

Two methods have been used to estimate the indirect costs associated with productivity losses: willingness-to-pay and the human capital approach. The method used most often to estimate indirect costs is the human capital approach. The *human capital approach* is based on the assumption that a person's productive contribution to society is measured through his or her earnings stream discounted to a present value. Relying as it does on earnings or market wages, the human capital approach is frequently criticized for failing to take into consideration imperfections within the labor market, such as job discrimination. As a result, the human capital approach underestimates indirect costs of disease for women, the young, elderly, and minorities. In addition, the human capital approach does not capture the value of nonmarket wages from activities, such as housekeeping or volunteer work. Despite its shortcomings, this approach still remains the most commonly used method for estimating the economic impact from lost productivity.

The *willingness-to-pay* approach has been used less frequently in cost-of-illness analysis to estimate indirect costs. Willingness to pay uses survey methods and involves asking individuals hypothetical questions regarding their willingness to pay to reduce their probability of death or morbidity. The advantage of willingness to pay is that it purports to measure the entire range of indirect and intangible benefits, including productivity, pain and suffering. However, it is difficult to apply this method in many instances. The willingness-to-pay approach also assumes that individuals are well informed and capable of comprehending small changes in the risk of significant events such as death. This approach also can be affected by a patient's earnings or wealth. Lower wage earners may not be willing to pay as much as higher wage earners, not because they value the alternative any less, but because their response is made within the context of their lower income.

Intangible or Psychosocial Costs

Intangible or psychosocial costs measure the effect disease has on a patient's quality of life. These effects might include the emotional stress from losing his or her job due to an illness, or the fear and anxiety experienced as a result of being diagnosed with a terminal illness. Numerous quality of life instruments have been developed to measure these intangible aspects of disease, many of these disease specific. However, assigning a cost to the intangible aspects of disease is difficult and, thus, rarely included in cost-of-illness analysis. The difficulty in valuing these intangible aspects of disease should not diminish their importance as a factor in the economic burden of disease. If quality of life is an important factor for a disease, researchers should consider, including quality of life information as a separate component of the analysis, if nothing else than to highlight the intangible burden of disease.

Summing It All Up

Once per patient costs have been obtained, these values are then applied or multiplied by the prevalence- or incidence-based estimates in the population of interest. Most cost-of-illness analyses are calculated from a societal perspective and, therefore, require population estimates of the prevalence or incidence of the disease. Estimates of the incidence and prevalence of disease are available from a variety of published studies and reports, many of which are based on regional or national surveys. Incidence and prevalence figures can be found in many publications available from the National Center for Health Statistics, an agency within the Centers for Disease Control and Prevention. The NCHS collects health data through personal interviews and through data collection systems taken from medical records.

Examples from the Literature

Several studies which illustrate the application and methodology of cost-of-illness analysis are discussed here.

Cost of Back Pain

One application of cost-of-illness analysis which appears in the literature involves use of a prevalence-based approach to estimate the total direct and indirect costs associated with back pain in the Netherlands for the year 1991. Data on use of health care resources and costs were obtained from a variety of national data sources, including Informatics in Health and Welfare, National Information of Social Insurance, and the Central Health Care Discharge Agency. Resource use for back pain was identified using the ICD-9 coding system for the diagnoses codes 720–724. The ICD-9 code 720 is classified as ankylosing spondylitis and other inflammatory spondylopathies; ICD-9 code 721 = spondylosis and allied disorders; ICD-9 code 722 = intervertebral disc disorders; ICD-9 code 723 = other disorders of cervical region; and ICD-9 code 724 = other and unspecified disorders of the back. These codes fall under the larger category of 'musculoskeletal' diseases, which include ICD-9 codes 710–739. Direct and indirect costs for this larger category of diseases also are estimated.

Direct medical costs included hospitalization, medical specialist care, general practice care, and paramedical care or physical therapy. Because back pain is not associated with a high risk of death, mortality costs were not included. Costs of absenteeism were calculated as the total number of sick days multiplied by the mean cost of one sick day. Costs of disablement were estimated by multiplying the total days of disability with the mean daily pension in 1991. Neither an estimation of the cost of back pain for nonwage earners (e.g., children, housewives, and the unemployed) nor intangible costs associated with pain and grief was included. The total *direct* medical costs of back pain were estimated to be $367.6 million (in United States dollars). Total *indirect* costs were calculated to be $4.6 billion, $3.1 billion due to absenteeism, and $1.5 billion represented by disablement. In total, indirect costs represented 93 percent of the total cost of back pain in the Netherlands which highlights the substantial economic burden back pain has on the labor economy.

Several assumptions were made in the estimation of resource use and costs; however, a sensitivity analysis was not conducted to determine whether final cost-estimates varied with respect to variation in these assumptions. For example, in estimating the costs of general practice care for back pain, estimates were only available for the larger category of musculoskeletal diseases for the year 1987. Data were available on hospitalization costs for back pain and hospitalization and general practice care for musculoskeletal diseases. Thus, it was assumed that the ratio of costs of hospitalization to general practice care for back pain was "about the same" as for musculoskeletal diseases in 1987. A second critique is not directed at the study per se, but is offered as a precautionary note to the reader. The estimate of the direct medical costs of hospitalization relies solely on the actual number of cases and number of hospital days reported through the ICD-9 coding system. This method may be appropriate for a country such as the Netherlands, but is not appropriate for the United States. In the Netherlands, insurance coverage for serious and prolonged disability and sickness is compulsory for the whole population. Thus, the data sources used in the study capture resource use for a large proportion of the population in the Netherlands, close to 100 percent for some diseases. In addition, as reported by the authors, the Netherlands is a country for which strict government guidelines exist in payment systems and reporting of health events. This uniformity in reporting systems does not exist in the United States.

Alzheimer's Disease

Several studies have been conducted measuring the economic burden of Alzheimer's disease to society. In one study, the authors use a prevalence-based approach to estimate the total formal and informal care costs of Alzheimer's disease based on a sample of community and institutionalized patients in California. Estimates of indirect costs associated with productivity losses were not estimated. Formal care services were defined as those services "rendered for a price in the traditional medical and social service marketplace". These services included costs for hospital, nursing home care, physician services, social services, drugs, and other items or services associated with the care of the patient with Alzheimer's disease. Charges for these services were used as a proxy for costs. Informal care services refer to services that fall outside of the labor market and for which providers are not reimbursed. These services are those provided by caregivers to assist the patient with activities of daily living (ADL), and instrumental activities of daily living (IADL). The annual average per-person cost for caring for a patient with Alzheimer's disease was about $47,000 ($47,083 for community and $47,591 for institutionalized patients). Although the total costs were similar between the two settings, a breakdown of costs by type of care (formal and informal) showed significant differences. Seventy-three percent of the total costs for community patients were represented by informal costs, whereas 88 percent of the total costs of caring for institutionalized patients were represented by formal care costs. This study is a good example of how, within a disease category, differences in the pattern of cost-of-illness exist by setting and/or severity of disease.

In another study, estimating the costs of Alzheimer's disease, the authors present per-case, prevalence prevalence-based estimates of the costs of Alzheimer's disease in 1991. Alzheimer's disease costs identified were those associated with nursing home care, mental hospital, community care, physicians' services (e.g., diagnosis and regular care) hospitalization, and caregiver costs. Unlike the study previous studies investigators of this study estimated the lost labor income of patients with Alzheimer's disease discounted at 4 percent. These costs were estimated at $50,380 per person. Study investigators used secondary data sources to estimate the direct and indirect costs. To calculate lifetime costs associated with the disease, study investigators assumed that patients diagnosed with Alzheimer's disease would survive on average 4.3 years for women and 3.3 years for men. On a per-case basis, direct costs of Alzheimer's disease were $47, 581 and total costs were $173,932 per patient. These values were then multiplied by the prevalence of Alzheimer's disease to obtain prevalence-based direct and total costs for 1991, which were $20.6 billion and $67.3 billion, respectively. The lifetime costs of care or incidence-based cost of-illness for patients with Alzheimer's disease diagnosed in 1991 were estimated to be $536 billion in direct costs and $1.75 trillion in total costs.

Conclusion

Cost-of-illness analysis is a valuable tool for policy-makers and other health care providers in setting priorities for research funding. Cost-of-illness analysis will continue to provide valuable baseline measures for pharmacoeconomic analysis, including cost-benefit and cost-effectiveness studies. When appropriate and feasible, incidence-based estimations of cost-of-illness should be considered.

For further application, see *Pharmacoeconomics and Outcomes: Applications for Patient Care,Case Studies,* Case Study: Calculation of the Cost of Migraine Within a Managed Care Organization to Work Through Estimation of the Cost of Migraine Within a Managed Care Organization.

Annotated Bibliography

1. Drummond M. Cost-of-illness studies: a major headache? Pharmacoeconomics 1992;2:1–4.

   This paper was published as a guide for evaluating and interpreting published costs-of-illness studies. Two approaches to costs-of-illness studies are discussed:

prevalence and incidence. Incidence-based approaches are more useful because they provide a baseline against which interventions may be assessed. The prevalence-based approach typically is not useful unless the full effects of an intervention are experienced within a single year. However, of the two approaches, the prevalence-based approach is the most commonly used. Inferences that may be soundly made by costs-of-illness studies are discussed. A critical review of several costs-of-illness studies also is provided. Finally, suggestions are made to improve the methods used in cost-of-illness research endeavors.

2. Ernst RL, Hay JW. The US economic and social costs of Alzheimer's disease revisited. Am J Public Health 1994;84(8):1261–4.

   This study estimates the per-case and prevalence-based costs of Alzheimer's disease in the United States. Alzheimer's disease costs included were nursing home care, mental hospital care, community care, physicians' services (diagnosis and regular care), hospitalization and caregiver costs. The authors estimated the lost labor income of Alzheimer's patients discounted at 4%. These costs were estimated at $50, 380 per person. The authors used secondary data sources to estimate the direct and indirect costs. To calculate lifetime costs associated with the disease, the authors assumed that patients diagnosed with Alzheimer's would survive on average 4.3 years for women and 3.3 years for men. On a per case basis, direct costs of Alzheimer's disease were $47, 581 and total costs were $173, 932 per patient. These values were then multiplied by the prevalence of Alzheimer's to obtain prevalence based direct and total costs for 1991, which were $20.6 billion and $67.3 billion, respectively. The lifetime costs of care or incidence based cost-of-illness for Alzheimer's patients diagnosed in 1991 were estimated to be $536 billion in direct costs and $1.75 trillion in total costs.

3. Hartunian NS, Smart CN, Thompson MS. The Incidence and Economic Costs of Major Health Impairments: A comparative analysis of cancer, motor vehicle injuries, coronary heart disease, and stroke. Lexington, MA: Lexington Books, 1981.

   This book reports the results of a 3-year study of the economic costs of four major health impairments. The costs of all illnesses were conducted using an incidence-based approach. In addition to estimating the cost of these illnesses, the text also provides a detailed explanation of the methodology and data sources used in calculating disease costs. Costs are disaggregated to a greater degree than previous cost-of-illness analyses. In addition to presenting costs by cost category (e.g., indirect and direct), costs also are presented by subconditions, age and gender.

4. Hellinger FJ. The lifetime cost of treating a person with HIV. JAMA 1993;270(4):474–8.

   This study presents results of the treatment costs for people infected with HIV. Costs are estimated for four different stages of the illness and highlights how the distribution of resource use can shift as a disease progresses. For example, 68 percent of the total cost of treating people with AIDS was composed of inpatient hospital costs, while only 19 percent of total costs were spent on inpatient costs for HIV-positive patients without AIDS and with a T cell count of 0.50 x 10^9/L or higher. Resource use and cost-data were taken from a large multisite survey, the AIDS Cost and Service Use Survey. Total costs of care for each disease stage were estimated by multiplying the mean time in months spent in each stage by the average cost per stage per month.

5. Hodgson TA, Meiners MR. Cost-of-illness methodology: a guide to current practices and procedures. Milbank Q 1982;60:429–62.

   This paper is frequently referenced and provides an overview of the methods used to estimate cost-of-illness. The paper discusses in detail the cost components included within cost-of-illness studies and the procedural methods used to calculate these costs. Direct costs for medical and nonmedical expenditures are identified and discussed as are the indirect costs from reductions in productivity due to morbidity and mortality. Two methods for estimating indirect costs are identified and discussed: willingness to pay and human capital. The advantages and disadvantages of both methods for estimating indirect costs are discussed. This paper also presents several procedural recommendations for conducting costs-of-illness studies and provides a useful glossary of cost-of-illness terms.

6. Levit K, Smith C, Cowan C, Lazenby H, Martin A. Inflation spurs health spending in 2000. Health Aff 2002;21(1):172–81.

   This article compiles figures on health expenditures in the United States from several sources to present a profile of health care spending in the United States from 1970 through 2000. Tables are presented which present actual spending and growth rates within multiple categories of health spending. Costs are broken down by categories, including health services and supplies (i.e., spending for hospital care, physician services, nursing homes, dental, and pharmaceuticals) in addition to investment costs (i.e., spending for health care research and construction). The authors also discuss legislative and market forces shaping health policy and, therefore, health expenditures.

7. Rice DP. Estimating the cost of illness. Am J Public Health 1967;57:424–40.

   This study was one of the original works estimating cost-of-illness by diagnostic category. The study presents the distribution of health expenditures for many services. Diagnostic groups were identified through what was then the International Classification of Diseases, Adapted, now referred to as ICD-9. The study describes the estimation procedure and methodological framework for calculating single-year cost-of-illness for several different disease categories. Estimation of direct costs of illness rests primarily on the use of specific types of services. Indirect costs are losses of output to the economy brought about by illness, death, or disability. Potential methodological problems are identified: presence of multiple diseases, mortality losses, population groups, and gaps in statistical data. The total economic costs of illness, disability and death was estimated at $58 billion (United States dollars in 1963).

8. Rice DP, Hodgson TA, Kopstein AN. The economic costs of illness: a replication and update. Heath Care Financ Rev 1985 Fall;7(1):61–80.

   This article provides an update to the previously estimated economic burden from illness, disability, and premature death. The total economic costs of illness, disability, and death in 1980 was estimated at $455 billion . Of this figure, $211 billion were direct costs, $68 billion for morbidity, and $176 billion for mortality. A review of the costs-of-illness methods are provided. Two approaches for estimating indirect costs are presented: willingness to pay and human capital. The paper also discusses the incidence- and prevalence-based methods for determining costs of disease.

9. Rice DP, Fox PJ, Max W, et al. The economic burden of Alzheimer's disease care. Health Aff 1993 Summer;12(2):164–76.

This study estimates the costs of caring for those with Alzheimer's disease. This study uses a prevalence-based approach to estimate the total formal and informal care costs of Alzheimer's disease based upon a sample of community and institutionalized patients in California. Indirect costs associated with productivity losses were not estimated. Formal care services were defined as those services "rendered for a price in the traditional medical and social service marketplace". These included costs for hospitalization, nursing home care, physician services, social services, medications, and other items or services associated with the care of the Alzheimer's patient. Charges for these services were used as a proxy for costs. Informal care services refer to services that fall outside of the labor market and for which providers are not reimbursed. These services are those provided by caregivers to assist the patient with activities of daily living (ADL), and instrumental activities of daily living (IADL). The average annual per person cost for caring for an Alzheimer's patient was about $47,000 ($47,083 for community care patients and $47,591 for institutionalized patients). Although the total costs were similar between the two settings, a breakdown of costs by type of care (formal and informal) showed significant differences. Seventy-three percent of the total costs for community patients were represented by informal costs, while 88% of the total costs of caring for institutionalized patients were represented by formal care costs. This study is a good example of how, within a disease category, differences in the pattern of cost-of-illness exist by setting and/or severity of disease.

10. van Tulder MW, Koes BW, Bouter LM. A cost-of illness study of back pain in The Netherlands. Pain 1995;62:233–40.

This study presents a prevalence-based approach to estimating the costs of back pain. This study presents a prevalence-based approach to estimating the total direct and indirect costs associated with back pain in the Netherlands for the year 1991. Data on utilization of health care resources and costs were obtained from a variety of national data sources. Resource use for back pain was identified using the ICD-9 coding system. Direct medical costs included hospitalization, medical specialist care, general practice care and paramedical care or physical therapy. Since back pain is not associated with a high risk of death, mortality costs were not included. Costs of absenteeism were calculated as the total number of sick days multiplied by the mean cost of one sick day. Costs of disablement were estimated by multiplying the total days of disability with the mean daily pension in 1991

Self-Assessment Questions

1. Which one of the following costs are *not* assessed in cost-of-illness analysis?
   A. Intangible costs.
   B. Incremental costs.
   C. Direct costs.
   D. Indirect costs.

2. Which one of the following is true of the incidence-based approach for estimating cost of illness?
   A. Useful for estimating the cost-effectiveness of alternative therapies.
   B. Only useful when the impact of an intervention occurs within a single year.
   C. Used in determining the lifetime costs resulting from a disease or illness.
   D. Does not require projections of treatment patterns past 1 year.

3. Which one of the following best describes the human capital approach to estimating indirect costs?
   A. Uses wage earnings as an estimate of lost productivity.
   B. Requires the determination of marginal and incremental costs.
   C. Uses medical care capital investments as indicators of indirect costs.
   D. Requires the determination of overhead and production costs.

4. The results of cost-of-illness analysis can assist decision-makers in many different arenas. Which one of the following is not an application of cost-of-illness studies?
   A. Used to estimate the proportion of costs by cost categories within a disease and between diseases.
   B. Assists policy-makers in establishing priorities for research funding.
   C. Indicates areas of inefficiency within the health care system.
   D. Provides baseline data for pharmacoeconomic analysis.

5. Which one of the following is true of prevalence-based approaches for estimating cost-of-illness?
   A. More difficult to undertake than incidence-based approach.
   B. Requires estimation of the lifetime disease costs.
   C. Requires a knowledge of the characteristics of a disease.
   D. Is more useful to health care policy-makers than the incidence-based approach for allocating funds to chronic diseases.

6. Which one of the following is a criticism of the human capital approach to estimating indirect costs?
   A. Assumes that an individual's lost productivity is accompanied by a decrease in GNP.
   B. Overestimates the value of lost productivity of women and minorities.
   C. Assumes that individuals are able to comprehend small changes in their risk of dying.
   D. Does not capture the value of losses from nonmarket activities.

7. Which one of the following best describes intangible costs?
   A. Used to determine the monetary value placed on the deterioration in quality of life due to a disease.
   B. Includes costs of hospitalization.
   C. Used in estimating overhead costs.
   D. Includes costs of lost productivity due to disease.

8. Which one of the following is suggested as the first step in conducting cost-of-illness analysis?
   A. Complete identification of all cost-generating components of a disease.
   B. Understanding of the dollar value to place on all resources consumed.
   C. A thorough understanding of all epidemiological aspects of a disease.
   D. Determining whether to use an incidence-versus a prevalence based method.

9. Which one of the following is not considered a direct cost?
   A. Costs due to hospitalization.
   B. Clinic visit charges.
   C. Prescription drug expenditures.
   D. Costs of pain and suffering.

10. Which one of the following is not considered a resource for defining or identifying a disease or condition?
    A. American Heart Association.
    B. International Classification of Diseases coding system.
    C. American Cancer Society.
    D. Local Oncologist.

COST-MINIMIZATION ANALYSIS

Emily Cox, Ph.D.

Outline

I. Definition

A. A pharmacoeconomic tool for comparing all of the relevant costs and consequences of two or more therapeutic interventions.

B. Distinguishing criteria: consequences of the interventions are shown to be equivalent.

C. Objective: choose the least cost alternative among equivalent, or equally efficacious, alternatives.

II. Methodological Approach

A. Search the literature to determine if the economic answer already exists.

B. Follow a structured process.

1. Ten-step method for conducting pharmacoeconomic analysis which includes: 1) defining the pharmacoeconomic problem, 2) determining the study's perspective, 3) determining the alternatives and outcomes, 4) selecting the appropriate pharmacoeconomic method, 5) placing monetary values on the outcomes, 6) identifying resources, 7) establishing the probabilities of the outcome event, 8) use of decision analysis, 9) discounting costs, or performing a sensitivity, or incremental cost analysis, and, finally, 10) presenting the results.

2. CMA and CEA

a. Similarity: costs measured in dollars and consequences, often measured in natural units

b. Difference: consequences are not equivalent in CEA

3. CMA and cost-analysis

a. Similarity: costs measured in dollars

b. Difference: outcomes are not measured in cost-analysis, regardless of whether outcomes are equivalent

III. Verifying the assumption of equivalent consequences

A. Outcomes, or consequences, should be assumed unequivalent until proven equivalent.

1. An incorrect assumption of equivalent outcomes leads to biased, and misleading conclusions, since no adjustment in costs are made for differences in effectiveness.

B. Several methods are available for establishing equivalence of outcomes which depends on how many alternatives, and how outcomes are measured.

1. Generic versus brand name

a. Use a published source of equivalency rating, such as *Approved Drug Products with Therapeutic Equivalence Evaluations, 16th edition.*

2. Products in a similar therapeutic class

a. Meta-analysis: a technique for "systematically" combining the results of many studies to reach a conclusion on an overall effect size.

i. Data retrieval should follow the stated objective of the economic analysis.

ii. Process of data retrieval and eligibility criteria for study inclusion should be clearly stated prior to beginning the search.

iii. Factors to consider in a literature review: type of study design; year of publication; language of the publication; other restrictions to sample size or follow-up; similarity of treatment and/or exposure; and the completeness of information.

iv. Meta-analysis would be conducted to determine an effect size for each alternative.

b. Testing for differences in effect size involves the use of statistical tests.

c. Use of meta-analysis and statistical tests to establish equivalence is encouraged.

C. Equivalency should also take into consideration safety factors: side-effect profiles.

1. Assuming differences in the side-effect profiles, ask, "What impact do the side effects have on patient morbidity and ultimately costs?" And, "what influence could they have on the primary endpoint?"

2. Side effects can cause patients to discontinue, or become less compliant with medication, thereby decreasing the effectiveness of treatment, which may not be evidenced from clinical trial data.

3. If differences exist in side-effect profiles across alternatives, CMA should not be the method chosen.

4. Choice of alternatives and outcomes

a. Include all alternatives appropriate to address the economic question.

b. Example: to determine the least costly alternative for treating recurrent urinary tract infections (UTIs) include all alternatives used to treat UTIs; if outcomes are equivalent, CMA is used to evaluate the data.

IV. Measurement of cost

A. Measurement of costs is in dollars.

B. Resource utilization captured in resource units; number of physician visits, number of doses of medication administered, or number of bed days.

C. A factor influencing the identification and inclusion of costs is the perspective of the analysis.

1. Objective of CMA (choosing the least cost alternative among equally efficacious alternatives) tends to favor the perspective of the payer (either individual, group or institution).

D. Due to equal efficacy, differences between products are related primarily to differences in costs.

E. Identification and valuation of costs is a detailed procedure.

1. Time and motion analysis track the personnel costs associated with preparing and administering therapies.

2. CMA allows decision makers to compare the order of magnitude of resource utilization between the competing alternatives: what are the cost drivers for different therapies; ingredient cost, or the cost of administration and/or testing?

V. Measurement of consequences

A. Although equivalent, consequences are measured, or addressed, in CMA.

B. Measured in natural units of effectiveness such as mm Hg decreased, clinical success, or infections averted.

VI. Presentation of results

A. Presented as average or per patient costs.

B. Include a breakdown of costs for each alternative.

1. Example: in a study comparing ampicillin/sulbactam and clindamycin/gentamicin therapy for the treatment of intra-abdominal infections, the authors presented seven different cost categories: including acquisition; intravenous (IV) administration supplies; drug administration; pharmacokinetic consultation; laboratory; pharmacist/technician and total hospital.

C. Important to present evidence supporting equivalence of outcomes as well (e.g., any statistical tests that were conducted or references from the literature).

VII. Applications of CMA

A. Application of CMA is reserved for situations that involve the analysis of alternatives with equivalent outcomes.

B. Generic versus brand name

1. Most often referred to in CMA.

2. Equivalence of outcomes can be confirmed through published bioequivalence ratings.

3. Differences are usually in acquisition costs alone.

4. Rarely published in the literature.

C. CMA of different routes of administration

1. CMA comparing IV versus intramuscular (IM) administration of imipenem-cilastatin.

2. Study conducted retrospectively, using data from a previously reported clinical trial.

3. Equivalency of outcomes was based on the authors' claim that "the failure rates between the two groups were not statistically different."

a. One failure out of 19 total patients in the IV group, and three failures out of 19 total in the IM group.

b. These findings of equivalency are questionable, given the small sample size in each group.

4. Costs presented as mean per patient and were categorized by drug acquisition costs, supplies, drug administration (nursing time), and pharmacist preparation time, as well as total cost.

5. Time and motion analysis used to determine nursing time required for reconstitution, preparation, and administration of the drug. Time factor was then multiplied by a mean hourly nurse wage to estimate the cost of administration. A similar time and motion analysis was used to estimate the pharmacist and pharmacy technician's time to manufacture and check a piggyback.

6. T-tests used to determine difference in costs across cost categories.

7. Authors' conclusions: costs of administering imipenem-cilastatin IM was significantly lower than IV administration.

D. Cost-minimization of different administration settings

1. CMA to compare the costs of hospital versus at-home management of narcotic infusions in cancer patients.

2. Conducted in Canada, all costs measured from the perspective of the Ministry of Health.

3. Several different types of cancer patients were included in the analysis (lung, colo-rectal, breast, prostate, and others) as were different narcotic medications (morphine, hydromorphone and meperidine).

4. Consequences measured as survival rates; which is a questionable measure of the consequences of narcotic therapy. A more appropriate measure might have been symptom-free days.

5. Study conducted retrospectively through a review of medical records.

6. Detailed assessment by cost category was conducted and the non-parametric Mann-Whitney U test was used to analyze differences in costs between treatment setting.

7. Conclusion: "it is less expensive for a central funding agency...to manage a patient who requires a narcotic infusion at home rather than in hospital."

E. Cost-minimization of different antibiotic therapies

1. Analyzed the management of postsurgical antibiotic therapy of patients with perforated or gangrenous appendicitis.

2. Two treatment alternatives were compared: ampicillin 2 g /sulbactam 1 g by IV infusion for 30 minutes, or 900 mg clindamycin admixed with 1.5 mg/kg gentamicin by IV infusion for 30 minutes.

3. Consequences measured as treatment failure.

4. No statistically significant differences in treatment failures between the two groups were found.

a. No statistical tests were identified or presented. This implies that efficacy was based solely on clinical opinion.

5. Costs were presented as mean patient treatment costs divided into seven cost categories (acquisition, IV administration supplies, drug administration, pharmacokinetic consultation, laboratory, pharmacist/technician, and total for all hospital days).

a. Student t-tests used to test for differences in costs.

b. Conclusion: no significant differences between therapies for mean total treatment costs. However, analyzing each category separately did show significant differences in costs.

6. CMA to compare ceftazidime versus tobramycin/ticarcillin in the treatment of hospital-acquired pneumonia and bacteremias.

7. Efficacy data were obtained via retrospective chart review on 121 patients in three different institutions.

8. Claims of equal efficacy are highly suspect, given the small sample sizes, differences in case mix of infections treated, and differences in the dose of tobramycin.

9. Time and motion studies conducted to determine both pharmacy and nursing personnel costs.

10. Costs were measured from the perspective of the individual hospitals.

11. Treatment costs for each therapy were presented as cost per patient day, categorized by total drug and laboratory costs; differences in costs were related to supplies, lab tests and personnel time.

12. Conclusion: the cost of treatment with ceftazidime was less than treatment with tobramycin/ticarcillin.

VIII. Conclusion

A. CMA remains an important tool in the evaluation of pharmaceuticals, even though its applicability is limited to those situations where comparisons are made between equally efficacious products.

B. Potential for CMA's applicability to expand given the growing number of "me-too" products, generic competition and changes in health care technology.

1. Technology has increased the ability to provide health-care services in a variety of settings using different administrative approaches.

2. Strength of CMA is that it is simple and many times straightforward, given that outcomes, or consequences of alternative therapies, are assumed equivalent.

C. The primary issue within CMA continues to be establishing the criteria for equal efficacy.

Learning Objectives

1. Distinguish the difference between cost-minimization analysis (CMA), cost-analysis and cost-effectiveness analysis (CEA).
2. Briefly discuss the steps in conducting CMA.
3. Discuss methods of establishing equivalence in outcomes.
4. Discuss how results are presented in CMA.
5. Describe the types of situations most appropriate for CMA.

Abbreviations in this chapter

ANOVA	analysis of variance
CMA	cost-minimization analysis
CEA	cost-effectiveness analysis
CI	confidence interval
COX-2	cyclo-oxygenase-2
CUA	cost-utility analysis
CTZ	ceftazidime
GI	gastrointestinal
IM	intramuscular
IV	intravenous
NSAIDs	non-steroidal anti-inflammatory agents
P&T	pharmacy and therapeutics
UTIs	urinary tract infections
TRx$	total drug therapy cost
T/T	tobrmycin/ticarcillin

Cost-minimization Analysis

Cost-minimization analysis (CMA) is a pharmacoeconomic tool for comparing all of the relevant costs and consequences of two or more therapeutic interventions. A requisite of CMA, which distinguishes it from other pharmacoeconomic methodologies, is that the consequences of the interventions are shown to be equivalent. Thus, the objective of CMA is to choose the least costly alternative among interventions with equivalent outcomes.

The requirement of equivalent outcomes limits the application of CMA to those situations for which equivalency is established. These situations include, but are not limited to, the comparisons between brand and generic products, different routes of administration of the same drug and, different settings for the administration of the same drug therapy (e.g., inpatient versus home therapy). In these instances, the evidence supporting equal efficacy should be clearly stated, and where appropriate, statistically confirmed. Within this chapter we will discuss the methodological issues unique to CMA and present examples of the application of the technique.

Methodological Approach

Before beginning any pharmacoeconomic analysis, a complete search of the literature should be conducted to determine if studies exist to answer the economic question. If the information is not there, is incomplete, or is irrelevant based on the perspective or variation in practice patterns, then the analysis should be carried out. Conducting a pharmacoeconomic evaluation, including CMA, is a structured process. Guidelines were developed to assist the researcher through this process and are discussed in more detail later in the book. These guidelines outline a ten-step method for conducting pharmacoeconomic analysis, and include: 1) Defining the pharmacoeconomic problem, 2) determining the study's perspective, 3) determining the alternatives and outcomes, 4) selecting the appropriate pharmacoeconomic method, 5) placing monetary values on the outcomes, 6) identifying resources, 7) establishing the probabilities of the outcome event, 8) use of decision analysis, 9) discounting costs, or performing a sensitivity or incremental cost analysis, and, finally, 10) presenting the results.

CMA is often confused with two other types of analyses: cost-effectiveness analysis (CEA) and cost-analysis. CMA is most similar to CEA in that costs are measured in dollars, and consequences are usually measured in natural units. The similarity of the two methods leads some researchers to "mislabel" findings as "cost-effective" when, in fact, the study is either a cost-analysis or cost-minimization analysis. The misuse of the term "cost-effective" is documented in the literature. In a study reviewing the pharmacoeconomic literature, it was reported that over half of the articles using the term "cost-effective" were labeled as such "based solely on the fact that it saved money." A product shown to be the least costly among equivalent alternatives is not necessarily "cost-effective" compared to other alternatives, rather it is the "least costly" alternative. CMA is also closely related to cost-analysis. In cost-analysis, the researcher's task is to identify and measure the costs associated with alternative therapies, regardless of whether outcomes are equivalent.

Figure 1 is presented as an aid in distinguishing between cost-minimization and other pharmacoeconomic methods. To determine whether CMA is the appropriate method to use, the researcher must determine whether outcomes will be measured. There can be situations where measuring outcomes is not of concern to the decision maker, and it is in these instances that cost-analysis is applied. However, if outcomes or consequences will be measured, the next question to address is, "Are the outcomes equivalent?" If the answer is "yes", then CMA is the appropriate method to use. If outcomes are not equivalent then, depending on how outcomes are measured, another method of analysis should be chosen: CEA for outcomes measured in natural units; cost-benefit analysis for outcomes measured in monetary units; and cost-utility analysis for outcomes measured in quality-adjusted life years.

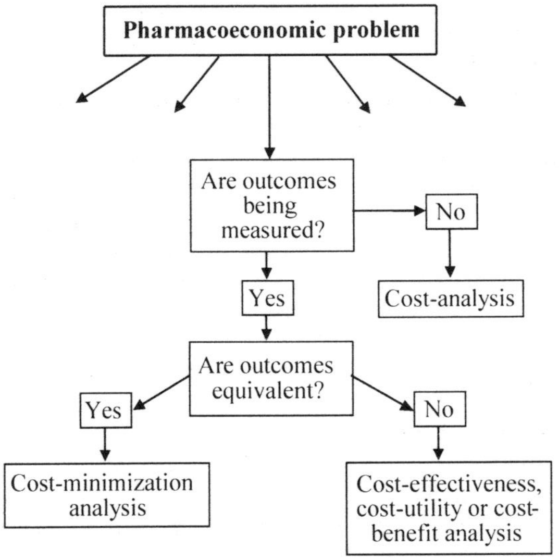

Figure 1: Cost-minimization Analysis Decision Framework

Verifying the assumption of equivalent consequences

One of the most important issues in CMA is verifying the equivalence of alternative consequences. Within the literature, very little is written about CMA, and what is written provides little guidance on accepted standards for determining equivalent outcomes. How is it confirmed whether the outcomes are equivalent? What does it mean when two or more alternatives have equivalent consequences? What about those situation when the primary outcomes are equivalent, but the alternative therapies vary in their side-effect profile?

Every attempt should be made to establish equivalency of outcomes before the analysis is conducted. Outcomes should be assumed unequivalent until proven equivalent. Making an incorrect assumption of equivalent outcomes leads to biased and misleading conclusions since no adjustment in costs are made for differences in effectiveness. Many CMA studies were conducted and published with claims of equivalency based on clinical assumptions, rather than published findings with head-to-head comparisons. Studies have also measured outcomes (prospectively or retrospectively) as part of the analysis and report that outcomes were "not significantly different." The error often made in these instances is that the power of the test was insufficient to detect a difference in effectiveness. The sample size was too small to reliably test for differences.

How does a researcher go about establishing equivalency? Several methods can be used, depending on the type of comparison being made, how outcomes are measured, and the number of alternatives compared. To establish equivalency in the simple case of brand versus generic products, a published equivalency rating from a source such as *Approved Drug Products with Therapeutic Equivalence Evaluations, 16th edition*, published by the U.S. Department of Health and Human Services, also known as the "Orange Book," could be used.

Establishing equivalency between products in a similar therapeutic class can be a bit more complicated. The first step involves gathering evidence on the effectiveness of the treatment alternatives. The process of retrieving data and summarizing the results is called meta-analysis. Meta-analysis is a technique for "systematically" combining the results of many studies to reach a conclusion on an overall effect size (e.g., the summary relative risk of stroke in users of estrogen replacement therapy from nine separate studies conducted from 1976 to 1992 was 0.89, 95 percent confidence interval [CI] = 0.77-1.03). In the process of retrieving data from published studies, the researcher should confirm that the published study's objective follow the stated objective of the economic analysis (e.g., determining the least costly alternative for treating hospital-acquired pneumonia involves identifying all studies testing antibiotics in that setting and for that condition). In many instances, the researcher has narrowed the search to only two or three alternative therapies. Even so, the number of studies published on the effectiveness of those alternatives in treating hospital-acquired pneumonia can still number in the hundreds. To make the task more manageable, the process of data retrieval and eligibility criteria for study inclusion should be clearly stated prior to beginning the search. Consideration should be given to the type of study design (e.g., randomized versus nonrandomized), year and language of the publication, other restrictions to sample size or follow-up, similarity of treatment and/or exposure and the completeness of information. In CMA, meta-analysis would be conducted to obtain a relative effect size for each alternative.

The test for differences in effect size between two alternatives involves, in essence, testing the null hypothesis that outcomes are equivalent (H_0: $\mu1-\mu2=0$). Table 1 shows statistical tests used to test for differences, depending on the number of alternative therapies evaluated. To test the difference in mean effectiveness between two alternatives, tests such as the two sample t test or χ^2 can be used depending on whether outcomes are measured on a continuous or interval level scale, or are measured as counts of the number of cases. Examples of continuously measured variables include mm HG or cholesterol levels. Clinical outcome measured as counts include number of successful outcomes, such as the number of infections averted.

When more than two alternatives are measured the researcher can use tests, such as analysis of variance (ANOVA) for variables measured on a continuous scale, or χ^2, for the number of cases.

Table 1: Examples of Statistical Tests Used to Test for Mean Differences in Effectiveness

Outcomes variable measured as:	Test statistic
2 alternatives	
Continuous	t-test
Categorical/frequency	χ^2
More than 2 alternatives	
Continuous	ANOVA
Categorical/frequency	χ^2

ANOVA= analysis of variance

The researcher uncertain as to which statistical techniques are appropriate should seek assistance from individuals trained in this area. These individuals can ensure that appropriate methods of analysis are used.

Equivalent, but different, side-effect profile

Although it is rarely, if ever, addressed, equivalency should also take into consideration safety factors, or the side-effect profile of alternative therapies. In pharmacoeconomic analyses, differences in side effects are often captured on the cost side of the equation. However, there are a growing number of "me-too" type products, in which the primary endpoint is equivalent, but the side-effect profile may differ from existing products. Questions to ask are, what impact do the side effects have on patient morbidity and, ultimately, costs? Also, could these side effects make a difference in primary endpoints once the product hits the market? This goes back to the discussion on the difference between efficacy and effectiveness. In the "real world" evaluation of drug therapies, the side-effect profile of a product can cause patients to discontinue, or become less compliant, with their medication, thereby decreasing the effectiveness of a treatment. In the controlled environment of the clinical trial this effect is not always captured. Thus, while the efficacy of two or more alternatives may appear equivalent from clinical trial results, the side-effect profiles may be quite different. If there are differences across alternatives in a common side effect that could influence effectiveness, then the appropriate method of analysis would not be CMA.

Differences in side effects can also have a substantial impact on costs. Case in point are the differences in non-selective and selective non-steroidal anti-inflammatory agents (NSAIDs) (i.e., cyclo-oxygenase-2 [COX-2]). COX-2 inhibitors and non-selective or traditional NSAIDs (e.g., ibuprofen, naproxen) were shown to have similar clinical efficacy at equipotent doses for the management of acute pain and other conditions associated with pain. However, there are important differences in their side-effect profiles, particularly for patients taking these medications on a chronic basis. These adverse events are primarily related to gastrointestinal (GI) upset, including everything from mild dyspepsia to more serious GI perforation. The economic evaluations of these agents reflect this understanding of equal efficacy and have, therefore, focused on the differences in GI side effects as the measure of outcome. Thus, the economic evaluations present results as cost per GI adverse event avoided. While it might appear to be a CMA due to equal efficacy, a CEA is more appropriate to adjust total costs for differences in side-effect profiles.

The choice of alternatives and outcome measures is also an important step in CMA. This step involves choosing all relevant alternatives which would address the pharmacoeconomic problem. If the problem is to determine the least costly alternative for treating recurrent urinary tract infections (UTIs) in women, then all alternatives indicated for the treatment of UTIs should be evaluated. If there exists evidence that therapies are equivalent, then the researcher would choose CMA as the appropriate method of analysis. In some instances, the researcher might want to focus on only those alternatives that are equivalent for the treatment of UTIs to determine the least costly among equivalent alternatives.

In establishing equivalency between therapies it is important to consider the timeline of the analysis. Although the consequences of alternatives are equivalent, the time to achieve those outcomes for each of the alternatives may be measurably different. The timeline should be based on the natural course of the clinical condition, and the time to achieve outcomes for each alternative. The time interval for one therapy may require a 10-day course, and another, a 21-day course of therapy to evaluate clinical efficacy or effectiveness. Thus, researchers can not assume a fixed time interval over which to measure costs and consequences.

Measurement of cost

CMA measures costs in dollars. The steps taken in cost measurement include identifying and valuing all relevant resources consumed. The measurement of costs involves capturing resource utilization in units: The number of physician visits, doses of medication administered, bed days, etc. After resources are identified, an appropriate cost is assigned to each resource unit.

As in all pharmacoeconomic analyses, an important factor influencing the identification and inclusion of costs is the perspective of the analysis. If the assumption of equal efficacy is confirmed, the primary objective becomes which alternative consumes fewer resources. Thus, the objective of CMA tends to favor the perspective of the payer (either individual, group or institution) since differences between products are related primarily to differences in costs.

Differences between products may be determined solely on administrative or preparation costs. To measure these differences, studies include time and motion analysis to track the personnel costs associated with preparing and administering the medications. In addition to a comparison of the costs and consequences of alternative therapies, CMA also allows decision makers to compare the order of magnitude of resource utilization between competing alternatives. This helps determine the cost drivers (e.g., highest proportion of costs coming from ingredient costs, cost of administration, or laboratory tests).

This level of detail in costs is presented in a study comparing the costs associated with various methods of preparing and administering intravenous (IV) cimetidine delivery systems. In this study, a detailed identification of the pharmacy and nursing personnel activities involved in the preparation and administration of five delivery systems. The authors detail each step in preparing the delivery systems, from obtaining an IV pole to opening a syringe package. This level of detail in identifying activities is not as common in other pharmacoeconomic methodologies, such as CEA or cost-utility analysis (CUA).

Measurement of consequences

CMA falls under the guise of a "full" economic evaluation, which entails evaluation of both costs and consequences. Although the consequences are equivalent, this does not mean that measurement is not necessary. The purpose in measuring consequences in CMA is to verify that outcomes are, in fact, equivalent. Similar to CEA, consequences in CMA are often measured in natural units of effectiveness, such as mm Hg decreased, clinical success, or infections averted.

Presentation of results

Results in CMA are not presented as cost per unit of outcome, given that consequences are equivalent. The results from CMA are presented the same for cost-analysis: average per-patient costs for each alternative therapy. Additionally, presenting results by cost category is helpful for decision makers to determine where differences in costs lie across alternatives. In a study comparing ampicillin/sulbactam and clindamycin/gentamicin therapy in treating intra-abdominal infections, the authors presented seven different cost categories. These included acquisition costs, IV administration supplies, drug administration costs, pharmacokinetic consultation costs, laboratory charges, pharmacist/technician costs and total hospital costs (Table 2). From these cost categories, researchers were able to identify where the differences in costs occurred. This example also highlights the variability in costs across cost categories. Although the difference in hospital costs across alternatives was quite large, more than $450, the variability, or standard deviation around the mean was also quite large. Thus, this difference was not found to be significant.

Conducting statistical tests to determine differences in costs is not always meaningful to decision makers. In this instance the difference of roughly $59 per patient (i.e., $433 minus $374) between the two therapies may not be different statistically, but may be quite significant to an administrator. When extrapolated to 100 patients treated monthly, there are substantial differences in costs.

Table 2: Per Patient Treatment Costs Between Two Antibiotic Treatment Strategies*

	Ampicillin/ Sulbactam	Clindamycin/ Gentamicin	p value
Acquisition costs	258.73 ± 144.71	244.61 ± 61.1	
IV administration supplies	104.6 ± 47.8	67.9 ± 16.7	p=0.001
Drug administration costs	16.5 ± 9.1	10.7 ± 2.6	p=0.001
Pharmacokinetic consultation costs	N/A	36.1 ± 11.5	
Laboratory charges	N/A	18.7 ± 11.5	
Pharmacist/ technician costs	13.3 ± 4.3	15.4 ± 4.0	p=0.001
Total cost all	7486.9 ± 3488.0	7012.1 ± 3596.3	p=0.48
Hospital days			
Total treatment cost	433.3 ± 58.5	373.8 ± 86.2	p=0.24

*All values are mean ± standard deviation.

Presentation of costs are often the focus in CMA, but the evidence gathered must support the equivalence of outcomes. This would include, where applicable, results from meta-analysis, statistical tests that were conducted, or references from the literature supporting equivalent effectiveness.

Applications of CMA

As previously stated, the applications of CMA include comparisons between brand and generic products, different routes of administration of the same drug and different settings for the administration of the same drug therapy (e.g., inpatient versus home therapy). This section discusses CMA as it has been applied within the literature.

Generic versus brand name

The application of CMA most often referred to in the pharmacoeconomic literature is the simple and straight forward comparison between generic and brand-name products. The assumption of equivalent outcomes is easily established through confirmation from published bio-equivalence ratings. These types of analyses usually involve differences in acquisition cost only, and are rarely published in the literature.

Cost-minimization analysis of different routes of administration

A 1989 cost-minimization analysis was conducted comparing IV versus intramuscular (IM) administration of imipenem-cilastatin. The IV group was given 500 mg every 6 hours, and the IM group was given 750 mg every 12 hours. The study was conducted retrospectively, using data from a previously reported clinical trial. Equivalency of outcomes was based on the authors' claim that "the failure rates between the two groups were not statistically different." However, it is questionable whether the author was able to detect differences in failure rates, given the small sample size within each group; one failure out of 19 total patients in the IV group, and three failures out of 19 total in the IM group. How, or if, the study was powered to detect differences was not discussed. This is a common criticism of many CMAs. If equivalence of outcomes is to be based solely on retrospective review of charts, or one prospective study, the study must have sufficient power to detect a significant difference.

Costs were presented as mean per patient and were categorized by drug acquisition, supplies, drug administration (nursing time), and pharmacist preparation time. A time and motion analysis was used to determine nursing time required for reconstitution, preparation, and administration of the drug. This time factor was then multiplied by a mean hourly nurse wage to estimate the cost of administration. A similar time and motion analysis was used to estimate the pharmacist and pharmacy technician's time to manufacture and check a piggyback.

Differences in costs across the two methods of administration were determined by means of statistical tests (e.g., the mean cost of administration supplies for the IV group was significantly greater than that for the IM group

[$30.60 ± $7.90 versus $0.90 ± $0.03]). Overall, the authors conclude that costs of administering imipenem-cilastatin IM was significantly lower than IV administration.

Cost-minimization of different administration settings

In 1991 a CMA was conducted to compare the costs of hospital versus at-home management of narcotic infusions in cancer patients. All costs were measured from the perspective of the Canadian Ministry of Health. The study was conducted retrospectively through a review of medical records. Several different types of cancer patients were included in the analysis (lung, colo-rectal, breast, prostate, and others), as were different narcotic medications (morphine, hydromorphone and meperidine). Consequences of the two administration settings were measured by survival rates, and it was concluded that no significant difference in survival existed between inpatient and outpatient administration. A researcher might question the measurement of consequences of narcotic therapy in terms of survival rates. A more appropriate outcome measurement would have been pain-free days, or some other measure of pain relief.

A detailed assessment by cost category was conducted and the non-parametric Mann-Whitney U test was used to analyze differences in costs between treatment settings. The authors conclude that, "it is less expensive for a central funding agency...to manage a patient who requires a narcotic infusion at home rather than in a hospital."

Cost-minimization of different antibiotic therapies

Several CMA studies involving antibiotics have been published in the literature. One study in particular compared two treatment alternatives in the management of post-surgical treatment of perforated or gangrenous appendicitis: ampicillin 2 g/sulbactam 1 g by IV infusion for 30 minutes, or clindamycin 900 mg admixed with gentamicin 1.5 mg/kg by IV infusion for 30 minutes. The consequence, or outcome, measured was treatment failure. It was concluded that there were no statistically significant differences in treatment failures between the two groups (four for the ampicillin/sulbactam group, n=58, and three in the clindamycin/gentamicin group, n=58). However, no statistical tests were identified, or presented. This implies that efficacy was based solely on clinical opinion. Although 58 patients per group may appear to be a sufficient number to detect a difference in effectiveness, this cannot be assumed. The authors also reference previously published studies on both ampicillin/sulbactam and clindamycin/gentamicin, each reporting that the agents were effective in treating intra-abdominal infections. However, this should not be interpreted to mean that the agents are equally efficacious in each treatment setting. Costs were presented as mean patient treatment costs divided into seven cost categories (acquisition, IV administration supplies, drug administration, pharmacokinetic consultation, lab charges, pharmacist/technician, and the total of all hospital days). Statistical tests were used to test for differences in costs between antibiotic regimens. The authors conclude that there were no significant differences between therapies for mean total treatment costs. However the analysis of each category did show significant differences in costs.

In 1988 a CMA was published comparing ceftazidime (CTZ) with tobramycin/ticarcillin (T/T) in the treatment of hospital-acquired pneumonia and bacteremias. Data were gathered via retrospective chart review on 121 patients in three separate hospital sites. The data were gathered on patients who were enrolled in a clinical trial within each site. Data gathered from the chart review included duration of therapy, number of doses of the antibiotic administered, side effects, and laboratory tests.

Reported efficacy at each site were 88 percent versus 83 percent, 93 percent versus 76 percent and 93 percent versus 88 percent for CTZ and T/T, respectively. From these three studies the authors claim that no significant difference in the efficacy of CTZ and T/T was demonstrated. This claim is highly questionable based on several factors. First, the studies had small sample sizes, in one study as few as 13 patients in the T/T arm. Second, the studies evaluated efficacy for different types of infections, and, finally, the dose of tobramycin varied across each study: 95 mg versus 90 mg versus 105 mg. The authors could have incorporated meta-analysis to summarize the findings across the three studies, and tested for differences in effect size between the two products. A search of the literature for other studies documenting the effectiveness of CTZ and T/T would also have been of value.

Time and motion studies were conducted to determine both pharmacy and nursing personnel costs. Costs were measured from the perspective of the individual hospitals. Treatment costs for each therapy were presented as cost per patient day, categorized by total drug and laboratory costs. Differences in costs were related to supplies, lab tests and personnel time. The authors concluded that when these factors were considered, the cost of treatment with CTZ was less than treatment with T/T.

Conclusion

CMA can be an important tool in the evaluation of pharmaceuticals. However, its applicability is limited to those situations in which equivalence of outcomes can be established. Although, this in and of itself, is not a limitation. There is the potential for CMA's applicability to expand, given the growing number of "me-too" products, generic competition, and changes in health-care technology. Technology has increased the ability to provide health-care services in a variety of settings using different administrative approaches. Decision makers continue to search for ways of providing health-care services at the lowest cost. The advantage of CMA is its simplicity and straightforward approach, particularly given that outcomes, or consequences, of alternative therapies are equivalent.

The primary issue within CMA continues to be establishing the criteria for equal efficacy. Many studies claiming equal efficacy of alternatives base these claims on questionable supporting evidence.

Annotated Bibliography

1. Bootman JL, Townsend RJ, McGhan WF. Principles of pharmacoeconomics, 2nd ed. Cincinnati, OH: Harvey Whitney Books, 1996.

   This recently published 2nd edition is an excellent introductory text for students of pharmacoeconomics, or for those who desire a working knowledge of the subject. Very little is presented on cost-minimization analysis (CMA), other than a brief description and definition.

2. Chin A, Gill MA, Ito MK, et al. A cost comparison of intramuscular versus intravenous imipenem. Hosp Pharm 1989;24:905-09.

   This study presents an application of cost-minimization analysis to different modes of administering the same drug therapy; imipenem-cilastatin, intramuscular (IM) versus intravenous (IV). The study is conducted retrospectively, by chart review of patients presenting to a hospital for treatment of perforated, or gangrenous, appendicitis. The authors measured outcomes between the two administration methods as failure rates, and mean hospital lengths of stay, neither of which was shown to be statistically different. In addition to categorizing and analyzing costs per category, the authors also discuss the formula used to calculate total drug therapy cost (TRx$). The administration of imipenem-cilastatin, IM was found to cost less than administration IV.

3. Chin A, Gill MA, Ito MK, et al. Treatment of intra-abdominal infections: Cost comparison of ampicillin/sulbactam and clindamycin/gentamicin. Hosp Formul 1990; 25:295-305.

   This article presents an example of the application of CMA to different "equally efficacious" antibiotic regimens. The purpose of the article is to compare the costs associated with the administration of ampicillin/sulbactam versus clindamycin/gentamicin in the treatment of perforated, or gangrenous, appendicitis. Although entitled a "cost comparison," some attempt to measure or claim equal efficacy is made, thus categorizing this study as a cost-minimization analysis, rather than a cost-analysis. This study is also a good example of how dominating hospital costs can be in the final equation. Significant differences are noted in every cost category (acquisition costs, IV administration supplies, and pharmacist/technician costs) except total cost of all hospital days. Because hospital costs where such a large component of total costs, no significant differences in total treatment cost between the two therapies were found. The difference in mean treatment cost per patient was approximately $60.

4. Evans D, Freund D, Dittus R, Robertson J, Henry D. The use of economic analysis as a basis for inclusion of pharmaceutical products on the Pharmaceutical Benefits Scheme, Commonwealth of Australia, Department of Health, Housing, and Community Service, Canberra, Australia: 1990.

   This document is written for the Australian government to provide a review of pharmacoeconomics and its application within the literature. This document is used by the Commonwealth of Australia to develop guidelines for the inclusion of pharmacoeconomic support material necessary for inclusion onto the Pharmaceutical Benefits Scheme. The paper presents a brief discussion of the four types of pharmacoeconomic analyses, and the advantages and disadvantages of each. The authors present a bibliography of the pharmacoeconomic literature as applied to pharmaceutical therapies. This is categorized by type of method and application to specific disease categories, or therapeutic categories.

5. Ferris FD, Wodinsky HB, Kerr IG, Sone M, Hume S, Coons C. A cost-minimization study of cancer patients requiring a narcotic infusion in hospital and at home. J Clin Epidemiol 1991;44(3): 13-327.

   This study provides an example of the application of cost-minimization analysis to analyze the costs of managing narcotic therapy in cancer patients between different treatment settings (home versus hospital). The study was conducted in Canada, and all costs are measured from the perspective of the Provincial Government or Ministry of Health. This article documents the breakdown of costs by setting, and provides a detailed assessment of costs in the management of cancer patients. A sensitivity analysis is also conducted on all of the cost categories individually, and in combination. The sensitivity analysis did not change the final conclusion that costs of managing narcotic therapy for cancer patients were less when provided at home compared to management of patients in a hospital.

6. Ford LC, Hammil HA, Lebherz TB. Cost-effective use of antibiotic prophylaxis for cesarean section. Am J Obstet Gynecol 1987;157:506-510.

   This study is another example of a CMA mislabeled as "cost-effective." The study evaluates five different antibiotics in the prophylaxic treatment of infection in women undergoing cesarean section. The study was conducted prospectively. The response rates for each antibiotic (piperacillin, cefoxitin, ceftazidime, cefazolin, cefotaxime and ampicillin) were not found to be significantly different from each other. What is different about this particular study is that the costs identified were not those associated with treatment but rather with antibiotic failure. These costs were measured as the minimum mean charges of treating infections after cesarean section, and included hospital room charges, lab tests and fees, drug costs, pharmacy preparation, and IV equipment. This total cost was then extrapolated to estimate the cost of treatment failure for 100 patients. This is a somewhat different approach in the analysis of costs of therapy. However, without knowing what the initial outlays were (cost of treatment), the costs of failure provide an incomplete picture of total resources consumed, and thus, can be misleading to decision makers.

7. Jolicoeur LM, Jones-Grizzle AJ, Boyer JG. Guidelines for performing a pharmacoeconomic analysis. Am J Hosp Pharm. 1992;49:1741-1747.

   This article defines the different types of pharmacoeconomic analyses and discusses the fundamental principles as outlined in a 10-step process. The 10-step method is provided as a guide to researchers in conducting pharmacoeconomic analyses and includes: 1) defining the pharmacoeconomic problem, 2) determining the study's perspective, 3) determining the alternatives and outcomes, 4) selecting the appropriate pharmacoeconomic method, 5) placing monetary values on the outcomes, 6) identifying resources, 7) establishing the probabilities of the outcome event, 8) use of decision analysis, 9) discounting costs, or performing a sensitivity or incremental cost analysis, and, finally, 10) presenting the results.

8. Lau NC, Cladwell RD, Arford PH. Cost comparison of oral, nasogastric, and intramuscular cimetidine drug delivery systems. Hosp Pharm 1992;27:946-947,950-952,954,956,962.

This study presents a cost comparison of different delivery systems for cimetidine drug delivery. The study compares six different delivery systems: unit dose tablet, unit dose elixir, pharmacy prepared suspension administered nasogastric, nursing prepared suspension administered nasogastric, unit-dose liquid via nasogastric tube and an IM premixed syringe. This study is not a cost-minimization study, but it is included for its thorough presentation of pharmacy and nursing personnel preparation, and administration activities.

9. Lee JT and Sanchez LA. Interpretation of "cost-effective" and soundness of economic evaluations in the pharmacy literature. Am J Hosp Pharm 1991;48:2622-2627.

This paper presents the results of a study conducted to examine the "soundness" of pharmacoeconomic evaluations published within the literature from January 1985 to December 1990. Ten criteria were used to evaluate the studies. The authors found that 55 percent of the articles were misinterpreted as cost-effective, therapies, which yielded cost savings only. Many of the studies were also found lacking from a methodological standpoint.

10. Parr MD, Hansen LA and Rapp RP. Cost comparison of ceftazidime versus tobramycin/ticarcillin therapy in three hospitals. Drug Intell Clin Pharm 1988;22:628-631.

This study presents an example of the application of CMA to antibiotic therapy. This study compares the costs of ceftazidime (CTZ) versus tobramycin/ticarcillin (TT) in the treatment of hospital-acquired pneumonias. The authors reviewed charts for patients who had participated in an earlier clinical trial comparing CTZ and TT in three hospital settings. Data collected included duration of therapy, number of doses administered, side effects and non-protocol laboratory parameters pertinent to the monitoring of the drugs. The perspective of the study was the hospital. The authors also preformed a time and motion study of pharmacy and nursing personnel. Results were presented as total costs for each hospital by therapy as well as cost per patient day. The authors conclude that the cost of CTZ was less than the cost of TT. They also note substantial variation in non-drug costs across hospitals. It is not certain that the economic data gathered included all original randomized subjects, and if not, why were only 121 patients or only the three institutions selected.

11. Pellissier JM, Straus WI, Watson DJ, Kong SX, Harper SE. Economic evaluation of rofecoxib versus nonselective nonsteroidal anti-inflammatory drugs for the treatment of osteoarthritis. Clin Ther 2001;23:1061-1079.

This study evaluates whether cost savings from lower rates of gastrointestinal (GI) side effects offsets the increased costs of rofecoxib, compared to nonselective nonsteroidal anti-inflammatory drugs. The authors used a decision-tree model to estimate the expected annual GI-related health care utilization of patients with osteoarthritis receiving either rofecoxib or other non-steroidal anti-inflammatory agents (NSAIDs).

12. Petitti DB. Meta-Analysis, Decision Analysis and Cost-Effectiveness Analysis. New York; Oxford University Press: 1994.

This text provides a thorough guide to conducting meta-analysis, from the process of information retrieval, to the statistical methods used to calculate an overall effect size. Additionally, the text provides an overview of decision analysis and cost-effectiveness analysis.

13. Sochalski A, Sullman S, Andriole VT. Cost-effectiveness study of cefotetan versus cefoxitin and cefotetan versus combination antibiotic regimens. The American Journal of Surgery 1988;155(5A):96-101.

This study compares the cost of cefotetan versus cefoxitin and cefotetan versus combination antibiotic regimens in the treatment of pathogenic anaerobic organisms. Although entitled as "cost-effectiveness," the study is, in fact, a cost-minimization analysis given the authors' findings of no statistical difference in success rates among therapies. The study was conducted through retrospective chart review and analyzed costs from the perspective of the institution, although this is not clearly stated in the text. Costs included for analyses were only those associated with ingredient, administration costs and administration time. Cefotetan was found to cost less than Cefoxitin, and other combination antibiotics, in the treatment of anaerobic infections.

Self-Assessment Questions

1. What is the primary difference between cost-minimization analysis and cost analysis?
   A. Cost analysis assumes that consequences are identical and, thus, are not measured.
   B. Cost-minimization analysis measures consequences and cost analysis does not.
   C. The perspective in cost-minimization analysis is usually from that of the payer, or institution.
   D. Cost analysis involves determining the least costly alternative among competing therapies.

2. Which one of the following statements regarding cost-minimization analysis is not true?
   A. Establishing equivalent outcomes is based solely on one's own expert clinical judgment.
   B. Cost-minimization analysis often involves a very detailed assessment of cost.
   C. Time and motion analysis is sometimes used to estimate personnel costs of drug administration.
   D. Differences between alternatives are related to cost differences alone.

3. Which one of the following statements is true regarding the process of researchers confirming equivalency of outcomes in cost-minimization analysis?
   A. Researchers should follow established guidelines within the literature.
   B. Equivalency should not be established through a prospectively conducted study.
   C. Confirming equivalency of outcomes is a subjective process.
   D. Researchers should incorporate techniques such as meta-analysis followed by statistical tests.

4. Which one of the following statements does not represent how outcomes are presented in CMA?
   A. Cost per unit of equivalent outcome.
   B. Total cost for each alternative.
   C. Classification of costs by cost category (e.g., acquisition costs or administration costs).
   D. Average per patient costs.

5. Cost-minimization analysis is applied to situations in which the outcomes of alternatives are equally efficacious. Which one of the following situations is not appropriately analyzed using cost-minimization analysis?
   A. Fluoxetine versus sertraline for the treatment of depression.
   B. Equipotent doses of naproxen and ibuprofen for osteoarthritis.
   C. Inpatient versus outpatient administration of the same medication (assume that differences in compliance is not an issue).
   D. Generic and brand-name product for the treatment of hypertension.

6. The following statements are factors to consider when conducting a cost-minimization analysis prospectively. Which one of the following statements is not true?
   A. Researchers should choose a fixed timeline to ensure that fair comparisons of outcomes among alternatives are made.
   B. An attempt to establish equivalency prior to conducting the analysis should be made.
   C. It is important to identify and measure all relevant costs and consequences.
   D. The perspective of the analysis should be determined prior to measuring costs and consequences.

7. Meta-analysis was described as a technique to summarize data on outcomes or effectiveness. Which one of the following statements concerning the use of meta-analysis in cost-minimization analysis is not true?
   A. In retrieving information, studies should be identified based on the pharmacoeconomic problem and established criteria for study inclusion.
   B. Using the results on effect size, statistical tests should be performed to determine equivalency.
   C. In cost-minimization analysis, meta-analysis is performed across all alternatives to obtain one overall effect size.
   D. Meta-analysis should be conducted prior to identifying and measuring costs.

8. Cost-minimization analysis and cost-effectiveness analysis are often confused within the literature. Which one of the following is the primary distinction between cost-minimization analysis and cost-effectiveness analysis?
   A. Consequences are measured in cost-effectiveness analysis, but not in cost-minimization analysis.
   B. In cost-minimization analysis, equivalence of outcomes takes into consideration both side effects and measures of effectiveness.
   C. Cost-minimization analysis includes a detailed assessment of costs.
   D. In cost-minimization analysis, outcomes are shown to be equivalent, while in cost-effectiveness analysis they are assumed unequivalent.

9. Establishing equivalency of outcomes is an important step in cost-minimization analysis. Which one of the following is not a factor influencing the method chosen to determine equivalence?
   A. The number of alternatives.
   B. Whether data are being gathered prospectively, or synthesized, from the literature.
   C. How outcomes are measured: continuous or categorical.
   D. The researcher's level of expertise in statistics.

10. Guidelines are available to assist researchers in conducting cost-minimization analysis. Which one of the following statements is *not* consistent with the guidelines presented?
   A. One step in conducting cost-minimization analysis is to identify the alternatives that would address the pharmacoeconomic problem.
   B. The presentation of results is an important step in cost-minimization analysis and often involves classifying costs into categories.
   C. If the timeline of the analysis goes beyond 1 year, researchers should discount costs.
   D. Seek the opinion of a local clinical expert when determining equivalency of outcomes.

Exercise

Exercise 1

You are a member of the P&T committee for a large urban hospital. A new third generation cephalosporin antibiotic has come onto the market called Cephamore® and the committee is scheduled to review the product in two weeks. Clinical studies have found that Cephamore® has a broad spectrum coverage, including gram positive, gram negative, and good anaerobic coverage. The advantage of Cephamore® is that it can be administered on a once daily IV dosing schedule. Additionally, no dosage adjustments are necessary for renal or hepatic impairment. The disadvantage is that it comes at a significantly higher price than comparable antibiotics on the formulary.

Results from clinical trials suggest that Cephamore® would be similar in efficacy to these products. Based on this and Cephamore's® higher cost, the committee is interested in conducting a CMA to determine the least cost alternative.

Your task for the P&T committee is to conduct a cost-minimization analysis (CMA) of Cephamore® compared to other equally efficacious antibiotics currently on the formulary. Given that the committee needs this information in two weeks, the study will be conducted retrospectively.

Please answer the following questions as a guide to conducting the analysis.

What products could potentially be used to compare with Cephamore®? What sources of information would you use to verify the assumption of equal efficacy? Assuming the analysis is from the perspective of the institution, what costs should be included in the analysis? Use the grid below to identify cost categories and the units of each cost that would be consumed per patient episode. After costs are identified, place a check in the appropriate box to indicate whether this cost would be incurred for each alternative.

What products could potentially be used to compare with Cephamore®?

The choice of alternatives is directed, in part, by the type of infectious agents these products would be used to treat. Because these agents would treat numerous infectious organisms, note the most common types of infections these agents are used to treat, or avert. It would be helpful to check with the hospitals micro lab (i.e., infectious disease team) to determine local organisms, and local patterns of resistance. Depending on the type of organism(s) to be evaluated, the choice of alternatives would include second or third generation cephalosporins, and possibly, other antibiotics, including aminoglycosides, or extended spectrum penicillins.

What sources of information would you use to verify equal efficacy?

Given the short time frame of the analysis, the primary source of information for existing antibiotics would be the literature. Clinical trial data available from the maker of Cephamore® would complete the information requirements.

Assuming the analysis is from the perspective of the institution, what costs should be included in the analysis?

Place a check mark in the appropriate column to indicate whether this cost would be incurred for each alternative. Also indicate the number of units that would be needed for each episode of care.

The cost categories identified in this analysis would include acquisition, personnel to prepare and administer the product (IV admixture procedures), and pharmacokinetic services. Pharmacokinetic services could be a potential area for cost differences, given that no dosage adjustments are necessary in cases of renal or hepatic impairment for Cephamore®. Finally, efficiencies in nurse time could be achieved, given the lower dosing frequency for Cephamore®. Efficiencies may not necessarily result in overall cost savings for the hospital, unless reductions in staffing results, which is unlikely.

The next step would be to identify the number of units per episode of care (e.g., if dosing of Cephamore® is to be done daily and the typical course of therapy lasts 5 days, then the number of units per episode for Cephamore® would be five). For nursing time, the unit might be measured as the number of minutes required for administration.

Cost Category	Cephamore®		Alternative 1		Alternative 2	
	Include	Units*	Include	Units*	Include	Units*

*Units per episode of care

COST-BENEFIT ANALYSIS

Jamie Barner, Ph.D., and
Karen Rascati, Ph.D.

Outline

I. Overview of cost-benefit analysis (CBA)

A. Definition

1. Cost-benefit analysis is an economic analysis that assesses whether the outcome (benefits) outweighs the inputs (costs) of a program or intervention.
2. This type of direct assessment can be made with CBA because both costs and benefits are quantified in monetary (e.g., United States dollar) terms.

B. Theory/History

1. The theoretical roots of CBA stem from welfare economics, which incorporates individual preferences and values to improve social welfare while balancing the effective use of resources.
2. CBA methodology was first used to help set policy for issues related to the environment (e.g., irrigation and flood control).
3. The first use of CBA in health care dates back to the 1960s when the benefits of a vaccination program for children were based on future productivity or earnings lost.

C. Examples of questions CBA may address

1. Do the benefits outweigh the costs of a program or intervention?
   a. Because costs and benefits are monetized, CBA can use a single measure to determine if the costs exceed the benefits.
2. Which program will provide the greatest benefit?
   a. When choosing among many health care programs, CBA can help decision makers understand which programs will
   give the greatest return on investment.

D. Advantages and disadvantages compared to other types of pharmacoeconomic studies

1. Advantages—CBA is unique because the costs and benefits are both valued in dollars. Measuring both costs and benefits in monetary terms has two major advantages:
   a. Decision makers can determine whether the benefits of a program or intervention exceed the costs of implementation.
   b. Decision makers can compare multiple programs or interventions with similar or unrelated outcomes.
2. Disadvantages—The unique aspect of placing a dollar value on the outcome or benefit (e.g., life-year saved) in CBA presents a challenge.
   a. Controversy arises regarding the methodology used to place a dollar value on a case prevented or a human life.
   b. It is difficult for researchers and decision makers to determine the value of a year of life saved.

II. Identify program or intervention and alternatives

A. Identify program or intervention

1. Before conducting a CBA, careful consideration must be given to the type of program or intervention to be implemented.
2. Several factors (e.g., organization goals, needs, and constraints) must be considered.

B. Identify alternatives

1. Alternatives must be considered and compared to the program or intervention of interest.
   a. "Do nothing" alternative is used in most cases. Thus, the new program or intervention is compared to not having the program or intervention.

b. Another alternative is to compare the program of interest to a similar program that is either smaller or larger in scale.

c. Another alternative is to implement a different program.

III. Types of costs and benefits

A. Categories

1. There are two categories of costs (medical and nonmedical) and three categories of benefits (direct benefits, indirect benefits, and intangible benefits).

B. Difference between costs versus benefits

1. In CBA, both costs and benefits are measured in dollar values. This can sometimes cause confusion because benefits are also "cost savings" or "costs avoided." It is important to make the distinction between the costs and benefits and to make sure that the two are properly placed within the equation.

C. Costs

1. Direct medical

a. Direct medical costs are the medically related inputs directly used to provide the treatment.

b. Examples of direct medical costs include the costs associated with the pharmaceuticals, laboratory tests, physician visits, pharmacist visits, emergency department visits, and hospitalizations.

2. Direct nonmedical

a. Direct nonmedical costs are costs directly associated with treatment, but are not medical in nature.

b. Examples of direct nonmedical costs would include the cost of traveling to and from the physician's office or the hospital, babysitting for the children of a patient, and food and lodging required for the patient and the patient's family during out-of-town treatment.

c. Other types of direct nonmedical costs include the costs of implementing a program or intervention. These costs include nonmedical personnel, space, advertising, supplies, and materials.

D. Benefits (Cost Savings)

1. Direct medical and direct nonmedical

a. As with direct costs, direct benefits encompass both direct medical and nonmedical expenditures. The difference between direct benefits and direct costs is that a direct benefit is the "cost avoided" or "potential savings" because of the program or intervention.

2. Indirect

a. Indirect benefits (cost savings) are the increased earnings or productivity gains that occurred because of the program or intervention.

b. Human capital (HC) is a method used to measure indirect benefits.

3. Intangible

a. Intangible costs include the costs of pain, suffering, anxiety, or fatigue that occur because of an illness or the treatment of an illness. Intangible benefits are the "cost savings" that result from a reduction in pain and suffering related to a program or intervention.

b. Although it is difficult to measure or assign values to intangible benefits, willingness to pay (WTP) is a method that is used to place a dollar value on these intangible outcomes.

IV. Measuring indirect and intangible benefits

A. Human Capital

1. Basic components for calculating HC: wage rate and missed time (days or years) because of illness.

2. Wage rate calculations—Depending on the type of study, a yearly wage rate or a daily wage rate is calculated.

a. A yearly wage rate (income/year) is calculated for a program or intervention that reduces long-term disability or death.

b. A daily wage rate (income/number of days worked per year) could be calculated for a program or intervention targeted at an acute or chronic illness with short-term disability.

3. Missed time (days or years) because of illness

a. If a yearly wage rate is calculated, then an assessment of the number of years lost because of a disease or illness is made.

b. If a daily wage rate is calculated, an assessment of the number of missed days because of illness is calculated.

i. Missed days because of illness fall into four groups: missed work, missed housekeeping, restricted activity days, and caregiver time.

4. Advantages

a. Straightforward and easy to measure

b. Income estimates are obtained or estimated from publicly available sources and days lost from illness are readily obtained from the patient or some other secondary source.

5. Disadvantages

a. Biased against various groups that, in general, are unemployed (e.g., children and the elderly)

b. Biased against low income individuals

c. Biased against disease states or conditions that have low or no impact on productivity (e.g., menopause)

B. Willingness to pay (WTP)

1. Willingness to pay is a method that can value both the indirect and intangible aspects (e.g., quality of life and satisfaction) of a disease or condition.

2. WTP determines how much people are willing to pay to reduce the chance of an adverse health outcome.

3. Contingent valuation, a direct method used to elicit the dollar values or the WTP amounts, includes two general elements: a hypothetical scenario and a bidding vehicle.

a. The hypothetical scenario should include a description of the health care program or intervention with the intent of providing the respondent with an accurate description of the good or service that they are being asked to value.

b. Bidding vehicles are designed using a variety of formats: open-ended questions, closed-ended questions, bidding game, or payment card.

4. Advantages

a. The main advantage of the WTP approach is that this approach places a dollar value on intangible benefits. Willingness to pay also incorporates patient preferences.

5. Disadvantages

a. There are several disadvantages to the WTP methodology. Many critics question the validity of the WTP responses because of the various methods used to elicit dollar values, as well as the hypothetical nature of the health benefit. It is difficult for people to place a dollar value on a health benefit or an increase in quality of life or satisfaction.

V. Calculating results of costs and benefits

A. Discounting

1. If costs and/or benefits are estimated based on dollars spent or saved in future years, an adjustment called *discounting*, is needed.

2. The discount rate typically used for health care interventions is 5 percent, but it is recommended that a sensitivity analysis of various rates be employed to determine whether the results are robust.

B. Net benefit (net cost) calculation

1 The net benefit (or net cost) calculation presents the difference between the total costs and benefits. Net benefit = total benefits – total costs; Net costs = total costs – total benefits.

2. For a program to be cost-beneficial using the net calculations: Net benefit ≥ 0 or Net cost < 0.

C. Benefit-cost (or cost-benefit) ratio calculations

1. If the time horizon for the project is 1 year or less, CBA can be calculated simply by summing up the total benefits and dividing by the total costs. The ratio may be expressed as BC or cost-benefit.

2. Depending on how the ratio is calculated, programs are cost-beneficial if: BC ≥ 1 or cost-benefit < 1.

D. Internal rate of return (IRR)

1. The internal rate of return is the rate of return that equates the PV of benefits to the PV of costs.

2. The decision rule for IRR is to accept all projects with an IRR greater than the "hurdle rate" or a specified discount rate.

3. Calculation of IRR is difficult to do by hand. Computer programs and special functions on calculators are available for determining the IRR.

E. Net present value (NPV)

1. Net present value is a method to determine the present value of a stream of costs (C) and benefits. The following formula can be used:

$$\sum_{t=0}^{n} \frac{B_t}{(1+r)^t} - \sum_{t=0}^{n} \frac{C_t}{(1+r)^t}$$

2. The decision rule for NPV is to accept all projects with a positive NPV and reject the rest. If two projects have a positive NPV, the project with the higher NPV is more cost-beneficial.

VI. Cost-benefit analysis in the literature

A. Of the four pharmacoeconomic methodologies, CBA is employed the least.

B. A review of the health care literature on CBA studies found that the most common application of CBA focuses on five broad areas: prevention strategies (58 percent); pharmaceuticals (25 percent); education and counseling (21 percent); screening strategies (18 percent); and diagnostic tests (17 percent).

VII. Evaluation of CBA articles

A. When evaluating a pharmacoeconomic study, the following 10 issues should be considered: title, study objectives, alternatives, perspective, valuation of costs, discounting, assumptions, sensitivity analyses, limitations, and potential bias.

VIII. Summary

A. Cost-benefit analysis differs from other pharmacoeconomic methods in that both the costs and benefits are measured in dollars.

B. Cost-benefit analysis can be useful in determining which program or intervention has the greatest benefit. In addition, it is a useful method for comparing multiple programs with varying outcomes.

C. Although CBA has the advantage of valuing indirect and intangible benefits, it is also a disadvantage because of the difficulty involved in valuing outcomes (e.g., productivity and quality of life).

Learning Objectives

1. Distinguish among cost-benefit analysis (CBA) studies and other types of pharmacoeconomic studies (e.g., cost-minimization analysis [CMA], cost-effectiveness analysis [CEA], and cost-utility analysis [CUA]).
2. Calculate the present value (PV) of a stream of costs and benefits.
3. Perform and interpret cost-benefit calculations—cost-benefit/benefit-cost ratios versus net benefit/net cost calculations.
4. Classify examples of cost information into the appropriate category (e.g., direct medical, direct nonmedical, indirect, or intangible).
5. Calculate productivity costs using the human capital (HC) approach.
6. Distinguish problems with both the HC and willingness-to-pay (WTP) methods of evaluating productivity costs.
7. Evaluate an abstract of a CBA study using the guidelines outlined in the text.

Abbreviations in this chapter

AIDS	acquired immunodeficiency syndrome
ADE	adverse drug event
BC	benefit-cost
CBA	cost-benefit analysis
CE	cost-effectiveness
CEA	cost-effectiveness analysis
CMA	cost-minimization analysis
CSP	clinical staff pharmacist
CUA	cost-utility analysis
HC	human capital
IRR	internal rate of return
NPV	net present value
PCSP	pharmaceutical care services program
PV	present value
WTP	willingness to pay

Overview of cost-benefit analysis

Definition

Cost-benefit analysis (CBA) is an economic analysis that can assess whether the outcomes (benefits) of a program or intervention outweigh the inputs (costs). This type of direct assessment can be made with CBA because both costs and benefits are quantified in monetary (dollar) terms. Cost-benefit analysis also can be defined using the following equation:

$$\frac{\text{Value of resources consumed (costs) from a program or intervention}}{\text{Value of outcome (benefits) from a program or intervention}}$$

Theory/History

The theoretical roots of CBA stem from welfare economics. Welfare economics is used to help make decisions regarding public policy by incorporating individual preferences and values to improve social welfare while balancing the effective use of resources. Some of the early social welfare issues in which CBA was used to help set policy involved the environment. In the 1800s and 1900s, CBA methodology was first used to help set policy for water projects, such as irrigation and flood control. Cost-benefit analysis was later applied to other public goods, such as wildlife, air quality, public parks, and health care. The first use of CBA in health care dates back to the 1960s. The costs and benefits of a vaccination program for children were assessed in 1961, where the benefits of the program were monetized by using wages to value lost productivity and reduced survival. (Note: This is referred to as the human capital [HC] approach, which is discussed in more detail in the Measuring indirect and intangible benefits: Human Capital section).

Examples of Questions CBA May Address

As the cost of health care continues to rise, many decision makers must decide which programs will be implemented. Pharmacists are working in many areas of health care, providing clinical services and developing specialty clinics in areas such as anticoagulation, diabetes, asthma, osteoporosis, human immunodeficiency *virus*, and acquired immunodeficiency syndrome (AIDS). Although clinical pharmacy programs have shown improvements in clinical outcomes such as glycemic control and bone density, financial pressures are forcing decision makers to consider the following questions: 1) Do the benefits of a program or intervention outweigh the costs?; and 2) Which program will provide the greatest benefit? Cost-benefit analysis is a tool that can be used to address these questions.

Advantages and Disadvantages Compared to Other Types of Pharmacoeconomic Studies

There are four types of pharmacoeconomic studies: cost-minimization analysis (CMA), cost-effectiveness analysis (CEA), CBA, and cost-utility analysis (CUA). Each method measures costs in dollars, but they differ regarding how outcomes are measured. Cost-minimization analysis has the advantage of being the easiest to conduct because the outcomes are assumed to be equivalent; thus, only the costs of the intervention are compared. The advantage of the CMA method is also its disadvantage: CMA cannot be used when outcomes of interventions are different. Thus, the type of interventions that can be evaluated with this method may be limited. The most commonly used pharmacoeconomic method, CEA, measures outcomes in natural units (e.g., mm Hg, cholesterol levels, symptom-free days, and life-years saved). The main advantage of this approach is that the outcomes are easier to quantify compared to CBA or CUA. The main disadvantage of CEA is that programs with different types of outcomes cannot be compared. Cost-utility analysis measures outcomes based on utilities or preferences. The advantage of this method is that it incorporates patient and/or society preferences for specific health states. The main disadvantage is that there is no consensus on how to measure the reliability and validity of these preferences or utilities.

When comparing the four economic methods (e.g., CMA, CEA, CBA, and CUA), CBA is unique in that not only are costs valued in dollars, but benefits also are valued in dollars. Measuring both costs and benefits in monetary terms has two major advantages: 1) decision makers can determine whether the benefits of a program or intervention exceed the costs of implementation; and 2) decision makers

Table 1. Comparison of CEA and CBA

Programs or interventions	Cost-effectiveness ratio	Benefit-cost ratio
AIDS prevention and awareness program	$230,000/case prevented	8.4
Vaccination program for children	$104,000/case prevented	0.3
Smoking cessation intervention	$3,700/patient who quit	6.7
Diabetes drug adherence program	$67/normoglycemic patient	15.1
Breast cancer screening program	$50,000/life-year saved	2.4

AIDS = acquired immunodeficiency sydrome; CBA = cost-benefit analysis; CEA = cost-effectiveness analysis can compare multiple programs/interventions with similar or unrelated outcomes. Table 1 shows examples of various programs/interventions, and their corresponding cost-effectiveness and cost-benefit ratios (Note: CBA ratios are expressed as benefit-cost (BC), where the higher the number, the more cost-beneficial).

A decision maker must choose one program from Table 1 to implement in the organization. The decision maker may only have cost-effectiveness (CE) ratios available to help make the choice. How would the choice be made? It can be seen quickly that it would be difficult to compare the programs using only CE ratios because of the varying types of outcomes (e.g., case prevented or life-years saved). On the other hand, the BC ratios can be ranked and programs with similar, as well as dissimilar outcomes can be compared. In addition, the decision maker can determine which programs' costs will exceed the benefit and vice versa. If the goal of the decision maker is to maximize the investment, the program with the highest BC ratio (i.e., diabetes drug adherence program) is chosen. If only the CE ratios are available, it is more difficult to compare the value of the various programs.

The unique aspect of placing a dollar value on the outcome or benefit in CBA also presents a challenge or disadvantage of the method. For example, when comparing the CE ratios for an AIDS prevention and awareness program and the vaccination program for children, it appears that the vaccination program is the most cost-effective. But when examining the BC ratios, the AIDS program is more cost-beneficial. Cost-benefit analysis uses methods (which are discussed in more detail in the Measuring indirect and intangible benefits: Human Capital section) to value morbidity or mortality lost from a human life. In this example, the benefit (case prevented) was valued higher for AIDS patients than for children. The controversy arises regarding the methodology used to place a dollar value on a case prevented or a human life. Thus, the advantage of placing a dollar value on the benefit or outcome is also a disadvantage of the method.

As previously discussed, CBA has some advantages over the other pharmacoeconomic methods. Conducting a CBA involves several steps. Figure 1 provides an overall view of steps required to conduct a CBA.

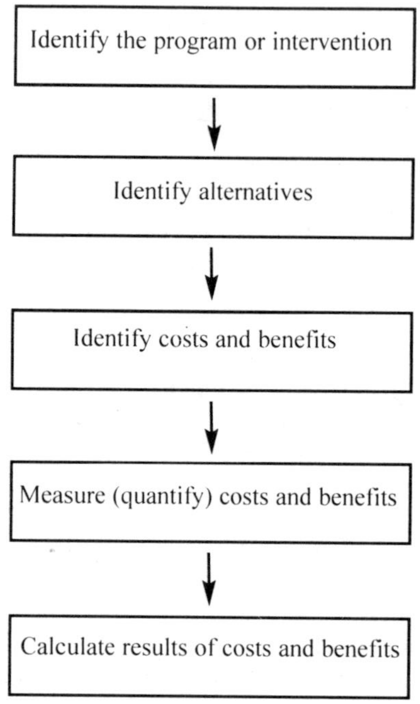

Figure 1. Steps in conducting a cost-benefit analysis

Identify program or intervention and alternatives

The first step in a CBA is to determine the type of program or intervention to be considered; the second step is to identify alternatives. In many cases, the alternative is to "do nothing." In other cases, the alternative could be to implement a similar program that is smaller or larger in scale, or to implement a different program. For example, a clinical pharmacist would like to start an asthma clinic. The alternative could be to compare the costs and benefits of having an asthma clinic to not having an asthma clinic. Another alternative could be to compare implementing an asthma clinic for all people who had an asthma-related emergency department visit. A third alternative could be to compare implementing an asthma clinic to implementing a diabetes clinic.

To illustrate the components of a CBA, the example of an asthma clinic is used. The clinic will focus on people with asthma who have had an asthma-related emergency department visit. These people automatically would be referred to a clinical pharmacist, who would provide education on managing asthma. These clinical pharmacy services could include education on triggers, drug adherence, and use of peak flow meter and inhaler. In this example, the alternative is no asthma clinic. Once the program or intervention and alternatives are identified, the next step is to identify the costs and benefits.

Types of costs and benefits

Figure 2 shows the basic components of CBA. There are two categories of costs (medical and nonmedical) and three categories of benefits (i.e., direct benefits, indirect benefits, and intangible benefits). Cost-benefit analysis can incorporate as few as one category of benefits, or as many as all three of the benefit categories. When only costs and direct benefits are measured, some researchers do not consider this to be a "true" CBA. This type of measurement is sometimes categorized as a "cost-comparison." Some researchers only consider an analysis to be a "true" CBA if, in addition to the direct benefits, either the indirect benefits and/or the intangible benefits are incorporated into the analysis. Before starting any pharmacoeconomic analysis, the perspective of the study should be determined. Because of its focus on social welfare and policy and the incorporation of indirect and/or intangible benefits, CBA should be conducted from the societal perspective.

Difference between costs versus benefits

In CBA, both costs and benefits are measured in dollar values. This can sometimes cause confusion because benefits are also "cost savings" or "costs avoided." Costs and direct benefits are categorized as medical or nonmedical (see Figure 2). For example, in the asthma program, a cost to the program could be an increase in medical costs related to visits to the pharmacists. A "cost saving" or benefit as a result of the program could be a reduction in medical costs for an asthma-related emergency department visits. The distinction between the two must be made and clinicians should make sure that costs and benefits are properly placed within the equation. The Costs section discusses the four types of "costs" (direct medical, direct nonmedical, indirect, and intangible). In CBA, these "costs" also can be "cost savings" or benefits, depending on the intervention or program.

Costs

Direct Medical

"Direct medical costs" are the most obvious costs to measure. These are the medically related inputs used directly to provide the treatment. Examples of direct medical costs include the costs associated with the drugs, laboratory tests, physician visits, pharmacist visits, emergency department visits, and hospitalizations.

Using the example of the asthma clinic, patients are automatically referred to the pharmacist for a visit. The pharmacist may order additional laboratory tests or suggest additional drugs, or counsel patients about drug adherence. Thus, the direct medical costs would include pharmacist visits, laboratory tests, and drugs.

Direct Nonmedical

"Direct nonmedical costs" are costs directly associated with treatment but are not medical in nature. Examples of direct nonmedical costs include the cost of traveling to and from the physician's office or the hospital, babysitting for the children of a patient, and food and lodging required for the patient and the patient's family during out-of-town treatment. Other types of direct nonmedical costs include the costs of implementing a program or intervention (e.g., nonmedical personnel, space, advertising, supplies, and materials).

Using the example of the asthma clinic, patients would have increased travel and time costs related to visiting the pharmacist. Additional nonmedical personnel may be needed in addition to space (or renovation), as well as supplies and materials (e.g., peak flow meter, videotapes, and brochures).

Benefits (Cost Savings)

Direct Medical and Direct Nonmedical

In CBA, the outcome variable, benefits, is also measured in dollars. There are three categories of benefits: direct, indirect, and intangible (see Figure 2). Direct benefits, similar to direct costs, encompass both direct medical and nonmedical expenditures. The difference between the two is that a direct benefit is the "cost avoided" or "potential savings" because of the program or intervention.

For example, assume that the clinical pharmacy services provided in the asthma clinic resulted in better patient self-management. The result of better self-management could be related to a decrease in physician visits, emergency department visits, or hospitalizations, resulting in a "potential savings" or a direct medical benefit.

Indirect

Indirect benefits (cost savings) are the increased earnings or productivity gains that occurred because of the program or intervention. "Indirect costs" involve the costs that result from the loss of productivity because of illness or death. For example, the asthma clinic may help decrease the number of days lost from work or days in bed because of complications from asthma, such as attacks or increased susceptibility to upper respiratory tract infections. Indirect benefits can be measured using the HC approach (Note: The methodology for calculating these benefits is discussed in the Measuring indirect and intangible benefits: Human Capital section). The accounting term "indirect costs", which is used to assign overhead, is different from the economic term, which

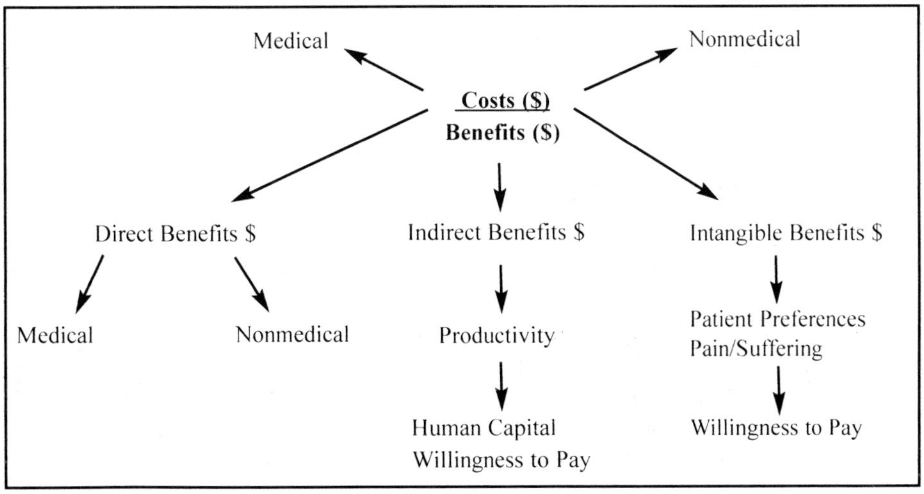

Figure 2. Components of cost-benefit analysis

refers to a loss of productivity of the patient or the patient's family because of illness.

Intangible

Intangible costs include the costs of pain, suffering, anxiety, or fatigue that occur because of an illness or the treatment of an illness. Intangible benefits are the "cost savings" that result from a reduction in pain and suffering related to a program or intervention. One intangible benefit of the asthma clinic may be avoiding the panic and fear that are associated with an asthma-related emergency department visit. Another intangible benefit may include the benefit of being able to participate in sports activities or other physical events. Although it is difficult to measure or assign values to intangible benefits, willingness to pay (WTP) is a method (details of the method are discussed in the Measuring indirect and intangible benefits: Willingness to Pay section) that is used to place a dollar value on these intangible outcomes.

Treatment of an illness may include all four types of costs and benefits. For example, the cost of surgery would include the direct medical costs of the surgery (e.g., drugs, room charges, laboratory tests, and physician services), direct nonmedical costs (e.g., travel and lodging for the pre-operation day), indirect costs (e.g., cost because of the patient missing work during the surgery and recuperative period), and intangible costs (because of pain and anxiety). Most studies only report the direct medical costs, which may be appropriate, depending on the objective of the study. For example, if the objective is to measure the costs to the hospital for two surgical procedures that differ in direct medical costs (e.g., using high-dose versus low-dose aprotinin in cardiac bypass surgery), but that are expected to have similar nonmedical, indirect, and intangible costs, measuring all four types of costs may not be warranted. The next section discusses the methods used to measure indirect and intangible benefits.

Measuring indirect and intangible benefits

Human Capital

As previously discussed, indirect benefits are increases in productivity or earnings because of a program or intervention. The HC approach is one way to measure indirect benefits. Human capital estimates wage and productivity losses because of illness, disability, or death. The HC approach assumes that the value of health benefits equal the economic productivity that those values permit. There are two basic components to calculating HC: wage rate and missed time (days or years) because of illness. Because the HC approach is based on wages, it is necessary to have some estimate of income. Income estimates can be obtained from several sources: the Census Bureau, the Bureau of Labor and Statistics, self-report, or any other data source that provides income estimates based on gender, age, or occupation. Missed time (days or years) because of illness can be obtained by self-report from either primary or secondary data sources.

Wage Rate Calculations

Depending on the type of study, a yearly wage rate or a daily wage rate can be calculated. A yearly wage rate (income/year) is calculated for a program or intervention that reduces long-term disability or death. For example, a pneumococcal vaccination program for the elderly might result in preventing premature death. Thus, it is appropriate to use a yearly wage rate and assess the value of the number of years saved because of the intervention. Income or wages should include fringe benefits.

A daily wage rate (income ÷ number of days worked per year) could be calculated for a program or intervention targeted at an acute or chronic illness with short-term disability. A person may not be adversely affected by the disease state on a continual basis, but may have short-term periodic disability. For example, asthma, a chronic disease state, may include episodic asthma attacks. Thus, a person may only experience problems with the disease state on a periodic basis. For this type of disease state, a daily wage rate would be calculated. To calculate a daily wage rate (income ÷ number of days worked per year), both income and number of days worked per year must be assessed. It is assumed that the average person works 240 days a year when accounting for weekends, vacation, and sick leave. A formula to calculate number of days worked per year is:

number of days in a year (365) – number of weekend days (104) – number of vacation days (14) – number of sick leave days (7) = 240.

Missed Time (Days or Years) Because of Illness

If a yearly wage rate is calculated, then assessment of the number of years lost because of a disease or illness must be made. If a daily wage rate is calculated, an assessment of the number of missed days because of illness must be calculated. Because most pharmaceutical interventions involve chronic disease states with intermittent episodes, an example calculating the daily wage rate and number of missed days will be used. Missed days because of illness fall into four groups (see Table 2). For housekeeping and caregiving, estimates of productivity loss are estimated

Table 2. Categories of missed days

Categories	Definition
Missed work	Days missed from work (for employed)
Missed housekeeping	Days missed from housekeeping (for unemployed)
Restricted activity days	Percent of time where work/housekeeping was restricted Did not miss an entire day of work/housekeeping but not productive for part of the day
Caregiver time	Time spent by a relative or friend providing care for a person suffering from an illness.

(imputed) even though no payments are directly associated with these activities.

Using the asthma clinic example, an indirect benefit is calculated. If the population served by the clinic are adults with an average income of $40,000 and 240 days worked per year (365 – weekends – 2 weeks vacation – 1 week sick leave), the daily wage rate (average income/number of days worked per year) is $40,000 ÷ 240 = $167/day. An average of 20 days a year were missed from work before participating in the asthma clinic and an average of 7 days a year were missed from work after participating in the asthma clinic. Multiplying the daily wage rate times the number of missed days results in the value of lost productivity. In other words, the value of 20 days lost from work is $3340 and the value of 7 days lost from work is $1169. The difference between before and after the program is $2171, which is the cost savings or the indirect benefit of the program or intervention. See Table 3 for the calculation.

Advantages

Measuring indirect benefits using the HC approach has several advantages. It is fairly straightforward and easy to measure. Income estimates can be obtained or estimated from publicly available sources, and days lost from illness can be readily obtained from the patient or some other secondary source.

Disadvantages

The HC approach has several disadvantages. The primary concern with using the HC approach is that it is biased against specific groups of people, namely the unemployed. It assumes that if a person is not working, that person has little or no economic benefit. Bias can occur regarding children and the unemployed elderly. In the example (see Table 1) of BC ratios for the AIDS awareness and prevention program (BC = 8.4) and the vaccination program for children (BC = 0.3), using the HC method, the value of productivity gained from the AIDS program is higher than the vaccination program, simply because the economic value of children is zero (i.e., they are not employed). A similar situation could occur with a program to prevent or manage hip fractures in the elderly because many elderly are unemployed or receive lower wages compared to adult nonelderly.

The HC assumption that the value of health benefits equals the economic productivity they permit also may be biased. The earnings for some individuals may not equal the value of their output. For example, there is a large difference between the daily wage rate of a professional football player compared to a school teacher.

The HC method also does not incorporate values for pain and suffering if it does not impact productivity. There may be certain disease states or conditions (e.g., menopause or hair loss) that may not impact productivity, but affect a person's quality of life. For example, many women experience problems with menopause, including moodiness, hot flashes and irregular cycles. Although this condition may have a significant impact on quality of life, most women do not miss a day of work because of complications from menopause. Thus, the HC method is not sensitive enough to capture the benefits of a pharmacist-provided menopause clinic. Although biases exist with this method, it is the most commonly used method to measure indirect benefits.

Willingness to Pay

Willingness to pay is a method that can value both the indirect and intangible aspects of a disease or condition. Willingness to pay determines how much people are willing to pay to reduce the chance of an adverse health outcome. The WTP method is grounded in welfare economic theory and incorporates patient preferences and intangible benefits such as quality of life. Contingent valuation, where the respondent is asked to value a contingent or hypothetical market, is a direct method that is used to elicit the dollar values or the WTP amounts. Willingness-to-pay values can be collected through face-to-face interviews, mail, telephone, or through the Internet. To elicit WTP values, respondents are presented with a hypothetical market describing the benefits of a particular health care intervention (e.g., program, drugs, and equipment). Respondents are then asked to value the health care intervention in a dollar amount, percent of income, or health care premium. Measuring WTP using the contingent valuation method should include two general elements: a hypothetical scenario and a bidding vehicle. Additional information on contingent valuation is available (Reference 5).

Hypothetical Scenario

The hypothetical scenario should include a description of the health care program or intervention (e.g., disease state management program and new drug therapy). The intent of the scenario is to provide an accurate description of the good or service that the respondent is being asked to value. In addition, the scenario should detail the amount of time the respondent should expect to spend to receive the health care program, as well as the benefit (e.g., percentage of

Table 3. Calculation of indirect benefit—missed work

	Daily wage rate	Number of missed days/year	Value of lost productivity
Before	$167	20	$3340
After	$167	7	$1169
		Indirect benefit per person (value of increase productivity)	**$2171**

improvement in their condition) of the intervention. An example of a hypothetical scenario for the asthma clinic might read:

Patients with asthma have improved their condition by learning more about their disease and by taking their drugs as directed. Pharmacists can help people with asthma understand their condition and the drugs used to treat it. In addition, pharmacists can:

- Help the patients learn how to use a peak flow meter and an inhaler.
- Help the patients better manage the drugs used to treat asthma.
- Help the patients recognize and handle situations when asthma attacks occur.
- Monitor the patient's asthma by keeping a record on file and following up on a regular basis to assess progress.
- Contact the patient's doctor and report any changes in the patient's health.

An initial visit with your pharmacist would include an educational program on managing your disease state. This type of service is available by appointment only and would last about 1 hour. Assume that the program would result in a 50 percent improvement in your asthma.

Bidding Vehicles

Once the program or intervention has been adequately described, respondents are then asked to "bid" or place a value on the program or intervention. Bids can be obtained through a variety of formats: open-ended questions; closed-ended questions; a bidding game; or a payment card. The following sections contain brief descriptions of each of the methods.

Open-ended Questions

Open-ended questions simply ask how much the respondent would be willing to pay for the program or intervention. This question should immediately follow the hypothetical scenario.

Example: What is the maximum amount that you would be willing to pay for a 1 hour consultation with a pharmacist? ________________

The respondent would then write in a maximum WTP amount. This method is least used because it results in WTP values that vary widely. Many people do not know how to value health care programs because they do not normally pay the full amount out of pocket. The other methods discussed provide the respondent with more guidance in determining their maximum WTP.

Closed-ended Questions

Closed-ended questions also are called "take-it-or-leave-it" or dichotomous choice questions. The question asked is whether the respondent will pay a specified dollar amount for the program or intervention.

Example: Would you be willing to pay $60 for a one-hour consultation with a pharmacist?

___Yes ____No

This method more closely resembles the market place. When consumers shop for products, they must decide based on the price of the product whether to "take-it-or-leave-it." One drawback to this method is that only one question and, thus, one WTP value can be elicited from a respondent. Thus, a large sample is required to determine the overall WTP value.

Bidding Game

The bidding game resembles an auction, in that several bids are offered to reach a person's maximum WTP amount. Before soliciting a second response, the bids are adjusted based on the first response. This iteration could go on many times, but it is suggested that three times is optimal.

Example: Would you be willing to pay $60 for a one-hour consultation with a pharmacist?

___Yes
___No

If "yes," would you be willing to pay $80?

___Yes
___No

If "no," would you be willing to pay $40?

___Yes
___No

This method is useful to arrive at a person's maximum WTP value. It is time consuming and is best conducted face to face or via the Internet. In addition, the WTP values can be biased depending on how high (or low) the first bid is. This is called starting point bias.

Payment Card

The payment card method provides the respondent with a list of possible WTP amounts (i.e. payment card) from which to choose.

Example: What is the maximum amount that you are willing to pay for a one-hour consultation with a pharmacist? Please circle your choice.

$150	$90	$30
$130	$70	$10
$110	$50	$0

This method is easy to use and it provides the respondent with a range of values from which to choose. The advantages of the method also can result in disadvantages. Providing respondents with a range of values can bias their WTP values. The range provided can "suggest" the value of the intervention and influence the response. Also, starting point bias can influence the WTP amount. For example, if the range of values was $0 – $75 versus $0 – $150, the respondents' WTP amount can vary depending on which range or starting point was provided.

The National Oceanic and Atmospheric Administration Recommendation

The National Oceanic and Atmospheric Administration (NOAA) convened an expert panel in 1993 to determine guidelines for conducting contingent valuation. Although the organization is primarily concerned with environmental issues, the panel's recommendations apply to the health care sector. The NOAA recommends face-to-face interviews and the dichotomous choice (closed-ended questions) bidding vehicle. Face-to-face interviews are time consuming and cost prohibitive for most studies. The use of the dichotomous choice format requires a large sample size to accommodate the varying bid levels. Although these are the preferred methods, most studies in the literature have used mail surveys and the payment card format.

Advantages

The main advantage of the WTP approach is that it places a dollar value on intangible benefits. It is also grounded in welfare economic theory, which embodies patient preferences and choice.

Disadvantages

There are several disadvantages to the WTP methodology. Many critics question the validity of the WTP responses because of the various methods used to elicit dollar values as well as the hypothetical nature of the health care benefit. It is difficult for people to place a dollar value on a health benefit or an increase in quality of life or satisfaction. Because a "hypothetical" scenario is presented, it is possible that respondents might give a "hypothetical response" or that the value of the market (e.g., pharmaceutical care program) being presented may not be understood. The methodology for collecting valid and reliable WTP values is ongoing.

Another disadvantage of this method is the bias involved in measuring WTP. Compliance bias occurs when the respondent wants to "please" the interviewer and may overstate the respondent's WTP values. Strategic bias occurs when respondents over- or understate the WTP values to strategically impact the outcome. For example, a respondent may understate a WTP value so that the respondent will not have to pay as much. Other biases with the bidding vehicles (e.g., range bias and starting point bias) were explained in the Bidding Game and Payment Card sections.

Calculating results of costs and benefits

Once all costs and benefits have been identified and quantified, the results of the analysis must be presented in ways that help decision makers understand the value of the program or intervention. Cost-benefit analysis can be presented in the following three formats: net benefit calculations, BC ratios, and internal rate of return (IRR). When evaluating programs, the method used must be assessed. Another issue that should be considered when choosing a method for displaying the results is the time horizon for the project. If the project spans for more than 1 year, it is important to use discounting.

Discounting

If costs and/or benefits are estimated based on dollars spent or saved in future years, an adjustment called *discounting*, is needed. There is a time-value associated with money. Most people (and businesses) prefer to receive money today, rather than at a later time. Therefore, a dollar received today is worth more than a dollar received next year. Using a "discount rate" that estimates the time-value of money, the present value (PV) of future expenditures and savings can be calculated. This calculation is presented in the following section.

Another issue that also must be considered when discounting is what rate to use. The discount rate typically used for health care interventions is 5 percent, but it is recommended that a sensitivity analysis of various rates be used to determine whether the results are robust.

Net Benefit (Net Cost) Calculation

The net benefit (or net cost) calculation simply presents the difference between the total costs and benefits. Net benefit = total benefits - total costs, Net costs = total costs - total benefits. For a program to be cost-beneficial using the net calculations:

Net benefit ≥ 0 or Net cost < 0.

If the time horizon for the project is more than 1 year, then discounting (or PV) should be used to take into account the time-value of money.

The following formula can be used to determine the net benefit or net present value (NPV):

$$\sum_{t=0}^{n} \frac{B_t}{(1+r)^t} - \sum_{t=0}^{n} \frac{C_t}{(1+r)^t}$$

The discount factor is equal to $1 \div (1 + r)^t$, where r is the discount rate and t is the year the cost or savings occur. The decision rule for NPV is to accept all projects with a positive NPV and reject the rest. If two projects have a positive NPV, the one with the higher NPV is more cost-beneficial.

For example, if the costs of a new pharmaceutical care program are \$5000 per year for the next 3 years, and the discount rate is 5 percent, the present value of these costs is \$14,297 [the sum of \$5000 for the beginning year + \$5000 $\div$ 1.05 for the next year + \$5000 $\div (1.05)^2$ for the third year]. This means that the *PV* of these costs is \$14,297 (less than the total of \$15,000 if costs were all due now). For benefits, a similar calculation can be conducted. If it is expected that \$5000 in benefits will be reaped the beginning year, but \$10,000 the next year and \$15,000 the third year, the total present value of these benefits would be \$ 28,129 [the sum of \$5000 for year 1 + \$10,000 $\div$ 1.05 for year 2 + \$15,000 $\div (1.05)^2$ for year 3]. The PV of benefits minus the PV of costs is a positive NPV = \$13,832 [\$28,129 - \$14,297]. Thus, the project could be accepted.

Benefit-cost (or Cost-Benefit) Ratio Calculations

If the time horizon for the project is 1 year or less, CBA can be calculated simply by summing up the total benefits and dividing by the total costs. The ratio may be expressed as BC or cost-benefit. Depending on how the ratio is calculated, programs are cost-beneficial if:

BC ratio ≥ 1 or cost-benefit ratio < 1.

Example Using BC and Net Benefit Calculations

A decision maker has to choose between two proposals for implementation. The projects are for 1 year; thus, discounting is not needed.

Proposal A: Cost = \$1000 Benefit = \$2000
Proposal B: Cost = \$5000 Benefit = \$7500

Table 4 shows the ratio and net benefit calculations for both proposals. Although four calculations are shown in the table, the *BC ratio* (compared to the cost-benefit ratio) and the *net benefit calculation* (compared to the net cost calculation) are used most often because the higher the result, the more cost-beneficial.

Table 4. Comparison of two proposals using ratios and net calculations

	Proposal A	Proposal B
Benefit-cost	\$2000 ÷ \$1000 = 2.0	\$7500 ÷ \$5000 = 1.5
Cost-benefit	\$1000 ÷ \$2000 = 0.5	\$5000 ÷ \$7500 = 0.7
Net benefit	\$2000 – \$1000 = \$1000	\$7500 – \$5000 = \$2500
Net cost	\$1000 – \$2000 = –\$1000	\$5000 - \$7500 = –\$2500

Using the criteria previously discussed for cost-beneficial programs, it is apparent that both programs are cost-beneficial using the ratio method. However, proposal A is more cost beneficial than proposal B (BC ratio = 2.0 vs. 1.5). When using the net calculation, it also is apparent that both programs are cost-beneficial (net benefit $\geq$ 0), but proposal B becomes more cost-beneficial compared to proposal A (net benefit = \$2500 versus \$1000). Thus, the ratio and the net calculation may produce different results.

In this example, where both proposals are cost-beneficial, the decision maker may consider other issues, such as the amount of money available for investment. Proposal A would require input costs of \$1000, whereas proposal B would require \$5000. Another consideration may involve the return on investment. Proposal A, with a 2:1 BC ratio, has a higher return than proposal B (i.e., 1.5:1 BC ratio). A third consideration is the actual net benefit amount. Proposal B has a higher net benefit than proposal A (\$2500 vs. \$1000). The choice between Proposals A and B depends on the goals (both programmatic and financial) of the organization.

If the time horizon for the project is more than 1 year, then PV should be used to take into account the time value of money. The following is a formula to calculate the BC ratio using PV or discounting calculations:

$$\sum_{t=0}^{n} \frac{B_t}{(1+r)^t} \div \sum_{t=0}^{n} \frac{C_t}{(1+r)^t}$$

For the example presented in the "net benefit" section, the PV of benefits was \$28,129 and the PV of costs was \$14,297. The benefit-to-cost ratio is 1.97 (\$28,129 ÷ \$14,297).

Internal Rate of Return

The internal rate of return is the rate of return that equates the PV of benefits to the PV of costs. The goal is to find the rate of return that makes the costs and benefits equal. Once the IRR is calculated, it is compared to a specified "hurdle rate," or a discount rate. The decision rule for IRR is to accept all projects with an IRR greater than the "hurdle rate" or discount rate. If the IRR is greater than the "hurdle rate," then the project can yield a higher rate of return compared to some other investment. Calculation of IRR is difficult to do by hand. Computer programs and special functions on calculators are available for determining the IRR. The IRR for the pharmaceutical care program previously discussed is 6.3 percent. If the market rate of return is 4.5 percent, this is the "hurdle rate." Because 6.3 percent exceeds 4.5 percent, the pharmaceutical care program should be chosen because it will yield a greater return than investing it on the market.

Cost-benefit analysis in the literature

Of all of the four pharmacoeconomic methodologies, CBA is used the least. A review of the health care literature on CBA studies found that the most common application of CBA focuses on five broad areas: prevention strategies (58 percent); pharmaceuticals (25 percent); education and counseling (21 percent); screening strategies (18 percent); and diagnostic tests (17 percent) (Reference 2). Preventive strategies include various types of vaccination programs for infections such as influenza and hepatitis B. Most of the studies that were categorized as pharmaceutical comparisons were studies that involved the vaccine in the preventive strategies studies. Education and counseling included both asthma and diabetes education programs. Screening strategies focused on cancer screenings and more recently screening for HIV/AIDS, particularly in pregnant women.

Because of the difficulties in measuring and in incorporating indirect and intangible benefits, many of the studies in the literature measured direct costs and direct benefits only. As previously discussed, some researchers do not consider this to be a "true" CBA. There are many studies that just focus on measuring HC (indirect costs) or WTP (intangible costs) without incorporation into a CBA. The following section provides the methods for evaluating pharmacoeconomic studies in the literature.

Evaluation of CBA articles

Several authors cite methodology to assist in systematically reviewing the pharmacoeconomic literature (Reference 13). If a study is carefully reviewed to ensure the author(s) included all meaningful components of an economic evaluation, the likelihood of finding valid and useful results is high. When evaluating a pharmacoeconomic study, the following ten issues should be considered: title; study objectives; alternatives; perspective; valuation of costs; discounting; assumptions; sensitivity analyses; limitations; and potential bias. The following questions illustrate what type of questions should be raised when reviewing pharmacoeconomic studies.

1. Is the title appropriate? From reading the title, can it be determined what is being compared and what type of study is being conducted (CMA, CBA, CEA, CUA, or a combination of these)?
2. Is a clear objective stated? Was a well-defined question posed in an answerable form? The specific questions and hypotheses (if applicable) should be clearly stated at the beginning of the article.
3. Were the appropriate alternatives considered and explained in detail? Ideally the most effective

treatments or alternatives should be compared. In pharmacotherapy evaluations, many times the makers of innovative new products will compare or measure themselves against a standard (i.e., older, more well established) therapy. This selection should include the best clinical options and/or the options that are used most often in that setting at the time of the study. If a clinician is considering a new treatment option, comparing it with an outdated treatment or a treatment with low efficacy rates is a waste of time and money. This new treatment should be compared with the next best alternative or the alternative it may end up replacing. The alternatives may include drug treatments and nondrug treatments. Head-to-head comparisons of the best alternatives provide more information than comparing a new product or service with an outdated or ineffective alternative. In many CBAs, the options may be thought of as a "with or without" option. The comparison of a service or a preventive therapy (e.g., a vaccination or immunization) is compared to the alternative of not implementing this service or providing the preventive therapy. Was a comprehensive description of the competing alternatives given? If products are compared, dosage and length of therapy should be included. If services are compared, explicit details of the services make the paper more useful. Could another researcher replicate the study based on the information given?

4. Is the perspective of the study addressed? From whose perspective will analysis be conducted? The perspective will determine the costs to be evaluated. Is the analysis being conducted from the perspective of the patient or from the hospital, clinic, insurance company, or society? Depending on the perspective assigned to the analysis, different results and recommendations based on those results may be identified. The perspective should be explicitly stated, not implied.
5. Were all the important and relevant costs and outcomes included? All resources consumed and outcomes assessed in each alternative should be identified and measured in monetary value. The costs and benefits for each alternative should be listed and estimated. If these costs are estimated from other research or source material, these should be referenced. Are all pertinent costs and benefits mentioned? The authors' list should be compared to the readers' practice situation. Was there justification for any important costs or consequences that were not included? Sometimes, the authors will admit that although certain costs or consequences were important, they were impractical (or impossible) to measure in the study. It is better that the authors state these limitations than to ignore them.
6. Was discounting appropriate? If so, was it conducted? If the costs or benefits are extrapolated more than 1 year out, the time-value of money must be incorporated into the cost estimates.
7. Are assumptions stated? When a precise number is not available, an estimate might be used. These estimates may be referred to as "assumptions." Many of the values used in pharmacoeconomic studies are based on assumptions. For example, authors may assume the side effect rate is 5 percent or that compliance with a regimen will be 80 percent. These types of assumptions should be stated explicitly. For important assumptions, was the estimate varied within a reasonable range of values?
8. Were sensitivity analyses conducted for these assumptions? A *sensitivity analysis* allows researchers to determine how the results of an analysis would change when these "best guesses", or assumptions are varied over a relevant range of values. For example, if the researcher makes the assumption that the appropriate discount rate is 5 percent, this estimate should be varied from 0 percent to 10 percent to determine if the same alternative is still chosen within this range. This method helps determine the "robustness" of the analysis. Do small changes in estimates produce significant differences in the results?
9. Were limitations addressed? No study is perfect; hence, the authors should mention the most important limitations. Using retrospective data may increase the possibility of selection bias. Using a specific population may limit generalizability of results. Small sample sizes or missing data may limit statistical comparisons. It is better for the authors to address these limitations than to leave them unstated.
10. Was an unbiased summary of the results presented? Sometimes, the conclusions seem to overstate or overextrapolate the data presented in the results section. Did the authors use unbiased reasonable estimates when determining the results? In general, are the results of the study believable?

Summary

Cost-benefit analysis differs from other pharmacoeconomic methods in that both the costs and benefits are measured in dollars. Cost-benefit analysis can be useful in determining which program or intervention has the greatest benefit. In addition, it is a useful method for comparing multiple programs with varying outcomes. Cost-benefit analysis values indirect benefits using the HC approach and intangible benefits using the WTP approach. Both methods have several advantages and disadvantages, which can lead to biased or inaccurate estimates of indirect and intangible benefits. Although CBA has the advantage of monetarily valuing indirect and intangible benefits, it is also a disadvantage because of the difficulty involved in valuing outcomes such as productivity and quality of life.

Annotated Bibliography

1. Blumenschein K, Johannesson M. Use of contingent valuation to place a monetary value on pharmacy services: an overview and review of the literature. Clin Ther 1999;21(8):1402–17.

This article reviewed studies published between 1970 and 1999 that used the contingent valuation method (i.e., willingness-to-pay [WTP] method) to place a dollar value on pharmacy services. The authors provide a brief overview of the use of cost-benefit analysis (CBA) in valuing pharmacy services. A more detailed review of the contingent valuation method, including how to elicit WTP values (i.e., format of questions) and potential biases with the method, is provided. The 10 studies that met the inclusion criteria for the review were discussed. Their methodologies were compared to the National Oceanic and Atmospheric Administration (NOAA) expert panel recommendations on the use of contingent valuation, and suggestions for future research were provided.

2. Zarnke KB, Levine MAH, O'Brien BJ. Cost-benefit analyses in the health-care literature: don't judge a study by its label. Clin Epidemiol 1997;50(7):813–22.

   This article provides an overview of the quantity and content of CBA studies in the literature. The article reviewed CBA studies published between 1991 and 1995. The main purposes of the review were to determine whether studies labeled as CBA actually met the criteria for CBA and to determine whether and how indirect and/or intangible benefits were quantified. According to their inclusion criteria, the authors found 95 studies "labeled" as CBA, 80 of which were actually CBA. Of those classified as CBA by the authors, 50 measured only direct costs and direct benefits. The remaining 30 studies (classified as bona fide CBA) measured indirect and intangible benefits, with the human capital (HC) method being used most often. This article also highlights an area of consensus and debate regarding the definition of a "true" or bona fide" CBA—some researchers do not consider a study to be a CBA unless either indirect and/or intangible benefits are measured.

3. McIntosh E, Donaldson C, Ryan M. Recent advances in the methods of cost-benefit analysis in healthcare: matching the art to the science. Pharmacoeconomics 1999;15(4):357–67.

   Cost-benefit analysis in health care is the least used pharmacoeconomic method, primarily because of the difficulty in placing a monetary value on indirect and intangible benefits. This article reviews this controversy and offers solutions for overcoming these obstacles. Some of the solutions offered are to use a balance sheet approach and conjoint analysis, both of which are discussed. This article also provides a brief review of the debate on measuring indirect benefits. This article is useful, in that it highlights potential future directions in conducting CBA.

4. Keith PK, Haddon J, Birch S, et al. A cost-benefit analysis using a willingness-to-pay questionnaire of intranasal budesonide for seasonal allergic rhinitis. Rhinocort Study Group. Ann Allergy Asthma Immunonol 2000;84:55–62.

   Few CBA studies in the health care literature have incorporated intangible benefits (measured by WTP methodology). This study used a double-blind, randomized, controlled design to evaluate the costs and benefits of using an inhaled corticosteroid for seasonal allergies. The study measured indirect costs using the HC method by valuing time lost from work or school. Intangible costs using the WTP method were assessed using the contingent valuation method. A copy of the WTP hypothetical scenario is included with the article along with a detailed methodology on how all costs and benefits were quantified.

5. Mitchell RC, Carson RT. Using surveys to value public goods: the contingent valuation method. Washington, DC: Johns Hopkins University Press, 1990.

   This textbook is a vital resource for information on how to construct WTP questions using the contingent valuation method. The text provides many examples to illustrate various hypothetical scenarios and bidding vehicles. In addition, it provides the advantages and disadvantages of the methods. As the title indicates, the text is focused on public goods and has few examples related to health care programs or interventions. Nonetheless, it is a great tool for understanding the theory and methods behind the contingent valuation method.

6. Sias JJ, Cook S, Wolfe T, et al An employee influenza immunization initiative in a large university managed care setting. JMCP 2001;7(3):219–23.

   The purpose of this study was to determine the direct and indirect cost savings associated with an initiative aimed at immunizing university employees. The team responsible for the initiative included pharmacists, nurses, a nurse practitioner, a physician, and a health educator. The average salary of university employees, including fringe benefits, was used to value productivity gained or lost. A model from a previous study was used to estimate costs and benefits. The *direct costs* and benefits measured included the vaccination program (cost), the medical care associated with side effects of the immunization (cost), and the medical care avoided for upper respiratory illnesses (benefit). The *indirect*, or productivity, costs and benefits included work time lost for immunizations (cost), work loss because of side effects of the immunization (cost) and work loss avoided because of a decrease in respiratory illnesses (benefit). The net benefit of the program was estimated at $90 per employee who was vaccinated.

7. Nesbit TW, Shermock KM, Bobek, MB, et al. Implementation and pharmacoeconomic analysis of a clinical staff pharmacist practice model. Am J Health-Syst Pharm 2001;58:784–790.

   The objective of this study was to evaluate the direct medical costs and benefits associated with a clinical staff pharmacist (CSP) practice model. Direct costs of the practice model included estimates of salaries (plus fringe benefits) of the CSPs and the cost of the equipment used to record their clinical interventions. Direct benefits included two estimates. The first was calculated for prescription therapy changes by subtracting what the therapy would have cost without the CSP intervention from the cost of the therapy after the intervention. The second was calculated based on the probability that some interventions would avoid an adverse drug event (ADE) multiplied by the average cost of an ADE. Probabilities associated with the interventions were assigned based on previous literature and an expert panel. Sensitivity analyses on probabilities and costs were conducted. The benefit-to-cost ratio of the practice model was estimated at 3.1:1.

8. Schrand LM, Elliott JM, Ross MB, et al. A cost-benefit analysis of RSV prophylaxis in high-risk infants. Ann Pharmacother 2001;35:1186–93.

   The authors conducted a retrospective cohort study assessing the costs and benefits of using RSV-IG (respiratory syncytial virus-immunoglobulin) and palivizumab in high-risk infants at their institution. Costs were compared for patients admitted from 1994 to 1995 when RSV prophylaxis drugs were not available to those patients admitted from 1998 to 1999 when prophylactic treatment was administered to high-risk patients. Costs for the 1994–1995 cohort consisted only of RSV-related hospital costs. Costs for the 1998–1999 group included acquisition costs of the prophylaxis drugs, pharmacy time, nursing time, clinic costs associated with administration of the drugs, and hospitalization costs. The benefit-to-cost ratio was $3985:$3461, or 1.15:1. Sensitivity analyses on hospitalization rates were conducted.

9. Lai LL, Sorkin AL. Cost benefit analysis of pharmaceutical care in a Medicaid population–from a budgetary perspective. JMCP 1998;4:303–8.

The objective of the study was to compare direct medical costs and benefits of a pharmaceutical care services program (PCSP) from the perspective of Maryland Medicaid. During the first year after implementation, PCSP clinical services were provided at four inner-city Baltimore hospitals to more than 1000 patients. Data were available for 437 of these patients (the intervention group). Another 437 patients who did not receive these services served as a control group (matching was based on age, gender, and ambulatory care group classification). Direct medical costs paid by Medicaid for those who received PCSP services in the year after the intervention increased by $80 per patient, whereas they increased by $477 per patient in the control group, a difference of $397. When the costs of the PCPS (about $193 per patient) are factored in, the savings are estimated at about $204 per patient.

10. Liljas B. How to calculate indirect costs in economic evaluations. Pharmacoeconomics 1998;13 (1 pt.1):1–7.

This article provides an overview of how to calculate indirect costs. It provides a conceptual framework for indirect costs and the measurement of these costs using the HC approach. In addition, a new method for valuing productivity, the friction cost method, is presented. This method assumes that the productivity lost during a short-term absence can be made up, resulting in no loss of production. The article also discusses the use of quality-adjusted life-years as a method to estimate indirect costs. This article not only provides information on how to calculate indirect costs, it provides a good discussion of other methods (includes both the advantages and disadvantages) that have been suggested as methods to measure indirect costs.

11 Schumock GT, Meek PD, Ploetz PA, Vermeulen LC. Economic evaluations of clinical pharmacy services—1988–1995. Pharmacotherapy Vol. 16, No. 6, 1996;16(6):1188–208.

The American College of Clinical Pharmacy (ACCP) published a position paper on the value of clinical pharmacy services that summarized the literature up to 1988. This 1996 paper is a follow-up literature review that summarizes literature from 1988 to 1995. Thirty-three studies that considered the cost of providing service were categorized as: 1) reports of net savings for the time period of the study or an annualized total (n = 21); 2) reports of net savings per patient day or per patient admission (n = 8); 3) calculations of BC ratios (n = 7). Each study could be included in more than one category. For the studies that reported it, BC ratios ranged from 1.08:1 to 75.84:1 (mean = 16.70:1; median = 4.09:1). The large difference between the mean and the median was because of one study with a large BC ratio; therefore, the median may be a better indicator of average savings. The article's appendix is an extensive grid of the evaluation of 104 articles.

12. Schumock GT, Butler MG, Meek PD, Vermeulen LC, Arondekar BV, Bauman JL. Evidence of economic benefit of clinical pharmacy services: 1996–2000. Pharmacotherapy 2003;23;1:113–32.

This is an update of reference 11. The ACCP Task Force on Economic Evaluations of Clinical Pharmacy Services again evaluated published articles on the economic benefits of clinical services. The update included articles published from 1996 to 2000. Fifty-nine articles were fully reviewed. The reviewers noted an improved quality of research (more studies included a comparison group and more measured both costs and outcomes). Although most studies were still conducted in the traditional hospital setting (52 percent), a large percentage of studies were now conducted in community pharmacies and clinics (41 percent). (The previous review indicated only 18 percent in community/clinic settings). Most studies reported a positive economic impact. For the studies that reported it, BC ratios ranged from 1.74:1 to 17.01:1 (mean = 5.54:1; median = 4.68:1). This median was similar to the previous review.

13. Draugalis JR. Assessing pharmaceconomic studies. In: Bootman JL, Townsend RJ, McGhan WF, eds. Principles of Pharmacoeconomics. 2nd ed. Cincinnati: Harvey Whitney Books Company, 1996:278-89.

This chapter discusses the assessment of pharmaceconomic studies. Outlined are questions to ask when reviewing an article. An example of a critique also is provided.

Exercises

Exercise 1: Identify program and alternatives

You have noticed that many of the patients with diabetes in the outpatient pharmacy are unaware of how to manage their diabetes. You would like to develop a diabetes self-management program to help them.
What would be the goals of your clinic? What alternatives might you consider?

Exercise 2: Identify costs and benefits to set up a diabetes clinic

What costs would be incurred with starting the program? What benefits would be derived from the program?

Exercise 3: Use wage and productivity data to calculate indirect benefits using the human capital approach

For your patient population, the average income/year is $44,000. Before your patients participated in the diabetes clinic, they missed work on average 3 days per month because of complications from their diabetes. After several visits with you, the patients on average missed work 1 day every other month because of their diabetes. What is the indirect benefit (i.e. the value of the productivity gained)?

Exercise 4: Write a hypothetical scenario and willingness-to-pay (WTP) question to assess the intangible benefits of a diabetes program.

Exercise 5: Calculate net present value

As supervisor of a new hospital outpatient pharmacy, you are asked to estimate the costs and benefits that would be associated with offering a drug "brown bag" counseling session once a week for all hospital employees. Employees would be advised to make an appointment with the pharmacist and bring all of the drugs they are currently taking (and any drug-related questions they have). This should increase the number of hospital employees who fill their prescription at your pharmacy (you accept the pharmacy plan that most hospital employees have as part of their benefits package). The costs of implementing this is mainly time by pharmacy personnel making appointments and counseling patients on "brown bag day." You estimate the following based on about 4 hours of personnel time once per week for the first year and slight increases over the following 3 years. You expected that increased sales from revenues would be about $5,000 for the first year, and growing each of the following 3 years. Using the numbers in the following table and a discount rate of 5 percent, calculate the net present value of the benefits minus the costs of "brown bag day."

Year	0	1	2	3
Costs	$10,000	$12,500	$15,000	$17,500
Benefits	$5,000	$12,500	$20,000	$25,000

Exercise 6: Calculate BC ratios

Using the data presented in exercise 5, calculate the BC ratio of the brown bag day. Then compare it to a list of other programs that might be implemented. Based on this information, which program would be implemented?

Service	Benefit-cost ratio
Drug information service	2.0:1
Durable medical equipment sales	2.7:1
Brown bag day	???:1
Discharge counseling	1.5:1

Self-Assessment Questions

1. Which one of the following is a *disadvantage* of conducting a cost-benefit analysis (CBA)?
   A. A comparison of the effects of different types of programs can be conducted.
   B. A dollar value must be placed on health outcomes.
   C. Quality-adjusted life-years must be measured.
   D. Outcomes must be measured in the same natural units.

2. Which one of the following is an *advantage* of conducting a CBA?
   A. A comparison of different types of programs can be conducted.
   B. A dollar value must be placed on health outcomes.
   C. Quality-adjusted life-years must be measured.
   D. Outcomes must be measured in the same natural units.

Question 3 pertains to the following case.

St. Elsewhere Hospital is considering starting an asthma clinic. The costs and benefits for the next 3 years are outlined below:

Costs associated with starting and maintaining the clinic are estimated at $7500 for clinic overhead each year and $50,000 per year salary *plus 25 percent for fringe benefits* for the pharmacist who staffs the clinic.
Benefits (Cost savings) are estimated to be $70,000 for the first year, $80,000 the second year and $100,000 the third year because of decreased use of emergency visits and hospitalizations.

3. Assuming a 10 percent discount and rounding to the nearest $1000, which one of the following is the calculated net present value (NPV) of the clinic *costs and benefits* over the next 3 years?
   A. Costs $210,000; benefits $250,000.
   B. Costs $191,000; benefits $225,000.
   C. Costs $225,000; benefits $250,000.
   D. Costs $200,000; benefits $237,000.

Questions 4 and 5 pertain to following case.

The costs for clinic A are $ 350,000 and the benefits for clinic A are $475,000, whereas the costs for clinic B are $275,000 and the benefits for clinic B are $350,000.

4. Which one of the following is the calculated estimated net benefit and benefit-to-cost ratio (BC) for clinic A?
   A. Net benefit = $75,000; BC = 1.36.
   B. Net benefit = - $75,000; BC = 0.74.
   C. Net benefit = - $125,000; BC = 0.74.
   D. Net benefit = $125,000; BC = 1.36.

5. Which one of the following is the calculated estimated net benefit and BC ratio for clinic B?
   A. Net benefit = $75,000; BC = 1.27.
   B. Net benefit = - $75,000; BC = 0.79.
   C. Net benefit = - $125,000; BC = 0.79.
   D. Net benefit = $125,000; BC = 1.27.

6. A patient must pay for parking at a clinic for a medical visit. Which one of the following types of cost is being measured?
   A. Direct medical cost.
   B. Direct nonmedical cost.
   C. Indirect cost.
   D. Intangible cost.

7. A patient receives an immunization given by their community pharmacist. Which one of the following types of cost is being measured?
   A. Direct medical cost.
   B. Direct nonmedical cost.
   C. Indirect cost.
   D. Intangible cost.

Questions 8 and 9 pertain to the following case.

The standard for chronic year round allergic rhinitis is daily drug. You are trying to decide whether it is cost-beneficial to provide a new once-a-year long-acting allergy injection to reduce the effects of allergic rhinitis compared to daily drugs. The perspective of the study is society. Use the following costs in 2002 United States dollars for your calculations.

With the standard daily oral drug, the patient needs to drive to the clinic for a physician visit once per year and purchases the drug year round through a mail-order pharmacy. This visit takes place in the morning and the patient does not miss any work as a result of this visit. The average patient has four more productive work days per year than if the patient had not received treatment for allergic rhinitis. With the yearly injection, the patient needs to drive to the clinic once per year for the physician visit along with the injection. This visit takes place in the morning and patients do not miss any work for this visit. The average patient has six more productive work days per year than if the patient had not received treatment for allergic rhinitis.

COSTS IN 2002 UNITED STATES DOLLARS

Cost of each allergy injection (lasts 1 year)	$290/injection
Cost of administering injection	$10/administration of injection
Daily wage of patients	$200/day
Physician visit (allergist)	$50/visit
Oral drug	$20/month x 12 months = $240
Drive to clinic for visit (gas and parking)	$10 per visit

8. Using the human capital (HC) approach, which one of the following is the calculated BC ratio for oral therapy?
   A. 2.8:1.
   B. 0:4:1.
   C. 3.0:1.
   D. 2.7:1.

9. Using the HC approach, which one of the following is the calculated BC ratio for injection therapy?
   A. 2.7:1.
   B. 0.3:1.
   C. 3.3:1.
   D. 2.8:1.

10. Which one of the following is a *disadvantage* to valuing health by using the HC approach?
    A. How much a person says he or she is willing to spend may not correspond to what that person will actually spend.
    B. It does not estimate any value for the provision of childcare and/or housekeeping activities.
    C. A person's earnings may not reflect that person's true value to society.
    D. Unemployed elderly are valued more highly than the adult worker.

11. Which one of the following is a disadvantage to valuing health by using the willingness-to-pay (WTP) approach?
    A. How much a person says he or she is willing to spend may not correspond to what that person will actually spend.
    B. It does not estimate any value for the provision of childcare and/or housekeeping activities.

C. A person's earnings may not reflect that person's true value to society.
D. Unemployed elderly are valued more highly than the adult worker.

Questions 12 and 13 pertain to the following abstract:

Based on the guidelines for evaluating cost-benefit studies, choose one positive and one negative aspect of the following abstract.

Title: Pharmacoeconomic Analysis of Ultraceph and Megaceph

Background: Indicated uses for two new antibiotics, Ultraceph and Megaceph, recently were approved by the Food and Drug Administration. Both have similar spectrums of activity. Ultraceph is dosed orally (50 mg once per day). Ultraceph is affected by liver functioning, so monitoring is needed. Megaceph is also dosed orally (25 mg 2 times/day) and is associated with a 1 percent chance of hearing loss, which is reversible if caught within the first 2 days of treatment.

Methods: The purpose of this study was to calculate the net BC when comparing Ultraceph and Megaceph. Costs paid by third-party payers were assessed. Costs of the drugs, administration time, and laboratory test monitoring were included as input costs. The average number of hospital days was assessed for patients on each drug. An estimated cost of $1500 per hospital day was used to calculate the outcome costs.

Results: The net savings of using Ultraceph compared to Megaceph was $700 per patient. The average cost estimates of hospitalization are varied from $500 to $2000 per day and results still favored Ultraceph (range of $200 – $950 net savings).

Conclusion: Although the costs associated with administering Ultraceph are higher than Megaceph, Ultraceph may allow patients to leave the hospital sooner; thus, third-party payers may realize a net benefit.

The names of actual drugs were not used: assume these are appropriate alternatives for this condition.

12. Which one of the following is a positive aspect of the abstract?
    A. Title is appropriate.
    B. Perspective is stated.
    C. Discounting is conducted.
    D. Limitations are addressed.

13. Which one of the following is a negative aspect of the abstract?
    A. Sensitivity analyses were not conducted.
    B. Objective was not stated.
    C. Dosing of alternatives were not described.
    D. Limitations were not addressed.

COST-EFFECTIVENESS ANALYSIS

Jeff Lee, Pharm.D., FCCP;
Connie McLaughlin-Miley, Pharm.D.; and
Mary Lou Chatterton, Pharm.D.

Outline

Balancing what is practical with what is ideal is a challenge whenever clinicians try to incorporate economic analysis into medical decision-making. Variations in settings, diseases, treatments, and constraints imposed by lack of time, money, and data will always be present.

I. Background

II. Definition

A. Cost-effectiveness analysis is a form of economic evaluation whose goal is to identify, examine, and compare the relevant costs and consequences of competing drug regimens and interventions

1. Costs are expressed in monetary terms
2. Consequences are measured in their natural units, such as lives saved, cases cured, and years of life saved

B. Cost-effective therapies are those that have outcomes worth their corresponding costs relative to competing alternatives

1. Alternatives that are less expensive and at least as effective as other alternatives
2. Alternatives that are more expensive than alternative therapies with an additional benefit worth the additional cost
3. Alternatives that are less expensive and less effective in instances where the extra benefit provided by the competing therapy is not worth the additional expense

C. Results are expressed as a cost-effectiveness ratio, such as cost per case cured, cost per life saved, or cost per infection avoided

D. Alternatives studied must have primary, measurable effects on one clear clinical outcome parameter because treatment outcome is expressed in terms of achieving this primary outcome

E. Examples

1. Compare the costs and outcomes of two or more antihypertensives because the primary treatment outcome for each agent can be expressed as decreases in blood pressure in mm Hg
2. Compare two programs designed to prevent excess mortality, as each program's effectiveness can be presented as lives saved
3. Restricts the use of CEA compared to cost-benefit analysis because in cost-benefit analysis outcomes for disparate programs are compared in monetary terms
4. Cost-utility analysis is a special form of CEA, where the scope of effectiveness is broadened by assessing the impact of an intervention on patients' functional status, health status, or health-related quality of life by including a utility in the analysis

F. The term cost-effective is commonly misused in the pharmacoeconomic literature

III. Steps for designing and conducting a cost-effectiveness analysis

A. Define the problem— The problem should be stated but the perspective and objectives of the question also should be specified.

1. Drummond example

2. "Is a long-term home care program worth it?" versus "From the perspective of (a) both the Ministry of Health and the Ministry of Community and Social Services budgets, and (b) patients incurring out-of-pocket costs, is a long-term home care program preferable to the existing program of institutionalized, extended care in designated hospital wards?"

3. Perspectives of evaluations may vary considerably

B. Identify treatment alternatives and outcomes

1. All clinically relevant treatment options and feasible outcomes should be identified and investigated

2. Primary clinical outcomes often have a direct relationship to patient morbidity and mortality

3. Primary outcomes typically are preferable to intermediate outcomes, but some are not easily measured examples of primary clinical outcomes include the cure of acute conditions such as infections or ketoacidosis; control of chronic conditions, such as diabetes mellitus, Parkinson's disease, or hypertension; improved functioning and reduction in disability; and lives saved or years of life saved

4. Intermediate outcomes should be identified when primary outcomes cannot be measured

5. Intermediate outcomes are measurable effects of treatment that are thought to be indicative of a specific long-term, primary outcome

6. More easily measured

7. Require extrapolation of clinical significance to primary outcomes

8. Examples of intermediate and corresponding primary outcomes include reductions of hypertension as measured in mm Hg and reduction in stroke, forced expiratory volume in 1 second as a predictor of acute exacerbations of asthma, and CD_4 lymphocyte counts as a predictor of stage of infection with the human immunodeficiency virus

9. Economic outcomes include outcomes associated with use of health care resources, such as length of hospital stay, length of intensive care unit stay, frequency of physician visits, drug use, and other services or treatments used

10. Humanistic outcomes are those reported by patients from their own point of view, such as patient satisfaction with health and health-related quality of life

11. After review of the literature, it is advisable to produce a comprehensive list of important clinical, economic, and humanistic outcomes and then determine which of these parameters are most relevant to include in the analyses (Reference Figure 1)

C. Select a study design

1. Experimental designs
   - Piggyback randomized, controlled, clinical trial
   - High internal validity and scientific rigor
   - Efficient and relatively inexpensive way to collect data
   - Limitations
   - Not enough data points to determine significant differences in measures of cost-effectiveness
   - Resource use is often protocol-driven; specific types of patients are included and excluded and frequency and types of interactions with health care providers are dictated by the study protocol; certain adverse events may result in hospitalization that outside the study would not
   - Alternatives are assessed under perfect conditions, which are not indicative of every day clinical practice
   - Prospective, randomized, economic-clinical trial (naturalistic trial)
   - Probably the best experimental study design for conducting a cost-effectiveness evaluation
   - Provides an opportunity to observe the effects of an alternative on outcomes of interest in conjunction with clinical practice patterns in a specific practice setting
   - Randomization occurs in the practice setting being studied
   - The usual course of clinical practice proceeds in this setting
   - Permits observation and collection of clinical, resource use, and quality-of-life data at predetermined time points
   - Maximizes external validity and generalizability to the practice site
   - Limitations
   - Loss of internal validity
   - Require large study populations to provide adequate statistical power
   - Duration is measured in years
   - Costly to conduct

2. Observational designs
   - Claims data analysis—refer to "Investigating the Outcomes Research Question" for information about this type of study

3. Simulations (modeling)
   - Combine data from the medical literature, traditional clinical trials, meta-analyses of clinical trials, epidemiologic studies, expert opinion, and data from one's own practice setting
   - Makes it possible to estimate treatment costs and outcomes when conducting a prospective or observational study is not practical
   - Typically involves a mathematical, computer-based portrayal of the problem
   - Inexpensive compared to experimental and observational studies
   - Can be adapted to represent most diseases and treatments over long time periods
   - Decision trees are a common form of simulation
   - Whatever design is chosen should best suit the disease being studied and the goals, time constraints, and resources available

D. Select and measure costs and outcomes

1. Selecting relevant parameters
   - Narrow the scope of the analysis by determining the critical cost and consequence parameters to include; should be measured realistically
   - Select relevant and reliable intermediaries if there are no primary outcomes to measure
   - Measuring and valuing relevant costs and outcomes
   - Cost-data should be derived from site-specific sources whenever possible
   - Cost-data generated from national databases, published literature, or expert opinion can provide useful estimates of treatment costs
   - Results should be presented as the various differences in resource use between alternative treatments and as the value of these costs in monetary terms
   - A transparent presentation of data allows others to review the work with a clear understanding of how cost-data were collected, valued, and integrated into the analysis
   - This allows readers to vary the costs assigned to various health care resources to better reflect the true costs of providing a specific treatment in their own settings

E. Report the results

1. Costs and consequences considered
   - Present an explicit description of the costs and consequences considered
   - Present the perspective of the analysis
   - Present the methods and sources used to place monetary value on costs
2. Cost-effectiveness ratios
   - Typically presented in the form of a cost-effectiveness ratio, where treatment costs comprise the numerator and the effectiveness measure serves as the denominator
   - Average cost-effectiveness ratio provides an estimate of the treatment costs of one alternative divided by its effectiveness measure
   - Example—if treatment cost of $500 results in an effect 10 cases cured, the cost-effectiveness ratio is the cost divided by the effectiveness, or $500 divided by 10 cures, which is equal to $50 per case cured
   - Incremental cost-effectiveness ratios provide a more meaningful comparison among treatments; calculated by dividing the difference in costs of two treatments by the difference in effectiveness
   - Example—if total treatment costs for drug A are $700 for 15 cases cured, and drug B treatment costs are $400 for 12 cases cured, then the incremental cost-effectiveness ratio is calculated as:
   - Incremental C/E = $700 - $400 ÷ 15 cures - 12 cures
     = $300 ÷ 3
     = $100 for each additional case cured with drug A
   - Incremental cost-effectiveness ratios estimate the cost per unit of effectiveness of switching from one treatment to another, or the cost of using one treatment in preference to another
   - Provides data that are most relevant to formulary and treatment decisions, when comparative information is of primary importance
   - Detsky example—treatment costs for low-osmolar contrast media were $36.98 to achieve an effectiveness measure of 29.9996 quality-adjusted life-years; high-osmolar contrast media treatment costs were estimated as $14.39 to achieve 29.9986 quality-adjusted life-years. The average cost-effectiveness ratio for the low-osmolar contrast media is $36.98 ÷ 29.9996 quality-adjusted life-years which is equal to $1.23 per quality-adjusted life-year; the incremental cost-effectiveness of using low- versus high-osmolar contrast media was calculated as the differences in the costs, $36.98 minus $14.39, divided by the differences in effectiveness, 29.9996 quality-adjusted life-years minus 29.9986 quality-adjusted life-years, which is equal to $22,600 per quality-adjusted life-year. In other words, for low-osmolar contrast media to achieve an increase of 1 quality-adjusted life-year in outcome, $22,600 in additional costs need to be expended. The choice of which type of ratio to report can strongly affect the decision made; the incremental analysis provides information that is more useful and accurate for making a decision regarding what agent to use
3. Limitations in interpreting cost-effectiveness ratios

- A cost-effectiveness ratio alone is of limited value in the absence of explicit criteria for making allocation decisions; an incremental cost-effectiveness ratio of $70 per additional case cured for a new drug is less useful if decision-makers do not agree ahead of time regarding what an acceptable cost per additional case cured is
- These ratios depend entirely on the quality of the data used to generate them
- Because there are many methodologic options for measuring costs and outcomes, comparisons of cost-effectiveness ratios generated from multiple studies in the literature must be undertaken with caution
- It is inevitable that some assumptions around uncertain variables will have to be made when performing a cost-effectiveness analysis

F. Application of sensitivity analysis

- Example—if a researcher uses an average cost per hospital day of $800 in an analysis but knows in practice the value can range from $600 to $1500 in a particular patient group, it is prudent to explore the effects of inputting values across this range to assess the robustness of the results of the analysis to changes in this parameter

IV.Conclusion

Cost-effectiveness analysis is distinct from other methods of economic evaluation in that the valuation of outcomes is presented in natural units specific to a desired clinical objective. Cost-effectiveness data provides useful information to augment traditional clinical data in clinical and formulary decision-making.

Learning Objectives

1.Define cost-effectiveness analysis (CEA) and differentiate it from other forms of economic analysis.
2.Identify opportunities for using CEA.
3.Compare and contrast strengths and limitations of various study designs used to conduct CEAs.
4.Calculate and interpret cost-effectiveness ratios.

Abbreviations in this chapter

CEA	Cost-effectiveness analysis
ECHO	Economic, clinical, and humanistic outcomes
QALY	Quality-adjusted life-year

Cost-Effectiveness Analysis

Background

Issues surrounding the demonstration of the tangible value of pharmaceuticals continue to swirl as governments, managed care organizations, and employers strive to manage the costs of providing pharmaceuticals to their constituencies. Current cost-management initiatives by these payer groups and consideration of future drug coverage initiatives such as a Medicare prescription benefit bring a significant focus to methods for evaluating the costs and consequences of competing therapeutic alternatives. All of these environmental factors have raised the consideration of the role of cost-effectiveness analysis (CEA) in therapeutic decision-making. Although these recent trends have enhanced the exposure of CEA in forming health policies, its use in the health care sector is not new.

Cost-effectiveness analysis has been used to study various health care issues since the late 1960s. In 1975, the possibility of using CEA to assess costs associated with health screening was raised with a published article that was an excellent example of the use of marginal CEA applied to a series of inexpensive tests used for cancer screening (see Reference 21). Since then, methods and applications of CEA applied to health care decisions have appeared in the published literature with increasing frequency. This increased attention to balancing costs and outcomes is a response to the limited resources available to meet the rising demand for medical services. If the benefits of new technologies are to be maximized, assessments must be used to enhance our ability to make rational and appropriate health care decisions and to help direct health resources toward their most productive uses.

In the early 1980s, a series of journal articles stated that CEA should be a component of medical decision-making whenever resources are scarce, and that it should not be used to identify areas to cut costs, but as a way to identify opportunities to use resources better (see references 15–20).

In spite of 30 years of using CEA in health care, most authors agree that no true gold standard methodologic approach exists for conducting CEAs. Variations in settings, diseases, treatments, and constraints imposed by lack of time, money, and data will always be present. All of these factors affect the design and subsequent analysis of CEA studies. Lack of a gold standard methodology provides a unique challenge to researchers to balance what is practical with what is ideal when incorporating economic analysis into medical decision-making.

Definition

Cost-effectiveness analysis is a form of economic evaluation whose goal is to identify, examine, and compare the relevant costs and consequences of competing drug regimens and interventions. Costs are expressed in monetary terms, and consequences are measured in their natural units, such as lives saved, cases cured, and years of life saved. The results of cost-effectiveness studies offer information that assists in sound decision-making.

A cost-effective therapy is one that has an outcome worth its corresponding cost relative to competing alternatives. This definition includes therapies that are: less expensive and at least as effective as other alternatives; more expensive than alternative therapies with an additional benefit worth the additional cost; and less expensive and less effective in instances where the extra benefit provided by the competing therapy is not worth the additional expense.

Overall, cost-effectiveness depends on the value placed on a health outcome relative to its cost. Unlike cost-benefit analysis, CEA does not place a dollar value on human life or health. Cost-effectiveness analysis includes valuation of life in nonmonetary terms, in the form of units of effectiveness. These units are measured by describing specific clinical objectives, such as lives saved, cases cured, or decreases in blood pressure. Valuation of costs is in monetary units. Results of CEA are then expressed as a cost-effectiveness ratio, such as cost per case cured, cost per life saved, or cost per infection avoided.

Cost-effectiveness as a term implies value for money, meaning neither the drug having the lowest acquisition cost nor the most effective therapy is necessarily the most cost-effective. Rather, the relative costs and consequences of each alternative must be considered together when determining the most cost-effective option.

The primary requirement for conducting a CEA is that alternatives studied must have primary, measurable effects on one clear clinical outcome parameter because treatment outcome is expressed in terms of achieving this primary outcome. For example, CEA is suitable to compare the costs and outcomes of two or more antihypertensives because the primary treatment outcome for each agent can be expressed as decreases in blood pressure in mm Hg. Alternatively, CEA can be used to compare two programs designed to prevent excess mortality because each program's effectiveness can be presented as lives saved. This requirement restricts the use of CEA compared to cost-benefit analysis because in cost-benefit analysis outcomes for disparate programs are compared in monetary terms.

Cost-utility analysis is considered by most experts a special form of CEA, where the scope of effectiveness is broadened by assessing the impact of an intervention on patients' functional status, health status, or health-related quality of life by including a utility in the analysis. Cost-utility analysis is discussed later in the cost-utility analysis section.

The term "cost-effective" is commonly misused in the pharmacoeconomic literature. Often, "cost-effective" is used to describe the results of a partial economic analysis, such as a comparison of the costs of two treatment alternatives. Other times, "cost-effective" has been used to describe the results of a cost-minimization analysis. It is important to make the distinction that a true CEA compares both the costs and the consequences of competing alternatives whose outcomes are not equal, but are measured using common units.

Steps for Designing and Conducting a Cost-Effectiveness Analysis

The initial steps involved in designing a CEA are similar to those for all methods of economic evaluation. This discussion will discuss these steps, which have already been discussed in the Types of Economic and Humanistic Outcomes Assessments chapter, as they pertain specifically to CEA.

Define the Problem

The first task in conducting a CEA is similar to that for any investigation. First, the research question must be clearly defined in a manner that is concise and measurable. The question should be framed within specific parameters and should include the use of concise operational definitions that describe the fundamental components of the question. The problem should be stated but the perspective and objectives of the question also should be specified. An excellent example of the contrasts between vague and explicit research questions is provided in Reference 5. In reference to a study assessing the benefits of a long-term home care program based in the United Kingdom, it is suggested that a preferable alternative to the research question, "Is a long-term home care program worth it?" to be, "From the perspective of (a) both the Ministry of Health and the Ministry of Community and Social Services budgets, and (b) patients incurring out-of-pocket costs, is a long-term home care program preferable to the existing program of institutionalized, extended care in designated hospital wards?" The latter study question is clearly preferable because the perspective of the analysis is clearly stated and the program alternatives are clearly identified.

The perspectives of the evaluation may vary considerably. The perspective chosen for a study delineates the viewpoint from which the analysis is performed and indicates the types of cost and outcomes data that will need to be collected. Potential perspectives for use in CEA are the same as those that can be used for other methods of economic assessment. One or a combination of viewpoints may be adopted when conducting a CEA. Many experts suggest that the perspective of society is best to select because this perspective allows for complete evaluation of the impact of a drug or technology on the system as a whole. However, adopting a more narrow perspective allows researchers to assess specific questions using more relevant comparisons for a given setting.

Patients and their caregivers are concerned with availability of care and expenses not covered by third-party payers for which they will be charged. Providers need information that allows them to act as patient advocates in gaining access to beneficial drugs and technologies, whereas third-party payers are concerned with minimizing costs while offering services that allow them to maintain competitiveness in the marketplace. A benefits manager in private industry may be particularly concerned with the direct medical costs of providing therapy to employees and the productivity of an employee. Regardless of the perspective chosen, it should reflect the objectives of the study and should match the final consumer of the results of the study.

Identify Treatment Alternatives and Outcomes

All clinically relevant treatment options and feasible outcomes should be identified and investigated. In medical applications, CEA almost always begins with a thorough review of the literature to determine previously published work relevant to the research question. MEDLINE is a good starting point to identify important primary and secondary publications that detail therapeutic options. Any available cost-of-illness studies that report estimates of the monetary and societal burden of the disease in question also should be noted. It also is desirable to study the results of well-conducted clinical trials and meta-analyses of clinical trials that studied the alternatives in question. From the literature, researchers will need to determine each alternative's reported efficacy or effectiveness rates, and incidence of clinically important adverse advents. The researcher also may wish to investigate the availability of costs and effectiveness rates of pertinent alternatives in the practice setting where the study is to be conducted and the results are to be applied.

During this phase, the objective is to identify all relevant economic, clinical, and humanistic outcomes associated with the disease and its treatment. Primary clinical outcomes often have a direct relationship to patient morbidity and mortality. Primary outcomes typically are preferable to intermediate outcomes, but some are not easily measured because they occur at time points far in the future. Examples of primary clinical outcomes include the cure of acute conditions such as infections or ketoacidosis; control of chronic conditions, such as diabetes mellitus, Parkinson's disease, or hypertension; improved functioning and reduction in disability; and lives saved or years of life saved.

When primary outcomes cannot be used or are not available for use, intermediate outcomes should be identified. Intermediate outcomes are measurable effects of treatment that are thought to be indicative of a specific long-term primary outcome. Intermediate outcomes typically are more easily measured and, if used in a CEA, require extrapolation of clinical significance to primary outcomes. Some examples of intermediate and corresponding primary outcomes include reductions in blood pressure as measured in mm Hg and reduction in stroke, forced expiratory volume in 1 second as a predictor of acute exacerbations of asthma, and CD_4 lymphocyte counts as a predictor of stage of infection with the human immunodeficiency virus.

Economic outcomes include outcomes associated with use of health care resources, such as length of hospital stay, length of intensive care unit stay, frequency of physician visits, drug use, and other services or treatments used. From the employer's perspective, absenteeism and productivity have an economic impact, and are often included as economic outcomes. These resource use parameters form the basis of the cost component of the cost-effectiveness equation. When selecting relevant economic outcomes for inclusion, the parameters should be those that can be readily converted to monetary units.

Humanistic outcomes are those reported by patients from their own point of view. Examples of these outcomes include patient satisfaction with health and health-related quality of life. These outcomes are not explicitly incorporated into a CEA, except in the special case of cost-utility analysis, although humanistic outcomes frequently are assessed in conjuntion with CEAs.

After review of the literature, it is advisable to produce a comprehensive list of important clinical, economic, and humanistic outcomes and then determine which of these parameters are most relevant to include in the analyses. Figure 1 illustrates one method of organizing information by applying the economic, clinical, and humanistic outcomes (ECHO), model to help identify mediators and outcomes in the treatment of unipolar depression. In this example, a researcher might determine that changes in depressive symptomatology, perhaps measured using scores on a symptom index as the effectiveness parameter, could serve as a primary clinical outcome, whereas resources used to manage depression, such as physician visits, hospitalizations, and drug treatments, could be selected as the most important economic parameters to include in the CEA.

The ECHO model provides a useful framework to organize what can be a vast amount of information in a clear and simple format. Although most researchers have a good idea of the important parameters to consider based on the research question, this process, in addition to helping organize available data, can highlight important parameters that may not have been readily identified otherwise.

Select a Study Design

Selection of a suitable study design is a crucial step when conducting a CEA. To assist in determining the best study design, background research should include attention given to previously conducted CEAs and epidemiologic studies. Background research will aid in gaining a better understanding of relevant populations and incidence of disease. Clinical outcomes, confounding factors, and methods used by other researchers can provide insight into what previous researchers have studied, and may help avoid problems that other studies have identified.

Three fundamental designs are used when determining cost-effectiveness: experimental and observational designs and simulations, also known as modeling. Combinations of these techniques also are used depending on the requirements of the question asked. Selection of the best design depends on the disease being treated, the goals of the study, time constraints, and available financial and manpower resources. These designs are discussed in detail in the Investigating the Outcomes Research Question chapter of this book.

Two experimental designs are of particular use when studying cost-effectiveness. The first involves "piggybacking" collection of economic or health-related quality-of-life data onto a randomized, controlled, clinical trial. These types of studies have high internal validity and scientific rigor. Because the trial may already be funded to determine safety and efficacy, this can be an efficient and relatively inexpensive way to collect data.

However, there are some notable limitations to evaluating cost-effectiveness using this study methodology. First, many clinical trials do not enroll enough patients to provide enough data points to determine significant differences in measures of cost-effectiveness. The number of patients needed to find a statistical difference in a clinical outcome may not be enough to show a difference in an economic or humanistic outcome. Second, resource use is often protocol-driven in a randomized, controlled, clinical trial. Specific types of patients are included and excluded and frequency and types of interactions with health care providers are dictated by the study protocol. Certain adverse events may result in hospitalization, even though, in a normal patient care environment, they would not. This design type assesses alternatives under perfect conditions, which are not indicative of every day clinical practice. Thus, resources saved or expended, and outcomes observed, often are not accurate reflections of typical patient care.

The prospective, randomized, economic-clinical trial, also known as a naturalistic trial, is probably the best experimental study design for conducting a cost-effectiveness evaluation. This design provides an opportunity to observe the effects of an alternative on outcomes of interest in conjunction with clinical practice patterns in a specific practice setting. Patient randomization occurs in the practice setting being studied, with patients assigned to a study arm when they receive a specific intervention. The usual course of clinical practice proceeds in this setting. Patients may or may not be adherent to therapy, doses and therapies may change or be discontinued, and adverse events may occur. Events happen just as they occur in routine practice. This design allows the researcher to investigate actual practice without adhering to the restrictions imposed by a randomized, controlled trial protocol. The naturalistic study design permits observation and collection of clinical, resource use, and quality-of-life data at predetermined time points throughout the study. This design maximizes external validity and generalizability to the practice site. However, there is some loss of internal validity with this design. Also, these designs require large study populations to provide adequate statistical power and, because they are conducted longitudinally, often have a duration measured in years. This makes a prospective, randomized, economic-clinical trial costly to conduct.

One type of observational study design that has been used when evaluating cost-effectiveness is claims data analysis. This design is well described in the Investigating the Outcomes Research Question chapter of this text and is not discussed in detail here.

A third family of designs often combines data from the medical literature, traditional clinical trials, meta-analyses of clinical trials, epidemiologic studies, expert opinion, and data from individuals' own practice settings through the use of simulations. Modeling makes it possible to estimate treatment costs and outcomes when conducting a prospective or observational study is not practical. Modeling typically involves a mathematical, computer-based portrayal of the problem. Modeling typically is less expensive than conducting experimental and observational studies. Models are flexible and can be adapted to represent most diseases and treatments over long time periods. A commonly used type of model is the decision tree, which is discussed in detail later in the Decision Analysis chapter. In addition, a decision tree is used as the study design in the problem exercise in the case study book.

Other types of study designs may be appropriate to evaluate cost-effectiveness. Whatever design is chosen should best suit the disease being studied, goals, time constraints, and resources available.

Select and Measure Costs and Outcomes

Selecting Relevant Parameters

Once the various economic, clinical, and humanistic intermediaries and outcomes have been identified and a study design selected, the researcher must narrow the scope of the analysis by determining the critical cost and consequence parameters to include based on the study perspective and the primary goals of the study. It is imperative to select outcomes that can be measured realistically and that are most relevant to the study. For example, it is impractical to use a cost per life-year gained ratio to compare two drug treatments when data describing effects on life expectancy do not exist in the published literature and are not feasible to determine using an experimental, observational, or simulation study. If measuring intermediate outcomes is the only reasonable assessment available, then selection of relevant and reliable intermediaries is the obvious choice. Costs associated with care needed after discharge from a hospital may not be particularly relevant if the study perspective is tightly defined as that of an inpatient provider. The researcher must ensure that selection of costs and outcomes are conducted with an emphasis on practical, but relevant and comprehensive, assessment.

Measuring and Valuing Relevant Costs and Outcomes

The methods of measuring and valuing cost parameters in a CEA are similar to those used in all methods of economic evaluation. In general, cost data should be derived from site-specific sources whenever possible to provide data that are most reflective of actual treatment costs. However, in the absence of site-specific data, cost data generated from national databases, published literature, or expert opinion can provide useful estimates of treatment costs. This approach provides less internal validity, but may provide cost-estimates that are more generalizable than institution-specific cost data.

Regardless of the methods of measuring and valuing cost data, it is crucial that these two processes be initiated and presented as two distinct steps. Results should be presented as the various differences in resource use between alternative treatments and as the values of these costs in monetary terms. This method of presentation relates to the concept of transparency (i.e., data should be presented in such a way that other researchers can review the work with a clear understanding of how cost data were collected, valued, and integrated into the analysis). This method of presentation or approach allows readers to vary the costs assigned to various health care resources to better reflect the true costs of providing a specific treatment in their own settings.

The method of assessing consequences in a CEA is the key point of differentiation relative to other techniques of economic evaluation. In a CEA, consequences are collected in natural clinical units such as cases cured, lives saved, or percentage of improvement in serum cholesterol. Thus, the primary consideration is to select the most relevant and measurable indicator of clinical effectiveness, whether it is a single clinical parameter or an index of effectiveness, such as quality-adjusted life-years (QALYs), that provides an index of outcome based on many disease effects.

Report the Results

Costs and Consequences Considered

An explicit description of the costs and consequences considered in a CEA is an important first step in reporting the results of an analysis. Before the results can be adequately reported and interpreted, the reader must understand the scope of the analysis, specifically the types of costs and consequences included, the perspective of the analysis, and the methods and sources used to place monetary value on the cost side of the cost-effectiveness equation. As previously discussed, this step addresses the concept of transparency, allowing informed decisions to be made based on the analysis. It also allows readers to more easily tailor the results of an analysis to their own specific practice settings.

Cost-Effectiveness Ratios

Results of a CEA typically are presented in the form of a cost-effectiveness ratio, where treatment costs comprise the numerator and the effectiveness measure serves as the denominator. Thus, if treatment costs C of $500 result in an effect E of 10 cases cured, the cost-effectiveness ratio is the cost divided by the effectiveness, or $500 ÷ 10 cures, which equals $50 per case cured.

This type of ratio is defined as an average cost-effectiveness ratio because it simply provides an estimate of the treatment costs of one alternative divided by the effectiveness measure. These ratios can be of some use as they provide an integrated picture of the costs and outcomes of a given treatment. That is, these ratios can provide a better sense of the treatment costs associated with achieving a desired outcome. However, although average cost-effectiveness ratios are relatively simple to calculate, they are not particularly useful in assisting in treatment and formulary decision-making because they do not provide an assessment of the relative costs and consequences of alternative treatment strategies for a given health state. Therefore, use of these ratios in comparative decision-making can be misleading.

To reflect more accurately the relative costs and consequences of competing alternatives, incremental cost-effectiveness ratios should be used because they provide a more meaningful comparison among treatments. Incremental cost-effectiveness ratios are calculated by dividing the difference in costs of two treatments by the difference in effectiveness. Specifically, these ratios are calculated as:

incremental C/E = Cost A – Cost B ÷ Effectiveness A – Effectiveness B

For example, if total treatment costs for drug A are $700 for 15 cases cured, and drug B treatment costs are $400 for 12 cases cured, then the incremental cost-effectiveness ratio is calculated as:

incremental C/E = $700 – $400 ÷ 15 cures – 12 cures
= $300 ÷ 3 cures
= $100 for each additional case cured with drug A

Incremental cost-effectiveness ratios estimate the cost per unit of effectiveness of switching from one treatment to another, or the cost of using one treatment in preference to another. This ratio provides data that are most relevant to formulary and treatment decisions, when comparative information is of primary importance.

An interesting comparison of average versus incremental cost-effectiveness ratios is demonstrated by evaluating the use of low- versus high-osmolar contrast media in high-risk patients (see Reference 5). In this analysis, the outcome of interest was QALYs. Treatment costs for low-osmolar contrast media were $36.98 to achieve an effectiveness measure of 29.9996 QALYs. High-osmolar contrast media treatment costs were estimated as $14.39 to achieve 29.9986 QALYs. The average cost-effectiveness ratio for the low-osmolar contrast media is $36.98 ÷ 29.9996 QALYs, which is equal to $1.23 per QALY. However, the incremental cost-effectiveness of using low- versus high-osmolar contrast media was calculated as the differences in the costs, $36.98 minus $14.39, divided by the differences in effectiveness, 29.9996 QALYs minus 29.9986 QALYs, which is equal to $22,600 per QALY. In other words, for low-osmolar contrast media to achieve an increase of 1 QALY in outcome, $22,600 in additional costs need to be expended.

Obviously, the choice of which type of ratio to report strongly affects the decision made in this example. The incremental analysis provides information that is more useful and accurate for making a decision regarding what contrast agent to use in this patient group.

Limitations in Interpreting Cost-Effectiveness Ratios

Cost-effectiveness ratios can provide useful information that supplements clinical decision-making. However, regardless of the type of ratio used, there are inherent limitations in interpreting and using cost-effectiveness ratios in practice. First, a cost-effectiveness ratio alone is of limited value in the absence of explicit criteria for making allocation decisions. For example, calculating an incremental cost-effectiveness ratio of $70 per additional case cured for a new drug is a less useful exercise if decision-makers do not agree ahead of time what they think an acceptable cost per additional case cured is. Second, these ratios depend entirely on the quality of the data used to generate them. Incomplete or assumption-laden cost data can result in inaccurate cost-effectiveness ratios.

Third, because there are many methodologic options for measuring costs and outcomes, comparisons of cost-effectiveness ratios generated from multiple studies in the literature must be undertaken with caution. The manner in which data are collected and presented can result in remarkably different results. Finally, it is inevitable that some assumptions around uncertain variables will have to be made when performing a CEA. In evaluating cost-effectiveness ratios, it is critical that the effects of altering the values of these variables are explored.

Application of Sensitivity Analysis

Sensitivity analysis allows the researcher to evaluate the stability of the conclusions of a CEA to assumptions made in the analysis. Sensitivity analysis is performed by varying the values of uncertain variables across a range of plausible estimates to assess how changing assumptions affects the result of the analysis. For example, if a researcher uses an average cost per hospital day of $800 in an analysis but knows in practice the value can range from $600 to $1500 in a particular patient group, it is prudent to explore the effects of inputting values across this range to assess the robustness of the results of the analysis to changes in this parameter. Sensitivity analysis is discussed in detail in the Sensitivity Analysis chapter of this book.

Conclusion

Cost-effectiveness analysis offers health care practitioners an important tool for assessing the relative costs and consequences of alternative treatments. It is distinct from other methods of economic evaluation in that the valuation of outcomes is presented in natural units specific to a desired clinical objective. Essential prestudy work to define the problem, determine the study perspective, identify the most relevant economic and clinical parameters, and determine the best study methodology is critical to conducting a well-done CEA.

When reporting the results of a CEA, it is essential that the costs and consequences considered in the analysis and the specific methods of valuing treatment costs are explicitly presented. Average cost-effectiveness ratios are of limited value because they do not compare one alternative to another. Incremental cost-effectiveness ratios prove useful in presenting the incremental costs per unit of outcome for a more costly alternative, although care must be used when interpreting these ratios. Sensitivity analysis is an important technique used to assess the stability of results to variation of parameter estimates. Cost-effectiveness data provide useful information to augment traditional clinical data in clinical and formulary decision-making.

Annotated Bibliography

1. Baltussen R, Leidl R, Ament A. Real world designs in economic evaluation: bridging the gap between clinical

research and policy-making. Pharmacoeconomics, 1999;16(5): 449–58.

This paper identifies the information that economic evaluation should provide to adequately inform policy-makers. Three conceptual approaches to economic evaluation are discussed: clinical trials, observational studies, and modeling. A three-step approach, comprising successive assessment of internal validity, external validity, and net impact at the system level, is described.

2. Boyer JG, Pathak DS. Establishing value through pharmacoeconomics: the emerging third objective in clinical trials. Top Hosp Pharm Manage 1994;13:1–10.

The authors discuss some of the important issues that must be considered when conducting pharmacoeconomic research in conjunction with clinical trials. Key questions that pharmacoeconomic components of clinical study protocols must answer are listed. Valuable insight into the methods and considerations of integrating pharmacoeconomic studies into the drug development process is provided. This paper also includes practical suggestions for approaching a piggyback trial.

3. Cahill NE. Caveats in interpreting and applying pharmacoeconomic data. Am J Health-Syst Pharm 1995;52(Suppl):S24–8.

The author advises readers to use caution when interpreting the results of pharmacoeconomic studies because study methods can be manipulated to support preordained conclusions. Legal and practical issues surrounding the interpretation and use of economic evaluations by health care providers are presented. Issues that should be considered when making policy decisions based on the results of economic analyses are discussed.

4. Data JL, Willke RJ, Barnes JR, DiRoma PJ. Re-engineering drug development: integrating pharmacoeconomic research into the drug development process. Psychopharmacol Bull 1995;31:67–73.

Pharmaceutical companies are establishing well-integrated pharmacoeconomic research programs that can respond to the changing health care environment and plan programs to optimize patient care. The authors discuss how pharmacoeconomic research has been incorporated into the drug development process at one pharmaceutical company. It provides a brief review of the role pharmacoeconomic research plays in regulatory approval and reimbursement of pharmaceuticals internationally and domestically. A detailed description of the integration of pharmacoeconomic research into the various phases of drug development and approval is provided along with a short discussion of controversies surrounding pharmacoeconomic studies.

5. Detsky AS, Naglie IG. A clinician's guide to cost-effectiveness analysis. Ann Intern Med 1990;113:147–54.

This paper includes a review of fundamental concepts involved in pharmacoeconomic analyses, using previously published study results to illustrate their points. The authors describe the evaluation of new health care interventions beginning with demonstration of efficacy through resolving policy issues related to distribution of results. Also presented are the types of economic analyses used to demonstrate the efficiency of interventions. A good discussion and examples are provided to illustrate the difference between average and incremental cost-effectiveness ratios.

6. Doubilet PM, Weinstein MC, McNeil BJ. Use and misuse of the term "cost-effective" in medicine. N Engl J Med 1986 Jan 23;314(4):253–6.

This paper contains a thorough discussion of the definition of "cost-effective" and outlines some of the typical misuses of the term. Some of the common misuses of the term equate "cost-effective" with "cost-saving" or "more effective". The authors define an appropriate definition of "cost-effective" as "having an outcome worth its cost compared to other alternatives".

7. Drummond MF. Economic evaluation of pharmaceuticals: science or marketing? Pharmacoeconomics 1992;1:8–13.

The author discusses the differences between clinical trials and economic studies as methods of technology assessment. He considers whether economic studies are more marketing than science, as economic analyses often are not held to the same standards as clinical studies that are used for regulatory approval. Issues of bias, ethics, the perceived value of economic endpoints, and the need to set methodological standards for scrutinizing the results of economic studies are addressed specifically.

8. Drummond MF, Stoddart GL, Torrance GW. Methods for the economic evaluation of health care programmes. Oxford: Oxford University Press, 1987.

This textbook includes detailed descriptions of the methodologic principles of economic evaluation of health care. The authors concentrate on practical issues that researchers need to consider when undertaking an economic evaluation. Methods for critical assessment of the pharmacoeconomic literature are provided. Critical appraisal of published articles of economic evaluations is used to illustrate the important points made in each chapter.

9. Gold MR, Siegel JE, Russell LB, Weinstein MC. Cost-effectiveness in health and medicine. New York, NY: Oxford University Press, 1996.

This book, a report of a United States Public Health Service appointed expert panel, makes a significant contribution toward improving the methods of CEA. Each chapter of this book is dedicated to standardization of conducting and reporting CEAs. Chapter 9 gives recommendations to investigators on how to report and submit a cost-effective analysis for publication.

10. Horn SD, Sharkey PD, Levy R. Managed care pharmacoeconomic research model based on the managed care outcomes project. J Pharm Prac 1995;8:172–7.

The authors describe and discuss the major components of a clinical practice improvement study. Clinical practice improvement, as defined by the authors, is a methodology that creates a clinical laboratory, built into every day practice settings, to find and test the best practices. The four main components (planning, monitoring, process stabilization, and improving) of a clinical practice improvement study are described in detail. Also described is the Managed Care Outcomes Project, a multisite clinical practice improvement study that examines the variations in clinical status and resource use of patients in health maintenance organizations with either acute of chronic conditions over a 1-year period.

11. Jolicoeur LM, Jones-Grizzle AJ, Boyer JG. Guidelines for performing a pharmacoeconomic analysis. Am J Hosp Pharm 1992;49:1741–7.

The four basic types of pharmacoeconomic analysis and 10 steps for constructing a well-designed study are described. Each pharmacoeconomic method measures costs in monetary terms; the differences lie in the valuation of outcomes for each of the different types of analyses: cost-benefit analysis, cost-effectiveness analysis (CEA), cost-minimization analysis, and cost-utility analysis. A hospital-related example of designing a CEA after the 10-step process is described to assist the pharmacist undertaking a pharmacoeconomic evaluation.

12. Kobelt G. Health economics: an introduction to economic evaluation, 2nd ed. London: Office of Health Economics, 2002.

This new text sponsored by the Office of Health Economics in London provides a good overview of the issues associated with multiple approaches to economic evaluation. The primary feature of this introduction to economic evaluation is the use of practical examples to show how the techniques can be applied in different types of studies.

13. Kozma CM, Kirchdoerfer LJ. Obtaining pharmacoeconomic data in health care organizations. Top Hosp Pharm Manage 1994;13:23–30.

The process and techniques of obtaining and collecting pharmacoeconomic data in various health care organizations, specifically in hospitals, physicians offices, and pharmacies, are illustrated. The authors also discuss the strengths and weaknesses of each type of data, and the role that pharmacoeconomic data has in the decision-making process. The relationship between the health care organization and the primary components needed to conduct a complete pharmacoeconomic analysis (clinical, humanistic, and economic outcomes) also is described.

14. Lee JT, Sanchez LA. Interpretation of "cost-effective" and soundness of economic evaluations in the pharmacy literature. Am J Hosp Pharm 1991;48:2622–7.

The authors present a systematic assessment of 65 studies concerned with cost issues published between 1985 and 1990. Each study was evaluated according to 10 methodologic criteria based on the 10 questions generated by previous investigators (see Reference 8). In 55 percent (36) of articles reviewed, cost-effectiveness was misinterpreted as cost-savings. Only three of the 10 criteria were fulfilled by 50 percent or more of the studies evaluated. Many pharmacoeconomic studies incorrectly used the term cost-effective and inadequately addressed basic methodologic components of an economic evaluation.

15. Mooney GH, Drummond MF. Part I: what is economics? Br Med J 1982;285:949–50, 1024–5.

16. Mooney GH, Drummond MF. Part II: financing health care. Br Med J 1982;285:1101–2, 1191–2.

17. Mooney GH, Drummond MF. Part III: developing health care policies. Br Med J 1982;285:1263–4, 1329–31.

18. Mooney GH, Drummond MF. Part IV: organizing health care resources. Br Med J 1982;285:1405–6, 1485–6.

19. Mooney GH, Drummond MF. Part V: assessing the costs and benefits of treatment alternatives. Br Med J 1982;285:1561–3, 1638–9.

20. Mooney GH, Drummond MF. Part VI: challenges for the future. Br Med J 1982;285:1727–8, 1983;286:40–1.

This six-part series is a summary of basic economic issues pertinent to the delivery of health care and how economic principles can contribute to financing, planning, organizing, and evaluating health services. Although this series was published in 1982, much of the information is still useful. Part I includes a description of economics and discusses the application of economic evaluations to health care. Part II provides a discussion of the differences between health care and other goods and services. There also is a brief discussion of the complex relationships influencing the supply and demand for health care services. Parts III and IV include discussions of economic issues encountered in developing health care policy and organizing health care resources using the national Health Service in the United Kingdom for illustration. Part V provides a brief description of the types of economic evaluations used to evaluate the costs and consequences of alternatives. Part VI focuses primarily on problems and challenges facing the National Health Service in the 1980s.

21. Neuhauser D, Lewicki A. What do we gain from the sixth stool guaiac? N Engl J Med 1975;293:226–8.

This study is a classic example of the difference between average and marginal cost-effectiveness. The goal of the study was to evaluate the marginal cost of performing multiple sequential stool guaiac tests as a screen for colon cancer. The analysis uses direct medical costs associated with the screening test, as well as the cost of confirmatory testing with barium-enema studies. A sensitivity analysis is performed to determine the effect of lower stool guaiac test sensitivity on marginal cost. Results of the analysis of using six stool guaiac tests show the dramatic difference between the average cost-effectiveness ratio calculated as $2,451 for each case of colon cancer identified, and the marginal cost-effectiveness for the six tests calculated as $47,107,214 for each new case identified.

22. Pettiti DB. Meta-analysis, decision analysis, and cost-effectiveness analysis: methods for quantitative synthesis in medicine. Oxford: Oxford University Press, 1994.

This book presents detail of the more practical aspects of conducting a meta-analysis, decision analysis, and CEA. The three analyses are covered together in this one text because they are conceptually related quantitative methods for combining information to arrive at a summary conclusion. Authors discuss how to design, conduct, analyze, and interpret these three analyses. In each chapter, several practical issues illustrating critical concepts of these three methodologies are presented. A basic understanding of statistical principles is needed to understand some of the statistical issues related to meta-analysis.

23. Revicki DA, Luce BR. Methods of pharmacoeconomic evaluation of new medical treatments in psychiatry. Psychopharmacol Bull 1995;31:57–65.

These authors review some basic concepts of outcomes research and present the types of designs used in pharmacoeconomic evaluation. A brief review of CEA and health-related quality-of-life measurement is provided along with a detailed description of prospective and retrospective pharmacoeconomic research designs.

24. Rubenstein EB, Elting LS. Pharmacoeconomic analyses: whose perspective counts and costs the most? Am J Hosp Pharm 1994;51:1564–71.

This paper is a commentary as well as a review and update of principles for performing economic analyses. The authors indicate that stating the perspective, costs, and benefits of the alternatives considered in an analysis is not enough. New standards are proposed stating that patient and physician perspectives should always be included in the analysis. The authors also indicate that costs and benefits of therapy should be clinically relevant, reflect medical decisions as they are actually made, and should represent the standard of excellent care.

25. Sacristan JA, Day SJ, Navarro O, Ramos J, Hernandez JM. Use of confidence intervals and sample size calculations in health economic studies. Ann Pharmacother 1995;29:719–25.

The calculation, advantages, and use of confidence intervals in pharmacoeconomic analyses are discussed. Calculation of confidence intervals around cost-effectiveness ratios is complicated because of the sampling error in the numerator and denominator of the ratio. Using Fieller's theorem, the authors describe a method for calculation of confidence intervals around a cost-effectiveness ratio. The authors believe that the use of confidence intervals and sensitivity analysis makes it possible to determine uncertainty related and unrelated to variability in sample data, allowing for use of the most objective information available.

26. Sacristan JA, Soto J, Galende I. Evaluation of pharmacoeconomic studies: use of a checklist. Ann Pharmacother 1993;27:1126–32.

The authors review basic concepts underlying pharmacoeconomic analysis and provide a 12-question checklist that can be used to systematically evaluate the quality of pharmacoeconomic studies. A detailed description of the criteria used in the 12-question checklist is provided.

27. Sanchez LA. Conducting pharmacoeconomic evaluations in a hospital setting. Hosp Pharm 1995;30:412–6, 428.

The author presents a 14-step guideline for conducting pharmacoeconomic evaluations that is based on the 10-step approach presented in Reference 11. This approach differs in that it expands the 10-step process to accommodate a hospital-based setting. The particular limitations of conducting pharmacoeconomic research within the hospital environment also are presented.

28. Weinstein MC, Fineberg HV. Clinical decision analysis. Philadelphia, PA: W.B. Saunders Company, 1980.

This book is an in-depth text on the theory involved in clinical decision-making and decision-analysis. It was published in 1980 but is still a valuable resource when undertaking a pharmacoeconomic study using modeling techniques. The authors present decision trees for structuring decisions, a discussion of probabilities in decision-making, the value of clinical judgments in the decision-making process, and utility analysis. Examples are provided to illustrate important points in each chapter. Exercises with solutions at the end of each chapter also are provided.

Self-Assessment Questions

1. A cost-effectiveness study comparing two alternatives for treating rheumatoid arthritis was conducted. The incremental cost-effectiveness ratio of drug B in comparison to drug A was reported to be $32 per symptom-free day. Which one of the following is the best interpretation of this ratio?

   A. It costs $32 per case to treat rheumatoid arthritis with drug B.
   B. drug B is more cost-effective than drug A.
   C. For every extra symptom-free day gained by using drug B, it costs an additional $32 over drug A.
   D. It costs $32 per case more to treat rheumatoid arthritis with drug B than with drug A.

2. All except which one of the following are advantages of a conducting a cost-effectiveness study as part of a randomized, controlled trial?

   A. Provides good internal validity.
   B. Potentially low cost.
   C. Provides results that are generalizable and reflect accurately actual practice patterns and broad patient populations.
   D. Excellent credibility.

3. All except which one of the following are general characteristics of cost-effectiveness analyses (CEAs)?

   A. At least two drugs or therapeutic interventions which have the same clinical objective are compared.
   B. Costs are measured in economic terms and the outcome of interest is measured in natural units.
   C. In special cases, may include the incorporation of functional status, health status, or quality of life.
   D. Uses the human capital approach to place a dollar value on outcomes.

4. A retrospective, case-control design was used to evaluate the cost-effectiveness of two alternatives for preventing fractures because of osteoporosis in postmenopausal women. The total costs for drug A were found to be $ 2400; drug A saved 200 years of life. Total costs for drug B were $1800; drug B saved 134 years of life. Which one of the following is the incremental cost-effectiveness ratio for drug A?

   A. $0.11 per life-year saved.
   B. $9.10 per life-year saved.
   C. $12.00 per life-year saved.
   D. $13.40 per life-year saved.

5. Which one of the following sets of costs and outcomes might be included in a cost-effectiveness study that is conducted from the perspective of a benefits manager for a large corporation?

   A. Direct medical and indirect costs; clinical, economic, and humanistic outcomes.
   B. Direct medical costs only; clinical outcomes only.

C. Direct medical and direct nonmedical costs; clinical and humanistic outcomes.
D. Direct medical costs; clinical, and economic outcomes.

6. All except which one of the following are true regarding simulation designs used to conduct a CEA?
   A. Simulations provide data that are as reliable as those obtained though an economic clinical trial.
   B. Simulations allow for estimation of costs and consequences without the trouble of a prospective trial.
   C. Simulations are relatively inexpensive.
   D. Simulations can be adapted for alternate questions.

7. Which one of the following is true of naturalistic trials?
   A. They reflect costs and outcomes in actual practice.
   B. Compared to a piggyback, randomized, controlled trial, they are less expensive to conduct.
   C. They require a small study population.
   D. Data collection occurs over a long duration.

8. Which one of the following is an advantage of a cost-effectiveness study using an observational design?
   A. It has good internal validity.
   B. It requires a small number of patients.
   C. There is good external validity.
   D. One is able to assess effectiveness parameters in monetary terms.

9. Which one of the following study designs may be best if resources and timeframe are limited?
   A. Observational study.
   B. Simulation design.
   C. Epidemiologic design.
   D. Piggyback, clinical trial.

COST-UTILITY ANALYSIS

Duska Franic, Pharm.D., Ph.D.; Dev Pathak, D.B.A.;
W. Jacqueline Kwong, Pharm.D., M.S.; and
Jerome Pierson, R.Ph.,Ph.D.

Outline

I. Definitions
  A. Cost-utility analysis (CUA) is an economic evaluation that integrates both costs and consequences of health programs within the utility analysis framework
    1. May be considered a variation of cost-effectiveness analysis
    2. Differences between cost-utility and cost-effectiveness analyses
      a. cost-utility analysis requires the measurement of final outcomes in terms of changes in life expectancy adjusted for patient preferences
      b. intermediate outcomes are not appropriate to use in cost-utility analysis
    3. Outcomes of cost-utility analysis are often expressed in quality-adjusted life years (QALY) gained
  B. Utilities are the numbers representing the strength of individual preferences for particular outcomes when faced with uncertainty
    1. Based on rational decision-making utility theory (Reference 9)
  C. Results of a cost-utility analysis are not expressed in cost per utility because utility values are difficult to comprehend
    1. Results expressed as cost per quality-adjusted life years (QALY) gained, per healthy year equivalents (HYE), per well-years gained, per time without symptoms and toxicity (TWiST), and others
    2. Other units of outcome proposed for use include function years, value-adjusted years, and quality-adjusted life expectancy
    3. Units of outcome/effectiveness are comprehensive measures of both quantity and quality

II. Applications of cost-utility analysis
  A. Cost-utility analysis is the most difficult and expensive economic evaluation method to use
  B. A recent guideline recommends the following applications (Reference 9)
    1. Quality of life is the important outcome
      a. example—psychological well-being, physical, and social function are important in the treatment of arthritis
    2. Quality of life is an important outcome
      a. example—chemotherapy may increase survival but decrease well-being; both quality and quantity of life are important
    3. The program in question affects both morbidity and mortality
      a. example—postmenopausal estrogen therapy improves patient quality of life, but may increase or decrease mortality

4. The programs being compared have a wide range of different kinds or outcomes and a common unit of output is desirable
    a. example—choice between an expansion of the neonatal intensive care unit or establishing a hypertension clinic
5. Comparing a program to others that have already been evaluated using cost-utility analysis

C. Cost-utility analysis should not be used when:
1. Only immediate output effectiveness data can be obtained
2. Data have shown the alternatives are equally effective
3. Quality of life is important, but can be captured using a single variable measured in easily understood units
4. The extra cost of obtaining and using utility values is judged to be in itself not cost-effective

D. United States Public Health Service says cost-utility analysis is appropriate to use when:
1. Evaluating mutually compatible health interventions
    a. example—comparing childhood vaccinations, alcohol and drug rehabilitation, and hypertension screening within a constrained budget to decide which program(s) to fund
2. Choosing the magnitude of selected health interventions—how much should an intervention be pursued?
    a. examples—applying treatment to a larger pool of individuals, or applying treatment to same number of individuals but increasing the number of physician visits per patient
3. Evaluating mutually exclusive health interventions
    a. example—treatment of gallstones with surgery versus drug therapy

III. Measurement of Costs

A. As with other types of economic evaluations, should consider direct medical costs, direct nonmedical costs, indirect costs, and intangible costs
1. The specific costs considered vary with the study perspective
2. Discounting should be performed to account for the time value of money for costs incurred over a period longer than 1 year
3. Costs should reflect resources consumed by the health intervention (opportunity costs); costs in accounting may not reflect resource utilization completely

B. Opportunity costs—the value of the forgone benefits when the resource is not available for its best alternatives

IV. Measurement of utility

A. Quality-adjusted life years
1. Quantity of life (Y)
    a. often measured in years, but can also be expressed in months, days, hours, or other units of time
    b. usually is the outcome measure in cost-effectiveness analysis (e.g., life expectancy)
2. Quality of life (Q)
    a. main differentiation of cost-utility analysis from cost-effectiveness analysis
    b. Q is the quality level of health states perceived by an individual, or the individual preferences (utilities) of health states
    c. Q is usually equal to 1.0 for normal health and 0 for death
    d. Q is expressed as a negative value for health states considered worse than death (e.g., some individuals may consider quadriplegia a fate worse than death)
3. Quality-adjusted life years
    a. is a multiple of quantity (Y) and quality (Q) of life
    b. example one—20 years of normal health
        i. life expectancy = 20 years
        ii. quality of life = 1.0 util
        iii. QALY = 20 years x 1.0 util = 20 QALYs
    c. example two—20 years of chronic illness
        i. life expectancy = 20 years
        ii. quality of life = 0.5 util
        iii. QALY = 20 years x 0.5 util = 10 QALYs (see Figure 1)
4. Assumptions underlying quality-adjusted life years (Reference 37)
    a. full healthy life and death are used as reference states for utility values and they represent all and none respectively in the health domain
    b. interpersonal utility comparisons are restricted to only the health domain because quality-adjusted life years only captures health-related utility
    c. utility value for a full healthy life is set equal for each individual at birth
        i. example—one QALY gained for a 20-year-old person is counted equally as that for a 80-year-old person
5. (mutually) utility independent assumption

a. attributes of quality and quantity must be independent of each other (see Figure 2)

6. In addition to (mutually) utility independent assumption two other assumptions for QALYs are described (1) constant proportional trade off assumption and (2) risk neutrality. Discussion of these assumptions are beyond the scope of this paper. Interested readers are referred to Reference 33 for further discussion.
   a. For example—an individual is indifferent about living either 14 years with mild angina and playing a lottery in which there is a 0.5 chance of living 10 years with mild angina or a 0.5 chance of living 20 years with mild angina. In this tradeoff, all health outcomes are such that while alive the individual has mild angina. The tradeoff involves quantity of life only and not quality of life while alive (i.e., quality of life is held constant); according to utility independence assumption, the individual would have the same preferences over length of life if, in making a choice among these health outcomes, mild angina is replaced by another health state at each endpoint, for example, no angina for each health state

B. Methods for obtaining utility values
   1. Three sources of utility values
      a. literature
         i. do the health states and subjects used in past studies match those of your study?
         ii. were the measurement instruments used in the literature valid? (see Table 1)
      b. judgment values
         i. estimates of utility values based on judgments from health professionals or experts
         ii. often subjective and require extensive sensitivity analysis
      c. direct measurement from subjects

C. Exercise 1: Calculation of Quality-Adjusted Life Years

D. Obtaining utility values directly from subjects
   1. Decision theory approach to measurement of utility
      a. based on utility theory of rational decision making that a rational person would choose an alternative with the highest expected utility
      b. three fundamental axioms
         i. transitivity
         ii. if A > B, and B > C, then A > C
         iii. continuity (see Figure 3)
         iv. if A > B and B > C , there is a probability p at which an individual is indifferent between receiving A with
            a) probability of p or C at a probability of 1 – p versus getting B for certain
      c. substitutability
         i. refer to the following for a detailed description (Reference 37) if interested
   2. standard gamble
      a. classic method to measure cardinal preferences
      b. subject is offered choice between two alternatives that lead to three health states
      c. subject is asked to align the health states in an order of preference
         i. most preferred health state = state h
         ii. least preferred health state = state j
         iii. between most preferred and least preferred = state i
      d. to study the utility value for state i in reference to state h and state j
      e. Alternative 1: two possible outcomes
         i. probability p to be in state h
         ii. probability 1 - p to be in state j
      f. Alternative 2 is to be in state i with 100 percent certainty (pi = 1.0) (see Figure 4)
      g. the value of p is altered until the subject becomes indifferent between Alternative 1 and 2
      h. equating multiples of utility values and probabilities:
         i. $h_i\ p_i = h_h\ p + h_j\ (1 - p)$ and simplify to $h_i = h_h\ p + h_j\ (1 - p)$ (equation 1)
      i. example—obtaining utility values for chronic asthma by standard gamble
      j. begins with ranking health states by preference; for example, healthy (state h) > chronic asthma (i) > death (j)
         i. choose one of two alternatives
            a) Alternative 1: probability p to be healthy for life and probability 1 – p to die immediately
            b) Alternative 2: chronic asthma for life for certain
         ii. begin with p = 1.0
            b) Alternative 1: a gamble of probability of p = 1.0 (or 100 percent) to be healthy for the rest of his life or probability of 0 to die immediately
            c) Alternative 2: chronic asthma for life for certain
         iii. because healthy is preferred to chronic asthma, Alternative 1 is chosen
      h. choose between the two alternatives when probability is changed to 0
         i. Alternative 1: probability 0 of being healthy and probability of 1.0 for immediate death

ii. Alternative 2: chronic asthma for life for certain
iii. because chronic asthma is preferred to death, Alternative 2 is chosen

i. probability p is alternately changed by a predetermined discrete percentage, such as 10 percent decrements from 1 and 10 percent decrements from 0 until the subject is indifferent between the two alternatives
   i. the following gambles of Alternative 1 included:
      a) 0.90 chance to be healthy or 0.10 chance to die immediately
      b) 0.10 chance to be healthy or 0.90 chance to die immediately
      c) 0.80 chance to be healthy or 0.20 chance to die immediately
      d) 0.20 chance to be healthy or 0.80 chance to die immediately
   ii. assume subject is indifferent between Alternative 1 and 2 at p = 0.60
      a) Alternative 1: probability 0.6 to be healthy or probability 0.40 to die immediately
      b) Alternative 2: chronic asthma for life for certain
      c) substitute p = 0.60 into equation 1, $h_{chronic\ asthma} = h_{healthy}\ (0.6) + h_{death}\ (1 - 0.6)$
      $h_{chronic\ asthma} = (1.0)(0.6) + 0\ (1 - 0.6)$, $h_{chronic\ asthma} = 0.6$
   iii. if preference is switched between p = 0.60 and p = 0.50—at p = 0.60, Alternative 1 is preferred to Alternative 2 and at p = 0.50, Alternative 2 is preferred to Alternative 1, then substitute p = (0.60 + 0.50) ÷ 2 = 0.55 into equation 1; thus hasthma = p = 0.55

j. probability wheel is an adjustable disk divided into two sectors with two different colors to represent state h and state j to facilitate subject's understanding of probabilities

3. time tradeoff
   a. subject chooses between two alternatives
   b. exact method depends on whether the health state in question is preferred to death or worse than death
   c. time tradeoff for a chronic health state i preferred to death (see Figure 5)
      i. Alternative 1: to be in health state i for time t followed by death (area CEFGC)
      ii. Alternative 2: to be healthy for time x which is equal to or shorter than t, and followed by death (area CABDC)
      iii. duration of time x is varied until subject is indifferent between the two alternatives
      iv. utility of health state i (hi) is obtained by equating the areas under the curve outlined by the two alternatives as appeared in Figure 5; hi = x ÷ t
   d. similar to standard gamble, except with varying duration of health state instead of probabilities
      i. example—using time tradeoff to measure utility values of an amputated state
   e. begin with determining order of preference: healthy > post-amputation > death
      i. method to determine utility values for health state preferred to death is used
   f. choose one of the two alternatives beginning with x = t = life expectancy
      i Alternative 1: to live remaining life being amputated for 30 years (t = 30 years)
      ii. Alternative 2: to live in perfect health for 30 years (x – t), then die without complications
      iii. because healthy is preferred to amputated, Alternative 2 is chosen
   g. choose one of the two alternatives again:
      i. Alternative 1: to live remaining life being amputated for 30 years (t = 30 years)
      ii. Alternative 2: to die immediately (x = 0)
      iii. because amputated state is preferred to death, Alternative 1 is chosen
   h. time x is then alternately decreased from t and increased from 0 by a predetermined number of years (e.g., 5 years) until the subject is indifferent between the two alternatives for Alternative 2; Alternative 1 remains the same throughout the time tradeoff method
      i. descriptions for Alternative 2 are: to live in perfect health for 25 years and die; to live in perfect health for 5 years and die; to live in perfect health for 20 years and die; to live in perfect health for 10 years and die; etc.
      ii. if the subject becomes indifferent between Alternatives 1 and 2 when x = 20 years, then h amputated = 20 ÷ 30 = 0.67
4. utility values obtained from different methods are often different from each other
5. standard gamble is the only true measure of utility
6. utility values from standard gamble, time tradeoff, and rating scale can be considered equated at the population level
7. Psychometric theory approach to measurement of utility

E. Quality of Well-Being Scale (QWB)
   1. Quality of Well-Being Scale categorizes individuals according to their symptoms and functioning levels
      a. utility weights for loss of subject mobility, physical activity, social activity, and symptoms are standardized
   2. overall well-being score is computed by adding the standardized utility weights for subject mobility, physical activity, social activity, and symptoms and substituted into the following equation:
      WY = [No. of persons x (1.0 + CPXwt + MOBwt + PACwt
   + SACwt) x time] (see Tables 2 and 3)

a. example—a hypothetical program incurs total costs of $20,000 per year to prevent 200 patients from suffering a self-limiting illness that results in excessive anxiety (CPX-27), inability to drive a car due to health-related reasons (PAC-2), and limited primary role activity (SAC-3) due to poor health which lasts for 10 days
   i. loss of utility weights are CPX-27 = -0.257, PAC-2 = -0.060, and SAC-3 = -0.061
   ii. patient well-being score = 1.0 + (-0.257) + (-0.060) + (-0.061) = 0.622
   iii. number of well-years gained from this program = (1 – 0.622) well being per patient x 10 days ÷ 365 days/year x 200 patients = 2.07 well-years
   iv. cost per well-year ratio = $20,000 ÷ 2.07 well-years = $9662 per well-year

3. Exercise 2: Calculation of Well-Years

F. European Quality of Life (EQ-5D or EuroQol)
1. Generic nondisease specific quality-of-life instrument
2. Designed to complement other quality-of-life instruments
3. Use multicenter, multidisciplinary, international quality-of-life studies
4. EuroQol is a 6-item quality-of-life questionnaire consisting of 2 sections:
   a. First section of EQ-5D describes health related quality of life according to five aspects or dimensions of health: mobility, self-care, usual activities, pain/discomfort and anxiety and depression
   b. Each dimension of health is composed of three levels and respondents are asked to select the level for each dimension that best reflects their own health state. For example respondents can self report their mobility as no problems walking about, some problems walking about, or confirmed in bed
   c. Respondents select of one of the three alternatives for each of the five different health states
   d. EQ-5D can theoretically describe up to 243 health states (i.e., 35) in addition to death and unconscious
   e. Numbers obtained can be converted to a single score for use in CUA using values derived from general population. Full health and death are scaled to 1.0 and zero, respectively (See figure 3b—EQ-5D instrument)
5. EQ-VAS is a 20cm vertical thermometer scale anchored at zero—worst imaginable health state and 100—best imaginable health state. (See figure 3c—EQ-VAS instrument)
   i. Administration: self-, interviewer-, or proxy administered
   ii. Time to complete: 2 - 3 minutes to complete
   iii. Example of (1) assessment of health using EQ-5D instrument and computation of EQ-5D utility

G. Health Utilities Index (HYI)
a. Developed by McMaster's University (Reference 11)
b. Based on utility theory. Since it contains many attributes (dimensions) referred to as multiattribute and also based on utility theory, therefore foundations lie in multiattribute utility theory (MAUT)
c. HUI is a family of generic nondisease specific quality-of-life instruments
d. Family consists of three instruments HUI I to HUI III
   i. HUI instruments can be used alone or in combination with other quality-of-life instruments including each other (e.g., HUI II with HUI III) since the different "family" members cover differ attributes of health
   ii. This chapter focuses on HUI III
      a) Eight-item quality of life questionnaire consisting of eight dimensions: vision, hearing, speech, ambulation, dexterity, emotion, cognition, pain
      b) Each attribute is composed of five to six levels
      c) EQ-5D can theoretically describe up to 972,000 different health states
      d) Numbers obtained can be converted to a single score for use in CUA
      e) Full health and death are scaled to 1.0 and zero, respectively
      f) Use:
         1) Popular in Canada used in population health studies
         2) 1990 Ontario Health Survey
         3) National Population Survey
         4) National Longitudinal Health Survey of Children in Canada
         5) Clinical and program evaluation studies – pediatrics and adults
         6) AIDS, cancer, stroke, alzheimers, lupus, liver transplant, osteoporosis (see figure 3d)
      g) Administration: self-, interviewer-, or proxy administered
      h) Time to complete: three to five minutes to complete
      i) Example of computation of HUI utility from CHEPA working paper series #92-18 (example also listed on CHEPA Web site *www.healthutilities.com*)

H. Short Form 36 (SF-36)
1. Widely used measure assessing health status
2. Consists of eight dimensions each scored 0 to 100.
3. Dimension scores cannot be combined to produce value to use in CUA

G. Alternative—SF-6D

1. An approach based on HUI® to estimate a single index from SF-36 that can be used in CUA (Reference 5)
2. Six Dimensions: physical functioning, role limitation, social functioning, bodily pain, mental health vitality
3. Produce a preference score (0 to 1.0) to estimate QALYs

V. Expression of Results
   A. Results of cost-utility analysis usually expressed in cost per quality-adjusted life years gained or cost per healthy year equivalents gained rather than cost per utility
   B. Results of cost-utility analysis are similar to cost-effectiveness analysis. Only final output effectiveness data will suffice as effectiveness measures in a cost-utility analysis (e.g., number of lives saved, disability days averted)
   C. Effectiveness in cost-utility analysis incorporates simultaneously both the change in quality (morbidity) and quantity of life (mortality)
      1. Example of CUA comparing two treatments (Reference 8)
         a) Treatment A: chemotherapy after surgical resection
         b) Treatment B: surgical resection only
         c) Utility values are in reference to perfect health (1.0) and death (0) (see Table 4)
         d) Incremental analysis finds the additional costs for an additional unit of outcome between two interventions
         e) incremental cost-effectiveness ratio is: ($20,000 - $10,000) ÷ (4.5 years – 3.5 years) = $10,000 per life-year gained
         f) incremental cost-utility ratio is: ($20,000 – $10,000) ÷ (3.6 QALY – 3.15 QALY) = $22,222 per QALY gained
   D. Cost-utility analysis is more comprehensive as it reflects patient preferences or quality of life in addition to quantity of life; cost-utility analysis is gaining popularity as a method to compare clinical interventions

VI. Guidelines for policy implementation
   A. If cost per well-year gained is < $20,000, it is a cost-effective intervention; if cost per well-year gained is $20,000 – $100,000, the program is controversial but justifiable; if cost per well-year gained is >$100,000, the intervention is of questionable value
   B. Discounting nonmonetary benefits such as the quantity of life-years gained is still controversial
      1. Discounting to account for individual time preference because people usually prefer to receive benefits earlier than later
      2. Some question whether a future expectation of quantity of life can be exchanged for life now
      3. It is argued that quantity of life should be discounted to remain consistent with the discounting of future monetary costs
      4. Lack of discounting gives equal weight to life-years generated now or in the distant future
      5. Discounting results in lowering the value for future life years, which in turns lowers the value of program designed for future generations
   C. Perspective
      1. Three general perspectives
         a. Patients
         b. Societal (General Public)
            i. Recommended by:
               a) United States Cost Effectiveness Panel (1996)
               b) The General Health Policy Model (Reference 20)
         c. Physicians or "expert" panel
      2. Use of Proxy or caregivers to acquire utility estimates
      3. Which perspective is correct?
      4. When to use which perspective

VII. League Tables or "QALY" league tables
   A. Definition: table listing (marginal) cost per QALY gained
   B. Assumptions:
      1. QALYs adequately measure health benefits
      2. No other forms of benefit
   C. How are they used:
      1. Priority setting: compare benefits versus costs of different health care interventions
      2. UK National Institute for Excellence (NICE)
      3. World Health Organization (WHO) development of a list of 100 health interventions worldwide
   D. Examples:
      1. The first league table was published on coronary artery bypass graft (CABG) surgery in 1985 in the British Medical Journal
   E. Controversy

1. Oregon Experiment
2. Should be treated with care even if it is assumed that QALYs adequately measure utility

VIII. Strengths, limitations, and controversies of cost-utility analysis

A. Strengths
1. Similar to cost-benefit analysis, the primary strength of cost-utility analysis is its ability to integrate both quantity and quality into a common unit of measure
2. cost-utility analysis avoids the problem encountered by cost-benefit analysis to translate patient-reported outcomes into monetary units
3. cost-utility analysis is often criticized as being biased towards people in the workforce or those who are wealthy, especially when the human capital approach is used
4. cost-utility analysis can incorporate multiple outcomes simultaneously; it accounts for the quality or desirability of outcomes

B. Limitations and controversies with quality-adjusted life years
1. different measurement methods of utility values often yield different utility weights; because methods to measure utility values are not comparable, a QALY may not be comparable to another QALY
2. the numerical value of QALY gained from a program to prevent acute conditions of short duration is so small that decision makers may mistakenly undervalue the contribution of such a prevention program
   a. example— a patient receives chemotherapy six times a year and suffers emesis episodes for 24 hours after each round of therapy
      i. utility value for having cancer = 0.60
      ii. utility value for having emesis = 0
      iii. Drug A can prevent emesis occurring within 24 hours after chemotherapy
      iv. QALY gained from Drug A = 0.60 x 6 days ÷ (365 days/year) = 0.0098 QALY per patient
3. quality-adjusted life years assumes during the conversion of ill health to full health takes place in a linear fashion; this risk neutrality assumption may not hold in reality, resulting in an underestimation of potential value of health interventions (see Figure 6)
   a. example—forty years of healthy life is same as QALY = 40
      i. if utility of chronic health state = 0.75, then quality-adjusted life years under risk neutrality assumption = 40 x 0.75 = 30 QALYs; and quality-adjusted life years under subject indifference curve = 15 QALYs
      ii. the maximum potential gains in QALY brought by a health intervention are undervalued by the risk neutrality assumption:
      iii. risk neutrality assumption: 40 QALYs – 30 QALYs = 10 QALYs gained
      iv. indifference curve risk averted: 40 QALYs – 15 QALYs = 25 QALYs gained

C. Alternative approaches to quality-adjusted life years
1. healthy year equivalents has been suggested to be an alternative to QALY
2. healthy year equivalents stems directly from the_individual's utility function and, thus, fully reflects an individual's preferences

D. Other limitations include spillover effects in patients with multiple disease states, relationship between healthy and other domains of life, the link between preferences from judgment response and the final choice

VIV. General limitations of cost-utility analysis

A. cost-utility analysis can be challenged on moral grounds
1. even though the cost-utility ratio is larger for childhood vaccinations than alcohol rehabilitation programs, should the alcohol rehabilitation program be funded and not childhood vaccinations?

B. uncertainties on clinical efficacy due to limited precision in biological and medical technology cannot be resolved by cost-utility analysis

C. the apparent sophistication of cost-utility analysis may mislead readers to neglect its limitations

D. more resources are needed to conduct a cost-utility analysis; the measurement of quality is challenging

E. when using utility values from the literature the decision maker must ask if the intents, perspectives, study subjects, and theory used in the original studies the same as those of the current study

F. when obtaining utility values directly from subjects, a considerable investment of time, energy and resources is needed. Investigators may not be familiar with measurement techniques

G. health care providers are able to readily understand the description of various health states, but their preferences may be biased

H. obtaining utility values from a patient or the general population is difficult; too much respondent burden may exist in standard gamble and time tradeoff techniques

I. it may be considered offensive to quantify or assign numbers to quality of life

J. requires extensive development of instrumentation means for data collection (e.g., visual aids, trained interviewers, interviewer manuals, response recording forms)

K. data may require statistical transformation

X. Evaluating the cost-utility analysis literature
   A. Criteria for reviewing cost-utility analysis literature
   B. Concrete symptoms and dysfunctions of health states should be described
   C. The source of utility weights should be mentioned
   D. Implication in terms of equivalence numbers and their plausibility should be described
   E. The composition of the gain in QALYs in terms of the relative contributions of increased quantity and quality should be discussed
   F. Sensitivity analysis should be conducted on utility weights
   G. All data, assumptions, and procedures behind each estimate of a QALY should be clearly presented so that the decision maker can perform alternative calculations based on different assumptions
   H. Additional information from the authors should be readily available

XI. Conclusion
   A. Researchers must recognize that regardless of how carefully real preferences are measured, they are not choices nor do they always materialize in choices. Hence, decisions to allocate resources based on preference measures alone require faith in inferential leaps.

Learning Objectives

1. Understand and explain the theoretical foundations of cost-utility analysis.
2. Apply and interpret cost-utility analysis studies.
3. Compare and contrast major sources for obtaining measures of utility with regard to ease of obtainment and potential applications.
4. Demonstrate how to calculate quality-adjusted life years using preference-based measures.
5. Compare and contrast major quality-of-life instruments.
6. Evaluate the strengths and limitations of a cost-utility analysis study.
7. Evaluate critically published literature using cost-utility analysis

Abbreviations in this chapter

CABG	Coronary artery bypass graft
CPX	symptom problems
CUA	Cost-utility analysis
EQ-5D or EuroQol	European Quality of Life Instrument
EQ-VAS	European Quality of Life Visual Analogue Scale
HUI	Health utilities index
HYE	Healthy year equivilant
MAUT	Multiattribute utility theory
MOB	mobility
PAC	physical activity
RS	rating scale
SAC	social activity
SAUT	single attribute utility theory
SF-36	Short Form 36
SG	standard gamble
TTO	time trade-off
TWiST	Time without symptoms and toxicity
QALE	Quality-adjusted life expectancy
QALY	Quality-adjusted life years
Q-TWiST	Quality-adjusted time without symptoms toxicity
QWB	Quality of well-being scale
WHO	World Health Organization

Definitions

Cost-utility analysis (CUA) is a form of economic evaluation that integrates both the costs and consequences of health programs within the utility analysis framework. Due to its similarity to cost-effectiveness analysis, it is sometimes regarded as a variation of cost-effectiveness analysis. The primary distinguishing feature between cost-effectiveness and cost-utility analyses is the measurement of outcomes. Outcomes of cost-utility analyses often are expressed in terms of gains in quality-adjusted life years (QALYs). Cost-utility analysis requires the measurement of final outcomes in terms of changes in life expectancy, such as number of life years gained or disability days reduced, adjusted for patient preferences, or utility. In contrast to cost-effectiveness analysis, intermediate outcomes are not appropriate for use in cost-utility analysis because they cannot be converted into quality-adjusted life years gained.

Utility in health care evaluation is based on a theory of rational decision making proposed in the 1940s. In utility theory, utilities do not mean usefulness as they do in everyday language; rather utilities are numbers representing the strength of an individual's preferences for particular outcomes when faced with uncertainty. Furthermore, the theory is *"normative."* This means it described how a rationale person should make decisions under conditions of uncertainty, not necessarily how they actually do in real life. Since health outcomes are uncertain, utility theory is regarded as the most appropriate to be adopted in healthcare. Although the underlying rationale for conducting cost-utility analysis is based on utility theory, results of cost-utility analysis are not expressed as cost per utility due to problems with interpretation of utils by decision makers. Instead, results typically are expressed as cost per QALY gained independent of how QALY metric was estimated. Other variants for labeling the denominator in a cost-utility ratio apart from QALY, depending on how the outcome unit was estimated, include; cost per healthy year equivalents (HYE), per well year gained, quality-adjusted time without symptoms toxicity (Q-TWiST), function years, value-adjusted years, and quality-adjusted life expectancy (QALE) gained. All of these units are proposed as comprehensive measures of both quantity and quality of treatment effectiveness. Because quality-adjusted life year is the most commonly used unit of outcome measurement in cost-utility analysis, it serves as the focus of this discussion.

Applications Of Cost-Utility Analysis

When compared to other types of economic evaluation, cost-utility analysis is the most difficult and expensive method to use. Therefore, cost-utility analysis is recommended when certain situations exist. First, cost-utility analysis is used when quality of life is *the* important outcome. When improvement in patients' psychological well-being and physical and social function are the main focus, such as in evaluating the treatment of arthritis, cost-utility analysis is appropriate. Second, use cost-utility analysis when quality of life is *an* important outcome. For example, a chemotherapeutic regimen may increase survival but decrease a patient's well-being. Because the quality-adjusted life year incorporates both the quantity and quality of treatment outcomes, cost-utility analysis is appropriate.

Third, cost-utility analysis also should be employed when the program affects both morbidity and mortality and it is desirable to have a common unit of outcome that combines both variables. For example, estrogen therapy for menopausal symptoms improves patient quality of life by relieving symptoms, but may increase the risk of mortality (or decrease survival) from endometrial cancer or decrease the risk of mortality from hip fracture.

A fourth situation in which to use cost-utility analysis is when the programs being compared have a wide range of outcomes and a common unit of output for comparison is desirable. An example is the choice between expanding the neonatal intensive care unit or establishing a clinic to treat hypertension. Finally, cost-utility analysis is used when comparing a program to others that have been evaluated using cost-utility analysis.

Four situations have been listed in the literature as inappropriate for cost-utility analysis (Reference 9). These include, when only immediate output effectiveness data can be obtained; when data have shown the alternatives are equally effective; when quality of life is important but can be captured by a single variable measured in easily understood units; and when the extra cost of obtaining and using utility values is judged to be in itself not cost effective.

Cost-utility analysis is not appropriate for intermediate output effectiveness because intermediate effectiveness measures cannot be converted into quality-adjusted life years. An example of an intermediate effectiveness measure is blood pressure. Although control of blood pressure can reduce the risk of cardiovascular disease, an intermediate outcome of reduction in blood pressure cannot be converted to quality-adjusted life years.

In a report to the Office of Disease Prevention and Health Promotion of the United States Public Health Service, another framework was provided to apply when deciding if cost-utility analysis is an appropriate tool. Three general applications for the use of cost-utility analysis are described. They include evaluating mutually compatible programs, choosing the magnitude of selected health interventions, and evaluating mutually exclusive programs.

First, cost-utility analysis is used to evaluate mutually compatible health interventions. For example, decision makers on a county board of health may be faced with the choice of funding childhood vaccinations, alcohol and drug rehabilitation, and hypertension screening within a constrained budget. These interventions are mutually compatible—that is, all of the interventions are feasible and the costs and health benefits of any of the interventions are independent of each other. Cost-utility analysis can be used in this type of scenario to select interventions for funding. However, should cost-utility analysis be used in this scenario? Herein lies one of the sources of controversy concerning its use. Even though cost-utility analysis provides an objective evaluation of compatible alternatives, the economic efficiency criterion by itself may not be sufficient to reflect societal perspectives for making resource allocation decisions.

Second, a variation of the use of cost-utility analysis to mutually compare compatible interventions is its application to choose the magnitude of health interventions. Many types of interventions can be expanded or contracted in scale. One way a health intervention can be expanded in scale is by applying a given treatment or prevention to a larger pool of individuals. Another way a health intervention can be altered in scale is by varying the intensity of the treatment per individual. For instance, the number of visits to a psychologist per week can be altered. The issue is not only whether a given intervention should be pursued, but also to what degree it should be pursued. The question is not only "whether" but also "how much."

Finally, the report also states that cost-utility analysis can be used to evaluate mutually exclusive health interventions. This application of cost-utility analysis is what most pharmacists are exposed to at the institutional level. Mutually exclusive health interventions include situations such as a patient suffering from a particular illness that may be treated either by drugs or surgical intervention. It may not make sense to do both. For example, treatment of gallstones may involve drugs and lithotripsy to dissolve and break down the gallstones. Alternatively, it may involve surgery to remove the gall bladder. It would be redundant to treat a given individual with both modes of therapy.

Measurement of Costs

Because approaches to cost measurement are discussed in the Types of Economic and Humanistic Outcomes Assessments and the Cost-of-Illness Analysis chapters, they are not discussed in detail in this chapter. Nevertheless, the same cost measurement principles apply to cost-utility analysis. All four categories of costs—direct medical costs, direct nonmedical costs, indirect costs, and intangible costs—are identified, measured, and valued. The types of cost vary with the perspective of the study. Because of the extensive resources required to conduct a cost-utility analysis, the perspective is usually that of a policy maker. However, cost-utility analysis does not have to be limited to policy decisions. Also, discounting must be performed on costs incurred over a period longer than 1 year to account for the time value of money.

The goal of many cost-utility analysis studies is to evaluate the resource utilization of an intervention. Therefore, the monetary costs recognized in accounting should be distinguished from resource utilization costs. Also, it is important to understand the concept of opportunity cost when measuring costs in cost-utility analysis. Opportunity cost is the value of the foregone benefits when the resource is not available for its best alternative. For example, land is considered a non-depreciable asset because it maintains its value. Although an investment in nondepreciable land will return the original capital sum when sold, there is still a cost. This cost is the lost opportunity to invest the sum in some other venture yielding positive benefits.

Measurement of Utility

Quality-Adjusted Life Years

Quality-adjusted life years have become popular in outcomes measurement due to its simplicity and ease of calculation. Quality-adjusted life years estimation involves the multiplication of two numbers: quantity of life Y and the quality of life, Q weight. Although the term quality-adjusted life years implies quantity of life is measured in years, and typically is, it also is measured in months, days, hours, or other units of time. The value of Y reflects the life expectancy of an individual for chronic conditions or the duration of the intervention for acute conditions. Q weight or utility is scaled from zero, Q=0, to full or perfect health with a Q weight of 1.0. However, occasionally when a health state is considered worse than death, utility is expressed as a negative value. An example of the interpretation of the QALY unit is presented graphically in Figure 1. If a healthy person is expected to live for 20 years (Y = 20 years) and places a value on his or her health state as being equivalent to full health (Q = 1.0), then the resultant quality-adjusted life year estimation is equal to Q x Y = 1.0 x 20 years = 20 QALYs. However, if the same person was suffering from a chronic condition such as arthritis, then one would expect the resultant desirability of that health state to be much less than perfect health. Suppose the same individual rated this health state as having a Q weight of 0.5. Then the resultant QALY estimation would be 0.5 x 20 years = 10 QALYs. This is interpreted as this particular person living for 20 years with arthritis is equivalent to living for 10 years but with full-health (i.e., 10 quality-adjusted life years). This concept of quality-adjusted life years also is graphically represented as the shaded area in Figure 1. Due to the intuitive appeal of quality-adjusted life years, it is understood why QALY has become so popular as a single index incorporating mortality and morbidity in health care.

The differentiation between cost-utility and cost-effectiveness analyses is the inclusion of respondent or patient preferences in the denominator of the ratio in the form of quality of life or Q weights in the former, and the use of natural units such as millimeters of mercury (mm Hg) reduced or reduction of adverse drug events observed in the latter. As a result cost-utility analysis is referred to as a special type of cost-effectiveness analysis. However, there

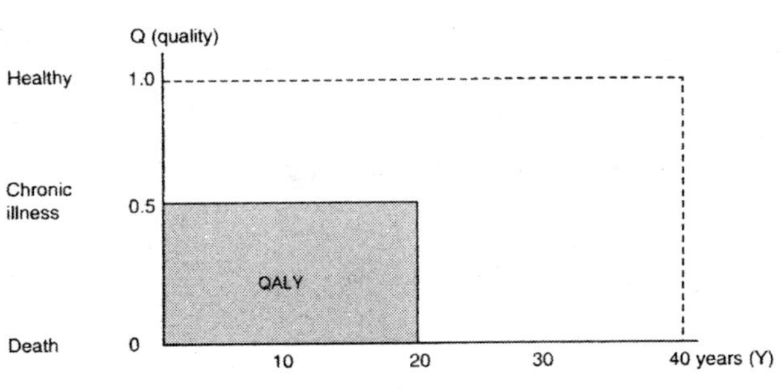

Figure 1: Graphical Presentation of the Concept of Quality-Adjusted Life Years (QALYs)

is substansive difference between the two metrics. Cost-utility analysis incorporates individual preferences, while natural units or laboratory results, although important in treatment, do not capture patient preferences.

Assumptions underlying quality-adjusted life years

Four assumptions have been proposed to underlying the concept of quality-adjusted life years (Reference 37). First, a full healthy life and death are used as reference states for utility values, as they represent all (1.0), and nothing (0) in the health domain. Second, quality-adjusted life years only capture health-related utility. Therefore, interpersonal-utility comparisons are restricted to the health domain. Third, the utility value of a full healthy life is set equal for each individual at birth. One full healthy year gained counts as 1.0, regardless of the individual. Therefore, one quality-adjusted life year gained for a 20-year-old is counted equally as that for an 80-year-old. Finally, the attributes of quality and quantity must be mutually utility independent. In other words, trade-offs between quantity of life are not affected by quality of life, and similarly, trade-offs between quality of life are not affected by the quantity or the length of life.

Mutual utility independence can be divided into two types: utility independence with respect to quality of life and utility independence with respect to quantity of life.

Utility independence with respect to quality of life can be further explained by the following example. Consider first the trade-offs between length of life and quality of life. Assume an individual is indifferent about living either 14 years with mild angina or playing a lottery, in which there is a 0.5 chance of living either 10 or 20 years with mild angina. This trade-off is illustrated in Figure 2. Note that in this trade-off, all health outcomes are such that the individual has mild angina while alive. The trade-off here involves quantity of life only and not quality of life while alive. According to the assumption of utility independence with respect to quality of life (i.e., quality of life is held constant), the individual has the same preferences over length of life even if, in making a choice among these health outcomes, the individual had no angina instead of mild angina. The individual must be indifferent between living 14 years with no angina versus a lottery in which there is a 0.5 chance of living 10 years with no angina and a 0.5 chance of living 20 years with no angina.

Alternately, according to the utility independence assumption with respect to time, if an individual is

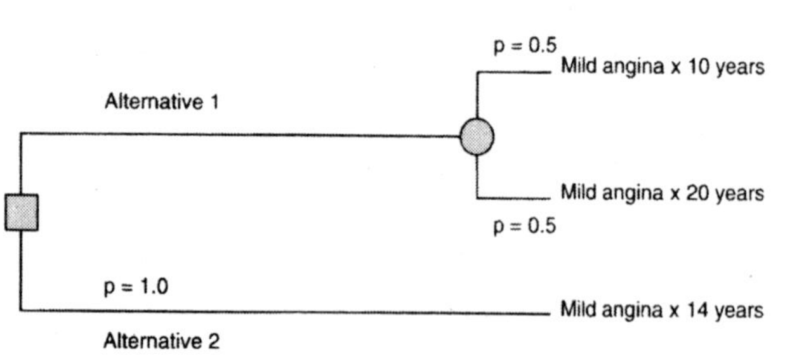

Figure 2: Utility Independence Between Quantity and Quality of Life

indifferent between Alternative 1, a lottery between perfect health (p = 0.5) and immediate death (p = 1 – 0.5) and Alternative 2, a certain health state angina when the time horizon for perfect heath and angina is 20 years, then, the same individual should still be indifferent between the two alternatives when the time horizon is 1 hour. In other words, the same individual should be indifferent to the gamble of risking death when the time frame for perfect health is only 1 hour versus the risk of immediate death versus angina.

Theory underlying quality-adjusted life year estimation is based on a normative model, or how a rational person should behave under conditions of uncertainty as opposed to how people actually behave. The underlying theory for quality-adjusted life year does not claim to describe how people actually behave under conditions of uncertainty.

Utility Value Sources

Utility or Q weights can be obtained by a number of sources: patients, their proxies, the public, experts, or the literature depending on resources available and the research question to be addressed. The source used determines the resultant perspective of cost-utility analysis. Perspectives described in the literature include, patient, societal/general public, and government.

Various methods are used to elicit Q weights or utility values. One source of Q weights is the literature. An example listing utilities of several states of health is provided in Table 1. If Q weights are borrowed from the literature, it is important to ensure the health states and subjects used in the studies are similar to those of your study population. It is also important to ensure that the authors identified the methods used to establish validity and reliability of the measurement instruments they used. Second, Q weights are obtained from a convenience sample of health care professionals or other experts who are asked to estimate the Q weights. Such preference scores are known as judgment values. Because judgment values are often subjective, extensive sensitivity analysis should be performed to determine how changes in Q weights affect the study results. Third, the most expensive method is to measure Q weights directly from patients—resulting in the patient perspective. Fourth, instead of using patients Q weights are elicited from healthy subjects—resulting in the societal perspective. Finally, another method seen increasingly in the literature is the use of proxies or patient surrogates to elicit Q weights. This is used in cases when patients cannot be used directly and represent the most vulnerable patient population. Examples include, victims of severe stroke, patients with schizophrenia, sufferers of Alzheimer, and pediatric patients. Proxy Q weights are intended to represent patient preferences and, therefore, intended to produce the patient perspective. However, empirical research indicates proxy Q weights differ from those of patients more so for emotional than physical dimensions. More recently empirical research was conducted to investigate the impact of health care interventions on patient caregivers. In these cases, the patient caregivers, or patient spouse is asked to provide Q weights for the impact the condition has had on their own quality of life. Therefore, this is conceptually different to the use of proxy measures and is consistent with being a component of the societal perspective—capturing the impact of an intervention or condition on the society as a whole, which also includes patients, general public, government, industry, and patient caregivers.

Exercise 1: Calculation of Quality-Adjusted Life Years

To practice calculating quality-adjusted life years from a literature-reported source, turn to the end of this chapter for Exercise 1: Calculation of Quality-Adjusted Life Years.

Now that you have some experience with calculating quality-adjusted life years based on literature values, consider how you might obtain utility values directly from subjects.

Obtaining Q weights for QALY

Two different methods used to obtain individual preferences or Q weights are utility-based/decision theory/preference and psychometric/nonpreference-based approaches.

The first method, preference based approach, can be further subdivided into holistic and decomposed models. Holistic approaches include rating scale (RS), standard gamble (SG), time trade-off (TTO), person trade-off, and magnitude estimation. The most commonly used techniques reported are RS, SG and TTO. The latter two, derive preference values implicitly based on a subject's direct response to decision situations, while rating scale derives Q weights directly. Rating scale, standard gamble and time trade-off techniques are described in detail in the Standard Gamble, Time Trade-off and Rating Scale sections. Holistic approaches are sometimes referred to as single attribute utility theory (SAUT) approaches. Holistic approaches can be time consuming and cognitively demanding for respondents, as a result the decomposed or multiattribute utility theory (MAUT) approaches have gained popularity. MAUT theory approaches require respondents to answer a series of questions regarding a number of different health dimensions or attributes in a survey format. The most common MAUT systems include United States Quality of Well-being scale (QWB), Canadian Health Utilities Index (HUI), European EQ-5D (formerly EuroQoL) and more recent utility scoring algorithms derived for Short Form 6 (SF-6) from SF-36. These four metrics also are known as generic health related quality-of-life instruments.

The second method, psychometric based approach, as advocated by behavioral scientists, derives weights for each of the multiple quality of life dimensions tested. Depending on the instrument the scores for each dimension may or may not be "added" to provide an overall Q weight for health for use in cost-utility analysis. The most common psychometric-

Table 1. Mean Daily Health State Utilities in the General Population Sample

Duration	Health State	Observations		Mean Daily Health State Utility	Standard Error
		Total	Useable		
	Reference State: Perfect Health			1.00	
3 months	Home confinement for tuberculosis	246	239	0.68	0.020
3 months	Home confinement for an unnamed contagious disease	246	240	0.65	0.022
3 months	Hospital dialysis	246	243	0.62	0.023
3 months	Hospital confinement for tuberculosis				
3 months	Hospital confinement for an unnamed contagious disease	246	242	0.56	0.023
3 months	Depression	246	243	0.44	0.024
8 years	Home dialysis	246	240	0.65	0.018
8 years	Mastectomy for injury	60[a]	56	0.63	0.038
8 years	Kidney transplant	246	242	0.58	0.021
8 years	Hospital dialysis	246	240	0.56	0.019
8 years	Mastectomy for breast cancer	60[a]	58	0.48	0.044
8 years	Hospital confinement for an unnamed contagious disease	246	241	0.33	0.022
Life	Home dialysis	197[b]	187	0.40	0.031
Life	Hospital dialysis	197[b]	189	0.32	0.028
Life	Hospital confinement for an unnamed contagious disease	197[b]	192	0.16	0.020
	Reference state: dead			0.00	
	Total	3171	3093		

[a] This scenario was presented to 41–79-year-old females only.
[b] This scenario was presented to 18–65-year-old females only.
Reprinted with permission from Sackett DL, Torrance GW. The utility of different health states as perceived by the public. J Chronic Dis 1978;31:697–704.

based measure used in the United States is Short Form 36 (SF-36). Because SF-36 health profile does not provide Q weights which can be used to estimate quality-adjusted life year, however, a recent publication showed how to convert dimension scores from SF-36 to QWB weights (Reference 10). Since these preferences can be used in quality-adjusted life year estimates, this model is discussed in the Nonpreference Based Measures section. The following section focuses on preference-based approaches—both holistic and decomposed approaches used to derive Q weights for use in quality-adjusted life year estimation.

Preference-Based Approach to Measurement of Utility.

The decision-theory approach is based on utility theory of rational decision making. It is assumed that a rational person will choose an alternative with the highest expected utility. Rational behavior is characterized by three fundamental axioms: preference transitivity, continuity, and substitutability. First, preferences exist and are transitive. For example, if A is preferred to B and B is preferred to C, then A is preferred to C. Second, preferences are continuous. If A is preferred to B and B is preferred to C, there is a probability p at which an individual is indifferent between getting B with certainty versus receiving A at a probability of p or C at a probability of (1 – p). This axiom is presented graphically in Figure 3. The third axiom, substitutability, is not discussed in this chapter in detail because of its technical complexity. Those who are interested should consult Reference 37.

Standard Gamble

Standard gamble is the classic method used to measure cardinal or interval-scale metric preferences. Since standard gamble is directly based on utility theory continuity axiom, it is regarded as the "gold standard" for measuring utilities under conditions of uncertainty in health care. In this method, a subject is given a choice between two alternatives that lead to three different health states. The subject is first asked to rank the three health states from the most preferred to the least preferred. The most preferred health state is labeled as state h and the least preferred health state is labeled as state j. The health state that lies between state h and state j is labeled as state i. The standard gamble technique is illustrated in Figure 4.

Alternative 1 is a treatment that leads to two possible outcomes: probability p to be in state h (h_h) and probability (1 – p) to be in state j for a certain period of time. Alternative 2 is 100 percent certainty (p_i = 1.0) to be in disease state i. Probability p is varied until the subject is indifferent between the two alternatives. Utility or Q weight for state i (h_i) is then computed by equating the multiples of utility and probability of health states at each decision node as shown by the following equation:

$$h_i p_i = h_h (p) + h_j (1 - p)$$

Because p_i = 1.0, the equation is reduced to:

$$h_i = h_h (p) + h_j (1 - p) \quad \textit{(equation 1)}$$

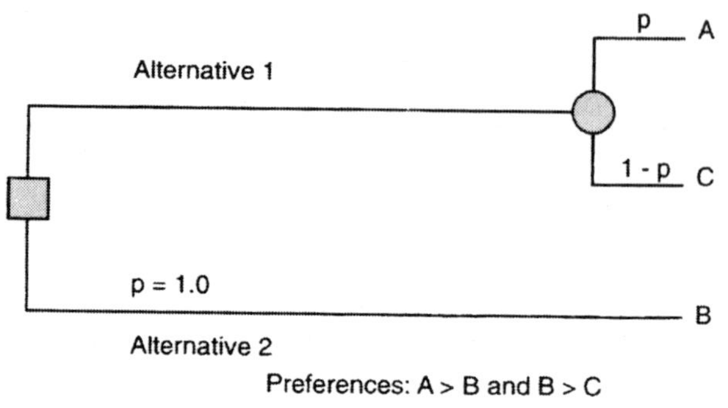

Figure 3: Continuity of Preferences

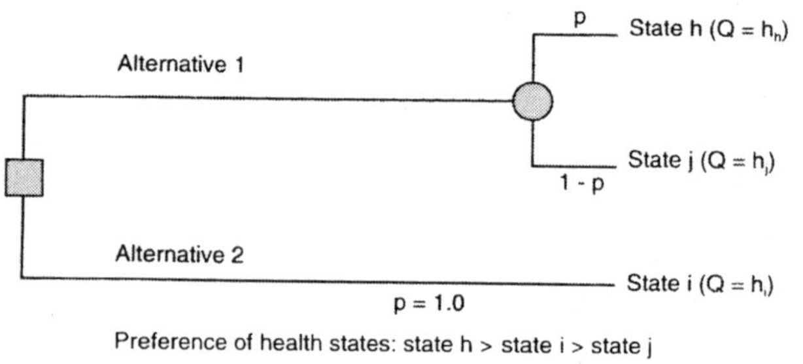

Figure 4: Standard Gamble Technique for Obtaining Utility Weights for Health State i
Reprinted with permission of Torrance G, McMaster University
Originally published in Torrance G. Measurement of health state utilities for economic appraisal. J Health Econ 1986;5:1–30.

In most cases, a Q weight of a health state is measured in reference to full health and death. Therefore, the three health states used in standard gamble studies are healthy, state i, and death.

To further illustrate the application of the standard gamble technique, look at an example to determine the utility value of chronic asthma relative to full health and death. The subject is first asked to rank the three health states healthy, death, and chronic asthma by preference. Next, subjects are provided with a rating scale as a prop to rate the health states relative to each other. Rating scales are used to familiarize respondents to the health state and help them to think about valuing health states—an exercise probably unfamiliar to them. The corresponding location of each health state using standard gamble in Figure 4 depends on the subject's preference ranking as described in the ranking and rating scale procedures. Assume that the subject prefers healthy to chronic asthma to death. Therefore, state h is healthy, which is preferred to state i, (chronic asthma), which is preferred to state j (death).

The health states are written on cards and displayed in front of the subject. The subject is asked to choose between the two alternatives. For example, Alternative 1 is to have a probability p to be healthy for life and probability of (1 – p) to die immediately. Alternative 2 is a certainty of chronic asthma, state i, for life (p = 1.0). Begin with p = 1.0 for

Alternative 1. If the subject chooses Alternative 1, there is a probability of 1.0 to remain healthy for life and a probability of 0 of immediate death. On the other hand, if the subject chooses alternative 2, there is a certain probability of 1.0 to have asthma for the remainder of life.

Assume the subject chooses Alternative 1; a probability of 1.0 of full healthy life and probability of 0 of immediate death. Probability p is changed to 0 for healthy life and 1.0 for immediate death, and the subject indicates a preference again. The subject chooses Alternative 2, to have asthma for the remainder of life. The subject perceives asthma health state as preferable to guaranteed death. Probability p for healthy life and the complementary probability (1 – p) for death is then modified until the subject is indifferent between the two alternatives. For example, assume, the next gamble is a probability of 0.9 (p) of healthy for life and 0.1 (1 – p) for immediate death, and Alternative 2 is chronic asthma for life with certainty. If the subject prefers Alternative 1 over 2, then the gamble is altered by changing Alternative 1 to have a probability of 0.1 to remain healthy and a probability of 0.9 of immediate death. If the subject prefers Alternative 2, certain asthma, Alternative 1 becomes a 0.8 probability to remain healthy and a 0.2 probability of immediate death. The probabilities of healthy life (p) and death (1-p) are modified back and forth until the subject's indifference point is reached between the two alternatives.

Assume the subject is indifferent between the two alternatives when p = 0.6. This means the subject prefers the two alternatives to the same extent and cannot choose one or the other alternative. Under Alternative 1, there is a probability of 0.6 of a healthy life and a 0.4 probability of immediate death. In this case, the subject's preference, or utility values, for chronic asthma are computed by substituting p into equation 1 as shown below:

$$h_{asthma} = h_{healthy}(p) + h_{death}(1 - p)$$
$$= 1.0\,(0.6) + 0.0\,(1 - 0.6) = 0.6$$

The utility of a full healthy life and death is always equal to 1 and 0, respectively. Therefore, equation 1 can be simplified to become:

$$h_{asthma} = p = 0.6.$$

On the other hand, if the subject prefers Alternative 1 at p = 0.6 but changes preference to Alternative 2 at p = 0.5, then p is taken as the midpoint between 0.60 and 0.50; that is, p = 0.55. Utility for chronic asthma then becomes:

$$h_{asthma} = p = 0.55$$

In practice, because it is difficult for subjects to relate to probability, the standard gamble method is usually supplemented with a probability wheel, which an adjustable disk divided into two sectors; each is painted with a different color to represent the health states h and j. The area of each color is then adjusted to represent the probabilities for the two health states.

Time Trade-off

Another technique commonly used to measure utility values directly from subjects is the time trade-off developed to be a less cognitively demanding alternative to standard gamble, however, whether time trade-off met this aim has been questioned. Similar to the standard gamble, the subject is offered a choice between two alternatives. However, the technique varies depending on whether the health state in question is worse than death. Figure 5 illustrates the time trade-off for a chronic health state i that is preferred to death. In this time-trade-off, Alternative 1 is to be in health state i for time t followed by death—that is, the area joined by points CEFG in Figure 5. Alternative 2 is to be healthy for time x that is shorter than t—that is, x > t—followed by death—area CABD. Instead of varying probabilities, duration of x is varied until the subject is indifferent between the two alternatives. Utility of state i (hi) is then obtained by equating the areas under the curve outlined by the two alternatives—that is, area CABD is equal to area CEFG. After algebraic manipulation, the resulting equation is:

$$hi = x \div t.$$

The application of time trade-off in measuring utilities is illustrated by the following example that obtains the utility value for post amputation, a chronic health state that is preferred to death, using the time trade-off technique. Assume that a subject is told they have an additional 30 years of life. The time trade-off technique begins with equating t to anticipated life expectancy. The subject is asked to decide on a preference for two alternatives: Alternative 1, to live her remaining 30 years of life with an amputation (t = 30); or Alternative 2, to live in perfect health for 30 years (x = t), then die without complications. Because the patient prefers the healthy state to the amputated state, she chooses Alternative 2.

The subject is asked to decide again between the same Alternative 1, but this time, Alternative 2 is to die immediately (x = 0). Alternative 1 is chosen because the subject prefers the amputated state to death. Time x is alternately increased from 0 or decreased from t by a predetermined number of years; for example, 5 years for

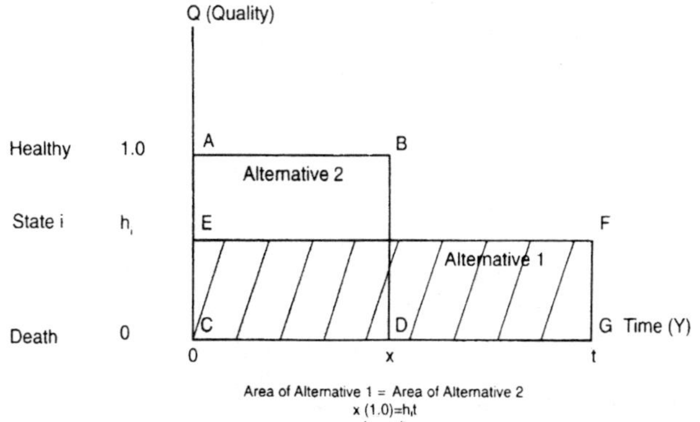

Figure 5: Time Trade-off for a Chronic Health State i Preferred to Death

Alternative 2 while Alternative 1 remains unchanged throughout the time trade-off technique. The subject is asked to make a choice until she is indifferent or encounters difficulty in choosing between the two alternatives.

The next options offered to the subject are Alternative 2, to be healthy for 25 years and then die or Alternative 1, to live 30 years with an amputation and then die. Alternative 2 is changed to full health for 5 years and then die, or Alternative 1. Alternative 2 is altered to healthy for 20 years and then die, followed by healthy for 10 years and then die, and so on. If the subject becomes indifferent between the two alternatives when x = 20 years, then the utility value for the amputated state is equal to 20 ÷ 30 = 0.67.

Time trade-off also is used to obtain utility values for temporary health states relative to each other. It also is used to calculate the utility of states that subjects may consider worse than death (References 35 and 38).

Rating Scale

Rating scale (RS) also is commonly referred to as thermometer scale, barometer scale and visual analogue scale (see Figure 6). RS theoretical foundations are attributed to disciplines of decision sciences, economics and psychology, and can describe measurement of differences on an interval scale. RS Q weights are obtained by asking respondents to rate health states on an 100-point scale. To achieve an interval scale respondents are asked to place the health state (hi) on rating scale calibrated from 0 (least desirable) to 100 (most desirable), such that the distance between placements reflects the difference between the health states (Figure 6). If the respondent does not regard death as the least desirable health state, scale is standardized with death as zero by using the following formula:

$$RS_{standardized} = RS_{raw} - RS_{death}/(1 - RS_{death})$$
(equation 2)

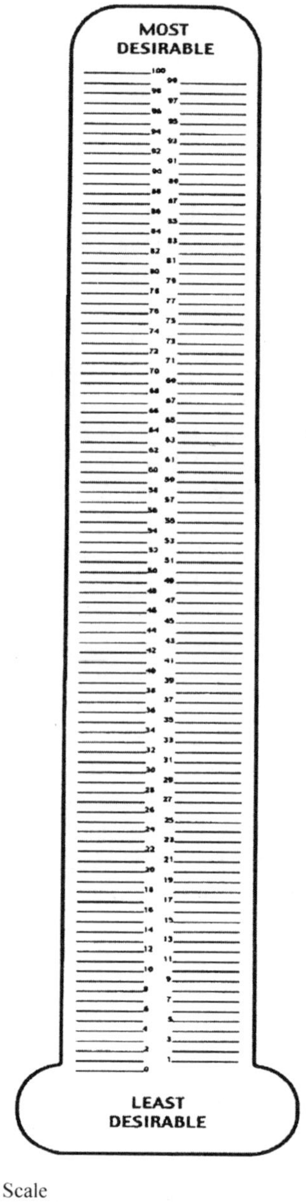

Figure 6: Rating Scale

The scale is converted to a 0 to 1.0 scale by dividing $RS_{standardized}$ by 100 (i.e., Q weight is equal to hi or $RS_{standardized}$ divided by 100). The RS does not measure preferences under conditions of uncertainty, and therefore is not considered a true measure of utility. Since RS measures health preferences under conditions of certainty it is referred to as a value. Although RS does not provide true utilities, it is the most commonly used technique for measuring health preferences. This is attributed mostly to its ease of use. In a 2001 paper on the value of rating scale in eliciting health preferences, the authors suggest their role was predominately in familiarizing health states to patients (e.g., prior to administering time trade-off or standard gamble) and recommended that they not be used as the only measure of individual's preferences.

Q weights generated by these different techniques are often different from each other. Typically Q weights derived from standard gamble method are higher than those from time trade-off method, which in turn are higher than those from RS methods due to the incorporation or lack thereof of uncertainty. The only measure of true utility is the standard gamble. The time trade-off and rating scales are not true measures of utility because the scenario is not presented under uncertainty; therefore, the numbers obtained from these methods are often referred to as values rather than as utility. However, this matter has been extensively studied and one group concluded that for practical purposes, Q weights derived from the standard gamble, time trade-off, and rating scale methods can be equated at the population level. The authors proposed mathematical equations for converting these values into utilities. Unfortunately, these conversions do not hold up under different situations. As a result, care must be taken in comparing quality-adjusted life years developed from different methods.

Decomposed Approach to Measurement of Utility

Sometimes, instead of measuring utility values directly by the standard gamble or time trade-off method, the value of Q weight for use in quality-adjusted life year estimation is obtained by using multiattribute utility theory based instruments, such as the QWB. Formerly known as the Health Status Index and Index of Well Being, it is one of the first multiattribute systems developed. The QWB scale is a quality-of-life instrument composed of four dimensions: mobility (MOB), physical activity (PAC), social activity (SAC), and symptom problems (CPX). The scale categorizes individuals according to symptoms and functions levels for each of the four dimensions. The standard weights of different dimensions and symptoms are provided in Tables 2 and 3. Although the exact method of obtaining the overall well-being score (W) is rather detailed, the instrument is easy to score. Respondents are required to answer four questions in order to provide a W value. A simplified explanation is that an overall well-being score is computed by adding the standardized utility weights for each of the four dimensions as shown by the equation provided in Table 2. The resultant "W" score can be used as a Q weight for estimation of "well-years" in cost-utility analysis. Instrument boundaries for W range from zero (death) to 1.0 (full health).

For example, consider a hypothetical program that incurs a total cost of $20,000 a year. What is the number of well-years obtained from the program assuming it prevents 200

Table 2. Elements and Calculating Formulas for Quality of Well-Being

Step No.	Step Definition	Weight
	Mobility Scale (MOB)	
5	No limitations for health reasons	-0.000
4	Did not drive a car, health-related; did not ride in a car as usual for age (younger than 15 years, health-related, *and/or* had or would have used more help than usual for age to use public transportation, health-related)	-0.062
2	In hospital, health-related	-0.090
	Physical Activity Scale (PAC)	
4	No limitations for health reasons	-0.000
3	In wheelchair, moved or controlled movement of wheelchair without help from someone else; or had trouble or did not try to lift, stoop, bend over, or use stairs or inclines, health-related; *and/or* had any other physical limitation in walking, or did not try to walk as far as or as fast as others the same age are able, health-related	-0.060
1	In wheelchair, did not move or control the movement of wheelchair without help from someone else, or in bed, chair, or couch for most or all of the day, health-related	-0.077
	Social Activity Scale (SAC)	
5	No limitations for health reasons	-0.000
4	Limited in other (e.g., recreational) role activity, health-related	-0.061
3	Limited in major (primary) role activity, health-related	-0.061
2	Performed no major role activity, health-related, but did perform self-care activities	-0.061
1	Performed no major role activity, health-related, and did not perform or had more help than usual in performance of one or more self-care activities, health-related	-0.106
	Calculating Formulas	

Formula 1. Point in time well-being score for an individual (W):
W = (1 + CPXwt) + (MOBwt) + (PACwt) + (SACwt)

Where "wt" is the preference-weighted measure for each factor and CPX is Sympton/Problem complex. For example, the W score for a person with the following description profile may be calculated for one day as:

CPX-11	Cough, wheezing, or shortness of breath, with or without fever, chills, or aching all over	-0.257
MOB-5	No limitations	-0.000
PAC-1	In bed, chair, or couch for most or all of the day, health-related	-0.077
SAC-2	Performed no major role activity, health-related, but did perform self-care	-0.061

Formula 2. Well-years (WY) as an output measure:
WY = [No. of persons x (1.0 + CPXwt + MOBwt + PACwt + SACwt) x Time]

Reprinted with permission from Kaplan RM, Anderson JP, Ganiats TG. The quality of well-being scale: rationale for a single quality of life index. In: Spilker B, ed. Quality of life assessments in clinical trials. New York: Raven Press, 1990.

patients suffering from a self-limiting illness that lasts 10 days in which patients have excessive anxiety, are not able to drive a car for health-related reasons, and experience limited primary role activity due to poor health, but have no mobility limitations. To determine the well-being of a patient suffering from this illness, the first step is to obtain the loss of well-being weights from Tables 2 and 3. Excessive anxiety is listed in Table 3 as symptom problem complex CPX-27; not being able to drive a car for health-related reasons is listed in Table 2 as PAC-2 on the physical activity scale; and having limited primary role activity is SAC-3 on the physical activity scale. Since there are no limitations from the mobility scale of Table 2, the step number for that category is MOB-5. The loss of well-being weights are listed adjacent to the symptoms. By substituting these weights into the equation provided at the bottom of Table 2, a patient suffering from this illness has a well-being score W equal to 1.0 plus the sums of the utilities or 0.622. Because this program is preventing a loss of well-being from full health to 0.622, the magnitude of the gain is calculated as 1 minus 0.622, or 0.378. The number of well-years gained from this program are gained utility of 0.378 multiplied by the portion of the year involved, 10 days divided by 365 days per year multiplied by 200 patients, or 2.07 well-years. The cost per well-year gained ratio of the program is $20,000 divided by 2.07 well-years, which is equal to $9662 per well-year.

Table 3. Symptom Problem (CPX) with Calculating Weights

CPX No.	CPX Description	Weights
1	Death (not on respondent's card)	-0.727
2	Loss of consciousness, such as seizure (fits), fainting, or coma (out cold or knocked out)	-0.407
3	Burn over large areas of face, body, arms, or legs	-0.387
4	Pain, bleeding, itching, or discharge (drainage) from sexual organs - does not include normal menstrual (monthly) bleeding	-0.349
5	Trouble learning, remembering, or thinking clearly	-0.340
6	Any combination of one or more hands, feet, arms, or legs either missing, deformed (crooked), paralyzed (unable to move), or broken—includes wearing artifical limbs or braces	-0.333
7	Pain, stiffness, weakness, numbness, or other discomfort in chest, stomach (including hernia or rupture), side, neck, back, hips, or any joints or hands, feet, arms, or legs	-0.299
8	Pain, burning, bleeding, itching, or other difficulty with rectum, bowel movements, or urination (passing water)	-0.292
9	Sick or upset stomach, vomiting, or loose bowel movement, with or without chills, or aching all over	-0.290
10	General tiredness, weakness, or weight loss	-0.259
11	Cough, wheezing, or shortness of breath, *with* or *without* fever, chills, or aching all over	-0.257
12	Spells of feeling upset, being depressed, or crying	-0.257
13	Headache, dizziness, ringing in ears, spells of feeling hot, nervous or shaky	-0.244
14	Burning or itching rash on large areas of face, body, arms, or legs	-0.240
15	Trouble talking, such as lisp, stuttering, hoarseness, or being unable to speak	-0.237
16	Pain or discomfort in one or both eyes (such as burning or itching) or any trouble seeing after correction	-0.230
17	Overweight for age and height, or skin defect of face, body, arms, or legs, such as scars, pimples, warts, bruises, or changes in color	-0.188
18	Pain in ear, tooth, jaw, throat, lips, tongue; several missing or crooked permanent teeth—includes wearing bridges or false teeth; stuffy, runny nose; or any trouble hearing—includes wearing a hearing aid	-0.170
19	Taking medication or staying on a prescribed diet for health reasons	-0.144
20	Wearing eyeglasses or contact lenses	-0.101
21	Breathing smog or unpleasant air	-0.101
22	No symptoms or problem (not on respondent's card)	-0.000
23	Standard symptom/problem	-0.257
x24	Trouble sleeping	-0.257
x25	Intoxication	-0.257
x26	Problems with sexual interest or performance	-0.257
x27	Excessive worry or anxiety	-0.257

Note: x (i.e., x24) indicates a standardized weight and is used because preference studies have not been completed

Reprinted with permission from Kaplan RM, Anderson JP, Ganiats TG. The quality of well-being scale: rationale for a single quality of life index. In: Spilker B, ed. Quality of life assessments in clinical trials. New York: Raven Press, 1990.

Exercise 2: Calculation of Well-Years

To apply the quality of well-being approach in a problem-solving scenario, turn to the end of this chapter for Exercise 2: Calculation of well-years.

Health Utilities Index (HUI®)

Health utilities index (HUI®) is actually a family of decomposed, generic health related quality of life measures, Mark 1 (HUI1), Mark 2 (HUI2) and Mark 3 (HUI3). HUI® was developed based on Quality of Well-being index multiattribute model at McMaster's University (Reference 11). HUI1 has basically been superseded by the latter two versions. HUI2 /HUI3 is used alone or concurrently since the two instruments cover different dimensions and are regarded as complementary. Like other generic quality of life measures, HUI is used in combination with other generic or disease specific quality of life measures depending on the desired research question. For example, the emotion dimension or attribute in HUI2 focuses on items regarding worry, anxiety and depression, while HUI3 focuses on happiness. While pain attribute in HUI2 focuses on analgesics use for pain alleviation, HUI3 emphasizes impact of pain on long-term disability. As a result, the authors recommend use of HUI2 for clinical study use or when impact on fertility is important (follow up for chemotherapy) and HUI3 for long term follow-up use and also if dexterity is an important factor.

This section focuses on HUI2 and HUI3 due to their prevalent use (see Tables 4 and 5). HUI2 consists of seven attributes (domains): sensation, mobility, emotion, cognition, self-care, pain and fertility. HUI3 is composed of eight attributes: vision, hearing, speech, ambulation, dexterity, emotion, cognition, and pain. Instrument developers prefer the term attribute over dimension since this emphasizes the theoretical foundations of HUI in multiattribute utility theory. Although there is some overlap with attribute labels and variations in attribute labels, careful comparison of the two instruments is required to note

Table 4: HUI2 Multiattribute Health Status Classification System

Attribute	Level	Description[a]
Sensation	1	Able to see, hear and speak normally for age.
	2	Requires equipment to see or hear or speak.
	3	Sees, hears, or speaks with limitations even with equipment.
	4	Blind, deaf or mute.
Mobility	1	Able to walk, bend, lift, jump, and run normally for age.
	2	Walks, bends, lifts, jumps, or runs with some limitations but does not require help.
	3	Requires mechanical equipment (such as canes, crutches, braces or wheelchair) to walk or get around independently.
	4	Requires the help of another person to walk or get around and requires mechanical equipment as well.
	5	Unable to control or use arms and legs.
Emotion	1	Generally happy and free from worry.
	2	Occasionally fretful, angry, irritable, anxious, depressed, or suffering "night terrors."
	3	Often fretful, angry, irritable, anxious, depressed, or suffering "night terrors."
	4	Almost always fretful, angry, irritable, anxious, depressed.
	5	Extremely fretful, angry, irritable, anxious or depressed usually requiring hospitalization or psychiatric institutional care.
Cognition	1	Learns and remembers school work normally for age
	2	Learns and remembers school work more slowly than classmates as judged by parents and/or teachers.
	3	Learns and remembers very slowly and usually requires special educational assistance.
	4	Unable to learn and remember.

Table 4: HUI2 Multiattribute Health Status Classification System (continued)

Attribute	Level	Description[a]
Self-Care	1	Eats, bathes, dresses, and uses the toilet normally for age.
	2	Eats, bathes, dresses, or uses the toilet independently with difficulty.
	3	Requires mechanical equipment to eat, bathe, dress, or use the toilet independently.
	4	Requires the help of another person to eat, bathe, dress, or use the toilet.
Pain	1	Free of pain and discomfort.
	2	Occasional pain. Discomfort relieved by nonprescription drugs or self-control activity without disruption of normal activities.
	3	Frequent pain. Discomfort relieved by oral medicines with occasional disruption of normal activities.
	4	Frequent pain; frequent disruption of normal activities. Discomfort requires prescription narcotics for relief.
	5	Severe pain. Pain not relieved by drugs and constantly disrupts normal activities.
Fertility	1	Able to have children with a fertile spouse.
	2	Difficulty in having children with a fertile spouse.
	3	Unable to have children with a fertile spouse.

[a] Level descriptions are worded here exactly as presented to respondents in HUI2 preference survey.

Reprinted with permission from Feeny D, Furlong W, Boyle M, Torrance GW. Multi-attribute health status classification systems: health utilities index. Pharmacoeconomics 1995;7:490–502.

Table 5: HUI3 Multiattribute Health Status Classification System

Attribute	Level	Description
Vision	1	Able to see well enough to read ordinary newsprint and recognize a friend on the other side of the street, without glasses or contact lenses.
	2	Able to see well enough to read ordinary newsprint and recognize a friend on the other side of the street, but with glasses or contact lenses.
	3	Able to read ordinary newsprint with or without glasses but unable to recognize a friend on the other side of the street, even with glasses or contact lenses.
	4	Able to recognize a friend on the other side of the street with or without glasses but unable to read ordinary newsprint, even with glasses or contact lenses.
	5	Unable to read ordinary newsprint and unable to recognize a friend on the other side of the street, even with glasses or contact lenses.
	6	Unable to see at all.
Hearing	1	Able to hear what is said in a group conversation with at least three other people, without a hearing aid.
	2	Able to hear what is said in a conversation with one other person in a quiet room without a hearing aid, but requires a hearing aid to hear what is said in a group conversation with at least three other people.
	3	Able to hear what is said in a conversation with one other person in a quiet room with a hearing aid, and able to hear what is said in a group conversation with at least three other people with a hearing aid.
	4	Able to hear what is said in a conversation with one other person in a quiet room without a hearing aid, but unable to hear what is said in a group conversation with at least three other people even with a hearing aid.
	5	Able to hear what is said in a conversation with one other person in a quiet room with a hearing aid, but unable to hear what is said in a group conversation with at least three other people even with a hearing aid.
	6	Unable to hear at all.
Speech	1	Able to be understood completely when speaking with strangers or people who know me well.
	2	Able to be understood partially when speaking with strangers but able to be understood completely when speaking with people who know me well.
	3	Able to be understood partially when speaking with strangers or people who know me well.
	4	Unable to be understood when speaking with strangers but able to be understood partially by people who know me well.
	5	Unable to be understood when speaking to other people (or unable to speak at all).
Ambulation	1	Able to walk around the neighbourhood without difficulty, and without walking equipment.
	2	Able to walk around the neighbourhood with difficulty; but does not require walking equipment or the help of another person.
	3	Able to walk around the neighbourhood with walking equipment, but without the help of another person.
	4	Able to walk only short distances with walking equipment, and requires a wheelchair to get around the neighborhood.
	5	Unable to walk alone, even with walking equipment. Able to walk short distances with the help of another person, and requires a wheelchair to get around the neighbourhood.
	6	Cannot walk at all.
Dexterity	1	Full use of two hands and ten fingers.
	2	Limitations in the use of hands or fingers, but does not require special tools or help of another person.
	3	Limitations in the use of hands or fingers, is independent with use of special tools (does not require the help of another person).
	4	Limitations in the use of hands or fingers, requires the help of another person for some tasks (not independent even with use of special tools).
	5	Limitations in use of hands or fingers, requires the help of another person for most tasks (not independent even with use of special tools).
	6	Limitations in use of hands or fingers, requires the help of another person for all tasks (not independent even with use of special tools).
Emotion	1	Happy and interested in life.
	2	Somewhat happy.
	3	Somewhat unhappy.
	4	Very unhappy.
	5	So unhappy that life is not worthwhile.
Cognition	1	Able to remember most things, think clearly and solve day to day problems.
	2	Able to remember most things, but has a little difficulty when trying to think and solve day to day problems.
	3	Somewhat forgetful, but able to think clearly and solve day to day problems.
	4	Somewhat forgetful, and has a little difficulty when trying to think or solve day to day problems.
	5	Very forgetful, and has great difficulty when trying to think or solve day to day problems.
	6	Unable to remember anything at all, and unable to think or solve day to day problems.
Pain	1	Free of pain and discomfort.
	2	Mild to moderate pain that prevents no activities.
	3	Moderate pain that prevents a few activities.
	4	Moderate to severe pain that prevents some activities.
	5	Severe pain that prevents most activities.

Reprinted with permission from Feeny D, Furlong W, Boyle M, Torrance GW. Multi-attribute health status classification systems: health utilities index. Pharmacoeconomics 1995;7:490–502.

similarities and differences. Each attribute in HUI2 (HUI3) is composed of three to five (five or six) levels. Since any combination of different levels of health states from each attribute is theoretically possible even though perhaps clinically unlikely, HUI2 (HUI3) defines 24,000 (972,000) possible unique health states. When revising the HUI2 developers noted that some combinations of health levels were unlikely if not impossible as a result HUI2 was subsequently modified. In addition, fertility dimension was dropped, dexterity and fine motor skills were added, and the attribute sensation was subdivided into three: vision, hearing and speech. The HUI survey system adopts a "within the skin" approach in defining quality of life. As a result, questions regarding social interactions were omitted from the instrument. If needed researchers using HUI may add these items separately.

Both HUI2 and HUI3 scale death at zero and full health at one, however, unlike the Quality of Well-being index, both of the HUI instruments allow for negative utilities or fates worse than death. Scores for HUI2 (HUI3) can range from -0.03 to 1.0 (- 0.36 to 1.0)

Formula for calculating HUI2 utilities is listed in equation 3, where bi is weight for each of the seven attributes at their corresponding attribute level xi (see Table 6). This formula looks more complicated than that for the QWB index Q weight. This is because the QWB "W" score is based on an "additive" model which means that the value attributed to each dimension is simply added to provide the preference score. Additive models require adherence to the stringent assumptions based on multiattribute utility theory. Adherence to these stringent assumptions enables simple calculations of "W" or Q weight. HUI does not conform to additive model assumptions and follows less strict assumptions resulting in a multiplicative model. This means that attribute scores cannot be added as with QWB index but instead are multiplied.

Example of HUI2 scoring—best possible health state.

If a respondent scored level 1 for each of the 7 attributes for HUI2, the resultant predicted Q weight, u*, for this health state would equal:

$$u^* = 1.06(b1 \times b2 \times b3 \times b4 \times b5 \times b6 \times b7) - 0.06$$ *(equation 3)*

Where death and perfect health are scaled at 0 and 1.0, and bi is the level score for attribute i from Table 4. The b weights are substituted from Table 4 for the appropriate attribute level of xi (see Table 6). An example for perfect health is provided below.

$$u^* = 1.06\,(1 \times 1 \times 1 \times 1 \times 1 \times 1 \times 1 \times 1) - 0.06$$
$$= 1.0 \text{ for perfect health}$$

Example of HUI2 scoring—chronic condition: arthritis

Assume individual health states for HUI2 are described by the following vector notation: x1, x2, x3, x4, x5, x6, x7. If a young patient was suffering from frequent pain due to arthritis, with some physical dysfunction, this is represented by the following vector: 1, 2, 1, 1, 1, 3, 1. The resultant Q weight for HUI2 equals:

$$u = 1.06\,(1 \times 0.97 \times 1 \times 1 \times 1 \times 0.85 \times 1) - 0.06 = 0.81.$$

As previously discussed, resultant Q weights or utilities from HUI2 are scored such that perfect health and death are equal to 1.0 and zero respectively with allowance for negative utilities.

The formula for estimating HUI3 utilities is similar to that of HUI2 except there are eight instead of seven attributes (b weights). For example:

$$u^* = 1.371\,(b1 \times b2 \times b3 \times b4 \times b5 \times b6 \times b7 \times b8) - 0.371.$$ *(equation 4)*

Table 6: Scoring weights for calculating HUI2 utilities.

Sensation		**Mobility Fertility**		**Emotion**		**Cognition**		**Self-Care**			**Pain**		
x_1	b_1	x_2	b_2	x_3	b_3	x_4	b_4	x_5	b_5	x_6	b^6	x7	b_7
1	1.00	1	1.00	1	1.00	1	1.00	1	1.00	1	1.00	1	1.00
2	0.95	2	0.97	2	0.93	2	0.95	2	0.97	2	0.97	2	0.97
3	0.86	3	0.84	3	0.81	3	0.88	3	0.91	3	0.85	3	0.88
4	0.61	4	0.73	4	0.70	4	0.65	4	0.80	4	0.64		
		5	0.58	5	0.53					5	0.38		

Where x_i is the attribute level and b_i is the attribute utility score.

Reprinted with permission from Torrance GW, Feeny DH, Furlong WJ, Barr RD, Zhang Y, and Wang Q. Multi-Attribute Preference Functions for A Comprehensive Health Status Classification System: Health Utilities Index Mark 2. *Medical Care* 1996; 34(7):702-22.

Table 7: Scoring weights for calculating HUI3 utilities

Vision		Hearing Pain		Speech		Ambulation		Dexterity		Emotion		Cognition			
x_1	b_1	x_2	b_2	x_3	b_3	x_4	b_4	x_5	b_5	x_6	b_6	x_7	b_7	x_8	b_8
1	1.00	1	1.00	1	1.00	1	1.00	1	1.00	1	1.00	1	1.00	1	1.00
2	0.98	2	0.95	2	0.94	2	0.93	2	0.95	2	0.95	2	0.92	2	0.96
3	0.89	3	0.89	3	0.89	3	0.86	3	0.88	3	0.85	3	0.95	3	0.90
4	0.84	4	0.80	4	0.81	4	0.73	4	0.76	4	0.64	4	0.83	4	0.77
5	0.75	5	0.74	5	0.68	5	0.65	5	0.65	5	0.46	5	0.60		0.55
6	0.61	6	0.61			6	0.58	6	0.56	6			0.42		

Where x_i is the attribute level and b_i is the attribute utility score.

Reprinted with permission from Feeny D, Furlong W, Torrance GW, Goldsmith CH, Zhu Z, DePauw S, Denton M, Boyle M. Multiattribute and Single-Attribute Utility Functions for the Health Utilities Index Mark 3 System. Medical Care 2002;40(2):113–28.

Where death and perfect health are scaled at 0 and 1.0, and bi is the level score for attribute i from Table 5. The b weights are substituted from Table 7 for the appropriate attribute level of xi. An example of HUI3 scoring for the worst possible health state is provided below.

Assuming a fate worse than death for the following vector (6, 6, 5, 6, 6, 5, 6, 5) would result in the following utility based on weights presented in Table 7 using equation 4.

$u^* = 1.371(0.61 \times 0.61 \times 0.68 \times 0.58 \times 0.56 \times 0.46 \times 0.42 \times 0.55) - 0.371 = -0.36$, i.e., the lowest negative utility possible based on HUI3 scoring system

European quality-of-life instrument (EQ-5D)

EQ-5D formerly known as EuroQol is an extensively used multiattribute generic, nondisease specific health-related quality-of-life instrument which can produce Q weights for quality-adjusted life year estimation. Similar to QWB index and health utilities index, EQ-5D is used in combination with other generic and disease specific metrics. Furthermore, developers designed EQ-5D to complement other health-related quality of life measures, and not to be used alone. EQ-5D quality of life questionnaire consists of 2 sections. The first section, EQ-5Dindex or EQ-5D self classifier, enables respondents to describe their health-related quality of life using five dimensions or attributes of health: mobility, self-care, usual activities, pain/discomfort, and anxiety/depression (see Figure 7). Each dimension is composed of three ordinal levels—none, some/moderate, unable/extreme—consistent with other multiattribute instruments. EQ-5D self classifier can theoretically describe up to 243 unique health states (i.e., 35) in addition to death and unconscious, totaling a possible 245 health state descriptions. Preference numbers obtained using EQ-5D can be converted to a single score for use in cost-utility analysis using values derived from general population. Similar to other metrics described, perfect health and death are scaled to 1.0 and zero, respectively, and fates worse than death are permitted with the lowest instrument boundary at -0.59.

By placing a tick in one box in each group below, please indicate which statements best describe your own health state today.

Mobility

I have no problems in walking about ❑
I have some problems in walking about ❑
I am confined to bed ❑

Self-Care

I have no problems with self-care ❑
I have some problems washing or dressing myself ❑
I am unable to wash or dress myself ❑

Usual Activities *(e.g., work, study, housework, family or leisure activities)*

I have no problems with performing my usual activities ❑
I have some problems with performing my usual activities ❑
I am unable to perform my usual activities ❑

Pain/Discomfort

I have no pain or discomfort ❑
I have moderate pain or discomfort ❑
I have extreme pain or discomfort ❑

Anxiety/Depression

I am not anxious or depressed ❑
I am moderately anxious or depressed ❑
I am extremely anxious or depressed ❑

Figure 7: EQ-5D classification of health states as listed on page 2 of EQ-5D Health Survey.
Permission to reproduce was granted by EuroQol Group.

The second section of EQ-5D, EQ-VAS, captures respondent self rating using a 20cm 100-point vertical thermometer scale anchored at zero—worst imaginable health state and 100—best imaginable health state (see Figure 8). Since EQ-VAS is based on a rating scale the instrument provides values not utilities.

For both QWB index and HUI system instruments developers provided level weights for each of the attributes and based on the multiattribute utility theory adopted were either *additive* or *multiplicative* to produce their respective Q weights. EQ-$5D_{index}$ is an additive model, therefore, Q weights are estimated similar to QWB index model by subtracting negative dimension scores depending on which level the respondent selected for each item. Attribute level weights were found to be robust and valid cross-culturally for utility assessment and are available for EQ-$5D_{index}$ using two methods. The first option is to contact instrument developers for weights consistent with population under study. The second option available to the researcher is to produce utility weights specific for the study population by administering an additional set of questions to respondents known as the "common core." Common core questions require respondents to rate 16 health states on a rating scale. If Q weights are not needed, then health state descriptions produced using EQ-5D are described in terms of a 5 level vector: x1x2x3x4 x5 , where xi represents the 1-3 score for dimension i. For example, the 5 digit vector 21121 means the respondent has some problems walking about, no problems with self-care, no problems with performing usual activities, moderate pain or discomfort and is not anxious or depressed.

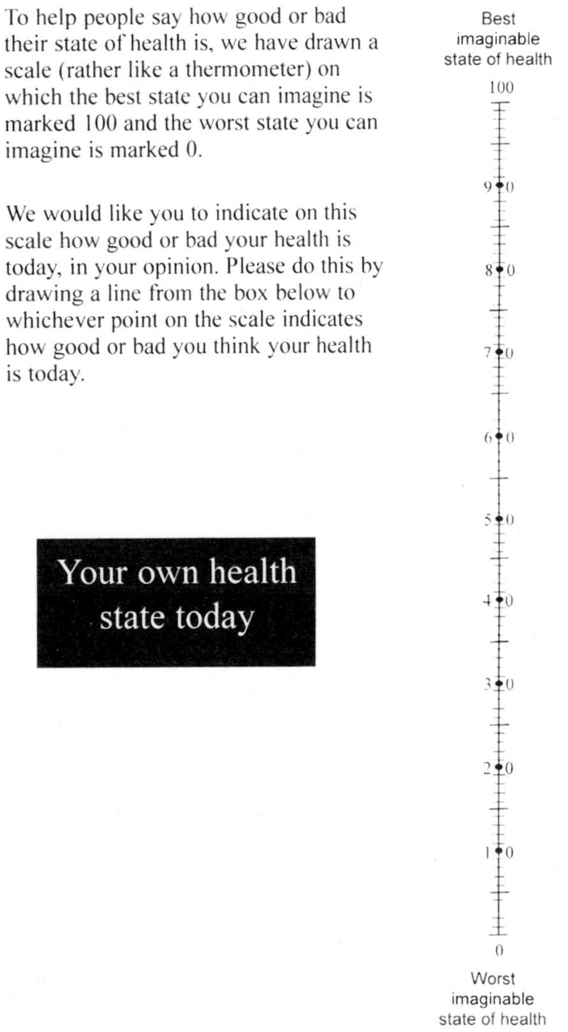

Figure 8: EQ-VAS as listed on page 3 of EQ-5D Health Survey. Permission to reproduce was granted by EuroQol Group. Copyright is held by the EuroQol Group. For all inquiries please contact Frank de Charro at *fdecharro@compuserve.com*.

League Tables

Quality-adjusted life years gained can be estimated using preference based scores such as standard gamble, rating scale, time trade-off, HUI® or QWB index. Resulting quality-adjusted life years gained, can be incorporated into cost per additional quality-adjusted life year ratios. Resultant marginal cost per quality-adjusted life year gained ratios from multiple studies can be listed in a tabular format to produce quality-adjusted life year "league" tables. The rationale behind league tables is that resources are limited; therefore, it is not possible to fund all potential health care interventions. However, due to budget constraints decisions must be made on which health care programs to fund. To assist in this process of allocative decision making, cost utility ratios are listed in descending order, starting with the lowest cost per quality-adjusted life year concluding with the highest cost per quality-adjusted life year in chronological order. Since the lowest cost per additional quality-adjusted life year is assumed to provide the most value for money, the decision maker adopts all programs in sequential order until the health care budget is depleted. Intuitively, the concept has appeal. However, it has met with much criticism. Table 8 lists the first quality-adjusted life year league table. This seminal paper is regarded as the "most influential" paper by a health economist published in 1985.

The marginal cost per quality-adjusted life year league tables assume: quality-adjusted life years adequately measure health benefits, there are no other important benefits and costs and quality-adjusted life years were measured in a way that makes them comparable. If the objective of an intervention was birth control, then less, not more, quality-adjusted life years would be desirable. Furthermore, how the Q weight was elicited can affect the resultant quality-adjusted life year gained estimate; however, studies are not always transparent in how they measured quality-adjusted life years. In addition, how costs were estimated and which costs were included, which also can vary depending on the study perspective, standards of care in used in different health care settings and discount rates incorporated.

Although the league table format permits a "cut-off" point where no more interventions will be funded greater than a certain cost per quality-adjusted life year, many researchers use the table to determine how their intervention fares with others—ratios of already accepted programs or interventions. The argument would be that if the ratio for the tested program is lower than that for already accepted programs it should be accepted since it provides value for money. However, if it is higher the program is too expensive and therefore should not be adopted based on the cost-utility ratio. Although some thresholds are quoted in the literature, one in 1982 suggested any intervention with a marginal cost per quality-adjusted life year of no more than $20,000 per quality-adjusted life year gained can be considered "cost-effective by current standards," but those interventions in excess of $100,000 per quality-adjusted life year gained did not provide value for money or "questionable in comparison with other health care expenditures" (Reference 20). Marginal costs per quality-adjusted life year gained between the two extreme cut-offs were regarded as tolerable "controversial but possibly justifiable." Ten years later, another group decided on the same cut-off criteria for economic decisions when comparing drug therapies.

In 1991 the Ontario Ministry for Health, which makes formulary decisions for drug reimbursement, adopted the above guidelines. Evidence in support of adding a drug to the formulary was regard as strong, moderate, or weak, if the marginal cost per quality-adjusted life year gained as less than $20,000, between $20,000—$100,000, or greater than $100,000, respectively (Canadian Dollars, 1990). However, these cut-offs were subsequently removed in later editions leaving the decision at the discretion of the decision maker. Curiously, again, these same cut-off values are still used even though they were originally formulated using 1982 United States dollars and inflation meant that the buying power of United States dollars had halved.

Controversy over league tables also was fueled by the Oregon experiment. In the early 1990s the state of Oregon charged the Health Services Committee to prioritize health care interventions in order of importance for their Medicaid patients. The goal was to rank-order health care services in chronological order from most to least important acknowledging that the state had limited resources. The Committee elected to use cost-utility analysis. The league table was developed using community inputs for Q weights. QWB index was used to estimate well-years weights by phone interviews with a 1000 of community members. The state acknowledged the importance of community preferences in the decision making process. Costs were based on direct costs to the state not necessarily those to the community. Although the Committee's original rational to incorporate community values was sound, their methodology and subsequent listings were flawed. The first ranking produced was criticized due to counter-intuitive rankings. The Committee produced three additional lists. The final 1993 list did not include quality-adjusted life years, due to concerns that QALYs violated the Americans with Disabilities Act. How Q weights were incorporated in the decision-making process was misunderstood by administrators. Quality-adjusted life year estimates are based on changes in Q weights. Therefore a low Q weight being assigned to a person with a disability did not mean their life had less value, in contrast it meant that interventions that improved quality of life producing higher Q weights would in fact be more highly rated.

Table 8: League table

Procedure	Present value of additional cost per marginal unit of QALY gained (£)
Pacemaker implantation for heartblock	700
Hip replacement	750
Valve replacement for aortic stenosis	900
CABG for severe angina with left main vessel disease	1040
CABG for moderate angina with triple vessel disease	2400
Kidney transplant (cadaver)	3000
Heart transplant	5000
Home hemodialysis	11000
CABG double vessel disease	12600
Hospital hemodialysis	14000

CABG = Coronary artery bypass graft.
Reprinted with permission from Elsevier Science. Drummond MF. Resource allocation decisions in health care: a role for quality of life assessments? J Chronic Dis 1987;40(6):605–19.

More recently, use of league tables for comparing acute—short lived and intense—with chronic interventions has been criticized. The rational for the critique lies in the computation of QALYs, multiplication of Q by Y, where Y is measured in years. Treatment of acute conditions can have substansive affects on quality of life, resulting in large changes of Q. However, any time horizon less than 1 year will result in fractionating quality-adjusted life year estimates, independent of perceived benefit as represented by Q weight. For example, if the change in Q weight is 0.5 utils, which is very large, but the time horizon is only 3 days, which would apply to acute conditions such as chemotherapy induced nausea and vomiting then estimated gain in quality-adjusted life years is only 0.004 QALYs (0.5 X 3 / 365). To produce the cost utility ratio for the league table the cost of therapy would be divided by a number approaching zero. In summary, league tables should be treated with care even if it is assumed that quality-adjusted life years adequately measure utility.

Nonpreference-based Measures

In the previous section, it was discussed that nonpreference-based measures cannot be used to estimate Q weights directly; however, they can be used indirectly. This section will briefly discuss the Short Form-36 (SF-36) health related quality-of-life instrument followed by two suggested models to convert SF-36 to a preference-based measure.

SF-36 is a widely used generic measure assessing health status. The SF-36 consists of 36 items divided into 8 dimensions: physical functioning, role functioning, bodily pain, mental health, role – emotional, social functioning, energy and fatigue, and general health perceptions. Each dimension is scored from 0 to 100, where a higher score means the respondent perceives the health state as more desirable. However, with SF-36, unlike preference instruments, dimension scores cannot be combined to produce a value to use in cost-utility analysis, nor are dimension scores comparable. Furthermore, unlike preference-based approaches, zero and 100 scores cannot be interpreted to mean death and perfect health. Therefore the scores are not anchored like utility scores and are conceptually different.

One solution to convert a nonpreference-based measure SF-36 to a preference-based measure (QWB) was published in 1997 by use of an algorithm resulting in Quality of Well-being index scores (W scores) (Reference 10). As part of the Beaver Dam Health Outcomes Study, researchers administered both instruments simultaneously to a random sample of adults over 45 in the Wisconsin community. Authors used multiple-linear regressions to predict QWB scores from SF-36 dimension scores. In the regression model, authors considered,all eight dimension scores, their squares and cross-product of dimension scores. The aim was to produce the best predictive algorithm for QWB scores while also making the model as simple as possible. The result was a six variable regression model to predict QWB scores using SF-36 dimension score (Adjusted R squared = 51.9 percent. The model produced a good fit or estimate of QWB or W scores. In other words, a linear combination of the six variables—dimension scores and combinations of dimension scores—was able to explain 51.9 percent of the variance in QWB scores. Since researchers using secondary data sources don't have access to individual patient scores, the model can be used using average SF-36 dimension scores.

$$QWB_{predicted} = 0.59196 + PF\ (0.0012588) - MH\ (0.0011709) - BP\ (0.0014261) + (GH \times RP) \times (0.00000705) + (PF \times BP) \times (0.00001140) + (MH \times BP) \times (0.00001931)$$
(equation 5)

Where,
QWB = average predicted Quality of Well-being score
PF = average physical functioning score
MH = average mental health score
BP = average bodily pain score.
GH = average general health perception score
RP = average role physical score,

For example, suppose the following scores were obtained from a sample of arthritis patients. Please note that only five of the eight dimension scores are listed. That is all that is needed to use equation 5.

PF = 75
MH = 75
BP = 60
GH = 70
RP = 80

Based on equation 5;

$$QWB_{predicted} = 0.59196 + (75) \times (0.0012588) - (75) \times (0.0011709) - (60) \times (0.0014261) + (70 \times 80) \times (0.00000705) + (75 \times 60) \times (0.00001140) + (75 \times 60) \times (0.00001931)$$

= 0.69, on a scale where death is equal to zero and perfect health is equal to one.

An alternative solution to converting SF-36 to a preference based score is available in the literature. The authors derived an approach based on HUI to estimate a single index. First, since eight dimensions and 36 items can generate millions of potential health states, the scale was simplified by removing potentially redundant questions to a six dimension scale: physical functioning (six items), role limitation (two items), social functioning (five items), bodily pain (six items), mental health (five items), and vitality (five items). Twenty of the 29 items are identical to those from the original SF-36; therefore, as long as these questions were completed then a preference score can be estimated using a computer algorithm available from the authors.

Expression of Cost-Utility Analysis Results

Results of cost-utility analyses are normally expressed in terms of cost per quality-of-life years gained or cost per healthy-year equivalents gained rather than cost-per utility. This is primarily because utility values alone are more difficult to comprehend than a unit such as cost per quality-of-life years. The approach to calculate cost per quality-adjusted life year is basically the same as that used in cost-effectiveness analysis. In the case of cost-utility analysis, the health effects are gains in quality-adjusted life years. In cost-effectiveness analysis, the health effect is a gain in some outcome of natural units, such as lives saved or cases of disease averted.

The difference between cost-effectiveness analysis and cost-utility analysis is the measurement of health outcomes. Both techniques require valid effectiveness data, but in the case of cost-utility analysis, only final output effectiveness data, with adjustments based on preferences will suffice. Intermediate output data, such as cases found or patients treated appropriately, are unsuitable because they cannot be converted into quality-adjusted life-years gained. By converting the effectiveness data to a common unit of measure such as quality-adjusted life years gained, cost-utility analysis is able to incorporate simultaneously both the change in quality of life, that is changes in morbidity, and the change in quantity of life, which can be measured as changes in mortality.

To illustrate the differences in expression of cost-effectiveness analysis and cost-utility analysis results, an example is presented in Table 9.

In this table, two methods of treating patients with Disease X are compared. To illustrate, Disease X is designated as lung cancer. The treatments are designated Treatment A, aggressive chemotherapy after surgical resection, and Treatment B, no chemotherapy after surgical resection. The table displays the average cost of treating patients with the two interventions in the first column. The next two columns show measures of effectiveness (life expectancy) and utility of health status outcomes associated with the two treatment strategies.

In this example, utility is based on the patients' preference for a given health state relative to perfect health on a scale from 0 to 1, with the value of 1 being equivalent to perfect health and the value of 0 being equivalent to death. For a patient who receives Treatment A, the utility value is 0.80 and for patients who receive Treatment B, the utility value is 0.90. Quality-adjusted life years are calculated by multiplying the life expectancy in years by the utility value for the given health state. Therefore, quality-adjusted life years are 3.6 (4.5 yrs x 0.80) and 3.15 (3.5 yrs x 0.90) quality-adjusted life years for Treatments A and B, respectively. The cost-effectiveness ratio is obtained by dividing the cost of the programs by the life expectancies. The cost-utility ratio is found by dividing the costs for each treatment program by the quality-adjusted life years.

Because a cost-utility analysis is usually conducted to compare one program to another, the results are expressed in terms of the incremental differences in terms of both costs and health effects. One could simply compare the ratios of costs to outcomes for two alternatives, but the correct comparison is of incremental costs over incremental outcomes. For example, by comparing the average ratios, it can be concluded that the cost-effectiveness of Program B compared to Program A is:

$4444 – $2587 = $1587 per life-year gained

and the cost-utility of Program B compared to Program A is:

$5555 – $3174 = $2381 per quality-adjusted life year gained.

The incremental change is the additional amount paid for one additional unit of outcome between different interventions. From Table 9, compare the incremental cost-effectiveness and cost-utility ratios. The incremental cost-effectiveness ratio is $10,000 per life-year gained, and the incremental cost-utility ratio is $22,222 per quality-adjusted life years gained.

Although effectiveness, when measured by life expectancy, may be easier to understand than utility, it does not reflect patient preferences or quality of life. The quality of life-years gained as a result of treatment is different between the two modalities. For example, the use of chemotherapy after resection of a lung tumor may have a considerable effect on quality of life. This effect is missed if one uses life expectancy alone as a measure of outcome. Thus, cost-utility analysis is more comprehensive and is gaining popularity as a method to compare clinical interventions. In 1986, from a policy implementation perspective, the developers of the General Health Policy Model proposed that health care programs with a cost-utility ratio less than $20,000 per well-year be considered cost-effective. In the author's classification, programs with a cost-utility ratio between $20,000 and $100,000 were identified as controversial, but still justifiable. The value of any program with a cost-utility ratio greater than $100,000 per well-year was considered questionable. The author's dollar figures do need adjustment to reflect accurately 1997 dollars.

There is considerable debate as to whether nonmonetary outcomes of an intervention should be discounted. Discounting is usually performed to account for individuals'

Table 9. Cost-Effectiveness Analysis and Cost-Utility Analysis of Two Alternative Treatment Interventions

Intervention	Costs	Effectiveness (Life Expectancy)	Utility of Health Status Outcome	Quality-Adjusted Life-years (QALYs)
Treatment A	$20,000	4.5 years	0.80	3.60
Treatment B	$10,000	3.5 years	0.90	3.15
	Cost-Effectiveness Ratio	**Incremental Cost-Effectiveness**	**Cost-Utility Ratio**	**Incremental Cost-Utility**
Treatment A	$4444/life-year gained	$10,000/life-year gained	$5555/QALY	$22,222/QALY
Treatment B	$2857/life-year gained		$3174/QALY	

Reprinted with permission from Detsky AS, Naglie IG. A clinician's guide to cost-effectiveness analysis. Ann Intern Med 1990;114:147–54.

time preferences. That is, patients usually prefer to receive benefits of therapy earlier rather than later.

It is generally accepted that costs incurred over a period longer than 1 year should be discounted to reflect the time value of money. However, it is a matter of debate whether health benefits, such as the quantity of life-years gained, should be discounted. Unlike money, it is questioned whether a future expectation of quantity of life can be exchanged for life now. However, another perspective states quantity of life should be discounted in an economic analysis of health care programs to remain consistent with the discounting of future monetary costs and benefits. Lack of discounting gives equal weight to life-years generated now or in the distant future. On the other hand, discounting results in lowering the value of future life-years, which in turn, lowers the value of programs designed to yield benefit in future generations.

Strengths, Limitations, and Controversies of Cost-Utility Analysis

Strengths

The primary strength of cost-utility analysis is the integration of both quality and quantity of life into a common unit of measure. Interventions that affect both quality and length of life can be compared. Use of a common unit of measure also enables comparison of effects of interventions on different dimensions of quality of life, such as comparing depression with pain.

Presenting comparisons between interventions based on cost-utility analysis is inherently appealing to decision makers because, when used appropriately, cost-utility analysis provides the decision maker with a tool that has advantages over cost-benefit and cost-effectiveness analyses. Although cost-benefit analysis also has the potential for integrating quality and quantity of consequences into a common unit of measure, it suffers from the difficulty of translating patient-reported outcomes, such as quality of life, into dollars. In addition, if the cost-benefit analysis is conducted using the human capital approach, it carries the potential for discrimination because the value of livelihood is equated with the value of life.

When comparing cost-utility analysis to cost-effectiveness analysis, cost-utility analysis has the advantage of being able to incorporate simultaneously multiple outcomes. Cost-effectiveness analysis is limited to comparisons of interventions with the same measurement of outcomes. Cost-utility analysis is capable of placing a value on the consequence or outcomes in terms of quality or desirability.

Limitations and Controversies

There are many limitations and controversies surrounding cost-utility analysis. In addition to the practical limitations of cost-utility analysis, there are a host of limitations based solely on the calculation of quality-adjusted life years.

Limitations and Controversies with Quality-Adjusted Life Years

Different approaches have been used to measure utility values. However, utility weights obtained by one method may differ from those obtained using another method. Therefore, the fact that users are allowed to choose their own way of measuring the weights is problematic because the results of quality-adjusted life years generated by the proposed measurement methods may be different. An underlying reason for these differences is that only one of the proposed measurement methods meets the axiomatic functions outlined by the utility theory. Although an advantage of using quality-adjusted life years gained as a comprehensive unit of outcome is that it incorporates both quality and quantity, this advantage is only true if all methods of measurement are comparable. Therefore, not all quality-adjusted life years are comparable.

In addition, violating the assumptions involving quality-adjusted life years also results in some more practical concerns regarding their application. By virtue of the fact that the name "quality-adjusted life years" specifies years, it becomes readily apparent that this measure is biased against interventions designed to improve quality of life due to acute conditions duration.

For example, consider a patient with cancer on chemotherapy who experiences severe episodes of emesis for 24 hours after each round of therapy with the patient receiving the described therapy six times a year. Assume the patient assigns the utility value of 0.60 to his health state with cancer, but considers the agony of having emesis for 24 hours after each treatment to approach a state as bad as being dead. Therefore, the utility of this emesis period is equal to 0.

Evaluate the benefits of Drug A, which is capable of allowing a patient to avoid the postchemotherapy emesis episodes. Because Drug A can prevent the health state utility from dropping from 0.60 to 0 for the 24 hours after chemotherapy, the quality-adjusted life years gained from drug A are equal to 0.60 multiplied by 6 days divided by 365 days/year or 0.0098 QALY. A decision maker or clinician may

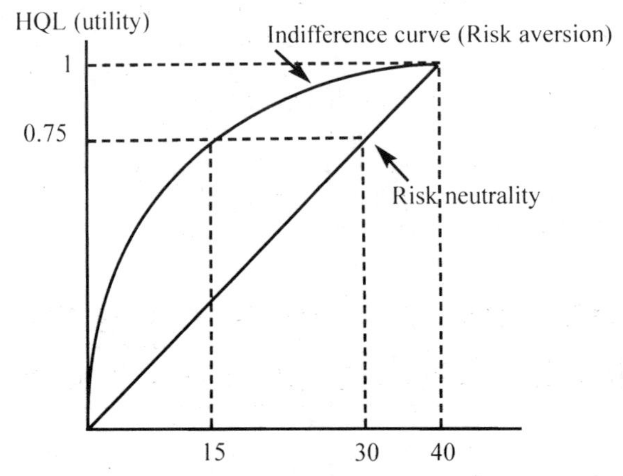

Figure 9. A Comparison of Indifference Curves Between Risk Neutrality and Risk Aversion Assumptions

mistakenly interpret 0.0098 QALY as an insignificant improvement and assign a low priority to funding such a drug with an apparently small numerical value. However, if patients receiving chemotherapy are willing to pay significant amounts to prevent emesis of short duration, the technique used to arrive at quality-adjusted life years is too restrictive and may undervalue the contribution of a health care technology, and lead to a misallocation of resources. The application of the quality-adjusted time without symptoms and toxicity could overcome some of the specific problems associated with measuring quality-adjustments of short duration.

The major reason for the low quality-adjusted life year values associated with acute conditions of short duration is that contemporary utility theory is designed to measure utility in use or utility based on experience; it does not take into account anticipated utility, or disutility, of a health state. Contemporary theory, upon which quality-adjusted life year measurements are based, is not consistent with market reality because patients are willing to pay large amounts of money to avoid the anticipated disutility resulting from emesis and other short duration health problems.

Another limitation of utility theory is that the risk neutrality assumption restricts the conversion of ill health time into full health time in a linear fashion only. The net effect of this inherent limitation of the quality-adjusted life years method is that it underestimates the potential value of health care technologies. The linearity assumption results in overvaluation of quality-adjusted life years associated with the current health state and, hence, underestimation of the potential value of health care technologies.

For example, an individual who has a life expectancy of 40 years of normal health, quality-adjusted life years is 40 QALYs. However, if he has to live with a chronic disease that he perceives to have a utility of only 0.75 for 40 years, under the risk neutrality assumption, his quality-adjusted life years will be 0.75 multiplied by 40 years, or 30 QALYs. Therefore, the maximum improvement any technology can provide is equal to 10 QALYs. However, if his personal preference is not linear, but instead follows the indifference curve of risk aversion as shown in Figure 9, his perceived quality-adjusted life years is only 15 QALYs, which is much lower than that predicted by the risk neutrality assumption line. With the risk averse assumption, the maximum improvement available from a given technology is now 40 QALYs minus 15 QALYs or 25 QALYs. Because it is commonly believed that individuals are risk averse in most situations, the current approach of measuring quality-adjusted life years under the risk neutrality assumption limits the available gain from medical technology to 10 quality-adjusted life years in this example.

Alternative Approaches to Quality-Adjusted Life Years

Although there are many unresolved issues with the current approaches used in measuring quality-adjusted life years, there is still a great deal of interest in developing measures of output of health care programs that combine the impact of both quantity and quality of life.

One approach, proposed as an alternative to quality-adjusted life years, is the use of healthy year equivalents (Reference 25). The authors claim that numbers represented by the current quality-adjusted life-years measures do not represent the real preferences of patients. This is because, when clinicians use quality-adjusted life years, they must assume that the numbers used to represent quality of life for a particular health state are independent of the time spent in the state and that patients are risk neutral. The authors assert that healthy year equivalents fully represent patients' or other individuals' preferences because they are calculated directly from each individual's utility function. By fully representing individual preferences, the use of healthy year equivalents avoids some of the major problems of quality-adjusted life years, because no assumptions are needed to equate the healthy year equivalents with utility.

These claims have generated a heated debate in the literature from the defenders of both concepts. Regardless of the theoretical advantage of healthy year equivalents, the measurement procedure to obtain healthy year equivalent values is much more complex and costly because it requires the subject to choose between two lottery questions as opposed to one to obtain weights for quality-adjusted life-years calculation. Unfortunately, not many studies have compared the results obtained from the healthy year equivalents and quality-adjusted life years approaches.

Another theory has been proposed based on generic utility theory that weakens some of the strong assumptions of the utility theory. Unfortunately, both the theory and scaling of utility functions for the given outcome domain are more complicated in the generic utility theory framework than with the expected utility theory. Another approach is to recognize that there is no single quality-adjusted life years formula. There are various bivariate functions for quality-adjusted life years, and depending upon which assumption holds true for a given study, the appropriate quality-adjusted life years function may be different.

Many other issues related to the measurement of quality-adjusted life years are not discussed in this chapter. Some of these issues include measuring quality-adjusted life years for patients with multiple disease states and multiple therapies; accounting for the intra- and inter-individual spillover effects in the measurement of quality-adjusted life years; implications of the relationship between health and other domains of life for the measurement of quality-adjusted life years; and, above all, the question of link between preferences determined from judgmental responses and the final choice. However, it also has been posited that global utility scores have an advantage by accounting for patients' response for their entire health experience, including multiple disease states.

Regardless of many of these unresolved issues, it is clear that the technology of measuring quality-adjusted life years is still in its evolutionary stage. It must be emphasized that using quality-adjusted life years to account for multiple disease states requires further research at the individual level. Hence, at this time, quality-adjusted life years, if used, should be viewed as only one more input that is available to assist decision makers in allocating resources. For more information regarding these models, interested readers are referred to a detailed synopsis in the literature (References 27 and 28).

General Limitations of Cost-Utility Analysis

There are important limits to what cost-utility analysis can tell a policy analyst when it comes to moral or ethical judgments about health care. The example of the county health board faced with choosing among childhood vaccinations, alcohol and drug rehabilitation, and hypertension screening is one of many scenarios where decisions based solely on the application of cost-utility analysis may be challenged on moral grounds. Although the mathematics and logic of the cost-utility analysis may be clearly defensible in the minds of investigators, translation of that rationale into a reasonable explanation to appease those who are left disenfranchised by a resource allocation decision may not be as straightforward.

Therefore, the domain in which cost-utility analysis can be applied should not be exaggerated. There are still many uncertainties in health care decisions because biological and medical science cannot yet indicate with precision the magnitude of an intervention's likely health outcome. Even though substantial uncertainty exists about the effects of a health intervention, it does not mean that cost-utility analysis cannot be used; the conclusions of a cost-utility analysis may still be valuable if placed in the proper context. But, the more uncertain the effects of a health intervention, the more uncertain the conclusion of a cost-utility analysis will be. Cost-utility analysis cannot resolve or eradicate uncertainties about basic clinical efficacy. Moreover, there is a danger that the seeming sophistication of a cost-utility analysis may give an undeserved aura of precision to its conclusions and that caveats about the uncertainty of the conclusions will be lost.

A practical limitation to cost-utility analysis is the challenge conducting this type of study poses. For a pharmacist interested in conducting a cost-utility analysis to address a particular decision in a given practice setting, the following questions should be taken into consideration. First, are the resources to measure the quantity of costs and effects of various alternatives available? If the resources are available, the researcher must then overcome the challenge of measuring preferences or utility for quality of life.

The next step is to decide on the strategy to measure utility. As previously discussed, three approaches can be considered: using utility weights reported in the literature, measuring utility directly from health care providers, or measuring utility directly from patients or the general public. The researcher must reconcile the limitations with these strategies. When employing the option of literature-based utility values, the researcher has to make sure the intents and perspectives of the original investigators, the study subject population, and theory used by the investigators match those of the current study. If the available literature is not sufficient to answer the questions mentioned, consideration should be given to primary data collection.

Difficulties have been reported in the literature associated with primary data collection. The authors note that assigning preferences to health states can involve a considerable investment of time, energy, and resources, especially if the investigator is not experienced in different measurement techniques. One major issue is who should serve as the potential population of subjects? Health care providers can readily understand the description of various health states, but they also represent a degree of bias. If the general population and subjects representative of the disease of interest are used, respondent burden becomes an issue. Experience shows that people often resist judgment tasks. They find probabilities or time difficult to work with, making the use of standard gamble and time trade-off techniques difficult. Other people find it offensive to assign numbers to quality of life.

Other practical considerations concern the need to develop extensive instrumentation means—visual aids, trained interviewers, interviewer manuals, and response-recording forms. Data, sometimes requiring statistical transformation, must be entered and analyzed. Measurement must be standardized in scaling studies to ensure precision, to help interviewers administer the preferences assignment task, and to increase confidence in the study results.

Evaluating the Cost-Utility Analysis Literature

Although the difficulties encountered in measuring utility may discourage investigators from pursuing the use of cost-utility analysis as a study methodology, it is still important to understand these limitations from a more pragmatic perspective. In the pharmacy field, clinicians are often presented with information from a variety of sources that use cost-utility analysis studies to promote one product as an alternative to others. Therefore, the ability to assess these arguments critically allows participants in this program to make informed decisions regarding the relative merits of cost-utility analysis studies.

Although the critical examination of quantity and cost information is crucial for review of all types of economic evaluations, cost-utility analysis presents another dimension to the challenge of evaluation. The unique measurement of quality or utility in cost-utility analysis leads to another source of controversy. A list of criteria has been provided by one group based on a literature review that expresses results in cost per quality-adjusted life year (Reference 30). These criteria are as follows:

1. All states of health that are assigned utility weights should be described in terms of concrete symptoms and dysfunctions so that nonmedical decision makers can independently judge the disutility of the state.

2. The source of each weight should be indicated. For example, is it taken from a previous scientific publication, is it obtained by applying an established instrument for valuing health states, or is it simply a judgment made by the authors or someone who they have consulted?

3. Analysts should point out what the weights imply in terms of equivalence numbers and discuss whether these implications are plausible because there is much confusion about what quality-adjustment weights actually mean.

Although utility values look like cardinal measures of utility or strength of preference, they are often not intended as such by the subjects from whom they are elicited. Uncritical application of such weights in a conventional quality-adjusted life years algorithm can lead to erroneous estimates of the social value of health care programs. Therefore, weights should be supported by a theoretical argument.

4. To further enhance understanding, the composition of the gain in quality-adjusted life years, in terms of the relative contributions of increased life expectancy and increased quality of life, should be given in plain language. One reason for this requirement is if the increase in quality is small, there is less reason for concern about the utility weights.

5. Sensitivity analysis should be performed over a wide range of alternative utility weight values.

6. All of the data, assumptions, and procedures behind each estimate of quality-adjusted life years should be clearly presented so that the decision maker can easily check the estimates and perform alternative calculations based on different assumptions. Ideally, the exact mathematical equation underlying each estimate should be given so that readers are spared all guesswork.

7. Additional information from the authors should be readily available.

The abovementioned criteria should be carefully considered by researchers as they develop their study methodologies and by readers of the cost-utility literature as they attempt to make informed interpretations of published studies.

Conclusion

This chapter provides the background and tools necessary to know when to use cost-utility analysis, practical considerations for the application of cost-utility analysis as an economic evaluation technique, and what elements or criteria to consider when reviewing published cost-utility analysis studies. It should now be obvious as to why cost-utility analysis is the most challenging type of economic analysis to conduct and why it is also the source of the most controversial dialogue among researchers and policy makers. Researchers must recognize that regardless of how carefully real preferences are measured, they are not choices nor do they always materialize in choices. Hence, decisions to allocate resources based on preference measures alone require faith in inferential leaps.

Annotated Bibliography

1. Anderson JP, Moser RJ. Parasite screening and treatment among Indochinese refugees, cost-benefit/utility and the general health policy model. JAMA 1985;253:2229–35.

The authors provide a detailed step-by-step demonstration of the application of the Quality of Well-Being scale (QWB) and the calculation of well-years as part of the General Health Policy Model. The authors refer to their cost-utility analysis as a cost-benefit/utility analysis that expands conventional cost-effectiveness methods to include social utility as measured by prevented morbidity and mortality. This approach also permits a more complete assessment of a health program than is possible under the more limited cost-benefit approach.

2. Beck JR, Pauker SG, Gottlied JE, et al. A convenient approximation of life expectancy (the DEALE). Am J Med 1982; 73: 889–97.

This paper provides a methodology for determining the Y, (i.e., quantity of years) in quality-adjusted life years calculations. This method, the declining exponential approximation of life expectancy (DEALE), enables the clinician to collate various survival data with information on morbidity to determine a quality-adjusted expected survival for a potential management plan. The key to the DEALE approach is the approximation of survival by a simple exponential function. This approximation makes it possible to translate data from various literature sources (life expectancy tables, 5-year survival rates, survival curves, and median survival) into a single unified mortality scale.

3. Bisonnie RS, Lawler FH, Pierce L. Recurrent otitis media: a cost-utility analysis of simulated treatment using tympanostomy tubes vs antibiotic prophylaxis. Fam Prac Res J 1991;11:371–88.

This study is an example of the application of cost-utility analysis to evaluate mutually exclusive alternatives. Of particular interest is the similarity in utility scores for the alternatives, which indicates the importance of sensitivity analysis.

4. Bootman JL, Townsend RJ, McGhan WF. Principles of pharmacoeconomics, 2nd ed. Cincinnati, OH: Harvey Whitney Books, 1996.

This is a review of the basic principles of pharmacoeconomics. This book systematically presents the techniques, tools, and strategies necessary to evaluate the economic contribution of specific drug therapies from the policy level down to individual patient needs. A thorough treatment of cost-utility analysis is included.

5. Brazier J, Usherwood T, harper R, Thomas K. Deriving a preference based single index from the UK SF-36 Health Survey. Journal of Clinical Epidemiology 1998;51(11): 1115–1128.

This study describes how to convert SF-36 to a preference based measure based on HUI®. Useful resource if a utility weight is needed and all you have are dimension scores from the Short Form 36 (SF-36). Includes a thorough explanation of methods used.

6. Culyer AJ, Wagstaff A. QALYs (quality-adjusted life-years) versus HYEs (healthy year equivalents) J Health Econ 1993;12:311–23.

In this paper, the authors explore the claim that quality-adjusted life years are liable to misrepresent consumer preferences and hence lead decision makers to choose options that are not those preferred by the public. They also consider the claim that healthy year equivalents do not suffer from this defect. The authors argue that none of the examples offered to date demonstrate the alleged tendency of quality-adjusted life years to misrepresent preferences. It also is shown that healthy year equivalents are identical to quality-adjusted life year scores obtained from a time trade-off experiment and, therefore, that the assumptions about preferences underlying healthy year equivalents are just as restrictive as those underlying time trade-off based quality-adjusted life years.

7. Department of Health and Human Services. Public Health Service. Office of Disease Prevention and Health Promotion. Kamlet MS. A framework for cost-utility analysis of government health care programs: the comparative benefits modeling project. Washington, DC: U.S. Department of Health and Human Services, 1992.

This reference reviews the methodological concerns of the application of cost-utility analysis. It describes the requirements for appropriate application from the perspective of public policy decision making.

8. Detsky AS, Naglie IG. A clinician's guide to cost-effectiveness analysis. Ann Intern Med 1990;114:147–54.

This concise primer of cost-effectiveness analysis contrasts the results of cost-effectiveness analysis to cost-utility analysis and cost-benefit analysis. It gives a thorough explanation of incremental analysis versus comparison of average cost-effectiveness ratios.

9 Drummond MF, Stoddart GL, Torrance GW. Methods for the economic evaluation of health care programmes. Oxford: Oxford University Press, 1986.

This textbook presents the methodological principles of economic evaluation by concentrating on the necessary practical issues that users need to understand as they either review papers or prepare to embark on their own evaluations. The case examples at the end of each chapter supplement the text.

10. Fryback DG, Lawrence WF, Martin PA, Klein R, Klein BEK. Predicting Quality of Well Being scores from the SF-36. Medical Decision Making 1997,17:1–9.

Useful paper to predict QWB scores from SF-36 dimension scores. Please see table 3 on page 6 for regression model. Authors clearly explain assumptions and also present validation of model.

11. Furlong W, Feeney D, Torrance G, Barr R. The Health Utilities Index (HUI®) System for Assessing Health-Related Quality of Life in Clinical Studies: A Technical report, McMaster University Center for Health Economics and Policy Analysis Working Paper 01-02, March 2001.

The latest in the series of HUI System working papers by the developers of the HUI®. This report describes the validation and development of the entire system, HUI1, HUI2 and the most recent version in the series HUI3. The review is comprehensive and also includes copies of HUI2 (Table 1, page 46–47) and HUI3 (Table 2, pages 48–51) attributes.

12. Furlong W, Feeney D, Torrance GW, Goldsmith CH, DePauw S, Zhu Z, Denton M, Boyle M. Multiplicative Multi-Attribute Utility Function for the Health Utilities Index Mark 3 (HUI3) System: A Technical report, McMaster University Center for Health Economics and Policy Analysis Working Paper 98–11, December 1998.

This report is a reference document authored by instrument developers and explains in detail the development of Health Utilities Index Mark 3. Scoring function (weights) needed to formulate HUI scores are located in Appendix B (pages 95–96). HUI3 items is located on pages 61–63.

13. Gabriel SE, Campion ME, O'Fallon WM. A cost-utility analysis of misoprostol prophylaxis for rheumatoid arthritis patients receiving nonsteroidal antiinflammatory drugs. Arthritis Rheum 1994;37:333–41.

This example of the application of cost-utility analysis demonstrates the importance of incorporating patient preferences into economic evaluations. Probabilistic sensitivity analysis demonstrated that, on average, prophylaxis resulted in modest additional costs and no additional quality of life benefits.

14. Gafni A. The standard gamble method: what is being measured and how it is interpreted? Health Serv Res 1994;29:207–24.

The author demonstrates inappropriate interpretation of time dimension at the individual level; issues stemming from the aggregation of individual utility values measured using different time horizons, the potential for double counting of the time preference effect when discounting future quality-adjusted life years, and problems associated with using the standard gamble technique to measure temporary health states.

15. Gerard K, Dobson M, Hall J. Framing and labeling effects in health descriptions: quality-adjusted life years for treatment of breast cancer. J Clin Epidemiol 1993;46;77–84.

This study investigated the impact of framing and labeling effects in 180 subjects randomly allocated to one of nine different presentations of two breast cancer health descriptions. There were no significant differences in the valuations placed on these descriptions when framing and labeling effects were taken into account. A significant difference was found in the particular values of descriptions that were written in the third person that differed in terms of whether the word "cancer" was used.

16. Hornberger JC, Redelmeier DA, Peterson J. Variability among methods to assess patients' well-being and consequent effect on a cost-effectiveness analysis. J Clin Epidemiol 1992;45:505–12.

These researchers interviewed 58 patients with chronic renal failure to determine the level of agreement among six methods for assessing well-being, and to determine the effects of variation in assessed well-being on the results of a cost-utility analysis of in-center hemodialysis. Patients reported well-being using the Sickness Impact Profile, Campbell Index of Well-Being, Kaplan-Bush Index of Well-Being, categorical scaling, standard gamble, and time trade-off. Correlations among assessment methods were poor and the cost per quality-adjusted life-year saved varied from $34,893 to $42,254 according to the Sickness Impact Profile and the standard gamble technique, respectively. The authors conclude that the substantial variability in patients' stated quality of life may preclude the use of a single method to analyze the cost-effectiveness or cost-utility of a health program.

17. Johannesson M. The ranking properties of healthy-years equivalents and quality-adjusted life-years under certainty and uncertainty. Int J Technol Assess Health Care 1995;11:40–8.

This paper investigates the theoretical properties of healthy year equivalents and quality-adjusted life years. A distinction is made between ex ante healthy year equivalents and expected healthy year equivalents and between risk-neutral quality-adjusted life years and risk-adjusted quality-adjusted life years.

In the case of certainty, healthy year equivalents always rank health profiles according to individual preferences, whereas quality-adjusted life years only rank health profiles according to individual preferences if a constant proportional trade-off holds for all health states and if additive independence of quality in different periods holds.

18. Johannesson M. QALYs, HYEs and individual preferences—a graphical illustration. Soc Sci Med 1994;39:1623–32.

The author graphically illustrates the underlying preferences and assumptions of quality-adjusted life years and healthy year equivalents. For quality-adjusted life years, the assumptions of mutual utility independence, constant proportional trade-off, and risk neutrality are explained. For healthy year equivalents to be a valid cardinal function, the somewhat less restrictive assumption of risk neutrality over life-years in full health has to be made. This paper demonstrates that, by estimating the certainty-equivalent number of healthy year equivalents, it is possible in theory to obtain a measure that will always rank risky health profiles according to individual preferences.

19. Johannesson M. Quality-adjusted life-years versus healthy-years equivalents—a comment. J Health Econ 1995;14:9–16.

This is a continuation of the quality-adjusted life years versus healthy year equivalents debate. The author questions the underlying assumptions of healthy years equivalents.

20. Kaplan RM. Quality of life assessment for cost/utility studies in cancer. Cancer Treat Rev 1993;19(suppl A):85–96.

The General Health Policy Model (GHPM) is proposed as a method to resolve issues related to balancing the desire to extend life expectancy and to improve the quality of life in the years before death. The model adjusts life expectancy for diminished quality of life, which is measured using a standardized instrument known as the Quality of Well-being Scale. The model expresses the effect of treatment in well-years or quality-adjusted life years. The paper compares the GHPM to similar methods, such as the quality-adjusted time without symptoms and toxicity (Q-TWIST).

21. La Puma J, Lawlor EF. Quality-adjusted life-years: ethical implications for physicians and policymakers. JAMA 1990;263:2917–21.

The authors discuss six ethical assumptions regarding quality-adjusted life years: quality of life can be accurately measured and used, utilitarianism is acceptable, equity and efficiency are compatible, projections of community preferences can substitute for individual preferences, the old have less capacity to benefit than the young, and physicians will not use quality-adjusted life years as clinical maxims. The use of quality-adjusted life years signal two shifts in the locus of control and the nature of the clinical encounter. First, formal expressions of community preferences and societal usefulness will counterbalance patient autonomy. Second, formal tools of resource allocation and applied decision analysis will counterbalance the use of clinical judgment. The authors conclude that using quality-adjusted life years for health policy decisions is problematic and speculative; using quality-adjusted life years at the bedside is dangerous.

22. Loomes G, McKenzie L. The use of QALYs in health care decision making. Soc Sci Med 1989;28:299–308.

The authors highlight some of the critical issues concerning the use of quality-adjusted life years to measure the outcome of health care choices in decisions related to both individual patient care and social resource allocation. Specific attention is given to the practical interpretation of the assumptions of quality-adjusted life year calculations.

23. McNeil BJ, Weichselbaum R, Pauker SG. Fallacy of five year survival in lung cancer. N Engl J Med 1978;229:1397–401.

This report provides a detailed interpretation of the practical considerations of 5-year survival data in lung cancer. The authors conducted an empiric study to determine the extent to which patients were willing to take risks regarding their life expectancy. The results suggest that patients routinely violate the utility assumption of constant proportional trade-off.

24. Mehrez A, Gafni A. Healthy-years equivalents versus quality-adjusted life years: in pursuit of progress. Med Decis Making 1993;13:287–92.

The authors respond to the contention that healthy year equivalents do not fulfill claims made previously. Developers of healthy years equivalents compare and contrast their metric to quality-adjusted life years and holistic methods used to estimate utility.

25. Mehrez A, Gafni A. Preference based outcome measures for economic evaluation of drug interventions: quality-adjusted life years (QALYs) versus healthy year equivalents (HYEs). PharmacoEconomics 1992;1:338–45.

The authors provide a critical overview of quality-adjusted life years and healthy year equivalents. Problems discussed include the fact that quality-adjusted life years do not fully reflect individual preferences and the fact that different (not necessarily comparable) methods of measurement can be used to generate quality-adjusted life-year weights. Healthy year equivalents are presented as an alternative measure that does not suffer from some of the major limitations of the quality-adjusted life-year measure.

26. Mehrez A, Gafni A. Quality-adjusted life years, utility theory, and healthy-years equivalents. Med Decis Making 1991;11:140–6.

The authors respond to the contention that healthy year equivalents do not fulfill previously made claims. The examples demonstrated in earlier papers are shown to be conclusive, and the authors respond to arguments about the practical aspects of using healthy year equivalents versus quality-adjusted life years.

27. Miyamoto JM, Eraker SA. A multiplicative model of the utility of survival duration and health quality. J Exp Psychol 1988;117:3–20.

In this introduction to generic utility theory, the authors investigate the hypothesis that utility (subjective value) of survival duration and health quality are determined by a multiplicative model. The generic utility theory overcomes the limitations based on the strong assumptions of the utility theory.

28. Miyamoto JM, Eraker SA. Parametric models of the utility of survival duration: tests of axioms in a generic utility framework. Organizational Behav Human Decis Processes 44;1989:166–202.

The authors describe an experiment that tests risk posture with respect to survival duration to determine if utility function is a linear, exponential, logarithmic, or power function relationship. Results show that these models are all violated by a substantial proportion of subjects. Qualitative analyses of the pattern of violations suggest that the linear and exponential utility models are better approximations of subjects' preferences than the logarithmic and power utility models.

29. Nease RF, Kneeland T, O'Connor GT, et al. Variation in patient utilities for outcomes of the management of chronic stable angina—implications for clinical practice guidelines. JAMA 1995;273:1185–90.

    In this study of 220 subjects with chronic stable angina, considerable variation in the tolerance for angina symptoms was found as measured by patient utilities using the standard gamble, time trade-off, and rating scale methods. These findings suggest that guidelines for managing ischemic heart disease should be based on the preferences of the individual rather than on symptom severity alone.

30. Nord E. Toward quality assurance in QALY calculations. Int J Technol Assess Health Care 1993;9:37–45.

    The utility weights used in published scientific articles for assessing benefits in terms of quality-adjusted life-years gained often have a weak theoretical and empiric basis. This review of 15 published studies, which all reported results in terms of quality-adjusted life years, highlights the need for cautious reading. The author describes basic criteria for appropriate use of quality-adjusted life years and finds that many journal articles fail to meet these standards.

31. O'Connor AMC, Boyd NF, Warde P, et al. Eliciting preferences for alternative drug therapies in oncology: influence of treatment outcome description, elicitation technique and treatment experience on preferences. J Chron Dis 1987;40:811–8.

    Methodologic issues in the measurement of health preferences are described. Examples include selecting appropriate descriptions of treatment outcomes and elicitation techniques and a comparison of patients' anticipated preferences for treatment versus actual preferences once they have experienced treatment. This study demonstrates the difference in patient preferences before and after exposure to chemotherapy treatment. The results raise questions about the extent to which patients are willing, at the time of decision making, to trade-off survival rate for improved quality of life.

32. Pathak D, MacKeigan L. Assessment of quality of life and health status: selected observations. J Res Pharm Econ 1992;4:31–52.

    The authors overview the issues related to quality of life assessment. The importance of sound methodological principles for conducting studies is emphasized, and several examples are provided to demonstrate their claims.

33. Pathak DS. QALYs in health outcomes research: representation of real preferences or another numerical abstraction? J Res Pharm Econ 1995;6:3–27.

    This paper includes details of the assumptions and axioms involved in utility and quality-adjusted life year calculations. It also examines how violations of these assumptions affects the interpretation of real preferences. Approaches such as healthy year equivalents and generic utility theories are presented as alternatives to the shortfalls in quality-adjusted life years. The author concludes that, because the preferences measured in quality-adjusted life years are not choices, decisions to allocate resources based on preference measures alone requires faith in inferential leaps.

34. Richardson J. Cost-utility analysis: what should be measured? Soc Sci Med 1994;39:7–21.

    The author re-examines the issue of the appropriate unit for measuring output in cost-utility analysis. The first theme of the paper is that utility, as is often conceived and quantified, is not an appropriate basis for measurement. The question then arises as to what is the appropriate unit of measurement. The second theme is the author's proposed criteria for evaluating measurement units.

35. Sackett DL, Torrance GW. The utility of different health states as perceived by the general public. J Chron Dis 1978;31:697–704.

    The authors describe the results of random sampling of the general public to determine their social utility. A series of scenarios describing the physical, social, and emotional characteristics; limitations; and durations of different health states was presented to subjects. The resulting mean daily health state utilities differed among disorders and varied with age, the duration of the disorder, the label used to describe the disorder, and the health status of the respondent.

36. Spilker B, ed. Quality of life assessments in clinical trials. New York: Raven Press, 1990.

    In this book are a number of tests and methods available for measuring quality of life. Readers are encouraged to consult Chapter 3 for a detailed description of the Quality of Well-being scale and the GHPM. The components and data sources of the GHPM are explained in detail. Also, several diverse clinical examples of well-year calculations are described. For generic preference and non-preference based instrument descriptions interested are provided for Health Utilities Index (HUI) (Chapter 26), EQ-5D, formerly, EuroQol (Chapter 22), and SF-3) (Chapter 34).

37. Torrance GW, Feeny D. Utilities and quality-adjusted life years. Int J Technol Assess Health Care 1989,10:559–75.

    Utilities and quality-adjusted life years are reviewed, with particular focus on their use in technology assessment. The authors provide a broad overview and perspective of the interrelationship between utilities and quality-adjusted life years. The historical development, assumptions, strengths, weaknesses, and applications of each are summarized.

38. Torrance GW. Measurement of health state utilities for economic appraisal. J Health Econ 1986;5:1–30.

    The author provides a detailed description of how to elicit utility values by the standard gamble, time trade-off, and magnitude ranking methods.

39. Weinstein MC, Stason WB. Foundations of cost-effectiveness for health and medical practices. N Engl J Med 1977;296:716–21.

    This is one of the first papers describing the use of cost-utility analysis in health care. The principles presented in this paper have stood the test of time and are the required practice of any study in the economic analysis of health care. Particularly noteworthy are the descriptions of discounting and sensitivity analysis. The authors present cost-utility analysis as an extension of cost-effectiveness analysis.

40. Weinstein MC. A QALY is a QALY is a QALY—or is it? J Health Econ 1988:7:289–90.

    In this editorial, the author articulates his concerns of making broad generalizations about the results of quality-adjusted life year calculations from one setting to the next. The author points out the need to sharpen the ability of generalized quality-adjusted life year scales to reflect age- and context-specific variations in the relative value of health states.

41(A). Zbrozek AS, Cantor SB, Cardenas MP, et al. Pharmacoeconomic analysis of ondanestron versus metoclopramide for cisplatin-induced nausea and vomiting. Am J Hosp Pharm 1994;51:1555–63.

41(B). Rubenstein EB, Elting LS. Pharmacoeconomic analyses: whose perspective counts and costs the most? Am J Hosp Pharm 1994;51:564–9.

This study and commentary demonstrates the importance of critical evaluation when reading the literature. Most of the methodology of this analysis was fundamentally sound, but the results must be tempered within the limitations stated by the authors. The authors obtained utility values through a meta-analysis of clinical trials of ondansetron and metoclopramide. Furthermore, the analysis did not include metoclopramide in combination therapy (as is usually the case in practice). The authors call into question the assumptions used in Reference 41(A) and the appropriateness of the cost-utility analysis in selecting therapy for chemotherapy-induced nausea and vomiting. The rebuttal also is included.

Self-Assessment Questions

1. Which one of the following statements is an example of a direct cost (such as those included in the exercise) that can be included in a cost-utility analysis?
   A. Lost income due to illness.
   B. Cost of drug administration.
   C. Cost of living.
   D. Cost for patient to access medical care.

2. In which one the following situations is cost-utility analysis the correct tool for economic analysis of health care programs?
   A. When quality is not an important outcome.
   B. When the outcomes of the program are similar.
   C. When the programs being compared have a wide range of different outcomes, and you wish to have a common unit of output for comparison.
   D. When the programs can only be measured by intermediate outcome variables.

3. What is the major difference between cost-effectiveness analysis and cost-utility analysis?
   A. Cost-utility analysis and cost-effectiveness analysis measure costs differently.
   B. Intermediate outcomes can be used in cost-effectiveness analysis, whereas final outcomes are required in cost-utility analysis.
   C. Cost-effectiveness analysis can be performed from secondary data sources, whereas cost-utility analysis requires primary collection of data.
   D. Results of a cost-utility analysis carry more weight for policy makers than results from a cost-effectiveness analysis.

4. Which one of the following methods provides values not utilities?
   A. Visual analogue scale.
   B. Standard gamble.
   C. Health Utilities Index.
   D. EQ-5D index.

5. In what form are results from cost-utility analysis studies normally expressed?
   A. As cost per utility.
   B. As cost per quality-adjusted life year.
   C. As utility dollars.
   D. As cost per percentage change in quality of life.

6. What do incremental differences explain when comparing alternative cost-utility analysis ratios?
   A. The simple difference in the cost-utility analysis ratios of the competing alternatives.
   B. The distance from zero benefit of a cost-utility analysis ratio.
   C. The relative effectiveness of one alternative compared to another alternative.
   D. The additional amount paid for one additional unit of outcome between the competing alternatives.

7. Which one of the following is an example of mutually compatible alternatives?
   A. Screening for hypertension versus vaccinating infants.
   B. Lithotripsy to reduce gallstones versus surgery to remove gallstones.
   C. Dietary changes to treat hyperlipidemia versus pharmacologic interventions to treat hyperlipidemia.
   D. Building more prisons versus hiring more police.

8. Which one of the following is the most appropriate form of economic analysis to use when quality of life is the most important outcome?
   A. Cost-effectiveness analysis.
   B. Cost-utility analysis.
   C. Cost-benefit analysis.
   D. Cost analysis.

Questions 9–13 pertain to the following case.

Two treatment alternatives, Treatment A and Treatment B are available for rheumatoid arthritis relief. Compared to the "do-nothing" alternative, Treatment A results in an additional four QALYs and Treatment B results in a five gain of QALYs compared to the do nothing alternative. Treatment A and Treatment B have associated costs of $28,000 and $30,000, respectively. Each treatment cost includes all direct medical expenses such as physician visits and drug costs.

9. What is the cost-utility ratio of Treatment A?
   A. $28,000 per QALY
   B. $14,000 per QALY
   C. $7000 per QALY
   D. $7000 per HYE

10. What is the cost-utility ratio of Treatment B?
    A. $30,000 per QALY
    B. $15,000 per QALY
    C. $6000 per QALY
    D. $6000 per HYE

11. What is the average difference between Treatments A and B?
    A. $2000 per QALY
    B. $2000 per HYE
    C. $1000 per QALY
    D. $1000 per HYE

12. What is the incremental difference between Treatments A and B?
    A. $2000 per QALY
    B. $2000 per HYE
    C. $1000 per QALY
    D. $1000 per HYE.

13. What is the opportunity cost of shifting resources from Program A to Program B with given resources of $100,000 if Program A yields 10 QALYs and Program B gives six QALYs?
    A. six QALYs
    B. six HYEs
    C. four QALYs
    D. four HYEs

14. The term quality-adjusted life year is a multiple of which one of the following components?
    A Q for quantity and Y for number of years.
    B. Q for quality and Y for number of months.
    C. Q for quality and Y for number of days.
    D. Q for quality and Y for number of years.

15. Which one of the following is a correct assumption of the expected utility theory?
    A. Quality-adjusted life years captures only health-related utility.
    B. Interpersonal utility comparisons are restricted to the health domain.
    C. Utility independence.
    D. The utility value of a full healthy life is set equal for each individual at birth.

16. Which one of the following is regarded as the gold standard method for measuring utility?
    A. Standard gamble.
    B. Time tradeoff.
    C. EuroQol.
    D. Rating scale.

17. Which one of the following is a basic assumption based on the utility theory of rational decision making?
    A. A rational person will choose an alternative with the highest expected utility.
    B. A rational person will choose an alternative with the greatest number of years.
    C. A rational person will choose an alternative with the least amount of risk.
    D. A rational person will choose an alternative with the most options.

18. What is meant by transitivity of preferences?
    A. If A is preferred to B and B is preferred to C, then there is a probability p at which an individual is indifferent between getting B with certainty versus receiving A at a probability of p or C at a probability of 1-C.
    B. If A is preferred to B and B is preferred to C, then A is preferred to C.
    C. If A is preferred to C and B is preferred to A, then there is a probability p at which an individual is indifferent between getting A and C.
    D. If A is preferred to C and B is preferred to C, then B is preferred to A.

19. The Quality of Well-Being Scale (QWB) used for obtaining utility is based on which type of theory?
    A. Decision theory.
    B. Psychometric theory.
    C. Adaptive reasoning.
    D. The QWB is atheoretical.

20. The standard gamble method for obtaining utility is based on which type of theory?
    A. Decision theory.
    B. Psychometric theory.
    C. Adaptive reasoning.
    D. The standard gamble is atheoretical.

21. The categories used in the QWB do not include which one of the following?
    A. Mobility.
    B. Interpersonal.
    C. Physical.
    D. Social activity.

22. What is the primary strength of cost-utility analysis?
    A. Its capacity to integrate quality and quantity of life into a common unit of measure.
    B. Its ability to provide decision makers with a definitive tool that can justify decisions.
    C. Its capacity to provide a solution for any problem.
    D. The relatively low requirement for time, money, and other resources compared to other types of economic analyses.

23. Which one of the following is an advantage of cost-utility analysis when compared to cost-effectiveness analysis?
    A. Cost-effectiveness analysis is limited to comparisons involving the same disease.
    B. Cost-effectiveness analysis is limited to comparisons of the same treatment modality.
    C. Cost-effectiveness analysis is limited to comparisons of the same dollar amount.
    D. Cost-effectiveness analysis is limited to comparisons of the same outcomes.

24. When using quality-adjusted life years as an outcome measure to compare alternatives involving chronic conditions to alternatives of short duration, which one of the following is possible?
    A. Completely unbiased analysis.
    B. Analysis potentially biased in favor of diseases of short-term duration.
    C. Analysis potentially biased in favor of chronic conditions.
    D. Completely invalid comparisons.

25. Which one of the following is true concerning the measurement of utility in the general population?
    A. People often resist judgment concerning risks.
    B. The general population readily identifies with probabilities.
    C. The general population has no reservations concerning assignment of numbers to quality of life.
    D. Finding subjects willing to spend 30 minutes participating in a survey is not a problem.

26. Q weights can be measured by using one of two different types of health related quality-of-life instruments—single attribute utility theory (SAUT) and multiattribute utility theory. Which one of the following sets includes an example of one of each?
    A. Standard gamble, HUI®
    B. HUI®, EQ-5D
    C. SF-36, EQ-5D
    D. SF-36, HUI®

27. Health related quality-of-life instruments can be divided into two groups those that provide utility scores that can be used to estimate quality adjusted life years, and those that provide dimension score only. Which one of the following measures provides dimension scores only?
    A. QWB
    B. HUI2
    C. SF-36
    D. HUI3

28. Proxies or patient surrogates can be used instead of patients to acquire utility scores when?
    A. Patient is unable to speak for him or herself.
    B. Never—scores deviate too much from true patient preferences.
    C. Patient's physician is unavailable.
    D. Patient is a minor.

Exercises

Exercise 1: Calculation of Quality-Adjusted Life Years

To gain practical experience in calculating quality-adjusted life years (QALYs), a variety of different interventions are presented for you to solve. The first question is a straightforward scenario. However, as you go on to the second and third questions, think for a moment about how the scenario is presented and how the questions are framed. Also, it is necessary to use the utility values from Table 1 in the chapter to answer the questions. Assume there is no discounting necessary for this exercise.

1. How many QALYs are gained if a person achieves a 13-year life extension with a kidney transplant?

2. How many QALYs are gained by preventing a 3-month episode of depression?

3. How many QALYs are gained if a patient is placed on home dialysis for 12 years and then dies as opposed to being placed on hospital dialysis for 8 years followed by death?

Exercise 2: Calculation of Well-Years

This exercise is based on the report of Anderson JP, Moser RJ. Parasite screening and treatment among Indochinese refugees, cost-benefit/utility and the general health policy model. JAMA 1985;253:2229-35.

At the Center of Indochinese Health Education at the University of California Medical Center, 6000 Southeast Asian refugees were screened for intestinal parasites. Ten percent of those screened were found to have the Strongyloides stercoralis parasite. It was estimated that if untreated, five percent of those found infected would have to be hospitalized for 10 days within the next 12 months. The other 95 percent of the infected refugees would remain asymptomatic. The average Quality of Well-Being Scale (QWB) results for the refugees hospitalized with the parasite were as follows: CPX-7, MOB-2, PAC-1, and SAC-1. The cost of hospitalization was estimated at $500 per day per patient. The costs of treatment of each refugee with the parasite were $20 for drugs and $35 for one visit to the physician. The cost of screening was $30 per screening evaluation.

Using your knowledge of the QWB, and assuming patients receiving drug treatment have no reduction in well-being, answer the following questions. Use the worksheets provided to help organize your approach to this problem.

1. How many well-years gained was produced by the screening program in this sample?

2. What is the incremental cost-utility ratio of the screening program as compared to no screening?

Worksheet 1: Screening and Treatment Costs

A	No. Screened	
B	Cost of screening examination ($)	
C	Total screening cost ($) (A X B = C)	
D	Parasite	
E	No. positive (prevalence)	
F	Cost for drugs ($)	
G	Cost per doctor visit ($)	
H	Treatment cost = [E X (F +G)]	
I	Screening cost = (A X B)	
J	Total Program Cost = [E X (F+G) = H]	

Worksheet 2: Costs of Not Screening

	Parasite	
A	No. of persons positive	
B	Percent of persons hospitalized	
C	No. of persons hospitalized (A x B = C)	
D	CPX and Function weights	CPX-7 = MOB-2 = PAC-1 = SAC-1 = Total =
E	No. of days hospitalized	
F	Total no. of Well-years reduced (C x D x E = F)	
G	Cost per day	
H	Cost Total Saved (C x E x G = H)	

Worksheet 3: Results of Final Cost-utility Ratio Analysis

A	Screening and Treatment Costs, $ (Column J, Worksheet 1)	
B	Prevented Hospitalization Savings, $ (Column H, Worksheet 2)	
C	Cost Minus Total Savings, $ (A – B = C)	
D	# of Well-years gained by preventing hospitalization (Column F, Worksheet 2)	
E	Cost/Utility Ratio C/D = E	

Worksheets 1, 2, and 3 adapted with permission of Anderson JP, Moser RJ. Parasite screening and treatment among Indochinese refugees: cost benefit/utility and the general health policy model. JAMA 1985;253:2229–35.

DECISION ANALYSIS

Judith Barr, Sc.D.; and
Gerald Schumacher, Pharm.D., Ph.D.

Outline

We use our intuition to guide us through complicated decisions, but multiple factors must be combined and considered when making a decision. We frequently fail to consider all the things that could happen when we select one option over another and also fail to incorporate into our thought process the uncertainty inherent in most decisions. Therefore, when making important decisions, we need help in identifying, organizing, and prioritizing all factors that affect the decision and its outcome.

I. Definition
- A. Decision analysis is an explicit quantitative approach to decision-making under conditions of uncertainty
  1. Combines the benefits of an organizing structure with the explicitness of this process
  2. Provides a visual road map to link each decision option to identified outcomes
- B. Decision analysis is more than a structure; it is a way of thinking about a problem that incorporates the values and beliefs of the decision-maker
- C. Definitions and conventions of Weinstein and Fineberg provide guidance for conducting decision analysis

II. Origins and applications of decision analysis
- A. Origins
  1. Early work in economics and game led investigators to consider how probabilistic estimates of future events could be combined with economic investment.
  2. In World War II, the Allied Forces used these formal analytical tools to optimize military decisions involving scarce allocation of limited resources
  3. Raiffa popularized the use of decision analysis in the business world and early leaders in medical decision-making introduced it to the medical community
  4. By the early 1970s, decision analysis had reached the medical literature
- B. Applications
  1. By 1987, more than 200 studies had been published in which investigators applied decision analysis to a wide range of medical and surgical questions
  2. In 1995, Barr and Schumacher identified 81 published articles involving the application of decision analysis to questions involving pharmaceutical products; applications involved a wide variety of clinical situations
     - To conduct a cost-effectiveness comparison between two antibiotics
     - To determine whether to use BCG vaccine for tuberculosis in a homeless shelter
     - To identify what patients receiving chemotherapy would benefit most from hematopoietic growth factor
     - To determine the effects of infarct location and the likelihood of infarction on cost-effectiveness of intravenous streptokinase for suspected acute myocardial infarction
     - To determine treatment for deep-vein thrombosis

3. Within the past 5 years (July 1998-July 2003), the MEDLINE database identified 725 articles indexed by the medical subject heading terms "decision analysis" or "decision analytic"; 240 of these also were indexed by the medical subject heading term "drug".

4. Major roles for decision analytic modeling in health economic evaluations:

   a. Extending results from a single randomized, controlled trial to relevant comparators: used to model the decision compared to "normal care" or "best alternative care" rather than the placebo comparator of the randomized, controlled trial

   b. Extrapolating outcomes to the longer term: used when the decision requires a longer comparison period than present in available randomized, controlled trials

   c. Translating from intermediate to final outcomes: used to model the extension of clinical physiological or functional results to meaningful final outcomes such as survival, life-years extended, or quality-adjusted life-years.

   d. Generalizing from highly selective randomized, controlled trial populations to general populations: used to adjust randomized, controlled trial efficacy results derived from selected subpopulations, tightly controlled protocols, drug administration and monitoring procedures to the effectiveness conditions of a general population.

III. Case study: The decision analytic approach

A. The case-Spondorex or Moodlift

B. Steps in a decision analysis (Using Data 4.0)

1. Step 1: Identify the decision, including selection of the decision options to be studied. Bound the time frame of the decision and determine from what perspective the decision is to be made

2. Step 2: Structure the decision and the consequences of each decision option over time

- A decision tree is a graphic structure similar to a flow diagram that displays the options and events that unfold over time
- Begins with the decision options
- Continues with the consequences of decision options as they sequentially develop over time
- Includes associated probabilities of occurrence, valuations of each possible outcome, and the expected valuation of each decision option
- Leads to identification of the preferred decision alternative
- Choice nodes (decision nodes) indicate that what follows in the decision tree is under the control of the decision-maker
- Decision-maker selects one of several options and must make a decision at this point in the tree
- Initial choice node is placed at the left of the tree
- Additional decision nodes are embedded in the tree whenever the decision-maker has control of events and can make a decision
- Choice nodes are represented by a small square
- Branches grow out of each node; one for each decision option or possible event
- (Reference Figure 1)
- Chance nodes indicate that what follows in the decision tree is beyond the control of the decision-maker and is subject to probabilistic occurrence
- Structure the rest of the tree based on the information presented in the case. Use Figure 1 as the beginning of the tree, add chance nodes to both treatment arms, and have effective and ineffective branches growing out of each. Using the sequence of events that is across the top of the tree, complete the structure of the decision tree to include the occurrence and nonoccurrence of adverse events and whether the patient was compliant.
- A decision path is a sequence of actions and events beginning at the initial choice node that follows a particular course of events and outcomes until reaching the designated outcome
- (Reference Figure 2)

3. Step 3: Assess the probability that each consequence will occur

- All probabilities associated with the same chance node must sum to 100 percent
- The probabilities in the case are entered adjacent to their respective chance nodes on the tree
- Probabilities in this case are obtained from meta-analysis of randomized, controlled trials
- Using Figure 2, place the probabilistic information provided in the case around each of the chance notes. Be sure that all information is accounted for and that all the branches originating from chance nodes have an attached probability. Check that the specification of each chance node to be sure the probabilities sum to 100 percent.
- (Reference Figure 3)
- Path probabilities are the combined probabilities of following a specific decision path
- Using Figure 3, determine path probabilities of each of the eight paths of the decision tree. Determine what drug has the higher probability of patients being treated effectively.

- (Reference Figure 4)

4. Step 4: Determine the value of each outcome
   - Decide to use patient-derived utilities as outcome measures. Now, create eight multidimensional scenarios, one for each of the eight paths, and conduct a standard reference gamble assessment for each scenario using patients. On average, the patients give the paths with effective treatment and no adverse events the highest utility value; both drugs yield a utility value of 0.90. Patients rate ineffective therapy and noncompliance the lowest value or 0.5 for both drugs. Patient-derived utilities for the remainder of the paths are 0.85 for effective therapy with Moodlift, which has minor adverse events; and 0.60 for effective therapy with Spondorex, which has more severe adverse events.
   - Options can be measured as dollars, quality-adjusted life-years saved, utilities, or quality-adjusted life-years
   - The utilities for different clinical states are entered at the end of their respective decision paths on the tree
   - Add the appropriate utility to each of the eight paths in Figure 4.
   - (Reference Figure 5)
5. Step 5: Identify the assumptions
   - Meta-analysis of randomized, controlled trials are really efficacy, not effectiveness rates. These rates will have to be varied in sensitivity analysis to determine results within potential ranges of effectiveness as the drugs are used outside general practice, outside randomized, controlled trials.
   - Noncompliance was only associated with side effects
   - Side effects developed only after effectiveness/ineffectiveness was determined; therefore, side effects were not incorporated into the ineffective arms
   - Patients receiving Spondorex only had severe side effects and those receiving Moodlift only had mild side effects
   - The disutilities of the several forms of mild side effects were perceived as equal to each other; therefore, only one composite utility assessment was performed for presence of mild side effects (same for the severe side effects)
6. Step 6: Select the option with the higher expected outcome
   - Expected value is the weighted average of outcomes of each path weighted by their probability of occurring
   - Use averaging-out-and-folding-back to determine option with higher value
   - Starting from the furthest right chance node, the path outcome values from that node are weighted by their respective probability of occurrence; at node 6 there is a 50 percent possibility that a utility of 0.60 will occur and a 50 percent probability that a utility of 0.5 will occur; therefore, the weighted average or expected utility of the events originating from node 6 is:[(0.5 x 0.60 utility) + (0.5 x 0.5 utility)] = 0.55 utility
   - This value is now connected to node 6 and serves as the expected utility as you move to the left and calculate the expected utility for events that originate from node 4
   - This process continues until a choice node is reached
   - Using Figure 4, average-out-and-fold-back to combine the structure, probabilities, and outcome valuations of the tree. Use Figure 5 to check your work.
7. Step 7: Determine the robustness of the decision by conducting sensitivity analyses and varying the values of probabilities and outcomes over a range of likely values
   - Sensitivity analysis is a systematic variation of the different structural assumptions built into a decision tree (i.e., factors included or excluded) and the quantitative assumptions (i.e., probabilities and outcome valuations) to see if the conclusion changes
   - Perform a partial sensitivity analysis based on the following scenario. If some type of treatment could reduce the severity of Spondorex's adverse events so that the utility of Path 2 is now 0.8 and only 20 percent of effectively treated patients become noncompliant, would Moodlift still produce the higher expected utilities? Change the indicated probability and utility values in Figure 4 and repeat the averaging-out-and-folding-back process with these new values.
   - (Reference Figure 6)

IV. Controversies in the use of decision analytic modeling in pharmacoeocnomic studies
- Clash of two cultures: randomized, controlled trial versus modeled analysis
- Modeled decision analyses can provide information when an additional randomized, controlled trial would take too much time and cost too much money.
- The problems with the generaliziability of data from randomized, controlled trial to routine clinical practice.
- However, based on the perception of bias, the New England Journal of Medicine has a policy instituted in 1994 of excluding modeled analyses if any author is associated with a pharmaceutical company. Also, the Food and Drug Administration has a policy of not permitting cost-effectiveness claims based on modeled analysis

- These controversies have prompted several international best practices and guidelines for modeled analysis. The recommendations from these efforts have been incorporated into a discussion of consideration for the seven steps.

V. Considerations within a decision analysis
   A. Identifying the question
      1. What is the decision and its options?
         - Inclusion of usual care as an option
         - Intra- versus intertherapeutic class comparison
         - Options limited to within one drug class
         - Need to include a "do-nothing" strategy
      2. What perspective should be taken?
         - Societal in national health insurance countries
         - Third-party payer
         - Institutional
         - Pharmacy department
         - Individual
      3. What patient population is to be studied?
         - All with the clinical condition in question
         - Subpopulations encouraged based on gender, age, or severity of clinical condition
      4. Over what period will the analysis apply?
         - Selection of time frame depends on several factors
         - Nature of clinical question and drug considered
         - Time necessary to achieve therapeutic effectiveness, detect adverse events, resolve medical sequelae
         - For chronic conditions, researchers may need to model the analysis beyond what is available from clinical trial information
      5. Perspective of the decision-maker
         - Availability of data to support analysis
         - Time frame also can depend on objectives of a study or an administrative period such as a budget cycle
      6. What are the decision criteria?
         - What metric will capture the effect of the intervention?
         - To what degree will the conclusion be compared to other resource allocation decisions?
         - Value of general health or preference measure versus disease-specific
         - Quality-adjusted life-years for comparison across disease states and treatment options
   B. Structuring the consequences of alternative options
      - Decision tree based on a series of "if, then" questions
      - Provides the graphic structure around which discussions about treatment options and consequences of interventions can occur
      - Several errors in structuring may occur
      - Conditioning of actions on unobservable states involves the difference between sensitivity and predictive positive value for a test
      - Violations of symmetry occur when the option branches are not structured similarly
      - Failure to apply consistent bias occur; if have to make simplifying assumptions, always make them in the same direction
   C. Assessing probabilities
      - Sources of probabilities
      - Large randomized, clinical trials
      - Problems with the efficacy focus of randomized, controlled trials versus the effectiveness needs of drug selection decisions
      - Trials might not be large enough to detect rare, but costly, adverse events
      - Administrative data sets such as pharmacy computer records and insurance files
      - Expert opinion
      - Experts underestimate the occurrence of common events and overestimate the occurrence of rare events
      - Delphi technique or nominal group process can be used to reach consensus among a panel of experts; the conclusion can then be subjected to a "reality check" by a panel of practicing clinicians
      - Use caution with diagnostic probabilities because most are based on sensitivity and specificity; investigators must convert these to predictive value
   D. Valuing outcomes
      - Can place multiple outcomes at the end of each path to permit the same structure to be used for economic and noneconomic outcomes measures

- Economic evaluations include the cost of ingredients of care for each path
- Noneconomic outcomes can be measured as natural units of outcomes (effectiveness) or as utilities

E. Identifying the assumptions
- Identify all assumptions that have been incorporated into the model to create as transparent an analysis as possible

F. Determining preferred options
- Averaging-out-and-folding-back
- Starting from the right and working left, the outcomes and probabilities are combined by weighing outcomes by their probabilities
- Expected value is the weighted value at a chance node; it is the expected, but not certain, value based on the probabilistic estimates that events of different valuations will occur

G. Conducting a sensitivity analysis
- Data elements with a high degree of uncertainty are varied over their range of possibilities

VI. Revisit the teaching case
- Incorporated the guidelines in the teaching case
- Step 1-Include usual care, extend the analysis to 1 year
- Step 2-Include initial compliance, major and minor side effect (SE) in all arms, possibility of relapse, possibility of suicide
- Step 3-Structured expert opinion for the probabilities beyond the usual randomized, controlled trial time period. Identify probabilities that affect the decision the most and develop better probability estimates
- Step 4-Include utilities from the general managed care population
- Step 5-Unchanged
- Step 6-Identify additional assumptions

VII. Applications of decision analysis
A. Framework for cost-of-illness studies
B. Framework for disease state management
C. Forms the backbone for any type of pharmacoeconomic analyses

VIII. Conclusion
- Decision analysis is only as good as the options considered and the model specified. All types of pharmacoeconomic methodologies can be strengthened by structuring the decision options and their consequences over time.
- Comparison of the quality of 10 decision analytic models for treatment options of major depressive disorders; five decision models for type 2 diabetes
- Decision analysis (DA) used for product development and drug portfolio management

Learning Objectives

1. Identify the seven steps involved in performing decision analyses.
2. Given a brief clinical scenario with accompanying data, properly construct a decision tree to include a temporal display of the options and events and the assignment of probabilities and outcome values.
3. Given a decision tree with probability and outcomes inserted, calculate the path probabilities and the expected values of each option and select the option preferred by the decision-maker.
4. Given a constructed decision tree, analyze if the tree is properly constructed or if errors of logic and/or structure and/or calculations occurred.
5. Perform a sensitivity analysis and interpret its graphic representation.
6. Given a pharmacoeconomic article that uses a decision analytic approach, analyze the appropriateness of each of the six steps as designed by the investigators.

Abbreviations in this chapter

BCG	Bacillus of Calmette-Guérin
MCO	Managed care organizations
MDD	Major depressive disorder
RCT	Randomized, controlled trial
SE	Side effect

Introduction

Decisions are a part of everyday life. From mundane decisions about to what to wear or have for dinner, to important personal economic decisions about which car or house to buy, to major life decisions about professional careers and marriage, decisions are constantly with us. Our clinical decisions frequently have life and death consequences. Although we use our intuition and logic to guide us through both simple and complicated decisions, we probably are not making the best decisions because we fail to recognize the multiple factors that must be considered and combined in the decision-making process. We often fail to consider all that could happen if we select one decision alternative over others. In addition, we ignore or fail to give proper weight to the uncertainty inherent in most decisions. For us to achieve the maximal benefit or outcome from our decisions, we need help in identifying, structuring, incorporating, and prioritizing all factors involved in the decision-making process.

This chapter will:

1. Define the decision analytic method to model decisions.
2. Discuss the origins of decision analysis and why and when modeling is necessary and appropriate
3. Present a simplified and abbreviated teaching case to demonstrate the seven steps involved in the decision analytic process.
4. Examine the controversy surrounding the use of modeling, specifically decision analytic modeling, in pharmacoeconomic studies and the need to standardize such studies.
5. Discuss methodologic issues to be considered in each step of the decision analytic process and the guidelines written in response to this controversy.
6. Expand the abbreviated teaching case to incorporate guideline recommendations.
7. Survey applications of decision analysis to pharmacoeconomic studies.
8. Apply guidelines to an analysis of a decision analytic pharmacoeconomic study published in Pharmacotherapy.

Definition

Decision analysis is defined as an explicit quantitative approach to decision-making under conditions of uncertainty. Using a modeling process, it is explicit because it forces the decision-maker to structure the decision faced as well as identify the consequences of the possible decision options. It is quantitative because it forces the assignment of probability estimates to areas of uncertainty within the decision and to assign monetary or nonmonetary values to all possible outcomes. When faced with uncertainty about the possible consequences of actions and how the outcomes will be valued, decision analysis (also referred to as decision analytic modeling) can be used to provide an organizing structure, a visual road map, around which decision options can be structured, consequences of those options considered, and outcomes valued. Then, by combining the probabilities that events will occur with the value of each possible outcome, decision analysis prescribes which option to select to maximize the outcome of the decision.

Without such a structured process, decisions involving multiple factors often are flawed when the decision-maker implicitly attempts to juggle and combine important elements. Errors occur because it is difficult to intuitively combine complex information, generate and revise probabilities, and give proportional weight to events of differing importance that occur at differing times. Decision analysis provides the structure to explicitly identify these factors and to quantitatively combine the various sources of information to identify the decision option that has the best chance for the desired outcome.

In addition, decision analysis is more than a systematic approach to solving problems under conditions of uncertainty. It creates a fundamental change in the way in which a decision is approached. The use of decision analysis engenders an attitude toward the problem or decision. It helps the decision-maker to think more analytically and forces the consideration of consequences of actions. Decision analysis helps to explicitly recognize that uncertainty is present, to estimate the degree of uncertainty, and to assess attitudes toward risk. Finally, it helps determine what the relevant outcome measures are and to value preferences for the alternative outcomes.

The definitions and conventions of clinical decision analysis (see Reference 25) are used throughout this chapter.

Origins and Applications

Early theoretical work involving economic and game theory led investigators to consider how probabilistic estimates of future events could be combined with economic investment. During World War II, the Allied Forces used these formal analytical tools to optimize military decisions involving scarce allocation of limited resources. Raiffa popularized the use of decision analysis in the business world and early leaders in medical decision-making introduced it into the medical community. By the early 1970s, decision analysis had reached the medical literature.

Applications

By 1987, more than 200 published studies had been published in which investigators applied decision analysis to a wide range of medical and surgical questions (see Reference 15). By 1996, more than 80 published articles had been identified involving the application of decision analysis to questions involving pharmaceutical products (see Reference 2). Many of these papers used a decision analytic approach to organize and conduct their cost-effectiveness or cost-utility analyses. Several examples of these decision analytic studies are listed below.

- a cost-effectiveness comparison between two antibiotics
- a decision analysis concerning whether Bacillus of Calmette-Guérin (BCG) vaccine should be used to vaccinate a homeless shelter population against tuberculosis
- an analysis of which patients receiving chemotherapy would benefit most from hematopoietic growth factors

- a determination of the effects of infarct location and of the likelihood of infarction on the cost-effectiveness of intravenous streptokinase for suspected acute myocardial infarction
- a determination of the optimal treatment for deep-vein thrombosis

The use of decision analytic modeling continues to expand. Within the past 5 years (July 1998-July 2003), the MEDLINE database identified 725 articles indexed by the medical subject heading terms "decision analysis" or "decision analytic"; 240 of these also were indexed by the medical subject heading term "drug". For the same period, a MEDLINE search identified 190 articles that were indexed with "cost", "drugs", and "decision analysis".

Given that the randomized, controlled trial (RCT) is the gold standard for clinical evaluation of pharmaceutical products, why would decision analysis be used rather than RCTs to answer pharmacoeconomic questions? The principal reason is that decision-makers frequently have to make decisions (e.g., formulary inclusion) before information is available from head-to-head RCTs of an innovator product with the current standard of care. They cannot wait for the time and expense needed to conduct such trials so they turn to decision analysis to model the considerations in their decision-making process: What are the options? What are the clinical consequences of each option? What is the rate at which these consequences occur? How are the outcomes of each consequence valued?

In a background paper for a 1999 Consensus Conference on Decision Analytic Modeling in Economic Evaluation of Health Technologies, the major roles for decision analytic modeling in health economic evaluations were identified:

1. Extending results from a single RCT to relevant comparators: used to model the decision compared to "normal care" or "best alternative care" rather than the placebo comparator of the RCT
2. Extrapolating outcomes to the longer term: used when the decision requires a longer comparison period than present in available RCTs
3. Translating from intermediate to final outcomes: used to model the extension of clinical physiological or functional results to meaningful final outcomes such as survival, life-years extended, or quality-adjusted life-years.
4. Generalizing from highly selective RCT populations to general populations: used to adjust RCT efficacy results derived from selected subpopulations, tightly controlled protocols, drug administration, and monitoring procedures to the effectiveness conditions of a general population.

Teaching Case: The Decision Analytic Modeling Approach

As an introduction to the terminology and mechanics involved in performing a decision analysis, a simplified teaching case is presented. A fictional formulary decision is developed following the seven major steps of the decision analytic approach. Later, the case is revisited and expanded after an examination of new guidelines for the use of decision analytic modeling in pharmacoeconomic studies.

The Teaching Case

As chief clinical pharmacist at a managed care organization (MCO), you are evaluating two agents in a new class of antidepressant therapy for inclusion in your formulary. Your decision involves selecting only one of these agents-Spondorex or Moodlift-for inclusion. From meta-analysis of several placebo-controlled, RCT data, you learn that Spondorex is 90 percent effective for treating major depressive disorder (MDD). However, over a 3-month period of use in these trials, 20 percent of patients develop severe adverse events and 50 percent of these patients are noncompliant and discontinue their drugs. Results from a meta-analysis of several other placebo-controlled, RCTs indicate that Moodlift is 82 percent effective for treating MDD and has a 5 percent incidence of the mild adverse events also over a 3-month period; 10 percent of patients with mild adverse events are noncompliant and discontinue their drugs. Based on the RCT data, all effectively treated patients without side effects in both trials adhere to their drug schedule.

Although an economic assessment is an essential component of the decision, for this teaching case, your primary considerations are focused on the effectiveness of therapy and the drug's impact on patient quality of life. Your first outcome measure will be used to determine which drug, on average, has the higher percentage of effectively treated patients; your second measure will capture the averaged impact of each drug and its sequelae on patient health-related quality of life. Based on patient-derived utilities obtained during standard reference gamble interviews with patients after 3 months of treatment, average patient preferences associated with each outcome are summarized in Table 1.

Your two options have different advantages and disadvantages. Spondorex is more effective, but Moodlift has fewer and milder adverse events, resulting in a higher compliance rate. Which drug should you select to optimize your two objectives of having more patients effectively treated and producing the higher averaged patient utility?

Table 1. Treatment Outcomes and Utilities Associated with Treatment with Moodlift and Spondorex for Major Depressive Disorder

Treatment Outcomes	Utilities
Effective treatment with no side effects	0.9
Effective treatment with Moodlift-induced side effects	0.85
Effective treatment with Spondorex-induced adverse events	0.6
Ineffective treatment related to the drug	0.5
Discontinuation due to adverse events	0.5

Steps in a Decision Analysis

As the steps involved in structuring and solving a decision analysis are discussed, readers will be asked to stop, complete the instructions, check answers, and then continue with the case. The best way to master the techniques of decision analysis is by actually trying to work through the tasks posed. Readers should take advantage of these breaks and do the work on their own before continuing with the next section.

Step 1: Identify the Decision, Including Selection of the Decision Options to be Studied. Bound the Time Frame of the Decision and Determine from What Perspective the Decision is to be Made

The decision options are whether to include Spondorex or Moodlift in the MCO formulary. In this teaching case, the time period is limited to 3 months, the study length of the available clinical trials. Although a patient perspective could be used for the analysis, the economic impact of the decision to the MCO will be added later, and it is best to have all aspects of the study conducted from the same perspective. Therefore, the perspective is that of the MCO trying to produce the best health outcomes for its members.

Step 2: Structure the Decision and the Consequences of Each Decision Option over Time

In this stage of the analysis, the decision is modeled using the structure of the decision tree. It starts with the initial decision and then is structured to reflect the events that sequentially develop over time. Events that happen first are placed to the left of the tree and others are placed to the right as they develop. Data 4.0 software (TreeAge Software, Inc; Williamstown MA) will be used to develop the decision tree. In addition, the sequence of the four major actions or events in this case (i.e., the decision options, effectiveness, safety, and compliance) is displayed across the top of the tree.

A decision tree is a graphic structure, similar to a flow diagram, that displays the options and events that unfold over time. It begins with the decision options, and continues with the consequences of those options as they sequentially develop. The associated probabilities or rates at which the events occur, the valuations of each possible outcome, the expected valuation of each decision option, and the preferred decision choice also are placed in the decision tree.

The decision tree starts with a choice or decision node. A choice or decision node indicates that what follows in the decision tree is under the control of the decision-maker. The initial choice node is placed at the left of the tree. Additional decision nodes can be embedded in the tree whenever the decision-maker can control events and can make a decision. All choice nodes are represented by a small square.

In the teaching case, the decision tree starts with a choice node, designated node 1 in Figure 1. The two options, Spondorex and Moodlift, grow as branches from the choice node on the left side of the tree. A branch originates from a node; one for each decision option, action, or consequence.

If Spondorex is selected, in a population of patients with MDD, some will be treated effectively and some will not respond. The same is true for Moodlift. The decision-maker can select the drug but then has no control over subsequent events. To indicate a point in time when the decision-maker has no control over the consequences, a chance node is inserted into the tree. A chance node indicates that several possible events can occur that are beyond the control of the decision-maker and are subject to probabilistic occurrence. A chance node is indicated by a small circle.

Now, readers should try to structure the rest of the tree based on information presented in the case. Figure 1 should be used as the beginning of the tree, and chance nodes should be added to both Spondorex and Moodlift, and effective and ineffective branches should be growing out of each. Using the sequence of events that is across the top of the tree, the completed structure of the decision tree should include the occurrence or nonoccurrence of adverse events and whether the patient was compliant. When the tree is completed, readers should check Figure 2 to see the complete structure.

In Figure 2, the possible responses to Spondorex originate from node 2; those for Moodlift, from node 3. Following the course of Spondorex therapy, it is apparent that it is ineffective for some of the population. Within the bounds of this case, this particular decision path labeled Path 1 is complete. A decision path is a sequence of actions and events that begin at the initial choice node and follow a particular course of events and actions within the time frame of the decision.

On the other branch originating from node 2, the rest of the patients will respond to Spondorex, but some will develop side effects. This is indicated at node 4. For those without adverse events, their decision path is complete and is labeled Path 4. For those with adverse events, some will continue the drug; this is indicated by Path 2. For others, the adverse events will be so severe they will discontinue their drug as is indicated in Path 3. The structure of the tree is similar for Moodlift and is indicated by decision paths 5 through 8 in Figure 2.

From a patient population of 200 chronically depressed patients, researchers randomized 100 patients to Spondorex and the other 100 to Moodlift at the initial choice node. The number of patients who eventually end up in each of the eight decision paths is a function of probability, but the decision tree identifies all the possible paths that the 200 patients entering the initial choice node might follow. As each of the two patient populations moves from left to right through the tree, their numbers split at each chance node. Ultimately, each of the 200 patients will reach the end of one of the eight paths

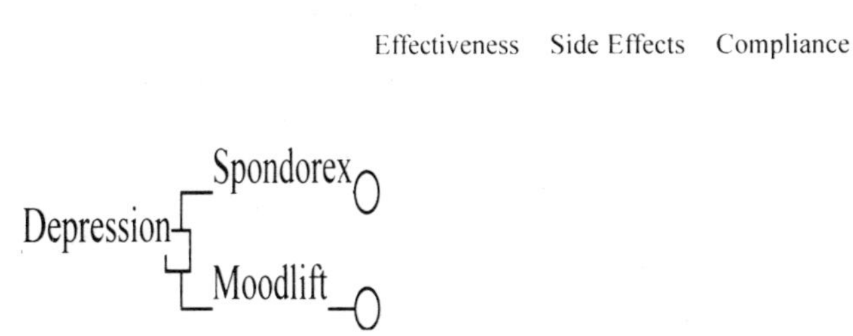

Figure 1. Choice node of Spondorex and Moodlift with time frame

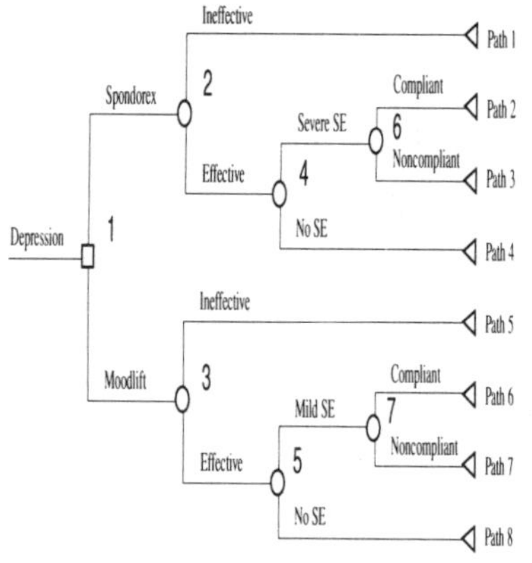

Figure 2. Structure of simplified decision tree of Spondorex and Moodlift with numbered nodes and paths.

Step 3: Assess the Probability That Each Consequence Will Occur

At each of the chance nodes, different events will occur and it is necessary to estimate the probability of each event happening. Now, the information presented earlier in the teaching case can be used to provide probability estimates. In this case, probabilities were based on fictional meta-analyses of placebo-controlled trials; probabilities for a real decision analysis in a clinical situation require special consideration and are discussed in the "Considerations within the Modeled Decision Analysis" section. Spondorex is 90 percent effective; 20 percent of effectively treated patients develop severe adverse events, and 50 percent of those with severe adverse events discontinue their drugs. Moodlift is 82 percent effective; 5 percent of effectively treated patients develop mild adverse events, and 10 percent of individuals with mild adverse events discontinue their drugs.

At each chance node, there is a 100 percent probability that something will happen. Therefore, if 90 percent of the patients treated with Spondorex are effectively treated, that leaves 10 percent who are not effectively treated. Also, probabilities are rates or proportions that consist of numerators and denominators. The numerator is the population with the characteristic of interest; the denominator is the population being studied.

Readers should now stop and place the probabilistic information provided in the case around each of the chance nodes in Figure 2. All the information in the case must be accounted for and all branches originating from chance nodes must have an attached probability. The specification of each chance node must always be checked to be sure the probabilities sum to 100 percent. If the probabilities around a chance node do not sum to 100 percent, the information used to obtain the probabilities assigned to that node needs to be reassessed.

Readers should now check Figure 3 and compare how the probabilistic information was entered. The probabilities at nodes 2 and 3 are associated with the effectiveness rates of Spondorex and Moodlift, respectively. Chance nodes 4 and 5 indicate the rate of adverse events that occur in the effectively treated portion of the two populations, whereas chance nodes 6 and 7 are the rates of noncompliance in that portion of the effectively treated populations who experience adverse events.

The probability that a patient will arrive at the end of one of the eight decision paths is a path probability determined by the product of the probabilities along the specific path. For example, the probability that a patient will be in Path 3, the path related to patients effectively treated with Spondorex with accompanying adverse events that caused noncompliance, is determined by combining the probability of effective Spondorex treatment, the probability that adverse events will occur in that population, and the probability that given the adverse events, the patient will become noncompliant. This path probability is 0.9 x 0.2 x 0.5 = 0.09. A path probability is the combined probabilities of following a specific decision path and represents the proportion of that population in that decision arm who follow that clinical course.

Readers should stop here and calculate the path probabilities of the remaining seven paths.

Readers should check their results with the calculated path probabilities on the right of the tree in Figure 4. Now, if readers had decided to base their selection only on the drug with the higher probability of effectively treating chronic depression, they must decide if they would select Spondorex or Moodlift? Effective treatment includes effectively treated patients without adverse events as well as those who are effectively treated but continue to take the drug while experiencing adverse events. For Spondorex, the sum of the path probabilities of paths 2 and 4 results in a probability of effective treatment of 0.810; for Moodlift, the sum of probabilities for paths 6 and 8 is 0.797. Therefore, based on the goal of maximizing the probability of effective treatment, readers must decide if they would select Spondorex.

Step 4: Determine the Value of Each Outcome in Units Such as Dollars, Quality-adjusted Life-years Saved, Utilities, and Quality-adjusted Life-years

In the teaching case, patient-derived utilities were selected as outcome measures. Eight multidimensional scenarios, one for each of the eight paths, must now be created and utility assessment using standard reference gamble assessment for each scenario must be conducted. On average, patients give the paths with effective treatment and no adverse events the highest utility value; both drugs yield a utility value of 0.90. Patients rate ineffective therapy and noncompliance the lowest value or 0.5 for both drugs. Patient-derived utilities for the remainder of the paths are 0.85 for effective therapy with Moodlift, which has minor adverse events; and 0.60 for effective therapy with Spondorex, which has more severe adverse events.

Based on the information just presented, readers should add the appropriate utility to each of the eight paths in Figure 4.

Figure 5 shows the utilities on the right of the tree correctly assigned to each path.

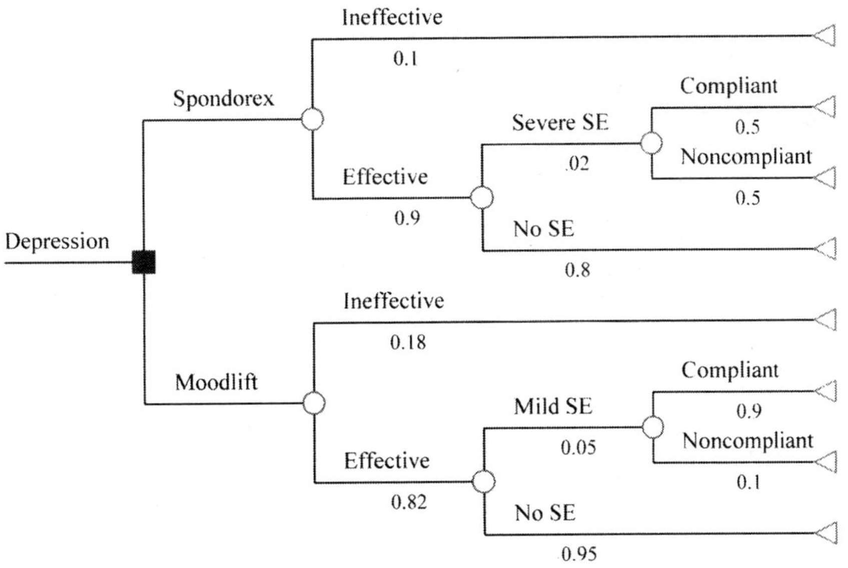

Figure 3. Decision tree with Spondorex and Moodlift probability information

Step 5: Explicitly State All Assumptions of the Model

Given that complete information is not available about all aspects of the decision options and their consequences (if complete information was available, why would a decision analysis be necessary?), the decision analyst must make certain assumptions as the analysis is performed and information is missing. However, these assumptions must be explicitly identified so that readers of the decision analysis can determine whether the assumptions are appropriate from their decision perspective and for their patient population.

Several assumptions in this case are:

- Meta-analysis of RCTs really determines efficacy, not effectiveness, rates. These rates will have to be varied in sensitivity analysis to determine results within potential

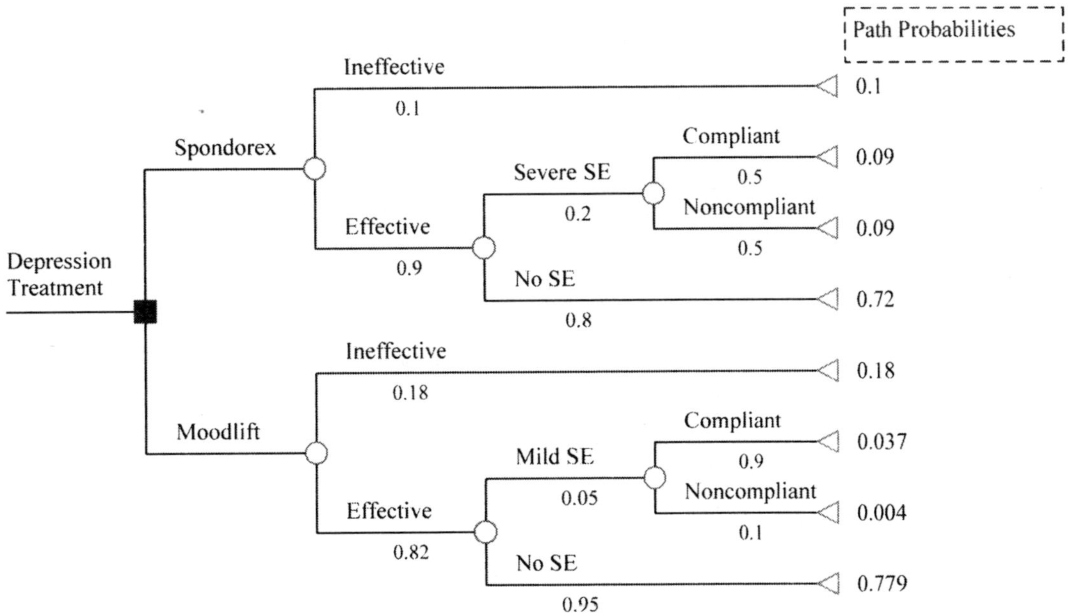

Figure 4. Decision tree with path probabilities for Spondorex and Moodlift

ranges of effectiveness as the drugs are used outside RCTs

- Noncompliance was only associated with side effects
- Side effects developed only after effectiveness/ ineffectiveness was determined; therefore, side effects were not incorporated into the ineffective arms
- Patients receiving Spondorex only had severe side effects and those receiving Moodlift only had mild side effects
- The disutilities of the several forms of mild side effects were perceived as equal to each other; therefore, only one composite utility assessment was performed for presence of mild side effects (same for the severe side effects)

Step 6: Select the Option with the Highest Expected Outcome

In this step, to solve the decision tree and determine which option will yield the higher expected value of utility (one of the designated outcomes), the average utility for the events that are the consequences of Spondorex treatment and Moodlift treatment must be determined. The term, "expected value", is used to indicate the average of outcomes of each path weighted by the probability of each path occurring.

The technique of averaging-out-and-folding-back is used for this purpose. Starting from the furthest right chance node, the path outcome values from that node are weighted by their respective probability of occurrence. For example, at node 6 there is a 50 percent probability that a utility of 0.60 will occur and a 50 percent probability that a utility of 0.5 will occur. Therefore, the weighted average or expected utility of the events originating from node 6 is:

[(0.5 x 0.60 utility) + (0.5 x 0.5 utility)] = 0.55 utility.

This value is now connected to node 6 and serves as the expected utility as the decision-maker moves to the left and calculate the expected utility for events that originate from node 4:

[(0.2 x 0.55 utility) + (0.8 x 0.9 utility)] = 0.83 utility

The averaging-out-and-folding-back continues until a choice node is reached. At a choice node, the decision-maker selects the option that maximizes his or her preferred outcomes; in this case, the option which has the higher utility. Readers should stop now and complete the averaging-out-and-folding back to determine the expected value of both decision options.

Based on how the tree has been structured, probabilities have been assigned, and outcomes have been valued, the decision analysis indicates that Moodlift should be selected because it has a higher average utility of 0.825 utilities compared to Spondorex, which has an average value of 0.796 utilities. When patient utilities are added to the decision process, Moodlift, with mild adverse events and higher compliance rates, becomes the preferred course of action.

However, now there is a conflict between the two outcome measures. Spondorex yields a higher proportion of patients who are effectively treated, but Moodlift is associated with a higher expected utility. Because the determination of the expected utility incorporates both the probability of effectiveness weighted by the utility associated with the treatment's effect in each decision path, the expected utility outcome dominates the percent effectiveness variable. Therefore, based on the higher expected utility, Moodlift is the preferred choice.

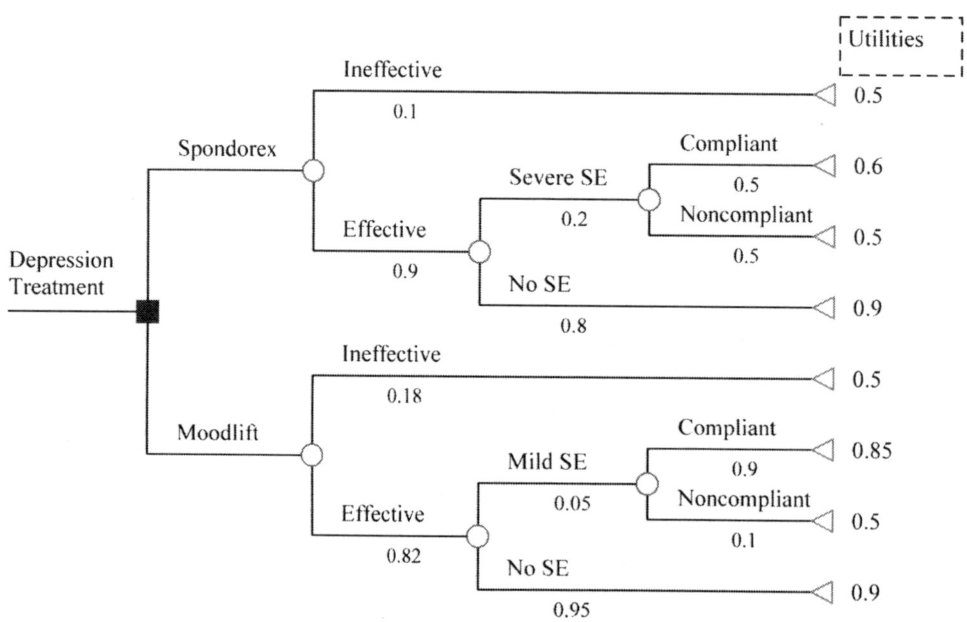

Figure 5. Spondorex and Moodlift decision tree with path outcome valuations

The completed decision tree is displayed in Figure 6. A double hatch is placed on the branch leading to Spondorex, indicating that the decision-maker should not go down the Spondorex path and instead, select Moodlift.

Step 7: Determine the Robustness of the Decision by Conducting Sensitivity Analyses and Varying the Values of Probabilities and Outcomes over a Range of Likely Values

Sensitivity analyses are performed at this stage to determine if the decision changes when probabilities or outcome valuations are varied. Sensitivity analysis is used to conduct a systematic variation of the quantitative assumptions concerning probability estimation and outcome valuations.

If only one variable is varied across the range of possible values, it is called a one-way sensitivity analysis; if two are varied simultaneously, it is called a two-way sensitivity analysis. For example, the "effectiveness" rates that were used in the analysis are really efficacy rates derived from RCTs with tight protocols, selected populations, specialist physicians, and adherence monitoring programs. It is unlikely that these efficacy rates are generalizable to routine practice with patients with multiple conditions, general practice physicians, and a lack of adherence monitoring. Sensitivity analysis can vary the base case "effectiveness" rates over a range of more reasonable values that would likely to be seen in routine practice.

Readers should stop now to perform a partial sensitivity analysis based on the following scenario. If some type of treatment could reduce the severity of Spondorex's adverse events so that the utility of Path 2 is now 0.8 and only 20 percent of effectively treated patients become noncompliant, would Moodlift still produce the higher expected utilities? Change the indicated probability and utility values in Figure 4 and repeat the averaging-out-and-folding-back process with these new values.

The answer is displayed in Figure 7. The utility assigned to Path 2 is changed from 0.6 to 0.8 and the probability of compliant behavior on that path is changed from 0.5 to 0.8. This forces the researcher also to change the probability of noncompliance from 0.5 to 0.2 because the probability of actions at a chance node must total 100 percent. These changes shift the preferred decision option. Now, Spondorex is preferred over Moodlift, 0.831 versus 0.825.

In Monte Carlo analysis, all variables can be varied simultaneously based on their probabilistic distributions across reasonable ranges of the variables.

Controversies in the Use of Decision Analytic Modeling in Pharmacoeconomic Studies

The controversies surrounding the use of decision analytic modeling in pharmacoeconomic studies can be applied equally to any type of retrospective pharmacoeconomic analysis-they are just more visible in decision analytic modeling because of the explicit and quantitative nature of the methodology and the use of the decision tree.

The controversies have their roots in two different paradigms of investigation: randomized, clinical trials and modeling. Some researchers have called it a clash of two cultures. The argument for the RCT is that only it can generate the type of true knowledge, free from bias, and

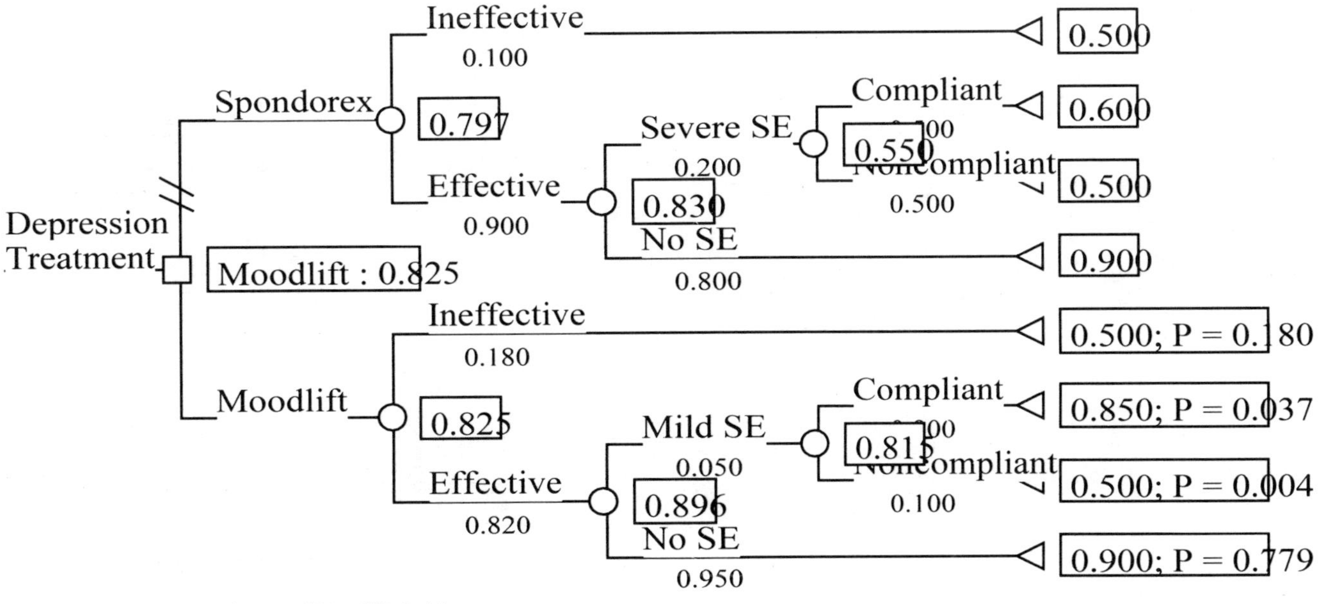

Figure 6. Completed Spondorex and Moodlift decision tree

based on hypothesis testing that is needed for advancement. The modeling proponents recognize "the necessity of various types of analytical models to enrich and broaden results from experimental research when it is available and to find substitutes for experimental data when it is not available" (see Reference 16).

Even if pharmacoeconomic analyses were based on RCTs, they would have problems. Seven threats to validity have been identified when the economic evaluations of pharmaceuticals are added to RCTs, the primary purpose of which is to establish clinical efficacy (e.g., inappropriate choice of comparison therapy and outcomes, inadequate time period and patient follow-up, excessive costs associated with the RCT protocol, and selected patient and provider populations) (see Reference 18). Although not perfect, and at times producing an awkward "Frankenstein model", the decision analytic approach of "pulling together the many needed pieces of information from multiple sources and then stitching them together into a (hopefully) cohesive whole" is an important approach (see Reference 18). Modeling, in general, and decision analytic modeling, in particular, can represent the real, non-RCT world with a decision tree and a synthesis of data from multiple disparate sources for approximations of effectiveness, consequences, and outcomes. A health care evaluation model has been defined as "an analytic methodology that accounts for events over time and across populations, that is based on data drawn from primary and/or secondary sources, and whose purpose is to estimate the effects of an intervention on valued health consequences and costs" (see Reference 27). When decisions need to be made before comprehensive data are available, a decision analytic model, incorporating the options and their consequences over time for the selected population, is the more efficient and effective method to assist the decision-making process.

But, based on the perceived potential and incentives for bias in modeled analyses, two important policy decisions have affected the credibility of modeling use in pharmacoeconomic analysis. In 1994, the editors of the New England Journal of Medicine announced that the journal would not publish any modeled cost-effectiveness analyses if any of the authors were associated with a pharmaceutical company; if the grant/contract to conduct such a study was awarded directly to an individual rather than to an institution; and if, in the opinion of their reviewers, all assumptions were not identified and models not disclosed. With the implementation of Section 114 of the Food and Drug Administration Modernization Act of 1997, the Food and Drug Administration continues to require RCTs, and restricts use of the results from modeled pharmacoeconomic analyses, to support cost-effectiveness claims.

These two actions, as well as worldwide interest in standardizing modeled analyses, have led to the development of guidelines, consensus conferences, and modeling frameworks: the Inter-Patient Outcome Research Teams Group, the Panel on Cost-Effectiveness in Health and Medicine, Consensus Conference on Guidelines on Economic Modeling in Health Technology Assessment, and the International Society for Pharmacoeconomics and Outcomes Research Task Force on Good Research Practices-Modeling Studies. These guidelines, consensus conferences, and modeling frameworks are discussed in more detail in the Annotated Bibliography. Incorporating these guidelines into the design and conduct of pharmacoeconomic analyses, particularly decision analytic models, will improve the validity of the analysis and reduce the potential for bias and conflict of interest. The following section further develops the considerations in each step of the decision analytic process.

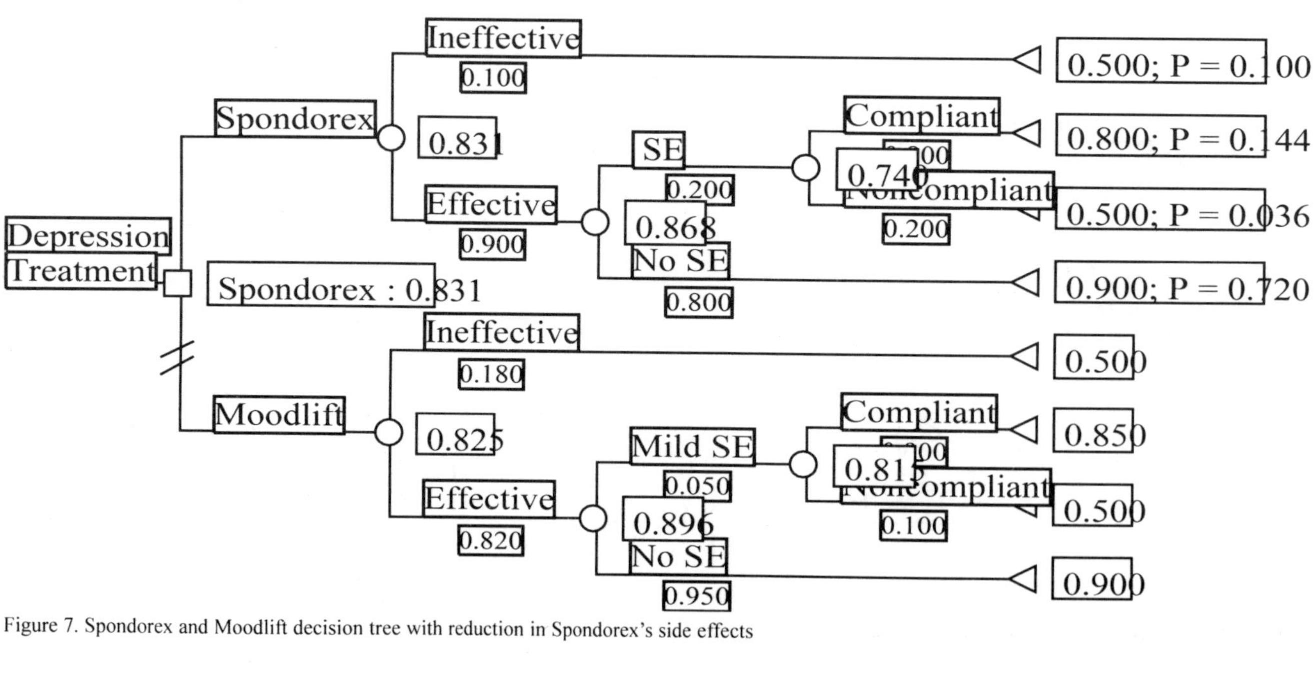

Figure 7. Spondorex and Moodlift decision tree with reduction in Spondorex's side effects

Considerations Within the Modeled Decision Analysis

Given the controversies with using decision analytic modeling in pharmacoeconomics and the resulting guideline developments to standardize the process, what are the considerations in the design and conduct of a pharmacoeconomic study using decision analysis? What are the methodologic issues in each of the seven decision analytic steps and how can the application of guidelines improve the decision analytic pharmacoeconomic model and its results?

There are strong similarities between these concerns and methodologic issues important to all forms of pharmacoeconomic evaluation. As in all pharmacoeconomic studies, it is essential to clearly identify all assumptions in the model and the sources of all inputs into the model. The analysis must be transparent; that means that another person would be able to replicate the study given the information presented.

Although decision analysis itself is a methodology, it also serves as the organizing framework for all of the pharmacoeconomic methods. In the antidepressant selection teaching case, utilities were used as the outcome measure. But, if cost also had been included as a second outcome column in Figure 5, the information needed to perform a cost-utility analysis would have been available. If outcomes had been measured as disability days and cost, a cost-effectiveness analysis could have been performed. And if both a cost-utility and cost-effectiveness study were to be performed, there would have been three outcome column-cost, disability days, and utilities. For whatever type of pharmacoeconomic analysis that is performed, the decision tree structure remains the same, but the units of outcome valuations differ. These examples suggest that decision analysis, and especially the decision tree, is a powerful and unifying methodology for any type of pharmacoeconomic study.

Step 1: Identify the Question

All pharmacoeconomic studies require that a series of questions be answered before data collection begins. The answers to these questions establish the ground rules for the analysis. What is the decision and what options will be considered? Who will be the decision-maker and whose perspective will be considered? What patient population will be studied and will subpopulation analyses be performed? Over what time horizon will the consequences be analyzed? What type of pharmacoeconomic evaluation is to be used? What units of outcome measurements will be included in the decision? The answers to these questions are necessary to properly frame the analysis, structure the decision, and collect the appropriate data.

What is the Decision and What are the Decision Options?

Depending on the scope of the decision, the decision model may require a large or small number of decision options. If the goal of the analysis is to determine the best treatment strategy for a condition, then all reasonable treatment options should be included. However, only two or three options may be needed when the question is more limited in nature.

Pharmacoeconomic evaluations can be comprehensive and examine options across treatment modalities, or be more limited and focus on interclass or intraclass pharmaceutical treatments. For example, for treating depression, should the decision-maker consider both counseling psychotherapy as well as pharmaceutical interventions? And within pharmacological therapy, should both tricyclic antidepressants and selective serotonin reuptake inhibitors be included, or should the analysis be limited to just an intraclass comparisons of the latter? An advantage of the intraclass comparison is that it is focused. But the focus may be so narrow that advantages or disadvantages of other approaches are excluded. By limiting the decision to a within-class comparison, the broader question of what is the most effective intervention is not examined.

All guidelines recommend that a "usual care" option be included in the study. The Inter-Patient Outcome Research Teams Decision Modeling work group also recommends that decision options include extreme strategies to represent the range of possibilities from passivity to aggressiveness in clinical treatment. An example of a passive comparison is the "do-nothing" or no-treatment strategy. Incorporating a no-treatment option is particularly useful in providing baseline information for marginal cost-effectiveness studies and other economic analyses of alternative treatment strategies. With no treatment as an option within the decision analysis, the outcomes of the least costly treatment option can be compared to those of a strategy of doing nothing. When the no-treatment option is omitted, an artificial situation is created in which all the costs and benefits are attributed to the least costly alternative. But even the do-nothing strategy frequently has associated costs and benefits. For example, a no vaccination strategy not only has costs associated with the disease not being prevented, but also has resources saved when major and minor reactions to the vaccines do not occur. Therefore, the no-treatment strategy should be included as a decision option to serve as a point of comparison to enable the analyst to calculate the marginal cost of the least costly alternative.

What Perspective Should be Taken?

Specifying the pharmacoeconomic analysis depends on identifying the decision-maker and the perspective from which the analysis is to be conducted. Frequently, it is argued that to achieve maximal societal good, all allocative decisions must be made from a societal perspective. That argument is particularly relevant for countries with a national health system where allocative decisions are made centrally and do affect society. Although the Panel on Cost-effectiveness in Health and Medicine recommends a societal perspective, in the United States, patients, providers, departments, and institutions frequently make decisions based on the unique perspective of each. The International Society for Pharmacoeconomics and Outcomes Research guidelines state that the model should be structured from the perspective of the decision-maker. It must be clearly established whether the decision analysis is being performed to select the preferred course of care for an individual patient care decision, to determine the composition of a managed care formulary, or to determine national health policy. Is it from the point of view of the pharmacy department, the hospital, an insurance company, a health maintenance organization, a corporation, or society?

Identifying the decision-maker and the perspective of the decision determines downstream factors such as the time frame, costs, and outcomes to be considered. For example, if a decision is limited to the perspective of a pharmacy department, only pharmacy and pharmacy-related costs will be included. However, if the analysis is conducted from the perspective of the hospital, all relevant costs over the length of the hospital stay will be collected. And if the perspective is that of an MCO, all costs related to the episode of illness will be incorporated into the analysis. Unfortunately, investigators in pharmacoeconomic studies frequently fail to identify the perspective of their analyses. This oversight hampers others when they try to determine if the results of a study are generalizable to their population of interest.

What Patient Population is to be Studied?

Disease severity and rates of drug effectiveness and adverse events can vary across populations. Therefore, the analyst must determine not only the perspective of the study, but also the patient population to be studied. Should the decision be structured to relate to an individual patient; to selected patient subpopulations based on variables, such as gender, age, or disease severity; or to all with a clinical condition? According to the International Society for Pharmacoeconomics and Outcomes Research guidelines, "When appropriate, modeled populations should be disaggregated according to strata that have different event probabilities, quality of life, and costs." Although subgroup analysis can be built into the structure of the decision tree, data may not be available at the subgroup level, but it can be estimated and evaluated through sensitivity analyses. Ultimately, identification of the patient population depends on the objectives of the study and the compatibility of the data, or modeling necessary, to achieve those objectives.

Over What Period Will the Analysis Apply?

Selection of the time horizon for the analysis bounds the period over which the decision and its consequences are to be studied. The selection of that time period depends on the nature of the clinical question and the drug class considered; the time period required to achieve therapeutic effectiveness, detect adverse events, and resolve drug sequelae; and the perspective of the decision-maker. If data are not available for the time frame selected, the decision can be modeled and the data estimated; both are then examined with sensitivity analyses. Depending on the clinical question, the time horizon for the evaluation can be selected to incorporate only the immediate near-term effects or be extended to include the more comprehensive assessment of the long-term sequelae and consequences of the drug decision. Natural time periods, such as days, weeks, months, and years; administrative times, such as budget periods; or functional periods, such as episode of illness and remainder of life; can be considered.

When a decision analytic study uses clinical trial data, the investigation was considered limited to the time period of the clinical trial. For example, in one study, pharmacoeconomic assessment of alternative treatments for persistent gastroesophageal reflux disease "was limited to a 7-month period to reflect the specific time frame of published controlled trials, which typically used a 4- or 8-week treatment period followed by 6 months of follow-up". Please If a randomized, clinical trial is of sufficient duration to detect both efficacy of the drug as well as safety concerns, the time period should be adequate and the trial's data suitable for inclusion in an evaluation. However, the chronicity of the disease also should be considered in the selection of the time analysis. The new International Society for Pharmacoeconomics and Outcomes Research (ISPOR) guidelines encourage modeled analysis to incorporate the time frame necessary for the decision, and model the unknown time period. As stated in the ISPOR guidelines, "The lack of long-term follow-up data should not be used as a rational for failing to extend the time horizon as long as is relevant to the decision under analysis."

What Are the Decision Criteria?

Two considerations face the investigator when selecting the decision criteria or outcome measures for the decision analysis: what metric will capture the effect of the interventions and to what degree should the conclusions be comparable to other resource allocative decisions. If costs and disease-specific outcome measures are selected, the results may be limited to the comparison of resource allocation only within the treatment options for this specific clinical condition. If the investigator includes a new metric as an outcome measure in a new study, unless other more recognized measures also are included, that study may not be comparable to any other analysis because the measure of outcome valuation is different. On the other hand, if an investigator wishes to assess patient preferences or to compare the relative resource use of the considered interventions to similar disease or other intervention programs, then utilities can be determined or estimated and a cost-utility analysis performed. Most of the guidelines recommend the selection of quality-adjusted life-years as one of the outcome measures to ensure comparison of analyses across all disease types.

Of 81 published decision analyses involving pharmaceutical interventions through 1996, 75 percent of the studies included cost as a decision criterion. Of these, 47 percent were cost-effectiveness studies; 28 percent were cost analyses; 21 percent were cost-utility; and 3 percent were cost-benefit. All cost-utility studies determined some quality-adjusted period (e.g., quality-adjusted life-years or quality-adjusted days) thus, permitting broad cross-study comparisons. However, the cost-effectiveness studies used a variety of both general measures, such as life-years saved, or disease-specific outcome measures, such as gastrointestinal events averted.

One early study demonstrates the interaction between the selection of the outcome measure and the intervention option preferred by the decision analysis. Decision analysis was used to answer the question, "Which of four options is the best treatment for dyspepsia?" The analysis did not reveal any best approach; rather, the preferred option depended on which outcome measure was most valued by the decision-maker. If mortality was to be minimized, the upper gastrointestinal series before selection of therapy yielded highest survival. However, if weeks of pain were to be minimized, ulcer therapy begun immediately provided the most pain-free days. On the other hand, if the direct costs were to be minimized, symptomatic therapy could be implemented with the lowest costs.

It is critical that these five questions be answered before proceeding with the decision analysis. They establish the foundation about what data are needed and can be used in the analysis. For example, unless the decision perspective, patient population, and time frame of the study are clearly specified, the analyst will not know whether data from a 2-month general population study conducted from a societal perspective are of value to the clinical question and patient population being considered at another institution. Without *a priori* establishing the bounds and characteristics of the analysis, investigators are likely to create conflicts within their models when data from different perspectives, different time horizons, or different patient populations are combined inappropriately during the analytic process.

Step 2: Structuring the Consequences of Alternative Options

Although decision analysis is a systematic and quantitative approach to decision-making under conditions of uncertainty, the decision model itself is the most powerful feature of decision analysis. The decision tree focuses the decision-maker to convert the intuitive decision-making process into an explicitly structured and detailed series of "if, then" questions. If one option is selected, then what are the possible consequences that will happen first? If the first consequence happens, then what is likely to happen next? If the second consequence happens, then what will happen as a follow-up consequence?

This process, and the resulting decision tree, changes the unexamined, intuitive decision process into one in which the thought process is clearly detailed. Structuring the tree forces the decision-maker to identify the relationships that exist between the decision options and the consequences of selecting each of the alternative options. The tree becomes a tool to assist in thinking through a decision as well as a tangible, graphic representation of factors to be considered in the decision. The tree can serve as a talking piece around which communications can be improved among individuals and departments working on the same project. With a decision tree, co-workers can identify where they agree or disagree about the alternatives and consequences to be considered, suggest additional consequences that must be included in the tree, or recommend that a branch be trimmed. Depending on the case, an approach could be to consider the construction of the tree to be a group effort from the beginning

To conduct a comprehensive pharmacoeconomic study, the decision-maker must structure the decision tree to include both the effectiveness and adverse events of the drug. At a minimum, this ensures that both the cost of the drug as well as the induced costs associated with adverse events are included in the analysis.

Decision models are prone to errors of both logic and structure. Three common errors have been identified by the Inter-Patient Outcome Research Teams Decision Modeling work group.

The first is conditioning of action on unobservable states, which frequently occurs when the results of diagnostic tests are incorporated into the decision tree. Investigators assume that positive tests indicate that patients have a condition without appreciating that most diagnostic tests are associated with some degree of classification error (i.e., false-positives and false-negatives). Investigators then condition the decision by using faulty information that does not represent the unobserved true status of the patient. Test results must be interpreted based on the estimate of the test's sensitivity and specificity, as well as the underlying prevalence of disease.

The second common error occurs as a violation of symmetry. All options must model prognosis the same way. For example, consider a tree where one option incorporates different levels of severity of disease outcomes, each associated with different utility values. The other options do not model the prognosis the same way and only have one level of outcome. If the underlying distribution among the different levels of severity of outcomes changes, the expected value of the first option will change, but not those of the other options because their branch structure failed to indicate a difference in the severity of the outcome. To make valid comparisons between decision options, the decision tree must incorporate symmetrical prognostic branches for each decision option.

Failure to apply consistent bias is the third common error identified by the work group. When constructing a decision analytic model, it is frequently necessary to make simplifying assumptions that may introduce biases. The Inter-Patient Outcome Research Teams group and Blue Ribbon panel recommend that all biases should go against the strategy that proves to be optimal according to the model, so that relaxing them will not affect the decision. If the decision tree includes biases that apply in opposite directions, it is impossible to say how the simplifying assumptions affect the results of the analysis. As always, these internal decisions must be clearly stated so that the decision model is transparent.

Step 3: Assessing Probabilities

A computer program, based on these and other rules of model construction (BUNYON), has been developed to critique the structure of decision trees automatically. The computer program can automatically identify many common errors based on purely structural characteristics, without the need for knowledge of the subject content (see Reference 28). Although not a comprehensive critique of all steps within the decision analytic process, BUNYON is an important way to improve the structure of decision analyses.

Each chance node indicates where events will occur that are not under the control of the decision-maker and the probability at which these events will occur. In decision analysis, a probability is the rate at which an event will occur within a specified population. A rate has a numerator and a denominator; the numerator is the number of times an event occurs within the denominator, the specified population. Pharmacoepidemiological studies can provide valuable assistance in determining the probabilities or rates at which events occur. Other sources of probabilistic information include large randomized, clinical trials (using either intention-to-treat or on-treatment data), meta-analysis of the results from several clinical trials, administrative data sets, expert opinion, and expert opinion combined with clinical reality.

A large RCT, providing information on the options and consequences of the options being considered, would provide an ideal database to determine probabilities. However, clinical trials typically are efficacy or safety studies, and most decision analyses are conducted for application to effectiveness work. The clinical trial is conducted under tight protocols and maintains high drug adherence rates, thus biasing upward the probabilities for drug effectiveness and patient adherence. Whereas these data might provide the best probability estimates, the investigator should lower the probabilities in the sensitivity analysis to determine if they affect the preferred decision. Also, clinical trials may be of insufficient size to detect rare events. Incorporation of data from clinical trials of inadequate size leads to distortions in the model, especially when a rare event occurs and is associated with great cost. To obtain more robust probability estimates, several similar clinical trials can be combined through the technique of meta-analysis.

In a more limited manner, administrative databases and clinical registries can serve as a source of probability estimates. Pharmacy databases can be used to identify patients receiving drugs of interest. Then insurance files can provide information about the frequency with which various procedures or admissions occur within the identified population. When using these databases or information from clinical trials, investigators must be careful to match the source of the estimates with the population being studied. If the decision analysis is comparing the costs and effects of two drugs for postmenopausal women, it might not be appropriate to use in estimating clinical effectiveness and adverse events in teenage girls. The same caution should be raised with the combination of trial results for meta-analysis. Trial results should be combined only if they are based on similar patient populations.

Expert opinion can be sampled for probability estimates, but psychologists say that people in general are poor estimators of probabilities. Most people tend to overestimate the occurrence of rare events and underestimate the frequency with which common events happen. Experts, basing their estimates on their atypical and more seriously ill patient population, also overestimate the frequency of the uncommon. The International Society for Pharmacoeconomics and Outcomes Research guidelines recommend using formal methods such as Delphi or nominal group techniques. These estimates are then subjected to a "reality check" by asking practicing clinicians if they concur with the expert estimates. If there are disagreements in opinion, investigators should provide feedback to both sources and ask both groups to reexamine their conclusions.

Until pharmacoepidemiological data from Phase IV trials are available to determine the rates at which the effectiveness and consequences following the decision options occur, probability estimates based on efficacy trials, meta-analyses of efficacy trials, administrative data sets, and Delphi techniques involving expert opinions will serve as the best approximations.

A computer program, based on these and other rules of model construction (BUNYON), has been developed to critique the structure of decision trees automatically. The computer program can automatically identify many common errors based on purely structural characteristics, without the need for knowledge of the subject content (see Reference 28). Although not a comprehensive critique of all steps within the decision analytic process, BUNYON is an important way to improve the structure of decision analyses.

Step 4: Valuing Outcomes

All forms of pharmacoeconomic analyses require that the economic costs and other outcome valuations be determined for different treatment options. One or more methods of outcomes valuation can be used to assign values to each decision path-dollars, utilities, or other noneconomic valuations. If more than one method of outcomes valuation is selected, separate columns are inserted at the end of each decision path. Economic values need to be adjusted for inflation and discounted to present value.

It is critical to remember that the economic valuation of each of the decision paths is determined by the perspective of the decision-maker. Decision analytic studies involving pharmaceutical products have used a variety of sources for cost estimates. Examples include labor costs estimated by industrial engineering studies, medical resources estimated by the author's best judgment and subjected to extensive sensitivity analyses, a cost-accounting software package used during a clinical trial, a step-down allocation using indirect costs and cost-to-charge ratios of revenue-producing cost centers to determine unit costs of hospital resources, estimates from diagnosis-related groups weights, Medicare data for terminal cancer care, average wholesale prices for drugs, and Delphi and investigator estimates. As with any pharmacoeconomic study, the investigator must clearly differentiate among the costs. If a cost-to-charge conversion is used, the method must be described.

Valuations for noneconomic decision criteria also are necessary. In a cost-effectiveness analysis, the investigator values the outcomes of each of the decision paths in some natural unit of measurement, such as life-years saved or infection prevented. If the study is a cost-utility analysis, utilities must be determined for each path. Through time tradeoff and standard reference gamble techniques, patients can be directly questioned about the utility they associate with or preferences they have for each of the clinical paths. However, in a review of 13 cost-utility studies using decision analysis to evaluate pharmaceutical products, only one included utilities generated from patients. In the other 12, patient utilities were derived from the study investigators; previously published expert opinion; oncology staff; oncology and nursing focus groups; Torrance and Feeney utility values; and faculty, residents, and medical students. The degree to which these individuals can empathically and accurately value the selected outcome (utility estimates of patient preferences for different disease states) must be determined.

Step 5: Determining Preferred Options

As seen in the Spondorex versus Moodlift Teaching Case, the decision tree is solved by averaging-out-and-folding-back. This process provides a quantitative combination of the outcome valuations and their probability of occurrence. Decision-makers move from the right to the left, averaging-out-and-folding-back until the choice node is reached. It is called averaging-out-and-folding-back because each path's outcome value is weighted by its probability of occurrence, the averaging-out component, working from right to left, from outcomes to options, the folding-back component. The weighted value at the chance node is called an expected value because it is the expected, but not certain, value based on probabilistic estimates that events of different valuations will occur. With the expected value of each decision option identified, the decision-maker can select the option that will yield the highest value defined by that individual.

If the decision analysis has only one choice node, the averaging-out-and-folding-back process continues until the expected values are determined for the options originating from the original choice node. If one or more choice nodes are embedded in the analysis, the option with the highest expected value is selected at each choice node within the decision tree, and this value is carried to the left to the next chance node.

Step 6: Identifying the Assumptions

All guidelines emphasize the need to be explicit and detailed about the assumptions that the decision-maker made in the previous five steps of the process. With the potential to bias the outcome of an analysis by assumptions behind the structure, rates, and valuations within the model, the guidelines collectively force analysts to detail assumptions and limitations of the models. Only then will analysts be able to assure clinical decision-makers, policy decision-makers, and journal editors of the transparency and soundness of decision analytic studies.

Step 7: Conducting Sensitivity Analyses

Sensitivity analysis is used to challenge the robustness of the conclusions of the decision analysis by determining if the preferred option will change when the estimated probabilities and outcomes of the base case analysis are varied. Although investigators use the most reasonable point estimates in the base case, the probabilities and outcome values have their own ranges of uncertainty. Therefore, in sensitivity analysis, these values are varied over their range of reasonable values. If available, confidence intervals of the variables serve as a convenient range over which the probability and outcome estimates can be varied.

Monte Carlo computer simulations can simultaneously vary the base case estimates of all probability and outcomes values across their probability distributions so that the uncertainties in all values are collectively considered. For each run of the simulated model, a value for each variable is randomly selected from within its population distribution, and the expected values of each option are recalculated. This random assignment of values from within the distribution to all probability and outcomes estimates is repeated a specified number of runs. Monte Carlo simulations provide a powerful estimate of the robustness of the decision analysis, and their use is increasing in pharmacoeconomic studies.

The Case Revisited: Application of Guidelines to the Teaching Case

Given the guidelines for modeled analysis, how can the teaching case be improved? A critical review of 10 published economic modeling studies in depression provides much insight to this question (see Reference 13).

Step 1: Identify the Decision, Including Selection of the Decision Options to be Studied. Bound the Time Frame of the Decision and Determine from What Perspective the Decision is to be Made

The decision-maker is that of an MCO considering the impact of two new antidepressant drugs on a cohort of patients with MDD in the MCO. Rather than only comparing the two options (Moodlift and Spondorex), the model could be improved by the addition of a "usual care" option such as the principal selective serotonin reuptake inhibitor (SSRI) used in that organization. Another improvement would be to extend the time frame of the analysis to at least 1 year, rather than the 3 months. This extension would permit a more accurate modeling of depression, a chronic illness.

Step 2: Structure the Decision and the Consequences of Each Decision Option over Time

Several additions have been made to the decision tree to more accurately capture the course of the disease over 1 year. Modeling the decision and the consequences over time, the decision now starts with three options: Moodlift, Spondorex, and a selective serotonin reuptake inhibitor. Decision analysis rarely accounts for the different types of noncompliance seen over the course of chronic diseases; these have now been included. As seen in Figure 8, the decision tree now includes: initial compliance/noncompliance; effective therapy leading to major, minor, or no side effects; continued effectiveness; and relapse. In the ineffective arm, titration upward of an ineffective dose is included followed by effective or ineffective therapy. In the ineffective and noncompliant arms, four possibilities are modeled: the patient's MDD continues, it spontaneously resolves, the drug is changed, or the patient commits suicide. Because this portion of the tree represents about 3-4 months, additional modeling is needed using either decision analysis or a recursive form of modeling called Markov modeling, which is discussed in the Markov Modeling chapter of this book.

Step 3: Assess the Probability That Each Consequence Will Occur

The more accurate level of modeling detail included in the revised tree does come as a cost. Published clinical trials will rarely have this level of detail; therefore, structured expert opinions are needed to derive the probabilities for the initial estimate. These probabilities should be extensively challenged with sensitivity analysis. As the new agents are incorporated into clinical practice, prospective epidemiological information can be collected to derive more accurate probability estimates.

Step 4: Valuing Outcomes

Quality-adjusted life-years, derived from standard reference gambles of patients with MDD from the MCO, were used to value outcomes in the teaching example. Given that the decision analysis is to guide allocative decisions within the MCO, the utilities derived from MCO members rather than society in general seems appropriate. However, the MCO budget must cover all services for all patients; therefore, following the Blue Ribbon recommendations, the utilities of a cross section of members of this MCO should be obtained.

Step 5: Determining Preferred Options

Preferred options remain unchanged.

Step 6: Identifying the Assumptions

The expanded decision tree and its associated probabilities and outcome valuations add more assumptions to the teaching case. Some of these would include:

- o Expert panel can distinguish among different forms of noncompliance and can accurately and reliability assess their rates
- o Initially noncompliant patients can be identified and followed up
- o Ineffectively treated patients will have two attempts at upward titration to a therapeutic dose before switching to an alternative mediation
- o Patients will not have both major and minor side effects

Step 7: Conducting Sensitivity Analyses

The expansion of the decision tree to include a third option, more consequences, and their associated additional probabilities create more opportunities for sensitivity analyses. The decision-maker can use the results of these analyses to identify the variables that most affect the decision and target those variables for prospective data collection.

In summary, decision-makers need to make decisions, and they often can neither take the time nor afford the expense to collect all necessary information. So, they turn to a model, in this case a decision analytic model, to structure their decisions, to synthesize data from multiple disparate sources, and to replicate as closely as possible the consequences of options, the expected rates of those consequences, and the estimated values of the outcomes. Decisions will continue to be made. The question is how can decision analytic modeling improve those actions. With the use of the guidelines and recommendations, their decision analytic models will be improved and expanded so that they are more representative of the clinical condition and the other inputs involved. Ultimately, their decisions will be better informed and the decisions will improve.

Applications of Decision Analysis in Pharmacoeconomics

Decision analysis has been used to structure issues, such as vaccination policies; interpretation of therapeutic drug monitoring results; and treatment of a variety of clinical condition including, but not limited to antithrombolytic therapy, cancer, hyperlipidemia, human immunodeficiency virus, diabetes, migraine, upper gastrointestinal disease, community-acquired pneumonia, MDDs, and cytomegalovirus infection.

Decision analysis also can provide a framework to develop disease state management protocols and to conduct cost-of-illness studies. Disease state management protocols can use the decision tree format to structure the natural course of the disease under study. Then, the investigator can insert various intervention strategies as decision options and determine how each intervention modifies the structure of the tree, the probabilities, the outcome valuations at each path, and the expected valuation of that intervention option. When economic values are attached to the ingredients of care for each decision path, the same structure can be used to support cost-of-illness studies. These techniques recently were used to evaluate the soundness of the International Gastro Primary Care Group guidelines for treating upper gastrointestinal symptoms. Using a decision analytic framework, one researcher concluded that the guidelines would save 15 percent of drug costs in the United Kingdom (see Reference 11). Again using decision analysis, another researcher compared the guidelines to five competitor treatment strategies and also concluded that the guidelines were the preferred option for reducing costs (see Reference 9).

Two recent studies have evaluated the quality of decision analytic models within the same type of clinical condition. Ten decision analytic studies modeling different treatments of major depressive disorder were critiqued (see Reference 13). In the second study, five decision analytic models for the treatment of type 2 diabetes were examined (see Reference 8). In both studies, the authors encouraged future investigators to be clear about the perspective of the analysis, to include a usual treatment option, to be more transparent, and to expend the analysis by modeling the clinical condition beyond the RCT time frame to a length of time that is clinically meaningful for such chronic disease conditions.

Decision analysis has been used to select drug projects and manage portfolios during the drug development process. One investigator presented decision analysis as the ideal framework for implementing real option valuation techniques because the technique can model the potential for additional future options such as label extension and the possibility of second generation drugs (see Reference 20).

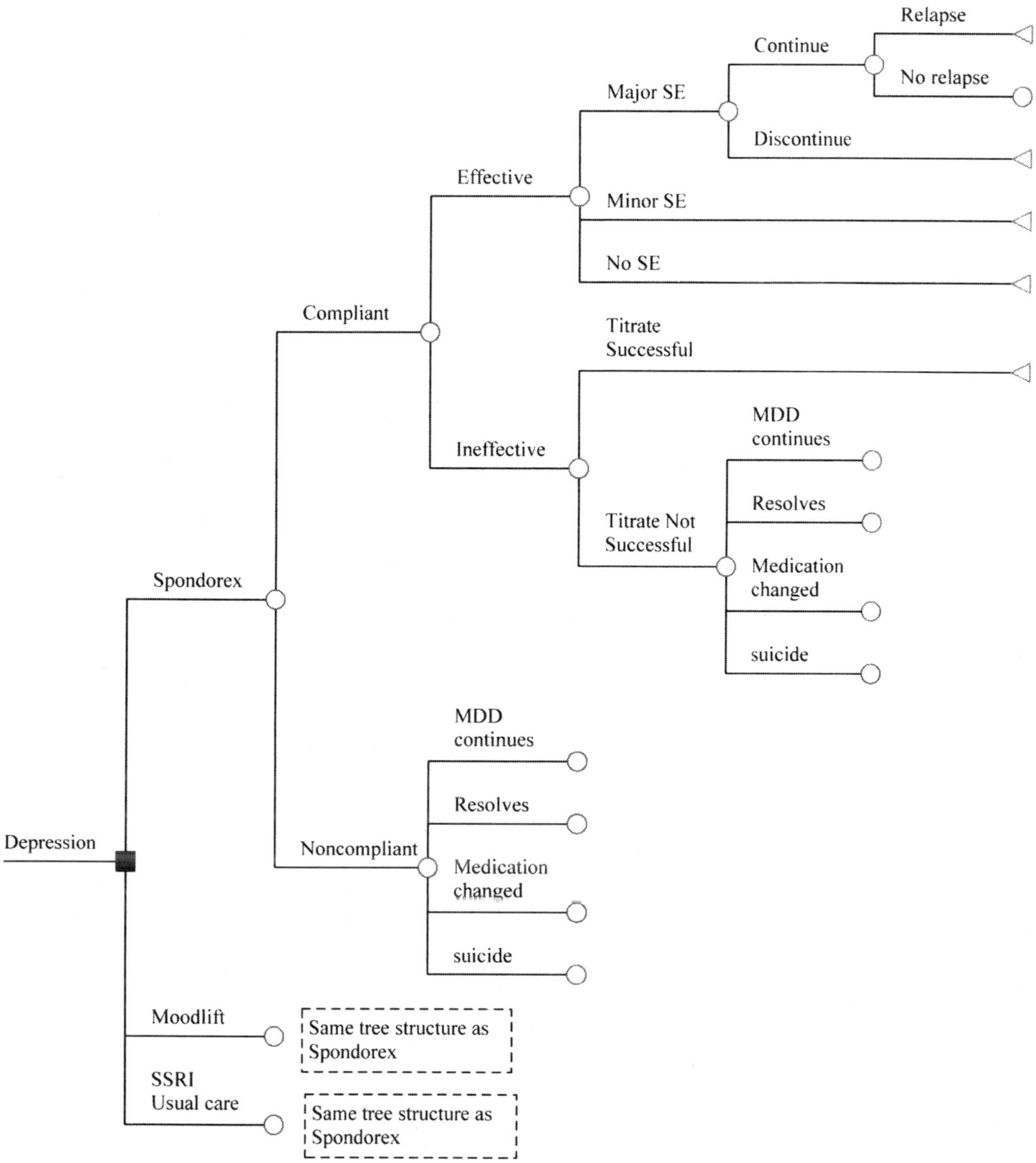

Figure 8. Application of guidelines to the structure of Spondorex and Moodlift case

Conclusion

Decision analysis is decision-making under conditions of uncertainty. In this chapter, it has been demonstrated how a question can be transformed into a decision analysis by identifying the issues surrounding the question, identifying the consequences of the decision options, estimating their probabilities of occurrence, and valuing all possible outcomes. The analysis then prescribes the decision option that will yield the greatest expected value based on how the outcomes have been valued.

However, the usefulness of decision analysis is only as good as the options considered and the model specified. If all relevant options are not included for consideration, if probability estimates are not derived from comparable populations, or if all costs of the ingredients of care are not included, the decision analysis will be flawed and potentially worthless. As with any pharmacoeconomic study, decision analysis can be subject to many overt and unintentional biases. It is the responsibility of the analyst to fairly construct the study from the perspective of the decision-maker and make the analysis transparent by clearly specifying all assumptions and generalizations that have been incorporated into the model.

Decision analysis provides the framework for all of the pharmacoeconomic approaches presented in this book. Whether it is a cost-effectiveness study, or cost-utility study, or even a benefit-cost study, all will be strengthened by explicitly structuring the decision options and their consequences. And even if readers do not continue and perform a complete pharmacoeconomic study, the process of constructing and discussing that underlying decision tree will improve their decisions by providing a method to systematically organize and integrate many factors impinging on a decision.

Annotated Bibliography

1. Akehurst R, Anderson P, Brazier J, et al. Consensus Conference on Guidelines on Economic Modelling in Health Technology Assessment. Decision analytic modeling in Economic evaluation of health technologies: a consensus statement. Pharmacoeconomics 2000;17:443–44.

   This article discusses a consensus statement resulting from a conference at the University of Sheffield, Sheffield, United Kingdom, April 22, 1999, on the properties of good decision analytic models. Models should be transparent, have internal consistency, be reproducible, be interpretable, and explore uncertainty in the model's parameters.

2. Barr JT, Schumacher GE. Using decision analysis to conduct pharmacoeconomic studies. In Spilker B, ed. Quality of life and pharmacoeconomics in clinical trials, 2nd ed. Philadelphia, PA: Lippincott-Raven Press, 1996.

   This chapter contains a comprehensive summary of 81 articles that used decision analysis to examine decision options related to pharmaceutical products. Sixty-one of the studies incorporated some type of economic evaluation into the decision analysis. The authors examine each step of the decision analytic process with particular attention given to issues and methodologic problems associated with these 81 articles.

3. Barr JT, Schumacher GE. Decision analysis and pharmacoeconomic evaluations. In: Bootman JL, Townsend RJ, McGhan WF, eds. Principles of pharmacoeconomics, 2nd ed. Cincinnati, OH: Harvey Whitney Books, 1996.

   This introductory chapter to decision analysis includes a fully developed case comparing two fictional antibiotic products being considered for formulary inclusion. Derivation of probability estimates from pharmacoepidemiology data is explored. Treatment costs are determined using an ingredient of care costing method.

4. Biddle AK, Shih YC, Kwong WJ. Cost-benefit analysis of sumatriptan tablets versus usual therapy for treatment of migraine. Pharmacotherapy 2000;20:1356–64.

   Conducted from a societal perspective, this decision analytic model examined the costs and benefits of oral sumatriptan versus usual care for treating migraine headache. Costs included drugs and other medical costs; benefits were derived using the human capital approach of dollars saved (wages) by preventing lost work time associated with an effectively treated migraine attack.

5. Brennan A, Akehurst R. Modeling in health economic evaluation. What is its place? What is its value? Pharmacoeconomics 2000;17:445–59.

   This article is a background paper for the 1999 Consensus Conference on Guidelines on Economic Modeling in Health Care Assessment. It discusses the problems inherent in using randomized, controlled trials (RCTs) and their data for health care evaluations. The authors present six major categories in which modeling in health economic evaluations is appropriate and of value.

6. Briggs AH. Handling uncertainty in cost-effectiveness models. Pharmacoeconomics 2000;17:479–500.

   A thorough discussion of the role of uncertainty in decision analytic models used for cost-effectiveness analyses. Uncertainty can be modeled by using empirical Bayesian methods to synthesize data. The use of probabilistic sensitivity techniques such as Monte Carlo and the determine of the distribution of the incremental cost-effectiveness ratio are described.

7. Brophy DF, Wallace JF, Kennedy DT, Gehr TW, Holdford DA. Cost-effectiveness of sevelamer versus calcium carbonate plus atorvastatin to reduce LDL in patients with chronic renal insufficiency with dyslipidemia and hyperphosphatemia. Pharmacotherapy 2000;20:950–7.

   This article discusses a modeled decision analytic study of the cost-effective of two treatment regimens to reduce low-density lipoprotein in patients with renal insufficiency complicated by dyslipidemia and hyperphosphatemia. The analysis was conducted from the perspective of a third-party payer. Drug costs were based on average wholesale price, and other treatment costs were derived from Medicare reimbursement rates. Effectiveness was defined as reaching a goal of at least a 35 percent reduction in low-density lipoprotein.

8. Coyle D, Lee KM, O'Brien BJ. The role of models within economic analysis: focus on type 2 diabetes mellitus. Pharmacoeconomics 2002;20 Suppl 1:11–19.

   This article reviews five complex disease models for the economic evaluation of treatment options for type 2 diabetes. Although the models were similar in structure and sources for data, they differed in inclusion of disease complications and the complexity of the analysis. The authors recommend that models be improved by increasing the transparency of the analysis and by using data relevant to only type 2 diabetes.

9. Duggan AK. Modelling different approaches to the management of upper gastrointestinal disease. Pharmacoeconomics 1998;14 Suppl 2:25–37.

   This article examines the present cost of treatment for upper gastrointestinal disease, the base case treatment recommended by the International Gastro Primary Care Group, and five alternative treatment guidelines. The time period is 1 year; the perspective is that of the National Health Service. Outpatient costs were the only variable included in the analysis; effectiveness was not considered. The original International Gastro Primary Care Group guidelines were the least costly approach. Modeling the competing therapies to determine their economic impact led to an economic validation of the guidelines.

10. Gold MR, Siegel JE, Russell LB, Weinstein MC, eds. Cost-effectiveness in health and medicine. New York: Oxford University Press, 1996.

An international panel of experts developed guidelines for a reference and base case for cost-effectiveness analysis with attention to framing the decision, assessing the effectiveness of the intervention, identifying and valuing outcomes, and estimating the costs. Support is given to the use of models, incorporating the panel's recommendations, in the performance of cost-effectiveness analyses.

11. Haycox A, Butterworth M, Walley T, Barton S. Development of an economic model for the management of upper gastrointestinal disease in primary care: preliminary findings. Pharmacoeconomics 1998;14 Suppl 2:11–23.

The authors developed a model to assess the economic impact of the clinical guidelines of the International Gastro Primary Care Group. The perspective was that of the National Health Service in the United Kingdom; the time period was 12 months of diagnostic treatment and follow-up for new patients presenting with upper gastrointestinal symptoms. The effectiveness measure was time without symptoms or toxicity. The model predicts that using the guidelines appropriate for the presenting symptom will reduce drug costs by about 15 percent.

12. Hughes DA, Bagust A, Haycox A, Walley T. Accounting for noncompliance in pharmacoeconomic evaluations. Pharmacoeconomics 2001;19:1185–97.

This article is a comprehensive review of the different forms, measures, and consequences of noncompliance. Noncompliance plays a major role in the effectiveness of therapy, but it is rarely adequately incorporated into a decision analysis. The authors suggest methods to distinguish among different forms of noncompliance and to incorporate assumptions about noncompliance into the decision analytic process.

13. Jones MT, Cockrum PC. A critical review of published economic modelling studies in depression. Pharmacoeconomics 2000;17:555–83.

This article is a critique of the various attributes of 10 modeled pharmacoeconomic analyses of antidepressant agents published between 1994 and 1997. While acknowledging that the analysis should be structured based on the perspective of the decision-maker, recommendations include a 5-year time frame (several popular antidepressants are coming off patent during this time period); a "usual care" comparison as a decision option; incorporation of subpopulation characteristics (e.g., severity of depression, age, and gender); quality-adjusted life-years as the outcome measure generated from appropriate cohort of patients; probability estimates of effectiveness (not efficacy); and a more thorough treatment of the various forms of compliance.

14. Kassirer JP, Angell M. The Journal's policy on cost-effectiveness analyses. N Engl J Med 1994;331:669–70.

This reference is an editorial describing the policy of the New England Journal of Medicine related to the publication of modeled cost-effectiveness studies. Considerations forming the decision were: the potential bias inherent in formulating models and identifying costs, the potential conflict of interests that arise when a pharmaceutical firm financially supports the authors of the analysis, and the resulting assumptions and selective use of data in such studies. The journal will accept for review only those articles where the authors attest to independence from a pharmaceutical company.

15. Kassier JP, Moskowitz AJ, Lau J, Pauker SG. Decision analysis: a progress report. Ann Intern Med 1987; 106:275–91.

This comprehensive review article classifies almost 200 clinical decision analytic studies published before 1987 into 13 types of difficult clinical problems (e.g., choosing among treatments, preventing disease, and preventing complications of established disease). This paper demonstrates the widespread use of decision analysis in many different clinical situations.

16. Luce BR. Policy implications of modeling the cost-effectiveness of health care technologies. Drug Info J 1995;29:1469–75.

This article is an analysis of the origin and effect of the controversy between the use of RCTs and modeling techniques to inform pharmacoeconomic decisions. The author tracks the roots of the New England Journal of Medicine's 1994 decision to not publish industry-supported, modeled pharmacoeconomic studies.

17. Najib MM, Stein GE, Goss TF. Cost-effectiveness of sparfloxacin compared with other oral antimicrobials in outpatient treatment of community-acquired pneumonia. Pharmacotherapy 2000;20:461–9.

This article discusses decision analysis modeling comparison of the cost per community-acquired pneumonia for six oral antimicrobials used in monotherapeutic treatment of community-acquired pneumonia. Cost estimates were derived from medical claims and Medicare reimbursement schedules, and were limited to outpatient treatment costs. Probability estimates of treatment success and other rates for the model were derived from published randomized trials, other medical literature, and expert opinion. The analysis was conducted from the Medicare perspective.

18. O'Brien B. Economic evaluation of pharmaceuticals: Frankenstein's Monster or Vampire of trials. Med Care 1996;34:DS99–108.

This paper identifies and discusses the impact of seven threats to validity when an economic "piggyback" component is added to an RCT for the purpose of conducting a pharmacoeconomic evaluation. The author argues that pharmaceutical evaluations "piggybacked" on to RCTs of drug studies create artificial and restrictive conclusions. The decision analytic modeling approach can more realistically answers to question raised in routine clinical settings.

19. Raiffa H. Decision analysis: introductory lectures under uncertainty. Reading, MA: Addison-Wesley Publishing Company, 1968.

This series of lectures for a Harvard Business School audience serves as the seminal publication in the field. The author used these lectures to introduce the business community to decision analysis. Over time, the concept has diffused into decision-making involving health care practices.

20. Rosati N. Decision analysis and drug development portfolio management: uncovering the real options value of your projects. Expert Rev Pharmacoeconomics Outcomes Res 2002;2:179-87.

This article describes the present methods used in the drug development process and the rising use of decision analysis to guide the management of drug development portfolios within pharmaceutical companies. The concept of economic value of additional information is presented and examples are given of how decision analysis can provide that information and determine when it is worth investing to obtain additional information to guide a drug development decision.

21. Sculpher M, Fenwick E, Claxton K. Assessing quality in decision analytic cost-effectiveness models: a suggested framework and example of application. Pharmacoeconomics 2000;17:461-77.

Written as a background paper for the 1999 Consensus Conference on Guidelines on Economic Modeling, the authors identify issues involved in assessing the quality and validity of modeling studies in pharmacoeconomics and make recommendations for improving cost-effectiveness analyses. Guidelines are presented for the model structure, the sources of data, the incorporation of data into the model, and the internal and external consistency and validity of the models.

22. Sonnenberg FA, Roberts MS, Tsevat J, et al. Toward a peer review process for medical decision analysis models. Med Care 1994;32:JS52-64.

Authored by a team of decision analytic specialists who have served on Inter-Patient Outcome Research Teams, this paper includes discussion of the general principles of correct structure for decision analytic models. Specific discussion centers on choice of model type, perspective, utility scheme, and identification of strategies. Events that should be modeled are identified. A set of rules to assist in developing a correct decision model structure and to guide reviewers in judging the adequacy of the model is presented.

23. TreeAge Software, Inc. Data™ 4.0 for healthcare user's manual. Williamstown MA: TreeAge Software, Inc., 2001.

This user-friendly guide to decision analytic software contains a primer on decision analysis as well as instructions for computerized decision analytic and Markov modeling, sensitivity analyses, threshold analyses, and Monte Carlo simulations. Instructions are provided to import data from Windows and Macintosh files into the model.

24. Tversky A, Kahneman D. Judgment under uncertainty: heuristics and biases. Science 1974;185:1124-31.

The authors provide an excellent discussion of the biases and heuristics used in formal and informal estimations of probability values. Intuitive estimates are faulty because individuals tend to underestimate the frequency of common occurrences and overestimate the occurrence of rare events. The message of this article is that it is important to remember that errors in estimations can occur when investigators rely on expert opinions, rather than empiric data, to estimate probability values. This is a classic and readable paper from the field.

25. Weinstein MC, Fineberg HV, eds. Clinical decision analysis. Philadelphia, PA: W.B. Saunders & Company, 1980.

This classic text describes both theoretical and practical aspects of all phases of decision analysis. Definition of the question, identification of consequences, estimation of probabilities, and valuation of outcomes are described. Many examples are provided from, and with applications to, clinical practice. Many practice exercises are included.

26. Weinstein MC, Toy EL, Sandberg EA, et al. Modeling for health care and other policy decisions: Uses, roles, and validity. Value Health 2001;4:348-61.

This article is an overview of the use of, and controversies associated with, modeling to guide decisions within public policy agencies: environment, national defense, and health administrations. The authors examine the position of the Food and Drug Administration and its interpretation of Section 114 of the Food and Drug Administration Modernization Act as applied to the acceptability of results from pharmacoeconomic models in cost effectiveness claims and their use as aids in decision-making.

27. Weinstein MC, Hornberger J, Jackson J, et al. Principles of good practice for decision analytic modeling in health care evaluations: report of the ISPOR Health Science Committee Task Force on Good Research Practices-Modeling Studies. Value Health 2003 Jan-Feb;6(1):9-17.

A series of recommendations written by members of a task force of the International Society for Pharmacoeconomics and Outcomes Research. The guidelines are designed to improve the structure of models, the identification and incorporation of data into the models, the identification of model assumptions, and the validation of models. The authors acknowledge that not all guidelines are appropriate for every modeled analysis, but their aim is to synthesize the present evidence to assist decision-makers in understanding the implications of structure and inputs into the model that affect the model's results.

28. Wellman MP, Eckman MH, Fleming C, et al. Automated critiquing of medical decision trees. Med Decis Making 1989;9:272-84.

The authors present a description of their decision tree-critiquing program, BUNYON. This program identifies and assists in correcting modeling errors in clinical decision trees. The program can be used by beginning analysts to critique structural features of clinical decision model under development. Awareness of structural elements of model construction to consider when modeling the question, specifying its options, and identifying the consequences of each decision option is raised.

29. Zabinski RA, Burke TA, Johnson J, et al. An economic model for determining the costs and consequences of using various treatment alternatives for the management of arthritis in Canada. Pharmacoeconomics 2001;19 Suppl 1:49-58.

This article discusses the development of a decision analytic model, funded by the Pharmacia Corporation, to compare the costs and consequences of treatment alternatives for Canadian patients with arthritis, both osteoarthritis and rheumatoid arthritis, from the perspective of a provincial minister of health. Eight Phase III trials provided probabilities; resources were estimated by experts in five Canadian provinces. Contains a break-even analysis.

Self-Assessment Questions

1. Which one of the following factors is least likely to be affected by different perspectives for the same study?
   A. Time frame.
   B. Valuation of each path in the decision analysis.
   C. Probability estimates.
   D. Need for sensitivity analysis.

2. Which one of the following is the best source for obtaining probability estimates for use in a decision tree?
   A. Expert opinion.
   B. Randomized, efficacy trials.
   C. Randomized, effectiveness trials.
   D. Retrospective chart review.

3. Which one of the following is premature to determine when first constructing a decision analysis?
   A. Identification of the decision options.
   B. Outcome valuation of the decision paths.
   C. Identification of the decision-maker.
   D. Determination of the time period.

4. You are comparing Yeast-be-Gone, a new topical treatment for candidiasis, to standard therapy. Structure a tree and solve a decision tree based on the following information. In the Yeast-be-Gone arm of the decision tree, you structure pertinent information. Ten percent of patients develop contact dermatitis and immediately discontinue treatment. Of those who do not develop contact dermatitis, 70 percent have the potential to be effectively treated, but 20 percent do not complete the full treatment and experience treatment failure. Which one of the following is the path probability of an effectively treated and adherent patient?
   A. 0.126.
   B. 0.504.
   C. 0.620.
   D. 0.700.

5. You are deciding between two sedatives, drug A and drug B. From the literature, you obtain the probabilities of various side effects as well as patient utilities for the side effects. You construct the decision tree shown to the right, but before you can even label the branches, your friend tells you that there is something wrong with what you have done so far. Which one of the following indicates where the error occurs?
   A. A.
   B. B.
   C. C.
   D. D.

The partial cost-utility decision tree shown to the right pertains to Questions 6-8.

6. Which one of the following is the expected utility at node B?

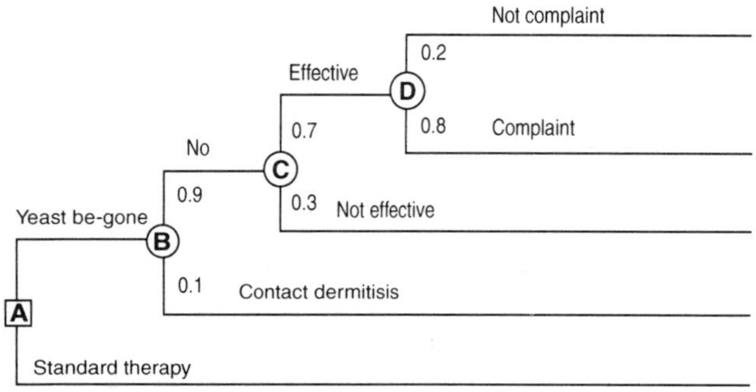

Figure for Question #5.

   A. 0.50 utility.
   B. 0.74 utility.
   C. 0.48 utility.
   D. 1.29 utility.

7. Which one of the following is the expected cost of the branch at node B?
   A. $990.
   B. $1210.
   C. $1830.
   D. $3150.

8. Which one of the following is the cost-utility ratio of the branch at node B?
   A. $1040 per utility.
   B. $1252 per utility.
   C. $1338 per utility.
   D. $1806 per utility.

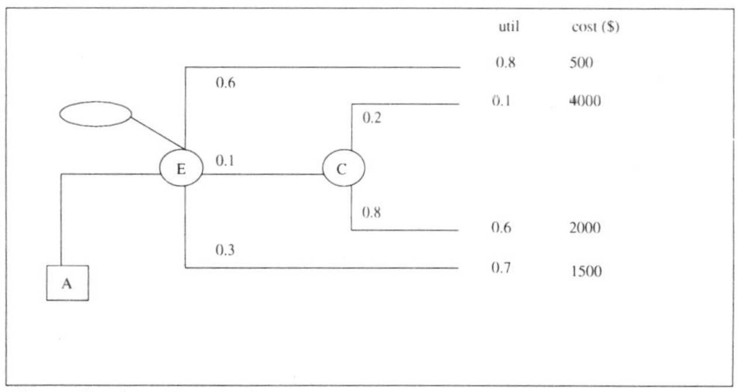

Figure for Questions #6-8.

MARKOV MODELING

Daniel Touchette, Pharm.D., M.A.; and
Daniel Hartung, Pharm.D.

Outline

I. Introduction
   A. Decision analysis is an explicit method for making choices under uncertain conditions.
   B. Decision analysis can be displayed visually, in the form of a decision tree, which illustrates the temporal and probabilistic relationship between options and outcomes.
   C. There are two commonly used methods of decision analysis.
      1. Simple decision analysis is well suited for comparing alternative options with relatively immediate impacts.
      2. Markov models efficiently manage outcomes with time-dependent risk changes, making them well suited for modeling chronic decisions.
      3. Markov models can be stand-alone models or may be combined with simple decision trees to predict the long-term effects of therapies.

II. Overview of Markov Model
   A. A Markov model typically is designed to simulate the most important aspects of a disease and can be used to estimate the long-term clinical, humanistic, and economic dimensions of the disease.
   B. The disease or condition is divided into numerous mutually exclusive health states termed *Markov states*.
   C. Simulated "patients" are sent through the model and experience some or all of the health states as they progress from health to eventual death or other outcomes of interest.
   D. The rate at which patients move from one state to another is determined by transition probabilities that can be either static (do not change over time) or dynamic (allowed to change over time).
   E. The time spent in each state and value attributed to that state contributes to the simulated patient's life expectancy, quality-adjusted life expectancy (QALE), health care costs, or other important outcome measure.
   F. At the end of the simulation, the total time spent by a cohort in each state is added up to determine the average life expectancy, QALE, costs, and other relevant outcomes.

III. Types of Markov Models
   A. Two distinct types of Markov models exist.
      1. Markov chains have transition probabilities that remain constant over time.
      2. A Markov process allows transition probabilities to vary each cycle, allowing for a more realistic model.

IV. Steps in Developing or Interpreting a Markov Model
   A. The initial step of building and interpreting a Markov model is to describe all discrete health states of the disease.

1. The characteristics of each health state and the probability per unit time of moving from one state to the next should be identified.
2. States should be mutually exclusive.
3. Although not absolutely necessary in every model, a state from which it is impossible to leave, termed the absorbing state, should be defined to allow for proper termination and solution of the model.

B. Transition probabilities should then be estimated.
   1. Transition probabilities represent the probability that a patient will move from one state to another in a given time period, termed a cycle.
   2. The sum of the transition probabilities exiting a particular state must equal one.

C. Initial state probabilities should be assigned.
   1. The initial state probability is the likelihood of being in a particular state at the start of the model and depends on the question being addressed by the model.

D. Cycle length and time horizon should be assigned next.
   1. The cycle length is the duration of each cycle in the model and depends on the duration of the disease or condition being modeled, the available literature estimates, and the need for precision in the estimate.
   2. The time horizon is the total duration for which the model is run and depends on the disease or condition being modeled and on the perspective of the analysis.

E. Assign rewards (costs and benefits).
   1. The costs or benefits that patients incur for being in a particular state for a given cycle are attached to each state.
   2. These rewards may be monetary costs, utilities, or some other outcome of interest.
   3. These rewards may change over time, according to the model cycle, in a Markov process.

F. If the purpose of the model is to compare therapies, the next step is to identify treatment options and how they affect important model parameters.
   1. Treatments may impact costs, benefits, and transition probabilities.

G. Run the model according to the predetermined time horizon.
   1. Calculate the costs and benefits associated with each treatment in the model and estimate the incremental cost-effectiveness ratio (ICER) in a treatment model.
   2. Estimate the cost of illness and outcomes associated with a disease or condition in a nontreatment model.

H. Perform sensitivity analysis on each of the model parameters, independently and as a group.
   1. One-way sensitivity analyses should be performed on all model parameters.
   2. The overall variability of the model should be estimated using a Monte Carlo simulation or similar approach.

V. Model Assumptions

A. When designing Markov models, several assumptions are made to keep the calculations simple that may be technically unrealistic for a disease.
   1. Simulated patients in a Markov process are restricted to moving between states only at the end of cycles.
   2. The half-cycle correction factor may be used to address this limitation by mathematically shifting the cycle to make movements between states occur toward the middle of the cycle.
   3. The process of transitioning from one health state to another is independent of all previous transitions, termed the Markovian assumption.
   4. Transition states, tunnel states, tracker variables, using additional states, and limiting the transition process are methods that can be used to create a "memory" in the model to overcome the Markovian assumption.

B. Transition states.
   1. States that accommodate short-term resource use and morbidity, termed transition states, can be introduced into the model to simulate short-term resource use or events.
   2. Transition states ensure that patients who enter them will pass on to subsequent health states within the same cycle.
   3. Costs and benefits can be assigned to the transition state and are only counted during a cycle in which a simulated "patient" passes through that state.

C. Tunnel states.
   1. Tunnel states are specialized states that can only be traversed in a fixed sequence.
   2. Once a patient has entered the tunnel, he or she must continue through the tunnel in one direction.
   3. The patient may exit the tunnel at any point.
   4. Tunnel states differ from normal Markov states in that the costs and benefits can be time-dependent based on when the patient enters the tunnel as opposed to being based on the model cycle.

VI. Assignment of Transition Probabilities and Converting Rates to Probabilities

A. Time-dependent transition rates can be incorporated in two distinct ways.
   1. Each transition probability can be made to be a function of both the present health state and time.
   2. A reference table of values by cycle is a second useful method.

B. Probabilities typically are derived from the published literature or from epidemiologic, health care, or administrative databases.

C. When using data from published literature, an author may have collected and reported the data using a time period that is different than the one that was chosen for the model cycle.

   1. The most appropriate method of determining the annual transition probability from a probability for another time frame is to convert the probability to a rate and then back to a probability for the new time period using this equation: $P[t_1] = 1 - (1 - P[t_t])^{1/t}$ where $P[t_1]$ is the probability we wish to determine, $P[t_t]$ is the probability from the literature, and t is the time period for which the literature probability is reported.

D. The estimates that are entered into the model should resemble the population for which the model applies as closely as possible to produce the best predictions.

E. Sensitivity analyses provide a formal method of testing the impact of model inputs on the predictions of the model.

VII. Solving the Model

A. A Markov model can be solved in three distinct ways: matrix algebra, Markov cohort analysis, and individual probabilistic simulation (Monte Carlo analysis).

   1. The matrix solution for a Markov model requires constant transition state probabilities and thus is only usable for Markov chains.
   2. The matrix method typically is less used in favor of the cohort or Monte Carlo method, which is now possible through decision analysis software.

B. Cohort method.

   1. In the Cohort method a large number or cohort of patients are tracked through the model.
   2. Given a sufficiently long time horizon, most of the cohort will eventually enter the absorbing state.
   3. It is common to apply termination criteria to a cohort when a critical proportion of the cohort has been absorbed or when the incremental rewards fall below a certain threshold (e.g., < 0.001 quality-adjusted life-years [QALY]).
   4. The average lifetime expected costs can be calculated by applying the costs of being in each state by the average amount of time in each state and summing them.
   5. The average QALY per person can be calculated by multiplying the annual utility for being in each state by the average number of cycles spent in each state and summing them.

C. Monte Carlo simulation.

   1. Second order Monte Carlo simulation is another method of calculating variability in a model.
   2. This method of Monte Carlo simulation allows clinicians to enter probability distributions around each of the transition probabilities and rewards.
   3. From this simulation, the mean costs and benefits can be estimated.
   4. 95 percent and other certainty intervals also may be calculated and used in a similar manner to confidence intervals in statistics.
   5. Because the distributions and base case values are subject to the investigator's own biases, caution must always be used in the interpretation of certainty intervals.

D. Half-cycle correction factor.

   1. The assignment of rewards at either the beginning or end of the cycle may result in under- or overestimation of life expectancy and other outcomes of interest, respectively.
   2. The half-cycle correction can be accomplished by assigning only half the reward for the first cycle.
   3. If the model is run for a specific number of cycles, the remaining half-cycle must be made up by adding another half of the reward to the remaining cohort at the end of the model.
   4. Models that run until there is no additional incremental benefit do not require this final step.

E. Discounting.

   1. Discounting is required when looking at outcomes and costs that are incurred in the future.
   2. Discounting is a method of incorporating a time preference to outcomes and costs to estimate what they would be worth in today's terms, called their present value (PV).
   3. Discounting should not be confused with inflation adjustment, which is a method of standardizing past costs so that they represent a consistent amount of purchasing power.
   4. Rates used in analyses have varied widely, from 2 percent to 10 percent for costs, although 3 percent or 5 percent is the most commonly used figure.
   5. Discounting should be applied for each year that the model is run, converting that year's costs (future value [FV]) to a PV according to the following equation:
      $PV = [FV_1 / (1 + r)^1] + [FV_2 / (1 + r)^2] + \ldots + [FV_n / (1 + r)^n]$.

VIII. Example

A. The Case.

Chronic hepatitis C (CHC) is a chronic disease in which important clinical outcomes (e.g., liver cancer and cirrhosis) are often delayed for many years. Markov models have been used extensively to estimate the long-term impact of therapy on CHC. Most existing models of CHC have included the following outcomes: chronic hepatitis

(CH), compensated cirrhosis, decompensated cirrhosis, hepatocellular carcinoma (HCC), orthotopic liver transplantation (OLT), and death. Combination therapy with interferon-α2b (IFN) and ribavirin (RBV) has been established as the treatment of choice for most patients. The addition of a polyethyleneglycol molecule to IFN (PEG) has markedly increased the half-life, allowing for once weekly dosing and an improved response rate.

B. Setting up the model.
   1. For the sake of educational simplicity, the model will only contain CH, cirrhosis, OLT (represented as two separate states to model the changing mortality and costs over time), and death.
   2. The tree structure for the model states is shown in Figure 1.
   3. Similarly, the model can be presented using a tree structure (Figure 2). Branches in the tree to the right of the decision node (blue square) indicate the therapies being compared. The Markov node (circled M) indicates where the Markov process begins. Branches in a Markov decision tree indicate possible states that a patient may enter. Each Markov state is represented by a branch immediately to the right of the Markov node.
   4. The next step is to add further branches from each Markov state that will represent transition paths (Figure 3). Chance nodes (green circle) indicate a chance event that occurs during a cycle (e.g., patient progresses to cirrhosis or dies). The chance event is labeled as a transition state. States emanating from the same decision node should be mutually exclusive and their probabilities should sum to 1. The terminal node (red triangle) indicates the end of the Markov process for a given cycle. At the end of each cycle, patients are redistributed to the state indicated at the right of the terminal node, according to the respective transition probability.
   5. Next, the initial state probabilities are added under the Markov states (Figure 4). Transition probabilities are also added under the transition states as variables. Cycle-specific costs and utilities are attached to each state in the model but are not shown in a tree structure model such as this one. They typically are incorporated using another window.
   6. Finally, the actual initial state probability, transition probability, cost, and utility estimates can be applied to the model variables. These can be entered as numbers for estimates that do not change over time or as tables for those that do change over time.
   7. Estimates of treatment efficacy, abstracted from randomized, controlled trials, are shown in Table 1.
   8. Transition state probabilities, health-related utilities, and cost estimates were obtained from previously published models and are shown in Table 2.
   9. Cost estimates, adjusted to reflect United States dollars in 2002 using the consumer price index for medical services, and utility estimates are shown in Table 3.
   10. The half-cycle correction may be applied by allowing only half the costs and benefits to accumulate in the first cycle.
   11. The model can then be "rolled back" or solved, and the expected values for each treatment calculated.
   12. When solving the model for a cohort of 100 patients and using the half-cycle correction, the costs and utility estimates shown in Table 4 are obtained.

C. Alternatively, the model can be constructed using a spreadsheet program.
   1. After defining the Markov states, the first step in conducting a spreadsheet Markov model is to set up the transition matrix.
   2. The Markov state matrix is developed using the transition matrix and describes the proportion or number of simulated patients that are in each state for each cycle.
   3. The Markov state matrix is set up so that the number of patients in each Markov state in one cycle is the starting point for the next cycle.
   4. Rewards matrices that indicate the costs and utilities for each state and each cycle of the model can then be set up.
   5. The Markov state matrix, cost matrix, and utility matrix should all contain the same number of rows and columns when completed.
   6. The Markov state matrix is then multiplied by the cost matrix and by the utility matrix to create two solution matrices, one for costs and one for utility.
   7. Finally, the solution matrices can be summed to provide the total costs and utility of each therapy and the incremental cost-utility calculated.

D. Interpreting the results.
   1. The entire modeling process is a retrospective one and is subject to the investigator's biases, whether intended or not.
   2. Sensitivity analyses should always be performed to assess which variables are the most critical to the model.
   3. Critical variables that have the ability to influence the decision should be noted and their impact discussed by the model's developers.
   4. If consensus regarding the estimates of those variables in the population cannot be reached, the policy that is developed from this model should reflect that uncertainty.
   5. The model should be easily interpretable and make clinical sense.
   6. All assumptions should be explicitly stated.

7. For a cost-effectiveness or cost-utility analysis, the results should always be presented both separately and as an ICER.
8. Although there is debate on what the threshold is for therapies to be considered cost-effective, there typically is agreement that interventions costing less than $20,000 per QALY should be universally adopted and that those more than $100,000 per QALY should be passed over in favor of more cost-effective therapies.
9. Political issues, an organization's ability to cover costly interventions, and several other factors may play a role in what an organization considers cost-effective.
10. In the analysis, PEG/RBV dominated IFN/RBV, meaning that it is less costly and more effective; this is contrary to what would be expected if only drug costs had been examined.
11. Several limitations existed in the analysis, including potentially overestimating the effectiveness of the two regimens through the use of efficacy studies.
12. Other important differences in costs and patient populations should be investigated by end users of a model such as this one.
13. Furthermore, sensitivity analyses were not included for this demonstration analysis; these would enlighten the end user of the model's limitations.
14. Policies developed from models such as this should be consistent with the results of the model and sensitivity analyses and should not be overly restrictive if sufficient uncertainty in the model's base results exists.

Learning Objectives

1. Differentiate between when to apply a simple decision analysis or a Markov decision analysis to a problem.
2. Develop a Markov decision tree to simulate a disease process.
3. Apply clinical and economic inputs to a Markov decision model using the best available methods.
4. Convert inputs from clinical studies or other sources of information into usable formats for incorporation into a Markov decision model.
5. Compute the expected value of a Markov decision model using a spreadsheet program.
6. Interpret the results obtained from a Markov decision model.

Abbreviations in this chapter

CH	Chronic hepatitis
CHC	Chronic hepatitis C
DATA	Decision analysis by TreeAge
HCC	Hepatocellular carcinoma
FV	Future value
ICER	Incremental cost-effective ratio
IFN	Interferon-α2b
OLT	Orthotopic liver transplant
PEG	Peginterferon
PV	Present value
QALE	Quality-adjusted life expectancy
QALY	Quality-adjusted life year
RBV	Ribavirin
SVR	Sustained virological response
WHO Class	World Health Organization Classification

Introduction

Decision analysis is an explicit method for making choices under uncertain conditions. It accomplishes this by identifying and analyzing all available options, probabilities, and potential outcomes in a quantitative fashion. While the origins of decision analysis lie in economic and game theory, the methodology has gained popularity for assisting decision makers in the field of medicine, where the situations can be complex and the outcomes are life threatening and costly. Most decision analysis can be displayed visually, in the form of a decision tree, which illustrates the temporal and probabilistic relationship between options and outcomes.

There are two commonly employed methods of decision analysis. Simple decision analysis is well-suited for comparing alternative options with relatively immediate impacts. For instance, the clinical approach to treating a patient with community-acquired pneumonia, where the outcomes are usually immediate, is well-suited for simple decision analysis. A more comprehensive overview of simple decision analytic methods is provided in the Decision Analysis chapter of this book.

Chronic conditions are difficult to model using simple decision trees for several reasons. First, clinical outcomes are usually time dependent. For example, the risk of nonsteroidal anti-inflammatory induced gastrointestinal bleeding is not constant with time and is known to increase as a person ages. While it is entirely possible to incorporate time dependent probabilities in a simple decision tree, branch structure quickly becomes organizationally complex and cumbersome to work with. In addition, it is difficult to incorporate a time preference for beneficial and harmful outcomes using simple decision trees. Markov models are an alternative way to arrange the decision process so that it efficiently manages clinical outcomes and time dependent risk changes. Although Markov models can be stand alone models of progression through various health states, they are often combined with simple decision trees in order to predict the long-term effects of therapies.

Overview of Markov Models

A Markov model is designed to simulate the most important aspects of a disease, and can be used to estimate the long-term clinical, humanistic, and economic dimensions of the disease. In a Markov model, the disease is divided up into numerous mutually exclusive health states (Markov states). Simulated "patients" are sent through the model and experience some, or all, of the health states as they progress from health to eventual death or other outcome of interest. The rate at which patients move from one state to another is determined by transition state probabilities that can either be static (do not change over time) or dynamic (allowed to change over time). The time spent in each state and value attributed to that state contributes to the simulated patient's life expectancy, quality-adjusted life expectancy (QALE), health care costs, or other important outcome measures. At the end of the simulation the total time spent by a cohort in each state is added to determine the average life expectancy, QALE, costs, and other relevant outcomes. This may then be compared to another cohort of patients with different model inputs, such as those receiving some type of therapy for the condition.

Types of Markov Models

Two distinct types of Markov models exist. The most simplistic Markov model, the *Markov chain*, has transition probabilities that remain constant over time. This allows for a much greater simplicity in the calculations for solving the Markov chain, but seems unrealistic for most natural disease processes. Markov chains are typically only appropriate for diseases with a short-time horizon, or when the time dependent transition probabilities are not known. When a longer time horizon is considered, time-dependent variability in the transition rates becomes a much greater factor in the estimation error.

The second type of Markov model is termed a *time-dependent Markov process*. In this type of model, transition probabilities are a function of the cycle and can vary. They may be entered directly as a function or changed cycle by cycle in the form of a reference table. In this way, actual numbers, such as population mortality figures, can be entered directly into the model. This type of model is computationally more complex, but is relatively simple to set up using computer programs that are readily available, such as spreadsheet or decision modeling programs.

Steps in Developing or Interpreting a Markov Model

Markov States

The initial step of building and interpreting a Markov model is to describe all discrete health states of the disease. Markov health states have several important features. First, they should be clearly defined and clinically translatable. Second, the characteristics of each health state, and the probability per unit of time of moving one state to the other, should be reasonably well-described in the medical literature. Third, states must be mutually exclusive. This means that a patient could not possibly be in more than one state at any one time. Finally, there should be one state from which it is impossible to leave. This state is termed the *absorbing state* and is necessary for termination (and solution) of the Markov models. In most clinical models simulating a disease process, death is usually the absorbing state. This allows us to calculate lifetime costs, life expectancy, and other important outcome measures.

Transition Probabilities

Transitions occur as patients move from one state to another. These transitions are entered into the model as *transition probabilities* and represent the probability that a patient will move from one state to another in a given period of time. The probability that a patient will remain in a state for that same period of time is also a transition probability.

The period of time over which the transition state probabilities are based is termed the *Markov cycle*.

For a given state in a given cycle, the sum of the transition probabilities exiting that state must equal one. Thus, all simulated patients currently in a particular state must be assigned to a state at the end of the cycle.

Initial State Probabilities

Simulated patients may start in any of the Markov states at the beginning of the simulation. The model may be run with the intent of seeing how a cohort of patients starting in the model in a particular state of health would move through the model. One may want to determine the total costs and utility of patients starting in a particular initial state and allowed to transition until a predetermined proportion of patients have died. Alternatively, one may wish to take a cross-section of the population (e.g., all 60-year-olds) and place them into the model according to the population prevalence for the disease.

Cycle Length and Time Horizon

The choice of cycle length will depend on the disease state being modeled. A common cycle length for lifelong models is 1 year, since most inputs that are available are estimated in 1-year increments. Occasionally, longer cycles such as 5- or 10-year increments may be used if inputs were estimated in longer increments. Conditions with a short life expectancy should be modeled with a relatively short cycle length such as 1, 3, or 6 months to reduce estimation error. Shorter cycles add less error due to the modeling process. However, if shorter cycles are used, it may be more difficult to estimate the transition probabilities and rewards.

The *time horizon* is the total duration for which the model is run. A model may be run until all patients in the model have expired, or for some predetermined period of time. For example, a managed care organization may wish to know the 1-, 2-, and/or 5-year costs associated with a particular disease or therapy to help them manage the costs. However, an academic model may prefer to address lifetime costs from the societal perspective, to better assess the impact of a new therapy on an entire population.

Developing the Model

As mentioned above, disease is depicted by a series of discrete, mutually exclusive states of health (*Markov states*) with a certain probability to move, or transition, to another state (*transition probability*) within a given time frame (Markov cycle). For example, one can imagine that for a particular disease three distinct health states exist: (1) WELL, (2) SICK, and (3) DEAD. A diagrammatic representation of this model is shown in Figure 1. This simplistic model serves as the backbone for the remainder of the chapter from which a larger, more realistic model is built.

In this model, each patient would start in a particular state such as WELL. There are three possible transitions that can occur from the well state: 1) Back to WELL (k_1); 2) To SICK (k_2); or 3) To DEAD (k_3). All transitions from one state to another occur only when the cycle changes. Note that the sum of the transition probabilities k_1, k_2, and k_3 should equal one.

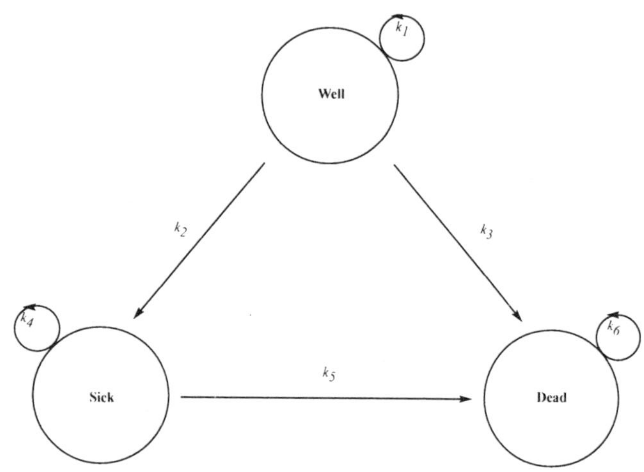

Figure 1. Simple Markov model illustrating 3 Markov states (Well, Sick, and Dead) and the probabilities of transitioning from one state to another each cycle (kn).

For patients in the SICK state, only two transitions are possible: 1) Back to SICK (k_4); or 2) To DEAD (k_5). The way this model has been designed, it is not possible to transition from SICK to WELL, although for some diseases it may be more realistic and desirable to include this transition. The sum of the transition probabilities k_4 and k_5 should equal one.

Finally, for the absorbing state (DEAD) the only transition allowed is back to DEAD (k_6). Transition probability k_6 should equal one, meaning that all patients who are DEAD will transition back to DEAD at the end of the cycle (short of some miraculous future cure for being DEAD).

The model is then run for a predetermined number of cycles, or until a predetermined proportion of patients have entered the absorbing state. The number of cycles each patient remains in each state or the number of people in each state at the beginning of a cycle can be determined. If the model is allowed to run until all patients have died, we can derive the life expectancy of patients with this condition. By attaching a weighted value to each state, such as a utility value or cost, we can easily determine the quality-adjusted life expectancy, or mean expected lifetime cost of the disease.

Rewards: Costs and Benefits

Markov models can yield useful information about life expectancy and the impact of potential therapies without applying rewards to Markov states. However, the true power of a Markov model is in its ability to simulate the costs and health related quality of life incurred over a lifetime based on short-term or incomplete longer-term data. In a Markov model lifetime expected costs may be calculated by applying estimated mean annual costs to each of the states included in the model and allowing the model to run until all patients have died. In the model depicted in Figure 1, we would determine the cost that patients incur for a given cycle in the WELL and the SICK states. We would not expect there to be any costs for patients who reside in the

DEAD state, although there may be some additional costs when transitioning into that state.

Similarly, we can assign utility values to being in a particular state for a cycle. Utility is a comprehensive dimensionless measure of quality of life that is (usually) anchored by 0 and 1. Death is assigned a utility value of 0, while patients in a state of perfect health are assigned a utility score of 1. Other states typically fall somewhere between these two extremes. The most commonly utilized measure in pharmacoeconomic analyses is the quality-adjusted life year (QALY), which is a measure of life expectancy (time) and the quality of life during that time. Other measures of utility * time, such as the years of healthy living, do exist. A more comprehensive discussion of these measures is presented in Chapter 10. If the total QALY gained is divided by the number of simulated patients, an estimate of average utility gained per person can be obtained.

It is also easy to calculate the average life expectancy of the cohort using this method. Assigning a reward of 1 to each state other than death, and a reward of 0 to patients who are dead, will yield the total life-years for the cohort. Dividing this number by the number of patients in the model will give the average remaining life expectancy of the cohort.

Assumptions of Markov Models

There are several assumptions that are made when designing Markov models, to keep the calculations simple, which may be technically unrealistic for a disease. These assumptions, and the limitations that they impose, should always be remembered when evaluating a Markov model. While these assumptions often may lead to inaccuracies in estimation, they do not necessarily invalidate the model as a predictive tool. However, the effects should always be examined and the impact on the model understood, where possible.

For example, the simulated patients in a Markov process are restricted to moving between states at the end of cycles only. Realistically, people with diseases have the capability to move from one health state to another, and then back again at any given time. In fact, it is possible for a real patient to be in multiple states in a period of 1 year (or whatever cycle length is chosen). When the simulation is run for a large number of patients, it is assumed that some of these simplifications average out. The timing at which costs and utilities are assigned also is important. These rewards can be assigned at the beginning, or the end of each cycle. Both of these methods can lead to an over- or under-estimation of the true costs and utility gained. One method developed to reduce this potential estimation bias is called the half-cycle correction factor. It is discussed later in the Half-Cycle Correction Factor section.

A second notable assumption of Markov models is that the process of transitioning from one health state to another is independent of all previous transitions. As a result, the model has no memory of the previous states each patient was in. This characteristic is frequently termed the *Markovian Assumption*. The Markovian Assumption dictates that, regardless of how different individuals arrived in particular health state, their probabilities of transitioning out are all uniform. This can create some difficulties for estimation of diseases where the outcomes for a patient are dependent on the previous states in which that patient has been (e.g., patients with osteoporosis who develop a hip fracture have a higher mortality rate for the first year, and a higher fracture risk that may extend for several years). These types of association with history are common in clinical medicine. Fortunately, there are procedures that can be employed to deal with states that have transition probabilities dependent on past events. *Transition states, tunnel states, tracker variables,* using additional states, and limiting the transition process can all be employed to create a "memory" in the model to overcome the Markovian assumption.

Transition States

Because it is rarely possible for simple Markov models to incorporate the wide range of states in the human condition, specialized Markov states were developed to better simulate health and disease. Many clinical conditions are known to be associated with acute use of resources and decrements to quality of life and life expectancy. For example, the resources consumed and disability incurred immediately after a stroke can be substantial. However, in some patients medical intervention and rehabilitation can return patients to a health state that is at, or near, their health prior to the stroke. Therefore, there is a need for a temporary state that can incorporate the high costs and impact on quality of life associated with the acute hospitalization and rehabilitation associated with having a stroke. States that accommodate short-term resource use and morbidity, termed transition states, can be introduced into the model. Transition states ensure that patients who enter them will pass on to subsequent health states within the same cycle. By doing this, transition states accomplish two goals: 1) assign health qualities and costs that are specific to acute events; and 2) possess transition probabilities that are unique to the acute state.

Figure 2 demonstrates a transition state (ACUTE EVENT) outlined by a dashed line. Patients who are WELL may remain well, experience an acute event, or die. Patients who experience the acute event quickly pass through the event at the end of the cycle and do not remain in the acute event for an entire cycle. They transition to SICK or DEAD where they spend the subsequent cycle according to transition probabilities k_8 or k_9.

We can assign costs or benefits to the transition state ACUTE EVENT just as we would to a Markov state. The difference is that the full rewards are applied one time as patients move through the acute event. This is different from Markov states, where patients can remain in the state for a number of cycles, accruing rewards. The reward is applied at the end of the cycle, just prior to the transition to a new Markov state and simulated patients also accrue the full reward for being in the Markov state for that cycle.

Tunnel States

As mentioned above, one of the main limitations of Markov processes is the lack of a memory. Patients entering a state are treated as every other patient entering that state, regardless of how they got there, or how long they have spent in that state. One method of bypassing the Markovian assumption is the creation of multiple states that determine a patient's progress through the disease. Patients can be forced to follow a set path once a particular event occurs. However, if the transitions are time-dependent and based on how long a patient was in a particular state, this method of creating memory in the model can quickly become unwieldy, resulting in the need for many additional states.

An alternative method for creating memory in a model is to use tunnel states. Tunnel states are specialized states that only can be traversed in a fixed sequence. Figure 3 shows how tunnel states can direct the experience of a patient through progressive disease states in a model. Once a patient has entered the tunnel, she must continue through the tunnel in one direction. However, the patient also may exit the tunnel at any point, which is indicated in this demonstration by transition probabilities k_6, k_9, and k_{11}, where the patient may die. While these states appear to be similar to normal Markov states, they differ in that the costs and benefits can be time-dependent, based on when the patient enters the tunnel, as opposed to being based on the model cycle.

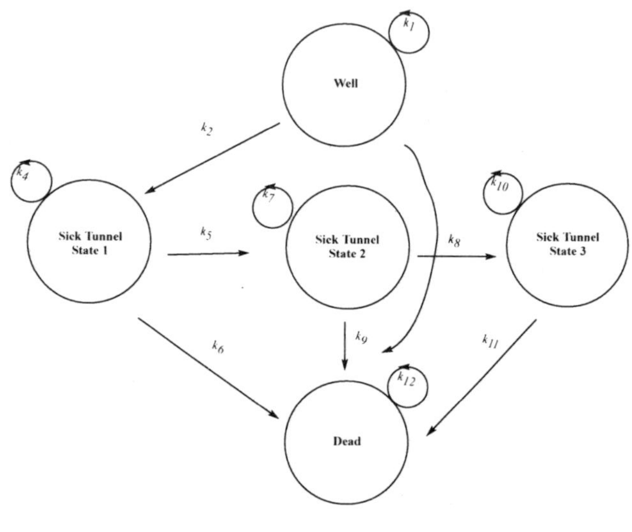

Figure 3. Simple Markov model illustrating a tunnel state (Sick Tunnel State 1 - 3). Once patients enter a tunnel, they must progress through the tunnel in the predetermined manner. Rewards can be assigned to patients in the tunnel according to when they entered the tunnel, instead of according to the number of cycles the model was run creating a "memory" of where a patient was in the model.

Tracker Variables

Decision Analysis by TreeAge (DATA) offers another method of adding memory to a model through tracker variables. These tracker variables act as a flag whenever a patient passes through a particular state. The variables can be used to assign new transition probabilities to patients who passed through a particular state, or can count the number of times a patient passes through a state. One limitation of tracker variables is that they only can be used in association with first order Monte Carlo simulations, since cohort simulations cannot track individual patients.

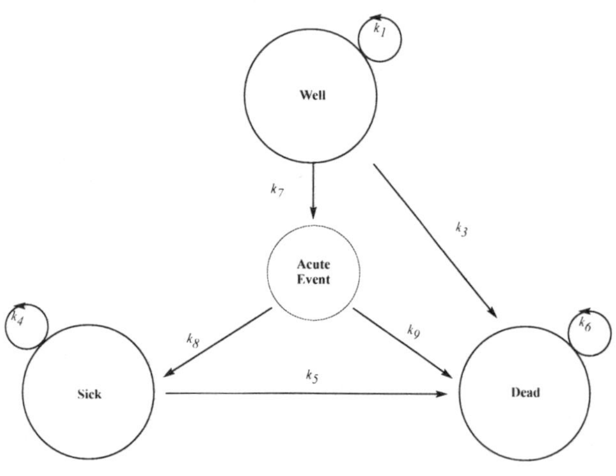

Figure 2. Simple Markov model with 3 Markov states (Well, Sick, and Dead) and 1 transition state (Acute Event) with transition probabilities (kn). Patients do not remain in the transition state for an entire cycle as they do for other states. They move through the transition state at the end of the cycle, and accumulate the respective rewards, and then into another Markov state for the start of the next cycle.

Assignment of Transition Probabilities and Converting Rates to Probabilities

In a previous section we introduced two types of Markov models: those with uniform transition probabilities, and those with time-dependent ones. Time-dependent transition rates can be incorporated in two distinct ways. First, each transition probability can be made to be a function of both the present health state and time. A second method makes use of a reference table of values. This second method is slightly more complicated to incorporate into a model, but can result in much more accurate results, provided sufficient information exists to completely fill in the table.

Until now, we primarily have discussed the generalities surrounding transition probabilities and how they are handled in the modeling process. However, the specifics on how these estimates are derived were not discussed. These probabilities are typically derived from the published literature, or from epidemiologic, health care, or administrative databases. Each data source poses unique strengths and difficulties that must be overcome when estimating transition probabilities.

When using data from published literature, an author may have collected and reported the data using a time period that is different than the one that was chosen for the model cycle. For example, an event of importance (such as patient mortality) may be collected or measured at 2 years, but the model may be designed using an annual cycle. It would be inappropriate to take half of the event rate at two years for the model, as this would overestimate the transition probability due to compounding (see figure 4). One way to think of this compounding effect is as interest on a deposit. If on a \$100 investment the interest rate is 10 percent compounded continuously, the investment will be worth more than \$120 after 2 years. It will actually be worth \$100 x $e^{(0.1)(2)}$ or \$122. Similarly, the effect of continuous compounding on an improperly calculated transition probability could lead to differences in the observed versus the modeled outcome that increase with the number of cycles.

The most appropriate method of determining the annual transition probability from a 2-year probability is to convert the probability to a rate and then back to a probability for the new time period using this equation: $P[t] = 1 - e^{-rt}$ where P[t] is the probability as a function of time, *r* is the rate, and *t* is the time period to which the transition probability is associated. This equation can be simplified to calculate the new probability using a single equation: $P[t_1] = 1 - (1 - P[t_t])^{1/t}$ where $P[t_1]$ is the probability we wish to determine, $P[t_t]$ is the probability from the literature, and *t* is the time period for which the literature probability is reported.

Another important consideration is whether the estimates used in the model can be extrapolated to the population of interest. For example, many models use data from clinical efficacy studies to estimate the impact of a new drug on a health plan, for which effectiveness estimates are more desirable. However, clinical efficacy studies usually have restrictions on patient entry, provide more intense monitoring and follow-up, and enforce patient compliance with therapy by conducting pill counts. If not otherwise altered to account for these potential sources of estimation error, the estimates produced by the model would typically produce higher benefits than what is expected for a health plan population. Adverse event estimates may be higher in a clinical trial due to closer patient monitoring or might be lower due to improved compliance with therapy than is expected in a health plan population.

The estimates that are entered into the model should resemble the population for which the model applies as close as possible to produce the best predictions. As such, an alternative to using clinical trial data is to use the health plan's own data to provide better estimates, noting the limitations of administrative databases. Alternatively, a well-done retrospective analysis from a validated database likely would provide the best input for the model.

If a high-quality estimate is not available, modeling provides the ability to change the estimates entered into the model to test the effect of different assumptions. Therefore, one could test the effect of a lower compliance rate on outcome by lowering the effectiveness of a therapy. *Sensitivity analyses* provide a formal method of testing the impact of model inputs on the predictions of the model. The effect of all inputs on a model's predictions should be systematically tested incorporating all available data. Sensitivity analysis is discussed in detail in the Sensitivity Analysis chapter of this book.

Frequently, inputs into a model are not available from either the clinical literature or from obtainable databases. For example, a model designed to estimate life expectancy of a new therapy in lung cancer may require toxicity probabilities from lung cancer studies. These toxicities are frequently reported using World Health Organization Classifications

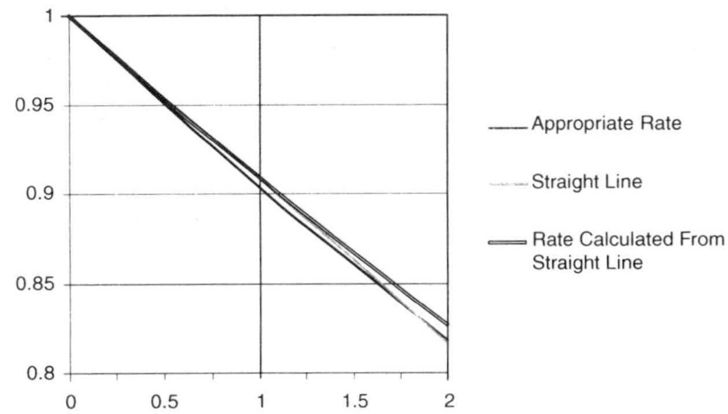

Figure 4. The effect of compounding when estimating a one-year probability from a 2- year probability. The black line represents the way a Markov model would arrive at the 2-year probability and the actual 1-year probability that should be used in the model. The dark gray straight line crosses the black line at the end of the second cycle and represents the rate that would be calculated if we took half of the 2-year probability. The light gray line represents the way the model would run using the probability calculated from the incorrect 1-year probability. If the model were extended beyond the second cycle, the lines would continue to diverge, adding more error into the model with additional cycles.

(WHO Class). Estimating the costs of toxicities from these trials are difficult in the absence of studies that associate WHO Class toxicities with cost. Since the therapy is new, there may be little or no information on resource utilization, or incidence of toxicities of the drug from clinical studies, or from any other databases. In these situations, reasonable inputs may not be available and there are two choices: 1) to prospectively determine the costs through a study or; 2) to use a proxy cost and incidence of toxicity from the studies, understanding the estimates may not be accurate. The decision on which of these approaches to take depends on the impact of a poor input estimate on the model. For inputs that have little impact, it may not be worth the cost of a trial to obtain a better estimate, but for those that affect the model predictions a great deal, a better estimate is essential. Sensitivity analyses should utilize a wider range when the uncertainty associated with an input is higher.

Time-dependent changes in disease progression may be entered into models, but typically require more detailed information of disease progression. While improvements may be made in model estimation when good estimates are available, the potential for increased estimation error exists if there are too few patients in any of the subgroups for a reasonable estimate.

Assignment of State-Related Benefits and Costs

The assignment of state-related benefits and costs, called *state rewards* carries similar pitfalls to the assignment of probabilities, and some additional ones specific to costs and utilities. The states are usually defined according to natural distinct divisions in the disease or, occasionally, according to disease-specific disability scales.

When determining state costs, care should be taken to observe that the perspective is maintained. There are several perspectives from which to choose including the societal, insurer's, patient's, or health system's perspective, but costs should be appropriate to the end users of the model.

Costs should be estimated using the best available sources. There are different methods of estimating costs including micro-costing methods, use of surveys, retrospective analysis of administrative databases using ICD-9 and other disease-specific codes, analysis of hospital cost and charge data, or a mix of these and other methods. Micro-costing methods typically piece together a patient's resource utilization from a variety of sources such as clinical trials and "best practice," and apply costs to these resources to estimate the total cost of care. The cost data may be obtained from fee schedules, administrative claims data, hospital cost and charge data, and published catalogs of drug or equipment prices. Labor costs may be estimated where appropriate by performing time-motion studies and applying salary schedules including overhead costs to the results of these studies. Micro-costing methods have the advantage of focusing on disease-specific costs, but may give estimates of best practice models only, omitting the costs of co-morbid conditions and the inefficiencies of practice in a real-world setting.

Surveys and Delphi methods (expert opinion through polling) also can be used to estimate disease specific costs. These methods are most useful for estimating resource utilization associated with direct non-medical costs, or occasionally, for outpatient costs when no other costing method is available. These methods are subject to memory and other biases and, therefore, should be used only when methods of directly assessing costs are not available.

Retrospective analysis of administrative databases, such as claims data and hospital cost and charge data are another practical method of estimating disease costs. This method typically uses ICD-9 codes, laboratory tests, and/or medications to identify patients with diagnoses similar to the disease of interest. The use of appropriate retrospective statistical techniques, such as multivariate regression can reduce confounding in estimates obtained from administrative databases. Administrative databases have the advantage of estimating all the disease related costs in a real-world setting, but suffer from problems associated with real-world settings. More specifically, patient information may be truncated, or have gaps due to enrollment and eligibility criteria, and ICD-9 codes may not be accurately coded, or may not have enough definition to apply directly to the Markov state. There is often a time lag that must be considered in administrative databases, and they are subject to other problems of accuracy. Ideally, the accuracy of the claims data should be confirmed against another source before being used to estimate costs.

Solving the Markov Model

A Markov model can be solved in three distinct ways: matrix algebra, Markov cohort analysis, and individual probabilistic simulation (Monte Carlo analysis). The matrix solution for a Markov model requires constant transition state probabilities and, thus, is only usable for Markov chains. In the past, matrices provided a quick way to "hand" calculate Markov solutions. This method of solving Markov chains will not be covered in this chapter.

With the advent of the high-speed personal computer and designer decision analysis software, the matrix method is generally less used in favor of the Cohort or Monte Carlo methods, which are more flexible. In addition to being able to handle models with time dependent transition state probabilities, Cohort and Monte Carlo methods offer other distinct advantages over the matrix method. In the Cohort method, a large number, or cohort, of patients are tracked through the model. For each cycle, portions of the cohort are channeled, as dictated by the transition probabilities, to the various Markov health states. Given a sufficiently long-time horizon, most of the cohort eventually enters the absorbing state of death. As the number of cycles increase, a greater proportion of the cohort is absorbed until only a few remaining individuals are alive. It is unlikely that the transitions of these remaining few individuals, frequently referred to as the tail of the cohort, will significantly contribute to the overall costs of illness or life years accrued. It is common to apply termination criteria to a cohort when a critical proportion of the cohort is absorbed, or when the incremental rewards fall below a certain threshold (e.g., $\leq$ 0.001 QALY). Consider applying the transition probabilities in Table 1 to the model illustrated in Figure 1. This model describes a disease process that has a sustained latent period, but also is rapidly fatal upon initial symptoms.

First, notice that transition probabilities from a particular state must equal one. If the probabilities to a theoretic cohort of 1000 diseased individuals who are all initially in the WELL state are applied, how the cohort traverses to the absorbing state of death in Table 2 can be found.

The average life expectancy for this disease is the sum of the time spent in the WELL state, and the sum of the time spent in the SICK state, divided by the number of patients in the model. Table 2 shows that out of a cohort of 100,000 patients, 500,000 life-years were spent in a living state (400,000 in WELL + 100,000 in SICK). The average life expectancy is therefore approximately 5 years (500,000/100,000). The information presented in Table 2 can be presented graphically as shown in Figure 5.

The average lifetime expected costs can be calculated by applying the costs of being in each state by the average amount of time in each state and summing them. Similarly, the average QALY per person can be calculated by multiplying the annual utility for being in each state by the average number of cycles spent in each state and summing them. An example of this is shown in Table 3.

Table 1: Transition probabilities for the simple Markov model.

Transition From	Transition To		
	Well	Sick	Dead
Well	0.75	0.2	0.05
Sick	0	0.2	0.8
Dead	0	0	1

Table 2: Matrix showing how patients with each successive cycle using the simple Markov model.

Cycle	Disease State Well	 Sick	 Dead	Total
1	100000	0	0	10000
2	75000	20000	5000	10000
3	56250	1900	24750	10000
4	42188	15050	42763	100000
5	31641	11448	56912	100000
6	23730	8618	67652	100000
7	17798	6470	75733	100000
8	13348	4853	81798	100000
9	10011	3640	86348	100000
10	7508	2730	89761	100000
....				
25	100	36	99863	100000
....				
50	0	0	100000	100000
Sum expected average time (sum/100,000)	400000 4	100000 1		

Frequently, the purpose of a Markov model is not to estimate the life expectancy, utility, and costs of a disease, but to estimate the incremental cost-effectiveness ratio (ICER) of a new drug, device, or clinical program. The costs of the drug easily can be added into the model as an additional cost for being in a particular state. Likewise the benefits of the drug can be modeled as a risk reduction in the particular event occurring. The model in Figure 1 and the inputs in Table 1 are used to estimate the effects of a hypothetical drug on this disease. Assume the drug slows the progression of the disease and results in a relative risk reduction of death of 0.5. If the drug is taken as prescribed, the probability of dying once contracting the disease drops from 0.8 to 0.4. Assume that the cost of the drug is $12,000 per year. From this information, the ICER of the drug can be calculated by running the model with these new inputs (Tables 4 and 5). The ICER for this drug is:

($46,000 - $12,000)/(5.2 - 4.6 QALYs) =
$56,667 per QALY gained

The final method for evaluating Markov models is the individual or Monte Carlo simulation. Instead of modeling a large cohort, the *first order* Monte Carlo method sends individual patients through the model a large number of times (usually 10,000 or more). The path a patient takes through the model is randomly determined based on the transition probabilities using a random number generator. If the random number generator selects a number less than the transition probability, the patient remains in their current state. If a number larger than the transition probability is selected, the patient moves to the corresponding state. As a result, each simulated patient will take a different path through the model, as actual patients with the disease do. This process is repeated 10,000 or more times, the mean time spent in each state tabulated, and all the rewards calculated to determine costs, life expectancy, and other outcomes of interest. Because the Monte Carlo simulation is governed to some extent by random variation (as determined by the probability distribution), no two simulations of the same probabilities will yield the same estimates, nor will they precisely match the results of the Cohort simulation. However, unlike the cohort analysis, the Monte Carlo method will also quantify the variability and precision around each estimate. Unfortunately, this method may underestimate the population variability, since the only parameters that are affected are the transition probabilities.

Second order Monte Carlo simulation is another method of calculating variability in a model. This method of Monte Carlo simulation allows you to enter probability distributions around each of the transition probabilities and rewards. This process results in a smaller variability than a first order Monte Carlo simulation does, and is more synonymous with the standard error of the mean (the variability of expected value estimates around the base-case expected value). From this simulation, 95 percent and other certainty intervals may be calculated, used in a similar manner to confidence intervals in statistics. Since the distributions and base case values are subject to the investigators' own biases, caution must always be used in the interpretation of certainty intervals. This method is described in more detail in the Sensitivity Analysis chapter of this book.

Half-Cycle Correction Factor

Markov model rewards can be assigned at the beginning or the end of each cycle. In the model calculated above, the rewards were assigned to patients at the beginning of the cycle (i.e., the full rewards were applied to all 100,000 simulated patients in the first cycle as if all 100,000 went one cycle in the WELL state before transitioning out). The reality is that patients will move in and out of health states throughout the cycle, with an average value somewhere in the middle of the cycle. Therefore, assignment of rewards at either the beginning, or end, of the cycle may result in an

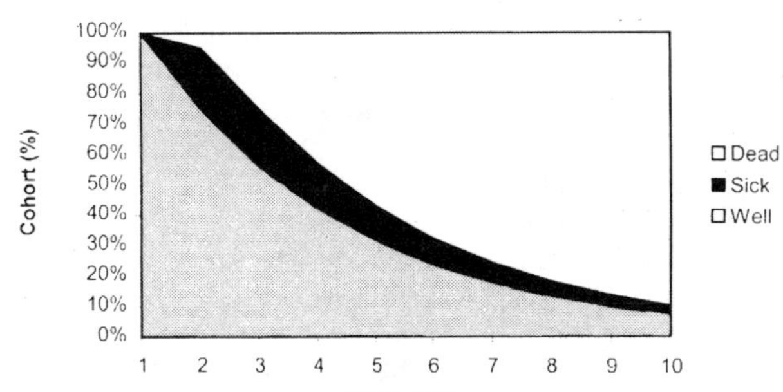

Figure 5: Proportion of cohort in each Markov state of the simple model by cycle.

Table 3: Application of cost and utility rewards to the simple Markov model

WELL Value per Cycle	Number of Cycles	SICK Value per Cycle	Number of Cycles	Avg. per Person
Cost $500	400,000	$10,000	100,000	$12,000
Utility 1.0	400,000	0.6	100,000	4.6000 QALYs

QALY = Quality-adjusted life year

under- or over-estimation of life expectancy and other outcomes of interest respectively.

The half-cycle correction can be accomplished by assigning only half the reward for the first cycle. If the model is run for a specific number of cycles, the remaining half-cycle must be made up by adding another half of the reward to the remaining cohort at the end of the model. Models that run until there is no additional incremental benefit do not require this final step. The impact of this modification is shown in Figure 6. Table 6 shows the model from Figure 1 using the probabilities from Table 1 incorporating the half-cycle correction.

The half-cycle correction is an approximation that hypothetically results in better estimates than if no correction was used.

Discounting

Discounting is required when looking at outcomes and costs that are incurred in the future. Discounting is a method of incorporating a time preference to outcomes and costs to estimate what they would be worth in today's terms, called their present value (PV). It should not be confused with *inflation adjustment*, which is a method of standardizing past costs so that they represent a consistent amount of purchasing power. Discounting looks towards the future and what a particular cost incurred today and/or in the future is worth today.

Since the actual discount rate is seldom known in pharmacoeconomic analyses, there is considerable variability in opinion on what discount rate to use. Rates used in analyses have varied widely, from 2 percent–10 percent for costs, although 3 percent or 5 percent are the most commonly used figures. For outcomes, the appropriate discount rate is even more controversial. In fact, one school of thought is that a discount rate should not be applied to clinical outcomes. However, discounting is inherently applied by populations on clinical outcomes. An extension of life by 1 year is worth more to someone whose mortality is imminent than by someone whose death is 20 years off, despite the equivalent duration of the increased survival. We continuously make life choices that provide immediate satisfaction despite the long-term health consequences, such as smoking. However, when these choices begin to impact our health we often choose to stop doing them indicating that our immediate health is likely of more importance than the lifestyle choices. As a result, consensus appears to be that clinical outcomes should be discounted, although the actual discount rate was not established. In many analyses, the discount rate that was applied to the costs is the one that is used for the clinical outcomes.

Practically, discounting should be applied for each year that the model is run, converting that year's costs to a PV. These costs, called future values (FVs), are added together to come up with the PV for that model variable.

$$PV = [FV_1 / (1 + r)^1] + [FV_2 / (1 + r)^2] + [FV3 / (1 + r)^3] + \ldots + [FV_n / (1 + r)^n]$$

Discounts should be applied to the first year if this year represents a program that would be started the following year or started in the second year if the program is one that is already being offered or could be immediately made available (such as a new therapy). The results of discounting using a rate of 3 percent and 5 percent on the model in Figure 1 using the inputs from Table 1 (with discounting started in the second cycle) is shown in Table 6.

Table 4: Matrix showing how patients transition with each cycle when receiving therapy in the simple Markov model.

Cycle	Disease State Well	Sick	Dead	Total
1	100000	0	0	100000
2	75000	20000	5000	100000
3	56250	27000	16750	100000
4	42188	27450	30363	100000
5	31641	24908	43452	100000
6	23730	21273	54997	100000
7	17798	17510	64692	100000
8	13348	14065	72586	100000
9	10011	11109	78880	100000
10	7508	8668	83824	100000
...				
25	100	36	99767	100000
...				
50	0	0	100000	100000
Sum	400000	200000		

Table 5: Application of cost and utility rewards to the simple Markov model for patients receiving treatment.

WELL Value per Cycle	Number of Cycles	SICK Value per Cycle	Number of Cycles	Avg. per Person
Cost $500	400,000	$22,000	200,000	$46,000
Utility 1.0	400,000	0.6	200,000	5.2000 QALYs

QALY = Quality-adjusted life year

A Clinical Example

Chronic hepatitis C (CHC) is an ideal disease to be modeled using a Markov process since it is a chronic disease in which important clinical outcomes (e.g., liver cancer, cirrhosis) are often delayed for many years. The long term follow-up of treated patients to determine terminal outcomes and cost-effectiveness through clinical trials would be difficult and very costly. Therefore, Markov models were used extensively to estimate the long-term impact of therapy on CHC. Most existing models of CHC include the following outcomes: chronic hepatitis (CH), compensated cirrhosis, decompensated cirrhosis, hepatocellular carinoma (HCC), orthotopic liver transplant (OLT), and death. To date, the inteferons are shown to be the most potent pharmacologic therapy for the treatment of CHC. Combination therapy with interferon-α2b (IFN) and ribavirin (RBV) were established as the treatment of choice for most patients. However, a sustained virological response (SVR), the standard indicator of treatment success, is only achieved in 30 percent–40 percent of IFN naïve patients. The addition of a polyethyleneglycol molecule to IFN to create peginterferon (PEG) was shown to markedly increase the half-life, allowing for once weekly dosing, and an improved response rate. Peginterferon plus RBV were shown in a large randomized controlled trial to be superior to IFN/RBV, and are considered by many to be the new standard of care for CHC. Throughout the remainder of the text, this example will be used to illustrate various technical aspects of Markov modeling.

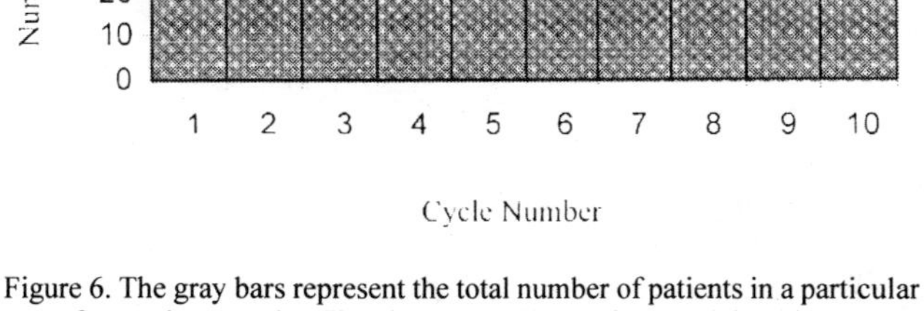

Figure 6. The gray bars represent the total number of patients in a particular state for a given cycle. The time that all people spend in this state is calculated as the area under the curve. The effect of the half-cycle correction factor on this curve is shown as a semi-transparent overlay (darker gray). Notice that without the half-cycle correction, there is an over-estimation of time spent in this state, shown by the area in which there is no overlap.

Setting up Markov Models Using Spreadsheet Programs

Simple Markov cohort simulations can be readily solved using spreadsheet programs. The process is presented in the following section using Microsoft Excel, but can be easily adapted to any other spreadsheet programs. Setting up the spreadsheet makes use of matrices as presented in Table 1 and relative and absolute cell references.

The hepatitis C example introduced in the previous section is used to illustrate the computer exercise. Prior to setting up the computer model, it is often useful to make a Markov-state diagram to describe the disease process. The model used for this demonstration is shown in Figure 7.

The first step in conducting a spreadsheet Markov model is to set up the transition matrix. We are using a 1-year cycle and running the model for 10 cycles. The transitions were obtained from the published literature, and the mortality rates for healthy individuals approximated for individuals 45–55 years of age from the National Center of Health Statistics vital statistics report. The transition matrix for this is shown in Table 7.

The next step is to set up the Markov state matrix. This matrix shows how many patients are in what state at each cycle. The initial number of patients that are entered into this model is 100, a round figure that approximates the number of patients that may be treated within a health care system. All patients will start out in the CHC state. They will transition through the model according to the probabilities in the transition matrix, so to determine the number of

Table 6: Results of the simple Markov model with and without discounting.

	No Discount	3% Discount	5% Discount
Cost	$12,000	$10,703	$9,985
Utility (QALYs)	4.6000	4.2104	3.9941

QALY = Quality-adjusted life year

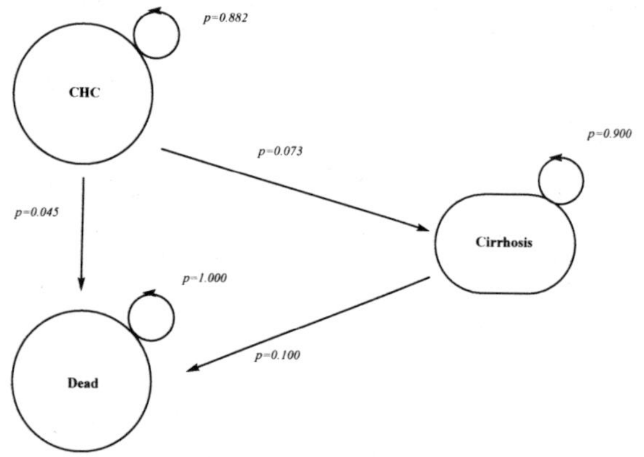

Figure 7: A simple three-state rendition of the chronic hepatitis C model with associated probabilities.

patients in each state in the next cycle we must set up a series of equations that moves them to the appropriate Markov state. These equations are shown in Table 8. (This matrix makes use of Excel's relative and absolute cell references. See the Microsoft Excel instruction manual for more detailed explanations of these useful features.)

The matrix is set up so that the number of patients in each Markov state in one cycle is the starting point for the next cycle. The initial cycle has the 100 patients that are starting in the CHC state. The number of patients remaining in CHC in the second cycle is the number in CHC in the first cycle multiplied by the transition rate (0.882). The number of patients who are in cirrhosis during the second cycle can be calculated by the number of patients in CHC, multiplied by the transition rate for CHC to cirrhosis, added to the number of patients in cirrhosis, multiplied by the transition for cirrhosis to cirrhosis and so on. Once the equations are set up for the first row, you can use the auto-fill feature to drag the calculations down to the tenth cycle. If the equations are entered correctly, the sum of patients in all three states should equal 100 at all cycles. You can provide a quick check by using the auto-sum feature at the end of the row to ensure that each cycle sums to 100 patients.

The next step is to create rewards tables based on literature values, one for costs and one for utility. The annual

Table 7: Transition matrix for the simple CHC model.

Transition From	Transition To		
	CHC	Cirrhosis	Dead
CH	0.882	0.073	0.045
Cirrhosis	0	0.9	0.100
Dead	0	0	1.00

CH = Chronic hepatitis

cost of CHC is $364 and cirrhosis has an annual cost of $25,194. Utility values for CHC and cirrhosis are 0.82 and 0.72, respectively. The tables for these inputs are shown in Tables 9 and 10. The tables should be formatted similar to these to make the *rollback* calculations, the calculations of the expected values, easier.

The first and last rows are different from the others due to application of the half-cycle correction factor (they are divided by a factor of 2). Remember that if the half-cycle correction factor is used, you must include an additional cycle at the end in which half of the normal reward is applied. This is why there are 11 cycles instead of 10 in this model.

The last column contains the adjustment for discounting. The equations in each of the cells refer to the discount row so that the appropriate discount is applied to each of the rewards according to the cycle.

The next step is to calculate the expected value of the model by multiplying the discounted stage reward by the number of people in that state for that cycle. A *solution matrix* is set up as shown in Table 11. These values are then added together to determine the 10-year cost and utility of CHC infection. This sum refers to the costs associated with 100 people, therefore dividing by 100 gives you the expected mean cost per person with CHC infection.

The same process is repeated for the utility inputs and the expected value for 10-year utility calculated. Set up the utility inputs and calculate them as an exercise. The model should yield a cost estimate of $43,442, and a utility estimate of 5.3625 if a 3 percent discount rate is used.

Constructing a Markov Model in DATA

As models become more complicated, and assumptions less reliable, the use of spreadsheet programs to model the decision becomes more difficult and time consuming. Several commercially available computer software programs were developed to help construct and evaluate Markov models. DATA (DATA; TreeAge Software, Inc.) is one of the most widely used decision analysis software available. Along with the ability to perform simple decision analysis, DATA also has Markov modeling, first and second order Monte Carlo simulation, and other advanced sensitivity analysis capabilities. The following exercise expands on the model presented in the previous section to provide a more comprehensive estimate of the cost of hepatitis C and introduce two comparative therapies to the disease. For the sake of educational simplicity our model only contains CH, cirrhosis, OLT, and death. A diagrammatic illustration of the model to be constructed is shown in Figure 8.

The model described below compares the incremental cost-effectiveness of 48 weeks of PEG/RBV to 48 weeks of standard IFN/RBV. Potentially important clinical details such as viral genotype, hepatic histology, and viral load are ignored again for maintaining simplicity of this demonstrative model. Estimates of treatment efficacy were abstracted from randomized controlled trials and are shown in Table 12.

Transition state probabilities, health-related utilities, and cost estimates were obtained from previously published models (Table 13). Cost and utility estimates are shown in Tables 14 and 15. Cost estimates are adjusted to reflect 2002

Table 8: Matrix showing the number of patients in each state at each cycle.

	A	B	C	D	E
1	Cycle	CH	Cirrhosis	Dead	Total
2	1	100	0	0	100
3	2	=B2*0.882	=B2*0.073+C2*0.9	=B2*0.045+C2*0.1+D2*1	=SUM(B3:D3)
4	3	= B3*0.882	=B3*0.073+C3*0.9	=B3*0.045+C3*0.1+D3*1	=SUM(B4:D4)
……					
11	10	= B10*0.882	=B10*0.073+C10*0.9	=B10*0.045+C10*0.1+D10*1	=SUM(B11:D11)

CH = Chronic hepatitis

US dollars using the consumer price index for medical services. The average wholesale prices were used to estimate the acquisition cost of IFN/RBV and PEG/RV.

It is assumed that patients who have a SVR to either interferon-α2b product are considered cured and standard US life tables will determine transition probabilities to death.

Model Structure

Markov models are graphically represented as recursive cycle trees. In other words, they are decision trees that cycle back on themselves, rather than terminate at the end of the branch. At first glance they appear very similar to standard decision trees. However, their properties are distinctly different. The first step in constructing the Markov model in DATA, similar to other types of decision analysis, consists of a decision node that branches into the two comparator arms: PEG/RBV and IFN/RBV. In a normal decision analysis the process would then consist of adding the appropriate chance nodes and populating the model with probabilities and payoffs. Markov modeling utilizes a unique node type, the Markov node, to indicate the entrance into the Markov portion of the tree. Choosing "change node type" from the Options menu can be used to select the Markov node.

The branches following a Markov node should represent all health states in the model. Therefore, the model of hepatitis C shown in Figure 8, with six possible health states, can be represented in DATA as having six branches emanating from the Markov node (Figure 9). Branches can be added, changed, and removed using procedures identical to those for standard decision tress.

The next step is to add further branches from each state that will represent transition paths. For example, patients not having a SVR, will automatically enter the CH state from which they can either traverse to the cirrhosis state or remain in CH. Thus, we should create two branches originating from CH, one to cirrhosis, and one back to CH. After creating the two branches, and labeling them appropriately, change the node on the right to a terminal node. Unlike traditional decision trees, terminal nodes do not necessarily represent the final end point of the model. Because the final common state for most Markov models is the absorbing state, the terminal nodes represent linkages

Table 9: Matrix showing costs for each state at each cycle including dicounting.

	A	B	C	D	E
14	Cycle	CH	Cirrhosis	Dead	Discount
15	1	=364/2/E15	=25194/2/E15	0	1
16	2	=364/E16	=25194/E16	0	=1.03*E15
17	3	=364/E17	=25194/E17	0	=1.03*E16
……					
24	10	=364/E24	=25194/E24	0	=1.03*E23
25	11	=364/2/E25	=25194/2/E25	0	=1.03*E24

CH = Chronic hepatitis

Table 10: Matrix showing utility for each state at each cycle including dicounting.

13	G	H	I	J	K
14	Cycle	CH	Cirrhosis	Dead	Discount
15	1	=0.82/2/K15	=0.72/2/K15	0	1
16	2	=0.82/K16	=0.72/K16	0	=1.03*K15
17	3	=0.82/K17	=0.72/K17	0	=1.03*K16
………					
24	10	=0.82/K24	=0.72/K24	0	=1.03*K23
25	11	=0.82/2/K24	=0.72/2/K24	0	=1.03*K24

back to a main branch, or state, in the model. At the terminal node, the cirrhosis transition branch should jump to the cirrhosis Markov state, and the CH transition branch should jump back to the CH Markov state. Repeat this process for all of the remaining nodes. All states will have at least two transition branches, except for the absorbing state of death. The DEAD chance node can be changed to a terminal node without creating any emanating branches.

Notice that OLT is represented by two distinct health states. This is done to facilitate the incorporation of unique costs, utility, and transition probability to death immediately (year 1) after a liver transplant and for subsequent years. The state labeled OLT (year 1) is a temporary state because it can only be passed through once. This unique situation can be handled in several ways by DATA. Only one is discussed in this section. Obviously, remaining in OLT (year 1) for more than one cycle should not be allowed. Therefore, when choosing states when transitioning from OLT (year 1) select OLT (year>1) and DEAD as appropriate. After finishing, your Markov model should appear similar to Figure 10.

Recall from previous discussions, Markov processes will continue indefinitely and incremental rewards accumulated will asymptotically approach zero as the cohort is absorbed. Therefore, a termination criterion needs to be defined for each Markov process. A Markov termination point can be set when a certain threshold in incremental costs/utility is gained or for a specific cycle number. Select the main Markov node and under the "Values" menu select "Markov Termination…" We are simulating a model with life table probabilities for 60 years (from age 40–100), therefore the termination criteria should be set to terminate when the cycle reaches 60 (_stage >59).

Transition State Probabilities

The next step involves populating the model with the appropriate data. Rather than entering raw data, DATA allows unique variables to be entered that represent point

Table 11: Results matrix for the simple CHC Markov. This matrix is obtained by multiplying the matrix in Table 8 by the cost or utility matrix.

26	A	B	C	D
27	Cycle	CH	Cirrhosis	Dead
28	1	=B2*B15	=C2*C15	=D2*D15
29	2	=B3*B16	=C2*C16	=D3*D16
30	3	=B4*B17	=C4*C17	=D4*D17
………				
37	10	=B11*B24	=C11*C24	=D11*D24
38	Total			=SUM (B28:D37)/100

CH = Chronic hepatitis

estimates and any range that the user wishes to vary in the sensitivity analysis. Transition state probabilities are indicated by variables underneath the line of the branch. For bookkeeping purposes, some users prefer to preface variable names with a letter that indicates the variable type, such as the letter "p" before the variable that represents a transition state probability or a "c" prior to a cost variable. Let us designate the transition probability of going from CH to cirrhosis as "pCirrhosis_CH." You can add the actual base-case and sensitivity analysis data by choosing the "define values" option under the values menu. Because all transition probabilities must sum to 1, the other transition probability is simply 1-pCirrhosis_CH. The pound (#) symbol can be entered in the variable area to indicate this when using DATA.

Follow a similar process to define the other transition probabilities for the remaining transition probabilities in the model leaving branches from the SVR state blank for now. Probabilities for living or dying after having a SVR are derived from a life table and will change with each cycle. DATA uses the special notation suffix, "[_stage]," to invoke a table reference for probabilities. Under the alive branch following SVR, type in the variable "normal_life[_stage]," to create a table with this name. Tables in DATA have two columns, one to index the cycle number and the other for the value associated with that cycle. Tables can either be entered by hand, or from other spreadsheets using the cut and paste feature. For the CHC model we shall assume that the average age of patients starting therapy is 40, therefore, the life table should begin at age 41.

Again, you can indicate that the probability of living as "1- normal_life[_stage]" or simply using the pound sign. Finally, the initial probability of having SVR after therapy should be entered using the point estimate and 95 percent confidence interval for the proportion of patients having a SVR from the major clinical trial shown in Table 14. We

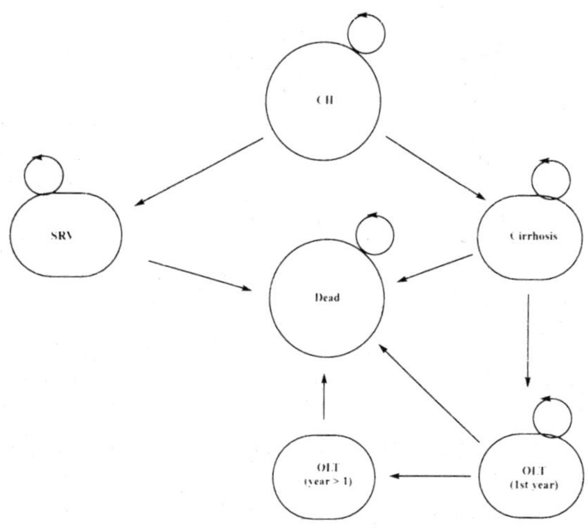

Figure 8. A more structurally complex CHC model, including SVR, CH, Cirrhosis, OLT for the first year, OLT for every year after the first, and Dead.
CH = chronic hepatitis; CHC = chronic hepatitis C; OLT = orthotopic liver transplant; SVR = sustained virologic response.

Table 12: Efficacy of therapy options from a randomized, controlled trial.

Treatment	N	SVR	95% CI	Reference
PEG/RBV	511	0.54	0.49–0.58	Manns MP, 2001.
IFN/RBV	505	0.47	0.42–0.51	Manns MP, 2001.

CI = confidence interval; IFN = interferon; PEG = peginterferon; RBV = ribavirin; SVR = sustained virologic response.

Table 13: Transition rates as estimated from the literature.

	Baseline	Range	Reference
CH			
• To cirrhosis	0.073	0.05 - 0.1	Kim WR, 1997. Bennett WG, 1997.
Cirrhosis			
• To Death	0.1	0.05 - 0.15	Kim WR, 1997. Younossi ZM, 1999.
• To OLT (year 1)	0.03	0.01 - 0.06	Kim WR, 1997. Younossi ZM, 1999.
OLT (year 1)			
• To Death	0.21	0.06 - 0.42	Bennett WG, 1997.
• To OLT (year >1)	0.79	0.94 - 0.58	Bennett WG, 1997.
OLT (year >1)			
• To Death	0.057	0.024 - 0.11	Bennett WG, 1997.

CHC = chronic hepatitis C; OLT = orthotopic liver transplant.

Table 14: Costs associated with CHC as estimated from the literature.

State	Cost	Range	References
CH	$364	$273 - $455	Kim WR, 1997.Younossi ZM, 1999.Bennett WG, 1997.
Cirrhosis	$25,194	$400 - $30,000	Kim WR, 1997.Younossi ZM, 1999.Bennett WG, 1997.
OLT (year 1)	$306,742	$230,057 - $383,428	Kim WR, 1997.Younossi ZM, 1999.Bennett WG, 1997.
OLT (year >1)	$29,537	$22,153 - $36,921	Kim WR, 1997.Younossi ZM, 1999.Bennett WG, 1997.
Cured (SVR)	$150	$100 - $200	Kim WR, 1997.Younossi ZM, 1999.Bennett WG, 1997.
IFN/RBV (48wks)	$21,330	$15,998 - $26,663	DrugTopics Red Book
PEG/RBV (48 wks)	$26,342 $	19,757 - $32,928	DrugTopics Red Book

CH = chronic hepatitis; IFN = interferon; OLT = orthotopic liver transplant; PEG = peginterferon; RBV = ribavirin; SVR = sustained virologic response.

Table 15: Utility associated with CHC as estimated from the literature.

State	Utility	Range	References
CHC	0.82	0.6-0.9	Kim WR, 1997.Younossi ZM, 1999.Bennett WG, 1997.
Cirrhosis	0.72	0.3-0.88	Kim WR, 1997.Younossi ZM, 1999.Bennett WG, 1997.
OLT (year 1)	0.5	0.1-0.7	Kim WR, 1997.Younossi ZM, 1999.Bennett WG, 1997.
OLT (year >1)	0.7	0.2-0.87	Kim WR, 1997.Younossi ZM, 1999.Bennett WG, 1997.
Cured (SVR)	1	0.8-1	Kim WR, 1997.Younossi ZM, 1999.Bennett WG, 1997.

CHC = chronic hepatitis C; OLT = orthotopic liver transplant; PEG = peginterferon; SVR = sustained virologic response.

will assume that patients who fail IFN first traverse to the CH state. Therefore, the probability transitioning to any other state will be 0. When finished, new unique variables for response from PEG/RBV and IFN/RBV are created.

Incremental Rewards Accounting

Recall that a basic principle of Markov modeling is that differing costs and levels of wellness are associated with various Markov health states. The next step in constructing our model involves the assignment of rewards to the states in our model. The utility and costs to be used in the model are shown in Tables 15 and 16. Similar transition state probabilities, and variables for stage costs, drug costs, and stage utilities can be created. This can be done prior to assigning them to the stages, or as you proceed through each branch. Select the CH branch of the model and open "Markov State Information" option under the values menu to create the variable "cCH" and "uCH" to represent the costs and utility associated with CH respectively.

State rewards, both costs and effects, are stored in the fields labeled: "Init," "Incr," and "Final." The field labeled "Rewards" allows up to four rewards to be entered. In our model, reward one is used to indicate costs; reward two to indicate health utility. The field labeled "Incr" (incremental) assigns that reward for every passage through the state. The fields labeled "Init" (Initial) and "Final" will assign that reward only the first time and last time the state is entered, respectively. The initial state reward is useful for assigning initial costs associated with a one-time intervention such as a drug regimen or surgery. It also is used when making half-cycle correction adjustments. The most basic application of the created cost and utility variables would be indicating

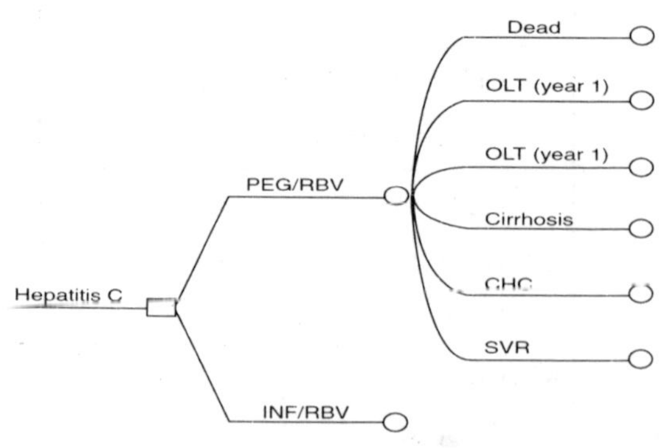

Figure 9.

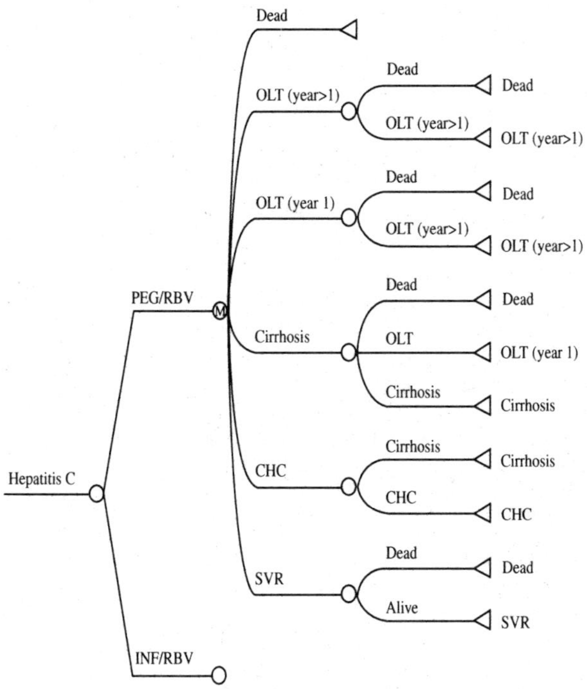

Figure 10.

them in the appropriate incremental reward box. However, because it is standard practice to discount both future costs and benefits, cycle dependent adjustments must be made to each variable. DATA automatically makes these adjustments by incorporating the "UtilDiscount" tool, found under the "Function-medical" button. Within the parentheses the user will then need to specify the reward, discount rate, and time. The discount rate can be entered either as decimal (e.g. 0.03 for 3 percent a year) or variable (e.g., "rDiscount"). It is preferable to use the variable form to allow for sensitivity analysis on the discount rate. The time of discount is typically each cycle and is indicated by the term "_stage." For example, to indicate that the costs of CH discounted for each yearly cycle the following statement would be entered in the incremental field: "UtilDiscount(cCH, rDiscount, _stage)." To indicate that health utility should be discounted, select reward two in the rewards field, and insert the statement "UtilDiscount(uCH, rDiscount, _stage)."

To account for the substantial upfront drug costs in the model, include the variable labeled cPEG/RBV in the initial cost reward field. Repeat this basic process for the remaining states in the tree remembering to include drug costs in the SVR health state also. Because the remaining states can only be reached after passing through the CH first, it is not necessary to incorporate these drug costs into any other states.

The disease process for patients who fail therapy is identical for patients treated with both therapies. Therefore, this initial Markov structure may be simply copied and pasted to the other treatment arm. Once the Markov process is pasted to the other treatment arm the variable for the probability of having SVR to IFN/RBV needs to be defined. The alternative, CH, can be defined as 1-CH, or with the pound sign convention. Also, it is necessary to enter zero probabilities for states other than CH and SVR for initial entry into the Markov process, since the cohort can only enter the model through the states CH and SVR. The finished structure should resemble the one pictured in Figure 11.

Half-Cycle Correction

The final step in completing the PEG/RBV arm of the model adjusts for the half-cycle correction that is necessary for Markov models. Recall, the Markov process calculates the incremental rewards at discrete points either at the beginning or end of each cycle. The half-cycle correction is an adjustment that shifts all transitions one-half step to the left and, in essence, assumes that all transitions occur halfway through the cycle. This is a relatively simple procedure that involves including an initial reward that is half of the incremental reward incurred after cycle one and adding one-half of the incremental reward to the final cycle. Because in this model we are interested in simulating the remaining life of the cohort we can disregard subtracting a half-cycle from the final rewards. To accomplish the half-cycle correction, open the Markov State Information dialog box for each state that accumulates rewards during the first cycle (i.e. CH, SVR) and add the quantity "(0.5 variable of interest)" to the initial rewards field for both costs and effects. For example, the state CH would require the addition of the statement "(0.5 uCH)" for the utility reward and "(0.5 cCH)" for the cost reward. CH and SVR are the only two stages that can be entered in cycle one and, therefore, the only two stages that require the half-cycle correction. If it is expected that a substantial portion of the cohort are not absorbed before cycle termination then similar half-cycle subtraction is required in the final rewards field of each cycle that is entered during the last cycle.

Table 16. Cost, effectiveness, and incremental cost-effectiveness of peginterferon/ ribavirin compared to interferon/ribavirin.

Strategy	Cost	Incremental Cost	Effectiveness	Incremental Effectiveness	Average Cost-effectiveness	Incremental Cost-effectiveness
PEG/RBV	$107.3K		16 QALYs		$6,715/QALY	
IFN/RBV	$114.0K	$6.7K	15 QALYs	-1 QALYs	$7,598/QALY	Dominated

CER = cost-effective ratio; ICER = incremental cost-effective ratio; IFN = interferon; PEG = peginterferon; QALY = quality-adjusted life year; RBV = ribavirin.

Markov Analysis

Assuming all variables are entered correctly and the mathematical statements make sense, evaluation of the Markov model is relatively simple. Prior to analysis, it is helpful to first enter the "preferences" dialog box under the edit menu and make a few adjustments. Under calculation method, select "Cost-Effectiveness," with costs as "1" and effectiveness as "2." It also is possible to specify accuracy of decimal reporting and any units such as dollar signs, or QALYs, using some other functions in the preferences dialog box. The finished Markov model can be evaluated in several different ways. The cost-effectiveness analysis is the most straightforward and quickest analytic tool to evaluate the ICER of this new therapy. Simply select "cost-effectiveness analysis" under the analysis menu. An efficiency plot of costs and benefits will appear. Select text report from the graph menu. The text report will display standard calculations, such as incremental costs, effectiveness, and incremental cost-effectiveness. This can be exported to numerous spreadsheet or word processing applications. Table 16 shows the results of the cost-effectiveness analysis for the two CHC treatment regimens.

The average lifetime treatment costs are $107,300 and $114,000 for the PEG/RBV and IFN/RBV products, respectively. The total QALYs accrued are 16 and 15, respectively. Thus, the model predicts PEG/RBV to exhibit dominance over standard IFN/RBV (less costly, more effective). A more detailed analysis of the model can be obtained if one first selects the Markov node of interest and then selects "Markov analysis" from the analysis menu. A report of the incremental and net costs and benefits accrued over each cycle in addition to a graphical representation can be obtained and exported for further examination. Sensitivity analysis can be performed in a manner similar to that of other decision trees. Feel free to experiment with the finished model to see how changing variables affects the model results!

Interpretation of the Results

Once the model is run and the base-case results obtained, it is important to interpret the results cautiously. The entire modeling process is a retrospective one, and is subject to the investigator's own biases, whether intended or not. Beliefs regarding which studies should be used to estimate the clinical effectiveness of drugs or devices can strongly influence the results, as can populations studies, and methods of obtaining costs. Sensitivity analyses should always be performed to assess which variables are the most critical to the model. Those variables that are critical, and have the ability to influence the decision should be noted and their impact discussed by the users of the model. If consensus regarding the estimates of those variables in your population cannot be reached, the policy that is developed from this model should reflect that uncertainty.

Finally, the model should be transparent and make clinical sense. Transparency refers to the ability to see how each individual variable and equation interact with the rest of the model and how they influence the final results of the model. Ideally, a person should be able to change variables and intuitively predict how the results would change or be able to track the changes. This indicates that the model should be kept as simple as possible, while retaining clinical validity. A model that does not follow the disease's progression, as we understand it, will be of little value in predicting the expected costs and outcomes associated with that disease.

In our clinical example, we used estimates obtained from clinical studies to calculate the impact of PEG/RBV and IFN/RBV on patients with CHC. Therefore, our estimates are likely biased in that the impact of therapy is greater than what would be expected in a naturalistic setting. Cost estimates were obtained from a variety of sources and also may be biased, but not likely in a consistent manner. More importantly, cost estimates may be different from those in another institution or health system. These estimates were predominantly obtained from tertiary teaching hospitals using a variety of methods. These costs should be compared to those of the reviewers' institution(s) and the impact of these costs on the model results assessed. Differences in

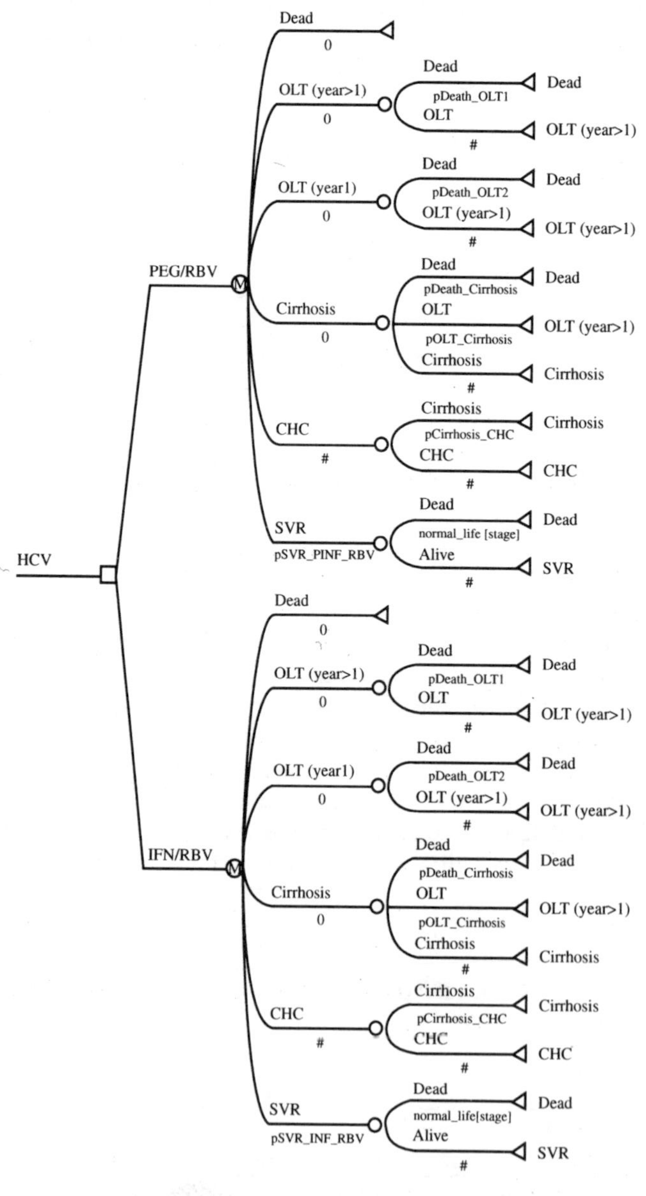

Figure 11.

patient populations between the reviewers' and investigators' institutions also should be closely examined.

Once all sources of bias are critically evaluated, the results of the model can be finally be interpreted. For a cost-effectiveness or cost-utility analysis, the results should always be presented both separately, and as an ICER. Presenting them separately allows the reviewer to determine both the monetary and clinical impact a therapy might have on the population of interest. Knowing these values separately will help to prioritize interventions when limited funding is available or when political pressures come to bear. The results of two competing therapies should always be presented as incremental ratios, since average cost-effectiveness ratios have little or no meaning in the absence of a true baseline.

There is considerable debate on what should and should not be considered cost-effective. Generally, there is agreement that interventions costing less than $20,000 per QALY should be universally adopted, and that those more than $100,000 per QALY should be passed over in favor of more cost-effective therapies. However, most therapies fall somewhere in the "gray zone" between these two extremes. In addition, political consideration must be given to therapies that are novel or unique, and to those that affect politically sensitive areas such as oncology and HIV therapy. These considerations actually underlie some of the debate on what is "cost-effective." Other important considerations are the financial stability of the reviewers' organization, corporate mission, and other corporate and cultural beliefs that may dramatically affect which therapies are adopted. All of these uncertainties emphasize the fact that decision analysis is a very useful *tool* to help make informed decisions, but cannot actually make the decisions for an organization.

This analysis, found that PEG/RBV dominated IFN/RBV, and was less costly and more effective. This analysis is a good example of how pharmacoeconomic analyses can be useful in informing decision makers. If only drug costs were examined, similar conclusions may not have been reached. Although sensitivity analyses were not conducted on this model, PEG/RBV would at least be recommended for inclusion as a treatment option in a health plan. Sensitivity analyses would help to further define the certainty of this result and might lead to the elimination of IFN/RBV from the available treatment options in favor of using PEG/RBV as first line therapy for all patients.

Annotated Bibliography

1. Petitti DB. Meta-Analysis, Decision Analysis, and Cost-Effectiveness Analysis. 2nd ed. New York, NY: Oxford University Press; 2000.

   This textbook covers the principles of decision analysis, including a short section on Markov models. It is a good introductory text that covers most of the relevant topics in a practical manner. One of the strengths of this textbook is its coverage of methods of estimating probabilities including several chapters dedicated to meta-analysis.

2. Eddy DM. A Manual for Assessing Health Practices & Designing Practice Policies: The Explicit Approach. Philadelphia, PA: American College of Physicians; 1992.

   This manual covers the principles of developing practice policies. Chapters include information on types of evidence and biases, collecting and interpreting evidence, combining evidence, use of decision models, and objective methods of comparing health outcomes. Written by one of the leaders in the field, this manual provides an excellent and concise resource for anyone involved in developing practice policies using explicit methods.

3. Beck JR, Pauker SG. The Markov process in medical prognosis. Med Decis Making 1983;3:419–58.

   This is likely the first review of Markov processes in the medical literature. This review covers the fundamentals of developing and solving a Markov model. Model solutions are discussed utilizing matrix algebra.

4. Sonnenberg FA, Beck JR. Markov models in medical decision making: a practical guide. Med Decis Making 1993;13:322–38.

   This journal article covers the basic theory behind Markov models, and provides an overview of how to construct a model. It also provides a clinical example of using a decision tree to aid with clinical decision making. This paper is one of the cardinal papers introducing Markov models to the medical community, although the specifics of how to conduct the analyses are not covered in detail. It updates terminology from the earlier paper by Beck and Pauker.

5. Briggs A, Sculpher M. An introduction to Markov modeling for economic evaluation. Pharmacocconomics 1998;13:397–409.

   This paper is one of the most recent updates and reviews of Markov models in the medical literature. Many of the concepts and terminology are updated, and another illustrative example of a Markov model is offered. This article is well written and easy to read for those who are not familiar with this methodology.

6. Miller DK, Homan SM. Determining transition probabilities: Confusion and suggestions. Med Decis Making 1994;14:52–58.

   This paper discusses the differences between rates and risks, including probabilities, as they apply to medical decision making and other disciplines. It also covers current misuse of these terms and potential sources of this confusion.

7. Doubilet P, Begg CB, Weinstein MC, Braun P, McNeil BJ. Probabilistic sensitivity analysis using Monte Carlo simulation. A practical approach. Med Decis Making 1985;5:157–77.

   This paper addresses the use of Monte Carlo analysis as a type of sensitivity analysis in medical decision making. The concepts of how to apply distributions to point estimates in a model are discussed. Although this paper is mathematically intense, there is an excellent section on selecting appropriate distributions to apply when limited information exists on a parameter's true distribution.

8. Bennett WG, Inoue Y, Beck JR, Wong JB, Pauker SG, Davis GL. Estimates of the cost-effectiveness of a single course of interferon-α2b in patients with histologically mild chronic hepatitis C. Ann Intern Med 1997;127:855–65.

The first of two papers published in the same issue of *Annals of Internal Medicine* estimating the cost-effectiveness of several interferon α-based treatment regimens for chronic hepatitis C. The purpose of this analysis was to estimate the long-term cost and clinical outcomes of a single 6-month course of interferon-α2b. The Markov model describing the natural history of chronic hepatitis C was constructed using 16 distinct health states associated with the disease (e.g., hepatocellular carcinoma [HCC], variceal hemorrhage, ascites, death). Base-case cost-effectiveness figures for a 35 year-old person resulted in an incremental cost-effectiveness ratio of $1900/life year gained and $430/quality-adjusted life years (QALYs), both comparing favorably with currently accepted medical practices.

9. Kim WR, Poterucha JJ, Hermans JE et al. Cost-effectiveness of 6 and 12 months of interferon-alpha therapy for chronic hepatitis C. Ann Intern Med 1997;127:866–74.

   The objective of this analysis was to compare clinical and economic outcomes for 6 and 12 months of interferon-α2b in four simulated age-specific cohorts. The simulated cohorts consisted of 1000 patients age 30, 40, 50, and 60 (4000 total) in a model described by six transition states: chronic hepatitis C, compensated cirrhosis, decompensated cirrhosis, orthotopic liver transplant (OLT), HCC, and death. It was found that compared to no treatment, 6 months of interferon-alpha was slightly more cost-effective than 12 months ($4000/QALY versus $5000/QALY). However, both treatment regimens, compared to no treatment, and the 12 months compared to the 6 months were well within currently accepted thresholds for other health technologies. This was one of the initial published Markov models of hepatitis C that was validated and performed well against a previously published clinical cohort. Other models that describe the natural history of hepatitis C have used similar structured models.

10. Younossi ZM, Singer ME, McHutchison JG, Shermock KM. Cost effectiveness of interferon alpha2b combined with ribavirin for the treatment of chronic hepatitis C. Hepatology 1999;30:1318–24.

    The costs and outcomes of five different treatment strategies, including initial genotyping, were compared in this Markov-based decision analysis. The model of disease progression is similar to others previously published and validated with available long-term data. It was found that a strategy involving initial genotyping to direct length of therapy was the most cost-effective, with an incremental cost-effective ration (ICER) of $7500/QALY. This was one of the first analyses to examine the cost-effectiveness of combination therapy. Also, unlike previous analyses, some utilities were obtained directly from patients using the health utility index mark III.

11. Wong JB, Poynard T, Ling MH, Albrecht JK, Pauker SG. Cost-effectiveness of 24 or 48 weeks of interferon alpha-2b alone or with ribavirin as initial treatment of chronic hepatitis C. International Hepatitis Interventional Therapy Group. Am J Gastroenterol 2000;95:1524–30.

    This cost-effectiveness anaylsis of combination therapy of interferon-α2b and ribavirin for 24 or 48 weeks uses the previously described model of hepatitis C by Bennett WG, et. al. Experts using a delphi technique estimated utilities. Costs were determined using a combination of expert opinion, health resource fee schedules, and published cost estimates. Base-case results indicate that the ICER for 24 or 48 weeks of combination therapy versus 48 weeks of monotherapy was $5400/QALY and $7700/QALY, respectively. This study suggests combination therapy for 24 and 48 weeks are both cost-effective compared to monotherapy for 48 weeks.

12. Manns MP, McHutchison JG, Gordon SC et al. Peginterferon alfa-2b plus ribavirin compared with interferon alfa-2b plus ribavirin for initial treatment of chronic hepatitis C: a randomised trial. Lancet 2001;358:958–65.

    This is the pivotal clinical trial that demonstrated the superiority of peginterferon α-2b in combination with ribavirin over standard interferon-α2b in combination with ribavirin. A total of 1530 patients were randomized to three different treatment regimens: interferon-α2b 3 million units (MU) SQ three times a week plus ribavirin 1000-1200 mg/day, peginterferon α-2b 1.5 mcg/kg/week, plus ribavirin 800 mg/day, or peginterferon α-2b 1.5 mcg/kg each week for 3 weeks then 0.5 mcg/kg/week, plus ribavirin 1000-1200 mg/day for 48 weeks. At the studies end, the primary end point of SVR was achieved in significantly more patients who received high dose peginteferon (54 percent) compared to both lower dose interferon-α2b (47 percent) and standard interferon-α2b (47 percent). The proportion of patients having a sustained virological response (SVR) in this trial is the highest of any published study to date, and has established peginterferon as the new standard of care for patients with chronic hepatitis C.

13. Drug Topics. Red Book. Montavill, NJ: Medical Economicx Co. Inc.; 2002.

    List of pharmaceutical products, recommended pricing, and average wholesale pricing. Frequently used in pharmacoeconomic analyses as a reference price for pharmaceutical products.

14. National Center of Health Statistics: Vital statistics of the United States. Washington, D.C.: Centers for Disease Control and Prevention; 1998.

    Source of vital statistics and life tables used for estimating transition probabilities from a "healthy" state to a "dead" state.

Self-Assessment Questions

1. Developing a Markov decision model is most useful for which one of the following scenarios?

   A. Estimating the effectiveness and/or costs of a single-treatment alternative, including short-term differences in outcomes.
   B. Comparing the effectiveness and/or costs of two-treatment alternatives, including short-term differences in outcomes.
   C. Estimating the effectiveness and/or costs of a single-treatment alternative, including long-term differences in outcomes.
   D. Comparing the effectiveness and/or costs of two-treatment alternatives, including long-term differences in outcomes.

Questions 2–4 pertain to the following case.

You are developing a Markov model that will determine the cost-effectiveness of a novel, more effective and costly treatment (Drug 1) compared with an existing alternative (Drug 2). There was a significant difference in effectiveness in the one available comparative study showing that Drug 1 reduced hip fractures. You also have information demonstrating differing annual costs between patients living posthip fracture and those who remain healthy. There is also a difference in mortality for patients suffering from a hip fracture.

2. Given the following simplistic start of the Markov tree, which one of the following sets of branches is best for node 1?

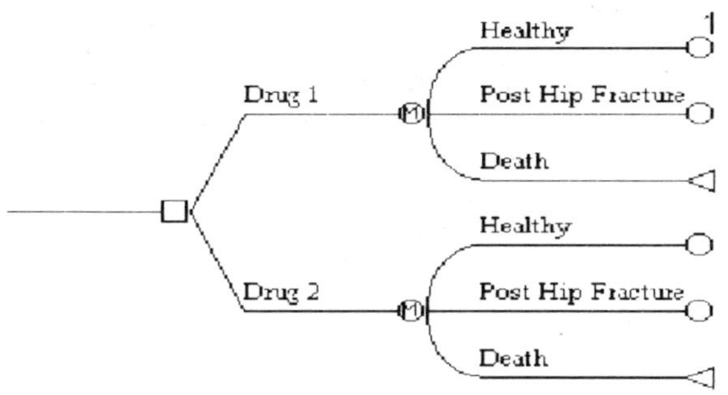

A.

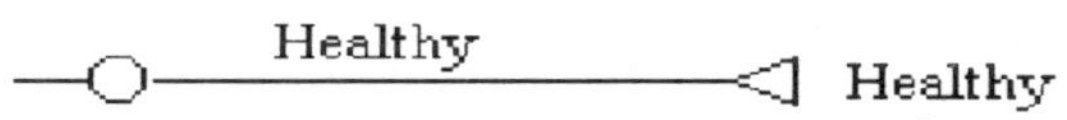

B.

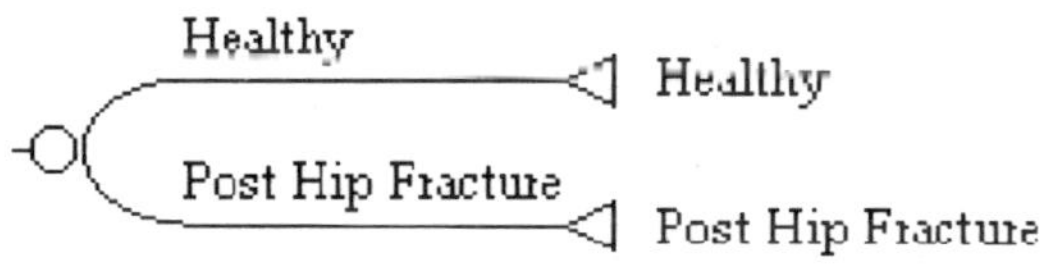

C.

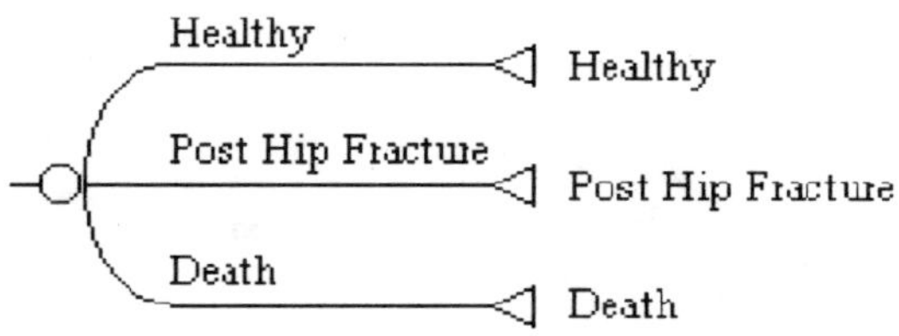

D.

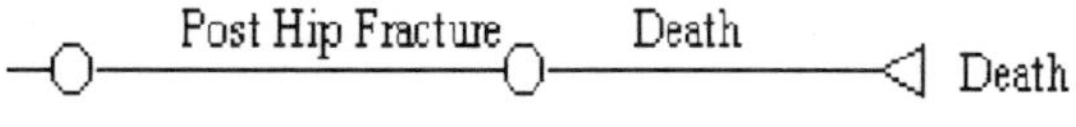

3. The actual event of a hip fracture is associated with a one-time increase in cost and reduction in quality of life. Which one of the following is the best method of applying the cost and reduced utility to the Markov decision tree?
   A. Apply them as initial rewards for the "post hip fracture" state.
   B. Apply them as incremental rewards for the "post hip fracture" state.
   C. Create a temporary state and apply them as transition rewards.
   D. Create a new Markov state and apply them as incremental rewards.

4. After conducting a systematic review of the literature, you have found several clinical trials involving Drug 1 and Drug 2. All of the studies are of similar quality but resulted in differing estimates for the effectiveness of each drug. Which one of the following is the best method of selecting the best base-case estimate for your model?
   A. Select the study with the most conservative estimates.
   B. Select the study with the least conservative estimates.
   C. Use a weighted average of the effects from all studies.
   D. Plot each of the estimates and their variability and select the one study with the smallest variability.

5. You have completed a Markov decision model that compares two drugs for an outpatient condition from the insurer's perspective. You wish to include drug cost estimates in this model that you are aiming to submit for publication. Which one of the following costs is the best to use in the model?
   A. Patient co-payments.
   B. Actual cost of the drugs to a local insurance plan.
   C. A proportion of average wholesale price.
   D. Actual cost of the drugs to a national retail pharmacy chain.

6. You are developing a Markov model that compares the effects of two cancer drugs. The study reports the proportion of deaths in the study after 5 years, but the cycle length you wish to use in your model is 1 year. If the 5-year mortality with one drug is 85 percent, which one of the following is the 1-year mortality (assume that the death rate is constant over the time period of the study)?
   A. 31.6 percent.
   B. 37.9 percent.
   C. 17.0 percent.
   D. 46.1 percent.

7. You wish to discount the costs included in your model over time. The cycle length of your model is 1 year. If the cost of a drug remains constant at $5000 per year and the discount rate is 5 percent, which one of the following is its discounted cost in the fifth cycle of your model?
   A. $5625.
   B. $4114.
   C. $4375.
   D. $6078.

8. Given the following cycle matrix from a Markov cohort simulation, which one of the following is the life expectancy of the cohort?

Cycle	Well	Disabled	Dead	Sum
1	10000	0	0	10000
2	2000	1000	7000	10000
3	400	300	9300	10000
4	80	70	9850	10000
5	16	15	9969	10000
6	3	3	9994	10000
7	1	1	9999	10000
8	0	0	10000	10000

A. 1.25 cycles.
B. 8 cycles.
C. 6.61 cycles.
D. 1.39 cycles.

9. Given the following cycle and utility matrices, which one of the following is the expected utility for this Markov cohort simulation?

Cycle Matrix

Cycle	Well	Disabled	Dead	Sum
1	10000.00	0.00	0.00	10000
2	500.00	500.00	9000.00	10000
3	25.00	50.00	9925.00	10000
4	1.25	3.75	9995.00	10000
5	0.06	0.25	9999.69	10000

Utility Matrix

Cycle	Well	Disabled	Dead
1	1	0.5	0
2	1	0.5	0
3	1	0.5	0
4	1	0.5	0
5	1	0.5	0

A. 1.0803.
B. 1.0526.
C. 1.1080.
D. 1.5000.

10. The process of adjusting a Markov model so that transitions occur continuously throughout the cycle rather than at the beginning or end of the cycle is called which one of the following?

A. Cohort simulation.
B. Monte Carlo simulation.
C. Incremental reward.
D. Half-cycle correction.

11. A Markov model assessing the cost-effectiveness of two antibiotic therapies was performed. Efficacy data were obtained from a prospective, randomized, blinded study that compared the two therapies head to head. Cost data were collected from a retrospective cost-analysis, adjusted for potential confounders. The cost data were listed in a table, but some of the estimates do not appear to be similar to your institutions costs. Sensitivity analyses were not performed. The results are shown in the following table:

Therapy	Cost (U.S. Dollars)	Effectiveness (Life-years saved)	ICER (U.S. Dollars per life-years saved)
A	250	0.53	
B	5000	1.22	6884

If you were asked to interpret the results of this analysis, which one of the following statements is the best summary?

A. Therapy B is definitely cost-effective because the ICER is well below the threshold of $20,000 per life years saved (LYS).
B. This analysis cannot be trusted because cost data were obtained from a retrospective analysis.
C. The use of sensitivity analysis would help to determine if a therapy is truly more cost-effective by providing an estimate of the ICER range.
D. Therapy A is definitely cost-effective because the ICER is well below the threshold of $20,000 per LYS.

SENSITIVITY ANALYSIS

Edward P. Armstrong, Pharm.D., BCPS, FASHP

Outline

I. Purposes of Sensitivity Analysis
- A. Definition of sensitivity analysis.
  - 1. Sensitivity analysis is a process whereby the soundness or robustness of the results and conclusions of economic evaluations are tested by varying the underlying assumptions and variables over a range of plausible values.
  - 2. A sensitivity analysis is not a change in study design but a mathematical manipulation of the study variables.
- B. Used to determine the effect of data uncertainty or assumptions on study conclusions.
  - 1. Finding sensitivity can greatly influence a researcher's interpretation of results and thereby serves as a critical step in conducting pharmacoeconomic evaluations.
- C. Used to identify the most important study assumptions.
  - 1. By identifying sensitive variables, sensitivity analysis can pinpoint areas where additional research is needed to clarify the contribution of specific variables.
- D. Situations when sensitivity analysis should be used.
  - 1. Data elements that are uncertain because no known facts are available and estimates must be used.
  - 2. Data elements that are not precise.
  - 3. Data elements that are unknown because of pharmacoeconomic methodology controversies.
- E. Sources to identify high and low variable ranges.
  - 1. Methodologies and results from previous research.
  - 2. Current literature to identify the usual ranges for variables of interest.
  - 3. Feedback from decision makers who will make health care choices

II. Uncertainty in Pharmacoeconomic Analysis
- A. Variability in the data.
  - 1. If a distribution is available for a specific data element, the 95 percent confidence interval around the mean may be used as the plausible range for sensitivity analysis testing.
- B. Generalizability of results.
  - 1. Researchers must consider how applicable the study results are to different patient populations and within different health systems.
  - 2. Clinical trials impose a range of inclusion and exclusion criteria, as well as specific treatment protocols.
  - 3. Generalizability also is difficult when pharmacoeconomic evaluations are conducted in countries other than that of the health care decision maker.
- C. Extrapolation of results.
  - 1. Extrapolation attempts to predict the final results of pharmacoeconomic studies over time, as well as the role intermediate outcomes play in predicting those results.
- D. Choice of analytical methods.
  - 1. Examples of this type of uncertainty include selection of the discount rate, whether indirect costs were included in the evaluation, and how health outcomes were valued.
  - 2. A large amount of the uncertainty involving analytical methods can be minimized by authors clearly stating the methodologic approaches and assumptions used.

III. Types of Sensitivity Analysis
- A. Simple sensitivity analysis.
  - 1. Simple sensitivity analysis is by far the most common form of sensitivity analysis.
  - 2. In the one-way sensitivity analysis, a single variable is modified over a range of plausible values and the remainder of the variables are held constant.

3. A multiple-way, or multiway, simple sensitivity analysis varies more than one variable simultaneously to determine the effect on the results.

4. Simple sensitivity analyses can be particularly helpful in improving the generalizability of a pharmacoeconomic evaluation.

B. Threshold analysis.

1. Threshold analysis is a modification of a one-way sensitivity analysis where the value of a single variable is varied until the alternative treatment option has the same outcome and there is no advantage between treatment options in the calculated outcome.

2. Threshold analyses are often used to plot variables to demonstrate the circumstances when one treatment option is more cost-effective than another.

C. Analysis of extremes.

1. The analysis considers the upper and lower cost estimates, as well as the upper and lower effectiveness estimates, to determine the best-case and worst-case scenarios.

2. Analysis of extremes is especially useful when data elements are derived from expert panels or whenever the distribution of data points within a range is unknown.

D. Monte Carlo simulation techniques.

1. These analyses have the strength to compute confidence intervals for mean costs, mean effects, and net health benefit (NHB).

2. Monte Carlo simulation allows researchers to assign plausible ranges, as well as an estimate of the distribution of data points, to each variable.

3. Monte Carlo simulation techniques are becoming increasingly popular because they randomly assign values from the variable ranges and estimate outcomes from models with large numbers of hypothetical patients.

IV. Newer Issues in Sensitivity Analysis

A. Net health benefit.

1. The incremental cost-effectiveness ratio is crucial when comparing two products; however, caution should be to excercised when trying to estimate confidence intervals for these ratios.

2. To resolve some of the confusion with the incremental cost-effectiveness ratios, the term "net health benefit" (NHB) was developed.

3. Net health benefit avoids the ratio concerns and incorporates willingness to pay.

4. Because NHB is linear in both cost and effectiveness, statistical inference is more understandable than using a ratio.

5. An "acceptability curve" can be calculated by determining the probability that one treatment was cost-effective relative to the alternative treatment.

V. Limitations of Sensitivity Analysis

A. Need for transparency in study methodology.

1. Because the strength of sensitivity analyses relies on the use of realistic variables, it is important for researchers to state how their variable ranges were selected and to be reasonable in how the ranges within which parameters are varied are chosen.

B. There are no hard and fast rules for interpretation of a sensitivity analysis.

1. There is no standard for what variation in results is reasonable for a study to be considered robust or powerful.

C. Investigators frequently have used sensitivity analysis in suboptimal ways.

1. Improved use of these techniques is necessary to increase readers' confidence in pharmacoeconomic study results.

VI. Examples from the Literature

A. Example of simple sensitivity analysis.

B. Example of threshold analysis.

C. Example of analysis of extremes.

VII. Conclusion and Exercise: Sensitivity Analysis in Formulary Decision Making

Learning Objectives

1. Perform sensitivity analysis and describe its role in evaluating the results of pharmacoeconomic investigations.
2. Detect sources of uncertainty that can be found in pharmacoeconomic assessments.
3. Distinguish between the strengths and limitations of various types of sensitivity analyses.
4. Apply sensitivity analysis to evaluate the results of an economic investigation.
5. Assess the benefits of Monte Carlo simulations in sensitivity analysis.

Abbreviations in this chapter

ADR	Adverse drug reaction
ICER	Incremental cost-effectiveness ratio
NHB	Net health benefit

Introduction

Methodological controversies and assumptions are inherent in many pharmacoeconomic evaluations. Often, there are uncertainties in determining accurate values for cost and outcome variables. Although inferential statistics are an important component of data analysis when conducting and evaluating clinical trials, inferential statistics often cannot be used to test for statistical significance when conducting a pharmacoeconomic evaluation involving decision-analytic modeling. In building models, data from various sources often are combined to produce the probabilities and outcomes. These methodological problems are best addressed by using the technique of sensitivity analysis, which serves as a means to determine the researcher's confidence in a study's results.

Sensitivity analysis is a process whereby the soundness or robustness of the results and conclusions of economic evaluations are tested by varying the underlying assumptions and variables over a range of plausible values. By using sensitivity analysis, a researcher can determine the extent that uncertainty in important variables has influenced conclusions regarding the economic impact of specific clinical decisions. If the conclusions are "sensitive" to the assumptions or biases of the study, then the researcher must ask whether the evaluation was conducted to measure specifically the effects of those assumptions and biases. Finding sensitivity can greatly influence the researcher's interpretation of results and thereby serves as a critical step in conducting pharmacoeconomic evaluations.

In this chapter, the types of data uncertainty that exist in the assessment of economic outcomes, as well as the types of sensitivity analyses that can be used to deal with the uncertainties, are reviewed. Finally, examples of sensitivity analyses found in the literature are reviewed.

Purposes of Sensitivity Analysis

Sensitivity analysis is used to determine the effect of data uncertainty or assumptions on study conclusions. A sensitivity analysis is not a change in study design, but a mathematical manipulation of the study variables. If the study results do not vary substantially when using a range of plausible values in the study variables, confidence in the study results is strengthened and the analysis is described as being insensitive to that variable. On the other hand, if the assumed value in the sensitivity analysis alters the study conclusion, the analysis is described as being sensitive to that variable. Different types of sensitivity analyses can be used to calculate the results separately using different values for particular cost or outcome elements within studies. Sensitivity analyses can be used in conjunction with cost-minimization, cost-effectiveness, cost-utility, and cost-benefit evaluations.

A sensitivity analysis also can be used to identify the most important study assumptions. If the study results change by varying the value of data points within a plausible range for specific variables, the study conclusions are sensitive to the effects of that variable. It is possible that the results of a cost-effectiveness analysis could change simply by selecting different antibiotic cure rates or by using different frequencies of adverse drug reactions (ADRs). By identifying these sensitive variables, sensitivity analysis can pinpoint areas where additional research is needed to clarify the contribution of specific variables. A sensitivity analysis also can identify under what conditions one product is more cost-effective, or with what group of underlying assumptions there is a net benefit to placing a product on a drug formulary. These threshold values between two products can be identified through sensitivity analyses.

Variables tested most often in sensitivity analyses include measures of drug effectiveness or efficacy; prevalence of adverse effects; resource unit costs, such as physician visits, emergency department visits, urgent care visits, laboratory costs, and drug costs; and discount rates.

Three basic factors have been identified (Reference 8) for consideration when determining when to conduct a sensitivity analysis. Examples of situations where these factors occur include: 1) data elements that are uncertain because no known facts are available and estimates must be used (e.g., the frequency of uncommon but expensive adverse effects); 2) data elements that are not precise (e.g., when actual costs for congestive heart failure hospitalizations are not available for a health system); and 3) data elements that are unknown because of pharmacoeconomic methodology controversies (e.g., the selection of the best discount rate).

Identifying high- and low-limit variable ranges for all variables by reviewing methodologies and results from previous research, reviewing the literature to identify the usual ranges found for variables of interest, and obtaining feedback from decision makers who will make health care choices based on the study results also have been suggested. By combining the information from these sources, researchers should be able to arrive at plausible ranges for variables that can then be varied within the sensitivity analysis.

The study results are then recalculated using the most likely estimates as well as the best-case and worst-case scenario estimates. By following this procedure, one treatment choice may dominate other options. However, it is important to recognize that further comparisons may reveal that one agent is preferred in one setting and another agent is preferred in a different setting. When this occurs, it is necessary to determine the point at which one product becomes more cost-effective than another. Decision makers can then review the threshold estimates to determine their real world implications. To use the sensitivity analysis optimally, it is important to state clearly any underlying assumptions, identify areas of uncertainty, and demonstrate how different assumptions may alter the study results.

Uncertainty in Pharmacoeconomic Analysis

The role of sensitivity analysis in assessing potential types of uncertainty was reviewed and four main areas where uncertainty can be introduced were identified (Reference 3). These areas are listed in Table 1 and include uncertainty in the variability of the data, difficulties in generalizing study results to a wider patient population, the challenge of extrapolating results of short-term studies to longer time periods, and the choice of analytical methods used.

Table 1. Sources of Uncertainty in Assessment of Economic Outcomes

Variability in the data
Generalizability of the results
Extrapolation of results
Choice of analytical methods

Sources of Uncertainty

Variability in Data

The first type of uncertainty occurs with *variability in the data.* This is the most obvious reason to perform a sensitivity analysis. Although quite unlikely, if there was no variability or uncertainty in any data element of a study, there would be no need to perform a sensitivity analysis. A pharmacoeconomic evaluation often includes estimates of clinical outcomes, health state indices, resources consumed, or estimates of resource unit costs. If a distribution is available for a specific data element, the 95 percent confidence interval around the mean may be used as the plausible range for sensitivity analysis testing. Another example is when a literature review or expert panel provides a range for a data element, such as rates of drug cure or drug side effects. In this case, the range of cure rates or adverse event rates can be used as the plausible range for sensitivity analysis testing.

However, there are instances when only a single value is available for a data element in an analysis. For example, a value obtained from a single expert or a resource unit cost from one health plan does not provide a range in values. In these settings, sensitivity testing can still be used by changing the value by a reasonable amount, such as raising and lowering the value by 25–50 percent to determine its effect on the study results.

Generalizability of Results

A second type of data uncertainty is *generalizability of the results.* An evaluation often describes the results of an analysis conducted within a specific population of patients in a specific health system. Researchers must consider how applicable the study results are to different patient populations and within different health systems. This type of uncertainty also is referred to as the external validity of the study. A critically important concern of health care decision makers is whether the results conducted in one setting are applicable to another setting. Sensitivity analysis can be quite useful in addressing these generalizability concerns; however, it may not completely answer the question because it is not able to account for limitations in generalizability introduced by the underlying study design.

Generalizability can be difficult if the pharmacoeconomic study was conducted as part of a clinical trial. Clinical trials impose a range of inclusion and exclusion criteria, as well as specific treatment protocols. It is difficult for health care decision makers to determine whether pharmacoeconomic data from clinical trials are applicable to their own treatment settings. Following specific treatment protocols may impose more extensive laboratory monitoring or exclude patients with comorbidities commonly seen in clinical practice. In addition, clinical trial efficacy data, collected under ideal situations, may be both qualitatively and quantitatively different from effectiveness data that measure what real patients and health care providers do in real life. Translating efficacy data to effectiveness data, in part, may be accomplished by use of sensitivity analysis.

Generalizability also is difficult when pharmacoeconomic evaluations are conducted in countries other than that of the health care decision maker. Practice patterns and resource use unit costs may differ greatly among different countries. In addition, patients in different parts of the world may place different values on specific health states or quality of life. A sensitivity analysis is particularly helpful when incorporating international data into a pharmacoeconomic analysis conducted in the United States.

Extrapolation of Results

A third type of uncertainty involves *extrapolation of results.* Extrapolation attempts to predict the final results of a pharmacoeconomic study over time as well as the role intermediate outcomes play in predicting those results. In these situations, intermediate outcomes measured in a 1- or 2-year clinical trial are extrapolated through use of a model over a long-term period such as the next 30 years to predict final outcomes for a hypothetical patient population. For example, a clinical trial might document that a certain treatment regimen is effective in producing blood pressure control; however, a pharmacoeconomic trial will seek information on long-term morbidity and mortality by using the intermediate outcome of reduced blood pressure to develop a model for predicting long-term outcomes. This modeling process introduces uncertainty into the evaluation that becomes greater over time. Sensitivity analysis is important for determining whether the effects of different values for the outcome measures change the results over the 30-year period of the model.

An example of uncertainty with intermediate outcomes is the controversy surrounding selection of the best clinical effectiveness measure for patients with asthma. Some researchers have selected forced expiratory volume in 1 second or peak expiratory flow rates as measures of intermediate outcomes, whereas others have selected symptom-free days, absenteeism from school or work, or histamine-provocative dose testing as intermediate measures. Depending on which intermediate outcomes are chosen, different models with different accuracy for predicting long-term morbidity and mortality may be developed. Uncertainty in these areas may produce large ranges in cost-effectiveness ratios. Sensitivity analysis is clearly an important way to assess extrapolation uncertainty.

Choice of Analytical Methods

The last major type of variance involves *uncertainty in analytical methods*. Examples of this type of uncertainty include selection of the discount rate used, whether indirect costs were included in the evaluation, and how health outcomes were valued. Other sources of uncertainty involve the difficulty in determining opportunity costs. Is it always possible to know what the next best alternative is and its value? It also is difficult to determine the exact cost of some resources. For example, the cost of a capitated primary care physician visit typically is more difficult to determine than if the physician practiced under a fee-for-service system where the charge and the cost are the same. Because there is debate involving optimal methodological approaches, uncertainty is introduced into pharmacoeconomic analyses.

When conducting an economic assessment, a large amount of the uncertainty involving analytical methods can be minimized by clearly stating the methodologic approaches and assumptions used. Although decision makers will not always agree with the methodology, they will know what the methodology was and will be able to make informed decisions based on this transparency in methodology. When evaluating methodology issues, sensitivity analysis is especially useful to determine the impact of different discount rates, different resource unit costs, and the value of including and excluding indirect costs.

Understanding these four sources of uncertainty helps identify instances when sensitivity analysis can be useful.

Types of Sensitivity Analyses

There are four general approaches to sensitivity analysis that can be used to address uncertainty in pharmacoeconomic assessments. Table 2 lists these types of analyses and summarizes some of their important characteristics.

Simple Sensitivity Analysis

Simple sensitivity analysis is by far the most common form of sensitivity analysis and is the type discussed most frequently in review articles. In a simple sensitivity analysis, one or more variables are modified over a range of likely values. The simple sensitivity analysis can be divided into one-way and multiple-way analyses. In a one-way sensitivity analysis, a single variable is modified over a range of plausible values and the remaining variables are held constant. For example, the average cost could be determined by changing an antibiotic cure rate from the highest to lowest range or reasonable values based on the literature. These results could be plotted graphically, demonstrating the change in average cost across the range of cure rates. Figure 1 is an example of a one-way sensitivity analysis by varying a cure rate.

By conducting this analysis across the variables, a one-way sensitivity analysis identifies the separate effect for each variable in the study. If the variables are independent, a series of simple sensitivity analyses may be adequate. An example of a one-way sensitivity analysis is conducting a cost-effectiveness analysis using a range of different discount

Table 2. Four General Approaches to Sensitivity Analysis

Type of Analysis	Characteristics
Simple sensitivity analysis	Most commonly used Useful for generalizing results
Threshold analysis	Finds point at which two options are equal Needs actual data; does not work well with ratios
Analysis of extremes	Compares best- and worst-case scenarios Useful when extremes of data are known or when actual distribution of data is unknown
Monte Carlo simulation analysis	Varies multiple variables within plausible ranges according to the usual distribution of data points

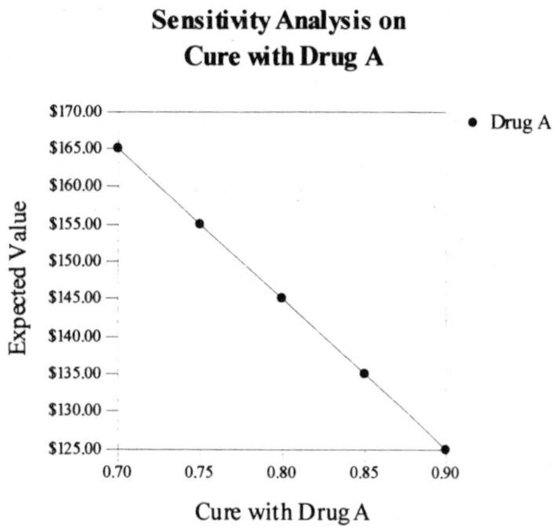

Figure 1. One-way Sensitivity Analysis

rates. If there is a major change in the results, the analysis is said to be sensitive to the effect of the discount rate.

When evaluating a series of one-way sensitivity analyses in a given model, a tornado diagram may be created. A tornado diagram graphically displays a series of one-way sensitivity analyses from the variables which change the answer from the greatest extent to those variables that have the most minor impact on the answer. When the answer ranges for several variables are stacked from lowest to highest, the results mimic a tornado. Computer software can be useful in creating tornado diagrams. Figure 2 provides an example tornado diagram across a range of variables.

A multiple-way, or multiway, simple sensitivity analysis varies more than one variable simultaneously to determine the effect on the results. Computer software, such as Data (TreeAge Software, Inc, Boston, MA), is available to simplify the calculations for multiway sensitivity analyses. For example, a multiway sensitivity analysis may vary a drug side effect rate and the cost to treat a side effect simultaneously. These results may be graphically displayed to demonstrate which treatment alternative is less costly while simultaneously changing at least two variables. For example, Figure 3 summarizes a two-way sensitivity analysis comparing variations in the cure rate with Drug A versus changes in the ADR rate with Drug B. In addition, a multiway analysis may include evaluating the effects of different treatment regimens in the presence of comorbidities. Scenario analysis is another name for multiway simple sensitivity analysis.

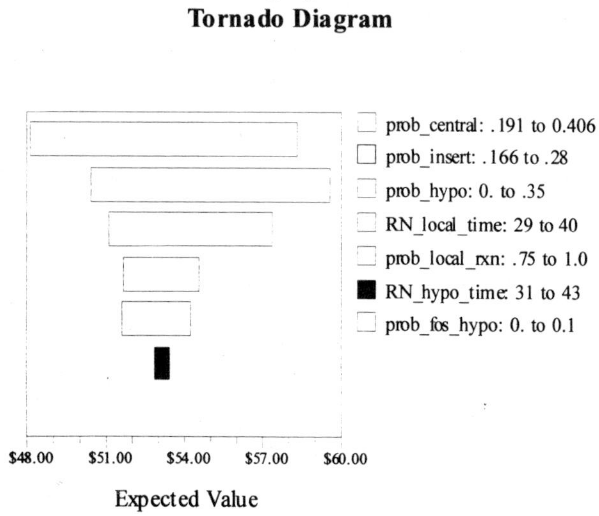

Figure 2. Tornado Diagram Example

For sensitivity analysis to be most useful to decision makers, a rationale or reference for why variable ranges were selected should be provided. Simple sensitivity analyses can be particularly helpful in improving the generalizability of a pharmacoeconomic evaluation. There may be significant differences in resource unit prices between teaching hospitals and community hospitals or between traditional fee-for-service health systems and managed care organizations. Simple sensitivity analyses can be performed over the range of costs of resource units that may be found in these different health systems. In addition, depending on the study perspective, the analysis can be calculated with or without indirect costs. By conducting a sensitivity analysis using different resource unit costs, researchers allow the results to be interpreted by other health systems to determine whether the study is generalizable to their practice settings.

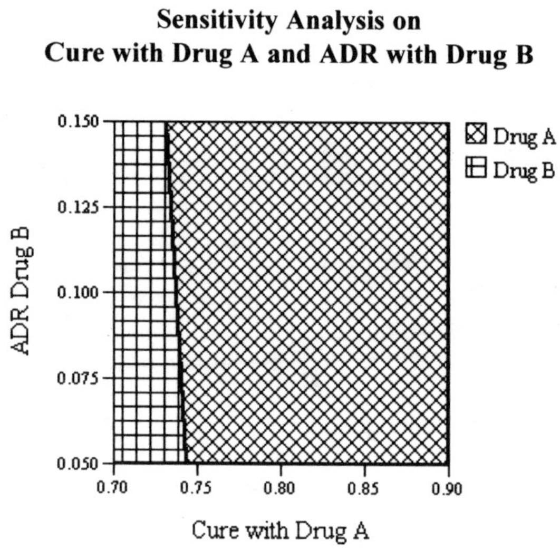

ADR = adverse drug reaction

Figure 3. Two-way Sensitivity Analysis

For example, consider a cost-minimization analysis (Reference 17) to examine the direct costs of monotherapy with carbamazepine, phenytoin, and divalproex for treating complex partial seizures. Two potentially sensitive variables were identified: the cost of drug therapy and the cost to treat ADRs. Using mean values for drug cost, phenytoin (dilantin) was less expensive than either brand name or generic carbamazepine or divalproex. Simple sensitivity analysis was performed by discounting the drug acquisition costs to see if a different agent became less expensive. When altering this single variable, it was found that generic carbamazepine became less expensive than phenytoin only at the low end of the carbamazepine dosage range, indicating that the results were relatively insensitive to drug acquisition costs.

A more detailed example of a study that used simple sensitivity analysis is provided in the "Examples from the Literature" section of this chapter.

Threshold Analysis

Threshold analysis is a modification of a one-way sensitivity analysis where the value of a single variable is changed until the alternative treatment option has the same outcome and there is no advantage between treatment options in the calculated outcome. This threshold also is described as the break-even point in the analysis. It is calculated by altering a variable (e.g., a drug's effectiveness rate) until the model predicts the same answer (e.g., equal average cost) as predicted with the alternative product. Threshold analyses often are used to plot variables to demonstrate the circumstances when one treatment option is more cost-effective than another.

Returning to a literature example (Reference 17) for an illustration of threshold analysis, it is important to recall that the cost to treat ADRs was identified as a potentially sensitive variable, with phenytoin having the lowest cost and divalproex the highest. Only when the cost of treating adverse effects with phenytoin were held constant, and the costs of treating adverse effects for the other two agents were lowered by 50 percent, was carbamazepine found to be less expensive than phenytoin in this regard. In other words, for carbamazepine to be superior to phenytoin, the costs to manage carbamazepine adverse reactions must be reduced by 50 percent of the mean, with phenytoin costs unchanged. Because this is unlikely, the analysis adds strength to the conclusion that phenytoin is less expensive and equally effective to carbamazepine in treating complex-partial seizures.

Threshold analysis is less useful in cost-effectiveness or cost-utility analyses that are focused on incremental cost-to-outcome ratios in which the actual values of data are lost and have been converted into ratio data. However, threshold analysis can be quite useful in cost-minimization analysis by allowing researchers to identify the point when one treatment option becomes less costly than another, as was done in the antiepileptic drug example (Reference 17). With cost-benefit analysis, threshold analysis can be used to identify at what point a NHB is possible with a particular treatment option.

A detailed example of the use of threshold analysis is provided in the "Examples from the Literature" section of this chapter.

Analysis of Extremes

The type of sensitivity analysis known as analysis of extremes is first conducted by using the initial assumption estimates, and is then repeated using variables at their plausible extreme values. The analysis considers the upper and lower cost estimates, as well as the upper and lower effectiveness estimates to determine the best-case and worst-case scenarios. The best-case scenario is found by using the lowest costs for each unit resource along with the highest effectiveness estimates for the outcome unit. Similarly, the worst-case scenario is determined by using the highest cost resource unit estimates combined with the lowest effectiveness estimates. If the same intervention is preferred using initial assumption estimates, the best-case scenario, and the worst-case scenario, there can be a high degree of confidence in the study results.

Analysis of extremes is especially useful when data elements are derived from expert panels or whenever the distribution of data points within a range is unknown. Although analysis of extremes can be useful even when specific data points within a range are unknown, it is not useful for evaluating most types of analytical methodology issues. For this form of analysis to be most useful to decision makers, it is necessary for sufficient detail to be provided so they can decide whether the extremes being evaluated are similar to their own situations. To help readers determine whether their health plan's data are within the range being evaluated, articles should present resource unit costs separately from resource units.

Using the epilepsy example (Reference 17), although researchers did not conduct an analysis of extremes, they could have by using the least and most expensive drug acquisition costs in combination with the least and most expensive costs for managing adverse drug effects, respectively, to evaluate the worst- and best-case scenarios.

A detailed example of how analysis of extremes can be used to compare two drug products is provided in the "Examples from the Literature" section of this chapter.

Monte Carlo Simulation Analysis

Traditional sensitivity analyses have many limitations. In practical application, this type of analysis may be awkward to conduct when varying a few parameters simultaneously. Typically, the results cannot easily be presented graphically when changing several parameters at the same time. Another potential concern is that bias may be introduced (intentionally or unintentionally) because the researcher can choose the variables and ranges to include in any sensitivity analyses. Furthermore, interpretation of sensitivity analyses is not always completely clear as there is not an established benchmark with which to determine variation in results are either robust or sensitive. Finally, changing only one parameter at a time does not take into account possible interactions that may exist if more than one parameter is varied.

Because of the limitations in traditional sensitivity analyses, researchers have developed a probabilistic sensitivity analysis by Monte Carlo simulation. These analyses have the strength to compute confidence intervals for mean costs, mean effects, and NHB. Monte Carlo simulation allows researchers to assign plausible ranges, as well as an estimate of the distribution of data points, to each variable. This is an improvement over the analysis of extremes which does not consider the distribution of data points within a variable range. In clinical settings, it is unlikely that all the worst-case or best-case findings will ever occur at the same time. Monte Carlo analysis can be used to model the distribution of variables when a decision analysis is used as a model. The distribution could be assumed to be uniform across the variable range.

Monte Carlo simulation techniques are becoming increasingly popular because they randomly assign values from the variable ranges and estimate outcomes from models with large numbers of hypothetical patients. Monte Carlo simulation also can be used by rerunning the model in different scenarios, such as including and excluding indirect costs or selecting different resource unit costs for the principal cost drivers. Through Monte Carlo simulations, it is possible to identify the percentage of patients where each treatment option is the preferred treatment choice.

There are two primary approaches in conducting Monte Carlo simulations. There are "first-order" and "second-order" simulations. First-order simulation describes sampling uncertainty that is the random variation in individual patient outcomes within a model. Second-order simulation describes uncertainty in the individual parameters of the model. Recently, authors have suggested cautions with first-order simulations and suggested that second-order simulations are preferred. In second-order simulations each variable has a known range and has a distribution function. Here, the analyst conducting the research randomly samples each parameter in the model and holds these constant while a specific patient is processed through the model. The analyst then randomly selects the next parameters for the variables and the next patient is processed through the model. This process is then repeated a large number of times (often at least 1000 patients) to produce a distribution of mean costs and effectiveness rates for each treatment strategy.

Until recent upgrades were available, software packages did not optimally apply second-order simulations. As of this time, to optimally use second-order simulations, analysts should use DATA 4.0 or DATA Pro by TreeAge.

A limitation to Monte Carlo simulation analysis is that it is unable to address analytical methodology issues. However, its strength is its ability to focus on unknowns in data elements, which are the major concerns for most health care decision makers. As the discipline of pharmacoeconomics and outcomes research expands to include more disease and therapy intervention modeling, Monte Carlo simulations are expected to become more commonly used.

Newer Issues in Sensitivity Analyses

Net Health Benefit

The most common method of comparing two different treatment alternatives is the incremental cost-effectiveness ratio (ICER). When comparing Drug A and Drug B, the ICER formula uses their respective mean values and is calculated as follows:

$$ICER = Cost_B - Cost_A / Effectiveness_B - Effectiveness_A$$

In this equation, the numerator and denominator are the incremental cost and the incremental effectiveness of Drug B relative to Drug A. The ICER is the additional money needed for each additional unit of effectiveness.

Because the ICER is crucial when comparing two products, much attention has focused on estimating uncertainty with this ratio. Different parametric and nonparametric approaches have been described in the literature. However, some authors have raised concern with trying to estimate confidence intervals for ICERs. Cautions include ICERs not having a parametric distribution, the sign of the ICER alone does not identify in which cost-effectiveness "quadrant" the ratio lies, and negative ICER values have no clear meaning. Figure 4 demonstrates a scatterplot of ICERs between two drugs.

Incremental Cost-Effectiveness Scatterplot of Drug A versus Drug B

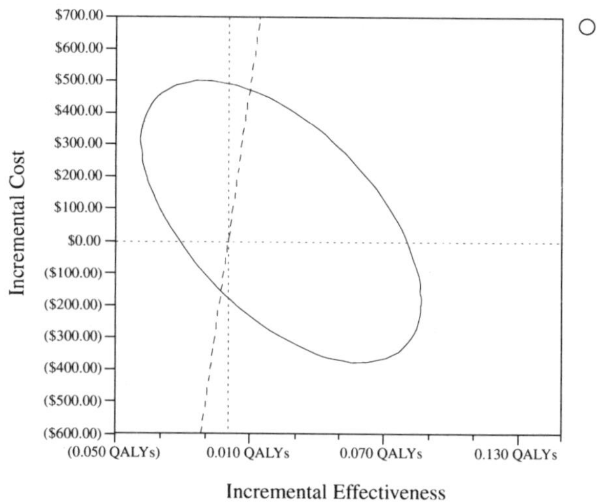

QALY = quality-adjusted life years

Figure 4. Incremental Cost-Effectiveness Scatterplot

To resolve some of the confusion with ICERs, the term net health benefit (NHB) was developed. Although related to ICERs, NHB avoids the ratio concerns by incorporating willingness to pay. In this setting, willingness to pay represents the maximum amount that society (or a health system) is willing to pay for an incremental gain in effectiveness. The strength of NHB is that it represents the net benefit (measured in units of health) of spending resources on one intervention rather than another. The formula for NHB incorporates willingness to pay and is calculated as follows:

$$NHB = (Effectiveness_B - Effectiveness_A) - [(Cost_B - Cost_A) / willingness\ to\ pay]$$

The willingness-to-pay value can be determined by various processes. Because the willingness-to-pay value is not precisely known, it is recommended that the NHB be calculated over a range of different values. Monte Carlo simulation is useful in determining the variability in NHB with one treatment versus another.

Because the NHB is linear in both cost and effectiveness, statistical inference is much more understandable than using ICERs. The meaning of the NHB sign is clear. A positive

NHB indicates favorable value for the product and indicates that it is cost-effective relative to the alternative treatment. Similarly, if the NHB is negative, it indicates a greater improvement in effectiveness could be obtained by avoiding the treatment versus the comparator.

In addition, an "acceptability curve" can be calculated by determining the probability that one treatment was cost-effective relative to the alternative treatment. This is defined as determining the probability that NHB is greater than zero for different willingness-to-pay values. Figure 5 presents an acceptability curve between two products.

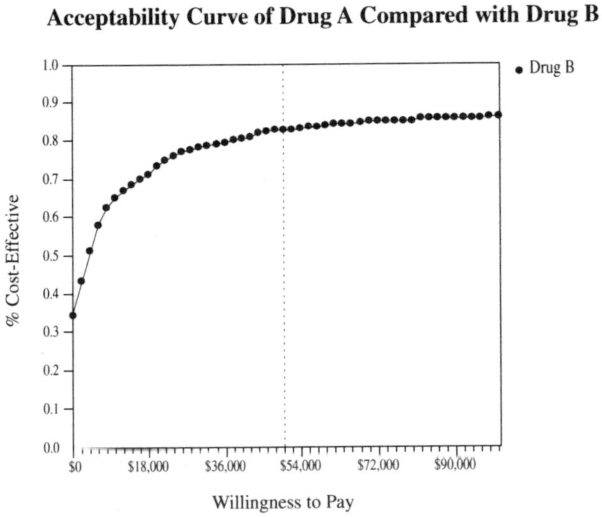

Figure 5. Acceptability Curve Between Two Products

Limitations of Sensitivity Analysis

Although researchers conducting a pharmacoeconomic study have complete freedom to select the variables and range of plausible choices for each variable, this freedom has the potential to introduce bias, whether unintentional or otherwise. Therefore, to minimize the likelihood of researcher bias, models need to be as transparent as possible. Because the strength of a sensitivity analysis relies on the use of realistic variables, it is important for researchers to state how their variable ranges were selected and to be reasonable in how the ranges within which parameters are varied were chosen. For example, if any values are reported using means and standard deviations, researchers could elect to conduct the sensitivity analysis using values within two standard deviations around the sample mean of a specific parameter. It also is reasonable to use the 95 percent confidence interval for a data element as a way to identify a range within which to vary the values of parameters.

Another limitation is that there are no hard and fast rules for interpreting a sensitivity analysis. What one person may believe to be an important finding may not be considered significant by another. This becomes an issue because there is no standard for what variation in results is reasonable for a study to be considered robust or powerful. Certainly, dramatic changes in results can indicate an analysis is sensitive to a specific variable. However, other studies may produce smaller changes, making it less clear to either researchers or readers whether the study should be considered robust.

In addition, although one-way simple sensitivity analysis is the most frequently used form of sensitivity analysis, it has limitations related to its inability to identify interactions between independent parameters. Multiway analysis may be helpful in overcoming this limitation.

A final limitation is that many investigators have used sensitivity analysis in less than optimal ways. A comprehensive review evaluated the use of sensitivity analysis in published health economic evaluations. Ninety-three studies published in 1992 were evaluated by rating the methods used to assess uncertainty systematically and comprehensively in their analyses. Twenty-two of these studies included no assessment of uncertainty, 35 used a sensitivity analysis that the authors judged as being too limited, 36 studies used an adequate sensitivity analysis, and 13 provided a good account of uncertainty in their analysis.

Furthermore, it was found that 51 studies did not consider uncertainty involving the value of resource unit costs and an additional 23 studies did not document their source for resource unit costs. Almost one-third did not generalize results beyond the specific study setting. Sixty-three of these articles did not clearly state the viewpoint of the analysis. One-way simple sensitivity analysis, used in 42 of these studies, was most commonly used, whereas multiway sensitivity testing was used in 15 articles. Threshold analysis was used in 12 reports, five used an analysis of extremes, and one study conducted a Monte Carlo simulation analysis. This review demonstrates that sensitivity analyses are either under reported or underused in many settings. Improved use of these techniques is necessary to increase reader confidence in pharmacoeconomic study results.

Examples from the Literature

Sensitivity analysis is a critically important issue in most pharmacoeconomic publications. The following section discusses three examples from the published literature. The first example illustrates a one-way simple sensitivity analysis. The second example discusses issues of long-term models and the inclusion of indirect costs. Finally, the third study discusses how a sensitivity analysis can be used to make a formulary decision.

Example of Simple Sensitivity Analysis

A recent drug-related morbidity and mortality article (Reference 16) is an excellent example of the use of sensitivity analysis. Investigators developed a conceptual model for drug-related morbidity and mortality and demonstrated that drug-related problems may produce treatment failures, new medical problems, or both as possible negative therapeutic outcomes. In the model, patients experiencing a drug-related problem could have eight possible events as end points: no further attention from a health care professional, another visit to a physician, another prescription drug, an urgent care visit, an emergency department visit, a hospital admission, a long-term care facility admission, or death. These end points were mutually exclusive; that is, their respective probabilities sum to one. This model emphasized ambulatory care and did not attempt to measure drug-related problems within the institutional setting.

No literature or health care databases are available to provide probability estimates for these drug-related problems and their respective costs. Thus, study investigators identified a panel of 15 pharmacist experts in the United States. The panel provided an estimate of the likelihood that treatment failure, a new medical problem, or a combination of both would occur from drug therapy in a typical ambulatory health care setting were pharmacists not able to provide the current level of pharmacy practice. The panel then estimated the percentage of patients who, if they experienced one of these three negative therapeutic outcomes, would require further attention and use of additional health care resources.

Investigators identified the cost-generating outcomes, such as another prescription drug or emergency department visits, and developed a resource unit price list from previous literature and statistical reports. The analysis took the perspective of a third-party payer, such as a managed care organization, and only considered health care costs that were directly associated with treating preventable drug-related morbidity and mortality. Costs for other medical problems and for indirect costs were *not* considered.

Probabilities for each of the therapeutic outcomes were derived from the panel members and placed into the decision-analysis model. The branches on the decision tree were then folded back to determine the average costs for each pathway. The resultant scenario costs provided a weighted average cost of the likely outcomes.

Health care resources consumed with each of the negative therapeutic outcomes were estimated and the total direct costs were calculated by multiplying the unit cost of each service by the total number of health care resources consumed by each pathway. Because the data were largely based on estimates provided by an expert panel, a series of one-way sensitivity analyses were needed. Investigators conducted sensitivity analyses over the range of plausible values for the following variables: ranges for negative therapeutic outcomes provided by the panel, each estimated cost in the model, and prescription noncompliance estimates.

The study indicated that 23.4 percent ± 13.2 percent (mean ± standard deviation of patients would experience some type of treatment failure from drug-related problems; 10.5 percent ± 5.4 percent would have a new medical problem; and 6.5 percent ± 4.1 percent would have both a treatment failure and a new medical problem. When the model was estimated for the ambulatory population of the United States, the estimated cost of drug-related problems was $76.6 billion.

Table 3. Sensitivity Analysis of Drug-related Problems

Scenario	Estimated Cost
Mean values	$ 76.6 billion
Best-case scenario	$ 30.1 billion
Worst-case scenario	$136.8 billion

The results of this study are summarized in Table 3. When the probabilities of negative therapeutic outcomes were varied throughout the ranges provided by the panel, the costs associated with drug-related problems ranged from $30.1 billion for the best-case scenario to $136.8 billion in the worst-case scenario. Study investigators found the analyses were sensitive to the cost assumptions included in the model, particularly costs of hospital and long-term care admissions. For example, using an arbitrary hospitalization cost range of $1000 to $20,000 per hospitalization, drug-related problem costs varied from $37.9 billion to $204.3 billion. Here, the sensitivity analysis demonstrated the need for additional research to clarify the hospital resource costs from drug-related problems. Investigators clearly state the thoroughness of the sensitivity testing and that the cost definitions were transparent.

Example of Threshold Analysis

The literature example of sensitivity analysis involves hormone replacement therapy to prevent hip fractures; in addition, it is an example of a study that did not separate direct and indirect costs in the analysis. A model was developed to calculate health care cost savings by targeting a specific subgroup of 100,000 Caucasian women who were 50 years of age to receive estrogen/progestogen replacement therapy to prevent osteoporosis. The model included an evaluation of the health care costs and cost savings of conducting bone mineral density screening at the time of menopause and treating high-risk women with hormone replacement therapy. The model adjusted for compliance and assumed that 90 percent of the high-risk women, 70 percent of the mid-risk women, and none of the low-risk women would receive hormone replacement therapy for 15 years. Cost savings in the model included both savings in health care costs, such as savings from fewer hip fractures *and* the value of lost productivity. Possible cardiovascular benefits were not included. Therefore, because the cost of lost productivity was included, indirect cost was accounted for and the study was conducted from a societal perspective. The estimate for lost earnings was adjusted to decrease with increasing age. Costs of screening and hormone replacement therapy also were included to obtain the net cost savings.

The model assumed no decrease in fractures would occur until hormone replacement therapy had been used for 5 years. The fracture risk was adjusted for the age of patients and bone mineral density, with higher risk existing in older women and those having lower bone density.

The study results are summarized in Table 4. The study found the net present value of hormone replacement therapy

Table 4. Threshold Sensitivity Analysis of Hormone Replacement Therapy Compliance Rates

Compliance Rate by Risk Group	Results
90 percent of high-risk patients, 70 percent of mid-risk patients, 0 percent of low-risk patients	$5.1 million cost-of-illness savings
77 percent of high-risk patients only	Breakeven cost of illness; screening and therapy costs match health care cost savings
70 percent of high-risk patients, 40 percent of mid-risk patients, 0 percent of low-risk patients	Breakeven cost of illness; screening and therapy costs match health care cost savings

in these 100,000 women for a 40-year period would be $42.9 million and the cost of bone mineral density screening would be $15 million. However, these costs were balanced by a reduction in medical expenses from fewer fractures and lost income after hormone replacement therapy of $63 million, resulting in an overall savings in cost of illness of $5.1 million for women treated according to this model. By conducting threshold sensitivity analyses, it was found that the model was sensitive to compliance. The break-even point could be achieved by screening and treating only the high-risk patients if 77 percent of these patients were compliant with their hormone replacement therapy regimens. The break-even point also could be reached if compliance rates were 70 percent in the high-risk group and 40 percent in the mid-risk group.

No other sensitivity analyses were reported in the article. Although the model adjusted for fracture rates with age, there was no mention of sensitivity analyses involving the range of fracture rates for different age groups. In addition, investigators did not separate out direct and indirect costs. The model estimated a net cost savings of $5.1 million; however, it is not clear if the savings included any direct health care costs. This is an important question for health care decision makers who must generalize these results to their own settings.

Example of Analysis of Extremes

This example of simple sensitivity analysis combined with analysis of extremes is a study, comparing the cost-effectiveness of enoxaparin versus warfarin prophylaxis against deep vein thrombosis after total hip replacement. The acquisition cost of enoxaparin for this indication was $19.55 per day, which was much higher than warfarin's cost of 30 cents per day. An efficacy meta-analysis was performed as no head-to-head comparisons were available in the literature. Investigators developed a cost-effectiveness decision analysis for each product that included data elements for typical patient management information from the published literature and an expert panel of six physicians. The model addressed both clinical and diagnostic probabilities of deep vein thrombosis, including false-positive and false-negative test results, as well as the costs of prophylaxis, diagnosis, and treatment.

From these data, a cost-effectiveness model was developed for a hypothetical cohort of 10,000 patients receiving either enoxaparin or warfarin as deep vein thrombosis prophylaxis. For each regimen, the expected costs associated with prophylaxis, diagnosis, and treatment of thromboembolic events, expected cases of confirmed deep vein thrombosis, expected cases of confirmed pulmonary embolism, and expected deaths from pulmonary embolism were calculated. The ICER was then determined by comparing the differences in cost to the differences in discounted life expectancy between enoxaparin and warfarin. Sensitivity analyses were then done to test the confidence in their results under a range of variable data inputs.

The pooled rates of deep vein thrombosis overall and of distal deep vein thrombosis were lower with enoxaparin than with warfarin. The 95 percent confidence interval for differences between the respective rates of deep vein thrombosis did not include zero, meaning that enoxaparin use resulted in significantly fewer distal thromboses. However, for proximal deep vein thrombosis, the difference between regimens was not significant.

The calculated cost of enoxaparin prophylaxis per patient was more than twice that for warfarin, $245 versus $114. However, because enoxaparin was more effective in preventing thromboembolism, the expected cost for diagnosing and treating deep vein thrombosis and pulmonary embolism was about $10 lower for each patient receiving enoxaparin ($110/patient for enoxaparin versus $120/patient for warfarin). When the costs of prophylaxis were combined with the costs for diagnosis and treatment, the total cost of the enoxaparin regimen was $355, or $121 per patient more than the cost of the warfarin regimen.

The model found that for every 10,000 patients, enoxaparin's higher efficacy would result in three fewer cases of confirmed and treated pulmonary embolism and four fewer deaths than would occur with warfarin. The incremental cost-effectiveness of enoxaparin relative to warfarin was $29,120 per life-year gained. A sensitivity

Table 5. Sensitivity Analysis of Different Enoxaparin Efficacy Rates

Scenario	Cost per Life-Year Saved
Mean values	$29,120
Best-case scenario	$6,000
Worst-case scenario	Model changes to warfarin being both more effective and less costly; warfarin dominates enoxaparin in this scenario

analysis was conducted that revealed the model was most sensitive to the assumption range of enoxaparin's efficacy. These results are summarized in Table 5. Investigators found that if the lower limit, or best-case scenario, of the 95 percent confidence interval for the overall rate of deep vein thrombosis with enoxaparin was used, the ICER decreased to $6,000 per life-year gained. However, if the upper limit, or worst-case scenario, for the rate of deep vein thrombosis with enoxaparin was used, the model favored warfarin, because in this scenario, warfarin became both less costly and more effective. Overall, it was concluded that enoxaparin is more effective than warfarin in lowering the overall incidence of deep vein thrombosis, in spite of its much higher acquisition cost. Again, using mean data, it was estimated that the additional cost per life-year saved would be $29,120 Canadian dollars.

This study addresses a common dilemma of formulary committees. A new drug is available that is better than placebo; however, there are no published head-to-head comparisons with existing agents. Formulary committee members must decide at least two questions based on the analysis. First, they must decide how much they trust the assumptions in the model. Overall, the model demonstrates that enoxaparin may be useful; however, because the sensitivity analysis using enoxaparin's efficacy at the lower range of the 95 percent confidence interval flipped or reversed the study results, it certainly raises an important concern for formulary committees. In addition, because enoxaparin was more effective in preventing distal, but not proximal, vein thromboses, it would have been interesting if a sensitivity analysis had been conducted examining only distal thromboses. The second question relates to the cost-effectiveness ratio. Is $29,120 per life-year saved a reasonable figure? This is a difficult question. Values under $20,000 are often considered desirable; $30,000 is similar to what is observed for some other commonly used therapies such as some antihypertensive regimens. Overall, this study demonstrated that enoxaparin may be a useful product; however, the sensitivity analysis should cause formulary committees to view the results with some caution.

Conclusion: Sensitivity Analysis in Formulary Decision Making

Sensitivity analysis is a critically important step necessary to assess uncertainty within pharmacoeconomic evaluations. By determining the strength of conclusions, researchers and readers can apply their results in ways that are most likely to yield reproducible results in their own practice settings. As the use of sensitivity analysis increases, it is imperative that practitioners have a thorough understanding of its application.

Annotated Bibliography

1. Anon. How to read clinical journals: VII. To understand an economic evaluation (part A) and (part B). CMAJ 1984;130:1428–34,1542–9.

   This two-part article outlines the most important features of pharmacoeconomic evaluations. It provides important questions to ask when reviewing pharmacoeconomic publications. One of these questions is whether a sensitivity analysis was performed. The principal issues concerning sensitivity analysis are nicely highlighted.

2. Briggs A, Sculpher M. Sensitivity analysis in economic evaluation: a review of published studies. Health Econ 1995;4:355–71.

   The authors conducted a methodological review of journal articles published in 1992 to determine whether recently published economic evaluations dealt systematically and comprehensively with uncertainty. They found that 24 percent of studies failed to consider uncertainty at all and 38 percent used sensitivity analysis in an inadequate manner. This is a useful article that demonstrates the failure of researchers to adequately document the sensitivity analyses.

3. Briggs A, Sculpher M, Buxton M. Uncertainty in the economic evaluation of health care technologies: the role of sensitivity analysis. Health Econ 1994;3:95–104.

   The authors of this excellent review of sensitivity analysis discuss the types of data uncertainty found within pharmacoeconomic studies and the different types of sensitivity analyses. Also discussed are the roles different types of sensitivity analysis play when testing the soundness of study results. This article provides an outstanding analysis of the topic.

4. Briggs AH, O'Brien BJ, Blackhouse G. Thinking outside the box: recent advances in the analysis and presentation of uncertainty in cost-effectiveness studies. Annu Rev Public Health 2002;23:377–401.

   This article discusses working with patient level data on both costs and effects. It discusses the cost-effectiveness quadrant plane in comparing the difference in costs and effectiveness between two products. The article emphasizes the issues when either the cost difference or effectiveness difference overlaps a quadrant. In addition, the authors emphasize the usefulness of estimations, the use of net benefit, and the development of cost-effectiveness acceptability curves. This is a useful article that discusses net benefit and issues of sensitivity analyses across different quadrants.

5. Carter BL, Butler CD, Bakht F, Miller JW. Decision analysis as a quality-assurance screening tool. Fam Med 1992;24:362–7.

   The article provides an example of a decision-analysis technique that uses prescribing of antihypertensive drugs and includes a sensitivity analysis. These techniques were used in a clinical quality assurance program. The results suggest that computerized decision-analysis techniques may be useful as an adjunct to other clinical quality assurance procedures in residency training programs.

6. Dao TD. Cost-benefit and cost-effectiveness analysis of drug therapy. Am J Hosp Pharm 1985;791–802.

This is an excellent article summarizing cost-benefit and cost-effectiveness analyses of pharmaceutical products. The article contains a good section that discusses the role of sensitivity analysis and the need to establish boundaries, as with best-case and worst-case analysis.

7. Dittus RS, Roberts SD, Wilson JR. Quantifying uncertainty in medical decisions. J Am Coll Cardiol 1989;14:23A–8A.

   This article emphasizes the importance of effectively handling uncertainty as a principal issue in medical decisions. Sources and effects of uncertainty in medical decision making, and approaches for addressing these problems are reviewed. Branching probabilities and node utilities for probability trees for alternative treatment options are presented. In addition, the article discusses a public domain software package that can be used to create probability trees.

8. Drummond MF, O'Brien B, Stoddart GL, Torrance GW. Methods for the economic evaluation of health care programmes. 2nd ed. Oxford: Oxford University Press, 1998.

   This is one of the most well-known references on pharmacoeconomic analysis and is an outstanding reference text. It includes useful examples of sensitivity analyses.

9. Freund DA, Dittus RS. Principles of pharmacoeconomic analysis of drug therapy. Pharmacoeconomics 1992;1:20–32.

   The authors note the recent value placed on economic analyses with pharmaceutical products. The basic principles of pharmacoeconomic analysis, including study perspective and the four primary analysis techniques, are outlined. The authors emphasize that all modeling assumptions should be described, and that the role of uncertainty in model assumptions and data must be evaluated. Within this article is a helpful discussion of sensitivity analysis.

10. Jolicoeur LM, Jones-Grizzle AJ, Boyer JG. Guidelines for performing a pharmacoeconomic analysis. Am J Hosp Pharm 1992;49:1741–7.

    This useful overview discusses pharmacoeconomic methods and an approach to pharmacoeconomic research. The authors also address uncertainty in economic analyses. Included in the steps are a discussion and an example of using a sensitivity analysis.

11. O'Brien BJ, Drummond MF, Labelle RJ, Willan A. In search of power and significance: issues in the design and analysis of stochastic cost-effectiveness studies in health care. Med Care 1994;32:150–63.

    This article includes a review of two primary types of economic evaluations: models based on assumptions and retrospective data, and prospective economic data obtained in association with clinical trials. The authors included an excellent section on reviewing the limitations of nonsampled data elements and the use of standard sensitivity analysis. The feasibility and desirability of creating statistical tests using 95 percent confidence intervals are discussed in the context of economic hypotheses and estimation of cost-effectiveness ratios, with emphasis on clinical trial data.

12. Sacristan JA, Soto J, Galende I. Evaluation of pharmacoeconomic studies: use of a checklist. Ann Pharmacother 1993;27:1126–33.

    These authors review the fundamental concepts used in pharmacoeconomic analysis and establish a simple model to evaluate systematically the quality of pharmacoeconomic studies. Although the checklist format may be criticized as too simplistic, the article identifies many important issues to consider. Part of this review discusses assumptions and limitations of pharmacoeconomic studies.

13. Stinnett AA, Mullahy J. Net health benefits: a new framework for the analysis of uncertainty in cost-effectiveness analysis. Med Decis Making 1998;18(Suppl):S68–S80.

    These authors discuss the concerns with the general approach of using confidence intervals to explain information with incremental cost-effectiveness ratios (ICERs). The authors recommend, in its place, using a net health benefit (NHB) approach that is more widely applicable and avoids problems associated with ICERs. This is an extremely important topic. When the NHB is positive, the treatment is cost-effective and should be selected in place of the alternative treatment.

Published Studies that Provide Examples of Using Sensitivity Analysis

14. Clark AP, Schuttinga JA. Targeted estrogen/progestogen replacement therapy for osteoporosis: calculation of health care cost savings. Osteoporosis Int 1992;2:195–200.

    Threshold sensitivity analysis was used in this study that examined the effect of different patient compliance rates on the cost of illness for osteoporosis.

15. Edelson JT, Weinstein MC, Tosteson AN, Williams L, Lee TH, Goldman L. Long-term cost-effectiveness of various initial monotherapies for mild to moderate hypertension. JAMA 1990;263:407–13.

    The authors provide an example of using various cost-effectiveness values for a commonly accepted treatment, essential hypertension.

16. Johnson JA, Bootman JL. Drug-related morbidity and mortality: a cost-of-illness model. Arch Intern Med 1995;155:1949–56.

    This article is a good example of extensive sensitivity analysis of a study using an expert panel and literature analysis.

17. Navarro RP, Ashraf T. Cost analysis of carbamazepine, phenytoin, and valproate for use in complex partial seizures. Med Interface (now Managed Care Interface) 1993;6:113–8.

    These authors used threshold sensitivity analysis to evaluate the roles of various anticonvulsant treatments.

18. O'Brien BJ, Anderson DR, Goeree R. Cost-effectiveness of enoxaparin versus warfarin prophylaxis against deep vein thrombosis after total hip replacement. CMAJ 1994;150:1083–90.

    This study provides an example of sensitivity analysis that demonstrated a change in study results within a range of drug efficacy rates.

Self-Assessment Questions

1. Which one of the following is meant when a sensitivity analysis finds that a study's results are sensitive to a specific variable?
   A. The study results vary when using a range of values for the variable, thereby strengthening confidence in the study results.
   B. The study results vary within the range of the values used for the variable, thereby weakening confidence in the study results.
   C. The analysis was not useful for the variable range.
   D. It was an inappropriate variable to be used in a sensitivity analysis.

2. Because of the data variability, a sensitivity analysis is most useful for which one of the following data sources?
   A. Precise cost figures from a large data set.
   B. Average wholesale drug prices for a recently approved product.
   C. Efficacy results from a randomized, clinical trial.
   D. Effectiveness data obtained from an expert panel.

3. Sometimes models must be created to predict long-term final outcomes based on intermediate clinical outcomes. This type of uncertainty is summarized within which one of the following categories?
   A. Analytical method uncertainty.
   B. Extrapolation uncertainty.
   C. Data variability uncertainty.
   D. Generalizability uncertainty.

4. Which one of the following types of sensitivity analysis is used when one variable in a model is varied over a range of plausible values and the remainder of the variables is left unchanged?
   A. One-way analysis.
   B. Threshold analysis.
   C. Multiway analysis.
   D. Analysis of extremes.

5. Modifying the effectiveness rate of a drug in a cost-effectiveness analysis is described as which one of the following types of sensitivity analysis?
   A. One-way analysis.
   B. Threshold analysis.
   C. Multiway analysis.
   D. Analysis of extremes.

6. Which one of the following types of sensitivity analysis is being conducted when a single variable is modified in a model until the same outcome is obtained as with an alternative treatment, and there is no advantage between treatment options in the outcome?
   A. Probabilistic sensitivity analysis.
   B. One-way analysis.
   C. Analysis of extremes.
   D. Threshold analysis.

7. Sensitivity analysis is important in models incorporating data from expert panels. Which one of the following types of sensitivity analysis is especially useful for these types of data?
   A. One-way sensitivity analysis.
   B. Simple analysis.
   C. Analysis of extremes.
   D. Threshold analysis.

8. Monte Carlo simulation techniques are becoming more popular and may be categorized as which one of the following types of sensitivity analysis?
   A. Probabilistic sensitivity analysis.
   B. Simple analysis.
   C. Analysis of extremes.
   D. Threshold analysis.

9. Which one of the following represents a tornado diagram?
   A. A three-way sensitivity analysis graph.
   B. A series of one-way analyses within a single graph.
   C. A cost-effectiveness ratio graph.
   D. A threshold value graph.

10. A break-even point is calculated in which one of the following types of sensitivity analysis?
    A. Probabilistic sensitivity analysis.
    B. Multiway analysis.
    C. Analysis of extremes.
    D. Threshold analysis.

Exercise

Sensitivity Analysis in Formulary Decision Making

Pharmacy and therapeutics committees face numerous challenges. One challenge is to take published pharmacoeconomic data from an outside source and apply it in their own settings. Even more difficult, they must often apply costs and outcomes that were obtained from clinical trials not specifically designed to yield pharmacoeconomic data. Pharmacy and therapeutics committees frequently must decide whether to add products to their formularies before full pharmacoeconomic evaluations have been published. In these settings, medical literature may provide the information needed to create an economic model. Hospital-specific costs can then be applied to the model and results estimated.

The following case illustrates how data can be gathered to build a model for evaluating an expensive, but potentially lifesaving, drug. You will be asked to evaluate the strength of the conclusions drawn by performing a sensitivity analysis.

Formulary Decision Making Case Study

Abciximab is a glycoprotein integren IIb/IIIa platelet inhibitor used as an adjunct to percutaneous transluminal coronary angioplasty in patients at high risk for abrupt closure of the treated coronary vessel. John, a pharmacist on the pharmacy and therapeutics committee at a local hospital, wants to evaluate the impact on costs and outcomes of adding abciximab to the formulary. John decides to use the hospital perspective for his evaluation and will use high-risk patients undergoing angioplasty as the entry point to the model he will construct. The principal treatment options are simply whether or not abciximab is used in these patients. Under his hospital's normal percutaneous transluminal coronary angioplasty treatment processes, all patients receive heparin and warfarin.

Important processes that John decides to include in his model include the drug (abciximab costs when used), ADRs (primarily bleeding and subsequent need for transfusions), and fewer complications with abciximab (nonfatal myocardial infarction and emergency angioplasty).

John searched the literature and concluded that the best clinical information is published in the Evaluation of 7E3 for the Prevention of Ischemic Complications (EPIC) trial (Use of a monoclonal antibody directed against the platelet glycoprotein IIb/IIIa receptor in high-risk coronary angioplasty. The EPIC Investigation. N Engl J Med 1994;330:956–61). This trial included 56 institutions and 2099 patients undergoing angioplasty who were at high risk for abrupt vessel closure, but not at high risk for bleeding. The 30-day results of an abciximab bolus plus infusion included a statistically significant reduction in composite primary end points defined by the study. When analyzed separately, abciximab resulted in a reduction in nonfatal myocardial infarctions and emergency angioplasties. In the abciximab group, 5.2 percent of patients had a nonfatal myocardial infarction compared to 8.6 percent in the placebo group. In the abciximab group, 0.8 percent of patients had an emergency angioplasty compared to 4.5 percent in the placebo group. However, this study also found significantly more bleeding with abciximab versus placebo. In addition, patients receiving abciximab received more transfusions (red blood cells, 15 percent; platelets, 6 percent) than patients receiving placebo (red blood cells, 7 percent; platelets, 3 percent). The EPIC study concluded that about 17 percent of angioplasties are high risk in nature.

John notes that his hospital performs about 200 angioplasties per year. He uses the 17 percent figure from the EPIC trial to estimate that his hospital will have 34 patients each year who will be high-risk candidates. The cost of abciximab for each patient is $1450, including the filter cost. John knows there will be some drug wastage during the year. After reviewing other expensive therapies used by cardiologists in his hospital and determining their wastage rate, he estimates that five doses of abciximab will be wasted each year.

John then attempts to estimate the cost to treat bleeding in his hospital. The clinical laboratory estimates the costs of cross-matching and transfusing blood for each episode of transfusion as $350 for red blood cells and $750 for platelets.

From the perspective of the hospital, he then estimates the potential costs avoided. In meeting with his hospital's cost accountants to receive figures for the hospital's cost estimates (*not charges*) for different diseases, he is told the hospital cost for a nonfatal myocardial infarction after an angioplasty is $14,220 (95 percent confidence interval $10,360–18,080). The cost for an emergency angioplasty is $24,665 (95 percent confidence interval $16,880–32,450).

John develops a table to record his results (summarized in Table 1 below) and then estimates the impact of using abciximab in 25 high-risk patients undergoing percutaneous transluminal coronary angioplasty. The predicted drug cost, including filters and wastage, is $39,150. The transfusion requirements for 25 patients receiving abciximab are estimated to be $2600. It is expected that one patient receiving abciximab would have a nonfatal myocardial infarction, costing an estimated $11,500. John concludes it to be unlikely for an emergency angioplasty to be necessary within the next year in patients receiving abciximab based on the incidence reported in the EPIC study. He finds that total health system costs for the 25 patients receiving abciximab would be $53,250.

Next, he estimates the impact of *not* using abciximab in these same 25 high-risk patients undergoing percutaneous transluminal coronary angioplasty. In this case, there would be no hospital cost for the drug, filters, or wastage. Transfusion requirements would be lower ($1300). However, if abciximab was not used, there would be more adverse clinical complications. John estimates the cost of nonfatal myocardial infarction as $23,000 and the cost of emergency angioplasties as $16,000. The total health system costs to not use abciximab would be $40,300.

Average Costs to Use or Not Use Abciximab in 34 High-Risk Patients Undergoing Angioplasty

Resource Unit	**Abciximab**	**No Abciximab**
	(No. of patients)	(No. of patients)
Abciximab (drug, filter, wastage)	$56,550 (34)	$0 (0)
Transfusion requirements		
Red blood cell	$1,750 (5)	$700 (2)
Platelet	$1,500 (2)	$750 (1)
Nonfatal myocarial infarction	$28,440 (2)	$42,660 (3)
Emergency angioplasty	$0 (0)	$24,665 (1)
Health system costs	$88,240	$68,775
Net change	$19,465	

Thus, John has estimated there would be a net increase in hospital costs of $19,465 ($88,240 less $68,775) to use abciximab to prevent one nonfatal myocardial infarction and one emergency angioplasty, and recommends that abciximab not be added to the formulary.

Task

1. Identify the sources of uncertainty in this example and describe how sensitivity analysis could be helpful in this evaluation.
2. Perform a sensitivity analysis by using the best-case and worst-case scenarios for both the abciximab and no abciximab groups.
3. What conclusions can you draw from this analysis of John's work?

EVALUATING ECONOMIC OUTCOMES LITERATURE

C. Daniel Mullins, Ph.D., and Louis R. Flowers III, Pharm.D

Outline

Literature about economic outcomes is expanding. However, there is considerable debate over the standardization of guidelines for economic evaluation. In this evolving field of pharmacoeconomics with an emphasis on methods for conducting and reporting outcomes, creating a set of standardized methods to be used when evaluating economic-outcomes literature may help the reader to effectively judge the appropriateness and applicability of results.

I. Importance of Economic Evaluation
- A. Decision Making
  - 1. Government
  - 2. Pharmaceutical Industry
  - 3. Managed Care Organizations
  - 4. Health Care Providers
- B. Lack of Universally Accepted Guidelines

II. Economic Evaluation of Health Care
- A. Measurement of costs and outcomes
  - 1. Type of Pharmacoeconomic Assessment
  - 2. Perspective
- B. Essential Elements
  - 1. Comparators
  - 2. Sensitivity Analysis
  - 3. Costs
  - 4. Outcomes
  - 5. Modeling
  - 6. Time Horizon
  - 7. Discounting
  - 8. Disclosure
  - 9. Generalizability

III. Checklists for Pharmacoeconomics Literature Evaluation
- A. British Medical Journal checklist
- B. Checklist to evaluate pharmacoeconomic studies
- C. Checklist for assessing economic evaluations
- D. Six principles
- E. Panel on Cost-Effectiveness Checklist
- F. PhRMA Principles
- G. Comparative Review

IV. Analyze and Critique Pharmacoeconomics Literature
- A. Tools Needed
- B. Application of Skills

V. Controversies with Pharmacoeconomics Literature

A. Inconsistent Reporting

B. Disagreement over Methodology

VI. Exercise 1: Critically evaluate the attached economic and outcomes study using one of the checklists for pharmacoeconomics literature evaluation.

VII. Exercise 2: Use the two-part scoring instrument (general and pharmacoeconomics) to evaluate the same study and calculate a summary quality score. Compare your checklist evaluation with the summary score in an overall assessment of the study.

VIII. Conclusion

Learning Objectives

1. Illustrate the importance of pharmacoeconomics literature evaluation.
2. Explain key topics for pharmacoeconomic evaluation.
3. Differentiate critical appraisal checklists for pharmacoeconomics literature evaluation.
4. Demonstrate how to analyze and critique pharmacoeconomics literature.
5. Summarize the controversies associated with pharmacoeconomics literature evaluation.

Abbreviations in this chapter

ACCP	American College of Clinical Pharmacy
AMCP	Academy of Managed Care Pharmacists
BMJ	British Medical Journal
CBA	cost-benefit analysis
CCA	cost-consequences analysis
CEA	cost-effectiveness analysis
CUA	cost-utility analysis
FDA	Food and Drug Administration
FTEs	Full-time equivalents
IFPMA	International Federation of Pharmaceutical Manufacturers Associations' Survey
ISPOR	International Society for Pharmacoeconomics and Outcomes Research
MCO	managed care organization
PBAC	Pharmaceutical Benefits Advisory Committee
PBM	pharmacy benefit management companies
PE	pharmacoeconomic
PhRMA	Pharmaceutical Research and Manufacturers of America
RCT	randomized, controlled clinical trial

Introduction

Today economic outcomes (e.g., expenditures for hospital stays, office visits, emergency department visits, and drug therapy, as well as the value of lost productivity because of absenteeism) have become an integral part of disease management. Pressures to contain health care expenditures provide the impetus for demanding economic-outcomes data. Traditionally, formulary decisions were typically based on data collected from relevant clinical literature and drug information from the pharmaceutical industry. The data collected were incorporated into a drug monograph summarizing the efficacy, safety, and acquisition cost of a drug relative to its alternatives. To control the cost of providing drug therapy for a particular disease, cost-containment programs were implemented. The manner of cost-containment often involved reviewing the acquisition cost and selecting the least expensive medication from a specific therapeutic drug class for formulary addition. Now, decision makers are abandoning the silo mentality of cost-containment programs based solely on drug acquisition costs. They are transitioning to using economic outcomes and the results of pharmacoeconomics research in making drug therapy decisions. As a result, it is imperative that pharmacists and other health care practitioners involved in formulary decision making are able to evaluate the study design and results of the economic-outcomes literature.

During the last two decades there has been an explosion in the number of journals publishing pharmacoeconomics articles. For example, in 1978 only seven articles on cost-effectiveness of drugs/pharmacoeconomics were published in journals indexed by MEDLINE whereas in 1998 there were several thousand articles. As a result, an increasing number of medical and health journals are publishing economic-outcomes studies, exposing a growing number of health practitioners, formulary committee members, and public decision makers to pharmacoeconomics information. A subset of outcomes research, pharmacoeconomics is a tool used in performing outcomes research that deals with the economic and humanistic outcomes of pharmaceutical care. The explosion of pharmacoeconomic literature suggests that pharmacoeconomic research can help in addressing the challenges of delivering high-quality health care cost-effectively. For organizations with fixed budgets, such as hospital pharmacies, pharmacoeconomic information may be used to implement strategies to control pharmacy expenditures. However, before making formulary decisions or implementing guidelines based on pharmacoeconomic literature, the decision makers must have a thorough understanding on how to evaluate, interpret, and disseminate the findings from the literature.

There is considerable debate about the standardization of guidelines for economic evaluation. In the evolving pharmacoeconomics field, which has an emphasis on methods for conducting and reporting outcomes, creating a set of standardized methods to be used when evaluating economic-outcomes literature may help decision makers to effectively judge the appropriateness and applicability of results. However, at this time there is no standardized way in which pharmacoeconomic studies are conducted. As a result, there is considerable variance in the structure, process, and complexity of applying the concepts and methods of pharmacoeconomic research to economic-outcomes evaluation in the published literature.

Because methods for evaluating pharmacoeconomics literature historically were not taught in school, many health care organizations may find it labor-intensive to introduce this practice and difficult to discern between high-quality and low-quality studies. In this chapter, we will provide material to develop the participant's knowledge and skills of evaluating economic-outcomes literature in such a way that it eases the burden of using pharmacoeconomic information in making drug-therapy decisions within health care organizations.

Importance of Economic Evaluation

Because of the global rise in health care costs, government, the pharmaceutical industry, managed care organizations (MCOs), and health care providers have invested time and money in the evaluation of economic-outcomes literature. The demand for pharmacoeconomic information suggests that the returns from their investment have paid dividends in controlling cost and providing a comprehensive care-management package. The increased demand for pharmacoeconomic data by MCOs has contributed to the growth of pharmacy benefit management companies (PBMs). As a result, the growth of the PBMs in the 1990s transformed the distribution of pharmaceuticals.

Decision Making

The purpose of evaluating economic-outcomes literature is to determine which health care interventions best improve the health status of a particular population and, in the process, determine how to better allocate health care resources to achieve that goal. Knowledge gained from evaluating economic-outcomes literature provides evidence-based data for pharmacists to support formulary decision making.

Government

Government decision makers who develop and implement national health insurance programs have a stake in the cost-effective use of drug products. For countries with national health insurance, pharmacoeconomic research may provide a mechanism for controlling government expenditures on pharmaceuticals. For instance, in 1990 pharmaceuticals were the fastest growing item in the Australian health care budget. As a result, in 1992 Australia became the first country to introduce national guidelines for conducting economic evaluations for pharmaceutical companies submitting drugs to the Pharmaceutical Benefits Advisory Committee (PBAC). The PBAC is an independent nongovernmental committee of physicians, researchers, and pharmacists that advises government decision makers about setting the national formulary for Medicare. The Australian guidelines were revised in November 1995, requiring mandatory evidentiary standards for all pharmaceutical companies wishing to make submission to the PABC. Others countries such as Canada, Spain, Italy, and the United Kingdom have developed national guidelines for the economic evaluation of pharmaceuticals. Although there is not a national health insurance program in the United States, pharmacoeconomics may be considered valuable for ensuring that funds are spent in the best possible way for Medicaid and other government-supported health programs. Moreover, the emerging use of pharmacoeconomics data in promotional materials has forced the Food and Drug Administration (FDA) rather than just focusing on assessing the safety and clinical efficacy of new drugs into evaluating the merit of pharmacoeconomic claims.

Pharmaceutical Industry

Pharmaceutical companies are pressured to demonstrate that their products offer greater value, in terms of price and quality, compared with competitors' products. Consequently, these companies are providing promotional materials to insurers, health care providers, and patients about the value of their products. To incorporate pharmacoeconomic claims such as "improves health-related quality of life" in the labeling of a drug, pharmaceutical companies must provide valid and substantial pharmacoeconomic evidence about its value. This "fourth hurdle" may constitute an additional burden for the pharmaceutical industry, above the demand to demonstrate efficacy, safety, and quality. From the perspective of the pharmaceutical industry, undertaking economic-outcomes evaluations makes sense if such analyses are required by the government or are used by MCOs to set formularies.

Managed Care Organizations

The challenge for MCOs is to effectively manage the risks and costs of care for their members in an increasing competitive market. Prescription drugs are a significant expenditure for MCOs. As a result, MCOs focus primarily on containing costs in their pharmaceutical budgets. However, to maintain high-quality care at reduced costs, MCOs are taking a comprehensive view of the cost of patient care and are using economic-outcomes research to assess the total cost of providing that care. Pharmacoeconomic analysis can be used by MCOs as a tool in the decision making process, such as for implementing treatment protocols for drug therapy, structuring the total benefit of a program, determining the amount of patient copayments, and providing the foundation for allocating scarce resources. Because of their knowledge and ability to assess claims databases, MCOs are clearly in the position to evaluate economic outcomes for making drug therapy decisions, thereby identifying the best choice of drugs for patients as well as for providers.

Health Care Providers

Health care providers such as pharmacists often base the formulary decisions on clinical and pharmacoeconomic studies. Health care providers not only have a responsibility to ensure positive patient outcomes but also need to be concerned about the costs of treatments and outcomes. The commitment that health care providers entering the profession make to promote the health of patients is one of the most compelling reasons for them to be concerned about patient outcomes. Health care providers can evaluate and apply pharmacoeconomic literature to benefit patients. Ultimately, the results will not only lead to positive patient outcomes but also provide the opportunity for patients to purchase and consume medications at a lower total cost of care.

Lack of Universally Accepted Guidelines

Before economic-outcomes literature is used in the decision making process, the evaluator of the literature must be aware of the issues concerning the lack of universally accepted guidelines. Researchers have held several conferences on the topic of guidelines, including those conducted by the University of North Carolina, Duke University, and the International Society for Pharmacoeconomics and Outcomes Research (ISPOR). Several publications have also been written on this topic. One basic issue surrounding the debate for development of methodological and ethical guidelines is the potential for bias in cost-effectiveness research. To contend with the suspicion of bias and improve credibility, it may be helpful to use a set of basic standardized guidelines when performing an economic evaluation. Implementing a set of standardized pharmacoeconomic guidelines may limit the introduction of bias into economic-outcomes studies and aid in promoting the credibility of pharmacoeconomic assessments that are methodologically and ethically sound. Moreover, standardization may increase generalization of pharmacoeconomic studies, therefore rendering them more applicable to decision makers. Before implementing any set of guidelines, the purpose of the guidelines should be clearly articulated.

Economic Evaluation of Health Care

To effectively evaluate the validity and usefulness of pharmacoeconomic literature, health care decision makers must be aware of the essential elements of a pharmacoeconomic study. It is important to remember that there are no universally accepted guidelines or principles for conducting pharmacoeconomic research; therefore, the following is only an analysis of a dozen key topics of pharmacoeconomic assessments.

Measurement of Costs and Outcomes

Pressures to contain health care spending mandate that decision makers consider cost in relation to expected benefits. Pharmacoeconomics research has emerged in response to this need. In deciding whether to add a new drug to their formularies, MCOs, government entities, and health care providers are evaluating not only the clinical efficacy of drugs but also the various costs and outcomes associated with the use of drugs.

Type of Pharmacoeconomic Assessment

The selection of an appropriate pharmacoeconomic evaluation method is based on the type of comparison being made. Cost-effectiveness analysis (CEA) and cost-benefit analysis (CBA) are models used to evaluate the costs and consequences of medical interventions. In CBA, all costs and consequences are expressed in monetary terms. In CEA, the costs are expressed in monetary terms, and consequences are measured in their natural units, (e.g., life-years saved, number of days of hospitalization avoided, or number of treatment successes). Although CEA is the most frequently used form of economic evaluation, researchers have argued that CBA may be superior to CEA from a theoretical perspective; nevertheless, the advantages of CBA come at the expense of difficult measurement issues, such as the monetary valuation of life. Placing a dollar value on life is not only methodologically challenging but also politically difficult to justify; thus CBA is passed over in favor of CEA for drug evaluations. However, for program evaluations, such as the evaluation of pharmaceutical care services, CBA may be preferred.

Decision makers who need to assess many outcomes may wish to conduct cost-consequences analysis (CCA). This variant of CEA presents a range of costs and consequences that may provide for decision makers a variety of outcomes ranging from clinical to humanistic. Unfortunately, it is difficult, if not impossible, to calculate a cost-consequence ratio using CCA. Another extension of CEA is cost-utility analysis (CUA), which incorporates consequences of medical interventions using patient preferences. Before evaluating an economic study, the evaluator should be able to distinguish among the different types of analysis.

Perspective

When choices about the allocation of health resources are considered, who is affected? On whose behalf are decisions made? The answers to these questions define the perspective of the analysis. The choice of perspective of the analysis is very important. Most literature states that the societal perspective is the best. However, the majority of government payers adopt the public-payer perspective. The public-payer perspective is identical to the societal perspective, except it places less attention on the indirect costs and benefits. Furthermore, the public-payer perspective places less attention on the value (utility) to family members and individuals other than the patient. In the United States, most pharmacoeconomic studies use the managed-care perspective because that is the intended audience for many published articles. Although the patient perspective is almost never mentioned as a preferred option, this perspective is significant to the pharmaceutical industry. The pharmaceutical industry assesses patient-reported outcomes in its studies and incorporates favorable findings in labeling and promotion claims. For example, a claim that a drug is indicated for lowering cholesterol may state "Expect a bright future." Because the patient perspective is of great importance to the audience members who make decisions about drug use, pharmaceutical companies have begun to promulgate the patient perspective in advertisements.

Essential Elements

Economic evaluation of health care interventions employs a variety of methodologies, and the outcomes of the evaluation may vary across perspectives. Although a pharmacoeconomic analysis can be undertaken from a number of perspectives, the common goal of all analyses is to assess the outcomes and costs of health care interventions. Regardless of the target audience for the study, the following key elements are common to a pharmacoeconomic study.

Comparator

When evaluating economic-outcomes literature, the evaluator must take into account the selection of the appropriate comparator. Guidelines for conducting pharmacoeconomic research recommend comparing a new treatment with current practice. Although most payers of health care favor comparing the new intervention or treatment with existing practice, numerous pharmacoeconomic studies are based on randomized, controlled clinical trials (RCTs) that compare active treatment with placebo. In this case, when the new treatment is not compared with the existing practice, the results may be deceptive. For example, if a new therapy for diabetes is compared with placebo, it may appear more cost-effective than it should. Moreover, comparing a new therapy with standard care is useful for evaluating the effects of replacing an existing therapy with an alternative.

Sensitivity Analysis

Many of the articles in the pharmacoeconomic literature use sensitivity analysis to assess uncertainty in data. For example, investigators modify the primary variables through a range of worst-case or best-case outcomes to assess their effect on the overall decision. This analysis provides some indication of how sensitive the results would be to change if an extreme value occurred. However, two limitations are associated with using sensitivity analysis: (1) The researcher may choose which variables and what alternative values are included in the sensitivity analysis, which may create selection bias; and (2) sensitivity analysis tests the robustness of conclusions to variations, but there is no standard way to determine whether a cost-effectiveness ratio is robust. During the last few years, there has been substantial debate over which statistical methods to employ when conducting pharmacoeconomic studies. Most of this literature focused on assessing the variability of cost-effectiveness ratios, calculating confidence intervals, and formal hypothesis testing with cost-effectiveness ratios.

Costs

When evaluating economic-outcomes literature, the evaluator must determine which specific types of costs were included, how the costs were measured and reported, and whether these reflect accurate and complete information. There are many recommendations for defining costs in a pharmacoeconomic study, but the preferred method is to document unit cost rather than just aggregate costs and calculate marginal costs as well as total costs. However, there is no consensus on what cost components should be included in an analysis. For example, many guidelines agree on the relevance of including direct medical costs and direct nonmedical costs in the study. Some guidelines do not recognize the importance of including indirect medical costs in analyses. Researchers should not only state whether indirect costs are included but also justify the reason for including or not including indirect medical costs. Furthermore, for the purpose of transparency, the direct and indirect costs should be reported in a disaggregated form before being combined into a single index or ratio. The relevance of reporting friction cost (direct nonhealth care costs, [i.e., transaction costs associated with the replacement of a worker]) has received a great deal of attention in the indirect-costs literature. For example, when training costs are associated with hiring a replacement worker, friction costs accrue to the employer, and these real societal costs must be reported. Pharmacoeconomic analysis may be used as a tool for making decisions about resource allocation beyond the health care system in the workplace; therefore, it is essential that the evaluator understand all cost components and units of measurement.

Outcomes

An increasing number of medical journals and pharmaceutical advertisements are publicizing terms such as outcomes, outcomes assessment, outcomes research, and outcomes management. These words and phrases have received national attention because of the strong desire by health practitioners, formulary committee members, and public decision makers to know which health interventions best improve the health status of a particular population and to estimate the overall cost for providing this intervention. Outcomes are direct measures of improvements or declines in a patient's health status. In a well-designed pharmacoeconomic study, the outcomes selected are appropriate to the treatment or disease state, measurable, and identified as either primary or secondary outcomes. For example, in considering alternative therapies for patients with elevated serum cholesterol, a primary objective may be to determine which alternative is most cost-effective in terms of reducing mortality, and a secondary objective may be to determine which alternative is most cost-effective in terms of quality of life. In terms of measuring outcomes, most guidelines suggest using a quality-adjusted outcomes measure because these outcomes may capture important changes in health status and make comparisons between different types of treatments easier. Furthermore, for the purpose of transparency, the improvement in quality of life should be reported in a disaggregated form before being combined into a single index or ratio. Finally, when evaluating economic-outcomes literature, the evaluator must recognize not only that the outcomes selected should relate to the objective of the study but also that all outcomes, both positive and negative, should be reported for each treatment alternative.

Modeling

As the demand for pharmacoeconomic data at product launches increases, so will the need for and interest in modeling, especially for long-term endpoints that cannot be captured in short-term RCTs. A well-designed model provides a framework for linking choices, actions, and outcomes, (i.e., modeling can provide structure for connecting intermediate outcomes to final outcomes). Furthermore, models can use efficacy data from clinical trials to estimate effectiveness. Some sets of pharmacoeconomic guidelines recommend using modeling but provide little information about which modeling techniques to use for an analysis. However, there is a consensus that all modeling assumptions should be based on published, peer-reviewed literature or current medical expert opinion and should be justified in the publication. One of the popular models seen in the literature for scenario-building is the Markov model, which is supported by a variety of computer software packages. Markov modeling allows for greater complexity of assumptions with the potential to more accurately reflect disease progression, but the models are only as good as the assumptions. In some cases, when the objective is to predict real-world effectiveness, the models are complex and offer little benefit over existing data from RCTs. Moreover, the information used in these models is usually not available for critical review. Often the greatest contribution of modeling in the pharmacoeconomic field is its ability to document a range of plausible outcomes and ratios using sensitivity analysis. In an ideal world, follow-up pharmacoeconomic studies would be performed once long-term data on real-world outcomes are available.

Time Horizon

The time horizon of a study is the period during which cost and outcome data are collected or projected. In general, the time horizon should be appropriate for the disease and long enough to capture the full effects of the treatment. An unresolved limitation related to the time horizon is how to incorporate the effects of treatment on diseases other than the principal focus of the study (e.g., how diabetic therapy may affect hypertension as well). It is well established that treatments that prolong life will result in costs and benefits that are unrelated to the specific disease being followed; therefore, it is not necessary to model these costs and benefits associated with prolonged life into a pharmacoeconomic study.

Discounting

When conducting a pharmacoeconomic study, most researchers consider discounting in their analysis. The general consensus among pharmacoeconomic guidelines is to discount future costs and possibly benefits. The rule of thumb is to discount at either 3 percent or 5 percent and to carry out a sensitivity analysis using rates between 0 percent and 10 percent. The upper limit becomes more significant when the study costs or benefits occur in the distant future or when patterns of resource utilization vary between alternatives being compared.

Disclosure

To ensure independence and integrity, disclosure of any relationships between investigators and sources of funding should be clearly stated in the pharmacoeconomic study. Most journals require disclosure of the funding sources for research and the financial relationship between authors and the industries whose products are being studied. When evaluating economic-outcomes literature, take the time to read the disclosures and critically evaluate them.

Generalizability

Most pharmacoeconomic guidelines do not address the issue of generalizability. However, in evaluating economic-outcomes literature, the studies should be conducted and reported clearly so they are transparent and can be replicated by the reader. This will allow decision makers to determine whether the study's assumptions and estimations are generalizable to their setting.

Checklists for Pharmacoeconomics Literature Evaluation

As payers for health care moved toward evidence-based approaches to patient care, they demanded evidence that pharmaceutical products and services added value. Although this movement caused an increased interest in the economic evaluation of health care interventions, there was ongoing debate concerning the lack of methodological and ethical guidelines among pharmacoeconomic studies. As a result, the checklists or principles described below were published to review the basic elements of a pharmacoeconomic analysis and to establish schemes to evaluate the quality of pharmacoeconomic studies.

British Medical Journal checklist

During the past decade, the number of pharmacoeconomic studies being published in medical journals has risen. However, few medical journals had explicit guidelines for peer review of economic evaluation. As result, in January 1995 the BMJ organized a working party on economic evaluation to improve the quality of submitted and published economic-evaluations articles. Consequently, a checklist for evaluating outcomes literature was published for the referees and authors. The BMJ checklist contains 35 sections grouped under three headings: study design, data collection, and analysis and interpretation of results (Table 1). Under the study design section, the economic importance of the research question, the viewpoint for the analysis, the alternatives being compared, and the form of evaluation used are addressed. Under the data collection section, effectiveness data, primary outcome measure, costs information, and modeling are addressed. The section on analysis and interpretation of results addresses time horizon of costs and benefits, discount rate, allowance for uncertainty, and presentation of results. Results should be reported in incremental analyses. Major outcomes, such as impact on quality of life, should be reported as disaggregated as well as aggregated data. The authors emphasized that transparency in reporting can help decision makers generalize results from one setting to another. However, in the checklist, generalizablility was not specifically addressed.

Checklist to evaluate pharmacoeconomic studies

The authors devised a checklist to review the basic concepts used in health economics analysis and to establish an easy and coherent method to systematically evaluate the quality of published pharmacoeconomic studies. The authors reviewed the most relevant studies on the subject and created a checklist similar to those already in existence for evaluating clinical trials. The checklist presents 12 general steps to follow in an economic evaluation and was created from three perspectives: hospital, local government, and the pharmaceutical industry. Each general section of the checklist contains several subsections. After evaluating each subsection, each of the 12 general sections is qualified as correct, acceptable, doubtful, incorrect, or not applicable (Table 2). From this qualitative evaluation, aspects that have been dealt with correctly and those needing improvement will become apparent. According to the authors, the following aspects should be considered when evaluating pharmamacoeconomic studies: (1) aim of the study; (2) characteristics of the patients; (3) comparison of all relevant alternatives; (4) is the perspective justified (depending on the goal of the study)?; (5) measurement of benefits in suitable terms (e.g., by clinical trial, literature data, and expert opinion); (6) measurement of costs under real conditions is ideal (but may use models based on expert opinions or literature); (7) type of analysis should depend on problem being examined; (8) results should be expressed in terms of increases, such as marginal costs and benefits; (9) discussion of the evaluation suitability if carried out within a clinical trial (e.g., whether randomization was performed, losses were taken into account, and suitable statistical tests were used); (10) assumptions, limitations, and possible bias; (11) ethical considerations; and (12) conclusion should be justified and able to be generalized. The authors suggest that using a checklist enables the evaluator to verify whether the results have been correctly obtained and, therefore, whether the conclusions are valid.

A checklist for assessing economic evaluations

The authors, well-known pioneers in economic evaluation, published several outstanding manuscripts about evaluating economic-outcomes literature. One such publication, Methods for the Economic Evaluation of Health Care Programmes 2nd Edition, contains a checklist for readers of economic evaluations. The checklist identifies and discusses 10 questions to ask in order to critically evaluate economic-outcomes literature (Table 3). According to the authors, these are the elements of a sound economic evaluation: (1) a well-defined question posed in an answerable form; (2) a statement of the primary objective of each alternative, which is critical to selecting the type of assessment (note: the type of assessment was not specially addressed in the checklist); (3) evidence that the programs' effectiveness had been established (i.e., if the economic evaluation assumes effectiveness, some indication of the prior validation of effectiveness should be reported); (4) relevant cost and consequences for each alternative are identified; (5) costs and consequences are measured accurately in appropriate physical units; (6) costs and consequences are valued credibly; (7) costs and consequences are adjusted for differential timing; (8) incremental analysis of costs and consequences of alternatives was performed; (9) allowance was made for uncertainty in the estimates of costs and consequences; (10) the presentation and discussion of study results include all issues of concern to users. According to the authors, it is important to remember that for a variety of reasons it is unlikely that every study will satisfy all criteria. However, the use of the checklist as a screening device should help

Table 1. BMJ Checklist

Referee's checklist (also to be used, implicitly, by authors) ITEM	Yes	No	Not clear	Not appropriate
STUDY DESIGN				
(1) The research question is stated	❑	❑	❑	
(2) The economic importance of the research question is stated				
(3) The viewpoint(s) of the analysis are clearly stated and justified		❑	❑	❑
(4) The rationale for choosing the alternative programmes or interventions compared is stated	❑	❑	❑	
(5) The alternative being compared are clearly described	❑	❑	❑	
(6) The form of economic evaluation used is stated	❑	❑	❑	
(7) The choice of form of economic evaluation is justified in relation to the question addressed	❑	❑	❑	
DATA COLLECTION				
(8) The source(s) of effectiveness estimates used are stated		❑	❑	❑
(9) etails of the design and results of effectiveness study are given (if based on a single study)	❑	❑	❑	❑
(10) Details of the methods of synthesis or meta-analysis of estimates are given (if based on an overview of a number of effectiveness studies)	❑	❑	❑	❑
(11) The primary outcome measure(s) for the economic evaluation are clearly stated	❑	❑	❑	
(12) Methods to value health status and other benefits are stated	❑	❑	❑	❑
(13) Details of the subjects from whom valuations were obtained are given	❑	❑	❑	❑
(14) Productivity changes (if included) are reported separately	❑	❑	❑	❑
(15) The relevance of productivity changes to the study question is discussed	❑	❑	❑	❑
(16) Quantities of resources are reported separately from their unit costs	❑	❑	❑	
(17) Methods for the estimation of quantities and unit costs are described	❑	❑	❑	
(18) Currency and price data are recorded	❑	❑	❑	
(19) Details of currency of price adjustments for inflation or currency conversion are given	❑	❑	❑	
(20) Details of any model used are given	❑	❑	❑	❑
(21) The choice of model used and the key parameters on which it is based are justified	❑	❑	❑	❑
ANALYSI S AND INTERPRETATION OF RESULTS				
(22) Time horizon of costs and benefits is stated	❑	❑	❑	
(23) The discount rate(s) is stated	❑	❑	❑	❑
(24) The choice of rate(s) is justified	❑	❑	❑	❑
(25) An explanation is given if costs or benefits are not discounted	❑	❑	❑	❑
(26) Details of statistical tests and confidence intervals are given for stochastic data	❑	❑	❑	❑
(27) The approach to sensitivity analysis is given	❑	❑	❑	❑
(28) The choice of variables for sensitivity analysis is justified	❑	❑	❑	❑
(29) The ranges over which the variables are varied are stated	❑	❑	❑	❑
(30) Relevant alternatives are compared	❑	❑	❑	
(31) Incremental analysis is reported	❑	❑	❑	❑
(32) Major outcomes are presented in a disaggregated as well as aggregated form	❑	❑	❑	
(33) The answer to the study question is given	❑	❑	❑	
(34) Conclusions follow from the data reported	❑	❑	❑	
(35) Conclusions are accompanied by the appropriate caveats	❑	❑	❑	

 Drummond MF, Jefferson TO: Guidelines for authors and peer reviewers of economic submissions to the BMJ. Br Med J 1996;313:275-283.

Table 2. Sacristán et al. Checklist

Checklist to Evaluate Pharmacoeconomic Studies					
1. Definition of Study Aim	C	A	D	I	NA
Does a well-defined question exist?	☐	☐	☐	☐	☐
Are the perspective and alternatives compared clearly specified?					
2. Sample Selection	C	A	D	I	NA
Are the types of patients chosen suitable and are they specified?	☐	☐	☐	☐	☐
Are the diagnostic criteria adequately specified?					
3. Analysis of Alternatives	C	A	D	I	NA
Are all the relevant alternatives analyzed?	☐	☐	☐	☐	☐
Is/are the comparison alternative(s) suitable?					
Is this the most commonly used treatment, or one that will be replaced by the new drug?					
Is the indication the most relevant one?					
Are adequate dosages used?					
Are the treatments reproducible? (doses, intervals, duration, etc.)					
Is the "do-nothing" option analyzed or should it be analyzed?					
Is a decision analysis applied?					
4. Analysis of Perspective	C	A	D	I	NA
Is it clearly specified (society, patient, hospital, etc.)?	☐	☐	☐	☐	☐
Is it justified for the question asked?					
5. Measurement of Benefits	C	A	D	I	NA
Is it adequate for the question asked and the perspective?	☐	☐	☐	☐	☐
Are the data on the effectiveness of alternatives adequately established?					
Is the main assessment variable (endpoint) objective and relevant?					
Is the time fixed for the evaluation sufficient and is it specified?					
Are the results quantified by time?					
6. Measurement of Costs	C	A	D	I	NA
Is the measurement of costs suitable for the perspective?	☐	☐	☐	☐	☐
Are the costs up to date and are the prices those of the market?					
Is the adjustment of future costs and benefits performed?					
7. Is the type of analysis used suitable?	C	A	D	I	NA
Financial terms: cost-benefit	☐	☐	☐	☐	☐
"Physical" units: cost-effectiveness					
Quality of life/utility: cost-utility					
Equal benefits: cost-minimization					
8. Analysis of the Results	C	A	D	I	NA
If intermediate variables are used, are they representative of the end benefit?	☐	☐	☐	☐	☐
Is a marginal analysis performed?					
Are the costs and consequences of adverse effects analyzed?					
9. Is the evaluation suitable if made within a clinical trial?	C	A	D	I	NA
Is the suitable methodology employed?	☐	☐	☐	☐	☐
Are the statistical methods used adequate?					
Is an analysis according to "intention to treat" made?					
Are costs resulting from the trial, which differ from those in normal practice, taken into account?					
10. Are the assumptions and limitations of the study discussed?	C	A	D	I	NA
Is a sensitivity analysis performed?	☐	☐	☐	☐	☐
Do the assumptions have a basis?					
Is the exclusion of any important variable analyzed or justified?					
If intermediate endpoints are assumed, are limitations discussed?					
11. Are possible ethical problems discussed and identified?	C	A	D	I	NA
	☐	☐	☐	☐	☐
12. Conclusions	C	A	D	I	NA
Are they justified?	☐	☐	☐	☐	☐
Can they be generalized? Can they be extrapolated to daily clinical practice?					

A = acceptable; C = correct; D = doubtful; I = incorrect; NA = not applicable.

Reprinted with permission from Harvey Whitney Books Company. Sacristán JA, Soto J, Galende I: Evaluations of pharmacoeconomic studies: utilization of a checklist. Ann Pharmacother 1993;27:1126-33.

Table 3. Drummond et al. Checklist

A check-list for assessing economic evaluations

1. **Was a well-defined question posed in answerable form?**
   1.1 Did the study examine both costs and effects of the service(s) or programme(s)?
   1.2 Did the study involve a comparison of alternatives?
   1.3 Was a viewpoint for the analysis stated and was the study placed in any particular decision-making context?

2. **Was a comprehensive description of the competing alternatives given (i.e. can you tell who did what to whom, where, and how often)?**
   2.1 Were any important alternatives omitted?
   2.2 Was (Should) a do-nothing alternative (be) considered?

3. **Was the effectiveness of the programmes or services established?**
   3.1 Was this done through a randomized, controlled clinical trial? If so, did the trial protocol reflect what would happen in regular practice?
   3.2 Was effectiveness established through an overview of clinical studies?
   3.3 Were observational data or assumptions used to established effectiveness? If so, what are the potential biases in results?

4. **Were all the important and relevant costs and consequences for each alternative identified?**
   4.1 Was the range wide enough for the research question at hand?
   4.2 Did it cover all relevant viewpoints? (Possible viewpoints include the community or social viewpoint, and those of patients and third-party payers. Other viewpoints may also be relevant depending upon the particularly analysis.)
   4.3 Were capital costs, as well as operating costs, included?

5. **Were costs and consequences measured accurately in appropriate physical units (e.g. hours of nursing time, number of physician visits, lost work-days, gained life-years)**
   5.1 Were any of the identified items omitted from measurement? If so, does this mean that they carried no weight in the subsequent analysis?
   5.2 Were there any special circumstances (e.g. joint use of resources) that made measurement difficult? Were these circumstances handled appropriately?

6. **Were costs and consequences valued credibly?**
   6.1 Were the sources of all values clearly identified? (Possible sources include market values, patients or client preferences and views, policy-makers' views and health professionals' judgments.)
   6.2 Were market values employed for changes involving resources gained or depleted?
   6.3 Where market values were absent (e.g. volunteer labour), or market values did not reflect actual values (such as clinic space donated at a reduced rate), were adjustments made to approximate market values?
   6.4 Was the valuation of consequences appropriate for the question posed (i.e. has the appropriate type or types of analysis — cost-effectiveness, cost-benefit, cost-utility - been selected)?

7. **Were costs and consequences adjusted for differential timing?**
   7.1 Were costs and consequences which occur in the future 'discounted' to their present values?
   7.2 Was any justification given for the discount rate used?

8. **Was an incremental analysis of costs and consequences of alternatives performed?**
   8.1 Were the additional (incremental) costs generated by one alternative over another compared to the additional effects, benefits, or utilities generated?

9. **Was allowance made for uncertainty in the estimates of costs and consequences?**
   9.1 If data on costs or consequences were stochastic, were appropriate statistical analyses performed?
   9.2 If a sensitivity analysis was employed, was justification provided for the ranges of values (for key study parameters)?
   9.3 Were study results sensitive to changes in the values (within the assumed range for sensitivity analysis, or within the confidence interval around the ratio of costs to consequences)?

10. **Did the presentation and discussion of study results include all issues of concern to users?**
    10.1 Were the conclusions of the analysis based on some overall index or ratio of costs to consequences (e.g. cost-effectiveness ratio)? If so, was the index interpreted intelligently or in a mechanistic fashion?
    10.2 Were the results compared with those of others who have investigated the same question? If so, were allowances made for potential differences in study methodology?
    10.3 the study discuss the generalizability of the results to other settings and patient/client groups?
    10.4 Did the study allude to, or take account of, other important factors in the choice or decision under consideration (e.g. distribution of costs and consequences, or relevant ethical issues)?
    10.5 Did the study discuss issues of implementation, such as the feasibility of adopting the 'preferred' programme given existing financial or other constraints, and whether any freed resources could be redeployed to other worthwhile programmes?

users of economic evaluations to quickly identify the strengths and weaknesses of studies.

Six principles

During the last decade, readers of pharmacoeconomic literature have become increasing knowledgeable about cost-effectiveness and cost-benefit analyses in the medical literature. However, many readers were unaware of any existing information that indicated whether the methods of economic analysis had been successfully incorporated into the medical literature. As a result, the authors examined whether studies in the medical literature that focused on cost-effectiveness and cost-benefit analyses used and reported methods appropriately. Before reviewing the studies, the authors identified six basic principles that should be followed in conducting economic evaluation (Table 4). The six principles were derived from reviewing recommendations cited in articles and textbooks describing appropriate methods for CEA and the economic evaluation of health care settings. The authors chose the six principles that were consistently recommended in these sources; therefore, the six principles should be interpreted as minimum requirements rather than an inclusive set of methods necessary to conduct all economic analyses. The authors used the following six principles to determine whether published cost-effectiveness and cost-benefit analyses adhered to basic analytic principles: (1) the perspective should be given; (2) a description of the benefits should be given; (3) describe the type of costs used; (4) discounting should be used to adjust for differential timing; (5) sensitivity analyses should be done, and (6) unless there is one dominant alternative (i.e., it saves money and has greater benefit) a summary measurement of efficiency, such as a cost-effectiveness ratio, should be expressed in marginal or incremental terms. By evaluating the literature using these six principles, the authors concluded that studies in general medical journals were more likely to adhere to the analytic principles than studies published in the general surgical or medical subspecialty journals.

Table 4. Six basic principles for conducting economic evaluations

Principle 1. An explicit statement of the perspective for the analysis should be provided.

Principle 2. An explicit description of the benefits of the program or technology being studied should be provided.

Principle 3. Investigators should specify what types of costs were used or considered in their analysis.

Principle 4. If costs and benefits accrue during different periods, discounting should be used to adjust for the differential timing.

Principle 5. Sensitivity analyses should be done to test important assumptions.

Principle 6. A summary measurement of efficiency, such as a cost-benefit or cost-effectiveness ratio, should be calculated and preferably expressed in marginal or incremental terms unless one alternative or strategy is dominant.

Panel on Cost-Effectiveness

The Panel on Cost-Effectiveness in Health and Medicine was a multidisciplinary panel composed of economists, ethicists, psychometricians, and clinicians appointed by the United States Public Health Services. The panel was directed to assess the science of CEA and move the field forward so that decision makers would have access to robust information with respect to CEA. The panel designed a checklist (Table 5) for authors to summarize all major features of a CEA for journal publication. The panel outlined its recommendation for journal reporting in four sections: (1) the framework of the analysis (report target population, description of comparator, time horizon, and perspective); (2) methods and data (report effectiveness, modeling assumptions, discount rates, outcome values, and costs); (3) results (report incremental costs and effectiveness, sensitivity analyses, aggregate cost and effectiveness data, and relevant disaggregated results) and (4) discussion (report limitations and relevance of study results for specific policy decision). Although most CEA follow a format similar to this one, the panel offered this general structure as a guide for authors, as consumers and reviewers of analyses will find it easier to locate needed information when it is placed in predictable parts of the publications.

The Pharmaceutical Research and Manufacturers of America (PhRMA)

The PhRMA developed for its members a set of voluntary general principles for conducting and evaluating pharmacoeconomic research (Table 6). These principles were based on recommendations from academic and industry experts in pharmacoeconomics. These principles were designed to minimize the potential for bias in conducting and reporting pharmacoeconomic studies and to provide transparency on study methodology. The PhRMA principles contain 21 subsections that are grouped under seven headings: (1) research design, (2) protocol/report, (3) contents of protocol/report, (4) costs/resources, (5) effectiveness/benefits, (6) data sources, and (7) extrapolation of results to other settings. Under the research design and protocol/report section, the researcher should be free to choose from multiple research designs and data source options. Study objectives and rationale for the outcome measures should be stated. In the contents of the protocol/report section, the target population, alternative treatments, and time horizon should be addressed and uncertainty should be tested by sensitivity analysis. Under the costs/resources section, the perspective of the analysis should be stated, categories of costs should be identified, and resources should be presented as increments (difference between alternatives) as well as totals. In the effectiveness/benefits section, consequences being evaluated and their sources should be clearly stated. Under the data sources section, the quality of the database should be documented. Finally, in the extrapolation of results section, generalizability should be discussed. The PhRMA suggests that following these recommended principles

Table 5. Panel on Cost-Effectiveness Reporting Checklist

Reporting Checklist

1. Framework
- Background of the problem
- General framing and design of the analysis
- Target population for intervention
- Other program descriptors (e.g., care setting, model of delivery, timing of intervention)
- Description of comparator programs
- Boundaries of the analysis
- Time horizon
- Statement of the perspective of the analysis

2. Data and methods
- Description of event pathway
- Identification of outcomes of interest in analysis
- Description of model used
- Modeling assumptions
- Diagram of event pathway/model
- Software used
- Complete information on the sources of effectiveness data, cost data, and preference weights
- Methods for obtaining estimates of effectiveness, costs, and preferences
- Critique and data quality
- Statement of year of costs
- Statement of method used to adjust costs for inflation
- Statement of type of currency
- Source and methods for obtaining expert judgment
- Statements of discount rates

3. Results
- Results of model validation
- Reference Case results (discounted and undiscounted): total costs and effectiveness, incremental costs and effectiveness, and incremental cost-effectiveness ratios
- Results of sensitivity analyses
- Other estimates of uncertainty, if available
- Graphical representation of C/E results
- Aggregate cost and effectiveness information
- Disaggregated results, as relevant
- Secondary analyses using 5% discount rate
- Other secondary analyses, as relevant

4. Discussion
- Summary of Reference Case results
- Summary of sensitivity of results to assumptions and uncertainties in the analysis
- Discussion of analysis assumptions having important ethical implications
- Limitations of the study
- Relevance of study results for specific policy questions or decisions
- Results of related CEAs
- Distributive implications of an intervention

Reprinted with permission from Gold MR, Siegel JE, Russell LB, et al., eds: Cost-Effectiveness in Health and Medicine. New York: Oxford University Press; 1996.

should yield methodologically sound results in quantifying the value of pharmaceutical products and services.

Comparative Review

A checklist for evaluating economic-outcomes literature may be useful for government decision makers, the pharmaceutical industry, MCOs, and health care providers when designing, reading, or adapting economic-outcomes studies to their organizations. Although all checklists encourage a standard regarding what should be assessed when evaluating economic-outcomes literature, there are some slight differences among checklists. For example, both the BMJ and the "Checklist to evaluate pharmacoeconomic studies" specifically addressed the time horizon, modeling, and the type of assessment used in the economic evaluation, whereas "A Checklist for assessing economic evaluations" did not specifically address these elements. On the other hand, "A Checklist for assessing economic evaluations" and the "Checklist to evaluate pharmacoeconomic studies" discussed generalizability, but BMJ did not specifically address this element. Neither "A Checklist for assessing economic evaluations" nor BMJ discussed the issue of disclosure, but the "Checklist to evaluate pharmacoeconomic studies" recommended that every economic study include a section for the identification and discussion of possible ethical problems. Moreover, both the Panel on Cost-effectiveness and PhRMA addressed modeling, generalizability, and time horizon, whereas the authors using the six principles did not specifically address these elements. Out of these three sets of checklists, only the Panel on Cost-effectiveness addressed the issues of disclosure. Despite their differences, for the most part the checklists share a common thread: the basic criteria for the evaluation of pharmacoeconomic literature. Nevertheless, the evaluator who uses a checklist should realize that just because all the criteria have been met does not mean the study has validity. Thus, the checklist is not a substitution for critical and informed thinking on the appropriateness and validity of methods chosen by the investigator. The checklists may be useful to help health care providers interpret and use the results of pharmacoeconomic studies to inform local decision making. Table 7 presents a summary of the six sets of checklists with respect to the 11 essential elements discussed in this chapter.

Analyze and Critique Pharmacoeconomics Literature

Today's cost-sensitive health care environment has been the impetus behind the increasing numbers of pharmacoeconomic analyses conducted and published. For pharmacoeconomics to flourish as a mature area of research and application, it requires expert and skilled professionals. Therefore, practitioners, especially pharmacists, must face the challenge of providing demonstrated evidence that pharmaceutical products and services add value. To be prepared for this challenge, pharmacists must acquire the tools to analyze and critique pharmacoeconomic literature.

Table 6. PhRMA general principles for conducting and evaluating pharmacoeconomic research

Research design:

1. Individual researchers should be free to choose from multiple research design and data source options that have been described in the literature.

Protocol/report:

2. Study objectives and rationale for the outcome measures, data sources, and analysis methods chosen should be stated in a research proposal or protocol.
3. A final report that describes all assumptions, methods, and data sources should be available.

Contents of protocol/report:

4. The study should clearly specify the target population or patient subgroups.
5. Alternative treatments should be stated in the study design, including a discussion of their costs, frequency of use, and relevance for the population of interest.
6. Time horizons for the analysis should be stated and should be based on the likely use and effect of the drug.
7. The study should clearly define the type of and rationale for the analyses.
8. Uncertainty should be demonstrated by statistical analysis to address random events and sensitivity analysis to cover a range of assumptions.

Costs/resources:

9. The perspective of the analysis (societal, third-party payer, etc.) and clear reasons for its selection should be stated.
10. Resources should be relevant to the perspective and described in natural units before a cost analysis is performed.
11. Categories of costs should be identified and presented separately.
12. Resources/costs should be presented as increments (difference between alternatives) as well as totals.
13. Costs should be discounted for analyses with time horizons greater than 1 year.
14. The source(s) and methods of deriving the costs/charges should be clearly stated and validated.

Effectiveness/benefits:

15. Consequences being evaluated and their sources should be clearly stated.
16. Effectiveness/benefit measures should be discounted, when appropriate, for analyses with time horizons of greater than 1 year.
17. Effectiveness/benefit measures should be presented as increments (differences between alternatives) as well as totals.

Data sources:

18. Clinical trial and other databases relevant to the research question may be used; all data need to be statistically controlled for confounding variables through randomization or other modeling techniques.
19. The quality of the database should be documented.
20. Expert clinical opinion may be used for certain limited purposes when other data sources are not available.

Extrapolation of results to other settings:

21. Effectiveness and resources data from one setting may be extrapolated to other settings if differences in medical intervention, treatment patterns, outcomes of existing treatment, and populations are addressed.

Tools Needed

The debate about education and skills needed for conducting, interpreting, and using pharmacoeconomic evaluations in health care decisions has existed for almost as long as the field of pharmacoeconomics. Several conferences have dealt with training qualified professionals, including those sponsored by the American College of Clinical Pharmacists (ACCP), Academy of Managed Care Pharmacy (AMCP), International Federation of Pharmaceutical Manufacturer Associations' Survey (IFPMA), and ISPOR. Various published surveys also have been produced with respect to the teaching of pharmacoeconomics at the university level. As the field of pharmacoeconomics continues to evolve, analyzing and critiquing pharmacoeconomic literature will require: (1) effective application and understanding of pharmacoeconomic terminology; (2) familiarity with the principles, methods, and applications of pharmacoeconomics; (3) attendance at conferences and acceptance of training opportunities; and (4) reading current literature and conversing with other professionals about research development in the field. Regardless of their health care environment, practitioners can benefit from applying the principles and methods of pharmacoeconomics to their daily practice settings.

Application of Skills

The primary purpose of applying skills to evaluating economic-outcomes literature is to determine or document that pharmaceutical products and services add value to a real-world practice setting. These skills center on developing three levels of expertise, awareness, application, and conceptualization extracted from the ISPOR Advisory Panel Report, February 1998: (1) awareness is defined as an exposure to and factual knowledge of pharmacoeconomics that allows trained practitioners to converse and understand research data in the field; (2) practitioners who are effective at applying their skills should be able to critically compare, evaluate, and make decisions based on pharmacoeconomic data. Furthermore, they should have the ability to initiate pharmacoeconomic analyses based on standard methodologies; (3) practitioners who are at the conceptualization level should use their skills to create new methodology, develop theory and assimilate relevant methodologies and theories from related disciplines.

Moreover, applications of skills, regardless of level, are enhanced by the incorporation of real-world data and exposure. Continuing professional education programs offer one avenue to receive training that may involve applying skills in a real-world scenario, with case studies and live datasets.

Table 7. Comparison of checklists with respect to 11 essential elements discussed in the chapter.

Elements	BMJ	Sacristán et al.	Drummond et al.
Type of assessment	The form of economic assessment used is stated and the choice of economic assessment is justified in relation to the questions addressed.	Is the type of analysis used suitable for the problem being examined?	Not specifically addressed
Perspective	The perspective of the analysis is clearly stated and justified.	Is the perspective clearly specified?	Was the perspective stated?
Comparator	The alternatives being compared are clearly described and justified.	Is the alternative compared clearly specified?	Did the study involve a comparison of alternatives?
Sensitivity Analysis	The approach to sensitivity analysis is given and choice of variables for sensitivity analysis is justified.	Is a sensitivity analysis performed?	If a sensitivity analysis was employed, was justification provided for the ranges of values?
Costs	Quantities of resources are reported separately from their unit costs. Methods for the estimation of quantities and unit costs are described. Currency and price data are recorded, and details of currency of price adjustments for inflation or currency conversion are given.	Is the measurement of costs suitable for the perspective? Are the costs up-to-date, and are the prices those of market?	Were all costs for each alternative identified? Were costs measured accurately in appropriate physical units? Were costs valued credibly? Was an incremental analysis of costs of alternatives performed?
Outcomes	The primary outcome measure for the economic evaluation is clearly stated. Incremental analysis is reported. Major outcomes are presented in a disaggregated as well as an aggregated form.	Is the main assessment variable (endpoint) objective and relevant? Is a marginal analysis performed? Are the costs and consequences of adverse effects analyzed?	Were consequences for each alternative identified? Were consequences measured in appropriate physical units?
Modeling	Details of any model used are given. The choice of the model used and the key parameters on which it is based are justified.	Is a decision analysis applied?	Not specifically addressed
Time Horizon	Time horizon of costs and benefits is stated.	Is the time fixed for the evaluation sufficient and is it specified?	Not specifically addressed
Discounting	The discount rate is stated and choice of rate is justified. An explanation is given if costs or benefits are not discounted.	Is an adjustment of future costs and benefits performed?	Were costs and consequences that occur in the future discounted to their present value? Was any justification given for the discount rate used?

Disclosure	Not specifically addressed	Are possible ethical problems discussed and identified?	Not specifically addressed
Generalizability	Not specifically addressed	Can results be generalized?	Did the study discuss generalizablity?

Elements	**Udvarhelyi et al.**	**Panel on Cost-Effectiveness**	**PhRMA**
Type of assessment	CEA and CBA	CEA	Researcher is free to choose based on the literature.
Perspective	Perspective stated	Statement of the perspective	Clearly state perspective.
Comparator	Not specifically addressed	Description of comparator programs	State alternative treatments.
Sensitivity Analysis	Sensitivity analysis should be done.	Results of sensitivity analyses	Results of sensitivity analyses
Costs	Researchers should specify what types of costs were used.	Complete information on the sources of cost, methods for obtaining estimates of costs, statement for year of costs, statement of method used to adjust costs for inflation, and statement of type of currency	Identify categories of costs and present costs as increments as well as totals.
Outcomes	Summary measurement of efficiency should be expressed in marginal or incremental terms unless one alternative is dominant.	Complete information on sources of effectiveness and methods for obtaining estimates of effectiveness	State consequences and present as increments as as well as totals.
Modeling	Not specifically addressed	Description of model used	Use standard techniques (e.g., Markov).
Time Horizon	Not specifically addressed	State time horizon.	State time horizon.
Discounting	Discounting should be used.	Statement of discount rates	Costs should be discounted.
Disclosure	Not specifically addressed	Ethical implications	Not specifically addressed
Generalizability addressed	Not specifically	Discussion of the limitations is intended to guide the reader in generalizing the results.	Extrapolation of results to other settings

Abbreviations: CEA = cost-effectiveness analysis; CBA = cost-benefit analysis

Controversies with Pharmacoeconomics Literature

Because pharmacoeconomics is a relatively new science without strong consensus on all methods, numerous publications have highlighted the inconsistent reporting and disagreement on methodology of pharmacoeconomic analyses. The widespread and highly visible disagreement among leading researchers in the field may contribute to external skepticism. Consequently, end users may be lackluster in their application pharmacoeconomic analyses, and findings may not be used as extensively as they could be in the decision making process. Ultimately, assessment of economic outcomes without consideration for all of the evidence will lead to inefficient decisions that adversely affect the distribution of health care resources.

Inconsistent Reporting

There is a need to develop a consensus on reporting pharmacoeconomic studies so that decision makers may be convinced of their reliability and relevance. However, the multidisciplinary nature of this field of research makes it challenging to resolve this controversial issue. For example, pharmacoeconomic information may be delivered to decision makers by way of pharmaceutical companies or their representatives (e.g., research organizations) in support of a particular drug therapy. There may be very little consistency in how this information is offered because each company and each researcher may present a different view of the research and the results. Consequently, pharmacoeconomic analyses are viewed skeptically and are considered to have limited applicability in the decision making process. To resolve the controversial issue of inconsistent reporting, a standard form of providing clinical, economic, and outcomes data to decision makers should be developed to consistently communicate the necessary data and results. Creating a standard scheme for reporting all types of pharmacoeconomic analyses will help end users maneuver through the information available, more quickly comprehend the bottom line, and be able to compare results across studies for decision making purposes.

Disagreement on Methodology

Another controversy stems from disagreement on economic evaluation methodology (e.g., researchers disagree about the inclusion of indirect costs and benefits, choice of discount rate for health benefits, and method of measuring the utilities of health status). There are different expectations among those who produce and those who interpret pharmacoeconomic studies. That is, the methods may be geared toward societal decision making but practical applications are at a different level (e.g., clinical decisions, formulary management, drug use policy, disease management, and resource allocation). Also undermining the methodology is the potential for bias in pharmacoeconomic analyses. In addition to the traditional concerns surrounding threats to internal and external validity, reliability, and self-selection into clinical trials, this issue addresses the controversy over funding of studies by pharmaceutical companies. Pharmaceutical companies' primary interest in economic-outcomes research is to promote the cost-effectiveness of their products. They fund research with a high probability of producing favorable findings. As a result, there is a perception that financial sponsorship may bias the study results. Bias may be introduced throughout the process of conducting a pharmacoeconomic analysis, and it may be intentional or unintentional. For example, the bias may result from an overemphasis on cost savings. Bias in economic-outcomes research leads to a systematic suppression of information that is needed by decision makers to determine how to allocate resources more effectively. Implementing a set of standardized methods to be used when conducting a pharmacoeconomic analysis will help limit the introduction of bias as well as assure decision makers that the analysis is methodologically and ethically sound.

Annotated Bibliography

1. Gold MR, Siegel JE, Russell LB, et al., eds. Cost-Effectiveness in Health and Medicine. New York: Oxford University Press; 1996.

   This book, a report of a U.S. Public Health Service-appointed expert panel, makes a significant contribution toward improving the methods of cost-effectiveness analysis (CEA). Each chapter of this book is dedicated toward standardization of conducting and reporting CEAs. Chapter nine gives recommendations to investigators about how to report and submit a CEA for publication.

2. Pauly MV. Valuing health care benefits in money terms. In: Sloan FA, ed., Valuing Health Care. New York: Cambridge University Press;1995:99–124.

   In Chapter six, the author explores in depth the relationship and differences between two commonly used methods cost-benefit analysis (CBA) and CEA for measuring the value of pharmaceutical products and services. He presents a thorough and intelligent argument for how CBA may be superior to CEA from a theoretical perspective.

3. Mullins CD, Ogilvie S. Emerging standardization in pharmacoeconomics. Clin Ther 1998;20(60):1194–1202.

   The authors performed a comprehensive literature review of the pharmacoeconomics guidelines from the United Kingdom, Spain, Italy, Australia, Canada, and the United States to determine areas of emerging standardization. The authors discuss general principles for which there is consensus across guidelines and the various differences detected across guidelines.

4. International Society for Pharmacoeconomics and Outcomes Research (ISPOR). Pharmacoeconomics: Identifying the Issues Advisory Panel Reports, 1998, from *http://www.ispor.org/workpaper/adpanel/index.html.*

   Cosponsored by the U.S. Health and Human Services, the Agency for Health Care Policy and Research, and the Health Outcomes Work Group of the Pharmaceutical Research Manufacturer's Association, ISPOR convened the Advisory Panel Meeting and Conference on Pharmacoeconomic Issues in February 1998. The objective of this interdisciplinary conference was to identify the issues involved in conducting pharmacoeconomic studies in interpreting the results of these studies, and in using pharmacoeconomic information in health care decisions. The results of this meeting and conference are summarized.

5. Drummond MF. Guidelines for pharmacoeconomics studies: The ways forward. Pharmacoeconomics 1994;6(6):493-497.

   The author presents a description of how economic studies can play a role in pricing decisions in countries that have universal health care coverage. This article provides a detailed discussion of the various parties with a stake in guidelines for the provision of economic information, explores the purposes served by such guidelines, and recommends ways to move forward.

6. Hillman AL, Eisenberg JM, Pauly MV, et al. Avoiding bias in the conduct and reporting of cost-effectiveness research sponsored by pharmaceutical companies. New Engl J Med 1991;321(19):1362–1365.

   This is a controversial article exploring the conduct of industry-sponsored pharmacoeconomic analyses. The underlying issue driving the need for the development of methodological and ethical guidelines in conducting and reporting pharmacoeconomic analyses is the potential for biases that may occur because of the behavior of the investigator, the sponsoring company, or both. The authors offer recommendations for building relationships between industry and academia to limit the introduction of bias into evaluations.

7. Burke LB. US Regulation of Pharmaceutical Outcomes Research. Presented at the ISPOR 5th Annual International Meeting, Crystal City, VA, 24 May 2000. Value in Health 2001;4(1):5–7.

   The author presents an enlightened discussion about how pharmaceutical companies use the patient perspective to market the value of their drug to formulary decision makers. This article deals with a series of issues that involve the future of outcomes research in drug development and the role of the Food and Drug Administration (FDA) in reviewing outcomes measures used in pharmaceutical product promotion.

8. Drummond MF, Jefferson TO. Guidelines for authors and peer reviewers of economic submissions to the BMJ. Br Med J 1996;313:275–283.

   The authors give readers a behind-the-scenes look at why the British Medical Journal (BMJ) set up a working party on economic evaluation. This is an excellent article that examines BMJ guidelines for improving the quality of submitted and published economic articles. Together with comprehensive supporting statements and a checklist, the guidelines reflect a broad consensus among the BMJ working party and are comprehensive and readable by both specialists and nonspecialists.

9. Sacristán JA, Soto J, Galende I. Evaluations of pharmacoeconomic studies: utilization of a checklist. Ann Pharmacother 1993;27:1126–33.

   The authors performed a thorough and impressive MEDLINE search for articles that evaluated the methodology of health economics. The article contains an excellent discussion about the similarities and differences between clinical trials and clinical economics studies. The authors introduce fundamental concepts used in clinical economic analysis in the form of a checklist.

10. Drummond MF, O'Brien B, Stoddart GL, et al. Methods for the Economic Evaluation of Health Care Programmes, 2nd ed. Oxford University Press; 1997.

    This is a classic publication that serves as an introductory text for those contemplating, undertaking, commissioning, or using an economic evaluation. The book discusses the terminology and points out the building blocks for an economic evaluation. Chapter three concentrates on the appropriateness of the methodology employed in economic evaluation and was designed to assist readers in assessing the validity of the results they encounter.

11. Udvarhelyi S, Colditz GA, Rai A, et al. Cost-effectiveness and cost-benefit analyses in the medical literature: are the methods being used correctly? Ann Intern Med 1992;116:238–244.

    This comprehensive review article found that, out of 77 articles published from 1978 to 1980 and from 1985 to 1987, 70 focused on CEA, and seven focused on CBA. Only three of these 77 articles adhered to the authors' six fundamental principles of analysis. This paper demonstrated that greater attention should be devoted to ensuring the appropriate use of analytic methods for economic analyses.

12. The Pharmaceutical Research and Manufacturers of America (PhRMA). Methodological and conduct principles for pharmacoeconomic research. Washington, DC: PhRMA; 1995.

    The PhRMA published guidance, enumerating the principles for conducting and evaluating pharmacoeconomic research. The guide gives an informative description of the key differences between clinical and pharmacoeconomic analyses. It examines in detail each step of a pharmacoeconomic analysis intended for use in the promotion of pharmaceuticals and provides a succinct discussion about how this document is pertinent to pharmaceutical companies as well as other researchers in the discipline.

Self-Assessment Questions

1. Which one of the following factors was *not* likely the purpose of the study discussed in Reference 13?

   A. To assess adverse reactions of pravastatin therapy.
   B. To assess the benefit of pravastatin therapy.
   C. To assess the cost of pravastatin therapy.
   D. To assess the effectiveness of pravastatin therapy.

2. From the study discussed in Reference 13, which one of the following costs was included in the cost-effectiveness ratio?

   A. Indirect costs.
   B. Intangible costs.
   C. Direct nonmedical costs.
   D. Direct medical costs.

3. Which one of the following best describes the characteristics of the comparator from the study discussed in Reference 13?

A. Active treatment, which is useful for decision makers.
B. Active treatment, which is not useful for decision makers.
C. Placebo-controlled trial, which documents the cost-effectiveness of a statin.
D. Placebo-controlled trial, which helps with the selection of a particular statin.

4. Which one of the following *least* represents the purpose of Markov models from the study discussed in Reference 13?

A. To estimate the probability of going from health to death.
B. To estimate effectiveness from efficacy data obtained in a clinical trial.
C. To analyze the likelihood of one event following another.
D. To estimate lost productivity associated with hospitalizations.

5. The discount rate in the study discussed in Reference 13 was based on which one of the following factors?

A. Medical care component of the Consumer Price Index for costs plus three percent per year of life.
B. Medical care component of the Consumer Price Index for both costs and years of life.
C. Three percent for all costs and years of life.
D. Medical care component of Consumer Price Index for costs only.

6. Who benefits the most from checklists for pharmacoeconomic studies?

A. Relatively untrained decision makers.
B. Highly trained pharmacoeconomists.
C. Doctorate of Pharmacy students.
D. Patients.

7. Generalizability is best described by which one of the following?

A. The ability to quantitatively synthesize the literature.
B. The ability to incorporate patient-subjective measures.
C. The extent to which results apply to other patients/health care settings.
D. The extent to which the patients will typically adhere to therapy.

8. Every pharmacoeconomic study should do which one of the following?

A. Describe all relevant drugs and insurance options available to patients.
B. List all dosage forms available to patients.
C. Describe the competing treatments, costs, and consequences.
D. Perform a cost-minimization analysis in addition to other calculations.

9. Which statement best describes pharmacoeconomic studies that are sponsored by drug manufacturers?

A. They should be illegal.
B. They never contain promotional claims because claims are edited during peer review.
C. They are relatively uncommon.
D. They should be evaluated for potential bias.

10. Which statement best describes guidelines for conducting pharmacoeconomics?

A. They should be avoided until one worldwide guideline is selected.
B. They should be periodically updated as pharmacoeconomics evolves.
C. They exist in fewer than five countries.
D. They have been universally adopted.

11. For what reason is evaluation of the pharmacoeconomics literature critical?

A. Ensuring clinical relevance.
B. Ensuring correct methodology.
C. Planning sensitivity analysis.
D. Planning selection of outcomes.

12. Which one of the following is an obstacle to implementing pharmacoeconomics literature evaluation within a health care system to control costs?

A. It limits the pharmacy budget.
B. It minimizes the role of pharmacists.
C. It puts full-time equivalents (FTEs) at risk when the budget is not met.
D. It requires training.

13. Which one of the following statements best describes the scheme discussed in Reference 11 for conducting economic evaluations?

A. It reflects six basic principles that are common among other checklists.
B. It can be used to determine the highest quality health outcomes studies.
C. It is one of the most recently published checklists.
D. It provides the most detailed guidance.

14. The publication that discusses methodological controversies the most is by which group?

A. The British Medical Journal.
B. The Panel on Cost Effectiveness.
C. The group discussed in Reference 9.
D. The group discussed in Reference 11.

Exercise 1

Critically evaluate the economic and outcomes study (Appendix A) using one of the six checklists for a pharmacoeconomics literature evaluation.

Exercise 2

Review the Economic Evaluation of Health Care section and use what you have learned from this chapter to critically evaluate the same study. Then, using the two scoring instruments (general and pharmacoeconomics), evaluate the same study and calculate a summary quality score. Finally, compare your checklist evaluation from Exercise 1 with the summary score in an overall assessment of the study.

Scoring System for Exercise 2

The scoring system for Exercise 2 has two scoring instruments (general and pharmacoeconomics). The general instrument consists of 15 common questions applicable to any study type and design, such as, "Was the study question sufficiently well described?" The pharmacoeconomics instrument consists of 12 questions, which evaluate topics ranging from the perspective of the study to the analysis of benefits and costs. The instruments, a relatively quick and simple scoring system, were developed to rate the quality of studies. Each question in the rating system is allocated a "positive" 1, 2, or 3 point(s) if answered "yes." One "positive" point is allocated to questions with a "partial" response. Furthermore, each question is allocated either a "negative" 1, 2, or 3 point(s) if answered "no," and zero points are allocated for a "not applicable" response. The study begins with a baseline score of 45 points. Points are added or subtracted from the baseline, based on the previously discussed allocation of points, (i.e., add a point for a "yes" or "partial" response, subtract a point for a "no" response, or add zero points for a "not applicable" response. The point system for the general scoring instrument ranges from "negative" 30 (if all questions were answered "no") to "positive" 35 (if all questions were answered "yes"). The point system for the pharmacoeconomics scoring instrument ranges from "negative" 15 (if all questions were answered "no") to a "positive" 20 (if all questions were answered "yes"). When points from the scoring instruments are combined, the total points for the article ranges from a minimum of zero to a maximum of 100. A combined score of less than 70 is considered bad, scores between 70 and 79 are fair, scores between 80 and 90 are good, and a score above 90 is excellent. The development of these instruments resulted from a review of previously published instruments, with adaptation to the evaluation of pharmacoeconomics articles.

Conclusion

The applications, principles, and methods for evaluating economic-outcomes literature were discussed in this chapter. Evaluators, such as pharmacists who understand these concepts, will be adequately prepared to evaluate a pharmacoeconomics study to determine and quantify the value added from pharmaceutical products and services relative to their alternatives.

SCORING INSTRUMENT (General)

Article Title: ______________________________

____

Author(s): ______________________________

____

Study Design:

What did the study assess? Check all that apply.

☐ Risks ☐ Benefits ☐ Costs

In the space below, please provide a synopsis or short summary of the article that you are reviewing (use additional paper if necessary):

____

____

____

____

____

____

____

____

____

____

1. Was the study question sufficiently well-described?

☐ Yes (2) ☐ Partial (1) ☐ No (-1)

2. Was the study population clearly specified (e.g., inclusion and exclusion criteria)?

☐ Yes (2) ☐ Partial (1) ☐ No (-2) ☐ N/A (0)

3. Were subjects appropriate to the study question?

☐ Yes (2) ☐Partial (1) ☐ No (-1)

4. Were comparator drugs/controls (subjects)/treatment options appropriate?

☐ Yes (3) ☐ Partial (1) ☐ No (-3) ☐ N/A (0)

5. If blinding of investigators to intervention was possible, was it reported?

☐ Yes (1) ☐ No (-1) ☐ N/A (0)

6. Was measurement bias accounted for by methods other than blinding?

☐ Yes (3) ☐ Partial (1) ☐ No (-3) ☐ N/A (0)

7. Were other biases in the data and/or confounders accounted for by methods other than blinding, such as study design or analysis?

☐ Yes (3) ☐ Partial (1) ☐ No (-3) ☐ N/A (0)

8. Were post hoc power calculations or confidence intervals reported for statistically nonsignificant results?

☐ Yes (2) ☐ Partial (1) ☐ No (-1) ☐ N/A (0)

9. Were the statistical tests/analyses stated (e.g., descriptive statistics and frequencies)?

☐ Yes (2) ☐ Partial (1) ☐ No (-1) ☐ N/A (0)

10. Did the test/analysis relate to the research question?

☐ Yes (3) ☐ Partial (1) ☐ No (-3)

11. Were the statistical analyses appropriate?

☐ Yes (2) ☐ Partial (1) ☐ No (-3)

12. Were statistical results such as exact P-values or confidence intervals reported for each test?

☐ Yes (2) ☐ Partial (1) ☐ No (-1)

13. Were exact results completely reported?

☐ Yes (2) ☐ Partial (1) ☐ No (-1) ☐ N/A (0)

14. Overall, was the study design appropriate?

☐ Yes (3) ☐ Partial (1) ☐ No (-3)

15. Do the findings support the conclusion?

☐ Yes (3) ☐ Partial (1) ☐ No (-3)

SCORING INSTRUMENT (Pharmacoeconomics)

Article Title: ______________________________

____

Author(s): ______________________________

____

Study Design

1.1 Is the perspective clearly stated?

☐ Yes (2) ☐ No (-1)

1.2 If the perspective is stated, is it appropriate for the question asked?

☐ Yes (1) ☐ No (-1) ☐ N/A (perspective not reported) (0)

Analysis of Benefits

2.1 Is the measurement of benefits adequate or appropriate for the study question or the stated perspective?

☐ Yes (2) ☐ Partial (1) ☐ No (-1)

2.2 Are the specified endpoints appropriate and justified?

☐ Yes (3) ☐ Partial (1) ☐ No (-2)

2.3 Is the time horizon for the benefits appropriate?

☐ Yes (1) ☐ No (-1)

Analysis of Costs

3.1 Are the cost variables adequate and appropriate for the stated perspective?

☐ Yes (1) ☐ No (-1)

3.2 Do the cost estimates seem reasonable?

☐ Yes (1) ☐ No (-1)

3.3 If the time horizon is greater than 1 year, are future costs discounted?

☐ Yes (1) ☐ No (-1)

Analysis Type

4.1 Identify the type of analysis used.

☐ Cost analysis ☐ Cost-benefit analysis
☐ Cost-effectiveness analysis ☐ Cost-utility analysis ☐ Cost-minimization analysis
☐ Cost-consequences analysis

4.2 Is this type of analysis appropriate?

☐ Yes (2) ☐ No (-2)

4.3 Was sensitivity analysis performed?

☐ Yes (3) ☐ Partial (1) ☐ No (-3)

4.4 Was an incremental analysis performed?

☐ Yes (3) ☐ No (-1)

Clinical Investigations

Secondary Prevention and Rehabilitation

Cost-effectiveness of pravastatin therapy for survivors of myocardial infarction with average cholesterol levels

Joel Tsevat, MD, MPH,[a] Karen M. Kuntz, ScD,[b,c] E. John Orav, PhD,[c,d] Milton C. Weinstein, PhD,[b,d] Frank M. Sacks, MD,[c] and Lee Goldman, MD, MPH[e] *Cincinnati, Ohio, Boston, Mass, and San Francisco, Calif*

Background The objective of this study was to assess the cost-effectiveness of pravastatin therapy in survivors of myocardial infarction with average cholesterol levels.

Methods We performed a cost-effectiveness analysis based on actual clinical, cost, and health-related quality-of-life data from the Cholesterol and Recurrent Events (CARE) trial. Survival and recurrent coronary heart disease events were modeled from trial data in Markov models, with the use of different assumptions regarding the long-term benefit of therapy.

Results Pravastatin therapy increased quality-adjusted life expectancy at an incremental cost of $16,000 to $32,000 per quality-adjusted life-year gained. In subgroup analyses, the cost-effectiveness of pravastatin therapy was more favorable for patients >60 years of age and for patients with pretreatment low-density lipoprotein cholesterol levels >125 mg/dL. Results were sensitive to the cost of pravastatin and to assumptions about long-term survival benefits from pravastatin therapy.

Conclusions The cost-effectiveness of pravastatin therapy in survivors of myocardial infarction with average cholesterol levels compares favorably with other interventions. (Am Heart J 2001;141:727-34.)

Coronary heart disease (CHD) is the leading cause of death in developed countries. In the United States, approximately 460,000 people die of CHD each year, and the annual cost of treating CHD is $55.2 billion.[1] Patients with CHD are at especially high risk of having fatal or nonfatal ischemic events. Because hypercholesterolemia is a major risk factor for such events, there is widespread agreement based on data from randomized trials that secondary prevention of CHD should include aggressive treatment of hypercholesterolemia.[2-7]

Treatment of hypercholesterolemia among patients who have had myocardial infarction not only reduces morbidity and mortality rates but is also relatively cost-effective.[8-13] However, the majority of survivors of acute myocardial infarction have average rather than high serum cholesterol levels.[14] Recently, the Cholesterol and Recurrent Events (CARE) trial[3] demonstrated that aggressive cholesterol-lowering therapy with pravastatin reduced the risk of fatal coronary events, nonfatal myocardial infarctions, revascularization procedures (coronary artery bypass surgery and angioplasty), and strokes among survivors of myocardial infarction with average cholesterol levels (eligibility criteria for the CARE trial included a total serum cholesterol level <240 mg/dL [6.2 mmol/L] and a low-density lipoprotein [LDL] level between 115 and 174 mg/dL [3.0 to 4.5 mmol/L]). It is not known, however, whether treating survivors of myocardial infarction who have average cholesterol levels with statin (HMG-CoA reductase inhibitor) drugs, which are relatively expensive, compares favorably in an economic sense with other therapies for such patients. The purpose of this study was to determine the cost-effectiveness of pravastatin therapy for survivors of myocardial infarction with average cholesterol levels by using data on effectiveness of therapy, resource use, and health-related quality of life directly from the CARE trial.

Methods

Patient characteristics

The cost-effectiveness analysis pertains to survivors of myocardial infarction similar to those enrolled in the CARE

From the [a]Section of Outcomes Research, Division of General Internal Medicine, Department of Internal Medicine and Center for Clinical Effectiveness, Institute for Health Policy and Health Services Research, University of Cincinnati Medical Center; [b]Center for Risk Analysis, Department of Health Policy and Management, Harvard School of Public Health; the [c]Department of Medicine, Brigham and Women's Hospital, Harvard Medical School; the [d]Department of Biostatistics, Harvard School of Public Health; and the [e]Department of Medicine, University of California, San Francisco.

Supported by a grant from Bristol-Myers Squibb. The funding agreement ensured the authors' independence in designing the study, interpreting the data, and writing and publishing the manuscript.

Submitted April 17, 2000; accepted February 1, 2001.

Reprint requests: Joel Tsevat, MD, MPH, Section of Outcomes Research, Division of General Internal Medicine, University of Cincinnati Medical Center, 231 Bethesda Ave, Cincinnati, OH 45267-0535.

E-mail: joel.tsevat@uc.edu

0002-8703/2001/$35.00 + 0 4/1/114805

doi:10.1067/mhj.2001.114805

Figure 1

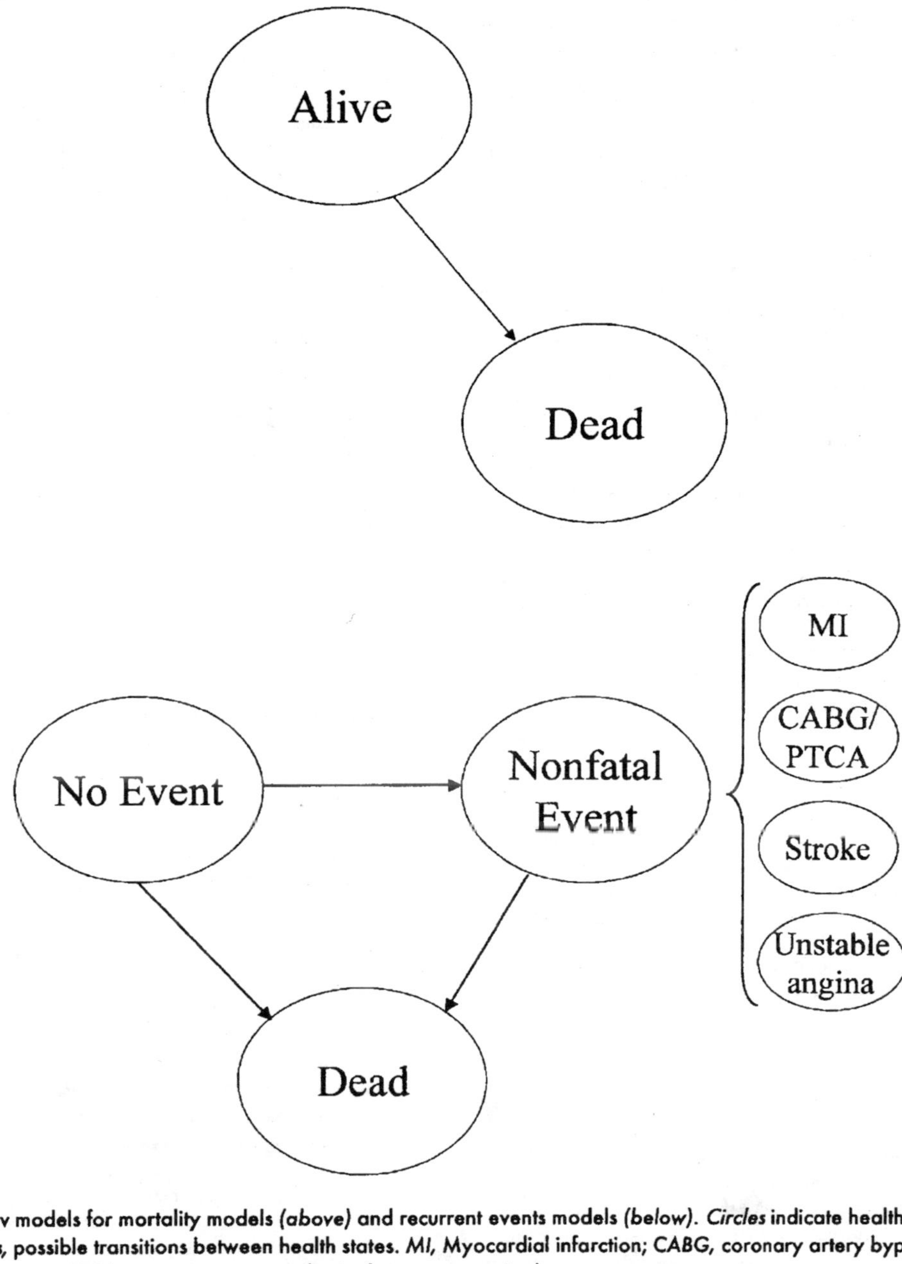

Markov models for mortality models *(above)* and recurrent events models *(below)*. *Circles* indicate health states; *arrows*, possible transitions between health states. *MI*, Myocardial infarction; *CABG*, coronary artery bypass graft surgery; *PTCA*, percutaneous transluminal coronary angioplasty.

trial. In CARE, the mean (SD) age was 59 (9) years. Eighty-six percent of patients were men; among patients assigned to the pravastatin arm, 93% were white, whereas among patients assigned to placebo, 92% were white. The mean cholesterol level at study entry for each group was 209 mg/dL (5.4 mmol/L), with a mean LDL fraction of 139 mg/dL (3.6 mmol/L).[3]

Effectiveness of therapy

To model the effectiveness of therapy, we developed two pairs of Markov models,[15] one pair based on all-cause mortality data from CARE (mortality models; Figure 1, *top*) and one based on recurrent event data from CARE (recurrent events models; Figure 1, *bottom*). The advantage of the mortality model is that it directly calculates quality-adjusted life-years (QALYs) gained with pravastatin therapy; QALYs are the standard denominator for reference case cost-effectiveness analyses.[16] The drawback of the mortality models is that they are based on an end point (all-cause mortality) that was not a primary end point in CARE and that was not statistically significantly different between treatment arms. The advantage of the recurrent events models is that they more closely simulate the primary end point of the CARE trial; their disadvantage is that they require further extrapolation to yield QALYs.

Mortality models

The mortality models incorporated all-cause mortality data for years 1 through 6 for the pravastatin and placebo groups from all 4159 trial patients. Because annual mortality rates fluctuated and because there was a 2-year lag to the effect of pravastatin therapy, we smoothed mortality rates for years 1 through 2 and years 3 through 6, weighting by the number of patients at risk in each year.

Survival beyond the end of the trial was simulated in the Markov model, which distinguished between CHD-related deaths and other-cause deaths. Age-specific other-cause mortality rates were obtained from US life tables and incorporated into the Markov model.[17] Age-specific CHD mortality rates for patients with a history of myocardial infarction were obtained from the Coronary Heart Disease Policy Model,[18,19] adjusted for the disease severity of CARE patients.

In the first of the two mortality models (mortality model 1), we incorporated actual CHD-related and non-CHD-related mortality data from CARE, stratified by treatment group. For years 1 through 2, the all-cause annual mortality rate was 0.0143 for the pravastatin group and 0.0144 for the placebo group. For years 3 through 6, the rates were 0.0209 (pravastatin group) and 0.0224 (placebo group). In mortality model 2, we assumed that non-CHD-related mortality rates were equal in both groups. In both models, we assumed that the survival benefit found in CARE would persist indefinitely as long as patients continued their therapy, but we examined various other assumptions regarding the long-term benefit of therapy in sensitivity analyses.

Recurrent events models

In the recurrent events models, we modeled fatal coronary events and nonfatal events (myocardial infarction, unstable angina, revascularization, and stroke) from the CARE data. Event rates were stratified by study arm and smoothed for years 1 through 2 and years 3 through 6. For years 1 through 2, the event rate was 0.0813 for the pravastatin group and 0.0841 for the placebo group. For years 3 through 6, the rates were 0.0654 (pravastatin group) and 0.0796 (placebo group). We estimated event- and group-specific case-fatality rates for patients who had a nonfatal event. Although in the trial, case-fatality rates for events were higher in the pravastatin arm than in the placebo arm, we assumed that after 10 years the case-fatality rates in the two treatment arms would be equal; we relaxed this assumption in a sensitivity analysis. Then, as with the mortality models, we developed one model that incorporated actual (unequal) group-specific non-CHD-related mortality rates (recurrent events model 1) and one that

Table I. Costs and health-related quality of life

	Pravastatin group	Placebo group
Annual direct medical cost		
Pravastatin therapy ($)*,†	925	0
Other cardiac medications ($)*,†	1295	1227
Hospitalizations, 1st y ($)*	1752	1804
Hospitalizations, 2nd y ($)*	1434	1663
Hospitalizations, 3rd y ($)*	1566	1690
Hospitalizations, 4th y ($)*	1315	1695
Hospitalizations, 5th y ($)*	1641	2191
Hospitalizations, 6th y ($)*	1698	2050
Myocardial infarction, 1st y ($)†	5087	6521
Subsequent y ($)†	3254	2661
Unstable angina, 1st y ($)†	4320	4345
Subsequent y ($)†	2424	2545
Revascularization, 1st y ($)†	3109	3601
Subsequent y ($)†	1614	2121
Stroke, 1st y ($)†	3913	2748
Subsequent y ($)†	2808	2530
Utility*	0.968	0.965

*Value used in mortality models.
†Value used in recurrent events models. (See text for details.)

assumed equal non-CHD-related mortality rates (recurrent events model 2).

Subgroup analyses

To parallel the subgroup analyses in the CARE trial, we determined the cost-effectiveness of pravastatin therapy for the following groups: men; women; pretreatment LDL level <125 mg/dL (3.2 mmol/L); pretreatment LDL level 125 to 150 mg/dL (3.2 to 3.9 mmol/L); pretreatment LDL level >150 mg/dL (3.9 mmol/L); age <60 years; and age ≥60 years.

Health-related quality-of-life adjustments

To incorporate health-related quality of life into the analyses, we assessed health ratings serially from all patients in CARE (Table I). Patients were asked to rate their health on a scale ranging from 0 (dead) to 100 (perfect health).[20] Health ratings were obtained annually; the mean number of ratings per patient was 5.1 (range, 1 to 7). Because quality-of-life weights in cost-effectiveness analysis should be based on health utilities rather than health ratings,[16] we transformed the mean patient ratings (r) to a mean utility (u), stratified by group, by using the McMaster power transformation[21]: $u = 1-(1-r)^{2.29}$. In the mortality models, as a simplification, we used the mean utility for each treatment group throughout the model (rather than year-specific utilities). In the recurrent events models, we used separate utilities for each health state, stratified by treatment group.

Costs

The analysis was performed from the societal perspective[16] with the use of costs rather than charges.[22] Cost estimates for the model were based on actual resource utilization of trial patients (Table I). We included direct medical costs only.

Detailed hospitalization data were obtained for all US patients enrolled in CARE. For each hospitalization, a trained medical records coder, blinded to treatment assignment, converted the International Classification of Diseases (ICD-9-CM) codes into Diagnosis-Related Groups (DRGs) and assigned the appropriate DRG reimbursement rate for 1996. Then, to account for professional fees associated with hospitalizations, we used Medicare's ratio of part B to part A expenditures for hospitalizations in 1995 (J. Wandishin, written communication, June 24, 1997); on the basis of that ratio, we added 16.6% to the DRG reimbursements to calculate total costs of hospitalization. For hospitalization costs after year 6, we averaged annual costs for years 1 through 6. In the recurrent events model, we used costs for the first year and for subsequent years after an event, stratified by treatment group.

The cost of pravastatin therapy was based on a dose of 40 mg daily (the target dose in CARE) and consisted of the average wholesale price (RedBook for Windows, Micromedex, Inc, Englewood, Colo)—reduced by 18.3% to reflect the overestimate of actual pharmacy acquisition costs of brand name drugs[23]—plus a monthly dispensing cost of $5.47.[24] On the basis of pill counts from CARE, we factored into the cost an adherence rate of 91.2%, calculated as the proportion of time patients were receiving active treatment (94.6%) times the proportion of pills taken while receiving active treatment (96.4%).

We also included the costs of other cardiac medications by using data from all 100 patients enrolled at one study site. Other cardiac medications included aspirin and anticoagulant medications; diuretics; cardiac glycosides; antianginal agents; antiarrhythmic agents; calcium channel blockers; β-blockers; centrally acting antihypertensives; vasodilators; angiotensin-converting enzyme inhibitors; and antihyperlipidemics. Because information on doses of those medications was not available, for each cardiac medication we determined the cost of a prototypic dose, defined as the midpoint of the range of maintenance doses as listed in *Drug Facts and Comparisons*.[25] For medications whose doses are adjusted on the basis of laboratory tests, we assigned a prototypic dose (eg, for warfarin, 7.5 mg/d). For medications dosed by patient weight, we used the dose for a 70-kg person. In cases of medications with multiple indications (eg, after myocardial infarction and hypertension), we used the dose most appropriate for CHD. Because we did not have data on pill counts for these cardiac medications, we assumed full adherence with medication. As with pravastatin, we used adjusted average wholesale prices (that is, average wholesale prices discounted by 18.3% for brand names and 42.5% for generic formulations)[23] and added a dispensing cost of $5.47 per 1-month supply.

All costs were assumed to continue to accrue over the patient's lifetime. Costs of outpatient tests were assumed to be equal under both strategies and thus were not modeled explicitly. To the extent that patients not receiving pravastatin therapy may have had more outpatient visits and undergone more outpatient tests (eg, electrocardiograms, echocardiograms, thallium stress tests) because they had more cardiovascular events, our analysis would be biased against the pravastatin strategy.

All costs were converted to 1996 US dollars by means of the medical care component of the Consumer Price Index. All costs and years of life were discounted at 3% per year.[16]

Sensitivity analyses

To examine the robustness of the cost-effectiveness results, we varied the assumptions and model parameters widely in sensitivity analyses. We also did a sensitivity analysis on the hospitalization costs in which we considered only those hospitalizations related to cardiovascular disease (eg, CHD, congestive heart failure, and stroke). For simplicity, most of the sensitivity analyses we present relate to mortality model 1.

Data analyses

The difference in health ratings between the pravastatin and placebo groups was tested for significance with the use of a regression model in which the dependent variable was health rating and the independent variables were group (pravastatin or placebo) and number of observations per patient. Statistical analyses were performed with SAS version 6.12 (SAS Institute, Cary, NC), and cost-effectiveness analyses were performed with Decision Maker version 7 (Pratt Medical Group, Boston, Mass).

Results

Costs and health-related quality of life

The cost of pravastatin therapy, based on the average dose taken by patients in the active treatment arm in CARE, was $925 per year. The mean cost of other cardiac medications was $1295 per year in the pravastatin group and $1227 per year in the placebo group. The excess medication costs in the pravastatin group were partly offset by savings in hospitalizations (Table I).

Mean health ratings were approximately 1% higher among patients receiving pravastatin: 77.8 versus 77.0 (utility, 0.968 vs 0.965; n = 4159; $P < .03$). Health ratings were also slightly higher for the pravastatin group among patients who did not have an event: 79.8 versus 79.4 (utility, 0.974 vs 0.973); among patients who had a nonfatal myocardial infarction: 74.6 versus 71.3 (utility, 0.957 vs 0.943); among patients who underwent a revascularization procedure during the study: 76.2 versus 74.6 (utility, 0.963 vs 0.957); among patients who had a stroke: 72.3 versus 70.2 (utility, 0.947 vs 0.937); among patients who had unstable angina: 72.8 versus 72.4 (utility, 0.949 vs 0.948); and among patients who had a nonfatal myocardial infarction and a revascularization procedure: 76.7 versus 72.9 (utility, 0.964 vs 0.950; P = not significant for all comparisons within subgroups).

Baseline cost-effectiveness analysis

With the use of the base case cost and health-related quality-of-life data and assuming a persistent survival benefit of 9% with pravastatin therapy but unequal non-CHD-related mortality rates (mortality model 1), pravastatin therapy increased quality-adjusted life

Figure 2

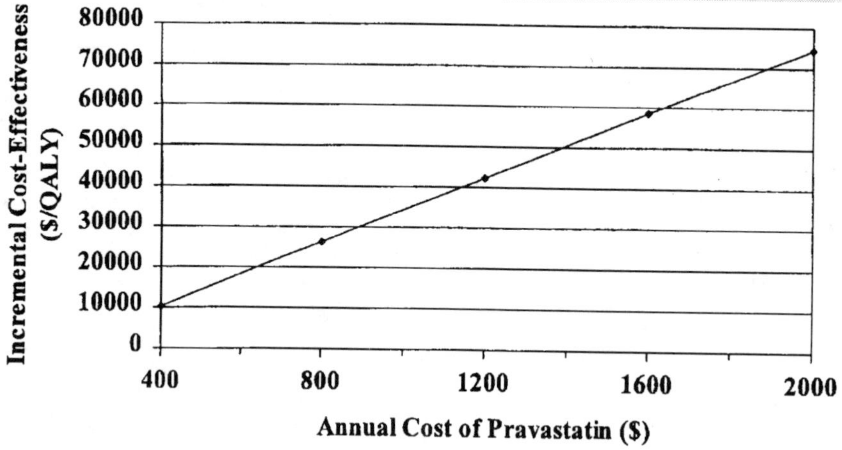

Sensitivity analysis of cost of pravastatin therapy in mortality model 1. In the base case analysis, the annual cost of pravastatin therapy was $925 per year.

Table II. Incremental cost-effectiveness of pravastatin therapy: Base case results

Model	Average discounted cost for pravastatin strategy ($)	Average discounted cost for no-pravastatin strategy ($)	Average discounted quality-adjusted life expectancy for pravastatin strategy (QALY)	Average discounted quality-adjusted life expectancy for no-pravastatin strategy (QALY)	Incremental cost-effectiveness of pravastatin therapy ($/QALY)*
Mortality model 1	53,177	42,223	13.62	13.27	31,000
Mortality model 2	54,359	41,788	13.92	13.13	16,000
Recurrent events model 1	48,734	37,435	12.99	12.64	32,000
Recurrent events model 2	49,087	37,224	13.10	12.55	22,000

*Incremental cost-effectiveness ratios are rounded to two significant figures.

expectancy at an incremental cost of $31,000 per QALY gained (Table II). By assuming equal non-CHD-related mortality rates (mortality model 2), the incremental cost-effectiveness ratio fell to $16,000 per QALY. In the recurrent events models, the incremental cost-effectiveness ratio was $32,000 per QALY, assuming unequal non-CHD-related mortality rates (recurrent events model 1), and $22,000 per QALY, assuming equal non-CHD-related mortality rates (recurrent events model 2).

Sensitivity analyses

Survival benefit and case-fatality rates. In mortality model 1, we assumed a 9% long-term survival benefit from pravastatin. The recently published Long-term Intervention with Pravastatin in Ischaemic Disease (LIPID) trial[4] found a 22% survival benefit from pravastatin therapy in similar patients. With the use of a 22% long-term survival benefit in our analysis, the incremental cost-effectiveness ratio drops to $14,000 per QALY.

In the recurrent events models, we assumed that the case-fatality rates in the pravastatin arm were higher than in the placebo arm (as observed in the CARE trial) and allowed this difference to persist for 10 years. If, however, this difference persisted for 30 years, the incremental cost-effectiveness ratio of pravastatin therapy increased to $80,000 per QALY in recurrent events model 1 and $34,000 per QALY in recurrent events model 2.

Costs of pravastatin therapy. The outcome of the analysis was somewhat sensitive to the cost of pravastatin therapy (Figure 2). In mortality model 1, at annual costs of pravastatin therapy <$146 per year (base case cost, $925 per year), the pravastatin strategy is both less costly and more effective than a no-pravastatin strategy (ie, the pravastatin strategy is dominant). The annual

Table III. Incremental cost-effectiveness of pravastatin therapy by subgroup

Patients	Mortality model 1 ($/QALY)*	Mortality model 2 ($/QALY)*	Recurrent events model 1 ($/QALY)*	Recurrent events model 2 ($/QALY)*
Men	31,000	16,000	37,000	21,000
Women	32,000	13,000	17,000	22,000
Age <60 y	†	†	†	2.0 million
Age ≥60 y	9100	10,000	10,000	12,000
LDL <125 mg/dL (3.2 mmol/L)	†	†	†	†
LDL 125-150 mg/dL (3.2-3.9 mmol/L)	16,000	16,000	18,000	18,000
LDL >150 mg/dL (3.9 mmol/L)	7900	8000	20,000	12,000

*Incremental cost-effectiveness ratios are rounded to two significant figures.
†Pravastatin strategy is both more expensive and less effective than alternative (placebo).

cost would have to exceed $1389 for the incremental cost-effectiveness ratio to exceed $50,000 per QALY.

Subgroup analyses. In the CARE trial, pravastatin therapy was shown to be relatively more effective among women by virtue of a larger reduction in event rates. However, because of small differences in survival, the incremental cost-effectiveness of pravastatin therapy for women was substantially better than for men in only 1 of our 4 mortality and recurrent events models (recurrent events model 1; Table III).

The incremental cost-effectiveness ratio for patients ≥60 years of age ranged from $9100 to $12,000 per QALY. For patients <60 years, the trial showed that pravastatin prevented recurrent events. Nevertheless, the point estimates for mortality rates were higher in the pravastatin group and thus the pravastatin strategy was not cost-effective for that age group.

Similarly, in the CARE trial, mortality and recurrent event rates were slightly higher in the pravastatin arm for patients with pretreatment LDL levels <125 mg/dL (3.2 mmol/L); hence the pravastatin strategy was more expensive and less effective. The incremental cost-effectiveness ratio for patients with pretreatment LDL levels of 125 to 150 mg/dL (3.2 to 3.9 mmol/L) was $16,000 to $18,000 per QALY; for patients with LDL levels >150 mg/dL (3.9 mmol/L), it was $7900 to $20,000 per QALY.

Other sensitivity analyses. The results were generally not sensitive to changes in other costs or to the difference in utilities between groups. The outcome was also not affected much by excluding noncardiovascular-related hospitalization costs. If long-term hospitalization costs were based on projections from years 5 and 6 (as opposed to years 1 through 6), the incremental cost-effectiveness of pravastatin therapy would be $27,000 per QALY.

Discussion

Over the last decade, evidence from epidemiologic studies and clinical trials has supported aggressive treatment of hypercholesterolemia and now of average cholesterol levels in patients with CHD.[3-7] Over the same period, statin drugs have surged in popularity because they are effective, well tolerated, and can be taken once or twice a day. Given the expense of statin drugs, however, it has not been clear whether treating patients with CHD who have average cholesterol levels with a statin is economically worthwhile. Our study found that at an incremental cost-effectiveness ratio of $16,000 to $32,000 per QALY, the cost-effectiveness of pravastatin therapy in survivors of myocardial infarction with average cholesterol levels compares favorably with other interventions for patients with CHD.[24,26,27] Our study also suggests that statin therapy in survivors of myocardial infarction with average cholesterol levels is as cost-effective or more cost-effective than it is in primary prevention for most patients with high cholesterol levels and multiple risk factors.[8,28]

A few other studies have assessed the cost-effectiveness of statin therapy for patients with CHD. By using the Coronary Heart Disease Policy Model, Goldman et al[8] estimated the cost-effectiveness of lovastatin therapy for prevention of CHD. For secondary prevention among patients with pretreatment cholesterol levels <250 mg/dL (6.5 mmol/L), 20 mg/d of lovastatin therapy had incremental cost-effectiveness ratios of $26,000 per year of life saved for 55- to 64-year-old men and $55,000 per year of life saved for 55- to 64-year-old women (in 1996 dollars). Higher doses of lovastatin were relatively less cost-effective.

By using data from two plaque regression trials[29,30] and the Framingham Heart Study[31] together with estimated costs of medications, hospitalizations, and follow-up, Ashraf et al[9] determined the cost-effectiveness of pravastatin therapy for men with CHD. They found that the incremental cost per year of life saved for secondary prevention with pravastatin therapy ranged from $7400 for men with ≥3 risk factors to $13,000 for men with 1 risk factor.

Several studies of the cost-effectiveness of statin therapy in secondary prevention have been based on primary data from the Scandinavian Simvastatin Survival Study (4S) trial.[10-13] Jönsson et al[10] calculated the net costs of treatment on the basis of the cost of simvastatin therapy and the savings in hospitalizations and procedures. They then estimated gains in life expectancy over the first 5.5 years of follow-up and assumed an average life expectancy of 10 more years for those surviving to the end of the trial. The incremental cost-effectiveness ratio for simvastatin therapy was 56,400 Swedish kronor (approximately $8800 in 1996 dollars) per year of life saved. Johannesson et al[11] incorporated data on coronary events and resource use from 4S in a Markov model to estimate the cost-effectiveness of simvastatin therapy for various subgroups of patients with CHD. When considering direct costs only, they found that the cost-effectiveness ranged from $3900 per year of life saved for 70-year-old men with pretreatment cholesterol levels of 309 mg/dL (8.0 mmol/L) to $28,000 per year of life saved for 35-year-old women with pretreatment levels of 213 mg/dL (5.5 mmol/L).

Our analysis was similar to that of Johannesson et al in several respects. Both analyses were based on actual resource use in their respective clinical trials and both used Markov models to estimate life expectancy. Both found that statin therapy is relatively more cost-effective for older patients than for younger patients and for patients with higher pretreatment lipid levels.

There were also several differences between our analysis and that of Johannesson et al. Our analysis included costs of other cardiac medications, whereas theirs considered the costs of lost productivity associated with morbidity. Their 4S analysis assumed that therapy would be discontinued after a coronary event and that the benefit of simvastatin therapy would end after 5 years. The 4S trial was conducted in Scandinavia, whereas CARE took place in North America; to the extent that there exist differences in practice patterns, the cost-effectiveness ratio could be affected. For example, patients in 4S were less likely to have had a coronary revascularization procedure before study entry, and fewer patients in 4S took aspirin; both of these factors would be expected to increase the risk of a subsequent coronary event in 4S and therefore favor the cost-effectiveness of lowering cholesterol levels. Similarly, patients in 4S had higher pretreatment cholesterol levels, which would be expected to favor the cost-effectiveness of the 4S intervention over the CARE intervention.

In our analysis, pravastatin therapy was found to have a small salutary effect on health-related quality of life. Average health ratings were approximately 1% higher in the pravastatin arm than in the placebo arm. To examine whether this was caused by a reduction in the number of cardiac events or by some other benefit of the medication, we analyzed health ratings among patients who did not have a trial event and among those who did. Health ratings were slightly higher for patients taking pravastatin irrespective of what kind of cardiovascular event they had, if any. Also, to project the potential long-term effects of pravastatin therapy on health-related quality of life, we compared the final health ratings obtained from patients receiving pravastatin therapy versus those from patients taking placebo. Except among patients who had both a revascularization procedure and a nonfatal myocardial infarction, final health ratings were slightly higher for patients taking pravastatin (data not shown).

Although relatively cost-effective in the aggregate, our results varied by patient sex, age, and pretreatment LDL level. Because of the small sample sizes of patients in certain subgroups, interpretation of the subgroup cost-effectiveness analyses should be undertaken cautiously. The results of our analyses also depended on whether mortality differences were modeled directly or through recurrent event rates; results of the two models differed, especially for patients <60 years of age. In the mortality models, we chose to model differences in all-cause mortality rates, even though this was not the study's primary end point, because it enabled us to calculate directly the incremental cost per quality-adjusted year of life saved; QALYs are preferred as a denominator to other "intermediate outcomes" such as events averted because QALYs serve as a common denominator for comparing the cost-effectiveness of all sorts of interventions.[16] The difference in all-cause mortality rates in CARE was not statistically significant, but because cost-effectiveness analysis is intended to inform decisions and not to prove hypotheses, the preferred approach is to use the best point estimates of probabilities and costs and then perform extensive sensitivity analyses.[32,33] On the other hand, for relatively short clinical trials, some experts believe that death is a less reliable end point when assessed directly than when assessed through the relative reduction of intermediate outcomes such as CHD events,[34] as captured in our recurrent events models. The recurrent events models more closely paralleled the clinical trial but required an extra extrapolation to calculate QALYs. Which model is the most appropriate is debatable. Future studies should examine the impact on cost-effectiveness of different ways to model outcomes from trials.

Conclusions

The cost-effectiveness of pravastatin therapy in survivors of myocardial infarction with average cholesterol levels compares favorably with other interventions, including cholesterol reduction in persons with significantly elevated cholesterol levels but no clinical CHD.

We thank Eugene Braunwald, MD, Marc Pfeffer, MD, PhD, and Lemuel Moye, MD, PhD, for helpful

input into the analyses; Mae Lipps, RRA, for coding the hospitalization data; Karen Mandell, PharmD, for assigning medication costs; and Loretta Simbartl, MS, for assisting with statistical analyses.

References

1. National Institutes of Health. NHLBI morbidity and mortality chart-book, 2000. Available at: http://www.nhlbi.nih.gov/resources/docs/cht-book.htm.
2. Summary of the second report of the National Cholesterol Education Report (NCEP) Expert Panel on Detection, Evaluation, and Treatment of High Blood Cholesterol in Adults (Adult Treatment Panel II). JAMA 1993;269:3015-23.
3. Sacks FM, Pfeffer MA, Moye LA, et al. The effect of pravastatin on coronary events after myocardial infarction in patients with average cholesterol levels. N Engl J Med 1996;335:1001-9.
4. Long-term Intervention with Pravastatin in Ischaemic Disease (LIPID) Study Group. Prevention of cardiovascular events and death with pravastatin in patients with coronary heart disease and a broad range of initial cholesterol levels. N Engl J Med 1998;339:1349-57.
5. Miller DB. Secondary prevention for ischemic heart disease: relative numbers needed to treat with different therapies. Arch Intern Med 1997;157:2045-52.
6. Marchioli R, Marfisi RM, Carcini F, et al. Meta-analysis, clinical trials, and transferability of research results into practice: the case of cholesterol-lowering interventions in the secondary prevention of coronary heart disease. Arch Intern Med 1996;156:1158-72.
7. Gaziano JM, Hebert PR, Hennekens CH. Cholesterol reduction: weighing the benefits and risks. Ann Intern Med 1996;124:914-8.
8. Goldman L, Weinstein MC, Goldman PA, et al. Cost-effectiveness of HMG-CoA reductase inhibition for primary and secondary prevention of coronary heart disease. JAMA 1991;265:1145-51.
9. Ashraf T, Hay JW, Pitt B, et al. Cost-effectiveness of pravastatin in secondary prevention of coronary artery disease. Am J Cardiol 1996;78:409-14.
10. Jönsson B, Johannesson M, Kjekshus J, et al. Cost-effectiveness of cholesterol lowering: results from the Scandinavian Simvastatin Survival Study (4S). Eur Heart J 1996;17:1001-7.
11. Johannesson M, Jönsson B, Kjekshus J, et al. Cost-effectiveness of simvastatin treatment to lower cholesterol levels in patients with coronary heart disease. N Engl J Med 1997;336:332-6.
12. Pharoah PDP, Hollingworth W. Cost effectiveness of lowering cholesterol concentration with statins in patients with and without pre-existing coronary heart disease: life table method applied to health authority population. BMJ 1996;312:1443-8.
13. Pedersen TR, Kjekshus J, Berk K, et al. Cholesterol lowering and the use of healthcare resources: results of the Scandinavian Simvastatin Survival Study. Circulation 1996;93:1796-1802.
14. Kannel WB. Range of serum cholesterol values in the population developing coronary artery disease. Am J Cardiol 1995;76:69C-77C.
15. Sonnenberg FA, Beck JR. Markov models in medical decision making: a practical guide. Med Decis Making 1993;13:322-38.
16. Gold MR, Siegel JE, Russell LB, et al. Cost-effectiveness in health and medicine. New York: Oxford University Press; 1996.
17. Sonnenberg FA, Wong JB. Commentary: fine-tuning life-expectancy calculations using Markov processes. Med Decis Making 1993;13:170-2.
18. Weinstein MC, Coxson PG, Williams LW, et al. Forecasting coronary heart disease incidence, mortality, and cost: the Coronary Heart Disease Policy Model. Am J Public Health 1987;77:1417-26.
19. Hunink MGM, Goldman L, Tosteson ANA, et al. The recent decline in mortality from coronary heart disease, 1980-1990: the effect of secular trends in risk factors and treatment. JAMA 1997;277:535-42.
20. Tsevat J, Goldman L, Lamas GA, et al. Functional status versus utilities in survivors of myocardial infarction. Med Care 1991;29:1153-9.
21. Torrance GW, Feeny DH, Furlong WJ, et al. Multiattribute utility function for a comprehensive health status classification system: Health Utilities Index Mark 2. Med Care 1996;34:702-22.
22. Finkler SA. The distinction between cost and charges. Ann Intern Med 1982;96:102-9.
23. AWP overstates actual pharmacy invoice cost for brand name drugs by average of 18.3% nationwide, HHS IG concludes; generic AWP overstates cost by 42.5%. F-D-C reports: "The Pink Sheet, Jan 13," 1997. p. 7.
24. Tsevat J, Duke D, Goldman L, et al. Cost-effectiveness of captopril therapy after myocardial infarction. J Am Coll Cardiol 1995;26:914-9.
25. Threlkeld DS, Hagemann RC, editors. Drug facts and comparisons. St Louis: Facts and Comparisons; 1997.
26. Kuntz KM, Tsevat J, Goldman L, et al. Cost-effectiveness of routine coronary angiography after acute myocardial infarction. Circulation 1996;94:957-65.
27. Mark DB, Hlatky MA, Califf RM, et al. Cost-effectiveness of thrombolytic therapy with tissue plasminogen activator as compared with streptokinase for acute myocardial infarction. N Engl J Med 1995;332:1418-24.
28. Caro J, Klittich W, McGuire A, et al. The West of Scotland coronary prevention study: economic benefit analysis of primary prevention with pravastatin. BMJ 1997;315:1577-82.
29. Pitt B, Ellis SG, Mancini GB, et al. Design and recruitment in the United States of a multicenter quantitative angiographic trial of pravastatin to limit atherosclerosis in the coronary arteries (PLAC I). Am J Cardiol 1993;72:31-5.
30. Crouse JR, Byington RP, Bond MG, et al. Pravastatin, lipids, and atherosclerosis in the carotid arteries: design features of a clinical trial with carotid atherosclerosis outcome. Control Clin Trials 1992;13:495-506.
31. Framingham Study. Section 35. Survival following initial cardiovascular events. US Department of Health and Human Services: NIH Publication No. 88-2969. 1998;37-204.
32. Weinstein MC, Fineberg HV, Elstein AS, et al. Clinical decision analysis. Philadelphia: WB Saunders; 1980.
33. Roberts MS, Angus DC, Clermont G, et al. From efficacy to effectiveness: problems in translating the results of clinical trials into cost-effectiveness analyses [abstract]. Med Decis Making 1997;17:540.
34. Collins R, Peto R. Antihypertensive drug therapy: effects on stroke and coronary heart disease. In: Swales JD, editor. Textbook of hypertension. Oxford: Blackwell Scientific Publications; 1994. p. 1156-64.

TOOLS FOR MEASURING HUMANISTIC OUTCOMES

Michelle M. Chapman, Pharm.D., BCPS

Outline

I. Introduction

Humanistic outcomes, by the nature of the assessment, are obtained directly from the patient or population of interest. Collecting data directly from patients introduces a need for standardized methods of asking questions and recording answers that are different from clinical and economic assessments

II. The elements of questionnaires

- A. Questionnaires, instruments, measures, surveys, and tools are interchangeable terms to describe the tools to measure humanistic outcomes
- B. Structure of questionnaires
  1. item
     - a. fundamental element of a questionnaire
     - b. an item, or item stem, is a single question or statement that is paired with its response options
  2. response options
     - a. the response options follow the item stem and are the choices by which respondents indicate their answer to the item stem
     - b. domain or dimension is a group of items that measures similar concepts that is an area of behavior or experience that is being measured
     - c. a scale is formed when the items that represent a domain are combined to produce a single score
     - d. profile is graphical representation of scale scores
     - e. an index is an aggregate score of multiple scales created to serve as a multidimensional measure
     - f. battery is a collection of measures used to obtain a comprehensive understanding on the impact of a disease or intervention
- C. Static versus dynamic questionnaires
  - a. static questionnaires ask respondents the same questions, regardless of the respondent's answer
  - b. dynamic questionnaires use computer technology to have a respondent answer only the questions that are pertinent to that individual based on the respondent's answer

III. Methods of questionnaire administration

- A. Administration methods for static questionnaires-the best method depends on a variety of considerations
  1. self-administration
     - a. traditional pencil and paper
     - b. mail-out/mail-back administration
  2. interview administration
     - a. traditional face-to-face interviews
     - b. telephone interviews
     - c. audio-assisted interviews
  3. technology-enhanced administration of static questionnaires
     - a. computer-assisted data collection
     - b. other technologies to assist static questionnaire administration

B. Dynamic questionnaire administration

1. computer-adapted testing (CAT), also known as dynamic testing, is a strategy that matches specific items to individual patients
2. a computer interface using artificial intelligence to select the fewest number of items for the desired level of precision
3. advantages of CAT include reduced respondent burden, increased score precision, elimination of ceiling and floor effects, individual-specific confidence intervals, the ability to monitor data in real time, and decreased data collection costs
4. disadvantages of CAT are the need for a large pool of items and the large representative data sets

C. Mixed administration modes

1. mixing administration modes within a study adds a level of complexity
2. results obtained from the different administration modes vary
3. particularly important if longitudinal assessments are being made and if change over time is important to the study design

IV. Identifying and evaluating existing questionnaires

A. Define measurement goals

1. discriminative instruments are used to discriminate among individuals or groups, describe differences in health status, or identify areas of need
2. predictive instruments are used to identify groups or individuals who have or will develop a medical condition or outcome and can be used to predict future needs
3. evaluative measures are used to measure the magnitude of longitudinal changes in individuals or groups

B. Locating existing questionnaires

1. standard bibliographic databases (e.g., Medline) other literature databases, textbooks and compendia, Web sites, etc

C. Critically evaluate the literature

1. standards for reviewing the clinical literature apply
2. assess general characteristics
    a. determine if the questionnaire is discriminative, predictive, or evaluative
    b. determine if a questionnaire is generic or disease specific
    c. assess the domains and range
3. assess psychometric properties, including reliability, validity, sensibility, responsiveness, response bias, and interpretability
4. caveats for reviewing patient-based assessments
    a. fully understand the original validation sample, along with the original purpose for which the questionnaire was designed
    b. additional areas include the scoring procedure, the subjects, how the population was sampled, and the statistical and psychometric methods used

D. The strategy for using a questionnaire

1. combine a generic and a disease-specific questionnaire
2. be aware of total length and time to complete questionnaire
3. augment published measures by adding scales that have already met psychometric criteria
4. pilot testing of a revised instrument is absolutely necessary if any changes or additions are made to a published questionnaire

E. Practical considerations

1. burden of questionnaire administration—administering a questionnaire adds effort both on the part of the patient and the research or clinical staff. It is important to assess and minimize that burden to ensure quality data collection
2. population characteristics—disease or treatment itself, education level, literacy rate, and language spoken
3. data collection and entry, results reporting, and cost

V. Conclusion

This chapter reviewed the process of selecting questionnaire administration modes, critically reviewing questionnaires, and assessing practical considerations. Deciding which administration mode to use depends on a variety of factors that must be evaluated for each patient group to be surveyed

Learning Objectives

1. Compare and contrast questionnaire administration methods.
2. Devise an appropriate plan for administering a questionnaire in a given situation or population.
3. Identify and evaluate published questionnaires to determine the appropriateness of their use in specific patient groups.
4. Assess the impact of computer-based technology on questionnaire administration.
5. Understand the role of evolving technologies in health status assessment.
6. Devise a strategy to minimize administration pitfalls in a given situation or patient population.

Abbreviations in this chapter

CAT	Computer-adapted testing
CHEQ	CHOICE Health Experience Questionnaire
IQOLA	International Quality of Life Assessment
KDQOL	Kidney Disease Quality Of Life Questionnaire
SF-36	Medical Outcomes Study Short Form-36

Introduction

Measuring humanistic outcomes has gained importance as the concept of outcomes assessment has expanded to include not only the traditional clinical indicators of care, but also health status, patient satisfaction, cost-effectiveness, and productivity. As these concepts have gained importance, it is necessary to use the correct data sources and tools to measure them.

The data source for traditional clinical indicators includes assessments from health care providers and the acquisition of samples or images that reflect a patient's organ functioning. Using the example of a patient's sera, the sample, or data source, is analyzed using clinical laboratory technology (the tool) whose use is dictated by standards. In contrast, economic outcomes use databases as the data source and the tools are a variety of analytic techniques and methodologies that were discussed earlier in chapters 5-10. However, humanistic outcomes, by the nature of the assessment, are obtained directly from the patient or population of interest. Collecting data directly from patients introduces a need for standardized methods of asking questions and recording answers that are different from clinical and economic assessments. This chapter discusses in detail the tools necessary for conducting humanistic outcomes assessments, comparing and contrasting the various questionnaire administration modes, and identifying what type of administration is best for various patient groups. In addition, readers will learn how to identify and evaluate questionnaires.

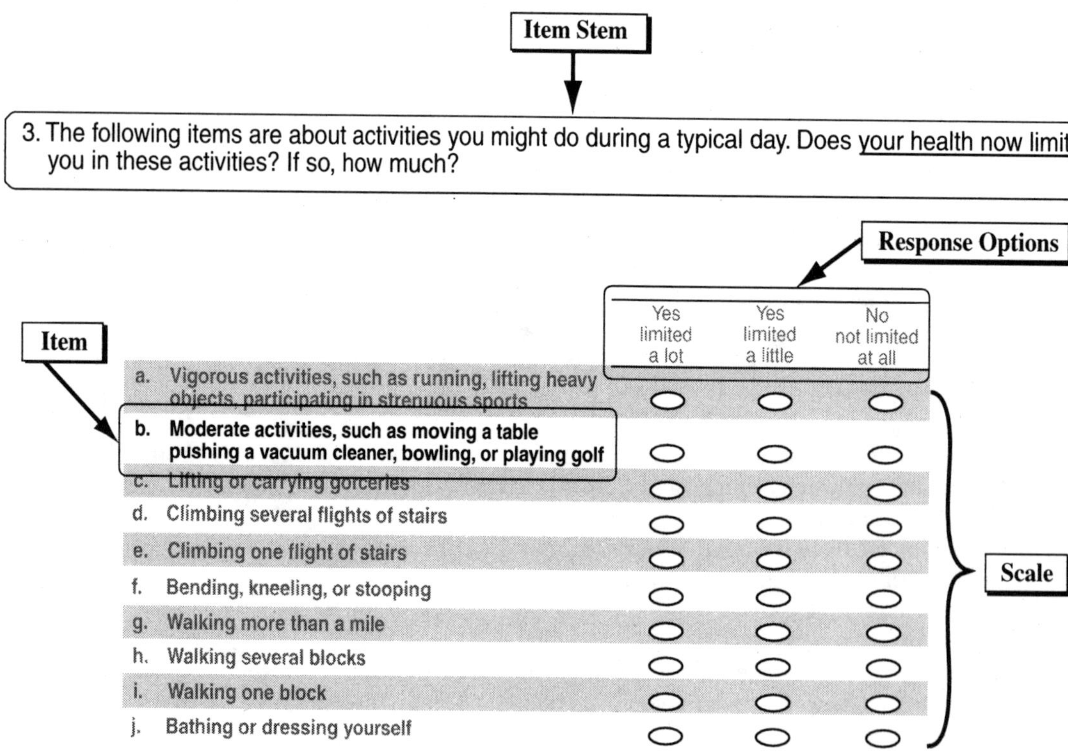

Figure 1. Elements of a questionnaire using select aquestions from the SF-36 Health Survey as an example.
 Ware, J.E., Snow, K.K., Kosinksi, M. *SF-36® Health Survey: Manual and Interpretation Guide*. Lincoln, RI: QualityMetric Incorporated, 1993, 2000.

The Elements of Questionnaires

In any measurement situation, the appropriate tool is necessary to accurately assess the desired attribute. For instance, if a person needs to measure a table, a tool called a ruler allows him or her to measure the table's attributes of height, width, and depth. The same is true for measuring the attributes of humanistic outcomes. In this case, the correct measurement tool is called a questionnaire, instrument, or survey. These terms are used interchangeably to describe the way in which patient-based information is obtained and measured from the population of interest. Other synonyms include measures or tools.

The fundamental element of a questionnaire is the item. An item, or item stem, is a single question or statement that is paired with its response options. The response options follow the item stem and are the choices by which respondents indicate their answer to the item stem. In their simplest form, measures of humanistic outcomes use only one question to measure a concept. These simple questionnaires are called single-item measures. An example of a single-item measure is "How satisfied are you with the health care you received today?" Although an overall answer is elicited, it is general and no specific information is obtained. Single-item measures may have limited usfulness. However, single-item pain measures may be effective and provide significant information. Multi-item measures contain multiple questions to measure a concept. A group of items that measure similar concepts represents a domain or dimension, which is an area of behavior or experience that is being measured. Examples of domains include physical functioning, mental health, and bodily pain. A scale is formed when the items that represent a domain are combined to produce a single score. Figure 1 represents the relationship among these questionaire items. When many different domains are measured, they can be displayed graphically as separate scores for each domain, which is then called a profile. When scales are combined to produce an aggregate score, they are referred to as an index. An index is an attempt to create a multidimensional measure by combining all scales or dimensions into one aggregate number. Several instruments, when combined, can give a comprehensive understanding of the impact of a disease or intervention on humanistic outcomes. A combination of instruments is called a battery. Finally, respondents are the individuals who complete the questionnaires. The definitions of these questionnaire elements and examples are listed in Table 1.

Static versus Dynamic Questionnaires

Traditionally, questionnaires asked respondents the same questions, regardless of the respondents' answers. These types of questionnaires are now referred to as static. A static questionnaire is one that poses a predetermined list of questions to respondents, regardless of their responses to previous questions. The traditional pencil-and-paper versions of questionnaires are considered static. All respondents, regardless of their responses, answer all questions. For instance, the SF-36 includes 10 questions about limitations in performing physical activities. Using the traditional paper version of the SF-36, respondents answer all 10 questions regardless of their physical ability. Whereas a dynamic questionnaire uses computer technology that limits the number of questions that respondents have to answer. The software determines the pertinent questions to

Clearly define the overall measurement goals, rationale, and outcomes of interest
↓
Identify available questionnaires
↓
Decide if using generic and/or disease-specific questionnaire
↓
Assess each questionnaire for the appropriate domains and ranges
↓
Assess the psychometric properties of the questionnaire
↓
Decide how, when, and where the questionnaire will be administered
↓
Assess unique characteristics of the population
↓
Assess respondent burden
↓
Determine costs of using health status questionnaire
↓
Decide how data will be collected, entered, analyzed, and reported
↓
Begin pilot administration of the questionnaire

Reprinted with permission from PSAP 4th ed. American College of Clinical Pharmacy, Kansas City MO, 2002. Chapman MM. Assessing Health Status and Patient Satisfaction. In: Mueller BA, Bertch KE, Dunsworth TS, et al, eds. Pharmacotherapy Self-Assessment Program, 4th ed. The Science and Practice of Pharmacotherapy II Module. Kansas City: ACCP; 2002:291-317.

ask based on respondents' previous answers. For instance, if respondents answered that they are severely impaired walking a block, the computer logically would not ask if they could walk a mile or perform vigorous activities. The many advantages to dynamic questionnaires are discussed in more detail in the Dynamic Questionnaire Administration section later in this chapter.

Methods of Questionnaire Administration

Administration Methods for Static Questionnaires

There are essentially two methods to collect health status information using static questionnaires. The first method is for respondents to complete the questionnaires by themselves, which is called self-administration. The other option is for respondents to be interviewed. The best method depends not only on practical considerations, such as cost and the amount of time needed to complete the questionnaire, but also on concerns about data quality. How patients are recruited, how long and how often follow-up needs to occur, whether patients will return to the clinic site, and a multitude of other factors affect the strategy chosen for data collection. There are many appropriate ways to collect health status data. All of the strategies discussed are appropriate when data requirements, study design, and constraints of the situation are considered. It is essential to evaluate all aspects of a protocol or program carefully before the onset of full-scale data collection. Often, a pilot study will be an important determinant of how well the proposed data collection methods work within the confines of the situation. It is clear that computers and other technology provide important alternatives to the traditional methods of questionnaire administration. The advantages and disadvantages of various administration methods are presented in Table 2.

Self-administration

Self-administration of questionnaires is often the most desirable and simple way to obtain health status information. Because respondents answer the questions independently, they tend to report socially undesirable information more readily than when they are interviewed. This tendency is especially important to consider if it is vital to obtain accurate reporting of sensitive or highly personal information.

Self-administration also has some disadvantages. It is commonly thought that self-administered questionnaires have lower rates of completeness and lower quality of data compared to interviewer-administered questionnaires. One solution to this potential problem is to have the questionnaire checked for incomplete data when it is collected. This way, patients are still available and can be asked if they would like to complete the questions that were skipped. Patients with decreased visual acuity or blindness from diabetes mellitus, cytomegalovirus retinitis, and other diseases often cannot complete the forms themselves and require assistance or interview. However, this problem can be overcome by reformatting the questionnaire so that the words are in a larger type (18 point or larger). Often, these formatting changes allow patients to self-administer a questionnaire.

Mail-out/Mail-back Administration

One adaptation of self-administration is to mail the questionnaires to respondents and have them return the

Table 1: The elements of a questionnaire

Element	Description	Example
Item	A single question or statement paired with its response options	Question 3a of the SF-36: "How limited are you in performing physical activities?"
Domain, dimension	A grouping of items intended to assess a concept	Questions 3a through 3j of the SF-36 measure the domain of physical functioning
Scale	Multiple items, representing a domain, that are combined to produce a score	The responses to questions 3a through 3j of the SF-36 can be scored to produce a single physical functioning scale score
Profile	Multiple scales are each displayed as individual scores	Eight regular scales of the SF-36 can be collectively displayed as individual scores
Index	An aggregate score of multiple individual scale scores	The Physical Component Score of the SF-36 includes multiple domains such as Physical Functioning, Role-Physical, and Bodily Pain.
Battery	Several questionnaires or scales from a variety of sources used in combination to obtain a comprehensive understanding of a condition or intervention	

Table 2: Advantages and disadvantages of administration methods		
	Advantages	**Disadvantages**
Traditional paper and-pencil	-Respondents answer questions on their own (self-administration) -Respondents more readily report socially undesirable information -Decreases or eliminates possible bias introduced with interviewer administration -Depending on numbers of respondents, least expensive	-Lower rates of completeness and poorer data quality compared to interviewer-administered questionaires -Data quality threatened secondary to need for data cleaning, transcription, and entry - Manifestations of certain diseases make it difficult or impossible for patients to self-administer questionaires -Difficult to receive useable answers to narrative questions
Mail-out/mail-back administration	-Less expensive than interview administration -Can be coordinated from a central office -Eliminates potential bias introduced by interviewers -Effective way to reach a large number of people	-Need to motivate the recipient to complete the questionaire -Difficult to obtain demographic information to compare responders with non-responders -Logistically more complicated -Lower response rates
Traditional interview	-Sure of respondent -Time intensive -Decreases missing data -Interviewer can ascertain any problems patient is having in understanding -For patients whom English is a 2nd language, they may understand spoken language better than reading it -Complicated questionnaires can be made more manageable -Visual aids can be used to help patients understand response choices -Effective in eliciting narrative responses -Maximizes response rates	-More expensive -Training required for interviewers -Inter-rater reliability among interviewers must be assessed -Necessary to schedule interview with the patient -May introduce bias between interviewer and interviewee -Respondents may be less willing to answer personal questions or discuss sensitive topics
Telephone interviews	-Same as traditional interviews -Less expensive than traditional interviews -Nonrespondents may be willing to provide some demographic information -Individuals from a large geographical area can be interviewed effectively by a few interviewers in a centralized setting	-Cannot reach participants who do not have a telephone -May be difficult for participants who have hearing difficulties and for those whose first language is not English -Cannot use visual aids or difficult response alternatives unless they are mailed in advance or respondent is asked to write them down -Small risk that someone in the household is prompting the respondent -Cannot verify the identity of the respondent -Time of call may be potential source of bias -Multiple calls may be needed to contact the desired individual
Audio-assisted interviews	- Respondents who have difficulty reading can essentially participate in a self-administration nprocess -Multiple languages can be made readily available on audiotapes -Eliminates need and cost to hire, train, and supervise bilingual interviewers -Using headphones makes the question and answer process confidential	-Need to maintain and keep track of audiotapes and equipment -Potentially not as effective for patients with hearing difficulties
Technology-enhanced/ Computer assisted administration	-Administer to several people at once -Decreased data transcription and entry errors -More difficult to omit or improperly respond to questions -People may respond more honestly -Less time consuming for staff -Lower data entry costs -Simplifies question sequences and skip patterns	-Computer itself may alter reliability and validity -Expense of equipment and/or software -Researcher/staff perception patients may be aprehensive about ptient's abilities to use computers -Special implementation considerations
Computer-adapted testing/Dynamic testing	-Reduced respondent burden -Increased score precision -Elimination of ceiling and floor effects -Individual-specific confidence intervals -Monitor data in real time	-Requires large pool of items -Large representative data sets needed -Equipment and software expense

completed questionnaires by mail. Mailing questionnaires is an effective way to reach many people, but motivating recipients to complete questionnaires can be difficult. Often, a cover letter explaining the purpose of the questionnaire is included in the mailing. Participants may decide not to complete a form they receive in the mail, whereas, if asked in person, they may be more receptive to complete it. If respondents decide not to return the questionnaire, it is often difficult to obtain any demographic information to compare responders with nonresponders. Mailing questionnaires is logistically complicated as a mechanism is needed to track respondents who return the questionnaire and to send out reminder cards in a timely fashion to those who have not. Maintaining adequate response rates requires using methods such as personalizing all mailings, giving advanced warning that a questionnaire will be arriving, providing a token of appreciation, assuring anonymity, enclosing self-addressed stamped envelopes, and conducting follow-ups.

The Medical Outcomes Study used a sophisticated method for mailing questionnaires to study participants to increase the response rate. The questionnaire was mailed with a personalized cover letter and a small monetary incentive. Seven days after the original mailing, a reminder card was sent thanking those who completed the questionnaire and encouraging those who did not to complete the questionnaire. Three weeks after the initial mailing, a reminder letter was sent to the nonrespondents with an additional questionnaire. Two weeks after the second mailing, the nonrespondents received a follow-up telephone call. The last resort was to send the short-form version of the questionnaire followed by a final telephone call. This effort resulted in an amazing 85 percent response rate. Although most studies do not use such extensive methods, this is an example of how a high response rate with mail surveys can be achieved.

Interview Administration

Traditional Face-to-face Interviews

Interview administration is an option when patients cannot complete the questionnaires independently or if a questionnaire is complicated. Verifying the identity of respondents is an advantage of face-to-face interviews. Although this may seem obvious, it may not be the case with telephone interview or mail administration. In these situations, anyone can answer the questions or provide opinions that may change the respondent's initial answer. Questionnaires that are too complicated as self-administered surveys can be made manageable with an interview. Unlike self-administered questionnaires, interview administration is effective in eliciting narrative responses as highly skilled interviewers can probe and clarify the patients' response.

There are some disadvantages of face-to-face interview administration, predominantly that it is more expensive. Using interviewer-administered questionnaires requires health care personnel to hire, train, and supervise the interviewers. Because of the amount of training and skill required, there may be real advantages to using professional interviewers as opposed to available staff, such as nurses or receptionists. When training interviewers, role-playing is essential. The interviewers must ask questions exactly as they are worded, probe inadequate answers in nondirective ways, train respondents in their role in a consistent way, and maintain a neutral, nonbiasing relationship with the respondents. These steps are important to minimizing bias. Many popular questionnaires have scripted interviewing guidelines to ensure consistency.

In addition, quality control procedures are needed to ensure standardization among interviewers. To maintain these standards, interviewers must be supervised. One approach to supervising interviewers is to monitor all initial interviews and then periodically and systematically supervise subsequent interviews to maintain high-quality data collection. In situations where supervisors cannot be available at all times, interviews can be tape-recorded and reviewed later. Obviously, the intensive training and monitoring of interviewers increases the cost of data collection and may introduce potential bias into a study or protocol. Attributes of interviewers may affect respondents' answers, which may be caused by biases of interviewers or by their ethnic or social characteristics. Adequate training can overcome the subtle bias interviewers may communicate that indicate which answers they want to hear. The second, and more difficult problem, is that differences in gender, possibly age, and especially race among interviewers and respondents may affect respondents' answers. Whenever possible, the race of interviewers and respondents should be the same.

Telephone Interviews

An alternative to face-to-face interviews is telephone interviews. The advantages of face-to-face interviewing also apply to telephone interviewing. Telephone interviews can decrease the expense associated with face-to-face interviews as central coordination allows for more consistent supervision. Telephone interviews can be conducted using computer systems that prompt the interviewer to ask the next question and allow for direct data entry. This technology simplifies complicated interviews, allows for immediate access to the data, and can be linked directly to a records management system to track respondents.

One of the disadvantages of telephone interviewing is that participants who do not have telephones cannot be interviewed. Although most Americans have telephones, this may be of concern in certain populations. There are solutions to some of the disadvantages listed in Table 2. Respondents can be sent visual aids to assist with difficult response options. However, it may be problematic if respondents cannot locate the aids at the time of the call or do not understand how to use them. If there is more than one set or type of response options, respondents are likely to become confused and less willing to participate or may resort to endorsing the first option. Another consideration for telephone interviews is that bias may be introduced by the time chosen for the interview. For some populations, researchers have identified significant differences in the characteristics of individuals reached during the daytime versus those reached in the evening.

Audio-assisted Interviews

In audio-assisted interviewing, questions are read aloud in person, on tape, or with a computer through headphones to respondents who then enter their answers into a computer or record them on paper. The advantage of this administration method is that people who have difficulty reading can participate in an essentially self-administered questionnaire process. People who do not speak English can use audio that recorded is in their language. This system eliminates the need to hire, train, and supervise bilingual interviewers. Finally, using headphones makes the question and answer process confidential.

Technology-enhanced Administration of Static Questionnaires

Computer-assisted Data Collection

Computer technology and software are available to assist with data collection for both interview-administered and self-administered questionnaires. Direct data entry by either the patient or the interviewer saves time and money. Software can be programmed so that a question must be answered before another question comes up on the screen which decreases missing data. In this case, respondents should have the option of indicating they wish to skip the question. Computer programs also can eliminate illogical responses by prompting respondents that their current answer is inconsistent with previous responses. Finally, people may be more honest in their reporting of socially undesirable behavior to a machine than to a person.

Computer technology also is available that allows direct entry of responses into the software program by using a light pen or touching the screen. A potential disadvantage of computerizing preexisting questionnaires is that the effect that computer technology has on the reliability and validity of the questionnaire may be unknown. Another disadvantage is that health care professionals may make assumptions about the willingness of their patient population to complete computer-based questionnaires, thinking the patients are unwilling or unable to work with the technology. However, if technical assistance is available, respondents who can complete self-administered questionnaires should be able to complete computerized questionnaires. An interesting use of computer technology is to have an interviewer use the computer to conduct the interview. The interviewer still asks the questions to the respondent, but the respondent enters their answer using the computer. When a sensitive question is asked, the interviewer can turn the computer monitor away from the interviewer and toward the respondent. The interviewer also is able to instruct participants about how to enter their response.

Several factors should be considered when implementing computerized questionnaire administration. First, because adequate computer equipment and support is needed to make the system feasible and easy to use, cost of the equipment is an important factor. Also, software may have to be developed if it is not commercially available, adding to both the expense and time required. Respondents must be able to stop answering the questions and return to the spot where they stopped with ease and without losing data or having to answer questions they have already completed. Provisions should be in place to allow respondents to change their current response as well as previous responses. Finally, respondents should be able to indicate that they do not wish to answer a particular question.

One study compared pen-based electronic questionnaires and conventional paper questionnaires in a randomized, crossover design. Forty-six patients, 17–81 years of age, participated. There was a high degree of acceptability for the pen-based electronic questionnaires; 57 percent preferred electronic questionnaire administration, 30 percent had no preference, and the remainig 13 percent preferred paper questionnaires. Age, gender, and familiarity with technology had no association with patient preference for computer or conventional questionnaires. The investigators also found that both types of questionnaires were easy to use, but that data handling procedures were greatly simplified with the electronic questionnaire. Other investigators have more recently confirmed these findings.

Other Technologies to Assist Static Questionnaire Administration

As technology has advanced, interest in using computerized questionnaires to facilitate questionnaire administration and data entry has increased. Several technologies are available that can accommodate static questionnaire administration. Software can be installed onto personal digital assistants, other hand held computers, and on the Internet to facilitate administration of questionnaires. Essentially any electronic device on which software can be loaded is an option for facilitating questionnaire administration. Other technologies also are available to aid data entry. Some questionnaires, such as the Dartmouth Cooperative Charts, use the traditional pencil-and-paper method but have bar coding on the response options as a technology to facilitate data entry.

The main concerns regarding computerized questionnaire administration are patient acceptance, changes in reliability and validity, and security. Patient acceptance of the technology is essential. Several studies have shown that patients are likely to accept technology as a questionnaire administration mode. Respondents must be able to use the technology and population characteristics must be considered. For instance, most personal digital assistant screens are small. As a result, the text may be too small and not clear enough for patients with visual impairments. Knowing the reliability and validity of the questionnaire using technology also is important. Most studies that have been conducted have not shown technology to affect the reliability and validity of a questionnaire, but there are not many studies to support a universal statement that computerization does not affect the reliability and validity of all questionnaires. Finally, security of these technologies is of concern. Small electronic devices are sometimes difficult to keep track of and may be easily stolen. Security issues must be considered before purchasing expensive electronic devices.

Dynamic Questionnaire Administration

The most recent and exciting advance in questionnaire research is computer-adapted testing (CAT) which also is known as dynamic testing. Computer-adapted testing is a strategy that matches specific items to individual patients. A computer interface tailors the items to the unique functional level of the respondent. Using artificial intelligence, items are selected based on the individual. The number of items asked is determined by the software to achieve the desired measurement precision. The score is based on a standard metric so that results can be compared. Traditional or static questionnaires require respondents to answer all of the questions, even if questions do not apply, whereas CAT chooses questions specific to respondents. For instance, if a patient is not able to walk 1 block, the questions from the SF-36 regarding walking several blocks or walking a mile are not asked. Instead, items are asked to ascertain what level of function below walking 1 block applies. Initial questions address the middle of the range with additional questions being determined based on the initial response. This tactic results in asking the fewest number of questions while maintaining the desired precision.

The advantages of CAT include reduced respondent burden, increased score precision, elimination of ceiling and floor effects, individual-specific confidence intervals, the ability to monitor data in real time, and decreased data collection costs. The primary disadvantages are that for CAT to be effective, a large pool of items is required as are large representative data sets.

Mixed Administration Modes

Depending on study design, more than one questionnaire administration mode may be needed. Mixing administration modes within a study adds a level of complexity to the study design that needs to be anticipated before any questionnaires are administered. Because the results obtained from the different administration modes vary, choosing to mix administration modes must be carefully considered. Mixing administration modes is particularly important if longitudinal assessments are being made and if change over time is important to the study design.

The McMaster Health Index Questionnaire was studied in 96 patients who were randomly assigned to one of three administration mode study groups. A single mode of self-completion was superior to mixed administration modes in terms of the magnitude of change in mean scores the investigators were able to measure. Another study compared the mean SF-36 scale scores for telephone and mail-administered questionnaires. Investigators found that respondents who received the questionnaire by mail reported significantly worse SF-36 scores and more chronic conditions than respondents who were interviewed over the telephone. If the administration modes change over the course of a study, statistical adjustments must be made to compensate for the changes in mean scores over time. Although mixing administration modes may simplify data-collection strategies, it complicates interpretation of any scale score changes over time. The changes in mean scores seen with differing administration modes may not be the same with different questionnaires. Before deciding to mix administration modes, review the literature to determine if any information is available for that particular questionnaire. Consulting experts and statisticians also is advised before beginning data collection.

Identifying and Evaluating Existing Questionnaires

Regardless of whether a single item or a battery of measures is being used, questionnaires to measure humanistic outcomes are designed using complicated and time-intensive methods. Experts suggest that researchers and clinicians use existing questionnaires whenever an adequate instrument is available. Often, it is easy to be overly critical of available measures and to underestimate the effort required to develop a new questionnaire. Developing tools to measure humanistic outcomes is not an easy task and requires significant investments of time and financial resources. The steps to assess questionnaires are listed in Figure 1.

Define Measurement Goals

Before attempting to identify a questionnaire, the goals for measuring humanistic outcomes must be clearly defined. Examples of measurement goals may include comparing the health status of patients in a randomized, clinical trial; evaluating a clinical service; or assessing the health of a population. Having identified a specific goal greatly simplifies the process of identifying and evaluating measures of humanistic outcomes.

Locating Existing Questionnaires

Assuming that the purpose for using a humanistic outcomes measure has been clearly defined and, as a result, the type of questionnaire needed is known, researchers can begin identifying published measures using standard bibliographic databases, such as Medline. However, the search should not be limited to Medline. The measurement of health status has evolved from many disciplines, including social sciences, psychology, education, and medicine. Therefore, published instruments often can be found in literature databases other than one that is medicine-based. Consulting with a reference librarian for other available databases that are pertinent to the search may be helpful. In addition, several textbooks and compendia include information about various measurement tools that are available.

Critically Evaluate the Literature

Once several instruments have been identified, they must be critically evaluated to determine if they meet the measurement goals of the study or program. A critical review of the published literature supporting the instrument, in combination with the reviewer's judgment of the appropriateness of the scale for the population being measured, will guide the decision regarding which instrument best suit the specific goal of the study or program.

The criteria in the following discussion serve as a list of characteristics that should be evaluated when reviewing the literature regarding an existing questionnaire. The effort spent reviewing the literature to find an appropriate measure is important and may save the time and energy required developing a new measure. Even if one decides to develop a new measure, critical review of the literature provides a solid foundation on which a new measure can be based.

Published questionnaires can be found for common disease states. In fact, several questionnaires may be available, especially for diseases such as asthma, cancer, and kidney disease. In concert with locating the actual questionnaire, the publications describing the original development methods and validity testing need to be retrieved.

Many of the same standards for reviewing the clinical literature apply to reviewing health status literature. Authors should describe the questionnaire development process clearly and adequately. Sufficient information should be provided so that the evaluative steps discussed in the following sections can be followed. It is likely that more than one article will need to be reviewed to meet all the steps; however, all the information should be available after a complete literature review.

Assess General Characteristics

Determine if the Questionnaire is Discriminative, Predictive, or Evaluative

Several characteristics of identified questionnaires need to be carefully evaluated. The first is to determine the purpose of the health status instrument. Instruments that measure humanistic outcomes can be discriminative, predictive, or evaluative. Discriminative instruments differentiate among individuals or groups at one point in time. Results from discriminative instruments can be used to describe differences in health status or can identify areas of need. Predictive instruments by definition are used to determine the likelihood of an event occurring. The results from predictive instruments may be used to identify groups or individuals who have or will develop a medical condition or outcome and can be used to predict future needs. Evaluative measures assess differences within subjects over time. Evaluative measures results are used to measure the magnitude of longitudinal changes. It is possible that an instrument may be categorized as more than one of these types, but it is unlikely that any one instrument will fulfill all three categories.

Determine if a Questionnaire is Generic or Disease-specific

The next step is to establish if the questionnaire is generic or disease-specific. Table 3 compares the advantages and disadvantages of generic and disease-specific questionnaires. Generic instruments are designed to apply to general populations regardless of their demographic or medical characteristics. A popular generic questionnaire is the SF-36. It is comprised of 36 items that are scored to create eight scales. The eight scales are Physical Function, Role-Physical, Bodily Pain, General Health, Vitality, Social Functioning, Role-Emotional, and Mental Health. The SF-36 is considered to be a generic questionnaire because none of the 36 questions refer to a specific disease entity. However, just because it is a generic questionnaire does not mean that the SF-36 cannot be used in patients with disease. There are many advantages of generic questionnaires. One of them is the ability to compare the mean scale scores of different populations and thereby determine the burden of a disease relative to other disease states. For example, comparing the mean scale scores of the dialysis patient to the general population, the burden of dialysis is clearly in

Table 3: Comparison of generic and disease-specific health status questionnaires

Questionnaire Type	Examples	Advantages	Disadvantages
Generic	-SF-36 -Dartmouth Cooperative Charts	-Compare relative health status of populations -Compare the relative burden of health of various disease states -Summarize range of basic concepts -Detect unexpected effects	-Need to address multiple domains of health status may increase respondent burden -Scoring algorithms generally more complicated than summing responses -Do not address particular concerns of a specific population -May or may not be sensitive to change -Results may be more difficult to interpret
Disease-specific	-Kidney Disease Quality of Life Questionnaire -CHOICE Health Experience Questionnaire	-More sensitive to specific disease effects -Patients may view as more relevant to their problems -Potentially more responsive to change	-Not as generalizable as general health status measures -If administered in addition to general health status measure, increase respondent burden -Computer printouts, interpretation guides, and scoring programs generally not as available as with more established generic questionnaires

Reprinted with permission from PSAP 4th ed. American College of Clinical Pharmacy, Kansas City MO, 2002. Chapman MM. Assessing Health Status and Patient Satisfaction. In: Mueller BA, Bertch KE, Dunsworth TS, et al, eds. Pharmacotherapy Self-Assessment Program, 4th ed. The Science and Practice of Pharmacotherapy II Module. Kansas City: ACCP; 2002:291-317.

the physical domains of health. In contrast, disease-specific questionnaires are created with the intent to understand the impact of certain disease states. These questionnaires are only appropriate to be completed by patients experiencing a particular disease state. Examples of disease-specific questionnaires for patients with kidney disease include the Kidney Disease Quality Of Life Questionnaire (KDQOL) and the CHOICE Health Experience Questionnaire (CHEQ). These questionnaires contain questions that are specific to patients with kidney disease and do not apply to people without the disease. For instance, it is not pertinent to ask the general population of the United States about the impact of restricting high-potassium foods or fluid intake. Items such as these are not in generic questionnaires because they have limited applicability and do not apply to the population at-large. However, for patients with kidney disease, these items are extremely pertinent because of the impact on patients' lives.

Assess the Domains and Range

An additional characteristic to be assessed includes the domains measured by an instrument. Domains are the dimensions or major topics of health that a questionnaire is intended to measure. Most modern generic instruments contain domains that measure physical, social, and mental functioning. The most commonly used generic questionnaires also assess pain, general health, and vitality. Despite the lack of consensus on the essential domains in a generic questionnaire, the domains previously discussed tend to be the most commonly assessed. Domains included in disease-specific instruments vary depending on the disease characteristics and the aspects of health most affected. Many disease-specific instruments include generic domains in addition to the disease-specific domains. Full descriptions of the domains measured by an instrument should be explained in the original publication of the instrument development process.

It is important to make certain that the domains assessed meet the measurement goals of the study or clinical program. For example, the KDQOL, a disease-specific instrument for patients undergoing dialysis, contains the SF-36 scales and the disease-specific domains of: symptoms, effects of kidney disease, burden of kidney disease, work status, cognitive function, quality of social interaction, sexual function, sleep, social support, dialysis staff encouragement, and patient satisfaction. Table 4 illustrates the domains of the generic SF-36 as compared to the disease-specific CHEQ.

After assessing the domains an instrument measures, the range of health states that the items measure must be assessed. The current convention is for items to cover the full array of health from the positive aspects of wellness, to the negative aspects of infirmity. It does not matter if a questionnaire is generic or disease-specific, items should still cover a full range. For example, items in a mental health scale should not ask only about depressive-type symptoms because depression is the negative aspect of disease. To fully assess the range of mental health states, other items should inquire about happiness to extend the range into positive health states. Common generic instruments fully measure the range of health states, but disease-specific instruments may only measure the more negative aspects of health. It may be acceptable to have a negative range depending on the measure and the disease state. However, the range of items should be evaluated based on the intended measurement goals.

Assess Psychometric Properties

If an instrument has passed through the previously discussed steps and is still deemed acceptable, the psychometric properties of the questionnaire must be carefully considered. A complete discussion of psychometrics is in the Interpretations of Humanistic Assessments chapter. The summary in this chapter is intended to provide the reader with a cursory understanding necessary to evaluate an instrument; it is not intended to be a guide to how to actually test an instrument.

Reliability

Determining the reliability and validity of a questionnaire is essential to critically evaluating its psychometrics. These reports are often contained in the first published articles. Reliability refers to how consistent a measure is, but a measure cannot be considered reliable unless all of its scales meet the criteria for reliability. There are several ways to measure the reliability of a scale. One of the most commonly reported methods is the internal consistency method. This method is based on a single administration of the instrument. Internal consistency measures the correlation between one item and the other items which address the same domain. The assumption is that there are multiple items evaluating the same domain and that it is reasonable to expect that the scores on each item to be correlated with the scores on the other similar

Table 4: Examples of generic domains and disease-specific domains

Generic domains (SF-36)	Disease-specific domains (CHEQ)
Physical Functioning	Physical Functioning (from SF-36)
Role-Physical	Role-Physical (from SF-36)
Bodily Pain	Bodily Pain (from SF-36)
General Health	General health (from SF-36)
Vitality	Vitality (from SF-36)
Social Functioning	Social Functioning (from SF-36)
Role-Emotional	Role-Emotional (from SF-36)
Mental Health	Mental Health (from SF-36)
	Pain
	Travel
	Diet
	Dialysis Access
	Finances
	Sleep
	Symptoms
	Freedom
	Cognitive Functioning
	Recreation
	Body Image
	Global Quality of Life
	Sexual Functioning

items. Internal consistency is reported as Cronbach's alpha, Kuder-Richardson, or split halves. Although there is no consensus about the minimum acceptable level of reliability for internal consistency reliability, it is recommended that Cronbach's alpha be greater than or equal to 0.7 (on a scale of 0 to 1) for group comparisons. Certain references suggest that internal consistency reliability should exceed 0.8. For longitudinal individual patient comparisons, a controversial minimum of 0.9 has been suggested as the required Cronbach's alpha. Measures of internal consistency are from a single administration and do not assess day-to-day or interobserver variation.

Day-to-day and observer variation can be assessed by determining the stability of a measure. The stability or reproducibility of a measure is an indication of how the same measure administered on different occasions performs. If a measure requires multiple observers, the inter-rater reliability is important. Alternatively, intraobserver reliability is important if the agreement between observations of the same person on two different occasions needs to be assessed. Test-retest reliability assesses the agreement in observation of a patient on two occasions separated by some interval of time. Stability measurements over time should have a reliability of 0.5 or greater. Assessing the reliability of an instrument requires consideration of both internal consistency and stability.

Validity

In addition to assessing reliability, validity also must be assessed. Reliability assesses that the results are reproducible or consistent, whereas assessing validity gives an indication of what is being measured. However, a questionnaire should not be used if it is not valid in a patient population. Judgement is necessary in evaluating all types of validity. An expert should be consulted if the validity of a scale or instrument is in question.

There are several types of validity. Face validity is a subjective assessment determined by assessing if the instrument measures the important domains for the population of interest. The important domains are determined by querying health care professionals, patients, and the literature. Once face validity has been established, the questionnaire's content validity needs to be assessed. Content validity assesses how comprehensively the items examine the domain of interest. The reviewer needs to assess if there are enough questions to fully cover the domain. A minimum of one item should be included for each important content area or domain.

Although there should be at least one item per domain, there are advantages to having multiple items assess each content area. Increased reliability and validity, along with increased score variability and, therefore, responsiveness, are characteristics of multi-item measures. Further advantages of multi-item measures include the ability to estimate scale scores in the setting of missing data and minimize acquiescence. Acquiescence is the tendency of respondents to agree with any item, regardless of the question.

Responsiveness

Responsiveness, or the ability of an instrument to demonstrate change over time, is a particularly important criterion if you are reviewing an evaluative instrument. Responsiveness is the ability of a questionnaire to detect small changes over time. These changes may occur spontaneously or as a result of an intervention. It may be difficult to assess an instrument's responsiveness because there is often little published information. Reasons for this include the original purpose for most questionnaires was not evaluative and a lack of methods to evaluate responsiveness. However, new techniques recently have been developed to evaluate responsiveness. If there is no specific information on an instrument's responsiveness, researchers initially can evaluate it by determining the floor and ceiling effects of an instrument. Floor effects are determined by the percent of patients who score the lowest possible score on the scale. Clearly, these respondents are not able to show worsening over time because they already have the lowest possible score. The opposite is true with ceiling effects. The ceiling is the highest possible score. If researchers were testing the ability of a drug to result in improvements in health, they would not be able to demonstrate improvement over time in patients who already had the highest score. Another indication that an instrument may be able to detect change over time is the number of response options that are available for each item. Measures with more refined grading of the response options, such as several levels of endorsement, severity, or frequency, are more likely to show small differences over time than are yes or no response options. Finally, having a measure that includes items that are expected to show change over time improves the responsiveness of the instrument.

Sensibility

Some subjectivity is involved when assessing face and content validity as the two are often tested without formal statistical analysis. Criteria for evaluating the sensibility of questionnaires have been devised to structure the assessment of face and content validity. Sensibility encompasses a variety of aspects, including the applicability of the questionnaire, its clarity and simplicity, the likelihood of bias, its comprehensiveness, and the presence of redundant items.

Do not prematurely dismiss a scale or questionnaire based only on the subjective judgments of face and content validity. Many older published instruments have not been proven to have face or content validity. Two things to keep in mind are that face and content validity are educated peer judgments and even though a measure may be valid for its original measurement goals, it cannot be assumed that it is valid for a different purpose.

More structured assessments of validity include criterion validity and construct validity. Criterion validity assesses the validity of a scale or questionnaire by comparing it to an existing instrument that is considered to be the gold standard. Criterion validity is met if the hypothesized domains compared in the two instruments are correlated and the correlation coefficient is greater than 0.4. If the correlation is less than 0.4, there is an unacceptable level of agreement. There are two potential reasons for the disagreement: either one measure has a low level of reliability or different concepts are being measured by the two instruments.

When there is no gold standard, construct validity is used because it is the most rigorous approach to examining an instrument's validity. Reports of construct validity should include both the hypotheses and the underlying model for testing them. Confirming the hypotheses strengthens the validity of the instrument. The opposite also is true. For instance, developers of the CHEQ, a disease-specific questionnaire designed to detect differences in health status among patients undergoing hemodialysis and peritoneal dialysis, performed tests of content validity. Based on information from focus groups and clinician input, the researchers hypothesized, a priori, that the scale scores for patients undergoing peritoneal dialysis would be higher in the domain of freedom. If this hypothesis were proven true, then the domain of freedom would have construct validity. In the original paper describing the preliminary reliability and validity results, patients receiving peritoneal dialysis did have statistically significant better scores than patients receiving hemodialysis. Therefore, the authors concluded that the CHEQ has construct validity in the domain of freedom. Other domains can be tested in a similar fashion.

Response Bias

Response bias is a source of systematic error in humanistic outcome measures and may be a result of the instrument's design or the patient. Form-based bias results from respondents being influenced by the wording of a question. An example of form-based bias is acquiescence where respondents tend to agree with any item, regardless of its content. Combining positively and negatively worded items within a scale can minimize acquiescence. Patients can be influenced by a variety of factors that result in patient-based bias and are often unaware of this bias. Socially desirable response sets, which can occur when respondents do not want to report socially undesirable feelings or behaviors or when they want to be perceived as a good patient, are an example of this type of bias. Response bias is especially prevalent when a member of the health care team is interviewing the patient.

Interpretability

Understanding all the concepts previously discussed is important so that the results of humanistic assessments can be properly interpreted. Interpretability determines what the results actually mean. Criterion-based interpretation is based on comparing health status results to external variables. Clinicians most often use clinical data to assist in interpreting health status scores. Laboratory values, mortality rates, lengths of stay, and numbers of hospitalizations are examples of external variables that can aid in interpretation. In patients undergoing dialysis, those patients with a SF-36 Physical Component Score of less than 34 were twice as likely to die and 1.5 times more likely to be hospitalized than patients whose score was above the median of 34. These results suggest that a clinical intervention should take place when the Physical Component Score is less than 34 to decrease the likelihood that the patient will die or be hospitalized.

Comparing known normative data is another example of criterion-based interpretation and is one advantage of generic questionnaires. Norms are calculated on the group or individual level, but most often comparisons are made at the group level. Norms from the group level are developed from a representative sample of the population. The SF-36 scales have norms for both the general healthy population and for many different chronic disease states. Additional comparisons with normative data can enhance understanding of specific disease states and the health status differences between genders and among different age groups. Currently, most normative data are derived from cross-sectional studies. However, interpreting changes over time requires longitudinal norms and is especially important in disease states where a progressive and known decline in health status exists.

Caveats for Reviewing Patient-based Assessments

Although the standard criteria for evaluating literature apply to health status measures, there are some caveats. Fully understanding the patient population in which the questionnaire was originally validated is important, as is knowing the original purpose for which the questionnaire was designed. These factors aid in determining if the questionnaire will perform reliably and validly in the patient population of interest. For example, the authors of the KDQOL reported in the original validation article that the population in which the questionnaire was validated was similar to the overall dialysis population. Users of the KDQOL can then be reassured that the KDQOL will perform in a similar manner, as it did in the original validation sample, if their population characteristics are similar to, or representative of, the overall population. Do not assume that a frequently used instrument has been demonstrated to be a reliable and valid measure in a patient population.

The population in which the instrument is tested is important as is the rationale of the developers for designing the instrument. For example, in developing the CHEQ, the authors clearly state that there were three goals in designing the instrument: complementing the generic SF-36, being sensitive to differences between dialysis modalities, and being useful for longitudinal data collection. A clear understanding of the original questionnaire goals aids in determining if the measurement goals will be met. For instance, if the current measurement goal is to assess the health status of only patients undergoing hemodialysis, the CHEQ may not be an appropriate measure because one of its original measurement goals is to differentiate between hemodialysis and peritoneal dialysis. There will be questions or scales that may not be relevant to the population of interest. This is not to say that the CHEQ would be dismissed immediately. However, it is a valid concern that requires more in-depth review of the actual questionnaire in relation to the measurement goals.

Additional areas that should be clearly described are the domains included in the questionnaire, the scoring procedure, the subjects, how the population was sampled, and the statistical and psychometric methods used.

The Strategy for Using a Questionnaire

Although the previously discussed approach to critically reviewing published questionnaires may seem cumbersome and time consuming, it is well worth the time and effort. The process is important and ultimately may save the time and expense required to develop a new measure. If a new questionnaire must be developed, a comprehensive literature review is necessary to provide the foundation for the new measure.

After following the process described, more than one questionnaire may be found that meets the defined measurement goals. In general, researchers and clinicians want to measure as much as possible without overburdening the patients. A common approach to obtain the most information is to combine a generic and a disease-specific questionnaire. The generic questionnaire allows comparisons to other populations, yet the disease-specific influence on health status also can be measured. Two questionnaires for patients with kidney disease (the KDQOL and the CHEQ) combine the generic SF-36 and disease-specific components.

Researchers and clinicians should be aware of the potential pitfall of combining general health status measures with a disease-specific measure. The increased length of the combined questionnaire will increase respondent burden and potentially decrease participation and or response rates. It also is important to be aware of the psychometric properties of each questionnaire alone and in combination.

In a combined questionnaire, the generic questionnaire items should come first. This approach is recommended so that patients think generally about their health when responding to the generic questions and then become narrower in focus when responding to the disease-specific items. Otherwise, patients may already be focusing on their specific disease state, and that would alter their responses to the generic questions.

It is possible that a published questionnaire, or combination of published questionnaires, may not fully meet the measurement goals. In this case, it is permissible to augment the published measure. The advised approach is to add scales that have already met psychometric criteria. It is not advised to make changes to existing instruments. Changes in the order of items or wording of a specific item have the potential to alter the original psychometric properties of the instrument. Any changes made to an existing instrument require that the revised instrument undergo rigorous testing to ensure it continues to meet psychometric standards. In addition, altering an existing questionnaire may violate copyright regulations and doing so without the author's permission may violate intellectual property laws. However, adding questions or scales at the end of an existing instrument is acceptable.

Pilot testing of a revised instrument is absolutely necessary if any changes or additions are made to a published questionnaire. The pilot test can be both formal and informal. Simply having patients complete the questionnaire and provide feedback is informal, but usually informative. This process identifies features, such as format, ease of readability, and patient interpretation of the items. Experience dictates that regardless of how perfect a clinician or researcher thinks a scale or questionnaire is, patient input can always improve the measure. Formal testing includes initial assessments of reliability and validity that is usually beyond the purview of the reader.

Regardless of the simplicity or complexity of a measure, humanistic outcomes instruments are designed using complicated and time-intensive methods. If published questionnaires are available, researchers and clinicians should choose to use them. While reviewing the literature, it is relatively easy to be overly critical of published instruments. In addition, it is a common mistake to underestimate the magnitude of the effort required to develop a new questionnaire. When done correctly, developing new instruments is a complicated, lengthy, and expensive proposition.

Practical Considerations

Methods for administering questionnaires and locating and evaluating questionnaires were discussed previously; however, there are practical considerations that are equally important and must be considered to ensure effective use of health status measures.

Burden of Questionnaire Administration

Administering a questionnaire adds effort both on the part of the patient and the research or clinical staff. It is important to assess and minimize that burden to ensure quality data collection.

Respondent Burden

Patient or respondent burden is an important point in instrument evaluation and is another survey characteristic that must be evaluated. Respondent burden takes into account not only the number of items, but also the difficulty in responding to those items and the total time it will take respondents to complete the questionnaire. It is important to assess if the amount of time that is required to complete the questionnaire is practical taking into account the setting in which the respondent will complete it. As questionnaires increase in length, patients are more likely to tire and choose not to respond. A balance needs to be achieved between meeting the defined measurement goals and the level of respondent burden. A general rule of thumb is 30 minutes or less is an acceptable amount of time to minimize respondent burden.

Patient characteristics affect the level of patient cooperation or willingness to complete a questionnaire. Although little is understood about the impact of age, education, and health status on questionnaire completion, it is known that respondent cooperation depends on what patients perceive as the loss or gain from completing the questionnaire. Losses include costs in terms of time and effort, direct monetary costs of participating, loss of income from time spent participating, and loss of privacy. Gains that patients perceive when completing a questionnaire include altruism, positive feelings about participating, and positive interactions with staff. There are effective methods to obtain and maintain respondent cooperation. These methods include personalizing the questionnaire, giving monetary incentives or gifts, promoting positive contacts with respondents, providing telephone numbers to contact in case of problems, sending holiday cards, and producing and mailing newsletters to the respondents.

Staff Burden

In addition to respondent burden, questionnaire administration also may cause staff burden. Planning a research study involving a questionnaire should include a dedicated person, at least initially to explain to respondents the purpose of the questionnaire, answer questions, and ensure data completeness. The level of research staff involvement in this process depends on the administration method chosen. Interview administration has the greatest staff burden of all the administration methods.

Population Characteristics

Characteristics of the population of interest have significant impact on the process of questionnaire administration and need to be carefully assessed in advance. For instance, patients undergoing dialysis are tethered to a dialysis machine and one arm is essentially not functional during the dialysis session. Tubing is predominantly, but not always, connected to patients' nondominant arm. Assessing health status in this patient population requires ensuring a hard surface on which to write (usually a clipboard) and providing assistance to patients whose dominant arm is unavailable. Decreased visual acuity is common in these patients because diabetes is one of the most common causes of kidney failure and is highly prevalent in elderly patients. Providing reading glasses and larger print forms is necessary to ensure questionnaire completion.

It also is important to consider the population's education level, literacy rate, and language spoken. Depending on the patient population, there may be a high rate of illiteracy. Often, patients who are functionally illiterate can respond using interview-administered questionnaires. In general, questionnaires should be written at no more than an eighth-grade reading level. Preferably, the reading level should be sixth-grade or lower. However, there will still be patients who are unable to read or understand the items. Additional considerations must be made for patients who are non-English speakers or not native speakers of English. Many of the commonly used generic questionnaires have been translated into a variety of foreign languages. Special considerations need to be made when assessing the foreign-language version of a questionnaire. It is important to know exactly how the questionnaire was translated and how cultural differences were taken into account. The methodology used by International Quality of Life Assessment (IQOLA) project is comprehensive. The iterative approach includes translations, both forward and backward, and assessments of the cultural applicability of the questionnaire. The project's standardized approach allows for scoring comparisons across countries. However, this standardization is time and resource intensive. Ensuring questionnaire equivalence is not an easy task and questionnaire developers strongly recommend that inexperienced individuals do not create their own translations of instruments.

Proxy Reports

Proxy reports or surrogate respondents are sometimes used in situations where the intended respondent is incapacitated or is otherwise unable to respond to the questions. These reports are especially relevant in patients with progressive cognitive disorders such as Alzheimer's disease. In these situations, responses can be generated through an informed third party, such as a spouse or relative. For analytic purposes, the third party must be clearly defined.

Although proxy reports provide information that is not otherwise available, studies have shown that, in general, proxy responses tend to differ from patients' responses. In one study the Sickness Impact Profile was administered to both terminally ill patients who were still able to complete the questionnaire and to a close relative. Investigators found only a moderate correlation (r=0.55) in responses between the respondent and the close relative. For more than half of the comparisons, the difference between the two sets of respondents was more than six points on a 100-point scale. The variance primarily depended on the domain assessed and the choice of surrogate. Patients and surrogates are much more likely to agree on observable domains such as physical functioning, although proxy respondents tend to rate patients' functional limitations lower than the patients do. This discrepancy is especially true with surrogate respondents who are close to the patients. With regard to morbidity, patients tend to report the most dysfunction and clinicians the least, with surrogates' reports positioned somewhere in between.

Data Collection and Entry, Results Reporting, and Cost

Other concerns that should be addressed before questionnaires are administered include how data will be processed and analyzed. Traditionally, self-administration has used paper-based questionnaires and after patients completed the questionnaire, the data were entered manually or scanned into a database. Recent technological advances have allowed for completed questionnaires to be faxed for processing. The results are then returned to the clinic within minutes of the initial fax. As previously discussed, computer systems and software have been developed that allow for direct response entry by the patient.

Furthermore, the data analysis needs for a researcher differ from the needs of a clinician. Researchers are primarily interested in group-level data and typically wait until all respondents complete the questionnaire before entering the data and analyzing it. This process is typically unacceptable to clinicians who are interested in individual patient data at the time of the clinic visit. Their needs are more urgent so that the data can be applied immediately to patient care. Data formatting and presentation also are important to clinicians. The data need to be readily available and easily interpretable for use in a busy clinic environment.

Another consideration when deciding which method of data collection to use is how are the results going to be reported. A practical example is seen in the dialysis population. In one health status assessment program, the traditional paper-and-pencil administration method is used and all the questionnaires processed at a central site. Once the questionnaires are processed, the results are downloaded into the medical information system and are readily available to all health care providers in the dialysis unit. This form of results reporting is effective primarily because patients undergoing dialysis frequent the clinic 3 times/week. However, in traditional outpatient settings, patients do not visit the clinic as frequently. In those settings, it is vitally important that the results be available during the patient's actual visit. Therefore, any decisions on how the data should be collected and entered need to take the results reporting into consideration.

Once a questionnaire and administration methods have been determined, it is necessary to decide exactly how the data are going to be collected and entered into a database. A recent cost comparison of the various methods to collect health status data assessed the annual fixed and variable costs needed to build, maintain, and generate SF-36 reports for a pain management clinic. The analyses revealed wide variations in cost based on questionnaire volume, personnel availability, access to necessary equipment, how quickly the results were needed, and the acceptable level of data error. Faxing questionnaires to a central repository was the least costly when there was a low volume of questionnaires. However, if more than 1250 surveys were administered annually, the costs of the faxing method and computer touch screen approach were similar. Once the annual questionnaire volume exceeded 1500, computer touch screen became the least costly.

A significant amount of time and effort goes into selecting the best questionnaire and an equal amount of time is necessary to determine how, when, and where to administer the questionnaire. Although the process is time consuming, it is essential to data quality and ultimately to interpreting the results.

Conclusion

This chapter reviewed the process of selecting questionnaire administration modes, critically reviewing questionnaires, and assessing practical considerations. Deciding which administration mode to use depends on a variety of factors that must be evaluated for each patient group to be surveyed. It is time consuming to critically review the literature to determine if a questionnaire is available for the intended purpose. However, the time spent is worthwhile. The process of developing a questionnaire is one that should not be undertaken lightly. Questionnaires are invaluable ways to learn how patients function and feel about their health and the health care they receive. Using questionnaires that are valid, reliable, and responsive is essential to collecting data that yield meaningful results. Administering questionnaires in ways that maximize patient ability to answer questions accurately and completely is equally essential.

Exercise 1: Selecting the Questionnaire Administration Mode

You are considering measuring the health status of patients who are seen by a group of physicians in a general medicine clinic attached to a large tertiary care hospital located in the center of an urban area. The goal of the project is to use the results of the health status measure to improve clinical care. Preliminarily, it is decided to use the SF-36 Health Status Survey. There are 20 physicians total who are divided into teams of four. There are two teams per floor of the building. Each team has a clinic secretary, a nurse practitioner, a file clerk and a phlebotomist. The demographics of the patients are: all adults, 45 percent of the patients having Medicare insurance, and 25 percent have Medicaid insurance. One of the physicians has a predominant Human Immunodeficiency Virus-infected population; one has a geriatric panel. The others have a mixed panel of patients. While planning your project, analyze the logistics of how the questionnaire will be administered. What steps must be taken to plan a successful project?

Annotated Bibliography

1. Adler DA, Bungay KM, Cynn DJ, Kosinski M. Patient-based health status assessments in an outpatient psychiatry setting. Psychiat Serv 2000;51:341–8.

   This article is an excellent description of how to implement health status assessment into routine clinical practice. Although the authors describe integration of the SF-36 into a psychiatric clinic, their points are valid for any questionnaire being implemented in any medical clinic. This article also is a good representation of how to present psychometric information about a questionnaire. The authors' explanations are concise and meaningful.

2. Chambers LW, Haight M, Norman G, MacDonald L. Sensitivity to change and effect of administration mode on health status measurement. Med Care 1987;25:470–80.

   The authors used the McMaster Health Index Questionnaire in 96 patients visiting a physiotherapy clinic to determine sensitivity to change and the effect of administration mode. They studied self-administration and telephone interview administration modes using random assignments to one of three groups. This study is a good example of how to assess two important measurement properties.

3. Drummond HE, Ghosh S, Ferguson A, Brackenridge D, Tiplady B. Electronic quality of life questionnaires: a comparison of pen-based electronic questionnaires with conventional paper in a gastrointestinal study. Qual Life Res 1995;4:21–6.

   This article examines one of the earliest published studies to compare conventional pencil-and-paper questionnaire administration with pen-based electronic questionnaires. Unfortunately, the authors do not compare the reliability and validity for the questionnaire when administered using the two methods.

4. Guyatt GH, Feeny DH, Patrick DL. Measuring health-related quality of life. Ann Intern Med 1993;118:622–9.

This article is a basic review of the science of measuring humanistic outcomes. The authors, who have significant experience in the field, discuss administration modes, the criteria for a good instrument, measuring validity, types of measures, and choosing an appropriate measure.

5. Lofland JH, Schaffer M, Goldfarb N. Evaluating health-related quality of life: cost comparison of computerized touch-screen technology and traditional paper systems. Pharmacotherapy 2000;20:1390–5.

This article is one of the few available that compares the costs of the options for collecting health status data. Three methods of administering the SF-36 (computer touch-screen, faxing completed questionnaires to an outside vendor, and scanning) as part of routine care in a pain management clinic were compared. The authors calculated the annual fixed, variable, and total costs per survey. The results demonstrated that cost was based on volume. Although these data are from a specialty clinic, they should be applicable to a variety of outpatient clinics.

6. McCusker J, Stoddard AM. Use of a surrogate for the Sickness Impact Profile. Med Care 1984;22:789–95.

In this article, the authors compare the responses to the Sickness Impact Profile provided by 66 terminally ill or homebound and chronically ill patients to those provided by surrogates. The Sickness Impact Profile was already known to be a valid and reliable measure for self-administration and interview administration. The authors wanted to compare responses of patients and their caregivers and determine which characteristics influenced agreement in scores.

7. McHorney CA, Kosinski M, Ware JE. Comparisons of the costs and quality of norms for the SF-36 Health Survey collected by mail versus telephone interview: results from a national survey. Med Care 50 1994;32:551–67.

This study is one of the most rigorous evaluations of the effects of administration mode on cost, response rate, data quality, and scale scores. The authors randomly assigned adults to receive either a mail survey or computer-assisted telephone survey. Data collection costs per case for the telephone survey were 77 percent higher than the costs of the mail survey. Although mail survey had a significantly higher response rate than did the computer-assisted telephone survey, the authors also found that the rate of missing data was greater for mailed surveys than for telephone surveys. Scale scores were lower and the report of chronic conditions higher among those who were mailed the questionnaire. In the discussion, the authors present an excellent discourse on the trade-offs in selecting the various administration modes.

8. Patrick DL, Chiang YP, eds. Health outcomes methodology: symposium proceedings. Med Care 2000;38(suppl II):II-1–II-209.

This supplement is the proceedings of a 1999 symposium where experts addressed contemporary methodologic issues in measuring health status. The main themes addressed at the symposium included: item response theory (the basis of computerized adaptive testing), longitudinal construct validity, health status assessments in diverse populations, the validity and interpretation of preference-based instruments, and quality of life outcomes interpretation. The entire supplement is peer reviewed. The supplement addresses critical issues in the field and contains a comprehensive glossary listing standardized terms, ending with a summary of the symposium and future recommendations.

9. Spilker B, ed. Quality of life and pharmacoeconomics in clinical trials, 2nd ed. Philadelphia: Lippincott-Raven, 1996.

This classic book contains a wealth of information about administration methods, questionnaire selection, and questionnaire development. It also is a tremendous resource of published instruments. Experts in the field author chapters. However, it has been several years since the most recent edition.

10. Stewart AL, Ware JE, eds. Measuring functioning and well-being: the Medical Outcomes Study approach. Durham, NC: Duke University Press, 1992.

This book contains information about the Medical Outcomes Study approach to measuring humanistic outcomes. The Medical Outcomes Study was the first large-scale study to measure humanistic outcomes. The approach to measurement and the experiences of the investigators are detailed in this book. It is an excellent resource for understanding administration modes and questionnaire development. It also contains several scales and their reliability and validity information.

11. Streiner DL, Norman GR. Health measurement scales: a practical guide to their development and use. 2nd ed. Oxford: Oxford University Press, 1995.

This textbook is a good reference for developing and/or evaluating questionnaires. Chapter 2 is a comprehensive discussion of how to critically evaluate health status literature and questionnaires. Chapter 3 is an excellent review of devising the items for a particular measure. Chapter 4 is devoted to the concept of scaling responses. The authors detail the process of selecting response options for items. Chapter 13 explains the different methods to administer measures and gives the advantages and disadvantages of each.

12. Wilkin D, Hallam L, Doggett M. Measures of need and outcome for primary health care. Oxford: Oxford University Press, 1992.

This book is an excellent reference both for individuals new to measuring humanistic outcomes and for those with prior experience. It is a particularly good starting point for individuals seeking a better understanding of how to identify and develop measures of humanistic outcomes. This book is particularly helpful in describing the process of critically reviewing the literature. The authors also describe the process of developing a questionnaire.

13. Wu AW, Rubin HR, Mathews WC, et al. A health status questionnaire using 30 items from the Medical Outcomes Study. Med Care 1991;29:786–98.

This article is an excellent example of a high-quality first publication of a newly developed instrument. The authors describe the development of a questionnaire to measure health status in human immunodeficiency virus-infected patients. There are good explanations of construct validity and examples of how internal consistency reliability is reported.

Self-Assessment Questions

1. You are assessing a disease-specific questionnaire for use in patients with diabetes mellitus. In the original development article, the authors report the highest Cronbach's alpha of any scale to be 0.6. Which one of the following is a correct interpretation of the questionnaire?
   A. It is a good choice for a longitudinal study.
   B. It is a reliable measure for patients with diabetes mellitus.
   C. None of the scales meet the necessary criteria.
   D. It is not a valid measure to predict needs or outcomes.

2. Using a questionnaire where 34 percent of respondents scored the highest possible score is of concern for which one of the following objectives?
   A. Determining in a cross-sectional study if differences in humanistic outcomes exist between patients who are taking a drug and those who are not.
   B. Evaluating an exercise program's effect on humanistic outcomes in respondents with a chronic disease.
   C. Predicting which respondents are at risk for having a disease.
   D. Describing the areas of need and potential interventions for respondents with a medical condition.

3. Which one of the following is a disadvantage of face-to-face interviews?
   A. Respondents are less likely to report sensitive information.
   B. More complicated patterns of questions can be asked.
   C. Face-to-face interviews are less expensive to administer.
   D. Clinic staff can administer face-to-face interviews.

4. When assessing humanistic outcomes in patients with Alzheimer's disease, which one of the following methods of administration is the least effective?
   A. Proxy reports from the primary caregiver.
   B. Face-to-face interview administration.
   C. Telephone-administered interviews.
   D. Mail-out/mail-back surveys.

5. You are selecting a humanistic outcomes instrument for a clinical trial comparing an active agent to a placebo. When identifying instruments in the literature, you are most interested in which one of the following types of instruments?
   A. Predictive.
   B. Discriminative.
   C. Evaluative.
   D. Descriptive.

6. As part of a study, you are interested in developing a questionnaire to determine which humanistic outcomes domain patients feel is most affected by their drug therapy. Little prior research has been done in this area and you chose to make the question open ended. Which one of the following is the best administration mode for this questionnaire?
   A. Self-administration.
   B. Face-to-face interview administration.
   C. Mail-out/mail-back administration.
   D. Computerized administration.

7. When evaluating a study that has used mixed administration modes, which one of the following does not need to be considered before changes in scores over time can be evaluated?
   A. The order of administration.
   B. Differences in scores based on type of administration.
   C. The rationale for mixing administration modes.
   D. The demographic background of the respondents.

8. Which one of the following considerations will not influence the choice of questionnaire administration mode?
   A. The budget for the project.
   B. Data quality needs.
   C. The amount of time to complete the questionnaire.
   D. The availability of an existing instrument.

9. The number of items in a questionnaire, the physical location where respondents will complete the questionnaire, and the age and level of education of respondents are all important because they influence which one of the following?
   A. Respondent burden.
   B. Sample size.
   C. Project duration.
   D. Result display.

10. A patient with lung cancer is completing a questionnaire using CAT software. The first question asked was the patient's ability to walk 1 mile. The response entered into the computer indicated that the patient was severely limited in his ability to walk 1 mile. Which one of the following items is chosen next by CAT software?
    A. Do you have difficulty bathing and dressing yourself?
    B. Do you feel full of energy?
    C. How would you rate your health overall?
    D. How limited are you in climbing one flight of stairs?

MEASURING HEALTH STATUS

Eleanor M. Perfetto, Ph.D., M.S.; Bryce Reeve, Ph.D.; Prasun Subedi, B.S.; Angeline M. Carlson, Ph.D.; and Lisa Stockwell Morris, Ph.D.

Outline

As drug therapy continues to play an increasingly prominent role in the management of disease, it is important that pharmacists and other health care providers become proficient in evaluating how drug therapy impacts the health status of the patient. This chapter focuses on the tools and applications of health status measurement and provides guidance for identifying, assessing and using these measures.

I. Changing perspective over time
    A. Historical origins
        1. Morbidity and mortality
        2. Function and disability
        3. Outcomes assessment and accountability
        4. Emphasis is on the patient
    B. Utility of health status instruments
        1. In addition to clinical measures when making treatment decisions
        2. See trends in well-being of populations beyond the disease level
        3. Outcomes research
        4. Policy making

II. Terminology
    A. A proliferation of terms and confusion
    B. Definitions
        1. Health status
        2. Quality of life
        3. Patient-reported outcomes
    C. Structure of a health status instrument
        1. Domains
        2. Subdomains
        3. Items

III. Health Measurement Taxonomies and Models
    A. Cocentric Model of Health Status
        1. Disease
        2. Personal functioning
        3. Well being

4. General health perceptions
5. Social/role functioning

B. Three Dimensional Model of Health Status
1. One component of quality of life
2. Health status combined with subjective perceptions results in quality of life

C. ECHO Model
1. Economic
2. Clinical
3. Humanistic

IV. Descriptive measures of health status: General vs. Disease-specific instruments

A. General health status instruments
1. Applied to patients in all health states
    a. Various types of medical conditions
    b. Differing levels of severity
    c. Different medical treatments
    d. Different demographic subgroups
    e. Different cultural subgroups
2. Summarize a wide spectrum of factors
    a. Duration of life
    b. Impairments
    c. Functional states
    d. Perceptions
    e. Social opportunities
3. Develop normative data to allow for comparisons of relative health status between groups of patients and populations
4. Permit comparisons across interventions and diagnostic conditions; importance to policy makers
5. Medical Outcomes Study Short Form 36
    a. Multi-item scale that measures eight dimensions of health
        i. Physical functioning
        ii. Role limitations because of physical health problems
        iii. Bodily pain
        iv. Social functioning
        v. General mental health
        vi. Role limitations because of emotional problems
        vii. Vitality
        viii. General health perceptions
    b. Single-item health transition measure
    c. Various scoring methodologies
6. Sickness Impact Profile
    a. Sickness is an individual's experience of illness
    b. Disease is a professional definition (diagnosis) of disease
    c. Assesses how illness experience changes daily activities and behavior
7. Concerns associated with the use of general instruments
    a. Length because of necessity of addressing multiple aspects of health status
    b. Increased respondent burden
    c. Decreased acceptability to patients
    d. Scoring instruments may be complex
    e. Do not address particular concerns of a specific population
    f. May not be sensitive to changes

B. Disease-specific health status instruments
1. Past use has been associated with clinical assessment and patient classification; do not typically incorporate input from patients
    a. Karnofsky Performance Status Scale for level of physical activity impairment among patients with cancer
    b. American Rheumatism Association Functional Classification to assess activities of daily living for arthritis patients
    c. New York Heart Association grading of angina to classify angina patients
    d. Mini-Mental State Examination for classification of cognitive functioning
2. Present use is more patient-oriented; self-administered instruments allow for more patient input
3. Newer instruments are designed to address health status issues when a specific disease, condition, or treatment is present

a. More sensitive to targeted effects
b. Not able to detect unanticipated effects
c. Not as generalizable as general health status measures; results can be compared across subpopulations only
d. Some concepts addressed in disease-specific instruments may apply across several unrelated conditions

4. Disease-specific instruments may be easier to administer, use fewer questions, and may be easier to score compared to general health status instruments
5. Decreased respondent burden improves acceptability to patients
6. More relevant to patient problems
7. Less costly to incorporate into clinical practice
8. May have the ability to distinguish between disease-specific functional changes and functional changes because of comorbid conditions
9. Number of instruments are available in different disease states
   a. Asthma Quality of Life Questionnaire: measures functional impairments important for adults with asthma
   b. Health Assessment Questionnaire: evaluates the severity of functional limitations because of rheumatoid arthritis by considering the patient's ability to perform daily life activities
   c. Functional Assessment of Chronic Illness Therapy: set of instruments (both general and disease specific) used to assess impact of cancer treatment on functional capacity

C. Overlap between general and disease-specific health status instruments
1. Disease-specific instruments developed from general instruments
2. Major differences in level of detail concerning specific conditions or functional abilities
3. Should include both general and disease-specific health status instruments in a study
   a. General instruments have decreased relevance but increased ability to make comparisons with other populations
   b. Disease-specific instruments have increased relevance but decreased ability to make comparisons with other populations
   c. Using both ensures that strengths of each one are included
4. Incorporating both general and disease-specific instruments can be accomplished in several ways
   a. Use two separate instruments
   b. Use a battery of instruments
   c. Modify terms in general instrument to make them more disease-specific
5. Suggestion: include two separate, valid, reliable, established instruments in a study
   a. Most practical
   b. Provides basis of comparison to existing literature
6. Use a battery of instruments
   a. Battery is a collection of disease-specific and general instruments
   b. Will not result in overall score
   c. Difficult to determine relative importance of each dimension of health when several different instruments are used
7. Adding questions to a general instrument or modifying a general instrument to make the focus more disease-specific requires considerable effort
   a. Could affect validity and reliability
   b. Could be construed as violation of copyright

V. Preference-based measures of health status

A. Health status and quality of life are complex constructs
1. As a result, instruments with varying degrees of subjectivity, reliability and validity have been developed
2. Reflects the fact that effects of disease or medical intervention will differ markedly according to values and preferences of individual patients
3. Individual expectations, values and judgments also play a role in how clinical symptoms are perceived by a patient
4. Health Belief Model: explanatory framework of preventative health behavior
   a. Personal susceptibility to a health consequence
   b. Level of severity associated with consequence that affects valued component of life
   c. Taking action will reduce consequence or severity
   d. Has been used to examine a variety of health behaviors including drug compliance

B. Role of expectations, values and judgments in quality of life and health status is important in HBM and other psychosocial theories
1. Researchers agree that it is possible to identify health concepts of importance to patients
   a. Long life
   b. Normal function

c. Free of pain and other physical, psychological, and social symptoms
d. Not have reduced health because of treatments
e. Financially stable after medical expenses paid
2. These dimensions are combined into a framework known as the Hierarchy of Patient Outcomes
a. Useful structure for planning health status measurement strategy
b. Global outcome examined in relation to patient-oriented factors
c. Consists of five dimensions, which are then broken down into subdimensions and items
3. Framework provides organized means of ensuring all subcomponents of an outcome are identified
C. Quantitative assessment of patient expectations, values and judgments
1. Recent efforts have focused on a shift from qualitative to quantitative measurement of expectations
2. Utility: value of a particular health state to patients or the general population
a. Assigned value reflects perceived quality or desirability of health state
b. Measured by assigning preferences
c. Preferences range from death to perfect health
d. Numerical assignment is 0 (death) and 1.0 (perfect health)
e. Possibility of health states worse than death
3. Utility assessment: method of integrating values attributed to life at given points in time with the quality of life spent in these health states
a. Leads to determination of a single index representing the combinations of different levels of functional status and perceptions
b. Index allows trade-offs between domains to be assessed over time
c. Average improvement or deterioration can be identified
4. Formation of a single index allows for comparison of tradeoffs and changes (improvement/deterioration) across domains over time

VI. Criteria for selecting a standardized health status instrument
A. Availability/assessment
1. Many instruments are available
2. No gold standard by which to compare instruments
3. Many instruments have not undergone adequate psychometric testing
4. Potential selection of inappropriate measure becomes a critical issue
B. Several key points in patient-focused health status assessment
1. Health assessment instruments must be selected that will measure and detect change in components relevant to an overall outcome
a. Understanding of overall purpose of study, rationale, and outcomes of interest
b. Clear articulation of research questions and hypotheses
c. Understanding of why and how health status measures contribute to study purpose
d. Only include measures necessary to meet stated purpose of study
2. Outcomes identified for health status assessment are different than those typically identified as clinical measures
a. Some diseases may not have clear relationship between clinical and patient outcomes
b. Examples of traditional clinical measures and patient-centered outcomes
3. Identify outcome, dimensions, subdimensions, and components before selecting health status instrument
4. Availability of an instrument should not determine the outcomes for a study
5. Several instruments may be needed to appropriately measure an outcome
a. Avoid 'cherry picking' of items
b. Identifying all key dimensions, subdimensions, and components provides a checklist from which to evaluate instruments
c. Consider decision to include general and disease-specific instruments
6. Measurement of health status may occur at multiple levels in a study
C. Patient-focused health status instrument includes measures of patient perceptions of health
1. A truly patient-focused health status instrument includes measures that reflect the unique perspective of the patient
2. Measures have meaning and relevance in the global context of patients' lives and their life in a diminished state of health
3. Should possess five important characteristics
a. Measures the effect of a disease, condition, or treatment on aspects of life considered by patients to be of greatest importance
b. Allows patients to rate the extent to which various aspects of life are affected by a disease, condition, or treatment
c. Measures changes in health over time

d. Allows patients to judge the value of changes in health over time
e. Relates the study population's changes in health to other populations of patients

D. Methodological considerations for selecting a health status instrument
1. Validity is the extent to which an instrument measures what it is intended to measure and does not measure what it should not
2. Four types of validity
a. Face validity judges whether the instrument measures what it says it does
b. Content validity judges whether the aspects of health measured in the instrument are relevant and includes all important aspects of health through expert opinion
c. Construct validity judges whether the instrument correlates with other related constructs as expected
d. Criterion validity judges the extent to which the instrument predicts or agrees with constructs external to those which are being measured
3. Reliability relates to the consistency of results obtained when using an instrument repeatedly
a. Internal consistency
b. Test-retest assessment
4. Sensitivity to change is the ability of an instrument to detect changes when it is administered before and after an event or period of time
a. Instrument may be able to detect large differences readily
b. Small differences (between treatment groups, for example) can go undetected
c. To detect expected small differences, an instrument with high sensitivity or a large sample would be needed

E. Practical administrative considerations in instrument selection
1. Costs associated with using health status instruments
a. Some instruments can be used freely
b. Permission/fees are required for others
c. Costs of reproducing the instrument for every patient
d. Data collection costs
e. Data entry/analysis costs
2. Respondent burden is the time and effort needed to complete the instrument
a. May increase when patients are in a poor state of health
b. Large respondent burden could influence the quality of data collected
3. Potential for response bias
4. Requirements to score the instrument and analyze results
a. Standardized instruments must be scored in a similar manner or results will not be comparable
b. Some instruments require complex scoring algorithms that can more easily be produced by computer
c. Computer-assisted scoring may be valuable in studies with large sample sizes
d. Computer capabilities may be required
e. Statistical analysis may require skills of a statistician

F. Advantages of using an established instrument
1. Ability to make comparisons with published literature
2. Increased confidence and credibility for the results
3. Accumulation of knowledge about an existing instrument
4. Advancement of knowledge about applicability of existing instruments in different populations and diseases
5. More judicious use of research funds

VII. Psychometric modeling
A. Need for balance between methodological and practical concerns
B. The field of psychometrics
1. Combines cognitive and quantitative psychology
2. Multidisciplined, scientific approach to human behavior
3. Emphasis on development from key constructs
C. Tools of psychometric theory
1. Focus groups
a. Designed to discover recurrent themes
b. Led by well-trained moderator
c. Offers participants the opportunity to listen and to be heard
2. Cognitive interviews
a. Allows for pre-testing of instrument
b. Interviewers probe to identify problems with items that might not have been readily apparent
3. Both focus groups and cognitive interviews address content validity
4. Tools of measurement theory

        a. Factor analysis
        b. Item response theory
    D. Future of health status measurement: item banking

VIII. Critically reading the literature about health status instruments
    A. Researchers and clinicians must review literature concerning health status assessment, outcomes research, quality of life, and quality assurance
        1. Outcomes, research questions, hypotheses, and likely instruments should help guide literature review
        2. Need to review two bodies of literature
            a. Literature concerning the development and psychometric testing of instruments
            b. Literature describing reports of research in which instruments were used
        3. Relevant literature may be found in areas other than health sciences
            a. Sociology literature
            b. Psychology literature
    B. Description of patient group from which results were obtained
        1. Researcher or clinician determines how proposed sample of patients are alike or different from research report
        2. If proposed study sample is different from study sample reported in the literature, the use of the instrument is not advised (unless psychometric testing is completed)
    C. Review of conditions under which instrument was tested
        1. Use of instrument under conditions different from those originally tested can affect validity and reliability
            a. Instruments originally used in mail survey may not be appropriate for use in a telephone survey
            b. Instruments tested in general population may not be appropriate for clinical trial
            c. Instrument tested in English-speaking population may not be easily translated into another language
    D. Consideration of results of validity, reliability, and sensitivity should be reviewed
            a. Were domains adequately measured?
            b. Did repeated administration produce similar (or expected) results?
            c. In situations where change was likely to occur, was it detected?
    E. Components of a well-written research report describing use of an instrument

IX. Conclusions and Excercises

Learning Objectives

1. Distinguish between and discuss similarities and differences of various terms used to refer to health measurement such as health status, health-related quality of life, and patient-reported outcomes.
2. Detect differences between generic and disease-specific health status instruments, and discuss the necessity for including both types of health-related instruments in health status assessment.
3. Evaluate the influence of patient expectations, values, and judgments on health status measures.
4. Demonstrate an understanding of the field of psychometrics and its application to measuring health and health-related applications for psychometric modeling.
5. Assess issues to be considered when selecting an appropriate health status instrument for use in studying various patient populations.
6. Discover and evaluate resources to assist in selecting health status measures.
7. Demonstrate use of typical health status measures.

Abbreviations in this chapter

ECHO	Economic, Clinical, and Humanistic Outcomes (model)
FDA	Food and Drug Administration
HBM	Health Belief Model
IRT	Item response theory
SF-36	Medical Outcomes Study short form, 36 items
PRO	Patient-reported outcomes
SIP	Sickness Impact Profile
WHO	World Health Organization

Changing Perspectives Through Time

The past several decades have brought many changes in both the focus and measurement of health. Although objective clinical and diagnostic measures (e.g., laboratory tests) remain important indicators of health, over time the role of subjective, personal measures of health has grown. The need for indices of personal health that rely on subjective judgments first came about in conjunction with World War II manpower demands. The influx of large numbers of military recruits resulted in a need for a large-scale screening system. The screening tests for physical capacity and psychological stability that were developed at this time formed the early basis for more modern techniques. Continued efforts during the 1960s led to refinements in health status assessment as measures of morbidity became available and widely used. These measures supplemented mortality counts as an indicator of the health of populations. In the United States, national measures of known and diagnosed illnesses were established with the National Health Interview Survey; unknown and undiagnosed illnesses were estimated with the National Health Examination Survey; health service use was estimated using the National Medical Expenditure Survey; and drug abuse was estimated using the National Household Survey on Drug Abuse.

During the 1970s, emphasis shifted from mortality and morbidity toward measures of function and disability. These efforts stressed process of care evaluations and assessment of quality of care. The 1980s brought recognition of the central role that the patient's point of view should play in assessing medical technologies. Throughout this period, concerns increased regarding how quality of care and patient well-being were affected by widespread efforts to control expenditures and reorganize health care delivery. In today's era of outcomes assessment and accountability, the focus on patients has been expanded further through efforts to identify and examine patient-reported health outcomes. Although many survey instruments used today to assess overall (general) health status and quality of life were developed during the 1970s and 1980s, newer instruments, especially those designed to assess specific disease states, are being constructed at a rapid pace. Measures of health status can prove useful in many settings. When used in conjunction with clinical measures, these instruments can provide detailed information to help health care professionals and patients make treatment decisions. These measures allow researchers to observe trends among different populations and over time. They also allow policy makers to consider the patient perspective when crafting health policy.

The increased availability and wider acceptance of health status instruments, combined with the increasing importance of the patient's role in health care, has resulted in the need for health care professionals to understand, select, use, and interpret the results of health status assessments. The team approach to health care delivery requires the participation of all health care professionals in patient care. The prominent role that drug therapy plays in treating disease means that pharmacists in particular must become experts in evaluating health status instruments to assess how drug therapy affects the patient's overall health and quality of life.

Terminology and Structure

Although the terms *health status* and *quality of life* represent two distinct concepts, these terms have been used interchangeably in the medical literature. For the purposes of this chapter, it is important to distinguish between them. The most common definition of *health status* comes from the World Health Organization (WHO), which describes it as "a state of complete physical, mental, and social well-being, and not merely the absence of disease or infirmity". More recently, Academy for Health Services Research and Health Policy has defined it as the "state of health of a specified individual, group or population". Health status incorporates functional status, morbidity, well-being, and physiologic outcomes. Using this view, health status is synonymous with personal functioning and role functioning. *Personal functioning* is defined as the performance or capacity to perform the kinds of tasks that most people perform every day, such as self-care and physical activities. *Role functioning* is defined as the performance or capacity to perform activities associated with a specific individual, such as attending school and accomplishing work activities.

Although the term *quality of life* has multiple meanings, most involve the particular knowledge, experience, and values of each individual. The WHO defines quality of life as a multidimensional concept that incorporates subjective perceptions of health. Others have expanded on this definition, stating that quality of life "encompasses the physical, emotional, and social components associated with an illness or treatment". Quality of life addresses subjective value judgments placed on the satisfaction a person has with a particular situation or overall experience of living. In addition, quality of life involves a wide range of experiences, states, and perceptions.

To clarify confusion both within and outside the Food and Drug Administration (FDA) regarding this terminology, the phrase patient-reported outcomes (PRO) has been offered as a generic-term under which all of those measures would fall. The FDA's Division of Drug Marketing Advertising and Communications refers to the term PROs to clarify the confusing misuse of the term *quality of life* which has often been applied to disparate terms such as *well-being, health status, function, symptoms, bothersomeness,* and *satisfaction*. Patient-reported outcomes are subjective assessments, self-assessed by patients and can range from a unidimensional construct such as physical functioning to multidimensional concepts such as quality-of-life or health status. Table 1 provides definitions for these and other important terms frequently used in health status measurement. Those unfamiliar with the lexicon of health status should refer to the table while reading this chapter.

Health status instruments can be dissected into many components. The most general division separates an instrument into a set of *domains* or dimensions. These are the generic elements of health status represented by both individual and groups of questions asked in the survey. Each domain of health can be measured through both objective assessments of functioning or health status and more subjective perceptions of health. For example, four major domains that are commonly used in health status measurement have been identified: 1) physical status and functional abilities, 2) psychological status and well-being, 3) social interactions, and 4) economic and/or vocational status and factors. Domains can be subclassified into *subdomains*, which represent more specific elements of health status. The most detailed level of health status instruments are its *items* or questions. Items address specific aspects of domains, and are the operationalized forms of both domains and subdomains. A single instrument can have any number of items, depending on the level of detail needed to adequately address all the domains and subdomains of interest.

Health Measurement Taxonomies and Models

To place the measurement of health status in context, begin with a brief discussion of outcomes measurement taxonomies and models. Outcomes of disease are multidimensional; taxonomies remind researchers of the multidimensional attributes that must be considered in a comprehensive approach to measuring disease burden and treatment effectiveness. As a brief review and background, the following sections discuss relevant taxonomies and models.

Concentric Model of Health Status

In 1984, a concentric model for conceptualizing health status was introduced. Disease is located in the center and is surrounded by layers of domains. The layers emanating from the center (disease) are personal functioning, well-being, general health perceptions, and social/role functioning, respectively. Disease includes the measurable physiologic and biologic parameters that represent the diagnostic definition of that condition. From disease, subsequent measures focus on personal, physical, and psychological distress and function, which then lead to general perceptions of health. Finally, distress in these aspects results in problems with social and role functioning, such as the inability to work, go to school, or care for children.

Three-dimensional Model of Health Status

In contrast to the concentric model, a three-dimensional model of quality of life, of which health status is one of three primary components, was introduced. When health status is combined with subjective perceptions and expectations, quality of life is derived. In this model, health status is one component of quality of life. Using this framework leads to better understanding of individual differences in reported quality of life under circumstances of similar health status. The focus of this discussion is health status, as defined by personal functioning and role functioning. However, most of the material presented is pertinent to both health status and quality of life.

Economic, Clinical, and Humanistic Outcomes Model

In 1993, a theoretical model for medical decision-making that included economic, clinical and humanistic outcomes (ECHO) was published. The ECHO model incorporates traditional clinical-based outcomes along with more contemporary measures that examine economic and quality-of-life issues. The purpose for developing the model was to assist and encourage practitioners to move beyond familiar clinical indicators to examine a more holistic relationship among disease, health outcomes, and decisions about medical care interventions. Clinical outcomes are limited to medical events or objective measures indicating a diagnosis or disease change (e.g., laboratory test and physical signs of disease). Humanistic outcomes include such things as functional status or quality of life. Economic outcomes, such as the total cost of treatment for a medical condition or the cost-effectiveness ratio of a drug, are increasingly being considered in tandem with clinical and humanistic outcomes.

Descriptive Measures of Health Status: Generic Versus Disease-specific Instruments

Researchers have wrestled with the question of whether it is more important to obtain information about general health status in a population that may or may not have a disease or to obtain information about health status related to a specific disease or condition within a defined population. Each involves a different way of viewing health. The first, a global or generic view, requires obtaining information about health status in a general way that could be applied to anyone. The second, a focused or specific view, requires obtaining information about health status in the context of a specific disease. Instruments have been developed to address both views.

Generic Health Status Instruments

Generic health status instruments are designed such that they can be applied to patients in all health states. Ideally, they can be used across various types and severity levels of conditions and treatments, or demographic and cultural subgroups. The utility of generic instruments across multiple populations led to the development of normative data, which allow for comparison of the relative health status between groups of patients and populations. For example, generic health status scores for patients with hypertension can be compared with scores from arthritis patients or from a "healthy" group of individuals. The results can then be used to compare the health status of patients with hypertension relative to these groups. The ability to make comparisons among various populations is one of the key advantages of generic instruments.

One reason comparisons can be made is that generic instruments summarize a wide spectrum of factors associated with health status, including duration of life, impairments, functional states, perceptions, and social opportunities. Generic instruments are designed to address one or more of these domains. Multiple questions are frequently asked for each domain addressed. The appropriate questions comprising specific domains are then most often converted to domain scores by applying scoring algorithms designed specifically for an instrument. For some generic instruments, an overall health status score (such as a domain or index score) can be calculated. These scores can then be compared across various populations. This ability for comparison can prove useful to policy makers, who often must make decisions for a heterogeneous population of individuals.

Table 2 lists some commonly used generic instruments. Two of the most familiar are the Medical Outcomes Study short form, 36 items (SF-36) and the Sickness Impact Profile (SIP). The SF-36 includes multi-item scales to measure eight dimensions of health: physical functioning, role limitations because of physical health problems, bodily pain, social functioning, general mental health, role limitations because of emotional problems, vitality, and general health perceptions. When the scale items are scored, they provide categorical measures of health status. A single-item, health transition measure designed to measure changes in health during the past year also is included and provides a global, or overall, measure of health status.

Table 1. Key Health Status Terms and Definitions

Term	*Definition*
Functional status	An individual's effective performance of or ability to perform those roles, tasks, or activities that are valued (e.g., going to work, playing sports, or maintaining the house). Most often, functional status is divided into physical, emotional, mental, and social domains, although much finer distinctions are possible. Deviations from usual performance or ability indicate dysfunction.
Health-related quality of life	The value assigned to duration of life as modified by the impairments, functional states, perceptions, and social opportunities that are influenced by disease, injury, treatment, or policy. Some measures include only one or two components with or without incorporation of survival or preference weights.
Health status	Most often defined by the World Health Organization's definition: "A state of complete physical, mental, and social well-being, and not merely the absence of disease or infirmity." Not included in this definition are physiological phenomena, the probability of health in the future, or the means for determining which states of well-being are more healthy or desirable than others. Nonetheless, the World Health Organization's popular definition encompasses most of the usual meanings given to health status, including functional status, morbidity, and well-being. A complete representation of health includes a definition of health and prognosis, or the probability of movement to future states based on all the evidence. May or may not incorporate preference weights and survival.
Internal validity	Evidence that findings are correct within the context of a single study.
Item bank	A large collection of questions that are organized, calibrated, and matched to a given construct or task (contrasted to "item pool").
Item response theory	A field of inquiry in the methodology of measurement in which the characteristics of the items composing a test, assessment, or scale are the locus of the study, and the characteristics of the items and the underlying individual abilities or traits can be analytically parsed. The application of the theory to data analysis that uses a set of generalized linear models and statistical procedures to ascertain the relationship between individuals' responses on a set of items in any given scale and their underlying abilities or traits. Numerous item response models have been developed to represent different mathematical forms of the item-characteristic function/curve (e.g.. the dichotomous models in which items have only two [yes/no] response categories, and the polytomous models in which items have multiple response categories) and the number of parameters specified in the models (e.g., one parameter representing the "difficulty" level of the items, another parameter representing the discriminatory power of the item, and yet another parameter representing guess or chance that a certain response is given).
Psychometrics	The field of psychometrics is rooted in a multidisciplined, scientific approach that uses both quantitative and qualitative methods to understand, measure, and model human behavior, emotions, and cognitions.

The SIP, introduced in the late 1970s, was developed to provide a measure that would be sensitive enough to detect changes in a person's behavior because of sickness. *Sickness*, conceptualized as an individual's illness experience, was differentiated from *disease*, which denotes a professional definition or diagnosis of physical disease using clinical parameters. The SIP measures health status by assessing how the illness experience changes daily activities and behavior. The behaviors included are considered significant from the individual, social, and health care points of view.

There are some concerns associated with the use of generic instruments, as they often are lengthy. This is, in part, because of the need to address multiple domains within a single instrument. Increased length leads to an increase in respondent burden, and may, therefore, decrease acceptability to patients. Another concern is scoring of the instrument. Psychometric testing has led to the development of scoring algorithms for some instruments that require more than simply summing or finding the average of the responses. Although the scoring can be performed by hand, it is an arduous task. Therefore, the instruments usually are scored with the aid of a computer program. Finally, generic health status measures are not designed to address the particular concerns of a specific population. The instruments may not be sensitive enough to detect changes that have relevancy only for that population. Generic instruments typically are more useful when making group-level decisions rather than patient-level decisions.

Disease-specific Health Status Instruments

Disease-specific measures of health status have been used extensively for several decades. However, much of their use

Table 1. Key Health Status Terms and Definitions (continued)

TERM	*DEFINITION*
Personal functioning	The performance or capacity to perform the kinds of tasks most people do every day, such as self-care and physical activities.
Quality of life	Encompasses the entire range of human experience, states, perceptions, and spheres of thought concerning the life of an individual or a community. Both objective and subjective, quality of life can include cultural, physical, psychological, interpersonal, spiritual, financial, political, temporal, and philosophical dimensions. Quality of life implies a judgment of value placed on the experience of communities, groups such as families, or individuals.
Reliability	The extent to which a measure is free of measurement error; the ratio of true score variance to observed score variance. Two basic forms of reliability are reproducibility and item homogeneity or consistency. Internal consistency reliability is a method for estimating reliability from the correlations among the items in a multi-item scale.
Role functioning	The performance or capacity to perform activities associated with a specific individual, such as attending school and work activities.
Sensitivity to change	The degree to which gradations in the metric of a measurement scale allow detection of important or meaningful differences. Sensitivity to change and responsiveness have been used interchangeably, but they may be separated. Sensitivity can be defined as the ability of an instrument to measure change in a state irrespective of whether it is relevant or meaningful, whereas responsiveness can be viewed as the ability of an instrument to measure a meaningful important change.
Validity	The extent to which a measure reflects the concept it is supposed to measure and does not reflect concepts that it is not supposed to measure. There are several aspects of validity. Content validity is the extent to which a measure or battery represents all aspects of a defined concept. Face validity is the extent to which a measure "looks like" what it is intended to measure. Criterion validity is the extent to which a measure corresponds to an accurate or previously validated measure of the same concept or to an external criterion established by the investigators. Construct validity is a process by which theory-based associations that are hypothesized between measures are confirmed through empirical testing. Convergent validity is a form of construct validity in which the strength of association between two measures of a similar construct is determined. Discriminant validity is a test of the extent to which measures are not associated with other measures that are hypothesized not to be associated. Predictive validity is a form of construct validity in which the hypothesis being tested is whether the measure can forecast the likelihood of another event or state (e.g., hospitalization). Concurrent validity similarly tests an association of measures that are both assessed at the same point in time.

Additional Resources: Glossary - Health Outcomes Methodology. Medical Care 2000;38 (9 SII): II7–13.; Kerlinger F. Foundations of behavioral research. New York: Harcourt Brace College Publishers, 1990.

has been associated with clinical assessment and patient classification. For example, the Karnofsky Performance Status Scale has been used to assess level of physical activity impairment among patients with cancer. The American Rheumatism Association Functional Classification aids in assessing activities of daily living for arthritis patients. An instrument that may be more well known is the New York Heart Association classification of angina severity, which is used to classify patients into one of four grade levels. Similarly, the Mini-Mental State Examination is designed to assess and classify the cognitive status of adults and can be used as a screening tool and an indicator of both changes in cognitive status over time and response to treatment. These instruments, and others like them, originally were developed for clinicians to assess patients. In general, they are arbitrary grading assignments that typically do not incorporate subjective input from patients.

Other more recent disease-specific measures are designed specifically to address health status issues that a patient may experience when a disease, condition, or treatment is present. Because of the specificity of the instrument, a disease-specific measure is more sensitive to targeted effects. Unanticipated effects that are not specific to the disease of interest, but which might be noticeable with more generic measures, may not be detected. For example, an arthritis-specific instrument that focuses on pain, physical function, and the potential gastrointestinal side effects from treatments, is unlikely to detect mental health symptoms. For these reasons, disease-specific measures are not as widely comparable as generic health status measures. When disease-specific instruments are used, the results can only be compared across various subpopulations. For example, an arthritis-specific instrument may be applicable to rheumatoid arthritis and osteoarthritis but not necessarily to other chronic pain conditions. Many of the concepts addressed in an arthritis-specific instrument, such as hand dexterity, are not concerns of patients with acute, low-back, or cancer-related pain. However, some concepts in an arthritis-specific instrument could be applicable to other conditions. For example, arthritis and asthma may both limit a patient's ability to run a mile or walk up several flights of stairs.

Because many disease-specific instruments were designed for application in a clinical setting, they may be easier to administer and score, and may use fewer questions compared with generic instruments. The decreased burden on respondents typically makes them more acceptable to patients. Patients consider the instruments to be more relevant to their problems because of the disease focus. In addition, the ease of administration can make disease-specific instruments less costly to incorporate into clinical practice and research. Disease-specific instruments also may contain a means for a patient to distinguish between disease-specific functional changes and changes because of comorbid conditions (e.g., the relationship pain may have with sleep). To have a clear understanding of the impact this relationship may have on health status, a patient may be asked to distinguish decreased sleep because of pain from a back injury or from worry about missing work days. The

Table 2. Examples of Generic Health Status Instruments

Name	*Sources*
Duke Health Profile	Parkerson GR Jr., Gehlbach SH, Wagner EH, et al. The Duke-UNC Health Profile: an adult health status instrument for primary care. Med Care 1981;19:806-28.
General Health Questionnaire	Goldberg D, Williams P. The Users Guide to the General Health Questionnaire. Windsor, England: NFER-Nelson Publishing, 1988.
Health Status Questionnaire	NCS Pearson Inc. Web site. NCS Assessments-Clinical and Career Assessments. Available at *http://assessments.ncspearson.com/assessments/tests/hsq_2.htm.*
Nottingham Health Profile	Hunt SM, McEwen J, McKenna SP. Measuring health status: a new tool for clinicians and epidemiologists. J R Coll Gen Pract 1985;35:185-8.
Medical Outcomes Study short form (8, 12, and 36 items)	Ware JE, Snow KK, Kosinski M. SF-36 Health Survey: Manual and Interpretation Guide. Lincoln, RI: QualityMetric Incorporated, 1993, 2000. *Available at http://www.sf36.com.*
Sickness Impact Profile	1) Bergner M, Bobbitt RA, Carter WB, et al. The Sickness Impact Profile: development and final revision of a health status measure. Med Care 1981;19:787-805. 2) Bergner M, Bobbitt RA, Kressel S, et al. The sickness impact profile: conceptual formulation and methodology for the development of a health status measure. Int J Health Serv 1976;6:393-415. See Medical Outcomes Trust Web site at *http://www.outcomes-trust.org/instruments/SIPpack.htm.*
World Health Organization Quality of Life Assessment	The World Health Organization Quality of Life Assessment (WHOQOL): position paper from the World Health Organization. Soc Sci Med 1995;41(10):1403-9.

ability to make this distinction does not exist with a generic instrument. Disease-specific changes may be especially important in an elderly population because few are diagnosed with a single disease entity.

Many disease-specific instruments currently are available, and new instruments are rapidly appearing in the medical literature. Certain diseases, such as asthma, arthritis, and diabetes, have seemingly held more interest and have spawned many instruments. In part, this may be because of the chronic nature of these conditions and the obvious impact they have on lifestyle and long-term health. Two examples of instruments in these areas are the Asthma Quality of Life Questionnaire, which measures functional impairments that are important for adults with asthma, and the Health Assessment Questionnaire, which evaluates the severity of functional limitations because of rheumatoid arthritis by considering the patient's ability to perform daily life activities.

Cancer also has received continued attention, most probably because of the large impact that both the disease and current treatments have on quality of life. The Functional Assessment of Chronic Illness Therapy measurement system is a set of instruments designed to assess the impact of cancer treatments on patients. The core of the system is the Functional Assessment of Cancer Therapy general instrument, which is supplemented in many subscales tailored for specific types of cancers (e.g., breast, lung, and cervical). Table 3 lists several examples of disease-specific instruments. Academic researchers have developed some of the instruments identified, whereas

Table 3. Examples of Disease-Specific Health Status Instruments

Disease/ Condition	*Instrument(s)*
Alzheimer's disease	• The Dementia Rating Scale • Dementia Quality of Life Instrument • Mini-Mental State Examination
Arthritis	• Arthritis Impact Measurement Scales • Health Assessment Questionnaire • WOMAC Osteoarthritis Index
Asthma/ respiratory	• Asthma Quality of Life Questionnaire • Asthma Quality of Life Questionnaire • Asthma Self-Efficacy Scale • Childhood Asthma Questionnaires • Life Activities Questionnaire for Adult Asthma • Life Activities Questionnaire for Childhood Asthma • Living with Asthma Questionnaire • Pediatric Asthma Quality of Life Questionnaire • St. George's Respiratory Questionnaire
Cancer	• Cancer Rehabilitation Evaluation System • European Organization for Research and Treatment of Cancer Quality of Life Questionnaire (EORTC-QLQ30) • QLQ-LC13 (lung cancer) • QLQ-BR23 (breast cancer) • QLQ-H&N35 (head and neck cancer) *Others in development* • Functional Assessment of Cancer Therapy (general) • FACT-B (breast cancer) • FACT-BMT (bone marrow transplantation)
Cancer	*Others in development (continued)* • FACT-BR (brain tumor) • FACT-C (colorectal tumor) • FACT-CX (cervical cancer) • FACT-E (esophageal cancer) • FACT H&N (head and neck cancer) • FACT-L (lung cancer) • FACT-O (ovarian cancer) • FACT-P (prostate cancer) • Rotterdam Symptom Checklist
Cardiovascular diseases	• Cardiac Depression Scale • Chronic Heart Failure Questionnaire • Duke Activities Status Index • Minnesota Living with Heart Failure Questionnaire
Diabetes	• Appraisal of Diabetes Scale • Diabetes Attitude Scale • Diabetes Empowerment Scale • Diabetes Self-Management Profile • Problem Areas in Diabetes Scale
HIV/AIDS	• Functional Assessment of HIV Infection • HIV/AIDS-Targeted Quality of Life • Multidimensional Quality of Life Questionnaire for Persons with HIV
Pain	• Brief Pain Inventory • Memorial Pain Assessment Card • McGill Pain Questionnaire • Visual Analog Pain Rating Scale

AIDS = acquired immune deficiency syndrome; HIV = human immunodeficiency virus.

others were produced by private and professional organizations. These instruments have varying degrees of reported validity and reliability; the listing in Table 3 is for illustrative purposes only and should not suggest endorsement of any specific instrument.

Overlap between Generic and Disease-specific Health Status Instruments

Although there are important differences between the two types of health status instruments, in many instances there is substantial overlap between generic and disease-specific instruments. This overlap may be related to the development process of many disease-specific instruments. For example, the Arthritis Impact Measurement Scales, a disease-specific instrument for arthritis, was developed from measures included in both the Quality of Well-Being Instrument and the Rand Health Insurance Experiment. The major differences between disease-specific and generic instruments are found in the level of detail concerning specific conditions or functional abilities. Although pain and functional status may be assessed in generic instruments, greater detail, direct attribution to the disease, and often more items are incorporated into disease-specific instruments. Disease-specific instruments tend to use word phrases or directions designed to focus the patient's thoughts on a specific disease or condition. Questions may include specifying attribution through phrases such as "because of my arthritis" or "as a result of having arthritis".

The general consensus found among researchers is that both generic and disease-specific measures should be included in any health status assessment. If a generic measure alone is used, there is decreased relevance for a specific group of patients but an increased ability to make comparisons with other populations. If a disease-specific measure alone is used, there is increased relevance for a specific group of patients but decreased ability to make comparisons with other populations. Using both types of measures ensures that the strengths of each are captured; however, as the number of measures used increases, so does the cost for data collection and analysis, and burden to the patient. Table 4 summarizes the strengths and limitations of both types of instruments.

Incorporating generic and disease-specific measures into an assessment can be accomplished by including two separate instruments or a battery of instruments, by adding disease-specific items to a generic instrument, or by modifying items in a generic instrument to make them disease-specific. Unless an experienced researcher with psychometric training is available to assist, the most practical option is to include two separate, valid, reliable, established instruments in a study, one generic and one disease-specific. This approach has the advantage of providing a basis to compare results to existing literature.

The next best option may be to include a battery of instruments. A *battery* is a collection of disease-specific and possibly generic instruments. A battery allows for assessment of many factors of importance to patients and for comparison among populations. However, the battery approach will not result in an overall score. In addition, it is not easy to determine the relative importance of each dimension of health when several different instruments are used. Therefore, interpreting the findings can be problematic and should be done cautiously. It should be noted that adding questions to a generic instrument or modifying a general instrument to make the focus more disease specific requires considerable effort to develop appropriate scoring algorithms and analyses. Altering established instruments also could influence validity and reliability. In addition, altering a published instrument without the consent of the developer could be construed as a violation of copyright. Finally, without adequate psychometric analysis of the newly developed or revised instruments, the results of the research study could be judged invalid.

Preference-based Measures of Health Status

The debate about generic versus specific measurement highlights the complexity of health status and quality of life as constructs. As a direct result of this complexity, instruments with varying degrees of subjectivity, reliability, and validity have been developed. One reason for this variation is that the effects of any disease or medical intervention, pharmaceutical or otherwise, will differ markedly according to the values and preferences of individual patients. For example, when measuring functional disability, a distinction must be made between

Table 4: Generic Versus Disease-specific Instruments

Type	Strengths	Weaknesses
General	Broadly applicable Summarizes range of concepts Detection of unanticipated effects	May not be responsive to change May not have relevance for specific population Length of instrument may be a problem Results may be difficult to interpret
Disease-Specific	Relevancy for a specific population More responsive to change	Cannot compare across populations Cannot detect unanticipated effects

Reprinted with permission from Patrick DL, Erickson P. Health status and health policy: allocating resources to health care. New York: Oxford University Press, 1993.

whether the patient can perform an activity and whether the patient has the desire to perform an activity. Failure to differentiate between ability and desire can lead to incorrect inferences about the relative importance of some functional outcomes to patients.

Individual expectations, values, and judgments also play a role in how clinical symptoms are perceived by a patient. Pain provides an excellent example. Numerous studies indicate that there is individual variation not only in the threshold for pain but also in the perceived disabling effect of various pain levels. What might be considered severe, crippling pain by one patient may not be evaluated as such by another. In addition, there is evidence to suggest that preemptively informing patients of the potential to experience pain may alter perceptions of pain intensity. These and other factors only recently have been considered in outcomes studies, though the effect that patient expectations, values, and judgments have on numerous processes within health care have been studied for some time. The Health Belief Model (HBM) integrates these factors conceptually and is familiar to many health professionals. A social and behavioral model, the HBM was designed to provide an explanatory framework for preventative health behavior on the part of the patient. Simply stated, the HBM explains that, for an individual to take health action, he or she needs to believe: 1) there is personal susceptibility to a health consequence; 2) there is some level of severity to the consequence that affects a valued component of life either in the present or in the near future; and 3) taking health action would be beneficial in reducing the consequence or the severity of it. Since its development almost four decades ago, considerable work with the HBM has been undertaken, primarily using the component parts of the model to examine a variety of health behaviors.

The role that expectations, values, and judgments play in relation to quality of life and patient assessment of health status is an explicitly stated aspect of the HBM and other psychosocial theories. Most researchers agree it is possible to identify health concepts of direct importance to patients relative to their health status, quality of life, and satisfaction with health care. A consensus of results suggests that patients would like to: 1) have as long a life as possible; 2) have normal function during that life; 3) be free of pain and other physical, psychological, or social symptoms; 4) not have reduced health because of treatments; and 5) be financially stable after medical expenses are paid. The relationships these five dimensions might have with one another and the smaller, discrete concepts that form them have been combined into a framework, the Hierarchy of Patient Outcomes. The hierarchy is a useful structure for planning a health status measurement strategy. Under this framework, a global outcome is examined in relation to patient-oriented factors. The framework consists of five dimensions: death, disability, discomfort, iatrogenic effects (dire events), and economics (debt). The dimensions are then broken into subdimensions, which can vary from those identified in the figure depending on the disease or condition under study. Finally, the subdimensions are broken into discreet, measurable parameters. All of the components should be of some importance to patients; some also will have clinical importance. Within the context of health status, the effect that a disease, condition, or treatment may have is multidimensional. A framework provides an organized means of ensuring that all subcomponents of an outcome are identified. Multiple outcomes may be incorporated into a study, each of which has a hierarchical framework.

Although the concepts of patient expectations, values, and judgments typically are thought of in qualitative terms, recent efforts have focused on quantifying them for the purposes of measurement. One way to do this is to measure utilities. A utility is the value of a particular health state or improvement in health status. The assigned value reflects the perceived quality or desirability of a health state to patients or the general population. Utilities frequently are measured by assigning the preferences of individuals or society to health states. To obtain utility measures, patients or members of the general public are asked about the worth of given health states. The health states range from death to perfect health. By convention, utility measures range from 0 for death to 1.0 for perfect health. However, it has been proposed that there are health states that could be valued as worse than death. *Utility assessment* is a method of integrating values attributed to life at given points in time with the quality of life spent in these health states. Assigning preferences leads to the determination of a single index that represents the combination of different levels of functional status and perceptions. Because of the formation of a single index, tradeoffs among domains, such as physical function and emotional function, can be addressed over time. Using health state preferences or utilities for changes between domains, allows identification of the average improvement or average deterioration of the health of a population. A more detailed discussion of utility measurement and cost-utility analysis can be found in the Cost-Utility Analysis chapter of this book.

Criteria for Selecting a Standardized Health Status Instrument

Increased availability of health status instruments can pose challenges in the selection of instruments for research or patient assessment. The interest in health status has resulted in many individuals and groups developing their own instruments. There is no gold standard with which to measure health status and many of the instruments have not undergone adequate psychometric analyses. Given the large number of instruments available, selection of an appropriate instrument becomes a critical issue. An inappropriate selection can seriously flaw an otherwise sound study design. A framework such as the Hierarchy of Patient Outcomes highlights several key points in patient-focused health status assessment: 1) health status instruments must be selected that will measure and detect changes in components relevant to an overall outcome; 2) identifying an outcome and the dimensions, subdimensions, and component parts of health status should precede selection of a health status instrument; 3) several instruments may be needed to adequately measure an outcome; and 4) measurement of health status may occur at multiple levels or over multiple time points within a study.

There must be an understanding of the overall purpose, rationale, and outcomes of interest by all individuals involved in the assessment effort. Early in project planning, there should be clear articulation of research questions and hypotheses to be tested. Included in this process should be a statement of the aspects of health being studied. Both clinicians and researchers should understand why and how health status measures can contribute to achieving the study goal. Too often, measures of this type are chosen hastily; only measures necessary to meet the purposes of the study should be included. Outcomes identified for a health status assessment are different than those typically identified as clinical measures. However, the Hierarchy of Patient Outcomes demonstrates that clinical measures can be included in a health status assessment. For example, in diabetes treatment, physicians tend to focus on serum glucose or hemoglobin A_{1C} levels. Patients may be more concerned about the long-term effects of uncontrolled diabetes, such as vision loss or loss of independence because of physical functioning problems. In some diseases, there may not be a clear relationship between objective and PROs. For example, among patients with asthma, improvements in forced expiratory volume in 1 second (FEV_1) values do not necessarily lead to perceived improvements in quality of life, or to a decline in hospitalizations or emergency department use. Some examples of clinical measures and the patient outcomes measures that may be identified for various conditions are listed in Table 5.

The second key point from the Hierarchy of Patient Outcomes framework addresses the order in which decisions are made regarding instrument selection. The availability of a health status instrument is an important consideration, but it should not be the determining factor to define the measures of a study. The driving force behind selecting a suitable health status instrument is the outcomes of interest identified for the study. It is not appropriate to select an instrument first and then use it to define outcomes. Although this seems intuitively basic, performing the two activities in reverse order happens more frequently than researchers would like to admit. The third key point highlighted in the hierarchy framework suggests that, given the domains identified for a single outcome, several instruments may be required for adequate measurement. However, it is important to avoid the mistake of selecting items from several instruments and arranging them together to produce a new instrument. Without appropriate and rigorous psychometric testing, this "cherry picking" of questions will not result in a valid and reliable instrument, even if the instruments from which the items were selected have been properly examined. Clearly identifying all key dimensions, subdimensions, and components provides a checklist from which to evaluate the selection of health status instruments for completeness of measurement. It also aids in the decision to include both generic and disease-specific instruments to ensure that all domains and outcomes are measured. The final key point from the

Table 5: Traditional Clinical Measures Versus Patient-centered Outcomes

Condition/Disease	Clinical Measure	Patient Outcomes Measure
Osteoporosis	Bone mineral density	Pain Height loss Fractures Quality of life
Cancer	Number and size of metastases	Pain Quality of life Quality-adjusted life years
Hypertension	Blood pressure	Quality of life Satisfaction
Diabetes mellitus	Serum glucose Hemoglobin A1C	Vision loss Physical functioning Quality of life
Asthma	FEV1 Peak expiratory flow rate	Symptom scores Quality of life Hospitalizations Emergency department visits

Reprinted with permission from Perfetto EM, Epstein RS, Baldwin R. What are the necessary research components for high quality, scientifically rigorous pharmaceutical outcomes research? Patient outcomes of pharmaceutical interventions: a scientific foundation for the future. Washington, D.C.: American Pharmaceutical Association, 1994.

hierarchy is that, to arrive at a complete understanding of the impact a disease, condition, or treatment may have on health status, measurement may be required at several levels, including the global, dimension, subdimension, and component levels. Including both generic and disease-specific instruments, perhaps as a battery, is one way to ensure this occurs.

Once a decision is made about the outcomes to be studied, the decision process moves to identifying the instruments that are used to measure them. A crucial aspect of health status measurement is that the patient provides the information; that is, the assessment relies on the patient's perception of health. A growing body of literature suggests that when clinicians or caregivers (i.e., proxies) are asked to assess a patient's health status, it typically is underestimated. A clinician's ability to assess the intensity of pain a patient experiences, and the subsequent effect that this may have on quality of life, has been the most frequent subject of this literature. A truly patient-focused health status instrument includes measures that reflect the unique perspective of the patient. Most important, the measures have meaning and relevance in the global context of patients' lives and their lives in a diminished health state. Important characteristics for the instruments include the ability to: 1) measure the effect of a disease, condition, or treatment on aspects of life considered by patients to be of greatest importance; 2) allow patients to rate the extent to which various aspects of life are affected by a disease, condition, or treatment; 3) measure changes in health over time; 4) allow patients to judge the value of changes in health over time; and 5) relate the study population's changes in health to other populations of patients.

Methodological Considerations

However, in addition to a patient orientation, critical issues from a research methodology standpoint also should be considered early in the selection process. These are addressed briefly here but are covered more fully in the Psychometric Instrument Development and Requirement section. One of these issues is that of validity. *Validity* refers to the extent an instrument measures the concepts it should measure and not reflect concepts it is not supposed to measure. The many aspects of validity have been discussed in depth (Reference 19); however, four types that must be addressed when considering instruments for inclusion in a study are discussed here. The first, *face validity*, as the name implies, is a judgment about whether the instrument appears to be measuring the domains of health the study intends to measure. For example, questions about a person's ability to walk up stairs appears to measure physical mobility. The second, *content validity*, judges whether the aspects measured are relevant and include all aspects needed to meet the study objectives. Third, *construct validity* judges whether hypothesized associations among measures in an instrument are confirmed through empirical testing (see the Factor Analysis section). Finally, criterion validity considers the extent to which the instrument predicts or agrees with constructs external to those that are being measured.

A second methodological issue, reliability, concerns the consistency of the results obtained when using an instrument repeatedly. A measure of reliability asks the following question: if the instrument is given to the same group of patients on two occasions, and the time frame is such that the results would not be expected to change, would the same results occur? *Internal consistency* considers the degree to which items within an instrument are correlated with one another. *Test-retest* reliability judges the reproducibility of the instrument's results by a process in which the instrument is administered to the same group of patients twice, and a determination is made about how close the results are to one another. The closer the results of the two administrations, the more reliable the instrument is considered. A specific statistical test, called Cronbach's alpha, has been devised to measure and report reliability in terms of internal consistency. Cronbach's alpha, which falls between 0 and 1 (with 1 indicating perfect reliability), typically is found in reports of research on health status instruments.

An additional issue, the *sensitivity* of the instrument, addresses the ability of the instrument to detect change. Sensitivity also may be referred to as responsiveness. Particularly in designing studies where the research questions relate to change because of some event such as initiation of a treatment or across some time period involving before or after events, an instrument must be able to detect change, if change occurs. Although an instrument may be able to detect large differences readily, it is possible that small differences, such as those that might occur between two treatment groups, can go undetected. If small differences are expected and considered important, instruments with high sensitivity are needed. Alternatively, a large patient sample, often not administratively or practically possible, would be required to detect a small difference.

From a methodological standpoint, selection of a health status assessment instrument requires a balance between the three issues of validity, reliability, and sensitivity. The most valid and reliable instrument may not be sensitive to changes over time. Clinicians and researchers may, of necessity, forego high reliability to have high sensitivity to change. Also, an instrument may be reliable, but not valid. However, a valid instrument assumes reliable measurement. Finally, several practical, administrative issues also should be considered in reviewing available instruments: cost to use the instrument, burden to the patient to respond to long questionnaires, and scoring and analysis complexities.

Practical Administrative Considerations in Instrument Selection

A primary consideration is cost. Some instruments are published and can be used freely; others require permission and payment of fees for their use. In addition, there are costs associated with reproducing the instruments, including: multiple applications for every patient; data collection such as postage expenses for mailed surveys, personnel expenses for face-to-face or phone interviews, and local and long distance phone charges for phone interviews; and data entry and analysis.

Another issue that should be considered carefully is burden on the patient–the time and effort to complete the instrument for patients who may be in a poor state of health. This may be as simple as considering whether asking patients with severe arthritis of the hands to respond to a mailed survey is an undue burden. Some patients, such as those who are terminally ill, may not be emotionally or psychologically able to discuss their disease. Large respondent burden can influence the quality of the data collected. For example, patients who are asked to complete extremely lengthy questionnaires, may hurry through them or skip questions to shorten the time. Patients also may elect not to participate because of the length of the instrument or their emotional state. Such reasons can create response bias; patients who agree to participate and are willing to complete lengthy forms may be different from patients who refuse.

Requirements to score the instrument and analyze the results also must be considered. Standardized instruments must be scored in a similar manner or the ability to compare results across studies and with published literature is lost. Some instruments require complex scoring algorithms that can be more easily produced by a computer. Even for easier scoring algorithms, such as summing the responses, computer-assisted scoring may be valuable in studies with large sample sizes. Computing capabilities, including programming expertise when standard scoring formats are not readily available, may be required to support these efforts. In addition, the selection and execution of appropriate statistical tests often require the assistance of a statistician. If this expertise is not available, the ability to evaluate the data collected may be severely hampered. Table 6 consists of a checklist of considerations for selecting an instrument.

A growing number of references are now available to help identify the health status instrument that can best fit the requirements of a study; several Internet sources for instruments can be found in the Annotated Bibliography. Use of an established instrument carries several benefits, which include the ability to make comparisons with population norms or the published literature, increased confidence and credibility in the results, accumulation of knowledge about an existing instrument, advancement of knowledge about applicability of existing instruments in different populations and diseases, and a more judicious use of research funds. Of these, perhaps the most important is the ability to have a basis of comparison. Interpretation of results is severely hampered when comparisons cannot be made among study populations with the same or different characteristics, diseases, conditions, or treatments. It is these comparisons that lead to further understanding about the effects and importance of outcomes.

Table 6. A Summary Checklist for Instrument Selection

✓	Is the instrument appropriate for the intended purpose of the study?
✓	Has the instrument previously been evaluated for validity and reliability?
✓	Does the instrument have appropriate content validity with regard to the outcomes to be measured?
✓	Does the instrument measure all outcomes of interest—are other instruments required?
✓	Does the instrument allow adequate representation of the patient's perspective?
✓	Does use of the instrument carry a reasonable respondent burden?
✓	Is the administration method required (e.g., mail survey, Web survey, telephone interview, or personal interview) appropriate for the patient population?
✓	Is the instrument readily obtainable?
✓	Does use of the instrument have associated costs?
✓	Is computer technology needed to administer, score, and analyze the instrument?
✓	Are additional personnel needed to administer, score, and analyze the instrument?

Psychometric Instrument Development and Refinement

The Need for a Balance between Methodological and Practical Concerns

This chapter has shown that there is a great need to use valid, reliable, and sensitive instruments that fully capture a population's health status as well as detect change in health because of disease, intervention, or life event. Generic health status instruments include questions that capture a wide range of health domains (or concepts), whereas disease-specific measures include only domains that are directly affected by the disease or its treatment. However, the need for psychometrically strong instruments must be balanced by the limitation of researchers to increase respondent burden with long questionnaires. A construct (such as physical functioning) can be assessed by a large number of instruments (such as the SF-36 or the McMaster Health Index Questionnaire), with each having its own strengths and limitations across subgroups. It is common to see multiple evaluations of a single intervention using different questionnaires, which hinders the ability to combine multiple study results. There is a great need to link the instruments measuring similar health domains on a common metric to allow scores from one instrument be converted (i.e., cross-walked or mapped) to scores on another instrument. Further, there is a need to have instruments that do not bias one group, having higher scores on a domain because of their group characteristics (e.g., language or race). But, researchers also want instruments that can detect differences in populations' cultures, beliefs, or perceptions about their health status.

Together, under the umbrella of psychometrics, the fields of cognitive psychology and quantitative psychology have made tremendous strides to provide tools and methodological procedures to develop and evaluate instruments that can better meet the needs of health status assessment. The field of psychometrics is rooted in a multidisciplined, scientific approach to understand, measure, and model human behavior, emotions, and cognitions.

Psychometricians place great emphasis on the whole process of developing instruments from defining key health constructs through focus groups, to revising items and response options through cognitive interviews, to evaluating item and scale functioning through statistical methods available from measurement theory. These tools are discussed in the following sections and outline the intricate steps of instrument development. The description is provided to illustrate the best processes to achieve robust instruments.

Focus Groups

Once the study objectives and target population are clearly defined, identification of key health domains to include in a questionnaire can be facilitated by conducting focus groups with a subset of patients and their caregivers. The purpose of a focus group is to hear the range of perceptions, insights, and experiences, and from these to discover what themes reoccur. These reoccurring themes, such as health problems (e.g., perceived body image for patients with breast cancer treated with mastectomy) or benefits (e.g., improved quality of life for patients in support groups), can be operationalized into domains to be measured by a health survey. A focus group includes a well-trained moderator who maximizes discussions and interactions among participants whereas gently guiding them though a predetermined set of open-ended questions. Participants have the opportunity to hear experiences of others and are encouraged to relate their own stories. Focus groups are beneficial when trying to identify which domains are important to patients and often are used when a new tool is being developed.

Cognitive Interviews

Once a questionnaire has been designed and reviewed by experts, it is extremely useful to pretest the questions on individuals who are representative of the population to be surveyed. Draft versions of questionnaires are tested in individual interviewing sessions by specially trained interviewers who probe respondents' understanding of the questions and respondents' thinking as they provide an answer. This allows interviewers to identify covert problems not otherwise apparent in the instrument design and review process. For example, an interviewer may ask the common general health question, "In general, would you say your health is: excellent, very good, good, fair, or poor?". The cognitive interviewer would then probe respondents as to how they rated their health status, what issues were involved in the decision, and their definition of health.

Inclusion of focus groups and cognitive interviews in the instrument development or revision process pulls in the patient perspective to address issues of content validity (i.e., to ensure the questionnaire captures the health domains that are relevant to the study population). Once pilot data are made available, or data are available from past administration of the same questionnaire in a separate study, the tools of management theory can be used to evaluate how well both the items and the set of items for measuring a health construct (i.e., a scale) function within the population of interest. There are many tools available, but the use of factor analysis to confirm the dimensionality of an instrument, and the applications of item response theory (IRT) to evaluate item and scale performance and to provide a framework for developing new health questionnaires using improved computer technology, is briefly discussed here.

Factor Analysis

Factor analysis is a statistical modeling tool that allows patients to confirm the placement of items in their respective health domains based on patients' responses to the questions. For example, questions from the SF-36 that ask, "Have you felt downhearted and blue?" and "Have you been a happy person?" should correlate (inversely) highly with each other and with other items that measure the domain of mental health. Also, factor analysis may be used to identify problematic items as well as relevant subdimensions that should be reported separately in study results. Setting up the model and analyzing the findings from a factor analysis should always include the input of a psychometrician (or statistician familiar with measurement theory) and content expert (i.e., someone familiar with the measured health domains and the study population) to help guide the interpretation of results. Factor analysis often is used in psychometric analyses to support the construct validity of a questionnaire.

Item Response Theory

Using responses from a large dataset, IRT models characterize each question in a scale with a set of properties that describe an item's relationship with a measured construct, such as depression or physical functioning, as well as how the item functions within the study population. This allows researchers to choose the most salient items that target a patient's health status. Because of its powerful features, applications of IRT modeling in health outcomes measurement have increased considerably because of its utility in instrument development and evaluation, scale scoring, identification of item bias, instrument linking, and computerized adaptive assessment. As a tool to revise questionnaires, IRT models can be used to choose the most reliable and informative items in a questionnaire, to identify redundancy in sets of items, to assess the appropriate number of response options per item, and to order response categories for developing the scoring system. At the scale level, IRT models allow researchers to evaluate the appropriateness (in terms of reliability) of the set of questions for the study population. In other words, IRT can estimate the precision of the item set, which varies across the different levels of function on the measured health domain. For example, a generic questionnaire designed for measuring the mental health status of the general United States population will not have high precision in measuring the mental health of a depressed population.

One important tool from applications of IRT modeling is the identification of item bias or differential item functioning. Differential item functioning occurs when one group responds differently to a question than another group despite controlling for differences between the two groups on the measured construct (such as mental health). Scales containing such items will have reduced validity for between-group comparisons because their scores are indicative of a variety of attributes other than those the scale is originally intended to measure. Differential item functioning analysis has been used to detect equivalence in item content across racial, gender, cultural, or treatment groups; between two administration modes such as telephone-interviewer administered versus self-administered questionnaires; and from one language translation of a questionnaire to another.

Future of Health Status Measurement: Item Banking

The increasing need for psychometrically strong instruments that are minimally burdensome to respondents is a call for better health measures than what exists today. New, adaptable instruments need to be created that are highly reliable; valid across different gender, cultural, or disease groups; and sensitive to change in health status. Using the methods of IRT modeling, the future of health status assessment rests with the development of what are called *item banks*. An item bank is a data resource that pools high-quality items from multiple instruments (i.e., includes the best items from many different questionnaires) to allow researchers or computer technology to pick the best set of questions from multiple domains that optimally measure the study population. Scores on item sets from the item bank are comparable on a similar metric (e.g., scoring method) despite groups of patients receiving different sets of questions. In addition, these measures are shorter and have lower measurement errors than traditional instruments. Using the item bank as a foundation, a computerized adaptive assessment can cover multiple health domains in a short amount of time and provide instant, accurate reports of a patient's health status to a caregiver or researcher. For a range of clinical and observational settings, these instruments can exist on multiple platforms, including laptop computers, hand held devices, and on the Internet, and through telephone interviews and interactive voice recognition technology.

Critically Reading the Literature about Health Status Instruments

To adequately assess a health status instrument for inclusion in a study, researchers and clinicians must turn to the growing body of literature related to health status assessment, outcomes research, quality of life, and quality assurance. It is easy to assume that accessing literature only from peer-reviewed journals will ensure the quality of the reported information. However, judging the quality of research reports and whether the published information is applicable for a proposed study goes beyond blindly accepting literature published in peer-reviewed journals. Particularly in research areas where theories come from many disciplines, there is a tendency for divergent views about the appropriate methods, instruments, variables, and analyses. This accounts, in part, for the proliferation of health status instruments and the numerous research reports about them. However, this chapter offers additional advice on the specific issues noted when reviewing publications on health status.

The outcomes, research questions, hypotheses, and likely instruments identified for study in the early stages of the planning process should help guide a search of the literature. A complete review should include two bodies of literature-the first concerning the development and psychometric testing of the instrument itself, and the second describing reports of research in which the instrument was used. Because health status assessment encompasses a variety of disciplines, relevant literature may be found in areas other than the health sciences; a good example is the need to review sociology and psychology references for relevant literature concerning value orientation and the measurement of values. Although journals may have different style requirements, the components of a well-written research report about health status instruments typically are the same and are listed in Table 7. These components include a description of the health status domains, the measuring instruments, the scoring requirements, the subjects, the sampling procedure, the sampling frame or population from which the sample was drawn, and the conditions under which the data were collected. Also included should be a discussion of the psychometric testing used with indications of validity, reliability, and sensitivity to change and a presentation and discussion of the results, the statement of conclusions, and description of the limitations.

A description of the patient group from which the results were obtained should always be reported. It is the responsibility of the clinician or researcher to determine how the proposed sample of patients is similar to or different from the patients identified for inclusion in the study, and whether any differences noted are likely to affect the research. In some instances, the proposed sample is so different from the study sample reported in the literature that use of the instrument is no longer advised unless supportive psychometric testing can be undertaken. A good example is the use of an instrument in a proposed pediatric sample when identified literature describes its use in adult study populations only.

Table 7. Components of a Well-written Research Report Describing Development and Validation of Health Status Instruments

✓	Description of health status domains
✓	Description of the measuring instruments
✓	Description of scoring requirements
✓	Description of subjects, the sampling procedure, and the sampling frame
✓	Description of the conditions under which the data were collected
✓	Discussion of the psychometric testing with indications of validity, reliability, and sensitivity to change
✓	Presentation and discussion of the results, statement of conclusions, and description of the limitations

The conditions under which the instrument was tested should be reviewed. Using an instrument under conditions different from those originally tested can affect the validity and reliability of the results. Instruments originally used in a mail survey may not be appropriate for use in a telephone survey or interview situation. Instruments designed and tested in a general population may not be suitable for a clinical trial. An instrument tested in an English-speaking population may not be easily translated into another language or adapted for another culture. The effect that different conditions may have should be considered so appropriate changes in the research design can be made.

The results of validity, reliability, and sensitivity testing should be reviewed carefully. Clinicians or researchers should ask themselves whether the results demonstrate that the domains were adequately measured; whether repeated administration produced similar and expected results; and, in situations where change was likely to occur, whether it was detected. The latter is often overlooked but should be considered carefully. If a clinician's experience suggests that treatment of a condition would result in changes in physical function, an instrument should detect that change; when it does not, the instrument and the clinician's experience are suspect. Clinicians and researchers also should review literature reporting the results of studies that used the instrument.

Often, the volume of available literature on an instrument can be used as an indicator of its quality. Instruments that have good validity, reliability, and sensitivity are used frequently. Frequent use also means that the instrument may have been used in a variety of settings, under different conditions, and among different groups of patients. These factors increase overall confidence in the instrument.

Conclusion

Assessing health status is a complex but necessary component of understanding outcomes measurement. As interest in the field of health status measurement grows and more instruments are created and psychometrically tested, it becomes increasingly important that health care professionals are able to critically appraise a given instrument and apply it properly to a patient population. Considerations such as understanding the basic differences and similarities between generic and disease-specific instruments along with their advantages and disadvantages should be considered when conducting an investigation. Finally, it is imperative that researchers critically assess research literature involving patient-based assessments before attempting to apply it to any new situation.

Annotated Bibliography

1. AcademyHealth. Glossary of terms commonly used in health care. Revised February 2002. Available at *http://www.academyhealth.org/publications/glossary.pdf.* Accessed May 15, 2002.

   A membership organization for health services researchers, AcademyHealth has published a glossary for researchers in the field. The complete document includes terms related to health care delivery and financing, epidemiological and statistical terms, and accounting and economic terms. Definitions related to the development and use of health status instruments are incorporated.

2. Burke L. Acceptable evidence for pharmaceutical advertising and labeling. Presentation at the Drug Information Association Workshop on Pharmacoeconomic and Quality of Life Labeling and Marketing Claims. New Orleans, LA, October 2, 2000. Available at *http://www.fda.gov/cder/ddmac/brkLDIAL00/tsLdooL.htm.*

   This presentation is where the author first proposed the term *patient-reported outcomes* (PROs) as an umbrella phrase to incorporate health-related quality of life, satisfaction with treatment, performance measures, and other patient-reported measures of health status, well-being, or functional status.

3. Bellamy N. WOMAC osteoarthritis index: a user's guide. London, Ontario: Victoria Hospital Corporation, 1995.

   This guide contains copies of the WOMAC Osteoarthritis Index using both visual analogue and Likert scales. Information about the development, administration, scoring, and analysis of the WOMAC Osteoarthritis Index is included. The reference list includes studies that used the instrument.

4. Bergner M. Measurement of health status. Med Care 1985;23:696–704.

   Although somewhat dated, this article provides an informative overview of the historic direction of health status measurement and an overview of the future focus of measurement issues.

5. Black TR. Evaluating social science research: an introduction. Thousand Oaks, CA: Sage Publications, 1993.

   The goal of this book is to provide the knowledge and skills necessary to read and evaluate research reports, journal articles, and conference papers. Exercises are included to allow the application of knowledge gained through reading.

6. Coons SJ, Kaplan RM. Quality of life assessment: understanding its use as an outcome measure. Hosp Formulary 1993;28:486–98.

   The second article in a three-part series, this article provides an overview of issues pertaining to the inclusion of quality-of-life assessment to evaluate existing and emerging medical technologies and health care practice. Key criteria of measurement instruments are discussed.

7. Cramer JA, Spilker B. Quality of life and pharmacoeconomics. Philadelphia, PA: Lippincott-Raven Publishers, 1998.

   In 1996, "Quality of Life and Pharmacoeconomics in Clinical Trials", a comprehensive guide to quality of life and pharmacoeconomic research, was published. These authors have taken that 1996 text and reduced it to seven chapters to provide a more concise guide to the topics. This book discusses social and psychological assessment, instruments, and pharmacoeconomics, and other topics.

8. Embretson, SE, Reise, SP. Item response theory for psychologists. Mahwah, NJ: Lawrence Erlbaum Associates, 2000.

   This book provides a comprehensive discussion of item response theory (IRT) models and their application to instrument evaluation and development. The book contrasts and compares IRT methods with traditional (or classical) methods used to evaluate item and scale psychometric properties. Also, the book provides an excellent introduction to the family of IRT models and methodological issues such as scoring and assessing IRT model fit. The book ends with a discussion of the application of IRT models for evaluating instruments and developing computerized adaptive tests.

9. Fowler FJ, Cleary PD, Magaziner J, et al. Methodological issues in measuring patient-reported outcomes: the agenda of the work group on outcomes assessment. Med Care 1994;32:JS65–76.

The authors identify several key methodologic issues concerning health status measurement. Insights into the decision process used by patient outcomes research teams to resolve the issues also are provided.

10. Fries JF, Singh G. The Hierarchy of Patient Outcomes. In: Spilker B, ed. Quality of life and pharmacoeconomics in clinical trials. Philadelphia, PA: Lippincott-Raven, 1996.

The hierarchical framework of patient outcomes described in this chapter is a useful way to view selection of one or several research instruments for health status assessment. This text is a useful resource.

11. Gill TM, Feinstein AR. A critical appraisal of the quality of quality-of-life measurements. JAMA 1994;272:619–26.

The authors present a meta-analysis of literature identified from the quality of life Bibliography and two MEDLINE searches. The process used by the authors to evaluate selected articles is a useful one for readers who must make decisions about the quality of information from the literature concerning health status, and then introduce that information into decision processes.

12. Guyatt GH, Cook DJ. Health status, quality of life, and the individual. JAMA 1994;272:630–1.

In this brief commentary, the authors provide a concise review of the definitions of health status and quality of life, arguing that they are two distinct concepts and should remain as such. Readers who have not yet made a clear distinction in their own minds about these concepts will find the commentary useful.

13. Kozma CM, Reeder CE, Schulz RM. Economic, clinical, and humanistic outcomes: a planning model for pharmacoeconomic research. Clin Ther 1993;15(6):1121–32.

The authors describe the framework for outcomes research, discussing the importance of weighing the relative strengths and weaknesses of pharmaceuticals in terms of economic and humanistic outcomes, as well as clinical outcomes. The authors' ultimate goal is to encourage practitioners to adopt a more complete model for health care decision making.

14. Read JL, Quinn RJ, Hoefer MA. Measuring overall health: an evaluation of three important approaches. J Chronic Dis 1987;40(Suppl 1):7S–21S.

The authors provide a review of three measures of overall health: the General Health Rating Index, the Quality of Well-Being Scale, and the Sickness Impact Profile. In addition to a comprehensive review of these instruments, the reader will gain insights into the process of evaluating health status instruments for use in research.

15. Lohr KN. Outcome measurement concepts and questions. Inquiry 1988;25(Spring):37–50.

This article provides a review of outcomes measurement and identifies four areas where work should concentrate: definitive evidence of process and outcome linkages; relationships between technology assessment and quality assessment; improved validity and reliability of outcomes measures; and continued development of health status measures. Useful insights into the linkages of objective indicators of health and subjective indicators of health status and quality of life are provided.

16. MacKeigan LD, Pathak DS. Overview of health-related quality-of-life measures. Am J Hosp Pharm 1992;49:2236–45.

The authors discuss the field of quality-of-life assessment with an emphasis on its relationship to pharmaceutical care and drug therapy. This article represents a useful first read from the perspective of pharmacy practice.

17. McDowell I, Newell C. Measuring health: a guide to rating scales and questionnaires. New York, NY: Oxford University Press, 1996.

This text is perhaps the most useful of any for insights into health status assessment and as a guide for selecting individual health status instruments. Key issues of research methodology are discussed; individual instruments are thoroughly analyzed.

18. Assessing health status and quality-of-life instruments: attributes and review criteria. Qual Life Res 2002;11(3):193–205.

The Scientific Advisory Committee of the Medical Outcomes Trust provides an in-depth discussion of the attributes and criteria for selecting a health status or quality-of-life instrument. The committee identifies eight key attributes to look for when reviewing an instrument: conceptual and measurement model; reliability; validity; responsiveness; interpretability; respondent and administrative burden; alternate forms; and cultural and language adaptations. It provides suggested guidelines for reviewing an instrument, as well as discusses methods of classical and modern measurement theory to evaluate these attributes.

19. Nunnally JC, Bernstein IH. Psychometric theory. New York, NY: McGraw-Hill, Inc. 1994.

The authors provide a comprehensive measurement design text for researchers. The text is broken into four parts: 1) explaining measurement as a general process; 2) discussing statistical foundations of measurement (explaining basic statistical concepts and correlation) and including an important discussion of validity; 3) addressing the problems associated with the internal structure of multi-item measures and aggregating items into scales; and 4) discussing exploratory and confirmatory factor analysis at length. Emerging topics in measurement also are presented.

20. Patrick DL, Deyo RA. Generic and disease specific measures in assessing health status and quality of life. Med Care 1989;27(Suppl):S217–32.

This paper provides a good overview of the issues surrounding generic and disease-specific measures. Differences and similarities between a generic measure approach and a disease-specific measure approach to assess health status are described. Four strategies for using generic and specific measures are identified and the advantages and disadvantages of generic and disease-specific measures, from a methodologic viewpoint, are discussed.

21. Patrick DL, Erickson P. Health status and health policy: allocating resources to health care. New York, NY: Oxford University Press, 1993.

    This book provides a systematic guide for developing and applying health status and quality-of-life measures. The primary focus is health care policy and research. The book explains how to allocate health resources by comparing costs and outcomes of alternative health policies. The authors provide an excellent overview of the concepts of health-related quality of life, types of health-related quality-of-life assessments, and assigning value to health states. Other topics covered in the book include selecting an instrument for primary data collection, calculating years of health life, concepts of health care costs, and health policy issues related to preventing disease and accessing care.

22. Perfetto EM, Epstein RS, Baldwin R. What are the necessary research components for high quality, scientifically rigorous pharmaceutical outcomes research? Patient outcomes of pharmaceutical interventions: a scientific foundation for the future. Washington, D.C.: American Pharmaceutical Association, 1994.

    This paper was prepared for an invitational conference sponsored by the American Pharmaceutical Association. The purpose of the conference was to advance the research base for patient outcome-oriented pharmacy practice. The focus of this paper is identifying design issues, research personnel, outcomes that should be measured, measurement issues, and analytical strategies relevant for conducting pharmaceutical outcomes research.

23. Revicki DA. Health-related quality of life in the evaluation of medical therapy for chronic illness. J Fam Pract 1989;29(4):377–80.

    This general review article that emphasizes the growing importance of quality-of-life outcomes to health care professions. The author provides a concise overview of health-related quality of life, and discusses its increasingly important role in clinical trials.

24. Riegelman RK, Hirsch RP. Studying a study and testing a test: how to read the health science literature, 3rd ed. Boston, MA: Little Brown Co., 1996.

    This text, now in its third edition, offers a step-by-step approach to thoughtful, critical, and efficient reading of the health sciences literature. The exercises provide a hands-on experience to the critical reading strategies presented by the authors.

25. Skaer TL. Applying pharmacoeconomic and quality of life measures to the formulary management process. Hosp Formulary 1993;28:577–84.

    This third article in a three-part series contains clinical case studies that incorporate pharmacoeconomic analysis and quality-of-life measures, and discusses the incorporation of research results into the formulary decision-making process.

26. Spilker B, ed. Quality of life and pharmacoeconomics in clinical trials, 2nd ed. Philadelphia, PA: Lippincott-Raven, 1996.

    This text is the standard text for industry provides an overview to quality-of-life research for those interested in clinical trials and, specifically, in pharmaceutical product development. The authors discuss in great detail the available tests and methods used in measuring quality of life, which tests have been validated for use, how investigators can choose which test to use in a specific situation, and, at present, the best quality-of-life measures to use in different therapeutic areas. Also included is a lengthy discussion of pharmacoeconomics and its relationship to quality-of-life research.

27. Stewart AL, Ware JE, eds. Measuring functioning and well-being: the Medical Outcomes Study approach. Durham, NC: Duke University Press, 1992.

    This text provides a discussion of the theory underlying the Medical Outcomes Study and the development of the Medical Outcomes Study short form, 36 items (SF-36). The scoring algorithms also are fully described in this book. Information about the psychometric analysis of the SF-36, including validity, reliability, precision, and norm-based results, are addressed.

28. Testa MA, Simonson DC. Assessment of quality-of-life outcomes. N Engl J Med 1996;334:835–40.

    Quality-of-life assessments and a conceptual scheme of quality of life are reviewed in this article. Quality of life incorporates both objective health status and subjective perceptions of health. The article also addresses properties of measurement scales, selecting an assessment instrument, and interpreting quality-of-life effects.

29. Ware JE, Brook RH, Davies AR, Lohr KN. Choosing measures of health status for individuals in general populations. Am J Public Health 1981;71:620–5.

    The authors identify general criteria that should be applied when selecting health status instruments and for data collection. A "shopper's guide" of issues to consider in the selection process is provided.

30. Ware JE. Methodology in behavioral and psychosocial cancer research. Conceptualizing disease impact and treatment outcomes Cancer 1984;53:2316–22.

    The author presents his model of quality of life, based on four primary dimensions of health status: physiologic status, personal (physical) functioning, mental health, and social well-being. Quality of life itself is described as a generic notion that includes the four primary domains, as well as other domains such as finances, housing, and employment.

31. Ware JE, Snow KK, Kosinski M, Gandek B. SF-36 health survey: manual and interpretation guide. Boston, MA: The Health Institute, New England Medical Center, 1993.

    This guide provides copies of the SF-36, along with information about developing and administering the instrument. The scoring algorithms also are fully described. Information about the psychometric analysis of the SF-36, including validity, reliability, precision, and norm-based results are addressed.

32. World Health Organization. Preamble to the Constitution of the World Health Organization as adopted by the International Health Conference, New York, NY, June 19-22, 1946; entered into force April 7, 1948.

    This document provides the basic definitions of health and quality of life as adopted by the World Health Organization.

Health Status Instrument Resources

There are many print sources that the interested researcher can refer to when trying to locate a health status instrument for inclusion into a study or practice; the advent of the Internet has made identification even simpler. The following are examples of computerized resources for health status instruments; appearance of a source on this list should not be viewed as an endorsement.

1. Online Guide to Quality of Life Assessment (OLGA) Web site: *http://www.olga-qol.com/*.

   This site offers a subscription-based service that includes detailed information regarding many major health status instruments. It provides information on instrument content, scoring, and psychometric properties, as well as supplemental references.

2. Health and Psychosocial Instruments. Available at *www.ovid.com*.

   This database is a subscription service that allows the user to search for health status instruments; results provide information pertaining to sources, domains, and psychometrics.

3. Quality of Life Instruments Database Web site. Available at *www.qolid.org*.

   This site was developed by the MAPI Research Institute; the Quality of Life Instruments Database provides free summary information (including full name, authors, administration mode, population, applicable diseases, and translated versions) for many health status instruments. Users can view a list of instruments by disease or search for specific terms. The site also has a section of restricted access for registered users.

4. American Thoracic Society Web site Quality of Life Resource. Available at *http://www.atsqol.org/*.

   This site offers a free service that lists quality-of-life instruments specific to respiratory diseases. Instruments are listed alphabetically. The site provides a description of the instrument, as well information on how to contact the developer, the instrument's cost and availability, number of domains and items, and psychometric properties.

Self-Assessment Questions

1. Which one of the following statements is *not* true?
   A. Patient-reported outcome (PRO) measures can be unidimensional.
   B. Quality-of-life measures can be unidimensional.
   C. Quality-of-life measures must be multidimensional.
   D. Health status is a PRO.

2. Including a generic instrument in a health status assessment allows which one of the following to be achieved?
   A. Gather pertinent data and determine cost-effectiveness ratios.
   B. Obtain information that may then be used as a basis of comparison to other populations.
   C. Provide a baseline measure for more intensive follow-up assessments.
   D. Increase response rates and decrease patient burden because general instruments are often short.

3. If specific effects have been identified for a treatment, a disease-specific instrument is a good choice because of which one of the following?
   A. It will be more sensitive to change.
   B. It will have low sensitivity to detect the treatment effect.
   C. It will be more sensitive for detecting unintended, related effects.
   D. It will provide a distinct baseline for future assessments.

4. Compared to disease-specific instruments, generic health status instruments have which one of the following sets of characteristics?
   A. Increased relevancy and decreased generalizability.
   B. Increased relevancy and increased generalizability.
   C. Decreased relevancy and increased generalizability.
   D. Decreased relevancy and decreased generalizability.

5. Which one of the following statements is *not* true?
   A. Instrument selection is not important because the SF-36 can be used for most projects.
   B. The method of administering the instrument should be appropriate for the patient population.
   C. One aspect of instrument selection involves an understanding of the intended purpose of the study.
   D. Established scoring algorithms for the instrument should be used rather than simply summing the responses.

6. The reliability of an instrument refers to its ability to accomplish which one of the following?
   A. Measure what it is purported to measure.
   B. Provide consistent results when used repeatedly.
   C. Detect the smallest level of change possible.
   D. Monitor large changes.

7. Respondent burden should be considered when assessing an instrument because of which one of the following?
   A. High respondent burden decreases significance in the results.
   B. High respondent burden decreases participation and affects the quality of results.
   C. High respondent burden increases participation and affects the quality of results.
   D. High respondent burden decreases participation but does not affect quality of results.

8. Utility assessment refers to which one of the following?
   A. Usefulness of a measure to detect change.
   B. Assigned value of a health state from a clinician's perspective.
   C. Desirability of a health state for a population.
   D. Use of publicly available health status instruments.

9. Use of an established instrument results in which one of the following?
   A. Decreased generalizability of results if populations with similar characteristics to the original are not used.
   B. Increased ability to add study-specific questions without affecting the instrument.
   C. Decreased respondent burden.
   D. Increased ability to provide comparative interpretation of results.

10. Which one of the following statements is true?
   A. All instruments reported in the peer-reviewed literature are valid and reliable and may be used with obtaining permission.
   B. The majority of relevant literature related to health status is found in the health sciences literature.
   C. Adequate description of the use of a disease-specific instrument in an adult population sets the stage for use of the instrument in both geriatric and pediatric populations.
   D. Critically reviewing the literature on health status instruments involves reviewing both the results of psychometric testing of the instrument and the studies using the instrument.

11. Which one of the following statements is false?
   A. A survey can be reliable but not valid.
   B. A reliable instrument can be multidimensional.
   C. Reliability measures the strength among item responses.
   D. A survey can be valid but not reliable.

12. Which one of the following benefits is not a good reason to develop computerized adaptive assessments of health-related quality-of-life constructs?
   A. The burden of responding to many questions is reduced.
   B. Assessments are cost beneficial on one-time assessment.
   C. Assessments can be used on multiple delivery platforms.
   D. Scores are comparable across different item sets.

13. Differential item functioning occurs when which one of the following is true?
   A. When two groups have a different mean score on a scale.
   B. When individuals from two groups, with similar levels on the measured construct, have different probabilities for endorsing a question.
   C. When the properties of the items are invariant to group membership.
   D. When two or more items function differently in a survey.

14. Applications of item response theory modeling are important tools to develop and evaluate health status instruments for all these reasons except which one of the following?
   A. To detect differences in the meaning of an item or construct across treatment groups.
   B. To model item and scale functioning along the construct continuum.
   C. To evaluate the construct validity of the scale.
   D. To calibrate items to be used for item banks and computerized adaptive assessments.

15. Which one of the following four dimensions is not a component of the Hierarchy of Patient Outcomes?
   A. Death.
   B. Iatrogenic effects.
   C. Religiosity.
   D. Discomfort.

PATIENT SATISFACTION

Jon C. Schommer, Ph.D.

Outline

I. What is Satisfaction?

A. Satisfaction is "an individual's *judgment* about the extent to which a product or service provides a pleasurable level of consumption-related fulfillment." Stated simply, satisfaction results from an *evaluation* of a product or service that nets some emotional reaction. A judgment is made by an individual as to how well the service was provided, and this judgment results in pleasure if satisfaction occurs or displeasure if dissatisfaction occurs.

B. Satisfaction is not to be confused with dimensions of quality, such as 1) quality of conformance or 2) *quality of design*. *Quality of conformance* is the consistency of how the product is manufactured or the service is delivered. *Quality of design* depicts how well the product or service meets the needs of consumers, or how well the product or service compares with those of the competitors in the eyes of the consumer.

C. Assessing satisfaction with services is different than evaluating the quality of products. Services are intangible; production and consumption of services are often inseparable; the way services are provided can vary from provider to provider even within the same organization; and variability among individual patients makes the provision of health care services an art that can vary from patient to patient.

II. Satisfaction as performance evaluation—Patient satisfaction can be viewed as a "personal evaluation of health care services and providers."

III. Satisfaction as disconfirmation of expectations—Satisfaction can be described as the result of an individual comparing an expectation to the actual service experience. This gap between the expectation and service experience then can impact how one feels about the service experience or the individual's satisfaction with the service.

IV. Satisfaction as affect-based evaluation—The focus in this conceptual framework is the degree of affective (emotional) response and not only how well expectations were or were not met.

V. Satisfaction as equity-based evaluation—This is a comparison of one's outcomes versus input with respect to someone else's outcomes versus input. An individual who perceives that a service provider has gained more than he or she has is likely to be less satisfied.

VI. Satisfaction as self-efficacy-based evaluation—Self-efficacy is the conviction that one can successfully execute a particular behavior required to produce desired outcomes. The extent to which pharmacists services contribute to patients' self-efficacy for managing their drug regimens could be an important component of their satisfaction with pharmacists services.

VII. Tools to measure patient satisfaction

A. Patient Satisfaction Questionnaire

B. Patient Satisfaction with Pharmacy Services Questionnaire

C. Other satisfaction measures in the pharmacy services domain and the evolution of the development of these measures.

VIII. A critique of patient satisfaction

A. Problems with its conceptualization and operationalization—Measures of patient satisfaction often are developed by researchers without patient input. Thus, patients are forced to limit descriptions of care to aspects selected by the researchers. This may not capture what the individuals would prefer to express.

B. Problems with its measurement—Many measures of patient satisfaction result in high scores that are skewed. Many measures are unable to capture the nuances which may be important to patients in the provision of health care.

C. Problems with its interpretation and use—Measures of patient satisfaction have been used to provide both descriptive and evaluative results. Both issues are potentially problematic. There is little justification for decisions about the allocation of resources to be determined only by satisfaction scores. An understanding about what is behind patients' positive and negative descriptions and/or evaluations of their health care experiences also is needed.

IX. Considerations for measuring patient satisfaction

A. Conceptualization to be consistent with research problem—Because many conceptualizations of patient satisfaction can be used, the measurement of patient satisfaction must fit the context of the overall research process. A research process involves six stages: 1) formulate the problem, 2) determine the research design, 3) design data collection method and forms, 4) select a sample and collect the data, 5) analyze and interpret the data, and 6) prepare the research report. Each stage is linked and decisions made at one stage affect decisions made at other stages.

B. Acknowledgment of limitations—When investigating patient satisfaction, one must also consider the requirements and limitations imposed by the research process itself. For example, the purpose of the research, potential users of the data, time and money available for the study, population of interest, and data collection methods all influence the type of satisfaction measure determined to be the best.

C. Measure development process—Because the meaning attributed to a satisfaction measure by the investigator may not be the same as the meaning given by the respondents, a systematic process for developing measures should be followed that includes: 1) specify the domain of the construct, 2) generate a pool of items and determine the format of the measure, 3) have the initial pool of items reviewed by experts, 4) consider inclusion of validation items, 5) administer items to a development sample, 6) purify the measure, and 7) optimize the practicality of the measure.

D. Acquiescence—When one is using existing measures of satisfaction or when developing new measures for a specific research purpose, acquiescence can be a problem. Acquiescence is a culturally based tendency to agree with others and could lead to invalid data in satisfaction surveys.

E. Case mix—When comparing satisfaction among groups of individuals who belong to different health plans or access different care providers within a health plan, it is important to control for case mix. *Case mix* refers to the different patient attributes that might be apparent in different settings.

Learning Objectives

1. Define patient satisfaction.
2. Identify dimensions of patient satisfaction.
3. Review popular satisfaction measures available for use in health care and pharmacy.
4. Critique patient satisfaction conceptualization, measurement, interpretation, and use.
5. Describe considerations for measuring patient satisfaction.

Abbreviations in this chapter

MTMM	Multitrait-multimethod
PES	Pharmacy Encounter Survey
PSPSQ	Patient Satisfaction with Pharmacy Services Questionnaire
PSQ	Patient Satisfaction Questionnaire
PSQ-18	Short-form Patient Satisfaction Questionnaire

Introduction

Patient satisfaction is a measure that is used to assess the performance of programs or personnel. It reflects the ability of the service provider to meet patients' needs. Satisfying patients is one important indicator of quality care because it demonstrates the ability of the provider to meet expectations and values of the patient. Industry reports about managed care organizations include patient satisfaction as one measure of service quality.

From a patient care view, satisfied patients are more likely than unsatisfied patients to continue using medical care services, maintain a relationship with a specific service provider, and comply with medical care regimens. In addition, patient satisfaction information can serve as a measure of service quality and as a predictor of health-related behavior. As pharmacist services evolve in sophistication and become more pervasive in health care systems, patient satisfaction will gain significance as a patient outcome for the purpose of performance assessment, reimbursement, and quality management.

What is Satisfaction?

Satisfaction is "an individual's *judgment* about the extent to which a product or service provides a pleasurable level of consumption-related fulfillment." Stated simply, satisfaction results from an *evaluation* of a product or service that nets some emotional reaction. A judgment is made by an individual as to how well the service was provided, and this judgment results in pleasure if satisfaction occurs or displeasure if dissatisfaction occurs.

Satisfaction is not to be confused with dimensions of quality, such as 1) quality of conformance or 2) quality of design. Quality of conformance is the consistency of how the product is manufactured or the service is delivered. For example, pharmaceutical tablets are manufactured to fit within Food and Drug Administration standards for dissolution. Each batch is tested to determine if tablets within that batch fit standards. Quality of design depicts how well the product or service meets the needs of consumers, or how well the product or service compares with those of the competitors in the eyes of the consumer. In the pharmaceutical tablet example, the manufacturer evaluates the quality of design by comparing the clinical outcomes provided by the product to the desired outcomes of the patients. Such factors as returning to "normal" health or avoiding side effects are used to evaluate quality of design. In addition, the product is compared to its competitors from the perspective of the consumer. The question to ask is, "Is the product perceived by consumers as safer and more effective than competitors' products?"

Quality of conformance and quality of design reflect the degree to which a product or service meets established standards. Satisfaction, on the other hand, should be viewed as an individual's judgment about the product or service and can vary from individual to individual. Thus, identical products (or services) would be rated as having the same quality when the same standards are used, but individuals satisfaction with the product (or service) could vary from individual to individual even if the products (or services) were identical in each evaluation.

Services possess unique characteristics from products which make evaluating them a greater challenge than evaluating products. First, for example, services are intangible, making classic quality engineering systems difficult to implement. Second, the production and consumption of services often are inseparable. Thus, an evaluation of services must include how well the service was delivered and how well the service met the needs of the patient. Finally, the way services are provided can vary from provider to provider even within the same organization. Although an institution or profession may develop standards for patient care, these standards often serve as recommendations and not absolute procedures. Also, variability among individual patients makes the provision of health care services an art that can vary from patient to patient.

In contrast to how quality is measured and evaluated, satisfaction is individual-specific and is based on the perceptions and judgments of individuals. Therefore, *patient satisfaction* is an individual's judgment about the extent to which a health care product or service provides a pleasurable level of consumption-related fulfillment. In the recent literature, satisfaction has been conceptualized in five ways: 1) performance evaluation, 2) disconfirmation of expectations, 3) affect-based evaluation, 4) equity-based evaluation, and 5) self-efficacy based evaluation (Table 1).

Table 1: Conceptualizations of Satisfaction

Conceptualization	Focus	Strengths	Weaknesses
Performance evaluation	Salient characteristics of a service	Can evaluate specific characteristics of a service	Characteristics are selected by the researcher and might not be reflective of individuals' views
Disconfirmation of expectations	Cognitive appraisal of a service experience	Provides and understanding of the physiological process of service evaluation	Results are sensitive to the type and level of expectations used for the study
Affect-based evaluation	Emotional response to a service and resultant actions by the individual	Allows the investigation of emotional responses to services, especially in the absence of prior expectations	Might be applicable to short-term evaluations but not to long-terms evaluations
Equity-based evaluation	Fairness in what is gained compared with what it cost the individual	Allows the investigation of the relationship between input and output of the individual and the service provider	Assumes that fairness is the key determinant of satisfaction
Self-efficacy-based evaluation	Extent to which a service leads to an individual's ability to execute a desired behavior	Allows the investigation of long-term outcomes that might be attained from the service	Assumes that satisfaction with a service is based primarily on long-term results that might be achieved

Satisfaction as Performance Evaluation

Some studies of patient satisfaction with health care services have been based on measures that evaluate the service experience on specific characteristics. These studies view satisfaction as: "personal evaluation of health care services and providers." The Patient Satisfaction Questionnaire (PSQ) was developed to evaluate health care services. Service characteristics were divided into eight categories: 1) interpersonal, 2) technical quality, 3) accessibility/convenience, 4) finances, 5) efficacy/outcomes, 6) continuity, 7) physical environment, and 8) availability. With this measure, a service is evaluated by asking patients to respond to statements using a five-point Likert scale, ranging from strongly agree to strongly disagree. Much of the literature on patient satisfaction has followed the PSQ approach and focused on identifying salient characteristics of health care services for evaluation by individuals. Some examples of items prepared for pharmacy services include: 1) "It takes me a long time to get to the pharmacy where I have my prescriptions filled" and 2) "The pharmacist often does not tell me how to take my prescription drug".

Viewing patient satisfaction as performance evaluation is most useful for services that have characteristics individuals can identify and understand. However, individuals might not have the expertise to assess unfamiliar or ambiguous services. Patients have a complex set of important and relevant beliefs which cannot be captured or described through a simple performance evaluation, because performance measures have been defined only from a health care system perspective and impose on the survey respondent an evaluation of satisfaction that is limited to what the system has decided is important and not necessarily what the individual considers important. Such measures of satisfaction may provide only an illusion of patient-centered care, producing results which tend to endorse the status quo. Questionnaires that are not based on an understanding of how and whether patients perceive and evaluate a service act as a form of censorship imposed on patients. Such an approach to questionaire design gives misleading results, limits the opportunity of patients to express their concerns about aspects of care, and can encourage professionals to believe that patients are satisfied when they are in reality highly discontent.

Therefore, a performance evaluation conceptualization of satisfaction might be limited to services with characteristics that are not ambiguous to patients. Researchers have shown that satisfaction with ambiguous product experiences (i.e., experiences with no clear end point or outcome) are not predicted by performance alone, but by comparing performance to consumer expectations. An example of an ambiguous pharmacist service could be pharmacists' efforts in evaluating the accuracy or appropriateness of prescription orders. Most patients are not likely to posses the expertise to make a determination about the performance of pharmacists in this regard. For services that have ambiguous or poorly understood components, a measure of satisfaction that can provide insight into the psychological process of evaluating a service experience is more useful.

Satisfaction as Disconfirmation of Expectations

Researchers have investigated the psychological process of service evaluation and have proposed the disconfirmation of expectations paradigm of satisfaction. This perspective views satisfaction as "a consumer fulfillment response" which occurs when the consumer associates the service with "a pleasurable level of consumption related fulfillment". Under this conceptualization, satisfaction results from a cognitive appraisal of the service experience which involves a comparison between the service experience and expectation. An example of a measurement item under this conceptualization could be: "Was the performance level of ________ less than you expected, about what you expected, or more than you expected?"

Patient satisfaction can be viewed as a positive evaluation of distinct dimensions of the service, resulting from a gap which exists between desires or expectations and what actually occurs. Theoretically, if the service provider fails to meet consumer expectations, dissatisfaction results. If the service provider meets or exceeds expectations, then satisfaction is realized.

The disconfirmation of expectations model has been tested and validated by various researchers. Although many researchers have accepted this view of satisfaction, they have retained different opinions about which expectations, or comparison standards, are most pertinent and about which interrelationships among variables are most important in the satisfaction process. Results from a recent study that focused on pharmacy services showed that cognitive services are best evaluated from the patients' perspective by asking how the services compared with what they think the services *should* be (e.g., some patients thought that they should receive no service at all, whereas others had the expectation that they should receive a high level of care). However, tangible aspects of services, such as informational leaflets or wait time, are best evaluated by asking patients about how recent experiences compare with *past* experiences. The authors suggested that satisfaction measures should be designed specifically to assess the type of services being studied.

Satisfaction as Affect-based Evaluation

Satisfaction also has been viewed as a pleasurable response to a service encounter. This type of conceptualization takes into consideration that individuals with moderate expectations of a health care service will likely be indifferent if those expectations are met. However, individuals with high expectations of a health care service might be delighted if a health care provider met their high expectations. Thus, the focus in this conceptual framework is the degree of affective response, not just how well expectations were or were not met. This conceptual view of satisfaction can be useful in cases when individuals have no prior expectations of a health care service. In the health care domain, individuals often do not know what to expect when experiencing a health care service. In these cases, how a person feels is an appropriate way to gauge patient satisfaction because knowledge about the service and prior expectations about the service are absent.

Although somewhat similar to the disconfirmation of expectations paradigm, affect can be independent from that view. For example, hypertensive patients were asked to evaluate services provided by physicians and pharmacists. When asked about specific service characteristics of the pharmacist, the proportion of respondents with no expectations ranged from 23 percent (knowledge about drug) to 41 percent (counseling about drug). Comparatively, a larger proportion of patients had some expectations with physician services with the range of no expectations from 3 percent (personality of the physician) to 27 percent (understanding the cost of the drug to the patient). In models of satisfaction that were tested, affect played an important role in patient satisfaction with pharmacy services, particularly when expectations did not exist. In that study, performance evaluation was a better predictor of satisfaction in cases for which expectations did exist.

Satisfaction as Equity-based Evaluation

A fourth conceptualization of patient satisfaction is an equity-based assessment. This assessment is a comparison of one's outcomes versus input with respect to someone else's outcomes versus input. The resulting perception of fairness has a direct relationship to satisfaction. An individual who perceives that a service provider has gained more than he or she has gained is likely to be less satisfied. Studies show that perceptions of fairness increased as the differences between input and output increased in favor of the individual.

Such an approach to understanding patient satisfaction assumes that fairness is the key determinant of patient satisfaction. An understanding of the key input and output of a health care service is required as well. There are only a few examples of this approach in the health care literature, but the approach could be quite useful in situations where equity is a primary consideration (e.g., satisfaction with insurance coverage for health care services).

Representative items that serve as examples of this conceptualization are given below:

1. Think of all you put into (invested) getting your last prescription of high blood pressure drug from your pharmacist, including waiting time in the pharmacy, attention you gave to the pharmacist's counseling, trust and faith you put into the pharmacist's knowledge, and the amount of money you spent to get the prescription filled. Now, rate how much you put into (invested) in your dealings with your pharmacist.

Maximum: 10 9 8 7 6 5 4 3 2 1 0 **:Minimum**

2. Think of all you received from your pharmacist who dispensed your last prescription for high blood pressure drug, including receiving the right drug in the right dosage, counseling about the drug, and personal attention. Now, rate how much you received from your pharmacist.

Maximum: 10 9 8 7 6 5 4 3 2 1 0 **:Minimum**

Some evidence supports this conceptualization of satisfaction. In a study of the relationships among preferences, equity, and fairness as determinants of consumer satisfaction, fairness was reflective of the consumer's evaluation of the input and output of both the consumer and the provider during the exchange process (i.e., equity). Fairness increased as the differences between input and output increased to favor the consumer. Fairness, in turn, was significantly related to satisfaction. In the pharmacy domain, researchers also reported that equity and fairness were significant predictors of patient satisfaction with pharmacists and physicians. Equity was related to fairness and fairness was directly related to satisfaction.

Satisfaction as Self-efficacy-based Evaluation

Self-efficacy is the conviction that one can successfully execute a particular behavior required to produce desired outcomes. Thus, the extent to which a pharmacist service leads to an individual's self-efficacy for a desired behavior can serve as a useful evaluative component for the service being studied. An example of a desired behavior that might result from a pharmacist service is the ability to self-manage one's drug regimen. The extent to which a pharmacist service contributes to an individual's ability to self-manage his or her drug regimen could be an important component of that individual's satisfaction with the pharmacist service.

Of the five types of evaluation reviewed in this chapter, self-efficacy evaluations have the most long-term focus. Some evidence supports the notion that such a long-term perspective could be useful for measuring patient satisfaction with some pharmacist services. Researchers have reported that self-efficacy was one of four distinct components of satisfaction for patients who had received pharmacist-conducted drug education classes at a tertiary headache clinic's hospital unit (the other three components were performance, disconfirmation of expectations, and equity). These findings suggest that both short-term and long-term perspectives could be useful for assessing patient satisfaction.

In summary, five conceptualizations of satisfaction were outlined: 1) performance evaluation, 2) disconfirmation of expectations, 3) affect-based, 4) equity-based, and 5) self-efficacy-based evaluations. The next sections review some popular satisfaction measures that have been used in health care.

Tools to Measure Patient Satisfaction

In the health care domain, the Patient Satisfaction Questionaire (PSQ) is a popular patient satisfaction measure for which psychometric properties have been investigated and reported. The most recent version, called the Short-form Patient Satisfaction Questionnaire (PSQ-18), can be obtained from RAND Corporation, Santa Monica, California. This version contains 18 items that focus on seven distinct areas: 1) general satisfaction, 2) technical quality, 3) interpersonal manner, 4) communication, 5) financial aspects, 6) time spent with doctor, and 7) accessibility/convenience. Acceptable reliability and validity have been reported for this measure. The PSQ-18 constitutes a widely used and accepted measure of patient satisfaction with medical care.

For the pharmacy services domain, many of the early studies used a single-item measure of performance evaluation as the conceptualization for satisfaction. Usually, a patient's overall satisfaction with a service or component of a service was assessed. It was a method by which pharmacist performance could be compared among different groups of pharmacists within a study. Although a single-item performance evaluation measure can be useful for comparisons among groups within a study, the validity of such a measure is suspect (i.e., what does satisfaction actually mean in these contexts?). Could it reflect how well the pharmacist is liked, how long the patient has patronized the pharmacy, or how long the patient waited for his or her prescription? Without a theoretical base on which the validity of the measure can be assessed, patient satisfaction is difficult to interpret within a study and difficult to compare among different study populations.

In 1989, a multiple-item performance evaluation perspective of patient satisfaction specific for pharmacy services was developed. This measure of patient satisfaction, called the Patient Satisfaction with Pharmacy Services Questionnaire (PSPSQ), was patterned after the PSQ measure. Items were designed to contain a personal referent (i.e., the focus was on an individual's personal experience rather than on the experience of people, in general). This measure of patient satisfaction was viewed as a multidimensional construct comprised of eight dimensions: 1) explanation, 2) consideration, 3) technical competence, 4) financial aspects, 5) accessibility, 6) drug efficacy, 7) over-the-counter product availability, and 8) quality of the drug product.

Developers of the PSPSQ recommended that future study of the questionnaire include item revision, testing in a broader population, and further testing of construct validity. Since that time, some researchers have modified and used the PSPSQ. For example, one study found four underlying dimensions of the PSPSQ: 1) professional communication, 2) physical/emotional comfort, 3) demographic issues, and 4) location/convenience. The researchers reported that the process they used to measure patient satisfaction can be replicated in other situations, but that its meaning might differ from market to market or even among pharmacies within a single market. That is, components that were relevant in one geographic area or pharmacy setting might be less relevant in another.

Other researchers applied six items from the PSPSQ and added three more of their own, resulting in a nine-item measure of satisfaction. The researchers treated satisfaction as a unidimensional construct and reported a reliability of 0.94 using Cronbach's coefficient alpha.

Developers of the PSPSQ built on their own work to help establish further the validity of their original PSPSQ measure. Their measurement of satisfaction was a slight modification of their 1989 version that resulted in 45 statements reflective of nine dimensions of satisfaction. Data were collected through telephone interviews of Iowa residents who had purchased one or more prescriptions in the 6 months before the study. A total of 454 contacts was made to acquire 180 completed interviews. The assessment of reliability and validity resulted in a final measure of 33 items reflective of seven dimensions.

In 2002, the PSPSQ was modified in order to focus more on the elements of pharmaceutical care services. Data were collected through a mailed survey of prescription patrons of eight community pharmacies in Iowa. A total of 428 responses was received. Based on analysis of 371 usable cases, support for instrument reliability and validity was found for a final measure of 20 items reflective of two dimensions: 1) friendly explanation and 2) managing therapy.

Various versions of the PSPSQ have been the most extensively used and validated measures of patient satisfaction in the pharmacy services domain. In addition to those useful measures, other researchers have introduced patient satisfaction measures that are likely to be helpful in some pharmacy service evaluations.

Some researchers in the pharmacy domain have endorsed the application of a flexible performance evaluation approach for developing satisfaction measures using a three-step process. First, build a pool of items by reviewing previous satisfaction instruments, talking with current patients about their concerns and interests, and tapping unique aspects of the service offering of interest. Second, select four to six items to represent each of five recommended domains: responsiveness, reassurance, empathy, assurance, and tangibles. Third, phrase survey items to rate each aspect of the service relative to normative or absolute standards, or to expectations of patients, depending on the purpose of the survey. This approach has been tested in different populations under three conditions (i.e., chronic illness, anticoagulation, and asthma). Preliminary reports suggest that this method can be successful for developing measures of satisfaction for different patient populations or for different pharmacist services.

Another example of a performance evaluation perspective of patient satisfaction is the Pharmacy Encounter Survey (PES), interviewers administered this measure to 260 consecutive people immediately after their visits to one of 26 randomly selected community pharmacies. Nine items rated from 1 (excellent) to 5 (poor) comprised the satisfaction measure. These items were used to ask respondents about specific features of their visit to a community pharmacy and were based on work reported in the health care domain. Satisfaction was treated as a unidimensional construct and reported a reliability of 0.94 using Cronbach's coefficient alpha.

In 1991, another type of conceptualization for patient satisfaction was introduced to the pharmacy domain. This conceptualization viewed satisfaction as a function of expectations disconfirmation and perceptions of equity. These views of satisfaction are rooted in the marketing literature as previously discussed. Others used the same type of conceptualization and identified an affective component of satisfaction and reported that satisfaction might be based on the perception of equity achieved in the service encounter. They showed that questions regarding affective components of satisfaction provided different results than questions which focused on performance evaluation.

The conceptualization of satisfaction proposed in the marketing literature has been applied to pharmacist consultation services. In one study, a three-item measure of satisfaction was used and in the other, a six-item measure was used. Each of the measures was based on the conceptualization that satisfaction is an affect-based response to a specific service encounter in which service performance is compared with a patient's prior expectations for that service. A patient's satisfaction, then, is a function of perceived performance and prior expectations. In each study, the measure of satisfaction was found to be reliable, valid, and responsive for discriminating among different categories of patients.

A problem with the marketing-based conceptualizations of satisfaction is the selection of the comparison standard of interest. This issue was addressed by investigating three different comparison standards: 1) prior experiences with the pharmacist services, 2) the best possible pharmacist services that should be provided (ideal expectation), and 3) pharmacist services provided by other pharmacies (market-based referent). The results showed that ideal expectations were better than prior experience referents when explaining satisfaction with a particular pharmacist service encounter, but prior experience referents were better than ideal referents when explaining satisfaction with cumulative pharmacist services (comprised of three categories: pharmacist performance, problem-solving performance, and written information). Market-based referents were not associated with pharmacist service encounter satisfaction or satisfaction with cumulative service encounters. Results revealed that ideal expectations are the comparison standard of choice when satisfaction with a specific service encounter is the focus. However, prior experience-based referents should be used when cumulative experiences with pharmacist services is the focus.

In subsequent analysis, it was found that cognitive services provided by pharmacists are best evaluated from the patient's perspective by asking the patient how the services compare with what they should be (i.e., ideal expectations serve as the comparison standard). Tangible aspects of pharmacist services, such as information leaflets, or wait times, are best evaluated by asking patients how recent experiences compare with past experiences (i.e., prior experiences serve as the comparison standard).

Recently, the previously discussed five conceptualizations of patient satisfaction were used simultaneously for evaluating a pharmacist service. Patient satisfaction with pharmacist-conducted education classes was assessed at a tertiary headache clinic's inpatient unit. The results showed that four of the five conceptualizations of satisfaction (e.g., performance, disconfirmation of expectations, equity, and self-efficacy) were useful for evaluating that particular pharmacist service.

In summary, the literature about patient satisfaction in pharmacy has followed two paths. One is rooted in the health care literature in which satisfaction is viewed as an experience-based performance evaluation of different pharmacist service dimensions. The other is rooted in the marketing literature in which satisfaction has an evaluative and an affective component and is focused on an individual's reaction to a particular service experience or the culmination of experiences.

It appears that a single, standard conceptualization of patient satisfaction with pharmacist services is not applicable to all pharmacy service situations. When one faces a decision about which conceptualization of patient satisfaction is best for a particular research question or situation, it is prudent to consider some of the critiques of patient satisfaction as an outcome measure. Such critiques of patient satisfaction in terms of 1) conceptualization, 2) measurement, and 3) interpretation and use are discussed in the A Critique of Patient Satisfaction section.

A Critique of Patient Satisfaction

One critique of patient satisfaction relates to its conceptualization. Measures of patient satisfaction often are developed by researchers without patient input. Thus, patients are forced to limit descriptions of care to aspects selected by the researchers. This method may not capture what the individuals would prefer to express. It also is assumed that the aspects of the service that are included in the measure are the ones that encompass each and every individual's expression of satisfaction—that the sum of all the responses represents an overall measure of satisfaction.

Another conceptual problem lies with the assumption that dissatisfaction is the opposite of satisfaction and the two concepts lie at either end of a continuum. Usually, this is not the case. Patients are able to be both satisfied and dissatisfied with the same aspects of care. For example, a patient may be typically satisfied or have a positive overall view of the clinical competence of a pharmacist, but still could pinpoint dissatisfying experiences or negative characteristics of that pharmacist. For some services or situations, an assessment of dissatisfaction, complaining behavior, changing service providers, negative word-of-mouth communication to other patients, or intentional nonadherence to medical advice might be more appropriate concepts to measure than patient satisfaction.

A second critique of patient satisfaction focuses on problems with its measurement. Many measures of patient satisfaction result in high scores that are skewed. Thus, these measures are unable to capture the nuances that may be important to patients in the provision of health care. The problems are not related so much to survey design or the validity and reliability of the instruments. Rather, the shortcoming lies in the limited capacity of some methods of measurement to capture a more comprehensive description of patients' experiences from their perspectives. There are times when a more qualitative assessment, using observational techniques, focus groups, unstructured interviews, or content analysis of patients' writings, would yield more useful data.

Finally, a third critique relates to problems with the interpretation and use of patient satisfaction data. Measures of patient satisfaction have been used to provide both descriptive and evaluative results. Patient satisfaction is a partial measure of the wide array of outcomes that can be achieved by health care services. Patient satisfaction should be viewed as one piece of a larger puzzle. Thus, there is little justification for decisions about the allocation of resources to be determined only by satisfaction scores. An understanding about what is behind patients' positive and negative descriptions and/or evaluations of their health care experiences also is needed for the decision-making process.

Considerations for Measuring Patient Satisfaction

With the critique of patient satisfaction in mind, how should one proceed when measuring it? First, one should acknowledge that no single, standard conceptualization of patient satisfaction is applicable to all situations. When selecting a conceptualization of satisfaction, the investigator must identify the research question. For example, if the primary research objective is to compare service providers in terms of how well individuals rate specific aspects of service performance, an experience-based evaluation of performance is appropriate. If the research is focused instead on the relationship between patients' evaluation of a service and their future commitment to the service provider, a satisfaction measure that reflects evaluative and affective reactions by the individual is appropriate. If the focus of the service is to help patients achieve a long-term outcome, then a self-efficacy-based evaluation might be the most useful.

Also, one should remember that patient satisfaction might not be the most relevant outcome for study. Performance, quality, loyalty, complaining behavior, trust, or some other outcome might be more useful for decision-making, planning, implementation, and evaluation related to health care products and services. It is important to link the construct being measured to the problem or decision that the study results will help address. Guidelines that can help one decide how to measure patient satisfaction are discussed in the next sections.

Conceptualization to be Consistent with the Research Problem

Because many conceptualizations of patient satisfaction can be used, the measurement of patient satisfaction must fit the context of the overall research process. A useful research process consists of six stages: 1) formulate the problem, 2) determine the research design, 3) design data collection method and forms, 4) select a sample and collect the data, 5) analyze and interpret the data, and 6) prepare the research report. Each stage is linked and decisions made at one stage will affect decisions made at other stages.

Acknowledgement of Limitations

When investigating patient satisfaction, consider the requirements and limitations imposed by the research process itself. For example, the purpose of the research, potential users of the data, time, and money available for the study; the population of interest; and the data collection methods will all influence the type of satisfaction measure determined to be the best. Limitations in these factors must be recognized, whether a new measure of patient satisfaction is being developed or an existing measure is being used.

Measure Development Process (if a New Measure is Needed)

Because the meaning attributed to a satisfaction measure by the investigator may not be the same as the meaning attributed to it by the respondents, a systematic process for developing measures should be followed that includes: 1) specifying the domain of the construct, 2) generating a pool of items and determine the format of the measure, 3) having the initial pool of items reviewed by experts, 4) considering inclusion of validation items, 5) administering items to a development sample, 6) purifying the measure, and 7) optimizing the practicality of the measure.

Specify the Domain of the Construct

Many researchers think they have a clear idea of what they wish to measure, only to find that their ideas are more vague than they thought. The researcher must be exact in delineating what is included in the pertinent domain and what is excluded. Proceed with the next steps of developing a measure only when an explicit definition of the satisfaction construct is outlined.

Address issues, such as the type of conceptualization of satisfaction that are best for the study. Should the focus be on performance evaluation of the consumption experience or on the patient and the decision process he or she uses to evaluate the service? Another issue to address when specifying the construct domain is whether satisfaction is encounter specific or reflective of cumulative experiences. Also, what is the most pertinent focus: satisfaction with the service itself, the pharmacist, or the pharmacy? Finally, an understanding of how and whether patients perceive and evaluate a service will help specify the domain. If a service is ambiguous to patients, an affective-based or equity-based approach might be best. If a service is well-defined and is salient to patients, a performance evaluation might be the best conceptualization of satisfaction.

Once the domain has been clearly articulated, the developer is ready to begin constructing the measure in earnest. If there is an existing measure that fits the construct domain of the study, that measure should be used. This provides replication of existing measures in different studies so that comparisons can be made between studies. Quite often, though, existing measures do not fit the purpose of the study and a new or modified measure must be developed as discussed in the Generate an Item Pool and Determine the Format for Measurement section.

Generate an Item Pool and Determine the Format for Measurement

At this point, a large pool of items that are candidates for eventual inclusion in the measure should be generated. Theoretically, a good set of items is chosen randomly from the universe of items relating to the construct of interest. The universe of items is assumed to be infinitely large, which precludes any hope of actually generating such a list of items and extracting items randomly. However, this ideal should be kept in mind. When generating items, think creatively about the satisfaction construct to be measured and represent all aspects of satisfaction as it is defined within the domain of interest.

Many methods can be used for item generation, such as literature searches, experience surveys, insight stimulating examples, critical incidents, focus groups, consultation with experts, and other measures. There should be redundancy of items related to the domain, and care should be given to the clarity, reading level, and wording of each item. An exhaustive list of potential items should be generated before moving to the next step.

As items are generated, the format for each item should be developed. Commonly used formats include Guttman scaling, Likert scales, itemized rating scales, semantic differential, visual analog, and binary options. A Guttman scale is a series of items tapping progressively higher levels of an attribute. Thus, a respondent should endorse a block of adjacent items until, at a critical point, the amount of the attribute exceeds that possessed by the subject. None of the remaining items should then be endorsed. For example, a series of questions might ask, "Did you wait for your prescription?" "Did you wait more than 1 minute?" "Did you wait more than 5 minutes?" and so on. This type of successive questioning could be especially useful for assessing different levels of satisfaction that are based on performance evaluation.

One of the most common formats is the Likert scale. Here, each item is presented as a declarative statement, followed by response options that indicate varying degrees of agreement or disagreement. It is useful for the statements to be fairly strong when used in Likert format because the moderation of opinion is expressed in the choice of response option (e.g., 1 = very strongly disagree, 2 = strongly disagree, 3 = disagree, 4 = neutral, 5 = agree, 6 = strongly agree, 7 = very strongly agree). In addition to the Likert scale, some researchers also provide a response signified "NA" and/or "unsure" so respondents can report that an item is not applicable or they are unsure about how to interpret the item.

Itemized rating scales are useful for performance evaluation measures of satisfaction. In general, individuals are asked to make a judgment about the person or object being rated in one of an ordered series of categories. For example, the PES previously discussed used an itemized rating scale from 1 (excellent) to 5 (poor):

In terms of your satisfaction, how would you rate each of the following:

	Excellent	**Very Good**	**Good**	**Fair**	**Poor**
How long you waited waited before seeing the pharmacist	1.☐	2.☐	3.☐	4.☐	5.☐

	Excellent	**Very Good**	**Good**	**Fair**	**Poor**
Getting through to the pharmacy by phone	1.☐	2.☐	3.☐	4.☐	5.☐

The semantic differential method identifies a target stimulus (e.g., a service encounter) followed by a list of adjective pairs. Each pair represents opposite ends of a continuum defined by adjectives. As shown in the examples below, there are several lines between the adjectives that constitute the response options:

	Extremely	Quite	Slightly	Neither	Slightly	Quite	Extremely	
Equitable	___ :	___ :	___ :	___ :	___ :	___ :	___	**Inequitable**

	Extremely	Quite	Slightly	Neither	Slightly	Quite	Extremely	
Fair	___ :	___ :	___ :	___ :	___ :	___ :	___	**Unfair**

The individual lines represent points along the continuum defined by the adjectives. The respondent places a mark on one of the lines to indicate the point along the continuum that best characterizes the identified stimulus.

Visual analog scales are similar to the semantic differential scale except that this format presents the respondent with a continuous line between a pair of descriptors representing opposite ends of a continuum. The individual is instructed to place a mark at a point on the line that best represents his or her opinion.

Equitable ______________________________ **Inequitable**

Fair ______________________________ **Unfair**

The fineness of differentiation in assigning scores to points on the continuum is determined by the investigator. A disadvantage of the visual analog scale is that a mark placed at a specific point along the line may not mean the same thing to different respondents even when the end points are identically labeled for all respondents.

Another common response format gives subjects a choice among binary options for each item. For example, subjects might be asked to check off all the adjectives on a list that they think apply to the pharmacist service being evaluated. Or, patients might be asked to answer "yes" or "no" to a list of emotional reactions they experienced in a specified service situation. Although extremely easy to answer, a limitation of the binary response format is that each item can have only minimal variability and limits data analysis options.

There are relative advantages and disadvantages for each format just presented. The type of scale chosen depends on the conceptualization of satisfaction used and the objectives of the study.

Have Initial Item Pool Reviewed by Experts

The next step is having a group of people who are knowledgeable in the content area review the item pool. Expert review can confirm or invalidate the definition of the construct. Panel members will rate how relevant they think each item is to what is intended to be measured. Also, reviewers can evaluate the items' clarity and conciseness. The content of an item may be relevant to the construct, but its wording may be problematic. Finally, expert reviewers can point out ways of tapping the construct that have not been included. There may be an approach that was overlooked or additional components that need to be included in the item pool.

Consider Inclusion of Validation Items

Validity is synonymous with accuracy or correctness. The overall validity of a measuring instrument is the extent to which differences in scores on it reflect true differences, rather than constant or random error. The goal of measurement is to accurately capture the characteristic of interest. For the purpose of validating a measure, some additional items should be included in the same questionnaire. There are two types of items to consider. The first type serves to detect flaws or problems. Respondents might not be answering the items the way in which would be assumed. There may be other motivations influencing their responses, such as social desirability. Evidence of this problem has been reported with satisfaction measures. By including a social desirability scale, the investigator can assess how strongly individual items are influenced by social desirability bias. Items in the satisfaction measure that correlate substantially with the social desirability score obtained should be considered candidates for exclusion unless there is sound theoretical reason that suggests otherwise.

The second type of items to consider including at this stage pertain to the construct validity (a component of overall validity) of the measure. If theory asserts that the phenomenon that is being measured relates to other constructs, the pattern of relationships between the satisfaction measure and these theoretically related constructs can provide support for claims of validity. For example, it may be expected that satisfied individuals are more likely to engage in positive word-of-mouth communication with others, and those who score low on the satisfaction measure are more likely to engage in negative word-of-mouth communication about the product or service being evaluated. Measuring word-of-mouth communication and correlating those behaviors with the satisfaction measure is one way to support the satisfaction measure's validity.

Administer Items to a Development Sample

Now, the questionnaire should be administered to a development sample. It should be large enough to conduct measure purification (see the Purify the Measure) and should be representative of the study population of interest. If this sample is too small or unrepresentative, patterns of covariation (degree of relationship) among measurement items may lead to erroneous conclusions. Without knowledge of results obtained in similar contexts of measurement, the exact number of subjects needed for this step cannot be determined. In the absence of such information, a sample of at least 200 subjects is a rule of thumb to provide sufficient stability to the analysis.

Purify the Measure

After an initial pool of items has been developed, scrutinized, and administered to an appropriately large and representative sample, it is time to evaluate the performance of the individual items so that appropriate ones can be identified to constitute the final form of the measure.

The process of assessing perfomance of individual items is called "measure purification" because changes are made to help improve the performance of the final measure that is accepted for use. Measure purification can include item reduction, item addition, and item rewording.

The purpose of any particular measurement is to estimate the score that is obtained if all of the hypothetically available items in the domain were used. In practice, only a sample of all potential items is used. Many techniques can be used to help select items for inclusion in the final measure. Most commonly, measure performance is viewed in terms of reliability and construct validity.

Reliability and construct validity are discussed briefly in their respective sections. For readers who are interested in learning more about reliability and validity, the annotated bibliography provides useful references.

Reliability

Most measures are composites formed from aggregating individual items into a scale. Internal consistency is a term used to describe estimates of reliability based on the average correlation among the measurement items. The recommended measure of the internal consistency of a set of items is provided by coefficient alpha. A low coefficient alpha (less than 0.70) indicates that the sample of items performs poorly in capturing the construct. If coefficient alpha is low, problematic items should be dropped from the measure.

A way to identify problematic items is to review item-to-total correlations, item variances, and item means. To arrive at a set of highly intercorrelated items, each individual item should correlate substantially with the collection of remaining items (item-to-total correlation). Another valuable attribute for an item is relatively high variance across subjects which suggests that the item response changes with varying levels of satisfaction. Also, homogeneity of variances among items is desirable which suggests that each item is contributing similarly to the measurement of a construct. Item means close to the center of the range of possible scores also are advantageous because items with means too near to an extreme of the response range are likely to have low variances and exhibit skewed distributions.

Construct Validity

The preceding steps should help produce an internally consistent set of items. Consistency is necessary but not sufficient for a good measure. The last step of measure purification is to assess the construct's validity. Construct validity is most directly related to the question of what the measurement is in fact measuring—what construct, trait, or concept underlies a person's score on a measure. To establish construct validity, the analyst must determine: 1) the extent to which the measure correlates with other measures designed to measure the same thing and 2) whether the measure behaves as expected.

A fundamental principle in construct validation is that any particular construct should be measurable by at least two different methods. Otherwise there is no way of knowing whether the construct is anything but an artifact of the measurement procedure. For example, suppose a self-administered patient satisfaction survey is distributed in a pharmacy by a friendly, well-liked pharmacist, and completed forms are returned to that same pharmacist. This method of administration might result in relatively high satisfaction scores because responses were influenced by who distributed and collected the survey. Another method (e.g., a mailed survey originating from the corporate headquarters and returned anonymously) might yield different results. Another example would be one survey in which items were worded positively compared to one in which the same items were used but now worded negatively. Again, different results could be obtained.

Two types of validity that can be used to support construct validity are convergent validity and discriminant validity. Convergent validity is the extent to which the measure correlates highly with other methods designed to measure the same construct. Discriminant validity is the extent to which the measure is indeed novel and not simply a reflection of some other variable.

There are many methods for assessing the convergent and discriminant validity of a measure but a discussion of each one would take the reader too far afield. Three methods are provided for interested readers. First, the traditional method of assessment is called the multitrait-multimethod (MTMM) matrix. The other methods that have been proposed to help overcome some of the limitations of the MTMM are: 1) confirmatory factor analysis and 2) the direct product model. Information about these methods is provided in the annotated bibliography (References 15-18).

The previous discussion of some measurement purification techniques has been provided to illustrate how prevalent and well developed measure purification tools are. The application of these techniques to patient satisfaction measures provides measures that lend evidence about the acceptability of a measure. The adoption of these techniques is important in patient satisfaction research so that decision-makers, such as administrators, benefit coordinators, and research colleagues can be confident in study results.

Optimize Practicality of the Measure

At this stage of the measure development process, the investigator has a carefully selected set of items that demonstrates acceptable reliability and validity. The final step before using the measure in the actual study is to assure that the measure is practical. For example, individuals' willingness to complete the questionnaire can be influenced by its length. Items might need to be dropped if the questionnaire is prohibitively long or complex.

Questionnaire length and complexity are not easily quantified. For example, the number of questions, number of pages, format and layout, print size, and level of cognitive effort needed to respond can contribute to a study subject's perception of the questionnaire's length and complexity. The main issue for the researcher is to design a questionnaire that most efficiently asks about all the elements that are important to the study. Pretesting and literature reviews will help in selecting questions that provide the information needed and also are clear, unambiguous, and interesting to the respondents. A rule of thumb is to ask only the questions that relate to the study's research question ... do not ask study subjects to answer additional questions just because the subjects' responses would be "interesting to know."

Often, reliability and validity are sacrificed when measures undergo item reduction. Thus, a balance between practicality and reliability/validity must be found. There should be a margin of safety maintained for reliability and validity when trying to optimize the length of a satisfaction measure.

Acquiescence

When using existing measures of satisfaction or when developing new measures for a specific research purpose, acquiescence can be a problem. Acquiescence is a culturally based tendency to agree with others. In most cultures, it is easier to agree than to disagree with someone when interacting with them. To illustrate this, researchers repeated an experiment seven times in which they asked respondents about whether proposals for increasing seat belt use would work. In their experiments, telephone respondents were significantly more likely than a comparable sample of mail respondents to agree with the proposals. Differences ranged from 5 to 23 percentage points in the seven experiments.

To overcome this problem, the use of a balanced multiple-item measure, asking several positively worded questions and several negatively worded questions, is something to consider for measuring patient satisfaction. This method tends to cancel out any systematic tendency to simply agree with items contained in the questionnaire and can help identify acquiescence in a study.

Case Mix

Finally, when comparing satisfaction among groups or individuals who belong to different health plans or access different care providers within a health plan, it is important to control for case mix. Case mix refers to the different patient attributes that might be apparent in different settings. To the extent that patients self-select or are assigned to different comparison groups in nonrandom ways, comparisons of satisfaction ratings may be biased by factors other than the provision of the health care services in the compared groups.

For example, relationships between health status and patient satisfaction have been reported. Thus, it is often prudent to control for the effects of health status when comparing patient satisfaction between or among groups. Other factors might account for differences in satisfaction scores, depending on the question being addressed in the study. Case mix control variables, such as age, gender, socioeconomic status, disease severity, physical functioning, service expertise, or service provider familiarity, also should be considered for inclusion in the study. Methods used to control or adjust for case mix variables can then be used (e.g., restriction, stratification, matching, and statistical adjustment).

Summary

Patient satisfaction is an individual's judgment about the extent to which a health care product or service provides a pleasurable level of consumption-related fulfillment. In the recent literature, patient satisfaction has been conceptualized in five ways: 1) performance evaluation, 2) disconfirmation of expectations, 3) affect-based evaluation, 4) equity-based evaluation, and 5) self-efficacy-based evaluation. Commonly used patient satisfaction measures include the PSQ and PSPSQ. However, no single standard measure of patient satisfaction is applicable to all situations. It is recommended that an existing measure of patient satisfaction, with demonstrated reliability and validity, should be used if it fits the construct domain of the study. Whenever a new satisfaction measure is needed, its conceptualization should be defined carefully and a systematic process for developing a measure should be followed.

Annotated Bibliography

1. Pasco GC. Patient satisfaction in primary health care: a literature review and analysis. Eval Program Plann 1983;6:185–210.
2. Hall JA, Dornan MC. What patients like about their medical care and how often they are asked: A meta-analysis of the satisfaction literature. Soc Sci Med 1988;27:935–9.

These articles (references 1 and 2) provide summaries for how patient satisfaction was viewed in the health care domain at about the time that Patient Satisfaction Questionnaire (PSQ) was developed. The authors showed that many patient satisfaction questionnaires did not sufficiently capture patients' true feelings about health care services and health care providers.

3. Schommer JC, Kucukarslan SN. Measuring patient satisfaction with pharmaceutical services. Am J Health-Syst Pharm 1997;54:2721–32.
4. Schommer JC, Wenzel RG, Kucukarslan SN. Evaluation of a pharmacist service for hospital patients. Am J Health-Syst Pharm 2002;59:1632-1637.

These articles (references 3 and 4) provide summaries for how patient satisfaction was viewed in the pharmacy services domain. The authors showed that there can be at least five conceptualizations of satisfaction including: performance evaluation, disconfirmation of expectations, affective-based evaluation, equity-based evaluation, and self-efficacy-based evaluation.

5. Ware, JE, Snyder, MK, Wright WR, et al. Development and validation of scales to measure patient satisfaction with medical care services. Vol I, Part A: Review of literature, overview of methods and results regarding construction of scales. Vol I, Part B: Results Regarding Scales Constructed from the Patient Satisfaction Questionaire and Measures of Other Health Care Perceptions Springfield, VA: National Technical Information Service; 1976. NTIS Publication No. PB 288-329.
6. Ware JE, Snyder MK, Wright R, and Davies AR. Defining and measuring patient satisfaction with medical care. Eval Program Plann 1983;6:247–63.

These articles (references 5 and 6) summarize the PSQ and provide background for how the measure was conceptualized and developed. The measure is based on salient aspects of a health care service and a health care provider's performance.

7. MacKeigan LD, Larson LN. Development and validation of an instrument to measure patient satisfaction with pharmacy services. Med Care 1989;27:522–36.
8. Larson LN, MacKeigan LD. Further validation of an instrument to measure patient satisfaction with pharmacy services. J Pharm Mark Manage 1994;8(1):125–39.
9. Larson LN, Rovers JP, MacKeigan LD. Patient satisfaction with pharmaceutical care: Update of a validated instrument. JAMA 2002;42(1):44–50.

These articles (references 7–9) summarize the PSPSQ and provide background for how the measure was conceptualized and developed. The measure is based on salient aspects of a health care service and a health care provider's performance. Recently, researchers further developed the measure so that it is applicable specifically to pharmaceutical care services.

10. Williams B. Patient satisfaction: a valid concept? Soc Sci Med 1994;38:509–16.
11. Hass M. A critique of patient satisfaction. Health Inf Manag 1999;29(1):9–13.

References 10 and 11 critique patient satisfaction. The validity of the satisfaction concept was critiqued based on the notion that many satisfaction measures do not adequately capture patients' true feelings and perspectives. Also, shortcomings in the conceptualization, measurement, and use of data related to patient satisfaction were proposed.

Measure Development

12. Churchill GA. Marketing Research Methodological Foundations. Orlando, FL: The Dryden Press; 1995.
13. DeVellis RF. Scale Development Theory and Applications. Newbury Park, CA: Sage Publications, Inc.; 1991.
14. Churchill GA. A Paradigm for Developing Better Measures of Marketing Constructs. J Mark Res 1979;16 (February):64–73.

References 12–14 are clear and easy to follow guides for developing measures for constructs, such as satisfaction.

Validity and Reliability

15. Peter JP. Construct validity: a review of basic issues and marketing practices. J Mark Res 1981;18(May):133–45.
16. Campbell DR, Fiske DW. Convergent and discriminant validation by the multitrait-multimethod matrix. Psychol Bull 1959; 56:81–105.
17. Bagozzi RP, Yi Y. Multitrait-multimethod matrices in consumer research. J Consum Res 1991;17:426–39.
18. Gerbing DW, Anderson JC. An updated paradigm for scale development incorporating unidimensionality and its assessment. J Mark Res 1988;25:186–92.
19. Nunnally JC, Bernstein IH. Psychometric Theory. New York, NY: McGraw-Hill; 1994.

References 15–19 are advanced discussions about validity and reliability. Not only do these authors discuss the definitions of validity and reliability, but also they outline different ways to assess validity and reliability of measures.

Data Collection

20. Mangione TW. Mail Surveys, vol. 40. Thousand Oaks, CA: Sate Publications, Inc.; 1995.
21. Dillman DA. Mail and Internet Surveys. New York, NY: John Wiley & Sons, Inc.; 1999.

Often, satisfaction questionnaires are administered through mailed survey. References 20 and 21 are valuable resources for the "how to" aspects of developing and administering mail surveys so that sample members will respond and give usable data.

Self-Assessment Questions

1. Which one of the following is not likely to differ between satisfied patients and unsatisfied ones ?
   A. Continued use of medical care services.
   B. Maintenance of a relationship with a specific service provider.
   C. Compliance with medical care regimens.
   D. Use of less expensive medical care services.

2. The consistency of how a product is manufactured or the service is delivered is called which one of the following?
   A. Quality of conformance.
   B. Quality of design.
   C. Quality of care.
   D. Quality improvement.

3. Compared to evaluating the quality of products, services possess unique characteristics from products, which make evaluating them a greater challenge. Services are which one of the following?
   A. Tangible, inseparable from production, and can vary from provider to provider.
   B. Intangible, inseparable from production, and are consistent from patient to patient.
   C. Intangible, inseparable from production, and can vary from provider to provider.
   D. Tangible, separable from production, and can vary from patient to patient.

4. Conceptualizations of patient satisfaction should not be based on which one of the following?
   A. Performance evaluation.
   B. Disconfirmation of expectations.
   C. Persuasion-based assessment.
   D. Equity-based assessment.

5. Which one of the following conceptualizations of satisfaction is best for a service that has characteristics that individuals can identify and understand?
   A. performance evaluation.
   B. Disconfirmation of expectations.
   C. Affect-based assessment.
   D. Equity-based assessment.

6. Which one of the following conceptualizations of satisfaction is best described as a "consumer fulfillment response" to a service experience?
   A. Performance evaluation.
   B. Disconfirmation of expectations.
   C. Affect-based assessment.
   D. Equity-based assessment.

7. Which one of the following conceptualizations of satisfaction is best described as the comparison of one's outcomes versus input with respect to someone else's outcomes versus input?
   A. Performance evaluation.
   B. Disconfirmation of expectations.
   C. Affect-based assessment.
   D. Equity-based assessment.

8. The patient satisfaction literature in pharmacy has followed two paths. One is rooted in the medical literature and the other is rooted in the marketing literature. Which one of the following statements is true about patient satisfaction literature in the pharmacy domain?
   A. The medical literature provides the best way to measure patient satisfaction because it views satisfaction as an experience-based performance evaluation of different service dimensions.
   B. The marketing literature provides the best way to measure patient satisfaction because it views satisfaction as having both an evaluative and affective component and is focused on an individual's reaction to a particular service experience.
   C. Neither the medical nor the marketing literature provides an acceptable way for measuring patient satisfaction with pharmacy services because they do not capture the unique aspects of these services.
   D. A single, standard conceptualization of patient satisfaction will not be applicable to all pharmacy service situations and, thus, many conceptualizations should be considered.

9. Which one of the following critiques of patient satisfaction measurement and research deals with the assumption that dissatisfaction is the opposite of satisfaction?
   A. Problems with conceptualization.
   B. Problems with measurement.
   C. Problems with interpretation.
   D. Problems with use.

10. A hospital-based headache clinic faced the decision concerning whether to retain a pharmacist who provided direct patient care about pharmaceuticals these patients take and how best to manage them. The clinic conducted a 1-year trial with the pharmacist actively counseling and caring for patients who were admitted as inpatients to the clinic. A patient satisfaction study that asked inpatients about their stay at the headache clinic indicated satisfaction with the clinic went down significantly from the year before the pharmacist was employed compared to the year the pharmacist was employed. The drop in satisfaction with the clinic suggested to one administrator that the pharmacist should not be retained. Which one of the following might be wrong with this conclusion?
    A. There is evidence that acquiescent response affected the results of this study.
    B. The wrong patient population was surveyed.
    C. There was no adjustment for case mix.
    D. The satisfaction measure was not a specific measure of patient satisfaction with the pharmacist.

11. A health insurance company measured patient satisfaction with services provided at 16 different pharmacist-managed anticoagulation clinics that had sent claims to them in the past year. An equity-based measure of satisfaction was used. The company found that six of the anticoagulation clinics exhibited significantly poorer satisfaction scores compared to the other 10 clinics. Based on site-visit data, the company had found no significant differences in procedures, or quality of care provided by the clinic personnel. However, the company did find that the six "lower satisfaction" clinics had patients with more comorbiditics, more drugs taken daily, and were more likely to have international normalized ratio values outside of target ranges at their first clinic visit. Such

information would highlight the need to consider which one of the following in the analysis of satisfaction scores?

A. Conceptualization of satisfaction.
B. Acquiescent response.
C. Case mix.
D. Measure development process.

Exercises

1. Choose a patient-oriented service. Think about which conceptualization of patient satisfaction is best for the evaluation of this service. Specify the domain of the satisfaction construct identified, generate a pool of at least five items, and determine the format of the measure. Then, have this initial pool of items reviewed by at least two colleagues. What was their reaction to the items? What changes to the items did the colleagues suggest? What was learned about the challenge of developing new satisfaction measures?

Explanation of the participant exercise: Expert review can confirm or invalidate the definition of the construct. The panel can be asked to rate how relevant they think each item is to what is the intended measure. Also, reviewers can evaluate the items' clarity and conciseness. The content of an item may be relevant to the construct, but its wording may be problematic. Finally, expert reviewers can point out ways of tapping the construct that have not been included. There may be an approach that was overlooked or additional components that need to be included in the item pool.

2. Choose a patient-oriented service. Prepare a definition of patient satisfaction with that service that is:

   A. Performance-based.
   B. Disconfirmation of expectations-based.
   C. Affect-based.
   D. Equity-based.

Which of these conceptualizations of satisfaction seems best? Why? Which aspect of the service was the focus as definitions were prepared? Which conceptualization of patient satisfaction would be best for the service?

Explanation of the participant exercise: When using patient satisfaction as an indicator of service quality, one must select an appropriate conceptualization of satisfaction that is relevant to decision-making and quality improvement. Any of these conceptualizations can be useful as the basis of satisfaction measurement depending on the anticipated use of the patient satisfaction measure.

MEASURING WORK OUTCOMES

Debra Lerner, M.S. Ph.D.,
Kathleen M. Bungay, Pharm.D.

Outline

I. Introduction/Background for Measuring Work Outcomes
  A. In the early 20th century, clinicians and scientists began studying how, and to what degree, illnesses and medical treatments affect ability to work.
  B. Within the last few decades, the impact of health problems and treatment on a person's ability to work has become a marker for functional health status and health-related quality of life. It has also become an important component of treatment cost-effectiveness analyses.
  C. Recently, the productivity loss of sick or injured employees gained currency, mainly among employer purchasers of health care, as a barometer for gauging the economic burden of health problems and the value of health improvement initiatives.
  D. Work outcomes (definition)—the degree to which a person's health status, or health-related interventions, have influenced the quantity and/or quality of a person's participation in the labor market.
  E. Four categories of work outcome indicators:
    1. Employment status,
    2. time loss,
    3. role function, and
    4. productivity loss.

II. Rationale for Measuring Work Outcomes
  A. The social importance of employment is a reason for studying labor market participation in relation to health.
    1. Paid work is considered a normative activity, while the absence of employment in some groups is regarded as deviant and even stigmatized.
    2. Work provides structure and a sense of purpose.
    3. Usually the main determinant of material wealth and a person's location in the social and economic strata.
    4. A source of social relationships and important social supports.
    5. A positive or negative assessment of work has a large influence on an individual's subjective perception of his/her quality of life overall.
    6. The social importance of work in societies is used to justify including "ability to work" as a criterion for determining what constitutes being "healthy," and a "good" health-related quality of life.
  B. Employment as an economic activity also provides a rationale for focusing on work outcomes in clinical care and research.
    1. Direct Costs
      a. Many who study health care financing and delivery issues have come to appreciate that illness has certain "direct costs."
        i. Utilization of services for medical diagnosis and treatment.
    2. Indirect costs
      a. In deliberations concerning the value of new technologies or specific medical interventions, consideration is given to the impact on "indirect costs."

i. Costs associated with a diminished capacity to work and be productive (sometimes called "indirect costs").

III. Work Outcomes Definitions; three major concepts:

A. The Work Role—work outcome measures differ with regard to how they operationalize work.

1. The work role is the prime context in which labor market participation occurs.

2. Measuring work outcomes inevitably involves formulating questions about a person's ability to perform work roles.

3. We usually think of work roles in terms of occupational categories (e.g., a registered nurse) or job titles (e.g., a hospital critical care unit nurse) which may mask the myriad of activities that make up a person's work; the activities that need to be measured to capture work outcomes.

a. The concept of work role is invoked in two principle ways in work outcomes measurement.

i. Global Work Indicators

A) Are general and ask about the impact of health problems on work (or "work activities").

B) Differ from the "role-level" questions because they do not ask the manner in which, or degree to which, health problems have affected performance of work or work activities.

C) The exact meaning of "work" or "work activities" is not defined.

D) Examples of global indicators: EuroQol; Quality of Well Being Scale (QWB); SF-36 role questions; Sickness Impact Profile (SIP).

E) Advantages: brief; practical; provide important summary information; useful information for identifying problems; targeting high-risk populations; and designing health-improvement strategies.

F) Disadvantages: by not specifying the meaning of work, it is up to the respondent to decide what are the exact parameters of his/her work role; lack of specificity introduces some risk of measurement error; additionally, role-level questions may provide too little detail about the specific aspects of work with which health problems interfere.

ii. Role Level Measures

A) Questionnaire items focus on the person's ability to perform specific job demands.

1) Occupations with the same names can involve very different activities and reward systems, and can be carried out in vastly different organizational settings.

2) Scientists have developed various methodologies for classifying and describing jobs and occupations according to the specific content; that is, what people do versus what they are called.

a) Many of the widely used approaches to classifying work disaggregate occupations and jobs into specific requirements or demands.

b) These classification systems permit more accurate specification of a person's work and group comparisons. (For examples see O*NET *http://online.onetcenter.org/main.html*)

c) O*NET replaced the Dictionary of Occupational Titles (*http://www.oalj.dol.gov/libdot.htm*)

B) Advantages

1) Work outcome measures focused on the demand-level of work better identify aspects of work affected by illness or treatment, and reduce error due to vague terminology.

2) More specific work outcome indicators tend to supply more variation in responses, which is important to detecting group differences and trends.

C) Disadvantages

1) If written too narrowly, they may not be relevant to certain groups of respondents.

2) Too many detailed items may increase respondent burden.

B. Work Disability

1. Multiple work outcomes measures attempt to assess apects of "work disability."

a. "Disability"

i. Refers to a unique dimension of health status with defined attributes.

ii. Is the result of a complex interaction between a person's functional limitations (health-related restrictions on a person's ability to perform social role tasks and obligations), and the physical and social environment.

A) Is defined as "the expression of a physical or mental limitation in a social context."

B) Implies a discrepancy or gap between a person's physical and mental capabilities, the demands associated with a particular role or environment, and the supports available to that individual.

C) Occurs when there is a lack of a "fit" between a person and a specific social role or context.

iii. The same pathology, impairment, or functional limitation may become a disability in some situations, but not in others.

iv. A disability may be reduced, or eliminated, by instituting health interventions, modifying role demands, improving supports, providing job retraining services, instituting job accommodations and the like.

b. Disability measures

i. Disability is an outcome of the person/role interaction, and not a characteristic of the person. Valid measures characterize the fit rather than an individual's attributes.

ii. The nature of disability suggests that work outcomes measures must employ criteria that are context-specific.

iii. Disabilities may range in duration from short-term, or temporary, to long-term or permanent; and vary by degree (i.e., from partial to total).

iv. Some people who can be considered to have disabilities may be totally unable to work, while others will be employed and have what might be termed "on-the-job disabilities."

v. Studies measuring work outcomes only in terms of disabilities may not adequately detect abilities.

vi. Measuring only work disabilities may also lead to the neglect of other work outcomes, such as subjectively assessed quality of working life or job satisfaction, which may be of value in studies of groups that are vulnerable to work disabilities.

C. Work Productivity

1. Work productivity is a third concept relevant to measuring work outcomes, in addition to work role and disability.

2. Assessing the productivity impact associated with health and medical care is fast becoming a main concern of employers.

3. While usually regarded as an employer issue, productivity loss is also a relevant concern for some employees, especially individuals whose opportunities for advancement and compensation are tied to their productivity.

4. Productivity losses may occur if:

a. A person stops working entirely (e.g., due to premature death or total disability),

b. Is prevented from working (e.g., by workplace safety regulations),

c. Reduces the time or effort spent on work activities,

d. Performs less than optimally while working, or

e. Leaves the job (e.g., turnover).

5. Measurement considerations for work productivity.

a. Productivity at the individual worker level (as distinct from the employer level) usually refers to the physical output of the worker, or the goods and services generated through paid work activity.

b. A related perspective defines productivity in terms of a ratio of the amount of physical outputs to the amount of input resources (e.g., labor hours, materials and management time).

i. Recent trends include efforts to incorporate measurement of the quality of goods and services generated, and not simply the amount.

c. Worker productivity is measured differently by different industries and employers.

d. How work productivity is already measured by the workplace has implications for work outcomes measurement.

e. Questions can be perceived as threatening:

i. Sensitive or threatening questions about personal productivity will tend to influence the accuracy of responses.

ii. Care must be used to ensure that questions about the impact of an illness on work productivity are neutral.

f. Timing of questions.

i. Need a timeframe that results in the most accuracy for reporting productivity.

ii. Productivity measurement can be especially sensitive to timing issues because of differences in the production processes associated with different positions, firms, and industries.

iii. A worker may experience problems carrying out certain role tasks for a short period. The problem may have no discernible effect on the output side (e.g., if the person can make up for lost time by coming in late, but working harder than usual until things get done).

V. Survey Measures of Work Outcomes

A. This section is an overview of the available work outcomes measurement tools.

B. There are four main classes of indicators that cover the conceptualizations of work role, disability, and work productivity: a) employment status, b) time loss, c) functional limitations, and d) productivity.

1. Employment status

a. Measures in this category include employment status, post-illness job loss, and post-illness or post-treatment return to work.

b. Employment status usually is measured by asking the respondent what he or she was mainly doing during a specific period of time (such as the past 4 weeks).

i. The choices might include categories such as employed full-time, employed part-time, unemployed, retired, or disabled.

c. In studies concerning populations that recently experienced a disruption of work activity after a health event (e.g., myocardial infarction, hospitalization or work injury), the scientist is usually interested in establishing whether the person has returned to his/her usual type, or level, of work activity.

i. Thus, pre- and post-event employment status questions may be supplemented with others (e.g., changes in full-time or part-time work, occupation, and job modifications).

d. Reasons for the popularity of measuring employment status as a work outcome.

i. It corresponds to the fact that it is relatively easy to ascertain.

ii. The categories represent socially and economically meaningful consequences (especially in cases of diminished work activity subsequent to a health event).

iii. Reports are considered "objective," not evaluative.

iv. Loss of paid employment in working-age populations is a credible indicator.

v. It serves as a basis for estimating productivity loss and associated costs.

vi. Scientists also find employment variables useful.

A) The large amount of normative and comparative data available is helpful for interpreting the results of a study.

B) Employment status variables can also be applied to both working and nonworking populations.

e. Weaknesses of employment status questions.

i. They are very coarse for describing outcomes.

ii. Loss of employment, or certain occupational transitions, usually can be interpreted as unsuccessful outcomes.

iii. "Employment" may hide partial work disabilities leading, in some cases, to diminished work productivity and job satisfaction.

iv. Employment also tells us nothing about the quality of the work experience from the worker's perspective and may misrepresent the "success" of the outcome.

v. Another issue concerning the use of employment status, as well as some other work outcomes, is that it may result from influences that are not related, directly or even indirectly, to the worker's health.

vi. Employment gains and losses can occur relatively infrequently in many groups.

2. Time Loss

a. The amount of time people miss from work due to health or medical care is frequently used to reflect work disability and lost productivity.

b. Several of the approaches used to measure time loss were based on "disability day" questions.

basis for many such measures.

A) The NHIS approach attempts to capture the number of full and part days missed attributed to health problems and, consequently, captures the complete inability to work during the time period (total disabilities), and days in which the worker was partially disabled.

ii. Self-reported lost work time was measured in a variety of chronic diseased populations.

A) Several versions of questions were developed, including those that ask respondents to report on the number of whole days and part days missed from work over a defined time period, the number of days they were late for work, or left work early due to illness, and the number of whole, or part, days spent in bed.

B) Questions vary with regard to the period of time referenced.

C) However, an important consideration in choosing a measure is the degree to which the time period will introduce recall bias.

1) Recall bias, errors due to faulty memory, is largely attributable to two types of errors:

a) Omissions of incidences of time missed within the reference period.

b) Inclusion of some that occurred before, or after, the period (i.e., "telescoping").

2) In addition to pre-testing measures, options for reducing recall bias include using time loss diaries and shortening recall periods.

a) Diaries tend to eliminate recall errors, but are expensive to administer, and respondents have to be reminded repeatedly to complete them.

3) The disadvantage of relatively short recall periods (e.g., 1- or 2-week intervals) is that they can skew the data in the direction of zero time loss (because little or no work time is missed), and constrain statistical power.

D) Time-based measures are fast becoming popular productivity/cost indicators, but clinicians and researchers interpreting the results should not overlook the human burden (real consequences of increased workloads, time pressures, lost pay) associated with missed work time.

3. Functional and Disability Measures
    a. Many questionnaires measure the degree to which health problems interfere with the ability to work.
    b. These questionnaires are of two types:
        i. Interviewer-administered,
        ii. Self-administered.
    c. Work outcome items are embedded in a more comprehensive health status assessment instrument.
    d. Examples
        i. The Euroqol Instrument now referred to as the EQ5D represents a global measurement approach.
            A) This is a health-related quality-of-life assessment tool, providing self-reported data concerning limitation in usual activities.
            B) It uses a three-level response scale to grade ability.
            C) A single set of items is used to address multiple roles.
            D) A single set of role-level items simultaneously addresses problems in employment, housework, schoolwork, family life, and leisure.
        ii. The QWB:
            A) Is administered by an interviewer in a semi-structured format;
            B) is based on NHIS items;
            C) aggregates data about activity limitations into an overall score; and
            D) the scale items are weighted to reflect heath-state preferences.
        iii. The Medical Outcome Study SF-36
            A) Contains one battery addressing role limitations due to physical health problems, and another for emotional health problems.
            B) Paid work activity is not addressed separately from other work activities.
            C) The role-physical health scale contains adapted, more detailed versions of the NHIS items.
            D) It also includes additional criteria for defining role limitation, and includes questions concerning inability to accomplish as much as usual, and difficulty performing roles described parenthetically as requiring extra effort.
            E) The emotional health scale excludes some of the physical scale items and adds a criterion; being unable to work as carefully as usual.
        iv. The Sickness Impact Profile (SIP)
            A) Contains a separate paid work question battery and reports a scale score to assess any disability.
            B) Role limitation criteria overlap with those embedded in the SF-36 and the NHIS.
            C) Two items address impact on the amount of work done (i.e., working shorter hours and doing part of job at home).
            D) Two items cover the kind of work (i.e., doing light work and working with some changes).
            E) Also asks about accomplishments and care in doing work and two additional issues, irritability toward others and interrupted work.
        v. Common features of the SIP and SF-36 questions:
            A) All are based substantially on the Activity Limitation battery of the NHIS and related surveys, such as the Current Population Survey administered by the U.S. Census Bureau.
                1) The NHIS ask respondents to name the condition(s) that caused any activity limitations. This methodology is designed to generate estimates of the number of people in the United States population who have severe work limitations (i.e., inability to work), or partial limitations (i.e., limits in amount, or kind of work performed).
            B) Both contain batteries to assess limitations in role activities, and distinct scale scores can be derived from these.
        vi. Common characteristics of all four Scales (Euroqol, QWB, SF-36, SIP).
            A) The role scales contained in these, and other health status questionnaires, generally have a high degree of validity and reliability across a range of different demographic groups, and a large body of comparative data is available.
            B) In addition, these measures are usually available in several formats (e.g., phone and mail), and are easy to administer.
            C) The major disadvantage of the role scales is that they are often not very discriminating with respect to social roles.

D) Except for the SIP, the rule scales tend to ask global questions (e.g., "Were [you] limited in the kind of work or other activities?"), which do not differentiate between paid and unpaid work.

E) In addition, some scales do not distinguish between gradations in level of work activity (e.g., mild, moderate and severe), and few employed respondents will tend to endorse the "unable to work" response. The results are often skewed toward high levels of functioning. Revisions in the SF-36 were developed to address these "floor effect" problems.

F) A final point about this group of instruments is that, except for the QWB, most of the items and the scale scores have no explicit economic interpretation.

G) They were developed as components of health status measures emphasizing the human burdens of health problems, rather than the economic implications.

H) The SF-36 and the SIP both address aspects of productivity (e.g., work quantity and quality), and with additional efforts, it may be possible to convert scores into an economic metric.

4. Work Productivity

a. Survey instruments are being developed to specifically measure productivity loss within the paid work domain.

i. Examples

A) Several, such as the Endicott Work Productivity Scale (EWPS),

B) the Migraine Work and Productivity Loss Questionnaire, and

C) the Angina Work Limitations Questionnaire (WLQ) are condition-specific.

ii. Content

A) Subjective assessments of effectiveness in performing work activities were used to assess work productivity loss in studies of depression and migraine headaches.

B) These surveys ask respondents to rate their effectiveness on the job on days they were symptomatic (e.g., during a migraine-headache episode).

C) Ratings scales run from 0 percent (not at all effective) to 100 percent (completely effective).

D) This information frequently is combined with time loss data (e.g., sickness absence data). Total productivity loss is estimated by the amount of lost wages. While easy to use, validation is limited.

iii. New Content

b. A small group of questionnaires is adding to the body of knowledge concerning two sources of productivity loss: losses due to missed work time ("absenteeism"), and those associated with an impaired ability to function while at work ("presenteeism"). Some studies estimate that productivity losses due to presenteeism are many orders of magnitude larger than those associated with missed work time. We focus on two questionnaires, but several are being tested.

i. Examples

A) The Health and Labor Questionnaire

1) Consists of four "modules," which address the following categories:

a) Work absences,

b) reduced on-the-job performance,

c) productivity in unpaid work, and

d) degree of trouble performing paid work.

2) Attempts to provide a comprehensive method for evaluating health-related productivity loss.

3) Tests of its performance are limited to small samples in the Netherlands, but results are encouraging.

B) The WLQ

1) A validated 25-item, self-administered, self-reported instrument measuring on-the-job work disability and productivity loss ("presenteeim").

2) Four scales reflect the multidimensional character of work roles.

a) The Time scale contains five items addressing time and scheduling demands.

b) The six-item Physical scale covers job tasks that involve bodily strength, movement, endurance, coordination and flexibility.

c) The Mental-Interpersonal Scale has nine items addressing cognitive and social tasks.

d) The Output Scale contains five items addressing diminished work productivity. Scale scores, which range from 0 (limited none of the time) to 100 (limited all of the time), represent the percentage of time in the past 2 weeks respondents had job performance limitations.

e) An empirically derived algorithm enables WLQ users to convert work limitation data into a productivity loss score.

3) The WLQ has demonstrated excellent psychometric performance.

V. Recommendations

A. Choosing the best measurement tool for the situation involves thinking about issues, such as the following:

1. Which aspects of work are hypothesized to be influenced by the illness or treatment being studied, and at what order of magnitude?
2. Over what period will these hypothesized effects occur, and how long will they last?
3. How important is it to be able to assign financial costs to these effects?
4. Are these guidelines for interpreting scores?

Learning Objectives

1. Define work outcomes.
2. Compare and contrast the various types of work outcomes that can be measured to assess health and health care.
3. Discuss the rationale for including work outcomes measures as endpoints in research.
4. Describe some available techniques for measuring work outcomes.
5. Devise applications for measurement of work outcomes in various settings.

Abbreviations in this chapter

EQ5D	Euroqol Instrument
EWPS	Endicott Work Productivity Scale
ICIDH-2	International Classification of Impairments, Activities, and Participation
IOM	Institute of Medicine
NHIS	National Health Interview Survey
QWB	Quality of Well-Being Scale
SF-36	Medical Outcomes Study SF-36
SIP	Sickness Impact Profile
WLQ	Work Limitations Questionnaire

Introduction

In the early 20th century, clinicians and scientists began studying how, and to what degree, illnesses and medical treatments affect ability to work. When physically-demanding work was more prevalent in the United States economy, a patient's return to work was regarded as a sign of successful recovery from physical illness. In the 1940's, employment was viewed as a sign of a patient's psychological adjustment to chronic illness and long-term treatment. Within the last few decades, the impact of health problems and treatment on a person's ability to work became a marker for functional health status and health-related quality of life. It has also become an important component of treatment cost-effectiveness analyses. Recently, the productivity loss of sick or injured employees is gaining currency, mainly among employer purchasers of health care, as a barometer for gauging the economic burden of health problems, and the value of health improvement initiatives.

Aims

This chapter will provide readers with the background for measuring work outcomes. As with other outcome measures used in clinical research, the term "work outcomes" refers to the end results of a process. Specifically, work outcomes indicate the degree to which a person's health status, or health-related interventions, have influenced the quantity and/or quality of a person's participation in the labor market. We discuss four categories of work outcome indicators. They include measures of employment, work time loss, role function, and productivity loss.

There are a variety of indicators and assessment tools used to measure work outcomes. The specific aims of this chapter are to: 1) indicate the rationale for including work outcome measures as endpoints in research; 2) describe the main concepts helpful to understanding, evaluating and improving measurement; and 3) identify some of the available techniques for measuring the four main types of work outcome indicators.

This chapter will focus on survey methods for eliciting information about the work impact of illness and treatment. This emphasis acknowledges that the perspectives of survey respondents, whether patients in medical settings, or employees in the workplace, are important to assess health status and the quality of care received. We do not address unpaid work, which has lagged behind the measurement of paid work outcomes, nor do we address provider-based assessment methods (e.g., work evaluations or functional capacity evaluations), or secondary data sources that may contain relevant information, but usually are not accessible for research (e.g., employer databases).

Rationale for Measuring Work Outcomes

There are several powerful reasons for monitoring and evaluating the impact of illness and/or treatment on the ability to work. Advocates for the use of such measures point to the social importance of employment as reason to study labor market participation in relation to health. In the United States and elsewhere, paid work is considered a normative activity, while the absence of employment, in some groups, is regarded as deviant, and even stigmatized. For many individuals, work provides structure and a sense of purpose. It is usually the main determinant of material wealth and a person's location in the social and economic strata. It is also a source of social relationships and, sometimes, important social supports. Not surprisingly, a positive or negative assessment of work has a large influence on an individual's subjective perception of his/her quality of life overall. Indeed, the social importance of work in various societies is frequently used as justification for including "ability to work" as a criterion for determining what constitutes being "healthy," and a "good" health-related quality of life.

The importance of employment as an economic activity also provides a strong rationale for focusing on work outcomes in clinical care and research. Many who study health care financing and delivery issues have come to appreciate that illness has certain "direct costs" related to the utilization of services for medical diagnosis and treatment, and costs associated with a diminished capacity to work and be productive (sometimes called "indirect costs"). A body of research is accumulating that carefully documents the productivity losses and costs associated with various chronic conditions, such as depression, allergies, arthritis, and heart disease, and even acute conditions such as the common cold. Thus, increasingly in deliberations concerning the value of new technologies, or specific medical interventions, consideration is given to the impact on indirect costs: the portion of total health care costs resulting from decreased productivity, mainly in paid work.

Work Outcomes Definitions

Developing survey instruments that are useful–in other words, that are reliable, valid, and practical and able to produce meaningful information, is invariably a complicated undertaking (this topic is addressed elsewhere in this volume). Work outcomes measurement has its own unique considerations. Work outcomes refer to the quantity, or quality, of labor market participation. There are three major concepts germane to how work outcomes are measured: work role, work disability, and work productivity.

The Work Role

The first concept is the "work role." The work role is the prime context in which labor market participation occurs. Thus, measuring work outcomes inevitably involves formulating questions about the ability to perform work roles.

The term "social role" frequently is used in health research with little attention to its meaning (sociologists also vary in the definitions of the concept). A "social role" generally refers to an aggregate set of actions, or shared expectations, for an action associated with a specific context. Within the sociological perspective, work roles are related to the broader concept of "social role." We usually think of work roles in ways that are relatively imprecise for measuring; occupational categories (e.g., a registered nurse), or job titles (e.g., a hospital critical care unit nurse). This everyday terminology masks the myriad of activities that make up a person's work; the activities that need to be measured to capture work outcomes.

The concept of work role is invoked in two principle ways in work outcomes measurement. One approach is the use of global indicators; the second approach is to measure the specific demands of the work.

Global work indicators are more general and ask about the impact of health problems on work (or "work activities"). The "role-level" questions address the manner in which, or degree to which, health problems affect performance of work or work activities. And the exact meaning of "work" or "work activities" is not defined. Global questions have the advantage of brevity and practicality. They can provide important summary information. However, by not specifying the meaning of work, it is up to the respondent to decide what are the exact parameters of his/her work role. Lack of specificity introduces some risk of measurement error. For instance, a person who has trouble commuting due to back pain may, or may not, consider it a "work" problem. Also, because work arrangements have changed dramatically in recent years, the divisions between work and home life are blurred. In addition, role-level questions may provide too little detail about the specific aspects of work with which health problems interfere. However, this type of information can be useful information for identifying problems, targeting high-risk populations, and designing health-improvement strategies. Examples of global indicators, such as the SF-36 role questions, are discussed later in this chapter.

A second approach to measuring work outcome indicators has emerged; it is more consistent with current concepts of work assessment in the social science disciplines. This approach is aimed at assessing work role performance, but uses questionnaire items addressing the person's ability to perform specific aspects of the job. Assessing role performance can be thought of as analogous to the health status conceptualization of the "disease" specific approach to health assessment. In this case, performance of a specific role is assessed. Accordingly, global work indicators are analogous to general (or generic) health status assessment. The premise for assessing role performance is that questions asking about the ability to perform specific job demands, such as participating in meetings or lifting heavy objects, will generate more information about the impact of health problems on a person's ability to work, if the items capture the relevant attributes of the work role.

Social scientists, and those involved in occupational health research, have provided various frameworks which assist in the specification of work roles. They have long recognized that occupations with the same names can involve very different activities and reward systems, and they can be carried out in vastly different organizational settings. To bypass some of the measurement issues inherent in studying work, scientists have developed various methodologies for classifying and describing jobs and occupations according to their specific content (i.e., what people do versus what they are called). Many of the widely used approaches to classifying work disaggregate occupations and jobs into specific requirements or demands. These classification systems permit a more accurate specification of a person's work and group comparisons (e.g., see O*NET *http://online.onetcenter.org/main.html*, which replaced the Dictionary of Occupational Titles *http://www.oalj.dol.gov/libdot.htm*).

Work outcome measures focused on the demand-level of work, or other job attributes may better identify aspects of work affected by illness or treatment and, thus, reduce the error due to vague terminology with work role-level questions. Additionally, more specific work outcomes indicators will tend to supply more variation in responses, which is important to detecting group differences and trends. However, drawbacks to demand-specific questions are that, if written too narrowly (e.g., a demand that is very specific to a particular line of work), they may not be relevant to certain groups of respondents, and too many detailed items may increase respondent burden.

Work Disability

Another conceptualization of work outcomes also can be characterized in terms of the degree to which they invoke the concept of disability. Not all do, but many measures contain items that capture aspects of disability. This conceptualization of work disability is in contrast to the conceptualizations of work role and work productivity as frameworks for measuring work outcomes. Several work outcomes measures are linked to the concept, "disability." In health research, the term "disability" refers to a unique dimension of health status with defined attributes. The concept "disability" is contained in several of the new health status taxonomies including the World Health Organization. These taxonomies were created in response to criticisms of the traditional biomedical model of health, which tended to define health as the "absence of disease." "Health" has evolved into a much broader, multi-dimensional concept, incorporating multiple health states such as impairment, functional limitation, and disability. See Table 1 for more details of the comparison of two such taxonomies.

For purposes of exploring the topic of work disability measurement, we will focus on the well-known Institute of Medicine (IOM) report on the subject. Accordingly, disability is "the expression of a physical or mental limitation in a social context–the gap between a person's capabilities and the demands of the environment." Disability is the result of a complex interaction between a person's functional limitations (health-related restrictions on a person's ability to perform social role tasks and obligations), and the physical and social environment in which such performances occur. A disability implies a discrepancy or gap between a person's physical and mental

Table 1. Definitions of Disability

Institute of Medicine Model

Pathology	Impairment	Functional Limitations	Disability
Interruption or interference of normal bodily processes or structures	Loss and/or abnormality of mental, emotional, physiological, or anatomical structure or function; includes all losses or abnormalities, not just those attributable to active pathology; also includes pain	Restriction or lack of ability to perform an action or activity in the manner or within the range considered normal that results from impairment (i.e., inability to climb stairs or read)	Inability or limitation in performing socially defined activities and roles expected of individuals within a social and physical environment (i.e., performance as a parent, spouse, partner, or employee)

World Health Organization Model

Disease	Impairment	Disability	Handicap
The intrinsic pathology or disorder (i.e., disease, injury, or congenital malformation)	Organic dysfunction (i.e., anatomic, physiologic, or psychological deficits)	Difficulty performing tasks of everyday life (i.e., both role functioning and physical functioning)	Disadvantages with respect to social roles or physical environment (i.e., restricted employment opportunities)

Adapted with permission. Disability in America: toward a national agenda for prevention. Washington, DC: National Academy Press, 1991 and from Verbrugge LM. The iceberg of disability. In: Stahl SM, ed. The legacy of longevity: health and health care in later life. Newbury Park, CA: Sage Publications, 1990. Copyright © 1991 by the National Academy of Sciences. Courtesy of the National Academics Press, Washington, D.C.

The World Health Organization has updated conceptualization of disability. It is included in a document called the International Classification of Impairments, Activities and Participation (ICIDH-2). At the time of this publication, a Beta-2 Draft was being tested in the field. For a formal reference and updates see *http://www3.who.int/icf/icftemplate.cfm.*

capabilities, the demands associated with a particular role or environment, and the supports available to that individual.

Disabilities are sometimes confused with functional limitations. Disabilities refer specifically to a person's performance of specific social roles (e.g., parent, spouse/partner, and employee), while functional limitations refer to the performance of tasks that may occur in many different settings (e.g., inability to climb stairs or read).

Disabilities occur when there is a lack of a "fit" between a person and a specific social role or context. Thus, the same pathology, impairment or functional limitation, may become a disability in some situations, but not in others. A person who has an impairment, such as a loss in cognitive function due to stroke, may be able to manage a household, but be disabled as a schoolteacher. A stroke may be highly disabling in an employee requiring long-term memory, such as a taxi driver, who needs to remember streets and routes, but not nearly as disabling as a supermarket cashier supported by computerized product codes. A disability may be reduced, or eliminated, by instituting health interventions, modifying role demands, improving supports, providing job retraining services, and instituting job accommodations.

Measuring disability has obvious applicability to studies that measure the effects of illness or treatment on labor force participation. However, adherence to definitions of disability can create measurement challenges (e.g., because disability is an outcome of the person/role interaction, and not a characteristic of the person, valid measures would characterize the fit, rather than an individual's attributes). Moreover, the nature of disability suggests that work outcomes measures must employ criteria that are context-specific and, thus, address employment. Additionally, current concepts of disability suggest there is a spectrum of levels and types of disabilities that could be measured. Disabilities may range in duration from short-term or temporary, to long-term or permanent; and vary by degree (i.e., from partial to total). Thus, some people considered to have disabilities may be totally unable to work, while others will be employed and have what might be termed "on-the-job disabilities."

The concept also may be limiting in that studies measuring work outcomes only in terms of disabilities may not adequately detect abilities. Finally, measuring only work disabilities also may lead to the neglect of other work outcomes, such as subjectively assessed quality of working life or job satisfaction, which may be of value in studies of groups that are vulnerable to work disabilities.

Work Productivity

Work outcomes measures can also be classified in terms of the degrees to which they are indicators of productivity. Work productivity is a third dimension characterizing work outcomes in addition to work role and disability. Assessing the productivity impact associated with health and medical care is fast becoming a main concern of employers. Productivity losses may occur if a person stops working entirely (e.g., due to premature death or total disability); is prevented from working (e.g., by workplace safety regulations); reduces the time or effort spent on work activities; performs less than optimally while working; or leaves the job (e.g., turnover). While usually regarded as an employer issue, productivity loss is also a relevant concern for some employees, especially individuals whose opportunities for advancement and compensation are tied to productivity.

Despite the acknowledged importance of productivity as a work outcome, measurement is difficult. Productivity at the individual worker level (as distinct from the employer level) usually refers to the physical output of the worker, or the goods and services generated through paid work activity. A related perspective defines productivity in terms of a ratio of the amount of physical outputs to the amount of input resources (e.g., labor hours, materials and management time). Recent trends include efforts to incorporate measurement of the quality of goods and services generated, and not simply the amount. In general, worker productivity is measured differently by different industries and employers.

Various properties of how work productivity is measured in the workplace have implications for work outcomes measurement. One implication is the great range of variation in productivity criteria, which makes it difficult to create questionnaires that apply to many different groups of employees. Another problem is that, in some job situations, productivity is difficult to define and individual's views within the same jobs may vary on what counts as being productive (e.g., a day spent writing [and rewriting] a book chapter may be regarded by some colleagues as a wasted day, but another colleague might regard it as quite productive).

Next, productivity can be a sensitive topic, and/or questions regarding personal productivity may be perceived as threatening. Sensitive or threatening questions will tend to influence the accuracy of responses. Thus, care must be used to ensure that questions about the impact of an illness on work productivity are neutral.

Finally, identifying appropriate frames of reference within which productivity is measured can be troublesome. While many survey questions benefit from including specific reference periods (e.g., the past 2 weeks), it is challenging to define the timeframe that results in the most accuracy for reporting productivity. Productivity measurement can be especially sensitive to timing issues because of differences in the production processes associated with different positions, firms and industries. Thus, a worker may experience problems carrying out certain role tasks for a short time period. These problems may have no discernible effect on the output side if, for example, the person can make up for lost time by coming in late, but working harder than usual until things get done.

Survey Measures of Work Outcomes

In this section, we offer an overview of the available work outcomes measurement tools. There are four main classes of indicators that cover the conceptualizations of work roles, disability, and work productivity. Those measuring: 1) employment status; 2) time loss; 3) role function; and 4) productivity loss.

Employment

Historically, in clinical research, characteristics of a person's employment were used in both studies of disability and/or productivity. Measures in this category include employment status, post-illness job loss, and post-illness or treatment return to work.

Employment status usually is measured by asking the respondent what he/she was mainly doing during a specific time period (such as the past 4 weeks). The choices might include categories, such as employed full-time or part-time, unemployed, retired, or disabled. Sometimes researchers also include questions to determine what the "not working" group is doing using categories such as "unemployed and looking for work," "temporarily laid off or on sick or other leave," "disabled," "retired," "homemaker," or "other."

In studies concerning populations that recently experienced a disruption of work activity after a health event (e.g., myocardial infarction, hospitalization or work injury), the scientist is usually interested in establishing whether the person has returned to his/her usual type, or level, of work activity. Thus, pre- and post-event employment status questions may be supplemented with others asking about changes in full- or part-time work, occupation, and job modifications.

The popularity of measuring employment status as a work outcome corresponds to the fact that it is relatively easy to ascertain, the categories represent socially and economically meaningful consequences (especially in cases of diminished work activity subsequent to a health event), and reports are considered "objective" not evaluative. Also, loss of paid employment in working-age populations is a credible indicator of disability, as well as lost productivity. It serves as a basis for estimating productivity loss and associated costs. Scientists also find employment variables useful because of the large amount of normative and comparative data available, which is helpful for interpreting the results of a study. Employment status variables also have the advantage of applying to both working and non-working populations. Some measures, such as time lost due to work absences, apply only to the employed.

However, employment status questions suffer from several weaknesses. First, they are very coarse with regard to describing outcomes. Loss of employment, or certain occupational transitions, usually can be interpreted as unsuccessful outcomes. However, it is not as easy to determine if employment represents a positive result. For example, "employment" may hide partial work disabilities leading in some cases to diminished work productivity and job satisfaction. Employment also tells us nothing about the quality of the work experience from the worker's perspective, and may misrepresent the "success" of the outcome.

Employment status also may not accurately reflect a person's outcome. This may not be a limitation of employment status questions; rather it is a feature of the tendency (in longitudinal studies) to measure employment status once, or only a few times, over a specified duration, and to omit questions about employment during interim periods. A study of work-related back injuries found that many workers post-injury move in, and out of, employment several times for health reasons and, thus, the measurement of impact is better served by creating variables for employment/disability trajectories.

Another issue concerning the use of employment status, as well as some other work outcomes, is that it may result from influences that are not related, directly or even indirectly, to the worker's health. The validity of the measure should be of concern in studies that do not, or cannot, take these other influences into account methodologically (e.g., using control groups). Survey questions that ask workers to report on job changes that are due to health or treatment may provide a solution, but attributions are subject to reporting problems.

Finally, employment gains and losses can occur relatively infrequently in many groups, and scientists who rely on employment indicators may not have adequate statistical power for certain analyses.

Time Loss

The amount of time people miss from work due to health or medical care is frequently used to reflect work disability and/or lost productivity. Several of the approaches used to measure time loss are based on "disability day" questions. The National Health Interview Survey (NHIS) approach, which is interviewer-administered, is the basis for many such measures. An NHIS interviewer asks respondents to report on the number of days during the past 2 weeks spent in bed all or most of the day because of a physical illness or injury. Follow-up questions ask specifically about days missed from work or school. The interviewer also asks about the number of days in that time period that the person cut down on things for as much as a day. The series is closed by asking about which condition(s) caused the person to miss days and cut down on activities. Thus, the NHIS approach attempts to capture the number of full and part days missed attributed to health problems and, consequently, captures the complete inability to work during the time period (total disabilities), and days in which the worker was partially disabled.

Self-reported lost work time was measured in a variety of study populations, including individuals with migraine headaches, angina pectoris, depression, anxiety, and other conditions. Several versions of questions were developed including those that ask respondents to report on the number of whole days and part days missed from work, over a defined time period, the number of days they were late for work or left work early due to illness, and the number of whole or part days spent in bed.

Respondents may be asked to report on the number of days any time was missed (frequency) and the total amount of time missed (quantity). The first approach, used in 1994, counts occasions of time loss, not total time missed (e.g., a 3-day absence is counted as one episode). It has particular applicability to studies that for practical reasons must rely on retrospective recall covering long time spans. The latter approach involves an actual count of days and/or hours missed, which is more typical in clinical research.

Results of studies measuring lost work time can report results as an absolute frequency of lost time, or as a ratio of the time lost divided by the amount of time a person was expected to work within a specified period. Relative measures (e.g., the percent of time lost) are superior, but acquiring the denominator can be tricky because of flexible work arrangements over time.

Questions vary with regard to the time period referenced. Surveys ask about time lost over periods of 7 days, 2 weeks, 4 weeks, 3 months, and 12 months. Determining which timeframe is the most appropriate depends partly on the course of an illness, or treatment effects (e.g., in migraine headache treatment studies, it may be desirable to determine how many hours were missed from work within a specific migraine episode). For groups such as chronic stable angina patients, who are expected to miss work infrequently or sporadically, it is more appropriate to ask about time loss during a period of weeks, or even months.

However, an important consideration in choosing a measure is the degree to which the time period will introduce recall bias. Recall bias, errors due to faulty memory, is largely attributable to two types of errors: omissions of incidences of time missed within the reference period; and inclusion of some that occurred before, or after, the period (referred to as "telescoping"). In a small pilot study, self-reported absences for four-week and three-month intervals were compared to employer records, and it was found that accuracy criteria were met. However, research in organizational psychology suggests that recall problems persist; especially the tendency to underreport work absences.

In addition to pre-testing measures, options for reducing recall bias include using time loss diaries and shortening recall periods. Although diaries tend to eliminate recall errors, they can be expensive to administer. In addition, given the response burden, respondents have to be reminded repeatedly to complete them. The disadvantage of relatively short recall periods (e.g., 1- or 2- week intervals) is that they can skew the data in the direction of zero time loss (because little or no work time is missed), and constrain statistical power. Time-based measures are fast becoming popular productivity/cost indicators, but clinicians and researchers should not overlook the human burden associated with missed work time. Many workers do not have the luxury of missing time without real consequences, in terms of increased workloads, time pressures, and/or lost pay. Thus, it is important not to lose the humanistic interpretation of the measure.

Functional and Disability Measures

Many questionnaires measure the degree to which health problems interfere with the ability to work. We mention a small number of these that represent the main characteristics. These questionnaires are of two types: interviewer-administered; or self-administered. Tables 2, 3, 4 and 5 briefly describe characteristics of four instruments used in outcomes research. In each case, work outcome items are embedded in a more comprehensive health-status assessment instrument.

The EuroQol Instrument (EQ5D) represents the most global measurement approach. This is a health-related, quality-of-life assessment tool, providing self-reported data concerning limitation in usual activities. It uses a three-level response scale to grade ability. Like many other instruments, a single set of items is used to address multiple roles. A single set of role-level items simultaneously addresses problems in employment, housework, schoolwork, family life and leisure.

The Quality of Well-Being Scale (QWB), the SF-36, and the Sickness Impact Profile (SIP), all are based substantially on the Activity Limitation battery of the NHIS and related surveys, such as the Current Population Survey administered by the United States Census Bureau. To ascertain activity limitations in the NHIS, an interviewer asks respondents whether they have an impairment or health problem that has prevented them from working entirely. For respondents answering "no" to this question, the interviewer

Table 2. Selected Questions: EuroQol Instrument Revised Classification: Role and Activity Limitations

We are trying to find out what people think about health. We are going to describe a few health states that people can be in. We want you to indicate how good or bad each of these states would be for a person like you. There are no right or wrong answers. Here we are interested only in your personal view.

But first of all, we would like you to indicate the state of your own health today.

Usual Activities

- ☐ I have no problems with performing my usual activities (e.g., work, study, housework, family or leisure activities)
- ☐ I have some problems with performing my usual activities
- ☐ I am unable to perform my usual activities

Adapted with permission. EUROQOL Instrument from Patrick DL, Erickson P. Health Status and Health Policy: Allocating Resources to Health Care. New York: Oxford University Press, 1993.

Table 3. Selected Questions: Quality of Well-Being Scale: Role and Activity Limitations

[Questions are asked of employed persons.]

		None	Day 1	Day 2	Day 3	Day 4	All 4 Days
3.	On which of the past 4 days, if any, did you work any time at your job or business?	0 (5)	1	2	3	4	5
[Ask for each day circled in 3.]							
4.	On *(day)*, were you limited in any way in the amount or kind of work done, such as not doing certain tasks, taking special rest periods, or working only part of the day?	1 [ ] Yes 2 [ ] No	1 [ ] Yes 2 [ ] No	1 [ ] Yes 2 [ ] No	1 [ ] Yes 2 [ ] No	1 [ ] Yes 2 [ ] No	1 [ ] Yes 2 [ ] No
[Ask for each day not circled in 3.]							
5a.	On *(day)*, were the reasons you did not work at your job or business related in any way to your health?	1 [ ] Yes 2 [ ] No	1 [ ] Yes 2 [ ] No	1 [ ] Yes 2 [ ] No	1 [ ] Yes 2 [ ] No	1 [ ] Yes 2 [ ] No	1 [ ] Yes 2 [ ] No
5b.	If you HAD worked at your job on *(day)*, would you have been limited in any way in the amount or kind of work done, such as taking special rest periods, working only part of the day, or not doing certain tasks?	1 [ ] Yes 2 [ ] No	1 [ ] Yes 2 [ ] No	1 [ ] Yes 2 [ ] No	1 [ ] Yes 2 [ ] No	1 [ ] Yes 2 [ ] No	1 [ ] Yes 2 [ ] No

Bush JW. General health policy model/Quality of Well-Being Scale. In: Wenger NK, Matison ME, Forberg C, Elinson J, eds. Assesssment of quality of life in clinical trials of cardiovascular therapies. New York: LeJarq, 1984.

Table 4: SF-36v2 Standard

4. During the past week, how much of the time have you had any of the following problems with your work or other regular daily activities as a result of your physical health?

	All of the time	Most of the time	Some of the time	A little of the time	None of the time
a Cut down on the amount of time you spent on work or other activities	☐ 1	☐ 2	☐ 3	☐ 4	☐ 5
b Accomplished less than you would like	☐ 1	☐ 2	☐ 3	☐ 4	☐ 5
c Were limited in the kind of work or other activities	☐ 1	☐ 2	☐ 3	☐ 4	☐ 5
d Had difficulty performing the work or other activities (for example, it took extra effort)	☐ 1	☐ 2	☐ 3	☐ 4	☐ 5

5. During the past week, how much of the time have you had any of the following problems with your work or other regular daily activities as a result of any emotional problems (such as feeling depressed or anxious)?

	All of the time	Most of the time	Some of the time	A little of the time	None of the time
a Cut down on the amount of time you spent on work or other activities	☐ 1	☐ 2	☐ 3	☐ 4	☐ 5
b Accomplished less than you would like	☐ 1	☐ 2	☐ 3	☐ 4	☐ 5
c Did work or other activities less carefully than usual	☐ 1	☐ 2	☐ 3	☐ 4	☐ 5

Table 5. Selected Questions: Sickness Impact Profile: Role and Activity Limitations

IF YOU ARE NOT WORKING AND IT IS *NOT* BECAUSE OF YOUR HEALTH, PLEASE SKIP THIS PAGE.

Now consider the work you do and respond to (check) *only* those statements that you are *sure* describe you today and are related to your state of health. (If today is a Saturday or Sunday or some other day that you would usually have off, please respond as if today were a working day.)

1. I am not working at all ______

(IF YOU CHECKED THIS STATEMENT, SKIP TO THE NEXT PAGE.)

2. I am doing part of my job at home ______
3. I am not accomplishing as much as usual at work ______
4. I often act irritable toward my work associates, for example, snap at them, give sharp answers, criticize easily ______
5. I am working shorter hours ______
6. I am doing only light work ______
7. I work only for short periods of time or take frequent rests ______
8. I am working at my usual job but with some changes, for example, using different tools or special aids, trading some tasks with other workers ______
9. I do not do my job as carefully and accurately as usual ______

Bergner M, Bobbitt RA, Carter WB, Gilson BS. The Sickness Impact Profile: development and final revision of a health status measure. Med Care 1981;19:787-805.

asks if, because of an impairment or health problem, they are limited in the kind or amount of work they can do. The NHIS also ask respondents to name the condition(s) that caused any activity limitations. This methodology is designed to generate estimates of the number of people in the United States population with severe work limitations (i.e., inability to work), or partial limitations (i.e., limits in the amount or kind of work performed).

An interviewer in a semi-structured format administers the QWB. It is based substantially on the NHIS items specified for each of the past 4 days. The QWB aggregates data about activity limitations into an overall score. Scale items are weighted to reflect heath-state preferences.

Both the SF-36 and the SIP contain batteries to assess limitations in role activities, and distinct scale scores can be derived from these. The SF-36 contains one battery addressing role limitations due to physical health problems and another for emotional health problems. (Table 4 depicts items in an updated version of the SF-36.) Paid work activity is not addressed separately from other work activities. The role-physical health scale contains more detailed versions of the NHIS items. It also includes additional criteria for defining role limitation, and includes questions concerning inability to accomplish as much as usual and difficulty performing roles described parenthetically as requiring extra effort. The emotional health scale excludes some of the physical scale items and adds a criterion; being unable to work as carefully as usual.

The SIP contains a separate paid work question battery and reports a scale score to assess any disability. Though using slightly different terminology, its role limitation criteria overlap substantially with those embedded in the SF-36 and the NHIS. Two SIP items address impact on the amount of work done (i.e., working shorter hours and doing part of the job at home), and two items cover the kind of work (i.e., doing light work and working with some changes). The SIP also asks about accomplishments and care in doing work, and two additional issues, irritability toward others, and interrupted work.

The role scales contained in these and other health status questionnaires, generally, have a high degree of validity and reliability across a range of different demographic groups, and a large body of comparative data is available. In addition, these measures are usually available in several formats (e.g., phone and mail) and are easy to administer.

The major disadvantage of the role scales is that they are often not very discriminating with respect to social roles. Except for the SIP, they tend to ask global questions (e.g.; "Were [you] limited in the kind of work or other activities?"), which do not differentiate between paid and unpaid work. In addition, some scales do not distinguish between gradations in level of work activity (e.g., mild, moderate and severe), and few employed respondents will tend to endorse the "unable to work" response, results are often skewed toward high levels of functioning. Revisions in the SF-36 were developed to address these "floor effect" problems.

A final point about this group of instruments is that, except for the QWB, most of the items and the scale scores have no explicit economic interpretation. They were developed as components of health status measures emphasizing the human burdens of health problems, rather than the economic implications. The SF-36, and the SIP, both address aspects of productivity (e.g., work quantity and quality), and with additional efforts, it may be possible to convert scores into an economic metric.

Work Productivity

Survey instruments are being developed to specifically measure productivity loss within the paid work domain. Several, such as the Endicott Work Productivity Scale (EWPS), the Migraine Work and Productivity Loss Questionnaire, and the Angina Work Limitations Questionnaire are condition-specific.

Subjective assessments of effectiveness in performing work activities were used to assess work productivity loss in studies of depression and migraine headache. These surveys ask respondents to rate the effectiveness on the job on days they were symptomatic (e.g., during a migraine headache episode). Ratings scales run from 0 percent (not at all effective) to 100 percent (completely effective). This information frequently is combined with time loss data (e.g., sickness absence data). Total productivity loss is estimated by the amount of lost wages. While easy to use, validation is limited.

A small group of questionnaires adds to the body of knowledge concerning two sources of productivity loss: losses due to missed work time ("absenteeism"); and those associated with an impaired ability to function while at work ("presenteeism"). Some studies estimate that productivity losses due to presenteeism are many orders of magnitude larger than those associated with missed work time. This chapter focuses on two questionnaires, but several are being tested.

The Health and Labor Questionnaire consists of four "modules" which address the following categories: work absences; reduced on-the-job performance; productivity in unpaid work; and degree of trouble performing paid work. This questionnaire is an attempt to provide a comprehensive method for evaluating health-related productivity loss. Tests of its performance, which are limited to relatively small samples in the Netherlands, show encouraging results.

The Work Limitations Questionnaire (WLQ) is a validated 25-item, self-administered, self-reported instrument measuring on-the-job work disability and productivity loss ("presenteeim"). The WLQ's four scales reflect the multidimensional character of work roles. The Time scale contains five items addressing ability to peform time and scheduling demands. The six-item Physical scale covers job tasks that involve bodily strength, movement, endurance, coordination and flexibility. The Mental-Interpersonal scale has nine items addressing cognitive and social tasks. The Output scale contains five items addressing diminished work productivity. Scale scores, which range from 0 (limited none of the time) to 100 (limited all of the time), represent the percentage of time over the past two weeks respondents had job performance limitations. An empirically-derived algorithm enables WLQ users to convert work-limitation data into a productivity loss score.

The WLQ has demonstrated excellent psychometric performance. Scale Cronbach alpha's results exceed the recommended level of .70 in both patient and employee populations. Construct validity tests show that WLQ scale scores vary with SF-36 measures of physical and mental health, type of chronic condition, and severity within condition groups, such as depression and osteoarthritis. A 2001 study of patients with depression found that the energy level, a hallmark depression symptom, predicted WLQ scores. Low energy corresponded to decreased work productivity, both cross-sectionally and longitudinally.

Criterion validity tests were performed in several settings. In a study of patients with rheumatoid arthritis, and in a second with a fibromyalgia sample, Wolfe and colleagues found that WLQ scores predicted patient income level. An important analysis conducted at a worksite involved repeat measures of approximately 900 employees. It determined that WLQ scores were significantly related to objectively measured employee work productivity and, thus, had validity as productivity indicators. A study is currently underway, which will obtain national normative WLQ data for population groups defined by demographic characteristics, work characteristics and health status.

Recommendations

We have addressed some of the available methods for evaluating the impact of health and treatment on the quantity and quality of labor force participation. In addition to the conventional concerns about an instrument's psychometric properties, choosing the best measurement tool for the situation involves thinking about issues such as the following:

1) Which aspects of work are hypothesized to be influenced by the illness, or treatment being studied, and at what order of magnitude?
2) Over what period will these hypothesized effects occur, and how long will they last?
3) How important it is to be able to assign financial costs to these effects?
4) Are there guidelines for interpreting scores?

Work outcome measurement is entering another era. A variety of survey instruments and scoring methods are available to meet the demand for work outcomes assessment. With an understanding of the same basic concepts and methods, researchers will be better able to choose the option(s) that are best suited to their aims.

Annotated Bibliography

1. Butler RJ, Johnson WG, Baldwin ML. Measuring success in managing work-disability: why return to work doesn't work. Industrial Labor Relations Review, April 1995.

   In this study, data from a survey of approximately 11,000 Canadian workers with permanent partial impairments resulting from work-related injuries were used to test the assumption that return to work indicates the end of the limiting effect of injury. Using longitudinal data, the rate of successful returns to work measured by first return to work was 85 percent. The rate of success was 50 percent when evaluated over a longer duration. This study increases awareness of a major pitfall in using employment status as an indicator of successful recovery.

2. Johns G. How often are you absent? A review of the use of self-reported absence data. J Applied Psychol 1994;79:574–91.

   This paper, written by an organizational psychologist, is a comprehensive review of self-reported absenteeism. It includes an overview of the reasons why self-report measures are being used increasingly in research, and the basic approaches used to measure absenteeism in studies. What is, and is not, known about the validity and reliability of self-reported absenteeism data is also discussed. This review is essential reading for those interested in measurement. However, the analysis does not explicitly address reporting by chronically ill groups or other patient populations.

3. Lerner D, Amick BC, Rogers WH, Malspeis S, Bungay KM, Cynn D. The Work Limitations Questionnaire Med Care 2001;39:72–85.

   This is the first report on a work outcomes measure, called the Work Limitations Questionnaire (WLQ). It was developed to fill the gap in measuring the on-the-job impact of chronic conditions and treatment. The paper reports on the original development, three pilot studies, and two psychometric field trials. The genealogy of the items is given. This report provides important evidence of the reliability and validity of the WLQ.

4. Lynch W, Reidel JE, eds. Measuring Employee Productivity: A guide to assessment tools, 2001 Edition. Denver: William M Mercer, Inc and Scottsdale: Institutue for Health & Productivity Management, 2001.

   A recent publication on the subject summarizes some of the newer health and work productivity survey instruments. The guide presents and reviews seven self-assessment instruments that were, or are, currently being used in a research setting to estimate work performance and detect the effects of health on performance and productivity. This guide can be used to learn about self-assessment of work performance, or to help users choose the best tool(s) for the specific purposes. The instruments identified in this guide were identified through literature searches, contact with researchers in related fields, and discussions with employers.

5. McCormick EJ, Jeanneret PR, Mecham RC. Position analysis questionnaire. Palo Alto, CA: Consulting Psychologists Press, Inc., 1989.

   U.S. Department of Labor, Employment and Training Administration. U.S. Employment Service. Dictionary of occupational titles. Washington, DC: Government Publications Office, 1991.

   These two publications and the O*NET website *(http://online.onetcenter.org/main.html)* reflect efforts to convert work role into a more useful analytic category. Each provides a taxonomic system of work roles that disaggregates each role into its constituent components or dimensions. They are useful for evaluating the comprehensiveness of work outcome measurement tools.

6. Mushet GR, Miller D, Clements B, Pait G, Gutterman DL. Impact of sumatriptan on workplace productivity, nonwork activities and health-related quality of life among hospital employees with migraine. Headache 1996;36:137–43.

   Osterhaus JT, Gutterman DL, Plachetka JR. Healthcare resource and lost labour costs of migraine headache in the US. PharmacoEconomics 1992;2:67–76.

   Reilly MC, Zbrozek AS, Dukes EM. The validity and reproducibility of a work productivity and activity impairment instrument. PharmacoEconomics 1993;4:353-65.

   These three studies are examples of relatively new approaches for measuring work consequences of chronic illness and treatment. Each assesses time spent working with symptoms and provides the measurement methods used. In the first two articles, the authors also discuss time loss measurement. The third article includes some psychometric analyses of one of the measures, although the analyses are limited.

7. Patrick DL, Erickson P. Health status and health policy: allocating resources to health care. New York: Oxford University Press, Inc., 1993.

   This comprehensive text addresses the basic concepts underlying the measurement of health status and health-related quality of life. Readers are provided with an understanding of the different measurement methods available, as well as examples of instruments. The authors explain how health status and health-related quality of life measurement can contribute to the process of making resource-allocation decisions. An in-depth discussion of economic valuation techniques is included.

8. Pope AM, Tarlov AR, eds. Disability in America: toward a national agenda for prevention. Washington, DC: National Academy Press, 1991.

   This report from an Institute of Medicine committee provides readers with a thorough understanding of the meaning of disability, and its significance to the United States population. It is an excellent handbook for gaining an understanding of the multiple dimensions of health status and how they differ. The book also includes policy recommendations for disability prevention. Ambiguities associated with the World Health Organization taxonomy are discussed in detail.

9. Van Roijen L, Essink-Bot, ML, Koopmanschap MA, Bonsel G, Rutten FF. Labor and health status in economic evaluation of health care. The health and labor questionnaire. Int Journal of Technology Assessment in Health care;12:3 (1996), 405–15.

This report describes the development of the Health and Labor Questionnaire (HLQ), which consists of four modules, to collect data on absence from work, reduced productivity, unpaid labor production, and labor-related problems. In this study researchers measured reduced productivity at paid work, time spent on unpaid labor, and impediments to work activities that were due to treatment.

10. Verbrugge LM. The iceberg of disability. In: Stahl SM, ed. The legacy of longevity: health and health care in later life. Newbury Park: Sage Publications, 1990.

In this classic paper, the author defines and discusses the disability concept and the limitations of statistics generated by national surveys to portray the full extent and scope of the problem. The author includes a discussion of the two dominant disability frameworks of Nagi and the WHO and enumerates different types of disabilities. A conceptual model explains the possible pathways linking chronic illness to work disability.

11. Yelin EH, Katz P. Making work more central to work disability. Milbank Quarterly 1994;72:592–619.

In this article, the labor market trajectories for people with and without disabilities, for the years 1981 through 1993, are compared using data from the Current Population Survey of the United States Census Bureau. It is an excellent resource for understanding measurement issues. It provides compelling evidence that the disabled experience a disproportionate share of unemployment.

12. Altman BM, Disability Definitions, Models, Classification Schemes and Applications. IN: Albrecht GL, Seelman KD, Bury M, eds. Handbook of Disability Studies. Thousand Oaks: Sage Publications, 2001.

This article is a comprehensive summary of multiple conceptualizations of disability with an emphasis on the application. It also provides a hard copy reference for the on-line references listed below.

On line References

The National Institute on Disability and Rehabilitation Research (NIDRR)—*http://www.ed.gov/offices/OSERS/NIDRR/*

Disability Statistics Center—*http://www.dsc.ucsf.edu/*

Created in 1978, The National Institute on Disability and Rehabilitation Research (NIDRR) is a national leader in sponsoring research. NIDRR is located in Washington, D.C., Its mission is to generate, disseminate, and promote new knowledge to improve the options available to disabled persons. As part of the scientific community, NIDRR makes an important contribution to the overall knowledge in rehabilitation medicine, engineering, psychosocial rehabilitation, integration, vocational outcomes, and the virtual and built environments.

One center is the Disability Statistics Center that produces and disseminates statistical information on disability and the status of people with disabilities in American Society and to establish and monitor indicators about how conditions are changing over time to meet their health, housing, economic, and social needs. The Center produces Disability Statistics Reports, a series of detailed research reports, and Disability Statistics Abstracts, a series of short research briefs, which are printed by NIDRR.

This report, which is updated periodically, provides statistics regarding the extent of activity limitation in the United States population by type of chronic condition. It is based on data from the National Health Interview Survey and contains a thorough discussion of measurement issues associated with the survey. A definition for activity limitations is provided.

Self-Assessment Questions

1. Which one of the following best describes a current application of work outcomes measures?
   A. Assessing degree of impairment.
   B. Measuring psychological adjustment to chronic illness.
   C. Assessing patient recovery from illness and response to treatment.
   D. Estimating the direct costs of health care attributable to illness.

2. Which one of the following statements is *not* true?
   A. Work outcomes refer to the direct or indirect consequences of a person's health problems, or treatment on the quantity, but not the quality, of labor force participation.
   B. Work outcomes are measured at an individual level, although the results are used at the aggregate or group level.
   C. Survey methods to measure work outcomes rely on the reports of individuals whose labor force participation is a concern.
   D. Work evaluations or functional capacity evaluations are principally used in rehabilitation settings.

3. All except which one of the following are fundamental reasons for including work outcomes in studies?
   A. Studies of adults' lives in the United States and elsewhere have demonstrated that paid work is an important activity around which our lives are organized.
   B. Work outcomes, such as employment status, serve as barometers of the economic gains and costs that may result from different treatment modalities.
   C. Attention to work outcomes promotes the view that people with chronic illnesses have low productivity.
   D. Increasingly in deliberations of the value of new technologies or specific medical interventions, consideration is given to their impact on the proportion of health care costs resulting from decreased productivity in paid work.

4. Which one of the following statements is true?
   A. Work performance and productivity are essentially the same concept.
   B. Work disability is the same as having an impairment.

C. In measurement, a distinction should be made between work role and work tasks.
D. A person's role at work is exactly the same as his/her social role.

5. Which one of the following statements about the measurement of work role as a type of work outcomes is *not* true?
   A. The Dictionary of Occupational Titles, the O*NET system, and the Position Analysis Questionnaire disaggregate work roles into constituent components, or dimensions, for rating purposes.
   B. Role-level questions are likely to elicit coarse assessments of ability to work, whereas demand-level questions will provide information about which specific dimensions of work are problematic.
   C. Typically, survey methods measure work outcomes at the role-level.
   D. Sociologists display general agreement regarding the definition of social role; this serves as a basis for extrapolation of a definition of work role.

6. Which one of the following is *not* addressed by questions contained in current tools for measuring work outcomes?
   A. Employment status and work loss.
   B. Time loss.
   C. Activity and role limitations.
   D. Unpaid work activities.

7. Which one of the following statements about the National Health Interview Survey, and its derived components, is *not* true?
   A. The National Health Interview Survey is interviewer administered and contains questions about disability days.
   B. The questions on the National Health Interview Survey are created specifically to allow comparisons across different populations with different illnesses.
   C. Many of the self-report batteries used to measure disability days in studies use National Health Interview Survey items and vary little in methodology from the National Health Interview Survey.
   D. The National Health Interview Survey approach attempts to capture the number of full and part days missed due to health problems and, consequently, captures the complete inability to work during the time period and days in which the worker was partially disabled.

8. Which one of the following statements about the measurement of work absences is *not* true?
   A. Work absences can be interpreted as a summary measure of disruptions in the performance of normative roles and diminished productivity.
   B. Work absence measurements are used more often as a health outcome than as an economic outcome.
   C. Although time-based measures are popular productivity and cost indicators, they often are not viewed as reflections for the human burden associated with missed work time.
   D. The use of work absence variables as individual-level productivity indicators requires a person to assume that time spent not working results in some net financial loss and does not account for these outputs efficiently.

9. Which one of the following statements about the Sickness Impact Profile and the SF-36, as they pertain to use as work outcomes measures, is correct?
   A. Both contain question batteries that assess limitations in role activities, and distinct scale scores can be derived from them.
   B. Both contain a separate paid work question battery.
   C. Both have been validated using data obtained from work sites as a criterion.
   D. Paid and nonpaid work roles are addressed separately.

INTERPRETATION OF HUMANISTIC ASSESSMENTS

San Keller, Ph.D.

Outline

Humanistic health assessments are derived from information provided by people about their functioning and well-being. Psychometrics is a set of methods that allow us to assign numerical values to characteristics of people (e.g., health) based on their responses to a test, or survey. This chapter first describes how personal information about functioning and well-being is quantified and then, how meaning is brought to those quantities (i.e., how these quantities are interpreted).

I. Scientific Methods used to Ensure the Accuracy of Patient-Based Assessment Data

A. Scaling

Scaling is the activity of assigning numbers to survey responses; these numbers are used to indicate qualities, or quantities, of people's health.

1. Scale Types

a. Nominal scales are rules of classification based on qualitative similarities, and differences, in health.

b. Ordinal scaling is used for the purpose of indicating better, or worse, health, and to assign order to health states.

c. Interval scaling is used to indicate how much greater, or less, an attribute of one person's health is compared to another's.

d. Ratio scaling indicates how much health differs in absolute magnitude, and requires the existence of a meaningful zero value (see Figure 1).

2. Scaling methods

a. Direct methods:

Assume an identity between the value placed on a response by a judge and the actual scale value

i. Nominal

ii. Ordinal

iii. Interval scales

b. Indirect scaling methods:

Transform the values obtained by judges into other values and these transformed values are considered to be the actual scale values. Can be used to create ratio scales based on ordinal data. Examples include methods based on utility theory and item response theory.

B. Reliability

Reliability reflects how confident one can be that a particular questionnaire score is the true score. It is estimated based on repeatability. The same score should occur with repeated administrations to an unchanging respondent (see Table 1).

1. Longitudinal Methods

The survey is administered to people in stable health at Time A, and then administered to the same group of people again at Time B. Statistics are then applied to the data to determine the degree to which scores at Time B are predictable from scores at Time A. Three statistical methods are commonly used.

a. Confidence interval

b. Pearson product-moment correlation

c. Intraclass correlation coefficient

2. Cross-sectional Methods

Used to estimate the reliability of scores by testing for repeatability of responses at one point in time by assessing the relationship between different, although equivalent, responses (see Table 2).

a. Alternate forms

b. Internal consistency

3. Standards of Reliability

For group-level analyses, reliability coefficients should be greater than 0.50 and, ideally, around 0.80. For individual-level analyses, reliability coefficients 0.90 and greater are desirable.

4. Scaling Effects :The method of scaling must be compatible with the cognitive capacity of the respondents to categorize information. The reliability of a scale indicates how reproducible the scale score is, but does not indicate whether that score provides the information it was designed to provide.

C. Validity: Validity is evidence that a survey, or questionnaire, measures what it is supposed to measure and does not measure what it is not supposed to measure; sensitivity, specificity, and responsiveness are all different terms that describe the validity of a scale. Sensitivity reflects the impact of all phenomena that may influence a measure. Specificity is the degree to which a measure responds to differences in what is being measured, but not to other factors. Responsiveness indicates the ability of a health measure to detect change in health, over time, in individuals whose health does, in fact, change.

1. Content validity depends on establishing logical links between the purpose of the questionnaire and the items and scales included in the questionnaire (see Table 3).

2. Construct validity is assessed by evaluating whether an instrument measures and can differentiate one construct from others within the survey; constructs are variables that are not measured directly, but are hypothesized to underlie the relationships between measured variables; which are "constructed" based on these relationships.

a. Factorial validity is a way to identify constructs based on the relationship of survey responses to one another. This can be done at the scale level by looking at the relationship between scale scores within, or among, questionnaires, or at the item level by looking at the relationship among all items on a questionnaire (see Table 4).

b. Convergent and discriminant validity are determined by comparing the relationship of the seven items to two factors. Convergent validity occurs when the items that should measure pain severity are highly related to the severity factor. Discriminant validity occurs when scales that should measure pain severity discriminate in their relationships to both the pain severity and pain interference factor; that is, both are less related to the interference than to the severity factor.

c. Known-groups validity looks at the relationship of scale scores to group membership among groups known to differ in the attribute being measured (see Figure 2).

3. Criterion validity is assessed by testing the relationship of scale scores to a measure considered to be the standard definition of that variable.

4. Standards of validity: Although statistically significant results are necessary, they are not sufficient evidence of validity; it is also important to assess the relevance, and the quality of the study (i.e., the external and internal validity of the results).

a. External validity refers to whether the results are applicable to situations external to the particular study and setting that generated them.

b. Internal validity refers to whether the results of the study can be unambiguously attributed to the influence of variables internal to the study.

5. Scaling Effects: Because scaling determines the precision of measurement, it also affects tests of the validity of a survey.

6. Effect of Reliability: Reliability is a necessary precondition for validity, but the opposite is not true; a measure can be reliable without being valid.

II. Bringing Meaning to Patient-Based Assessment Data

Interpretation methods focus on the meaning that can be assigned to any particular patient-rated outcome (PRO) score or score range.

A. Methods of interpreting PRO scores

There are three common methods of scale score interpretation:

1. Analysis of content: For single items, it is based on the content of the question and the response choices (see Table 5). For multi-item scales, the challenge lies with interpreting intermediate scale levels, because these can be obtained via a variety of response patterns (see Table 6 and Figure 3).

2. Normative Comparisons: Require the use of PROs for which there are existing data bases that can be used to calculate expected scores for different sociodemographic groups. This gives established PROs an interpretation advantage over PROs that are created expressly for use in a new study. In comparison to the item in Table 7, the item in Table 8 is much more useful from an interpretation standpoint because we know what scores are expected from this item (see Table 9).

3. Relationship to Causes and Consequences: The meaning of scale scores can be gauged by looking at likely causes and consequences of differences. To understand how this would work in relationship to causes consider the questions in Table 10 and 11. Figure 4 shows that lower overall health plan ratings mean that consumers have a problem with obtaining approval for health-care usage. Meaning is also brought to scale scores by looking at their relationship to future events. Figure 5 demonstrates the meaning of the responses to the "Problem with Health Plan Approval" item in terms of future consumer behavior.

B. Methods for Interpreting Differences in PRO Scores

Before describing methods that might be used to interpret score differences, it is helpful to define the major types of differences that may be of interest (see Table 12). The discussion of interpretation methods for differences in scores that follows draws heavily on recent reviews of methods for determining a minimal important difference (MID) [or sometimes called minimal clinically important difference, MCID] in a PRO score.

1. Judgment-Based Interpretation of Differences

In this section, some frequently mentioned approaches to identifying important differences that rely on subjective evaluations are characterized briefly.

a. Patient evaluations: Patients are asked whether their status has changed (e.g., is there a change in the severity of pain?) and, if so, how much? (See Figure 6). The average change score on a PRO for patients who indicate that they have gotten minimally better, or worse, is calculated, and this quantity is the MID. Moderate or large differences in the physical functioning (PF) PRO would be identified by calculating the average PF change score for people who responded at the mid, (± 3 to ± 5), or extreme (± 6 to ± 7) values, respectively.

b. Clinician evaluations: Similar to the methods described above, a physician global rating of patient change can be used to identify patients who are judged to have changed minimally; then the average change scores of patients can be calculated to derive an MID.

2. Statistical Approaches

a. Standard Error of Measurement (SEM): The SEM is used to calculate confidence bands around individual scale scores just as the standard error is used to calculate a confidence interval around the average score for a group of individuals (see Figure 7 and Table 13).

b. Standardized effect size: The size of the effect must be indexed against the variability one would expect in the scores of a clinically stable patient. Standardized effect sizes are calculated from changes, they are sometimes called responsiveness statistics. Figure 8 illustrates the value of standardized effect sizes in interpretation of differences. The graph on the left shows differences between the general population and people with migraines in raw score units. The graph on the right shows these differences expressed as standardized effect sizes. Since each scale differs from the general population by a different amount, and each scale has a different degree of variability in clinically stable respondents (see Table 14), it is difficult to judge how large the differences between scales are using raw score units.

3. Sources of Misinterpretation of Scale Score Differences: Occurs when standardization across comparisons made within groups over time, or among groups, at one point in time is lacking with regard to types of respondents surveyed, or methods used to collect the health status information (e.g., the answers to some health questions will be strongly influenced by how anonymous the patient feels he or she is when responding). (See Table 15, Figure 9, and Figure 10).

4. Scaling Effects: The number of levels of measurement in a scale, and the range of measurement for that scale, is important when interpreting scale scores because the ability of a scale to describe differences among people, and changes within people over time, increases with increased levels of measurement (see Figure 11, Figure 12 and Table 17). Some of the respondents who were forced to choose the "excellent" response to the item in Table 16, will choose "nearly excellent," "very good," and "good."

5. Effects of Reliability: Because reliability refers to how confident one can be that a particular score is the true score, scale score reliability is a pre-condition for interpretation. Differences in reliability between two PRO scores for the same patient are depicted in Figure 13. These differences lead to different conclusions about change between the second and third quarters.

6. Effects of Validity: The relevance of a questionnaire's content to a particular group of respondents affects the interpretability of scale scores (see Table 18).

Items that are not relevant will yield scores that are not responsive because the item content held little meaning for the respondents. The emotional behavior scale in Table 19 is sensitive to the effects of analgesics.

III. Summary and Conclusions

A. Patients reported outcome surveys (PROs) are important because they provide a vehicle for entering patients' voices into the medical data base, and thus, provide important information that is not otherwise available.

B. This chapter describes a rigorous set of methods used to ensure the reliability, validity and usefulness of data provided by PROs.

C. The information provided by this chapter should be considered a primer on this subject, and as a spring board for further learning.

D. The reader is encouraged to study the source material listed in the annotated bibliography, and in Table 20, to learn more about the appropriate use of PROs.

E. With regard to the use of particular health and health-care surveys, the reader is encouraged to consult manuals, the seminal peer-reviewed literature, and the survey developers.

Learning Objectives

1. Describe the scientific methods used to ensure the accuracy and usefulness of information provided by patient-based surveys.
2. Compare and contrast the various methods for testing reliability.
3. Compare and contrast the various methods for determining validity.
4. List and evaluate the four methods for interpreting scale scores..
5. Interpret scale scores that are reported in the published literature and measured in patients.

Abbreviations in this chapter

BPI	Brief pain inventory
CAHPS 2.0	Consumer assessments of health plans survey
ICC	Intraclass correlation coefficient
FEV	Forced expiratory volume
HIV	Human immunodeficiency virus
IRT	Item response theory
MID	Minimal important difference
MCID	Minimal clinically important difference
MHI-5	5-Item mental health inventory
MOS	Medical outcomes study
PBA	Patient-based assessment
PF	Physical functioning
PRO	Particular patient-related outcome
RCT	Randomized clinical trials
ROC	Response operator curve
SEM	Standard error of measurement
SF-36	SF-36 Health Survey
SIP	Sickness impact profile

The purpose of this chapter is to demonstrate methods for interpreting data derived from patient-rated outcomes. It begins with a brief discussion of the scientific methods used to ensure the accuracy of those data. This is done for two reasons: 1) the first step in interpreting health information is to assess how trustworthy and relevant that information is, and, relatedly; 2) properties of the data that limit precision will also limit interpretability.

Scientific Methods Used To Ensure the Accuracy of Patient-Rated Outcome Data

Patient-rated outcomes (PROs) are surveys, or questionnaires, administered to patients to determine their feelings, judgments, and perceptions. Because these data are derived from a source internal to the patient (are subjective) they are sometimes thought to be less reliable, or accurate, than other health data. However, this is not necessarily true. Developers of PROs can ensure the accuracy of the data by basing the construction of PROs on common, well developed, and thoroughly researched scientific methods. These methods come from the field of *psychometrics*, the science of quantifying characteristics of people based on their responses to a test or survey. In this discussion of psychometrics, the focus is on its application to health status outcomes, rather than to theory. In addition, the approach taken is conceptual, rather than statistical. Those interested in theoretical and statistical presentations of these methods are encouraged to consult the texts listed in the annotated bibliography.

In the course of this text, the reader will learn about: 1) Scaling-assigning numbers to survey responses; 2) Reliability-evaluating the stability of responses in an unchanging subject; 3) Validity-testing the ability of the numbers to provide information about patients' health; and 4) Interpretation-evaluating the importance of the information provided by these numbers.

Scaling

Scaling is the activity of assigning numbers to survey responses. Why do numbers need to be assigned to survey responses? Numbers are a simple and useful way to describe reality, and to summarize health information provided by people. Numbers can indicate qualities, or quantities, of people's health. Assigning numbers, rather than labels, allows the use of math to describe relationships among attributes.

Four basic relationships exist between numbers and qualities, or quantities. These four relationships, categorized as nominal, ordinal, interval, and ratio in nature, are referred to as levels of measurement because they are levels of resolution progressing from the grossest type of numbering (nominal) to the most fine-grained type of numbering (ratio). Figure 1 presents examples of scales corresponding to these four levels of measurement. *Nominal* scales are rules of classification based on qualitative similarities, and differences, in health. To assess the type of health condition a person has, nominal scaling can be used to assign people to categories. These categories, which differ qualitatively, cannot necessarily be ordered as greater or lesser (e.g., nominal scaling can be used to categorize people according to the type of pain they are experiencing, such as sharp versus throbbing). In this sense, nominal scales assign names to health states.

When it is important to know how people rank in terms of health, or who has better health, ordinal scaling is used. *Ordinal* scaling indicates better, or worse, health and assigns order to health states (e.g., a 5-point scale of pain may correspond to choices ordered according to intensity: no pain, a little pain, moderate pain, severe pain, and unbearable pain).

Interval scaling is used to indicate how much greater, or less, an attribute of one person's health is compared to another's. Furthermore, these category labels ideally are chosen based on research indicating a perception to be equal in distance from one another: A person might have pain that *prevents* functioning, pain that *moderately interferes* with functioning, or pain that has *no* impact on functioning.

Ratio scaling is used to indicate how much health differs in absolute magnitude, and requires the existence of a

Scale	Assignment of Numbers		
Nominal	Headache Stomach ache 1	Toothache 2	3
Ordinal	Less than average pain 1	Average pain 2	Greater than average pain 3
Interval	Not at all limited by pain 1	Moderately limited by pain 2	Completely limited by pain 3
Ratio	Minutes of pain 0 5 10 15 20 25 30 35		

Figure 1. Types of Scales

meaningful zero value. Because ratio scales require a known zero point, they are rarely found in subjective measures, and most patient-rated outcome scales are either nominal, ordinal, or interval measures. However, indirect scaling methods, such as those based on Item Response Theory (IRT) are increasingly used to translate ordinal and interval scales into ratio scales. Common examples of meaningful ratio scales used in health care are body weight scales, yardsticks for measuring height, seconds to walk 50 feet, and duration of pain in minutes.

Scaling Methods

Although many methods are available to assign numbers to responses, subject-matter experts are commonly used for this purpose at some point in the scaling process. These subject-matter experts, also called judges, can be health researchers, clinicians, or people similar to those who will eventually respond to the questionnaire. The choice of judge depends on the phenomenon being scaled. Judges can evaluate the responses by either placing the responses into categories, as in nominal scaling; ordering them in terms of magnitude, as in ordinal scaling; or indicating the distance between responses, as in interval scaling. Direct and indirect scaling methods are two basic procedures to assign numbers to survey responses. Direct methods of scaling assume an identity between the value placed on a response by a judge and the actual scale value. Indirect scaling methods transform the values obtained by judges into other values, and these transformed values are then considered to be the actual scale values.

Direct scaling methods

Direct scaling methods use a consensus among judges to assign quantities to health states. Nominal, ordinal, and interval scales can be created by direct scaling methods.

Nominal scales. In nominal scaling, judges are asked to group responses into meaningful categories, and these categories are then assumed to represent the scale values (e.g., responses to a question about type of cancer could be classified according to the cancer site. That is, breast, colon, lung, prostate, etc.).

Ordinal scales. Ordinal scales are developed when judges assign rank orders to stimuli and these rank orders are then averaged. The order of these averaged ranks indicates the scale value for the corresponding stimuli (e.g., 20 different judges could rank order five different activity statements in terms of the amount of leg strength required). The average of 20 ranks for each statement could be calculated and the statements could be ordered from 1-5, according to the magnitude of these average ranks. A scale value of 1, 2, 3, 4, or 5 would then be assigned to each statement, depending on the order. A comparison of these numbers would indicate whether the statement referred to greater, or lesser, leg strength. Staging systems for the severity of heart disease, or cancer, are examples of ordinal health scales.

Interval scales. For interval scales, judges assign a magnitude to a response choice along a continuum of response anchored by high and low health states. This is often done by asking judges to mark where they would place a particular response choice (e.g., severe pain) on a 10-centimeter line that is anchored on the right by the best health state possible (i.e., pain free), and of the left by the worst health state possible (i.e., unbearable pain). Generally, an average value is calculated across judges, and response choices that have average values that are ordinal, and differ from one another in approximately equal intervals of magnitude, are chosen (e.g., this process might result in the selection of the following response choice labels to measure pain severity: mild, moderate, and severe). This is a popular method of scaling called equal-appearing intervals, which forms the basis for Likert scales. This is the method used to develop response scales for the translated versions of questions on the SF-36 Health Survey (SF-36).

Indirect scaling methods. Scale scores based on utility theory, and item response theory, are common examples of PROs created using indirect scaling methods. Indirect methods transform judges' item evaluations based on a formula that relates such values to those on another scale.

The paired-comparison method, and method of successive intervals, are, perhaps, the best known of these procedures. Both transform the comparisons that judges make among stimuli into percentages, which are then transformed into normal curve deviates (e.g., in the paired-comparison method, judges rate which of the two responses is greater, according to a certain attribute. The normal curve is then used to transform the value into a z-score, the percentage of times a response is judged greater than other responses. This method transforms the greater than, and less than, values assigned by judges to a ratio scale.

Now that the types of scales and scaling methods, have been discussed, the methods used to ensure that the numbers assigned through scaling provide trustworthy and useful information will be reviewed.

Reliability

What does it mean to talk about the reliability of a survey instrument? All estimates of *reliability* describe, in one way or another, the degree of confidence a person can have in knowing that any particular score or reading is representative of the true reading. This estimate is based on repeated observations. Confidence that this score is the true score is enhanced if repeated administrations to an unchanging respondent yield the same score again and again. Any reading, or score, can be divided into that portion which is systematic — and, therefore, repeatable and predictable — and that portion which varies randomly, is spurious, or occurs by chance. Methods used to estimate the reliability of scale scores can be characterized according to whether they are used for longitudinal (over time) data collections, or for cross-sectional (point-in-time) data collections. These methods and the reliability question that each addresses are listed in Table 1.

Longitudinal Methods

Longitudinal tests of reliability are discussed first because the idea of testing for stability of scores, over time, is closest to the common sense notion of reliability. All longitudinal tests of reliability address the basic question; Do health scores change in people whose health is, in fact, stable over time? The procedure for longitudinal methods of reliability testing is to administer the health survey to people in stable health at Time A and then to administer the same survey to the same group of people again at Time B. A 2-week interval between Time A and Time B administrations is commonly chosen because this is thought to be long enough to minimize memory effects, yet short enough so that real change in health would not be expected to occur in stable subjects. Statistics are then applied to determine the degree to which scores at Time B are predictable from scores at Time A. The most commonly used statistics for this purpose are presented below.

Confidence interval

Confidence interval reliability of scale scores addresses the question: Are the scale scores at Time B different from those at Time A by too large an amount to be expected by chance alone? The mean scale score at Time A, and the 95 percent confidence interval around that score, is calculated. The percentage of Time B scale scores that fall outside of the 95 percent confidence interval around the Time A scores is an indicator of the unreliability of the scale.

Pearson-product moment

The reliability of scale scores estimated by Pearson product-moment correlations addresses the question: Are readings at Time B ordered the same as those at Time A? The Pearson product-moment correlation coefficient between the vectors of survey scores of a group of respondents from two test administrations is then calculated. This method of estimating reliability is not appropriate to use under circumstances where acute changes in health can be expected. This method also will not detect disagreement between scores at Time A and Time B, if Time B scores maintain the same order as Time A, but all scores change in magnitude (e.g., if each of 20 people gained 3 pounds from Time A to Time B, a Pearson-product moment correlation calculated between the weights would suggest that body weight remained stable across the two time periods). This method contrasts with the confidence interval and intraclass correlation methods, which can detect a mean shift in scores from Time A to Time B.

Intraclass correlation coefficient (ICC)

Determining the intraclass correlation coefficient is a method of testing the reliability of scale scores that addresses the question: How much of the difference in scale scores is due to differences between respondents, and how much is due to error? True differences among the scores of a group of

Table 1. Common Reliability Analyses

Method	Question Answered
Longitudinal	
95 percent confidence interval	Do the scores vary by more than is expected by chance?
Pearson product-moment	Are scores ranked the same over time?
Intraclass correlation coefficient	How much of the difference in scores is due to differences between respondents, and how much is due to error?
Cross-sectional	
Alternate forms	How similar are scores obtained from equivalent samples?
Internal consistency	Are responses to items in a scale equivalent?

respondents, are assumed to be due to questionnaire responses that are characteristic of the participant. Other sources of variation, including systematic changes in respondent means over time, are assumed to be error.

Of the three statistics presented, the most commonly reported in the literature are the Pearson product-moment and the intraclass correlation coefficient. Increasingly, the intraclass correlation coefficient is considered to be the superior method because it tests for agreement between Time 1 and Time 2, in both the ordering of scores, and in the absolute magnitude of scores.

Cross-Sectional Methods

Cross-sectional methods to estimate the reliability of scores test for the repeatability of responses, at one point in time, by assessing the relationship between different, although equivalent, responses. These responses are obtained from two equivalent surveys, or from equivalent items within a survey.

Alternate forms

Alternate forms reliability addresses the question: How similar are scores obtained from equivalent health surveys? At one point in time, all respondents fill out two different versions of the same survey. The correlation between scores for the two forms is then calculated. Because people actually respond to two different sets of questions, similarity between scores cannot be due to memory effects. Therefore, it is not necessary to wait several days between survey administrations. This method of testing the reliability of a survey requires proof that the two versions are truly equivalent, otherwise, a lack of relationship between scale scores could be attributed to nonequivalence of forms, rather than to unreliability. An example of the alternate forms method of testing reliability is presented in Table 2. In this example, two versions of a five-item mental health inventory were both administered to a group of respondents. From the table, it is clear that the mean scores and standard deviations are very similar, and the correlation coefficient between the scores for the two versions was 0.93, indicating the equivalent measures (a correlation coefficient of 1.0 indicates perfect redundancy between two measures, and a coefficient of 0 indicates no relationship whatsoever between two measures).

Internal consistency

The internal consistency method of testing reliability addresses the question: Are responses to items in a scale equivalent? That is, do the items in a scale function as repeated measures of one another? This is perhaps the most widely used method to estimate the reliability of scale scores because it cannot be affected by real change in the scale scores over time, or by memory. However, this method of testing will be affected by meaningful differences in the content of the items in a scale. To the degree that the meaning of scale items is not equivalent, the estimate of scale reliability will be low (e.g., a seizure severity scale might have low internal consistency reliability if it contains items that measure both frequency of seizures and type of each seizure). However, such a scale might have high test-retest reliability. The approach for estimating internal consistency reliability is similar to that of estimating the intraclass correlation coefficient. In both of these analyses, true variation is represented by differences between respondents, while differences due to repeated assessments (in this case, different items) are assigned to error.

Table 2. Alternate Forms of the Mental Health Inventory Scale

Abbreviated Item Content* (direction of item wording)	**MHI-5**	**Alternate MHI-5**
Anxiety		
Been a very nervous person (-)	X	
Felt tense or high strung (-)		X
Depression		
Felt downhearted and blue (-)	X	
Been in low or very low spirits (-)		X
Behavioral/emotional control		
Felt so down in the dumps nothing could cheer you up (-)	X	
Feel you had nothing to look forward to (-)		X
Positive affect		
Been a happy person (+)	X	
Felt calm and peaceful (+)	X	
Generally enjoyed the things you do (+)		X
Felt cheerful, lighthearted (+)		X
Mean	71.45	71.39
Standard deviation	21.10	20.68

MHI-5 = 5-Item Mental Health Inventory

* Items were preceded by, "How much of the time during the past month . . ." Response categories were: (1) all of the time; (2) most of the time; (3) a good bit of the time; (4) some of the time; (5) a little of the time; and (6) none of the time.

Adapted with permission from McHorney CA, Ware JE. Construction and validation of an alternate form general mental health scale for the Medical Outcomes Study Short Form 36-Item Health Survey. Med Care 1995;33:15-28.

The internal consistency method is the only test for reliability that requires a single administration of a single form. For this reason, internal consistency reliability is the most cost-efficient method of estimating reliability. In contrast, the other methods discussed require either two administrations of the questionnaire, with the additional expenses of printing and processing the second administration, or developing a second questionnaire that is psychometrically equivalent to the first, as with the alternate forms method. Developing a psychometrically equivalent form is very labor intensive and time-consuming. It requires an iterative process of testing the alternate form by administering it to a group of people, analyzing the data, revising the form, administering the revised form, analyzing those data, etc.

The internal consistency method is not appropriate to use when testing the reliability of scales having heterogeneous content. Internal consistency reliability requires that items in a scale measure one concept. This is why people would be expected to respond similarly to each item, and why the items can be thought of as repeated measures of one another. If, in fact, the items measure very different concepts, they do not serve as repeated measures of one concept — the responses that people make to those items are unlikely to be similar, and the internal consistency estimate of reliability will be low.

Standards of Reliability

All measures contain some error. Therefore, health scores of people in stable health are not expected to be identical across multiple observations. That is, reliability coefficients are not expected to be 1.0. Standards of reliability differ depending on whether the questionnaire is used to describe the health of a single individual, an individual-level analysis, or a group of individuals, a group-level analysis. In group-level analyses, reliability coefficients greater than 0.80 will not improve the precision of the measure for purposes of hypothesis testing. However, the precision of individual-level measures of health are greatly affected by the reliability of the measure, and so reliability coefficients of 0.90 and above are desired.

This difference in standards for reliable measurement at the group and individual levels is because different formulas are used to calculate the standard error for each level. On the group level, the standard error is the standard deviation divided by the square root of the sample size. Thus, as the sample size gets larger, the standard error gets smaller (e.g., given a standard deviation of 10, and a sample size of 100, the standard error is 1; whereas, given a standard deviation of 10, and a sample size of 25, the standard error is 2). At the individual level, the standard error is the standard deviation multiplied by the square root of the quantity one minus the reliability coefficient for the scale. With a standard deviation of 10, a scale has to have a reliability coefficient of 0.99 in order for the individual score standard error to be the same size (equal to 1), as would be the standard error on a scale score averaged over 100 patients.

Scaling Effects

How responses to a survey are categorized, or scaled, will affect the reliability of the responses. For example, a body weight scale with very gross levels of measurement that indicate whether someone's weight is greater, or less than, 100 pounds is likely to result in very repeatable measures of weight. However, very little information actually describing the weights is provided. With such a scale, it would be difficult to detect changes in weight over time, or compare the weights of two individuals. As the levels of measurement, or resolution for a scale increase, the chance of obtaining the same score on repeated measures decreases because the probability of fluctuation in scores due to real change in the phenomena of interest also increases (e.g., a scale that measures body weight to the nearest tenth of a pound is unlikely to yield equivalent measures from hour to hour, as a person's weight will change according to what they eat or wear).

When the phenomenon being measured is people's health reports, the method of scaling must be compatible with the cognitive capacity to categorize information; otherwise, the scale will be unreliable. Research indicates that it is difficult for people to hold more than seven pieces of information in immediate memory. Thus, visual analogue scales of pain intensity were found to be less reliable than pain intensity scales employing 5 to 7 graduated response categories, such as no pain, a little, moderate, severe, and unbearable pain.

The reliability of a scale indicates how reproducible the scale score is, but does not indicate whether that score provides the information it was designed to provide. For that, the scale's validity must be assessed.

Validity

Validity is evidence that a survey, or questionnaire, measures what it is supposed to measure, and does not measure what it is not supposed to measure. The most important questions to ask when reviewing documentation of a particular survey's validity are: 1) Does the evidence support the validity of the questionnaire for my purposes? and 2) Was the evidence gathered from a well-designed study?

Because validity refers to the appropriateness of a particular questionnaire and purpose, evidence must be gathered in relation to each specific purpose for which the questionnaire is used. Thus, validity is not an absolute property of a questionnaire established once and forever. Studies of the validity of a questionnaire may continue for as long as the questionnaire is applied within new situations.

Sensitivity, specificity, and responsiveness are all different terms used to describe the validity of a scale (e.g., a general health measure is sensitive to the degree that it reflects the impact of all phenomena that may influence health, such as age, disease state, eating habits, and stress level). A general health measure is specific to the degree that it responds to differences in health, and not other factors, such as reading ability. Responsiveness indicates the ability of a health measure to detect change in health, over time, in individuals whose health does in fact change.

Methods for testing the validity of a measure can be categorized according to the three broad approaches of content, construct, and criterion. Although it is convenient to discuss evidence for validity under these three headings, at the outset, a great deal of overlap exists among them.

Table 3. Content analysis of the Brief Pain Inventory

Potential Items	Sensory Dimension of Pain	Reactive Dimension of Pain
Worst pain	*	
Least pain	*	
Average pain	*	
Pain right now	*	
Pain interferes with general activity		*
Pain interferes with mood		*
Pain interferes with walking ability		*
Pain interferes with normal work		*
Pain interferes with relations with others		*
Pain interferes with sleep		*
Pain interferes with enjoyment of life		*

Content Validity

Content validity depends on establishing logical links between the purpose of the questionnaire and the items, and scales included in the questionnaire. Evidence of content validity is gathered to answer the question: Does this survey contain items that adequately describe the health state measured? This question is answered by comparing the health information in the survey to that presented in the peer-reviewed literature, or by consulting subject matter experts, such as clinicians, medical researchers, and individuals who are experiencing that health state.

If the purpose of a questionnaire is to measure pain, the content validity of the questionnaire will depend on whether the items and scales address the most essential components of pain. One way to identify these components is to conduct a review of the published literature to determine the consensus among experts regarding models of pain. When the developers of the Brief Pain Inventory (BPI) did this, they found that there was agreement that pain included at least two dimensions; a sensory dimension, and a reactive dimension. Thus, the developers generated items that would reflect the magnitude of pain and the reactions of people to pain. The asterisks in Table 3 show the logical links between the item content from the BPI (first column) and dimensions of pain frequently described in the clinical literature (i.e., sensory and reactive, second and third column, respectively).

Construct Validity

Constructs are variables that are not measured directly, but are hypothesized to underlie the relationships among measured variables, which are "constructed" based on these relationships (e.g., intelligence is a construct). It is a variable hypothesized to underlie the relationship between SAT scores and grade-point average. Whenever it is hypothesized that some unseen, unmeasured variable is responsible for the relationship among other variables, and the focus is to establish the validity of a measure of that variable, a *construct validity* study is being performed. Construct validity assessments of a measure of role functioning might determine the relationship between the role functioning scores and number of days missed from work, or the relationship of role functioning scores to scores from other measures of role functioning, such as those contained in the Work Limitations Questionnaire or the Sickness Impact Profile. Evidence of construct validity is gathered by testing hypotheses regarding relationships between measures that would be obtained if, in fact, these measures addressed the same construct. The hypotheses that are tested take the form of the assumption: If my questionnaire is measuring this construct, then I expect to observe certain [fill in the blank] significant relationships. There are two common forms of relationships that are tested: 1) within the questionnaire, the relationships of items to each other, and scales to each other are tested; 2) between the questionnaire and other measures, the relationships of scale scores to scores from other questionnaires measuring the same, or different constructs, and the relationships of scale scores to other indicators of health differences, are tested.

Suppose a person wants to test the construct validity of a scale to measure pain. First, administer the questionnaire to a group of people and calculate their scale scores. Then, look to see that all the items in the scale are related to each other. This would argue for the fact that all the items measure one concept. Next, look to see how the scale scores of these people are related to other indicators of pain. Find out whether the respondents to the patient questionnaire have any chronically painful conditions such as arthritis or migraine. It would be expected that those patients with chronically painful conditions would have worse pain scores than those without such conditions. If this were found to be the case, evidence for construct validity would exist.

Factorial, convergent, and discriminant construct validity methods

Factorial validity, including *convergent* and *discriminant validity*, is a way to identify constructs based on the relationship of survey responses to one another. This can be done at the scale level by looking at the relationships between scale scores within, or among, questionnaires or at the item level by looking at the relationship among responses to items in a questionnaire.

Table 4 presents the relationship of items on the BPI to underlying constructs or factors. The table shows that those items that ask patients to describe how strong their pain is are highly related to the first factor (the items converge on this factor — *convergent* validity), and have a much weaker relationship to the second factor (the items discriminate in

Table 4. Factor Analysis of the Brief Pain Inventory

0-10 ratings for items (0=no pain; 10=pain as bad as you can imagine)	Severity factor loadings	Interference factor loadings
Your worst pain	.73	.13
Your least pain	.59	.08
Your average pain	.61	.17
Your pain right now	.83	-.01
0-10 ratings for items (0=does not interfere; 10=completely interferes)		
Pain interferes with general activity	.31	.64
Pain interferes with mood	.08	.81
Pain interferes with walking ability	.26	.62
Pain interferes with normal work	.32	.62
Pain interferes with relations with others	-.04	.87
Pain interferes with sleep	.39	.46
Pain interferes with enjoyment of life	-.02	.89

their relationships to the two factors—*discriminant* validity). The pattern of the relationship of questionnaire content to underlying factors is used to define the factors. The first factor is highly related to items that describe the severity of pain, so it is labeled the "Severity" factor; whereas, the second factor is highly related to items that describe how pain interferes with different aspects of a person's life, so it is labeled the "Interference" factor. This is, in fact, the pattern of relationships of items to factors that is generally found for the BPI, and supports the construct validity of the Severity and Interference scale scores. While the BPI was developed for use in cancer patients, the data provided in Table 4 is from patients with a variety of non-cancer pain. These data, thus, argue that the Severity and Interference factors are valid in patients different from those for which the BPI was originally developed.

The method of convergent and discriminant validity to identify underlying factors, or constructs, is not only done to look at the relationship of items to scales, but to look at the relationship of measures to one another (e.g., if several questionnaires are administered to a patient, including several pain questionnaires, and several depression questionnaires, a person would expect the pattern of relationships among the scale scores to be such that the pain scores would be highly related to each other [convergent validity], and less related to the depression scores [discriminant validity]).

Known group validity methods

Known group validity is a common method of testing the construct validity of a questionnaire in which respondents are divided into groups that should have different scores on the questionnaire because the patients are known to differ in the attribute being measured. For physical health questionnaires, known groups are often created based on age categories with research that shows that physical health generally declines with age. Another simple way of creating known groups is to compare people with a particular diagnosis to those without it (e.g., those with and without arthritis). Suppose the validity of scores from a questionnaire are evaluated to measure the degree to which people get adequate sleep. The questionnaire would be given to respondents who are likely to differ in the quantity, and quality, of sleep, and see if, in fact, the questionnaire scores discriminate among these groups. A person may know from experience, and certainly there is a large scientific literature to back this, that attempting to sleep during daylight results in poorer quality sleep than sleeping at night. If the questionnaire is measuring sleep adequacy, hypothesize that the scores would be higher (better) for people working the day shift (i.e., sleeping at night) than for people working the night shift (i.e., sleeping during the day). The data presented in Figure 2 support the construct validity of our sleep adequacy measure, based on the method of known groups because they show that the people who work during the night have lower scores than those who work during the day.

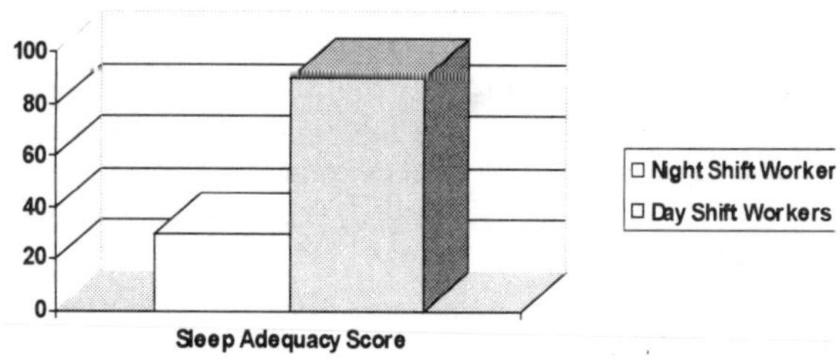

Figure 2. Sleep Adequacy Scores: Shift Workers

Criterion Validity

Criterion validity is assessed by testing the relationship of scale scores to a measure that is considered to be the standard measure for that variable (e.g., if wanting to provide evidence of the criterion validity of a dyspnea questionnaire, look at the relationship between patients' questionnaire scores and percent of normal forced expiratory volume in one second ($FEV_{1\%}$) levels).

Standards of Validity

Standards of validity assessments usually require detecting statistically significant relationships between patient-rated outcome scores and some other variable (e.g., statistically significant differences in health status scores at different levels of arthritis severity would be evidence for the validity of the scores). Whereas statistically significant results are necessary, they are not sufficient evidence of validity. It is also important to assess the relevance, and the quality, of the study. That is, are the results applicable to situations external to the particular study and setting that generated them? *External validity* refers to whether the results are relevant to populations and relationships other than those included in the validity study.

Internal validity refers to whether the results of a study can be unambiguously attributed to the influence of variables internal to the study. Suppose the relationship of health status scores to arthritis severity is due to a third variable — age. Those with the most severe arthritis are also the oldest, whereas those with the least severe arthritis are the youngest. The health status scores may not be sensitive to arthritis at all, but rather to age. In that case, the validity results would be due to the influence of a variable, not internal to the relationships that are the specific focus of the study. Thus, the internal validity of the results is compromised. A threat to internal validity is the influence of unanticipated variables. Wherever possible, attempts should be made to rule out the effects of other variables on the relationship between variables of interest.

Randomized clinical trials (RCTs) are examples of studies designed to have high internal validity. Great care is taken to rule out the effect of extraneous variables by applying stringent research protocols, including very specific inclusion and exclusion criteria for subjects. Because of this, the efficacy in the field, or external validity of the results of an RCT, is frequently questioned.

Scaling Effects

Scaling determines the precision of measurement and, thus, affects tests of the validity of a survey. Suppose the validity of a 5-level physical functioning scale was tested by relating it to a continuous measure of physical functioning. Very different scores on the continuous scale among respondents who are all at level 4 on the 5-level scale could be found. This lack of precision is likely to result in the 5-level scale demonstrating weaker relationships to other measures of physical functioning than would be obtained with the continuous scale.

Effect of Reliability

It is often difficult to grasp the difference between reliability and validity because most people intuitively understand that both attributes determine whether a measure provides information. Whereas validity has to do with whether the survey tells us what we want to know; reliability has to do with whether the survey yields stable answers in unchanging respondents. Reliability is a necessary precondition for validity, but the opposite is not true. A measure can be reliable without being valid. Although a measure can yield stable readings for an unchanging subject, the readings may have no relationship to the health of the subject (e.g., each time a tape measure is used to measure the circumference of someone's head, the same number is likely to be obtained. However, the number will tell nothing about how healthy that person is). The tape measure yields reliable readings. However, the readings are not valid measures of health. The readings provided by an instrument must be trustworthy, or reliable, in order to provide useful, or valid, information. There is also a practical relationship between reliability and validity. As indicated above, the amount of error in a measure, the unreliability, limits the precision with which estimates of validity for that measure can be made.

Bringing Meaning to Patient-Rated Outcome Data

One of the most frequently asked questions about patient-rated outcome scores has to do with interpretation; What do the numbers mean? Similar approaches are used in validation and interpretation, but the focus is slightly different. Validity assessments focus on the *magnitude* of the relationships between the PRO score and *indicators that the score should be related to* if it is indeed measuring what it is supposed to measure. The stronger the relationship between the PRO score and such an indicator, the more valid that PRO score is considered to be. Similarly, the more responsive the PRO score is to change in that indicator, the more valid that PRO score is considered to be.

Deriving interpretations for PRO scores is a bit more complicated than assessing their validity, because the experiences and values of the audiences for the PRO data play a role (e.g., a PRO score may be valid in that it changes when the health of the patient changes. However, those changes may or may not be meaningful to an individual patient, or be deemed worthy of reimbursement by the private or public insurers).

In understanding the difference between validity and interpretation, it helps to use the analogy of an outdoor temperature thermometer. The thermometer is valid when the numbers change in correspondence to the weather in a way that makes sense based on the weather. But how is the meaning of those numbers interpreted? This comes from experience. It is learned that when the numbers are at a certain magnitude, it will be cold when outside, at another magnitude, it will be hot and at another magnitude, it will be comfortable. It is learned that the numbers provide information about what should be worn and whether to take equipment (an umbrella or shovel). A Celsius and Fahrenheit thermometer may be equally valid, but the meaning of the numbers provided by one thermometer may be understood, and the meaning of the numbers provided by the other may not be understood. If a person is experienced with the Celsius thermometer only, the data provided by the Fahrenheit thermometer will be useless (even though reliable and valid). Time spent using the Fahrenheit thermometer is needed before the meaning of the numbers becomes intuitive. The meaning of a PRO score is understood through experience of how the score is related to other variables. Gathering information to interpret scores is an ongoing process for the life of a questionnaire. With accumulating experience, the understanding of the meaning of scores increases. Learning how to interpret these scores can allow users to determine their societal and economic implications, and whether a statistically significant difference exists between treatment groups that is meaningful in terms of how people are able to function in their daily lives.

Methods of Interpreting PRO Scores

Standard psychometric texts typically do not describe methods to interpret questionnaire scores. However, these methods are evident in the way the data are commonly presented to audiences. Common methods of scale score interpretation include: descriptions of scale content; comparisons of obtained scale scores to some normative standard for these scores (individual or group); and the relationship of the scores to phenomena thought to be causes or consequences of the score.

Analysis of Content

Content-based interpretation of PRO scale scores relies on the direct meaning of the items and response choices in the scale. That content determines what the respondents think about in replying to the question and, therefore, provides an indication of what the answers mean (e.g., a choice of excellent in response to the question, "In general, would you say your health is excellent, very good, good, fair, or poor?," defines the highest level of health possible. As defined in Table 5, where excellent is a score of 1, and poor is a score of 5, going from a score of 2 to a score of 1 is an improvement in health, from better than good, but not excellent, to excellent health).

In general, multi-item scales are preferred over single-item scales (e.g., Table 5) because the scores are almost always more reliable and valid. Compared to single item scales, multi-item scales have the potential to provide a more comprehensive sample of the universe of content, and, because they have more levels of measurement, they nearly always have greater reliability relative to single-item scales. However, content-based interpretation of the scores of multi-item scales is complex because most of the scores (with the exception of the top and bottom scores) can be achieved by a variety of response patterns (i.e., there are many ways to get the same score). Scores at the top or bottom of the scale are easy to interpret because they have unique response patterns: A person needs only to look at the items and response choices necessary to earn those scores to understand the health state of the person with that score (e.g., as displayed in Table 6, the top score of the SF-36 Physical Functioning scale is earned only one way: by being able to perform all physical activities mentioned, including vigorous activities, without limitations due to health. Conversely, the bottom score is assigned only to those individuals limited by their health in performing all physical activities, including bathing and dressing).

Table 5. Widely-used General Health Item

In general, would you say your health is:

	(Circle one)
Excellent	1
Very good	2
Good	3
Fair	4
Poor	5

The challenge in interpreting multi-item scales lies in bringing meaning to all of the scores between the highest and lowest. A useful method is to use responses to a single item from the scale to interpret scores across scale levels (e.g., what does it mean to improve from a score of 40 to 50 on the scale in Table 6?). To address this question, a question was chosen from the scale that would indicate whether a person could walk enough to engage in every day activities. Then people were separated into two categories according to whether a person could walk a block (item 9) with or without limitation (ignoring how limited the person was). Next, the percentage of people who responded that they could walk one block without difficulty for each of 10 levels of the Physical Functioning scale was calculated (see Figure 3). As the Physical Functioning scale scores increased from 40 to 50 points, 18 percent more people could walk one block without limitations. Therefore, a 10-point improvement at this level of the scale results in nearly

Table 6. Items in the SF-36 Physical Functioning Scale

The following items are about activities you might do during a typical day. Does your health now limit you in these activities? If so, how much?

(circle one number on each line)

Activities	YES, Limited a lot	YES, Limited a little	NO, Not limited at all
1. Vigorous activities, such as running, lifting, heavy objects, participating in strenuous sports	1	2	3
2. Moderate activities, such as moving a table, pushing a vacuum cleaner, bowling, or playing golf	1	2	3
3. Lifting or carrying groceries	1	2	3
4. Climbing several flights of stairs	1	2	3
5. Climbing one flight of stairs	1	2	3
6. Bending, kneeling, or stooping	1	2	3
7. Walking more than a mile	1	2	3
8. Walking several blocks	1	2	3
9. Walking one block	1	2	3
10. Bathing or dressing yourself	1	2	3

SF-36 = SF-36 Health Survey

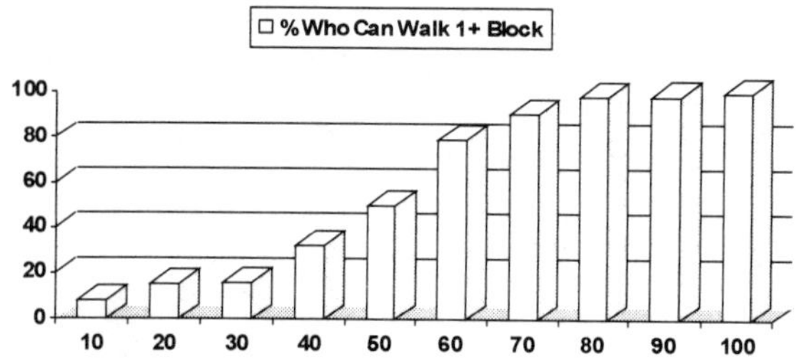

Figure 3. Percentage of Respondents Who Can Walk One Block or More at Each Scale Level

a 55 percent increase in the percentage of people reporting being unlimited by health in being able to walk a block. The graph also shows an important inflexion point at the score of 80 in that everyone who achieves that score can walk a block without difficulty. The graph also shows that most of the change in ability to walk a block occurs in the range of Physical Functioning scale scores between 30 and 80.

Normative Comparisons

With norm-based comparisons, scores are understood as departures from expected or typical scores. These expected, or typical scores, are called norms. Norm-based comparison is a common method for interpreting health data. Tables of normal ranges are given for different blood tests. Sometimes these ranges are stratified by gender. When calculating the average score of a group of individuals who respond to a PRO, does this average depart from what is expected based on the age, or diagnosis, of the respondents: that is, are these people healthier, or not as healthy as expected? PRO norms can be computed at the individual or group level. At the individual level, norms are the scores typical of the individual under stable conditions. At the group level, norms are the average values for the group and can be calculated based on a sample of the general population.

The availability of published norms would be a strong reason for using an existing PRO, rather than creating a new PRO specifically for a particular study. Suppose a study of the general health of a group of people is being conducted. If only interested in content-based interpretation, researchers could make up their own general health question to field in the study (for example, see Table 7). These data can be analyzed to see if the average score of the respondents is close to the value for "Extremely healthy," "very healthy," or "somewhat healthy," but it will not be known how typical that score is — whether the group of respondents is healthier or less healthy than would be expected.

By contrast, the item in Table 8 (and Table 5) is an established measure of health used for decades in many large national data collections, and so normative values can be calculated for this item based on population samples. It also is possible to obtain norms for this item stratified according to different sociodemographic characteristics and clinical conditions. Had this item been used, in addition to performing a content-based interpretation of the average score of the group, the group's score could be compared to the norms. Table 9 shows some averages calculated on data for that item that have been transformed so that higher scores mean better health and scores are expressed on a scale of 0-100. Based on the normative data in Table 9, an average group score of "72" may mean that the respondents enjoy health typical of well people in the age range of 25-44.

The usefulness of PRO data will be greatly enhanced with the availability of normative data to aid in interpretation. It is important to research whether norms exist for a PRO measure before deciding to use it. Because the health status of individuals is influenced by variables such as age and gender, normative values are often calculated separately for males and females, and for different age groups.

Table 7. Newly Drafted General Health Item

How healthy are you?	(Circle one)
Extremely healthy	1
Very healthy	2
Somewhat healthy	3
Not very healthy	4
Not at all healthy	5

Table 8. Established Measure of General Health

In general, would you say your health is:	(Circle one)
Excellent	1
Very Good	2
Good	3
Fair	4
Poor	5

Table 9. Normative Data for Established Measure of General Health

Age	18-24	76.54
	25-34	71.75
	35-44	72.00
	45-54	70.92
	55-64	69.35
	65+	68.77
Condition	Well	74.73
	Hypertension	66.43
	Depression	66.87
	CHF	54.92

CHF = Congestive heart failure

Relationship to Causes and Consequences

The meaning of scale scores can be gauged by looking at likely causes and consequences of differences. To understand how this would work in relationship to causes consider the questions in Tables 10 and 11. In Version 2 of the Consumer Assessments of Health Plans Survey (CAHPS 2.0), respondents are asked to rate their health plan on an 11-point scale starting with "0" to indicate the worst health plan possible, and going to "10" to indicate the best health plan possible (see Table 10).

Table 10. Overall Health Plan Rating on the CAHPS™ 2.0 Adult Core Questionnaire (October, 1998, Harvard, RAND, RTI International)

We want to know your rating of all your experience with your health plan. Use any number from 0 to 10 where 0 is the worst health plan possible, and 10 is the best health plan possible. How would you rate your health plan now?

☐ 0 Worst health plan possible
☐ 1
☐ 2
☐ 3
☐ 4
☐ 5
☐ 6
☐ 7
☐ 8
☐ 9
☐ 10 Best health plan possible

Table 11. Question from the Access-to-Care Composite on the CAHPS™ 2.0 Adult Core Questionnaire (October, 1998, Harvard, RAND, RTI International)

In the last 12 months, how much of a problem, if any, were delays in health care while you waited for approval from your health plan?

☐ A big problem
☐ A small problem
☐ Not a problem
☐ I had no visits in the last 12 months

While the overall rating of health plans is interesting, audiences for these data will want to know what specific features of the plan are associated with these ratings. Table 11 presents one such feature: How much of a problem, over the past 12 months, was waiting for plan approval in order to obtain health care?

Figure 4 shows that lower overall health plan ratings mean that consumers had a problem with obtaining approval for health care usage (data are hypothetical).

Meaning also is brought to scale scores by looking at the relationship to future events (e.g., it is possible to get an idea of the severity of scores for a general health PRO by plotting the scores of respondents against the percentage who develop a chronic illness or die five years hence). Figure 5 demonstrates how to bring meaning to the responses to the "Problem with Health Plan Approval" item by plotting the percentage of people who disenrolled from their health plan against their responses to that item a year before (data are hypothetical).

When interpreting the relationship of PRO responses to either causes, or consequences, it is important to take into account the potential influence of other variables (e.g., health plan disenrollment may have little to do with whether consumers are bothered by waiting for health plan approval; rather, it may be determined by a change in plan availability [sometimes people disenroll because the plan is no longer

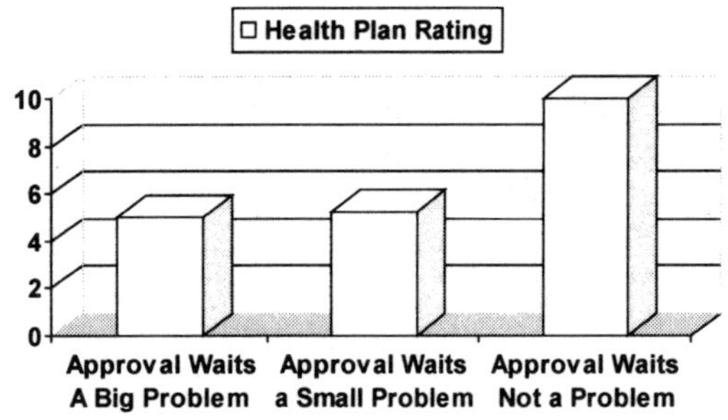

Figure 4. Problems with Health Plan Approval Waits Over Past 12 Months Plotted Against Overall Health Plan Rating Now

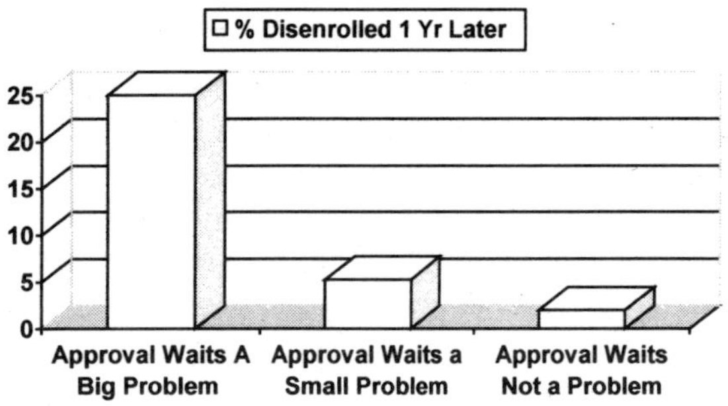

Figure 5. Problems with Health Plan Approval Waits Over Past 12 Months Plotted Against Percent Who Were Disenrolled From that Health Plan One Year Later

offered by the company, or because they move out of the region where the plan is located]).

Another way to interpret PROs, in terms of causes or consequences, is to identify a particular PRO score that most accurately separates patients into health-related categories of interest. Response Operator Curve (ROC) analysis was used to identify the score on the MHI-5 of the (SF-36) that would have the lowest overall error rate in classifying patients into those that were, or were not, clinically depressed, according to standard psychiatric interviews. This analysis found that an MHI-5 score of 52 correctly classified the greatest percentage of patients. In a similar fashion, a cut-off score for a physical functioning scale could be identified based on future employability. Suppose patients at an inpatient rehabilitation facility are administered a physical functioning PRO at discharge. One year later, data could be gathered regarding whether or not each patient is employed. ROC curve analysis could be used to identify the discharge physical functioning score that most accurately classifies patients, in terms of their employment status, 1 year later. In the future, those patients scoring near, or below, the cut-off score could then be assigned to more intense outpatient therapy, in order to improve chances of future employability.

Methods for Interpreting *Differences* in PRO Scores

In the discussion above, different methods of bringing meaning to a particular score, or to a range of scores were discussed. However, the meaning of the *magnitude of differences* in scores has not yet been addressed. In other words, using the thermometer analogy, it has been shown how to bring meaning to a temperature of 32 or 72 degrees Fahrenheit, but it has not directly been discussed how to know

Table 12. Types of PRO Score Differences

	Type of Data Collection Required	
Type of Comparison	**Cross-Sectional**	**Longitudinal**
Within patient(s) only		Change in pain score for each patient from beginning to end of treatment.
Between patients only	Comparison of pain scores of treated and untreated patients at end of treatment.	Comparison between treated and untreated patients' pain scores at two time points: the beginning of treatment, and again at the end of treatment.
Both within <u>and</u> between patients		Comparison between treated and untreated patients' <u>change in</u> pain scores from beginning to end of treatment.

whether a difference in temperature of 2 degrees is important, and how to determine what size difference in temperature would be important. Before describing methods that might be used to interpret score differences, it is helpful to define the major types of differences that may be of interest.

Score differences are any quantity that could be determined by subtracting the scores on the same PRO, and include comparisons within and/or between patients. Table 12 defines and gives examples of common types of score differences that a person might want to interpret. The type of difference is defined by the intersection of row and column headings, and an example of this difference for each appears in the table cells.

The following discussion of interpretation methods for differences in scores draws heavily on recent reviews of methods for determining a MID in a PRO score, also called minimal important difference (MCID). It is widely known that there is not a one-to-one correspondence between differences that can be detected statistically, and those that can be perceived, or experienced, or those that will have meaningful implications for the future. MID methods have grown out of a need to derive systematic and standardized approaches to determining whether a score difference is important. In the current era of health care cost containment, private and public insurers are asking for guidance from health services researchers to determine when a difference in health outcome is worth reimbursing. The promise of MIDs is that they would determine consequential differences in health, regardless of statistical significance, and so be a primary determinant to medical decision making. At present, it is not clear whether that promise will be fulfilled. The current consensus among reviewers is that the definition of MIDs requires much more methodological work before they could provide data that are reliable and valid enough to determine formularies or guide treatment protocols. Nevertheless, the MID literature is useful for the purpose of this learning module because the search for the MID has produced a taxonomy of interpretation methods that can be used to define the meaning, or importance, of PRO differences in general.

Judgement-Based Interpretation of Differences

Briefly characterized in this section are some frequently mentioned approaches to identifying important differences that rely on subjective evaluations.

Patient evaluations

Internal comparisons. With this method, patients are asked whether or not their status has changed (e.g., Is there a change in the severity of your pain?), and, if so, how much their status has changed? This method is an internal comparison because patients compare their current state with their previous state (e.g., at the beginning of treatment) in order to evaluate whether they've changed, and how much. Frequently, a 15-point scale is used where "0" indicates no change and -1 to -7 indicates increasing degrees, or change, for the worse, whereas +1 to +7 indicates increasing degrees of change for the better (see Figure 6).

The average change score on a PRO (e.g., on a physical functioning scale) for patients who indicate that they have gotten minimally better, or minimally worse, is calculated, and this quantity is the MID. However, when labels are not provided for all of the response choices, as in Figure 6, the choice of the value for minimally better or minimally worse is left up to the data analyst, and this introduces another source of judgment (the analyst's) into the process. The value chosen by analysts varies in the literature from ± 1 to ± 3. Moderate, or large, differences in a PRO could also be identified using this method (e.g., a person could calculate the average change score for people who responded at the mid [± 3 to ± 5] or extreme [±6 to ± 7] values, respectively, of the item in Figure 6).

At this writing, the literature provides no clear guidance for the meaning of these internal comparisons. The validity of the comparisons is often assessed by comparing actual baseline responses to retrospective responses. When this is done, the retrospective ratings sometimes suggest that "response shift" has occurred in that patients *remember* their baseline condition as less serious than they had, in fact,

-7	-6	-5	-4	-3	-2	-1	0	+1	+2	+3	+4	+5	+6	+7
Very much worse							The same							Very much better

Figure 6. An example of a 15-point Patients Self-rating of Change Scale

indicated at baseline. Response shift is theorized to occur either because patients adapt to feeling worse (e.g., more tired, greater pain) or, as a result of their health, they adapt their expectations for what they should do, so they no longer feel as limited (e.g., they cut back from working 12 hours a day to 8 hours a day, and so they feel less tired and have less pain). A recent qualitative study into what people mean when they say they have gotten better supports these theories. On the basis of extensive interviews, the study authors classified the meaning people gave for answering "Yes" to the question, "Are you better?" into three categories: 1) the condition resolved; 2) the condition did not resolve, but people practiced ignoring it; 3) the condition did not resolve, but people adjusted the demands made on them either by not doing what they were doing before, doing it differently, or doing it with help. Another curiosity with regard to internal comparisons is the frequent finding that changes for the worse are minimized, while changes for the better are exaggerated in retrospective evaluations. One explanation offered is that information that is counter to expectations is more salient than that which is consistent, and if people are prone to expect getting worse they will take more notice when they get better.

External comparisons. In contrast to the internal comparison method where patients compare themselves to an earlier time, the external comparison method asks patients to compare themselves to other patients. One way to do this is to randomly assign patients to dyads where they converse about their condition to each other. Then, in private, each patient rates her or himself relative to the dyad partner on an ordinal scale like the one in Figure 6. The average difference in PRO scores between those patients who rate themselves as minimally different than their partner (better or worse) is the MID. Again, moderate and large differences also could be identified using this method.

Clinician evaluations

Similar to the methods described above, a physician global rating of patient change can be used to identify those patients who are judged to have changed minimally; then the average change scores of those patients can be calculated to derive an MID. The source of change evaluation is likely to influence whether, and how much, change is perceived. Previous research indicates that, compared to patients, clinicians are likely to see more improvement, more frequently.

When the PRO is something with which clinicians are somewhat familiar (e.g., an 11-point global rating of pain intensity), group consensus techniques can be used to derive MIDs (e.g., expert clinician could be given average scores and standard deviations for PRO data obtained from groups of patients with different clinical profiles. They could then be asked, individually and anonymously, to give their opinion regarding what would be the smallest clinically meaningful difference on that PRO. These anonymous judgments would be reported to all participating clinicians and each would have an opportunity to anonymously revise her or his MID based on information provided by the group. The process could be repeated until consensus regarding the MID is achieved).

Statistical Approaches

Standard error of measurement

The standard error of measurement (SEM) is an estimate of the amount of variability a person would expect to find around any observed score — it can be used to determine whether a minimally noticeable change has occurred. The SEM is used to calculate confidence bands around individual scale scores just as the standard error is used to calculate confidence intervals around the average score for a group of individuals. The formula for SEM takes into account two estimates of variability: the standard deviation of scale scores (the standard deviation of a normative population will provide a stable estimate of such) and the reliability (r_{tt}) of the scale. The SEM equals the standard deviation multiplied by the square root of 1 minus the reliability (see Figure 7).

$$SEM = Std * \sqrt{1 - r_{tt}}$$

Figure 7. Formula for Standard Error of Measurement

This means that scores with smaller standard deviations and higher reliability estimates will have smaller SEMs. Suppose a patient had a pain score of 50 pre-treatment (scores are on 100-point scale with higher scores meaning better health [i.e., less pain]), how can the SEM be used to determine whether treatment has led to meaningful intra-individual change in pain? According to the formula in Figure 7, if the standard deviation for the scores on this pain measure is 10 and the reliability of the measure is .90 then the SEM will be 3.16. Individual change can be interpreted as the same, better, or worse if the individual's score at time two falls within the range of the baseline score plus or minus one SEM, is greater than the baseline score plus one SEM, or less than the baseline score minus one SEM, respectively (see Table 13).

Table 13. Interpretation of Intra-Individual Change in PRO Score Using SEM

Am I…	
Better	Time 2 Score > Time 1 Score + SEM
Same	Time 1 Score - SEM ≤ Time 2 Score ≤ Time 1 Score + SEM
Worse	Time 2 Score < Time 1 Score - SEM

SEM = Standard error of measurement

Standardized effect size

Everything discussed until this point has concerned the interpretation of "effect sizes." The size of an effect is simply another term for a difference between scores (e.g., if there is *no effect* of treatment, there is *no difference* between the scores of treated and untreated patients. If there is, in fact, *an effect* of treatment, there *is a difference of a certain magnitude* between the treated and untreated). It is useful to index the size of the effect against the variability a person would expect in the scores of a clinically stable patient. For the effect to be real, it must be greater than this variability.

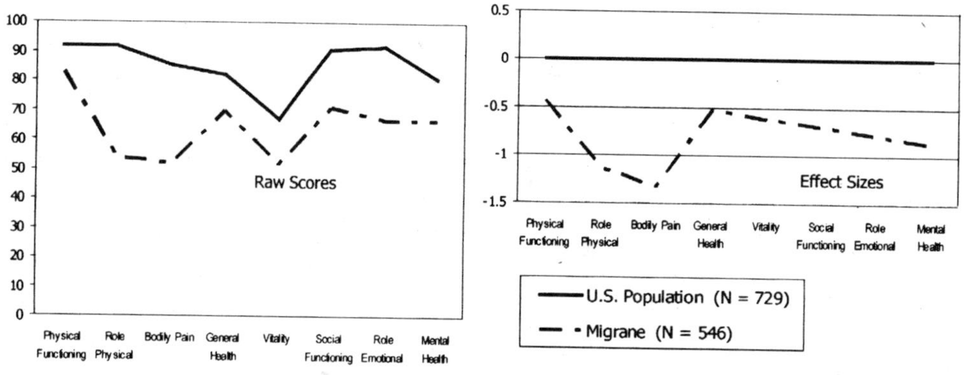

Figure 8. Interpretation of Differences Using Effect Sizes

Variability of scores is estimated in different ways, but the most commonly used estimate is the standard deviation for the scores within the stable population. When the difference between scores is divided by this standard deviation, the scores are expressed in z-scores, or normal curve deviates, and typically range from -3 to +3. PRO scores with different raw score ranges and standard deviations can be made comparable (i.e., transformed to have the same range and standard deviation) by expressing them as z-scores. These are also called *standardized effect sizes*. When standardized effect sizes are calculated from changes in scores, they are sometimes called *responsiveness statistics*.

The interpretation value of standardized effect sizes is that they enable valid comparisons among PROs that differ in raw score metrics as illustrated by the data in Figure 8. The graph on the left shows the difference between the general population and a group of patients with migraines in mean scores for eight different PRO scales. Since each scale differs from the general population by a different amount, and each scale has a different degree of variability in clinically stable respondents (see Table 14), it is difficult to judge how large the differences between scales are using raw score units. The graph on the right shows these differences expressed as standardized effect sizes. It clearly is shown that the effect of migraine is more pronounced on the Bodily Pain scale than any of the other PROs. Contrary to the impression given in the left-hand graph, the right-hand graph shows that the effect of migraine on the Mental Health scale is larger than it is on the Social Functioning.

Sources of Misinterpretation of Differences

Now that some standard methods of illustrating the importance of scale score differences were briefly described, it is important to be aware of some common mistakes that can be made in this endeavor.

Lack of standardization in Methods

Misinterpretation of *comparisons* over time within groups, and comparison between groups, can occur due to heterogeneity of survey methods. One important survey method is the mode, or medium, of question administration. Mode refers to how the questions are asked: Is there an interviewer? Is the interview conducted face-to-face, over the telephone, or by way of the Internet? Does the respondent answer the questions in privacy by filling out a paper, or electronic form, or by pressing the keys on a telephone? The mode of administration will affect scores when respondents lack literacy, such that those participants who must read the questions will be handicapped relative to those participants who are able to hear the questions read by someone else. The mode of administration also determines the privacy with which the respondent answers questions which can affect how respondents answer questions, particularly if the questions are of a sensitive nature (i.e., asking for information that people generally keep private because it might embarrass them. People are reluctant to admit to health behaviors that are known to be harmful, such as having unprotected sex, excessive eating or alcohol abuse, and they may be reluctant to admit to having a contagious, or potentially fatal disease, for fear of stigmatization).

Table 15 presents two questions from the Medical Outcomes Study (MOS) that ask people about their sexual functioning over the past 4 weeks. Such questions may be answered differently if the respondent has to talk to an interviewer, rather than filling out a form in private. A serious challenge to the interpretation of a treatment effect would occur if the mode of administration were changed from baseline to end of treatment. Suppose the baseline questionnaire was administered by an interviewer when the patient came into the clinic, but the end-of-treatment questionnaire was self-administered by the patient at home. The scores could indicate that sexual problems increased

Table 14. PRO Measures May Differ in their Standard Deviations

PRO Scale	Physical Functioning	Role Physical	Bodily Pain	General Health	Vitality	Social Functioning	Role Emotional	Mental Health
*US Gen. Pop StDev	23.28	34.00	23.69	20.34	20.96	22.69	33.04	18.05

PRO = Particular patient-related outcome
United States general population standard deviation

Table 15. Example Questions from the Medical Outcomes Study Health Survey

How much of a problem was <u>each</u> of the following during the past 4 weeks?

1. How much of a problem was lack of sexual interest for you over the past 4 weeks?

	(circle one)
Not a problem	1
Little of a problem	2
Somewhat of a problem	3
Very much a problem	4
Not applicable	5

2. How much of a problem was difficulty in becoming aroused for you over the past 4 weeks?

	(circle one)
Not a problem	1
Little of a problem	2
Somewhat of a problem	3
Very much a problem	4
Not applicable	5

Adapted with permission from Stewart, AL and Ware, JE (1992). Measuring Functioning and Wellbeing. Durham, NC: Duke University Press.

over the course of treatment (higher scores mean more problems). However, the increase could be because of the greater willingness of respondents to report problems in private (end-of-treatment survey), as compared to a face-to-face interview (baseline survey), and not to a paradoxical effect of treatment (see hypothetical data in Figure 9). Attributing this change to a paradoxical treatment effect could be an example of misinterpretation becuase of heterogeneity of methods.

Different or shifting demographic composition of respondents

Similarly, the demographic composition of the respondents to a survey can affect the scale scores. Age, gender and educational level may all affect the way people respond to health questionnaires, either because these variables are associated with health (older people tend to have poorer physical health) or because the variables affect the respondent's ability to understand the questions, or their comfort with the questions. This is why adjustments are made to normative scores so that they are based on samples that have a similar demographic composition to the comparison group. Figure 10 shows what might happen to the scores on the sexual functioning measure if the demographic composition of the respondent group were to change from baseline to end-of-treatment through the attrition of males from the study. Compared to females, males might report (or admit to) fewer sexual problems. If the baseline sample were mostly male, whereas the end-of-treatment sample were mostly female, the increase in scores over time might be because of the change in sample composition, rather than a paradoxical effect of treatment.

Sociodemographic variables, such as gender, age, education, income, and race/ethnicity, are shown to be associated with differences in health status; therefore, comparisons should be restricted to groups that are equivalent in terms of these background variables. Alternatively, statistical controls for these variables should be used.

Different types of respondents

The type of respondent also has an effect on scale scores. Proxies are often used to provide responses for those who cannot complete questionnaires becuase of disability and to recover patients who began the study but cannot complete subsequent administrations. Changing the survey respondent from self to proxy, and from proxy to self during longitudinal data collections is likely to lead to misinterpretation of survey results (e.g., authors of a review of studies examining the use of proxy data in health status assessment found that health care providers and significant others tend, in general, to underestimate patients' quality of

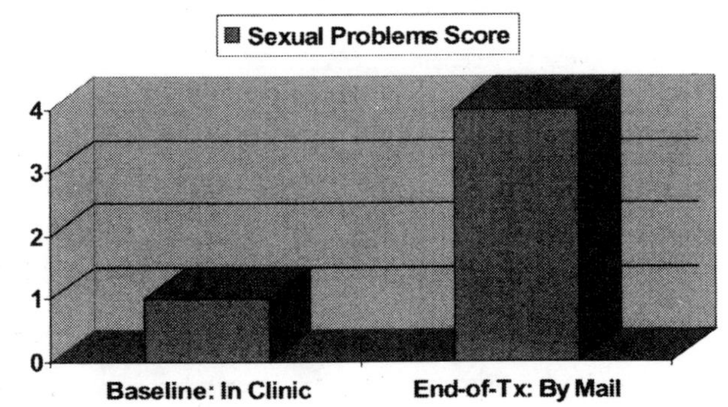

Figure 9. Possible Misinterpretation of Treatment Effects Due to Mode of Administration.

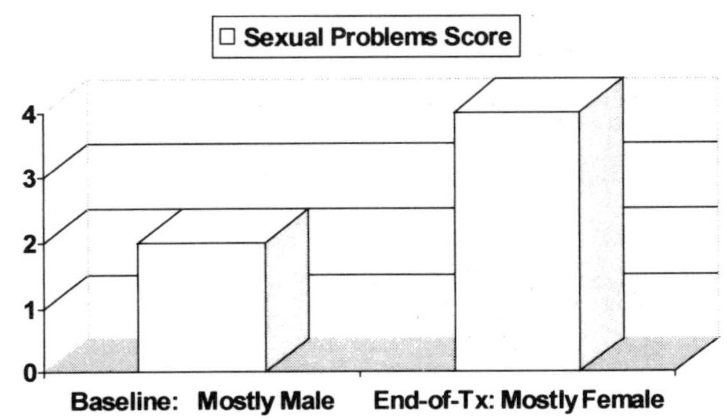

Figure 10. Possible Misinterpretation Due to Difference in Respondent Characteristics.

life; that health care providers tend to underrate the pain intensity experienced by their patients; and that proxy ratings tend to be more accurate when the information sought is concrete and observable. Thus, if proxy data are used, they should be used consistently throughout a study).

Standards for Interpretation

The interpretability of patient-rated outcome scores depends on the availability of data, or reports of data, in the public domain that can be analyzed to determine relationships to health status scores. Such data should include published norms for the general population, for different sociodemographic groups within that population, for different conditions, and for changes in conditions. Other data useful for interpretation include medical care utilization rates at various scale scores, diagnostic classifications associated with particular scale scores, and frequency of work disability associated with specific scale scores. At present, very few patient-rated outcome measures have data available for scale score interpretation. Standardization of measurement leads to the acquisition of these data. Each time the same measure is used in a new population, condition, or application, data are gathered to link the scale scores with new variables, yielding new interpretations for those scores.

All of the psychometric properties of scores considered, thus far, affect the interpretation of scale scores, including scaling, reliability, and validity. Each of these will be considered in the following sections.

Scaling Effects

The number of levels of measurement in a scale is important when interpreting scale scores because the ability of a scale to describe differences among people and changes within people over time increases with increased levels of measurement. For example, consider a walking scale with only two levels of measurement, 1) "I can walk," and 2) "I cannot walk." The majority of people in the general population would endorse the first statement, and it would be impossible to describe differences in walking ability among these people. The only change that could be detected among this group would be if someone was unable to walk. In contrast, consider the example of a scale with four levels of measurement, with 1) "I walk with no difficulty;" 2) "I walk, but with some difficulty;" 3) "I walk, but with a great deal of difficulty;" and 4) "I cannot walk." The group of people who endorsed the first response on the coarser scale would now be divided among responses 1, 2, and 3 on this finer scale. The possibility is greater to distinguish among people in terms of their walking ability and to describe change in people over time. Thus, the scale score has greater meaning or interpretability.

The following tables and graphs illustrate how the response scale to a single-item measure of health plan performance might influence the interpretation of results. Table 16 presents an item, which asks respondents how they would rate their health plan among choices of excellent, acceptable and poor. On the basis of Figure 11(data are hypothetical), it can be concluded that more than 90 percent of respondents felt that their health plan was excellent. However, if potential respondents are confronted with a response scale that has more choices falling between excellent and acceptable, a different interpretation of the data may result.

The item in Table 17 gives respondents a scale with three choices between "acceptable" and "excellent." Some of the respondents who were forced to choose the "excellent" response to the item in Table 16, will choose "nearly

Table 16. Satisfaction Question: No Levels Between Excellent and Acceptable

In general, how would you rate the performance of your health plan?

Poor	1
Acceptable	2
Excellent	3

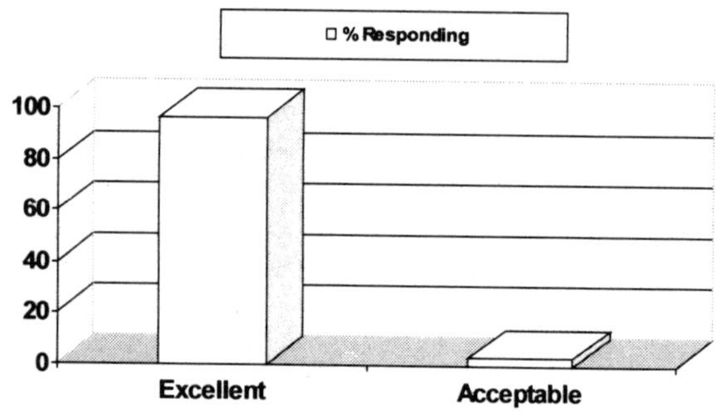

Figure 11: Percent of Patients Responding "Excellent"

Table 17. Patient Satisfaction Question: Three Levels Between Excellent and Acceptable

In general, how would you rate the performance of your health plan?

Poor	1
Acceptable	2
Good	3
Very good	4
Nearly Excellent	5

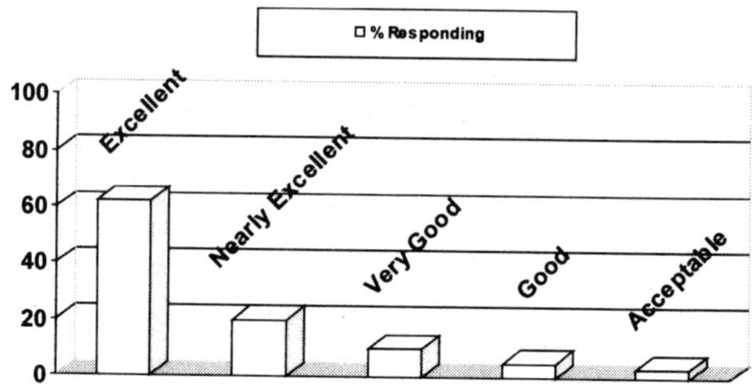

Figure 12: Percent of Patients Responding "Excellent"

excellent," "very good," and "good." It is likely that fewer people will choose the "excellent" response, and in this way, the scale will have affected how the data are interpreted (see Figure 12).

Effects of Reliability

Because reliability refers to how confident a person can be that a particular score is the true score, scale score reliability is a precondition for interpretation and researchers will have an effect on how differences in scores are interpretted. In an earlier section it was shown how the reliability of a score is part of the formula for its SEM. The SEM can be used to set confidence intervals around individual patients' scores. Use these confidence intervals to decide whether the difference between scores is real (e.g., the graphs in Figure 13 show data from two different PROs administered to the same patient).

Data were collected quarterly for 2 ½ years, and 10 data points were plotted to describe changes in the physical health of the patient over time. The PRO on the top differs from the PRO on the bottom in two ways: it has a lower reliability coefficient, and it has a larger standard deviation in a clinically stable sample. Therefore, according to the formula for SEM given in Figure 7, the confidence intervals around the data points for the PRO on the top will be wider than those for the PRO on the bottom. The PRO on the top indicates that there was no real improvement in health between the second and third data collection, whereas the PRO on the bottom indicates that there was. The different score reliabilities of the two PROs lead to different interpretations of the change in health between the second and third data collection.

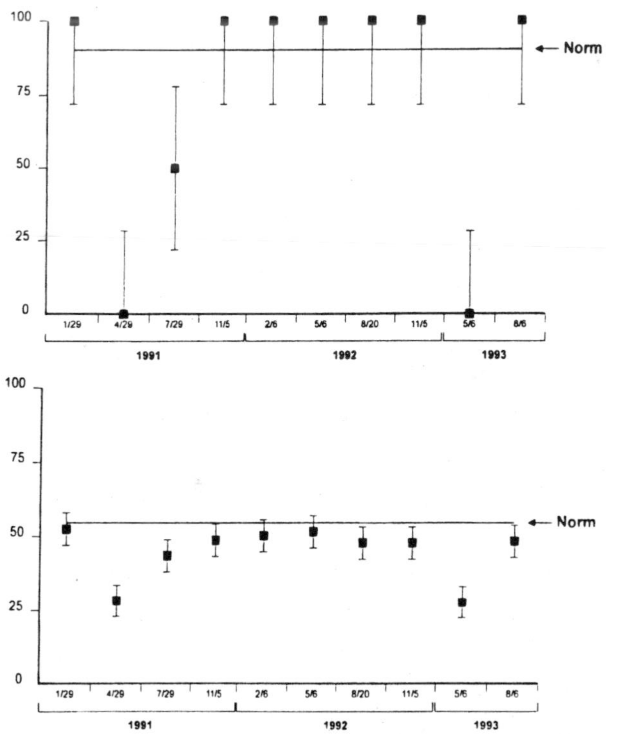

Figure 13. Reliability of Physical Health Status Scores Determines Whether You Can Detect a Real Change in Health Status

Table 18. Example of Questions that May not be Relevant to All Respondents

How often during the <u>past 4 weeks</u> did you experience joint pain during, or immediately following, vigorous exercise?

(circle one)

All of the time	1
Most of the time	2
Some of the time	3
A little of the time	4
None of the time	5

Table 19. Example of How Inconsistency Between Content and Title of a Measure May Lead to Misinterpretation

SIP: Emotional Behavior Scale

1. I say how bad or useless I am, for example, that I am a burden to others.
2. I laugh or cry suddenly.
3. I often moan and groan in pain or discomfort.
4. I have attempted suicide.
5. I act nervous or restless.
6. I keep rubbing or holding areas of my body that hurt or are uncomfortable.
7. I act irritable and impatient with myself, for example, talk badly about myself.
8. I talk about the future in a hopeless way.
9. I get sudden frights.

SIP = Sickness impact profile

Effects of Validity

Within the scope of this chapter, it is impossible to describe all the ways that validity may affect the interpretation of PRO scores. Certainly the most accessible aspect of PRO validity is the content validity of the scale. The following two examples illustrate the impact that content validity can have on score interpretation.

The relevance of a questionnaire's content to a particular group of respondents will affect the interpretability of scale scores. Suppose people who do not exercise are asked to indicate how often they experience pain during vigorous exercise (see Table 18). It is difficult to know what a response of, "None of the time" would mean for these people. Does it mean that they *do not* feel pain while exercising, or that they *do* feel pain, but not while exercising because they do not exercise?

The content validity of each item in a scale is important to interpreting the meaning of the total score for that scale. For example, Table 19 lists the items on the Sickness Impact Profile (SIP) Emotional Behavior scale. This scale was shown to be sensitive to the effects of analgesics. The content of the title of this scale might lead a person to interpret this finding as indicating that pain medication affects emotional behavior. However, looking at the shaded items, it can be seen that the relationship between this scale and analgesic treatment is probably due to scale content that is not consistent with the scale title (the shaded items).

Summary and Conclusions

This chapter deals with the subject of how to measure health and health care using PRO collected via questionnaires and surveys. The chapter begins with a discussion of scaling: that is, methods for assigning numbers to response choices to communicate categories (nominal), order (ordinal), or magnitude (interval and ratio). Next, methods for evaluating the trustworthiness of these numbers were presented including reliability estimates and validity studies. The second half of the chapter discusses ways to evaluate the meaningfulness of these numbers or to provide interpretations for these numbers to different audiences. The text also demonstrates the interdependence of each PRO attribute (i.e., scaling, reliability, validity, and interpretation). It was the author's intention to make the psychometrics behind the construction, and use of PRO's, accessible to practitioners, but also to demonstrate the complexity involved in developing, choosing, and using PRO's, and to encourage care in the interpretation of PRO data.

PROs are important because they provide a vehicle for entering patients' voices into the medical database and, thus, provide important information that is not otherwise available. For this reason, it is important that practitioners continue to use PRO's to document health and health care quality, but the task of doing so is not simple. This chapter is only an introduction to the subject. The reader is encouraged to obtain more detail on the research discussed in this chapter from the articles listed in Table 20, and to deepen his or her expertise by reading the articles referenced in the Annotated Bibliography. In addition, users of specific health and health care surveys should obtain and study the manuals for those surveys. In the absence of manuals, users should obtain articles from the peer-reviewed literature documenting the development and psychometric evaluation of the surveys, and contact the developers for further information on the appropriate use of the surveys, analysis of the data, and interpretation of results.

Annotated Bibliography

1. American Educational Research Association, American Psychological Association, and National Council on Measurement in Education. Standards for Educational and Psychological Testing. Washington, DC: American Psychological Association, 1985.

This work is a case-by-case summary of psychometric techniques, and standards, to guide the development and use of tests and surveys in various settings. Part I of the short volume outlines technical standards for validity, reliability, test development, scaling, norming, comparability, equating, and publication of test instruments and the application. Part II provides professional standards for test use in various settings, such as clinical, education, psychology, employment, and program evaluation. Part III addresses ways to handle socio-economic, cultural, or physical differences in standardizing test instruments. Part IV points out the procedural issues of test administration and the ethical issues of test-taker rights.

2. Beaton DE, Hogg-Johnson S and Bombardier C. Evaluating changes in health status: reliability and responsiveness of five generic health status measures in workers with musculoskeletal disorders. Journal of Clinical Epidemiology, 1997 Jan;50(1):79–93.

The authors describe a very thorough comparative study of the relative sensitivity of five common health status measures to detect change in health over time. This is an excellent tutorial on different statistics to evaluate the

Table 20. Additional Reading

• Beaton DE, Boers M, Wells GA. Many faces of the minimal clinically important difference (MCID): a literature review and directions for future research. Current Opinion in Rheumatology, 2002;Mar, 14(2):109-114.

• Beaton DE, Tarasuk, V. Katz, J.N., Wright, J.G. and Bombardier, C. "Are you better ?" A qualitative study of the meaning of recovery. Arthritis Care and Research, 2001;45:270-279

• Cohen J. Statistical power analysis for the behavioral sciences. Second Edition.Hillsdale, NJ: Lawrence Erlbaum Associates, 1988.

• McHorney CA, Ware JE. Construction and validation of an alternate form general mental health scale for the Medical Outcomes Study Short Form 36-item Health Survey. Medical Care, 1995;33(1):15-28.

• Meyer KB, Espindle DM, DeGiacomo JM, Jenuleson CS, Kurtin PS, Davies AR. Monitoring dialysis patients' health status. American Journal of Kidney Diseases, 1994;24(2):267-279.

• Osterhaus JT, Townsend RJ, Gandek B, Ware JE. Measuring the functional status and well-being of patients with migraine headaches. Headache 1994; 34(6):337-343.

• Sprangers MAG, Aaronson NK. The role of health care providers and significant others in evaluating the quality of life of patients with chronic disease: a review. Journal of Clinical Epidemiology 1992;45:743-60.

• Visser MRM, Smets EMA, Sprangers MAG and de Haes HJCJM. How response shift may affect the measurement of change in fatigue. Journal of Pain and Symptom Management, 2000; 20(1),12-18.

responsiveness of measures. It includes an evaluation of whether the different "responsiveness statistic" formulas will affect the relative rank ordering of the different measures in terms of the sensitivity to change over time in health status. This is also an excellent demonstration of the relationship between reliability and validity, and methods for describing, and presenting, the relative sensitivity of different measures to audiences.

3. Bowling A. Measuring disease: a review of disease-specific quality of life measurement scales. Philadelphia: Open University Press, 1995.

   Bowling discusses the most commonly used condition-specific measures of health-related quality of life. Each chapter contains an introduction to the methods of measuring health-related quality of life for a specific area and references the commonly used health-related quality of life measures for that area. The disease areas covered include: cancers; mental illness; respiratory conditions; neurological disorders; rheumatic problems; cardiovascular disease; and a catch-all chapter that contains scales ranging from human immunodeficiency virus (HIV)-infection to back problems. Disease-specific symptom items, and other indicators of the presence of ill health, also are presented. Last, measurement issues, such as reliability and validity, are discussed and an appendix that contains a list of scale distributors and addresses is provided.

4. McHorney CA. Health status assessment methods for adults: Past accomplishments and future challenges. Annual Review of Public Health, 1999, 20:309–335.

   The Annual Review of Public Health periodically publishes articles that summarize, and comment on, the current state-of-the-art of patient-based health status assessments. This chapter, which includes 120 citations to the literature, is the most recent. The author begins by providing a nice history of the past 30 years of research and development on this topic, then describes how patient-based assessments (PBAs) are used in health services research, public policy and clinical practice, and goes on to provide guidelines for selecting among PBAs for each purpose. The chapter ends by identifying and discussing current challenges in the use of PBAs and specific areas of methodological development that are required to increase the usefulness of PBAs.

5. McHorney CA, Kosinski M, Ware JE. Comparisons of the costs and quality of norms for the SF-36 Health Survey collected by mail versus telephone interview: results from a national survey. Medical Care 1994;32:551–67.

   The authors used the General Social Survey sampling frame to randomly assign respondents to mail survey or telephone interview in order to obtain adult (age greater than 17) population norms for the SF-36 Health Survey (SF-36) scale scores for each mode of data collection. Rate of missing data and internal consistency reliability estimates for each mode are presented. Norms are presented for each mode for the total sample and stratified by five age ranges. Results reveal different strengths and weaknesses associated with each mode of data collection. While the response rate was higher for mail surveys (79 percent versus 69 percent), the rate of missing responses within completed surveys was also higher for mail than telephone (1.59 versus 49 missing items, respectively). Per case data collection costs for mail surveys were nearly 50 percent of that for telephone and results indicate that respondents may have been more honest in answering questions by mail than over the phone (respondents were more likely to report problems with their emotional health and to report chronic health conditions by mail than over the phone).

6. McDowell I, Newell C. Measuring health: a guide to rating scales and questionnaires. New York: Oxford University Press, 1996.

   McDowell and Newell provide a comprehensive overview of health measurement methods and its applications. They begin by describing psychometric characteristics of measures (e.g., reliability and validity) within the context of health status and health-related quality of life assessment. The authors then provide a compendium of generic and condition specific health status and health-related quality of life measures including a summary of the development and testing of these measures, citations to relevant literature, and exact reproductions of the entire questionnaires. The writers also summarize the strengths and weaknesses of the measures, and provide guidance in choosing and scoring appropriate measures.

7. Nunnally JC, Bernstein IH. Psychometric theory. Second Edition. New York: McGraw-Hill, Inc., 1994.

   This book is the authoritative text on psychometric theory and its application to the development and evaluation of questionnaires and tests. The four major sections of the book explain measurement as a general process, discuss statistical foundations of measurement (including thorough explanations of basic statistical concepts such as variation and covariation), address the problems associated with the internal structure of multi-item measures and aggregating items into scales; and discuss exploratory and confirmatory factor analysis at length. Emerging topics in measurement are also presented.

8. Patrick DL, Erickson P. Health status and health policy: quality of life in health care evaluation and resource allocation. New York: Oxford University Press, 1993.

   The authors present a procedure to systematically evaluate the benefits of different health care programs. They offer the Health Resource Allocation Strategy to evaluate health care interventions. This text is a state-of-the-art reference for health-related quality of life research and treatment evaluation. Included are a taxonomy of important characteristics of health-related quality of life, a list of disease-specific measures, a table of selected health-related quality of life measures for older adults, and a discussion of child health assessment. Appendix I contains four health-related quality of life examples, and Appendix II contains a list of publications that review health-related quality of life measures, relevant databases, and Medline key words for literature searches on the topic.

9. Scientific Advisory Committee of the Medical Outcomes Trust. Assessing health status and quality-of-life instruments: Attributes and review criteria. Quality of Life Research, 2002;11:193–205.

   Eight years ago the Medical Outcomes Trust (MOT) convened a Scientific Advisory Committee (SAC) and tasked the SAC with developing criteria for evaluating the quality of humanistic assessments including PBAs of health status and quality of life. This publication presents the most up-to-date and second edition of these criteria. The criteria address the conceptual and measurement models that form the basis of the

PBAs, reliability, validity, interpretability, respondent and administrative burden, alternate forms, and cultural and language adaptations.

10. Spilker B, ed. Quality of life and pharmacoeconomics in clinical trials, 2nd ed. Philadelphia: Lippincott-Raven, 1996.

This voluminous text includes 127 chapters authored by experts in the use of humanistic assessments in pharmaceutical research. Chapter topics span methods for choosing and administering measures, review articles on specific health-related quality of life instruments (frequently written by the developers), the analysis and interpretation of the data, cross-cultural issues in the use of these measures, the use of these measures in specific populations and for specific diseases, and the application of the measures to health policy and pharmacoeconomics.

11. Stewart AL, Ware JE Jr, eds. Measuring functioning and well-being: the Medical Outcomes Study approach. Durham, NC: Duke University Press, 1992.

This book is a collection of chapters written by the architects of the Medical Outcomes Study (MOS) which together describe, in detail, the careful and thorough approach to assessing health status that was used in the MOS. Chapters cover the overall conceptual approach, the application of psychometrics to the development and evaluation of the MOS surveys, and discuss the research and development behind each of the specific domains of health assessed by the MOS surveys including general health perceptions and expectations, physical functioning, social functioning, family functioning, sexual functioning, societal role functioning, emotional health, cognitive functioning, energy and fatigue, pain, and sleep. An appendix includes a complete reproduction of the 136-item measure of functioning and well being that was fielded in the study.

12. Wells, GA, Beaton D, Shea B, Boers M, Simon L, Strand V, Brooks P, and Tugwell P. Minimal clinically important differences: Review of methods. The Journal of Rheumatology, 2001;28:2,406–412.

The purpose of this research was to classify and summarize the various approaches used to determine the minimal clinically important difference (MCID) for different measures of health outcome. From a review of more than 2,000 citations related to the topic of MCID the authors identified nine different approaches. These approaches are summarized in a table. The text provides very accessible descriptions of these approaches including examples.

13. Wilkin D, Hallam L, Doggett MA. Measures of need and outcome for primary health care. New York: Oxford University Press, 1993.

This reference provides a guide to 40 measures of need and outcomes of health care for use in primary health care, research, and practice, and includes a reproduction of all, or part, of the instruments, and a summary of the evidence supporting their validity and reliability. Also included is a basic discussion of defining needs and outcomes, and a review of theoretical and methodological issues in health assessment.

Self-Assessment Questions

1. Which one of the following answers the question of whether an observed score is typical?
   A. Content-based interpretation.
   B. Content validity.
   C. Factorial validity.
   D. Norm-based interpretation.

2. Which one of the following is the method for estimating reliability, based on the relationships among items in a scale?
   A. Alternate forms.
   B. Internal consistency.
   C. Confidence interval.
   D. Test-retest.

3. Which one of the following is NOT a method of interpreting the size of scale score differences?
   A. Calculating the responsiveness statistic.
   B. Calculating the standard error of measurement for a score.
   C. Nominal scaling of health states.
   D. Comparing scores from known groups.

4. Which one of the following validity methods requires a "gold standard?"
   A. Criterion validity.
   B. Internal consistency.
   C. Factorial validity.
   D. Content validity.

5. Which one of the following is an unmeasured variable hypothesized to be responsible for the relationship among measured variables?
   A. Correlation.
   B. Construct.
   C. Criterion.
   D. Reliability coefficient.

6. Which one of the following types of scaling indicates how much health differs in absolute magnitude?
   A. Nominal.
   B. Ordinal.
   C. Interval.
   D. Ratio.

7. Which one of the following characterizes the relationship between validity and reliability of scale scores?
   A. Reliability is a necessary precondition for validity to exist.
   B. Validity is a necessary precondition for reliability to exist.
   C. Reliability and validity both depend on the interpretability of the score.
   D. Validity is independent of reliability.

8. For which one of the following are subject-matter experts NOT used?
   A. Direct scaling.
   B. Factorial validity.
   C. Indirect scaling.
   D. Establishing content validity.

9. Which one of the following is synonymous with telling an audience what scale scores mean?
   A. Validation.
   B. Reliability testing.
   C. Interpretation.
   D. Scaling.

10. Misinterpretation of changes in health over time is LEAST likely under which one of the following conditions?
    A. When proxy respondents are used for patients who can no longer self-respond to the questionnaire.
    B. When the exact same procedures for administering the survey are used throughout the study no matter what.
    C. When data for patients who did not respond by mail are collected by telephone interview.
    D. When improvements to the format of the baseline survey are implemented in subsequent administrations.

USING PATIENT-BASED ASSESSMENTS FOR INDIVIDUAL PATIENT CARE

Anita K. Wagner, Pharm.D.

Outline

Although patient-based health status measures are widely used for research purposes, their application in the care of individual patients in clinical practice is still developmental in many ways.

I. Considerations for using health status assessment in clinical practice
  A. Practical concerns
    (See patient case regarding Mr. A)
    1. Clinic logistics
      a. this example highlights that one of the most important issues surrounding the use of patient-based assessments in clinical practice is that patient-based assessments must be feasible
      b. the processes of presenting and administering a questionnaire, entering and scoring the data, creating a report, and interpreting the results must be integrated into the logistics of the patient-clinician encounter (see Table 1)
      c. physicians, nurses, pharmacists, and other health care professionals should share the responsibility of gathering and evaluating health status data
      d. questionnaire administration guidelines should be prepared so all staff members understand the process and can answer questions from patients (see Table 2)
    2. Patient burden
      a. patients must be able to complete the questionnaires presented to them
      b. the practicality of five general health status surveys proposed for assessing individual patients were evaluated (see Table 3)
      c. all five instruments met the standards set for questionnaire administration time
      d. thus, patient burden should not be a concern for their use in most clinical practice settings
      e. language spoken; visual, writing, and cognitive abilities; and educational level of patients are other issues that should be addressed before administering a questionnaire
    3. Staff burden
      a. patients' answers to the health status questions should be available to clinicians for direct application to patient care
      b. issues that must be addressed so patient-based health assessments can be quickly incorporated into patient care activities
        i. a method for processing the completed questionnaires
        ii. a method for calculating scale scores
        iii. a method for providing results
      c. a list of companies that distribute software programs for administering the MOS SF-36 is posted at *www.sf-36.com*
    4. Data display
      (See patient case regarding Mr. A)
      a. the type of report desired and the amount of information presented must be considered when planning to use a health status questionnaire in clinical practice
        i. the clinician evaluating a patient's health status data needs to know whether the patient completed all questions, and if it was done consistently

    - ii. missing or inconsistent answers could indicate that the patient did not understand the questions or felt uncomfortable about answering them
  - b. information that will help the user interpret the results also should be available
    - i. a health status report is more informative when it presents age- and gender-adjusted normative data, as well as the patient's scale scores over time
    - ii. reports should be created that link historical data with the health status profile obtained when the patient comes in for follow-up visits

B. Psychometric issues

(See patient case regarding Mr. A)

1. Reliability
  - a. every measurement result contains some error
    - i. when interpreting an individual patient's health status scale scores, it is important to know if the observed scale score changes are because of the measurement error or true changes in the person's health status
    - ii. the reliability of a questionnaire indicates the amount of confidence that a particular score is a true score
  - b. a measurement procedure is reliable if, when changes did not occur, an individual scores the same on repeated administrations
  - c. the measurement error can be quantified and visually depicted as the confidence interval around the patient's score
    - i. the confidence interval depends on both the reliability of the score and the standard deviation of the score distribution in a particular population
    - ii. the reliability of the score determines the standard error of measurement (SEM), which in turn determines the size of the confidence interval according to the formula: $SEM = SD_t \div 1 - r_{tt}$
      - a) where r_{tt} is the reliability coefficient and SD_t is the standard deviation of the particular score
      - b) to be 95 percent certain that a particular score difference is not because of chance, and is a true score difference, clinicians should calculate the 95 percent confidence interval as being equal to two times the standard error of measurement (see Table 4)
  - d. a reliability coefficient of 0.90 or higher is recommended for measures used for making decisions at the level of the individual; most instruments do not meet this rigid criterion

C. Interpretation of health status results

1. Health status comparisons

   (See patient case regarding Mr. A)
  - a. normative data exist for health status measures and are influenced by age and gender, as well as other variables, most noticeably socioeconomic status and educational level
  - b. for a first estimate of where a person's health lies in relation to that of other patients, comparative evaluation of an individual's scores with normative data is useful
2. Health status and clinical data
  - a. to interpret health status scale score differences, the causal pathways that link clinical and health status concepts must be known
  - b. if clinicians know which key factors may be responsible for diminished functioning and well-being of a patient, they can design intervention strategies to improve functioning and well-being (see Figure 2)
3. Health outcomes are divided into five categories: biological and physiological factors; symptoms; functioning; general health perceptions; and overall quality of life
  - a. they are ordered left to right from the most "cellular" to the most "interactive" at the level of the individual in society
  - b. moving from left to right, increasingly more variables, not all of which can be controlled by clinicians, influence each domain
  - c. formal evaluation of the causative factors underlying health status changes should help clinicians and patients develop strategies to improve functioning and well-being

D. Potential benefits

1. Confirmation and discovery of knowledge

   (See patient case regarding Mr. A)
  - a. standardized health questionnaires offer the opportunity to confirm and quantify clinical impressions of patients and to increase the detection of functional limitations and psychological distress
  - b. two-thirds to three-fourths of United States adults have reported that physicians rarely or never ask about the extent of their limitations in performing everyday activities
  - c. physicians tend to underdetect functional and psychological disabilities
    - i. patient-completed health status information could help clinicians caring for patients with chronic conditions to detect limitations or declines in functioning and well-being

ii. primary care practitioners using the Dartmouth COOP Poster Charts indicated that for one out of every four patients, the COOP charts uncovered important information about the patient

iii. in treating patients with epilepsy, routine assessment of patient health-related quality of life using the MOS SF-36 resulted in increased clinician knowledge about their patients for more than 60 percent of the encounters

d. the five-item mental health scale of the MOS SF-36 has been advocated as a screening test for depression

e. the therapeutic implication of the test results must be determined

i. assessing health status in routine care is redundant when the test results are expected to have no effect on subsequent decision making

ii. the testing threshold depends on the efficacy and safety of the treatment that may be the consequence of a positive test

iii. in the case of health status assessment, the appropriate responses to a "positive" test have yet to be identified

iv. because patient-based health status measures are not intended to be specific for a particular disease, there may not be one appropriate treatment in response to a low social functioning score; health status measurement needs to be combined with other, more specific tests, and subsequent actions determined based on the diagnosis

f. adding health status measures to clinical practice is likely most beneficial in instances where alternatives for the patient and the clinician to share and elicit the information about the patient's general health do not exist

2. Changes in management

(See patient case regarding Mr. A)

a. neurologists have indicated that the availability and discussion of the MOS SF-36 profile with their patients prompted a change in therapy in 12.3 percent of the encounters

i. physicians rated the MOS SF-36 as being at least moderately useful for managing the care of patients in 8.4 percent of the encounters

ii. the lower patients' MOS SF-36 scale scores were (the worse their health status), the more useful the physicians rated the MOS SF-36 results for communication and management; these data may be more helpful for more severely ill patients, especially those who perceive their health as bad in areas that are not easily observable for clinicians, namely role and social functioning

b. in the Dartmouth COOP study, the new information clinicians learned resulted in specific clinical management actions in 40 percent of patients, indicating that improvement in detection can translate into changes in the processes of care

3. Enhanced communication

a. patient-clinician communication

i. in our case example, having access to MOS SF-36 results helped ensure that issues important for the patient, in addition to his seizures, were addressed within the time constraints of patient-clinician encounters

ii. standardized information about a patient's perceptions of health status provides the clinician and patient with an assessment of the overall effectiveness of the current regimen, and permits comparison of the functional status and well-being effects of the current treatment to those of previous regimens

iii. by quantifying the patient's subjective experience, health status assessment makes that experience more accessible to the clinicians who care for the patient

b. clinician-clinician communication

i. care by a multidisciplinary team is the optimal treatment approach to address the medical, surgical, pharmacological, educational, psychiatric, psychological, and social service needs of individuals with chronic conditions

ii. ideally, a team of clinicians from different specialties communicates about the provision of a patient's care, using the same language, and representing the patient's voice

a) standardized patient-completed assessment of physical, psychological, and social functioning may provide this language

iii. within multidisciplinary treatment programs, health status measurement can fulfill at least three potential purposes

a) to screen for those patients who will benefit most from multidisciplinary care

b) to communicate among the different providers about the progress patients are making

c) to measure whether the goals of multidisciplinary care are achieved for the individual

4. Improved adherence

a. clinicians' considerations of the outcomes of therapy may differ from quality of life considerations important to patients

b. appropriate health behavior should be thought of as actions that meet the person's goals and achieve some mutually definable outcome
i. there is considerable variability among patients with respect to preferences in the trade-offs between symptom control and adverse effects of therapy
ii. health status measures can provide useful information to assist the patient and the clinician in choosing desired treatment outcomes and quantifying progress toward their achievement
c. recent research shows that patient trust in the physician and physician's "whole-person" knowledge of their patients are the characteristics of the physician-patient primary care relationship most strongly associated with patient adherence to physician advice

5. Increased patient satisfaction
a. assessment of functioning and well-being is associated with increased patient satisfaction with care
i. eighty-nine percent of patients who participated in clinical studies using the Dartmouth COOP Poster Charts felt that information provided by the charts was important for the doctor to know
ii. at least 60 percent of respondents in a national survey wanted their physicians to ask about their physical functioning and emotional well-being or both, and more than half were willing to fill out a questionnaire concerning those aspects of health
b. although there are no data to support that routine health status measurement contributes to improving patient satisfaction with care, recent pilot study results favor this notion

6. Improved health
a. the ultimate goal for using patient-based assessments in clinical practice is to improve patient health
b. although participating clinicians typically believe that assessments are useful, a positive effect of routine health status measurement on patient functioning and well-being has not been consistently demonstrated

7. Development of an effectiveness research database
a. the public's request for relating clinical practice, the cost of care, and measurable improvements to patient health has resulted in a mandate to conduct medical effectiveness research
i. This focus is evidenced by the Agency of Health Cree Policy and Research's funding of Patient Outcomes Research Teams
ii. when patient-based health status data are a part of routine care, the crucial linkage of the process and patient-based outcomes databases is possible

E. Educational needs
1. Among reasons suggested for the failure of health status assessment to demonstrate a beneficial effect in clinical practice are physicians' unfamiliarity with patients' health status scale scores and the complexity of the health status measures used
2. Education before using a health status measure in clinical practice could include lectures and workshops that provide information about the administration of and the concepts underlying the measure, the content of individual items and scales, and the general interpretation of patients' scale scores compared to normative data
3. User-friendly training and reference materials should be provided, including information about the confidence intervals around patient scale scores
4. Clinicians also must identify suggested action in response to health status scale scores

F. Ethical and legal issues
1. Medical ethics
a. it has been argued that patient-based health status measurements are ethically indicated based on the assumption that health status measurement contributes to improvements in individual patient health status
b. another ethical principle relates to respect for people; implies that individuals should be treated as autonomous agents who need to know answers to the questions related to their well-being
c. still to be answered is whether health status measures that represent the values of groups of people will also appropriately reflect the values of individual patients

2. Potential liability
a. clinicians may be obligated to act on and document action in response to poor health status; this could potentially increase clinician liability

II. Questions yet to be answered (see Table 5)

III. Conclusion and Case Study: Interpreting Scale Scores for an Individual Patient
A. Although more questions can be raised than answered, the intuitive benefits of using patient-based health status assessments in clinical practice warrant this new application. Clinicians and health status researchers should collaborate to identify the best possible ways to realize and demonstrate the potential benefits of their use.
B. Turn to the case study, Interpreting Scale Scores for an Individual Patient, found at the end of this book. The case of Mr. B is presented and readers are asked to interpret his health status scale scores as they make decisions about his care.

Learning Objectives

1. Discuss six issues that must be addressed when using patient-based assessments to care for individual patients.
2. Consider how patient-based assessments of health status can be used to augment traditional clinical decision making.
3. List several potential benefits of using patient-based assessments in caring for patients.
4. Identify questions that have yet to be answered regarding the use of patient-based assessments for individual patient care.
5. Evaluate health status scores to help determine optimal patient care.

Using Patient-Based Assessments for Individual Patient Care

Clinicians should consider the last patient they saw in a practice setting. Perhaps it was a women with epilepsy taking anticonvulsant drugs. Her goal in seeking care, and the clinician's goal in providing it, is to restore this patient's health—that is, to restore her physical, mental, and social well-being. How is she doing? What does having seizures or side effects from the antiepileptic drugs actually mean for her in her daily life? Does the therapy restore her day-to-day functioning and well-being? In the patient's chart, the clinician could probably find data describing her seizure frequency, whether she felt drowsy, her serum drug concentrations, her liver function, and electroencephalographic changes recorded over the course of her illness. However, these data, do not tell how her illness and its therapy are influencing her daily life. Standardized patient-based health status assessments can help fill this gap in information.

When planning to use a patient-completed health status questionnaire in clinical practice, a practitioner needs to answer several questions. How do I get the questionnaire to the patient? How do I get the patient's answers in a timely manner? Can I trust the numbers? What do the results mean? What am I going to do with them? What good does it do me, the patient, the clinic to get health status information? What do I need to learn and teach patients and to maximize use of this information? Are there any ethical or legal implications of using health status measures in my practice?

Although patient-based health status measures are widely used for research purposes, their application in the care of individual patients in clinical practice is still developmental in many ways. Thus, answers to many of those questions are not readily available or cannot be answered in a straightforward manner at this time. In this chapter, considerations for the use of health status measures in clinical practice are discussed, and more questions are raised. It is hoped the discussion will help practitioners plan the steps necessary to implement using patient-completed health status assessments in their own practices. Issues related to using patient-based health status assessment in the care of individual patients can be classified into six categories and are displayed in Figure 1. These six issues include practical concerns, psychometric issues, interpretation, potential benefits, educational requirements, and ethical and legal issues. As these issues are most salient when discussing general health status measures, the discussion is focused in that way.

These topics are discussed in light of what is known and what still needs to be researched for patient-based health status measurement to become a part of clinical practice. In many of the examples presented, clinicians use the Medical Outcomes Study, short form 36 items (MOS SF-36) Health Survey. However, the issues discussed in this chapter are applicable to patient-based health status assessment in clinical practice in general.

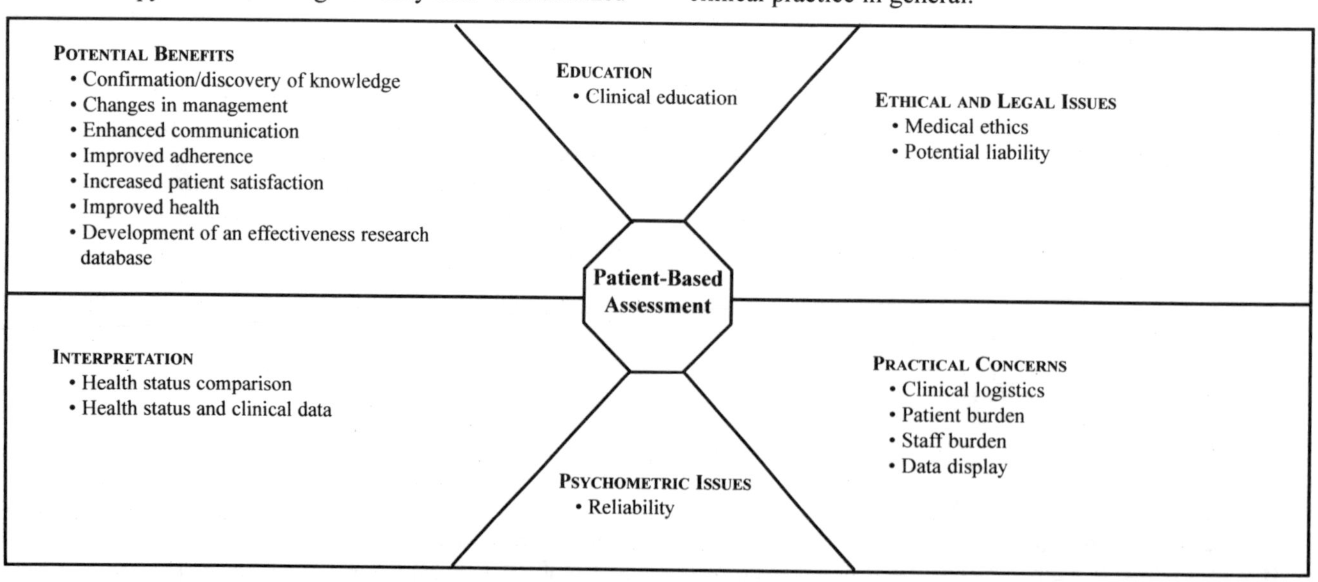

Figure 1. Considerations When Applying Patient-Based Assessments to Individual Patient Care

Considerations for Using Health Status Assessments in Clinical Practice

Practical Concerns

Mr. A is a 53-year-old Caucasian man with severe hemiparesis on the left and superimposed quadriparesis because of cerebral palsy. He operates a powered wheelchair with his right hand. He arrives for a follow-up visit at the outpatient neurology clinic where he receives care for his complex partial seizures with occasional secondary generalization. His current therapy is phenytoin 330 mg/day and carbamazepine 800 mg/day. After checking him in, the receptionist asks Mr. A to complete the optically scannable version of the MOS SF-36, displayed in Appendix D at the end of this chapter. She shows the form to Mr. A and explains to him what it is about. However, Mr. A says that he has trouble reading the fine print. And although he is able to write large printed letters with his right hand, he does not have the dexterity to darken the small ovals on the scannable form. Fortunately, the clinic is not busy and the clinic nurse offers to read the questionnaire to him. She finds an empty examination room and they spend about 30 minutes together, during which time the nurse reads the questions to him aloud and checks the responses according to his answers to the 36 questions. After accompanying Mr. A back to the waiting area, the nurse feeds the completed form into a computerized scanner. Within a few seconds, a printout of Mr. A's MOS SF-36 scale scores for today and from his previous assessment earlier this year are obtained. The receptionist clips the printout on the outside of Mr. A's clinic chart.

Clinic Logistics

This example highlights one of the most important issues surrounding the use of patient-based assessments in clinical practice. Using patient-based assessments must be feasible. The processes of presenting and administering a questionnaire, entering and scoring the data, creating a report, and interpreting the results must be integrated into the logistics of the patient-clinician encounter. First, someone must be responsible for presenting the questionnaire to the patient, explaining to the patient what the questionnaire is about and why the patient should complete it, and answering patients' questions. After questionnaire completion, data entry and response scoring must be conducted in a manner that allows creation of a report of the patient's health status in real time, so that patient-based data are available for the patient and the clinician at the point of the encounter.

An approach that integrates the different steps of patient-based assessment into the clinical office process has been advocated. This integrative approach ensures that all members of the practice collectively assume responsibilities in the interests of improving patient health. It also breaks the process of measuring health status into manageable tasks. Answering the questions listed in Table 1, which target the different steps in the administration process, should help clinicians establish who is responsible for each stage in the process.

Table 1. Questions to Ask When Integrating Patient-Based Assessments into the Clinic Process

- ✓ Who invites the patient to complete the questionnaire?
- ✓ When, where, and how is the questionnaire presented?
- ✓ Who explains the questionnaire to the patient?
- ✓ Where should the patient complete the questionnaire?
- ✓ Who answers questions the patient may have?
- ✓ Who assists patients in completing the questionnaire, if needed?
- ✓ If patients need the questionnaire read to them, where can this be done privately?
- ✓ Who processes (i.e., scans and scores) the completed questionnaire; when and where does this occur?
- ✓ How does a report of the data get created?
- ✓ How does the report get to the patient's clinician in time for the interaction?
- ✓ What happens with the report after the encounter?

In our case, the questionnaire presentation and administration process was the responsibility of several members of the clinic. To integrate everyone in the process, each staff member must understand the rationale for collecting patient-based information. General health status information is not specific to any particular discipline; rather, it falls within the purview of health care in general. Thus, physicians, nurses, pharmacists, and other health care professionals should share the responsibility of gathering and evaluating health status data.

Patients will have questions about the forms they are asked to complete. To enable and empower clinicians and administrative staff to answer the questions, questionnaire administration guidelines should be prepared that indicate what is needed. For example, personnel must know what to do when a patient cannot complete a questionnaire because reading glasses were forgotten or when patients are concerned about the confidentiality of their responses. A list of the "dos and don'ts" for administering the MOS SF-36 Health Survey is reprinted in Table 2.

Patient Burden

Patients must be able to complete the questionnaires presented to them. The number of questions on many patient-completed questionnaires restricts health status assessments to research settings because their length is thought to put undue burden on patients in routine encounters. The practicality of five general health status surveys was evaluated. Surveys included were the Functional Status Questionnaire and the Dartmouth COOP Poster Charts, which were designed for use in clinical practice; and the Nottingham Health Profile, the Duke Health Profile, and the MOS SF-36, which were designed for group-level applications, but also have been recommended for use in clinical practice. As shown in Table 3, the investigators found that all five instruments met the standards set for questionnaire administration time. Average self-administration times range from 5 minutes to complete the Duke Health Profile to 15 minutes to complete the Functional Status Questionnaire, according to the

Table 2. Questionnaire Administration DOs and DON'Ts

DOs	DON'Ts
• Do have the respondents fill out the questionnaire before they fill out any other health data forms and before they see their physicians	• Do not discuss respondents' health, health data, or emotions with them before they fill out the questionnaire
• Do be warm, friendly, and helpful	• Do not force or command respondents to fill out the questionnaire
• Do request and encourage respondents to fill out the questionnaire	• Do not accept an incomplete questionnaire without first encouraging the respondent to fill out unanswered questions
• Do read and repeat a question verbatim for the respondent	• Do not interpret or explain a question
•Do tell respondents to answer a question based on what they think the question means	• Do not force or command respondents to fill out a particular question
•Do have respondents fill out the questionnaire by themselves	• Do not allow spouses or family members to help the respondent fill out the questionnaire
• Do encourage respondents to fill out all the questions	• Do not minimize the importance of the questionnaire
• Do thank respondents for filling out the questionnaire	
• Do inform respondents if they will be asked to fill out the same questionnaire again at other clinic visits	

Reprinted with permission from Ware JE, Snow KK, Kosinski M, Gandek B. SF-36 Health Survey: manual and interpretation guide. Boston, MA: The Health Institute, New England Medical Center, 1993.

number of items they contain. Thus, patient burden should not be a concern for their use in most clinical practice settings. In general, clinicians are most in need of functioning and well-being assessments for those patients who are most difficult to communicate with. For a variety of reasons, barriers to communication exist. Before administering a questionnaire, each patient should be assessed for language spoken; visual, writing, and cognitive abilities; and educational level. Much progress has been made in the translation and evaluation of some general health status questionnaires. For example, the MOS SF-36 has been translated into about 40 languages, including Spanish and Chinese as spoken in the United States. The Nottingham Health Profile and the Dartmouth COOP Poster Charts are available in nonEnglish versions as well. A large-print version of the MOS SF-36 exists for people with visual problems. Advances in computer technology are being made constantly, which will facilitate questionnaire completion by allowing patients with motor coordination problems or other physical limitations to simply touch a computer screen to indicate a response.

Staff Burden

Patients' answers to the health status questions should be available to clinicians in a way that allows their use of the data. Single-item measures, such as the Dartmouth COOP Poster Charts, do not require scaling techniques. Other questionnaires, such as the others already mentioned, require aggregation of item values into scale scores. Thus, when planning to use a patient-completed questionnaire in clinical practice, clinicians need to develop a method for processing the completed questionnaires and establish who is responsible for doing so. The amount of effort involved in calculating scale scores is another aspect of the feasibility of using health status assessment in clinical practice. In the clinical practice setting, results need to be available quickly; therefore, computerized scoring is preferable over hand scoring. The five questionnaires evaluated did meet the scoring requirements for their use in clinical practice (see Table 3).

In the patient case, clinic staff scanned and scored Mr. A's questionnaire using a computer program. The process took less than 1 minute. Continuous advances in software development give clinic staff a range of options to process questionnaires. For example, more than 10 companies are currently developing and distributing various software programs for administering the MOS SF-36, including scanning, scoring, and the reporting of MOS SF-36 data for individual patients, as well as for an entire group of patients. A list of these companies with contact addresses is posted on the World Wide Web at *http://www.sf-36.com.*

Table 3. Comparison of Practical Features Across General Health Status Surveys

Feature	NHP	FSQ	COOP	DUKE	SF-36
Number of items	38	34	9	17	36
Average self-administration time (minutes)	10	15	6	5	10
Scaling method	Thurstone	Likert for 6; not needed for 6	Not needed	Likert	Likert

NHP = Nottingham Health Profile; FSQ = Functional Status Questionnaire; COOP = Dartmouth COOP Poster Charts; DUKE = Duke Health Profile; MOS SF-36 = Medical Outcomes Study short form, 36 items Health Survey

Reprinted with kind permission of Kluwer Academic Publishers. McHorney CA, Tarlov AR. Individual-patient monitoring in clinical practice: are available health status surveys adequate? Quality Life Res 1995;4:293–307.

Data Display

Mr. A's MOS SF-36 report provided for the clinician at the beginning of their encounter is shown as Profile 1. It shows a bar graph of each of his scores on the eight MOS SF-36 scales at two time points, on April 3, 1996, and on October 3, 1996. The actual scores are printed next to the bars. Data quality is listed, assessed as the percentage of the 36 items he completed, and how consistently he answered 15 pairs of MOS SF-36 questions targeting mutually exclusive states of health, such as feeling tired all the time and having a lot of energy all of the time.

In looking at the data quality section of the printout, the physician notices that item completeness is 72.2 percent and item consistency is 100 percent. Both times, Mr. A did not complete enough items in the physical functioning scale to get a score on that scale. The physician remembers that when Mr. A was listening to the physical functioning questions dealing with walking and climbing stairs that were read to him by the staff assistant during the last visit, both Mr. A and the staff assistant had felt awkward about those questions as Mr. A is wheelchair bound. Mr. A decided in both instances that he did not want to complete these questions. Therefore, missing data were generated and were reflected in the percentage of complete items being just above 70 percent.

Another aspect to be considered when planning to use a health status questionnaire in clinical practice is the type of report desired and the amount of information that should be presented. This is similar to reports that are generated from clinical laboratory results. To be able to interpret the information, the user needs to know how good the data are. Analogous to needing to know whether a serum sample analyzed for potassium was hemolyzed, clinicians evaluating patients' health status data needs to know whether patients completed all questions, and if they did so consistently. Missing or inconsistent answers can indicate that the patient did not understand the questions, or, as for Mr. A with respect to the questions on physical functioning, whether the patient felt uncomfortable about answering them.

Furthermore, information that will help the user interpret the results also should be available. For example, information about the range of normal values for a patient's age, weight, and height helps one interpret a patient's serum creatinine. Similarly, an individual's scale scores at a point in time can be considered with respect to the health status data of other people of the same age and gender, as well as to the person's own baseline. Thus, a health status report is most informative when it presents age- and gender-adjusted normative data, as well as the patient's scale scores over time. In addition, as with other clinical data, health status scale scores must be used in the context of other information. Ideally, a report is created that links historical data, such as the start of a drug or serum drug concentrations, with the health status profile obtained when the patient comes in for a follow-up clinic visit. The report created in the example above did not provide this information. However, as medical records become computerized, linkage of data from different sources, such as the health status questionnaire, the clinicians' dictations, the pharmacy records, and others, should be possible.

Psychometric Issues

Next, the clinician looks at Mr. A's scale scores. He knows that they range from 0 (worst health on each scale) to 100 (best health on each scale). He realizes that several of the patient's scale scores have declined since his last visit, most noticeably his role physical score decreased from 50 to 0, and his pain score from 62 to 10. His general health score declined by 12 points from 62 to 50, his social functioning score from 100 to 75, and his mental health score dropped by 24 points from 84 to 60. On the other hand, his vitality score improved by 5 points from 50 to 55. His role emotional score has remained stable at 66.7. The clinician wonders if the changes in scale scores reflect true changes in Mr. A's health.

Reliability

Every measurement result contains a certain amount of error. When interpreting an individual patient's health status scale scores, it is important to know if the observed scale score changes are because of the measurement error or to true changes in the person's health status. The reliability of a questionnaire indicates the amount of confidence one can have that a particular score is a true score. Indices of reliability of a measure give an indication of the extent to which scores produced by a particular measurement procedure are consistent and reproducible. A measurement procedure is reliable if, when changes did not occur, an individual scores the same on repeated administrations. Reliability can be compared to the reproducibility of a laboratory test. When the same plasma sample is submitted for analysis of the phenytoin concentration on two subsequent occasions, results of both assays are expected to be the same, indicating reproducibility of the test. A reliability coefficient is an estimate of how much of the variation of a scale score is real variation or measurement error. For example, a reliability coefficient of 0.80 indicates that 80 percent of the total measured variance is true score variation.

The measurement error can be quantified and visually depicted as the confidence interval around the patient's score. The confidence interval depends on both the reliability of the score and the standard deviation of the score distribution in a particular population. For an individual's scores, the reliability of the score determines the standard error of measurement (SEM), which in turn determines the size of the confidence interval according to the formula:

$$SEM = SD_t \div 1\text{-}r_{tt}$$

where r_{tt} is the reliability coefficient and SD_t is the standard deviation of the particular score. If clinicians want to be 95 percent certain that a particular score difference is not because of chance, but is a true score difference, they can calculate the 95 percent confidence interval as being equal to two times the standard error of measurement. Table 4 illustrates how different reliability coefficients lead to different confidence intervals around a given score for a 0 to 100 scale with an assumed standard deviation equal to 20. The calculations illustrate that the higher the reliability of a scale, the smaller the confidence interval around an individual patient's scale score. Therefore, a reliability coefficient of

Table 4. Effects of Differences in Reliability on the Standard Error of Measurement and the 95 Percent Confidence Interval for an Individual Score

Reliability Coefficient	SEM	95 Percent Confidence Interval
0.50	14.2	28.4
0.70	11.0	22.0
0.90	6.4	12.8
0.95	4.4	8.8

SEM = standard error of measurement; estimates of SEM and 95 percent confidence interval assume standard deviation is equal to 20.0 for a scale which ranges from 0 to 100

Reprinted with permission from Ware JE. Confidence intervals for individual scores. Medical Outcomes Trust Bulletin 1994;2:3.

0.90 or higher has been recommended for measures to be used in decisions at the level of the individual.

What this means is that for a scale score of 60, with a reliability coefficient of 0.90 and a standard deviation of 20, the confidence interval is 12.8, and it can be said with 95 percent confidence that the actual patient score is 60 plus or minus 12.8, and it falls within a range of scores from 47.2 to 72.8. If the scale has a reliability coefficient of 0.95, clinicians can be 95 percent certain that the patient's true score lies between 51.2 and 68.8. So the higher the reliability, the greater the confidence that a given score reflects the time score.

Most health status measures considered for use in clinical practice do not meet the strict reliability criterion of 0.9. For example, the reliability coefficients for the eight MOS SF-36 scales in the general United States population range from 0.63 to 0.94, with a median of 0.85. Application of the stringent criterion of 0.9 for measures to be used with individual patients requires improvements of the currently available general health status measures. Scale score reliability depends, among other variables, on the number of items in a scale. However, longer scales, which would have higher reliability, currently constitute a larger burden for the respondent. In practice, the 0.90 criterion may be too stringent for creating a balance between desired measurement precision and practical needs. In clinical decision making, the results of any one test are never used in isolation. For example, the measurements of systolic and diastolic blood pressure have reliabilities of 0.87 and 0.67, respectively. Therefore, repeated blood pressure measurements are done for an individual patient before a definite diagnosis of hypertension is made. Similarly, patient-based health status data are also only one piece of the information needed for patient assessment and care planning. Despite current health status questionnaires falling short of meeting the 0.90 reliability criterion, they nevertheless may be useful in clinical practice because, as some researchers argue, although the confidence interval around an individual patient's score is wider than clinicians might like, the interval is still tighter than that based on no information at all.

Looking at Mr. A's MOS SF-36 profile, one notices that the change in scale scores is 95 percent likely to reflect a true change in health for the role physical, the bodily pain, and the mental health scales. His general health scale score today, although 95 percent likely to differ from the general health scale scores of the comparison groups, may not reflect a true change as it is within the 95 percent confidence interval of his previous score on that scale. Similarly, his results on the vitality, social functioning, and mental health scales may not reflect true health status changes in these domains.

Interpretation of Health Status Results

Health Status Comparisons

The clinician takes a quick look at how Mr. A's scale scores compare to those of the general United States population and to those of other men his age. Whereas in April, most of his scores did not seem to differ much from those of the two normative groups, today's results suggest the health status burden he is suffering is quite different from that of other men his age or the population in general. On four of the eight scales—role physical, bodily pain, general health, and mental health—his scores today are significantly lower than both comparison groups', indicating that his health in these areas is worse than theirs. The physician wonders what prompted the changes over the past 6 months.

When clinicians evaluate biomedical data from a patient they do not yet know, they interpret the results in light of the expected results, also called normal or reference values, of people of similar age, gender, and possibly other characteristics, depending on the test. For example, a serum creatinine of 1.0 mg/L in a middle-aged man is considered to be within normal limits. However, the normal serum creatinine value is different for a thin, elderly woman. Similarly, normative data exist for health status measures which are equally influenced and therefore differ by age and gender, as well as other variables, most noticeably socioeconomic status and educational level. For a first estimate of where a person's health lies in relation to the general population, to others of equal demographic characteristics, and to other patients with the same disease, comparative evaluation of an individual's scores with normative data is useful. Also, just as with common clinical measures, comparison of patients' health status scores with their own baseline scores is valuable.

Health Status and Clinical Data

When interpreting differences between patients' scale scores and normative values, and between patients' own scores over time, clinicians must ask what accounts for the changes observed. To interpret health status scale score differences, the causal pathways that link clinical and health status concepts must be known. If clinicians know which key factors may be responsible for diminished functioning and well-being of a patient, they can design intervention strategies to improve functioning and well-being. To advance the assessment of causal pathways that lead to low functioning and well-being, a conceptual model was developed that

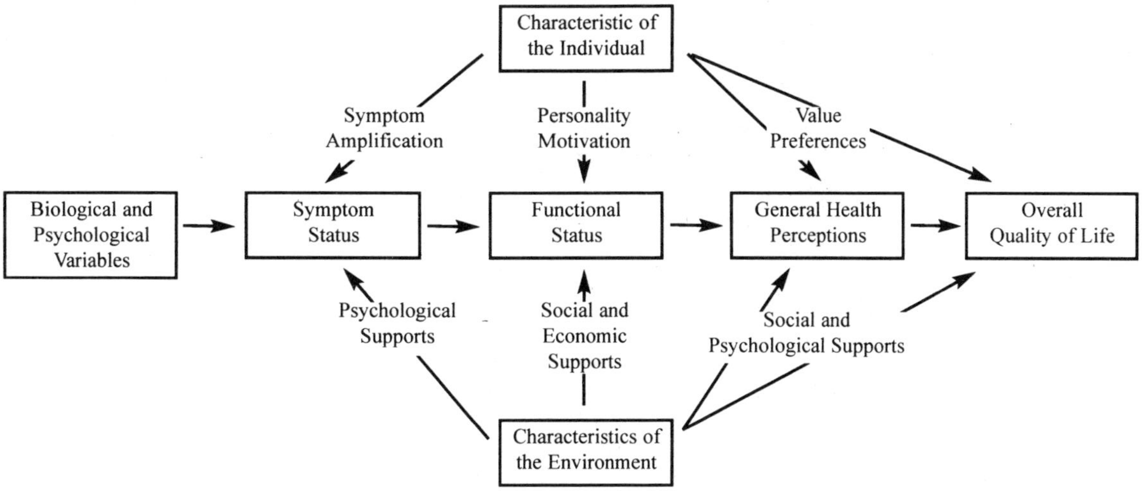

Figure 2. Relationships among measures of patient outcome in a Health-Related Quality of Life Conceptual Model.
Reprinted with permission from Wilson IB, Cleary PO. Linking clinical variables with health-related quality of life: a conceptual model of patient outcomes. JAMA 1995;273:59–65.

attempts to combine the biomedical model of clinicians and the quality of life model of health services researchers. This model is depicted in Figure 2.

In this model, health outcomes are divided into five categories which are biological and physiological factors, symptoms, functioning, general health perceptions, and overall quality of life. The categories are ordered from the most "cellular" to the most "interactive" at the level of the individual in society. In this direction, increasingly more variables, not all of which can be controlled by clinicians, influence each domain.

For Mr. A, the first category, biological and physiological variables, includes his electroencephalographic abnormalities and his diagnosis of cerebral palsy. Symptoms, the second category, are defined as a patient's perception of an abnormal physical, emotional, or cognitive state. Complex partial seizures, for example, are symptoms of the specific physiologic changes, possibly leading to changes in physical, social, role, and emotional functioning and well-being. Regarding the third category of functioning, change is quantified in Mr. A's decline in the role physical scale. According to the model, in addition to symptoms, patient-specific and environmental factors also can influence an individual's functioning. Another patient with a different personality and motivation may perceive a different impact in any functional domain while having the same symptoms. An individual's integration of the preceding health concepts, including additional person-specific and environmental factors, leads to the formulation of general health perceptions, the fourth category of health outcomes in the model. Finally, the authors of Figure 2 identify quality of life as the category influenced by individual perception of health and other life circumstances, which are not necessarily medical factors. This may seem obvious, as clinicians may automatically think their way through these sorts of associations; however, it serves a useful purpose in helping clinicians think through how the various factors and variables involved with a patient's condition interact and influence each other.

Formal evaluation of the causative factors underlying health status changes should help clinicians and patients develop strategies to improve functioning and well-being. For example, in a 3-year experience with dialysis patients, investigators combined chronologically all clinical events noted in the patients' charts by a multidisciplinary team, as well as further information they learned from patients by asking them about their MOS SF-36 scale score changes over time. For example, one dialysis patient was found to have hip pain that prevented him from doing his usual activities. Acetaminophen relieved the pain, resulting in improvement in pain and vitality scores. The combination of health status and clinical data helped the dialysis team identify the causes underlying the patient's scale score changes. In clinical diagnosis and decision making in general, data from multiple sources are combined routinely. Similarly, in clinical practice, general health status data need to be linked to changes in symptoms and physiologic variables, and the interventions that contributed to them, such as drug changes or surgical interventions.

Potential Benefits

The discussion so far has centered around issues a practitioner needs to consider before including a general health status measure in clinical practice. This chapter will discuss the potential benefits of patient-based health status data.

Confirmation and Discovery of Knowledge

Following his doctor who opens the door for him, Mr. A slowly maneuvers his wheelchair into the examination room. He bumps into the door frame before he can adjust the direction he is going. "How are things going for you, Mr. A?" Then, seeing Mr. A's bandaged foot, the clinician asks. "What happened to your foot?" Because of his speech impediment, it takes Mr. A a while to explain what happened. It turns out that he bumped his wheelchair into the elevator door when using public transportation last week and severely bruised his foot. Looking at the decrease in Mr. A's pain score, which indicates an increase in pain, the clinician asks, "It seems you are having quite a bit of pain lately. Is this what causes it?" Mr. A nods.

Noticing that the 50-point change in the role physical scale is 95 percent likely to reflect a true change, the clinician wonders what may have caused the decline. What is it that Mr. A could not do as well or as frequently during the past 4 weeks because of physical health issues compared to when the clinician saw him in April? In response to the physician's question, Mr. A explains that he usually reads a lot at home, but has had trouble doing so lately because his vision has gotten kind of blurry. "Did that cause you to bump into things more easily?" Mr. A responds that it did. Indeed, this was his second foot injury in the past 8 weeks, which is unusual for him. It turned out that these accidents and their consequences also made Mr. A feel kind of sad lately.

Standardized health questionnaires offer the opportunity to confirm and quantify clinical impressions of patients. This allows clinicians to keep track of these impressions in a measurable way over time. It also offers the opportunity to increase the detection of functional limitations and psychological distress. In a 1990 survey, two-thirds to three-fourths of United States adults reported that physicians rarely or never ask about the extent of their limitations in performing everyday activities, even in the presence of chronic conditions. In addition, studies have shown that physicians tend to underdetect functional disabilities in their patients, especially disabilities related to social activities. Differences in severity of psychological distress also are not apparent to treating physicians. Even the most severely psychologically distressed patients are unlikely to be recognized or treated.

Given the likelihood of underdetection of health status problems and the frequently marked disparity between physician and patient ratings of health status, patient-completed health status information can help clinicians caring for patients with chronic conditions to detect limitations or declines in functioning and well-being, and can serve as one step in the multistage diagnostic screening process. Longitudinal health status assessment in a dialysis clinic, for example, was found to reveal new information rather than merely restate clinicians' intuition about their patients' functioning and well-being, despite the fact that the dialysis clinicians had regular and frequent contact with their patients.

Primary care practitioners using the Dartmouth COOP charts in small private practices indicated that for one out of every four patients, the COOP charts uncovered important information about the patient. Similarly, in treating people with epilepsy, routine assessment of patients' health-related quality of life using the MOS SF-36 resulted in increased clinicians' knowledge about their patients for more than 60 percent of the encounters.

Patient-based health status measurement could be considered a screening test. For example, the five-item mental health scale of the MOS SF-36 has been advocated as a screening test for depression. Screening tests are done to identify individuals at risk of certain problems, usually followed by further testing. If one considers health status measurement a screening test, important questions that arise are, Who should be screened, and when? In answering these questions, it is important to know the significance of a positive screening, which is different in different populations. Depending on the sensitivity and specificity of the test, positive test results in a population with a low prevalence of the disease may frequently be false-positives, whereas in a population with a high prevalence of the disease, a positive result frequently is a true-positive. The concept of testing thresholds, which are benchmarks for the use of diagnostic tests, indicates that tests should be done based on the sensitivity and specificity of the test, the risk associated with the test, and the disease probability.

One could argue that the accuracy (reliability and validity) of health status measurement is relatively high, and the risks associated with it are very low. Which leaves disease probability as the determinant of the testing threshold. One could then argue that the probability of functional and emotional well-being problems is high, for example, in patients with chronic conditions, elderly patients, and patients taking multiple drugs. With such reasoning, specific patient populations that might be more likely to benefit from health status measurement than others could be suggested.

Another critical element in the decision to use a test is the therapeutic implication of its results.

It may be argued that assessing health status in routine care, just as carrying out diagnostic tests, is redundant when the test results are expected to have no effect on subsequent decision making. The testing threshold, therefore, also depends on the efficacy and safety of the treatment that may be the consequence of a "positive" test. In the case of health status assessment, the appropriate responses to a positive test have yet to be identified. To the extent that patient-based health status measures are general measures, they are not intended to be specific for a particular disease. There may not be one appropriate treatment in response to a low social functioning score. Rather, health status measurement needs to be combined with other, more specific tests, and subsequent actions determined based on the diagnosis.

Finally, adding health status measures to clinical practice will probably be most beneficial in instances where alternatives for the patient and the clinician to share and elicit the information about the patient's general health are unlikely. Possible alternatives to using health status measures could be an increase in the amount of time the patient and the clinician spend together, which is unlikely to happen in most settings; or an increase in patients' ability to share and ask questions about their functioning and well-being in general, which may not be likely for poorer, elderly, or less educated patients. However, even when patient-clinician communication allows for discussion of health status issues, applying standardized health status measures in clinical practice could serve the purpose of streamlining or focusing the communication toward topics relevant in the patients' point of view. Research, using decision analysis methods, will help clarify the optimal use of health status questionnaires in clinical practice.

Changes in Management

On neurologic examination, it is noted that Mr. A has a dense left field cut that has been present since 1950.

However, today he is unable to read from a standard near-vision card anything after 20/70-size letters. He feels that his vision problems started in the beginning of the summer. Although he had a severe seizure at the time, his drugs were not changed. He is wearing the same glasses he has had for 2 years, and his optometrist told him recently that there was no change in his vision. The examination also shows slight nystagmus. The clinician decides to refer him to an ophthalmologist for a second opinion. He also decides to reduce his phenytoin dose as his last phenytoin concentration measured last summer may have been borderline high for him.

Detection of the vision problems and their effect on the patient guided the clinician's care plan. The patient was referred to an ophthalmologist, and his antiepileptic drug therapy was changed. In a recent pilot study of the usefulness of the MOS SF-36 to the management of epilepsy patients' care, neurologists indicated that the availability and discussion of the MOS SF-36 profile prompted a change in therapy in 12.3 percent of the encounters. Therapy changes consisted of instituting, discontinuing, and changing the dose of an antiepileptic drug, instituting and discontinuing nonantiepileptic drugs, ordering tests, referring patients to other services, and counseling patients about lifestyle and other issues. Physicians rated the MOS SF-36 as being at least moderately useful for managing the care of patients in 8.4 percent of the encounters. The lower the patients' MOS SF-36 scale scores were, the more useful the physicians rated the MOS SF-36 results for communication and management.

Health status data may be more helpful for patients who are more ill, especially those patients who perceive their health as bad in areas that are not easily observable for the clinician, namely role and social functioning. Greater usefulness of health status information for patients with lower role and social functioning suggests that it may be more useful to field instruments that are somewhat richer in these areas. Advances in computer-adaptive testing will allow presentation of a list of questions exploring a particular domain of health status in more detail to those patients who indicate problems in that area, and not to others. Thus, only patients for whom detailed assessment is indicated would be subjected to the burden associated with a longer questionnaire.

In the Dartmouth COOP study, the new information clinicians learned resulted in specific clinical management actions in 40 percent of patients, indicating that improvement in detection can translate into changes in the processes of care. Many inputs lead to functional changes, not all of which can be implemented or controlled by one type of health care professional, or maybe even the traditional health care system. Thus, it may be necessary not only to identify clinical specialists who can help respond to a patient's poor health status, but also other sources of support. This process has been called resource linkage. To support resource linkage, clinicians and researchers at Dartmouth Hitchcock Medical Center developed the User's Index of the Functional Health Management Guide for Adults with Chronic Diseases. For example, to help patients who have problems with physical functioning, social and daily activities, and social support, which are determined to be related to problems getting rides from friends or family, the resource guide prompts the clinician to consider resources in the form of assisted transportation and support groups. These resources are listed in the respective chapter of the guide. Again, the collection of and response to more general, patient-based health status data may require collaboration of a multidisciplinary team of care givers.

Enhanced Communication

Patient-Clinician Communication

Turning once again to the conversation between Mr. A and his physician, an astute clinician would have noticed Mr. A's bandaged foot. An ensuing conversation may then have revealed he is having more accidents than usual and that the cause may be vision problems, which also affects his usual daily activities. Or it may not have. Following a seizure, he was in the emergency department in early summer. With increasingly shorter amounts of time allocated for patient-clinician encounters, the clinician and the patient may have been forced to limit their conversation to the most acute problem, his seizures. Having access to MOS SF-36 results aided in ensuring that issues important to the patient, in addition to his seizures, were addressed within these time constraints. Such issues include the impact of drug therapy on his functioning. As has been stated, "patients do not consult physicians because they are offended by sphygmomanometer readings. They have a much broader view of what it means to secure their well-being now and in their personal futures. What they really want to know is this: 'What is my life likely to be if I take these drugs? What will I be able to do? How will I feel? And what if I don't?'" Health status data from clinical trials should better equip clinicians to answer such questions more reliably and with more detail than is currently the case.

With health status becoming a part of patient assessment, the patient's questions of well-being are certain to be raised. Adding to the traditional database of signs and symptoms, standardized information about the patient's perceptions of his health status provides the clinician and patient with an assessment of the overall effectiveness of the current regimen, and permits comparison of the functional status and well-being effects of the current treatment to those of previous regimens. By quantifying the patient's subjective experience, health status assessment makes that experience more accessible to the clinicians who care for the patient. This could result in a more focused and effective clinician-patient interaction, which could promote patient participation in the decision making process. In turn, patients' participation in care may increase their sense of control over their illness, allay anxiety, and improve compliance, clinical outcomes, and satisfaction with care. In addition, routine use of standardized patient-completed health status questionnaires may even lead to savings in the time it takes clinicians to document patients' functional status and well-being, thus allowing for more time for patient-support and teaching interventions.

Clinician-Clinician Communication

Although physicians are equipped to address many of the problems that arise for patients, medical and surgical treatment alone do not resolve all health-related problems. Care by a multidisciplinary team is the optimal treatment approach to address the medical, surgical, pharmacological, educational, psychiatric, psychological, and social service needs of individuals with chronic conditions and those of their families. The patient Mr. A has multiple problems. Ideally, a team of clinicians from different specialties communicates about the provision of his care, using the same language, and representing the patient's voice. Standardized patient-completed assessment may provide this language. Within multidisciplinary treatment programs, health status measurement can fulfill at least three potential purposes. It can be used to screen for those patients who would benefit most from multidisciplinary care, to communicate among the different providers about the progress patients are making, and to measure whether the goals of multidisciplinary care are achieved for the individual.

Improved Adherence

The goal of therapy of patients with chronic conditions is to limit progression of the disease, control pain and discomfort completely without causing adverse treatment effects, and improve patient functioning and well-being. An increasing number of therapeutic options are available for clinicians and patients from which to choose. However, as long as there is no cure for chronic conditions, the task remains to choose from the available treatment options the regimen that provides the most benefits and the least adverse effects for an individual patient. Clinician considerations of the outcomes of therapy, however, may differ from quality of life considerations important to patients. The clinician's focus may be on freedom from symptoms, while concerns about the actual and potential side effects of the treatment or the financial burden associated with the therapy, may influence the patient's decision making.

It has been proposed that appropriate health behavior be thought of as actions that meet the person's goals and achieve some mutually definable outcome. As pharmacists and other clinicians are well aware, there is considerable variability among patients with respect to preferences in the trade-offs between symptom control and adverse effects of therapy. For example, one individual may not mind a drug regimen that causes occasional blurred vision but controls seizures, thereby permitting the patient to drive. For another person, blurred vision during the day is bothersome enough to warrant a change in therapy, at the risk of increased seizures. As life situations change for an individual, so may individual priorities for the goals and the individual evaluation of the outcomes of therapy. Health status measures can provide useful information to assist the patient and the clinician in choosing the desired treatment outcomes and quantifying the progress toward their achievement.

Recent research shows that patient trust in their physician and physician's "whole-person" knowledge of their patients are the characteristics of the physician-patient primary care relationship most strongly associated with patient adherence to physician advice. Conceivably, patient-completed general health status measures, through increasing the physician's whole-person knowledge of the patient, could promote adherence, including adherence to drug therapy regimens.

Increased Patient Satisfaction

It has been suggested that assessment of functioning and well-being is associated with increased patient satisfaction with care. Patients whose physicians underestimated their level of limitations in activities because of their condition were found to be more likely to report dissatisfaction with the treatment they received. Eighty-nine percent of patients who participated in clinical studies of use of the Dartmouth COOP charts in physicians' offices felt that information provided by the charts was important for the doctor to know. At least 60 percent of respondents in a national survey wanted their physicians to ask about their physical functioning and emotional well-being or both, and more than half were willing to fill out a questionnaire concerning those aspects of health, indicating patient preferences for comprehensive health care. These perceptions were found to be shared by patients with epilepsy and are likely to be shared by patients with other chronic conditions.

Although to date there are no data to support the assumption that routine health status measurement contributes to improving patient satisfaction with care, recent pilot study results favor this notion. It is suggested that a general health status questionnaire can open channels of communication to the physician about feelings from the patient perspective, and that this channel can enhance satisfaction noticeably. Although the experiment was too small to determine if this potential was realized, the results are indicative of such an effect, with a 6-point (on a 0 to 100 scale) improvement in satisfaction with interpersonal aspects of care.

Improved Health

The ultimate goal of the use of patient-based assessments in clinical practice is to improve patient health. Some researchers are starting to evaluate whether routine health status measurement and feedback of the data to clinicians improves patients' perceptions of their functioning and well-being. Although participating clinicians typically believe that assessments are useful, a positive effect on patient functioning and well-being has not been consistently demonstrated.

After a one-time, 2-hour multimedia educational session, investigators provided patient profiles on the Functional Status Questionnaire to an experimental group of physicians every 4 months for a year. The control group of physicians did not receive education on their patients' Functional Status Questionnaire scores. Almost all clinicians in the experimental group felt the questionnaire was accurate and useful, and that it would improve patient health and physician-patient communication about functional status. In addition, almost half of the experimental group physicians said that they had used results of the questionnaire to change therapy. However, no significant differences ($p>0.05$) in any dimension of function were detected between experimental and control groups of patients. When physicians received management and resource suggestions in addition to their patient profiles, as well as continued educational interventions, experimental patient mental health and social functioning scores were significantly ($p<0.02$ and $p<0.01$, respectively) better than those of control. The ultimate goal of the use of patient-based assessments in clinical practice is to improve patient health. Some researchers are starting to evaluate whether routine health status measurement and feedback of the data to clinicians improves patient perceptions of their functioning and well-being. Although participating clinicians typically believe that assessments are useful, a positive effect on patient functioning and well-being has not been consistently demonstrated.

Development of an Effectiveness Research Database

Increasingly more clinical trials of pharmacological and other treatments include patient-based health status measures. With this added outcome variable, measuring the efficacy and safety of an intervention is expanded to include its assessment from the patient point of view. By design, clinical trial results reflect an ideal setting, where age and gender differences, compliance issues, and difficult access to care for multiple reasons do not influence the outcomes of care. Data generated by clinical trials do not answer questions about the effectiveness of an intervention in normal, routine use.

The public's request for relating clinical practice, the cost of care, and measurable improvements to patient health has resulted in a mandate to conduct medical effectiveness research. This focus is evidenced by the Agency for Health Care Policy and Research's funding of Patient Outcomes Research Teams. Routine, standardized patient-based assessment of health status is a crucial outcome in the medical effectiveness research database. When patient-based health status data are a part of routine care, and as clinical process data are increasingly captured in computerized databases, the crucial linkage of both the process and patient-based outcomes databases is possible.

Thus, the database needed to answer questions about the effect of having a pharmacist participate in patient care has been built. General health status data in such a database allow comparisons of cost-effectiveness of different services within the scheme of treatment of a particular problem, such as the effects of eye care or foot care or diet counseling or glucose control for patients with diabetes. It also allows us to assess the aggregate impact of all of the services. Similarly, the effectiveness and cost-effectiveness of pharmacist services in the care of patients can be evaluated in terms of their impact on patient functioning and well-being.

Research on which treatment approach generates optimal outcomes, from the patient point of view, should be especially important for those patients who are not part of the traditional clinical trial population; that is, patients with multiple health and psychosocial problems.

Educational Needs

The clinician who cares for Mr. A is obviously knowledgeable about the content and interpretation of MOS SF-36 health status scores. She was trained in its use and has been evaluating results for some time. Among the reasons suggested for the failure of health status assessment to demonstrate a beneficial effect are physician unfamiliarity with patient health status scale scores and the complexity of the health status measures used. Many researchers have concluded that more intensive and prolonged training than what is provided in a typical one-time, 2-hour educational session is needed to result in measurable individual health status effects.

Education before using a health status measure in clinical practice could include lectures and workshops that provide information about the administration of and the concepts underlying the measure, the content of individual items and scales, and the general interpretation of patient scale scores compared to normative data. User-friendly training and reference materials should be provided that include information about the confidence intervals around individual patient scale scores. Regular discussions between clinicians who use the measure and the developers of the measure, in a case study format, can be extremely useful. More information about and experience with interpreting individual patient health status scores are needed. The onus to generate and share this knowledge is on health services researchers and clinicians alike. Although manuals that present normative data for people with different conditions greatly facilitate the interpretation of scale scores, clinicians using the measures must be able to gather and share their own experiences as to how to put the data into context with other clinical data and the overall process of care.

Beyond teaching about the science behind health status measurement, it is crucial that suggested actions in response to health status data be discussed. Clinicians know very well what to do in response to an abnormal hemoglobin. They will consider the differential diagnosis, order a battery of tests to rule out items on the differential diagnosis, and prescribe a therapy to treat the underlying problem. Similarly, differential diagnoses, steps to diagnosis, and therapeutic prescription in response to a low score on an energy/fatigue or social functioning scale need to be developed. Also, thresholds for intervention need to be established.

Currently, the process of including health status information in the patient-clinician encounter is different for each clinician. In a recent pilot study evaluating the impact of using the MOS SF-36 in clinical practice, one of the physicians discussed the MOS SF-36 results early in the visit while another waited until the end of the interaction. One physician devoted more time to considering MOS SF-36 data than the other. One physician found MOS SF-36 data to be more useful for communication and management than the other. Differences in practice and the differential indication of usefulness raise further questions. Do benefits of the routine use of health status information depend on clinician characteristics such as gender, training, experience, or beliefs? Is there an optimal process for including health status information in the patient-clinician encounter? If so, what is it, and can it be taught in health care professionals' courses of study? Multicenter studies involving a large number of clinicians are needed to answer these questions.

Ethical and Legal Issues

Medical Ethics

The overall goal of medicine, and the oath underwritten by its disciples, is to do good. The good sought by the physician for the patient, however, is "not merely to prolong life and to eliminate or reduce deviations in biologic functioning, but also to relieve pain and suffering, to ease fear and anxiety through compassionate interactions and acts of caring, and to improve general functioning and well-being." Patient-based assessments certainly provide a focus on the patient perspective of disease and treatment effects—the good done by medical care. A major argument in favor of the ethical value of patient-based health status measurement in clinical practice is based on the assumption that it will contribute to improvement in the health status of individual patients.

Respect for people is another ethical principle. It implies that individuals should be treated as autonomous agents. As such, individuals need to know, and clinicians need to provide, answers to the questions mentioned above, "What will my life be like if I take these drugs or if I have this surgery?" In helping both clinicians and patients in the pursuit of answers to these questions, health status assessment may fulfill another ethical requirement of medical care.

One ethical question that remains to be answered is whether health status measures that represent the values of groups of people also appropriately reflect the values of individual patients. If that is not the case, the clinician relying on the results of a measure might actually be less aware of an individual patient's values, rather than more so. It needs to be shown that discussions between patients and clinicians, when facilitated by standardized health status assessment, compared to traditional discussions, lead to improvements in medical decision making. Further, it remains to be shown that improved clinical decision making leads to better health and satisfaction with care or improved health care services.

The premise of using health status information in clinical practice is to arrive at the best decision for an individual patient. However, health status information about individual patients may conceivably be used to make decisions about individual patients with the collective outcome of a group of patients in mind. For example, managed care decisions about who is a candidate for expensive procedures, such as epilepsy or transplant surgery, might be influenced by the quantified health status data. Ethically, it could be argued that in this case, health status quantification meets the need to improve the functioning and well-being of the greatest number of people. On the other hand, using health status results to justify withholding or withdrawing care can be considered ethically hazardous. Severely restricting such use has been advocated.

It is clear that a great deal has yet to be determined about how best to use health status measures to care for individual patients from an ethical perspective.

Potential Liability

It is hoped that health status data, when routinely available, will help clinicians improve their diagnosis of problems of functional status and emotional well-being. As discussed above, such improvements remain to be demonstrated empirically. If they are demonstrated, however, health status measurement will be considered a medical technology of proven value and, therefore, become required on ethical grounds. Clinicians may then be obligated to act on and document action in response to poor health status. Potentially, this could increase clinician liability.

Questions Yet to be Answered

Patients like to share with their clinicians how they feel and function in their daily lives and clinicians seem to find such information useful. Standardized tools are available to measure functional status and well-being, and their use in clinical practice is feasible. However, the ability to measure general health status does not necessarily translate into the ability to treat problems and improve general health status. Ultimately, for health status data to be implemented in clinical practice, their benefits must be demonstrated to patients, clinicians, and payers. To demonstrate that standardized health status measures contribute to improve outcomes of care for patients is the current challenge to clinicians and researchers. Table 5 contains a list of some questions for further study that have been discussed and others that should be anticipated.

Conclusion and Case Study: Interpreting Scale Scores for an Individual Patient

Six areas of consideration when planning to use patient-completed health status measures in clinical practice have been discussed. Although more questions have been raised than answered, the intuitive benefits of using patient-based health status assessments in clinical practice warrant much wider investigation and use of this new application. Clinicians and health status researchers should collaborate to identify the best possible ways to realize and demonstrate the potential benefits of their use.

Turn to the case study, Interpreting Scale Scores for an Individual Patient, found in the back of this book. You will be presented with the case of Mr. B and asked to interpret his health status scale scores as you make decisions about his care.

Table 5. Research Questions for the Use of Patient-Based Health Status Measures in Clinical Practice

- Is the recommended reliability criterion of alpha of 0.9 adequate and necessary for using health status measures in individual patient care? And if so, how can reliability of existing measures be improved?
- For which patients is routine health status assessment most beneficial?
- What is the causal relationship between clinical status and an individual's functioning and well-being?
- How should health status scale scores of individual patients be interpreted?
- Are there scale score cut-offs that require action, and what is the appropriate response to low scale scores?
- Are there scale score cut-offs that require different action for different patients?
- Does an appropriate response differ for different patients, and how?
- What questionnaire administration and scoring techniques are least burdensome for the majority of patients and staff?
- How can the health status of patients who do not speak or read English be assessed routinely?
- Under what circumstances is health status assessment cost-effective?
- When should health status assessment be reimbursed?
- What is the value of health status assessment of individual patients to patients, clinicians, and payers?
- Does the value of health status assessment differ for clinicians in different specialties? Is it most valuable for generalists?
- What interventions should be instituted in response to low health status scores?
- Should health status data form a basis for assessment of individual clinician performance?
- Should health status data be a criterion for clinician reimbursement?
- Is there an optimal process to use health status data in the care of individual patients?
- How and when should health status measurement be taught to clinicians?
- Whose responsibility is it to act on individual patient health status results?
- How can potential abuse of health status data be prevented?

Acknowledgments

The author wishes to acknowledge her colleagues Kathleen Bungay, Pharm.D.; Bruce Ehrenberg, M.D.; Daniel Carr, M.D.; William Rogers, Ph.D.; Teresa Tran, M.D.; Barbara Vickrey, M.D.; and John Ware, Ph.D. for their collaboration and contributions to her study of the material described in this chapter and to Frank Massaro, Pharm.D., who developed the case study. She also acknowledges the Epilepsy Foundation of America for funding some of the research reported in this chapter.

Annotated Bibliography

1. Kazis LE, Anderson JJ, Meenan RF. Health status information in clinical practice: the development and testing of patient profile reports. J Rheumatol 1988;15:338–44.

   As an initial step in applying health status measures inclinical practice, the authors developed and tested profiles of patient scores on the Arthritis Impact Measurement Scales. Single-page summary reports of patient scale scores were given to 123 rheumatologists and arthritis health care professionals. These profile summary reports were found to be reliable and valid when used by the clinicians, supporting their possible use in clinical practice.

2. Kazis LE, Callahan LF, Meenan RF, Pincus T. Health status reports in the care of patients with rheumatoid arthritis. J Clin Epidemiol 1990;43:1243–53.

   In this paper, the authors describe a randomized, controlled trial to assess the usefulness of health status reports in clinical practice. More than 1900 patients from 27 community practice sites were randomly assigned to the intervention, the attention placebo, or the control group. Every 3 months over the course of a year, single-page, computer-generated summaries of scores from the Arthritis Impact Measurement Scales or the Modified Health Assessment Questionnaire were given to clinicians in the intervention group. Although 55 percent of physicians found the report to be at least moderately useful as an aid to patient management, no detectable differences were found among the three groups in drug compliance, number of physician visits, number of referrals, frequency of major drug changes, attitudes toward the physician, patient satisfaction, or change in health status over 1 year. Among other reasons, the authors offer physician unfamiliarity with health status scores as an explanation for the apparent failure to demonstrate benefits of health status measurement in clinical practice.

3. McHorney CA, Tarlov AR. Individual-patient monitoring in clinical practice: are available health status surveys adequate? Qual Life Res 1995;4:293–307.

   The authors propose six measurement standards for individual patient applications of health status measures: practicality, breadth of health measured, depth of health measured, precision for cross-sectional assessment, precision for longitudinal monitoring, and validity. They evaluated five health status surveys, namely the Functional Status Questionnaire, the Dartmouth COOP Poster Charts, the Nottingham Health Profile, The Duke Health Profile, and the Medical Outcomes Study short form, 36 items (MOS SF-36) Health Survey, for their application in caring for individual patients. Lack of precision was found to be the most problematic feature of the five instruments. In addition, little evidence was found for the validity of these measures for screening, diagnosing, or monitoring individual patients. The authors conclude that these health status measures may not be suitable for use with individual patients and advocate the development of new instruments or adaptation of existing measures and scaling methods for this purpose.

4. Meyer KB, Espindle DM, DeGiacomo JM, Jenuelson CS, Kurtin PS, Davies AR. Monitoring dialysis patients' health status. Am J Kidney Dis 1994;24:267–79.

The authors report 3 years of experience with quarterly assessment of the health status of dialysis outpatients using the MOS SF-36 Health Survey. Psychometric characteristics of the MOS SF-36 in this population are described. Mean initial MOS SF-36 scale scores of dialysis patients are compared to MOS SF-36 scale scores of the general United States population. The authors describe two patient scale scores and clinical events over the course of 4 years. Changes in scale scores frequently exceeded the 95 percent confidence intervals for patient-level scores. Comparing information obtained from the MOS SF-36 with the dialysis team's assessment of the patient as reported in the medical record, the authors conclude that MOS SF-36 data provide information that enhances, rather than merely restates, the health care professional's clinical impression of the patient.

5. Nelson EC, Berwick DM. The measurement of health status in clinical practice. Med Care 1989;27:S77–90.

Despite the availability of tools to measure health status that are practical, reliable, and valid, widespread adoption of the measures in the clinical world has not occurred. The authors analyze both the potential and the barriers to use of health status assessment tools in practice. They note the need for better scientific evidence of the clinical utility of these measures. They conclude that evidence is needed that application of health status measures in clinical practice actually improves patient health status.

6. Nelson ED, Landgraf JM, Hays RD, Wasson JH, Kirk JW. The functional status of patients: how can it be measured in physicians' offices? Med Care 1990;28:1111–26.

Results of the Dartmouth COOP Study are presented in this paper. For this study, nine pictorial charts were developed to efficiently measure patient function in the clinical practice setting. Each of the Dartmouth COOP charts has a 5-point scale, is illustrated, and can be self-administered or administered by office staff. When completed by more than 2000 patients in four different clinic settings, the COOP charts were found to be reliable and valid. Most clinicians and patients found the charts easy to use; clinicians considered them a valuable tool to measure overall function in a busy clinic setting. The charts helped uncover new information for 25 percent of the patients; for 40 percent of those, changes in clinical management were initiated. The authors conclude that the COOP charts are practical, reliable, valid, sensitive to the effects of disease, and useful for quickly measuring patient function.

7. Nerenz DR, Repasky DP, Whitehouse FW, Kahkonen DM. Ongoing assessment of health status in patients with diabetes mellitus. Med Care 1992;30:MS112–24.

As part of a program of outcomes management, the authors established a longitudinal database of patient-based health status assessments of adult patients receiving care for insulin-dependent diabetes mellitus or noninsulin-dependent diabetes mellitus. The following issues were addressed: 1) whether regular collection of health status data, using the MOS SF-36, plus clinical data is practical in routine care; 2) whether patients and physicians agree in their assessments of patient health status; and 3) whether the intensity of diabetes control is related to patient-reported health status. The authors conclude that health status measurement of patients with diabetes is practical in an ambulatory care setting. The MOS SF-36 data provided information new to treating physicians, related to the discrepancy between patient and physician assessments of health status. Perceived health status also seemed to be a function of tightness of diabetes control, educational status, presence of complications, and age.

8. Rubenstein LV, Calkins DR, Young RT, et al. Improving patient function: a randomized trial of functional disability screening. Ann Intern Med 1989;111:836–42.

This prospective, randomized trial was designed to test whether a 34-item functional status questionnaire measuring physical, psychological, and social function can be used by physicians in practice settings to help improve patients outcomes. Seventy-six internists in community office practices and 510 of their patients were randomized to either the experimental or the control group. Experimental group physicians received a 2-hour training session and four functional status reports of each of their patients over the course of a year. Control group patients received neither training nor reports. The functional status of both control and experimental group patients was evaluated every 4 months for 1 year. Use of health services was evaluated as well. Experimental group physicians answered an anonymous evaluation questionnaire 6 months after study entry. In the experimental group, 43 percent of physicians reported they had used the functional status questionnaire to change therapy. Most (95 percent) reported that it was useful and accurate. There were no differences between the experimental and the control group patients in number of drugs used, visits to health care professionals, equipment purchased, diet, or exercise programs. There were also no significant differences between experimental and control group patients' functional health status at exit from the study. The authors conclude that more powerful interventions than a 2-hour educational session and regular provision of functional status information are needed to help office-based internists improve patient outcomes.

9. Schor EL, Lerner DJ, Malspeis S. Physicians' assessment of functional health status and well-being: the patient's perspective. Arch Intern Med 1995;155:309–14.

The authors conducted a cross-sectional, population survey of adults in the United States to estimate how frequently physicians inquire about patient functional health status and emotional well-being, patient attitudes about such assessments, and the perceived use of such data in the therapeutic process. The majority of physicians rarely or never asked about the extent to which health limited the ability of their patients to perform everyday activities, or about limitations because of emotional problems. More than 60 percent of respondents wanted their physicians to ask about their functional health status and well-being. The authors conclude that the content of care may be less comprehensive than physicians believe to be the case.

10. Wagner AK, Vickrey BG. The routine use of health-related quality of life measures in the care of patients with epilepsy: rationale and research agenda. Qual Life Res 1995;4:169–77.

Increasingly, reliable and valid patient-completed questionnaires to assess the health-related quality of life of people with epilepsy are available. At present, they are not routinely used in the care of patients with epilepsy. The authors outline that the use of health-related quality of life measurement in clinical practice settings may improve the quality of care for patients with epilepsy through increasing the detection of patient problems with daily functioning and well-being, guiding therapeutic management, and leading to improvements in patient health-related quality of life and satisfaction with care. To realize these potential benefits, research into the feasibility of office-based use of health-related quality of life questionnaires, measurement quality, and the impact of routine health-related quality of life assessment on the quality of care patients with epilepsy receive needs to be undertaken. The conversion of health-related quality of life questionnaires from research tools into clinical tools requires the collaboration of social scientists, health services researchers, and clinicians. The authors conclude that health-related quality of life questionnaires have the potential to become a new clinical tool that could enhance the quality of care physicians are able to provide for their patients with epilepsy.

11. Ware JE. The status of health assessment 1994. Annu Rev Public Health 1995;16:327–54.

The author provides an overview of general health status measurement concepts and methods in the broader concept of quality of life assessment. Comprehensive assessment includes measures of physical, mental, social, and role functioning as well as general health perceptions. The 10 most widely used general health surveys are discussed. A schematic of the relationships among condition-specific and general health status measures is presented. Applications of general health status measures are discussed. In clinical practice, standardized health surveys have the potential to become new laboratory tests of medical practice. As such, standardized assessment of functional status and well-being would be useful to ensure that these concepts are considered routinely and comprehensively; to detect and monitor changes over time; to allow clinicians and patients to consider functional status and well-being comprehensively when choosing among alternative treatment strategies; to guide clinicians and patients in the use of resources; and to help predict the course of a chronic condition, in terms that are most important to the patient.

12. Wilson IB, Kaplan S. Clinical practice and patients' health status: how are the two related? Med Care 1995;33:AS209–14.

Wilson IB, Cleary PD. Linking clinical variables with health-related quality of life: a conceptual model of patient outcomes. JAMA 1995;273:59–65.

The authors compare and contrast the different conceptual models that physicians and social scientists use to understand health. They point out that conceptual models underlying current health status measurement approaches do not meet the needs of clinicians to understand causation and mechanisms, without which therapeutic decisions in response to the data is difficult. To facilitate the use of health status measurement in clinical practice, the authors describe a model that links clinical and health status concepts. The example of a model that unifies the clinicians' biomedical and the social scientists' quality of life models establishes five levels of patient care outcomes: biologic and physiologic variables, symptoms, functional status, general health perceptions, and overall quality of life. These outcome variables are hypothesized to be causally related. The authors propose to test hypothesized relationships to elucidate the genesis or pathogenesis of disorders of health-related quality of life. Once knowledge about the determinants of poor health status is gained, interventions to improve health status need to be identified. If these prerequisites are met, the measurement of health status is thought to become an increasingly useful clinical tool.

Additional References

13. Brody D. The patient's role in clinical decision making. Ann Intern Med 1980;93:718–22.
14. Brody DS. Physician recognition of behavioral, psychological, and social aspects of medical care. Arch Intern Med 1980;140:1286–9.
15. Calkins DR, Rubenstein LV, Cleary PD, et al. Failure of physicians to recognize functional disability in ambulatory patients. Ann Intern Med 1991;114:451–4.
16. Faden R, German PS. Quality of life: considerations in geriatrics. Clin Geriatric Med 1994;3:541–51.
17. Faden R, Leplege A. Assessing quality of life: moral implications for clinical practice. Med Care 1992;30:MS166–75.
18. Greenfield S, Kaplan SH, Silliman RA, et al. The uses of outcomes research for medical effectiveness, quality of care, and reimbursement in type II diabetes. Diabetes Care 1994;17(suppl):32–9.
19. Hanlon JT, Weinberger M, Samsa GP, et al. A randomized, controlled trial of a clinical pharmacy intervention to improve inappropriate prescribing in elderly outpatients with polypharmacy. Am J Med 1996;100:428–37.
20. Hays RD, Anderson R, Revicki D. Psychometric considerations in evaluating health-related quality of life measures. Qual Life Res 1993;2:441–9.
21. Hedrick SC, Taeuber RC, Erickson P. On learning and understanding quality of life: a guide to information sources. In: Spilker B, ed. Quality of life and pharmacoeconomics in clinical trials, 2nd ed. Philadelphia, PA: Lippincott-Raven Publishers, 1996.
22. Hirshfield-Bartek J, Hassey Dow K, Creaton E. Decreasing documentation time using a patient self-assessment tool. Oncol Nurs Forum 1990;17:251–5.
23. Hunt SM, McEwen J. The development of a subjective health indicator. Social Health Illn 1980;2:231–46.
24. Jette AM, Davies AR, Cleary PD, et al. The Functional Status Questionnaire: reliability and validity when used in primary care. J Gen Intern Med 1986;1:143–9.
25. Kassirer JP, Kopelman RI. Learning clinical reasoning. Baltimore MD: Williams and Wilkins, 1991.
26. Levine R. Quality of life assessment in clinical trials: an ethical perspective. In: Spilker B, ed. Quality of life and pharmacoeconomics in clinical trials, 2nd ed. Philadelphia, PA: Lippincott-Raven Publishers, 1996.
27. Liang MH. Compliance and quality of life: confessions of a difficult patient. Arthritis Care Res 1989;2:S71–4.
28. Lohr K. Applications of health status assessment measures in clinical practice. Med Care 1992;30:MS1–14.
29. Long AF, Scott DL. Measuring health status and outcomes in rheumatoid arthritis within routine clinical practice. Br J Rheum atol 1994;33:682–5.
30. The National Commission for the Protection of Human Subjects of Biomedical and Behavioral Research. The Belmont report: ethical principles and guidelines for the protection of human subjects of research. Washington, D.C.: Department of Health Education, and welfare, 1978. Publication No. (OS) 78–0012.
31. Nelson E, Conger B, Douglass R, et al. Functional health status levels of primary care patients. JAMA 1983;249:3331–8.

32. Nelson E, Wasson J, Kirk J, et al. Assessment of function in routine clinical practice: description of the COOP chart method and preliminary findings. J Chronic Dis 1987;40(suppl):55S–63S.

33. Nelson EC, Landgraf JM, Hays RD, et al. The COOP function Charts: a system to measure patient function in physicians' offices. In: WONCA Classification Committee. Function status measurement in primary care. New York: Springer-Verlag, 1990.

34. Nunnally JC, Bernstein IH. Psychometric theory, 3rd ed. New York: McGraw-Hill, 1994.

35. Parkerson GR, Broadhead WE, Tse CJ. The Duke Health Profile: a 17-item measure of death and dysfunction. Med Care 1990;28:1056–72.

36. Prisant ML, Carr AA, Bottini PB, Thompson WO, Rhoades RB. Repeatability of automated ambulatory blood pressure measurements. J Fam Pract 1992;34:569–74.

37. Rubenstein LV, McCoy JM, Cope DW, et al. Improving patient functional status: a randomized trial of computer-generated resource and management suggestions. Clin Res 1989;37:801A.

38. Safran DG, Tarlov AR, Rogers WH, et al. Linking primary care performance to valued outcomes of care. Paper presented at the Association for Health Services Research Annual Meeting, June 10, 1996, Atlanta, GA.

39. Slevin ML, Plant H, Lynch D, Drinkwater J, Gregory WM. Who should measure quality of life, the doctor or the patient? Br J Cancer 1988;57:109–12.

40. Sox HC. Probability theory in the use of diagnostic tests: an introduction to critical study of the literature. Ann Intern Med 1986;104:60–6.

41. Stewart MA, Buck CW. Physicians' knowledge and response to patients' problems. Med Care 1977;15:578–85.

42. Wagner AK, Cynn DJ, Ehrenberg BL, Tran TA, Bungay KB, Rogers WH. The impact of routine health status measurement on aspects of epilepsy patients' care. Epilepsia 1995;36:98.

43. Ware JE. Confidence intervals for individual scores. Med Outcomes Trust Bull 1994;2:3.

44. Ware JE, Kosinski, M, Keller SD. SF-36 physical and mental health summary scales: a user's manual. Boston, MA: The Health Institute, New England Medical Center, 1994.

45. Ware JE, Kosinski, M, Keller SD. SF-12: how to score the SF-12 physical and mental health summary scales. Boston, MA: The Health Institute, New England Medical Center, 1995.

46. Ware JE, Manning WG, Duan N, Wells KB, Newhouse JP. Health status and the use of outpatient mental health services. Am Psychol 1984;39:1090–100.

47. Ware JE, Sherbourne CD. The MOS 36-Item Short-Form Health Survey (SF-36): I. Conceptual framework and item selection. Med Care 1993;30:473–83.

48. Ware JE, Snow KK, Kosinski M, Gandek B. SF-36 Health Survey: manual and interpretation guide. Boston, MA: The Health Institute, New England Medical Center, 1993.

49. Wartman SA, Morlock LL, Malitz FE, Palm E. Impact of divergent evaluations of physicians and patients of patients' complaints. Public Health Rep 1983;98:141–5.

50. Wasson J, Keller A, Rubenstein L, et al. Benefits and obstacles of health status assessment in ambulatory settings. Med Care 1992;30:MS42–9.

51. Wells KB, Hays RD, Burnam MA, et al. Detection of depressive disorders for patients receiving prepaid or fee-for-service care: results from the Medical Outcomes Study. JAMA 1989;262:3298–302.

52. Wilson IB, Kaplan S. Clinical practice and patients' health status: how are the two related? Med Care 1995;33:AS209–14.

Self-Assessment Questions

1. For which one of the following reasons is routine collection and use of general health status information, such as Medical Outcomes Study, short form, 36 items (MOS SF-36) Health Survey data, in clinical practice being advocated?
   A. When used in individual patient care, general health status questionnaires can contribute to improved health and satisfaction with care of individual patients.
   B. When used in individual patient care, general health status questionnaires are reliable and valid.
   C. When used in individual patient care, general health status questionnaires contribute to the improvement in the general health status of individual patients.
   D. When used in individual patient care, general health status questionnaires provide a valuable mechanism for communication between clinicians and their foreign language patients.

2. Study of which one of the following hypotheses would contribute to the formal evaluation of the conceptual model that attempts to link clinical and health status variables?
   A. Inclusion of the MOS SF-36 in the routine care of patients with epilepsy increases patient satisfaction with their care.
   B. Valproic acid-induced weight gain and hair loss contribute to increased limitations in daily role functioning of patients as assessed by the MOS SF-36 role-emotional scale.
   C. Discussion of individual patient role-emotional scale scores increases the duration of patient-clinician encounters.
   D. Clinicians judge the availability of patient general health status data as most helpful for new patients.

3. Which one of the following statements best describes why patient-based health status assessments might be worthwhile for use in a particular practice setting?
   A. Patient-based health status assessments can help document a services' contribution to care.
   B. Patient-based health status assessments do not require much implementation effort.
   C. Patient-based health status assessments improve patient adherence to drug therapy.
   D. Patient-based health status assessments save resources.

4. Which one of the following represents the rationale behind a higher standard for reliability for individual patient applications of health status measures compared to group-level use?
   A. The higher the reliability coefficient of a scale score, the more responsive the scale is to changes in patient health status over time.
   B. The higher the reliability coefficient of a scale score, the more valid the scale is in assessing individual patient health status.
   C. The higher the reliability coefficient of a scale score, the larger the confidence interval is around that score.
   D. The higher the reliability coefficient of a scale score, the more precisely the scale score is in reflecting patient health status.

5. Of which one of the following should clinicians be aware when patient-completed general health status questionnaires are used in clinical practice?
   A. No questionnaire provides in-depth measurement of health concepts.
   B. All questionnaires are too burdensome for patients.
   C. No questionnaire meets stringent reliability standards for individual-patient assessment.
   D. No questionnaire differentiates among sicker patients.

6. Which one of the following steps is least necessary as a prerequisite to advancing the routine use of patient-based assessments of health in clinical practice?
   A. Demonstrating the impact of general health status questionnaires on health care outcomes.
   B. Educating clinicians about interpreting general health status data.
   C. Documenting the experiences of patients and clinicians with the use of general health status data.
   D. Creating a new generation of general health status questionnaires.

7. When asking a patient to complete a questionnaire, which one of the following questionnaire administration guidelines should be followed?
   A. If the patient has doubts about a question, interpret the question for him.
   B. If the patient forgets his reading glasses, have the questions read to him verbatim.
   C. If easier, have the patient's spouse or partner complete the questionnaire for him.
   D. If the patient does not speak English, have an interpreter translate the items for him.

8. You are in charge of designing a pilot study to evaluate the impact of patient-based health status assessment as a routine part of therapeutic drug monitoring in a comprehensive health system. Which one of the following practice settings or patient populations is not well-suited for your study?
   A. Acutely ill patients who receive drugs to cure infectious diseases, such as patients with community-acquired pneumonia.
   B. Patients who receive drugs for a chronic, not usually life-threatening condition, such as epilepsy.
   C. Patients who receive drugs for a chronic, life-threatening illness, such as cancer.
   D. Patients who receive drugs for multiple conditions, such as elderly patients.

9. A 25-year-old football player injured his right knee. His physical functioning score on the MOS SF-36 is 60 on a scale from 0 to 100 where 100 indicates best health, no limitations in even strenuous physical activities. A clinician quickly compares his score on those listed in Table 6 (located in the case study in the back of this book). Which one of the following statements is most correct?
   A. The patient has an average level of physical health limitations for his age.
   B. The patient's score is near the 50th percentile.
   C. Half of those studied score lower than he does and half score higher.
   D. No conclusions can be drawn.

CASE STUDY: CONDUCTING A PHARMACOECONOMIC EVALUATION

Lynn Jolicoeur Okamoto, Pharm.D.

Pharmacoeconomic analyses are tools that assess the value or worth of health care services, products, and interventions so that informed decisions about their use can be made. Today, it is imperative for health care providers, whether it be individual providers such as pharmacists or physicians or entire health care systems such as a managed care organization, to demonstrate they maximize available monies while providing effective outcomes. Pharmacoeconomic research can assist in assessing resources and outcomes by identifying, measuring, and comparing costs, risks, and benefits of programs, services, or therapies and determining which alternative produces the best health care outcomes for the resource invested.

Pharmacoeconomic research is widely used by industry and academia to support the use of new medicines and interventions. But pharmacoeconomic research is not limited to those practice settings and can be a valuable tool for all health care providers. Usually, the only data available to assess new medicines has been generated by the pharmaceutical industry using restricted study populations and therefore is not always generalizable to all practice settings. This makes it all the more important that pharmacoeconomic analyses be applied in your own practice setting to assess the clinical, economic, and humanistic outcomes of medicines and to make informed decisions relevant to your specific situation.

This case study presents the steps used in a pharmacoeconomic analysis. For any pharmacoeconomic analysis, there are many choices, and depending on your health care setting or the complexity of the question, there also can be a number of different outcomes. The steps used are basically guidelines to approach pharmacoeconomic research and can be used as a starting point for conducting you own pharmacoeconomic evaluations.

You are presented with information about a formulary decision coming up for the Pharmacy and Therapeutics (P&T) Committee of a hypothetical integrated health care system, Health Network. As you proceed through each step of the case, stop to answer the questions posed. Also, consider your own practice setting. How do the events of the case compare to what happens in your situation? If you don't directly participate on a Pharmacy and Therapeutics Committee, how do the events described impact upon your setting? At the end, you are encouraged to conduct an economic assessment in your own practice setting.

Step 1: Define the Problem

The first step of any pharmacoeconomic analysis is to clearly and concisely identify the problem. If the problem is not thoroughly defined, the resultant outcome may not fully address the original problem. For example, if the problem is not fully thought out, or the alternatives of comparison or perspective of the study are not correctly identified, results from your analysis may lead to an inappropriate decision. Thus, it is important to spend time identifying the problem.

Economic Assessment Case Study

You are a pharmacist practicing in an integrated health care system for Health Network, a managed care organization, with responsibilities in the asthma outpatient clinic. A year ago, the P&T Committee added a new inhaled corticosteroid, Wheezeless, to the health care system's (both hospital and clinic) formulary. The Health Network administration has announced it is reviewing expensive products at the P&T level to decide whether high-cost products should remain on the formulary. One of the therapeutic areas the P&T Committee has decided to review is inhaled corticosteroids. While it is clear that some inhaled corticosteroid must remain on formulary, currently two are included, Wheezeless and BreathX. The acquisition cost of Wheezeless is $32.00, which is $4.00 higher than for BreathX. The P&T Committee would like to know whether Wheezeless should remain on the formulary and, if so, with what recommendations for use? Your director comes to you for help because of your expertise in asthma. He wants you to prepare a recommendation for the P&T Committee.

- Given this scenario, what is the problem you are asked to address?

Answer: Define the Problem

Health Network's administration is looking for cost-containment opportunities. The P&T committee has asked your director to specifically address the issue of expensive, highly utilized products. The products under review are inhaled corticosteroids. You, the pharmacist, must not only address whether Wheezeless should remain on the formulary, but also compare Wheezeless and BreathX and make recommendations for use of this category of agents.

Step 2: Determine Resources Needed to Conduct the Assessment

To address a pharmacoeconomic problem, it is necessary to gather information and data from many areas within the medical setting. In addition, any outcomes or changes resulting from the analysis will potentially affect a number of health care providers. Because of this, it is essential to create a multidisciplinary task force or cross-functional team to assist in the development, implementation, and interpretation of the analysis. The team may consist of, but should not be limited to, physicians, pharmacists, nurses, hospital administrators, database analysts, financial staff, biostatisticians, and pharmacoeconomic researchers.

You also need to determine what resources are needed to carry out the assessment. The availability of key resources determines whether a pharmacoeconomic analysis is feasible and can be completed on schedule. The necessary data and resources vary from one setting to another and involve pulling together information from multiple sources, such as using clinical trial data in conjunction with data from your own setting.

Some types of resources to consider include 1) access to data, either from your organization, such as medical chart review, or from published prospective clinical trial data; 2) personnel needed to complete the project, such as biostatisticians or medical staff; and 3) budgetary support, such as a grant or designated time to support collection of data at your institution.

- What departments in this integrated health care system should be involved on the cross-functional team? Write down four departments that should be represented.
- List at least two types of resources that are needed to complete this project.

Answer: Determine Resources Needed to Conduct the Assessment

Many individuals could be involved in this cross-functional team. Each team member should bring a certain expertise for solving the problem. In this case study, we know that formulary decisions affect the way physicians practice medicine. Because of this, you should seek to include a prominent pulmonary physician who can provide information regarding care of asthma patients. The physician might be someone you already have a good relationship with, or someone who likes to use Wheezeless and would have a stake in the decision. Regardless of which physician is chosen, it should be someone whose judgment is respected by others, as this person will be key to backing up any recommendations your team ultimately makes.

You should also seek assistance on your team from a caregiver in the ambulatory setting, since this is where most inhaled corticosteroids are monitored. A nurse from a clinic where asthma patients are seen would be an ideal team member.

Knowing you also will need to collect data from patient medical records, you will need the assistance of someone from medical records. This should help facilitate access to patient charts and the electronic database, and provide insight into the most efficient ways to collect the information needed.

Others who could be included on the cross-functional team include a health care administrator, a respiratory therapist, or participants from the emergency department or utilization review. Whoever is chosen should have a stake in the findings and be able to offer a unique expertise to solving the problem.

To complete this cost-effectiveness analysis, the following resources are required. A review of the published literature regarding rates of asthma exacerbations and other areas of comparison for Wheezeless and BreathX is needed. The team will need access to computerized medical records to evaluate the use of Wheezeless in your setting. Finally, personnel time from the cross-functional team is needed in order to carry out the assessment.

You consulted the chief physician of the Section of Pulmonary Medicine, Dr. Jones, and the head nurse at the Pulmonary Clinic, Ms. Smith, to discuss P&T's request. Dr. Jones and Ms. Smith inform you that Wheezeless has been used mostly in patients with moderate to severe asthma. They also believe that patients who use Wheezeless have had fewer unscheduled clinic visits, emergency department visits, and hospitalizations during the past year compared to asthma patients treated with other inhaled corticosteroids. Because Dr. Jones and Ms. Smith have no objective data to support these claims, you agree that these observations need to be substantiated.

Another way to evaluate this possible decreased use of medical resources in patient's who use Wheezeless is through collection of data from patients' medical records. You contact the Head of Medical Records to discuss how you can use the electronic database to review medical care used by patients receiving Wheezeless.

You also consult with your Pharmacy Director to inform him of your preliminary findings and of the make-up of the cross-functional team involved in this project.

Step 3: Define the Study's Perspective

The perspective of a pharmacoeconomic analysis may be that of society, a patient, a department or institution, an integrated health care system, a third-party payer, or a combination of these. The point of view determines the scope of the analysis and the data required.

- From what perspective do you think this pharmacoeconomic analysis should be conducted?

Answer: Define the Study's Perspective

Health Network's P&T Committee is interested in saving dollars, providing quality medications, and managing their budget. Therefore, this group wants to know the overall cost and benefit of having Wheezeless on the formulary. In this case, costs of concern for treating asthma patients include unscheduled clinic visits, emergency department visits, hospitalizations, and drug therapy. The benefit of interest is to maintain asthma control and to prevent asthma exacerbations. When medical resources are used in the hospital and clinic, fewer dollars are available to treat other diseases, which can affect the budgets of other departments. Because the P&T Committee represents many areas of this integrated health system, the review of Wheezeless should be conducted from Health Network's point of view.

Step 4: Determine Treatment Alternatives and Outcomes

All likely treatment options for patients with asthma should be identified and investigated, with the alternatives representative of current clinical practice. Asthma can be treated with a number of therapies, either alone or in combination, and valid alternatives depend upon the clinical characteristics and lung function of the patient. Besides treatment with BreathX or Wheezeless, patients with asthma could receive a number of other treatments, including inhaled or oral bronchodilators (administered as necessary or scheduled, long- or short-acting in nature), oral corticosteroids, or cromolyn.

Your team must determine which inhaled corticosteroid should be included on the formulary for use in Health Network's patient population. The newer product, Wheezeless, is a more potent inhaled corticosteroid that requires fewer puffs per day to achieve effects similar to those received with BreathX. Published clinical data show significantly increased lung function with Wheezeless as compared with BreathX. In addition, hospitalizations and unscheduled clinic visits were fewer in asthma patients receiving Wheezeless. However, there was no difference between patients treated with Wheezeless and those treated with BreathX in the use of other asthma medications, such as bronchodilators or cromolyn.

For the outcomes side of the equation, both desired and adverse outcomes should be identified. A desired outcome is the benefit expected from a particular treatment, which is sometimes referred to as treatment success. In this example, you and the pulmonary physician, Dr. Jones, define treatment success as prevention of asthma exacerbations. You define an asthma exacerbation as an asthma event that requires medical attention in the form of an unscheduled clinic or emergency department visit, or hospitalization during a 6-month period. Adverse outcomes include adverse effects and complications that can be caused by a particular therapy. In this case, both inhaled corticosteroids have similar adverse event profiles.

- From the description above, what are the alternatives for this study and what are the outcomes to be assessed?

Answer: Determine Treatment Alternatives and Outcomes

From the perspective of Health Network, the alternatives to be assessed in this investigation are BreathX versus Wheezeless. Outcomes to be assessed include prevention of asthma exacerbations that require medical attention in the form of unscheduled clinic visits, emergency department visits, or hospitalizations within a 6-month period. Indirect costs such as time lost from work, patient discomfort from excessive shortness of breath, and expenses related to travel to health care facilities are not important from this perspective.

Step 5: Select the Appropriate Pharmacoeconomic Method

The next step is to choose the pharmacoeconomic method that is best suited to the problem. A cost-minimization analysis could be used if the products assessed had equivalent outcomes and consequences, leaving only the costs associated with therapy to be compared. If a cost-benefit analysis is used, all the outcome measures are converted to dollars and all associated costs are identified. Cost-benefit analysis is most often used when comparing the value of dissimilar programs where the outcomes are measured using different units. Cost-effectiveness analysis requires the use of the same measurement of desired outcome for both drugs, such as the improvement in blood pressure expressed as millimeters of mercury (mm Hg). A cost-utility analysis has to be based on patients' preferences and is often expressed as cost per quality-adjusted life-year gained.

Compare the outcomes associated with the use of Wheezeless to those observed with BreathX. Treatment success has been defined as the outcomes associated with preventing asthma exacerbations as measured by unscheduled clinic visits, emergency department visits, and hospitalizations.

- Take a few minutes to decide which pharmacoeconomic method is the most appropriate to employ in this study.

Answer: Select the Appropriate Pharmacoeconomic Method

Because the outcome measure, prevention of asthma exacerbations, has been defined and is a term expressed in terms of units of success for each alternative, the appropriate pharmacoeconomic method is a cost-effectiveness analysis. The cost-effectiveness analysis for this study is expressed as the cost-per-prevented asthma exacerbation throughout 6 months. Cost-minimization analysis is not appropriate because outcomes are not equivalent. For cost-minimization analysis to be used properly, outcomes must be equivalent so that only the cost side of the equation need be considered. Neither is cost-benefit analysis the best choice. This evaluation involves two similar treatments with outcomes measured using similar units; the strength of cost-benefit analysis is its ability to compare dissimilar costs and consequences. Cost-utility analysis involves use of patients' preferences, involving data that are not of concern for this particular evaluation.

Step 6: Place Monetary Values on Patient Care Resources

Resources consumed and outcomes observed need to be given dollar values; therefore, several factors need to be considered. Various monetary values can be used in a pharmacoeconomic evaluation. Acquisition costs, charges, current market prices, diagnosis-related group payments, and third-party reimbursements are all possible monetary inputs. Each of the values chosen can vary the results of the analysis. Whatever value is selected should be consistent across the alternatives chosen and should represent the perspective of the assessment.

- Given the alternatives and outcomes for this study, identify the costs associated with each and how you would identify these costs in this health care system.

Answer: Place Monetary Values on Patient Care Resources

From the chosen perspective of the health system, important costs are those for drug acquisition and for unscheduled clinic visits, care in an emergency department, and hospitalizations. Because published studies have shown that adverse drug reactions and use of other drugs remains constant, regardless of either BreathX or Wheezeless use, the costs of these outcomes are not assessed.

Monetary values associated with BreathX and Wheezeless prescriptions are taken from pharmacy costs. These include acquisition, storage, dispensing, and administrative costs. The monetary value for your alternatives are \$28.00/month for BreathX and \$32.00/month for Wheezeless.

If the treatment does not prevent asthma exacerbations and medical attention is required, additional costs are incurred for each alternative. These costs, taken from Health Network's database, consist of the following:

- \$197 for each unscheduled clinic visit, including the physician's charge and pulmonary function testing
- \$850 for each emergency department visit, including the physician's charge, pulmonary function testing, chest x-ray, blood gases, and medications
- \$2600 for each hospitalization, including physicians' charges, medications, pulmonary function testing, and ancillary charges for the bed, nursing, etc. for an average length of stay of 3 days

Step 7: Establish the Probabilities of the Outcome Events

This step involves identifying the probability of each outcome. Some key sources of information to obtain probabilities include published literature, national databases, and patient care records. Which source to use depends on the decisions made at the beginning of this process. For this example, the study is being conducted from Health Network's perspective. Therefore, probabilities obtained from the clinic and hospital will more accurately reflect the health care system and its patients. However, clinic and hospital records are often difficult to obtain and, when obtainable, do not always contain the needed information. Thus, published literature can be used to obtain probability data not captured by the health care system. When using published literature, the generalizability of the data must be determined as part of a critical review of the research design, its limitations, and the results.

- For this study, list what probabilities need to be identified to perform your pharmacoeconomic analysis.

Table 1. Percentage Rates of Medical Use for Patients Who Use Wheezeless and BreathX and Experience an Asthma Exacerbation

Medical Use	Wheezeless	BreathX
Unscheduled clinic visit	90 percent	84 percent
Emergency department visit	10 percent	16 percent
Hospitalization *(following clinic visit)*	1 percent	3 percent
Hospitalization *(following emergency department visit)*	2 percent	5 percent

Answer: Establish the Probabilities of the Outcome Events

The probabilities that need to be identified include percentage of patients with asthma experiencing an asthma exacerbation and the percentage rates of medical use associated with an asthma exacerbation, including unscheduled clinic visits, emergency department visits, and hospitalizations.

For this example, the percentage of patients with asthma experiencing an asthma exacerbation while receiving Wheezeless or BreathX is 20 percent (range 18 percent to 22 percent) and 22 percent (range 18 percent to 26 percent), respectively. These probability rates were identified by a literature review of both medications which included clinical trial data and observation or "real world" studies. Because there were a number of studies, an average number and range were calculated.

From the clinic's and hospital's electronic records, medical use associated with an asthma exacerbation was obtained. For all patients with asthma treated with Wheezeless or BreathX throughout a 6-month period, the use of unscheduled clinic visits, emergency department visits, and associated hospitalizations were extracted. Percentage rates of medical use for both groups are in Table 1.

Step 8: Use Decision Analysis, Part 1

When approaching pharmacoeconomic analyses, multiple outcomes are usually under consideration, with each outcome having a degree of uncertainty. For example, there can be uncertainty about how often a therapy is successful or how often a side effect will occur. Decision analysis is a tool used to assist a researcher in making decisions when uncertainty exists. Decision analysis can be used to 1) identify the available options when faced with a decision, 2) predict the consequences or outcomes of each option, 3) assess the likelihood or probability of the identified possible outcomes, 4) determine the value of each outcome, and 5) select the decision option that will yield the best payoff. Thus, decision analysis is performed using an orderly sequence of steps that includes framing the question, structuring the problem, assigning probabilities, valuing outcomes, and calculating the outcomes. A decision analysis can be graphically displayed using a decision-tree structure that lays out treatment options, outcomes, and associated probabilities.

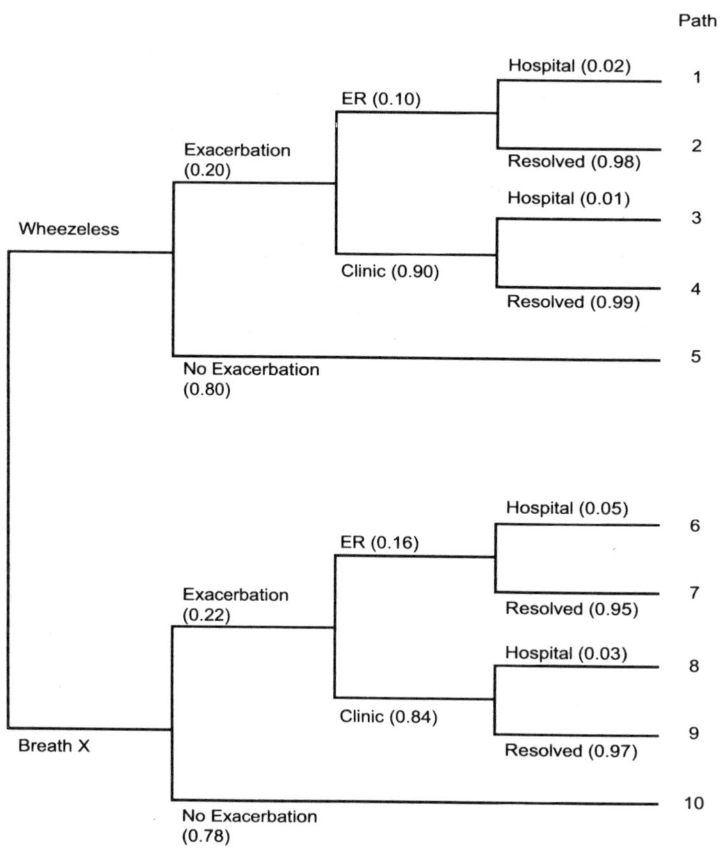

Figure 1. Decision tree for the prevention of asthma exacerbation using Wheezeless and BreathX

- Take time now to graphically display the decision analysis for this study and assign the associated probabilities to each outcome.

Answer: Use Decision Analysis, Part 1

The decision tree for Wheezeless and BreathX is shown in Figure 1. The branches of the decision tree represent the possible outcomes and probabilities of occurrence for that outcome. There are five possible paths a patient may follow in this example. The patient may experience an asthma exacerbation and seek medical assistance in the emergency department (ED) or at the clinic. If the exacerbation persists, the patient may be admitted to the hospital, otherwise the patient is sent home. The other possibility is that the patient does not experience an asthma exacerbation during the 6-month period (a treatment success).

Step 8: Use Decision Analysis, Part 2

To determine the cost-effectiveness ratio for Wheezeless and BreathX, the expected cost of treating an asthma patient with either drug must be calculated. The expected cost of treating a patient with Wheezeless is illustrated by following the paths in Figure 1. A patient with asthma treated with Wheezeless has a 20 percent probability of experiencing an asthma exacerbation during a 6-month period. There is a 10 percent probability that this patient will receive medical assistance from an emergency care facility and a two percent probability this patient is hospitalized for this asthma exacerbation event. Therefore, this patient has a 0.0004 (0.20 x 0.10 x 0.02) cumulative probability of following path 1. The cumulative probability calculated for each path is then multiplied by the path's cost, based on the cost of drug (either Wheezeless or BreathX) for 6 months plus the costs associated with an asthma exacerbation requiring medical attention such as unscheduled clinic visits, emergency department visits, and hospitalization.

- Calculate the cost and cumulative probability of each path, along the with the total expected costs for both Wheezeless and BreathX, using Worksheet 1.

Answer: Use Decision Analysis, Part 2

The cost and cumulative probability of each path, along with the total expected costs for both Wheezeless and BreathX, are presented in Table 2.

A treatment success associated with Wheezeless or BreathX occurs only if the patient with asthma does not experience an asthma exacerbation during a 6-month period. Treatment success is found in paths 5 and 10 for Wheezeless and BreathX, respectively.

Worksheet 1

Path	Drug Cost ($)	Clinic Cost ($)	ED Cost ($)	Hospital Cost ($)	Cumulative Probability	Cost of Path Outcome ($)
Wheezeless						
1						
2						
3						
4						
5						
						Total =
BreathX						
6						
7						
8						
9						
10						
						Total =

Table 2. Costs of Preventing Asthma Exacerbations using Wheezeless and BreathX

Path	Drug Cost ($)	Clinic Cost ($)	ED Cost ($)	Hospital Cost ($)	Cumulative Probability	Cost of Path Outcome ($)
Wheezeless						
1	192.00		850.00	2600.00	0.0004	1.46
2	192.00		850.00		0.0196	20.42
3	192.00	197.00		2600.00	0.0018	5.38
4	192.00	197.00			0.1782	69.32
5	192.00				0.8000	153.60
Total						250.18
BreathX						
6	168.00		850.00	2600.00	0.0018	6.51
7	168.00		850.00		0.0334	34.00
8	168.00	197.00		2600.00	0.0055	16.31
9	168.00	197.00			0.1793	65.45
10	168.00				0.7800	131.04
Total						253.31

Step 9: Calculate the Cost-Effectiveness Ratios for BreathX and Wheezeless

The cost-effectiveness ratios for Wheezeless and BreathX are calculated by dividing the expected cost of treating a patient by the probability of treatment success.

- Calculate the cost per prevented asthma exacerbation (the cost-effectiveness ratio) for each drug.

Answer: Calculate the Cost-Effectiveness Ratios for BreathX and Wheezeless

The cost for each prevented asthma exacerbation for each drug is determined by dividing the expected cost of treatment for each patient with each drug by each drug's respective effectiveness in preventing an exacerbation.

For Wheezeless, the cost to prevent an asthma exacerbation is $250.18 ÷ 0.80 = $312.73, and for BreathX, this cost is $253.31 ÷ 0.78 = $324.75.

Step 10: Discount Costs or Perform a Sensitivity or Incremental Cost Analysis

When the costs and benefits of a program extend over time, the future costs and benefits should be discounted to reflect their present value. Many researchers repeat the analysis, varying the discount rate to examine the effect on outcomes. Although there is no standard discount rate used in pharmacoeconomic evaluations, five percent is most commonly used. Alternatively, the current interest rate offered by banking institutions is often used. Discounting effectiveness outcomes is a controversial issue in cost-effectiveness analysis. If the effects and costs associated with cost-effectiveness outcomes occur over a period of less than 1 year; discounting is not required. Also, with some measures of effectiveness, such as life-years gained, it does not make sense to discount the effects.

Sensitivity analysis is used to determine what impact assumptions have on study results. To determine at what point the findings change, the values of key variables must be varied followed by recalculation of the findings. Common variables that are most likely to be varied in a pharmacoeconomic analysis are efficacy rates, adverse event rates, and estimates of key cost items. When the range of change is unknown, researchers occasionally vary the key variable by an arbitrary percentage such as five percent. By performing sensitivity analysis, researchers can express an appropriate degree of confidence in their findings.

Incremental cost analysis is another technique used to determine the degree of confidence in the original analysis. Incremental cost analysis assesses the additional cost one treatment imposes over another compared with the additional benefits it provides. Even though a comparison of simple ratios of costs to outcomes for two alternatives can be performed, the comparison of incremental costs over the incremental outcomes tells investigators how much they are paying to add the intervention or to gain the additional outcome.

In this case study, we apply only sensitivity and incremental analyses. For the sensitivity analysis, the key variable of interest is the probability of a patient with asthma experiencing an asthma exacerbation. From the literature, we know the minimum and maximum values of likelihood for patients to experience an asthma exacerbation

Worksheet 2

Path	Total Outcome Cost ($)	Cumulative Probability for Maximum	Cost of Path Outcome ($)	Cumulative Probability for Minimum	Cost of Path Outcome ($)
Wheezeless					
1	3,642.00				
2	1,042.00				
3	2,989.00				
4	2,389.00				
5	2,192.00				
		Total =		Total =	
BreathX					
6	3,618.00				
7	1,018.00				
8	2,965.00				
9	2,365.00				
10	2,168.00				
		Total =		Total =	

while being treated with Wheezeless and BreathX. Therefore, we can vary these exacerbation rates to the maximum and minimum range numbers reported. For Wheezeless, the sensitivity analysis modifies the exacerbation rate from 20 percent to a minimum of 18 percent and a maximum of 22 percent; for BreathX the minimum is 18 percent and the maximum is 26 percent.

- Recalculate the cost and cumulative probability of each path along with the total expected costs for both Wheezeless and BreathX using the minimum and maximum ranges for the exacerbation variable using the worksheet below. The total costs associated with the medical use for each path are provided for your convenience.
- Then calculate the maximum and minimum costs per prevented asthma exacerbation for 6 months for each drug.

Answer: Discount Costs or Perform a Sensitivity or Incremental Cost Analysis

The cost and cumulative probability of each path, along with the total expected costs for both Wheezeless and BreathX, are presented in Table 3.

Using exacerbation rates at the high end of the range, the cost for Wheezeless to prevent an asthma exacerbation is $255.95 ÷ 0.78 = $328.14, and for BreathX, this ratio is $269.00 ÷ 0.74 = $363.51.

Using minimum rates of exacerbation, the cost for Wheezeless to prevent an asthma exacerbation is $244.41 ÷ 0.82 = $298.06, and for BreathX, this ratio is $237.61 ÷ 0.82 = $289.77.

Thus, when the maximum exacerbation values are used, the cost-effectiveness ratio increases from $312.73 to $328.14 for Wheezeless and from $324.75 to $363.51 for BreathX; when minimum values are used, the cost-effectiveness ratio declines from $312.73 to $298.06 for Wheezeless and from $324.75 to $289.77 for BreathX. This sensitivity analysis highlights that Wheezeless is more cost-effective using mean or high rates of exacerbation; when the lowest asthma exacerbation rates of 18 percent for each are used, BreathX becomes more cost-effective.

Step 11: Perform Incremental Cost Analysis

Incremental cost analysis is performed by dividing the difference in costs of treatment by the difference in probability of preventing an exacerbation. In this situation, by subtracting the cost of treating asthma patients with BreathX from the cost of treating asthma patients with Wheezeless and dividing by the probability of preventing an asthma exacerbation with BreathX subtracted from the probability of preventing an asthma exacerbation with Wheezeless, one can determine the incremental cost of using Wheezeless.

$$\frac{\text{(cost of treatment for Wheezeless - BreathX)}}{\text{(efficacy rate for Wheezeless - BreathX)}}$$

- Take time now to calculate the incremental cost of using Wheezeless.

Answer: Perform Incremental Cost Analysis

By subtracting the cost of treating a patient with BreathX ($253.31) from the cost of using Wheezeless ($250.18) and dividing this by the difference in efficacy rates (0.80 - 0.78), a value of $-156.50 is obtained. The additional benefit gained by using Wheezeless outweighs the cost to the

Table 3. Costs of Preventing Asthma Exacerbations using Wheezeless and BreathX

Path	Total Outcome ($)	Cumulative Probability for Maximum	Cost of Path Outcome ($)	Cumulative Probability for Minimum	Cost of Path Outcome ($)
Wheezeless					
1	3,642.00	0.0004	1.45	0.0004	1.45
2	1,042.00	0.0216	22.51	0.0176	18.34
3	2,989.00	0.0020	5.98	0.0016	4.78
4	2,389.00	0.1960	76.25	0.1604	62.40
5	2,192.00	0.7800	149.76	0.8200	157.44
			Total = 255.95		Total = 244.41
BreathX					
6	3,618.00	0.0021	7.60	0.0014	5.07
7	1,018.00	0.0395	40.21	0.0274	27.89
8	2,965.00	0.0066	19.56	0.0045	13.34
9	2,365.00	0.2118	77.31	0.1467	53.55
10	2,168.00	0.7400	124.32	0.8200	137.76
			Total = 269.00		Total = 237.61

Health Network by $-156.50 per prevented asthma exacerbation. Therefore, Wheezeless produces no additional cost, but does produce savings of $156.50 for each asthma exacerbation that is prevented.

Step 12: Present the Results

The next step is to present your results to the P&T Committee. The presentation should clearly state the question posed followed by a clear and concise description of each of the steps as outlined in this example, beginning with creating a cross-functional team to conduct the sensitivity analysis.

- Prepare at least two key messages from this study that you would report back to the P&T Committee regarding the use of Wheezeless.

Answer: Present the Results

Based on your cost-effectiveness, sensitivity, and incremental analyses, you recommend that Wheezeless remain on the formulary. The presentation highlights the fact that, although the exacerbation rates for Wheezeless and BreathX are very similar, patients who received Wheezeless and experienced an exacerbation used less expensive resources over a 6-month period. A larger number of exacerbations with Wheezeless were managed on an outpatient basis; and a lower number required hospitalization or emergency department care. Therefore, there was an actual shift of hospital resources for these patients. In fact, this is not surprising because the published literature indicated that patients treated with Wheezeless have better lung function that translates into less severe asthma exacerbations. Overall, the cost-effectiveness analysis has confirmed the results already published on Wheezeless.

Step 13: Develop an Intervention or a Policy

The P&T Committee is excited about the results of the cost-effectiveness analysis and requests that Wheezeless and BreathX remain on the formulary. The committee feels that BreathX could still be used, especially in patients without a history of asthma exacerbations requiring medical attention. When discussing the use of Wheezeless, the P&T Committee suggests that you prepare a policy for prescribing Wheezeless.

- Outline treatment guidelines for the use of Wheezeless

Answer: Develop an Intervention or a Policy

After consulting with your cross-functional team, you recommend the following policy regarding use of Wheezeless and BreathX:

1. Newly diagnosed patients and those with no previous exacerbations of asthma requiring hospitalization or emergency department care should receive BreathX.
2. Patients currently receiving BreathX who experience an asthma exacerbation that requires emergency medical attention (unscheduled clinic use, emergency department visit, or hospitalization) should be considered for treatment with Wheezeless as it was found that Health Network patients who receive Wheezeless utilize fewer emergency department and hospital care resources than those who receive BreathX when they experience an asthma exacerbation.

Step 14: Implement the Intervention and Educate Key Professionals

After developing a policy, the next step is to implement it throughout your health care setting. Implementing a policy is not limited to just providing the information in a written format, but should be a dynamic process. Various methods are available to assist in implementing new policies. These can include verbal communication through inservices to the health care providers and face to face consults with key personnel affected by the new policy; written communication through newsletters, brochures, and information pocket cards; and online computer communication.

- List two methods you could use to implement this policy in your own practice setting. Who would you target with these methods?

Answer: Implement the Intervention and Educate Key Professionals

In this asthma example, it is important for the health care providers involved in treating patients with asthma to understand that the hospital's goal is to provide cost-effective treatments that are good for their patients. With this in mind, to implement this policy, the results of the cost-effectiveness analysis should be presented to key providers such as pulmonary physicians, emergency department providers, other pharmacists, nurses, and anyone else who plays a role in caring for these patients to assist their understanding of why the policy is being implemented. Without buy-in from the people involved, the policy will not be fully implemented and the cost-effective savings identified will not occur.

Case conferences, one-on-one interactions, newsletters, and working with the pharmaceutical sales representatives for Wheezeless and Breathless are effective ways to implement the P&T Committee's new policy.

Step 15: Document Quality of Care and Potential Cost Savings Through Follow-Up

In many cost-effectiveness analyses, assumptions are made or data are used in the decision model that may not always accurately reflect your patient population or health care setting. In addition, new products may be introduced over time or policies change within the health care setting. All of these scenarios affect the results or recommendations based on your cost-effectiveness analysis. Therefore, when you implement the results from your analysis, it is important to document and follow-up any promised cost-savings from your recommendation.

- List at least two follow-up projects that will support your findings and serve as a way to document the implementation of the new drug policy.

Answer: Document Quality of Care and Potential Cost Savings Through Follow-Up

Because the exacerbation rates used for your analysis were obtained from the literature for both Wheezeless and BreathX, you may want to develop a tracking system for assessing the number of exacerbations associated with each product during a 6-month period. This establishes the true exacerbation rates for your patient population and can be used to confirm your cost-effectiveness results. In addition, you will want to periodically document any changes in health care resource use associated with asthma exacerbations. For example, 1 year following the Wheezeless policy implementation, the resource use associated with asthma exacerbations should be identified by reviewing Health Network's medical record database, just as was done for your initial analysis. The new rates can then be reevaluated in your model using current costs of resources to determine if your analysis holds and whether Health Network has experienced a cost-savings as a result of your recommendations.

Step 16: What Needs to Be Done in Your Setting?

Although this example may appear straightforward, a pharmacoeconomic analysis is not a simple matter. To assess how many factors are involved in such a process, it is suggested that you prepare a case study example based on your own practice setting. Identify a question that needs to be answered, and begin to work through the steps in a systematic way. There are many factors and assumptions to address, and changing only one may cause substantial differences in a pharmacoeconomic analysis. As you work through your question, you will begin to see how you can pull together information from a variety of sources within your health care system, and you will begin to have increased confidence in your ability to make sound, informed recommendations that will affect the care of your patients.

CASE STUDY: FORMULARY DECISION-MAKING INCORPORATING HUMANISTIC OUTCOMES

Thomas F. Goss, Pharm.D.; and
Xiao Xu, Ph.D.

Outline

Previous chapters discussed using results of clinical trials to compare therapeutic regimens, the various methodologies used to assess the economic and humanistic impacts of these regimens, and interpreting results of economic and humanistic outcome assessments. This chapter is designed to incorporate what has been presented previously, and apply these skills to reviewing and interpreting the results of such studies to assist with policy- and decision-making. The exercise that is presented in this chapter builds on the economic assessment case study previously presented in the Case Study: Conducting a Pharmacoeconomic Evaluation chapter.

I. Relationship between humanistic outcomes data and formulary decision-making
   A. Audiences for humanistic outcomes data
      1. Audiences include society, patients, hospitals, managed care plans, government agencies, individual health care providers, insurers, and other payers.
      2. Each audience influences health care decisions or is affected by them.
   B. Humanistic outcomes data are often used in context with clinical and economic data for policy- and decision-making.
   C. Fundamental skills to review and evaluate humanistic outcomes information are necessary to optimize the decision- and policy-making process.
   D. For most formulary decisions, the following therapeutic alternatives and outcomes must be considered:
      1. Clinical outcomes
      2. Economic outcomes
      3. Humanistic outcomes

II. Case study for introducing steps of developing formulary decision-making
   A. The case study used in showing the steps is designed to allow readers to apply the skills previously learned for reviewing and interpreting the results of studies to develop formulary recommendations that incorporate humanistic outcomes data.
   B. This exercise builds on the economic assessment case study previously presented in the Case Study: Conducting a Pharmacoeconomic Evaluation chapter.
   C. The steps followed in this case study are the same steps followed in the "Case Study: Conducting a Pharmacoeconomic Evaluation" chapter. This basic approach also can be adapted for other formulary decisions that include evaluating humanistic outcomes data.
   D. Case study: Wheezeless and BreathX

III. Steps of developing formulary decision-making
   A. Step 1: Define the problem
      1. Based on the information presented, what is the problem that the pharmacy and therapeutics committee wants you to address?
         a. Your integrated health system is conducting a formulary review to identify opportunities to reduce costs.
      2. List some specific humanistic outcomes that may be affected by different treatments for asthma.
         a. Health-related quality of life
         b. Patient satisfaction with health care
         c. Work force participation and productivity
   B. Step 2: Determine resources needed to conduct the assessment
      1. The multidisciplinary team
         a. The team should include a pulmonary physician, a nurse from the asthma clinic, a medical records representative, a health care administrator, a respiratory therapist, and a representative from the emergency department.
      2. In addition to the multidisciplinary team, describe additional resources that will be needed to evaluate the humanistic outcomes important to this decision.
         a. Data providing objective information
         b. Staff to assist with the evaluation
         c. Time and a budget
   C. Step 3: Define the study's perspective
      1. Evaluation can be performed from the perspective of society, the provider, the health system, payers, or patients
      2. The point of view used will determine the scope of the analysis and the data that are required.
      3. From what perspective do you think this pharmacoeconomic analysis should be conducted? Should more than one perspective be considered?
         a. Health Network
   D. Step 4: Determine treatment alternatives and outcomes
      1. Asthma treatment regimens are highly individualized and often include many drugs, used alone and in combination.
      2. Inhaled corticosteroids can reduce asthma symptoms and the need for inhaled β-agonists and oral corticosteroids.
      3. Based on this information, for which treatment alternatives should you seek comparative humanistic outcomes data?
         a. Wheezeless and BreathX
      4. Based on these comparisons, hypothesize a model in which humanistic outcomes can be integrated with clinical and economic outcomes. (Figure 1)
   E. Step 5: Identify possible sources of data
      1. Consider the possible sources of humanistic outcomes data for patients with asthma treated with the inhaled corticosteroids, Wheezeless and BreathX. For each source identified, consider the possible strengths and limitations of data from that source.
         a. Peer-reviewed published studies

         Following factors need to be considered:
            i. Generalizability of the findings.
            ii. Comparison of Wheezeless and BreathX: direct or indirect?
            iii. Comparability of the patients with asthma' severity between published studies and patient population that you serve.
         b. Primary data collected in your clinics.

            Strength
            i. High internal validity
            ii. Reasonable generalizability

            Weakness
            i. Selection bias
            ii. Might not include information needed.
         c. Prospective, randomized data

            Strength
            i. High internal validity
            ii. Reasonable generalizability
            iii. Includes needed information

            Weakness
            i. Costly in terms of time and money
            ii. A recommendation before study might be required.

        iii. External funding might be needed.
        iv. Institutional review board approval might be needed.

F. Step 6: Select a data collection method
    1. Rank the major sources of health status and patient satisfaction information in terms of their desirability for your situation.
        a. Best data: prospective evaluations of health status and patient satisfaction in comparable groups taking either Wheezeless or BreathX
        b. Next best data: past measurements of patient satisfaction or health status in your setting
        c. Last resort: peer-reviewed published studies

G. Step 7: Review and interpret data (Tables 1 and 2)
    1. What do the results of the baseline evaluation indicate?
        a. All baseline SF-36 Health Survey (SF-36) scale scores in both treatment groups are significantly lower than the United States population norm but are not significantly different from one another.
    2. What do the results of this evaluation mean in terms of the therapies currently available to treat patients with asthma?
        a. Patients with asthma enrolled in this study experienced clinically and statistically significant decrements in health status in virtually every aspect of their daily lives and functioning.
        b. Corticosteroid treatment for asthma can lead to levels of functioning close to the general population, one of the obvious goals of therapy.

H. Step 8: Summarize your findings
    Points to consider when drawing conclusions
    1. List at least five strengths of the published study
    2. List any limitations of the study
    3. Summarize the conclusions that can be drawn from the study
    4. How would your conclusions change if BreathX demonstrated greater improvement in health status than Wheezeless

I. Step 9: Present the results
    1. Prepare at least three concise messages to report to the pharmacy and therapeutics committee to support your recommendation.
        a. Cost-effectiveness analysis
        b. Incremental cost-analysis
        c. Association between two drugs and asthma exacerbation
        d. Health-related quality of findings
        e. Patient satisfaction

J. Step 10: Develop a plan to monitor this decision
    1. Suggest two strategies to monitor the impact of the formulary decision made by the pharmacy and therapeutics committee.
        a. Performing periodic health status evaluations among patients with asthma
        b. Performing periodic patient satisfaction evaluations among patients with asthma

K. Step 11: What needs to be done in your setting?
    1. Think about the various questions of importance in your own practice setting.
    2. Try to identify a service you provide that you believe results in a significant improvement in a humanistic outcome. Work through the steps to document this improvement in a systematic way.

VI. Conclusion and self-assessment

Turn to the end of the chapter for questions to assess various potential applications of humanistic outcomes assessment in your setting. Please answer those questions as honestly as you can.

Learning Objectives

1. List and evaluate the general steps in formulary decision-making process required to incorporate humanistic outcomes.
2. Apply understanding of the formulary review process to identify other aspects of the case study population that should be considered for formulary decision-making besides humanistic outcomes.
3. Compare and contrast three possible sources of humanistic outcomes data for the case study population.
4. Analyze and list strengths and limitations of the published study data provided in the case study.
5. Develop strategies to monitor the impact of the formulary decision made.
6. Incorporate what has been learned in this case study in future formulary decision-making processes.

Abbreviations in this chapter

P&T	Pharmacy and therapeutics
FEV_1	Forced expiratory volume in 1 second
HCT	Hematocrit

Case Study

Several audiences are known to be interested in humanistic outcomes data—society, patients, hospitals, managed care plans, government agencies, individual health care providers, insurers, and other payers. Each audience either influences health care decisions, or is affected by them. Humanistic outcomes data provide important information on the impact of disease and treatment of physical, psychological, and social functioning and well-being. Although the use of humanistic outcomes data to make formulary and other policy decisions is an evolving discipline, these decisions often have far-reaching effects on individual patient outcomes.

Everyone is familiar with using results of clinical trials to compare therapeutic regimens, and in recent years, there has been increasing familiarity with the methodologies used to assess the economic impacts of these same regimens. However, it is safe to say that humanistic outcomes data rarely have been used in a quantifiable way to make policy or formulary decisions apart from their consideration in context with clinical and economic data. Yet, health care providers and administrators intuitively know that patient functioning and satisfaction play major roles in how patients view their care and certainly in other types of outcomes. Although the relationships between these different categories of outcomes are complex, policy and decision-makers must have the fundamental skills necessary to review and evaluate humanistic outcomes information to optimize the decision- and policy-making process.

Humanistic outcomes are documented in the product label, advertisement, peer-reviewed publications, and presentations for patient advocacy groups. One of the strongest indicators of the evolving nature of the use of outcomes data in formulary decision-making is demonstrated in product labels and/or promotional claims. Another strong indicator of the importance of humanistic outcomes data is evidenced by the formalization of recommendations related to the use of these data in policy decisions. For example, the United States Food and Drug Administration convened the first Quality of Life Subcommittee meeting to the Oncology Drugs Advisory committee on February 10, 2000, whose meeting findings have been disseminated for public review (*http://www.fda.gov/ohrms/dockets/ac/00/slides/3591s1c/*). Other advisory groups also have recommended the consideration of humanistic outcomes data, including the United Kingdom National Institutes for Clinical Excellence (*http://www.nice.org.uk*), and the Academy of Managed Care Pharmacy Guidelines for submission of dossiers (*http://www.fmcpnet.org/data/resource/formatv20.pdf*).

Pharmaceutical marketers often use implicit claims of health-related quality-of-life benefits to promote attributes of pharmaceutical products. Currently, at least 15 United States marketed products have health-related quality-of-life statements in their labels. For example, PROCRITÒ had this promotional claim in the March 2000 New England Journal of Medicine, "By increasing and maintaining hematocrit (HCT), PROCRIT significantly increases energy and work capacity so patients with early renal insufficiency can feel better and do more". Pharmacists and others involved in making formulary decisions increasingly are confronted with a variety of claims about quality of life when making these decisions. Also, pharmaceutical companies frequently use quality-of-life claims to formally demonstrate product value in relation to other competing treatments. It is possible that two treatment regimens might be essentially equal with regard to therapeutic and cost outcomes, yet different in how they are accepted by patients, when health-related quality of life and satisfaction outcomes are considered.

This case study is designed to allow readers to apply the skills they have learned for reviewing and interpreting the results of studies to develop formulary recommendations that incorporate humanistic outcomes data. This exercise builds on the Economic Assessment Case Study in the Case Study: Conducting a Pharmacoeconomic Evaluation chapter, and is adapted from health-related quality-of-life data from a comparative study. The treatment names have been changed to maintain confidentiality of sponsor data.

For most formulary decisions, many therapeutic alternatives and outcomes must be considered. The steps followed in this case study are the same steps discussed in the chapter Case Study: Conducting a Pharmacoeconomic Evaluation. This basic approach also can be adapted for other formulary decisions that include evaluating humanistic outcomes data.

This case study presents a hypothetical formulary decision in an integrated health system that provides inpatient and outpatient services. The integrated health system has a pharmacy and therapeutics (P&T) committee that manages formularies for both settings. Providers in your integrated health system agree to follow formulary recommendations or to obtain prior authorization before deviating from the formulary. As you proceed through the case, carefully consider each of the issues addressed. Also, consider how these issues may be different in your own practice setting. If you do not participate directly in P&T committee decision-making, consider what recommendation you would make to your colleagues representing the pharmacy perspective, if you were asked to do so.

Step 1: Define the Problem

As with any pharmacoeconomic and outcomes analysis, the first step involves clearly defining the issues. If the problem is not thoroughly defined, results from the analysis may lead to an incomplete or incorrect conclusion. Thus, it is important to spend time identifying the problem.

Humanistic Assessment Case Study

You are a clinical practitioner in an integrated health care system for Health Network, a managed care organization, with responsibilities in the asthma outpatient clinic. One year ago, the P&T committee added a new inhaled corticosteroid, Wheezeless, to the formulary. Six months ago, Health Network's administration requested the P&T (P&T) committee systematically review expensive therapies to determine whether any could be deleted from the formulary to help control costs without decreasing the quality of care received by patients in the health system. After completing reviews in other therapeutic areas, the P&T committee now focuses on respiratory products. The goal of the P&T committee, if justified, is to select the one best inhaled corticosteroid product. The formulary currently includes two inhaled corticosteroids, Wheezeless and BreathX. The acquisition cost of Wheezeless is $32 per inhaler, which is $4 higher than the acquisition cost for each BreathX inhaler. Based on the previous economic evaluation performed for inhaled corticosteroids, the incremental cost-analysis estimated a cost-savings of $156.50 for each asthma exacerbation prevented with Wheezeless.

The P&T committee is impressed with the results of the economic evaluation, but in keeping with its mandate "to determine whether there are any therapies that can be removed from the formulary to help control costs without decreasing the quality of care received by patients in the health system," you have been asked to consider other sources of data, including humanistic outcomes data.

- Based on the information presented, what is the problem you are being asked by the P&T committee to address?
- List some specific humanistic outcomes that may be affected by different treatments for asthma.

Answer: Define the Problem

Your integrated health system is conducting a formulary review to identify opportunities to reduce costs. Two of the expensive respiratory products are being reviewed to determine whether one of them could be deleted from the formulary. A systematic evaluation of the two therapies needs to be performed. As previously discussed, the influence of health care decisions thus far has been on clinical and economic outcomes. In our example, compared with BreathX, Wheezeless has $4 higher cost but has a favorable cost-effectiveness ratio for each asthma exacerbation prevented. Based on this clinical and economic information, each therapy has its own pros and cons. Therefore, given the P&T committee's mandate to control costs without reducing the quality of care received by patients in the health system, an evaluation of economic, clinical, and humanistic outcomes is necessary. Health-related quality of life, patient satisfaction with health care, and work force participation and productivity all are important patient-based humanistic outcomes, particularly in patients with asthma. Each of these outcomes is important to individual patients, society, and health care providers. Therefore, you must assimilate information that takes data derived from patient-based assessments into account with the clinical and economic data currently available to make a final recommendation to the committee regarding the formulary status of Wheezeless and BreathX.

Step 2: Determine Resources Needed to Conduct the Assessment

To address the formulary issue presented by the P&T committee, the evaluation must be undertaken within the framework of a multidisciplinary team that includes a pulmonary physician, a nurse from the asthma clinic, a medical records representative, a health care administrator, a respiratory therapist, and a representative from the emergency department. Because data to address the quality of care issues are needed, you may need to add members from other departments within the system to your team as well.

- In addition to participation from the multidisciplinary team, describe additional resources that will be needed to evaluate the humanistic outcomes important to this decision.

Answer: Determine Resources Needed to Conduct the Assessment

The specific resources needed to complete your review, in addition to participation of a multidisciplinary team, include the need for:

- human research review committee or institutional review board, to oversee data collection;
- data that provide objective information for any or all of the humanistic outcomes that bear on this decision;
- staff to assist with the evaluation, particularly if data collection will be necessary;
- a biostatistician to assist with data analysis; and
- time and a budget to allow you to complete this review in addition to your other responsibilities.

Step 3: Define the Study's Perspective

Your evaluation can be performed from the perspective of society, the provider, the health system, payers, or patients. The point of view used determines the scope of the analysis and the data that are required.

- From what perspective do you think this pharmacoeconomic analysis should be conducted? Should more than one perspective be considered?

Answer: Define the Study's Perspective

The P&T committee is interested in saving dollars and providing quality care. Therefore, this group wants to know the overall costs and benefits of having these agents on the formulary. In this case, costs of concern for treating patients with asthma include unscheduled clinic visits, emergency department visits, hospitalizations, and drug therapy. The consequences of interest are to maintain asthma control and prevent asthma exacerbations, to improve patient adherence with treatment recommendations to the extent this helps prevent exacerbations, to prevent patient disenrollment because of dissatisfaction with care, and to identify through patient satisfaction surveys and health status assessment specific interventions that can be implemented to improve quality. Because the P&T committee represents many areas of this integrated health system, the review of Wheezeless should be conducted from Health Network's point of view.

Selecting Health Network's point of view may seem at odds with the concept that underlies patient-based assessment because such assessments focus on what patients think and feel. Decisions about whether to include a given drug on a formulary have been based mainly on estimates of its costs and effectiveness relative to other treatment strategies. These decisions commonly are made from a societal perspective, as opposed to that of individual patients, which sometimes results in conflicts. Therefore, in the case of a formulary decision where the health system's policies affect many patients, it is appropriate that this evaluation be conducted from the health system's perspective. The health system's goal is to allocate finite resources to maximize population health. To assist in decision-making, health care systems are increasingly using health outcomes information and economic analyses, which has been emphasized in this chapter.

Step 4: Determine Treatment Alternatives and Outcomes

To compare humanistic outcomes, it is necessary to define appropriate treatment alternatives available for patients with asthma in your health system. Because asthma treatment regimens are highly individualized and often include many drugs, used alone and in combination, your integrated health system likely provides many alternative therapies, including inhaled and oral bronchodilators; inhaled and oral corticosteroids; and mast cell-stabilizing agents, such as cromolyn.

Better management from a clinical perspective may result in improved respiratory function, such as increased percentage forced expiratory volume in 1 second (FEV_1), reduced cough, and reduced wheezing. Because inhaled corticosteroids can reduce asthma symptoms and the need for inhaled β-agonists and oral corticosteroids, they also may improve patients' health-related quality of life.

- Based on this information, for which treatment alternatives should you seek comparative humanistic outcomes data?
- Based on these comparisons, hypothesize a model in which humanistic outcomes can be integrated with clinical and economic outcomes.

Answer: Determine Treatment Alternatives and Outcomes

Based on the objectives of Health Network's administration and the P&T committee's pending formulary decision, the treatment comparisons should be limited to Wheezeless and BreathX, if possible. These agents are of the same therapeutic category and often are considered interchangeable.

Differences in the clinical effects of inhaled corticosteroids may translate into measurable health-related quality-of-life differences, including improved physical and role functioning, and possibly better psychological functioning related to reduced anxiety and worry associated with frequent or severe asthma attacks. The model depicted in Figure 1 summarizes one possible hypothesis about the relationship between asthma therapy and economic, clinical, and humanistic outcomes.

A reduction in asthma symptoms and concurrent drugs that results in improved health should result in increased patient satisfaction with care. In turn, this increased satisfaction should theoretically influence participant willingness to continue to be cared for by Health Network. Another reason Health Network should be concerned with health status is that improved functioning among its members also should translate into improved patient satisfaction with care.

Although important, this evaluation is not being undertaken to satisfy the information requirements of an employer audience. Thus, measures of work force participation and productivity are not of primary importance in this evaluation, although some will be captured through measurement of health status. However, health status does include a broader definition of productivity, which includes ability to resume normal roles and activities, which, in turn, may affect patient satisfaction with care, and therefore, have to be considered.

Note that the proposed outcomes benefits typically are derived from a measurable clinical effect. The relationship between humanistic outcomes and potential clinical effects is an important relationship because one should not expect to demonstrate improved humanistic and economic outcomes without first demonstrating a reasonable clinical benefit. However, it also is worth noting that economic outcomes can be positive or negative, depending on many factors, including the price of a product or therapy relative to its competitors. In the situation where one therapy is associated with positive clinical, humanistic, and economic outcomes, that therapy dominates other therapies from the cost-effectiveness perspective as it provides superior

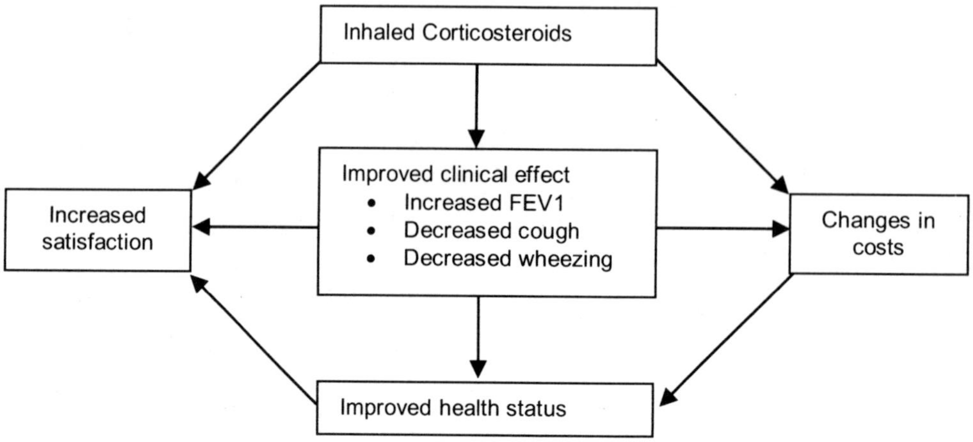

Figure 1. The Interaction of Economic, Clinical, and Humanistic Outcomes in Asthma Patients
FEV_1 = forced expiratory volume in one second.

benefits at lower costs. In the situation where a therapy is associated with superior clinical and humanistic outcomes but negative economic outcomes, such as being more costly, then the cost-effectiveness evaluation becomes a value judgment. The question then becomes, Are the improved clinical and/or humanistic outcomes worth the additional cost? The answer to this question may vary substantially, depending on the audience evaluating these outcomes.

Step 5: Identify Possible Sources of Data

Now that specific humanistic outcomes of interest have been identified, the next step is to identify potential sources of these data. Please review what you have learned in the Data Sources and Tools for Measuring Humanistic Outcomes chapter, if necessary.

- Consider the possible sources of humanistic outcomes data for patients with asthma treated with the inhaled corticosteroids, Wheezeless and BreathX. For each source you identify, consider the possible strengths and limitations of data from that source.

Answer: Identify Possible Sources of Data

In this case, there are several possible sources of health status and patient satisfaction information.

Peer-reviewed Published Studies

A well-established body of published literature describes the health-related quality-of-life effects of asthma and its treatments. Many of these reports provide an excellent foundation to evaluate the impact of asthma and its treatments on health-related quality of life; however, few studies to date report detailed information on patient satisfaction or work force participation. When considering the use of a published study as a source of data for a formulary evaluation, several factors should be considered.

- How generalizable are the findings from published studies to the patient population served in your practice?
- Do any studies provide a direct comparison of Wheezeless and BreathX? If not, are indirect comparisons available and appropriate?
- Is the asthma severity of the patients in published studies similar to the severity in the patient population you serve?

These are just some of the more important factors that should be considered before extrapolating data from published trials to your health system.

Primary Data Collected in Your Clinics

Many health systems conduct ongoing prospective outcomes monitoring projects through their quality assurance department or through other programs. For example, health-related quality of life and patient satisfaction commonly are measured to satisfy the accreditation standards of the National Committee on Quality Assurance. Therefore, you may be able to evaluate data already collected within your institution. Data collected in this manner have several possible strengths and limitations.

- Limitations of the data previously collected in your health system should be readily understood and be reasonably generalizable to the patients currently served.
- Data that were not collected from prospective, randomized patient cohorts may be subject to selection bias. For example, patients with more severe asthma may systematically receive one regimen over the other, resulting in a difference between treatment groups because of baseline disease severity and not to treatment effects.
- Data that have been collected already may not specifically include the information you are seeking for your evaluation.

Prospective, Randomized Data

It may be possible to collect data prospectively in your health system's clinics before making a final formulary decision. If time permits, this may be a realistic option. It will be important to coordinate any prospective data collection initiative through the multidisciplinary team assembled to review this formulary issue. Research grants may be available from industry sponsors for such projects; however, it is important to establish the independence of your research before pursuing potential sources of funding. This method of data collection also has several strengths and limitations.

- Data collected in a prospective, randomized study will be internally valid and generalizable for making formulary decisions within your health system.
- Data collected prospectively can be selected specifically for the needs of your evaluation. A prospective evaluation could incorporate health status and patient satisfaction, both of interest to the integrated health system.
- Prospective, randomized trials can be costly in terms of time and financial resources required.
- The P&T committee may require a recommendation before such a study can reasonably be completed.
- External funding may be needed to conduct such an evaluation.
- Institutional review board approval may be needed.

Step 6: Select a Data Collection Method

After completing a literature search, you know the major sources of data that you need for this portion of your formulary evaluation. Rank these sources in terms of their desirability for your situation. Please note that because of internal P&T committee deadlines, data to reach a decision are required within 2 months, which you must consider when selecting among potential sources of data.

Answer: Select a Data Collection Method

The best data that you could obtain for your evaluation would be prospective evaluations of health status and patient satisfaction in comparable groups taking either Wheezeless or BreathX. However, after discussing the time and expense that would be involved in this approach with the chairman of the P&T committee, you find that Health Network expects you to provide a recommendation at the next P&T committee meeting in 2 months. That will not be enough time to measure either patient satisfaction or health status prospectively.

The next best data would come from past measurements of patient satisfaction or health status in your setting. You know that patients have not been asked to complete health questionnaires while in the asthma clinic. Therefore, you decide to check with the quality improvement department to see if these data were obtained in some other way. You find that patient satisfaction has been measured in outpatient surgery patients and oncology patients, but not in any other patient groups thus far. Health status questionnaires have not been used because they have been viewed as being too great a burden without the addition of more staff.

Thus, seeking data from the published literature becomes your last resort. Through a MEDLINE search, you identify one study that evaluated health status in patients with asthma of comparable demographic characteristics as those of Health Network's members. However, neither this study nor any other that you located measured patient satisfaction in patients with asthma who received either BreathX or Wheezeless.

Step 7: Review and Interpret Data

In the published study that you found, the results of a Phase III clinical trial are detailed. The authors describe the trial as a prospective, randomized study comparing Wheezeless to BreathX. A total of 450 adult patients were enrolled in the trial, 225 to each treatment group. During the initial 4-week washout phase, patients were not allowed to use any inhaled or oral corticosteroid; they were allowed to use a β-agonist inhaler as needed to control wheezing. All patients met the American Thoracic Society diagnostic criteria for asthma. Inclusion criteria included FEV_1 measurements between 40 and 80 percent of predicted values. Written informed consent was obtained from all study participants.

Patients were randomized to receive inhaled Wheezeless 500 mcg/day or inhaled BreathX 1000 mcg 2 times/day. Pulmonary function tests were performed before the 4-week washout period, at the time of randomization (baseline), and after 16 weeks of therapy. Health-related quality of life was measured using the SF-36 health survey. The SF-36 was completed by study patients at baseline and at the 16-week evaluation. At baseline, patient demographics and asthma severity were similar between treatment groups.

In addition to the information provided below, the authors indicated that the SF-36 was selected for this study because it had been widely validated in the general population and in disease states other than asthma. The authors also stated that they evaluated the psychometric performance standards of the SF-36 in their patient sample using the baseline health-related quality-of-life measures and found that "each of the eight SF-36 scales met all recommended psychometric performance standards for performing group level comparisons. Internal consistency reliability estimates (Cronbach's alpha) ranged from 0.72 to 0.95 for each of the eight scales, and no significant scale ceiling or floor effects were observed".

The results of the health-related quality-of-life component of the study were provided. Table 1 summarizes baseline mean SF-36 scale scores for the 225 patients in each treatment group. The results of the week 16 health-related quality-of-life assessment for the 212 Wheezeless patients and 208 BreathX patients who completed the study are summarized by treatment group in Table 2, which also shows the United States population normative SF-36 scale scores, found in the SF-36 manual and adjusted for age and gender.

Table 1. Baseline SF-36 Scale Scores by Treatment Group

	PF	RP	BP	GH	VT	SF	RE	MH
Wheezeless (n=225)	71.2	68.0	69.5	64.1	49.5	72.1	67.0	66.5
BreathX (n=225)	70.9	69.1	69.7	63.7	50.1	72.3	68.0	67.0
United States population norm	84.2[a]	81.0[a]	75.2[a]	72.0[a]	60.9[a]	83.3[a]	81.3[a]	74.7[a]

[a] p<0.05 for differences between treatment groups and United States population norms.
BP = bodily pain; GH = general health; MH = mental health; PF = physical function; RE = role emotional; RP = role physical; SF = social function; VT = vitality.

Table 2. Week 16 SF-36 Scale Scores by Treatment Group

PF	RP	BP	GH	VT	SF	RE	MH	
Wheezeless (n=212)	80.9[a]	78.5	75.0	70.8[a]	58.5	84.0[a]	79.5	74.5
BreathX (n=208)	73.5[b]	74.2	71.2[b]	66.8[b]	55.6[b]	77.0[b]	74.0	71.0[b]
United States population norm	84.2	81.0	75.2	72.0	60.9	83.3	81.3	74.7

[a] p<0.05 for treatment group differences.
[b] p<0.05 for differences between treatment and United States Population Norms.
BP = bodily pain; GH = general health; MH = mental health; PF = physical function; RE = role emotional; RP = role physical; SF = social function; VT = vitality.

- Take a few minutes to consider what the results of the baseline evaluation indicate. Which domains are most significantly affected by asthma? Where are treatment-related improvements most likely to be observed?
- Based on the data you have reviewed, which therapy do you believe has the greatest impact on patients functioning and well-being?

Answer: Review and Interpret Data

These results indicate that all baseline SF-36 scale scores in both treatment group are significantly lower than the United States population norm but are not significantly different from one another. These findings suggest that the patients with asthma enrolled in this study experienced clinically and statistically significant decrements in health status in virtually every aspect of their daily lives and functioning.

After 16 weeks of treatment, patients treated with Wheezeless demonstrated statistically and clinically significant improvements in three of the SF-36 scales—physical function, general health, and social function—compared to patients treated with BreathX. Patients treated with Wheezeless also demonstrated health status scores substantially closer to those of the general population than patients treated with BreathX, indicating that corticosteroid treatment for asthma can lead to levels of functioning close to the general population, one of the obvious goals of therapy.

Step 8: Summarize Your Findings

After reviewing the study that compared health status associated with Wheezeless and BreathX therapy, you can now begin to draw some conclusions from this study. As you do, there are several points to consider.

- List at least five strengths of the published study.
- List any limitations of the study.
- Summarize the conclusions that can be drawn from the study.
- What conclusions would you draw if the measured scale scores and treatment effects were reversed; that is, how would your conclusions change if BreathX demonstrated greater improvement in health status than Wheezeless?

Answer: Summarize Your Findings

The published study has many strengths worth noting, including:

- The study sample size was adequate to detect clinically significant differences.
- The design of the study was prospective and randomized.
- Corticosteroids were withdrawn before enrollment, providing the opportunity to evaluate treatment effects associated with the therapies of interest.
- Patients met standard diagnostic criteria from the American Thoracic Society.
- Objective measures of lung function were obtained from all patients, allowing correlation to health status assessments.
- Written informed consent was obtained from all participants.
- A majority of patients enrolled (92–94 percent of patients randomized) completed the study.
- The study duration was long enough to demonstrate meaningful treatment effects.
- The study used a widely used, validated measure of health status.
- The psychometric performance of the measure was reported in the population studied.
- Normative comparisons were provided to allow readers to assess the burden of illness associated with the illness under study.

The study also had some limitations, which are summarized below:

- Treatment assignments were not blinded; thus, the potential for bias was increased somewhat.
- The results are not provided by individual strata based on lung function or other objective measures of disease severity.
- A 16-week evaluation may not be representative of the differences observed after longer therapy duration.
- Only adults were evaluated in this study; therefore, the results may not be generalizable to pediatric patients with asthma treated within Health Network.
- The report only summarizes the results of the evaluation based on SF-36 results and may not be comparable to results obtained with other general or disease-specific measures.
- Patient satisfaction, the outcome of most immediate interest to the P&T committee, was not measured in this study.

Conclusions that can be drawn from the results reported in the study include:

- The patients with asthma evaluated in this study experienced significant decrements in health-related quality of life when their usual asthma regimens were withdrawn.
- The SF-36 is a reliable and valid instrument to measure health-related quality of life in patients with asthma.
- Patients treated with Wheezeless demonstrated greater improvement in health status during the study compared to patients treated with BreathX.
- After a 16-week course of therapy, patients treated with Wheezeless did not demonstrate any significant decrements in health-related quality of life compared to age- and gender-adjusted population normative values.

If the treatment effect results were reversed, that is, if BreathX demonstrated greater health status improvement than Wheezeless, the first two conclusions listed above would remain unchanged but the last two would be reversed.

Step 9: Present the Results

Now that the humanistic outcomes comparison between Wheezeless and BreathX is complete, it is time to summarize all of these findings into a recommendation for the P&T committee of the integrated health system.

- Prepare at least three concise messages to report to the P&T committee to support your recommendation.

Answer: Present the Results

Based on your review of the published literature in conjunction with the results from the previous economic evaluation, the following statements can be made:

- The incremental cost-analysis demonstrated that Wheezeless saves $156.50 per asthma exacerbation prevented compared to BreathX.
- Wheezeless was associated with a slightly lower probability of asthma exacerbation compared to BreathX.
- Patients treated with Wheezeless reported significantly better health-related quality of life compared to patients treated with BreathX in the areas of physical function, general health, and social function. Health status reported by patients after 16 weeks of Wheezeless therapy was not different than United States population norms in any of eight domains measured with the SF-36.
- This improved health status with Wheezeless should translate into increased patient satisfaction with care for asthma, although it should be measured directly in future evaluations.

Based on the consistency of the economic, clinical, and humanistic outcomes, the P&T committee decides to remove BreathX from the formulary and continue to cover Wheezeless for patients who require an inhaled corticosteroid.

Step 10: Develop a Plan to Monitor this Decision

Now that the decision has been made by the P&T committee, you should consider how the impact of this decision can be monitored by the committee.

- Suggest two strategies to monitor the impact of the formulary decision made by the P&T committee.

Answer: Develop a Plan to Monitor this Decision

The integrated health system should consider performing periodic health status evaluations among patients with asthma. For patients who are discontinued from BreathX, a baseline health status evaluation performed before the switch and a follow-up evaluation after the switch may be useful to document that patient functioning remains the same or improves after therapy is switched. In addition to assessing health status, periodic assessments of patient satisfaction with the health system and the care patients receive in the asthma clinic will provide another valuable humanistic outcomes measure. Again, securing a baseline assessment from patients treated with BreathX before switching to Wheezeless may provide useful data to ensure that the formulary policy conforms to the mandate to the P&T committee that quality of care is assured.

Step 11: What Needs to be Done in Your Setting?

Although this example provided clinical, economic, and humanistic outcomes that aligned with each other, it is not always that simple. What choice do you suppose would have been made if the health status results had been the opposite of the findings of the economic assessment? What choice would your P&T committee have made?

Think about the various questions of importance in your own practice setting. Can you identify any situations where an expensive therapy results in favorable improvements in health status or patient satisfaction, but does not provide a significant clinical improvement?

- Check the answers that best describe the reasons why you would use outcomes information. What are the potential applications to your practice of the material you have learned thus far?

Potential Applications of Humanistic Outcomes Information for Me	**Not a Need (1)**	**A Small Need (2)**	**May be a Need (3)**	**Part of my Need (4)**	**A Major Need (5)**
Marketing; public relations; risk management; employee morale; salary increases; promotions	❑	❑	❑	❑	❑
Develop treatment guidelines and policies	❑	❑	❑	❑	❑
Advance research skills in methods pharmacoeconomics	❑	❑	❑	❑	❑
Validate information from published studies	❑	❑	❑	❑	❑
Document need for my position	❑	❑	❑	❑	❑
Make better formulary decisions	❑	❑	❑	❑	❑
Use for creative, prospective problem-solving	❑	❑	❑	❑	❑
Improve health care	❑	❑	❑	❑	❑
Improve community resources	❑	❑	❑	❑	❑
Find a way to be paid for my services	❑	❑	❑	❑	❑
Other: ______________	❑	❑	❑	❑	❑

- Check the answers that best describe how important each of the following requirements for obtaining and using humanistic outcomes information is to you in your current position.

Uses of Humanistic Outcomes Information for Me	**None (1)**	**Little Bit (2)**	**Some (3)**	**Moderate (4)**	**Great (5)**
Inexpensive to obtain	❑	❑	❑	❑	❑
Provides information of general interest	❑	❑	❑	❑	❑
Addresses practical issues	❑	❑	❑	❑	❑
Timely in nature	❑	❑	❑	❑	❑
Provides a standard for evaluation	❑	❑	❑	❑	❑
Yields unbiased results	❑	❑	❑	❑	❑
Yields valid information	❑	❑	❑	❑	❑
Yields reliable results	❑	❑	❑	❑	❑
Provides relevant information	❑	❑	❑	❑	❑
Easy to complete	❑	❑	❑	❑	❑
Comprehensive	❑	❑	❑	❑	❑
Other: ______________	❑	❑	❑	❑	❑

Try to identify a service you provide that you believe results in a significant improvement in a humanistic outcome. Work through the steps to document this improvement in a systematic way. As you work through your project, you will begin to see how you can use these assessments for a variety of purposes.

Finally, turn to the following questions to assess various potential applications of humanistic outcomes assessment in your setting. Please answer the questions as honestly as you can.

- Examine the items you have marked as a 4 or a 5. These items are your highest needs, desires, and priorities. Take a few more minutes now to specifically clarify what you hope to accomplish on your own behalf and on behalf of your practice setting. What needs to be done? What are the priorities? Make a list here of assessments that would have meaning for you.

Annotated Bibliography

1. Bungay KM. Methods to assess the humanistic outcomes of clinical pharmacy services. Pharmacotherapy 2000;20(10 Pt 2):253S-8S.

This paper describes selected scientific principles involved in designing self-administered patient questionnaires to assess humanistic outcomes. It gives several examples of successful uses of patient surveys and suggests possibilities for the use of the results by pharmacists in clinical care.

- Check the answers that best describe what information you would like to find out through the application of pharmacoeconomic principles.

What I Would Like to Find Out by Using Pharmacoeconomic Principles	**Not at All (1)**	**A Little Bit (2)**	**Maybe (3)**	**Probably (4)**	**Definitely (5)**
Results to show to my superiors	❑	❑	❑	❑	❑
Introduce proper research methods to my setting	❑	❑	❑	❑	❑
Statistical results to prove what I think is true	❑	❑	❑	❑	❑
Data to show to JCAHO and quality management	❑	❑	❑	❑	❑
Information I can use to change how things are done	❑	❑	❑	❑	❑
Relevant information for interest only	❑	❑	❑	❑	❑
Information to improve my credibility	❑	❑	❑	❑	❑
Information that will allow me to better serve as an advocate for my patients	❑	❑	❑	❑	❑
Other: ______________________	❑	❑	❑	❑	❑

JCAHO = Joint Commission on Accreditation of Healthcare Organizations.

- Check the answers that best describe what interventions you hope to accomplish by using the results of pharmacoeconomic data.

Interventions Resulting from Pharmacoeconomic Evaluations	**Not at All (1)**	**A Little Bit (2)**	**Maybe (3)**	**Probably (4)**	**Definitely (5)**
Design changes in my practice setting	❑	❑	❑	❑	❑
Respond to individual negative comments	❑	❑	❑	❑	❑
Evaluate current services	❑	❑	❑	❑	❑
Incorporate findings into practice	❑	❑	❑	❑	❑
Find problems	❑	❑	❑	❑	❑
Design solutions to problems	❑	❑	❑	❑	❑
Better consider the viewpoint of patients	❑	❑	❑	❑	❑
Incorporate findings into the medical record	❑	❑	❑	❑	❑
Justify what I do	❑	❑	❑	❑	❑
Develop a new service, program, or policy in my setting	❑	❑	❑	❑	❑
Other: ______________________	❑	❑	❑	❑	❑

2. Bungay KM, Wagner AK. Introduction to pharmacist participation in measuring and monitoring patients' health-related quality of life. Am J Health-Syst Pharm 1995;52(suppl 3):S19–23.

The authors introduce the concepts and scientific techniques used to measure health-related quality of life. A conceptual framework also is introduced that summarizes the complex interaction of factors influencing the relationship between therapeutic interventions and health outcomes.

3. Hulley SB, Cummings SR. Designing clinical research: an epidemiologic approach. Philadelphia, PA: Williams and Wilkins, 1988.

In this text, various study designs used in clinical research are reviewed. An excellent chapter on planning research with questionnaires is included. A good understanding of the fundamental design issues discussed in this text will assist in the review of many different types of clinical research, including humanistic outcomes research conducted as a component of a clinical trial evaluating a medical treatment or pharmaceutical product.

4. Kozma CM, Reeder CE, Schulz RM. Economic, clinical, and humanistic outcomes: a planning model for pharmacoeconomic research. Clin Ther 1993;15:1121–32.

This paper describes a comprehensive model for clinical decision-making, detailing the relevance and interaction of data supporting economic, clinical, and humanistic outcomes. The proposed model can be used by decision-makers to evaluate products and services using a systematic approach.

5. Revicki DA, Osoba D, Fairclough D, et al. Recommendations on health-related quality of life research to support labeling and promotional claims in the United States. Qual Life Res 2000;9(8):887–900.

This paper provides a detailed summary of the key issues and recommendations in health-related quality-of-life research. The authors outlined the selection of appropriate quality-of-life domain; considerations in measurement instrument, research design, and statistical analyses; the issues of clinical significance; and the evidences for product labels and promotional claims.

6. Rothermich EA, Pathak DS, Smeenk DA. Health-related quality-of-life claims in prescription drug advertisements. Am J Health-Syst Pharm 1996;53:1565–9.

The authors describe several uses of health-related quality-of-life information in pharmaceutical marketing and present examples of how marketers attempt to use quality-of-life data to promote products. Health-related quality-of-life claims from advertisements contained in three medical journals in three separate years, 1984, 1988, and 1992, were analyzed. The study examined whether the claims were explicit or implied; how the products were claimed to affect health-related quality of life; whether trends have developed in health-related quality-of-life advertisements with respect to drug products, drug classes, and advertisement characteristics; and whether health-related quality-of-life advertisements from 1992 complied with Food and Drug Administration regulations for prescription drug advertising. The authors found that health-related quality-of-life claims were more often implied than explicit, and they appeared to promote specific physiologic aspects of functioning, but not overall health status. Another finding was that 42 percent of advertisements appeared not to comply with Food and Drug Administration regulations for prescription drug advertising as recently as 1992.

7. Singhal PK, Raisch DW, Gupchup GV. The impact of pharmaceutical services in community and ambulatory care settings: evidence and recommendations for future research. Ann Pharmacother 1999;33(12):1336–55.

The authors did a comprehensive review of the research on pharmaceutical services in community and ambulatory care pharmacy settings from 1966 to 1998. They examined each of the 95 identified studies on the study objectives; sample size; study period and design; major tasks performed by pharmacists; and economic, clinical, and humanistic outcomes. Few studies were randomized and controlled, and few studies measured humanistic outcomes. Based on the research review, the authors provided recommendations to improve future research.

8. Staquet M, Berzon R, Osoba D, Machin D. Guidelines for reporting results of quality of life assessments in clinical trials. Qual Life Res 1996;5:496–502.

The authors provide a concise primer for reporting results of clinical trials investigating health-related quality of life. A systematic approach that is useful not only for authors, but also for readers and reviewers of this literature is presented. A helpful checklist is included as an appendix.

Self-Assessment Questions

1. Which one of the following documents the correct steps of developing formulary decision?
   A. Define the problem, define the study perspective, determine resources needed, determine treatment alternatives and outcomes, identify possible sources of data, select a data collection method, review and interpret data, present results, summarize findings, and develop plan for monitoring decisions.
   B. Define the problem, determine resources needed, define the study perspective, determine treatment alternatives and outcomes, identify possible sources of data, select a data collection method, review and interpret data, summarize findings, present results, and develop plan for monitoring decisions.
   C. Determine resources needed, define the problem, define the study perspective, identify possible sources of data, determine treatment alternatives and outcomes, select a data collection method, review and interpret data, summarize findings, present results, and develop plan for monitoring decisions.
   D. Determine resources needed, define the problem, define the study perspective, determine treatment alternatives and outcomes, identify possible sources of data, select a data collection method, review and interpret data, present results, summarize findings, and develop plan for monitoring decisions.

2. Which one of the following is <u>NOT</u> one of the resources that are needed to conduct assessment of the problems?
   A. The multidisciplinary team.
   B. Staff to assist with the evaluation.

C. Data providing objective information.
D. Chief executive officers of the companies producing the drugs.

3. Which one of the following shows a correct model of integrating humanistic outcomes with clinical and economic outcomes?
   A. Inhaled corticosteroids → improved clinical effects → changes in costs → improved health status → increased satisfaction.
   B. Inhaled corticosteroids → changes in costs → improved clinical effects → improved health status → increased satisfaction.
   C. Inhaled corticosteroids → increased satisfaction → improved clinical effects → improved health status → changes in costs.
   D. Inhaled corticosteroids → improved clinical effects → improved health status → changes in costs → increased satisfaction.

4. Which one of the following is the least objective a data collection method?
   A. Expert opinions.
   B. Peer-reviewed published studies.
   C. Primary data collected in the clinics.
   D. Prospective, randomized data.

5. One of the possible sources of data is the primary data collected in your clinics. Which one of the following is <u>NOT</u> one of the strengths for this type of data source?
   A. High internal validity.
   B. Reasonable generalizability.
   C. No selection bias.
   D. Time and money saving.

6. Which one of the following is <u>NOT</u> one of the strengths for prospective, randomized data?
   A. High internal validity.
   B. Allows direct head-to-head comparisons.
   C. No selection bias.
   D. Time and money saving.

7. Which of following should be considered when designing a study?
   A. Sample size of the study.
   B. Representativeness of the patient population.
   C. Reliability and validity of the instrument.
   D. All of the above.

8. In a randomized, clinical trial comparing drug A and drug B in preventing asthma attack, 50 patients were randomized into receiving either drug A or B for 2 weeks. At the beginning of the study and at 2 weeks, patients filled out a quality-of-life survey QOL-A. Study results showed that at baseline patients taking either drug had similar quality-of-life scores. At the end of the 2-week treatment period, patients taking drug A had significantly better quality-of-life scores. If you are presented with the above information, which one of the following conclusion will you draw?
   A. The QOL-A is a reliable and valid instrument to measure health-related quality of life.
   B. Drug A is more effective than drug B in preventing asthma attacks.
   C. After 2-week course of therapy, patients treated with drug A demonstrated greater improvement in health status as measured by QOL-A compared to patients treated with drug B.
   D. All of the above.

9. Which one of the following is important for formulary decision-making?
   A. Economics outcomes.
   B. Clinical outcomes.
   C. Humanistic outcomes.
   D. All of the above.

10. Which one of the following is <u>NOT</u> one of the factors that you should consider when using published studies as a source of data for a formulary evaluation?
    A. How generalizable are the findings from published studies to the patient population in your practice?
    B. Are those who published those studies well known in the area of your practice?
    C. Do any studies provide comparison of the drugs of your interest?
    D. Is the disease severity of the patient populations in the published studies similar to the severity in the patient population you serve?

EVALUATING AND JUSTIFYING CLINICAL PHARMACY SERVICES

Glen Schumock Pharm.D., M.B.A, BCPS and
Melissa Butler Pharm.D.

Outline

I. Introduction

II. Assessment of Clinical Pharmacy Services
- A. Basic model (input versus outputs, comparison)
- B. Structure of the evaluation
- C. Perspective
- D. Resource measurement
- E. Outcome measurement
  - 1. Clinical
  - 2. Humanistic
  - 3. Economic
- A. Study design
- B. Uncertainty

III. Types of Economic Evaluations
- A. Cost-benefit analysis

IV. Literature

V. Strategies
- A. Literature generalization
- B. Decision analysis
- C. Local evaluation
- D. Step approach

VI. Developing a Proposal for a Clinical Pharmacy Service
- A. Understanding the business environment
- B. Reviewing the literature
- C. Evaluating the market and competitors
- D. Identifying the proposed processes and operations
- E. Developing financial projections
- F. Writing the business plan and selling the proposal

VII. Conclusion

VIII. Definition of Terms

IX. Figures and Tables

X. Annotated Bibliography

XI. Self-Assessment Questions

Learning Objectives

1. Discuss the importance of evaluation of clinical pharmacy services (CPSs) as a means to make resource allocation decisions.
2. List the basic components associated with a rigorous economic evaluation of a CPS.
3. Compare and contrast the economic methods most commonly used for measuring the impact of CPSs.
4. Understand the use of clinical and humanistic measures in evaluations of CPSs.
5. Discuss the strategies and challenges for applying results of economic evaluations of CPSs.

Abbreviations in this chapter

ACCP	American College of Clinical Pharmacy
CBA	Cost-benefit analysis
CEA	Cost-effectiveness analysis
CMA	Cost-minimization analysis
CPS	Clinical pharmacy service
CUA	Cost-utility analysis
IMPROVE	Impact of Managed Pharmaceutical Care on Resource Utilization and Outcomes in Veterans Affairs Medical Centers Study
PDA	Personal data assistant
SWOT	Strengths, weaknesess, opportunities and threats

Introduction

Assessment of the costs and outcomes of clinical pharmacy services (CPSs) is a distinct application with the discipline of pharmacoeconomics that has many commonalities with other fields, such as health service research and technology assessment. The original definition of pharmacoeconomics (number 4 in Annotated Bibliography), clearly identified the evaluation of pharmacy services as a domain of pharmacoeconomics. That definition reads as follows: "the description and analysis of the costs and consequences of pharmaceutical products and/or services and their impact on individuals, health care systems, and society." Today, evaluation of CPSs remains a principal application of the discipline.

However, the evaluation of CPSs does require certain unique considerations and, therefore, differs from other applications of pharmacoeconomics, such as the evaluation of pharmaceutical products. The design of an evaluation of a pharmacy service is often restricted by problems with selecting appropriate comparators, the inability to eliminate selection bias because of issues with randomization, confusion about appropriate outcome measures and handling of economic variables, and inability to distinguish the effect of the intervention. Furthermore, the external validity of these evaluations is often confounded by the uniqueness of the study site, type of clinical service, and competency of the individual clinical pharmacist(s) involved.

Nevertheless, the need to evaluate CPSs is exemplified when contrasted to product-related pharmacy services. Product-related services are usually tied to reimbursement for a prescription. That is, the value of the pharmacist is included in the charge for the prescription (typically as a dispensing or professional fee). There is relatively little need to continue to justify the role of the pharmacist under this scenario because it is continuously reinforced by demand for the product and service. This is the same for physicians or other health care providers who charge for and are reimbursed for their professional services. However, CPSs are still largely not reimbursed, though in some cases this is changing. Therefore, the value of the clinical pharmacist is not routinely recognized monetarily. Therefore, its value must be assessed extemporaneously. In fact, the evaluation of CPSs is a vital ingredient to the continued success of the profession of pharmacy, particularly as the profession continues its evolution from one that focuses on products to one that focuses on patients.

There are other compelling reasons for the continued evaluation of CPSs. In the health care industry today, perhaps more than ever before, there is enormous pressure to hold down costs. In many cases, this means a reduction in personnel. At the same time, there is an ongoing shortage of pharmacists in the labor market, yet an expanding need for dispensing services secondary to higher use of prescription drugs and the aging of society. Collectively, these pressures work to prevent further expansion of CPSs or cognitive pharmacy services. Still, there is good evidence that CPSs may reduce other health care expenses while providing improved clinical and/or humanistic outcomes. As such, well-designed evaluations of CPSs are likely to provide the data to assist pharmacy managers and clinicians in the successful expansion, continuation, or justification of such programs.

Pharmacists must interface with those in health care organizations who make resource allocation decisions, to convince them of the value of CPSs. Thus, the ability to conduct, interpret, and use pharmacoeconomic evaluations of CPSs, and sell the results of those evaluations, is a vital skill for pharmacists. This chapter reviews methods for assessing the economic outcomes of CPSs. The chapter focuses on the importance of evaluations of CPSs as a means to make resource allocation decisions, and provides a framework for the design and methodologies that may be used in such evaluations. The chapter also provides examples of the economic methods most commonly used for measuring the impact of CPSs, including the measurement of clinical and humanistic outcomes. The chapter also provides practical strategies for applying results of outcome evaluations of CPSs to the local setting. Finally, the chapter details important concepts in gaining support for CPSs once the evaluation has been conducted.

Assessment of Clinical Pharmacy Services

Basic Model

The basic model of an economic evaluation of CPSs is shown in Figure 1. Most important in this model is the consideration or measurement of both costs (investment required to provide the service) and consequences (outcomes) of the service or program. Costs can be thought of as "inputs" or resources required to provide the service. Typically, the principal component on the cost side of the equation is personnel wages and benefits. Other costs may include equipment required to provide the service or overhead expenses associated with the program.

Consequences can be thought of as the "outputs" of the service or program - these are outcomes of the care provided. Consequences can be in the form of clinical outcomes, humanistic outcomes, or economic outcomes, each defining a unique type of evaluation (cost-effectiveness analysis [CEA], cost-utility analysis [CUA], and cost-benefit analysis [CBA], respectively). Considerations in the measurement of both costs and outcomes of CPSs are provided in the Types of Economic Evaluations section of this chapter.

Another key element of this model is the inclusion of a comparison(s) or alternative(s) to the service in question. For example, alternatives might include the absence of service (control). A comparator group is important to be able to attribute the intervention or "cause" (the pharmacy service) to the "effect" (outcome).

Although this basic model is ideal, on a percentage basis, relatively few published economic evaluations of CPSs comply with both these criteria. In fact, as reported in a recent systematic review of the literature, of 59 studies published between 1996 and 2000 (inclusive) only 23.7 percent measured both costs and consequences and included a comparator group.

Structure of the Evaluation

Based on the elements from the model previously discussed, analyses of CPSs can be characterized as partial or full as shown in Table 1. Analyses that measure both the costs and consequences and that include at least one alternative (e.g., control group) are sometimes termed "full evaluations" and are most desirable from a methodological standpoint. Full evaluations can be subdivided based on the outcome(s) measured and include: cost-minimization analysis (CMA; where outcomes are measured and found to be equivalent), CEA, CUA, and CBA. These have been previously discussed in chapters 7, 8, 9, and 10 of this textbook. Considerations of these methodologies pertinent to the evaluation of CPSs are discussed in Types of Economic Evaluations.

Partial evaluations can be subdivided into five groups. An evaluation that includes at least one alternative but only examines costs or consequences (but not both) is either a "cost-analysis" or "outcomes analysis", respectively. An evaluation that does not compare an alternative is called a "description." There can be of three types of descriptions, including a "cost description" (examines only costs, not consequences), an "outcome description" (examines only consequences not costs), and a "cost and outcome

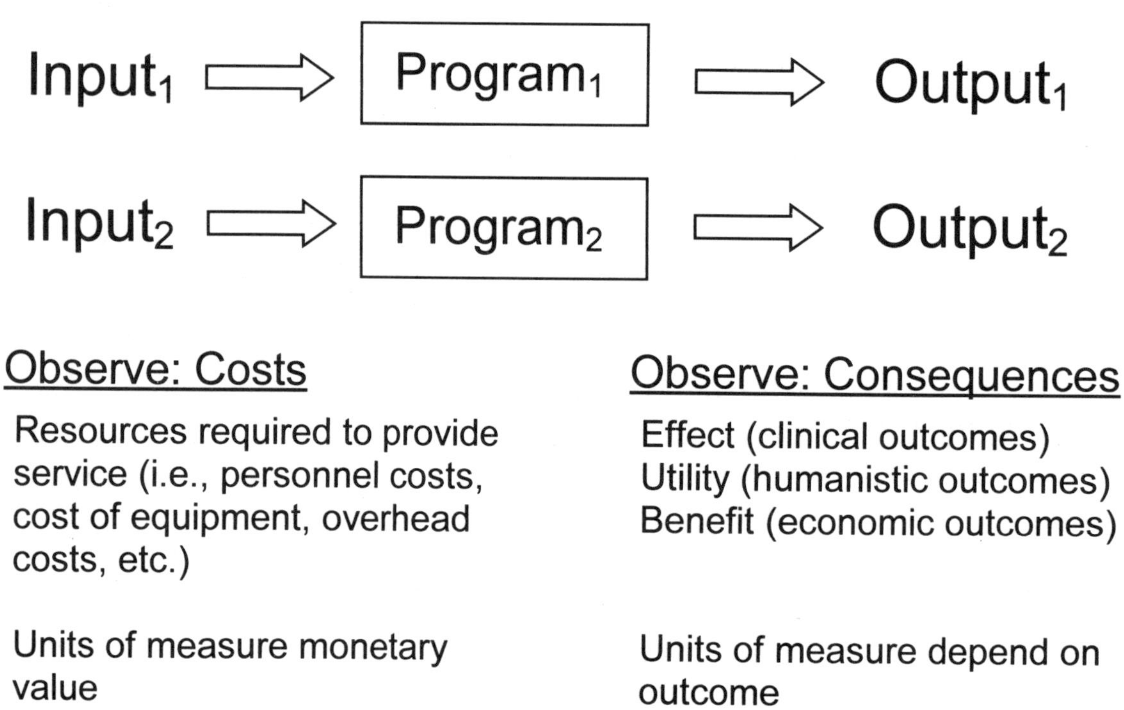

Figure 1.

Table 1. Criteria for Assessment of Type of Analysis

		Were both costs and outcomes considered? No	Were both costs and outcomes considered? Yes
Were two or more alternatives considered?	**No**	Cost description, or Outcome description	Cost and outcome description
	Yes	Cost-analysis, or Outcome analysis	Full economic analysis Subcategories Cost-minimization analysis Cost-benefit analysis Cost-effectiveness analysis Cost-utility analysis

Adapted with permission from Oxford University Press. Drummond MF, O'Brien B, Stoddart GL, Torrance GW. Methods for economic evaluation of health care programmes. 2nd ed. Oxford, UK: Oxford Medical Publications, 1997:10.

description" (examines both costs and outcomes). This discussion is important because economic evaluations of CPSs are often partial evaluations because of failure or inability to measure either costs or outcomes, or because of failure to include a control group. Although these evaluations may not be ideal, from a practical standpoint, they may represent the best or only option. The findings provided may be worthwhile as long as they are considered within the limitations of the study design.

In a majority of cases, authors of studies of CPSs fail to include in their analysis the cost to provide the service of the program evaluated. This would seem like a relatively simple variable to measure. Obviously, it is an extremely important variable. Even if a CPS appears to provide positive clinical or economic outcomes, without a comparison to its costs, no conclusion can be made regarding the economic impact. For example, the net benefit of a program (economic benefit less cost to provide program) cannot be determined. If the purpose of the evaluation is to economically justify CPSs, failure to include the investment required to provide the program is an obvious problem.

Likewise, authors of studies of CPSs include a comparator group in their analyses in only slightly more than 50 percent of cases. As previously discussed, a comparator group is an absolute requirement to determine a cause and effect relationship. Without a comparator group, no real conclusion can be made about the effect produced by the presence of the CPS studied. Studies of CPSs do pose a unique challenge for investigators with respect to comparator groups. It is often difficult to identify a reasonable comparator. Ideally, the comparison group is comprised of patients who have not been exposed to the CPSs. In many settings, such groups do not exist. The issue of randomization to the control group (no service) or intervention group (receive CPS) also is a difficult one. In the typical busy health care setting, whether it be a hospital, clinic, or community pharmacy, it often is not possible to randomize an individual patient. The need for a comparison group and randomization is discussed in more detail in the Study Design section of this chapter.

Perspective

Evaluations of pharmacy services are usually conducted from the perspective of the provider. This is because (at least as of the writing of this chapter) CPSs are rarely reimbursed either by patients or payers. Therefore, the economic objective of these services is typically the reduction of costs incurred by the provider organization. Some exceptions to this may occur and are even more likely in the future. Recently, there have been renewed efforts to seek reimbursement for CPS from Medicare. If successful, future evaluations of the benefit to the Medicare program would be conducted from the payer perspective. Likewise, in a growing number of states, Medicaid programs are reimbursing for "cognitive" pharmacy services. Evaluations of such programs, either as demonstration projects or after full implementation, should occur from the payer perspective. Finally, there are some examples where patients pay out of pocket for CPSs. Typically, these are education or counseling programs (e.g., brown bag programs) that would not be reimbursed by third-party payers. Evaluations of these programs should be conducted from the patient perspective.

As with any pharmacoeconomic study, it is important to establish the perspective of an evaluation of a CPS upfront. This will not only provide transparency for others, but also help the investigators in both the identification of applicable costs and in the correct categorization of costs and benefits.

Resource Measurement

As previously discussed, inclusion of the costs or investment required to provide CPSs, represents an important component of the evaluation. These costs typically can be categorized as either fixed costs or variable costs. Fixed costs are those that do not change with each unit of service provided. For example, equipment is typically considered a fixed cost. Consider a CPS where the pharmacist carries a personal data assistant (PDA) for accessing drug information databases. The cost of the PDA occurs regardless of the number of patients the pharmacist sees. Thus, the cost of the PDA is a fixed cost. Another way to think about fixed costs is that these are expenses that occur regardless of the volume of service provided. For example, rent payments for the facility leased by a program occur each month and must be paid regardless of the number of patients who received service by the program each month. Other examples of fixed costs common to CPSs are shown in Table 2.

Conversely, a variable cost is one that changes or reoccurs with each unit of service provided. An example might be the cost of a test strip used in a blood glucose-monitoring device used as part of the service provided by a pharmacist in a diabetes counseling program. Each patient the pharmacist sees requires a new test strip; thus, that cost is considered variable. Variable costs fluctuate with the volume of service provided. Other examples of variable costs common to CPSs are shown in Table 2.

Some expenses may be classified as fixed under one scenario but variable in another situation. For example, the classification of personnel wages as a variable cost assumes that those work hours can be titrated up or down to meet patient volume. In reality, some personnel costs may be fixed. For example, if a pharmacist is hired full-time to provide a specific clinical service or program, on days when the patient volume is not sufficient to keep that pharmacist busy, unless that pharmacist is sent home when no patients are scheduled, the personnel cost becomes fixed rather than variable. The same can be said for personnel benefits (e.g., health insurance) if these are paid at a set rate each pay period, rather than paid based on hours worked.

Outcome Measurement

The outcomes or consequences of a CPS can be categorized into three groups: clinical outcomes, humanistic outcomes, and economic outcomes. Previous chapters of this book have reviewed these categories of outcomes in detail. This chapter discusses considerations of outcome measurement specific to the evaluation of CPSs.

Ideally, any evaluation of a CPS should include consideration of both economic outcomes and clinical and/or humanistic outcomes. The inclusion of clinical or humanistic outcomes is important to the credibility of the economic analysis. Obviously, clinicians want to be able to show that a CPS is not only economically beneficial but also that clinical or humanistic outcomes are improved, or at least equivalent to the alternative (usually the absence of the program).

Clinical Outcomes

Clinical outcomes measured in the evaluation of CPSs can be either long-term outcomes or intermediate outcomes. The long-term or intermediate outcomes applicable to CPSs do not differ from those used in evaluations of pharmaceuticals or other medical interventions. A meta-analysis of studies that evaluated outcomes of CPSs was published in 2001 and is discussed in the annotated bibliography.

Long-term clinical outcomes are typically either mortality or morbidity, and are preferred over intermediate outcomes. Deaths (or the opposite: lives saved), myocardial infarctions averted, and strokes averted are examples of long-term clinical outcomes. These types of outcomes often require long-term monitoring and, therefore, may not be practical. Also, it is often difficult to differentiate the effect of CPSs (versus other factors) on these outcomes.

Intermediate clinical outcomes may be easier to measure and more easily attributed to the presence of CPSs. Furthermore, epidemiological studies have confirmed that certain intermediate outcomes are good surrogates for long-term outcomes. For example, the intermediate outcome of blood pressure is associated with the long-term outcome of stroke. Examples of intermediate outcomes measured in evaluations of CPSs include blood pressure measurement, serum lipid concentrations, serum creatinine level or creatinine clearance, and blood glucose concentration. Obviously, there are many others that could be applicable.

Humanistic Outcomes

Humanistic outcomes are another important category of consequences of CPSs, though humanistic outcomes have been less studied in this context. Humanistic outcomes applicable to the evaluation of CPSs typically can be categorized as those that measure either health-related quality of life or patient satisfaction. Studies that measure health-related quality of life may incorporate a variety of "instruments" (or questionnaires) that provides different types of results. Some instruments quantify quality of life in utilities, others produce summary scores, and still others provide specific health status results. As previously discussed in this book, quality-of-life instruments can measure general health or can be disease-specific. The selection of the type of instrument used in an evaluation of a CPS depends on the type of service, patient population, and other considerations. In general, it is thought that it is

Table 2. Examples of Fixed and Variable Costs Common to Clinical Pharmacy Services

Fixed Costs	Variable Costs
• Equipment that is reused (e.g., testing machines)	• Office supplies
• Computer(s) and software (e.g., drug information databases)	• Wages for employees
• Furniture	• Benefits paid for employees
• Rent	• Testing strips
• Housekeeping/maintenance	• Pharmaceuticals (if administered as part of the program, as in the case of a vaccine administration clinic)
• Energy costs for heating/lighting/electrical services	• Educational brochures/pamphlets/handouts
• Administrative overhead (allocation of managerial expenses if shared with other programs)	• Equipment or supplies that are single-use or provided to patients (e.g., peak flow meters)

difficult to detect differences in quality of life resulting from exposure to CPSs. This difficulty is likely due to limited durations of exposure of patients to CPSs (especially in acute care settings), inability of available instruments to detect differences, or lack of effect. A systematic review of studies that measured the effect of CPSs on health-related quality of life was published in 1999 and is discussed in number 13 of the annotated bibliography.

Another important humanistic outcome, and one that is perhaps more measurable and applicable to CPSs, is that of patient or customer satisfaction. Obviously, the level of satisfaction with services received is an important indicator of the success of the service. Patient satisfaction can greatly effect the desire on the part of the patient to return for continued care, and can affect the level of patient compliance with the therapy and/or recommendations imparted by the program. In a domino pattern, patient satisfaction and patient compliance can alter clinical and economic outcomes of the service provided.

Economic Outcomes

Assessment of the economic outcomes or economic consequences is the intent of a majority of studies of CPSs. Economics plays a major role in health care decision-making, and demonstration of the ability of pharmacy services to reduce health care expenses is often the justification used for initiation, expansion, or continuation of those services. The economic outcomes included in an evaluation depend on the perspective of the analysis. Typically, these reflect changes in resource use (and the corresponding monetary value of such) resulting from the presence of CPSs. Examples of resource use include drug use, office visits, and hospitalizations, among others. When resource use is the economic outcome of importance, the analysis is usually from the perspective of the payer or the provider, the perspective most common to evaluations of CPSs.

Economic outcomes also can be measured by determining the willingness of patients to pay for a service, or the reimbursement received for CPSs (from patients or payers). An important consideration with respect to economic outcomes is the differentiation or handling of economic variables (whether costs or consequences of the services provided) in the analysis. This topic is addressed later in the Cost-benefit Analysis section of this chapter.

Study Design

The design used in an evaluation of a CPS is extremely important. All too often, a CPS that is well planned and executed is evaluated using a suboptimal study design. It may be the case that a pharmacy program provides significant clinical, humanistic, or economic benefit; however, with a poor study design, investigators are unable to demonstrate a cause-and-effect relationship, or are unable to prove net benefits resultant from the service. A rigorous study design helps reduce the likelihood of reaching false conclusions.

Studies of CPSs depend on the ability of the study design to establish a relationship between the intervention(s) and the resulting observed outcome(s). Several archetypical study designs have been described and are illustrated in Table 3. Investigators and readers of articles describing evaluations of CPSs should understand these study designs, including the strengths and weaknesses of each. The design of a study typically can be classified as experimental, quasiexperimental, and pre-experimental. Pre-experimental designs are used in many published evaluations of CPSs but should be avoided.

Most of the designs shown in Table 3 are multigroup studies, meaning that there is at least one alternative or comparison (i.e., a control group) to which the CPS is being compared. Single-group studies, where all patients receive the intervention, do not allow for any conclusion about the effect of the intervention (or effect of the CPS) on the outcomes being measured. This is because there is no way to establish a causal relationship between the intervention and the effect. Some pre-experimental designs incorporate only a single group. Studies that aim to establish a causal relationship must address issues of internal validity.

Single-group studies are problematic because there are numerous threats to interval validity. In single-group studies, it is possible that events (other than the presence of the CPS) that take place during the study have an effect on the outcome (this is called "history effect"). It also is possible that the patients involved in the study will undergo changes unrelated to the intervention during the course of the study that might have an effect on the outcome (this is called "maturation effect"). In single-group studies, there also are potential problems related to the selection of patients. If patients selected for the study are those likely to have the worst outcomes, there is a greater likelihood that an effect will be observed regardless of the intervention. This is called statistical regression, or regression toward the mean. Single-group studies also may be subject to problems with the measurement of the outcomes. For example, when a subject is exposed to the measurement instrument more than once (i.e., a questionnaire taken before and after an intervention), they tend to score better the second time, independent of the intervention (this is called "testing effect"). Likewise, the evaluator may change the way he or she records data over the course of a study (this is called "instrumentation effect"). All of these problems can be mitigated by use of a multigroup study design.

The key question of internal validity is whether observed changes can be attributed to the program (or intervention) and not to other possible causes or alternative explanations. To answer this question requires use of an alternative group that is comparable on all characteristics except the presence of the CPS. This allows clinicians to isolate the effect of the intervention. These multigroup studies also must meet several additional conditions to establish a causal relationship. First, there should be a temporal relationship between the cause (CPS) and the effect. This relationship helps confirm that the program happened before the effect and not visa versa). Second, it should be demonstrated that when the program is present, the effect is present; and when the program is absent, the effect is absent (this is called co-variation of cause and effect). Finally, the study should allow the exclusion of other plausible explanations of the effect.

Although the inclusion of a comparison group mitigates many of the problems associated with single-group studies, there are still potential threats to internal validity. The most important of these is selection bias. Selection bias occurs when there is error in the way subjects are included in the study or assigned to groups. This may result in differences between groups that are not caused by the intervention. Randomization is used to reduce the potential for selection bias. Randomization removes any intentional or unintentional subjective biases of the investigators in the process of selecting patients to one group or the other. In the long run, it is expected that randomization increases the likelihood that groups will be comparable with regard to characteristics that may affect the outcome.

Randomization does not solve all problems, especially social interaction threats. These threats include, among others, diffusion (the control group receives the intervention), compensatory equalization (those who run the study try to do something good for the control group to compensate for the treatment the intervention group receives), and the Hawthorne effect (because subjects know they are a subject and are being watched, they act better). Although it is difficult to prevent or control social interaction threats, attempts can be made by isolating groups, explaining the importance of preserving group

Table 3. Study Designs Used for Evaluations of Clinical Pharmacy Services

Design Type, Subtypes, and Groups	Notation[a]	Strengths	Weaknesses
EXPERIMENTAL		Randomization reduces heterogeneity resulting from selection bias	Randomization may not be feasible; difficult and expensive to accomplish
Pretest–post-test			
Intervention	R O X O	Repeated measures allow assessment of baseline equivalence of groups	Subject to social threats to internal validity
Control	R O O		
Post-test only			
Intervention	R X O	Simplest of all experimental designs; does not use repeated measures; therefore, subject to less bias as a result or measurement error	Subject to social threats to internal validity
Control	R O		
QUASIEXPERIMENTAL		More feasible to perform when randomization is not possible	Lacks benefit of random assignment (i.e., baseline group equivalence); may be expensive to accomplish
Pretest–post-test			
Intervention	O X O	Repeated measures allow assessment of equivalence of groups at baseline	Subject to multigroup threats to internal validity
Control	O O		
PRE-EXPERIMENTAL		May help in generating hypotheses	Cause and effect between the intervention and outcome cannot be established
One-Group pretest–post-test	O X O		
Static Group comparison			Unable to adjust for baseline differences in groups
Intervention	X O		
Control	O		

[a] R indicates that the groups are randomly assigned; lack of an R indicates that the design is not randomized (nonequivalent groups). O denotes observations or measures (e.g., costs and clinical measures); vertical alignment of Os shows that measurements occur at the same time. X denotes the intervention (program); when there are two lines, one denotes the intervention group, the other represents the control group; time sequence (temporality) of variables is designated by the position of the variable (e.g., "to the left" occur before, and "to the right" occur after another variable in the sequence).

Adapted from Campbell DT, Stanley JC. Experimental and quasiexperimental designs for research. Chicago, IL: Rand McNally & Company, 1966. Copyright 1963 by the American Educational Research Association; reproduced with permission from the publisher.

membership to study subjects and investigators, and, ultimately, by blinding the subjects and investigators.

The issue of randomization is a difficult one with respect to CPSs. These evaluations are often conducted using a service that is already established, and it may not be possible to "assign" some patients to receive the service and some to not receive the service. Evaluations that are conducted before and after initiation of a new service may allow for easier grouping of patients. Furthermore, rather than randomizing individual patients, investigators may randomize groups of patient (i.e., by nursing unit or by specific clinic). Studies of cognitive pharmacy services in community pharmacies may even randomize whole stores to one group or another.

A study that includes a comparison group (multigroup) and incorporates randomization is considered an experimental design. There subtypes are two primary subtypes of experimental designs used in evaluations of CPSs, as shown in Table 3. These include the pretest–post-test multigroup design, and the post-test–only multigroup. The terms "pretest" and "post-test" refer to the timing of the observation in relation to the intervention. A pretest–post-test design (sometimes called "before-after") is a design that includes observation or measurement of the effect both before the intervention is implemented and after the intervention has been implemented. Many evaluations of CPSs use this design, though most are not randomized.

Studies that are not randomized are sometimes called "pre-experimental" or "quasiexperimental". An example of a quasiexperimental study is a nonrandomized, multigroup, pretest–post-test design (also called a nonequivalent group design). An example of a pre-experimental study is a nonrandomized post-test–only design, or a single-group pretest–post-test study. Both quasiexperimental and pre-experimental represent somewhat less rigorous designs compared to experimental studies. When it is impractical to develop an evaluation with a true experimental design, these designs may be useful (though quasiexperimental is preferred).

Uncertainty

As discussed in chapter 13, sensitivity analysis helps to determine the stability of results. This also is true for evaluations of CPSs. Uncertainty can be dealt with either through sensitivity analysis or through more traditional statistical testing.

The use of sensitivity analysis in evaluations of CPSs is no different than evaluations of pharmaceutical products. As previously discussed, there are several types of sensitivity analyses, such as one-way, two-way, and more rigorous forms, such as Monte Carlo simulations. Sensitivity analysis is more applicable to the evaluation of CPSs where cost data included in the evaluation were derived from aggregate values or from outside sources. For example, if the average pharmacist wage rate from the study hospital is used in lieu of the actual wage to the individual pharmacist providing the service, then it may be appropriate to adjust that value in sensitivity analysis to determine the impact or variation. If the average wage of pharmacists in the state is used, then sensitivity analysis would be even more important. Sensitivity analysis also can be applied to values collected from actual data in the study. For example, sensitivity analysis can be conducted to determine the effect of variation around a mean value using either the upper and lower extremes of the range or the 95 percent confidence interval.

Finally, sensitivity analysis also can be used to anticipate future changes in the variables included in an evaluation of a CPS (e.g., the impact of changes in reimbursement rates, changes in contracts or pricing of pharmaceuticals, or changes in rates of pay for personnel involved in the program). Observing how that future change may alter the results allows the investigator to make a more informed decision.

As is the case for other types of studies, determining if statistical differences exist between the intervention (presence of a CPS) and comparison group(s) may be appropriate. For example, statistical analyses may be used to compare outcomes measured in a CEA. Even if a positive effect is observed, a confidence interval that crosses zero (negative) indicates a nonsignificant result. Nonparametric tests should be used when the distribution of the data is not normal.

Statistical analysis may be important in CMA where outcomes are deemed equivalent. Using a *t* test to detect a statistical difference may not be adequate in determining equivalence. This is particularly true if a type II error has occurred. Evaluations of CPSs are at risk for committing type II error because the power and sample size are often not adequate. Before assuming equivalence because a t–test shows no difference, the adequacy of the sample size and power should be evaluated. An evaluator can have more confidence in a decision to use CMA instead of a CEA if more rigorous statistical analyses are performed.

Types of Economic Evaluations

As discussed throughout this book, pharmacoeconomic evaluations can be categorized based on the outcomes measured. Categories of types of evaluations include CEA, CMA, CUA, and CBA. All of these types may be applicable and have been used in evaluations of CPSs.

As previously discussed, CEA incorporates both costs and clinical outcomes or consequences into the analysis, and the results of CEA can be expressed as a ratio of cost per unit of outcomes. This ratio is then used to compare alternatives. Evaluations of CPSs have assessed, for example, cost per life saved. Cost-utility analysis is a subset of CEA where the consequences are a humanistic outcome. As with CEA, a ratio of cost per unit of outcomes is produced, in this case a humanistic outcome. Evaluations of CPSs, for examples, have reported cost per quality-adjusted life-year. Cost-minimization analysis is usually considered another special form of CEA, where the clinical outcomes are measured and determined to be equivalent. In this case, the only remaining differential variable is cost, which can be compared for the different alternatives (with that being least expensive being selected).

A problem with CEA, CUA, and CMA is that they do not help determine to what degree the outcomes are worth the cost, and this is the question most often asked of CPSs. To answer this question, CBA must be used. Cost-benefit analysis takes the analysis beyond clinical terms and forces an explicit decision as to whether the cost is worth the benefit. Cost-benefit analysis does this by measuring both the costs and consequences in the same units (currency).

Cost-benefit Analysis

Cost-benefit analysis is the method most commonly used in evaluations of CPSs because most often the intent of the evaluation is to demonstrate that the service is a worthwhile investment. What distinguishes CBA from other types of analysis is the unit of measure used for the output or consequences of the service. The unit of measure is dollars or other currency. This allows the inputs and outputs to be compared because they are in the same units of measure. Essentially, CBA allows clinicians to determine if the cost to provide the service is worth the benefits derived from the service.

The outcomes that are measured in CBA are most often economic outcomes or outcomes that can be easily converted to financial values. For example, if a CPS reduces length of hospital stay, that outcome can be easily converted into a financial value. Often, in evaluating CPSs the change in drug use (reduction) is measured, as an outcome, and subsequently the drug expenses saved or avoided.

It also is possible to measure clinical effects (as in CEA) or even humanistic outcomes (as in CUA) and then convert those to financial values. There are research methodologies such as "willingness-to-pay" or the "human capital" method that enable clinicians to convert clinical or humanistic results into economic values. For example, a researcher might survey patients to determine what amount of money they would be willing to pay for a CPS that promises to achieve a defined quality of life. Or, if a CPS is expected to save lives, then the potential additional lifetime earnings associated with those lives can be calculated and considered an economic benefit of the program.

The results of CBA are typically presented as a benefit-to-cost ratio. Cost-benefit analyses of CPSs often use a comparator of "no service". In the case of no service, there are neither costs nor benefits, so the incremental benefit-to-cost ratio and the average benefit-to-cost ratio for the intervention group may be the same. Other ways of expressing results include the net present value (benefits less costs) and the return on investment (benefits less costs divided by costs).

One of the first examples of a CBA of a CPS was published in the 1979 and compared the costs and consequences in a control group (no service) to a group of patients who received a pharmacokinetic dosing service. Costs measured were those related to providing the service, a majority of which were the wages of pharmacist personnel. In addition, the investigators included as a cost to provide the service, additional serum concentration tests required to closely monitor the drug, as well as indirect costs associated with administration and overhead. Consequences of the service measured were mortality and morbidity and these were converted to economic values. In this analysis, the benefits outweighed costs by 8.7:1, or for every dollar ($1) invested in the CPS, $8.70 in benefit was attained.

Literature

The first economic evaluations of CPSs were published in the late 1970s. As more and more pharmacy practitioners moved toward the provision of clinical services, increasing numbers of evaluations were conducted and published. Today, the body of literature contains hundreds of studies. These studies evaluate many different specialized CPSs, such as pharmacist-run anticoagulation clinics, and evaluate entire programs within health care organizations. Some are single-site evaluations and some are multisite evaluations. Although the most common setting in which studies have been conducted is the hospital, many evaluations have been conducted of pharmacy services in community pharmacies, clinics, long-term care facilities, managed care organizations, and others. Even within these different settings, there is variety. For example, studies have been conducted in different types of hospitals, including university hospitals, community hospitals, Veterans Affairs hospitals, county hospitals, military hospitals, rural hospitals, psychiatric hospitals, and others. The studies published tend to follow the trends that are seen in the practice of clinical pharmacy. For example, recently there have been an increasing number of studies published in community pharmacies and in managed care organizations.

In this chapter, it is not possible to review all of the different studies that have been published on the topic of CPSs. However, the reader should be aware of these studies. Knowledge of this body of literature can be valuable in understanding the successes and failures of those who have gone before us. These studies can be used as models (if well conducted) for future evaluations, or they can be used to determine the impact of CPSs in each practitioner's practice site. However, the sheer volume of articles in the literature makes access to pertinent publications challenging. Fortunately, there are tools to assist with this.

Many systematic reviews have been published that provide the reader with a summary of evaluations of CPSs and typically provide abstracted information from each included study. These reviews can serve as valuable resources for identifying studies pertinent to a particular project. Each of these reviews focuses on a slightly different aspect or section of the literature. For example, the American College of Clinical Pharmacy (ACCP) has sponsored a series of three such reviews, each inclusive of different publication time periods (1979–1987, 1988–1995, and 1996–2000). Other reviews also have been published. Some have focused on studies of specific areas of clinical pharmacy practice (e.g., ambulatory care) or pharmaceutical care. Others have focused on studies that evaluated specific outcomes of CPSs, such as clinical outcomes, humanistic outcomes, or economic outcomes. Key systematic reviews of published studies of CPSs are discussed in detail in the annotated bibliography.

In the annotated bibliography, there also are descriptions of some of the important individual studies of CPSs. These references were chosen because they are examples of either good study designs, or because they are considered landmark studies from the standpoint of the results and impact on the profession. The reader is encouraged to carefully review these studies.

Strategies

Although rigorous evaluations of CPSs are the best method to answer questions about value, in many scenarios such evaluations are not necessary or possible. For pharmacy practitioners and managers charged with determining the potential impact of a specific clinical pharmacy program in their own practice setting, there are other strategies that can be considered. These strategies are literature generalization and decision analysis. These two strategies are contrasted to the third strategy—to conduct a local evaluation. Literature generalization is the application of data from published studies of like services or practice sites to the local practice site. Typically, this strategy involves abstracting or projecting consequences from external data (e.g., previously published studies) and combining that with internal cost information. More structured decision analysis or modeling also may be used and again involves use of previously published literature and/or locally collected data, but is distinguished by use of a decision-analysis model to better define costs and consequences and to conduct sensitivity analysis. The last strategy, local evaluation, is the measurement of actual costs and actual consequences of an existing service using one of the study designs discussed in this chapter.

Literature Generalization

Literature generalization typically can be described as the extrapolation of results of studies from other sites to the environment in question. This process requires the identification of articles that describe the CPS in question. Preferably, these articles describe studies that were conducted in a similar environment to that being considered. There are some resources available (in the form of literature reviews) to help identify published assessments of CPSs that might be useful based on the type of service described, the practice site in question, and other pertinent similarities to the local practice environment. These are identified in the literature section and are discussed in detail in the annotated bibliography.

Extrapolation of the results of published studies requires careful consideration of not only the similarity of the practice site, service, but also the appropriate size of the expected benefit. For example, if a study reports the results of a CPS that used one pharmacist for 40 hours/week, is it appropriate to assume that the benefit would be doubled if expanded to two pharmacists for 40 hours/week? Furthermore, the reporting of results in published studies may take a variety of formats, such as benefit (savings) per patient-day, benefit (savings) per pharmacist, benefit (savings) per month (or annually), or as a benefit per dollar invested (benefit-to-cost ratio). Consider the best format for the situation. If results are not reported in the desired format, it may be possible to convert or calculate them, provided that necessary information is given.

Whenever possible, data from the local site that are known should be incorporated with the extrapolated results. The easiest example of this is to include the local costs required to provide the service. These costs should be estimated based on what is known about the proposed service. These cost values likely will be of different magnitude than those found in the published study because of differences in personnel wages and other costs, and because the costs reported in the published study are likely older (from a previous year) then those applicable currently.

An example of the use of literature generalization to estimate the benefit that might be obtained from CPSs was discussed in a recent report. As part of a hospital-wide reengineering program, a pharmacy department in a community hospital proposed and gained approval for implementation of a CPS as a cost-savings measure. Previously published articles that discussed CPSs in community hospitals were identified and reviewed. Articles that discussed a similar patient mix, similar drug use patterns, and similar types of services to those proposed were targeted. From each article, drug cost-savings/avoided and the number of clinical pharmacists work-hours associated with the savings were abstracted. By combining the results of applicable articles, the authors estimated that opportunities existed in this hospital to save about $500,000 (gross) annually in drug expenses. The authors also estimated the pharmacist work-hours that would be required to provide these services and used the average pharmacist salary at the hospital to calculate the investment required. Net benefits were projected to exceed $250,000 with about $2 in benefit achieved for every $1 invested.

There are advantages and disadvantages of this strategy. Literature generalization is relatively quick and easy to perform and, therefore, is inexpensive. Articles can be limited to those that are peer-reviewed to increase the quality of the results included in the projections. Because the original articles may use a variety of approaches, examine the effects of different approaches to the provision of the service and choose the best approach. Also, compare articles that describe different types of CPSs to ensure that the one in question is the best for the given situation. Most important, this strategy can be used even before resources are available to implement the service in question. Thus, it can be an extremely useful approach to use to gain approval for funding of CPSs.

Disadvantages of literature generalization relate primarily to the question of external validity. Clinical pharmacy services tend to be highly dependent on the environment and people involved; thus, it is difficult to ensure that the result will be the same in a different setting. Furthermore, it is recognized that the quality of much of the published literature on CPSs is of mediocre quality. This is usually because of methodology deficiencies in study design, a further reason to question the validity of literature generalization. Because of these deficiencies, literature generalization may not be convincing to financial decision-makers.

Decision Analysis

Decision analysis, or modeling, allows for a more structured and reliable approach compared to literature generalization, though it may use similar input data.

Modeling is a method of economic analysis that lies between literature generalization and conduction of a full study. Modeling allows use of literature data, usually to determine probabilities of certain outcomes, and this is typically then combined with internal cost data. Other sources of data, such as values derived from expert panels, also may be used in modeling. The use of a decision tree to confine the analysis to certain predetermined end points sets this strategy apart from others. Modeling is commonly used in pharmacoeconomic evaluations of pharmaceuticals but is less often used for evaluations of CPSs.

One example of the use of modeling in CPSs was a study that evaluated the cost-effectiveness of consultant pharmacists in nursing homes. The study compared outcomes of patients who received consultant pharmacist services versus those who did not. An expert panel determined probabilities for each of the outcomes included in the model. Costs were obtained from the Health Care Financing Administration (now known as the Centers for Medicare and Medicaid Services), and other sources. The cost to provide the service, based on pharmacist time, was estimated to be $10 per encounter. The authors determined that for each optimal outcome achieved with a consultant pharmacist, $1034 was saved by prevention of costly drug-related problems.

There are many advantages of decision analysis. As with literature generalization, the modeling approach is inexpensive because it can be conducted without actually having the service in place. Modeling is more complicated than just extrapolating so it can take longer to perform, but even still it is relatively time-efficient. Because modeling can include locally collected information, the results can be made more organization-specific than literature generalization. Most important, however, is the ability to perform sensitivity analysis in the modeling strategy. Through sensitivity analysis, the probability values of the outcomes in the model or the costs included in the model can be varied. This variation allows for a better understanding of the range of values within which the results will remain viable; thus, the validity of the results is stronger than can be achieved with literature generalization. Again, this strategy can be used even before resources are available to implement the service in question, a major advantage.

There also are disadvantages of the decision-analysis approach, which are related primarily to the model itself. In developing the decision model, potential consequences often have to be limited to those that are most obvious, otherwise the model becomes unmanageable. Furthermore, modeling, similar to literature generalization, requires assumptions to be made by the researchers about the likelihood of potential consequences. This creates potential for researcher bias to affect the results. Nevertheless, modeling is a good method to increase confidence in the expected results that might be obtained from a CPS given the data available.

Local Evaluation

Local evaluation is really just the conduct of an evaluation or study at the practice site of interest. Typically, such a study is done as part of a "pilot project" to determine the true impact of a CPS. The results are then used to justify the continuation and/or expansion of the service evaluated. The design of the evaluation can take any one of the forms previously discussed in this chapter. Obviously, the measurement of both the actual costs and consequences of the service is important. Often, this measurement is done before and after implementation of the program. Ideally, there also is some comparison or control group that is observed. The local evaluation approach is the best from a methodology standpoint because it uses data from the actual site and it, therefore, reflects the actual outcomes of the services.

There are many good examples of this approach published in the literature. One example was a study of CPSs in an ambulatory practice site. The CPS described recently was implemented to provide intensive monitoring and intervention on drug-related issues for ambulatory Medicaid patients visiting a clinic. The goal of the study was to determine the ability of the CPSs to reduce health care use and associated expenses. A control group that did not receive the monitoring was used to compare outcomes. The costs to provide the service for 1 year were $84,363 and were primarily represented by the personnel expenses. Overall health use was reduced by $173,651 in the intervention group. The benefit-to-cost ratio was just more than 2:1.

Again, there are advantages and disadvantages with the local evaluation strategy. Obviously, this strategy is the best in terms of yielding organization-specific results; thus, it has the highest internal validity. Because it is conducted postimplementation, it measures actual benefits and actual costs, and reflects actual or usual care. When conducted well, this strategy is the most likely to be accepted by financial decision-makers because the results are difficult to refute.

However, this strategy is expensive because the CPSs must actually be implemented. Implementation means that personnel must be hired, trained, and paid; and that expenses are incurred. The local evaluation strategy also is the one that is most time-consuming. A significant amount of time may be invested during implementation of the program. Also, time will be incurred during the course of the evaluation; this is especially true if the evaluation is well conducted and includes a sufficient sample of patients needed to make a valid conclusion. Other disadvantages of this strategy stem from the issue of study design. As previously discussed, it may be difficult to design the evaluation with an adequate control group and with all potential sources of bias being minimized.

Step Approach

There are some key steps to consider in any assessment of CPSs regardless of the strategy used. These steps have been published as guidelines and are available for more detailed review. Steps within each set of guidelines vary slightly. The steps most pertinent to this discussion are shown in Table 4.

Steps 1 through 3 relate to the purpose of the study. The first step is always to define the study question—this should be clear, concise, well explained, and measurable. From this, determine the specific objectives of the evaluation. Early on, it also is important to determine the perspective of the analysis. As previously discussed, determining the analysis perspective will help establish the costs to include in the analysis.

Table 4. Steps in Conducting an Economic Assessment of a Clinical Pharmacy Service

Step	Action
Step 1	Define study question (should be clear, concise, well defined, measurable)
Step 2	State specific objectives
Step 3	Determine perspective of analysis (e.g., provider, payer, patient, society)
Step 4	Identify alternatives if any (e.g., control group)
Step 5	Determine the methods and type of analysis (partial vs. full evaluation, CMA, CEA, CUA, CBA)
Step 6	Determine study design (modeling, decision analysis, randomization)
Step 7	Analyze consequences (benefits or effects) of alternatives (measure, obtain from literature)
Step 8	Analyze costs to provide service
Step 9	Perform discounting
Step 10	Conduct sensitivity analysis or statistical analysis
Step 11	Analysis results
Step 12	Summarize
Step 13	Present findings

CBA = cost-benefit analysis; CEA = cost-effectiveness analysis; CMA = cost-minimization analysis; CUA = cost-utility analysis.
Adapted with permission from Sanchez LA. Some techniques for adapting pharmacoeconomics and outcomes research to pharmaceutical care. New Medicine 1997;1:41–5.

Steps 4 through 6 related to the study methods and design, also were previously discussed in more detail. Again, a key element of the design is to determine which, if any, alternatives will be compared. Given this, the methodology that will best fit the evaluation (e.g., CBA and CEA) and whether a full economic evaluation is needed versus a partial analysis can be determined. The strategy and design of the evaluation also should be determined (e.g., if modeling is appropriate).

Steps 7 through 10 relate to the conduct of the evaluation. First, both costs and consequences must be measured, obtained from literature, determined by an expert panel, or otherwise identified. For long-term projects, or for projects that use economic values from different time periods, an adjustment for the time-value-of-money may be necessary. This practice is commonly referred to as discounting. Discounting has been discussed in other chapters of this textbook; however, in simple terms, it is adjusting up or down the value of money based on a discount rate. Sensitivity analysis or statistical analysis also should be considered. Again, sensitivity analysis allows confirmation of the results with a range of values, similar to confidence intervals in statistics.

The last steps are to analyze the results, make conclusions, and summarize and present the findings. An important part of a local economic evaluation of a clinical pharmacy program is the presentation of results. Typically, this is the point where decisions are made about the continuation, discontinuation, or expansion of the program. In this step, "selling" the service is important and there are certain skills needed to ensure success in selling or marketing the results. These skills are discussed in the Developing a Proposal for a CPS section.

Developing a Proposal for a Clinical Pharmacy Service

Understanding the Business Environment

One of the most important things that pharmacy managers and clinicians can do to ensure successful approval of CPSs is to understand the health care business environment. It is within this environment that decisions are made with respect to funding for new programs. Understanding the terminology and driving forces that impact decision making will better prepare the pharmacist to effectively communicate the value of CPSs to the financial decision makers within the health care organization. Included in this chapter is a section containing important terms pertinent to the health care business environment. The reader is encouraged to read and understand these terms.

In most health care organizations, decisions about new programs first require the development of a business plan. A business plan is a proposal that is structured and information-based. Depending on the type of health care organization, the program proposed, and the investment required, the plan might contain a greater or lesser amount of detail. There are different categories of information that may be included in a business plan, the most important of which is the financial projection. The plan may include other elements, such as an evaluation of the market, an evaluation of competitors, a definition of the clinical and quality requirements pertinent to the service, a description of the proposed processes required to operate the service, a strategy for marketing the service once it is implemented, an assessment of critical risk and opportunities that may affect the future of the program, and an action plan and timeline for implementing and monitoring the success of the program. There are books and other references available to assist the pharmacy manager or clinician in developing a business plan. One of these books, which is written specifically for business planning for CPSs, is discussed in number 17 of the annotated bibliography. Some of the basic considerations in business planning are explained in the following sections.

Reviewing the Literature

The first place to start in developing a business plan or proposal for pharmacy services is to understand published literature on the topic. The concepts of literature generalization were previously discussed and are pertinent to the planning process. The business plan should include a well-written summary of the literature on the topic, including descriptions of the successes obtained by others who have implemented similar programs. This type of information can provide a supportive backdrop to the proposal. In some cases, descriptions of other successful programs can be convincing to financial decision makers.

Evaluating the Market and Competitors

The market for pharmacy services is something that is often not considered by managers and clinicians. Yet, it is an element that should be a considered and will be important to the financial decision maker. The market is the population of patients from which the service or program will draw. For example, a proposed pharmacist-managed diabetes clinic would have a market of all patients with diabetes in the local area. Knowing the market will help in projecting the potential volume of business that the program might achieve. Within the general market, there may be market segments. These are subgroups that may be of interest to the program. For example, within the diabetes market there is a percentage of patients with insulin-dependent diabetes. This market segment may represent patients who are more likely to need the service as compared to those with noninsulin-dependent diabetes. Market segments can be defined by age, race, income, and proximity to the service, and by any other classification that is pertinent.

Going hand-in-hand with an understanding of the market is an assessment of competitors. Again, this is a topic often not considered by clinical pharmacists. Competitors should be broadly defined. Competitors may include other pharmacists providing the same service (i.e., another pharmacist-run diabetes clinic in the same town) or competitors may be other health care professionals, such as physicians or nurses, who provide closely-related services. Even in a hospital setting, there may be competitors to a CPS. For example, consider a pharmacist-run inpatient antibiotic dosing service. A potential competitor to this service may be a physician infectious disease specialist who provides consults to other physicians. Knowing the competitors, including their strengths and weaknesses, will help in developing strategies to ensure the success of the program. Also, knowing the market share of each competitor also is useful.

Identifying the Proposed Processes and Operations

Clearly, any business plan or proposal must contain a thorough description of how the program or service will work. This description should include the organizational structure and reporting relationships both within the program and within the greater organization. The description should include the physical requirements of the program, including space, equipment, supplies, and other important components. The description also should include the personnel requirements of the program. With respect to personnel, there should be detail as to the qualifications and training required, the number of staff by position, and specific job duties. The workflow envisioned for the program should be described, with emphasis on the interface between the customers and the program.

Developing Financial Projections

The financial analysis is the most important aspect of any business plan or proposal. The plan should clearly define the costs (expenses) that will be incurred by the program along with the expected economic benefit. The economic benefit may be in the form of revenue (if the program is one that can charge for its services) or may be in the form of savings that are incurred as a result of the program. The costs and benefits (expenses and revenue) should be estimated for the first year and through years three and five of the program. This requires assumptions to be made about the growth of the program and the effects of growth on both costs and benefits. The net benefit and return on investment should be determined at each time period. Typically, these financial projections are expressed in a tabular format. Standard financial statements may be used. The most useful of these is the revenue and expense statement (also known as a profit and loss statement).

Writing the Business Plan and Selling the Proposal

Decisions about new programs are usually made based on both a written proposal and a verbal presentation. The written proposal is the business plan document. The written business plan should address the key elements and be formatted in a business style. The writing style should be professional but not overly scientific (as is the habit of pharmacists). A good understanding of the audience is key to writing an effective proposal. The audience is usually the health care organization administrator. These individuals often are busy and appreciate documents that get to the bottom line quickly. Many business plans include an executive summary for this purpose.

The organization of the business plan depends on the specific program being proposed. The table of contents of many sample business plans include the following sections: executive summary, background and description, market analysis and strategy, operational structure and processes, financial projections, implementation action plan and milestones, critical risks and opportunities, exit strategy, conclusion, and supportive documents.

Although the business plan document is important, the presentation of the proposal can often be even more influential to the decision process. A convincing presentation can sometimes sway a decision even if the business plan itself is not perfect. Keys to an effective presentation include good visual aids (slides or overheads), good organization and flow of material, and keeping to the allotted time for the presentation. Always reinforce the message by repeating important points.

Conclusion

Pharmacy practitioners know the value of CPSs and that CPSs can improve clinical and humanistic outcomes of drug use and can reduce health care expenses. However, to prove these claims, sound techniques of evaluation and assessment are needed. As has been previously discussed, in any economic evaluation of CPSs there are certain key elements that should be included. The cost to provide the program should be included. Outcomes or consequences measured may be clinical, humanistic, or economic, depending on the goal of the evaluation. The perspective should be clearly stated and consistent with the analysis performed. To show a cause-and-effect relationship, the evaluation should include a control group or alternative to the service being assessed.

Although these basic elements should be included, there are different strategies for performing evaluations that vary in rigor of methods and intended purpose. Previously published literature can be used and generalized to the practice site. Alternatively, modeling and decision analysis can be used with input from the literature, expert opinion, and/or from locally collected costs and/or outcome data. Finally, actual costs and consequences resulting from the service can be assessed and compared.

Clinical practitioners and managers should use whatever method of evaluation best accomplishes the intended purpose of the assessment. Where that purpose includes gaining support of financial decision makers for implementation or expansion of services, a key element is an informative written proposal, or business plan. Also important to obtaining support is a well planned, persuasive, and effectively delivered presentation of the proposal.

Definition of Terms

allocate. To spread a cost from one account to several accounts, to several products, or activities, or to several financial periods.

benefit-to-cost ratio. The financial benefits of a program (in dollars or some other monetary unit) divided by the cost (investment) required to provide the program (in dollars). Benefits and costs should be calculated for the same time period. Ratio is expressed as benefit for every $1 invested in the program.

break-even analysis. A method to project the point where expenses (costs) and benefits (revenues) are equal.

break-even point. The volume of activity where expenses (costs) are equal to benefits (revenues).

budget. A financial plan that is used to estimate the results of future operations.

capital. Capital is most often defined as the permanent or fixed assets of a business, such as facilities and equipment. Capital assets are not recoverable in the short run unless the entire business is sold.

capital budget. A financial plan of proposed outlays for acquiring long-term assets, typically expensive equipment.

capital equipment. Equipment used to manufacture a product; provide a service; or sell, store, or deliver a product/service. This equipment will be used over many financial periods.

competitive advantage. Those aspects of the business that give it an edge over the competition.

competitor. A business competing for the same market dollars or customer base.

contribution margin. Revenue less variable expenses.

contribution per unit. Revenue less variable expense per unit of goods produced or service rendered (e.g., the income per patient seen minus the cost to provide service per patient seen).

cost. The expense required to produce goods or services, or the investment required to obtain a certain benefit. From the customer's standpoint, it is the price paid to receive the product or service.

cost-benefit. Some measure of costs compared to some measure of benefits for a proposed undertaking. If the benefits exceed the costs, the undertaking is judged worthwhile.

cost center. A unit of activity (or department) for which expenditures and expenses are accumulated. Sometimes the term "cost center" is used generically to mean a business unit for which expenses and revenues are tracked (this is the same as profit center).

cost of goods sold. This is the total expenditure on the production of goods or provision of service sold in a given period, also called product or service costs.

customer base. The mainstay of business for a program, the customers who are most loyal to the business.

demand. The desire for a product or service and the ability to pay for it, the amount customers are ready and able to buy at a certain price.

depreciation. The process of allocating the cost of an asset to the periods of benefit (life span of the asset).

differential cost. Same as *incremental* cost.

direct cost. In economics, a direct costs is one for which there is a definable transaction, or exchange of asset. In managerial accounting, direct costs are those incurred in production of a product or service, same as *variable cost.*

discount. The difference between the *future value* and *present value* of a payment.

discounted cash flow analysis. Analysis of projected cash flow over time, converts incremental (annual) amounts into their present value using a *discount* rate.

discount rate. Interest rate used to convert future payments to present values.

expenditure. The payment of cash for goods or services received.

expense. A past or current expenditure.

external validity. The degree to which the results of a study or evaluation are valid in a larger population, beyond the study group, similar to "generalizability".

financial statements. Documents that provide information about financial status, including the balance sheet, *income statement*, and statement of cash flows.

fixed budget. A *budget* that provides specified amounts of expenditures and income that do not vary with activity level. Different than a *flexible budget* where the plan varies by expected activity level.

fixed cost. An expenditure or expense that does not vary with the volume of activity, at least in the short run.

flexible budget. A plan that projects revenues and expenses as a function of anticipated activity levels. Health care

organizations typically use flexible budgets (as opposed to *fixed budgets*) that are based on expected level of patient volume.
forecasting. Estimating or projecting costs or revenues or both, or estimating the trends in the economy or any other variable.
future value. How much a certain dollar amount invested today will be worth in the future.
gross. Overall total before deductions.
gross profit. Net sales (sales or charges minus discounts or allowances) less the costs of goods or services.
income statement. A financial statement that provides revenues, expenses, and gains or losses for a period of time (past), ending with *net income*.
incremental. An adjective used to describe cost, expense, investment, cash flow, revenue, profit, or benefit if one more unit of service is provided, or of one option versus another.
indirect costs. Costs of production not easily associated with the production of specific goods or provision of service, related to fixed costs and *overhead costs*. In economic terms, indirect cost may refer to a cost for which there is no definable transaction, for example the cost of mortality.
intangible assets. Assets that are not physical entities or whose value goes beyond their physical presence and that do not have set values. Examples are brand names, patents, and customer loyalty.
interest. The charge or cost of using money, expressed as a rate per period, usually 1 year, called the *interest rate*.
interest rate. The rate of return that lenders expect on their investment to compensate them for their risk and lost opportunities to use the cash elsewhere.
life span. Duration of time for which the business or program is likely to be profitable, or during which the environment is favorable for the business.
margin. Revenue less specified costs.
marginal cost. The incremental cost of the last unit added to production or service.
market. The population of consumers for which the service/product is applicable. The market may be defined geographically, by specific characteristics (e.g., age, disease, profession, socioeconomic class, interests, or other demographics), or by a combination of factors.
market segment. A subgroup of the total market, a group of customers or potential customers whose members have a common characteristic relating to how and why they might use the good or service.
market share. The percentage share of the market that the business serves or desires to serve.
markup. The difference between the selling price and acquisition cost.
net. What is left after deductions from gross (e.g., deduction of expenses).
net income. The excess of revenues over expenses for a period of time. Negative net income is net loss.
net present value. Present value of all future cash inflows and outflows of a project or investment at a given discount rate.
operating budget. A formal budget for the operating cycle or for the fiscal year. Typically, this includes only the revenue and expenses of operating the business, not capital expenses.
opportunity cost. The present value of the income that could be earned from using an asset (investment) in its best alternative use to the one being considered.
overhead cost. Any cost not directly associated with the production or delivery of services, sometimes called indirect costs (e.g., rent, electricity, and management costs).
payback time. The time period to reach the break-even point. The time it takes for income to equal or exceed the initial investment and ongoing expenses in a program.
payer. Individual or entity that pays for services. In health care, payers typically are third-party insurance companies, managed care organizations, or the government.
payer mix. A list of payers, and the percentage of the total that each contributes to the annual operating revenue of a health care organization.
present value. Value today of an amount to be paid later, discounted at some interest or discount rate. Based on the principle of the *time value of money*; that money is worth more today than the same amount in some future period.
profit. The excess of revenues over expenses for a transaction, sometimes used synonymously with net income for the period.
profit and loss statement. Same as the revenue and expense report. The statement is defined by a time period and provides a listing of revenues and expenses for the business unit.
profit center. A unit of activity (department) for which both revenue and expense are accumulated, as opposed to a cost center.
pro forma statements. Hypothetical statements. Financial statements as they would appear if some event were to occur.
return on investment. Net income (or loss) divided by the amount invested.
revenue. The increase in equity caused by services rendered. Not the same as receipt of funds, which may occur before, when, or after revenue is recognized.
revenue and expense report. Same as the profit and loss statement. The statement is defined by a time period and provides a listing of revenues and expenses for the business unit.
risk. A measure of variability of the return on investment, the possibility of loss.
sensitivity analysis. The study of how the outcome of a decision-making process changes as one or more of the assumptions used in the decision changes, also called "what if" analysis.
strategic plan. A statement of the method for achieving an organization's goals.
SWOT analysis. A method of analyzing the business to identify it's strengths, opportunities, weakness, and threats. Used in market planning.
target market. The specific individuals or groups within the market that are most likely to be potential customers for the goods or services of the business.
useful life. The time period for which an asset will be of value to a company.
variable costs. Costs that change as activity levels change.
variance. The difference between the actual and budget amount.
window of opportunity. The time period within which the business opportunity is most likely to be taken advantage of or achieved.

Annotated Bibliography

1. Bond CA, Raehl CL, Franke T. Clinical pharmacy services and hospital mortality rates. Pharmacotherapy 1999;19:556–64.

   This is the first article of a series (references 2 and 3) of studies by the same authors that uses secondary data to examine associations between clinical pharmacy services (CPSs) and clinical and economic outcomes. In each study, data from hospitals across the country were obtained from secondary sources (American Hospital Association Abridged Guide to the Health Care Field, National Survey of Clinical Pharmacy Services, and/or Medicare) and analyzed through multiple regression for associations between the presence of CPSs and clinical and economic variables. Cost estimates were provided in 1992 United States dollars. In this study, the authors demonstrated an association among four specific types of CPSs (clinical research, drug information, admission drug histories, and CPR team participation) and reduced mortality. Cost-effectiveness ratios for these services also were estimated; these ratios ranged from $28.92 (clinical research) to $192.58 (drug information) per death avoided. This and the other related studies (references 2 and 3) are important because they represent large scale, ecologic-type evaluations. These types of evaluations require large databases and are not easily accomplished, making this series so much more impressive.

2. Bond CA, Raehl CL, Franke T. Clinical pharmacy services, pharmacist staffing, and drug costs in United States hospitals. Pharmacotherapy 1999;19:1354–62.

   This is the second study of the series by the same authors and it uses the same methodology as that was discussed in reference 1 In this study, the authors demonstrate an association between specific CPSs (e.g., in-service education, drug information, drug protocol management, and admission drug histories) and reduced hospital drug costs. Reductions in drug costs per occupied bed for hospitals with versus without these services ranged from $490.96 for in-service education to $1961.55 for drug information. The benefit-to-cost ratios for each service also were estimated and ranged from $23.80:1 (drug histories) to $83.23:1 (drug protocol management). As with references 1 and 3, this study is unique in the magnitude of data analyzed and for the significance to the results.

3. Bond CA, Raehl CL, Franke T. Clinical pharmacy services, pharmacy staffing, and the total cost of care in United States hospitals. Pharmacotherapy 2000;20:609–21.

   In a third study by these authors (references 1 and 2), again using the same methods, an association among six different CPSs and reductions in the total cost of hospital care (drug use evaluation, drug information, adverse drug reaction monitoring, drug protocol management, medical rounds participation, and admission drug histories) is shown. Benefit-to-cost ratios were estimated for each service; these ratios ranged from $31.92:1 (drug use evaluation) to $2,988.57:1 (adverse reaction monitoring). Although the benefit-to-cost values from these studies are impressive, they should be interpreted in the context of the study design, which was not to determine causation but rather to determine association between CPSs and cost reduction. Collectively, this and the studies discussed in references 1 and 2 represent an important contribution to the literature on CPSs.

4. Bootman JL, Townsend RJ, McGhan WF, eds. Principles of Pharmacoeconomics, 2nd ed. Cincinnati, OH: Harvey Whitney Books Co., 1996.

   The second edition of this book is a greatly expanded version of the first and includes discussions on pharmacoeconomic research in clinical trials, medical centers, community practice, and managed health care settings. The information is relevant for researchers, practitioners, and students; however, the primary audience is the beginning researcher. The book should stimulate health care providers and researchers to generate more pharmacoeconomic research and apply the results to prevent and treat disease.

5. Carter BL, Malone DC, Billups SJ, et al. Interpreting the findings of the IMPROVE study. Am J Health-Syst Pharm 2001;58:1330–7.

   The Impact of Managed Pharmaceutical Care on Resource Utilization and Outcomes in Veterans Affairs Medical Centers (IMPROVE) was a prospective, multisite, randomized, controlled trial that compared patients who received CPSs to those who received standard care. This paper summarizes the various findings from that study. These findings were originally reported in several papers that originated from this study. Nine Veterans Affairs medical centers participated in the IMPROVE study and more than 1054 patients were randomized to either an intervention or control group. The study identified no difference in patient satisfaction or quality of life in the two groups. Selected disease-specific processes of care were different. For example, there was an improved rate of measurement of hemoglobin A_{1c} and low-density cholesterol levels in the intervention group. Total health care costs increased over time in both groups and the difference between groups was not statistically significant. Overall, the findings of the IMPROVE study are rather unimpressive, and frankly disappointing. Yet, the study is important because it was one of the largest studies of CPSs ever conducted. It will continue to be important as practitioners seek to understand why the results were not more positive.

6. Gourley GK, Gourley DR, Rigolosi EL, et al. Development and validation of the pharmaceutical care satisfaction questionnaire. Am J Manag Care 2001;7:461–6.

   This article reviews the development and validation of a patient satisfaction questionnaire that specifically evaluates pharmaceutical care. Many other published patient satisfaction questionnaires are geared to evaluate dispensary roles of pharmacists and pharmacies. This questionnaire addresses duties of a clinical pharmacist and the pharmacist's impact on patient outcomes. Published data on this questionnaire are limited; however, it is an alternative that allows for evaluation of patient responses to pharmaceutical care.

7. Harrison DL, Bootman JL, Cox ER. Cost-effectiveness of consultant pharmacists in managing drug related morbidity and mortality at nursing facilities. Am J Health-Syst Pharm 1998;55:1588–94.

   As with the study in reference 5, this study is based on a cost-of-illness study that was published in the Journal Archives of Internal Medicine and conducted by the same authors. This study used data from the previous analyses to estimate the impact that consultant pharmacy services have in the nursing home setting. An expert panel was used to determine conditional probabilities, and health care use and associated costs were estimated and/or derived from available statistical reports. The authors found that the annual cost of drug-related problems per nursing home resident fell from an estimated $235 without consultant pharmacists to $162 with consultant pharmacists (in 1994 United States dollars). For all nursing facility residents in the United States, the total cost of managing drug-related morbidity and mortality was estimated to be $9.64 and $6.64 billion with and without consultant pharmacists, respectively. This study is extremely valuable for those justifying CPSs in the long-term care environment.

8. Hatoum HT, Akhras K. A 32-year literature review on the value and acceptance of ambulatory care provided by pharmacists. Ann Pharmacother 1993;27:1106–19.

   This article provides a systematic review of published evaluations of the value and acceptance of CPSs in the ambulatory care environment. Studies published between 1960 and 1992 were included. Studies included must have evaluated either cost of care, quality of care, or attitudinal outcomes of services provided by pharmacists in ambulatory settings. Of 170 articles identified, 104 were summarized in the review. The authors categorize studies based on outcomes reported. Because of the extensive time period covered by this review, the authors were able to record trends that occurred in the types of studies conducted. Based on the status of the literature reviewed, the authors made several recommendations for future research. This article is important because it focuses specifically on the ambulatory care environment. This article is widely cited and is one with which all pharmacists interested in this subject should be familiar.

9. Hatoum HT, Catizone C, Hutchinson RA, Purohit A. An eleven-year review of the pharmacy literature: documentation of the value and acceptance of clinical pharmacy services. Drug Intell Clin Pharm 1986;20:33–47.

   This paper represents the first large review of published evaluations of CPSs. The publication time period of the review spans from 1974 to 1984 (inclusive). Of 305 articles identified, 93 are reported in detail. These 93 articles represent original studies that assess one of the following: reduction in the cost of care, improvement in the quality of patient care, or acceptance of CPSs. Data are provided on each study in tabular format. Although this article provides useful information, it was written as a bibliography rather than a systematic review; thus, relatively few findings or analyses are presented. Though dated, this article remains a good secondary source of information of older literature on this topic.

10. Johnson JA, Bootman JL. Drug-related morbidity and mortality and the economic impact of pharmaceutical care. Am J Health-Syst Pharm 1997;54:554–8.

   This article is based on a landmark cost-of-illness study that was published in the Journal Archives of Internal Medicine and conducted by the same authors. This study used data from the previous analyses to estimate the impact that pharmaceutical care has in the ambulatory setting. An expert panel was used to determine conditional probabilities, and health care use and associated costs were estimated and/or derived from available statistical reports. The authors estimate that if all patients received pharmaceutical care in the ambulatory care setting, $45.6 billion in direct health care costs would be avoided (in 1995 United States dollars). Even when the fee associated with the provision of pharmaceutical care was increased 4-fold, the estimated cost avoidance changed only slightly. This article and reference 6 are good examples of the use of decision analysis and expert panels in evaluating CPSs.

11. Lai LL, Sorkin AL. Cost benefit analysis of pharmaceutical care in a Medicaid population–from a budgetary perspective. J Manag Care Pharm 1998;4:303–8.

   This study evaluated the impact of pharmaceutical care in a Medicaid population using a cost-benefit analysis (CBA). A quasiexperimental pretest–post-test design was used. The intervention and control groups were matched on different variables to reduce the possibility of dissimilar groups. Matching was used because the groups were not randomized. Only participants with continuous Medicaid eligibility 1 year before and after the start of the program were enrolled in the study. The inclusion criteria were that each subject had the same length of exposure to Medicaid and, therefore, reduced the history effect. This study provides an excellent example for reducing threats to interval validity when true experimental analyses are not possible.

12. Morrison A, Wertheimer AI. Evaluation of studies investigating the effectiveness of pharmacists' clinical services. Am J Health-Syst Pharm 2001;58:567–77.

   The authors of this study performed a meta-analysis of randomized trials of counseling, education, and other CPSs. A Medline search was conducted to identify studies describing pharmacist counseling of patients, counseling of both patients and physicians, and other patient care services. Outcomes of interest were measures of patient behavior, disease symptoms, and patient knowledge. The authors identified 32 trials that met the inclusion criteria. Findings included six studies of patient counseling, in all of which the outcomes favored the counseled patients over the control patients. In studies that evaluated pharmacist counseling of both patients and physicians, outcomes were better in the intervention group. Four trials of other patient care services by pharmacists were evaluated, all of which were inconclusive. The authors concluded that counseling of patients and their physicians by pharmacists can improve clinical outcomes. This meta-analysis is important because it focuses on clinical outcomes of pharmacy services. Also, it is one of only a few reviews that attempts to pool data from different studies.

13. Pickard AS, Johnson JA, Farris KB. The impact of pharmacist interventions on health-related quality of life. Ann Pharmacother 1999;33;1167–72.

   This article is a review of published literature on the impact of pharmacist interventions on health-related quality of life. The authors conducted a systematic literature review to identify pertinent articles. After reviewing each study, the authors found the impact of pharmacists improving health-related quality of life due to their interventions was inconclusive. The authors suggest several reasons for the results: use of an inappropriate quality-of-life measure, inadequate sample size, insufficient study length, and the possibility that pharmacists have no impact on health-related quality of life. The authors provide suggestions for future analyses to improve study methodology and design. This is an important article for anyone interested in the humanistic impact of CPSs.

14. Plumridge RJ, Wojnar-Horton RE. A review of pharmacoeconomic of pharmaceutical care. Pharmacoeconomics 1998;14:175–89.

   This review of the pharmacy literature sought to identify studies of "pharmaceutical care" that demonstrate economic impact. The authors note that the term "pharmaceutical care" is often used incorrectly, and they refer to the published definitions by Hepler and Strand. Studies identified from the literature search categorized as either pharmaceutical care or CPSs. Of the pharmaceutical care studies, none met the pharmacoeconomic criteria established by the authors. Identified articles are summarized in tabular format with key data elements abstracted and reported. The authors report many findings that are limitations of the literature, including failure to state perspective, lack of comparator groups, lack of randomization, failure to consider input costs, and many others. The authors also provide many recommendations for future research in this area. The value of this article is in the extensive listing of limitations of current research, and in the recommendations for future research.

15. Schumock GT, Butler MG, Meek PD, Vermeulen LC, Arondekar BV, Bauman JL. Evidence of the economic benefit of clinical pharmacy services: 1996–2000. Pharmacotherapy 2003;23(1):113-132.

This is the third, and most recent of the systematic reviews of the literature sponsored by ACCP. This paper summarizes original evaluations of the economic impact of CPSs published during the 5-year period from 1996 to 2000 (inclusion). There were 59 studies included from this time frame. The settings of these studies were hospitals (52.5 percent), community pharmacies and clinics (40.7 percent), health maintenance organizations (3.4 percent), and long-term or intermediate care facilities (3.4 percent). The types of CPSs studies were general pharmacotherapeutic monitoring (47.4 percent), target drug programs (20.3 percent), disease management programs (10.2 percent), and patient education or cognitive services (10.2 percent). Compared to the previous review (reference number 15), a greater proportion of evaluations was conducted in community pharmacies or clinics, and the types of services evaluated tended to be more comprehensive rather than specialized. Also, compared to the previous review, a greater proportion of studies used more rigorous study designs. In 16 of the studies reviewed, a benefit-to-cost ratio was reported by the authors, or was able to be calculated by the reviewers (these ratios ranged from 1.7:1 to 17.0:1, median = 4.68:1). This article represents the most recent systematic review published and is useful for its inclusion of contemporary studies.

16. Schumock GT, Meek PD, Ploetz PA, Vermeulen LC. Economic evaluations of clinical pharmacy services: 1988–1995. Pharmacotherapy 1996;16(6):1188-1208.

This article discusses the second of the systematic reviews of the literature sponsored by ACCP. This paper summarizes original evaluations of the economic impact of CPSs published from 1988 to 1995 (inclusive). The authors review 104 studies that were grouped into four categorizes based on type of service evaluated: disease state management (4 percent), general pharmacotherapeutic monitoring (36 percent), pharmacokinetic monitoring (13 percent), and targeted drug programs (47 percent). The study design of each article also was assessed and reported. Unfortunately, many studies were not well designed. In fact, a majority (68 percent) did not even include the cost of providing the service in the financial analysis. However, of the studies that were conducted appropriately, most reported positive financial benefits of the clinical services evaluated. Seven studies reported a benefit-to-cost ratio, ranging from 1.08:1 to 75.84:1 (mean = 16.70:1). As with the study discussed in reference 14, this article provides the reader with an easy access point to the literature on this topic. This paper is frequently cited, especially in reference to mean benefit-to-cost value reported.

17. Schumock GT. How to develop a business plan for clinical pharmacy services. 1st ed. Kansas City, MO: ACCP, 2001.

Although there are many books on the market that describe business planning, there are relatively few that deal with the health care environment. This text is the only one available that focuses specifically on CPSs. The publication is designed as a workbook and contains hundreds of questions that guide the reader through the important elements of developing a business plan. The book is divided into sections that represent the key components of a business plan and the key considerations important to the business planning process. These include: reviewing the literature, exploring the business concept, evaluating the market, evaluating competitors, assessing clinical and quality requirements, assessing the proposed processes and operations, developing a marketing strategy, assessing critical risks and opportunities, developing financial data and projections, identifying an action plan and time line, writing the business plan, and evaluating the proposal and presenting the case. Included in the text are sample financial statements that can be included in a business plan. Also included is a template for organizing the plan. The text comes with a computer disk that contains the questions in the book, a spreadsheet for generating financial statements, and the template for writing the business plan.

18. Schumock GT. Methods to assess the economic outcomes of clinical pharmacy services. Pharmacotherapy 2000;20(10Pt2):243S–52S.

This article provides a compelling argument for the need for economic evaluations of CPSs. The article reviews the clinical and economic burden of drug misadventuring, citing key studies that have added to our knowledge on the topic. By combining results of several large-scale studies, the article estimates the total economic burden of drug misadventuring to be in excess of $102 billion (based on 1999 United States dollars). The article describes evidence of the impact of CPSs on the problem of drug misadventuring, again describing key studies in this area. Methods to assess the economic impact of CPSs are described, beginning with the basic model of evaluation. A thorough discussion of CBA applied to CPSs is provided. Finally, the article describes different strategies that may be useful in the justification of CPSs. Taken together, the article provides a good overview of the topic of economic evaluations of CPSs.

19. Willett MS, Bertch KE, Rich DS, Ereshefsky L. Prospectus on the economic value of clinical pharmacy services. Pharmacotherapy 1989;9:45–56.

This article is the first of three systematic reviews sponsored by ACCP (along with references 14 and 15). It also represents the first real analysis of the literature on this topic. The authors summarize the literature that has attempted to document the economic value of CPSs. Studies included were published between 1979 and 1987 (inclusive). Fifty-nine studies are reviewed and described in tabular format. Studies are classified by type of service evaluated. Special attention is given to those that assess drug therapy monitoring, pharmacokinetic dosing, and primary care services. The authors discuss trends in the types of evaluations conducted over time and suggest strategies for future evaluations. The authors also provide an assessment of methodologies used in evaluations of CPSs and propose techniques to solve previous study design problems.

Self-Assessment Questions

1. Which one of the following best describes an evaluation of a clinical pharmacy services that includes measurement of both costs and outcomes but has no comparison or alternative?

   A. Cost and outcome description.
   B. Cost-minimization analysis.
   C. Cost and outcome analysis.
   D. Cost-effectiveness analysis.

2. Which one of the following is the best example of an economic outcome that might be measured in an evaluation of a clinical pharmacy service?

   A. Pharmacist salary and benefits.
   B. Length of hospital stay.
   C. Cost of drug information resources.
   D. Drug cost-savings.

3. In a cost-benefit analysis of a pharmacy immunization program, which one of the following best describes how the cost of the vaccine should be evaluated?

   A. Vaccine costs are excluded because they are not significant.
   B. Vaccine costs are excluded because they are incurred before the illness.
   C. Vaccine costs are included because they represent input costs.
   D. Vaccine costs are included because they are incurred with or without the program.

4. Which one of the following arguments best supports the need for conducting outcomes evaluations of clinical pharmacy services?

   A. The value of dispensing pharmacy services traditionally has been incorporated in the prescription price.
   B. Cognitive pharmacy services are increasingly "billable" and paid for by third-party payers.
   C. Patients are willing to pay for clinical pharmacy services.
   D. Health system administrators often have limited budgets for investment in new programs.

5. Which one of the following is not a typical example of an outcome that might be included in an economic evaluation of a clinical pharmacy service?

   A. Patient satisfaction.
   B. Patient preference.
   C. Mortality.
   D. Willingness to pay.

6. Which one of the following is <u>not</u> an example of an input that might be considered in a cost-benefit analysis of a pharmacist-managed refill clinic?

   A. Advertising expenses to promote the service.
   B. Drug cost-savings.
   C. Pharmacist salary and benefits.
   D. Overhead costs.

7. Which one of the following methods best allows for comparing different types of clinical pharmacy services to make the best investment decision?

   A. Cost-analysis.
   B. Cost-effectiveness analysis.
   C. Cost-benefit analysis.
   D. Cost-utility analysis.

8. Which one of the following is most true regarding the advantages of using literature generalization to justify clinical pharmacy services?

   A. Previously published studies have high external validity.
   B. Most published evaluations are complete.
   C. Literature generalization is usually convincing to financial decision-makers.
   D. Literature generalization can be conducted before implementation of the service.

9. Which one of the following is most true regarding the disadvantages of using decision analysis methods to justify clinical pharmacy services?

   A. Yields organization-specific result.
   B. Results may depend on assumptions.
   C. It is expensive.
   D. Can be conducted before implementation.

10. Which one of the following is not a key step in the process of conducting an economic evaluation of a clinical pharmacy service?

    A. State the study question.
    B. Conduct sensitivity analysis.
    C. Conduct a literature review.
    D. Identify alternative(s).

11. You are clinical pharmacist practicing in a hospital in Miami, FL. In 2 months, you will be starting to provide clinical services in a geriatric clinic owned by the hospital. The clinic has a large Caribbean population. To assess the impact of your services, you consider administering a patient-satisfaction questionnaire to the patients and to a control group both before and after implementation. Which one of the following is the least likely reason no difference is observed between the intervention and control groups?

    A. Cross-cultural differences.
    B. Timing of assessments.
    C. Length of questionnaire.
    D. Choice of instrument.

USING PHARMACOECONOMIC METHODOLOGIES TO DEVELOP HEALTH POLICY

Judith L. Glennie, Pharm.D., MSc, and Neil J. M[ac]Kinnon, Ph.D.*

Outline

I. Introduction to health policy
- A. Defining policy and health policy
  - 1. Public policy: a course of action or inaction chosen by (public/government) authorities to address a given problem or interrelated set of problems
  - 2. Overview of the policy analysis and development process
  - 3. Health policy: the framework that guides the approach to a range of activities in the field of health
- B. What constitutes the health policy environment?
  - 1. Description of the stakeholders in the health policy
  - 2. Description of the health policy environment and how it influences the manner in which health policy functions
  - 3. General description of the various decision points and decision makers in the health policy decision making spectrum/continuum
- C. Applications of health policy
  - 1. How health policy analysis links to the fundamental structure and processes in health care systems

II. The role of pharmacoeconomics in the health policy environment
- A. Goals in bringing discipline to health policy decisions—linkage between pharmacoeconomic assessments and the policy development process
  - 1. Goal of economic evaluation in encouraging decision making on the basis of costs and outcomes (rather than costs alone), helping to set priorities, choosing the most cost-effective treatment modality, establishing cost-effective prescribing policies
- B. Pharmacoeconomics and the formulary environment
  - 1. Historical review of factors which have led to the link between pharmacoeconomics and policy decisions regarding drug therapy
  - 2. Review of types of formulary/pharmacy and therapeutics committees (e.g., hospitals, government payers, private drug plans, pharmacy benefit management companies, and managed care organizations), including pressures on formulary decision makers
  - 3. Role of pharmacoeconomics in drug benefit management

III. The global emergence of pharmacoeconomic guidelines
- A. Brief historical overview of the development of pharmacoeconomic guidelines
- B. Purpose of pharmacoeconomics guidelines and pharmacoeconomic studies
- C. Overview of pharmacoeconomics guidelines available
  - 1. Australian guidelines, various Canadian guidelines, guidelines in health maintenance organizations in United States
  - 2. Linkages between pharmacoeconomic guidelines and formulary decision making requirements
- D. Barriers to the effective use of pharmacoeconomics and the guidelines

1. Gaps in transparency regarding use of pharmacoeconomic guidelines (and, thereby, pharmacoeconomic studies) by policy and decision makers

IV. The use of pharmacoeconomics in policy decision making

A. Applications of pharmacoeconomics

1. Increasing drug expenditures as a driving force for pharmacoeconomics

2. Appropriateness of expectations being placed on economic evaluations

3. Importance of evaluating the expected and unexpected consequences in the application of pharmacoeconomics in decision making

B. Organizations using pharmacoeconomics

1. Overview of some major health organizations around the world involved in the generation and use of pharmacoeconomic studies

C. Experiences using economic evaluation in health policy

1. Some examples of the scope of the application of pharmacoeconomic studies and their influence on health policy decision making

2. The Oregon experience as an example of the use of health economic principles in a health policy/prioritization process

V. Application of pharmacoeconomic methodologies in the health policy environment

A. The rationale for using pharmacoeconomics

1. Review of basic pharmacoeconomics methods and linkage to their utility in the health policy environment of constrained resources

2. Examples of when pharmacoeconomic studies can be helpful in addressing a wide range of health policy issues

3. Limitations of traditional pharmacoeconomic input for health policy decision making

B. What method and when?

1. Overview of health policy scenarios, potentially useful pharmacoeconomics methods and factors which contribute to the decision of which method to use

2. The utility of multiple economic analyses to reflect different perspectives within the health care system

3. The use of systematic reviews of health care interventions as a means of informing health policy makers

VI. Challenges in the use of pharmacoeconomic studies by health policy decision makers

A. Challenges in research/knowledge transfer

1. Challenge of bringing pharmacoeconomic researchers and policy and/or decision makers together

2. Suboptimal use of pharmacoeconomic information and, thus, undermining the goals of informed decision making

B. Challenges in the application of research results

1. Lack of decision maker knowledge in pharmacoeconomic methodologies, limitations, data interpretation, etc. limits ability to interpret and use the information

2. Need for transparency regarding the use of pharmacoeconomic information in the decision process

3. Lack of generalizability and/or transferability of information among jurisdictions as a barrier

4. Differing time lines and perspectives of formulary decision makers and pharmacoeconomic models/studies

VII. What is the future of pharmacoeconomics in health policy development?

A. The potential of studies to both inform health policy development as well as assess the impact of health policy decisions to determine effectiveness and assess unintended effects

B. Key issues that need to be addressed to ensure the continued development of pharmacoeconomics as a discipline

C. Need for good pharmacoeconomic practice guidelines to build rigor and credibility into economic evaluations

D. Eventual move towards standardized formats for reporting pharmacoeconomic studies

E. Need for improved data sources/inputs into economic assessments

F. Decision makers need to improve their level of knowledge so as to use pharmacoeconomic information in an informed manner

G. Need for decision makers to communicate their decision making processes as well as the decisions made

H. Need for pharmacoeconomics to continue to adapt to new technologies and methodologies

I. Increasing of importance of pharmacoeconomics as drug costs and proportion of health care spending on drugs continues to increase

J. Striving towards pharmacoeconomic evaluations contributing to a wide range of information for consideration in the decision making process

Learning Objectives

1. Describe the environment and the factors which influence health policy development.
2. Discuss the relationship between pharmacoeconomic studies and health policy development.
3. Explain the development of pharmacoeconomic guidelines around the globe.
4. Compare and contrast the use of pharmacoeconomic information in decision making within a range of health-related organizations.
5. Assess which pharmacoeconomic methodologies are most amenable to the health policy development environment.
6. Describe the challenges of using pharmacoeconomic information in the health policy environment.
7. Outline future developments in pharmacoeconomics and health policy.

Abbreviations in this chapter

AHRQ	Agency for Healthcare Research and Quality
CCOHTA	Canadian Coordinating Office for Health Technology Assessment
CONSORT Trials	Consolidated Standards of Reporting
HMO	Health maintenance organization
HRQOL	Health-related quality of life
ISPOR	International Society for Pharmacoeconomics and Outcomes Research
NHS	National Health Service
NICE	National Institute for Clinical Excellence
P&T	Pharmacy and therapeutics
R&D	Research and development

Introduction to Health Policy

Defining Policy and Health Policy

Public Policy

Before making assertions as to how pharmacoeconomics can contribute to health policy decision making, it is important to have a good grounding in the concepts which underlie policy, in general, and health policy, specifically. Courses in health policy are not typical in the curricula of most health practitioners, which is unfortunate considering the impact of health policy activities on their day-to-day work. The discussion herein touches only the surface of this topic; and although some key reference sources are provided in the Annotated Bibliography and in Table 1, readers are encouraged to seek out additional sources (e.g., government, university, and health professional association Web sites) to expand their knowledge of this important influence on their practice environment.

For purposes of this discussion, the term *policy* is used in the sense of *public policy* (the terms are used interchangeably), the latter of which is defined as "a course of action or inaction chosen by public [government] authorities to address a given problem or interrelated set of problems." (The focus on public policies as developed by public authorities or governments is of note, as policies also can be developed by private organizations, which is discussed in this section.) Understanding the policy environment is important, as public policy is a key mechanism by which societies address the management of issues that affect the public at large.

Policies are not synonymous with decisions—a single decision on a given issue may or may not be part of a series of interrelated decisions intended to address a concern or a direction in which the organization wants to move. It is hoped that most of the decisions of public authorities are made within the context or framework of an overarching policy or approach that the government has chosen to take on a given issue; but that is not always the case.

As previously discussed, the policy process described in this chapter is the basis by which public authorities as well as many nonpublic organizations (i.e., private enterprise) approach issue management (i.e., a structured approach to analyzing and addressing a problem within their environment). The general but key difference between the public versus the nonpublic approach is the context and factors which the organization needs to take into consideration (i.e., investors and stockholders in the case of the private sector), and, even then, the differences blur into similarities in terms of pressures faced by the public versus private sector organization. For instance, both organizations have stakeholders who have an interest in ensuring the most return for their investment, whether that investment be financial in the case of the private sector, or trust through democratic and supporting bureaucratic processes on the public side.

The Policy Analysis and Development Process

Policy analysis and development is essentially a problem-solving process, which can be differentiated into a series of steps. However, it would be a mistake to assume that there is a cookbook approach to developing policy that applies to all situations, as each issue is truly different by virtue of the problem itself and the stakeholders involved. As a result, policy analysis and development process is iterative in nature, such that problem definition (for instance) must be revisited as new information becomes available or as new stakeholders become involved. Some general steps and principles for policy analysis and development are listed in Table 2.

Health Policy

Given this basis for defining public policy, it is time to turn to the definition of health policy. In its simplest terms, health policy is defined as the framework that guides the approach to a range of activities in the field of health care. The following definition of health care serves as the context for the definition of health policy within this chapter: "health care is larger than medical care and involves influences on the health of a population, including medical care, public health measures, and broad social policies that improve overall social well-being." Taking such a broad approach is important to good health policy development. Unnecessary limiting of the definition to, say, medical care alone ignores a significant body of knowledge regarding determinants of health that cannot be denied if rigorous health policy for the population at large is to be developed.

The differentiation between public and private policy can be quite blurred within the health policy environment. While the responsibility for overall health policy rests clearly with national and/or regional government organizations in some countries (e.g., Canada and United Kingdom), in other jurisdictions health policy decisions of private health care organizations (e.g., the managed care approach) have a huge impact on a significant proportion of the public and, thus, drive public health status and outcomes to a large extent (e.g., United States). This is not to say that one approach is preferable to another; rather it is to point out that, depending on the environment, policy makers need to look at both public and private organizations to determine the overall approach to health policy in a given jurisdiction.

Table 1. Key references on health policy and pharmacoeconomics

Formularies/Pharmacy and Therapeutics Committees

Hepler CD. Where is the evidence for formulary effectiveness? Am J Health-Syst Pharm 1997;54:95.

Laupacis A. Inclusion of drugs in provincial drug benefit programs: who is making these decisions, and are they the right ones [commentary]? CMAJ 2002;166(1):44-7.

Sanchez LA. Pharmacoeconomics and formulary decision making. Pharmacoeconomics 1996;9(suppl 1);16-25.

Sullivan SD, Lyles A, Luce B, Grigar J. AMCP guidance for submission of clinical and economic evaluation data to support formulary listing in US health plans and pharmacy benefit management organizations. J Managed Care Pharm 2001;7(4):272-82.

Health Policy–Basic References

Folland S, Goodman AC, Stano M. Government intervention in health care markets and an introduction to regulation. In: The economics of health and health care. New York, NY: Macmillan Publishing Company, 1993:565-97.

Hadorn DC. Setting health care priorities in Oregon–Costeffectiveness meets the rule of rescue. JAMA 1991;265(17):2218-25.

Hadorn DC. The role of public values in setting health care priorities. Soc Sci Med 1991;32(7):773-81.

Health Canada. Health Canada Decision-Making Framework for Identifying, Assessing and Managing Health Risks, August 2000. http://www.hcsc.gc.ca/hpb/transitn/hcrisk_e.pdf. Accessed June 27, 2002.

Pal LA. Public policy analysis–An introduction. 2nd ed. Scarborough: Nelson Canada, 1992.

Health Policy–Impact of Health Policy Tools for Pharmaceuticals

Horn SD, Sharkey PD, Tracy DM, et al. Intended and unintended consequences of HMO cost-containment strategies: results from the Managed Care Outcomes Project. Am J Manage Care 1996;2:253-64.

Schneeweiss S, Walker AM, Glynn RN, Maclure M, Dormuth C, Soumerai SB. Outcomes of reference-based pricing for angiotensin-converting-enzyme inhibitors. N Engl J Med 2002;346(11):822-9.

Soumerai SB, McLaughlin TJ, Ross-Degnan D, Casteris CS, Bollini P. Effects of a limit on Medicaid drug reimbursement benefits on the use of psychotropic agents and acute mental health services by patients with schizophrenia. N Engl J Med# 1994;331(10):6505.

Soumerai SB, Ross-Degnan D, Fortess EE, Abelson J. A critical analysis of studies of state drug reimbursement policies: research in need of discipline. Milbank Q 1993;71(2):217-50.

Pharmacoeconomics–Basic References

Bootman JL, Townsend RJ, McGhan WF, eds. Principles of pharmacoeconomics. Cincinnati: Harvey Whitney Books Company, 1998.

Canadian Coordinating Office for Health Technology Assessment (CCOHTA). Guidelines for economic evaluation of pharmaceuticals: Canada. 2nd ed. Ottawa: CCOHTA,1997. Available at http://www.ccohta.ca.

Drummond MF, O'Brien B, Stoddart GL, Torrance GW. Methods for the economic evaluation of health care programmes. 2nd ed. Oxford: Oxford University Press, 1997.

Hill SR, Mitchell AS, Henry DA. Problems with the interpretation of pharmacoeconomic analyses: a review of submissions to the Australian Pharmaceuticals Benefit Scheme. JAMA 2000;283(16):2116-21.

Knight W. Too much or too little? The role of pharmaceuticals in the health care system. J Managed Care Pharm 1999;5(4):296,297,301,302.

Laupacis A, Feeny D, Detsky AS, Tugwell PX. How attractive does a new technology have to be to warrant adoption and utilization? Tentative guidelines for using clinical and economic evaluations. CMAJ 1992;146(4):47381.

Sanchez LA, Lee JT. Applied pharmacoeconomics: Modeling data from internal and external sources. Am J Health-Syst Pharm 2000;57:146-58.

Table 2. General Steps and Principles for Policy Analysis and Development

1. Recognizing and defining the problem or issue to be addressed

• a key step in the policy process, as poor definition of the problem leads to solutions that do not have the intended impact

• helps to clearly state why a policy needs to be developed (or adjusted, if one already exists); thus, problem definition is closely linked to the goal of the policy itself (i.e., what the policy is trying to achieve)

• this, as well as all the subsequent steps, may require the involvement of stakeholders to clearly assess the scope of the problem and to reach mutually acceptable solutions that work

2. Analyzing the problem

• developing an in-depth understanding of the problem/issue, and clearly documenting both known and unknown aspects related to the problem itself and the implications of solving the problem or maintaining the status quo

• also includes outlining the information known about the context within which the problem exists (e.g., known factors, such as how the health care system is funded, epidemiology of a disease, cultural or ethical issues, and the views of various stakeholders on the issue)

3. Developing options

• defining a list of possible approaches for how the problem is going to be solved

• need to include the instruments or specific means by which each policy option could be implemented (e.g., legislation, voluntary compliance, and education)

• need to define the costs, benefits, and impacts (positive and negative) for each option proposed

4. Selecting an option

• the purview of the decision maker, on the advice of the policy analyst and the documentation/evidence provided

5. Implementing

• implementation of the chosen policy option/instrument, as well as the monitoring process to facilitate assessment of the intended and unintended impacts of the policy on the issue initially identified

• although communication is a key component throughout the policy development process, it is particularly important in the implementation phase

6. Monitoring the impact of the solution implemented

• this includes using the information gathered through a formal monitoring and evaluation process (i.e., continuous quality improvement tool) so as to adjust the policy if required (i.e., going back to step 1)

Table 3. Key stakeholders in the health policy environment

Nongovernmental organizations

• Patient advocacy groups (e.g., Diabetes Association, antipoverty groups, and Cancer Society)

• Health care professional organizations (e.g., medical, nursing, and pharmacist associations)

• Vocal health care "champions" (e.g., Michael Decter and Ralph Nader)

• General public

Private sector

• Health care industries (e.g., pharmaceutical industry and insurance industry)

• Private sector (e.g., employers and health care benefit management industry)

• Liberal or conservative "think tanks"/research organizations (e.g., Fraser Institute, Canadian Policy Research Network, and The Commonwealth Fund)

• Media (e.g., health care reporter specialists)

Government organizations

• Politicians (e.g., opposition parties versus party in power)

• Government bureaucracies (e.g., health departments versus other government departments with competing interests)

• Other governments (e.g., state, provincial, and local governments)

What Constitutes the Health Policy Environment?

As previously discussed, a key factor in the development of any public policy is the context within which that policy is developed. Overall, that context is determined by the range of stakeholders and the political environment (i.e., not only the political party in power, but also the conservative versus the liberal mood of the general public) that exists at the time that policy is being developed. In the case of health care, the emotionally charged nature of the subject matter and the wide range of stakeholders from both the public and private policy sectors, as well as the public at large, make the health policy environment a particularly complex one. Policy analysis in this environment is not an academic exercise and the stakes are high: real people and their being are impacted by health policy decisions.

Within the health policy environment of most jurisdictions with well-developed health care systems, some generalizations are possible in terms of the groups or individuals who can influence the policy development process. The three groups involved in health policy development tend to be nongovernmental organizations, private sector organizations, and government organizations. Table 3 outlines some examples of individuals and/or organizations within each of these categories. A good policy analyst makes it his/her business to understand the various needs and biases of these groups, including the policy analyst's own and those of the relevant decision makers.

Within the health care system, there are several levels of decision makers and policy makers, and it is important to understand these various levels and the interactions therein. In general, there are at least three levels: the overarching health policy environment, the health care system environment, and the point of health care delivery environment. Figure 1 represents the relationships among these levels within the overall health care system and health policy environment, and reinforces one of the fundamental concepts in policy analysis and development (i.e., the multiplicity of layers that need to be taken into consideration in developing good policy, depending on where within the system the policy is being developed).

To understand some of the dynamics among the groups in the health policy environment, some broad generalizations, in terms of the roles they play, can be drawn. However, these roles can vary depending on their positioning within the various levels of the health care system. For instance, within the health care system, bureaucrats play the role of policy maker and administrators play the role of decision maker when it comes to determining the best approach to addressing the budgetary priorities of an institution. However, in other parts of the system, the role of policy maker or decision maker may be shared. For instance, at the point of care delivery, health care professionals and patients are increasingly taking a partnership approach to making decisions on the best approach to care for a given individual, within the set of policies and structures set out by the policy environment and the system overall.

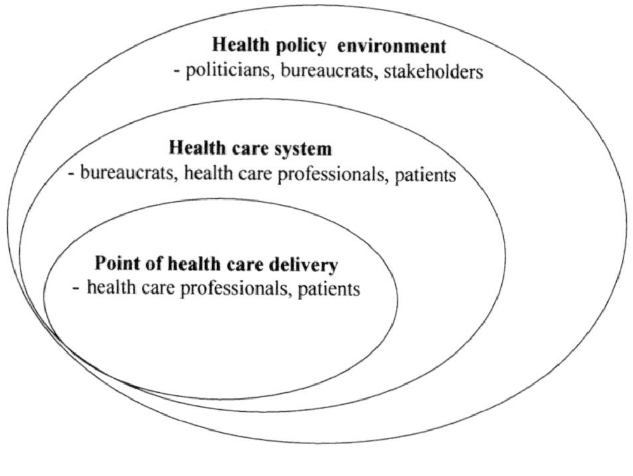

Figure 1. Relationships within the healthcare system.

In addition to the influence of the wide range of stakeholders involved, another factor which significantly influences the health policy environment is the general view held by most individuals in the Western world that health care is a human right. As such, considerable passion is generated in any discussions of changes or limits to that right. The introduction of a relatively intangible consideration to the policy environment creates additional challenges that need to be addressed both in the policy development process and in the final decision making process. These two features (i.e., stakeholders and the right to health care) introduce two significant factors that influence the manner in which health policy functions.

Applications of Health Policy

Provided later in the Use of Pharmacoeconomics in Policy Decision Making Section are specific examples of how pharmacoeconomics have been applied within the health policy environment. At a more general level, however, health policy initiatives (and the research and analysis that underpin them) have played a role in directly or indirectly affecting every aspect of the health care system, from front-line delivery of care to global approaches to funding the health care system, and the more fundamental, philosophical underpinnings of society's approach to health overall.

Health policy determines the respective roles and responsibilities of health care providers and how they differ from one jurisdiction to another (e.g., variation in the roles of midwives). It can determine the scope of services offered to patients (e.g., screening criteria for hepatitis B or C or familial hypercholesterolemia) and how the use of new ways of delivering service (e.g., telemedicine) is approached. Health policy defines how the funding of the system is addressed (i.e., through taxation versus private insurance versus out of pocket), who has access to the system, and whether society sees social and economic policy issues (e.g., unemployment and air pollution) as integral considerations in the development of a comprehensive health policy approach.

Thus, it is key that professionals in this field understand the basics of the policy environment that is part of the health care system overall. Although health care professionals may not deal with policy makers on a daily basis, these two parts of the system are inextricably linked; and an understanding of each other's environment is important for both good health policy and for good health care.

The Role of Pharmacoeconomics in the Health Policy Environment

Introduction

Although this section focuses on specifically addressing the role that pharmacoeconomic assessment can play in the overall health policy environment, it also is useful to demonstrate the linkage between such assessments and the policy development process discussed in the Introduction to Health Policy section (i.e., Table 2). Economic analyses can contribute to the deliberations in each step of the process, but they are particularly useful in developing and defining policy options in terms of transparently delineating the costs, benefits, and impacts of each of the options being considered. This linkage among steps of the policy development process and whether/what kind of an economic analysis may contribute is something that should be kept in mind as the reader proceeds through the remainder of this chapter.

The Goals in Bringing Discipline to Health Policy Decisions

Pharmacoeconomics certainly is more than just a tool to be used occasionally in the health policy environment. Indeed, it brings discipline to the entire decision making process. Accompanying this discipline is the strong and justifiable methodology of well-designed pharmacoeconomic evaluations. Overall, there are several goals of the economic evaluation of pharmaceuticals within the context of the health policy environment, four of which are presented below and discussed further in The Use of Pharmacoeconomics in Policy Decision Making section.

First, pharmacoeconomics encourages decision making on the basis of costs and outcomes, rather than costs alone. Outcomes data are seldom easy to collect, and, as a result, they are infrequently measured and typically bypassed in the policy development stages. Nonetheless, the importance of including outcomes data in the decision making process is clear. Some authors have argued that the first objective for health plans is to determine which health outcomes should be achieved, after which the focus should be on the cost of achieving those outcomes. Pharmacoeconomics, therefore, provides a vehicle by which both outcomes and cost data can be used together in both the planning and evaluation stages of health policy.

Second, pharmacoeconomics can help purchasing authorities set priorities. As previously discussed, the preferred outcomes of health policies and programs can be weighed in the context of their expected costs. Still, pharmacoeconomics is only one of several factors that should be used in helping to set priorities. Societal needs and the political environment also must be considered. In addition, deeper philosophical issues about medical ethics and intended objectives of health interventions are paramount. For example, even if lifestyle drugs have value in pharmacoeconomic models, their use begs the larger question of whether we are attempting to make society more homogeneous.

Third, pharmacoeconomics can help providers choose the most cost-effective treatment modality available for use. Information of this type may come in the form of published studies or in-house evaluations performed by health care organizations. The availability of published pharmacoeconomic evaluations that assess the cost-effectiveness of various treatments has rapidly increased in recent years. Organizations such as the National Institute for Clinical Excellence (NICE) in the United Kingdom are assisting decision makers by providing education on how to interpret pharmacoeconomic evaluations and by performing cost-effectiveness evaluations and compiling study abstracts that are available for free on the Internet. (The NICE and other organizations involved in producing pharmacoeconomic evaluations are discussed further in The Use of Pharmacoeconomics in Policy Decision Making section.)

Fourth, pharmacoeconomics also could help to establish cost-effective policies. However, there currently there exists a shortage of studies that document the cost-effectiveness of many of the principal approaches to health care today, including evaluations of total quality management, evidence-based medicine, performance measurement, and others. In the discussion of a proposed model of economic analyses of health policies, it has been argued that health policy cost-effectiveness is always less attractive than treatment cost-effectiveness. This may be why, to date, pharmacoeconomics has been used less frequently to evaluate policies rather than treatments. Nevertheless, given the promise of pharmacoeconomics in policy evaluation and advances in technology, this could soon change. For example, when used in combination with electronic physician prescribing systems, pharmacoeconomic information may contribute to more cost-effective prescribing, better adherence to preferred practice guidelines, and improved collection of data for postmarketing surveillance.

Pharmacoeconomics and the Formulary Environment

Several factors within the health care environment have caused many decision makers to turn to pharmacoeconomics to inform drug therapy policy decisions. One force driving this change is the large increase in prescription drug expenditures, both in total dollars and as a proportion of total health care costs. In the United States, drug-related expenditures are increasing 12–18 percent per year in most managed care plans, and controlling this rate of increase has become a critical focus for plan managers. This trend is not limited to the United States; other Western countries also are facing large increases in drug costs. For example, in Canada, prescription drugs are now the second largest health care expenditure after hospitals. In some health systems, educating the board of directors about this dramatic rise in drug costs is a major focus of the pharmacy department's efforts. Other factors driving the need for pharmacoeconomics includes the rise in the number of alternative therapies available in most drug classes; the growth of managed care in the United States and its emphasis on the efficient allocation of resources; and an increasing demand for program and product evaluation.

Yet, a majority of formulary decision makers still have not truly incorporated pharmacoeconomic considerations into their decision making processes. A recent article discussed the importance of factors in the decision making process in a survey of drug benefit decision makers. Efficacy and safety tied as being the most important factors weighed, followed by cost, pharmacoeconomics, health-related quality of life (HRQOL) effects of the drug, and physician demand for the drug. Moreover, in another survey of formulary decision makers, 83.8 percent of respondents reported that a pharmacoeconomist was not a member of the formulary or pharmacy and therapeutics (P&T) committee.

The structure and function of most P&T committees has changed considerably in recent years. Originally, a majority of these committees functioned in the inpatient setting and primarily consisted of physicians and the director of pharmacy services. An article based on three recent surveys provides a good overview of the current state of formulary committees. This article states that it was found that the mean size of P&T committees is 13 members, with typical participants including the medical director, physicians, the pharmacy director, drug information officer, nurses, use review specialists, risk management specialists, and others. The three types of individuals cited as being the most likely to be added to P&T committees within the next 2 years were a pharmacoeconomist, patient privacy/compliance officer, and information technology/informatics specialist. Activities that are a responsibility of a majority of P& T committees, as reported by the survey respondents, include: report/monitor adverse drug reactions and drug errors, make formulary inclusion/reimbursement decisions, develop/review treatment guidelines and protocols, develop drug use policies and procedures to meet regulatory/accreditation standards, conduct or approve drug use evaluations, provide drug use education programs for professional staff, and evaluate short-term medical savings for drugs under formulary review. To help prevent inappropriate prescribing patterns, some formulary committees are now attempting to proactively review new drugs rather than reactively reviewing them after a request from a physician or a pharmaceutical company.

Pharmacoeconomics has an important role in the evaluation of drug benefit management policies. Drug formularies are an effective tool to lower drug expenditures, but a 1996 study observed that managed care organizations with more restrictive drug formularies had higher overall health care costs. Although the study was widely criticized, other researchers also have concluded that the impact of drug formularies on overall health care costs cannot be determined with certainty at this time. Given that drug formularies are almost universally accepted as an important drug benefit management tool to help educate prescribers and direct appropriate use, it seems that evaluations are warranted. Pharmacoeconomic evaluations, which can provide the broad health system perspective needed for these evaluations, appear to have a significant potential role.

The Global Emergence of Pharmacoeconomic Guidelines

A Brief History of Pharmacoeconomic Guidelines

Australia has been a world leader in the development and health policy application of pharmacoeconomic guidelines and studies. It was the first country to develop and implement guidelines for the economic evaluation of pharmaceuticals, with a draft first released in 1990. Multiple revisions have been carried out since that time on the basis of increasing experience, as well as developments in the art and science of economic evaluations in a health care setting.

The Australian guidelines strongly influenced the move to examine potential uses of pharmacoeconomic evaluations in the Canadian health care sector, with the introduction of the draft Ontario guidelines for comment in the fall of 1991. Shortly thereafter, the Canadian Collaborative Workshop on Pharmacoeconomics was held with the goal of developing a set of Canadian guidelines that each province could adopt, with or without modifications, as they saw fit. Thus, the first edition of the Guidelines for Economic Evaluation of Pharmaceuticals: Canada was published in 1994, with an update published in 1997.

Initially, extramural projects contracted by the Canadian Coordinating Office for Health Technology Assessment (CCOHTA) required that the guidelines be used as a framework for the economic assessment portion of the research. This then expanded to the point where several provinces either mandated (e.g., Ontario and British Columbia) or strongly recommended that pharmaceutical manufacturers include with their formulary submissions the results of pharmacoeconomic evaluations based on the principles set out in the Canadian or Ontario guidelines. The same eventually became true of several private drug plan insurers and health care institutions, to facilitate formulary decision making.

Since these initial forays into guideline development, there has been an explosion of pharmacoeconomic research as well as the use of information from pharmacoeconomic studies. This has led to a wide variety of both public and private sector organizations around the world to publish their own policy statements and/or guidance documents on pharmacoeconomic analysis (see discussion in the Overview of the Pharmacoeconomic Guidelines Available section).

The Purpose of Guidelines and Pharmacoeconomic Studies

Pharmacoeconomic guidelines are usually developed to facilitate study design or to provide approaches for reporting to decision making bodies. Because pharmacoeconomic evaluation is simply a specific type of economic evaluation, such guidelines are often useful in other kinds of process as well as health care intervention evaluations and may contribute to the overall movement toward disease management in health care.

The purpose of health economic methods and studies also includes helping to inform policy decisions at a program (as opposed to total population) level regarding the appropriateness and availability of health care interventions, including drugs. Results of such programmatic decision making (e.g., formulary listings and clinical practice guidelines) often impact decision making for individual patients; but economic evaluations themselves are not usually targeted for use in bedside decision making.

It is important that decision makers recognize and use these studies for their intended purpose, and not look to pharmacoeconomic studies as a means to avoid making a decision. Studies do not provide a cookbook answer to difficult programmatic issues; and they cannot replace the careful consideration of data, the use of judgment, and the ultimate accountability of decision makers. Pharmacoeconomic evaluations provide additional input into the decision making process; and, in some cases, the comprehensive nature of the information may make that process more complex. The ultimate goal, however, is to ensure that the decision-maker has access to all the relevant information available to make an informed decision.

Overview of the Pharmacoeconomic Guidelines Available

This section provides a summary of some of the key pharmacoeconomics guidelines and their development throughout the past decade or so. The fundamental purpose of each of these guidelines is to facilitate overall policy decision making by providing a framework for both the submission of information as well as some standards by which the information should be assessed. In addition, the guidelines have evolved over time from being methodologic documents to becoming policies in and of themselves; and research is starting to appear related to evaluation of their impact on policy decisions to accompany this evolution. This latter subject is discussed briefly below, as well as in The Use of Pharmacoeconomics in Policy decision making section.

A recent review of the literature identified at least 25 formalized, informal, and/or health economic methods guideline documents in use around the world today. Academics, government commissions, professional organizations such as the International Society for Pharmacoeconomics and Outcomes Research (ISPOR), and many individual corporations (e.g., health maintenance organizations [HMOs]) and jurisdictions have developed guidelines to facilitate research and decision making using health economic methods and information. The boom in guidelines has been accompanied by a huge increase in research in developing and/or refining pharmacoeconomic methods and an increase in the volume of studies published.

There also has been an increase in attempts to use this information in a variety of decision making processes. The linkages are clear between the pharmacoeconomic guidelines developed and the requirements of the formulary decision making process for jurisdictions such as Canada (e.g., British Columbia and Ontario) and Australia; and for health maintenance organizations, as represented by guidelines from the Academy of Managed Care Pharmacy. The following sections outline some features and limitations associated with a few of the guidelines available; but readers should refer to the Annotated Bibliography for the most comprehensive assessment and level of detail. It also should be noted that over and above applying guidelines, some jurisdictions have started to evaluate the impact of pharmacoeconomic inputs on the formulary decision process, and others have begun to assess the impact of their policy decisions on patient and health system outcomes (see discussion in The Use of Pharmacoeconomics in Policy Decision Making section).

The Canadian Guidelines

The second edition of the Canadian guidelines was developed with the intent of providing assistance to those carrying out analyses, for the purposes of providing standardized and reliable information for their audience. Emphasis was placed on providing direction in areas where there was methodologic agreement and key areas where significant developments in theory and/or methodology had been made were explored in some depth. The guideline authors underscored two additional principles for the revised guidelines: there was significance placed on the guidelines remaining a guidance document; and they were written to be less prescriptive and provide information and advice in areas of controversy, but more prescriptive with sound direction in areas of general agreement. The CCOHTA Guidance Document for the Costing Process is an important partner document to the Canadian guidelines.

The CCOHTA has evaluated the extent to which submissions in response to its requests for proposals adhered to the Canadian guidelines. The study looked at the 2-year period (1995–1996) immediately after the publication of the first edition of the guidelines. Although the studies were found to be of variable quality, the majority were well presented, complete, and transparent, characteristics which were thought to be due in part to the guidelines.

One of the issues not addressed in the Canadian guidelines is their specific impact on the pharmaceutical industry. There are two sides to this issue: although economic evaluations are evolving as an additional information requirement (particularly at the provincial level) for firms to address, there also are potential benefits to this additional information from the perspective of decision makers. The pharmaceutical industry is grappling with the practical problems of funding and modifying clinical trials to collect economic data, while decision makers are striving to determine the impact of these pharmacoeconomic evaluations and related decision making within the Canadian health care system as a whole.

The British Columbia Approach

In British Columbia, clinical and economic assessments are carried out in parallel by two expert advisory groups (i.e., the Therapeutics Initiative and the Pharmacoeconomic Initiative of British Columbia), with the latter essentially applying the principles espoused in the Canadian guidelines.

Researchers have carried out assessments of economic evaluations which accompanied formulary listing submissions to the British Columbia Pharmacare program. Problems in compliance with the CCOHTA and/or Ontario guidelines have focused on areas such as missing sensitivity analysis and inappropriate comparators. Guideline conformance has consistently been associated with a greater likelihood of formulary listing, although the authors have suggested that the pharmaceutical industry may "be skeptical about the importance of cost-effectiveness and guideline compliance in decision-making."

The Australian Guidelines

As previously discussed, the Australians have the greatest experience in terms of development and application of pharmacoeconomic guidelines within the public health care sector, with a well established regulatory role for pharmacoeconomics in their pharmaceuticals program. A 1997 audit of the Australian Pharmaceuticals Benefit Scheme noted Australia's leadership in pharmacoeconomics and reimbursement strategies and the contribution this has made to the administrative effectiveness of the listing process. The national auditor also noted the role of guidelines in improving the quality of sponsors' submissions and the usefulness of the information therein. But the variability in quality noted in other jurisdictions plagues Australia as well. At the time of the audit, the Australian approach focused heavily on cost-effectiveness analysis and suggestions were made to shift to a method which would provide a basis for comparison of the value to the health system of drugs addressing different indications or medical problems. (Australia has since shifted its approach to accept cost-benefit and/or utility analyses under certain circumstances; however, the inclusion of indirect costs remains a point of contention.)

Barriers to the Effective Use of Pharmacoeconomics and the Guidelines

Some have argued that pharmacoeconomic information and the guidelines that are supposed to frame the generation of that information have not been used as effectively as they could be within the decision making process. There are many interrelated factors underlying this problem; and errors have been made on both the supply side (i.e., researchers and industry) and the demand side (i.e., policy makers and decision makers) in introducing pharmacoeconomics to the decision making process. This has resulted in what appears to be a flurry of activity without a stated sense of purpose. (The challenges associated with incorporating pharmacoeconomics into the health policy decision process are discussed in more depth in the Challenges in the Use of Pharmacoeconomic Studies by Health Policy Decision Makers section.)

On the demand side, pharmacoeconomic information has moved rapidly into the decision making realm. Unfortunately, decision makers have not planned the means by which they will assess and use the information provided, let alone the weight that this information should carry in the overall decision making process—or at least many have not done so in a manner that is transparent to those generating the information. Questions also have been raised as to whether decision makers have the skill sets to use pharmacoeconomic guidelines and the studies generated in an effective manner. The need for training arises as a recurring theme in the literature around this subject. Gaps in the transparency of the use of pharmacoeconomic guidelines (and, thereby, pharmacoeconomic studies) combined with the pressure to somehow use health economic information in an environment where there also is pressure to contain costs creates an environment of uncertainty for all parties. This reinforces the need for greater understanding of how decision makers use pharmacoeconomic information and guidelines in their decision processes, as well as the need for transparency in the rationale for decisions.

On the supply side, there are an equal number of problems in terms of the quality of pharmacoeconomic studies from both a design and data perspective. Although there have been improvements, problems in the quality of some studies can make decision makers question the validity of all studies, and a vicious cycle is created. Study relevance (as not every product necessarily requires a full economic assessment), the adequacy of input data, the relevance of the assumptions made, and other methodologic issues continue to be problems in many pharmacoeconomic studies.

A disconnect in expectations between doers and users is certainly a factor in this environment. Many in industry have a desire for consistent decision patterns and voice frustration when they perceive inconsistencies in decision makers' interpretations of pharmacoeconomic studies which they say undermine efforts in enhancing the profile of health economic units within their organizations. On the other hand, decision makers indicate their need for flexibility in using the information provided through economic assessments, as they interpret the clinical impact and "value" of a product on the basis of the population they serve, local practice and health care support service patterns (e.g., homecare), and the blunt reality of the resources that they have available to them. These differences in expectations of what studies can or should accomplish give rise to frustrations on the extent to which pharmacoeconomic studies are having their intended impact in improving the basis for decision making within the health care system. Some jurisdictions have started to publish data which get to the core of this issue.

There are potential solutions to all of the problems previously discussed, one of which is addressing the need for some fundamental research on decision making processes within the pharmaceutical policy environment. Understanding the barriers previously discussed and working collaboratively through frank, multilateral (i.e., consumers, industry, governments, hospitals, and third-party payers) discussions will help develop a long-term and cooperative approach to using pharmacoeconomic information effectively within the health policy environment.

The Use of Pharmacoeconomics in Policy Decision Making

Applications of Pharmacoeconomics

The variety of applications of pharmacoeconomic studies was discussed earlier. One of the chief concerns in the current health policy environment is the rate of increase as well as the absolute level of costs associated with the health care system. Many policies have been introduced with the goal of containing (if not reducing) health care costs, and drug expenditures in both the hospital and outpatient setting have been a particular target as the rate of rise in this category of expenditures has typically outpaced most other components of health care costs.

It is in this context of cost-containment that both public and private health care payers have looked to pharmacoeconomics as the shining path to decreasing drug expenditures. Despite warnings to the contrary, some policy makers have created unrealistic expectations of the role of economic analysis in the health care decision making processes. Far too frequently, both decision makers and industry alike expect pharmacoeconomic evaluations to provide answers to the challenging policy choices and trade-offs that must be made in the limited resource environment of the health care system. However, the role of pharmacoeconomics is merely to make transparent the data and relationships therein which must be considered in making choices. decision makers still need to make the decision based on additional contextual factors (i.e., ethical, political, and cultural considerations) that may impact on the policy issue at hand.

Notwithstanding the development of frameworks with which to interpret economic evaluations and identify additional information needs to support sound decision making, decision makers still have yet to shift their perception of economic assessments (i.e., from providing them with the answers to providing them with information to facilitate their decisions). Ironically, it has been suggested that, if an incremental cost-effectiveness approach is used as the basis for determining what will and will not be covered by a drug plan, by definition, plan costs will increase as cost-effective drugs are added to the formulary unless commensurate decreases are achieved by removing drugs that are not cost-effective. Other authors have raised similar concerns regarding the impact of successive decisions based on cost-utility methods in creating inefficient drug formularies that deliver suboptimal health benefits per dollar of expenditure.

Another concern related to the cost-containment application of pharmacoeconomics is the potential for unintended negative consequences on health outcomes and health expenditures. This means a commitment to evaluating microlevel outcomes (i.e., clinical and economic outcomes) associated with policy decisions that use pharmacoeconomic evaluations as part of an informed decision process (see British Columbia example in the Experiences Using Economic Evaluation in Health Policy section). A structured approach to evaluating drug benefit changes has been proposed, applying principles of observational research and the use of administrative databases in their assessment of the impact of reference-based pricing of angiotensin-converting enzyme inhibitors. These microlevel measurements are arguably more relevant to prescribers, drug plan managers, and patients and, although a challenge, may facilitate the appropriate use of economic evaluations into the decision making process.

Organizations Using Pharmacoeconomics

It is beyond the scope of this chapter to provide a complete inventory of all the organizations using pharmacoeconomic information in their policy and decision making processes. It is worthwhile to note some major organizations that are somewhat representative within the health policy environment, as a means of demonstrating the application of pharmacoeconomics as a tool.

In the United States, a variety of public authorities as well as private sector organizations pursue pharmacoeconomic studies in both the research context as well as the policy context. The Agency for Healthcare Research and Quality (AHRQ) spearheads a variety of research programs related to patient outcomes associated with pharmaceutical therapy, with the goal of understanding which agents work for which patients and at what costs. The role of pharmacoeconomics in HMOs, the Academy of Managed Care Pharmacy, academia, and health care institutions previously have been discussed.

The NICE, a government agency in the United Kingdom, is mandated with (among other things) providing the National Health Service (NHS) with advice on/appraisals of individual technologies based on rigorous analysis of available evidence on clinical effectiveness as well as cost-effectiveness. The usefulness of NICE's work, its impact on the health care system, and the system's ability to implement the advice generated have been questioned; as has the effect of pressure from lobby groups on NICE's evaluations, decisions, and/or its implementation. The issue of transparency (as discussed in The Global Emergence of Pharmacoeconomic Guidelines section) also has been a challenge for NICE, as some consumer organizations have called for the organization to be more explicit and open about how it arrives at decisions on whether drugs should be funded by the health service.

The CCOHTA is a nongovernmental organization funded by federal, provincial, and territorial governments to provide these governments with information about and assessments of a variety of health technology, including pharmaceuticals. For instance, a recent technology overview published by CCOHTA provided an economic analysis of two new products for rheumatoid and osteoarthritis. This information would then be used by a variety of federal, provincial, and territorial organizations (e.g., provincial Pharmacare committees and public health units) to address their decision making needs.

As previously discussed, pharmacoeconomic assessments play a key role in drug reimbursement decision making within the Australian health care system. The Australian approach sees an amalgamation of clinical and economic evaluation processes into an overall decision process. Problems with the validity of the methods used or the data input into those methods (e.g., assumptions and estimates) have been issues, which, in turn, can undermine the policy application of such studies in the decision making process. Despite these challenges in obtaining quality inputs into their policy process, the Australians remain committed to the application of pharmacoeconomics within their pharmaceutical benefits scheme.

Experiences Using Economic Evaluation in Health Policy

One of the more comprehensive experiences in using economic analysis as part of the health care resource allocation process was that undertaken by the state of

Oregon under its Basic Health Services Act of 1989. In an attempt to expand medical services to a broader population within the state and to support this expansion through rationalizing services to all Medicaid recipients, the state of Oregon developed a priority list of services. The list was based on assessments of the degree of improvement in quantity and quality of life that a given treatment was expected to produce per dollar expenditure (i.e., fundamentally, a cost-effectiveness league table). The list generated through this process resulted in what were thought to be strange conclusions (i.e., it seemed to favor minor treatments over life-saving treatments), reflecting less a problem with economic methods and more a conflict between the results using those methods and the desire to save lives. The process also introduced both positive and negative ethical considerations in terms of the population's access to needed health care services.

What the Oregon experience demonstrates most profoundly is the concept previously discussed: economic analysis can only inform decision making—it cannot replace it. Thus, the introduction of cost-effectiveness information can help to bring clarity to the relative impact of different health care interventions in terms of both costs and clinical outcome benefits; but judgment must still play a role in the decision making process, in terms of doing what makes sense and what is ethical in terms of delivery of health care services to the population at large. The experience also points out the significant influence that public input can and should have on decision makers, a fact particularly relevant to pharmaceutical resource allocation decisions.

As with the Oregon experiment, the issue of judgment and the need for decision makers to understand potential biases introduced by and limitations of economic methods has been demonstrated in an assessment of a home hemophilia treatment program. The authors developed a model which compared a pediatric and a young adult cohort, and compared productivity, societal return, and quality-adjusted life-years among other parameters. The pediatric cohort was favored in the cost-effectiveness analysis on the basis of longer survival and higher quality of life per year, whereas the young adult cohort was favored in the cost-benefit analysis on the basis of increased productivity and less impact of discounting. Decision makers need to be aware of the potential for introduction of such systematic biases, so that prioritization exercises like that in Oregon are not undermined by inappropriate use of information.

Over and above the need to assess the use of pharmacoeconomic information in the policy process, there also is a need to evaluate the longer term impacts of such policy decisions on the health system itself. A classic example of a policy decision that should have had some economic assessment as input from the beginning was the decision of the New Hampshire government to introduce a prescription payment limit for psychotropic drugs in noninstitutionalized patients with schizophrenia. The impact of this policy was evaluated and found not only an increase in the use of acute mental health services (let alone the pain and suffering on the part of patients), but also the estimated average increase in mental health care costs per patient during the cap ($1530) exceeded the savings in drug costs to Medicaid by a factor of 17. Despite the absence of an evidence-based approach in the initial decision making process, the evaluation of this natural experiment provided data sufficient to demonstrate to policy makers that the costs far outweighed any expected benefits.

In a similar vein of evaluating the impact of drug policy decisions, the impact of the reference-based pricing policy (based on the assumption of a class effect and, thereby, a cost-minimization analysis) introduced by the Government of British Columbia (as a means of containing the costs associated with angiotensin-converting enzyme inhibitors) was assessed. Through the use of administrative databases, the authors determined that there were no significant related changes in the rates of physician visits, hospitalizations, long-term care admissions, or mortality in the patient group affected. The importance of assessing offsetting changes in the use of other health care interventions due to significant health policy decisions cannot be overstated.

Systematic policy or program evaluation is more rare than common in the public policy environment, so jurisdictions which follow this path should be applauded for recognizing the importance of ensuring that their policy decisions are assessed for both the intended as well as unintended effects that may occur after implementation. The question of whether such evaluations will consistently result in adjustments to public policy is a question that remains mostly unanswered.

Application of Pharmacoeconomic Methodologies in the Health Policy Environment

The Rationale for Using Pharmacoeconomics

To determine the applicability of various pharmacoeconomic methodologies to the health policy environment, it is important to go back to first principles to reiterate the purpose of economic evaluations and their role in the decision making process.

Pharmacoeconomics involves the application of economic evaluation methodologies, originally developed in the context of health care programs, to interventions involving pharmaceutical products. By definition, in a full economic evaluation (i.e., cost-minimization, cost-effectiveness, cost-benefit, or cost-utility analysis) comparisons of costs and consequences are made so as to make choices between one pharmaceutical product and its relevant alternatives (including, in some cases, no treatment).

Partial economic evaluations also can provide the decision maker with important preliminary information in terms of the characteristics of a single agent and the costs associated with it (i.e., cost-outcome description) or the comparative monetary costs of using one agent versus another (i.e., cost-analysis). The absence of a comparator and information about consequences, respectively, limit the contribution of these partial analyses to making a fully informed decision. Cost-of-illness studies also can be valuable in terms of providing a good understanding of the natural course of a disease, and in creating a good basis for future pharmacoeconomic studies. However, none of these partial analyses are discussed here in detail.

But why are these comparisons necessary? If there were unlimited resources available for health care spending, there would be no need for pharmacoeconomic studies. However, the reality is that choices must be made because resources are limited and inadequate to support all treatments that might demonstrate efficacy in clinical trials. A choice for one effective treatment means that some other effective therapy cannot be listed; and the benefit that might have been achieved with this latter treatment is the opportunity cost of the former (i.e., the opportunity cost associated with rejecting the second effective treatment). That is what pharmacoeconomics is all about—explicitly documenting and comparing the benefits and costs of drug products so that decision makers can use this information in identifying treatments which may be more worthy of listing than others, such that the overall benefit to the population is maximized (i.e., the opportunity costs incurred are minimized) with the resources available.

In general, the most common application of pharmacoeconomics in the policy environment has been in making decisions on whether to list a product, be it in the context of a fairly self-contained hospital or HMO formulary or in the context of reimbursement for a product on a major public or private drug plan. There also have been population/public health applications of such analyses, usually in the context of making decisions regarding different immunization strategies and their subsequent funding. A less common application of these methods (or at least so it appears in the published literature) has been in the context of decisions to delist products. This reluctance to use pharmacoeconomic information for the purposes of delisting has been predicted in the literature, although in the context of an environment with limited resources (such as health care) such an application of these methods seems to be a natural outcome.

In addition to the formulary environment, there are a variety of other decision making situations where pharmacoeconomic studies can play a useful role within the health care system. Although less frequently reported in the literature, these methods can be applied to pharmaceutical industry research and development (R&D) processes (e.g., in identifying promising areas for R&D investment, in making "go"/"no go" decisions at critical points in a product's development); to pricing decisions by both industry and/or regulators; in the development of options within clinical practice guidelines; and in the postapproval environment (i.e., in monitoring real-life drug performance and shifting from efficacy to effectiveness-based measures of clinical outcomes and costs).

It is particularly in this context of applying pharmacoeconomics in the postmarketing setting that the limitations of pharmacoeconomic studies based on clinical/efficacy trials must be emphasized. Decision makers cannot forget that the majority of economic evaluations tends to be severely limited in their generalizability to the population at large, as well as their predictive validity in terms of cost-savings and the level of clinical improvements that can actually be achieved. Health policy research initiatives which provide population-based data for both baseline analysis and long-term outcomes/effectiveness assessments can only help to improve the confidence with which decision makers use pharmacoeconomic assessments in the future.

What Method and When?

Previous chapters have already reviewed in depth the basic analytic methods available for carrying out pharmacoeconomic assessments. In terms of policy decisions, the application of these instruments can depend on many factors, such as the question being asked by the policy-maker, the clinical comparability of the products in question, and the potential scope of use of the product(s). Table 4 describes these factors in further detail and

Table 4. Factors affecting the choice of applicable pharmacoeconomic method

Policy-maker questions

- Should I fund?
- Should I fund but restrict access?
- What is my perspective for making the funding decision (i.e., societal, individual patient, range of methods from cost-minimization to cost-utility, depending on perspective)?
- Am I interested in focussing on my own budget (i.e., silo approach), or am I willing to take a more horizontal approach to realizing benefits and costs (i.e., savings accruing across the department, government, or to society overall)?

Comparability of products

- Breakthrough product where no previous therapy existed (need for cost-of-illness analysis [i.e., "no treatment" comparator] as well as cost-effectiveness analysis)
- Many similar products for the treatment of the same disease (cost-minimization or cost-effectiveness analysis may apply, depending on the degree of difference in the outcomes associated with therapy)

Scope of product use

- Single, focused therapeutic application versus multiple potential applications; for instance, a biotechnology product designed only the treatment of multiple sclerosis versus a product that has application for the treatment of rheumatoid arthritis, Crohn's disease, and other immunologic disorders (the latter may require a cost-utility approach to capture the multiple clinical outcomes) proposes possible methodologies which might be applicable.

Table 5 provides an outline of the four types of analyses and examples of the policy scenarios where they might be used. (Additional examples are available throughout the text of this book.) Up until a few years ago, the cost-minimization approach represented the classic method by which choices between products were made; that is, a simple comparison among agents used for the same condition in terms of the cost of a course of treatment—only slightly more sophisticated than the previous approach of comparing unit prices of new versus old products. Although still a valid methodology in some cases, assumptions of equivalency in terms of all consequences (i.e., benefits and risks) of treatment will become increasingly difficult to justify with the more novel therapies coming to market.

Cost-benefit analysis, although a theoretically attractive approach, is still limited in its application within the health care sphere. A great deal of research has been published on contingent valuation/willingness to pay and other methodologies for cost-benefit assessments, but there is just as much discussion in the literature as to the validity and generalizability of this approach. Cost-utility analyses also have experienced some limits to their application in the health policy environment. To some extent, this is related to a lack of understanding by decision makers of the theories and methods which underlie HRQOL assessment. Decision makers in some jurisdictions have been hesitant to consider and/or pay for many drugs whose main impact is on HRQOL, although this trend may be shifting. In addition, however, some of the limitations have resulted from the inappropriate application of these methods in clinical studies that has ultimately undermined the credibility of these outcome measures in the eyes of health policy makers.

A given situation may call for more than one type of evaluation, as each method may provide a different aspect of the value of one product over another. For instance, a cost-effectiveness analysis which focuses on strictly objective clinical differences between two products for treating angina may not provide the same level of information as a cost-utility analysis of the same two products which introduces the differences in the side effect profile as reflected through the HRQOL/utility assessment. It is conceivable that the results of these analyses may demonstrate different relative results and, thus, a different policy might be pursued depending on the perspective taken by and inherent value system of the decision maker.

Finally, in a health policy context the range of pre-existing pharmacoeconomic information can range from no study (wherein the analyst might have to develop his/her own model), a single study (wherein the discussions above would apply), to a group of studies that needs to be synthesized in some manner. Methods have

Table 5. Application of pharmacoeconomic methods in different policy scenarios

METHOD	POLICY SCENARIO
Cost-minimization	**"Me-too" drugs** • All clinical outcomes (i.e., benefits and adverse events) are virtually identical between the two products such that only the cost differences (i.e., all aspects of treatment costs) to achieve that clinical outcome are taken into consideration • The decision is based on the least cost alternative
Cost-effectiveness	**Different drugs for the treatment of diastolic hypertension** • The outcome of interest is similar to all drugs being compared (i.e., decreasing blood pressure and related long-term outcomes), but the extent to which each product achieves that goal differs (i.e., clinical impact differences) • Assessment of costs per unit of effect allow for a congruent unit of comparison, such that the policy decision can be made as to which product is least expensive for the amount of clinical benefit gained
Cost-benefit	**Different treatments for different diseases** • Allows for comparison of disparate treatment scenarios (i.e., comparison of appendectomy to antianginal therapy) • Results in a common denominator (i.e., costs) that allows for such comparisons • Assumes that a dollar value can be attached to the effects derived from the interventions • Theoretically provides information on the absolute benefit of the intervention, in addition to information on the relative performance
Cost-utility	**Different utilities assigned to the outcomes of different treatments and/or disease states** • Value is assessed in terms of the preferences that individuals or society has for a given health state/outcome • Allows for health-related quality of life adjustments for treatment outcomes • Results in a common denominator (e.g., QALYs) that allows for comparisons of costs and outcomes of different treatments (expressed as cost per QALY gained)

QALY = quality-adjusted life year.

been proposed to summarize economic evaluations found in systematic reviews of health care interventions. This is increasingly a challenge, as there have been no standardized methods developed for carrying out systematic reviews of such data, as have been developed for systematic reviews of clinical trials. Although not yet vetted in the health economic community, the proposed approach is helpful in organizing and summarizing the information available in a coherent manner.

Challenges in the Use of Pharmacoeconomic Studies by Health Policy Decision Makers

Introduction

Note that in The Global Emergence of Pharmacoeconomic guidelines section, the barriers to the effective use of pharmacoeconomics were discussed, mainly in the context of the guidelines that have been developed to support the generation of rigorous economic analyses. In this section, the broader challenges of using pharmacoeconomic studies in the policy decision making environment are examined.

Challenges in Research/Knowledge Transfer

One of the major challenges facing pharmacoeconomics today is the ability (or lack thereof) to bring together the two principal stakeholders: the pharmacoeconomic researchers and the policy decision makers. Although pharmacoeconomic evaluations have progressed in rigor and in availability to the end users, their uptake by these same users remains suboptimal.

A good starting place in addressing this challenge is to ask what types of pharmacoeconomic evaluations formulary decision makers desire? This question was addressed in a survey of 409 formulary decision makers and the top five desired changes (in descending order of importance) in pharmacoeconomic evaluations were: conduct more head-to-head comparisons of competing drugs, make studies independent of drug manufacturer funding, conduct more studies in typical clinical practice patient populations, make study reports easier to understand, and encourage researchers to fully disclose study methods.

Unfortunately, many pharmacoeconomic researchers continue to work in isolation and produce research on the basis of what decision makers should be doing. This issue revolves around relevance: there exists a disconnect between what decision makers see as relevant versus the information that researchers perceive as relevant, thus undermining the goals of informed decision making and a better health care system. Pharmacoeconomics is both an art and a science and applying the science requires considerable prudence and professional judgment. To overcome the problems of relevance, some experts suggest modeling data from both internal and external sources. It is argued that this allows for the creation of results that are more specific to the organization in question.

Not all the blame can be placed on the shoulders of the researchers. Many health care decision makers do not want pharmacoeconomic evaluations of their policies performed. Health policies frequently are implemented without evaluation, for fear that they may do more harm than good or waste scarce resources, or because of the perception that simply conducting an evaluation is an admission of uncertainty. Thus, clearly there is room for both the researchers and end users to improve the current state of knowledge transfer of pharmacoeconomic evaluations.

Challenges in the Application of Research Results

Related to the problem of knowledge transfer is the problem of application of pharmacoeconomic research results. There are several factors contributing to this problem.

First, decision makers are not often well versed in pharmacoeconomic methodologies, limitations, data interpretation, etc., thus limiting their ability to interpret and use the information. Few policy makers have advanced training in pharmacoeconomics, and, as a result, most health policy decision makers are still inadequately prepared to interpret and apply pharmacoeconomic evaluations. A survey of 254 health system pharmacy management personnel in Canada asked the respondents to assess their own skill level of 61 managerial competencies. Of all the competencies that were ranked, two of the five greatest weaknesses dealt with outcomes analyses: *construct reports and recommend plans to improve outcomes based on conclusions drawn from analysis of financial and clinical outcomes data,* and *perform prospective and retrospective financial and clinical outcomes analyses*. (The three other weaknesses in the top five were *participate in the implementation of a marketing program, use an organized system for staying current with pertinent management and leadership literature,* and *understand the operating principles of managed care.*)

Second, decision makers are not typically transparent about how the information is used in the decision process. This is especially frustrating for the pharmaceutical companies who submit material to formulary committees when requesting a new drug to be added to the formulary and only receive a simple "yes" or "no" response without reasons for either response.

Third, the lack of generalizability and/or transferability of information from one jurisdiction to another are barriers to the use of pharmacoeconomic analyses. Typically, most pharmacoeconomic evaluations try to demonstrate the impact of a drug on overall health care costs, whereas many organizations are still focusing on silo management or the impact of the drug on the pharmacy/drug budget. Some authors argue that the primary reason pharmacoeconomic studies are not used by decision makers is that they fail to meet the needs of these users. It is suggested that those involved in conveying the results of pharmacoeconomic studies to local decision makers, such as P&T committees, prepare a pharmacoeconomic report. This report should explicitly review the usefulness and validity of existing pharmacoeconomic studies and summarize the data in a practical format for the end users. Still, these pharmacoeconomic reports have many common pitfalls. Listed are common mistakes made by those who prepare pharmacoeconomic reports: 1) they use terminology that is not appropriate for the end user; 2) the perspective used is either irrelevant or unrequested; 3) terms such as outcomes, costs, and effectiveness are not defined; 4) the methodology used is poorly described; 5) the methodology is incomplete, such as lack a sensitivity analysis; and, 6) the final pharmacoeconomic report is not in a format with which health policy makers are familiar.

Fourth, in many settings, the time lines and perspectives of formulary decision makers and pharmacoeconomic models/studies differ considerably. Scientific research does not accept time as a constraint as the scientist substitutes certainty for timeliness. Health care decision makers, on the other hand, often operate on belief instead of knowledge, and this behavior is acceptable and even unavoidable when time is of the essence. Political and corporate pressures may dictate that decisions must be made now with the available knowledge and in the context of a formulary committee and drug policy, this may mean not being able to wait for a full evaluation or pharmacoeconomic model to be developed.

What is the Future of Pharmacoeconomics in Health Policy Development?

The discipline of pharmacoeconomics has progressed considerably in recent years. It has become an accepted (and even a mandatory) part of clinical drug trials and the formulary submission process, pharmacoeconomics-specific graduate-level training is more widely available, and its methodologies have become increasingly sophisticated. Its development has been compared to that of pharmacokinetics by three of the pioneers in the discipline—Bootman, Townsend and McGhan. Yet, at this time, one area of weakness of pharmacoeconomics that remains is its usefulness to health policy decision makers.

Pharmacoeconomic studies have the potential to both inform health policy development and assess the impact of health policy decisions to determine effectiveness. Both intended and unintended effects of health policies can be evaluated by pharmacoeconomic evaluations in a total quality management approach. In fact, the need for these types of studies that incorporate economic, clinical, and humanistic outcomes is great. Well-designed evaluations of drug benefit management policies, including formularies, prior authorization programs, and other cost-containment or appropriate use strategies, currently are lacking. Nonetheless, to reach the point where pharmacoeconomics is an essential part of health policy decision making, some key issues need to be addressed from both the perspective of those who carry out pharmacoeconomic research and those who use the information to develop health policy and make decisions.

From the perspective of those who conduct pharmacoeconomic research, several things are required in the near future to continue the development of this discipline. First, there is clearly a need for good pharmacoeconomic practice guidelines to build rigor and credibility into the process of carrying out economic evaluations. This is somewhat analogous to good clinical practice guidelines for clinical trials (e.g., ISPOR statements), and includes an eventual move toward standardized formats for reporting (e.g., the Consolidated Standards of Reporting Trials [CONSORT] approach). The guidelines should not be limited simply to the methodology component of pharmacoeconomic evaluations, but also to the update of studies and their application in policy making. The recent Academy of Managed Care Pharmacy Format for Formulary Submissions is a positive step. Second, the quality of the data used for pharmacoeconomic analysis, especially for effectiveness evaluations, must be improved. The pharmacoeconomic literature recently has focused on the limitations of most health care databases for health policy analysis that continue to hinder this type of research. Third, further evaluations of organizations that perform pharmacoeconomic evaluations are essential to help establish credibility of these individuals.

Several things also are required from those individuals who use pharmacoeconomic information to develop health policy and make decisions. First, decision makers have a responsibility toward improving their level of knowledge so as to use the information provided in an informed manner.

A survey of 409 managed care drug benefit decision makers in the United States yielded mixed results about the perceived understanding and importance of pharmacoeconomics by these individuals. The respondents reported that efficacy, safety, and cost were all of higher importance in the drug benefit decision making process than pharmacoeconomics, and only 17 percent said that if pharmacoeconomic studies were no longer published that this would have a large impact on their drug benefit management activities. It also has been argued that considerable effort is still required to turn pharmacoeconomic evaluations into reliable tools for those involved in drug benefit management. Second, decision makers need to be prepared to communicate their decision making process (in advance) and their decisions and rationale (post hoc). Third, whereas the pressures on most health payers dictate that overuse of pharmaceuticals has been a major focus, underuse of health technologies, including pharmaceuticals, has been identified as a major quality problem in health care today, and pharmacoeconomic models could be used to address this problem as well.

In the future, the discipline of pharmacoeconomics must adapt to new trends and incorporate new approaches if it is to be embraced by health policy makers. For example, many believe that further real-world pharmacoeconomic evaluations are needed for products before they are adopted into clinical practice. There is a role for pharmacoeconomics to improve the reliability of physician profiling as pertaining to appropriateness of drug use and associated patterns of care. Neural networks may be able to improve the predictive abilities of pharmacoeconomic models. E-prescribing and electronic medical records may facilitate the use of pharmacoeconomic data by physicians at the point of prescribing.

These and other trends also suggest that pharmacoeconomics has the potential to increase in importance to decision makers. With the constant rise in pharmaceutical costs, health policy makers are focusing more attention on pharmaceuticals and look to tools such as pharmacoeconomics that can better help them to understand and manage these costs. Phase IV studies should continue to grow in importance to obtain effectiveness data. Finally, pharmacoeconomics has an important role to play in disease management and patient health management programs.

In conclusion, pharmacoeconomic analyses will never replace the need for decisions and neither side—those performing the analyses and those using the analyses—should expect, or hope for, that to be the eventual outcome. Rather, professionals in this field should strive to see such evaluations contribute to a wider range of information for consideration in the decision making process.

Annotated Bibliography

1. Bodenheimer TS, Grumbach K. Understanding Health Policy—A Clinical Approach. 1st ed. Norwalk, CT: Appleton & Lange, 1995.

   This book provides a good overview of a variety of health policy issues from a public health perspective. It is unique in that it tries to address issues of relevance to front-line health professionals, to help them understand how the overall health care system works. Although the book focuses on the United States health care system (particularly as it relates to the organization of health care), many general topics also are discussed (e.g., prevention, quality of care, medical ethics, and rationing); and the authors discuss the systems in and pull in many examples from other countries. A second edition of this book was published in 1998 and includes a discussion of managed care.

2. Hjelmgren J, Berggren F, Andersson F. Health economic guidelines—similarities, differences and some implications. Value Health 2001;4(3):225–50.

   The authors have provided a useful inventory of health economic guidelines and have carried out an excellent and detailed comparative analysis of the similarities and differences in the documents that have been issued in Europe, North America, and Australia by governmental, nongovernmental, and industry organizations. The similarities identified are reflective of the gradual development of accepted methods for pharmacoeconomic studies. Of particular interest, however, are the differences identified which, in turn, have a direct relationship to study design. For instance, key difference areas included: perspective of the evaluation, resources used and costs, and the valuation of resources (e.g., presence or absence of standardized price lists); and the authors speculate that these differences arise from differences in the health care system where the guidelines are used and/or the purpose for which the guidelines were developed.

3. Beutels P, Edmunds WJ, Autonanzas F, et al. Economic evaluation of vaccination programmes: a consensus statement focusing on viral hepatitis. Pharmacoeconomics 2002;20(1):1–7.

   This article is a classic example of the kind of challenge faced by policy makers in developing health policies and programs. As the authors note, incorporating data that have been derived from studies designed on the basis of pharmacoeconomic guidelines may introduce unexpected results in this public health scenario. Because of the significant influence of discounting on future health gains and future costs, the authors reinforce the need to present data as both discounted and nondiscounted values (as recommended by most guideline documents). Finally, the authors emphasize some key considerations addressed throughout the chapter: that economic evaluations are only one consideration in the decision making process concerning a given intervention; and, that such evaluations should be used as much for discontinuing inefficient practices or programs as they are for introducing new ones.

4. Lopert R, Lang DL, Hill SR, Henry DA. Differential pricing of drugs: a role for cost-effectiveness analysis? Lancet 2002;359:2105–7.

   In an interesting twist on the application of pharmacoeconomics and in response to growing controversies regarding drug prices and access to drugs in developing countries (e.g., human immunodeficiency virus and acquired immune deficiency syndrome drugs for Africa), the authors have proposed a method for establishing differential prices for patented pharmaceuticals based on the Gross Domestic Product (GDP) of a given country. In their methodology, rather than use the acquisition cost (as set by the manufacturer) as an input into calculation of the cost-effectiveness ratio, a desired incremental cost per life-year gained equal to a country's GDP is set, and then the cost-effective price is derived from the analysis. Such a method could be applied by policy analysts at the World Health Organization in relation to their essential drugs list, and in facilitating access to needed drugs to less developed countries around the world. This demonstrates an innovative application of well-established methods and tools!

5. McDonald R, Haycox A, Walley R. The impact of health economics on healthcare delivery: the health economists' perspective. Pharmacoeconomics 2001;19(8):803–9.

   One of the lingering questions surrounding the field of pharmacoeconomics and, more typically, health economics is whether it is having an impact on health care delivery; and, if so, whether that impact is as intended (or not) and positive (or negative) in nature. The authors provide a comprehensive overview of the conflicting perspectives of clinicians and health economists (i.e., individual versus population), as well as many other challenges also faced by health policy makers (e.g., rationing of services, limited availability of evidence, and extrapolating from efficacy data). It is important to understand these issues as they underlie many of the communications and credibility problems that face pharmacoeconomics in the health care environment.

6. Coyle D, Davies L, Drummond MF. Trials and tribulations: emerging issues in designing economic evaluations alongside clinical trials. Int J Technol Assess Health Care 1998;14(1):135–44.

   One of the key sources for generating pharmacoeconomic information to facilitate decision making is the randomized, clinical trial. Understanding the situations under which economic data can and should be derived from such trials is important not only for those who undertake such studies, but also those who interpret them. The authors discuss decision points that determine whether an economic evaluation is needed, what study design is best suited to answer the question at hand, what kinds of randomized, clinical trials are most amenable to incorporating a pharmacoeconomic assessment, and how to go about collecting and analyzing the data derived from such studies.

7. Campbell G, Sprague KL. The state of drug-decision-making: report on a survey of P&T committee structure and practices. Formulary 2001;36:644–55.

This study provides a nice overview of the structure and function of pharmacy and therapeutics (P&T) committees in a variety of settings. The survey pool consisted of the subscribers of the journal, Formulary, and the survey was divided into three subsurveys. The study noted a large degree of consistency in survey responses across the practice settings it examined. The results of the study should be weighed against its methodology—only Formulary readers were surveyed, and the response rate was only about 30 percent.

8. Crane VS, Hull BL, Hatwig CA, Teresi M, Croft CL. Presenting drug cost information to a board of directors: a case example. Formulary 2001;36:857–64.

An excellent example of applied pharmacoeconomics, this paper presents a model for P&T committees to use when presenting data to their respective boards of directors. An actual presentation that was delivered to the board of directors at Parkland Health and Hospital System in Dallas, Texas, by its P&T committee is described. The paper outlines tips on presenting pharmaceutical data to executives who are not versed in this area of business, as well as suggestions for presentation format and content.

9. Mason J, Freemantle N, Nazareth I, Eccles M, Haines A, Drummond M. When is it cost-effective to change the behavior of health professionals? JAMA 2001;286(23):2988–92.

Determining health program and policy cost-effectiveness is often a complex and difficult task for researchers and health decision makers, and this paper demonstrates a method that may be useful for these individuals. The authors apply their methods of calculating cost-effectiveness to a recent randomized, controlled trial regarding educational outreach, the Evidenced-Based Outreach study. In this study, community pharmacists provided educational sessions to promote changes in prescribing habits. After applying the authors' cost-effectiveness model, the outreach efforts showed "modest" effects. The authors identify the limitations to their model and discuss its implications in decision making.

10. McNeil BJ. Shattuck lecture—hidden barriers to improvement in the quality of care. N Engl J Med 2001;345(22):1612–20.

This paper was presented at the annual meeting of the Massachusetts Medical Society in May 2001, and is an overview of the many barriers that impede the quality of health care. The author examines the current status of this problem and discusses some of the flaws within the evidence that clinicians use in their decision making processes. Escalating costs, notably drug costs, are reviewed and the place for technology within health care is discussed. The author explores the underuse of current technologies and the reasons for it, as well as some potential solutions for the problem. The author also recognizes cost-containment issues and how this may affect decision making and use of medical technology.

11. Motheral BR, Grizzle AJ, Armstrong EP, Cox E, Fairman K. Role of pharmacoeconomics in drug benefit decision-making: results of a survey. Formulary 2000;35:412–21.

This article discussed a survey that was used to measure the extent to which pharmacoeconomics is used in drug benefit decision making in managed care settings. This article is recommended for those looking for a "snapshot" on what these formulary decision makers think about the usefulness of pharmacoeconomics. For example, 50 percent of those surveyed thought that pharmacoeconomic data are *important* in managing drug benefits, whereas 47 percent indicated that these data were *somewhat important*. The weaknesses of the methodology do limit this study somewhat: only subscribers to the journal Formulary were approached, with only a small percentage (14) actually responding to the survey.

12. Nuijten MJC, Berto P, Berdeaux G, Fricke F-U, Villar FA. Trends in decision-making process for pharmaceuticals in Western European countries: A focus on emerging hurdles for obtaining reimbursement and a price. Health Econ Prev Care 2001;2:162–9.

This paper serves as an overview to pharmaceutical pricing and decision making in the western European countries. The more traditional centralized decision making processes, reimbursement programs, drug pricing and cost-containment strategies are presented and reviewed. The paper identifies three major trends that are occurring with western Europe: Increasing data requirements centrally (i.e., cost-effectiveness data), decentralization of prescription requirements, and decentralization of decision making processes. The authors also discuss the limitations to decentralization, temporary reimbursement, use of databases to merge purchasing bodies, and drug-specific developments.

Self-Assessment Questions

1. Health policy in the public sector differs from health policy in the private sector in which one of the following ways?
   A. Health policy development in the public sector stresses decision making, selecting goals, and the best means for reaching them, whereas health policy development in the private sector does not.
   B. Health policy development plays a greater role in the private sector, compared to the public sector.
   C. Health policy development in the public sector is more of a political process, which is propelled by dynamic negotiations between groups with competing societal priorities and conflicting social ideologies.
   D. Health policy development in the private sector handles conflicting views about what should be done and allocates resources to address needs, whereas health policy development in the public sector does not.

2. L.M. is a junior policy analyst who has just been assigned the task of developing potential solutions to health policy issues related to reimbursement of drug products for treating human immunodeficiency virus/acquired immune deficiency syndrome. She comes to you with her plan for tackling this issue and asks for your advice on how to ensure that she covers

the most important aspects of the issue. Which one of the following statements **BEST** reflects a good general approach to health policy analysis that will help L.M. develop options from which senior management can select their preferred option to dealing with this issue?

A. The positions of various stakeholders should have no bearing on what the best approach to addressing this issue might be.
B. L.M. should start with a thorough pharmacoeconomic analysis to tell her what the best options are to present to senior management.
C. Implementation issues do not need to be considered in the analysis until the option is selected by senior management.
D. An investment should be made at the beginning of the policy analysis process to fully define the issue at hand and to understand the context within which this issue exists.

3. Which one of the following statements **BEST** describes the economic outcomes of drug formularies as a pharmacy benefit management technique?
   A. Drug formularies lower drug expenditures and lower overall health care costs.
   B. Drug formularies lower drug expenditures but do not lower overall health care costs.
   C. Drug formularies do not lower drug expenditures but do lower overall health care costs.
   D. Drug formularies do not lower drug expenditures and do not lower overall health care costs.

4. According to a recent survey of drug benefit decision makers, what were the two most important factors that are considered in the drug benefit management decision making process?
   A. Efficacy and safety.
   B. Safety and pharmacoeconomics.
   C. Efficacy and health-related quality of life effects of drug.
   D. Physician demand for drug and cost.

5. Which one of the following **BEST** describes the relationship of drug expenditures to total health expenditures in most Western countries?
   A. Prescription drug expenditures are rapidly increasing both as a total cost and as a proportion of total health care costs.
   B. Prescription drug expenditures are rapidly increasing as a total cost but not as a proportion of total health care costs.
   C. Prescription drug expenditures are slightly decreasing as a total cost and as a proportion of total health care costs.
   D. Prescription drug expenditures are slightly increasing as a total cost but are slightly decreasing as a proportion of total health care costs.

6. Which one of the following organizations was the first to develop pharmacoeconomic guidelines for formulary submissions?
   A. Canadian Coordinating Office of Health Technology Assessment.
   B. Academy of Managed Care Pharmacy.
   C. Regence Blue Shield of Washington.
   D. Australian Pharmacy Benefit Advisory Committee.

7. An ongoing controversy with the Australian Pharmacy Benefit Advisory Committee pharmacoeconomic guidelines has been which one of the following?
   A. The inclusion of indirect costs in pharmacoeconomic submissions.
   B. The requirement for submissions to compare subjects from clinical trials to typical Australian patients.
   C. Differing requirements from those of the Patented Medicine Prices Review Board.
   D. Failure to allow for comparative benefits and costs.

8. In 1991, the state of Oregon Health Services Commission created a list of 709 condition-treatment pairs to assign priorities and rank health care procedures for funding purposes. A key economic evaluation methodology problem experienced in this process was which one of the following?
   A. Life-saving, expensive procedures that benefited a few or that had questionable benefits were at the top of the list.
   B. Undertaking cost-benefit or cost-effectiveness analyses for so many conditions was difficult.
   C. Ethical issues were systematically part of the assessment process.
   D. Without rational explanation, minor conditions appeared at the bottom of the list.

9. Which one of the following statements **BEST** describes some of the key barriers to health policy makers when attempting to incorporate data from the pharmacoeconomic evaluations in the literature into the decision making process?
   A. Using data from the literature is far more time-consuming than conducting a prospective pharmacoeconomic evaluation.
   B. Using data from the literature enables policy makers to use studies that were tailored to reflect usual care in their organization.
   C. Using data from the literature often results in difficulty in determining the assumptions that were behind the published models.
   D. Using data from the literature means that the policy maker will have to rely on case-controlled studies rather than randomized, controlled studies.

10. J.S. is a member of the pharmacy and therapeutics committee for a third-party payer. He is having difficulty using pharmacoeconomic studies in the formulary decision making process. Which one of the

following statements likely **BEST** represents the reason for his difficulty?

A. J.S. is creating pharmacoeconomic models from both internal and external data.
B. J.S. does not understand the pharmacoeconomic methodologies described and used in the studies.
C. J.S.'s organization wants him to consider the impact of the drug on overall health care costs, whereas the pharmacoeconomic evaluations he is reading only focus on the impact of drug costs.
D. J.S. is unable to find any evidence-based summaries of the literature in this area.

11. Which one of the following characteristics of pharmacoeconomic evaluations do many formulary decision makers wish to see in the studies they review?

A. Pharmacoeconomic evaluations that are done in partnership with a pharmaceutical company.
B. Pharmacoeconomic evaluations that compare only the product in question with one sample comparator.
C. Pharmacoeconomic evaluations that provide simply a quick overview of the methods used.
D. Pharmacoeconomic evaluations that are based on typical clinical practice patient populations.

12. Which one of the following statements **BEST** describes how current trends will likely impact health policy development and pharmacoeconomics in the near future?

A. Pharmacoeconomics will likely increase in importance as drug expenditures (as a percentage of overall health care expenditures) continue to increase.
B. Phase IV studies will become increasingly irrelevant to health policy makers as pharmacoeconomic evaluations are incorporated with increasing frequency in Phase III studies.
C. Increased requirements for pharmacoeconomic components in formulary submissions by third-party payers will result in fewer formulary submissions by pharmaceutical companies.
D. The progression from silo management to patient health management will result in a decreased role for pharmacoeconomic evaluations.

ANSWERS

THE STRUCTURE OF THE UNITED STATES HEALTH CARE DELIVERY SYSTEM

Answers to Self-Assessment Questions

1. Answer: B

Copayment (Answer B) is correct. In a tiered copayment structure, when the patient is required to contribute a static amount (flat dollar amount) per prescription, the correct term to use is copayment. More often than not, in addition to the potential for a flat copayment, pharmacy benefit managers (PBMs) require a percentage copayment for outpatient prescription drugs.

2. Answer: C

Payment for prescription drugs is optional (Answer C). It seems unfathomable, yet outpatient prescription drug benefits are an optional coverage item under all state Medicaid programs. There is no coverage (optional or otherwise) in the federally sponsored public program, Medicare.

3. Answer: C

In third-party programs, PBMs pay pharmacists on a cost of the drug plus fee (cost plus fee) arrangement. Other responses listed are inaccurate, and thus incorrect.

4. Answer: B

Pharmacy benefit managers have used the approach of seeking to reduce reimbursement levels paid to participating pharmacies as a method of reducing drug expenditures. Because PBMs are paid on a capitated, per member per month basis, the more they can reduce reimbursement levels to participating pharmacies, the more profitable they will appear to investors and insurers.

5. Answer: D

Individuals older than 65 years of age inhabit long-term care facilities (LTCFs) or nursing homes in the vast majority of instances.

6. Answer: D

"PA" refers to prior approval. In the PA process, approval must be sought and obtained before the use of the drug with a patient (Answer D). Various PBMs and/or managed care organizations (MCOs) use PA programs to try to stem the rapid increase in the cost of drugs. Medicaid programs have begun to increasingly use PA criteria to try to decrease the cost of the drug component in Medicaid programs.

7. Answer: D

In PBM-sponsored drug formularies, dollar signs are indicative of the relative expense of a formulary item. So, the more dollar signs, the more expensive the drug therapy option in comparison with others drugs within the therapeutic class. Therefore, Drug D, $$$$ (Answer D) is correct.

8. Answer: A

Tragically, the number of deaths per year attributable to cigarette smoking is great than half a million people per year (Answer A). The preventive health behavior of smoking cessation should be stressed with smokers at every patient encounter. Reinforcement by varying health professionals could make a dramatic impact on subsequent untoward disease sequelae.

9. Answer: A

By far and away, general hospitals (Answer A) is the largest component of the classification of hospitals.

10. Answer: C

According to the new categorization of elderly patients, the following breakdown separates patients older than 65 years of age:

- young old age (Answer B). Those between the ages of 65 and 74 years of age;
- middle old age (Answer C). Those between the ages of 75 and 84 years of age;
- old old age (Answer D). Those older than 85 years of age. Currently, this segment of the elderly is the fastest growing.

TYPES OF ECONOMIC AND HUMANISTIC OUTCOMES ASSESSMENTS

Answers to Self-Assessment Questions

1. Answer: B

Pharmacoeconomics is part of the larger area of research known as outcomes research. The two are not synonymous; therefore, Answer A is incorrect. Not all outcomes research is pharmacoeconomic research (Answer D). Proponents of outcomes research include clinical, economic, and humanistic variables as dependent or as the outcome variables. Outcomes research includes clinical assessments, the patient's perspective about their functioning and wellbeing, as well as the economics of the intervention; therefore, Answer C is incorrect.

2. Answer: D

The economic, clinical, and humanistic outcomes (ECHO) model represents economic, clinical, and humanistic outcomes. Each of these endpoints involves intermediate steps or intermediate outcomes. Humanistic intermediaries can include specific behaviors of an individual or a group of people. The behaviors themselves are not outcomes in this model. One example is the behavior of patients' adherence to their drug regimen. Compliance can be affected by nonbehavioral factors also, such as the cost of the drug or the patient's belief system, or attitude toward taking drugs. All of these influences can have an impact on the outcome and the patients assessment of the outcome. In a statistical model, adherence to drug regimens is considered both a dependent and an independent variable. As an independent variable, adherence can be evaluated for its effect on the dependent variable of humanistic outcomes. In this way, it is an intermediary, or an intermediate step.

3. Answer: A

Economic outcomes have been defined as the total costs of medical care associated with treatment alternatives balanced against clinical or humanistic outcomes (see Reference 13). Clinical outcomes are defined as medical events that occur as a result of a disease or treatment (Answer B). Humanistic outcomes are defined as the consequences of disease or treatment on patient functional status or quality of life (Answer C). Researchers have proposed that the evaluation of pharmaceutical products should include an assessment of each of these three outcome types.

4. Answer: D

Direct medical costs are the costs incurred for medical products and services used for the prevention, detection, and treatment of a disease, such as transportation. Examples of other direct costs include drugs, supplies, and hospitalizations. Pain (Answer A) is an example of an intangible cost. Mortality (Answer C) is an example of an indirect cost. Transportation (Answer B) is a direct nonmedical cost.

5. Answer: C

Indirect costs are those costs resulting from morbidity and mortality. They are costs valued as real money that are not directly paid for the treatment of an illness or disease, such as transportation. Morbidity costs are incurred from missing work (lost productivity), whereas mortality costs are the costs incurred due to premature death.

6. Answer: B

Economic evaluations can be conducted from single (Answer A) or multiple perspectives, as long as it is clear what the perspective(s) is and the costs and consequences are relevant to the perspective(s) chosen. Popular perspectives for conducting economic evaluations include the patient (Answer C), provider, payer, and society. In countries with nationalized medicine, society is the predominate perspective; however, it is not the only valid perspective (Answer D).

7. Answer: D

Direct costs of importance to providers are expenses paid by the provider to care for patients. The amount paid out-of-pocket by patients directly to their physicians for a clinic visit is a direct expense to patients (Answer A). Patient charges for visits to an emergency department (Answer B) and the prescription cost of insulin at the community pharmacy (Answer C) both are direct expenses to third-party payers and to patients (for the amount of their co-payment). Salaries of clinical pharmacists who monitor patients' therapies are direct expenses from the perspective of the provider.

8. Answer: B

Indirect costs are composed of costs due to work loss and decreased productivity due to illness. From the perspective of an employer, costs related to lost days of work and decreased functioning of employees are pertinent indirect costs. A drug that reduces an employee's ability to function certainly falls into this category. Loss of income (Answer C) is an indirect cost from the perspective of the patient, whereas family care-giving expenses (Answer D) are direct nonmedical costs. The patient's share of hospitalization costs (Answer A) are a direct cost from the patient perspective.

9. Answer: A

Costs from a patient's perspective are essentially the uninsured portion of what they pay, or are charged, for a product or service. The provider's perspective is represented by the true cost of providing a service (Answer B). The charges allowed for a health care product or service (Answer C) represent cost from the perspective of a payer. Cost from a societal perspective includes the cost of giving and receiving medical care, including morbidity and mortality (Answer D).

10. Answer: B

A full economic evaluation is one that encompasses two basic characteristics: 1) a comparison of two or more treatment alternatives is made; and 2) both the costs and the consequences of the alternatives are examined (see Reference 7). A partial economic evaluation encompasses only one of these characteristics. A complete evaluation should identify, measure, and compare the costs and consequences associated with competing programs or treatment alternatives.

11. Answer: D

A partial economic evaluation provides a descriptive assessment of resource use or outcome. By definition, partial evaluations do not provide both a comprehensive assessment and comparison of the costs and consequences of competing alternatives; therefore, Answer A is incorrect. A simple cost comparison without regard for outcomes, as well as comparison of only outcomes without regard for costs, are both examples of partial economic assessments. A third example of partial economic assessment is the description of costs and outcomes for a single treatment alternative.

12. Answer: C

Although partial economic evaluations may serve as a useful starting point in outlining or describing the costs or consequences of drug therapy, they are not a component of a full assessment (Answer A). A full economic assessment necessitates evaluation of both the costs and consequences of competing alternatives. In the absence of a full evaluation, a partial evaluation may provide some insight into important cost and outcome parameters for a given disease state, but should never serve as the basis for selection of an alternative.

13. Answer: D

Cost-minimization analysis should not be used if there is any doubt regarding the therapeutic equivalence of two or more treatment alternatives being compared. This methodology does not take into account differences in clinical outcomes between agents. The appropriate use of this method could be to compare agents in the same therapeutic class with documented equivalence in safety and efficacy. Although the costs of these agents would be identified, measured, and compared, the analysis should extend beyond drug acquisition costs, and include all relevant costs incurred for administering, monitoring, and preparing the agent.

14. Answer: A

The results of a cost-benefit analysis are typically expressed as either a cost-benefit ratio, or as net cost or net benefit. When comparing two or more treatment alternatives, the alternative with the greatest cost-benefit ratio, or net benefit, is considered the most efficient use of resources. However, caution must be exercised when using cost-benefit ratios. The values can be misleading; therefore, the relative magnitude of the cost-benefit ratio must be considered. The net benefit associated with a program or treatment alternative is often the preferred expression of study results.

15. Answer: A

A cost-benefit analysis is the best economic evaluation method to compare two or more programs when it is best to translate benefits into a dollar value. For example, if quantifying the value of a new pharmacy service, such as a Therapeutic Drug Monitoring Service, the cost of implementing and managing the program (the pharmacist's salary, laboratory tests), and the benefit of the program (decreased drug costs, decreased patient lengths of stay), can both be translated into dollar values.

16. Answer: A

A product or service may be considered cost-effective compared to a competing alternative when any of the following three conditions are met: 1) the alternative is less expensive and at least as effective as the comparator; 2) the alternative is more expensive and provides an additional benefit that is worth the additional cost; or 3) the alternative is less expensive and less effective and the lost benefit was not worth the extra cost of the comparator. Cost-effectiveness analysis attempts to determine the optimal alternative, which is not always the least expensive alternative, for obtaining a desired effect.

17. Answer: A

Cost-effectiveness analysis is the best economic evaluation method to apply when two or more treatment alternatives have different efficacy and safety profiles. An appropriate application of this method could be to compare treatment alternatives from different therapeutic categories that are used to treat the same disease. A complete evaluation would identify, measure, and compare all of the costs and consequences relative to the perspective(s) chosen. Relevant costs assessed in this evaluation should extend beyond drug treatment costs, and include the costs of treatment failures and adverse drug reactions.

18. Answer: C

The incremental cost-effectiveness ratio represents the incremental or additional cost required to obtain an incremental or additional benefit when comparing a treatment alternative to the next most intensive or expensive treatment option. Summary measurements of efficiency Answer A) typically describe cost-effectiveness ratios. The cost per benefit of a new strategy independent of other alternatives (Answer B) describes the classic average cost-effectiveness ratio, where the average cost to obtain a specific therapeutic objective is spread over a large population. The cost per quality-adjusted life-year gained (Answer D) is a description of a cost-utility ratio.

19. Answer: A

Cost-utility analyses can compare cost, quality, and quantity of patient-years. Thus, when evaluating treatment alternatives that are life-extending with serious side effects, such as cancer chemotherapy, is the best economic evaluation technique. Cost-utility analysis is also an appropriate methodology to use when evaluating alternatives that produce reductions in morbidity instead of mortality, such as arthritis treatments.

20. Answer: C

The primary role of discounting in economic evaluation is to incorporate the effects of differential timing into the decision process. Whenever a cost or benefit is realized more than 1 year into the future, discounting should be performed. There is no standard discount rate to use, although 5 percent is commonly used.

21. Answer: C

There is no one standard discount rate for use in pharmacoeconomic analyses. Many investigators recommend that costs should be discounted to their present value using a rate of 3–8 percent per annum. However, a commonly used rate in recently published evaluations is 5 percent.

22. Answer: A

Sensitivity analysis is a standard approach to manage uncertainty in an economic evaluation. Due to the almost universal need to make assumptions when conducting economic evaluations, it is critical to perform sensitivity analyses. By varying sensitive variables over a range of plausible results, one can test the robustness of the study conclusions.

23. Answer: D

No one single factor can absolutely ensure that drug-use policies will have a positive effect on prescribing patterns. However, having pharmacoeconomic data to support the appropriate and cost-effective use of a pharmaceutical product typically increases its acceptance by health care providers and society. Strategic implementation of strategies using verbal, written, and on-line communication, based on sound pharmacoeconomic data, will also enhance the success of these policies in a health care organization.

24. Answer: D

For formulary management, the best uses of pharmacoeconomic data are for formulary decisions regarding the inclusion or exclusion of treatment options. Although a formulary is often viewed as a cost-containment tool, a formulary should not be a list of the cheapest alternatives. The purpose of today's formulary should be to optimize therapeutic outcomes while controlling the cost of pharmaceutical products. Contemporary formulary management decisions have begun to extend beyond an evaluation of only safety and efficacy, or only cost, and include an assessment of the pharmacoeconomic value of pharmaceutical products and services.

25. Answer: B

Health-related quality of life refers to those aspects of life dominated, or significantly influenced, by personal health and activities performed to maintain health. Health is only one aspect of quality of life. Quality of life encompasses more than a person's lifestyle (Answer A). There are 12 different domains of life proposed in the literature. Marital status, education, and religious beliefs more accurately describe quality of life, rather than health; therefore, Answer D is incorrect.

26. Answer: B

Only physical functioning is a dimension of health. Activities such as the ability to carry a bag of groceries (Answer A), playing sports (Answer C), and bathing and dressing (Answer D), are all items used to inquire about a degree or state of physical functioning. Knowing that a patient has no limitations in bathing or dressing, but has some limitations in playing sports, gives one information to describe a range of physical functions that the person can perform.

27. Answer: C

Distress and well-being describe two extreme points, or boundaries, in the range of mental health states. To be complete, it is recommended that the dimensions included within health status questionnaires go beyond the absence of the negative health state. For example, a patient who experiences relief of his psychological distress would not necessarily have achieved his ultimate health goal unless he achieved an experience of psychological well-being, or was happy, and not just not sad.

28. Answer: A

Traditional means of collecting clinical data, such as laboratory tests, radiographs, and physical examinations, are usually performed by a technician, a machine, or a clinician. Health status assessments, as described in this module, are patient self-administered questionnaires. Collection of information from patients is not a new phenomenon; what is new are the attempts to standardize the collection of this information; therefore, Answer B is incorrect. Clinicians can use the information from health status assessments in clinical decision-making; therefore, Answer C is incorrect. Although there is some controversy surrounding the application of the results of the questionnaires, the results are being used. The methods of assessing health status use the discipline of psychometrics, enabling one to assess objectively the subjective aspects of health. Thus, an argument can be made that health status measures are also "hard data;" therefore, Answer D is incorrect.

29. Answer: A

Measurement of health status across the spectrum of patient age, race, and socio-demographics is unique when using generic measures. If generic status measurements were applied to a disease population, the measurement would be too burdensome to the patient and include concepts that were not applicable to some patients in the population. The dimensions of health addressed in the measurement definitely need to be comprehensive, but cannot contain too many questions that would overburden the patient. Measurement frameworks (Answer C) should extend across the entire range of a dimension for *both* general and disease-specific assessments. In addition, measurements must be sensitive to change over time for *both* types of assessments; therefore, Answer D is incorrect.

30. Answer: B

Quality of care can be evaluated in areas of structure, process, and outcome (see Reference 5). This can be a confusing concept because one can achieve quality in the structure of a care setting, in the process of care, or in the outcome of care; however, Donnabedian proposed that to achieve true quality of care, quality must be achieved in all three areas. Although the categories are intimately related, success in one area does not imply success in another. Until the recent attention to outcomes assessment, the system had focused on achieving quality in structure and process only. Patient satisfaction with care (Answer A) is a component of quality outcomes, as is patient self-assessment of the health care system (Answer D). Although the information gained from knowing about the structure, the process, and the outcomes of a health care delivery system can give a representation of the quality of care, it is really only a starting point for changes in health policy (Answer C).

31. Answer: C

There are no national regulations for the use of patient-based assessments. The Joint Commission on Accreditation of Healthcare Organizations recommends patient satisfaction be assessed for accreditation; however, it is not a mandate; therefore, Answer A is incorrect. To date, there is no regulatory body that requires health-related quality-of-life measures for drug approval (Answer B); however, manufacturers must now provide evidence of scientifically valid conclusions to make labeling claims about quality of life. *Both* patient satisfaction and health status are measured using psychometric techniques; therefore, Answer D is incorrect.

32. Answer: A

Ware has proposed that everyday use of health status assessments could ensure that all important dimensions of functional status and well-being are considered consistently to detect, explain, and track changes over time (Answer B). Their use would make it possible to better consider the patients total functioning when choosing among therapies (Answer C). Health status assessments also could guide the efficient use of community resources and social services (Answer D), as well as more accurately predict the course of chronic disease. Although health status assessments have great potential to improve care, they are not meant to serve as a replacement for current, more detailed assessments of function, such as that used by physical therapists, or of emotional well being, such as is assessed by psychiatrists and social workers.

33. Answer: D

Existing health outcome assessments drawn from classic test theory, along with item response theory, offer exciting opportunities for appreciably expanding applications of patient based health assessments in biomedical and health services research, clinical practice, and decision-making, and policy developments. Answers A, B, and C all discuss true characteristics of the measurement and use of individual level patient self-reported health status information.

INVESTIGATING THE OUTCOMES RESEARCH QUESTION

Answers to Self-Assessment Questions

1. Answer: B

When initiating the research process, state the question (Answer B). Do not let available data drive the question (Answer A); that could lead to answering the wrong question. Ask the question in a narrow sense so that objectives can be clearly defined. The purpose of research is to try to answer a question. Perspective (Answer D) is important, but the question needs to be asked before the perspective is determined.

2. Answer: C

Measuring both processes and outcomes is a critical aspect of informed decision-making. It is certainly possible to measure processes without outcomes; therefore, Answer B is incorrect. For example, claims databases contain documentation of procedures and other interventions with no information about outcome. It also is possible to measure outcomes without linking them to process measures; therefore, Answer A is incorrect. Measuring change in a patient's health-related quality of life without any other information provides an outcome but no information to suggest why the outcome was achieved. Processes and outcomes are not mutually exclusive; linking them together allows for informed decision-making based on inferences that a specific process leads to a specific outcome. Therefore, Answer C is correct and Answer D is incorrect.

3. Answer: B

Biases to internal validity affect the accuracy of study results (Answer B). Patient selection (Answer A) bias exists when patients in two comparison groups differ in ways that could affect the outcome of interest. Errors in ascertainment of exposure (Answer C) occur when patients presumed to be exposed to an intervention were not. Errors in measurement (Answer D) can affect a study's results if the technique used to measure outcomes does not accurately measure the true outcome. Generalizability of study results beyond people who were studied is an external validity issue.

4. Answer: C

Biases to external validity affect the applicability of results to other settings. When the level of technology used in the study differs from the technology used in actual practice, an intensity bias may occur. If there are differences among the people studied and the people to whom the study is to be generalized, a population (Answer C) bias may exist. Crossover (Answer A) occurs either when patients in the control group receive the intervention or when patients in the study group do not receive the intervention. This is a bias to internal validity because it could affect the conclusions drawn for the study population. Patient selection bias (to internal validity) exists when patients in two groups to be compared differ in ways that could affect the outcome of interest.

5. Answer: A

It is not possible to look at people and determine how much pain they are experiencing. It is possible to observe some aspect of functional status, such as physical functioning. For example, a patient can be observed walking up a flight of steps. However because only patients (Answer A), not caregivers (Answer C), can answer specific questions about their mood or the level of discomfort they are experiencing, patients are the preferred source of health-related quality-of-life data. Databases (Answers B&D) do not provide patient reported outcomes.

6. Answer: C

Study design affects a variety of administrative issues surrounding the research question. The cost of the evaluation (Answer A) varies significantly, depending on whether the study design is retrospective or prospective. Collecting data for a specific purpose is almost always more expensive than reanalyzing data that has already been collected. The time required to conduct the evaluation (Answer B) also will be a function of whether the design is retrospective or prospective. If prospective, typically more time is necessary for a crossover design compared to a parallel design. The accuracy of the information gained (Answer D) also will be affected by the study design. Although all study designs have biases and limitations, each study design is weighted differently relative to the accuracy of the information provided. This accuracy is in part a function of the variance surrounding the estimates of the outcomes of interest. It also is more difficult to show causality in a retrospective analysis than in a prospective, randomized, double-blind study. The evaluation administered is more complex in a study that is blinded than in an open-label study. The study design will not affect the importance of the study (Answer C), although the importance of the study may affect the resources committed to the study and ultimately the design selected.

7. Answer: A

When measuring outcomes in a study, they should be quantified in their most natural units (Answer A). This might include clinical measures, such as a change in hemoglobin A1c or a blood pressure measure in millimeters of mercury. Quality of life may be measured using a general or disease-specific quality-of-life instrument where units are measured in terms of various dimensions of health. Because outcomes are measured in their most natural units, it is unlikely that a single data source (Answer B) is available for all outcome measures. Some are generated by the health care provider, others by the patient, and still others may come from an administrative database. Outcomes should be measured in their natural units first and then, if appropriate, a monetary value (Answer C) can be attached to them. Reporting only monetary values limits the generalizability of the information, as cost structures vary significantly in health care systems. Outcomes do not have to be measured before resources (Answer D) and may be measured simultaneously or may follow resource use measures, depending on the timing and conduct of the study.

8. Answer: A

When measuring resources, they should be counted in the units of service required to produce the intended benefit, such as hours of work, hospital days, and number of laboratory tests. In some cases, it is important to watch for substitution of resources (Answers A and C). If pharmacists are filling prescriptions when someone at a lesser wage could actually be providing that same service at the same level, one needs to consider the impact of such substitution. A technician substituting for a pharmacist would lower the cost of the process. If migration was from Drug A or B to Drug C that would be a concern. Substitution between Drug A and B would not be a problem if both are studied. Migration of resources (Answers B and D) also can occur. If comparing two interventions for managing a condition, other interventions may be used to manage the condition beyond the two that are being compared. If comparing Drugs A and B in an observational study, patients may be migrating to Drug C. Migration is a big concern if one is looking only at costs because the costs for Drugs A and B might drop, whereas costs are increasing for Drug C. Migration should be evaluated in a benchmarking study and, in general, any study design where there is a time factor for which there is no control group.

9. Answer: D

Data are analyzed to evaluate patients (Answer A), to discriminate among patients (Answer B), or to try to predict how patients may act (Answer C). If the goal is to evaluate patients, questions asked might include, What is the current situation? or What is the baseline? Descriptive statistics are often useful at this evaluative stage. Discrimination among patients might involve determining whether a health-related quality-of-life instrument can differentiate among patients based on levels of severity or presence or absence of a disease, or whether patients can be moved from one severity level to another based on appropriate treatment. If the goal is to predict behavior, a question might be, Can a patient's annual level of resource use be predicted based on a general health-related quality-of-life score? Predicting how patients might act is the most challenging of the three approaches and typically requires higher levels of statistics and more data. The goal would never be to incriminate patients, but to learn from them.

10. Answer: C

A research framework will assist the researcher in thinking clearly about what can be accomplished (Answer C). It will not necessarily guarantee that your study gets funded (Answer A) because as there are a host of other issues that can affect that; however, the lack of a framework may reduce chances of funding. A framework also does not force a researcher to collect both process and outcomes data (Answer D), but it should get the researcher to think clearly about what needs to be collected to answer the research question. A framework should get the researcher to think about prioritizing objectives, but not results (Answer B)

DATA SOURCES FOR ECONOMIC OUTCOMES ANALYSES

Answers to Self-Assessment Questions

1. Answer: B

The perspective or point of view used for the study is helpful when deciding what types of costs to use and where to obtain the data. For example, a study conducted from the perspective of the hospital should measure actual hospital costs using data from the hospital's cost accounting system. From the perspective of the third-party payer, it would be important to include the amount paid out for medical claims.

2. Answer: A

Quality of life data must be obtained prospectively from patients, as it is not usually recorded in patients' medical records. If a study is designed to evaluate differences in quality of life for two pharmaceutical products, these data are usually measured prospectively, preferably in a randomized study.

3. Answer: D

Published studies can serve as useful data sources if the study is credible and if the drug therapy used was applicable to the one in which the economic analysis will be performed.

4. Answer: C

Care should be exercised if there are few patients from which to draw the sample because the sample may then not be a true representation of the population. This could lead to misleading and inaccurate analysis results. When a health care organization has too few cases, the data can be evaluated in a preliminary fashion. A full analysis should include data from an external data source.

5. Answer: B

The best way to become familiar with the data source is to obtain an extract of the data and conduct a pilot analysis (Answer B). This helps assess the completeness of the data and the feasibility of using it for a full economic analysis. Publishing an economic analysis (Answer A) before becoming familiar with the data source would be a much more difficult approach.

6 Answer: D

Clinical financial information systems in hospitals usually contain detailed cost and resource use data (Answer D) for each hospital admission. These systems may also contain limited information on patient outcomes, such as morbidity and mortality (Answer C) or severity of illness data. Patient outcomes data, such as quality of life and satisfaction (Answer A and B), are not usually available.

7. Answer: A

Hospital costs more accurately represent the financial impact on the hospital and should be used if the study is conducted from the perspective of the hospital. Patient charges are the amounts of money requested by the hospital for the services provided. These charges are rarely paid in full, as most hospital contracts allow either a per diem charge or a discount from charges. Whereas charge data were often used in the past, these data have come into disfavor, since it is more widely recognized that there is little relationship between actual hospital costs and the amount charged for the service.

8. Answer: C

An important consideration in using managed care claims data is that the medical and pharmacy claims are not usually integrated into one database system (Answer C). Pharmacy prescription claims are often contracted out to an external pharmacy benefit management company. It often is necessary to obtain the pharmacy data and integrate them with the medical claims data before a full economic analysis can be conducted. The use of database query tools (Answer D) can greatly expedite the data evaluation process.

9. Answer: D

Database studies have an advantage in that they represent ordinary medical practice (Answer D) and not data from the selective patient populations that exist in randomized, clinical trials (Answer B). It is true that the data are always collected retrospectively (Answer A) when using a database; however, this is not an advantage. Only with a prospective design could one hope to establish cause and effect relationships or to randomly assign patients to different treatment options.

10. Answer: C

When patients are not randomly assigned to a treatment regimen, certain biases may exist in the data. Database studies must be carefully designed to control for confounding variables (Answer C), including patient differences such as comorbidities or severity of illness. Although a prospective study (Answer A) will reduce confounding factors, it is a time-consuming and expensive process. Informed consent (Answer D) from individual patients is not usually necessary when searching a database.

COST-OF-ILLNESS ANALYSIS

Answers to Self-Assessment Questions

1. Answer: B

Cost-of-illness analysis involves the identification and valuation of direct, indirect, and intangible costs (Answers C, D, and A, respectively). Incremental costs (Answer B) are used in pharmacoeconomic studies and defined as the additional costs incurred from using one alternative over another; they typically are not the focus of cost-of-illness analysis.

2. Answer: C

The incidence-based approach measures the lifetime disease costs (Answers C) and, therefore, in most cases, will need to project treatment patterns past the first year (Answer D). This type of analysis, in general, is not used to estimate the cost-effectiveness of alternative therapies (Answer A), but can serve as a baseline for pharmacoeconomic analysis.

3. Answer: A

The human capital approach is based on the premise that a person's wages can be used to estimate losses in productivity (Answer A). This approach does not require the determination of overhead and production costs or marginal or incremental costs (Answers D and B, respectively).

4. Answer: C

Cost-of-illness studies can disaggregate costs by cost category for a particular disease (Answer A), assist policy-makers in establishing priorities for research funding (Answer B), and also can provide baseline data for the future conduct of more sophisticated economic analyses (Answer D). However, cost-of-illness estimates alone are not an indication of whether resources are being used efficiently or effectively (Answer C).

5. Answer: C

Prevalence-based costs-of-illness studies are relatively easier to conduct than incidence-based costing and are only useful when the full effects of an intervention are experienced within a single year. Prevalence-based and incidence-based costing both require a knowledge of the disease process and other characteristics of the disease (Answer C) to obtain an accurate estimate of total costs.

6. Answer: D

A frequent criticism of the human capital approach is that it does not capture the value of lost productivity from such nonmarket activities as housekeeping and volunteer work (Answer D). The human capital approach to valuing indirect costs is based on the assumption that lost productivity affects GNP; however, this is an assumption, not necessarily a criticism (Answer A). The human capital approach undervalues rather than overvalues women and minorities (Answer B) due to job discrimination and it is the willingness-to-pay approach that is criticized on the basis that individuals can interpret small changes in risk of significant life events (Answer C).

7. Answer: A

Intangible costs are psychosocial costs which measure the emotional stress from losing a job or the fear and anxiety associated with illness and disease. These costs assign monetary value to deterioration in the quality of life due to a disease (Answer A). Hospitalization and capital equipment costs (Answers B and C, respectively) are considered direct medical costs.

8. Answer: D

Conducting cost-of-illness analysis requires all of the information identified in Answers A, B, and C. The identification and valuation of all cost-generating components of a disease is critical in cost-of-illness studies as is a thorough knowledge of the epidemiological aspects and progression of a disease.

9. Answer: D

The costs of pain and suffering (Answer D) are considered intangible costs. Costs due to hospitalization, clinic visits, and prescription drug expenses (Answers A, B, and C) are all considered direct costs.

10. Answer: D

The ICD-9 coding system (Answer B) is a well-established method of identifying patients with a particular condition. Medical offices use this coding system to identify patients with a particular condition. These data are then fed into medical claims data and other data systems and can be used to identify those with a particular condition. Assuming that the condition the clinician wants to identify or measure is related to cancer, the American Cancer Society (Answer C) certainly is the place to go to learn about specific diagnoses and diagnostic criteria. The same would apply for cardiovascular conditions and the American Heart Association (Answer A). Although a particular physician specialist may be well versed with accepted diagnostic criteria and could provide great insight into local treatment patterns, the opinion may differ from accepted criteria. Also, local or regional practice patterns and diagnostic techniques may not be representative.

COST-MINIMIZATION ANALYSIS

Answers to Self-Assessment Questions

1. Answer: B

The primary difference between cost-minimization analysis and cost analysis is that cost-minimization analysis measures consequences of alternative therapies to establish their equivalence. Cost analysis does not constitute a full economic evaluation, given that consequences are not measured (Answer A). It is true that many cost-minimization analyses are from a payer's perspective. However, many cost analyses are conducted from a similar perspective (Answer B). Answer D is also true, but is not considered the primary distinguishing feature between cost-minimization analysis and cost analysis.

2. Answer: A

Establishing equivalency of outcomes, either in retrospect or prospectively, should not rely solely on one's own clinical judgement, but should also include some objective evidence of equivalency. Many cost-minimization analyses include a detailed assessment of costs, and time and motion studies are used to estimate personnel costs (Answers B and C). Given that outcomes are equivalent, the difference between alternatives relate to differences in costs or resource utilization (Answer D).

3. Answer: D

Establishing equivalency of outcomes should include evidence from the literature together with appropriate statistical tests. Currently, no established guidelines exist within the literature to guide researchers in this process (Answer A). Every attempt should be made to establish equivalency prior to conducting an analysis. However, this is not always possible. Cost-minimization analysis can be conducted without having first established equivalency (Answer B). However, in these instances the researcher must ensure that the study is designed to detect differences in effectiveness (e.g., sufficient sample size) (Answer C).

4. Answer: A

Presentation of results in cost-minimization analysis focuses on the presentation of costs. There are numerous ways in which costs can be presented, depending on the objective of the analysis, and the alternatives being compared. However, in general, results can be presented as total, or average cost per patient, or per patient day categorized by cost category. Results are not presented as cost per unit of outcome, or cost per unit of effectiveness.

5. Answer: A

This answer is obtained through a process of elimination. It is more apparent that answers B, C and D are appropriate for cost-minimization analysis. Answer D is the application of cost-minimization analysis to the simple comparison of a generic versus brand name product. The analysis of fluoxentine versus sertraline would not be appropriate for cost-minimization analysis, due to questionable equal effectiveness, as well as side-effect profile. This comparison would be more appropriately analyzed using cost-effectiveness analysis or cost-utility analysis.

6. Answer: A

Because the time to reach effectiveness may differ markedly between alternatives, conducting cost-minimization analysis, prospectively, should not incorporate a fixed time line over which alternatives are compared. Some attempt to analyze the equality of outcomes prior to conducting the analysis should be made (Answer B). Additionally, the perspective should be clearly stated prior to identifying and measuring costs so that irrelevant costs would not be included, or relevant costs excluded (Answers C and D). Finally, the purpose of cost-minimization analysis is to identify and measure all relevant costs and consequences.

7. Answer: C

Meta-analysis is conducted separately to obtain an effect size for each alternative being compared (Answer D). The separate effect sizes are then compared by means of statistical tests to determine equivalency (Answer B). Studies included in meta-analysis should be chosen based on the pharmacoeconomic problem, and established criteria developed for study inclusion (Answer A).

8. Answer: D

The primary distinction between cost-effectiveness analysis and cost-minimization analysis is that in cost-minimization analysis outcomes are found to be equivalent, while in cost-effectiveness analysis they are assumed unequivalent. Both cost-minimization analysis and cost-effectiveness analysis are considered full economic evaluations and, therefore, costs and consequences are both measured (Answer A). Cost-minimization analysis should take into consideration a product's side-effect profile in establishing equivalency. However this is not the primary distinguishing feature between these two methods (Answer B). Cost-minimization analysis often involves a detailed assessment of costs, but a similar detailed assessment can be found in cost-effectiveness analysis (Answer C).

9. Answer: D

A researcher's level of statistical expertise should not be a factor in influencing the method chosen to determine equivalency. If the researcher is unfamiliar with statistical procedures, assistance should be sought from those trained in this area. Answers A-C can all influence the method chosen to establish equivalency. Answers A and C can influence the type of statistical test used, as can answer B, which will determine whether meta-analysis or individual level data is obtained from prospective analysis.

10. Answer: D

All three statements are true regarding the steps taken in conducting cost-minimization analysis. Identifying all the relevant alternatives is a critical step in cost-minimization analysis, as is discounting when the analysis goes beyond a calendar year. The presentation of results is key in aiding decision makers and is an important last step. Although local clinical experts can provide important insight into the clinical pathways and local treatment protocols, do not rely solely on their opinion to determine equivalency of outcomes.

Answers to Exercise

See grid below.

Cost Category	Cephamore®		Alternative 1		Alternative 2	
	Include	Units*	Include	Units*	Include	Units*
Acquisition costs						
Lab costs						
Personnel costs Pharmacy manufacturing pharmacy kinetic services Nursing						

*Units per episode of care

COST-BENEFIT ANALYSIS

Answers To Self-Assessment Questions

1. Answer: B

A dollar value must be placed on health outcomes (Answer B) is correct because it is difficult to place dollar values on clinical outcomes; therefore, it is a *disadvantage* of cost-benefit analysis (CBA). Both the human capital (HC) and willingness-to-pay (WTP) approaches of valuing outcomes in dollars are difficult to use and have disadvantages. A comparison of the effects of different types of programs can be conducted (Answer A) is an *advantage* of CBA. Quality-adjusted life-year must be measured (Answer C) is a disadvantage of cost-utility analysis (CUA). Outcomes must be measured in the same natural units (Answer D) is a disadvantage of cost-effectiveness analysis (CEA).

2. Answer: A

A comparison of the effects of different types of programs can be conducted (Answer A) is correct because it is an *advantage* of CBA. For example, benefits from an acquired immunodeficiency syndrome (AIDS) clinic can be compared to benefits from a diabetes clinic even though the clinical outcomes are different. Because it is difficult to place a dollar value on clinical outcomes (Answer B) is a *disadvantage* of CBA. Quality-adjusted life-years must be measured (Answer C) is a *disadvantage* of CUA. Outcomes must be measured in the same natural units (Answer D) is a *disadvantage* of CEA.

3. Answer: B

Based on the calculations below, the present value (PV) of costs is $191,000 and the PV of benefits is $225,000.

COSTS
Cost – year 1 = $7500 + $50,000 + .25($50,000) = $70,000 – no discounting for year 1
Cost – year 2 = $70,000/1.10 based on formula in text w/10 percent rate = $63,636
Cost – year 3 = $70,000/(1.10)^2 based on formula in text w/10 percent rate = $57,851
Total present value of costs for 3 years = $191,487 – Costs round to $191,000.

SAVINGS (BENEFITS)
Benefit – year 1 = $70,000 – no discounting for year 1
Benefit – year 2 = $80,000/1.10 based on formula in text w/10 percent rate = $ 72,727
Benefit – year 3 = $100,000/(1.10)^2 based on formula in text w/10 percent rate = $ 82,645
Total present value of benefits for 3 years = $225,372 – Benefits round to $225,000.

4. Answer: D

Based on the calculations below, the net benefits of clinic A are $125,000 and the BC ratio for clinic A is 1.36.

Clinic A costs = $350,000, benefits = $475,000.
net benefit = Net benefit = Benefits – Costs = $475,000 – 350,000 = $125,000
BC = Benefit to cost ratio = Benefits/Costs = $475,000/$350,000 = 1.36

5. Answer: A

Based on the calculations below, the net benefits of clinic B are $75,000 and the BC ratio for clinic B is 1.27.

Clinic B costs = $275,000, benefits = $350,000.
net benefit = Net benefit = Benefits - Costs = $350,000 - $275,000 = $75,000
BC = Benefit to cost ratio = Benefits/Costs = $350,000/$275,000 = 1.27

6. Answer: B

Direct nonmedical costs (Answer B) is correct because the costs are tied to medical services but are nonmedical in nature. Parking for a medical visit is tied to the visit but not medical in nature. It is not a direct medical cost (Answer A) because these are medical in nature. It is not an indirect cost (Answer C) because indirect costs are defined as productivity costs. It is not an intangible cost (Answer D) because intangible costs are related to pain and suffering.

7. Answer: A

Direct medical costs (Answer A) is correct because the costs are for medical services, and receiving an immunization is a medical service. It is not a direct nonmedical cost (Answer B) because it is medical in nature. It is not an indirect cost (Answer C) because indirect costs are defined as productivity costs. It is not an intangible cost (Answer D) because intangible costs are related to pain and suffering.

8. Answer: D

Based on the calculations below, the BC ratio for oral (daily) therapy is 2.7:1.

COST—ORAL DRUG
$50—Physician visit
$240—Drug $20 per month times 12 months
$10—Drive to clinic (direct nonmedical cost)
$300 total per year for oral drug.
BENEFIT—ORAL DRUG
$800 = 4 more work days times $200 per day
BC ratio Oral = BC = $800 ÷ $300 = 2.7:1

9. Answer: C

Based on the calculations below, the BC ratio for the once-a-year injection is 3.3:1.

COST – INJECTION

$50 – Physician visit

$290 – Injection

$10 – Administration of injection

$10 – Drive to clinic (direct nonmedical cost)

$360 total per year for injection.

BENEFIT – INJECTION

$1200 = 6 more work days times $200 per day

BC ratio Injection = benefit ÷ cost = $1200 ÷ $360 = 3.3:1

10. Answer: C

A person's earnings may not reflect that person's true value to society (Answer C) is correct because this is a major limitation of the HC approach. For example, teachers or childcare providers may not earn as much as other professions but may be more valuable to society than what their paycheck reflects. What people say they are willing to spend may not correspond to what they will spend (Answer A) is a disadvantage of the WTP approach not the HC approach. It does not estimate any value for the provision of childcare and/or housekeeping activities (Answer B) is not true because HC does estimate a value for this. Unemployed elderly are valued more highly than the adult worker is not true (Answer D). The opposite is true for the HC method, working adults are valued more highly than children and the unemployed elderly.

11. Answer: A

What people say they are willing to spend may not correspond to what they will spend (Answer A) is a disadvantage of the WTP approach. Some will overestimate or underestimate the value of a "hypothetical" product or service. Such biases include starting point bias, strategic bias, range bias, and compliance bias. It does not estimate any value for the provision of childcare and/or housekeeping activities is not true (Answer B) or relevant to this method. A person's earnings may not reflect that person's true value to society (Answer C) is a disadvantage of the HC approach. Unemployed elderly are valued more highly than the adult worker (Answer D) is not true or relevant to WTP.

For questions 12 and 13—A critique of the abstract for the questions outlined in the text is as follows:

1. Was the title clear and complete? The title was not complete. Although it tells you what is being compared (Ultraceph and Megaceph), it does not include the type of pharmacoeconomic analysis conducted.
2. Was the objective stated? The objective was stated in the first line of the methods section: "The purpose of this study was to calculate the net BC when comparing Ultraceph and Megaceph."
3. What was compared? Was the dosing clear? Comparisons and doses were clear (Ultraceph is dosed 50 mg once per day. Megaceph is dosed 25 mg 2 times/day).
4. Was the perspective stated? Yes the perspective was stated when the authors wrote: "Costs paid by third-party payers were assessed."
5. Were appropriate costs and consequences measured? With an abstract, it is difficult to determine if certain specific costs and benefits were included.
6. Was discounting conducted? Because of the short timeframe it was not needed or conducted.
7. Were assumptions stated? Were they reasonable? One assumption was that $1500 per day was a reasonable estimate for a hospital stay.
8. Was a sensitivity analysis conducted? Yes. "The average cost estimates of hospitalization are varied from $500 to $2000 per day."
9. Were limitations addressed? No limitations to data collection, analysis, or generalization were addressed in the abstract.
10. Was the article biased? In an abstract it is difficult to tell if parts of the article seemed biased. The abstract itself did not seem biased.

12. Answer: B

The perspective was stated (Answer B) when the authors wrote "Costs paid by third-party payers were assessed." This is a positive aspect of the abstract. The title is appropriate (Answer A) is not true because the type of pharmacoeconomic analysis was not contained in the title. Discounting was conducted (Answer C) is not true because discounting was not conducted; it did not need to be for a short-term study. Limitations were addressed (Answer D) is not true because the abstract does not include any limitations.

13. Answer: D

Limitations not being addressed (Answer D) is a negative aspect of the abstract. Sensitivity analyses were not conducted (Answer A) is false because the estimate of hospital costs was varied from $500 to $2000 per day (which is a sensitivity analysis). Objective was not stated is not true (Answer B) because the objective was stated: "The purpose of this study was to calculate the net BC when comparing Ultraceph and Megaceph." Dosing of alternatives not described is false (Answer C) because the dosing was described for both drugs.

Answers to Exercises

Exercise 1

Goals:

Clinic goals depend on the organization, the pharmacist, and the population being served. Some possible goals of the clinic may be:

Decrease glycosylated hemoglobin (HbA_{1c})levels

Educate patients on self-monitoring of blood glucose

Improve adherence to hypoglycemic agents

Decrease hospitalizations related to complications from diabetes

Alternatives:

One alternative is to do nothing

A second alternative is to consider developing a different type of clinic

A third alternative is to target the program to certain populations:

Patients with HbA_{1c} levels above a specified threshold

Patients requiring tight control of their diabetes

Patients who are not adherent to their hypoglycemic drugs

Patients who have been hospitalized because of complications from diabetes

Exercise 2

Costs:

Costs incurred from implementing the program would include:

Direct medical

Pharmacy services (pharmacist's time to provide the education)

Drugs (could increase because of increased drug adherence)

Direct nonmedical

Patient costs

Travel costs (cost to travel to clinic for program)

Time costs (time spent participating in the program)

Overhead costs

Personnel (other nonmedical personnel needed to administer the program)

Space rental (may need additional space or remodeling)

Advertising (may need to identify and recruit patients to participate)

Supplies (e.g., glucose meters, strips, and laboratory tests)

Materials (e.g., such educational materials as brochures and video tapes)

Benefits:

Benefits from the program could include:

Direct benefits

Decreased physician visits, emergency department visits, hospitalizations

Indirect benefits

Increased productivity (or decreased work loss)

Intangible benefits

Increased diabetes quality of life (or decreased pain and suffering from diabetes)

Exercise 3

The daily wage rate = income ÷ number of days worked per year: $44,000 ÷ 240 = $183.

Value of lost productivity daily wage rate times the number of days missed/year:

Before patients missed 36 days a year (3 days/month)

$183 X 36 = $6588.

After patients missed 6 days per year (1 day every other month)

$183 X 6 = $1098

Value of indirect benefit (increase productivity)

Before-after

$6588 - $1098 = $5490/person/year

Exercise 4

Below is an example of how to elicit a WTP value using the payment card method.

We would like to ask you about your interest in participating in programs that would be designed to help you manage your diabetes. Below is a description of a program that could be provided by your pharmacist.

Patients with diabetes have improved their condition by learning more about their disease and by taking their drugs as directed. Pharmacists can help people with diabetes understand the conditions and the drugs used to treat it. In addition, they can:

• Help you learn how to use a glucose meter and give yourself insulin
• Help you with dietary management techniques, such as carbohydrate counting
• Help you recognize and handle situations when diabetic crises occur
• Check your feet for signs of nerve damage
• Check your blood pressure
• Check your blood sugar
• Monitor your diabetes by keeping a record on file and following up with you on a regular basis to assess your progress
• Contact your doctor and report any changes in your health

An initial visit with your pharmacist would include an assessment of your needs and planning an educational program to manage your disease state. This type of service is available by appointment only. Consider the disease state management program previously discussed. Assume you had to pay for the initial needs assessment and educational appointment with the pharmacist. This visit would last about 1 hour. Your insurance will not cover any costs. Assume that this consultation would result in a 50 percent improvement in your diabetes. Below is a list of possible fees for the initial consultation visit. What is the maximum amount that you would be willing to pay for a 1-hour consultation visit? Please circle your choice.

\$150	\$90	\$30
\$130	\$70	\$10
\$110	\$50	\$0

Exercise 5

You would want to use the formula to calculate the net present value of the program.

$$NPV_i = \sum_{t=0}^{n} \frac{B_t - C_t}{(1+r)_t}$$

The present value of benefits are calculated as:

$$\frac{\$5{,}000}{1} + \frac{\$12{,}500}{1.05} + \frac{\$20{,}000}{(1.05)^2} + \frac{\$25{,}000}{(1.05)^3} =$$

\$5,000 + \$11,905 + \$18,141 + \$21,596 = \$56,642

And the calculation of the present value of costs is:

$$\frac{\$10{,}000}{1} + \frac{\$12{,}500}{1.05} + \frac{\$15{,}000}{(1.05)^2} + \frac{\$17{,}500}{(1.05)^3} =$$

\$10,000 + \$11,905 + \$13,605 + \$15,117 = \$50,627

And the net present value of the program =
\$56,642 – \$50,627 = \$6,015

Exercise 6

The BC ratio for "brown bag day" would be found by dividing the net present value of the benefit by the net present value of the costs.

= \$56,642 ÷ \$50,627 = 1.1:1

The greatest benefit for dollars invested would be selling durable medical equipment from the outpatient pharmacy, where for every dollar invested in the program, the hospital would receive \$2.70 in benefits.

COST-EFFECTIVENESS ANALYSIS

Answers to Self-Assessment Questions

1. Answer: C

An incremental cost-effectiveness ratio provides the cost for one additional unit of output of one alternative over another. In this case, the output is symptom-free days. The incremental cost-effectiveness ratio provides the cost associated with producing an extra symptom-free day with drug B. The value of an incremental cost-effectiveness ratio in and of itself does not say that one drug is more effective than another.

2. Answer: C

The study protocol of a randomized, controlled, clinical trial typically will dictate inclusion and exclusion of specific types of patients, when these patients will return for clinic visits, and what drugs or procedures will be used. Resources saved or expended, and outcomes observed, may not be an accurate reflection of actual practice patterns and broad patient populations that exist in the real world setting. Therefore, the results may have low external validity and may not be generalizable to the clinical practice environment. A piggyback, randomized, clinical trial provides good internal validity, potentially low cost, and excellent credibility.

3. Answer: D

A cost-effectiveness analysis (CEA) compares the cost and consequences of two or more alternative therapies that have the same clinical objectives. Costs are measured in monetary units and the common outcome is measured in natural units, such as lives saved or cases cured. Cost-utility analysis is considered to be a special case of CEA where the scope of effectiveness is broadened by assessing the impact of an intervention on patients' functional status, health status, or health-related quality of life by including a utility such as quality-adjusted life-years (QALYs) in the analysis. Unlike cost-benefit analysis, CEA does not place a dollar value on human life or health by using the human capital approach. Cost-effectiveness analysis includes valuation of life in nonmonetary terms as units of effectiveness measured as specific clinical objectives (e.g., lives saved, cases cured, and decreases in blood pressure).

4. Answer: B

To calculate the incremental cost-effectiveness ratio for drug A the following formula is used:

incremental C/E = cost Drugs (A – B) ÷ effectiveness Drugs (A – B)

= \$2400 - \$1800 ÷ (200 – 134) life-years saved

= \$600 ÷ 66 life-years saved

= \$9.10 per life-year saved

5. Answer: A

A benefits manager in a large corporation is concerned with the direct medical costs of proving care for employees and also about employee productivity. Therefore, the benefits manager is interested in direct medical costs associated with a treatment, including the amount spent on medical services as a direct consequence of an illness. Direct nonmedical costs, such as care provided by the family, child care, social services, and housekeeping, are not a concern to the corporation because these are costs borne by the patient alone. Indirect costs of therapy, such as lost productivity and absenteeism, are important to the corporation. The clinical and economic outcomes of therapy are of interest because the corporation is seeking the most effective outcome available for the lowest cost. Humanistic outcomes might also be of interest to the corporation because they influence worker satisfaction, quality of life, and potentially, productivity.

6. Answer: A

Simulation designs used to conduct CEAs make it possible to estimate the treatment costs and outcomes without the time and expense of conducting a prospective trial. The models used are flexible and can often be adapted to represent many diseases and treatments over long time periods. A major limitation of simulation designs is that the models created rely on the literature and expert opinion for data that may be incomplete or biased.

7. Answer: A

Naturalistic trials are an optimal way to conduct CEAs because they provide the opportunity to observe the effects of a therapy under typical clinical practice in the population in a specific setting. Therefore, a naturalistic trial represents the costs and outcomes in actual clinical practice. Large study populations typically are required to provide enough statistical power to determine differences between alternatives, and long time periods may be required to collect all information of interest causing these studies to be costly to conduct.

8. Answer: C

Observational studies have good external validity because they represent the costs and consequences of alternatives in actual clinical practice. Because this type of study is not experimental and does not contain any random assignment of interventions, confounding factors can be introduced, causing the internal validity of the study to be poor. Typically, the differences between alternatives are small requiring large sample sizes to demonstrate statistically significant differences. Observational studies are usually retrospective and therefore do not allow for assessment of quality-of-life outcomes (the exception is the prospective cohort design).

9. Answer: B

Simulation designs allow researchers to compare treatments based on a synthesis of existing data. This is a faster approach than any of the prospective designs because it obviates the need for patient recruitment and observation. The primary disadvantage of this approach is that the analysis is limited to data available.

COST-UTILITY ANALYSIS

Answers to Self-Assessment Questions

1. Answer: C

The costs appropriate for inclusion in a cost-utility analysis include direct medical and nonmedical costs, indirect costs, and intangible costs. The cost of living (Answer C), a concern for all consumers, is a constant that does not vary with alternative programs and lost income (Answer A) is not a direct cost. Lastly, patient access to health care (e.g., driving to a physician's office, taxi, or bust transport) (Answer D) is regarded as an indirect cost.

2. Answer: C

When programs being compared have a wide range of different outcomes, conversion to cost per quality-adjusted life years or cost per healthy years equivalents provides a means to compare the relative program outputs. Cost-utility analysis is only appropriate with final outcome variables; intermediate variables should not be used; therefore, Answer D is incorrect. When the outcomes are similar (Answer B), other less expensive and difficult methods, such as cost analysis or cost-effectiveness analysis, can be used. If quality is not an important outcome then cost-utility analysis is not appropriate; therefore, Answer A is incorrect.

3. Answer: B

Both techniques measure costs the same, (therefore, Answer A is incorrect) and require valid effectiveness data. But in the case of cost-utility analysis, only final output effectiveness data will suffice (e.g., lives saved, disability days averted). Intermediate outcomes data (e.g., cases found, patient days averted) are unsuitable in cost-utility analysis because they cannot be converted into quality-adjusted life years gained. The source of data (Answer C) bears no impact on the type of study, and neither type of study has an advantage in policy decisions; therefore, Answer D is incorrect.

4. Answer: A

Standard gamble (Answer B) is the gold standard for measuring utility and is therefore regarded as a utility. Health Utilities Index (Answer C) and EQ-5D$_{index}$ (Answer D) are based on multi-attribute utility theory and is therefore regarded by developers as a measure of utility also. Visual analogue scale (Answer A) does not include risk in measurement and is therefore not regarded as a measure of utilities but values.

5. Answer: B

Results of cost-utility analysis studies are normally expressed in terms of cost per quality of life years because utility values by themselves are more difficult to comprehend than a unit such as cost per quality-adjusted life year. Answers A, C and D are not used to express cost-utility analysis results.

6. Answer: D

Because a cost-utility analysis is usually conducted to compare one program to another, the results are expressed in terms of the incremental differences in terms of both costs and health effects. The correct comparison is that of incremental costs over incremental outcomes. The incremental difference is the additional amount paid for one additional unit of outcome between competing alternatives.

7. Answer: A

Mutually compatible interventions are those that are all feasible and whose costs and benefits are independent of each other. Screening for hypertension and childhood vaccinations are both feasible and one program does not depend on the other. The other three selections (Answers B, C, and D) represent comparisons of interventions where one intervention is dependent or related to the other intervention.

8. Answer: B

When quality of life issues, such as improvement in patients' psychological well-being and physical and social functions, are the main foci, cost-utility analysis is the most appropriate form of economic analysis. Cost-effectiveness (Answer A), cost-benefit (Answer C), and cost analyses (Answer D) cannot incorporate quality and quantity of life into a common unit of measure.

9. Answer: C

A cost-utility ratio is calculated as the costs per gain in quality-adjusted life years. Treatment A has a cost of $28,000 and resulted in a gain four QALYs. Dividing $28,000 by four QALYs is equal to $7000 per QALY; therefore, Answers A, B, and D are incorrect.

10. Answer: C

The same procedure used in the previous question applies. For Treatment B, the cost is $30,000 and there are five QALYs gained. Dividing $30,000 by five QALYs is equal to $6000 per QALY; therefore, Answers A, B, and D are incorrect.

11. Answer: C

Average differences in treatment programs examine only the difference in cost per QALY and do not consider incremental differences. The difference between $7000 and

$6000 per QALY is $1000 per QALY; therefore, Answers A, B, and D are incorrect.

12. Answer: A

An incremental difference examines the additional amount paid for one additional unit of outcome between two interventions. Expressing differences between treatment programs as the incremental difference considers the difference in both the costs the effects. Therefore, the answer to this question is calculated as ($30,000 – $28,000) ÷ (5 QALYs – 4 QALYs) = $2000 per QALY; thus, Answers B, C, and D are incorrect.

13. Answer: C

Opportunity cost is associated with not pursuing an available alternative. In this case, we lose the potential for any gain in quality-adjusted life years from Program A if the resources are provided to Program B. That opportunity cost expressed in quality-adjusted life years is based on the mathematical difference in quality-adjusted life years available from the two programs. Program A had the potential to provide 10 QALYs, Program B provides six QALYs. Therefore, the opportunity cost is equal to 10 QALYs – six QALYs = four QALYs; thus, Answers A, B, and D are incorrect.

14. Answer: D

A quality-adjusted life year is a combination of Q, the quality of life, and Y, the quantity of life in years; therefore, Answer A is incorrect. Although the condition of interest may span most any fraction of a year (days, weeks, months), those units are converted to years to provide a true quality-adjusted life year; therefore, Answers B and C are incorrect.

15. Answer: C

Direct assumptions for the expected utility theory includes transitivity and continuity and utility independence; therefore, Answer C is correct. Options A, B and D are the correct assumptions required beyond for the expected utility theory for quality adjusted life years. A quality-adjusted life year can only capture health-related aspects of life. Aspects outside of the health domain (marriage, professional career, hobbies), even though they may be affected by health problems, are not encompassed in quality-adjusted life years because there are many other factors outside of health that affect these domains.

16. Answer: A

Because standard gamble method is based directly on axiom of continuity (see Figure 3 in chapter) it is regarded as the gold standard for utility measurement in health care; therefore, Answers D (rating scale), C (EuroQol), and B (time trade-off) are incorrect.

17. Answer: A

The utility theory is predicated on the assumption that people choose alternatives with the highest expected utility (or payoff) based on rational behavior, characterized by three fundamental axioms: preference transitivity, continuity, and substitutability. Therefore, Answers B, C and D are incorrect.

18. Answer: B

The classic example of transitivity is: if A is preferred to B and B is preferred to C, then A is preferred to C. Probability does not play a role in transitivity; therefore, Answers A and C are incorrect, and Answer D is illogical and, therefore, incorrect.

19. Answer: B

The quality of well-being instrument is based on psychometric theory; therefore, Answer D is incorrect. The standard gamble is based on decision theory (Answer A). Adaptive reasoning is a behavioral theory unrelated to this topic (Answer C).

20. Answer: A

The standard gamble technique is based on decision theory (expected utility theory); therefore, Answers B, C and D are incorrect.

21. Answer: B

The categories used in the Quality of Well-Being Scale QWB) are mobility, physical activity, social activity, and symptom-problem complex.

22. Answer: A

A cost-utility analysis incorporates both quality and quantity into a common unit of measure. The final unit of measure, whether it be in cost per quality-adjusted life year, cost per healthy-year equivalent, or cost per quality-adjusted time without symptoms toxicity, is in a format that decision makers can readily grasp to compare alternatives. Cost-utility analysis is not a definitive tool (Answer B). It cannot provide a solution for all problems (Answer C), and it requires a great deal of resources compared to other forms of economic evaluation (Answer D).

23. Answer: D

Cost-effectiveness analysis is limited to comparison of alternatives of the same outcome. Cost-effectiveness analysis is capable of comparing alternatives involving different diseases, treatment modalities, and dollar amounts, as long as the outcomes are expressed in the same terms (e.g., lives saved, mm Hg lowered, cases reported); therefore, Answers A, B and C are incorrect.

24. Answer: C

By virtue of the fact that the name of the measure is quality-adjusted life years, it becomes readily apparent that quality-adjusted life years are biased against interventions designed to improve quality of life due to acute conditions of short duration; therefore, Answers A and B are incorrect. For example, a therapy that relieves the side effects of nausea and vomiting associated with 6 days of cancer chemotherapy per year may result in 0.0098 QALY, whereas treatment that relieves arthritis pain every day of the year may yield 0.1 QALY. Though the nausea and vomiting experienced by the cancer patient may be intolerable during the 6 days of the year, it provides about one-tenth the amount of QALYs as the arthritis treatment, which may relieve only moderate pain.

25. Answer: A

If the general population is used to obtain utility values, then respondent burden becomes an issue; therefore, Answer D is incorrect. Experiences show that people often resist judgment tasks; therefore, Answer B is incorrect. They find probabilities or time difficult to work with; therefore, standard gamble or time trade-off techniques are difficult to use. Some people find it offensive to assign numbers to quality of life; therefore, Answer C is incorrect.

26. Answer: A

Standard gamble is the only single attribute utility theory (SAUT) instrument listed; therefore, Answers B, C and D are incorrect. Health Utilities Index (HUI®) is multiattribute; therefore, only Answer A is correct.

27. Answer: C

Short Form 36 is the only measure listed that provides scores for each dimension that cannot be added in any meaningful way (directly) to provide utility scores; therefore, Answers A, B and D are incorrect. However, there are conversions listed in the literature (References 5 and 10).

28. Answer: A

Proxies have been used when utility elicitation has not been possible directly from patients such as the elderly, very young, and incapacitated patients (severe stroke or schizophrenia patients). Use of a patient's physician as a proxy is generally not recommended with preference given to a family member; therefore, Answer C is incorrect. Patient age is not a relevant issue; therefore, Answer D is incorrect. Some authors argue that true utilities are only available from patients not surrogates; however, a number of studies have supported the use of surrogates when patients are unavailable; therefore, Answer B is incorrect.

Answers to Excercises

Exercise 1: Calculation of Quality-Adjusted Life Years

For the person who receives a kidney transplant and gains a 13-year life extension, quality-adjusted life years gained is determined by multiplying the mean daily health state utility obtained from Table 1 for kidney transplant of 0.58 by 13 years of extended life, which equals 7.54 QALYs.

Prevention of a 3-month episode of depression is a little more complicated. With depression, the mean daily health state utility of 0.44. When depression is avoided, the gain is the difference between full health and the depressed state; therefore, the gain is equal to 1 minus 0.44, or 0.56. This gain is for one-fourth of a year; therefore, 0.14 QALYs are gained.

Home dialysis for 12 years followed by death versus hospital dialysis for 8 years followed by death can be depicted by the figure below.

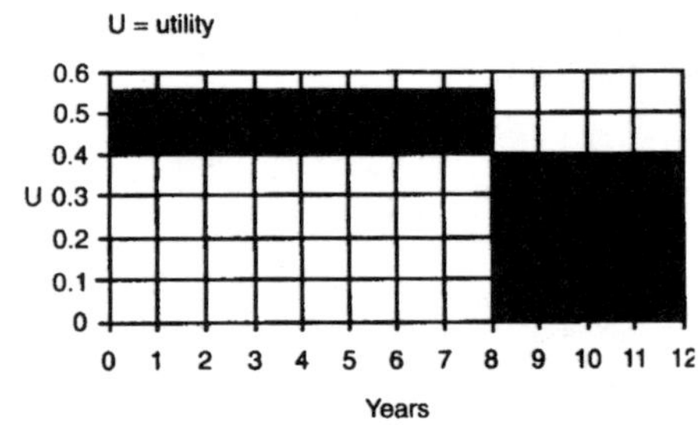

Home Dialysis for 12 Years versus Hospital Dialysis for 8 Years

The picture helps organize the calculation of the difference in QALYs. The shaded areas represent relative differences between the two alternatives. From Table 1, we see that home dialysis beyond 8 years—that is, for life—has a mean daily health state utility of 0.4. From the picture we see that the advantage gained is from years 8 to 12 for a total of 1.6 QALYs. The mean daily health state utility for hospital dialysis up to 8 years is 0.56. The difference between the utility for home dialysis at 0.4 and hospital dialysis at 0.56 for 8 years is 0.16 multiplied by 8 years, or 1.28 QALYs. From these calculations it is obvious that home dialysis for 12 years results in more QALYs (1.6 QALYs gained with 4 additional years of life minus 1.28 QALYs lost in quality of dialysis for first 8 years equals a difference of 0.32 QALY) than does hospital dialysis for 8 years.

Exercise 2: Calculation of Well-Years

This example of parasite screening and treatment among Indochinese refugees demonstrates the need for an organized approach to identify and categorize relevant information. First, the screening and treatment costs must be identified to find the costs of the screening programs and the no screening alternative.

Worksheet 1: Screening and Treatment Costs (Answers)

A	No. Screened	6000
B	Cost of screening examination ($)	$30
C	Total screening cost ($) (A X B = C)	$180,000
D	Parasite	Strongyloides stercoralis
E	No. positive (prevalence)	600
F	Cost for drugs ($)	$20
G	Cost per doctor visit ($)	$35
H	Total Program Cost = H + I	$33,000 (C + H = $213,000)

Worksheet 2: Costs of Not Screening (Answers)

	Parasite	Strongyloides stercoralis
A	No. of persons positive	600
B	Percent of persons hospitalized	0.05
C	No. of persons hospitalized (A x B = C)	30
D	CPX and Function weights	CPX-7 = 0.299 MOB-2 = 0.090 PAC-1 = 0.077 SAC-1 = 0.106 Total = 0.572
E	No. of days hospitalized	10 days 10/365 = 0.27 years
F	Total no. of Well-years reduced (C x D x E = F)	0.463
G	Cost per day	$500
H	Cost Total Saved (C x E x G = H)	$150,000

The benefits of the program are then identified both as costs avoided and the utility or well-years gained as a result of preventing hospitalization days.

As seen from Worksheet 3, once the costs and well-years are identified, calculation of the cost-utility ratio is a straightforward exercise. To make this analysis complete, the costs and utility estimates should be subjected to a sensitivity analysis. In addition, if the program is to have future years of costs or benefits, appropriate discount factors should be included before conducting the final calculation.

Worksheet 3: Results of Final Cost-utility Ratio Analysis (Answers)

A	Screening and Treatment Costs, $	$213,000
B	(Column J, Worksheet 1) Prevented Hospitalization Savings, $	$150,000
C	(Column H, Worksheet 2) Cost Minus Total Savings, $	$63,000
D	(A – B = C) # of Well-years gained by preventing hospitalization (Column F, Worksheet 2)	$0.463
E	Cost/Utility Ratio C/D = E	$136,069/ well year

DECISION ANALYSIS

Answers to Self-Assessment Questions

1. Answer: D

By definition, decision analysis involves making decisions under conditions of uncertainty. Therefore, sensitivity analysis should always be conducted around variables of uncertainty; therefore, Answer D is correct. The perspective of a decision can affect the time period selected (Answer A), the population of the analysis (and hence the rates or probabilities of disease occurrence within the population; Answer C), and the associated costs of the decision paths (Answer B). Regardless of the perspective, elements of the decision, such as probability estimates and outcomes valuations, will always have some degree of uncertainty attached to them and should be subjected to sensitivity analysis.

2. Answer: C

Probability estimates are best when obtained from prospectively conducted, randomized, controlled trials (RCTs), especially if they are of sufficient size to detect rare events. However, efficacy trials (Answer B), following rigid protocols with strict inclusion criteria, do not provide adequate testing of an intervention in a typical patient population. Therefore, population-based, controlled trials following effectiveness principles (Answer C) are most reflective of the rates of events within a representative population. Experts (Answer A) are notorious for overestimating rare events and underestimating common occurrences. Retrospective chart reviews (Answer D) depend on the quality of the recorded data, which are often incomplete.

3. Answer: B

The initial step of decision analysis involves identification of the decision-maker (Answer C) and the associated perspective, identification of decision options (Answer A), and identification of the time period (Answer D) over which the analysis is to be conducted. Only after the consequences are identified and the probabilities estimated should the outcome valuations of decision paths be determined (Answer B).

4. Answer: B

As diagramed in the Yeast-be-Gone arm of the tree, the probability of effective therapy is the combined probabilities of a 90 percent chance that the patient will not develop contact dermatitis, followed by a 70 percent probability that the agent is effective, and an 80 percent probability that the patient will use the drug. These probabilities are combined by multiplication-0.90 x 0.70 x 0.80 for a path probability of 0.504. All other arms of the Yeast-be-Gone branch of the tree lead to ineffective therapy or discontinuation of drugs.

5. Answer: B

Chance node B has been incorrectly specified because the probabilities arising out of this node total to more than 1.0. It is not possible to have greater than a 100 percent chance that something will happen.

6. Answer: B

The expected value at chance node B is calculated by averaging-out-and-folding-back, combining the path utilities with the associated probabilities. By first calculating the expected utility value at chance node C (a 20 percent chance of a 0.1 utility plus an 80 percent chance of a 0.6 utility), investigators find the expected value at chance node C is 0.5. This value is then used to calculate the expected utility value at chance node B by combining the expected values from the upper, middle, and lower paths:

[(0.6 x 0.8 utility) + (0.1 x 0.5 utility) + (0.3 x 0.7 utility) = 0.74 utility

7. Answer: A

This calculation is similar to what was done with the previous question; this time, the cost variables are the values that are averaged-out-and-folded-back. The expected cost value at chance node C is:

[(0.2 x \$4000) + (0.8 x \$2000)] = \$2400.

The expected cost value at chance node B is found by combining the expected cost values from the upper, middle, and lower paths:

[(0.6 x \$500) + (0.1 x \$2400) + (0.3 x \$1500) = \$990.

8. Answer: C

The two expected values can now be combined to yield a cost-utility ratio. This arm of the decision tree has an expected cost of \$990 and an expected utility of 0.74; therefore, the cost-utility ratio is \$990 ÷ 0.74 utility or \$1338 per utility.

MARKOV MODELING

Answers to Self-Assessment Questions

1. Answer: D

Markov decision models are best used for determining outcomes for chronic conditions, decisions in which options recur and in which the likelihood of the options occurring changes over time. In general, models should not be used to estimate effectiveness or costs (Answers A and C) because the model inputs may be inaccurate or biased leading to erroneous predictions. These biases and estimation errors tend to cancel out when comparing two treatments and using incremental costs and/or effects, leading to much smaller inaccuracies.

2. Answer: C

The branch in Answer C allows patients to move from the "healthy" state to any of the three states in the model. Answer A allows patients only to remain healthy and does not model hip fracture at all. Answer B is correct if healthy patients could not die. This could lead to inaccuracies in estimating the treatment difference in models that ran for an extended time period as only patients with hip fractures would be allowed to die, leading to an overestimate in the therapy that is more effective in preventing hip fractures. Answer D would have everyone have a hip fracture and die in the first cycle of the model.

3. Answer: C

Creating a temporary state allows the costs and reductions in utility to be applied as a one-time immediate "reward" for patients suffering hip fracture (Answer C). Applying them as initial rewards (Answer A) would have them only count toward people who started the model in the "posthip fracture" state. Applying them as transition rewards for the "posthip fracture" (Answer B) state applies the costs in the cycle following the event and for every cycle that a person remained in that state. Creating a new Markov state (Answer D) could potentially work if done correctly but adds unnecessary complexity to the calculations for the Markov tree.

4. Answer: C

Using a weighted average of the effects from all the available studies (Answer C) is the best method as it would take into account the size of the trials and the effect size seen from each trial. A formal meta-analysis is even more appropriate. Answers A and B would lead to biased estimates for the base-case but is appropriate for sensitivity analyses. Answer D may be appropriate for some instances but still suffers from the possibility that an extreme point estimate was obtained because of chance or differences in patient populations enrolled.

5. Answer: C

Using published prices along with performing adequate sensitivity analyses make it easier for other institutions to compare the results of your analysis with their own setting. Because the purpose of this paper is publication, actual drug cost (Answer B) is less appropriate than a proportion of the average wholesale price (Answer C). Depending on the ultimate use of the decision model, another method of pricing drugs may be entirely appropriate. For example, in an internal analysis for your hospital formulary committee, you might find that using your hospital's actual acquisition costs provide a much better estimate than average wholesale price. Patient co-payments (Answer A) and cost to retail pharmacy chains (Answer D) are inappropriate from the insurer's perspective.

6. Answer: A

The answer (31.6 percent) is derived by determining the instantaneous mortality rate (r=0.37942) and then calculating the new probability of dying after 1 year using the following equations:

$$r = \frac{-\ln(1-p)}{t} \qquad p = 1-e^{-rt}$$

7. Answer: B

The initial state does not require discounting. Therefore the present value of \$5000 given 4 cycles from now can be calculated using the following equation:

$$C_t = \frac{C_0}{(1+d)^t}$$

Where C_t is the present value of C_0 at time t
C_0 is the present cost
d is the discount rate
t is time

8. Answer: D

The life expectancy is determined by summing up the number of people-cycles spent in the "well" (12,500) and "disabled" (1389) states and dividing by the number of people (10,000) who started in the model.

9. Answer: A

The utility is determined by multiplying the equivalent cells of the two matrices to get a third matrix (shown below) and then summing all the cells (10,803.31) and dividing by the number of patients in the model (10,803.31/10,000 – 1.0803) to reach Answer A.

Cycle	Well	Disabled	Dead
1	10000	0	0
2	500	250	0
3	25	25	0
4	1.25	1.875	0
5	0.0625	0.125	0

Sum of all cells = 10803.31

10. Answer: D

Half-cycle correction (Answer D) is the correct term for the description. Cohort simulations and Monte Carlo simulations (Answers A and B) are different Markov approaches. Incremental rewards (Answer C) are rewards that are applied to being in a Markov state for a full cycle.

11. Answer: C

Markov models are a method of combining indirect evidence to aid in a decision for which there is no direct evidence. As such, a model is more prone to subjective judgments and assumptions, which should be tested using sensitivity analyses (Answer C). In the same way that we would not consider a point estimate in a clinical trial without confidence intervals or another measure of variability, we should not blindly accept the base estimate of a decision model without an adequate assessment of the variability in the model and the model's inputs. Answer A does not consider the potential variability that may be present in the model's cost-effectiveness estimate. Answer B is not correct since retrospective data is often the best source of available information and is the most appropriate data to use. Answer D is incorrect since therapy A is less effective than therapy B and the ICER is not less than $20,000 per LYS.

SENSITIVITY ANALYSIS

Answers to Self-Assessment Questions

1. Answer: B

If a study result is sensitive to changes in a variable, it means there is less confidence in the study findings. The results significantly change when the variable is modified within a range of plausible values. Answer A is incorrect because it would not strengthen the confidence in the results. Answer C is incorrect because it is useful to identify variable that significantly alter the findings. Answer D is incorrect because it is especially important to identify variables that significantly alter the study results.

2. Answer: D

Sensitivity analyses may be useful for a wide range of variable types. However, sensitivity analyses are especially useful for data obtained from expert panels (Answer D) because there are often wide ranges of data variability from expert panels. Answer A is incorrect because there would be less variation in a precise cost estimate. Answer B is incorrect because there typically is no variation in average wholesale prices of recently approved products. Answer C is incorrect because there may be less variability in efficacy results compared to less controlled analysis within naturalistic trials.

3. Answer: B

Extrapolation uncertainty (Answer B) describes the uncertainty in estimating long-term outcomes based on proxy outcomes. Answer A is incorrect because it is not an analytical method of uncertainty. Answer C is incorrect because it is not an issue of data variability uncertainty. Answer D is incorrect because it is not an issue of whether a study's findings can be generalized to another population.

4. Answer: A

A one-way sensitivity analysis (Answer A) changes the values for one variable in a model within a range of plausible values and leaves the remaining variables unchanged. Threshold analysis (Answer B) is incorrect because it does not determine when a parameter equals the other treatment alternative. Multiway analysis (Answer C) is incorrect because only one parameter is being varied at a time. Analysis of extremes (Answer D) is incorrect because it is not determining the impact of the highest and lowest values for a parameter.

5. Answer: A

A simple one-way sensitivity analysis (Answer A) describes changing the effectiveness rate in a cost-effectiveness analysis. Threshold analysis (Answer B) is incorrect because the break-even point of a variable is not determined. Multiway analysis (Answer C) is incorrect because multiple parameters are not being simultaneously manipulated. Analysis of extremes (Answer D) is incorrect because the greatest and lowest effectiveness rates are not being assessed.

6. Answer: D

A threshold sensitivity analysis (Answer D) described the changing of a single variable until the same outcome is obtained with an alternative treatment plan and there is no advantage between treatment options in the outcome described. Answer A is incorrect because a probabilistic analysis is not being performed. One-way analysis (Answer B) is incorrect because a single variable is being manipulated in a specific manner to determine the break-even point in outcome findings. Analysis of extremes (Answer C) is incorrect because the highest and lowest values are not being tested.

7. Answer: C

An analysis of extremes (Answer C) may be especially useful with data from expert panels to determine the greatest and lowest impact across the data collected from the expert panel. This is often useful as the range of plausible values is frequently larger with data from expert panels. One-way sensitivity analysis (Answer A) is incorrect because it may be important to determine the impact of multiple variables simultaneously. Simple analysis (Answer B) is incorrect because a single variable is being manipulated in a specific manner with the extreme ranges. Answer D is incorrect and the threshold analysis does not provide an estimate of the full values reported by the expert panel.

8. Answer: A

A Monte Carlo simulation is categorized as a probabilistic sensitivity analysis (Answer A) because this technique randomly assigns values from variable ranges and estimates outcomes from models with large numbers of hypothetical patients. Simple analysis (Answer B) is incorrect because often more than a single variable is manipulated simultaneously. Analysis of extremes (Answer C) is incorrect and it is not limited to extreme values of the range, but selects values within the range. Threshold analysis (Answer D) is incorrect because it is not determining the equivalence point between two treatments.

9. Answer: B

By definition, a tornado diagram is a series of one-way sensitivity analyses displayed simultaneously in a single graph (Answer B). Answer A is incorrect because it is not a three-way sensitivity analysis graph. Answer C is incorrect because it does not have to be a cost-effectiveness ratio graph. Answer D is incorrect because it is not a threshold value graph.

10. Answer: D

A break-even point is calculated in a threshold analysis. In this method, a variable (e.g., a drug cure rate) is modified until the answer equals the comparator. Answer A is incorrect because this does not describe a probabilistic analysis. Answer B is incorrect because does not manipulate more than one variable at a time. Answer C is incorrect because the highest and lowest cure rates are not being tested.

Answers to Exercise

1. There are numerous sources of uncertainty in this analysis. The pharmacist is basing several critical values on a single published study from a controlled, clinical trial. The patients and results from the clinical trial may not be generalizable to the patients in John's hospital. Specifically in John's calculations, there may be variation in the success rate for preventing nonfatal myocardial infarctions and emergency angioplasties in John's hospital. Based on this single study, John is assuming that abciximab will only be used in high-risk angioplasties. However, there may be more widespread use of abciximab in actual practice. In addition, there may be variation in the wastage rate of abciximab in actual practice. In addition, the requirements for red blood cells and platelets observed in the clinical trial may differ from that observed in John's hospital. In addition to the clinical parameters, there may be variation in the actual costs observed in John's hospital. The hospital's accountants may have provided John with reasonable estimates, but the true costs experienced in future practice may vary from the values they provided John.

2. A best-case and worst-case analysis would include using a sensitivity analysis of extremes. Within the data provided, the only ranges of data elements are with the 95 percent confidence interval costs for a nonfatal myocardial infarction and an emergency angioplasty. The tables can be recalculated using the highest and lowest cost values for both the nonfatal myocardial infarction and emergency angioplasty costs. The new data are summarized in the following tables:

Worst Case Scenario for Using Abciximab in 34 High-Risk Patients Undergoing Angioplasty

Resource Unit	**Abciximab**	**No Abciximab**
	(No. of patients)	(No. of patients)
Abciximab (drug, filters, wastage)	$56,550 (34)	$0 (0)
Transfusion requirements		
Red blood cell	$1,750 (5)	$700 (2)
Platelet	$1,500 (2)	$750 (1)
Nonfatal ($10,360@) myocarial infarction	$20,720 (2)	$31,080 (3)
Emergency ($16,880@)	$0 (0)	$16,880 (1)
Health system costs	$80,520	$52,410
Net change	$28,110	

Best Case Scenario for Using Abciximab in 34 High-Risk Patients Undergoing Angioplasty

Resource Unit	**Abciximab**	**No Abciximab**
	(No. of patients)	(No. of patients)
Abciximab (drug, filters, wastage)	$56,550 (34)	$0 (0)
Transfusion requirements		
Red blood cell	$1,750 (5)	$700 (2)
Platelet	$1,500 (2)	$750 (1)
Nonfatal ($18,080@) myocarial infarction	$36,160 (2)	$54,240 (3)
Emergency ($32,450@) angioplasty	$0 (0)	$32,450 (1)
Health system costs	$95,960	$88,140
Net change	$7,820	

When John used his best cost estimates, he estimated that cost to his institution would be $19,465 to save one nonfatal myocardial infarction and one emergency angioplasty. However, when John recalculated his cost estimates using the highest and lowest cost estimates, he noted that the cost could potentially vary between $7,820 and $28,110 to prevent these two adverse complications.

3. These analyses demonstrate there is a reasonably large variation in costs encountered to prevent two significant adverse complications. If the hospital only had to spend $7,820 to prevent two bad complications, John may change his mind and recommend that the abciximab be available for high-risk patients. On the other hand, realizing that the hospital could have to pay more than $28,000 to prevent these two complications, John reinforces his recommendation to not use abciximab and a wise use of hospital resources.

EVALUATING ECONOMIC OUTCOMES LITERATURE

Answers to Self-Assessment Questions

1. Answer: A

The purpose of the study was to assess the cost-effectiveness of pravastatin therapy in survivors of myocardial infarction with average cholesterol levels. The authors performed a cost-effectiveness analysis based on actual clinical, cost, and health-related quality-of-life data from the Cholesterol and Recurrent Events (CARE) trial. Although this study provided information on the benefit, cost, and effectiveness of pravastatin therapy (Answers B, C, and D), the authors did not consider the potential adverse reactions of pravastatin therapy (e.g., myopathy) in their analysis per se.

2. Answer: D

The authors included direct medical costs only, (i.e., payments for hospitalization and other medical services). Intangible, indirect, and direct nonmedical costs were not included (Answers A, B and C). Direct costs for health care resources are commonly included in the numerator of the cost-effectiveness ratio because direct costs have a direct financial effect on health care organizations that is easiest to measure and best understood by health care decision makers.

3. Answer: C

The authors used the placebo-controlled trial data from the CARE trial to assess the cost-effectiveness of pravastatin therapy. The authors did not compare pravastatin with an active comparator (Answer A and B), although decision makers often find it useful to look at studies that compare active treatment with existing practice rather than placebo (Answer D). However, the empirical literature still contains a large number of pharmacoeconomic studies based on randomized, controlled clinical trial data that compare active treatment with placebo, as did the study discussed in Reference 13.

4. Answer: D

To model the effectiveness of therapy, the authors used two pairs of Markov models, one pair based on all-cause mortality data from CARE trial and one based on recurrent event data from the trial. Also, survival beyond the end of the trial was simulated in the Markov model (Answers A, B, and C). The authors used a Markov model to estimate life expectancy, but the analysis did not include lost productivity associated with hospitalizations.

5. Answer: C

The authors converted all costs to 1996 U.S. dollars by means of the medical care component of the Consumer Price Index. All costs and years of life were then discounted at three percent per year. The general rule is to discount at either three percent or five percent. Therefore Answers A, B, and D are incorrect.

6. Answer: A

Many decision makers do not have the time or the training to fully evaluate all pharmacoeconomic studies, so having a checklist that helps them to categorize studies may be quite beneficial. Highly trained pharmacoeconomists (Answer B) probably do not need a checklist because they would be knowledgeable about how to perform and evaluate pharmacoeconomic studies. Doctorate of Pharmacy students (Answer C) benefit from training in pharmacoeconomics, but only those students who will be responsible for decision making will need to use checklists. Patients (Answer D) are generally not presented with pharmacoeconomic articles, so they would have little need for checklists.

7. Answer: C

For decision makers to believe that results will generalize to their population, they must be convinced that the results reflect their patients and health care setting. Although observing consistent results through a quantitative synthesis of the literature may help, it is not required for a study to be generalizable (Answer A). Knowing that a study has incorporated patient-subjective measures does not guarantee generalizability if the patient population differs significantly from the population observed by the decision maker (Answer B). If an efficacy-based study has documented that patients will in general adhere to therapy, the efficacy results may generalize to effectiveness results, but again those results do not generalize to another patient population (Answer D).

8. Answer: C

It is essential that the decision maker understand which treatments are being compared and what costs and consequences are being evaluated. Although it would be helpful if all relevant drugs were considered in a pharmacoeconomic study, it is impractical to address all insurance options and all dosage forms (Answers A and B). Cost-minimization analysis (CMA) assumes equal outcomes, so these results should be presented only if one plausible assumption is that the competing treatment options produce identical outcomes; therefore, Answer D is incorrect.

9. Answer: D

Drug manufacturers have an incentive to sponsor pharmacoeconomic studies because they can use the results to justify the use of their drug based on its relative cost-effectiveness. Manufacturers also have an incentive to try to manipulate such studies to highlight the most favorable aspects of their drug and downplay the less favorable aspects, which creates the potential for bias. The peer-review process can help to eliminate biased studies from being published, but the process is not guaranteed to eliminate biased studies (Answer B). Drug companies are often the only institutions that are willing to financially support pharmacoeconomic research, so industry-sponsored studies are fairly common (Answer C). Many of these studies are unbiased because of the nature of the contracts under which the studies are performed. Thus outlawing industry-sponsored studies would eliminate not only the few biased studies but also the plethora of high-quality studies funded by the industry (Answer A).

10. Answer: B

Current guidelines are helpful to decision makers who are interpreting pharmacoeconomic claims, but guidelines should be updated as agreement on additional principles emerges. To wait until there is agreement on one set of guidelines would provide no guidance to current decision makers (Answer A), which is arguably worse than offering only some guidance. As the number of guidelines worldwide continues to grow, more decision makers will use them, but at this point many decision makers have yet to adopt any guidelines (Answers C and D).

11. Answer: B

Early pharmacoeconomic studies, and occasional contemporary studies, are wrought with bad methodological design. Proper evaluation of pharmacoeconomic literature can help to ensure that misinformation is not used in decision making. Although pharmacoeconomic studies should have clinical relevance, ensuring clinical relevance does not require evaluation of the pharmacoeconomics literature (Answer A); clinical relevance can be ascertained from purely clinical literature. Evaluation of pharmacoeconomic literature should examine the sensitivity analysis and selection of outcomes, not be used to plan for them (Answers C and D).

12. Answer: D

Evaluating pharmacoeconomic literature to contain health care costs will not limit the pharmacy budget (Answer A). In contrast, it will provide the information necessary to track baseline costs and outcomes for disease management; therefore, it provides a more accurate cost profile for the pharmacy budget. Pharmacists who are able to evaluate the pharmacoeconomic literature will be more cognizant of the overall outcomes associated with drug therapy, thereby enhancing their role of meeting the demand for cost accountability (Answer B). Using pharmacoeconomics can help preserve full-time equivalents (FTEs) because it gives decision makers the tools to better plan their budgets (Answer C). To evaluate the pharmacoeconomic literature, evaluators must meet reasonable professional standards. This may be an obstacle because the evaluator must receive unfamiliar and time-consuming training on how to evaluate pharmacoeconomic literature.

13. Answer: A

The checklist cited in Reference 11 is fairly general and reflects the minimum standards for a pharmacoeconomic study. As such, its recommendations are in general consistent with other checklists but not as detailed (Answer D). The checklist was published more than a decade ago and helps to identify poor studies (Answer C). It does not, however, distinguish the quality of studies that surpass minimum standards (Answer B).

14. Answer: B

The Panel on Cost Effectiveness published an entire book to discuss the controversies surrounding the design, conducting, and reporting of health-outcomes studies. In addition to its recommendations, it discusses topics that did not reach consensus among panel members. Other checklists provide general guidance and less discussion surrounding controversial topics; therefore, Answers A, C and D are incorrect.

Answer to Exercise

See grid below.

Cost Category	Cephamore®		Alternative 1		Alternative 2	
	Include	Unit	Include	Unit	Include	Unit
Acquisition costs						
Lab costs						
Personnel costs						
Pharmacy						
manufacturing						
pharmacy kinetic services						
Nursing						

TOOLS FOR MEASURING HUMANISTIC OUTCOMES

Answers to Self-Assessment Questions

1. Answer: C

Although there is some controversy as to acceptable levels of reliability, the minimum acceptable level is 0.7. A reported Cronbach's alpha of 0.6 does not meet the minimum criteria and therefore, the scale does not reliably measure its domains (Answer C). Answers A, B and D are incorrect because the questionaire does not meet the minimum reliability criteria; therefore, it should not be used.

2. Answer: B

Ceiling effects, or the percent of respondents achieving the highest possible score, are of concern when evaluating the responsiveness of a questionnaire. The ability to detect change over time is especially important when assessing evaluative questionnaires. Cross-sectional studies, by definition, do not assess change over time (Answer A). Using questionnaires to predict who will develop a disease involves a single administration (Answer C). Finally, describing needs and identifying potential interventions are the purposes of discriminative questionnaires (Answer B).

3. Answer: A

In the presence of an interviewer, respondents are less likely to report sensitive information (Answer A). Being able to ask more complicated patterns of questions (Answer B) is an advantage of face-to-face interviews. Interviews are more expensive to conduct (Answer C), partly because they require trained interviewers and take longer to administer. Clinic staff typically do not have the additional time to be trained and conduct interviews in addition to their usual activities (Answer D).

4. Answer: D

The best method of administration depends on the severity of disease in the sample population. Both telephone-administered interviews and mail-out/mail-back surveys (Answers C and D, respectively) are difficult to conduct in an Alzheimer's disease population, but mail-out/mail-back administration is the least appropriate in this situation. During a telephone interview or face-to-face interfiew, the interviewer would at least be able to determine if the respondent does not comprehend the questions. Proxy reports may be the most appropriate for patients with a progressive neurological disease.

5. Answer: C

Because the trial in question is a longitudinal assessment comparing an active agent to a placebo, a predictive instrument (Answer A) is not the best choice to detect changes in humanistic outcomes over time. Predictive instruments are used to identify groups or individuals who have or will develop a medical condition or outcome and can be used to predict future needs. Discriminative instruments (Answer B) are used to differentiate between individuals or groups, describe differences in health status, or identify areas of need. This method may be an appropriate type of instrument depending on the other goals of the trial. However, evaluative measures (Answer C) determine the magnitude of longitudinal changes in individuals or groups. An evaluative measure is the best type of instrument for the purpose described. Descriptive (Answer D) is not a type of health status measure.

6. Answer: B

When asking open-ended questions, patients can provide detailed explanations of their answers and thought processes. Mailing questionnaires and computerized administrations (Answers C and D, respectively) are examples of self-administration. In self-administered questionnaires (Answer A), it is difficult to have respondents provide lengthy responses. However, during a face-to-face interview (Answer B), the interviewer can ask probing and clarifying questions to elicit the desired narrative responses.

7. Answer: D

Mixing administration modes complicates the interpretation of scores. The published literature for a specific instrument should be consulted to determine if there are known differences in scores based on administration mode. Also, clearly understanding the order of administration (Answer A) and any resulting differences in scores will aid in interpreting changes over time and any statistical adjustments that need to be made to accommodate mixing administration modes. Respondent demographics (Answer D) have very little to do with understanding the change in scores over time as demographics remain constant.

8. Answer: D

The choice of administration mode depends on a variety of factors, including the budget, data quality needs, and the amount of time needed to complete the questionnaire (Answers A, B, and C, respectively). Other factors influencing how the questionnaire should be administered include how patients will be recruited and how long followup will occur. All of these factors need to be taken into consideration so that the best administration method can be chosen. Answer D is correct because a questionaire must first be identified before a mode of administration can be selected.

9. Answer: A

The number of items in the questionnaire, the physical location where the questionnaire will be complete, and the age and level of respondent education all influence the level of patient cooperation and the perceptions of loss or gain from completing the questionnaire. Sample size, project duration, and result display (Answers B, C, and D, respectively) are all important considerations, but are not directly relevant to respondent burden.

10. Answer: D

The first question asked was in reference to a physical activity. Therefore, Answers B and C cannot be correct. Computer-adapted testing will ask a question in the same domain to determine the level of the patient's functioning. Although Answer D is an item that measures physical function, it is a drastic change from being limited in walking 1 mile. The software is most likely to ask a question of a lower physical ability before choosing a drastic change in function.

MEASURING HEALTH STATUS

Answers to Self-Assessment Questions

1. Answer: C

Quality-of-life measures (like patient-reported outcome [PRO] measures) may be uni- or multidimensional; therefore Answers A, B, and D are incorrect. There is nothing to say that a quality-of-life measure must be multidimensional (Answer C).

2. Answer: B

Generic health status instruments can prove useful to researchers because they allow for comparison of scores against other populations (Answer B), either from the published literature, or normative data often provided by instrument developers. Generic instruments per se do not provide C/E ratios (Answer A); they are not necessarily short (Answer D); and if used as a baseline, could not be followed up with only a disease-specific questionnaire (Answer C).

3. Answer: A

Because of their high level of specificity, disease-specific measures are more sensitive to small changes that might go unnoticed by a generic instrument (Answer A). They will have higher sensitivity to change than generic tools.

4. Answer: C

Because generic instruments are designed to be used across all types and severity levels of disease, they can lack the relevancy (Answers C and D) to a specific population that a disease-specific measure can offer. However, the generic instrument's general nature allows for comparison to different populations (Answers B and C).

5. Answer: A

Although the SF-36 is widely used and well accepted, its availability does not mean that other instruments (generic and disease-specific) should not be considered. Researchers should ask themselves many questions before selecting an instrument to ensure that the best measure is used (see Table 4). The burden to the patient of completing an instrument should always be considered, and the mode of administration is an integral part of the burden concept (Answer B). A clear understanding of the intended use of an instrument is critical (Answer C). Different instruments are designed to be scored in different ways; while some allowing for simple summation of responses, others require detailed and complex algorithms to be scored appropriately (Answer D).

6. Answer: B

Reliability is a measure of consistency (Answer B). If all else is equal across multiple administrations of an instrument in a given population, will the instrument scores be the same? If so, the instrument is deemed reliable. Validity is the assessment of whether the instrument measures the concepts and constructs it was designed to measure (Answer A). Answers C and D are unrelated concepts.

7. Answer: B

Increased burden decreases participation (Answer C) and has an impact on the quality of the results (Answer D). Issues that affect respondent burden such as sample size and quality issues must be considered. Researchers must consider the length of the survey, the administration mode, and the types of questions asked, as all three factors can impact the results of the survey. Burden is not related to statistical measures of significance (Answer A).

8. Answer: C

Utility assessment is a method by which patients can express their relative prioritization of many treatments based on the hypothetical health state they would be in as a result of taking that treatment. The definition of utility assessment does not indicate any ability to detect change (Answer A) or any relationship to the availability of instruments. As utility is a measure of individual preference, it should not be measured from a clinician's perspective (Answer B).

9. Answer: D

Because general instruments are often used in a variety of conditions and disease states, results from one population can be compared to another through published literature or normative data (Answer D). The population that an instrument is being administered to does not necessarily have to be similar to the population in which the instrument was developed in order for the instrument to be generalizable (Answer A). Established instruments should always be used as they were developed and validated; questions cannot be added on an ad-hoc basis without potentially impacting both validity and reliability (Answer B). There is no inherent relationship between whether an instrument is established and the level of burden associated with the instrument (Answer C).

10. Answer: D

Assessing the psychometric literature on an instrument allows the researcher to establish the reliability and validity of an instrument; considering other studies in which the instrument has been used allows for comparison of populations and results (Answer D). The peer-reviewed literature is full of instruments that have not been assessed for validity or reliability; simply because an instrument appears in the literature does not mean that it is a good measure. Different authors have different requirements regarding permission to use instruments; permission should always be requested before health status measures are used (Answer A). Given that health status is a concept that was developed from a number of social sciences, it is important to recognize that literature related to health status can be found in the literature of a number of disciplines (Answer B). If an instrument has been well described in one population (such as an adult population), it can be used in that population; but if the instrument has not been described and tested in other populations (i.e., pediatric or geriatric), it should not be used unless proper validation studies are undertaken.

11. Answer: D

Reliability is a necessary, but not sufficient factor for validity. A questionnaire first must be able to accurately measure the same construct repeatedly (i.e., it must be reliable); if a survey cannot fulfill this requirement, then by definition, it cannot measure what it was intended to measure (i.e., it cannot be valid) (Answer D). However, it is possible for a survey to meet the consistency requirement set forth by reliability, but still not measure what it was intended to measure. It is possible for measures to both be multidimensional and reliable at the same time; reliability does not require unidimensional measures (Answer B). Reliability does not make any assessment as to the relative 'strength' of a response (Answer C).

12. Answer: B

Reduction in respondent burden (Answer A), choice of delivery platforms (Answer C), and comparable scores across different item sets (Answer D) are the primary strengths of computerized adaptive assessments. Assessments may or may not be cost beneficial on one time assessment (Answer B).

13. Answer: B

Differential item functioning occurs when one group responds differently to a question than another group despite controlling for differences between the two groups on the measured construct (such as mental health; Answer B). Scales containing such items will have reduced validity for between-group comparisons because their scores will be indicative of a variety of attributes other than those the scale is originally intended to measure. By definition Answers A, C and D are not related to the concept in the text.

14. Answer: C

Applications of item response theory modeling can be used to evaluate the item and scale properties (Answer B) of an instrument, to detect differential item functioning across groups (Answer A), and to calibrate item properties (Answer D) for an item bank.

15. Answer: C

The Hierarchy of Patient Outcomes considers the following five dimensions: death (Answer A), disability, discomfort (Answer D), iatrogenic effects (dire events; Answer B), and economics. Religiosity is not a component of the Hierarchy of Patient Outcomes; therefore, Answer C is incorrect.

PATIENT SATISFACTION

Answers to Self-Assessment Questions

1. Answer: D

Satisfied patients are expected to be more actively involved in their health care an may, in some cases, use more health care services compared to those who exit the health care system. However, satisfied patients might also require fewer or less costly services. Thus, there might be no difference in costs.

2. Answer: A

For example, pharmaceutical tablets are manufactured to fit within Food and Drug Administration standards for dissolution and considered quality of conformance (Answer A). Quality of design (Answer B), on the other hand, focuses on how well the product or service meets the needs of consumer or how well the product or service compares with those of the competitors in the eyes of the consumer. Care relates to patients (Answer C). Quality improvement is a process of change not only consistency (Answer D).

3. Answer: C

Services are unique from products, which makes their evaluation difficult. They are intangible, inseparable from production, and can vary from provider to provider.

4. Answer: C

Persuasion-based should be affect-based assessment. Affect is rooted in emotions and can be a valuable conceptualization for patient satisfaction. Persuation is not related to the satisfaction concept in this paper. Persuation is related to decision making and attitude change.

5. Answer: A

Viewing patient satisfaction as performance evaluation (Answer A) is most useful for services that have characteristics individuals can identify and understand. Disconfirmation of expectations (Answer B), affect-based assessment (Answer C), and equity-based assessment (Answer D) might be more useful for services that have components that are poorly understood by patients. Using disconfirmation of expectations, affect-based, or equity-based assessments could provide insight into the psychological process of evaluating the service and are more useful.

6. Answer: B

The consumer fulfillment response results from a cognitive appraisal of the service experience which involves a comparison between the service experience and expectation. If the service fails to meet expectations, dissatisfaction results. If the service meets for exceeds expectations, then satisfaction will be realized. Performance evaluation (Answer A), affect-based assessment (Answer C), and equity-based assessment (Answer D) are based on performance, emotion, and fairness, respectively.

7. Answer: D

Comparing one's outcomes versus input to respecting someone else's outcomes versus input results in a perception of fairness (Answer D). The level of fairness (or equity) is a significant predictor of satisfaction with some services. Answers A-C are not based on fairness.

8. Answer: D

When selecting which perspective of satisfaction to take, one must identify the research question that is being addressed. For example, if the primary research question of interest deals with comparisons among different service providers as to how well clients rate defined aspects of service performance, an experience-based performance evaluation most likely is appropriate. However, if the research question is focused on understanding the relationship between clients' evaluation of a service and the clients' commitment to future interaction with the service provider, a satisfaction measure that reflects evaluative and affective reactions is appropriate. Also, satisfaction might not be the best construct to measure. Performance, quality, loyalty, complaining behavior, trust, or another outcome might be more useful for decision-making. It is important for the researcher to be able to link the measured construct to the decision problem the study results will help address. Medical, marketing or other literature cannot meet all needs. Do not dismiss Answers A-C, but one size does not fit all.

9. Answer: D

Patient satisfaction has been critiqued on many levels, including how it has been conceptualized, how it has been measured, and how it has been interpreted and used for decision-making. The dissatisfaction-satisfaction continuum deals specifically with its conceptualization (Answer A).

10. Answer: D

Many researchers think they have a clear idea of what they wish to measure, only to find that their ideas are more vague than they thought. The researcher must be exacting in delineating what is included in the pertinent domain and what is excluded. Only when an explicit definition of the satisfaction construct is outlined can one proceed with the next steps of developing a measure. One should address issues, such as the type of conceptualization of satisfaction that is best for the study. Should the focus be on performance evaluation of the consumption experience or should the focus be on the patient and the decision process he or she uses to evaluate the service? Another issue to address when specifying the construct domain is whether satisfaction is encounter specific or reflective of cumulative experiences. Also, what is the most pertinent focus; satisfaction with the service itself, the pharmacist, or the pharmacy? Finally, an understanding of how and whether patients perceive and evaluate a service will help specify the domain. There is no evidence provided in the scenario for Answers A-C.

11. Answer: C

Case mix refers to the different patient attributes that might be apparent in different settings. To the extent that patients self-select or are assigned to different comparison groups in nonrandom ways, comparisons of satisfaction ratings may be biased by factors other than the provision of the health care services in the compared groups. The evidence is leading to a case mix issue and not Answers A, B or D.

MEASURING WORK OUTCOMES

Answers to Self-Assessment Questions

1. Answer: A

Assessing functional performance and health related quality of life is the most current use, and the most recent subject of research in the area of work outcomes. Using work outcomes to measure psychological adjustment to chronic illness (Answer B) occurred in the 1940s, while using them as an indication that a patient recovered from physical illness and responded to treatment dates (Answer C) to a time when physically demanding work was prevalent in the United States. Work outcomes can be used to estimate the indirect costs of health care attributable to illness, but not the direct costs (Answer D).

2. Answer: A

Work outcomes are measured at an individual level, although the results are used at the aggregate or group level (Answer B). Survey methods to measure work outcomes rely on the reports of individuals whose labor force participation is a concern (Answer C). Work evaluations, or functional capacity evaluations, are principally used in rehabilitation settings (Answer D). In all of these cases, measurement is at the individual level, and use of the results is at the group level. In addition, work outcomes refer to the direct or indirect consequences of a person's health problems or treatment on both the quantity and quality of labor force participation.

3. Answer: D

Reasons for including work outcomes in studies are: the fact that paid work is an important activity around which our lives are organized (Answer A); and that work outcomes, such as employment status, serve as barometers of the financial gains and costs that may result from different treatment modalities (Answer B). Work outcomes are not studied to promote the view that allowances should be made for people with chronic illnesses who work (Answer C), but rather to promote the use of these measures so that health does not compromise one's ability, or opportunity, to work.

4. Answer: C

When measuring work outcomes, a distinction should be made between work role and work tasks. Work performance and work productivity refer to two different concepts (Answer A). Generally, performing a job role suggests implementing a set of actions in response to role demands, while productivity usually refers to the physical output of the worker, or the goods and services generated through paid work activity. Work disability and work impairment are also different (Answer B). According to the Institute of Medicine model, disabilities refer specifically to a person's performance of specific social roles, such as being a parent, a spouse, or an employee (Answer D). Impairment refers to loss and/or abnormality of mental, emotional, physiological, or anatomical structure or function; and includes all losses or abnormalities, not just those attributable to active pathology.

5. Answer: D

Sociologists do not agree on the definition of social role, thus, there are variations in the definition. In addition, scientists within the field of work-related research do not regard the role, either defined according to occupational category or job title, as a useful characterization of what a person does or is required to do. Efforts to overcome this include the Dictionary of Occupational Titles (now known as O*NET) and the Position Analysis Questionnaire. Each seeks to disaggregate work roles into their constituent components or dimensions for rating purposes (Answer A). Role-level questions are likely to elicit coarse reports of ability to work, whereas demand-level questions will provide information about which specific domains of work and work tasks are problematic (Answer B). Typically, survey methods measure work outcomes at the role-level (Answer C).

6. Answer: D

Unpaid work activities are one of the deficiencies of all conceptual frameworks and all measurement methods of work outcomes to date. Measures of work outcomes do include consideration of employment status and work loss, time loss, and activity and role limitations (Answers A, B and C).

7. Answer: C

The questions adapted from the National Health Interview Survey for these self-report measures vary on the reference period. That is, the newer measures ask questions about time loss over 7 days, 2 weeks, 12 months, etc. This is an important consideration when choosing an instrument or a battery of questions. The National Health Interview Survey is interviewer administered, and the questions are geared toward disability days (Answer A). The questions are created specifically to allow comparisons across different populations with different illnesses (Answer B). The National Health Interview Survey approaches attempts to capture the number of full and part days missed due to health problems and, consequently, captures the complete inability to work during the time period, and days in which the worker was partially disabled (Answer D).

8. Answer: B

Work absence measures are used both as a health outcome and an economic outcome. Although time-based measures are popular productivity and cost indicators, they often are not viewed as reflections for the human burden associated with missed work time (Answer C). The use of work absence variables as individual-level productivity indicators requires one to assume that time spent not working results in some net financial loss and does not account for these outputs efficiently (Answer D). Work absence measures can be interpreted as a summary measure of disruptions in the performance of normative roles and diminished productivity (Answer A).

9. Answer: A

Both the SF-36 and the Sickness Impact Profile contain question batteries that assess limitations in role activities with distinct scale scores. Only the Sickness Impact Profile contains a separate paid work battery (Answer B). There are no published data on validation of role limitations measured by either the SF-36 or the Sickness Impact Profile using work-site data (Answer C). The paid and not paid work roles are not addressed seperately (Answer D).

INTERPRETATION OF HUMANISTIC ASSESSMENTS

Answers to Self-Assessment Questions

1. Answer: D

The word "typical" implies a comparison to what would be the expected or normal. As the chapter indicates, "Norms" are the average scale scores for a particular group that resembles the study group and so represent the scores that would be expected. In contrast, "Content-based interpretation" and "Content validity" (Answers A and B) have to do with the meaning of the words used in the question stem and response choices; while factorial validity (Answer C) has to do with statistical covariation among item responses.

2. Answer: B

The key phrase is "items in a scale." This indicates that the reader is to consider multi-item scales (as opposed to single-item scales) when answering the question. According to the chapter, the only method listed that looks at the relationship of within-scale item values to each other, is the internal consistency method. Alternate forms, confidence interval and test-retest methods all consider relationships between scales. Alternate forms (Answer A) looks at the relationship of scale scores on form A to form B. Confidence interval and test-retest methods (Answers C and D) look at the similarity of scale scores from time 1 to those at time 2.

3. Answer: C

The important phrase here is, "...size of scale score differences," which indicates that the question refers to quantities. As discussed in the chapter, nominal scaling is the assignment of responses to categories, which are qualitatively, and not necessarily quantitatively different. The size of the score is not important in nominal scaling. In contrast, the size of scores is central to all of the other methods. The responsiveness statistic (Answer A) is a formula for calculating the size of an effect in standard units. The standard error of measurement (Answer B) is used to create a confidence interval around an observed score. If the compared score falls within that confidence interval it is considered to be the same size as the observed score. By contrast, if the compared score falls outside of that confidence interval, it is considered to be either larger, or smaller, than the observed score. A comparison of scores of known groups (Answer D) is used to gauge the size of the difference of scores from groups that are not known.

4. Answer: A

The term "gold standard" implies an external standard that is universally accepted as defining the phenomenon in question. This is the meaning of criterion. Internal consistency (Answer B) is a method for evaluating reliability, not validity. Factorial validity (Answer C) is the relationship of observed values to an underlying hypothesized phenomenon. Content validity (Answer D) is the meaning of the words used in the survey questions and their responses.

5. Answer: B

The important words here are "unmeasured" and "hypothesized." A construct is an unmeasured and unobserved variable. Indeed, it cannot be measured because it exists only in theory—it is a hypothesized variable. In contrast, correlation (Answer A) is a synonym for relationship, criterion (Answer C) is a standard or principle against which other things are evaluated, and a reliability coefficient (Answer D) is a statistic.

6. Answer: D

As discussed in the text, an absolute zero value is necessary in order to calculate absolute magnitude and a ratio scale is the only scale that contains an absolute zero. Nominal, ordinal and interval scales (Answers A, B and C) do not contain an absolute zero.

7. Answer: A

As discussed in the chapter, reliability is a necessary precondition for validity to exist; thus, Answer B is incorrect. Reliability refers to the consistency, repeatability or stability of a reading, measure or value. Validity is determined by studying that reading or value to see if it indicates what it is supposed to indicate. In order to study something, it must have some stability. For that reason, validity is dependent on reliability; thus, Answer D is incorrect. On the other hand, a reading can be repeatable, yet not be a valid indicator of something (e.g., a heart rate monitor can yield a reliable reading that is nevertheless invalid for the measurement of blood glucose levels). The interpretability of a measure or its value to any particular audience depends on its reliability and validity–not the other way around; thus, Answer C is not correct. By definition a measure is not valuable to anyone if it is not reliable or valid.

8. Answer: B

Content Validity, as well as direct and indirect scaling methods, are sometimes based on evaluations and judgements of persons (subject matter experts) who are familiar with the content of the questionnaire. The text discusses how content validity (Answer D), as well as direct and indirect scaling methods (Answers A and C) make use of subject matter experts. In contrast, factorial validity is based on statistical analysis of data.

9 Answer: C

While scaling, reliability, and validity influence the meaning of scale scores (Answer D, B, and A respectively), they are not methods whose purpose is directly concerned with providing meaning to the scores. The class of methods directly involved with communicating this meaning to different constituencies is interpretation.

10 Answer: B

It is logical to suppose that in order to rule out changes in health scores due to methodological artifacts, a person would need to keep the methods of measuring health constant across time. Indeed, research has shown that type of respondent (proxy versus self versus provider) (Answer A), and mode of administration (mail versus telephone) (Answer C), as well as some changes in the format of the questionnaire (Answer D), affect survey data.

USING PATIENT-BASED ASSESSMENTS FOR INDIVIDUAL PATIENT CARE

Answers to Self-Assessment Questions

1. Answer: A

When used in individual patient care, general health status questionnaires can contribute to improved health and satisfaction with care of individual patients. Although several potential benefits of the routine use of patient-based assessments of general health status have been proposed, data in support of these hypotheses are inconclusive. In addition, questions about whether the instruments meet reliability standards have been raised.

2. Answer: B

A model that combines the biomedical approach to a patient with that of health status researchers has been proposed. The model is intended to link specific symptoms to the more general evaluation of health by patients, so that causal pathways between specific symptoms and health status levels can be determined. Then interventions can be targeted to treat the cause of diminished health status, thereby improving health. In support of the model, more information about how symptoms and general health status levels are related is needed.

3. Answer: A

Measuring patient health status before and after implementing a protocol for a particular service would allow one to use patient health status as an outcome variable in the evaluation of the service. Implementing patient-based health status assessments in clinical practice requires thoughtful planning and collaborative efforts of several staff members. Whereas the use of patient-based health status questionnaires in clinical practice has many intuitive benefits, such as improved communication with patients, improved adherence to medication regimens, improved gathering of important information, aid in clinical decision making, and, ultimately, improved health status and satisfaction with care, those benefits have not been consistently demonstrated scientifically.

4. Answer: D

Validity and responsiveness are different from reliability. Reliability is a necessary, but insufficient, condition for validity. The higher the reliability coefficient, the smaller the confidence interval, and the more precisely a scale score reflects the patient's health status.

5. Answer: C

As investigated, the Medical Outcomes Study short form, 36 items (MOS SF- 36) Health Survey, the Functional Status Questionnaire, the Dartmouth COOP Poster Charts, the Nottingham Health Profile, and the Duke UNC Health Profile comprehensively measure health, meet practicality criteria, and differentiate well among sick patients; however, they do not meet the stringent reliability criterion of 0.9 for individual patient application.

6. Answer: D

Although reliability and validity of several general health status questionnaires for use with individual patients have been criticized, a more beneficial strategy to advance the routine use of these tools is to build on existing knowledge, rather than developing entirely new measures. Prerequisites for the transfer of health status questionnaires from research to practice include education, documenting experiences, and demonstrating their value in Module 3 470 this setting.

7. Answer: B

Patient-based assessments are intended to provide patients, but not spouse, clinician, or other opinions of health. Reading questions verbatim without interpretation to the patient is encouraged when visual problems inhibit the patient from completing a questionnaire. Questionnaire administration through an interpreter is not acceptable, because an impromptu translation cannot undergo the same stringent evaluation process the original questionnaire underwent before its use.

8. Answer: A

In considering the possible study populations, evaluate the hypotheses that could be formulated for such a study. For example, one could hypothesize that patient-based health status assessment as part of routine therapeutic drug monitoring identifies information about the effects of a medication regimen, positive as well as negative, on the patient's daily life that would not be known without it. Such information would be important in making therapeutic choices for chronic therapy and optimizing long-term drug therapy. In the case of acute illnesses that are cured by appropriate, usually short-term antibiotic therapy, patient-based assessments may not provide as much additional value to decision making in clinical practice.

9. Answer: D

Normative data displayed in Table 6 are for people with chronic obstructive pulmonary disease and hypertension, who are on average much older than 25 years. These normative data do not apply to a 25-year-old football player. For an assessment of the football player's health burden, the appropriate comparison score is that of largely healthy males of the same age. In fact, the physical functioning scale mean score for men 25-34 years old is 95 and the 50th percentile score is 100.

CASE STUDY: FORMULARY DECISION MAKING INCORPORATING HUMANISTIC OUTCOMES

Answers to Self-Assessment Questions

1. Answer: B

Answer B shows the steps that should be taken in the right sequence. In developing formulary decision, first you must define the problem, then determine resources needed, define the study perspective, determine treatment alternatives and outcomes, identify possible sources of data, select a data collection method, review and interpret data, summarize findings, present results, and develop plan for monitoring decisions.

2. Answer: D

The resources needed to conduct the assessment include the multidisciplinary team (Answer A), data providing objective information (Answer C), staff to assist with the evaluation (Answer B), time, and budget.

3. Answer: A

Both improved clinical effects and improved health status can increase patient satisfaction. Changes in costs can increase patient satisfaction through improved health status. To show improved health status, patients have to show their improved clinical effects first.

4. Answer: A

Expert opinions (Answer A) are the least objective of data collection methods provided. Objective data collections methods include peer-reviewed published studies (Answer B); primary data collected in the clinics (Answer C); and prospective, randomized data (Answer D).

5. Answer: C

This type of data source usually has selection bias (Answer C) and also might not include information needed. Prospective, randomized data can avoid selection bias through randomization. Retrospective methodologies typically are not considered to have high internal validity (Answer A) and suffer from many biases. However, the sample is drawn directly from the population of interest; therefore, results can be hypothesized to be generalizable to the clinic population better than a study from a different population (Answer B). Retrospective data collecting generally can be performed more efficiently and save time and money relative to prospective, randomized trials (Answer D).

6. Answer: D

These types of data usually are costly in terms of time and money (Answer D). One of the established strengths of data from prospective, random trials is high internal validity (Answer A), and because of the trial design, are deemed adequate for unbiased comparisons (Answers B and C).

7. Answer: D

Sample size of the study, representativeness of the patient population, and reliability and validity of the instrument (Answers A, B, and C, respectively) all need to be considered when designing a study.

8. Answer: C

Only Answer C can be derived from the information provided in the question above Based on the information given, it was not known whether the instrument QOL-A was valid (Answer A), and whether drug A is more effective in preventing asthma attack because no clinical data was provided (Answer B).

9. Answer: D

Economics outcomes, clinical outcomes, and humanistic outcomes (Answers A, B, and C, respectively) all need to be considered when formulating decision-making.

10. Answer: B

When using published studies as a source of data for a formulary evaluation, only the study designs and results (Answers A, C, and D), not the credentials of the authors (Answer B), are important.

EVALUATING AND JUSTIFYING CLINICAL SERVICES

Answers to Self-Assessment Questions

1. Answer: A

An evaluation of a clinical pharmacy service that includes measurement of both costs and outcomes, but has no comparison or alternative, is a "cost and outcome description"; therefore, Answer A is correct. Evaluations without comparators are termed "descriptions" and are considered partial evaluations. Evaluations that include a comparator are termed analyses. These can be either partial evaluations or full evaluations. A "cost-analysis" (Answer C) is a partial evaluation because it only measures costs (not outcomes) and includes a comparison; thus, Answer C is incorrect. By definition, cost-minimization analysis (Answer B) and cost-effectiveness analysis (Answer D) include a comparison and are consider "full economic evaluations" and are thus incorrect.

2. Answer: D

Drug costs savings (Answer D) is the only example of an economic outcome in the answer choices given. Pharmacist salary and benefits (Answer A) and cost of drug information resources (Answer C) are inputs, or resources consumed in the provision of a clinical pharmacy service, not economic outcomes; thus, Answers A and C are incorrect. Likewise, length of hospital stay (Answer B) is incorrect because it is not an economic measure, rather it is a measure of use (though it could be converted to an economic measure).

3. Answer: C

In a cost-benefit analysis of a pharmacy immunization clinic, vaccine costs should be included because they represent input costs (Answer C). Vaccines can be costly; thus, the cost of vaccines is obviously significant to the evaluation; therefore, Answer A is incorrect. Vaccine use may vary between the pharmacy group and whatever comparison group is evaluated; thus, vaccine costs need to be included even though they also are incurred in the comparison group; therefore, Answer D is incorrect. By nature, vaccines are intended to prevent illness, the timing of vaccine expenditures in relation to illness is irrelevant to this program; therefore, Answer B is incorrect.

4. Answer: D

Health system administrators often have limited budgets for investment in new programs and, thus, must make decisions between programs of seemingly equivalent importance. Outcomes and/or economic evaluations (e.g., cost-benefit analysis) of such programs can help evaluate the relative value of different options (Answer D is correct). Although perhaps true, Answer A (the value of dispensing pharmacy services traditionally has been incorporated in the prescription price) does not support the need for outcomes evaluations of clinical pharmacy services. Answer B (cognitive pharmacy services are increasingly "billable" and paid for by third-party payers) and Answer C (patients are willing to pay for clinical pharmacy services) are both true and may, in fact, be reasons to conduct an outcomes evaluation, but they are less important compared to Answer D.

5. Answer: A

Economic evaluations typically refer to cost-effectiveness analysis, cost-benefit analysis, cost-utility analysis, or cost-minimization analysis. Although patient satisfaction is an important outcome of clinical pharmacy services, it is not an example of an outcome that would typically be included in an economic evaluation of a clinical pharmacy service; therefore, Answer A is correct. Humanistic measures included in economic evaluations are typically based on patient preference in the form of a utility-based outcome (e.g., quality-adjusted life-years). Thus, Answer B is incorrect. Mortality (Answer C) is an example of a clinical outcome, and willingness to pay (Answer D) is an example of an economic outcome, used in cost-effectiveness analysis and cost-benefit analysis, respectively.

6. Answer: B

In this scenario, drug cost-savings (Answer B) is not an input; it is an economic outcome. Other possible economic outcomes of a pharmacist-managed refill clinic might include (but are not limited to) reduced hospitalization costs, reduced emergency visit costs, and reduced physician office costs. Advertising expenses to promote the service, the pharmacist salary and benefits, and overhead costs (Answers A, C, and D) are clearly resources consumed (or inputs) in providing the pharmacist-managed refill service.

7. Answer: C

Cost-benefit analyses (Answer C) are designed to compare investment options to facilitate resource allocation decisions. Because the outcomes is a monetary unit, cost-benefit analysis allows for comparison of programs the have completely different clinical end points. This would be the case in a comparison of different types of clinical pharmacy services. Cost-effectiveness analysis (Answer B) and cost-utility analysis (Answer D) allow for determining and comparing the additional cost to achieve a specific clinical or quality-of-life outcome. These methods do not provide information that would enable an investment decision. Cost-analysis (Answer A) only provides information on the cost to provide the program, it does not assist in understanding the financial impact or outcomes and, thus, is not sufficient to make an informed investment decision.

8. Answer: D

Literature generalization can be conducted before implementation of the service (Answer D), which is a major advantage of this strategy. Published outcomes studies of clinical pharmacy services typically do not have high external validity because outcomes often are specific to the setting, patient population, and practitioners; therefore, Answer A is incorrect. Furthermore, these studies are often not complete because they may not include the costs to provide the service, or may not have a comparator group; therefore, Answer B is incorrect. Literature generalization is usually not convincing to financial decision-makers because of the problems previously discussed; therefore, Answer C is incorrect.

9. Answer: B

A disadvantage of using decision-analysis methods to justify clinical pharmacy services is that the results depend on assumptions made about the probability of expected outcomes or the range of actual costs incurred; therefore, Answer B is correct. Answers A and D are advantages (not disadvantages) of decision analysis. This method can yield organization-specific results (Answer A) and can be conducted before implementation (Answer D). Decision analysis is not expensive (Answer C) compared to conducting an actual study.

10. Answer: C

Key steps in conducting an economic evaluation of a clinical pharmacy service are shown in Table 4 of the text. Among these key steps are the need to state the study question (Answer A), identify alternatives (Answer D), and conduct sensitivity analysis (Answer B). Although important, literature review (Answer C) is not necessarily part of the actual process of conducting an evaluation.

11. Answer: A

Although all of the responses may effect the results, the language in a humanistic instrument can have the greatest impact (Answer A). An English translation for a United States population may not have the same meaning as a translation for a Caribbean population. Likewise, translations of questionnaires to other languages may lose the intended meaning. If subjects are unable to interpret the questions, they are likely to respond with a neutral score or not respond at all. The timing of assessments (Answer B) with respect to the intervention could effect the results. For example, if the goal of the analysis is to evaluate long-term effects, an evaluation 3 months after the initiation of the service may be inadequate. The length of the questionnaire (Answer C) is least likely to effect observation of no difference; however, extremely long questionnaires may limit the number of patients who want to participate in the analysis. The choice of the instrument (Answer D) can impact the results because the instrument should be measuring the services that are provided. Many of the patient satisfaction instruments available for pharmacy services focus on the dispensing role of pharmacists. If these instruments are used to measure the impact of clinical pharmacy services there is a greater chance that no impact will be measured.

USING PHARMACOECONOMIC METHODOLOGIES TO DEVELOP HEALTH POLICY

Answers to Self-Assessment Questions

1. Answer: C

Health policy development in the public sector is more of a political process, as compared to the private sector, given the input of special interest groups, the fact that policy makers may not be the same individuals as the decision makers, and other factors. This is not to say that health policy development in the private sector is void of political considerations, however. Both private and public sector health policy development stresses decision making, selecting goals, and the best means for reaching them and handles conflicting views about what should be done and allocates resources to address needs. Health policy development plays an important role in both the private and public sectors.

2. Answer: D

Taking the time to clearly define the scope of an issue, the key stakeholders involved, the context within which that issue exists, and potential implementation issues are all part of this first important step in the policy process. Poor definition of the problem (and, thus, why a policy needs to be developed and what it is trying to achieve) can lead to solutions that do not have the intended impact on the issue that started the policy analysis and development process in the first place. As the policy development process moves forward, the analyst should be willing to go back and revisit and/or redefine the issue, as new information that is gathered through policy development may change the manner in which the issue is scoped.

3. Answer: B

The economic impact of drug formularies certainly has been one of the more controversial areas in the pharmacy literature in recent years. Although drug formularies are almost universally accepted as an important pharmacy benefit management tool to help educate prescribers and direct appropriate use, their impact on economic outcomes is less clear. It does appear that drug formularies do reduce drug expenditures; therefore, Answers C and D are incorrect. However, their impact on overall health care expenditures is less clear. A 1996 study of HMO cost-containment strategies stated that the opposite effect may be true, although their study methodology has been criticized. A number of reviews in the literature suggest that the impact of drug formularies on overall health care costs cannot be determined with certainty at this time.

4. Answer: A

In a survey of 409 drug benefit decision makers, a Likert-type scale was used (1 = not important to the decision making process; 5 = extremely important to the decision making process) to assess the perceived importance of various factors. Efficacy and safety tied for most important (4.8), followed by cost (4.1), pharmacoeconomics (3.9), health-related quality of life effects of drug (3.8), and physician demand for drug (3.3). The authors of this study conclude that although pharmacoeconomics does appear to be of importance to the survey respondents, the impact of pharmacoeconomics on decision making remains unclear.

5. Answer: A

In most Western countries, prescription drug expenditures are rapidly increasing both as a total cost and as a proportion of total health care costs. For example, in the United States, prescription drug expenditures are increasing 12–18 percent per year, and this trend is projected to continue for at least the next 10 years. In Canada, prescription drug costs now account for more than 15 percent of total health care costs and have replaced physicians as the second largest expense category, following hospital care.

6. Answer: D

Australia was a pioneer in pharmacoeconomic guideline development, with the Australian Pharmacy Benefits Advisory Committee being published in 1992, becoming effective in 1993. The Canadian Coordinating Office of Health Technology Assessment and the Ontario Ministry of Health followed shortly after that, both publishing guidelines in 1994. More recent developments have been the Academy of Managed Care Pharmacy guidance for submission of clinical and economic evaluation data to support formulary listing in United States health plans and the similar submission requirements by Regence Blue Shield of Washington.

7. Answer: A

The ongoing controversy has been the inclusion of indirect costs in the required pharmacoeconomic analyses and the pharmaceutical industry reaction to this. The guidelines do require comparisons from clinical trials to typical Australian patients but this has not been controversial. The Patented Medicine Prices Review Board is a regulatory body in Canada, not Australia. The Australian Pharmacy Benefit Advisory Committee guidelines do allow for comparative benefits and costs.

8. Answer: B

Conducting cost-benefit or cost-effectiveness analyses for so many conditions did prove to be too difficult with this large number of condition-treatment pairs. Expensive procedures that benefit a few or that have questionable benefits were at the bottom of the list and conditions, such as pneumonia, tuberculosis, and peritonitis, appeared at the top of the list; therefore, Answers A and D are incorrect. Allocation of funds for the program did have a relationship to how far down the list coverage would extend, which resulted in great controversy and debate for those condition-treatment pairs that did not quite make the "cut".

9. Answer: C

Depending on the quality of the published pharmacoeconomic analyses, often it will be difficult for the health policy maker to determine the assumptions that were behind the published models. Conducting a prospective pharmacoeconomic evaluation tailored to the organization is typically far more time-consuming than using results from the literature (therefore, Answer A is incorrect) but do enable the policy makers to tailor the prospective study to reflect usual care in their organization (therefore, Answer B is incorrect). Pharmacoeconomic evaluations continue to improve in quality and many are part of the randomized, controlled clinical trials; therefore, Answer D is incorrect.

10. Answer: B

Unfortunately, many recent papers continue to suggest that most health policy decision makers are still inadequately prepared to interpret and apply pharmacoeconomic evaluations. Relevance of the models to the decision makers is a problem in many settings. It has been argued that modeling data from both internal and external sources is helpful in tailoring results that are more specific to the organization in question. Typically, most pharmacoeconomic evaluations try to demonstrate the impact of a drug on overall health care costs, whereas many organizations are still focusing on silo management or the impact of the drug on the pharmacy/drug budget. Locating evidence-based summaries of the pharmacoeconomic evaluations was a problem even fairly recently, but with the development of the Cochrane Collaboration and other initiatives, many of these evidence-based summaries are now available for use by policy makers.

11. Answer: D

A recently published survey of 409 formulary decision makers asked respondents for their opinions on the role of pharmacoeconomics in drug benefit decision making. The respondents were asked about the types of pharmacoeconomic evaluations they desired. They asked for more pharmacoeconomic evaluations that conduct head-to-head comparisons of competing drugs, are independent of drug manufacturer funding) are conducted in typical clinical practice patient populations, and that fully disclose the study methods used.

12. Answer: A

With the constant rise in pharmaceutical costs, health policy makers are focusing more attention on pharmaceuticals and on tools like pharmacoeconomics that can better help them to understand and manage these costs. Phase IV studies should continue to grow in importance to obtain effectiveness data; therefore, Answer B is incorrect. Including a pharmacoeconomic component in formulary submissions is becoming part of the standard expectations of the formulary decision making process and should not distract future formulary submissions by pharmaceutical companies; therefore, Answer C is incorrect. Finally, pharmacoeconomics clearly has an important role to play in patient health management programs; therefore, Answer D is incorrect.